Reuben Fine

Reuben Fine

A Comprehensive Record of an American Chess Career, 1929–1951

AIDAN WOODGER

McFarland & Company, Inc., Publishers

Jefferson, North Carolina

The present work is a reprint, with corrections, of the library bound edition of Reuben Fine: A Comprehensive Record of an American Chess Career, 1929–1951 , *first published in 2004 by McFarland.*

All photographs in this book are courtesy of Edward Winter.

LIBRARY OF CONGRESS CATALOGUING-IN-PUBLICATION DATA

Woodger, Aidan.
Reuben Fine : a comprehensive record of an American chess career,
1929–1951 / Aidan Woodger.
p.   cm.
Includes bibliographical references and index.

ISBN 978-1-4766-7532-9 (softcover : acid free paper) ∞

1. Fine, Reuben, 1914–1993.   2. Chess players—United States—Biography.
3. Chess—Collections of games.   I. Title.
GV1439.F46W66 2018   794.1'092—dc22   2003017941

British Library cataloguing data are available

Printed in the United States of America

*McFarland & Company, Inc., Publishers
Box 611, Jefferson, North Carolina 28640
www.mcfarlandpub.com*

Contents

A BRIEF BIOGRAPHY

CAREER HISTORY AND COLLECTED GAMES

CAREER RESULTS TABLES

APPENDICES

BIBLIOGRAPHY

Acknowledgments

A project such as this necessarily relies on assistance from a range of other collectors and curators (particularly in view of the lack of a national chess library in the U.K.). It is my duty, and great pleasure, to thank Henk Chervet of the Koninlijke Bibliotheek for copying many pages from journals and books from the collection in the Hague, the late Ken Whyld for allowing me the use of his library, Vlastimil Fiala for placing a request for information in his *Quarterly for Chess History* (and for sharing some of his findings from his work on Fine, which should now be available and which will contain a great deal more information about Fine's early career), and also for sharing with me game scores he had uncovered in contemporary newspaper reports, Edward Winter for posting a request for games on the internet and for supplying the photographs used in this book, Dale A. Brandreth for supplying me with copies of Fine's notebooks from the Library of Congress, Peter Lahde who supplied game scores, some of which had been sent to him by Larry Parr and Neil Brennen, Jeremy Gaige who provided a number of crosstables and a copy of Fine's career record, Tony Gillam for game scores and support (and for not complaining about my desire to use another publisher), Patrick Kerwin of the Library of Congress for answering queries about the notebooks and sending me a copy of Fine's article on blindfold play from the *European Journal of Psychology*, Erik Osbun, John S. Hilbert and Jack O'Keefe for supplying me with difficult-to-find gamescores, and providing me with information to supplement the player biographies and tournament chronologies, Andy Ansel for information and gamescores supplied from Fred Reinfeld's papers, Richard James for printing a request for assistance with translation in *Chess Monthly*, Svend Aage Jensen and Øystein Brekke for information about the Oslo tournament, Bob Jones of Keverel books for photocopies of several tournament books written by Fred Reinfeld, Tony Peterson for helping me to find several out of print works, Ed Tassinari for supplying me with biographical material, Bernard de Bruycker for his assistance with translation from a few of the Dutch and German sources, Dr. Richard Cantwell for sharing some of his thoughts, and Timothy Harding for information from Walter Muir's autobiography. I would also like to thank the staff of the Colindale Newspaper Library, and the Halifax Public Library, Reference Section. I gratefully acknowledge suggestions from Andy Soltis, Arnold Denker, and Jon Speelman. I apologise if I have omitted anyone who should have appeared in the list above.

All errors and misrepresentations are solely the responsibility of the author.

Introduction

From the time I first started to study chess seriously, at the relatively late age of eighteen (this was about 1980), my favoured method of study has been playing over the games of the great masters, preferably with notes provided by the players themselves. For several years Reuben Fine's collection of his own games was an almost constant companion as I moved from place to place working for different employers on archaeological sites around England. Naturally at that time I knew many of his games by heart—Fine's collection *Lessons from My Games: A Passion for Chess* contained only about 45 of his tournament or match games in its 50 chapters.

Over the years I bought more of his books and sought out games from tournament books to supplement the small selection available in his autobiography. Judging by the Tournament and Match Record that Fine provided on pages xxi and xxii of the autobiography, I estimated that there were fewer than 500 games to be collected in total. This turned out to be a considerable underestimate, partly because Fine did not even include all of the tournaments he won in this list. Fortunately, Fine had donated a collection of his notebooks to the Library of Congress, copies of which I obtained from Dale A. Brandreth. These notebooks provided a rich source of games for the period 1931–1941. Sadly it soon became apparent that the collection of notebooks was incomplete (though everything donated by Fine to the library was still available). Nevertheless, with the help of other researchers, it has been possible to compile a collection of 659 tournament and match games (plus one exhibition game and one practice game), four fragments from tournament or match games, 28 rapid transit games from U.S. Lightning championship tournaments, 34 correspondence chess games (including nine fragments) and something over 120 miscellaneous exhibition, clock simultaneous exhibition, blitz and consultation games. All of these amount to substantially more than the 242 games available in, for example, ChessBase Mega Database '97, though I note ChessBase Big Database 2002 has increased the number to about 320.

My principal aim in this work has been to make available a comprehensive collection of Fine's games played at classical time limits and present them chronologically and in context. All other miscellaneous games are provided for the sake of comprehensiveness. I have included the United States Rapid Transit Championship games within the main body of text because of the quality of the opposition in the events.

The translations are largely my own. I cannot, however, claim fluency in any language other than my native English, and therefore the translated notes are necessarily often simplified in comparison to the originals upon which they were based. Apart from English-language sources, I have made use of materials from journals, biographies, games collections and tournament books in Russian, Ukrainian, Slovenian, Slovakian, Polish, Czech, Croat, Dutch, German, Swedish, Norwegian, Spanish and French. Notes have also been edited to conform with the English algebraic form of move notation and to regularize some spellings.

Wherever possible, I have tried to use good quality notes from sources other than *Lessons from My Games*. In cases where there are several good sources I have made a synthesis of the available material. Occasionally a single alternative source is of outstanding quality, in which case, I have principally made use of that source. I have corrected minor errors without comment, but in the case of certain contested conclusions or repeated errors I have indicated what I believe to be correct. Naturally, my own suggestions require testing, though I have run most of them through Fritz 5.32 on an IBM machine with a Pentium chip.

I hope this work can serve as a basis for further research, possibly leading to a new edition to celebrate Fine's centenary. There are plenty more games to be found, many good quality games without notes, more biographical material to be unearthed, tables to be found, and so on. Being remote in time and place from the events described, I am aware that the context and details of events could be more complete. There may well be plenty of sources which could provide additional useful data, and there are still a few people alive who could provide eyewitness accounts. I am confident that much more material will be found. However, there comes a time when a researcher has a duty to make the fruits of their labour more widely available, and I believe this time has come in this instance.

I have not made any overt attempt to analyse Fine's play during the various phases of the game, define his style or discuss his errors (I understand from Dr. Richard Cantwell that he is working on a book along those lines).

Games without reference to source from the period 1931 to 1941 are taken from Fine's notebooks, which have also been valuable for correcting errors of move order and providing a complete record of some games which have usually been quoted in abbreviated form (sometimes without indication that the game is incomplete).

Aidan Woodger
Halifax (England), May 2004

"God keep me from completing anything. This whole book is but a draught—nay, but the draught of a draught. Oh, Time, Strength, Cash, and Patience!"
—Herman Melville from "Cetology"
in *Moby-Dick or, The Whale*

"The knowledge of past times and places on the earth is both ornament and nutriment to the mind."
—Leonardo da Vinci

A Brief Biography

Introduction

Reuben Fine, the only child of businessman Jacob and Bertha Fine (*née* Nedner), was born on 11 October 1914, New York, New York, into a Russian-Jewish family who had emigrated to the United States around the turn of the century, and died there on 26 March 1993. Only 2 when his father abandoned the family, he grew up in impoverished circumstances in the East Bronx. His active international career was remarkably short, consisting of participation in Pasadena 1932, Syracuse 1934, Mexico City 1934-5, the Olympiads of 1933, '35 and '37, 15 major European tournaments in about 18 months of 1936 and '37, the A.V.R.O. tournament of 1938, the Pan-American Championship 1945, and two New York Internationals of 1948 and 1951. In addition he participated in numerous domestic events in the United States between 1929 and 1951 and played several matches against players of master and grandmaster quality.

Early Years

Fine learned the moves of the game at the age of about 8 from an uncle. When he enrolled in high school in 1927 he joined the chess club at Townsend Harris High School (a school for gifted students), but was not a strong player by the standards of his peer group at that time. In the spring of 1929, nearing graduation from high school (normally students would graduate high school at 17 or 18 years of age; Jack O'Keefe suggests that Fine might have taken examinations to accelerate his graduation by avoiding the need to take certain classes) he became a junior member of the Marshall Chess Club and was introduced to the Manhattan Chess Club, which, however, had no junior members. (Judging from the record in L.M. Skinner and R.G.P. Verhoeven *Alexander Alekhine's Chess Games, 1902–1946* it would

have been in 1929, and not 1928 as he wrote in his autobiography, that he was prevented from seeing Alekhine giving a display of blindfold chess at the Manhattan Chess Club.)

Fine wrote that it was then, shortly before his fifteenth birthday, that his passion for chess, which lasted for eight years, began. Fine found his college studies rather easy, and he therefore spent many of his weekends and evenings in the chess clubs. It seems that much of his time was spent playing rapid-transit chess at the Marshall Club, at which he made quick progress (the *American Chess Bulletin* of March 1930 reported that Rubin Fine (*sic*) shared second and third prizes with Professor Ismael Amado of the University of the Philippines at Manila behind Hermann Helms in a Marshall Chess Club rapid transit tournament) earning the nickname "Kid Gefaerlich" (dangerous), and "three-cornered pots" at the Manhattan. By 1931 he was regularly winning first prize in blitz tournaments, with only Capablanca, who rarely played, being his superior. (Pandolfini in *Chess Life* recorded that later on Flohr was also to prove superior, and a further story from the Soviet visit suggests that Tolush also defeated him, though this may have been in a single game.) During these early years his stake winnings, and nickels earned playing at a concession in Coney Island, helped to supplement the family income.

During 1929 and 1930 Fine participated in at least six minor tournaments organized by various of the New York chess clubs. His principal club was clearly the Marshall, with which he was to be associated for the remainder of his career, but he also took part in contests at the Manhattan Chess Club, and the Isaac L. Rice Progressive Chess Club. He had some success at first in the Marshall Club subsidiary events of 1929–30, but apparently fared less well during the main part of 1930. The tournaments recorded here may not be a comprehensive list, references to the events are few in contemporary sources, furthermore, the memories of the players involved concerning these tournaments were apparently not always accurate, as might be expected when recalling minor events decades later.

In his first non-club tournament, New York State Championship, Rome 1931, Fine placed second after Fred Reinfeld, but ahead of Arthur Dake, a member of the United States chess team at the Prague International Team Tournament earlier that year. He won the Marshall Club Championship in 1931-2, and then the Western Open (forerunner of the U. S. Open) in Minneapolis, ahead of Reshevsky, but fared badly in his first international tournament, Pasadena 1932 (though if his recollection of his adjourned game with Reshevsky is correct he might have placed 3rd and relegated the former prodigy to a tie for 7th–10th). It was only at this stage that he started to study the literature of the game, for which purpose he learned German in order to understand Tarrasch's *Dreihundert Meisterpartien*, Réti's *Die Meister des Schachbretts* and Nimzowitsch's *Mein System*. Feeling that these works were lacking in some aspects he then turned his attention to the games of Lasker, Capablanca and Alekhine and the writings of the latter. Around this time Fine was apparently able to defeat Alekhine in rapid chess.

Fine held onto his title of Marshall Club Champion in 1932-3 and then, by placing first in a selection tournament, qualified for board 3 on the United States chess team for the Folkestone International Team Tournament of 1933 (Kashdan and Marshall were pre-selected for the top boards). In his first, brief, trip abroad he made a significant contribution to the team's success (+6 –1 =6) as they held onto the Hamilton-Russell trophy. In June 1933, not yet 19, he graduated from the College of the City of New York (normally students would graduate at the age of 22), where he had studied mathematics and philosophy, with a B.S. degree. He decided to become a professional chess player, since the economic situation at the time made it difficult for young men to find well-paid, steady work. He became a contributing editor to *The Chess Review*, which was founded by Kashdan that year. Around August he defeated Arthur Dake (the U.S. board 4 at Folkestone) in a match and retained his Western Open title at Detroit in September, once more ahead of Reshevsky. America, however, was not a good place to make a living as a chessplayer, since players were required to pay their own expenses at tournaments and did not always receive their dues in prize money. For this reason Fine tried to obtain invitations to Zurich 1934 and Moscow 1935, but got no reply from the organizers. From about mid–April 1934, Fine started a number of correspondence chess games. These were apparently not part of an organized tournament, but, most probably, represent an attempt to make money from the game by offering his services as an opponent, as was certainly the case for some games played in the 1940s.

For the third time in a row, Fine won both the Marshall Club championship and the American Chess Federation (successor to the Western Chess Federation) Open, at Chicago 1934, once again ahead of Reshevsky. In two international tournaments that year he had reasonable success, at Syracuse 1934 he placed third equal with Dake, two points behind Reshevsky but only half a point behind Kashdan, and at Mexico City 1934-5 he shared first with Dake and Herman Steiner, each making a clean score against the ten local players, winning one and losing one in their personal encounters. During the visit to Mexico he played a brief match with Carlos Torre Repetto, winning one game and drawing the other.

In July of 1935 he won the Open title once more, at Milwaukee. On this occasion, though, Reshevsky was in England winning a relatively weak tournament at Yarmouth. All these successes led to his selection for the American team attempting to win the international team tournament for the third time, and so in August 1935 he left for Europe for the second time. He now found himself playing on top board for the United States team, which was successful once more in retaining the Hamilton-Russell Trophy. After Warsaw he was invited by his Polish hosts to his first individual tournament on European soil at Łódź. On his way back to the States he took part in the traditional Christmas tournament at Hastings, where he started by winning from a precarious position against the favourite, Salo Flohr.

In the spring of 1936 the first modern United States Championship tournament was held. The result was disappointing for Fine, but the first of four consecutive wins for Reshevsky, though for a long time it had looked like the winner would be Albert C. Simonson.

A Spell in Europe

In the summer of 1936 Fine returned to Europe and stayed for about eighteen months. While there he took part in 17 tournaments in the Netherlands, England, Norway, Sweden, Soviet Russia, Belgium, Latvia and Austria, finishing first or equal first in eleven, second in two, third equal in one (probably the strongest event). He did have a few failures, particularly towards the end of this period, but also helped the United States team to win the Hamilton-Russell trophy for the fourth time at the Stockholm Team Tournament of 1937. He also played a match with the leading Swedish player Gideon Ståhlberg, married for the first time and acted as a second to defending World Chess Champion Dr. Max Euwe in his match with Alexander Alekhine.

In Fine's first tournament of this period, Zandvoort 1936, he had the satisfaction of defeating Keres with the black pieces in their second meeting at the board. The ten meetings during the 1930s between these players ended with a minimal plus score for the Estonian, who had the advantage of the first move on seven occasions. At the Nottingham tournament which followed, the non–British players were largely of world champion or challenger class. Fine made steady progress to end up just half a point behind the winners Capablanca and Botvinnik, both of whom enjoyed some fortune against British Champion William Winter. After victories in three relatively minor tournaments, Fine showed his best side at Amsterdam, where he came back from a loss in the opening round to share top honours with World Champion Max Euwe. The next big event for Fine was the annual Hastings Christmas tournament, which he had won the year before. Here he scored seven wins in nine games but had to console himself with second prize: the once and future World Champion Alexander Alekhine played one of his best tournaments of the mid–1930s, defeating Fine in a much admired clash.

In the new year Fine travelled to Sweden where he topped a table composed largely of Olympiad team members of the host country. An excellent match showing against the leading Swedish player Gideon Ståhlberg preceded an easier workout against two lesser players, who took it in turn to have a day off while Fine faced their compatriot. A visit to Soviet Russia brought two further tournament victories, although there were occasional intimations of the future from the home players. On trips to England and Belgium, Fine shared first prize with Keres, and in the latter case also with Grob. The top three players at Ostend allowed only four draws between them in 27 games. All of Fine's games were decisive.

There followed a dip in form, perhaps caused by a year of almost non-stop chess activity. At Kemeri, Fine required a great deal of fighting spirit just to keep his head above water. At the International Team Tournament back in Sweden, however, the opposition on second board was not quite so tough and Fine made a major contribution to a winning score for the United States for the third time. The Semmering-Baden tournament provided another good result, but Fine enjoyed a considerable amount of luck against Ragozin, the only Soviet player other than Botvinnik to take part in a tournament outside of the U.S.S.R. during the 1930s. At the Hastings tournament at the end of the year, Fine had the black pieces against the strongest players and was unable to make much headway with white against Hugh Alexander. At the time there was much criticism of the so-called Fine-Flohr style of play, a supposedly technical exercise leading to a good many draws. Fine, unquestionably, found it tough to achieve anything against certain players, several of his games with Flohr and Capablanca being drawn in around twenty moves. This was, however, an exception to the rule, for the most part his games were hard fought.

Annus Mirabilis—1938

Fine returned to New York for a rest from full-time chess activity but tried once more to grab the national honours. The 1938 tournament was, however, Reshevsky's most solid effort of these early championship tournaments. Fine, with one more win to his name but two losses to lesser lights, needed to win their last round encounter to take the title. An enterprising pawn sacrifice in the opening turned out to be insufficient and Sammy took the draw from a position of strength.

Fine had intended to give up professional chess at this time, but he had signed a contract to participate in a tournament of the world's eight strongest players in the Netherlands in the late autumn. The organizers had hoped that the event would act as a candidates' tournament to select a challenger for a world title match. The field was made up of the reigning world champion, two past world champions, a future world champion, two future candidates, the F.I.D.E.'s official challenger, and Fine himself. Between them, the world champions who were present held the title from 1921 to 1963, apart from two brief spells in 1957–1958 and 1960–1961. Former World Champion Emanuel Lasker was apparently disappointed not to be invited. Fine led from the start, he won five of his first six games and achieved a winning position in the other. In round seven Keres did what was necessary to keep the contest alive and won with the black pieces. Fine, nevertheless, held a half-point advantage after the first cycle of the double-round event. The second cycle was less successful for the young American, but, in spite of a rather unfortunate loss to Reshevsky, he did enough to hold on to shared top place at the end. The two youngest players in the field, Paul Keres of Estonia and Fine himself, came ahead of their generally more celebrated colleagues. Keres was declared the winner on a pre-arranged tiebreak formula and duly issued a formal challenge to Alekhine. For various reasons the title match never took place. Indeed, Alekhine did not defend his title before his death in 1946 and a new champion was not crowned until 1948.

Back to College and Domestic Chess

Fine was fairly active in chess for a little over two and a half more years. Meanwhile he completed a master's degree, graduating from the City College of New York with an M.S. in education in 1939. He had, however, decided to forsake chess as a profession. Apart from tournament prizes and honoraria he had supplemented his income by giving lessons at $2.50 an hour (during the war Maurice Wertheim paid him $10 an hour) and around this time was charging $5 to play an opponent by mail. At this time he was only making a few dollars a year in royalties from his books. Despite the new academic degree, Fine apparently returned to professional chess, Denker describes him as having been unemployed in 1939–1941.

In 1939 Fine won the U.S. Open (in one of its various guises—the North American Championship) for the fifth time. In the finals he conceded but a single draw, to his great rival Reshevsky, who also shared the point with Al Pinkus. As had happened so often in the early 1930s, the year was rounded off by Fine's winning the prestigious Marshall Chess Club Championship. He lost in an early round, but following a winning streak, was able to coast home with draws against a couple of the stronger players in the last two rounds. In his game with Marshall he allowed simplification without weakening his position, whereas in the game with David Polland he was able to agree to a draw as Black from a position of strength.

In March and April of 1940, three wins in the New York Metropolitan League represented a reasonable warm-up for the main event of the year—the third U.S. Championship. As expected, both Fine and Reshevsky scored well, and as chance would have it, they were slated once more to meet in the final round. Reshevsky led by half a point, so Fine had to win. For a long time it looked as if he was going to manage it. Opening with the king's pawn he caught Reshevsky in an antiquated system in which Fine's knowledge of theory was superior. Reshevsky made an inaccurate move on his 11th turn and a further mistake ten moves later. On the 27th move, however, Fine failed to find the strongest continuation, his attack faded and the game reduced to a draw.

At the U.S. Open in August Fine conceded three draws in qualifying for the final, but then stormed through the field for a perfect eight out of eight. In his next tournament, held in Salt Lake City over the Labor Day weekend, he made another clean sweep. Just a week later in California he took his score to 17 straight wins before dropping a half-point to Herman Steiner. He did, however, win the short tournament with a round to spare.

In early 1941 Fine competed in the Marshall Club championship for the last time, winning as he had every time he had entered the main event since 1931. In July he finished ahead of a weaker than normal field in the U.S.C.F. Open. The strongest tournament of the year was, however, the New York State Chess Association Championship. Here Fine finished unbeaten, a clear point ahead of a field including his strongest rivals in the United States.

The years from 1938 to 1942 may well have been Fine's active peak. The period of rest he took after his European adventure, coupled with the study involved in writing the new edition of *Modern Chess Openings*, and, later, *Basic Chess Endings*, seems to have brought his play to a new level of maturity. His overall score in competitive games during these four years was 116 wins, as few as 29 draws and only six losses. In other words he won over 75 percent of his games, with an overall 86.4 percent score.

Beginning in the fall of 1941, Fine began a two-and-a-half-years stint working for the Federal Trade Commission as a translator and editor.

A Chess Amateur

In 1942 Fine effectively became an amateur. From this time on he participated in tournaments only very rarely, though not without success. During the war he became interested in psychoanalysis. He obtained a degree from the University of Southern California and by the late 1940s had set himself up in practice.

In the war years, chess events were few. Furthermore, Fine, now remote from the major chess centres and no longer a professional, did not need to seek out those which did take place. Because of his wartime work, and apart from the one-day National Rapid Transit Tournaments held in the summer, Fine only played in a single tournament during the years 1942 and '43, making a clean sweep in the Washington Divan Championship 1942.

In March 1944 he warmed up for the Fifth U.S. Championship by contesting a short practice match against old foe Herman Steiner. Without Reshevsky playing, Fine was a clear favourite to take the national title for the first time. Arnold Denker was, however, in phenomenal form against a relatively weak field, and Fine's attempts to play for complications, rather than adopt a safe continuation as Black in their crucial encounter, backfired. Denker won a magnificent attacking game which was the object of intensive post-mortem analysis, which ultimately seems to have come out in his favour. This was Fine's last attempt to win the title. His failure to do so has perhaps led, a little unfairly maybe, to his being considered clearly behind Reshevsky in the pecking order of the time.

With the war in Europe over, there was renewed interest and opportunity for international tournaments. The presence of Fine, who had relocated to the west to both study for his doctorate and teach at the University of Southern California at Los Angeles (some sources say U.C.L.A., but this seems to be a confusion with U.S.C.) from 1945 to 1948, Herman Steiner and Isaac Kashdan in California provided an impetus for a challenge to the domination of chess events by New York. In July and August 1945, a Pan-American Championship was held in Hollywood. Representatives from South and Central America battled with those from the United States for the title. Samuel Reshevsky came out a comfortable winner, Fine agreeing to too many draws.

In September of 1945, a radio match between the U.S.A., which had dominated Olympiads throughout most of the 1930s, and the U.S.S.R. ended in a crushing 15½–4½ win for the Soviets. Fine's single draw with Boleslavsky was the only success for the Americans on the top three boards. A return match was arranged for the following year in Moscow. On this occasion the Americans improved somewhat, but the U.S.S.R. team, strengthened by the presence of Paul Keres (Estonia having become a Soviet Republic), again ran out winners with a score of 12½–7½. It was clear which way the wind was blowing. Considering his lack of practice, Fine did not do too badly in his match with Keres, but it would not be surprising if these results did not have some effect on Fine's later decision not to take part in the world championship match-tournament. During the stay in Moscow he had lobbied hard for the world championship event to be held in 1947. It was cancelled for political reasons, and by 1948 requirements of work and study caused Fine to decide against participation. As it turned out, Fine's only games in 1947 were played in a match with Herman Steiner. He allowed his opponent just two draws in six games.

Fine did not play in 1948 until almost the end of the year. He drew a radio match game with Dr. Ossip Bernstein of France on 19 December, then played in the New York International tournament over Christmas and New Year's. This offered him a chance to show that he still deserved to be considered among the world's elite. His opponents included Dutch former World Champion Max Euwe and Miguel Najdorf of Argentina (whom he had encountered during the 1930s as Moishe Najdorf of Poland), who believed he should have been invited to the world championship tournament earlier in the year. Fine finished one and a half points clear of the field, allowing only two draws and defeating both of his main rivals. After a fortnight's break, he contested an extremely hard-fought match with Najdorf, who had been the second-placed player in the New York tourney. He got off to a flying start, winning the first two games. Najdorf, however, immediately struck back to level the score. The final four games ended in draws, though both players missed winning chances in the fantastically complicated seventh game.

In 1950 Fine's only international practice was in the radio match held in February between the United States and Yugoslavia, winners of the first post-war Olympiad. Fine played out two fairly solid draws with Vasja Pirc on second board. Turning out for the Marshall Club in the Metropolitan League once more in June, he played an exemplary game against Denker's Sicilian, inflicting a defeat which took him into the lead in scores in their personal encounters.

In February 1951 the team from the Marshall Club visited Havana, Cuba. In the match which resulted the hosts held their visitors to a draw, but Fine defeated Francisco Planas. A short tournament was arranged among six of the strongest players of the Marshall Chess Club in the spring. Fine shared first place with Larry Evans, then club champion (having won the title for the first time as a 15 year old in 1947) and soon to be United States champion.

Fine's final tournament, the Wertheim Memorial tournament of 1951, was a disappointment. He was working during the day and showed signs of tiredness during his evening playing hours. Losses in the first round to Euwe and the seventh to Najdorf, keeping him on a 50 percent score, meant that only by winning his last three games was he able to register a respectable result.

By this time it was clear he could no longer combine his two careers and so he gave up competitive chess completely at the age of just 36, when still among the strongest players in the world. He had a highly successful career in psychoanalysis, firstly in private practice as a psychologist and psychoanalyst in Los Angeles between 1945 and 1948. He returned east to teach at the City College of New York and work as a clinical psychologist for the Veterans Administration. In New York he continued in private practice, becoming an internationally respected Freudian psychoanalyst. He was the author of many books on the subject including A *History of Psychoanalysis* (1979), the standard work on the subject. With Theodore Reik, Fine helped to organize the National Psychological Center for Psychoanalytical Training, supervising the training of psychoanalytic candidates.

During the 1970s, Fine lived in Manhattan pursuing his interests in art, music, history and mathematics. In his later years Fine continued to write in spite of the effects of a series of strokes. In January 1993, however, he suffered a severe stroke and entered Saint Luke's–Roosevelt Medical Center, Manhattan, where he died from complications of pneumonia on 26 March 1993. He had been married five times, and was survived by his wife Marcia, his son Benjamin, his daughter Ellyn, and stepson Harry.

Appreciations and Assessments

Alexander Alekhine

"Dr. Alexander Alekhine, before leaving New York for Europe on September 5 [1933], told an interviewer that he regarded as specially likely future opponents Kashdan, Fine, and Flohr, with the two first-named the most probable. 'America's chances of possessing the next Champion' he said 'are excellent.'" He apparently already at that time considered Fine "a real threat" for the title. (BCM 1933, 477, 527).

David Bronstein

"... Working up forcing lines for use in the opening battle, a fearsome weapon in the hands of such players as Morphy, Chigorin, Pillsbury, Alekhine, Fine and Botvinnik, is a method that works equally well for White or Black." (Bronstein 1960, 291)

George Koltanowski

REUBEN FINE, THE THEORETICIAN
"Luna Park–!
"Shouting, hustling, screaming, noise.
"In this place of excitement, elephants, wrestlers, hot

dogs, and switchbacks a young lad stands behind a chess board, in a booth for all kinds of amusements, playing all comers for a few cents a game. This badly dressed youth, with his hair hanging over his left eye, rather short and thin, plays and beats everyone. Here is a genius in disguise.

"Nobody had heard of Reuben Fine then. But this young lad made good, and made the chess world sit up!

"Let me introduce our hero: he was born in New York City in 1914, of Russian-Jewish parents, and graduated from the College of the City of New York in 1933. At an early age he took a great interest in chess; together with this he had a great facility for picking up languages. Also he possesses a very great memory for everything he has read. These factors make Reuben Fine pre-eminent amongst the great young masters in his knowledge of theory. His style is clear-cut, and theoretically very sound; he avoids middle-game complications, but just like Reshevsky, he is a great master in the endgame.

"Recently he has changed somehow. He is now well-dressed and his hair is neatly parted so the boy of Luna Park would not now be able to recognise himself; he is still small but is getting stout.

"Although at the moment he is not considered a dangerous candidate for the world's title, I still maintain the chess world had better keep an eye on this walking Bilguer!" (G. Koltanowski BCM 1938, 162)

Max Euwe

The World Champion Dr. Euwe wrote in an article at the time of the 1936 Amsterdam International: "Reuben Fine surprising as it may seem to those who have studied the solidity of his play, is always taking risks. He is always risking the draw! He will not permit his opponent the ghost of a counter-chance, but by the exercise of a super-subtle positional sense seeks to draw minute advantages out of perfectly even positions: and these minute advantages serve, over and over again, to tip the scales in his favour in the endgame." (Dudley in the 1980 edition of Fine 1937)

What Do They Like—FINE: *SHARP POSITIONS*
"Fine is extremely gifted in the solving of technical problems such as the preservation of a small advantage; but this is a characteristic of the younger players which he shares with Flohr, and Reshevsky, not his own special perquisite. More typical is his readiness to go in for 'chancy' positions, often enough in the very opening. He is not a combinative

player like Alekhine, and his fondness for critical play is not so great as to make him take risks. No, he never takes risks! such is not his style, though his straightforward, downright methods often force him to make moves which appear risky on the surface and give his play a keen edge. Unlike Capablanca, Flohr, and Reshevsky, he likes to confront his opponents with tricky problems from the very first move; not, like Alekhine, so as to get an attack, or, like Botvinnik, to produce the opportunity for a surprise counter-attack but merely with an eye to position. Able technician that he is, he can exploit incidental chances as efficiently as he can through a routine attack. Above all, his play is logical. There was a striking instance of this in a tournament at Amsterdam, 1936, where he unexpectedly lost to one of the less fancied players in the first round. The tournament was a small one, so that he had little opportunity to make up his leeway. Another player might have played riskily, striving to wrest a little more out of his subsequent games—and very probably have overplayed his hand. Not so Fine; his play continued to exhibit just the same crystal-clear logic. He dropped a draw here and there, but by the last day he had reached the top place.

"Like Reshevsky, Fine is a highly experienced lightning player, and can achieve real marvels of efficacious play in the most severe time-trouble. One thing which does play him tricks now and then is his none too cool temperament, which bothers him more than the other masters; but if we are to make a considered decision, we must admit that his instinct for logic enables him to overcome this failing." (Euwe, 1940 8-10)

Yuri Averbakh

Interviewed by *New in Chess*, former U.S.S.R. champion and world championship candidate Yury Averbakh explained that he considered that there are essentially six different kinds of chessplayer, though with some players fitting in more than one category. Firstly, the killers: for example Botvinnik, Fischer and Korchnoi; secondly the fighters: Bronstein, Tal; thirdly the sportsmen: Spassky, Keres, Capablanca; fourthly the gamblers or "players"—Karpov, and all of these four types have very strong motivation. But there are two other types, the artists—Simagin, Rossolimo and lastly the explorers or investigators. Fine was an explorer as were Rubinstein, Nimzowitsch and Averbakh himself. ("Yury Averbakh: Interview" NiC 1997/4, 43-4)

Career History
and Collected Games

Junior Master in the New York Clubs, 1929–1932

During this period, which might be considered as Fine's chess apprenticeship, the teenaged student was almost exclusively involved in club tournaments in the New York area. His lifelong affiliation to the Marshall Chess Club was soon established, although he played in a few events at the Manhattan Chess Club, and occasionally represented them in team events, though not the New York Metropolitan League. A regular player of Fine's age was not as common as is now the case, and therefore even in junior events he often faced opposition a few years older, and more experienced, than himself.

By 1932 Fine was starting to show signs of developing into a genuinely strong player. Having placed second in the New York State Championship of 1931 he went on to defeat the victorious Fred Reinfeld in a short match. At the turn of the year he had his first success in the Marshall Chess Club championship (a result he repeated before the year was out). A match victory over a recent United States team member in the middle of the year provided further evidence that he was making big strides forward.

Many of the events recorded within this chapter are somewhat obscure. Consequently, details are often rather spare. It is possible that Fine participated in even more minor tournaments, details of which have yet to come to light.

Marshall Club Junior Championships, New York, 1929–1930

According to the *American Chess Bulletin* Fine was presented with a medal for winning the tournament. Reinfeld's

papers record two games between the players around this time, one on 10 October 1929 and a second on 1 November 1929 (Ansel *pers comm*), presumably played in this tournament and a second tournament mentioned immediately below. Fine drew with MacMurray in the first round, and they went on to lead with 2½ out of 3. His final score is not known. Gamescores unavailable. Crosstable unavailable.

Marshall Club Championships B Section, New York, 1929–1930

American Chess Bulletin reported that Fine won first prize with the score of 13–3. Robert Levenstein and Donald MacMurray divided second and third prizes, half a point behind. Gamescores unavailable. Crosstable unavailable.

Metropolitan Chess League, New York, 1930

In his first recorded outings in the Metropolitan League, Fine represented The College of the City of New York. He held down second board, playing on eight occasions. Clubs competing in the championship section included the Marshall Chess Club, Manhattan Chess Club, the Hungarian Chess Club. (Fiala, in preparation; ACB) Gamescores unavailable. Results unavailable.

Manhattan CC vs Philadelphia CC, New York, May 30, 1930

"Intercity relations between New York and Philadelphia were resumed on May 30, when, at the new rooms of the Manhattan Chess Club, a team selected by the Franklin

Chess Club, and which included the pick of Philadelphia, contested a match on twenty boards with the Manhattans. All but two of the games were decided. After adjudication by Lajos Steiner, the referee, the match went on record as a victory for Manhattan by 15 to 5. the home team succeeded in winning 13 games, drawing 5 and losing two. Similar teams will meet in Philadelphia next May. The visitors were the guests of the Manhattan Chess Club at luncheon before the match." (*ACB* 1930) Fine played on board 12. Other members of the Manhattan team included Tenner, Kupchik, Kevitz, Kashdan (on board 8!), Herman Steiner and Horowitz; the Philadelphia representatives included Sharp, Mlotkowski, Ruth and Winkelman. Board order in matches in the United States at this time often seem to bear no relationship to the ranking of the players. These contests began in 1895, the same year as the New York Metropolitan Chess League, when these were the two most powerful clubs in the States.

Everding 0   Fine 1

(1) EVERDING, H—FINE

Manhattan CC vs Philadelphia, New York, 1930 (30 May)
Vienna Game [C28]

1. e4 e5 2. Bc4 Nc6 3. Nc3 Nf6 4. d3 Be7 5. f4 d6 6. Nf3 Bg4 7. h3 Bxf3 8. gxf3 Nh5 9. Ne2 Bh4+ 10. Kd2 exf4 11. c3 Ne5 12. Kc2 Qf6 13. Nd4 Ng3 14. Rh2 0–0 15. Rg2 c6 16. Ne2 g5 17. Nxg3 fxg3 18. Bd2 Qxf3 19. Qxf3 Nxf3 20. d4 Rae8 21. Bd3 d5 22. exd5 cxd5 23. Rf1 Nxd2 24. Kxd2 Kg7 25. Rf5 Rd8 26. Rxg3 Bxg3 27. Rxg5+ Kh6 28. Rxg3 Rg8 29. Rf3 Rg2+ 30. Kc1 Re8 31. Rf1 Re3 32. Bf5 Reg3 33. Bc8 Rg1 34. Rxg1 Rxg1+ 35. Kc2 Rg2+ 36. Kb3 Rg8 37. Bg4 Kg5 38. Kb4 f5 39. Bf3 Rd8 40. Kc5 f4 41. b3 Kh4 42. c4 dxc4 43. Kxc4 Kxh3 44. Kd3 Kg3 45. Bxb7 f3 46. Ke3 Re8+ 47. Kd2 Re2+ 48. Kd1 Rxa2 49. Bxf3 Kxf3 50. d5 Ra5 0–1 Lahde

Marshall Club Handicap Tournament, New York, 1930

Fine started with one point in three games. No other details are available. Gamescores unavailable. Crosstable unavailable.

Manhattan Club Handicap Championship, New York, Summer, 1930

"Edward Schwartz, playing in class B, has been declared the winner of the annual handicap tournament at the Manhattan Chess Club, which has been hanging fire throughout the summer months. His winning score was 16 to 2.

Second prize was awarded to E.A. McGinnis, Class F, who scored 14 to 4. G. J. Belhoff and Reuben Fine were also in line for prizes, but their schedules were not completed." (*ACB* 1930) Fine started with three straight wins, but no other details of his score, or his class, are available. Gamescores unavailable. Crosstable unavailable.

Match with Croney, New York, July, 1930

Fine won both games in a brief encounter with Croney. (Fiala, in preparation) Gamescores unavailable.

	1	2	
Fine	1	1	2
Croney	0	0	0

Match with Forsberg, New York, July, 1930

Fine won all three games of a short match with Forsberg. (Fiala, in preparation) Gamescores unavailable.

	1	2	3	
Fine	1	1	1	3
Forsberg	0	0	0	0

Match with Forsberg, New York, ? August, 1930

Fine won the first game of another match with Forsberg. (Fiala, in preparation) Gamescores unavailable. Crosstable unavailable.

Rice Chess Club, Junior Masters, New York, September–October, 1930

This intriguing tournament took place during September and October at the Isaac L. Rice Progressive Club of 40 Union Square, New York. The other participants were Bartha, Cohen, Dake, Denker, Fajans, Gerrity, Dr. Kline, Kussman, Lessing, MacMurray, Newburger and Reinfeld, but not Schwartz (*contra* Denker and Fiala). First prize, won by Dake (8½–2½, possibly indicating a withdrawal, and not +4 –0 =2 as reported by Bush), was supposed to include a barrel of schmaltz herring, but this was withdrawn before the conclusion of the tournament. By round seven Fine had scored 4½–2½, but a later report, while not giving Fine's score, reported that only Kussman could catch Dake (which he did not). Fine, therefore, must have had at least one further draw or loss. Herman Helms' column of 18 September reported the list of entrants and the result of the first round. Dake reported that this tournament took place in late May, but O'Keefe's research demonstrates that it was played during September and October, probably at the rate of two games a week. Fine's game with Reinfeld reportedly came from a Marshall Club Junior Championship. In view of the coincidence of date and close similarity of title, and in the absence of a mention of the Rice Club tournament in Reinfeld's papers, I am assuming this to be a misattribution. (Denker, Bush, Denker & Parr, Hilbert & Lahde, Ansel *pers comm* and O'Keefe *pers comm*) Crosstable unavailable.

(2) Dake, A—Fine

Rice Club Junior Masters (?), New
Closed Sicilian [B24]

1. e4 c5 2. Nc3 Nc6 3. g3 g6
Nf6 6. d3 0-0 7. 0-0 d6 8.
10. a4 a6 11. Qd2 Re8 12. f4
14. a5! Qd8 The problem with 14
ning a piece. 15. e5! dxe5 16. fx
Dake intended 17 Bf4 and 18 Qe3
17. Bxh6 Bxe5 18. Bf4 Rf8 19
Qc7 21. Nd5 Qd6 22. Ng3 B
Bxd5 25. Bxd5+ e6 Dake state
better 25 ... Kh8 White still scores
Ne4. 26. Ne4! Qe7 27. Nxf6+
Rxf1+ 29. Rxf1 Re8 30. Be4
32. Bxg6 Rd8 33. h4 Kg7 34
1-0 *Washington Post, 5 April 1931*

(3) Reinfeld, F—Fine

Rice Club Junior Masters (?), New
French Defence, Alapin Variation [C

1. e4 e6 2. d4 d5 3. Nc3 Nf6
Nfd7 6. Bxe7 Qxe7 7. Nb5
c5 10. f4 Nc6 11. Nf3 Bd7 12
0-0 14. Ne3 cxd4 15. cxd4
Rfc8 18. Nc2 Qxd2+ 19. Kxd
21. Bxb5 Bxb5 22. a4 Be8 2
Rxc1 25. Kxc1 Nc8 26. Nd3
Ne7 29. g4 Kg7 30. Kd2 h5
Nh6 33. Nh2 Kf8 34. Kf3 K
36. hxg4 Kd8 37. Kh4 Kc7 3
Bd7 40. Ne3 Bc8 41. f5 gxf5
Kb5 44. Ng4 Kxa5 45. Nh6
47. Kg7 b6 48. Na4 b5 49. N
Kxd4 51. Kg6 Kxc5 52. f7 d4
54. Qxc8 Kxe5 55. Qxa6 1-0

14th Marshall C
Championship Pre
October–November, N

There were sixteen entrants for the preliminary tournament. In order to avoid a long qualification event, they

were divided into two groups of eight, the first three placed in each group to go forward to the final. With a slight negative score in his group, Fine failed to qualify for the championship tournament. A second section was won by Arthur Dake (5½–1½), who went on to take the title in the new year (scoring 3½–1½, again *contra* Bush). Second and third places, in the preliminary section, went to Nat Grossman and David Polland. (Information from Jack O'Keefe, who also constructed the crosstable, two missing Reinfeld scores supplied by Andy Ansel; ACB)

	1	2	3	4	5	6	7	8	
	*	1	1	1	1	½	1	1	6½
	0	*	1	½	½	1	1	½	4½
n	0	0	*	1	½	½	1	1	4
	0	½	0	*	½	1	½	1	3½
	0	½	½	½	*	0	1	1	3½
	½	0	½	0	1	*	1	0	3
	0	0	0	½	0	0	*	1	1½
	0	½	0	0	0	1	0	*	1½

NE—Wright, E

CC championship preliminaries, New York (1),
ct.)
of this game is not available. 1-0

IGELOW, H—Fine

CC championship preliminaries, New York (2),
ct.)
nce, Burn Variation [C10]

2. d4 d5 3. Nc3 Nf6 4. Bg5 dxe4 5. Nxe4
Nf3 Be7 7. Nxf6+ Nxf6 8. Bd3 0-0
6? 10. Bxf6 Bxf6 11. Be4 Rb8 12. Qd3 g6
5 14. h5 Bg7 15. hxg6 hxg6 16. Ne5! Bxe5
Re8 18. dxe5 Kf8 19. Qh8+ Ke7 20. Qf6+
0-0-0+ 1-0 *New York Post, October 1930.*

NE—Croney, T

CC championship preliminaries, New York (3),
ct.)
of this game is not available. 0-1

EINFELD, F—Fine

CC championship preliminaries, New York (4),
Nov.)
pening, Steinitz Defence Deferred [C73]

2. Nf3 Nc6 3. Bb5 a6 4. Ba4 d6 5. Bxc6+
d4 exd4 7. Nxd4 Bd7 8. 0-0 Nf6 9. Nc3
Be7 10. b3 0-0 11. Bb2 Re8 12. Qd3 Bf8 13. Rad1
g6 14. Rfe1 Bg7 15. f3 Nh5 16. Bc1 Qh4 17. Nde2
Be5 18. f4

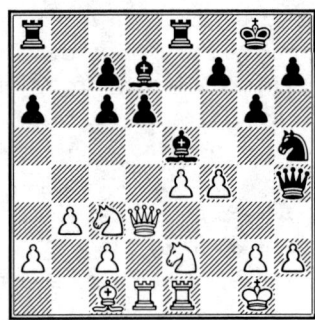

Position after White's 18th move

18 ... Bg7 19. Rf1 Re7 20. Be3 Nf6 21. Bf2 Qh6 22. Bd4 Rae8 23. Ng3 Bg4 24. Rd2 Bc8 25. h3 Bb7 26. e5 dxe5 27. Bxe5 Rd7 28. Qe2 Rxd2 29. Qxd2 Rxe5 30. Qd8+ Re8 31. Qxc7 Ba8 32. Rd1 Nd5 33. Qd7 Rf8 34. Nce2 Nxf4 0−1 *New York Sun Times*, November 1930

(8) FINE—BENTZ, D

Marshall CC championship preliminaries, New York (5), 1930 (Nov.)

The score of this game is not available. **0−1**

(9) FINE—THOLFSEN, E

Marshall CC championship preliminaries, New York (6), 1930 (Nov.)

The score of this game is not available. ½−½

(10) BERNSTEIN, S—FINE

Marshall CC championship preliminaries, New York (7), 1930 (Nov.)

The score of this game is not available. ½−½

Metropolitan Chess League, New York, 1931

In his first preserved outing in America's strongest chess league, formed in 1895, Fine drew an interesting game with W. J. Bryan. In the decisive match of the season he won with Black against Herman Steiner of the Manhattan Chess Club on Board 2, Bernstein beating L. Samuels on Board 1. The Marshall Club won all nine of their matches, amassing 57½ points out of a possible 62. According to the *American Chess Bulletin* other competing teams were Empire City, Stuyvesant, Scandinavian, Columbia, West Side, New York (*sic*), North Jersey and the Philidor Club.

Bryan	½	Fine	½
Steiner	0	Fine	1

(10A) BRYAN, W—FINE

Metropolitan League, New York, 1931
Nimzowitsch Indian Defence, Spielman Variation

1. d4 Nf6 2. c4 e6 3. Nc3 Bb4 4. Qb3 c5 5. dxc5 Nc6 6. Nf3 Ne4 7. Bd2 Nxd2 The Carlsbad Variation. 8. Nxd2 0−0 9. e3 Bxc5 10. Be2 b6 11. Nf3 Bb7 12. 0−0−0 f5 13. Rd2 Qe7 14. Rhd1 Rfd8 15. a3 Rac8 16. Kb1 f4 17. exf4 17 Ne4 is "practically a win" for White.—Bryan Bxf2 18. g3 Be3 19. Rc2 Na5 20. Qa2 Bxf3 21. Bxf3 Nxc4 22. Nd5 Nxa3+ 23. bxa3 exd5 24. Qxd5+ Kh8 25. Qxd7 Qf8 26. Rxc8 Rxc8 27. Bg4 Ra8 28. Ka2 Bc5 29. a4 Be7 30. Qc6 Bf6 31. Be6 a6 32. Rd7 b5 33. Rf7 Qe8 34. Qxe8+ Rxe8 35. axb5 axb5 36. Rb7 g6 37. f5 gxf5 38. Bxf5 Re2+ 39. Kb3 Rxh2 ½−½ *The Chess Correspondent*, 1950, 104 (Supplied by Jack O'Keefe).

(11) STEINER, H—FINE

Metropolitan League, New York, 1931
Slav Defence [D18]

1. d4 Nf6 2. Nf3 d5 3. c4 c6 4. Nc3 dxc4 5. a4 Bf5 6. e3 Nbd7 7. Bxc4 Qc7 8. 0−0 e6 9. Qe2 Be7 10. h3 h6 11. e4 Bh7 12. Bd2 0−0 13. Rac1 Rad8 14. Rfd1 e5 15. d5 Nc5 16. dxc6 bxc6 17. Be3 Rxd1+ 18. Qxd1 Nfxe4 19. Nxe4 Nxe4 20. Bb5 c5 21. Qd3 Bd6 22. b4 Nf6 23. Qa3 e4 24. Nd2 Rd8 25. bxc5 Be5 26. Nf1 Nd5 27. Qb3 Bg6 28. Rd1 Nf4 29. Rxd8+ Qxd8 30. c6 Qh4 31. Bxa7 Nxg2 32. Kxg2 Bh5 33. Ng3 Bf3+ 34. Kh2 Qe7 35. Be3 h5 36. Kg1 h4 37. Ne2 Bc7 38. Kf1 Qe5 39. Qc3 Bxe2+ 0−1 Fiala (in preparation).

Manhattan CC vs Philadelphia, February 23, New York, 1931

The *Bulletin* recorded "Instead of twenty, as last year, Philadelphia sent over eighteen players to do battle with the Manhattan Chess Club in the second of the new series of Washington's Birthday matches contested in Manhattan on February 23. The Manhattans were again powerfully represented and scored at a rate of 2 to 1. The final score gave the Manhattans eight wins, eight draws and two losses, the equivalent of 12 to 6. This was a slightly better showing for Philadelphia than last year, when the Manhattans won by 15 to 5." On this occasion Fine held down the top board ahead of Steiner, Horowitz, Pinkus, MacMurray, Kevitz, and Kupchik among others.

Fine	1	Goldstein	0

(12) FINE—GOLDSTEIN, M

Manhattan CC vs Philadelphia, New York, 1931 (23 Feb.)

The score of this game is not available. **1−0**

City College Alumni–Varsity Chess Match, City College Club, New York, 1931

The *American Chess Bulletin* reported that the varsity team won the match by 6–4. Rosenblatt, Fine, Borowitz, Beckhardt and Hellman winning, while Bernstein and Desind drew. Gamescore unavailable.

Match with Arthur Dake, June, 1931

This is reported as being a two-game match played before Dake left for Europe where he held down board 3, behind Kashdan and Marshall, for the victorious United States team. Annotations to one of the games, identified as game 3, in Casey Bush's biography of Dake, however, make it clear that Fine played White on two occasions. *American Chess Bulletin* states that Dake conceded the odds of the draw, and won two games in succession. Further information from Vlastimil Fiala (in preparation) suggests that the match was to be three games and that Fine would have been declared the winner had he scored at least one and a half points.

	1	2	
Fine	0	0	0
Dake	1	1	2

(13) FINE–DAKE, A

Match, New York (1), 1931 (June)
Nimzowitsch-Indian Defence [E43]

1. d4 Nf6 2. c4 e6 3. Nc3 Bb4 4. e3 b6 5. Bd3 Bb7 6. Nge2 Black did not take the pawn, but White eventually lost after 70 moves. **0–1**

(14) FINE DAKE, A

Match, New York (2), 1931 (June)
Nimzowitsch-Indian Defence [E43]

1. d4 Nf6 2. c4 e6 3. Nc3 Bb4 4. e3 b6 5. Bd3 Bb7 6. Nge2 In our first match game Fine played this same move but I did not play bishop takes pawn, and it took 70 moves for me to win that contest. 6 … Bxg2 In this game, I did my homework with the help of Al Horowitz. We decided that bishop takes pawn gives Black good play. 7. Rg1 Be4 8. Bxe4 This move is an error. Larry Parr, former editor of *Chess Life*, suggested the move 8 Qc2! giving White play for the loss of a pawn. 8 … Nxe4 9. Rxg7 Nxf2 A surprise for White. 10. Qc2 Qh4 11. Kf1 Ng4 After this move White is lost in all variations. The moral of this game is not to play dubious chess openings. 12. Ng3 Qf6+ 13. Kg1 Qxg7 14. Nb5 Na6 15. Qa4 c6 16. Qxa6 cxb5 17. Qb7 Rd8 White resigned. **0–1** Notes by Arthur Dake in Bush, 20–1.

Marshall Chess Club Summer Tournament, New York, June–July, 1931

In his autobiographical games collection Sidney Bernstein recalled that he and Fine tied for first place in this sub-

sidiary club tournament. The summer championship was for players of below championship class, the winners qualifying for the championship tournament which took place around the turn of the year. Andy Ansel (*pers comm*) reports that Reinfeld played five rounds in this competition on 26 June, 11, 16, 18 and 22 July. Crosstable unavailable.

(15) FINE–REINFELD, F

Marshall CC Summer Tournament, New York, 1931 (18 July)
Slav Defence, Exchange Variation [D10]

1. d4 Nf6 2. c4 c6 3. Nc3 d5 4. cxd5 cxd5 5. Bf4 Nc6 6. e3 Bf5 7. Qb3 Na5 8. Bb5+ Bd7 9. Qa4 e6 10. Bxd7+ Nxd7 and White went on to win. **1–0** Reinfeld's papers.

53rd New York State Chess Association Championship, Rome, August 17–22, 1931

Victory in the State championship at Rome was one of Fred Reinfeld's best results. He was a good solid player, which he demonstrated by winning ahead of a talented, largely youthful, entry. Seven of the twelve entries in the championship tournament were from the Marshall Chess Club. At the time Reinfeld was a student of the College of the City of New York, as were Fine, Sidney Bernstein and Robert Willman.

		1	2	3	4	5	6	7	8	9	10	11	12	
1	Reinfeld	*	½	½	1	½	½	½	1	1	1	1	1	8½
2	Fine	½	*	½	½	1	0	½	1	1	1	1	1	8
3	Dake	½	½	*	½	0	½	1	0	1	1	1	1	7
4	Santasiere	0	½	½	*	1	0	1	1	1	0	1	1	7
5	Lessing	½	0	1	0	*	0	0	1	1	1	1	1	6½
6	Bernstein	½	1	½	1	1	*	½	0	0	0	½	1	6
7	Polland	½	½	0	0	1	½	*	½	0	1	1	1	6
8	Grossman	0	0	1	0	0	1	½	*	0	1	1	1	5½
9	Guckemus	0	0	0	0	0	1	1	1	*	1	1	½	5½
10	Adams	0	0	0	1	0	1	0	0	0	*	0	1	3
11	Garfinkel	0	0	0	0	0	½	0	0	0	1	*	1	2½
12	Barron	0	0	0	0	0	0	0	0	½	0	0	*	½

(16) FINE–GROSSMAN, N

New York State Championship, Rome (1), 1931 (18 Aug.)
Nimzowitsch-Indian Defence [E43]

1. d4 Nf6 2. c4 e6 3. Nc3 Bb4 4. e3 b6 5. Bd3 Bb7 6. f3 0–0 7. Nge2 d5 8. 0–0 c5 9. cxd5 exd5 10. Qe1 Nc6 11. Qh4 Re8 12. g4 c4 13. Bc2 g6 14. Nf4 Be7 15. g5 Nd7 16. Nfxd5 Bxg5 17. Qg4 Nf8 18. f4 Bh6 19. f5 Bg7 20. f6 Bh8 21. Ba4 a6 22. Bxc6 Bxc6 23. e4 h5 24. Qh4 Ra7 25. Be3 b5 26. a4 Rd7 27. Ne7+ Rdxe7 28. fxe7 Qxe7 29. Qxe7 Rxe7 30. axb5 axb5

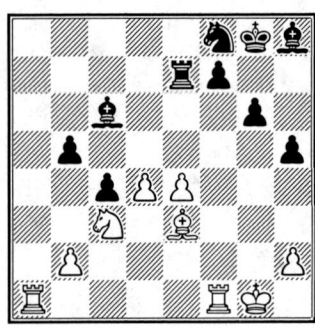

*Position after
Black's 30th move*

31. d5 Bxc3 32. bxc3 Bxd5 33. exd5 Rxe3
34. Ra7 Rxc3 35. Raxf7 Nh7 36. d6 Rd3 37. d7
c3 38. Re7 Nf8 39. Re8 Rxd7 40. Rexf8+ Kg7
41. Rc8 b4 42. Rf4 Rd2 43. Rxb4 c2 44. Rbc4
Kh6 45. h4 Black resigned. 1–0

(17) GARFINKEL, B—FINE

New York State Championship, Rome (2), 1931 (18 Aug.)
Queen's Gambit Accepted [D15]

1. d4 Nf6 2. Nf3 d5 3. c4 c6 4. Nc3 dxc4 5. e3 b5
6. a4 Nd5 7. Ne5 Nxc3 8. bxc3 Qd5 9. axb5 cxb5
10. Ra5 Qb7 11. Be2 Qb6 12. Ra1 Bb7 13. Rb1 Qa6
14. 0–0 f6 15. Nf3 e6 16. Qc2 Be7 17. e4 0–0
18. Bf4 Nd7 19. Bg3 f5

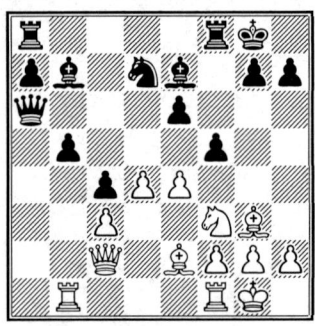

*Position after
Black's 19th move*

20. e5? Be4 21. Qd2 Bxb1 22. Rxb1 Nb6 23. Ng5
Nd5 24. f4 h6 25. Nf3 Rab8 26. Bh4 Bxh4
27. Nxh4 Qa3 28. Rc1 b4 29. cxb4 c3 30. Qe1
Nxf4 31. Bc4 Rbc8 32. Ra1 Rxc4 33. Rxa3 c2
34. Ra1 c1Q White resigned. 0–1

(18) FINE—DAKE, A

New York State Championship, Rome (3), 1931 (19 Aug.)
Vienna Game [C29]

1. e4 e5 2. f4 Nf6 3. Nc3 d5 4. fxe5 Nxe4 5. Nf3
Be7 6. Qe2 f5 7. g3 0–0 8. Bg2 Bc5 9. d3 Bf2+
10. Kf1 Nxc3 11. Qxf2 Ne4 12. Qe3 Nc6 13. c3 h6
14. Kg1 Ng5 15. Nxg5 hxg5 16. Qxg5 Nxe5 17. d4
Nf7 18. Qxd8 Rxd8 19. Bf4 c6 20. h4 Nd6
21. Bxd6 Rxd6 22. Re1 Re6 23. Rxe6 Bxe6 24. Kf2
Kf7 25. Kf3 Bd7 26. Re1 Re8 27. Rxe8 Bxe8

28. Kf4 Kf6 29. Bh3 Bg6 30. b4 b6 31. a3 Bh7
32. Bf1 Bg8 33. Ba6 Be6 34. Bb7 Bd7 35. b5
cxb5 36. Bxd5 g6 37. Bb7 Be8 38. d5 Bf7 39. Bc6
a5 40. d6 Bc4 41. d7 Ke7 42. Kg5 Bd3 43. Kh6
Kd8 44. Kg7 Ke7 45. Kg8 Be2 46. Kh7 Bd3 47. Kg7
b4 48. cxb4 axb4 49. axb4 Be4 50. Bb5 Bc2 51. Kh6
Be4 52. Kg5 Bc2 53. Kf4 Bb3 54. Ke5 Ba2 55. d8Q+
Kxd8 56. Kd6 Bb1 57. Kc6 Ke7 58. Kxb6 Kf6
59. Kc5 g5 60. hxg5+ Kxg5 61. Bc6 Bd3 62. Bf3
Kf6 63. b5 Ke7 64. b6 Kd7 65. Kd5 Kc8 66. Ke5
Kb8 67. Bd5 Bc2 68. Kf4 Bd3 69. Be6 Kb7
70. Bxf5 Be2 71. Be4+ Kxb6 72. Bf3 Bd3 73. Ke5
Kc7 74. Kf6 Kd8 75. g4 Ke8 76. Kg7 Ke7 77. Bd5
Be2 78. g5 Bd3 79. Bg8 Bb5 80. Bf7 Bd3 81. Bg8
Bb5 82. Bf7 Bd3 83. Bb3 Be4 84. Bc4 Bf5
85. Bg8 Bd7 86. Bf7 Bf5 87. Bc4 Be4 88. Ba2
Bd3 89. Bd5 Bf5 90. Ba2 Bd3 91. Bd5 Bf5
92. Bg8 Bd7 93. Bf7 Bf5 94. Bb3 Be4 95. Bg8
Bc6 96. Bb3 Be4 97. Bg8 Agreed drawn. ½–½

(19) BERNSTEIN, S—FINE

New York State Championship, Rome (4), 1931 (19 Aug.)
Sicilian Defence, Classical Dragon [B74]

1. e4 c5 2. Nf3 Nc6 3. d4 cxd4 4. Nxd4 Nf6
5. Nc3 d6 6. Be2 g6 7. Be3 Bg7 8. 0–0 0–0
9. Nb3 Bd7 10. f4 Rc8 11. Bf3 a6 12. a4 Na5
13. Nd2 Nc4 14. Nxc4 Rxc4 15. a5 Qc8 16. h3 h5
17. e5 dxe5 18. fxe5 Nh7 19. Nd5 Qe8 20. Nb6
Rc7 21. Bf4 Be6 22. Qe2 Qb5 23. Qxb5 axb5
24. Rfd1 g5 25. Bg3 g4 26. hxg4 Ng5 27. c3
Nxf3+ 28. gxf3 hxg4 29. fxg4 Bxg4 30. Rd5 b4
31. Rd4 bxc3 32. Rxg4 cxb2 33. Rf1 f5 34. Rc4
Rxc4 35. Nxc4 f4 36. Bf2 Rc8 37. Nxb2 Bxe5
38. Nd3 Bd6 39. Bb6 Kf7 40. Nxf4 Ke8 41. Ne6
Kd7 42. Nf8+ Ke8 43. Ne6 Kd7 44. Nd4 Rg8+
45. Kh1 Rh8+ 46. Kg2 Rh2+ 47. Kf3 Ra2 48. Ke4
e5 49. Nb5 Bb4 50. Rf7+ Kc6 51. Na7+ Kd6
52. Nc8+ Ke6 53. Rxb7 Bxa5 54. Ra7 Rc2 55. Bxa5
Rc4+ 56. Kd3 Rxc8 57. Bc3 e4+ 58. Kd4 e3
59. Bb4 e2 60. Re7+ Kf5 61. Rxe2 An adjourned
position was reached against Sidney Bernstein, where he had
rook and bishop against my rook. Neither of us knew the
best lines, but there was a gifted player there, David Polland,
who was quite expert in the endings. He coached us both,
just to make sure that he was fair, and we resumed play. We
followed the analysis for a long time, he threatening and I
defending in the prescribed manner. Unfortunately after
about forty or fifty moves (*sic*) without pawns had been
made I overlooked the best defence against a mating net,
and lost. RF 61 ... Rd8+ 62. Kc4 Kf4 63. Bc5 Kf3
64. Re7 Kf4 65. Bd4 Kf5 66. Kd3 Rg8 67. Ke2
Rg3 68. Kf2 Ra3 69. Re8 Rb3 70. Be3 Rb1 71. Kf3
Rf1+ 72. Bf2 Rb1 73. Rf8+ Ke5 74. Bg3+ Ke6
75. Bf2 Ke5 76. Ra8 Rb5 77. Rh8 Kd5 78. Rd8+
Ke5 79. Bd4+ Kf5 80. Rf8+ Ke6 81. Ke4 Rb1
82. Rf6+ Ke7 83. Rh6 Re1+ 84. Kd5 Rd1 85. Rh7+

Kf8 86. Ke5 Kg8 87. Rd7 Rc1 88. Kf5 Kf8 89. Be5 Kg8 90. Bf6 Rc2 91. Kg6 Rg2+ 92. Bg5 Rf2 93. Rd1 Rf3 94. Bh4 Rf4 A tactical slip, perhaps caused by tiredness. The game would still have been drawn after 94 ... Rf7. AW 95. Bf6 Rg4+ 96. Bg5 Black resigned. He cannot avoid Rd8+ without giving up his rook. 1–0 Notebook 1; Bernstein in "Combat," 3; Fine 1958, x.

(20) FINE—SANTASIERE, A

New York State Championship Rome (5), 1931 (19 Aug.)
Nimzowitsch-Indian Defence [E43]

1. d4 Nf6 2. c4 e6 3. Nc3 Bb4 4. e3 b6 5. Bd3 Bb7 6. f3 0–0 7. Nge2 c5 8. 0–0 d5 9. cxd5 Nxd5 10. Nxd5 exd5 11. a3 Ba5 12. dxc5 bxc5 13. Qc2 h6 14. Qxc5 Bb6 15. Qb4 Nc6 16. Qf4 Qg5 17. Qxg5 hxg5 18. Bb5 Na5 19. Ba4 Ba6 20. Re1 Rac8 21. Nd4 Rc4 22. b3 Rc7 23. Bb2 Nb7 24. Nf5 f6 25. b4 g6 26. Nd4 Kf7 27. b5 Nc5 28. Bc2 Bb7 29. a4 Ba5 30. Red1 f5 31. Ba3 Re8 32. b6 axb6 33. Nb5 Rd7 34. e4 fxe4 35. fxe4 d4 36. Rxd4 Rxd4 37. Nxd4 Bxe4 Agreed drawn. ½–½

(21) ADAMS, E—FINE

New York State Championship, Rome (6), 1931 (20 Aug.)
Sicilian Scheveningen [B84]

1. e4 c5 2. Nf3 e6 3. Nc3 d6 4. d4 cxd4 5. Nxd4 Nf6 6. Be3 a6 7. Be2 Be7 8. Qd2 0–0 9. 0–0 b5 10. a3 Bb7 11. Bf3 Nbd7 12. Rae1 Nc5 13. Bg5 Nfxe4 14. Bxe4 Bxg5 15. f4 Nxe4 16. Nxe4 Bh6 17. Kh1 g6 18. Nf3 Bg7 19. c3 Bd5 20. Rf2 Qb6 21. Neg5 Rad8 22. h4 h6 23. Nh3 Bxf3 24. Rxf3 d5 25. Qe2 d4 26. h5 dxc3 27. bxc3 Rc8 28. hxg6 fxg6 29. Qxe6+ Qxe6 30. Rxe6 Rf6 31. f5 gxf5 32. Rxf6 Bxf6 33. Rxf5 Bxc3 34. Rf2 Be5 35. g4 Rc3 36. Ng1 Bd4 37. Rd2 Bxg1 38. Kxg1 Rxa3 39. Kf2 b4 White resigned. 0–1

(22) FINE—BARRON, T

New York State Championship, Rome (7), 1931 (20 Aug.)
English Opening, Symmetrical Variation [A30]

1. Nf3 Nf6 2. c4 c5 3. g3 g6 4. b3 b6 5. Bg2 Bb7 6. Bb2 Bg7 7. 0–0 0–0 8. d3 d6 9. Nbd2 Nbd7 10. e4 e5 11. Qe2 Qe7 12. Ne1 Ne8 13. Nc2 Nc7 14. Rae1 Rae8 15. f4 f5 16. exf5 Bxg2 17. Qxg2 Rxf5 18. d4 Qd8 19. Ne4 Nf8 20. dxe5 dxe5 21. Rd1 Nd7 22. Nd6 exf4 23. Bxg7 Kxg7 24. Nxf5+ gxf5 25. Qc6 Re7 26. Rxf4 Ne5 27. Rxd8 Nxc6 28. Rd6 Nd4 29. Nxd4 cxd4 30. Rfxd4 Ne6 31. Rd7 Kf6 32. R4d6 Kf7 33. Rxe7+ Kxe7 34. Rxe6+ Kxe6 35. Kf2 a5 36. Ke3 Ke5 37. a3 h6 38. b4 axb4 39. axb4 h5

40. h4 f4+ 41. gxf4+ Kf5 42. c5 bxc5 43. bxc5 Kg4 44. c6 Kxh4 45. c7 Black resigned. 1–0

(23) FINE—REINFELD, F

New York State Championship, Rome (8), 1931 (21 Aug.)
Queen's Gambit Declined, Semi-Tarrasch Variation [D40]

1. c4 Nf6 2. Nf3 e6 3. d4 d5 4. Nc3 c5 5. e3 Nc6 6. Bd3 dxc4 7. Bxc4 Be7 8. 0–0 0–0 9. dxc5 Bxc5 10. a3 Qxd1 11. Rxd1 a6 12. b4 Be7 13. Bb2 b5 14. Bb3 Bb7 15. Kf1 Rfd8 16. Ke2 Rxd1 17. Rxd1 Rd8 18. Rxd8+ Bxd8 ½–½

(24) FINE—LESSING, N

New York State Championship, Rome (10), 1931 (21 Aug.)
English Opening/Benko Gambit [A15]

1. Nf3 Nf6 2. c4 b6 3. g3 Bb7 4. Bg2 d6 5. 0–0 Nbd7 6. d4 c5 7. Nc3 g6 8. d5 Bg7 9. e4 0–0 10. Bd2 a6 11. Qe2 b5 12. cxb5 axb5 13. Nxb5 Ba6 14. a4

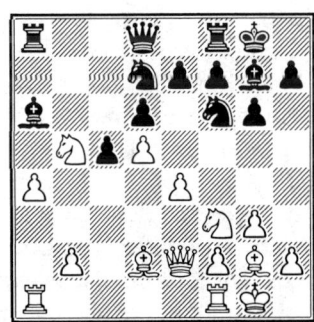

Position after White's 14th move

14 ... Qb6 15. Bc3 Rab8 16. Nd2 Ne8 17. Nc4 Bxb5 18. Nxb6 Bxe2 19. Nxd7 Bxf1 20. Nxb8 Bxg2 21. Kxg2 Bxc3 22. bxc3 Nf6 23. Rb1 Nxe4 24. a5 Nxc3 25. a6 Nxd5 26. a7 Nc7 27. Rb7 1–0 Fiala QCH3 1999, 442 (from *Brooklyn Daily Eagle*, September 3, 1931).

(25) GUCKEMUS—FINE

New York State Championship, Rome (11), 1931 (22 Aug.)
Sicilian Defence [B40]

1. e4 c5 2. Nf3 e6 3. c3 Nc6 4. Na3 d5 5. e5 Nge7 6. Bb5 a6 7. Qa4 Bd7 8. 0–0 axb5 9. Nxb5 Qb8 10. Qxa8 Qxa8 11. Nc7+ Kd8 12. Nxa8 Nc8 13. a4 Na5 14. d4 c4 15. Bg5+ Be7 16. Bxe7+ Nxe7 17. Nd2 Bc6 18. Ra3 Kd7 19. Nb6+ Kc7 20. b4 cxb3 21. Nxb3 Kxb6 22. Rb1 Nxb3 23. a5+ Kc7 24. Rbxb3 Ra8 25. g4 Ng6 26. Kg2 f6 27. exf6 gxf6 28. Kg3 Ne7 29. f4 Nc8 30. h4 Nd6 31. Ra1 Bb5 32. Rba3 Rg8 33. g5 h6 34. Re1 Ne4+ 35. Kg4 fxg5 36. hxg5 hxg5 37. fxg5 Rxg5+ 38. Kf4 Kd6 39. Rb3 Ba6 40. Rb6+ Ke7 41. c4 Rf5+ 42. Kg4 Nf6+ 43. Kh3 dxc4 44. Rbxe6+ Kf7 45. R6e5

Rxe5 46. Rxe5 c3 47. Rc5 Ne4 48. Rc7+ Ke6
49. Kg2 Kd6 50. Rh7 Bf1+ 51. Kxf1 c2 52. Ke2
c1Q 53. Rxb7 Qd2+ 54. Kf3 Qf2+ 55. Kg4 Nf6+
0–1 Fiala *QCH3* 1999, 442 (from *Brooklyn Daily Eagle*,
September 10, 1931)

Match with Fred Reinfeld, New York, July 25—August 9, 1931

Fred Reinfeld's papers indicate that the youngsters contested a six game match in the late summer. Fine won three games to Reinfeld's two, the other game being drawn. In addition to the match Fine and Reinfeld were involved in a consultation game on 17 September. Gamescores unavailable. Crosstable unavailable.

15th Marshall Club Championship, New York, October 1931–February 1932

Fine won the championship of the Marshall Chess Club, which had recently moved into new premises at 23 West Tenth Street, for the first time with a score of +10 =1 –2. Arthur Dake was unable to defend his title. Reuben's opponents, however, included two of his teammates from college and eight players whose careers included wins in either, or both, the Marshall Club championship or the New York State Chess Association championship. Fred Reinfeld defeated Reuben in the eleventh round, but it was insufficient for him to take the title as Fine drew one fewer game than his main rival, while Reinfeld lost to Rudolph Smirka and Nat Grossman.

		1	2	3	4	5	6	7	8	9	10	11	12	13	14	
1	Fine	*	0	1	1	1	1	0	1	1	1	1	1	½	1	10½
2	Reinfeld	1	*	½	0	1	½	1	0	1	1	1	1	1	1	10
3=	Hanauer	0	½	*	0	½	0	1	1	1	1	1	1	1	1	9
3=	Smirka	0	1	1	*	0	0	1	1	½	1	1	½	1	1	9
3=	Tholfsen	0	0	½	1	*	0	½	1	1	1	1	1	1	1	9
6	Bernstein	0	½	1	1	1	*	½	0	0	1	1	½	1	1	8½
7	Santasiere	1	0	0	0	½	½	*	½	½	1	0	1	1	1	7
8	Grossman	0	1	0	0	0	1	½	*	½	½	0	1	½	1	6
9	Cass	0	0	0	½	0	1	½	½	*	0	0	1	1	1	5½
10=	Dunst	0	0	0	0	0	0	0	½	1	*	1	1	½	1	5
10=	Levenstein	0	0	0	0	0	0	1	1	1	0	*	0	1	1	5
12	Bigelow	0	0	0	½	0	½	0	0	0	0	1	*	1	1	4
13	Croney	½	0	0	0	0	0	0	½	0	½	0	0	*	1	2½
14	Morton	0	0	0	0	0	0	0	0	0	0	0	0	0	*	0

(26) FINE—MORTON, H

Marshall Chess Club championship 1931/2, New York (1), 1931 (31 Oct.)

Gamescore unavailable. 1–0

(27) FINE—HANAUER, M

Marshall Chess Club championship 1931/2, New York (2), 1931 (7 Nov.)

Queen's Gambit Declined, Cambridge Springs Defence [D52]

1. d4 d5 2. c4 c6 3. Nf3 Nf6 4. Nc3 e6 5. Bg5
Nbd7 6. e3 Qa5 7. cxd5 Nxd5 8. Qb3 Bb4 9. Rc1
0–0 10. Bd3 Nxc3 11. bxc3 Ba3 12. Rd1 b6 13. 0–0
Ba6 14. c4 h6 15. Bf4 Be7 16. e4 Qh5 17. e5 Rfd8
18. h3 g5 19. Be3 Bb7 20. Be4 f5 21. exf6 Nxf6
22. c5 Nxe4 23. Qxe6+ Qf7 24. Qxe4 Rd5 25. Ne5
Qg7 26. f4 Rf8 27. fxg5 Bxg5 28. Rxf8+ Qxf8
29. Bxg5 hxg5 30. Rf1 Qh6 31. Ng4 1–0 Fiala *QCH3*
1999, 442 from *Brooklyn Daily Eagle*, December 3, 1931.

(28) SANTASIERE, A—FINE

Marshall Chess Club championship 1931/2, New York (3), 1931 (14 Nov.)

English Opening [A10]

1. c4 d5 2. cxd5 Qxd5 3. Nc3 Qd8 4. Nf3 g6 5. d4
Bg7 6. e4 Nf6 7. Bc4 c5 8. d5 0–0 9. h3 b5
10. Nxb5 Nxe4 11. 0–0 a6 12. Na3 Bb7 13. Qb3
Ra7 14. Bf4 Nd7 15. Rfe1 Nd6 16. Rad1 Nb6
17. Be3 Qc7 18. Be2 Rd8 19. Nh2 Ba8 20. Bf3 Nf5
21. Nf1 Bd4 22. Nc2 Bxd5 23. Bxd5 Rxd5
24. Nxd4 cxd4 25. Rc1 Qd6 26. Bd2 Rc7 27. Qd3
Rb5 28. b3 Nd5 29. Rxc7 Qxc7 30. Rc1 Qb7
31. Ng3 Nde3?! 32. fxe3 Nxg3 33. exd4 Ne4
34. Bh6 Rh5? 35. Qxe4 1–0 Denker & Parr, 289; Fiala
QCH3 1999, 443 from *Brooklyn Daily Eagle*, December 3,
1931.

(29) GROSSMAN, N—FINE

Marshall Chess Club championship 1931/2, New York (4), 1931 (?21 Nov.)

Réti Opening [A09]

1. Nf3 d5 2. c4 dxc4 3. Na3 c5 4. Nxc4 Nc6 5. g3
f6 6. Bg2 e5 7. 0–0 Be6 8. b3 Nge7 9. Bb2 Nd5
10. d3 Be7 11. e3 0–0 12. Qe2 Qe8 13. Nh4 g5
14. Nf5 Rd8 15. Nxe7+ Qxe7 16. Rfd1 Bf7 17. h4
Bg6 18. hxg5 fxg5 19. Qg4 Ndb4 20. Be4 Nxd3
21. Rxd3 Rxd3 22. Bxc6 bxc6 23. Nxe5 Rd5
24. Qc4 Qe6 25. Ng4 Kf7 26. Qa4 Ra8 27. Qa6
Qxg4 28. Qb7+ Rd7 29. Qxa8 Be4 30. Qh8 Rd1+
31. Kh2 Rh1+ 32. Rxh1 Qh5+ 0–1 Fiala *QCH3* 1999,
443 from *Brooklyn Daily Eagle*, December 10, 1931.

(29A) THOLFSEN, E—FINE

Marshall Chess Club championship 1931/2, New York (5), 1931 (28 Nov.)

Gamescore unavailable. 0–1

(30) BERNSTEIN, S—FINE

Marshall Chess Club championship 1931/2, New York (6), 1931 (?5 Dec.)

Italian Game [C54]

1. e4 e5 2. Nf3 Nc6 3. Bc4 Bc5 4. c3 Nf6 5. d4 exd4 6. cxd4 Bb4+ 7. Nc3 Nxe4 8. 0-0 Nxc3 9. bxc3 d5 10. Bb5 Be7 11. Rb1 0-0 12. Bd3 Bg4 13. Rxb7 Bd6 14. h3 Bh5 15. Qa4 Bxf3 16. Qxc6 Qh4 17. Re1 Rad8 18. Kf1 Bg3 19. fxg3 Qxg3 20. Rb2 Rd6 21. Qe8 Be4 22. Qxf8+ Kxf8 23. Rb8+ Ke7 24. Bxe4 dxe4 25. Ba3 e3 26. Bxd6+ Kxd6 27. Re2 f5 28. Rf8 f4 29. Kg1 Qg5 30. Kf1 Ke7 31. Rc8 Qg3 32. Rxc7+ Kd8 33. Rf7 Qh2 34. Rc2 Qh1+ 35. Ke2 Qxg2+ 36. Kd3 Qg6+ 0-1 *Brooklyn Daily Eagle*, 21 January 1932; Fiala (in preparation).

(30A) FINE—SMIRKA, R

Marshall Chess Club championship 1931/2, New York (7), 1931 (12 Dec.)

Gamescore unavailable. 1-0

(30B) FINE—CASS, A

Marshall Chess Club championship 1931/2, New York (8), 1931 (27 Dec.)

Gamescore unavailable. 1-0

(30C) BIGELOW, H—FINE

Marshall Chess Club championship 1931/2, New York (9), 1932 (?2 Jan.)

Gamescore unavailable. 0-1

(30D) FINE—LEVENSTEIN, R

Marshall Chess Club championship 1931/2, New York (10), 1932 (9 Jan.)

Queen's Gambit Declined, Slav [D18]

1. d4 Nf6 2. c4 c6 3. Nc3 d5 4. Nf3 dxc4 5. a4 Bf5 6. e3 Na6 7. Bxc4 Nb4 8. 0-0 e6 9. Qe2 Be7 10. e4 Bg4 11. Rd1 Qa5 12. h3 Bh5 13. g4 Bg6 14. Ne5 0-0-0 15. Bf4 Nd7 16. d5! exd5 [16 ... Nxe5!? Fritz] 17. exd5 Nxe5 18. Bxe5 Rhe8 19. Qf3 f6 20. Bg3 Bc5 21. Rac1 a6 22. h4 h6 23. g5! hxg5 24. Qg4+ f5 25. Qxg5 Bh7 26. Qh5 Rh8 27. dxc6 bxc6 28. Qf7 Rhe8 29. Rxd8+ Qxd8 30. Rd1 1-0 *Brooklyn Daily Eagle*, 28 January 1932 (Lahde).

(31) REINFELD, F—FINE

Marshall Chess Club championship 1931/2, New York (11), 1932 (23 Jan.)

Queen's Gambit Declined, Exchange Variation [D65]

1. Nf3 d5 2. d4 Nf6 3. c4 e6 4. Bg5 Nbd7 5. e3 Be7 6. Nc3 0-0 7. Rc1 c6 8. Qc2 a6 9. cxd5 exd5 10. Bd3 Qc7?? 11. Bxh7+ Nxh7 12. Bxe7 Re8 13. Bh4 Qf4 14. 0-0 Qg4 15. Bg3 Ndf6 16. Ne5 Qh5 17. Qb3 Ng5 18. f3 Ne6 19. Na4 Qh6 20. Nb6 Ra7 21. Rfe1 Ng5 22. Nxc8 Rxc8 23. Qb6 Raa8 24. h4 1-0 Denker & Parr, 303.

(31A) FINE—DUNST, T

Marshall Chess Club championship 1931/2, New York (12), 1932 (30 Jan.)

Gamescore unavailable. 1-0

(31B) CRONEY—FINE

Marshall Chess Club championship 1931/2, New York (13), 1932 (12 Feb.)

Gamescore unavailable. ½-½

Intercollegiate Championships, New York, 28–31 December, 1931

American Chess Bulletin reported the contest was held in the rooms of the Marshall Chess Club. Fine Played on Board 1 and made a clean sweep against B. Goldman of Brooklyn (Milton Avin top board player for Brooklyn, who finished with +3 –1 =1, did not play in this match), Ralph W. Borsodi, Jr., of Columbia, Milton Paul of Pittsburgh, Abraham Horwitz of Brown, H. D. Cutler of N.Y.U. and J. Rappaport of Pennsylvania. The rest of the team, which scored +23 =1 –0, comprised Sidney Bernstein, Nathan Beckhardt and Robert Levenstein. Henry Nissnewitz, the substitute, did not play. The team held for the year an "unique" trophy, donated by Harold M. Phillips, in addition to their individual medals, awarded by the same in his capacity as President of the Intercollegiate Chess League.

Bernstein relates the tale of the draw in his autobiography *Combat: My 50 Years at the Chessboard*—"The next event was the Intercollegiate Team Tourney. Reuben and I were on the City College Team—he at first board, I at second. With eight teams in all [sic], four boards per team, the maximum score was of course 28 points [sic]. The games were played mornings during the Christmas holidays. One morning I was awakened by my mother, who told me there was a phone call for me. My caller was a furious Reuben Fine, who informed me that the elapsed time on my clock was almost one hour. (In those days there was no time forfeit after one hour—only after two hours!) Without stopping to eat breakfast or to shave, I grabbed my overcoat and dashed to the club (by bus and subway—the trip took close to an hour!). When I finally appeared at the club, my opponent (Columbia University) claimed a time forfeit, pointing out that the hour hand and minute hand of the chess clock were both at 12 o'clock. The referee (Frank Marshall) ruled that I still had approximately 40 seconds. Reuben, who had an easily won game and plenty of extra time, sat down in my chair and kept score for me. I stood at the table, not daring to start removing my coat, and replied instantaneously to my adversary's moves (he had White). Playing the Budapest Defense to his Queen Pawn opening, I rattled off moves in rapid-fire style. My opponent could not have been a Psychology Major—he contented himself with playing a well-known line! I of course kept exchanging pieces whenever possible! After 38 moves, my aghast partner proposed a draw—which I of course accepted! I had used 37 seconds! ... When Fine grumbled that I had spoiled a 'no-hitter', I retorted that 27½–½ [sic] was absolutely overwhelming, far superior to a football score of 28–0! [sic]."

Apart from the occasional lapses of memory, this is slightly at odds with the account in the *American Chess Bulletin* which recorded that "Bernstein finished with 5½–½. His drawn game in the second round with W. G. Madow, Columbia, '32, was protested by the latter on the ground of infringement of the time limit rule. On the last day the Blue and White manager withdrew the protest before President Phillips had rendered a decision on the merits of the case and the game went on the record as a draw." Bernstein's version has the feeling of a tale that has improved somewhat in the telling, but containing a core of truth. It is worth noting that Madow also scored 5½–½.

Goldman	0	Fine	1
Fine	1	Borsodi	0
Paul	0	Fine	1

City College had the bye in round four

Fine	1	Horwitz	0
Cutler	0	Fine	1
Fine	1	Rappaport	0

(32) GOLDMAN, B—FINE

Intercollegiate Team Tournament, Marshall CC, New York (1), 1931 (28 Dec.)
French Defence, Classical Exchange Variation [C01]

1. e4 e6 2. d4 d5 3. Nc3 Nf6 4. exd5 exd5 5. Bd3 Bd6 6. Bg5 c6 7. h3 0–0 8. Nge2 Be6 9. 0–0 Na6 10. a3 c5 11. Bxa6 bxa6 12. dxc5 Bxc5 13. Nf4 h6 14. Bxf6 Qxf6 15. Nfxd5 Qe5 16. Qf3 Bd6 17. Rfe1 Qh2+ 18. Kf1 Rae8 19. Ne2 Bxd5 20. Qxd5 Qh1+ 21. Ng1 Bh2 0–1 Fiala QCH3 1999, 443–4.

(33) FINE—BORSODI, R

Intercollegiate Team Tournament, Marshall CC, New York (2), 1931 (29 Dec.)
Queen's Gambit Declined [D63]

1. d4 d5 2. c4 e6 3. Nf3 Nf6 4. Bg5 Nbd7 5. Nc3 Be7 6. e3 0–0 7. Rc1 a6 8. c5 c6 9. Bd3 Re8 10. 0–0 Nf8 11. Ne5 Bd7 12. f4 Rc8 13. Rf3 Rc7 14. Rh3 g6 15. Qf3 Bc8 16. Rf1 Bd7 17. Rh6 Kg7 18. Qh3 Bc8 19. g4 Ng8 20. Nxf7 1–0

(34) PAUL, M—FINE

Intercollegiate Team Tournament, Marshall CC, New York (3), 1931 (29 Dec.)

Sicilian Defence. The score of this game is not available. 0–1

(35) FINE—HORWITZ, A

Intercollegiate Team Tournament, Marshall CC, New York (5), 1931 (30 Dec.)

Queen's Gambit Declined. The score of this game is not available. 1–0

(36) CUTLER, H—FINE

Intercollegiate Team Tournament, Marshall CC, New York (6), 1931 (31 Dec.)

Queen's Gambit Declined. The score of this game is not available. 0–1

(37) FINE—RAPPAPORT, J

Intercollegiate Team Tournament, Marshall CC, New York (7), 1931 (31 Dec.)
Barnes Opening [A00]

1. f3!? d5 2. e4 e5 3. Nc3 c6 4. d4 dxe4 5. dxe5 Qxd1+ 6. Nxd1 exf3 7. gxf3?! Be6 8. Bh3 Bd5 9. Ne3 Bc5 10. c4 Bxe3?! 11. cxd5 Bxc1 12. Rxc1 Nd7 13. f4 cxd5 14. Rc7 Nb6 15. Rxb7 Ne7 16. Ne2 Nc6 17. Rg1 g6 18. Kf2 Ne7 19. Rc1 Nc4 20. b3 Na5 21. Rxe7+ Kxe7 22. Rc5 Nxb3 23. axb3 a5 24. Rc7+ Ke8 25. Nc3 Rb8 26. Nxd5 Kf8 27. e6 f5 28. Nf6 1–0 Fiala QCH3 1999, 444.

New York Metropolitan League, April, 1932

Fine lost to both Bloch and Alexander Kevitz, the latter in the match between the Manhattan Chess Club and the Marshall Club. In a rather wild and woolly Dutch Defence Fine, playing with the black pieces against Kevitz, overlooked a saving resource and resigned in a drawn position. Both players were in terrible time trouble. Other teams participating in the league were Hungaria International, Hungarian Workers, Rice Progressive, City College, New York University, Staten Island, Scandinavian, Empire City, West Side and Gramercy. The Marshall Chess Club, nevertheless, retained the Metropolitan Chess League title by winning all eleven of their matches.

Bloch	1	Fine	0
Kevitz	1	Fine	0

(38) BLOCH—FINE

Metropolitan League, New York, 1932 (April)
Scottish Opening [C45]

1. e4 e5 2. Nf3 Nc6 3. d4 exd4 4. Nxd4 Bc5 5. Be3 Qf6 6. c3 Nge7 7. f3 0–0 8. Bc4 d5 9. Nxc6 Bxe3 10. Nxe7+ Qxe7 11. Bxd5 Be6 12. Qe2 Qg5 13. Bxe6 fxe6 14. Nd2 Rad8 15. 0–0–0 Rxd2 16. Rxd2 Rd8 17. Rhd1 h6 18. Kc2 Rxd2+ 19. Rxd2 Bxd2 20. Qxd2 Qa5 21. Qd7 Qxa2 22. Qc8+ Kh7 23. Qxb7 Qc4 24. Qxa7 Qe2+ 25. Kb1 Qxg2 26. Qxc7 Qxf3 27. Qc4 e5 28. b4 h5 29. b5 Qh1+ 30. Kb2 Qxh2+ 31. Ka3 Qf2 32. Qd5 Qf6 33. Qc6 h4 34. Qxf6 gxf6 35. b6 h3 36. b7 h2 37. b8Q h1Q 38. Qb7+ Kg6 39. Qd5 Kg5 40. c4 Qa1+ 41. Kb3 Qb1+ 42. Ka4 Qa2+ 43. Kb5 Kf4 44. c5 Qxd5? 45. exd5 e4 46. d6 e3 47. d7 e2 48. d8Q e1Q 49. Qxf6+ Kg4 50. c6 Qb1+ 51. Kc5 Qc2+ 52. Kd6 Qd2+ 53. Ke7 Kh5 54. Qe5+ Kh4 55. c7 Qb4+ 56. Kd8 Qb6 57. Kd7 Qa7 58. Qe7+ Kh5 59. Qb4 1–0 *New York Sun, 8 April 1932.*

(39) KEVITZ, A—FINE

Metropolitan League, New York, 1932 (16 April)
Dutch Defence [A90]

1. c4 f5 2. d4 Nf6 3. g3 e6 4. Bg2 Bb4+ 5. Nc3 White could play 5 Bd2 to avoid the possibility of doubled c-pawns, in fact he does nothing to prevent this is in the following moves either. **5 ... 0–0 6. Nf3 Nc6 7. 0–0 Bxc3 8. bxc3** White has allowed Black to achieve his first strategic object in this variation. **8 ... Ne4 9. Qd3 b6 10. Ba3 Re8 11. d5 Na5 12. Bb4 Nc5 13. Qd4 d6 14. dxe6 Nxe6 15. Qd2 Bb7 16. Bxa5 bxa5 17. Rab1 Be4 18. Rb5 c6 19. Rb2 Nc5 20. Nd4 Bxg2 21. Kxg2 Qd7 22. Rfb1 Qf7 23. Nxc6 Qxc4 24. Qxd6 Na4 25. Rb7 Qe4+ 26. Kg1 Nxc3 27. h3 f4 28. Qc7 Qg6 29. Ne5 Rxe5 30. Qxc3 Rae8 31. Qc4+ Kh8 32. Qxf4 Rxe2 33. Rb8 h6 34. Rxe8+ Rxe8 35. Rc1 Qe6 36. Kh2 Qxa2**

The victorious College of the City of New York intercollegiate chess team of 1931 was composed entirely of young members of the Marshall Chess Club. Standing (left to right) Sidney Bernstein, Nathan Beckhardt, Robert Levenstein, seated Reuben Fine.

37. Rc7 Kg8 38. Qd4 Black resigned. Howell pointed out that 38 ... Re5! would draw after 39 Qxe5 Qxf2+. White can also try 39 Rxg7+ Kxg7 40 Qxe5+, when Kf7 draws. **1–0** ACB 1932, 69–70.

Match with Fred Reinfeld, New York, June, 1932

Fred Reinfeld's papers indicate that the friends contested a two game match in the spring. One of the games being played on 4 June. Reinfeld won one game, the other was drawn. Gamescores unavailable. Crosstable unavailable.

Match with Herman Steiner, June ?–July 18, 1932

By holding a slightly inferior middlegame and simplifying to an equal ending, Fine was able to share the point in the 10th game of a hard fought match and thus come out the winner by the odd point over the reserve player of the victorious United States chess team of the Prague 1931 Olympiad. The second game of this match is the first recorded in the second of the notebooks, and is so numbered. German algebraic notation is used. The base of the second page is inscribed Gift/Reuben Fine/Oct. 10. 1945.

	1	2	3	4	5	6	7	8	9	10	
Fine	½	1	½	0	1	1	0	0	1	½	5½
Steiner	½	0	½	1	0	0	1	1	0	½	4½

(40) STEINER, H—FINE

match, New York (1), 1932 (June)
Bogolyubov-Indian Defence [E16]

1. d4 Nf6 2. Nf3 e6 3. c4 Bb4+ 4. Bd2 Bxd2+ 5. Qxd2 b6 6. g3 Bb7 7. Bg2 0–0 8. Nc3 d6 9. 0–0 Nbd7 10. Rfe1 Qe7 11. e4 e5 12. Rad1 Rfe8 13. Nh4 g6 14. f4 Rad8 15. Nd5 Nxd5 16. exd5 Qf6 17. Bh3 Bc8 18. Qe3 e4 19. Qa3 h6 20. Bg2 g5 21. fxg5 hxg5 22. Rf1 Qh8 23. Nf5 Nf6 24. Ne3 Ng4 25. h3 Nh6 26. g4 f5 27. gxf5 Qf6 28. Ng4 Nxg4 29. hxg4 Rd7 30. Qe3 Rh7 31. Rfe1 Ba6 32. b3 b5 33. cxb5 Bxb5 34. Bxe4 Qh6 35. Rd2 Qh4 36. f6 Kf8 37. Rg2 Bd3 38. Bxd3 Qxe1+ 39. Qxe1 Rxe1+ 40. Kf2 Rhh1 41. Rg3 Ra1 42. Re3 Rxa2+ 43. Kg3 Raa1 44. Re6 Kf7 45. Bb5 Rhe1 46. Be8+ Kf8 47. Bg6 a5 48. Kf2 Rf1+ 49. Kg2 Rae1 50. Re7 Rg1+ 51. Kh2 Rh1+ 52. Kg2 Regl+ 53. Kf2 Rf1+ 54. Kg2 Rhg1+ 55. Kh2 Rxf6 56. Re8+ Kg7 57. Kxg1 Kxg6 58. Rg8+ Kh6 59. Rh8+ Kg6 60. Rg8+ Kh6 61. Rh8+ Kg7 62. Rc8 Rf4 63. Rxc7+ Kf6 64. Rd7 Rxg4+ 65. Kf2 Rxd4 66. Rxd6+ Ke5 67. Re6+ Kf5 68. Rd6 Ke5 69. Re6+ Kf5 70. Rd6 Rd3 71. Rd8 Rxb3 72. Rf8+ Ke5 73. d6 Kxd6 74. Rf5 a4 75. Rxg5 ½–½ ChessBase

(41) FINE—STEINER, H

match, New York (2), 1932 (1 July)
Nimzowitsch-Indian Defence [E41]

1. d4 Nf6 2. c4 e6 3. Nc3 Bb4 4. e3 c5 5. Bd3 Nc6 6. Nf3 b6 7. 0–0 Bxc3 8. bxc3 d6 9. e4 Qc7 10. Bg5 Nd7 11. d5 Nce5 12. Nxe5 Nxe5 13. f4 Nxd3 14. Qxd3 f6 15. Bh4 e5 16. Qg3 Ba6 17. fxe5 dxe5 18. Bxf6 0–0 19. d6 Qd7 20. Be7 Rxf1+ 21. Rxf1 Bxc4 22. Rf5 Re8 23. h3 h6 24. a3 a5 25. Rxe5 Kh7 26. Qf4 Kg8 27. Kh2 Be6 28. Qf3 a4 29. Qh5 Rc8 30. Rxe6 Qxe6 31. Qf5 Qxf5 32. exf5 b5 33. d7 Ra8 34. d8Q+ Rxd8 35. Bxd8 b4 36. cxb4 cxb4 37. axb4 Black resigned. 1–0

(42) STEINER, H—FINE

match, New York (3), 1932 (July)
Grünfeld Defence, Flohr Variation [D90]

1. d4 Nf6 2. Nf3 d5 3. c4 c6 4. Nc3 g6 5. cxd5 cxd5 6. Bf4 Bg7 7. h3 0–0 8. e3 Qb6 9. Qb3 Qxb3 10. axb3 Nc6 11. Be2 Bf5 12. 0–0 Rfc8 13. g4 Bc2 14. Rfc1 Nb4 15. Ra4 a5 16. Ra3 Bd3 17. Bd1 Ne4 18. Ne1 e6 19. f3 g5 20. Bh2 Nf6 21. Rca1 b6 22. Bd6 Ba6 23. Bxb4 axb4 24. Rxa6 Rxa6 25. Rxa6 bxc3 26. bxc3 Rxc3 27. Kf2 Rc6 28. b4 h5 29. Ba4 Rc4 30. Rxb6 Bf8 31. Nd3 Rc3 32. Nc5 Ra3 33. Bb5 Ra2+ 34. Ke1 h4 35. Be2 Kg7 36. b5 Ra1+ 37. Kf2 Ne8 38. Rb7 Bd6 39. f4 Kf8 40. Nd7+ Kg8 41. fxg5 Bg3+ 42. Kg2 Ra2 43. Kf1 Ra1+ 44. Kg2 Ra2 45. Kf1 Ra1+ 46. Kg2 Ra2 Fine claimed a draw by 3-fold repetition. The match referee eventually ruled in Fine's favour, but not before ordering the players to finish the game! ½–½ Denker & Parr, 245–6.

(43) FINE—STEINER, H

match, New York (4), 1932 (July)
Queen's Gambit Declined, Exchange Variation [D35]

1. d4 d5 2. c4 e6 3. Nc3 Nf6 4. Nf3 Nbd7 5. cxd5 exd5 6. Bf4 c6 7. e3 Be7 8. Bd3 Nf8 9. Ne5 Be6 10. 0–0 N6d7 11. Bg3 f6 12. Nf3 f5 13. Qb3 Qb6 14. Qc2 g6 15. Na4 Qd8 16. Qb3 Qc8 17. Rac1 Nf6 18. Nc3 a6 19. Na4 N8d7 20. Ne5 0–0 21. Rc2 Bd8 22. Rfc1 Nxe5 23. Bxe5 Nd7 24. Bd6 Rf7 25. g3 Bc7 26. Qb4 Qb8 27. Bxc7 Qxc7 28. h4 Kg7 29. Rc3 Re8 30. Rb3 Nf6 White lost by overstepping the time limit. He was in the process of making the move 31 Qb6. 0–1

(44) STEINER, H—FINE

match, New York (5), 1932 (7 July)
Schlechter Variation [D94]

1. d4 Nf6 2. c4 c6 3. Nc3 d5 4. Nf3 g6 5. e3 Bg7 6. Be2 0–0 7. 0–0 Nbd7 8. cxd5 cxd5 9. Qb3 Nb6 10. Bd2 Ne4 11. Rfd1 Bg4 12. Be1 Rc8 13. h3 Bxf3 14. Bxf3 Nxc3 15. Bxc3 Qd7 16. Qa3 White would appear to have at least equality with his two bishops and good development. 16 … Nc4 Setting a trap into which White plunges. 17. Qxa7?? Rc7!! Suddenly White discovers his queen is in danger. The immediate threat is … b6; Qa6, Ra7. 18. a4 The best try. 18 … Qd6! With the threat of … b5. White is now defenceless. 19. e4 dxe4 20. Bxe4 b5 21. Bb7 Qd7 Winning a piece and the game. 22. Bc6 Rxa7 23. Bxd7 Rxd7 24. axb5 Rb8 25. Ra6 Rdb7 26. Rc6 Nd6 27. Bb4 Nxb5 28. Bc5 Rd7 White resigned. 0–1 Fine 1958, 20–1.

(45) FINE—STEINER, H

match, New York (6), 1932 (July)
Nimzowitsch-Indian Defence, Classical Variation [E34]

1. d4 Nf6 2. c4 e6 3. Nc3 Bb4 4. Qc2 d5 5. Bg5 c5 6. cxd5 Qxd5 7. Bxf6 gxf6 8. dxc5 Qxc5 9. e3 Nc6 10. Nge2 Qa5 11. Ng3 Bd7 12. Be2 Rc8 13. 0-0 f5 14. Nh5 Ke7 15. Rfd1 Rhd8 16. e4 Bxc3 17. bxc3 fxe4 18. Qxe4 h6 19. Rab1 b6 20. Bb5 Qxc3 21. Rbc1 Qe5 22. Rxd7+ Rxd7 23. Qxe5 Nxe5 24. Rxc8 Rd1+ 25. Bf1 f5 26. Nf4 Kd7 27. Rc2 b5 28. Ne2 b4 29. Rc1 Rd2 30. Ra1 a5 31. Nc1 Rd1 32. Nb3 Rxa1 33. Nxa1 Kc6 34. Be2 a4 35. Kf1 Kc5 36. Ke1 Nc6 37. Kd2 e5 38. Bh5 Black lost by overstepping the time limit. He was in the process of making the move 38 ... Na5. **1-0**

(46) STEINER, H–FINE

match, New York (7), 1932 (July)
Four Knights Game [C49]

1. e4 e5 2. Nf3 Nc6 3. Nc3 Nf6 4. Bb5 Bb4 5. d3 d6 6. 0-0 0-0 7. Bg5 Bxc3 8. bxc3 Qe7 9. Bxc6 bxc6 10. Nd2 h6 11. Bh4 g5 12. Bg3 Ne8 13. d4 f6 14. Qe2 Qf7 15. Rfb1 Ng7 16. Qc4 Qxc4 17. Nxc4 Ne6 18. Rd1 c5 19. dxe5 fxe5 20. Ne3 Rb8 21. f3 Ba6 22. Rab1 h5 23. h4 gxh4 24. Bxh4 Kf7 25. Rb3 Nf4 26. Ra3 Rb6 27. g3 Ne6 28. Nd5 Rc6?! 29. Kf2 Rb8 30. Ne7 Rcb6 31. Nd5 Rc6 32. Ke3 Rb2 33. Kd2 Bc4 34. Ne3 Ba6 35. Ra1 Nd4 36. cxd4 cxd4 37. Kc1 Rb7 38. Nd5 Be2 39. Rb1 d3 40. Rxb7 **1-0** ChessBase

(47) FINE–STEINER, H

match, New York (8), 1932 (July)
English Opening, Symmetrical Variation [A14]

1. Nf3 d5 2. c4 e6 3. b3 Nf6 4. g3 Be7 5. Bb2 0-0 6. Bg2 c5 7. 0-0 Nc6 8. cxd5 Nxd5 9. Nc3 Nc7 10. Rc1 Rb8 11. Qc2 b6 12. Rfd1 e5 13. Qe4? f5! 14. Qb1 Qe8 15. d3 g5 16. Qa1 Bb7 17. Nd2 Rd8 18. Nc4 Bf6 19. a4 Ba8 20. Nb5 Nxb5 21. axb5 Nd4 22. Bxd4 exd4 23. Qxa7 Bxg2 24. Kxg2 Qxe2 25. Rd2 Qh5 26. f3 Rde8 27. Qxb6 Re7 28. Rf1 g4 29. fxg4 fxg4 30. Rdf2 Bg7 31. Rxf8+ Bxf8 32. Qf6 Re2+ 33. Rf2 Be7 34. Qf4 Re1 35. Rf1 Re2+ 36. Rf2 Re1 37. h4?? Qd5+ **0-1** Denker & Parr, 246.

(48) STEINER, H–FINE

match, New York (9), 1932 (July)
Alekhine's Defence [B03]

1. e4 Nf6 2. e5 Nd5 3. c4 Nb6 4. d4 d6 5. exd6 exd6 6. Be3 Be7 7. Bd3 0-0 8. Nd2 Nc6 9. a3 Re8 10. Ngf3 Bg5 11. Nxg5 Qxg5 12. Nf3 Qf6 13. d5 Ne7 14. Qc2 Bf5 15. 0-0 Qg6 16. Rad1 Bxd3 17. Rxd3 Nf5 18. Bxb6 axb6 19. Rd2 Qg4 20. h3 Qe4 21. Qc3 Nh4 22. Nxh4 Qxh4 23. Rd4 Qf6 24. Qd2 Re5 25. Rf4 Qe7 26. Rf3 Re8 27. b4

Re2 28. Qc3 Re1 29. Rxe1 Qxe1+ 30. Kh2 Qxc3 31. Rxc3 Kf8 32. c5 bxc5 33. bxc5 Ke7 34. Re3+ Kd8 35. cxd6 cxd6 36. Rb3 Kc7 37. Rg3 g6 38. Rf3 Re7 39. Rf6 Rd7 40. Rf3 Kb6 41. Rc3 Rc7 42. Rb3+ Ka5 43. g4 Ka4 44. Re3 b5 45. Kg2 Rc5 46. Rd3 Rc2 47. Rf3 Rd2 48. Rxf7 Kxa3 49. Rxh7 b4 50. h4 Rd4 51. Ra7+ Kb2 52. Kg3 Rxd5 53. Rb7 b3 54. g5 Kc2 55. f4 Rd3+ 56. Kg4 b2 57. Rxb2+ Kxb2 58. h5 gxh5+ 59. Kxh5 Rf3 60. Kg4 Rf1 61. Kf5 Kc3 62. Ke4 Kc4 63. f5 Re1+ 64. Kf4 Kd5 65. g6 Rg1 **0-1** ChessBase

(49) FINE–STEINER, H

match, New York (10), 1932 (18 July)
English Opening [A13]

1. Nf3 Nf6 2. c4 e6 3. b3 d5 4. Bb2 Be7 5. g3 0-0 6. Bg2 a5 7. 0-0 a4!? 8. d4!? c6 9. c5?! axb3 10. axb3 Rxa1 11. Bxa1 Na6 12. Ne5 Nd7 13. Nd3 e5 14. dxe5 Naxc5 15. Nxc5 Nxc5 16. Qc2 Qb6 17. Nd2 Bg4 18. Re1 f6 19. e3 fxe5 20. Bxe5 Bf5 21. e4 dxe4 22. Bxe4 Bxe4 23. Nxe4 Qxb3 24. Qxb3+ Nxb3 25. Rb1 Rf5 26. Bd6 Bxd6 27. Rxb3 Be7 28. Rxb7 Re5 29. f3 Kf7 30. Rc7 c5 31. Kf2 Ke6 32. Ke2 Kd5 33. Kd3 g5 34. Nc3+ Kd6 35. Ra7 Ke6 36. Ra6+ Kf7 37. Rh6 Kg7 38. Rc6 Kf7 39. Ne4 Rd5+ 40. Kc4 Rd4+ 41. Kc3 g4 42. Rc7 Ra4 43. Kb3 Rb4+ 44. Kc3 gxf3 45. Ng5+ Kf6 46. Nxf3 Ke6 47. Nd2 h5 48. Rc6+ Kf5 49. Nb3 Bf6+ 50. Kc2 c4 51. Nd2 Rb2+ 52. Kc1 c3 53. Rc5+ Kg4 54. Ne4 Bd4 55. Nxc3 Bxc3 56. Rxc3 Rxh2 57. Kd1 Rg2 58. Ke1 Agreed drawn. **½-½**

United States Open Champion and the Pasadena International, 1932–1933

In 1932 Fine stepped up his activity from the club level. Initially he made the transition to domestic tournament play, winning the Western Championship in Minnesota. After this came his first international tournament, with the participation of no less a figure than World Champion Alexander Alekhine. Although Fine was later disappointed with his result, in truth he put up a reasonable showing for a teenager. These events also marked Fine's first meeting with his long term rival Samuel Reshevsky, who was returning to chess after completing his own education, having started out as a Polish chess prodigy who traveled to the States to give exhibitions. It is unfortunate that the score of their second encounter has not survived, not only does it deprive us of an important part of the record of American chess, but it also means that it is impossible to verify Fine's statement that he had adjourned in a winning position. At the end of the year Reuben successfully defended his Marshall Club title, this time without the loss of a single game.

33rd Western Chess Championship, Minneapolis, July 30–August 7, 1932

	1	2	3	4	5	6	7	8	9	10	11	12	
1 Fine	*	½	½	1	1	1	1	½	1	1	1	1	9½
2 Reshevsky	½	*	0	½	1	1	1	1	1	1	1	1	9
3 Reinfeld	½	1	*	0	½	1	1	½	1	1	1	1	8½
4 Steiner	0	½	1	*	½	½	1	½	½	1	1	1	7½
5 Barnes	0	0	½	½	*	½	1	1	½	1	½	0	5½
6 Harris	0	0	0	½	½	*	0	1	1	1	0	1	5
7 Palmer	0	0	0	0	0	1	*	1	0	1	½	1	4½
8 Osher	½	0	½	½	0	0	0	*	1	0	1	1	4½
9 Factor	0	0	0	½	½	0	1	0	*	1	1	½	4½
10 Elison	0	0	0	0	0	0	0	1	0	*	1	1	3
11 Hermann	0	0	0	0	½	1	½	0	0	0	*	1	3
12 Hazard	0	0	0	0	1	0	0	0	½	0	0	*	1½

"The championship of the Western Chess Association, won by Samuel Reshevsky of Chicago, at Tulsa, a year ago, passed into the keeping of Reuben Fine, champion of the Marshall Chess Club of New York, at the Hotel West in Minneapolis, Minn., from July 30 to August 7. The latter went through with a score of eight wins, three draws and nary a loss for a total of 9½ points out of a possible 11. Reshevsky, but half a point behind, won second prize. Other contestants were Jacob Harris of Minneapolis, Marvin Palmer of Detroit, Samuel D. Factor, Seymour Osher and Charles Elison of Chicago, Arne Hermann of St. Louis, and Fred S. Hazard of Minneapolis. At the conclusion of the meeting, five of the players—Fine, Reshevsky, Reinfeld, Steiner and Factor—departed for Pasadena to participate in the California Congress." (ACB 1932) The Western Chess Association effectively became the American Chess Federation in 1934 and its principal tournament the ACF Open Tournament, later the United States Open. The National Chess Federation ran the U.S. Championship tournaments of 1936 and '38, the United States Chess Federation taking over the running of both the U.S. Championship and U.S. Open Tournaments from 1939. Further to a discussion of the poor state of chess organization in the States during the 1930s, Fine wrote of this tournament: "One bright spot in 1932 was the Western Chess Association, which held an annual tournament that attracted many of the top players. This came as close as a tournament could be at that time to a United States chess championship, but without the name. In 1931 the winner was the famous ex–boy wonder Sammy Reshevsky, who had just returned to chess after a period of exile in various educational institutions. It was reported that the managers of the Tulsa affair had failed to

pay out the promised prizes, which added to our trials and tribulations; would Minneapolis do the same? Fortunately they did not. ... I nosed out Reshevsky by half a point and became the proud possessor of a national title for the first time: Western Champion." (Fine 1958) The games are recorded in the German algebraic form in the notebook.

(50) REINFELD, F—FINE

Western Chess Association, Minneapolis (1), 1932 (31 July)
Four Knights Game [C49]

1.e4 e5 2.Nf3 Nc6 3.Nc3 Nf6 4.Bb5 Bb4 5.0–0 0–0 6.d3 d6 7.Bg5 Bxc3 8.bxc3 Bg4 9.Bxc6 bxc6 10.h3 Bxf3 11.Qxf3 h6 12.Bxf6 Qxf6 13.Qxf6 gxf6 14.Rab1 Rab8 15.Rb3 Rb6 16.Rfb1 Rfb8 17.Kf1 Kf8 18.Ke2 Ke7 19.Kd2 Kd7 20.Ke3 Ke7 Agreed drawn. ½–½

(51) FINE—FACTOR, S

Western Chess Association, Minneapolis (2), 1932 (31 July)
Semi-Benoni or Blockade Variation [A56]

1. d4 Nf6 2. c4 e6 3. Nc3 c5 4. d5 d6 5. e4 e5 6. f4 It is best to attack the black centre at once. 6 ... exf4 Hoping to be able to settle a piece at e5. White in turn will try to stop this plan, which leads to the ensuing struggle. 7. Bxf4 Nbd7 8. Nf3 Ng4 9. Qa4! Be7 10. h3 Ngf6 11. 0–0–0 0–0 12. Bd3 White is waiting for an opportunity to break with e4–e5. The immediate push is premature, for after 12 e5 Nxe5 13 Nxe5 dxe5 14 Bxe5 Bd6 Black's game is much freer. 12 ... Re8 With the queen's knight unpinned, 12 ... Nh5 looks playable. AW 13. Rhe1 13 Rde1 would save a tempo. Looking back almost a quarter of a century I am trying to remember whether I had the following sacrifice in mind. I doubt it; my tendency is to play such positions intuitively. 13 ... Bf8 14. e5 Otherwise ... Ne5 can follow. 14 ... dxe5 If 14 ... Nh5 15 Bg5 wins. 15. Bg5! h6 16. Bh4

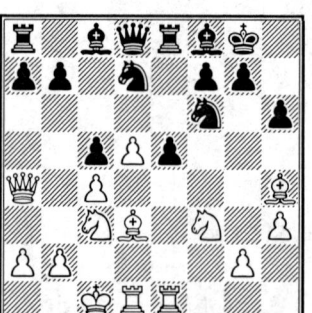

Position after White's 16th move

16 ... Bd6 (Fine claims the position is won (for example 16 ... g5 17 Nxg5! or 16 ... Be7 17 d6!), but I am not so sure. At no time does Black try to gain counterplay with ... a6 and ... b5, which would at least have muddied the waters. The game was, however, played well before the days of

Boleslavsky, Bronstein and Tal. AW) **17. Ne4 Qe7!**
18. Rf1 Qf8 To break the pin. **19. Bxf6 gxf6** On 19 ...
Nxf6 20 Nxf6+ gxf6 21 Nd2 and Black is no better off.
20. Nh4 Be7 21. d6 Bd8 22. Bb1 Nb6 23. Qc2
Qg7 24. Rf3 Kf8 25. Rdf1 Be6 26. Nf5 Bxf5
27. Rxf5 Re6 28. R1f3 Rc8 29. Rg3 Qh7 30. Qf2
Qh8 Not 30 ... Nxc4 31 Nxf6. **31. b3 Rc6 32. Qe3 Nc8**
33. Nxc5 Rexd6 34. Nxb7 Rd4 Or 34 ... Bb6 35 Qf3
Re6 36 Be4. **35. Nxd8 Rxd8 36. Rh5! f5 37. Rxf5**
Ne7 38. Qxe5! Qxe5 39. Rxe5 Rcd6 40. Bc2 Nc6
41. Re1 Nb4 42. Bh7! f6 43. Rg8+ Kf7 44. Rxd8
Rxd8 45. a3 Nc6 46. Be4 Ne5 47. Rd1 Rb8
48. Kc2 a5 49. Kc3 Rc8 50. Rd6 a4 51. Bd5+ Kg6
52. bxa4 Rc7 53. a5 Rc5 54. a6 Black resigned. **1–0**
Fine 1958, 8–11.

(52) HARRIS, J—FINE

Western Chess Association, Minneapolis (3), 1932 (1 Aug.)
Sicilian Defence [B33]

1. e4 c5 2. Nf3 Nc6 3. d4 cxd4 4. Nxd4 Nf6
5. Nxc6 bxc6 6. Bd3 e5 7. 0–0 Bc5 8. Nc3 0–0
9. Bg5 Be7 10. Qe2 d6 11. h3 Be6 12. Rad1 Qa5
13. Qe1 Qc7 14. Qe2 d5 15. Bxf6 Bxf6 16. b3 g6
17. Qf3 dxe4 18. Nxe4 Bc7 19. Qc2 Rac8 20. Bc4
Bc8 21. Qe3 Kg7 22. Nc5 Bd6 23. Ne4 Ba3 24. f3
f5 25. Nf2 Qb6 26. Qxb6 axb6 27. Kh1 e4
28. fxe4 fxe4 29. Be2 Bc5 30. Ng4 h5 31. Nh2
Rxf1+ 32. Rxf1 Rd8 33. Rd1 Rxd1+ 34. Bxd1 Kf6
35. g3 Bxh3 36. c3 Bd6 37. g4 Bxh2 38. Kxh2
Bxg4 White resigned. **0–1**

(53) FINE—HAZARD, F

Western Chess Association, Minneapolis (4), 1932 (2 Aug.)
Queen's Gambit Declined, Cambridge Springs Defence [D52]

1. d4 d5 2. c4 e6 3. Nf3 Nf6 4. Nc3 c6 5. Bg5
Nbd7 6. e3 Qa5 7. cxd5 exd5 8. Bd3 Bd6 9. 0–0
0–0 10. Qc2 h6 11. Bh4 Re8 12. a3 Qc7 13. Rac1
a6 14. Rfe1 Be7 15. h3 Qd8 16. Bg3 Nf8 17. Ne5
Be6 18. f4 Nh5 19. Bf2 Bd6 20. g4 Nf6 21. Bg3
N6h7 22. Rf1 f6 23. Nf3 Bf7 24. Rce1 Qc7
25. Ne5 Re7 26. e4 dxe4 27. Nxe4 Bd5 28. Nc4
Bxc4 29. Qxc4+ Kh8 30. Kg2 Rae8 31. Bb1 Nd7
32. d5 Nhf8 33. dxc6 bxc6 34. Rc1 Nb8 35. Rcd1
Rd8 36. Ba2 Nh7 37. Nxd6 Red7 38. Nf7+ Rxf7
39. Qxf7 Qb6 40. Rxd8+ Qxd8 41. Rd1 Black
resigned. **0–1**

(54) FINE—STEINER, H

Western Chess Association, Minneapolis (5), 1932 (2 Aug.)
Nimzowitsch–Indian Defence, Rubinstein Variation [E41]

1. d4 Nf6 2. c4 e6 3. Nc3 Bb4 4. e3 c5 5. Bd3
Nc6 6. Nf3 cxd4 7. exd4 d5 8. a3 Be7 9. c5 0–0

10. 0–0 Ne8 11. Bc2 f5 12. b4 Nf6 13. Ne5 a5
14. Nxc6 bxc6 15. Na4 axb4 16. axb4 Nd7 17. Re1
Rf6 18. Bg5 Rf7 19. Bf4 Rf6 20. Nc3 Rxa1
21. Qxa1 Rg6 22. Qa8 Bf6 23. Qxc6 Bxd4 24. Nb5
Nf8 25. Nxd4 e5 26. Qa8 exf4 27. Nxf5 Kh8
28. Ne7 Rxg2+ 29. Kh1 Rxf2 30. Bf5 f3 31. Qxc8
Qxe7 32. Rg1 g6 33. Qb8 Kg7 34. Qf4 Qe2
35. Bh3 h5 36. c6 Qe4 37. Qxe4 dxe4 38. c7 Rc2
39. c8Q Rxc8 40. Bxc8 e3 41. Ra1 g5 42. b5 Ng6
43. b6 Black resigned. **1–0**

(55) HERMANN, A—FINE

Western Chess Association, Minneapolis (6), 1932 (3 Aug.)
Slav-Grünfeld [D90]

1. Nf3 d5 2. d4 Nf6 3. c4 c6 4. Nc3 g6 5. cxd5
cxd5 6. Bf4 Bg7 7. Bxb8 Rxb8 8. Qa4+ Bd7
9. Qxa7 0–0 10. Nd2 Bc6 11. Qa3 Nd7 12. e3 e5
13. dxe5 Nxe5 14. Be2 d4 15. exd4 Qxd4 16. Nb3
Nd3+ 17. Bxd3 Qxd3 18. Nc1 Black announced mate in
four beginning with 18 ... Bxc3+. **0–1**

(56) BARNES, G—FINE

Western Chess Association, Minneapolis (7), 1932 (3 Aug.)
Queen's Gambit Declined [D66]

1. d4 Nf6 2. Nf3 d5 3. c4 e6 4. Nc3 Be7 5. Bg5
Nbd7 6. e3 0–0 7. Rc1 c6 8. Bd3 Re8 9. 0–0 a6
10. Qe2 dxc4 11. Bxc4 b5 12. Bd3 Bb7 13. Rfd1
Qb6 14. e4 c5 15. e5 Nd5 16. dxc5 Bxc5 17. Ne4
Bf8 18. Bd2 Red8 19. Neg5 g6 20. Ne4 Bg7
21. Nc3 Rac8 22. a3 Ba8 23. Nxd5 Bxd5 24. Bc3
Qh8 25. Re1? Bxf3 26. Qxf3 Bxe5 27. Bb1 Bxc3
28. bxc3 Ne5 29. Qe4 Nc4 30. Ba2 Rd2 31. Bxc4
Rxc4 32. Qe3 Qf4 33. Qb6 Qd6 34. Qe3 Rf4
35. g3 Rfxf2 36. Qxf2 Rxf2 37. Kxf2 Qxa3 38. c4
bxc4 White resigned. **0–1**

(57) OSHER, S—FINE

Western Chess Association, Minneapolis (8), 1932 (4 Aug.)
Slav Defence, Exchange Variation [D13]

1. Nf3 d5 2. d4 Nf6 3. c4 c6 4. cxd5 cxd5 5. Nc3
Nc6 6. Bf4 e6 7. e3 Bd6 8. Bg3 0–0 9. Bd3 Qe7
10. Ne5 Nd7 11. f4 Re8 12. 0–0 Nf8 13. Nb5 Bb8
14. Rc1 Bd7 15. Nc3 Rd8 16. Bb1 Be8 17. Qg4 f6
18. Bh4 g6 19. Ne2 Bd6 20. Qg3 Qg7 21. Nxc6
Bxc6 22. Qf3 Rac8 23. g4 Nd7 24. g5 Rf8
25. Qg4 Rce8 26. Kh1 Bc7 27. Ng1 f5 28. Qe2
Qe7 29. Nf3 Kg7 30. Be1 Rc8 31. Kg2 Bd6
32. Bc3 Rh8 33. Rh1 Nb6 34. h4 Na4 35. Be1 Bb5
36. Qd2 Rxc1 37. Qxc1 Qc7 38. Qxc7+ Bxc7
39. b3 Nb6 40. Bb4 Rc8 41. Rc1 Agreed drawn.
½–½

(58) FINE—PALMER, M

Western Chess Association, Minneapolis (9), 1932 (5 Aug.)
Queen's Gambit Declined [D43]

1. d4 d5 2. c4 c6 3. Nc3 Nf6 4. Nf3 e6 5. Bg5
Bb4 6. Qb3 Ba5 7. e3 0-0 8. Bd3 Nbd7 9. 0-0
Bc7 10. Rad1 Qe7 11. Rfe1 dxc4 12. Bxc4 e5 13. e4
exd4 14. e5 Nxe5 15. Nxe5 Bxe5 16. f4 dxc3
17. Rxe5 Qc7 18. Qxc3 Bg4 19. Rde1 Qd6 20. Kh1
Nd5 21. Bxd5 cxd5 22. Be7 Qd7 23. Bxf8 Rxf8
24. h3 Bf5 25. Qd4 Be6 26. Kg1 g6 27. h4 Rc8
28. f5 gxf5 29. b3 a6 30. R5e3 Qd6 31. h5 h6
32. Kh1 Kh7 33. Rf3 Rg8 34. Qf4 Qxf4 35. Rxf4
Rg4 36. Rxg4 fxg4 37. Kh2 Kg7 38. Kg3 Kf6
39. Kf4 Ke7 40. Ke5 f6+ 41. Kd4 Kd6 42. g3 b6
43. Rf1 Ke7 44. b4 Bf7 45. a3 Ke6 46. Rc1 Kd6
47. Rc8 Bxh5 48. Rd8+ Kc6 49. Rf8 Kb5 50. Rxf6
Be8 51. Rxh6 a5 52. Kxd5 axb4 53. axb4 Bf7+
54. Kd4 Bb3 55. Kc3 Bd1 56. Rh5+ Ka4 57. Re5
Bf3 58. Kc4 Bc6 59. Re6 b5+ 60. Kc3 Black
resigned. 1-0

(59) FINE—ELISON, C

Western Chess Association, Minneapolis (10), 1932 (5 Aug.)
Queen's Gambit Declined [D64]

1. d4 Nf6 2. c4 e6 3. Nc3 d5 4. Nf3 Nbd7 5. Bg5
Be7 6. e3 0-0 7. Rc1 c6 8. Qc2 Re8 9. a3 Nf8
10. Bd3 dxc4 11. Bxc4 Nd5 12. Bxe7 Qxe7 13. 0-0
Nb6 14. Ba2 Bd7 15. Ne5 f6 16. Nd3 Red8 17. Ne4
Be8 18. Qc5 Rd7 19. Qxe7 Rxe7 20. Ndc5 Rd8
21. f4 Bf7 22. g4 Nd5 23. Rce1 b6 24. Nd3 Bg6
25. Ndf2 Bf7 26. h3 h6 27. Nd3 Kh8 28. Re2 Bg6
29. Nef2 Nc7 30. Nb4 Rd6 31. Rc1 Nd5 32. Rxc6
Rxc6?! 33. Nxc6 Rc7 34. Bxd5 exd5 35. Nb4 Rc1+
36. Kg2 Bf7 37. f5 a5 38. Nbd3 Rc8 39. Nf4 g6
40. fxg6 Nxg6 41. N2d3 Kg8 42. Kg3 Kf8 43. Re1
Nxf4 44. Nxf4 Rc2 45. Re2 Rxe2 46. Nxe2 Ke7
47. Kf4 Bg6 48. Ng3 Bd3 49. Nf5+ Bxf5 50. Kxf5
Kf7 51. a4 Black resigned. 1-0

(60) RESHEVSKY, S—FINE

Western Chess Association, Minneapolis (11), 1932 (7 Aug.)
Bogolyubov-Indian Defence [E11]

1. d4 Nf6 2. Nf3 e6 3. c4 Bb4+ 4. Bd2 Qe7
5. Qc2 Bxd2+ 6. Nbxd2 d6 7. e3 0-0 8. Bd3
Nbd7 9. 0-0 a5 10. a4 b6 11. Ne4 Bb7 12. Nfd2
Rad8 13. Ng3 Rfe8 14. Qc3 e5 15. d5 Nc5 16. Bc2
e4 17. b4 axb4 18. Qxb4 Ra8 19. Nb1 Ng4 20. h3
Nh6 Fine missed a shot here: 20 ... Nxf2! 21 Qc3 (21 Rxf2
Qe5) Nfd3. AW 21. Nc3 Qh4 21 ... f5!? AW 22. a5!
Rab8 23. Nb5 Qe7 24. axb6 cxb6 25. Nd4 Ba8
26. Rfb1 g6 27. Ba4 Rf8 28. Bc6 f5 29. Bxa8 Rxa8
30. Qxb6 Rxa1 31. Rxa1 f4 32. Nge2 fxe3 33. fxe3

This game was played in the final round. I was half a point ahead of Reshevsky and had to at least draw to be first. In this position I managed to squeeze out with **33 ... Qf6!
34. Qc7** On 34 Nf4, 34 ... Nf5 is powerful. White now threatens Ra7. **34 ... Ng4! 35. hxg4 Qf2+** Agreed drawn. The black queen can administer perpetual check on h4 and f2. ½-½ Fine 1958, 21.

Pasadena International Tournament, August 15–28, 1932

American Chess Bulletin reported, "Abraham Kupchik of the Manhattan Chess Club has received an invitation.... Among interesting possibilities ... is ... William E. Napier of Brooklyn, who of late has shown a decided inclination to return to active practice. Among other likely contenders are Frank J. Marshall, Isaac I. Kashdan, Arthur W. Dake and Samuel Factor. ... [A] $5 season ticket will entitle the holder to entrance throughout the Congress." The May-June *Bulletin* indicated that Napier, Marshall and John Tippin of California were expected to attend (ACB 1932, 85). Neither John Hilbert, in his biography of Napier, nor Soltis, in his work about Marshall, threw any light on the non-participation of their subjects. "Three New Yorkers, Jacob Bernstein, Reuben Fine and Fred Reinfeld, tied with Samuel Factor of Chicago for seventh place. Bernstein, who has been State Champion four times, required time in which to find himself. This he finally did but lost three games in doing so. Thereafter in eight rounds he did not lose again. In contrast to that record Factor dropped three points in succession at the last and spoiled a promising chance of being very high. Reuben Fine, the new Western Champion who outranked Reshevsky at Minneapolis, did not come up to expectations, but made his presence felt, nevertheless." (ACB)

In discussing the break off of the 1961 Fischer-Reshevsky match, Fine wrote, "In my second game with Reshevsky at Pasadena in 1932, we adjourned in a position which was a clear win for me. The adjourned time fell on a Jewish Holiday and was therefore postponed, over my objections. For the second adjournment the game was rearranged for an earlier time, which I failed to keep. This time I was forfeited, in spite of my objections. The tournament Director, a Dr. Griffith, took me into the men's room and consoled me with a medicinal shot of Scotch (those were still the days of Prohibition). I was then 17 years old, about the same age as Bobby in his match with Reshevsky." (Fine 1973, footnote to page 30). The ACB reported that Reshevsky adjourned his first eight games. This Fine game is not in Gordon's comprehensive collection of Reshevsky's games, nor amongst Fine's papers. One might speculate that both scoresheets were placed in the adjournment envelope, which, upon non-continuation of the game, was not opened. If Fine's story is true he might have shared third place, relegating Reshevsky to seventh (a single point separated third place from tenth), but verification seems unlikely.

Fred Reinfeld recalled a four day road trip with Fine, Los Angeles to New York, likely in the wake of this tournament, with $10 between them. They had steak for 50 cents each in El Paso. Fine recalled, "Shortly thereafter *(after Pasadena—AW)*, Alekhine visited New York (*perhaps November 1932, the next Alekhine New York visit according to Skinner & Verhoeven—AW*). We played some skittles at the Marshall Chess Club, and I won most of them. At this he became very angry (he never did like to lose) and challenged me to a set 10-second-a-move match for $10, six games. This sum, unreachable for me at this time, was quickly put up by my supporters. As I recall, he managed to win, 3½ to 2½. I was surprised at his need to beat me, since I was still a comparatively unknown, and equally surprised by how well I did in the quick chess games. Years later, at the A.V.R.O. tournament in 1938, Alekhine and I would regularly play off-hand games for a guilder a game (55 cents at that time), and I won almost every time. But he insisted on playing." The games are in German algebraic in the notebook.

		1	2	3	4	5	6	7	8	9	10	11	12	
1	Alekhine	*	1	0	1	1	1	1	½	½	½	1	1	8½
2	Kashdan	0	*	½	1	1	½	½	1	½	½	1	1	7½
3=	Dake	1	½	*	0	½	½	½	1	½	1	0	½	6
3=	Reshevsky	0	0	1	*	½	0	1	½	1	0	1	1	6
3=	Steiner	0	0	½	½	*	1	½	1	1	½	1	0	6
6	Borochow	0	½	½	1	0	*	0	0	1	1	1	½	5½
7=	Bernstein	0	½	½	0	½	1	*	0	½	½	½	1	5
7=	Factor	½	0	0	½	0	1	1	*	½	0	½	1	5
7=	Fine	½	½	½	0	0	0	½	½	*	1	½	1	5
7=	Reinfeld	½	½	0	1	½	0	½	1	0	*	0	1	5
11	Araiza	0	0	1	0	0	0	½	½	½	1	*	0	3½
12	Fink	0	0	½	0	1	½	0	0	0	0	1	*	3

(61) Fine—Reshevsky, S

Pasadena (1), 1932 (15 Aug.)

The score of this game is not available. **0–1**

(62) Factor, S—Fine

Pasadena (2), 1932 (16 Aug.)
Queen's Gambit Declined [D30]

1. d4 Nf6 2. Nf3 d5 3. c4 c6 4. e3 e6 5. Bd3 Bd6 6. 0–0 0–0 7. Nbd2 c5 8. cxd5 Nxd5 9. dxc5 Bxc5 10. Bxh7+ Kxh7 11. Qc2+ g6 12. Qxc5 b6 13. Qc2 Bb7 14. e4 Nf4 15. Nc4 Qd3 16. Qxd3 Nxd3 17. Rd1 Nc5 18. Nd6 Bc6 19. b4 Nb7 20. Ng5+ Kg8 21. Bb2 Nxd6 22. Rxd6 Ba4 23. f4 Nd7 24. Rd3 Rfe8 25. Rh3 f6 26. Nf3 Rac8 27. e5 Rc2 28. Bd4 f5 29. Be3 Rc4 30. a3 Rd8 31. Rc1 Rxc1+ 32. Bxc1 Nf8 33. Kf2 Rd1 34. Bd2 Bc6 35. Bc3 Bd5 36. Nd2 Nd7 37. Re3 b5 38. Nf3 Nb6 39. Re1 Rd3 40. Re3 Rxe3 41. Kxe3 Nc4+ 42. Kd4 Nxa3 43. Kc5 Kf7 44. Nd4 Bxg2 45. Nxb5 Nxb5 46. Kxb5 Bf1+ 47. Kc6 a6 48. Kd6 Bc4 49. Be1 Agreed drawn. **½–½**

(63) Fine—Steiner, H

Pasadena (3), 1932 (17 Aug.)
Queen's Gambit Declined [D67]

1. Nf3 d5 2. d4 Nf6 3. c4 e6 4. Nc3 Be7 5. Bg5 0–0 6. e3 Nbd7 7. Rc1 c6 8. Bd3 dxc4 9. Bxc4 Nd5 10. Bxe7 Qxe7 11. 0–0 Nxc3 12. bxc3 e5 13. Qc2 e4 14. Nd2 Nf6 15. Rce1 Bf5 16. f3 Bg6 17. fxe4 Nxe4 18. Nxe4 Bxe4 19. Qd2 Kh8 20. Rf4 f5 21. Bd3 g5 22. Rf2 Rae8 23. Bc4 Rf6 24. Ref1 Rh6 25. Bd3?? Qd6 26. g3 Qxg3+ 27. Rg2 Qxg2+ 28. Qxg2 Bxg2 29. Kxg2 Rxe3 White resigned. **0–1**

(64) Reinfeld, F—Fine

Pasadena (4), 1932 (18 Aug.)
Queen's Indian Defence [E16]

1. d4 e6 2. Nf3 Nf6 3. c4 b6 4. g3 Bb7 5. Bg2 Bb4+ 6. Bd2 Qe7 7. 0–0 Bxd2 8. Qxd2 0–0 9. Nc3 d6 10. Qc2 Nbd7 11. e4 Rad8 12. a3 e5 13. d5 Ne8 14. b4 g6 15. Nh4 Ng7 16. Bh3 Qg5 17. Qc1 Qe7 18. Qe3 Ra8 19. Qd3 Rfb8 20. Ng2 Rf8 21. Ne3 Rae8 22. f3 a6 23. Rac1 Rc8 24. Rf2 Qg5 25. Rfc2 f5 26. Bg2 h5 27. Nf1 h4 28. Na4 hxg3 29. hxg3 fxe4 30. fxe4 Nf6 31. Qe3 Qh5 32. Nh2? Qxh2+ White resigned. **0–1**

(65) Fine—Kashdan, I

Pasadena (5), 1932 (20 Aug.)
Queen's Gambit Declined, Exchange Variation with 6 Bf4 [D35]

1. c4 Nf6 2. d4 e6 3. Nc3 d5 4. Nf3 Nbd7 5. cxd5 exd5 6. Bf4 c6 7. e3 Be7 8. Bd3 0–0 9. Qc2 Re8 10. h3 c5 11. dxc5 Nxc5 12. Bb5 Bd7 13. Bxd7 Qxd7 14. 0–0 Rac8 15. Rfd1 Nce4 16. Be5 Nxc3 17. bxc3 Qe6 18. Rab1 Nd7 19. Bf4 Nc5 20. Nd4 Qd7 21. c4 dxc4 22. Nb5 Nd3 23. Nc7 Red8 24. Qxc4 Qc6 25. Qxc6 bxc6 26. Bg3 h5 27. Na6 c5 28. Bc7 (Not 28 Rb7? c4! 29 Rxe7 c3. AW) **28 ... Rd5 29. Kf1 c4 30. Ke2 Ba3 31. Rd2 Rd7 32. Ba5 f6 33. Rc2 Rd5 34. Bc7 Nb2 35. Rcxb2 Bxb2 36. Rxb2 Rd7 37. Rc2** (White could play for a win with 37 Ba5.) **37 ... Rdxc7 38. Nxc7 Rxc7 39. Kd2 Kf7 40. Kc3 Ke6** Draw agreed. (Surely 41 Kd4 gives White chances. AW) **½–½** Gamescore supplied by Peter Lahde from a California chess website.

(66) Dake, A—Fine

Pasadena (6), 1932 (21 Aug.)
French Defence, Classical Variation [C14]

1. e4 e6 2. d4 d5 3. Nc3 Nf6 4. Bg5 Be7 5. e5
Nfd7 6. Bxe7 Qxe7 7. Qd2 0–0 8. f4 c5 9. Nf3
Nc6 10. g3 a6 11. Bg2 b5 12. 0–0 Nb6 13. Qf2 cxd4
14. Nxd4 Nxd4 15. Qxd4 Rb8 16. Nd1 Bd7 17. Ne3
Rfc8 18. c3 Qc5 19. Qxc5 Rxc5 20. Rf2 Nc4 21. Nd1
g6 22. Bf1 Kg7 23. Rc1 h5 24. Bxc4 dxc4 25. Rd2
Bc6 26. h4 Rd5 27. Rxd5 Bxd5 28. Ne3 Be4
29. Rd1 Bd3 30. Rd2 a5 31. a3 Agreed drawn. ½–½

(67) FINE–FINK, A

Pasadena (7), 1932 (23 Aug.)
Heinrichsen Opening [A00]

1. Nc3 d5 2. f4 d4 3. Ne4 Nf6 4. Nf2 Bf5 5. Nf3
Nc6 6. g3 Qd7 7. Bg2 0–0–0 8. 0–0 h6 9. a3 g6
10. b4 a6 11. Bb2 Bg7 12. c4 Ng4 13. Qa4 Nxf2
14. Rxf2 Bf6?! 15. b5 Nb8 16. Qb3 c5 17. bxa6
Nxa6 18. Ne5 Bxe5 19. fxe5 Qc7 20. d3 Rd7
21. Bc1 e6 22. Bd2 Nb8 23. Qb5 Nc6 24. Rb1 Nd8
25. Qa4 g5 26. Qa7 Qxe5 27. Ba5 Re7 28. Rb5
Nc6 29. Rxc5 Rc7 30. Bxc6 Black resigned. 1–0

(68) BERNSTEIN, J–FINE

Pasadena (8), 1932 (24 Aug.)

The score of this game is unavailable. ½–½

(69) BOROCHOW, H–FINE

Pasadena (9), 1932 (25 Aug.)
Alekhine's Defence [B03]

1. e4 Nf6 2. e5 Nd5 3. d4 Nc6? 4. c4 Nb6 5. d5
Nxe5 6. c5 Nbc4 7. f4 e6 8. Qd4 Qh4+ 9. g3 Qh6
10. Nc3 exd5 11. fxe5 Black resigned. 1–0

(70) FINE–ARAIZA, J

Pasadena (10), 1932 (27 Aug.)
English Opening, Classical Variation [A29]

1. c4 e5 2. Nf3 Nc6 3. Nc3 Nf6 4. d3 d5 5. cxd5
Nxd5 6. g3 Be6 7. Bg2 Be7 8. 0–0 0–0 9. Bd2
Qd7 10. Rc1 Nxc3 11. Bxc3 f6 12. d4 exd4
13. Nxd4 Nxd4 14. Qxd4 Qxd4 15. Bxd4 c6 16. a3
Rfd8 17. Rfd1 a6 18. Bb6 Rxd1+ 19. Rxd1 Kf7
20. f4 Ke8 21. Kf2 Bd8 22. Bxd8 Rxd8 23. Rxd8+
Kxd8 Agreed drawn. ½–½

(71) ALEKHINE, A–FINE

Pasadena (11), 1932 (28 Aug.)
Alekhine's Defence [B02]

1. e4 Nf6! With daring typical of youth. Alekhine had of
course introduced this defence, but then abandoned it. Its
correctness is not entirely established. 2. e5 Nd5 3. c4

Nb6 4. c5 Perhaps because he was playing an unknown.
The more usual 4 d4 is stronger. 4 ... Nd5 5. Nc3 Nxc3
6. dxc3 d6 7. Bc4 Preventing a capture, for if the queen
takes either pawn, 8 Bxf7+ wins. 7 ... d5! Forcing a
favourable simplification. (Simpler is 7 ... Nc6 and if 8 Nf3?
dxe5 for 9 Bxf7+ is unsound: Kxf7 10 Ng5+ Kg8! 11 Qb3+ e6
12 Nxe6 Na5! 13 Nxd8+ Nxb3 14 axb3 Be7 and White has a
winning advantage, MCO 7. 8. Qxd5 Qxd5 9. Bxd5 e6
The position is even, MCO. 10. Be4 Bxc5 White's game is
still freer, and Black must play carefully. 11. Nf3 h6 To
keep the king in the centre without fear of a check at g5.
12. h4 a5 13. h5 a4 Tit for tat! 14. Rh3 Nd7 15. Rg3
Kf8 Forced (if 15 ... Rg8?; 16 Bxh6). Black's game is none
too easy. 16. Bf4 Ra5! A dynamic conception which keeps
Black's game alive. 17. Rd1 Rb5 18. Rd2 By this time I
realized I had been thoroughly outplayed since the exchange
of queens. I had no choice but to hold on doggedly. 18 ...
Be7 To allow some development. 19. Bd3 Ra5 Continued
pressure against White's e-pawn is the idea. 20. Bc2 Nb6
Threatening ... Nc4. 21. Rd1 Bd7 At last this bishop can
move. 22. c4 The exposed position of the bishop makes
this advance possible. 22 ... Bc6 23. Rd4 Nd7 Tenaciously I hold onto my main defensive plan: pressure against
White's e-pawn. 24. Bd2 Rc5! Prepared to sacrifice the
exchange. On 24 ... Ra8 25 Bc3 Bc5 (or 25 ... Bxf3 26
Rxd7!) 26 Rdg4 with advantage. The position is now quite
complicated, and besides both players were in time pressure.
Alekhine exerts all his ingenious efforts to force a win.
25. Be3! On 25 Bb4 Rxe5+! 26 Nxe5 Bxb4+ 27 Ke2 Nxe5
28 Rd8+ Be8 29 Bxa4 is good for Black. (Fine continues 29
... c6, but I think this is dubious in view of 30 Rb3 Ba5 31
Ra8 b6 32 c5. However, 29 ... Ke7 is better for Black. AW)
25 ... Ra5! Avoiding the trap. If here 25 ... Nxe5 26
Rd8+!, and if 25 ... Bxf3 26 Rxd7 Rxc4 27 Bd3 win for
White. 26. Bd2 Rc5 Black is content to draw; White is
not. 27. Be3 Ra5 28. Be4! Another ingenious continuation. 28 ... Nb8 Fine reckoned that 28 ... Nxe5 29 Nxe5
Rxe5 30 Bxc6 bxc6 31 Rd7 Rxh5 32 Rxc7 would have give
White disastrous threats, but 32 ... g6 seems to hold out.
AW 29. Bd2 Ra8 Now 29 ... Rc5 would be countered by
30 Bb4. 30. Bc3 f5 In time pressure and fearful of what
the great man might have in store, I stumble. The correct
defence is 30 ... Bxe4! 31 Rxe4 Nc6 32 Reg4 (if 32 a3 Kg8!
33 Reg4 Bf8 and White cannot make progress [I'm not sure
about this, after 34 Nd2, threatening Ne4, it is difficult to
believe Black's tangled kingside will be able to unravel
before White can generate some kind of fatal threat somewhere. AW]) a3! 33 b3 (33 Rxg7 axb2 34 Bxb2 Rxa2 leads
nowhere for White) Rd8! and Black has numerous coun-
terthreats, for if 34 Rxg7 Bb4! 35 Bxb4+ Nxb4 White is in a
bad way. 31. exf6 Bxf6 32. Bxc6 Nxc6 Not 32 ... Bxd4?
33 Bxd4 Nxc6 34 Bxg7+. 33. Rf4 a3! Fine rightly saw that
this was the only chance, giving the alternatives 33 ... Ke7
34 Bxf6+ gxf6 35 Rg7+ or 33 ... Kf7 34 Bxf6 gxf6 35 Rg6 f5
36 g4 and wins. In the second line 36 ... Ra5 seems to give
Black chances. However, instead of 34 Bxf6, after 33 ... Kf7,
White wins simply by 34 Rxg7+, ending up a pawn ahead.
AW 34. bxa3 Under the circumstances (six moves in a few

minutes) it was very difficult to decide whether this was better than the more quiet 34 b3. After 34 b3 Ke7 35 Bxf6+ gxf6 36 Rg7+ Kd6 37 Rxf6 (I wonder about 37 c5+! Kxc5 38 Rxc7, for example, Kb6 39 Rf7 Ra5 40 R7xf6 Rxh5 41 Ra4 Rg8 42 g3 Rh1+ 43 Ke2 Re8 44 Rxa3 Kc5 45 Ra4 e5. AW) Nb4 analysis indicates that Black does have enough counter-play. After 38 Rff7 Rhd8 39 Rxc7 Nxa2 Black can at least draw. (Indeed, Black seems close to winning as it is not apparent how White can stop the a-pawn. AW) **34 ... Rxa3 35. Bxf6 gxf6 36. Rxf6+ Ke7 37. Rgg6 Rxa2 38. Rxe6+ Kd7 39. Ref6?** Here, however, Alekhine gives me a chance. Correct is 39 Rxh6 Rha8 40 Ne5+! Nxe5 41 Rxe5 Rc2 42 Rd5+ Ke7 43 Rd2 Rxc4 44 f3 followed by g4 and White's pawns get there first; Black has no perpetual. **39 ... Re8+ 40. Kd1** Not 40 Kf1?? Ra1+. **40 ... Ree2 41. Rg7+ Ne7!** Not 41 ... Kc8 42 Rf8+ Nd8 43 Rgg8. **42. Rxh6** With one last trap: if 42 ... Rxf2 43 Ne5+ Ke8 44 Rh8+ Rf8 45 Rxe7+ and with the threat of mate lifted the extra pawn wins. **42 ... b6!** After this precautionary move White cannot win. **43.** c5 Or 43 Rhh7 Kd6. **43 ... bxc5 44. Ra6 Rab2 45. Ra3 Rxf2 46. Rd3+ Ke6! 47. Rd2** Forced, for if 47 Re3+ Kf6 and the mate threat at b1 is deadly. **47 ... Rbxd2+ 48. Nxd2 Kf6 49. h6 Rf4** A last try; the threat is 50 Ne4+. **50. g4 Ng6 51. Rxc7 Rxg4 52. Nf3 Rg3 53. Ke2 Nf4+ 54. Kf2 Rh3 55. h7 Ne6 56. Ra7 Nf8 57. Ra6+ Kf5** Agreed drawn. Psychologically, this game was of crucial importance in my development. It taught me for the first time that I could hold my own in over-the-board play with the best in the world. If only I could master the openings, I felt, I could really make my mark in chess. It was from this point on that I began to devote a major proportion of my time to the study of the literature. ½–½ Fine 1958, 12–7.

16th Marshall Club Championship, New York, October 2–December 25, 1932

		1	2	3	4	5	6	7	8	9	10	11	12	13	14	
1	Fine	*	1	½	1	1	½	1	1	½	1	1	1	1	1	11½
2	Kevitz	0	*	0	1	½	1	1	1	1	½	1	1	0	1	9
3	Smirka	½	1	*	1	1	½	0	1	1	0	0	1	½	1	8½
4	Costa-Rivas	0	0	0	*	1	½	0	1	1	½	1	1	1	1	8
5=	Dunst	0	½	0	0	*	0	½	1	1	½	1	1	1	1	7½
5=	Polland	½	0	½	½	1	*	0	0	0	1	1	1	1	1	7½
5=	Tholfsen	0	0	1	1	½	1	*	0	0	0	1	1	1	1	7½
8=	Beckhardt	0	0	0	0	0	1	1	*	1	1	0	½	1	1	6½
8=	Chernev	½	0	0	0	0	1	1	0	*	1	1	0	1	1	6½
8=	Levenstein	0	½	1	½	½	0	1	0	0	*	0	1	1	1	6½
11	Simonson	0	0	1	0	0	0	0	1	0	1	*	0	1	1	5
12	Santasiere	0	0	0	0	0	0	0	½	1	0	1	*	1	1	4½
13	Cass	0	1	½	0	0	0	0	0	0	0	0	0	*	½	2
14	Frere	0	0	0	0	0	0	0	0	0	0	0	0	½	*	½

Fine retained his grip on the Marshall Club championship with an unbeaten score of 11½ out of 13. The games

were played on Sundays. A strong entry included recent Manhattan Club Champion Alexander Kevitz and three former Marshall Club Champions. Reuben started with 9½/10, which already practically guaranteed him first place. Draws with Smirka and Chernev in rounds 11 and 12 provided the necessary points to confirm the title. Prizes were awarded to the top seven finishers. The games are recorded in the German algebraic form in the notebook.

(72) Cass, A—Fine

Marshall CC championship 1932/3, New York (1), 1932 (2 Oct.)
Queen's Pawn Game [A56]

1. d4 Nf6 **2.** c4 e6 **3.** e3 c5 **4.** Nf3 cxd4 **5.** exd4 d5 **6.** Nc3 dxc4 **7.** Bxc4 a6 **8.** 0–0 Bd6 **9.** Be3 0–0 **10.** Rc1 b5 **11.** Be2 Nbd7 **12.** Qd2 Bb7 **13.** Rc2 Qe7 **14.** a3 Rfd8 **15.** Rd1 h6 **16.** Ne1 Nb6 **17.** Bf3 Rac8 **18.** Bxb7 Qxb7 **19.** Qe2 Nc4 **20.** Qf3? Qxf3 **21.** Nxf3 Nxb2 **22.** Rxb2 Rxc3 **23.** a4 b4 **24.** Bd2 Rd3 **25.** Rc1 a5 **26.** Rbc2 Ra3 **27.** Rc8 Rxc8 **28.** Rxc8+ Kh7 **29.** Kf1 Ne4 **30.** Ke2 Nxd2 **31.** Nxd2 Rxa4 **32.** g3 Ra2 **33.** Kd3 a4 **34.** Rc6 Be7 **35.** Rb6 b3 **36.** f4 b2 **37.** Kc3 a3 **38.** Ra6 Ra1 **39.** Kc2 Rc1+ White resigned. 0–1

(73) Fine—Kevitz, A

Marshall CC championship 1932/3, New York (2), 1932 (9 Oct.)
Benoni Defence, Schmid Variation [A60]

1. d4 Nf6 **2.** c4 e6 **3.** Nc3 c5 **4.** d5 exd5 **5.** cxd5 d6 **6.** Nf3 a6 **7.** a4 Prevents the liberating ... b5. **7 ... Be7** (7 ... g6 would, of course, lead to a Modern Benoni. AW) **8.** Nd2 0–0 **9.** e4 Re8 **10.** Bd3 Nbd7 **11.** f4 b6 **12.** 0–0 Qc7 **13.** Nc4 Bf8 **14.** Qf3 Rb8 **15.** b3 b5 **16.** axb5 axb5 **17.** Na5 Ba6 **18.** Nc6 Rb6

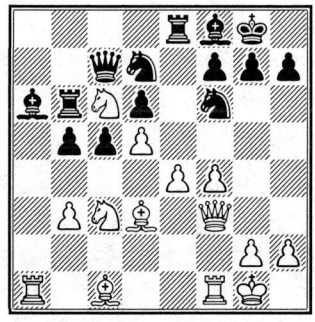

Position after Black's 18th move

White obviously has an overwhelming position, but how is he to continue? The break e5 will probably be decisive, so he sacrifices to make it possible. **19. Rxa6 Rxa6 20. Bxb5 Rb6 21. Bc4 Nb8** Hoping to free himself with exchanges. **22. Nb5 Qb7 23. e5** Finally. **23 ... Nfd7** Countersacrifices do not help: if 23 ... Nxd5 24 Na5 Qa6 25 Qxd5 wins. **24. Na5 Qc8 25. Bb2 Qd8** To take the pawn would open up the f-file with devastating effect. **26. Nc6 Qc8 27. e6! Nf6** There is nothing better: after 27 ... fxe6 28 dxe6 the discovered checks are killing. **28. Bxf6 gxf6 29. Qg4+ Bg7** Or 29 ... Kh8 30 exf7 Qxg4 31 fxe8Q. **30. Ne7+ Rxe7 31. exf7+ Kxf7 32. Qxc8** Black resigned. **1–0** Fine 1953, 372–4.

(74) BECKHARDT, N—FINE

Marshall CC championship 1932/3, New York (3), 1932
  (16 Oct.)

Sicilian Defence, Dragon Variation [B73]

1. e4 c5 2. d4 cxd4 3. Nf3 Nc6 4. Nxd4 Nf6 5. Nc3 d6 6. Be2 g6 7. 0–0 Bg7 8. Be3 0–0 9. f4 Bd7 10. Bf3 Rc8 11. Rc1 Qb6 12. Qd3 Qxb2 13. a3? Nb4 14. axb4 Rxc3 15. Qd2 Rxe3 16. Qxe3 Ng4 17. Qe2 Bxd4+ 18. Kh1 Nf2+ White resigned. **0–1**

(75) FINE—THOLFSEN, E

Marshall CC championship 1932/3, New York (4), 1932
  (23 Oct.)

English Opening [A15]

1. Nf3 Nf6 2. c4 g6 3. b3 Bg7 4. Bb2 0–0 5. g3 b6 6. Bg2 Bb7 7. 0–0 d6 8. d4 e6 9. Nc3 c5 10. dxc5 bxc5 11. Qc2 Nc6 12. Rad1 Qe7 13. Rd2 Rfd8 14. Rfd1 Ne8 15. e3 Nb4 16. Qb1 Bc6 17. h4 Qb7 18. Ne1 Bxg2 19. Nxg2 Nc6 20. Ne4 Bxb2 21. Qxb2 Ne5 22. Nxd6 Nf3+ 23. Kh1 Rxd6 24. Rxd6 Nxd6 25. Rxd6 Ne1 26. f4 Re8 27. Qf2 Nf3 28. Rd1 e5 29. Rd5 e4 30. Ne1 Nxe1 31. Qxe1 Qc8 32. Kg2 Qc7 33. Qd2 Re6 34. Rd7 Qb6 35. Rd8+ Kg7 36. g4 Qc6 37. Qb2+ f6 38. g5 Rd6 39. gxf6+ Rxf6 40. Qe5 Kf7 41. Rh8 Kg7 42. Re8 Black resigned. **1–0**

(76) RIVAS-COSTA, S—FINE

Marshall CC championship 1932/3, New York (5), 1932
  (30 Oct.)

Spanish Opening, Steinitz Defence Deferred [C73]

1. e4 e5 2. Nf3 Nc6 3. Bb5 a6 4. Ba4 d6 5. Bxc6+ bxc6 6. d4 exd4 7. Nxd4 Bd7 8. 0–0 Nf6 9. Nc3 Be7 10. Qd3 0–0 11. h3 Re8 12. b3 Bf8 13. Bb2 g6 14. Rae1 Bg7 15. f4 c5 16. Nf3 Nh5 17. Bc1 Ng3 18. Ne2 Nxf1 19. Kxf1 Bc6 20. Ng3 d5 21. exd5 Rxe1+ 22. Nxe1 Qxd5 23. Qe2 Re8 24. c4 Qd8 25. Qc2 Qh4 26. Ne2 Bd4 27. Nd3 Be4 28. g3 Qxh3+ 29. Ke1 Bf3 White resigned. **0–1**

(77) FINE—LEVENSTEIN, R

Marshall CC championship 1932/3, New York (6), 1932
  (6 Nov.)

Old Indian Defence [A53]

1. d4 Nf6 2. c4 d6 3. Nc3 Nbd7 4. e4 e5 5. Be3

Be7 6. Bd3 0–0 7. f3 c6 8. d5 Nh5 9. Nge2 g6 10. 0–0 Bg5 11. Bf2 Nc5 12. Bc2 cxd5 13. Nxd5 f5 14. h4 Bh6 15. b4 Ne6 16. exf5 gxf5 17. Qd3 Qd7 18. Rad1 Qf7 19. Ndc3 Nef4 20. Nxf4 Nxf4 21. Qxd6 Be6 22. Qxe5 Qg6 23. g3 Bxc4 24. Bb3 Bxb3 25. axb3 Rae8 26. Qb5 Nh5 27. Kh2 Be3 28. Qe2 Kh8 29. Qb2 Qg7 30. Na4 Rf6 31. Rfe1 Rg8 32. Rg1 f4 33. gxf4 Bxf4+ 34. Kh1 Qh6 35. Bd4 Ng3+ 36. Rxg3 Qxh4+ 37. Qh2 Bxg3 38. Qxh4 Bxh4 39. Nc5 b6? 40. Ne4 Rgg6 41. Ra1 Kg8 42. Bxf6 Bxf6 43. Rxa7 Bd4 44. Rd7 Be3 45. Nd6 Rh6+ 46. Kg2 Rg6+ 47. Kf1 h5 48. Nf5 Bg5 49. f4 Bf6 50. Rd6 Kh7 51. Rxb6 Rg4 52. Rxf6 Rxf4+ 53. Ke2 Rxb4 54. Rh6+ Kg8 55. Nd4 Rxd4 56. Rxh5 Kf7 57. Re5 Rd6 58. Re3 Re6 59. Kd3 Rxe3+ 60. Kxe3 Ke6 61. Ke4 Kd6 62. Kd4 Kc6 63. Kc4** Black resigned. **1–0**

(78) DUNST, T—FINE

Marshall CC championship 1932/3, New York (7), 1932
  (13 Nov.)

English Opening [D13]

1. Nf3 Nf6 2. c4 c6 3. g3 d5 4. cxd5 cxd5 5. Bg2 Nc6 6. d4 Bf5 7. Nc3 e6 8. Bg5 Bd6 9. 0–0 0–0 10. Rc1 Qb6 11. Bxf6 gxf6 12. Qd2 Rac8 13. Na4 Qa5 14. Nc3 Qb6 15. Na4 Qa6 16. b3 Ba3 17. Rcd1 Ne7 18. Nh4 Rc2 19. Qh6 Bg6 20. Rd2 Rxd2 21. Nxg6 hxg6 22. Qxd2 Rc8 23. Nb2 Qc6 24. Nd3?! 24 Nc4! was playable because of the pin on the d-pawn. **24 ... Nc3 25. Qf4 Nf5 26. Kh1 Qxd4 27. Qd2 b6 28. h3 Nd6 29. Rd1 Ne4 30. Qf4 Rc2 31. e3 Nxf2+ 32. Nxf2 Qxf4** White resigned. **0–1**

(79) POLLAND, D—FINE

Marshall CC championship 1932/3, New York (8), 1932
  (20 Nov.)

Bogolyubov Indian Defence [E16]

1. d4 e6 2. c4 Nf6 3. Nf3 Bb4+ 4. Bd2 Qe7 5. g3 b6 6. Bg2 Bb7 7. 0–0 Bxd2 8. Qxd2 0–0 9. Nc3 d6 10. Rfe1 c5 11. Rad1 Rd8 12. dxc5 bxc5 13. e4 Nc6 14. b3 Nb4 15. h3 Bc6 16. Nd5! exd5 17. exd5 Qc7 18. dxc6 d5! 19. cxd5 Rxd5 20. Qe2 Rxd1 21. Rxd1 Re8 22. Qc4 Qxc6 23. a3 Nbd5 24. b4 Nb6 25. Qxc5 Qa4 26. Rd3 Qa6 27. Ne5 h6 28. Re3 Qa4 29. Qc7 Rf8 30. Rd3 Qb5 31. Bc6 Qa6 32. Rd8 Rxd8 33. Qxd8+ Kh7 34. Qd3+ Qxd3 35. Nxd3 Kg8 36. a4 Kf8 37. a5 Nc4 38. Kf1 Ke7 39. Ke2 Kd6 40. Bb5 Kd5 41. f3 Kd4 42. Bc6 Nh5 43. g4 Ng3+ 44. Kf2 Nh1+ 45. Ke2 Ng3+ 46. Kf2 Agreed drawn. **½–½**

(80) FINE—FRERE, W

Marshall CC championship 1932/3, New York (9), 1932
  (27 Nov.)

French Defence, Nimzowitsch Advance Variation [C02]

1. d4 e6 2. e4 d5 3. e5 c5 4. Qg4 Nc6 5. Nf3 cxd4
6. Bd3 Qc7 7. Qg3 f6 8. exf6 Qxg3 9. f7+ Kxf7
10. hxg3 g6 After 10 ... e5! Black stands slightly better,
MCO 70. 11. Bf4 Nb4?! 12. Ng5+ Kg7 13. Be5+ Nf6
14. Rxh7+ Rxh7 15. Bxf6+ Kxf6 16. Nxh7+ Kg7
17. Nxf8 Nxd3+ 18. cxd3 Kxf8 19. Nd2 e5 20. Nf3
Bf5 21. Kd2 Re8 22. Re1 Bxd3 23. Kxd3 e4+
24. Kxd4 exf3 25. Rxe8+ Black resigned. 1–0

(81) SANTASIERE, A—FINE

Marshall CC championship 1932/3, New York (10), 1932
(5 Dec.)
Bogolyubov Indian Defence [E16]

1. d4 e6 2. c4 Nf6 3. Nf3 Bb4+ 4. Bd2 Bxd2+
5. Qxd2 b6 6. g3 Bb7 7. Bg2 0–0 8. Nc3 d6
9. 0–0 Qe7 10. Ne1 Bxg2 11. Nxg2 c5 12. d5 Nbd7
13. f3 exd5 14. cxd5 a6 15. e4 b5 16. Ne3 g6
17. a4 b4 18. Ne2 Rfe8 19. Rf2 Ne5 20. g4 a5
21. Ng3 c4 22. g5 Nfd7 23. f4 Nd3 24. Rff1 N3c5
25. Rae1 Nxe4 26. Qd4 Nxg3 27. hxg3 Qe4
28. Qxc4 Nb6 29. Qxe4 Rxe4 30. b3 Rae8 31. Kf2
Kg7 32. Rh1 R8e7 33. Rh6 Rc7 34. Rehl Rc3
35. Rxh7+ Kf8 36. Rh8+ Ke7 37. Re1 Nd7?!
38. Ra8 Rxb3 39. f5?! Ne5 40. Ra7+? Kd8 41. Ra8+
Kc7 42. Rc1+ Rc3 43. Rxc3+ bxc3 44. fxg6 fxg6
45. Nc2 Rxa4 46. Ke3 Ra2 47. Nd4 Rd2 48. Rh8
Ng4+ 49. Ke4 Nf2+ White resigned. 0–1

(82) FINE—SMIRKA, R

Marshall CC championship 1932/3, New York (11), 1932
(11 Dec.)
Two Knights Defence, Chigorin Variation [C59]

1. e4 e5 2. Nf3 Nc6 3. Bc4 Nf6 4. Ng5 d5 5. exd5
Na5 6. Bb5+ c6 7. dxc6 bxc6 8. Be2 h6 9. Nf3 e4
10. Ne5 Bd6 11. d4 Qc7 12. Bd2 0–0 13. Na3 Rb8
14. Nac4 Nxc4 15. Nxc4 Be7 16. 0–0 Nd5 17. Re1
f5 18. Bf1 Nf6 19. b3 Ng4 20. g3 g5 21. Ba5 Rb6?
22. Nxb6 axb6 23. Bc3 Nf6 24. d5 Nxd5 25. Bc4
Be6 26. Qh5 Kh7 27. Bb2 Bc5 28. Rad1 e3!
29. fxe3 Nxe3 30. Bd4 Bxd4 31. Rxd4 Qe5?
32. c3 Bd5 33. Kf2?! Simply 33 Bxd5 cxd5 34 Rd3 f4
35 gxf4 wins. 33 ... Ng4+ 34. Kf1 Ne3+ Now Black
could play for more: 34 ... Bg2+! 35 Kxg2 Qxe1 36 Kh3 Qf2
37 Rxg4 fxg4+ 38 Qxg4. One might surmise that both players had but seconds on their clocks at this point. 35. Kf2
Ng4+ 36. Kf1 Ne3+ Agreed drawn. ½–½

(83) CHERNEV, I—FINE

Marshall CC championship 1932/3, New York (12), 1932
(18 Dec.)
Colle System [D05]

1. d4 d5 2. Nf3 Nf6 3. e3 e6 4. Bd3 c5 5. c3 Nc6
6. Nbd2 Qc7 7. b3?! cxd4 8. cxd4 Nb4 9. Bb5+
Bd7 10. Bxd7+ Nxd7 11. 0–0 Rc8 12. Ne1 Bd6
13. Ndf3 Nc2 14. Nxc2 Qxc2 15. Qxc2 Rxc2
16. Bd2 Ke7?! 17. Rfc1 Rhc8 18. Ne1 Rxc1 19. Rxc1
Rxc1 20. Bxc1 Agreed drawn. ½–½

(84) FINE—SIMONSON, A

Marshall CC championship 1932/3, New York (13), 1932
(25 Dec.)
Clemenz Opening/Colle System [A00]

1. h3 d5 2. d4 c5 3. c3 Nc6 4. e3 e6 5. Nf3 Qc7
6. Nbd2 Nf6 7. Bd3 Bd6 8. 0–0 0–0–0 9. Qe2 Re8
10. e4 e5 11. exd5 exd4 12. Ne4 Nxd5 13. c4 Nde7
14. Re1 Bd7 15. Nfg5 Ng6 16. Qh5 h6 17. Nxf7
Kxf7 18. Bxh6 Rxe4 Or 18 ... Bh2+ 19 Kh1 Nce5 20
Ng5+ Kg8 21 Bxg6 Re7 22 Bh7+ Kf8 23 Be4 with a fierce
attack. 19. Bxe4 Nce5 20. f4 Rh8 21. fxe5 Rxh6
22. Bd5+ Black resigned. 1–0

The International Team Tournament at Folkestone, 1933

As a result of his success on the national scene over the previous nine months, Fine was invited to participate in a tournament to select the lower boards of the American team which was to defend their title as international team champions. By winning the tournament Fine qualified to repre-sent his home country and booked his passage for his first professional experience outside the United States.

New York Metropolitan League, February–April, 1933

Fine won an excellent attacking game against H. D. Cut-ler of N. Y. U. in February but was efficiently dispatched by Isaac Kashdan of the Manhattan Chess Club in an energet-ically played ending a couple of months later. At the time Kashdan was the foremost American player, holding down first board for the United States in the team tournaments of 1928, 1930, 1931 and 1933, in the latter two of which the Americans were victorious. In fact Kashdan was one of the best players in the world, having a much superior record against Alekhine than had Flohr, considered by many to be a worthy challenger for the crown. The inability of Kashdan's supporters to raise funds, in the poor economic climate of the times, for a match with Marshall probably deprived him not only of the deserved title of U.S. Champion, but perhaps indirectly of a chance to raise a purse for the higher laurels.

The teams expected to participate in the league in 1933 were: Marshall, Manhattan, Empire City, Rice Progressive, West Side, Scandinavian, Karl Marx, Queens, City College and New York University Chess Clubs. The games are recorded in the English descriptive form in the notebook.

Fine	1	Cutler	0
Kashdan	1	Fine	0

(85) FINE—CUTLER, H

Metropolitan League, New York, 1933 (Feb.)
Queen's Gambit Declined, Exchange Variation [D36]

1. d4 Nf6 2. c4 e6 3. Nc3 d5 4. Bg5 Nbd7 5. cxd5 exd5 6. e3 Be7 7. Bd3 0–0 8. Qc2 c6 9. Nge2 a5 10. 0–0–0 b5 11. Ng3 g6 12. h4 Ne8 13. Bh6 Ng7 14. h5 Bg5 15. hxg6 fxg6 16. Bxg6 hxg6 17. Qxg6 Bxh6 18. Rxh6 Rf6 19. Qh7+ Kf7 20. Nh5 Qf8 21. Nxf6 Nxf6 22. Qg6+ Ke7 23. e4 Be6 24. Qg5 dxe4 25. Nxe4 Nge8 26. Qc5+ Kf7 27. Ng5+ Kg8 28. Rh8+ Black resigned. **1–0**

(86) KASHDAN, I—FINE

Metropolitan League, New York, 1933 (April)
Slav Defence [D18]

1. d4 d5 2. c4 c6 3. Nf3 Nf6 4. Nc3 dxc4 5. a4 Bf5 6. e3 e6 7. Bxc4 Bb4 8. 0–0 0–0 9. Qb3 Qe7 10. Bd2 Fine quotes this as the main line in MCO and says that on other moves c5 is likewise best. **10 ... Nbd7? 11. Rfe1 h6 12. e4 Bh7 13. e5 Ne8 14. a5 Nc7 15. Ne4** As a harbinger of his style to come, Kashdan seeks a technical solution when he could have achieved an overwhelming advantage with the aggressive 15 Ra4. (I don't quite see this, especially after 15 ... c5 16 dxc5 Bxc3 17 Bxc3 Nxc5! AW) **15 ... Bxd2 16. Nfxd2 Rab8 17. Re3 c5 18. Nxc5 Nxc5 19. dxc5 Qxc5 20. Qa3 Qd4 21. Qc3 Rfd8 22. Nf3 Qxc3 23. Rxc3 Be4 24. Be2 Bc6 25. Rac1 Rd5 26. a6 Ne8 27. axb7 Bxb7 28. Ra3 a5 29. h3 Kf8 30. b3 Ke7 31. Rca1 Nc7?** Black would have drawing chances after 31 ... Rc5. **32. Bc4 Rd7 33. Rxa5 Bd5 34. Ra7 Nb5 35. Rxd7+ Kxd7 36. Ra5 Nc7 37. Bxd5 Nxd5 38. Ra7+ Nc7 39. Nd2 Rb6 40. Kf1 Rb8 41. Ke2 Rb5 42. f4 g5 43. g3 h5 44. Kf3! h4 45. gxh4 gxf4 46. Kxf4 Rb4+ 47. Kg3** A prettier, though not a speedier, win was 47 Ne4 Kc6 48 Rxc7+. **47 ... Rb5 48. Nf3 Rxb3 49. h5 Kc6 50. h6 Rb8 51. Ng5 Rg8 52. Kh4 Kb6 53. Rxc7 Kxc7 54. Nxf7** Black resigned. **1–0** Denker & Parr, 197–8.

U.S. Team Trial, New York, May 6–16, 1933

"In June 1933 an international team tournament was scheduled for Folkestone, England. For the United States team Kashdan and Marshall were seeded; the remaining three places were to be filled by a qualifying tournament among the leading players. I took first prize in this tournament which entitled me to play at third board for the team." (Fine 1958) The tournament was played at the Marshall Chess Club on May 6 and 7, the West Side Y. M. C. A. on May 8 to 13 and finished at the Manhattan Chess Club on May 14 to 16. In the second round Fine was defeated by Levenstein, who won a prize for this effort, and in the fourth his attempts to win against Willman almost backfired. From that point on, however, he dropped only half a point to finish a point clear of Arthur Dake and Al Simonson. The time limit was 50 moves in 2½ hours with five-hour sessions from 7.15 P.M. to 12.15 A.M., except on the weekend when the sessions were 2 to 7 P.M., with adjourned games 8 P.M. to midnight. The games are recorded in the German algebraic and English descriptive forms in the notebook (in one case changing from the former to the latter after one move).

		1	2	3	4	5	6	7	8	9	10	11	
1	Fine	*	1	1	1	½	1	½	0	1	1	1	8
2	Dake	0	*	1	½	1	1	½	1	1	0	1	7
3	Simonson	0	0	*	1	1	½	½	1	1	1	1	7
4	Denker	0	½	0	*	½	1	1	1	0	1	1	6
5	Willman	½	0	0	½	*	½	½	1	1	½	1	5½
6	Horowitz	0	0	½	0	½	*	1	½	1	1	1	5½
7	Reinfeld	½	½	½	0	½	0	*	0	½	½	1	4
8	Levenstein	1	0	0	0	0	½	1	*	½	1	0	4
9	Beckhardt	0	0	0	1	0	0	½	½	*	1	0	3
10	Schwartz	0	1	0	0	½	0	½	0	0	*	½	2½
11	Hassialis	0	0	0	0	0	0	0	1	1	½	*	2½

(87) FINE—BECKHARDT, N

U.S. team trial, New York (2), 1933 (7 May)
Nimzowitsch-Indian Defence [E43]

1. d4 Nf6 2. c4 e6 3. Nc3 Bb4 4. e3 b6 5. Bd3 Bb7 6. f3 c5 7. Nge2 Bxc3+ 8. bxc3 d6 9. 0–0 Nc6 10. e4 e5 11. d5 Na5 12. Ng3 g6 13. f4 Nd7 14. f5 Qh4 15. f6 0–0–0

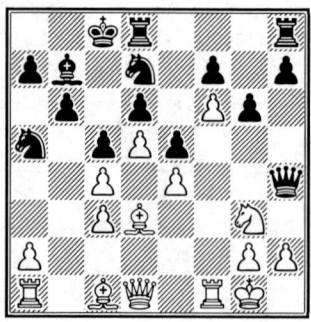

Position after Black's 15th move

16. Nh1 Nf8 17. Be3 Ba6 18. Rb1 Bxc4 19. g3 Qh3 20. Bxc4 Nxc4 21. Qe2 Nxe3 22. Qa6+ Kb8 23. Rxb6+ Black resigned. **1–0**

(88) LEVENSTEIN, R—FINE

U.S. team trial, New York (3), 1933 (8 May)
Queen's Indian Defence [E18]

1. c4 e6 2. Nf3 Nf6 3. g3 b6 4. Bg2 Bb7 5. 0–0
Be7 6. d4 0–0 7. Nc3 d6 8. Qc2 Nbd7 9. e4 e5
10. b3 c6 11. Bb2 Qc7 12. Rad1 b5 13. h3 bxc4
14. bxc4 Ba6 15. Ne2 Rfe8 16. Rfe1 Bf8 17. c5
exd4 18. cxd6 Bxd6 19. Nexd4 Bb4 20. Re3?! Bc5
21. Nh4 Bb6 22. Rc3 c5 23. Ndf5 Rad8 24. Nd6
Re6 25. Nhf5 Nb8 26. e5 Rxe5 27. Re3 Re6?!
28. Bxf6 gxf6 29. Re4 Nc6 30. Qd2 Qxd6 31. Qh6
Qf8 32. Rxd8 Black resigned. 1–0

(89) FINE—DAKE, A

U.S. team trial, New York (4), 1933 (9 May)
Nimzowitsch-Indian Defence, Classical Variation [E32]

1. d4 Nf6 2. c4 e6 3. Nc3 Bb4 4. Qc2 This is at
present considered White's best reply to Nimzowitsch's
Defence. 4 ... 0–0 5. a3 Bxc3+ Undoubtedly best. After
5 ... Be7 6 e4 White has decidedly the better of it. 6. Qxc3
d6 7. e3 Nbd7 8. Bd3 e5 9. Ne2 Re8 10. 0–0 Nf8
11. b4 exd4 This releases the tension in the centre,
enables White to post his knight very strongly at d4, and
opens up the diagonal of White's dark-squared bishop.
Preferable, therefore, was 11 ... Bd7 or 11 ... Ng6. 12. Nxd4
Ng6 13. Bb2 Ne5 14. Bc2 Qe7 15. f4 Ng6

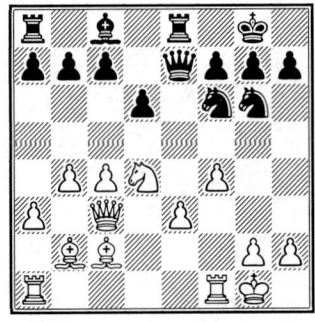

*Position after
Black's 15th move*

16. e4! Qf8 17. Rae1 Bd7 18. Qg3 Kh8 19. h3 If 19
e5 Nh5 20 Qg5 Nhxf4 21 Rxf4 dxe5 22 Bxg6 exf4! and
Black can defend himself successfully. 19 ... a5 20. b5
Rad8 21. Qf3 Bc8 22. g4 Ng8 23. Qg3 f6 Against
e5. 24. Kh2 Qf7 25. Bd3

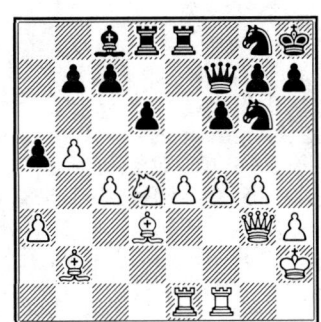

*Position after
White's 25th move*

*A portrait from 1933, Fine's final year at college. Not long after gradu-
ation he represented his country for the first time in the international
team tournament at Folkestone.*

25 ... Nf8 Intending Nf8-d7-c5. Against a more passive
defence White would continue with Rg1, Nf5, Re1-e2-g2,
and, finally, g5. 26. e5! dxe5 If 26 ... h6 27 exf6,
followed by g5 winning easily. 27. fxe5 h6 Against g5.
28. Re3 Qd7 29. Nf5 Nh7 If 29 ... fxe5 30 Bxe5 Ne6
31 Qh4 and White has no satisfactory defence to White's
chief threat, Nxh6. 30. Nh4 Nf8 If 30 ... g5 31 exf6 gxh4
32 f7+ Ngf6, White can win prosaically by 33 fxe8Q+, as
well as brilliantly by 33 Rxf6 hxg3+ 34 Kg1 Kg7 35 f8Q+
Nxf8 36 Rg6+ Kh7 37 Rg7+ Kh8 38 Rxd7+. 31. exf6
Nxf6 32. Rxf6! gxf6 33. Bxf6+ Kg8 34. Nf5! Kf7
35. Nxh6+ Kxf6 36. Qf4+ Black resigned. 1–0 Fine,
ACB 1933, 88.

(90) WILLMAN, R—FINE

U.S. team trial, New York (5), 1933 (10 May)
Réti Opening [A09]

1. Nf3 d5 2. c4 dxc4 3. e3 g6 4. Bxc4 Bg7 5. d4
Nf6 6. Nbd2 0–0 7. 0–0 Nbd7 8. b4 a6 9. Bb2
b6 10. Rc1 Bb7 11. Qe2 Nd5 12. a3 c5 13. e4
Nc7 14. Ba2 Nb5 15. Nb3 cxb4 16. axb4 e6
17. Na1 Qe7 18. Nc2 Nf6 19. Nd2 Rac8 20. Bc4
Nxe4 21. Nxe4 Rxc4!? (21 ... Bxe4 22 Bxb5 Rxc2 23
Rxc2 Bxc2 24 Bxa6 Bb3—AW) 22. Qxc4 Bxe4 23. f3
Bb7 24. Rfe1 Qh4 25. Rcd1 h5 26. Na3 Rc8
27. Qd3 Nxa3 28. Bxa3 b5 29. Bb2 Rc4 30. Bc3
Qd8 (30 ... Bf8!?) 31. Re2 h4 (31 ... Qc7!) 32. h3 Bd5
(32 ... Qc7!) 33. Rc2 Qc7 34. Rdc1 Qf4 35. Rd1 Bf8
36. Bd2 Qxd4+ 37. Qxd4 Rxd4 38. Rc8 g5?!

39. Kf2 Bb3 40. Ke3 e5 41. Ra1 Bc4 42. Be1 Be6
43. Rb8 Kg7 44. Bc3 Rd5 45. Rxa6 Bf5 46. Kf2
Be7 47. Rab6 Bd3 48. Ke3 Bf6 49. Rc8 Bc4
50. Ke4 Rd3 51. Bxe5 Bxe5 52. Kxe5 Agreed drawn.
½–½

(91) FINE—SCHWARTZ, E

U.S. team trial, New York (6), 1933 (11 May)
Queen's Gambit Declined, Tarrasch Defence [D34]

1. c4 e6 2. Nf3 Nf6 3. g3 c5 4. Bg2 Nc6 5. 0–0
Be7 6. d4 d5 7. cxd5 exd5 White now transposes
into a variation of the Tarrasch Defence to the Queen's
Gambit Declined very favourable to him. Preferable,
therefore, is 7 ... Nxd5. 8. dxc5 Bxc5 9. Nc3 0–0
10. Na4 Be7 11. Be3 Qa5 Loss of time. 11 ... Be6
should have been played. 12. a3 Bf5 13. b4 Qd8
14. Nc5 b6 15. Nb3 Rc8 16. Nbd4 Nxd4
17. Nxd4 Bg4 18. h3 Be6 19. Qd3 Qd7 20. Kh2
Rc4 21. f4 Ne4 22. f5 Rc3 23. Bxe4 Rxd3
24. Bxd3 Bf6 25. Rac1 Qa4 26. fxe6 fxe6 27. Rc3
a6 28. Bc2 Qd7 29. Bb3 h5 30. Rd3 Rd8 31. Nf3
Qc7 32. Bf4 e5 33. Rc1 Qb8 34. Rxd5 Rxd5
35. Bxd5+ Kf8 36. Bg5 Qd8 37. Bb7 Qd7
38. Bxa6

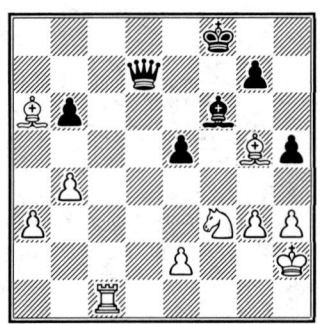

*Position after
White's 38th move*

38 ... Qa4 38 ... e4 gives better drawing chances. White
would continue with 39 Bxf6 gxf6 40 Ng1 Qa4 41 b5 Qxa3
42 Rf1 Ke7 43 Bb7. The win is then more difficult than in
the actual game. 39. Bd3 Qxa3 40. Rf1 Ke7 41. b5
Qb4 A blunder. The win, however, was only a question of
time. 42. Nxe5 Qc5 43. Nc6+ Kf7 44. Bxf6 gxf6
45. h4 Qe3 46. Nb4 Qc5 47. Rf4 Kg7 48. Nc6
Qe3 49. Rf5 Qe8 50. Bc4 Black resigned. 1–0 Fine,
ACB 1933, 89.

(92) HOROWITZ, I—FINE

U.S. team trial, New York (7), 1933 (12 May)
Réti Opening [D28]

1. Nf3 d5 2. c4 dxc4 3. e3 c5 4. Bxc4 e6 5. d4 a6
6. 0–0 Nf6 7. Qe2 Nbd7 8. Rd1 Qc7 9. a3 b5
10. Ba2 c4 11. e4 Be7 12. Nc3 Bb7 13. Bg5 Nb6
14. Rac1 0–0 15. Bb1 Rfe8

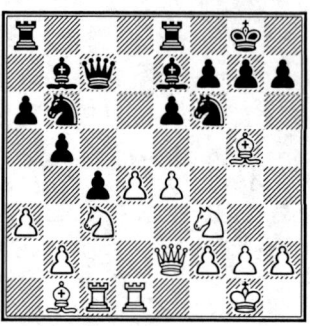

*Position after
Black's 15th move*

16. e5 Nfd7 17. Ne4 Bf8 18. Qc2 g6 19. Qd2 Nd5
20. Bh6 f6 21. Bxf8 Rxf8 22. exf6 Nf4 23. Ne5
Nxf6 24. f3 Nxe4 25. fxe4 Rad8 26. b3 Rxd4
White resigned. 0–1

(93) DENKER, A—FINE

U.S. team trial, New York (8), 1933 (13 May)
Schlechter Variation, Slav-Grünfeld [D90]

1. Nf3 Nf6 2. c4 c6 3. d4 d5 4. Nc3 g6 5. cxd5
cxd5 6. Bf4 Bg7 7. h3 0–0 8. e3 Qb6 9. Qc2 Nc6
10. Bb5 Ne4 11. Bxc6 Qxc6 12. Rc1 Nxc3 13. Qxc3
Qa6 14. Qb3 14 Qa3 would save valuable time. 14 ... Bf5
15. Qa3 Rfc8 16. Kd2 Not 16 Qxa6, because of 16 ...
Rxc1+ 17 Kd2 Rc2+. 16 ... Qb5 17. Nh4 Bd7 18. g4 g5
19. Bxg5 f6 20. Bf4 e5 21. dxe5 fxe5 22. Bh2 Bf8
23. Qb3

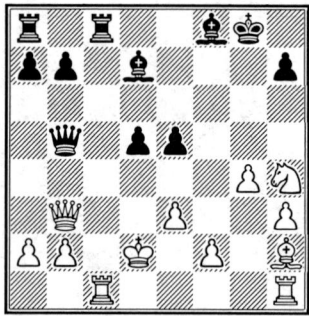

*Position after
White's 23rd move*

23 ... Bb4+ Fine thought that Black could not play 23 ...
Qa5+, attempting to trap the queen, because of 24 Ke2 Ba4
25 Qxb7 Rab8 26 b4 (which he thought was winning for
White). But 26 ... Bb5+ 27 Kf3 Qd8 28 Qxa7 Ra8 29 Qb7
Ba6 30 Rxc8 Qf6+ 31 Nf5 Bxb7 32 Rxa8 Bxa8 wins for
Black. 25 Rxc8 is also inadequate by reason of 25 ... Rxc8
26 Qxb7 Rc2+ 27 Kf3 e4+ 28 Kg3 Bd6+ 29 Kg2 Rxf2+! 30
Kxf2 Qd2+ 31 Kg1 Qxe3+ 32 Kf1 Qc1+ 33 Kg2 Qc2+ 34 Kf1
Qc4+ with a winning attack. AW 24. Kd1 This loses
quickly. After 24 Rc3 White can put up a sturdy resistance.
24 ... Qa5 25. Qd3 Rxc1+ 26. Kxc1 Qxa2 27. Bxe5
Rc8+ 28. Bc3 If 28 Kd1, 28 ... a6 wins the white queen.
28 ... Ba4 White resigned. Black threatened 29 ... Rxc3+.
0–1 Fine, ACB 1933, 90.

(94) FINE—REINFELD, F

U.S. team trial, New York (9), 1933 (14 May)
English Opening, Keres Variation [A12]

1. c4 c6 2. Nf3 Nf6 3. g3 d5 4. b3 Bg4 (The earliest Keres' game I can find in this system is Petrosyan–Keres, U.S.S.R. Club Team Championship, Tallinn 1964. The only earlier example of this position arriving seems to be Réti–Torre, Moscow 1925. AW) 5. Qc2 Nbd7 6. Bb2 e6 7. Bg2 Bd6 8. 0–0 0–0 9. d4 Bf5 10. Qd1 h6 11. Nc3 Qe7 12. Nd2 Ba3 13. Qc1 Bxb2 14. Qxb2 Bg6 15. Rae1 Rfd8 16. f4 Rab8 17. h3 h5 18. Kh2 Nh7 19. e4 dxe4 20. Ndxe4 Nhf6 21. Ng5 Qd6 22. Rd1 b5 23. d5 b4 24. dxe6 bxc3 25. Qxc3 Qe7 26. exd7 Rxd7 27. Qe5 Rc8 28. Rfe1 Kf8 29. Qa5 Qd8 30. Qc5+ Kg8 31. Rxd7 Qxd7 32. f5 Qxf5 33. Qxf5 Bxf5 34. Re7 Bd7 35. Kg1 Re8 36. Rxe8+ Bxe8 37. b4 Kf8 38. Kf2 Ke7 39. Ke3 Bd7 40. Kd4 Ne8 41. Ne4 Nc7 42. Nc5 Be8 43. a4 a6 44. h4 Bd7 45. Nxd7 Kxd7 46. Bh3+ Ne6+ 47. Ke4 Kd6 48. Bxe6 Kxe6 49. b5 axb5 50. cxb5 cxb5 51. axb5 Agreed drawn. ½–½

(95) FINE—HASSIALIS, M

U.S. team trial, New York (10), 1933 (15 May)

Default 1–0

(96) SIMONSON, A—FINE

U.S. team trial, New York (11), 1933 (16 May)
Nimzowitsch-Indian Defence [E43]

1. d4 e6 2. c4 Nf6 3. Nc3 Bb4 4. e3 b6 5. Bd3 Bb7 6. f3 c5 7. Nge2 cxd4 8. exd4 0–0 9. 0–0 d5 10. Bg5 dxc4 11. Bxc4 Nbd7 12. Ne4 Be7 13. N2g3 h6 14. Be3 a6 15. a4 Nd5 16. Bd2 f5 17. Nc3 Bf6 18. Nxf5 exf5 19. Nxd5 Bxd4+ 20. Be3 Bxe3+ 21. Nxe3+ Kh8 22. Be6 Nc5 23. Qxd8 Raxd8 24. Bxf5 Rde8 25. Rfe1 Rxe3 26. Rxe3 Rxf5 27. b4 Nd7 28. Rc1 Bd5 29. Rc7 Ne5

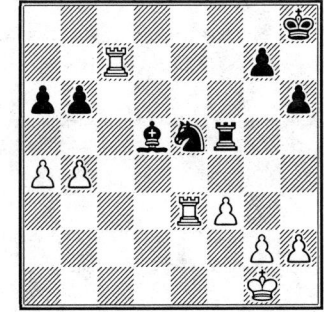

Position after Black's 29th move

30. f4?! Nc6 31. Re8+ Kh7 32. b5 axb5 33. axb5 Nd4 34. Ree7 Ne6 35. Rcd7 Bc4 36. Rd6?! Nxf4 37. Rxb6? Ne2+ White resigned. 0–1

Folkestone Olympiad, June 12–23, 1933

"The committee appointed by the National Chess Federation to select and organize the team to represent the United States in the International Tournament of FIDE which is to be held at Folkestone, England, June 12th to 24th, 1933, for the Hamilton-Russell Trophy now in our possession, is making progress and is endeavouring to underwrite the necessary attending expenses of a team of five players. This committee appeals to every lover and patron of the game in the United States to help us to retain the Trophy in this country. Subscriptions may be sent to the Secretary of the Committee, Mr. H. Helms, ... Our chance of winning again is excellent and we should not let it go by default." (ACB 1933)

The tournament was to take place in the palatial Leas Cliff Hall (designed by a chess player—J. L. Seaton Dahl) in Folkestone, Kent. The United States team set off from New York on Saturday 3 June aboard the steam ship *Champlain* of the French Line due to dock at Plymouth on 10 June. The American team, comprising Kashdan (+7 =6 –1), Marshall (+4 =6), Fine (+6 =6 –1, taking White only 4 times), Dake (+9 =2 –2) and Simonson (+2 =2 –2), won their matches against Lithuania (4–0), Iceland and Scotland (3½–½), Poland, Austria, France, Latvia, England and Belgium (3–1), Hungary and Italy (2½–1½), drew with Denmark and lost to the second and third placed teams Czechoslovakia (in the final round) and Sweden (1½–2½). The time limit was 36 moves in two hours. Fine, who played with the black pieces nine times out of thirteen, annotated four of his own games for the tournament book produced by Kashdan, who provided notes for a further two. He later recalled "In the team tournament my play was somewhat of a disappointment, although I did help the American team to win first prize. My best game from that period was a win in the qualifying tournament over Arthur Dake." (Fine 1958). In fact Fine's percentage score on third board was exceeded only by that of Lundin, who played all 14 games at board 3, since Sweden had no reserve, whereas Fine thrice played at board 2 when Marshall was rested.

Fine 1 Thorvaldsson (Iceland) 0
Fine 1 Page (Scotland) 0
Fine ½ Kahn (France)
Appel (Poland) ½ Fine
Fine rested in round 5
Petrovs (Latvia) 0—Fine 1
Winter (BCF) ½ Fine
United States scored 4–0 by Estonia's default
Glass (Austria) 0—Fine 1
Enevoldsen (Denmark) ½ Fine
Norcia (Italy) 0 Fine 1

Vistanetskis (Lithuania) 0 Fine 1
Havasi (Hungary) ½ Fine
Fine 0 Lundin (Sweden)
Rejfir (Czechoslovakia) ½ Fine

(97) FINE—THORVALDSSON, E

International Team Tournament, Folkestone (1), 1933 (12 June)
Queen's Gambit Declined, Exchange Variation [D36]

1. d4 Nf6 2. c4 e6 3. Nc3 d5 4. Bg5 Nbd7 5. cxd5 exd5 6. e3 Be7 7. Bd3 c6 8. Qc2 (8 Nge2 Nh5 9 Bxe7 Qxe7 10 g4 Nhf6 11 Ng3 Nb6 with an unclear position or 8 Nf3 Nh5 9 Bxe7 Qxe7 10 0–0 Nhf6 11 Qc2 0–0 12 Rfe1 g6 is slightly better for White, Burgess, NCO 393.) **8 ... h6?** Unnecessarily weakening his king's position. White can now easily open a file for his rooks. Better was 8 ... 0–0. This pawn move allows two possible combinative inroads: first along the g-file via a pawn storm, second along the b1-h7 diagonal, by means of a massing of the queen and bishop. White's plan is now clear: to storm the kingside with g2-g4-g5. **9. Bf4 0–0 10. 0–0–0** If White castled short the advance of the pawns would endanger his own safety. So he removes the king to the other side to have full freedom for the attack. In so doing White exposes himself to a counterattack on the queenside, but that is easily warded off. **10 ... b5 11. Nf3 a5 12. g4** (After this typical pawn sacrifice Fine assessed the position as slightly in White's favour (MCO, 146), which seems to contradict his opinion in *The Middle Game in Chess* that Black is strategically lost after his eighth move.) **12 ... Ne8** Trying to avoid opening the g-file. If 12 ... Nxg4 13 Rdg1 h5 14 h3 Ngf6 15 Rg5 Kh8 16 Rhg1 Rg8 17 Ne5 White regains his pawn with a very superior position. Again, if 12 ... Nb6 13 Rdg1 Bxg4 14 Ne5 h5 15 h3 (not 15 Nxc6 Qd7 16 Nxe7+ Qxe7 17 Bxb5 Bf3 etc.) Bd7 16 Bh6 Ne8 17 Qe2 and Black's position cannot be defended. **13. h4 Bd6 14. h5** Threatening of course g4-g5. **14 ... Bxf4** If 14 ... Be7 15 Rdg1 Bg5 16 Nxg5 hxg5 17 Bg3 White has a winning advantage, e.g., 17 ... Nb6 18 h6 g6 19 Bxg6 fxg6 20 Qxg6+ Kh8 21 Be5+ Rf6 22 Bxf6+ Qxf6 23 Qxe8+. **15. exf4 f6** Again an unnecessary weakening of the king's position; 15 ... Nb6 offered better defensive chances. Now White can win in either of two ways: by g4-g5, after safeguarding the knight (for if 16 g5? at once, ... fxg5, and the pawn cannot recapture because the knight is loose), or by the text. **16. Nh4**

16 ... f5 Desperation. The weaknesses on the diagonal make Black's position untenable. If 16 ... Rf7 17 Bg6 Re7 18 Bh7+ Kf7 19 Ng6 Re6 20 f5 Rd6 21 Rde1 Nb6 22 Re7+ wins the queen. Or still better is 22 Re3 Ra7 23 Rhe1 R6d7 24 Rxe8 winning easily. **17. Rdg1** Open lines are more important than the pawn. **17 ... Ndf6** If instead 17 ... fxg4 18 Bh7+ Kh8 19 Ng6+ Kxh7 20 Nxf8+ Kg8 21 Ng6 wins the exchange and preserves the attack. **18. Ng6 Rf7 19. Ne5 Rc7 20. Bxf5 Bxf5 21. Qxf5 Qc8 22. Qg6** Naturally avoiding exchanges. The game is now decided by the routine advance of the pawns. **22 ... Nh7 23. g5 Nf8** If 23 ... hxg5 a pretty queen sacrifice is possible; 24 fxg5 Nf8 25 h6!! **24. Qd3 Qe6 25. f5 Qd6 26. f6 gxf6 27. gxh6+** Equally good is 27 gxf6+ Kh8 28 Qg3 Qe6 29 f7. **27 ... Kh8 28. Qg3 Qe6 29. Ng6+ Nxg6 30. hxg6** There is now no defence against the pawn advance, so Black resigned.**1–0** Fine 1953, 357–60; Fine in Kashdan, 3–4

(98) FINE—PAGE, G

International Team Tournament, Folkestone (2), 1933 (13 June)
Budapest Defence [A52]

1. d4 Nf6 2. c4 e5 3. dxe5 Ng4 4. e4 Nowadays either 4 Nf3 or 4 Bf4 are considered the best way to retain the advantage—AW. **4 ... Nxe5 5. f4 Ng6 6. Bd3** Nunn's main continuation here is 6 Be3 Bb4+ 7 Nd2 Qe7 8 Qc2 0–0 9 0–0–0, with an unclear position. **6 ... Bc5 7. Nf3 d6 8. Nc3 Bg4** A good idea. By exchanging this bishop for White's valuable knight, Black gains the square d4 for his pieces and has good chances on the queenside. It would have been better, however, to defer this move until the occupation of d4 is more effective than in the actual game. Thus 8 ... 0–0 9 Qe2 Nc6 10 Bd2 Bg4. **9. h3 Bxf3 10. Qxf3 Nc6 11. Bd2 Nd4 12. Qg3 c6 13. 0–0–0 0–0** Better is 13 ... Qh4 14 Qxh4 Nxh4 15 Bf1, although White still has the advantage. **14. h4 Ne7** If 14 ... f5 15 exf5 Ndxf5 16 Bxf5 Rxf5 and the advance of the White kingside pawns is decisive. **15. f5 f6 16. Bb1** White plays to win the Black knight at d4, but this is not possible. Simpler and better therefore, was Qh3, followed by g2-g4-g5. **16 ... b5 17. Qd3 Qb6 18. Bf4** 18 Be3 is met by 18 ... Nb3+, while 18 Rhe1 is answered by Rab8. **18 ... Rfd8 19. Rhe1 a5 20. Rd2** 20 Be3 could be answered by 20 ... bxc4 21 Qxc4+ d5 22 exd5 Nb3+ 23 axb3 Bxe3+ 24 Kc2 cxd5 25 Nxd5 Nxd5 26 Rxd5 Kh8 and White cannot win. **20 ... a4 21. g4 bxc4 22. Qxc4+ d5 23. Qd3 Kh8** Better is dxe4. **24. e5**

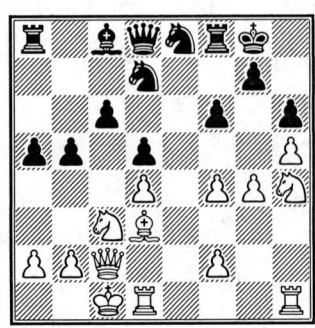

*Position after
White's 16th move*

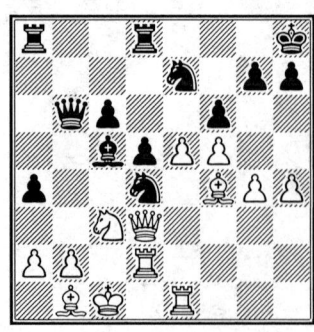

*Position after
White's 24th move*

24 ... Nb5 25. g5 Nxc3 26. bxc3 Ba3+ 27. Kd1 Rab8 28. Bc2 d4 29. c4 Bb4 There is nothing to be done against the coming attack on h7. **30. exf6 gxf6 31. gxf6 Bxd2 32. fxe7** Black resigned. **1–0** Fine in Kashdan, 16–7

(99) FINE–KAHN, V

International Team Tournament, Folkestone (3), 1933 (14 June)

This gamescore in unavailable. ½–½

(100) APPEL, I–FINE

International Team Tournament, Folkestone (4), 1933 (15 June)
Bogolyubov Indian Defence [E16]

1. d4 Nf6 2. c4 e6 3. Nf3 Bb4+ 4. Bd2 Bxd2+ 5. Qxd2 b6 (5 ... 0–0 6 g3 d5 7 Bg2 Nbd7 8 Qc2 b6 9 cxd5 Nxd5 10 0–0 c5! 11 Nc3 Bb7 12 Rfd1 Rc8 with equality, Stohl, NCO 452.) **6. Nc3 Bb7 7. g3** (7 Qc2!, Mueller) **7 ... 0–0** (7 ... Ne4, Mueller) **8. Bg2 Qe7 9. 0–0 d6 10. Rfe1 Rd8** (10 ... Ne4, Mueller) **11. e4 Nbd7 12. Rad1 Ne8** (12 ... e5 13 Nh4 or 13 Nd5, Mueller) **13. Nh4 Rab8 14. f4 c6 15. Qf2 Nc7 16. d5** "And after a few more moves White obtained a winning position." BCM 1933, 510–1. ½–½ Hans Mueller (Vienna) "Theoretical Novelties from the Folkestone Chess Olympiade (1933): Part IV—Queen's Gambit" BCM 1933, 506–13.

(101) PETROVS, V–FINE

International Team Tournament, Folkestone (6), 1933 (16 June)

This gamescore is unavailable. **0–1**

(102) WINTER, W–FINE

International Team Tournament, Folkestone (7), 1933 (17 June)

This gamescore is unavailable. ½–½

(103) GLASS, E–FINE

International Team Tournament, Folkestone (9), 1933 (19 June)
Queen's Gambit Declined, Tarrasch Defence [D30]

1. d4 Nf6 2. Nf3 d5 3. c4 e6 4. e3 c5 5. cxd5 Nxd5 6. Be2 Nc6 7. 0–0 Be7 8. dxc5 Bxc5 9. a3 0–0 10. Qc2 Be7 11. e4 Nb6 12. Bf4 f6 Black has played the opening weakly, and now can develop only with difficulty. **13. Rd1 Qe8 14. Nc3 e5 15. Be3 Be6 16. Nd5 Bd8 17. Bxb6** This exchange only strengthens Black's game. Preferable was 17 Bc5 Rf7 18 Rac1. **17 ... axb6 18. Bc4 Kh8 19. b4 Rc8 20. Qb3 Bg4 21. Be2 f5 22. Qd3 Qg6 23. exf5** If 23 Nd2 Nd4 24 Bxg4 fxg4 and Black stands well. **23 ... Bxf5 24. Qe3 Be4**

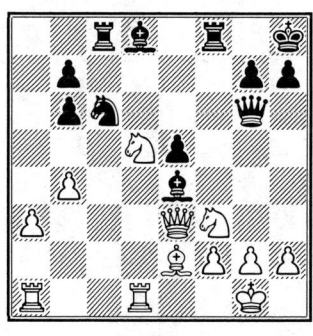

Position after Black's 24th move

25. b5 Forcing Black to make the winning move. It is difficult, however, to find an adequate defence. If 25 Nc3 Bxf3 26 Bxf3 Nd4 27 Kh1 (27 Be4 Rxc3! 28 Bxg6 Rxe3 29 fxe3 Ne2+ 30 Kh1 hxg6 31 Rd7 Bg5) 27 Nc2; 25 g3 seems best. (This seems to be well answered by 25 ... Qf5, in contrast 25 Kh1 looks quite promising. AW) **25 ... Nd4 26. Ne1 Bxd5 27. Qxe5 Bf6** White resigned. **0–1** Fine in Kashdan, 86.

(104) ENEVOLDSEN, J–FINE

International Team Tournament, Folkestone (10), 1933 (19 June)
Grünfeld Defence [D90]

1. d4 Nf6 2. c4 g6 3. Nc3 d5 4. Nf3 c6 5. Bf4 dxc4 The natural 5 ... Bg7 would enter a system reckoned to give Black a reasonable game (NCO, 436). AW **6. Be5!** (6 a4 Nd5 7 Be5 (7 Bd2 Nb4 8 Rc1 Bg7 9 Ng1 a5 10 Nh3 c5 is clearly better for Black, Euwe–Flohr, 6th match game, 1932) f6 8 Bg3 Bg7 9 e4 Nxc3 10 bxc3 b5 11 Be2 with excellent attacking prospects. Euwe) **6 ... Nbd7 7. e3 Nb6 8. Nd2 Be6 9. Be2 Bg7 10. Nce4 0–0 11. Nc5** with equality, MCO 218. **11 ... Qc8 12. 0–0 Ne8 13. Bg3 f5 14. a4 a5 15. Nxe6 Qxe6 16. Qc2 Nd6 17. Bxd6 exd6 18. Nxc4 Nxc4 19. Bxc4 d5 20. Bd3 f4 21. Rfe1 f3 22. g3 Qd7 23. Kh1 Rae8 24. Rac1 Rf6 25. Rcd1 g5 26. e4** It is too dangerous for White to open the h-file. AW **26 ... dxe4 27. Rxe4 Rd8 28. Bf1 Bf8 29. Re3 Kg7 30. Qb3 g4 31. h4 Bb4 32. Bc4 Re8 33. Qd3 Rff8 34. Bb3 Rxe3 35. Qxe3 Qe7 36. Qc1 h6 37. Bc4** ½–½ Gamescore provided by Tony Gillam.

(105) NORCIA, F–FINE

International Team Tournament, Folkestone (11), 1933 (21 June)
French Defence, Classical Variation [C14]

1. e4 e6 2. d4 d5 3. Nc3 Nf6 4. Bg5 Be7 5. e5 Nfd7 6. Bxe7 Qxe7 7. Qd2 The modern main line runs 7 f4 0–0 8 Nf3 c5. **7 ... 0–0 8. f4** 8 Nce2 c5 9 c3 f6 10 f4 cxd4 11 cxd4 fxe5 12 fxe5 Nc6 13 Nf3 Nb6 with equality, EMCO 1996, 134. **8 ... c5 9. dxc5** 9 Nf3 Nc6 10 0–0–0 f6 11 exf6 Qxf6 (11 ... Nxf6 is better, but after 12 Bd3 cxd4 13 Nb5 Qb4 (13 ... Nb4!?, Fritz) 14 Nbxd4 White retains the advantage) 12 g3 cxd4 13 Nxd4 and White stands slightly better, MCO 68. **9 ... Nc6 10. Nf3 a6 11. Na4 N×c5 12. N×c5 Q×c5 13. Bd3 Bd7 14. Qf2** Losing a pawn. Safer is 14 c3. **14 ... Qb4+** Of course this involves loss of time, but White's attack does not prove dangerous. **15. Qd2 Q×b2 16. 0−0 Qa3 17. Qe3 Qe7**

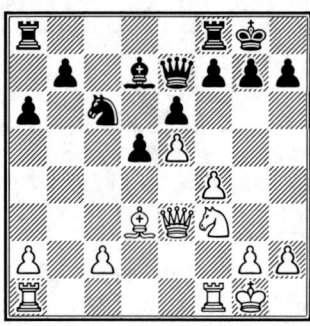

*Position after
Black's 17th move*

18. B×h7+ Very tempting, but Black has a defence. Better chances were offered by 18 Ng5 h6 19 Nh7 Rfe8 20 Rf3. **18 ... K×h7 19. Ng5+ Kg8 20. Qh3 Qc5+ 21. Kh1 Rfc8 22. Qh5** If 22 Qh7+ Kf8 23 Qh8+ Ke7 24 Q×g7 Rf8 25 f5 e×f5 26 e6 B×e6 27 Rae1 Kd6! and Black escapes. The text is also insufficient. **22 ... Nd8 23. Qh7+ Kf8 24. Qh8+ Ke7 25. Q×g7 Bb5 26. c4** Opening the file to get additional chances on the queenside. **26 ... B×c4 27. Rac1 Kd7 28. f5** If 28 N×f7 Qe7 wins the knight. **28 ... Qe7 29. f6 Qe8 30. Rfe1 Bd3 31. h4** White's hopes now lie in the advance of this pawn, but Black's extra piece enables him to work up a mating attack. **31 ... Bg6 32. g4 R×c1 33. R×c1 Rc8 34. Re1** If 34 R×c8 K×c8 35 h5 Bd3 36 h6 Qa4, and the attack will win. **34 ... Rc4 35. Rg1 Nc6 36. h5 Be4+ 37. Kh2** If 37 N×e4 R×e4 38 h6 N×e5 39 h7 Ng6, stops the pawns and wins. **37 ... N×e5 38. Kh3 Bf3 39. N×f3 N×f3 40. Rg3 Ne5 41. g5** The only way to advance, but it still further exposes the white king, allowing a quick finish. **41 ... Kc7 42. g6 Qa4 43. g×f7 Rh4+ 44. Kg2 Q×a2+ 45. Kg1 Qh2+ 46. Kf1 Rf4+** White resigned. **0−1** Kashdan, 101−2

(106) VISTANETSKIS, I—FINE

International Team Tournament, Folkestone (12), 1933
   (21 June)

King's Indian Defence [E70]

1. d4 Nf6 2. c4 g6 3. Nc3 Bg7 4. e4 d6 5. Bd3 0−0 6. Nge2 A fairly rare line, which has nonetheless appeared on and off since it was first tried in 1925 by Sämisch and Bogolyubov. Recent regular practitioners have included Seirawan, Pinter and Skembris. AW **6 ... e5 7. d5 Nbd7 8. f3 Nh5 9. 0−0** A game Miles–Hebden, Biel 1983, continued 9 Be3 f5 10 e×f5 g×f5 11 Qd2 Nc5 12 Bc2 a5 13 0−0−0, ending in a draw after 52 moves. Hebden has also played this variation as White. AW **9 ... f5 10. e×f5** Inconsistent. The text deprives f2-f3 of all point. Better was 10 Be3. (But compare the above game. AW) **10 ... g×f5 11. f4 Kh8** More precise is 11 ... e4, for after 12 f×e5,

White is not so bad off as in the actual game. **12. Bc2 e4 13. Be3 Ndf6 14. h3 Rg8 15. Qe1 Bd7 16. Nd4**

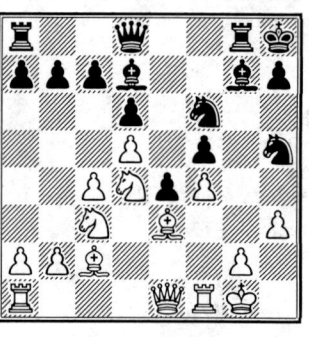

*Position after
White's 16th move*

16 ... a6 Black's plan is to bring all his pieces over to the kingside. He therefore safeguards the other wing against Nb5. **17. Rd1 Qe8 18. Kh2 Bf8 19. Nde2 Qg6 20. g3 Be7 21. Bd4 Rg7 22. Rg1 Rag8 23. Rg2 Qh6 24. b4** White's attack is too slow to be of any effect. **24 ... Rg6 25. c5 Ng7 26. Rg1 Qh5 27. Rf1 Rh6 28. Ng1 Ng4+ 29. Kg2 Bf6 30. Qe2 Ne8 31. Rfe1 B×d4 32. R×d4 Nef6!**

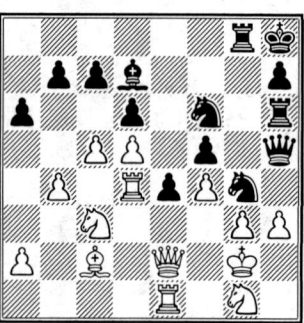

*Position after
Black's 32nd move*

33. h×g4 This loses quickly. It is interesting to note, however, that although Black's knight is lost in any case, and although he only gets one pawn for the piece, White cannot withstand the attack. 33 Kf1 Rhg6 34 h×g4 R×g4, and White is defenceless. **33 ... Qh1+ 34. Kf1 Rh2 35. g5 Ng4 36. B×e4** Desperation under time pressure. The game is, however, lost in any case. **36 ... f×e4** If 37 N×e4, Black mates in two by 37 ... Ne3+ 38 Q×e3 Qg2 or 38 ... Bh3 mate. **0−1** Fine in Kashdan 107−8

(107) HAVASI, K—FINE

International Team Tournament, Folkestone (13), 1933
   (21 June)

This gamescore is unavailable. **½−½**

(108) FINE—LUNDIN, E

International Team Tournament, Folkestone (14), 1933
   (22 June)

Queen's Gambit Declined, Tarrasch Variation [D33]

1. c4 e6 2. g3 c5 3. Bg2 d5 The Tarrasch Defence has been played so frequently in the last few years that one can talk of its "renaissance." New variations are constantly being found, many of them interesting gambits. Saviely Tartakower in Kashdan, 28–9. **4. cxd5 exd5 5. d4 Nc6 6. Nc3 c4** This, in combination with the next two moves, is an idea of Dr. Krause, Danish theoretician, first played between Réti and Dr. Tarrasch, Teplitz-Schonau, 1922. ST **7. Nf3 Bb4 8. 0–0 Nge7** This variation of the Tarrasch Defence was frequently played by the Swedish team at Folkestone. It seems to be very promising. **9. Ne5** With this move White obtains the initiative. Other moves tried, such as Bf4, Bg5, or at once e4, proved less effective. ST **9 ... 0–0 10. Nxc6 bxc6 11. e4** Now the advance is strong, as Black cannot exchange pawns without greatly weakening his formation. **11 ... Rb8 12. Be3** (In MCO Fine calls this weaker than 12 Bg5, as was played in the game Grünfeld–Ståhlberg from the third round.) **12 ... Be6 13. Qc2 f5! 14. exd5 Nxd5! 15. Nxd5 Bxd5 16. Bf4** White has played the opening correctly up to now, but here he goes astray. 16 Rfc1 Bd6 17 f4 Qa5 18 Bf1 Qb4 19 Rab1 etc. was better. **16 ... Bd6** Now Black is better, MCO 153. **17. Bxd5+ cxd5 18. Bxd6 Qxd6 19. Rfe1 f4** Here however Black overlooks the win of a pawn by 19 ... Qb6 20 Re5 (20 b3!? AW) Qxd4 21 Rxf5 Qxb2 22 Rxf8+ Kxf8 23 Qf5+ Qf6. **20. Re5 f3 21. h3 Rb6 22. b3 Qd7 23. Rh5** Not 23 Kh2 Rh6 24 h4 Qg4, threatening Rxh4+!. **23 ... g6 24. Rh4 Rc6 25. bxc4 Rxc4 26. Qd2 Qc7 27. Re1 Rc2 28. Qe3** If 28 Qg5 Rxf2! 29 Kxf2 Qc2+ 30 Ke3 Qc3+ 31 Kf2 Qb2+ 32 Ke3 Qa3+ 33 Kf2 Qxa2+ 34 Ke3 f2, and wins. **28 ... Rxa2 29. Rf4 Rxf4 30. gxf4 Re2 31. Rxe2 fxe2 32. Qxe2 Qxf4 33. Qe8+ Qf8 34. Qe5 Qf7 35. Qb8+ Kg7 36. Qe5+ Kh6 37. Qe3+ g5 38. Qa3 Kh5 39. Qd3 a5 40. Qe2+ Kh6 41. Qa6+ Kh5 42. Qxa5 Qf3 43. Qc7 h6 44. Qg7 Qf5 45. Qb7** If 45 Kg2 g4 46 h4 Qf4 wins for Black. In spite of the reduced material and the apparently simple position the endgame is won for Black. **45 ... Qe6 46. Kh2 Qf5 47. Kg1 Kh4** But here Black overlooks the correct manoeuvre. 47 ... Qe4 wins, for after 48 Qg7 Qf3! White is in Zugzwang. If 48 Qb6, also Qf3 49 Qc5 Kh4 wins, or 49 Qe6 Qd1+ and Qxd4. (In this last line it is not clear how Black wins after 50 Kg2 Qxd4 51 Qe2+, for example 51 Kh4 52 f4! threatens mate and prepares to check on e1 and e8, or 51 Qg6 Qe8+ and so on. AW) **48. Qb3 Qe4 49. Qg3+ Kh5 50. Qe3?** Miscalculating the results of the pawn ending. 50 Qc3 would have drawn. **50 ... Qxe3 51. fxe3 Kg6 52. e4 dxe4 53. Kf2 Kf5 54. Ke3 h5 55. d5 Ke5 56. d6 Kxd6 57. Kxe4 Ke6 58. Kd3 Kd5** White resigned. A remarkable ending, misplayed by both sides. **0–1** Kashdan, 132–3

(109) Rejfir, J–Fine

International Team Tournament, Folkestone (15), 1933
   (23 June)
Queen's Gambit Declined [D51]

1. c4 e6 2. Nc3 d5 3. d4 Nf6 4. Bg5 Nbd7 5. e3 c6 6. a3 This quiet move, whose main object is to avoid the Cambridge Springs Defence, should hardly promise White more than equality. It is simply played in order to get out of book variations as soon as possible. Alekhine **6 ... Be7 7. Nf3 0–0 8. Qc2** (8 Bd3 dxc4 9 Bxc4 Nd5 10 Bxe7 Qxe7 11 Ne4! N5f6 12 Ng3 c5 13 0–0 Nb6 [13 ... b6, followed by ... Bb7, seems preferable. RJ] 14 Ba2 cxd4 15 Nxd4 and White stands slightly better, Alekhine–Capablanca, 34th match game, 1927, MCO 144.) **8 ... h6 9. Bf4 Nh5 10. Bd3 Nxf4 11. exf4 dxc4 12. Bxc4 c5 13. dxc5 Qc7 14. 0–0 Nxc5 15. Ne5 Nd7 16. Nb5 Qb8 17. Rfe1 Nxe5 18. fxe5 Bd7 19. Rad1 Rd8 20. Nd6 Bxd6 21. Rxd6 Bc6 22. Red1 Rxd6 23. Rxd6 Qc7 24. Ba2 Rc8 25. h3 Qe7 26. Qd2 Kh8 27. Kh2 Qh4 28. Rd4 Qe7 29. Rd6 Qh4 30. Rd4 Qe7 31. b4 Qg5 32. f4 Qxg2+ 33. Qxg2 Bxg2 34. Bxe6!** If 34 Kxg2 Rc2+ 35 Kf1 Rxa2 36 Rd7 Rxa3 Black would be able to make White suffer for longer if he wished. **34 ... fxe6 35. Kxg2 Rc2+ 36. Kf3 Rc3+ 37. Kg4** At this point the American team had secured first place and so the game, which had been adjourned, was agreed drawn. (This contradicts the version in Soltis (1994), which suggests that Marshall's game with Treybal was the last of the games in this match to finish, thereby saving the Americans and winning the event. AW) **½–½** Pokorny, game 55.

Pushing to the Forefront of American Chess, 1933–1934

Having left college Fine took up the life of a professional chessplayer. In the fall he confirmed his improvement by overcoming in match play an opponent who had been hitherto an awkward customer, the Oregonian Arthur Dake. This excellent start to his career was immediately followed by a slight disappointment when he took third behind Reinfeld and the selfsame Dake at the New York State Chess Association meeting at Syracuse, where eleven rounds were apparently squeezed into five days, with but a single game on two of the days. There was, however, better to come. At the Western Championship Fine's insistence on playing for a complicated game, rather than early simplification, against Reshevsky cost him a point, but it was the only one he dropped, whereas the former prodigy was held to a draw on four occasions. Therefore, Fine kept the title he had won the year before, a feat he was to repeat, for the second time, at the annual Marshall Chess Club tournament at the turn of the year.

With the exception of club games there seems to have been very little activity in the first half of 1934. But around June Fine played two matches against strong opposition, defeating Al Horowitz, but suffering a rare loss in match play, to Arnold Denker. Fine certainly seems to have been a little rusty during the Western Championship (perhaps an indication that the match with Denker was actually played earlier in the year), losing in all three stages, but he was still able to tie with Reshevsky and thereby retain the title once more.

Match with Arthur Dake, Early August, 1933

"A match of nine games between Reuben Fine and Arthur W. Dake, members of the United States team at Folkestone, was contested during the first two weeks in August at the rooms of the Manhattan and Marshall Chess Clubs in New York and was won by Fine by the score of 4–2, with 3 games drawn. The first, sixth, seventh and ninth games were won by Fine, who also drew the third, fifth and eighth. Dake, who had the better of the first half, won the other two." (ACB 1933)

	1	2	3	4	5	6	7	8	9	
Fine	1	0	½	0	½	1	1	½	1	5½
Dake	0	1	½	1	½	0	0	½	0	3½

(110) FINE—DAKE, A

Dake–Fine, Match, New York (1), 1933 (Aug.)
Nimzowitsch-Indian Defence, Classical Variation [E32]

1. d4 Nf6 2. c4 e6 3. Nc3 Bb4 4. Qc2 0–0 5. a3 Bxc3+ 6. Qxc3 d6 7. e3 b6 8. Bd3 Bb7 9. f3 Nh5 10. Nh3 Qh4+ 11. Nf2 f5 12. 0–0 Nd7 13. Bd2 e5 14. d5 a5 15. b4 g6 16. Nh3 Qe7 17. Qb2 axb4 18. axb4 Nhf6 19. e4

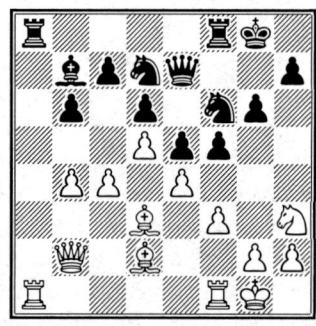

Position after White's 19th move

19 ... f4 20. Ng5 Rfb8 21. Ne6 Nf8 22. Nxf8 Qxf8 23. Rxa8 Rxa8 24. Ra1 Nd7 25. h3 Kf7 26. c5 bxc5 27. Bb5 Rxa1+ 28. Qxa1 Ke7 29. Bxd7 Kxd7 30. bxc5 Ke7 31. Bb4! Bc8?? 32. cxd6+ cxd6 33. Bxd6+ Black resigned. 1–0 ACB 1933, 120.

(111) DAKE, A—FINE

Dake–Fine, Match, New York (2), 1933 (Aug.)
Catalan System [E06]

1. c4 e6 2. Nf3 d5 3. g3 Nf6 4. Bg2 Be7 5. 0–0 0–0 6. d4 c5 7. cxd5 Nxd5 8. e4 Nc7 9. Nc3 Nc6 10. Be3 cxd4 11. Nxd4 Nxd4 12. Bxd4 Bd7 13. Qh5 Qe8 14. Bxg7 Kxg7 15. Qe5+ f6 16. Qxc7 Bc6 17. e5 Bxg2 18. exf6+ Rxf6 19. Kxg2 Rc8 20. Qxb7 Rb8 21. Qxa7 Qc6+ 22. Kg1 Rb7 23. Qa4 Qc5 24. Qc2 h5 25. Rae1 h4 26. Re3 Qh5 27. Qe2 Qg6 28. Nd5 hxg3 29. Rxg3 exd5 30. Rxg6+ Rxg6+ 31. Kh1 Bf6 32. b3 d4 33. Rg1 Rxg1+ 34. Kxg1 Rb8 35. Qg4+ Kf7 36. Qe4 Rd8 37. Qd3 Rc8 38. Qh7+ Kf8 39. Qf5 Rc6 40. a4 Ke7 41. a5 Rc3 42. a6 d3 43. Qd5 Black resigned. 1–0 ACB 1933, 120.

(112) FINE—DAKE, A

Dake–Fine, Match, New York (3), 1933 (Aug.)
Queen's Indian Defence [E16]

1. Nf3 Nf6 2. c4 b6 3. d4 Bb7 4. g3 e6 5. Bg2 Bb4+ 6. Bd2 Bxd2+ 7. Qxd2 Ne4 8. Qc2 Qc8 9. 0–0 0–0 10. Rd1 f5 11. d5 c5 12. Nc3 Nxc3 13. bxc3 exd5 14. cxd5 d6 15. Bh3 g6 16. e4 Qd8 17. exf5 Bc8 18. Nh4 Qf6 19. Qd2 Na6 20. Re1 Nc7 21. Re2 Bxf5 22. Bxf5 gxf5 23. Rae1 Rae8 24. Qd3 Rxe2 25. Rxe2 f4 26. c4 fxg3 27. hxg3 Re8 28. Rxe8+ Nxe8 29. Qe2 Ng7 30. Qg4 Kf7 31. Kg2 Qe5 32. Nf3 Qf5 33. Qh4 Ke8 34. Qh6 Qg6 35. Qe3+ Kd8 36. Ng5 h6 37. Ne4 Nf5 38. Qf4 Ke7 39. Nc3 Nd4 Draw offered by Fine, who had slightly the better of the position. ½–½ ACB 1933, 120–1.

(113) DAKE, A—FINE

Dake–Fine, Match, New York (4), 1933 (Aug.)
English Opening, Classical Defence [A25]

1. c4 e5 2. Nc3 Nc6 3. g3 d6 4. Bg2 Be6 5. d3 Qd7 6. f4 f6 7. Nf3 Nge7 8. e4 Bh3 9. 0–0 Bxg2 10. Kxg2 h5 11. f5 g6 12. Nd5 Bg7 13. Nh4 gxf5 14. Nxf5 Nxf5 15. Rxf5 Nd4 16. Rxh5 0–0–0 17. Ne3 Bh6 18. Nf5 Nxf5 19. Rxf5 Bxc1 20. Rxc1 Qh7 21. h4 Rdg8 22. h5 Rg7 23. Rxf6 Rhg8 24. Rg6 Rxg6 25. hxg6 Qxg6 26. Qf3 Kb8 27. Rf1 Qh6 28. Qf6 Qxf6 29. Rxf6 b6 30. Rf7 Kb7 31. b4 Kc6 32. Kf3 a5 33. a3 Rh8 34. b5+ Kb7 35. Kg2 Rg8 36. Rh7 Rg6 37. Rh4 Rg7 38. g4 c6 39. Kg3 cxb5 40. cxb5 Rc7 41. g5 Rc3 42. Rh7+ Black resigned. 1–0 Bush, 53

(114) FINE—DAKE, A

Dake–Fine, Match, New York (5), 1933 (Aug.)
English Opening, Classical Four Knights Variation [A28]

1. c4 e5 2. Nf3 Nc6 3. Nc3 Nf6 4. d4 exd4 5. Nxd4 Bb4 6. Bg5 h6 7. Nxc6 bxc6 8. Bh4

Bxc3+ 9. bxc3 0–0 10. e3 c5 11. Bd3 Bb7 12. 0–0 Re8 13. Qe2 Be4 14. Rad1 d6 15. f3 Bxd3 16. Qxd3 Rb8 17. Rd2 Qe7 18. e4 Qe6 19. Bxf6 Qxf6 20. f4 Re7 21. Re2 Rbe8 22. e5 dxe5 23. fxe5 Qg5 24. Qd5 Rxe5 25. Qxf7+ Kh7 26. Qxe8 Rxe8 27. Rxe8 Qd2 28. Re7 Qxa2 29. Rxc7 Qxc4 30. Rxa7 Qxc3 31. Raa1 c4 32. Rac1 Qe3+ 33. Kh1 c3 34. Rc2 Qd3 35. Rfc1 Qe3 36. Rxc3 Qd2 37. Rc7 Qf4 38. h3 Kh8 39. Rc8+ Kh7 40. Rd1 Qf5 41. Re8 Qf7 42. Rde1 Qf6 43. R8e4 Qc6 44. R1e3 Qc7 45. Rf3 Kh8 46. h4 Qc6 47. Rg4 Qe6 48. Rfg3 Qe7 49. Kg1 Qe1+ 50. Kh2 Qe7 51. Rf4 Kh7 52. Rgf3 Qe5 53. Kh3 Qe6+ 54. g4 h5 ½–½ Fiala QCH3 1999, 468–9 from *Brooklyn Daily Eagle*, 17 August, 1933.

(115) DAKE, A—FINE

Dake–Fine, Match, New York (6), 1933 (Aug.)
English Opening, Symmetrical Variation [A31]

1. c4 Nf6 2. Nf3 c5 3. d4 cxd4 4. Nxd4 e5!?
5. Nb5 Bb4+ 6. Bd2 Bc5 7. Bc3 Qb6 8. e3 a6
9. N5a3 Nc6 10. Bd3 0–0 11. 0–0 d6 12. Nc2 Be6
13. e4 Ng4 14. Qf3 g6 15. Nd2

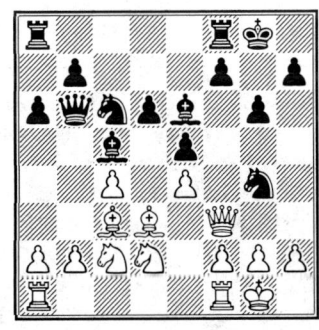

*Position after
White's 15th move*

15 ... Nxf2 16. Rxf2 f5 17. exf5 Bxf5 18. Bxf5 Rxf5
19. Qd5+ Kg7 20. Ne4 Bxf2+ 21. Kh1 Raf8
22. Nxd6 R5f6 23. Ne4 Rd8 24. Nxf6? Rxd5
25. Nxd5 Qc5 26. b3 b5 27. Nf4 Qd6 28. Rf1 Bd4
29. Nxd4 Nxd4 30. Nd5 bxc4 31. bxc4 Qc5
32. Bb4 Qxc4 33. Bf8+ Kh8 34. Ne3 Qe2 35. Bh6
Nf5 0–1 Fiala QCH3 469; Fine 1953, 121–2.

(116) FINE—DAKE, A

Dake–Fine, Match, New York (7), 1933 (Aug.)
Queen's Gambit Declined [D64]

1. d4 d5 2. c4 e6 3. Nc3 Nf6 4. Bg5 Be7 5. Nf3
0–0 6. e3 Nbd7 7. Rc1 c6 8. a3 Re8 9. Qc2 a6
10. cxd5 exd5 11. Bd3 Nf8 12. 0–0 Ne4 13. Bxe7
Qxe7 14. Na4 Bg4 15. Ne5 Nf6 16. Nc5 Bc8 17. b4
g6 18. f4 N6d7 19. Rce1 f5 20. a4 Nxe5 21. fxe5
Ne6 22. Nxe6 Bxe6 23. Qc5 Qxc5 24. bxc5 Rad8
25. Kf2 Re7 26. Ke2 a5 27. h4 h5 28. Rb1 Kg7
29. Rb6 Rf8 30. Kf3 Kh6 31. Kf4 Bc8 32. Be2

Re6 33. Rfb1 Rf7 34. R1b2 Rc7 35. Rb1 Rf7 36. Rh1
Rf8 37. Bd3 Rf7 38. Rb2 Ree7 39. Be2 Be6 40. Ra1
Bc8 41. Rba2 Re6 42. Rb1 Ree7 43. Rab2

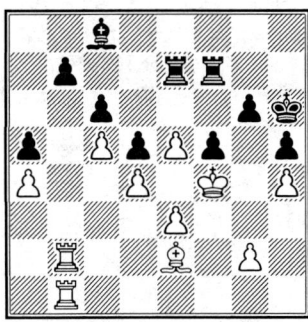

*Position after
White's 43rd move*

43 ... Be6 44. Rb3 Bc8 45. Rb6 Re6 46. Kg3 Ree7
47. Rf1 Be6 48. Kf4 Bc8 49. Rfb1 Re6 50. Bf3
Rd7? 51. R1b5 Rxe5 52. Kxe5 cxb5 53. Rxb5
Re7+ 54. Kxd5 Rxe3 55. Kd6 Rd3 56. d5 f4

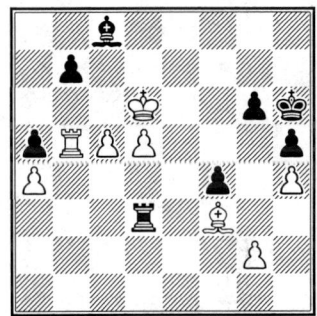

*Position after
Black's 56th move*

57. Kc7 Bg4 58. Bxg4 hxg4 59. d6 f3 60. gxf3
gxf3 61. d7 f2 62. Rb1 Kh5 63. d8Q Rxd8
64. Kxd8 Kxh4 65. Kc7 g5 66. Rh1+ Kg3 67. Kxb7
Kg2 68. Ra1 g4 69. c6 g3 70. c7 f1Q 71. Rxf1 Kxf1
72. c8Q 1–0 Gamescore provided by Peter Lahde.

(117) DAKE, A—FINE

Dake–Fine, Match, New York (8), 1933 (Aug.)
Grünfeld Defence [A34]

1. c4 Nf6 2. Nf3 c5 3. Nc3 d5 4. cxd5 Nxd5 5. e4
Nxc3 6. bxc3 g6 7. Bb5+ Nd7 8. 0–0 Bg7 9. d4
0–0 10. Ba3 cxd4 11. cxd4 a6 12. Bd3 b5 13. Qe2
Nb6 14. Rad1 Bg4 15. h3 Bxf3 16. Qxf3 Rc8 17. d5
Qd7 18. Rc1 Na4 19. Bb4 Bh6 20. Rc2 Qa7 21. Qg4
Nc5 22. Be2 a5 23. Ba3 b4 24. Bb2 Qb7 25. Qh4
Bg7 26. Bxg7 Kxg7 27. Rfc1 b3 28. axb3 Nxb3
29. Rxc8 Rxc8 30. Rxc8 Qxc8 31. Qxe7 Qc1+
32. Kh2 Qf4+ 33. Kg1 Qc1+ 34. Kh2 ½–½ Gamescore provided by Peter Lahde.

(118) FINE—DAKE, A

Dake–Fine, Match, Manhattan Chess Club, New York (9), 1933 (?16 Aug.)

Catalan System [D30]

1. d4 d5 2. Nf3 c6 3. c4 e6 4. Nbd2 Nf6 5. g3
Be7 6. Bg2 0–0 7. 0–0 Nbd7 8. b3 b6 9. Bb2
Bb7 10. Ne5 Nxe5 11. dxe5 Nd7 12. f4 g6 13. Nf3
dxc4 14. bxc4 c5 15. Qc2 Qc7 16. Rad1 Rad8
17. g4 Nb8 18. Rxd8 Rxd8 19. f5 Bxf3 20. exf3
Nc6 21. fxe6 fxe6 22. f4 Nd4 23. Qe4 Qd7

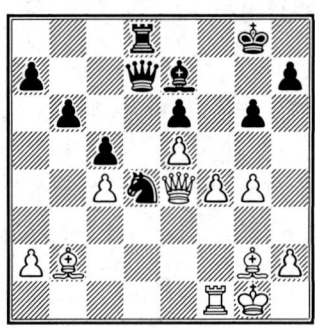

*Position after
Black's 23rd move*

24. Kh1 Bf8 25. Bxd4 Qxd4 26. f5 Qxe4 27. Bxe4
gxf5 28. gxf5 Rd4 29. Bc6 exf5 30. Bd5+ Kh8
31. Rxf5 Bg7 32. e6 Rd1+ 33. Kg2 Re1 34. Kf2
Bc3 35. Rf3 Bd2 36. Rd3 Ba5 37. Re3 1–0
Gamescore provided by Erik Osbun.

55th New York State Championship, Syracuse, August 21–26, 1933

The *American Chess Bulletin* of July-August announced
that the New York State Chess Association would hold its
annual midsummer meeting for the week of August 21–25
at the roof garden of the Hotel Onondaga in Syracuse under
the auspices of the Syracuse Chess Club. It was reported
that play would begin at one o'clock on Monday 22 August.
The *Bulletin* reported "Emerging first from a strong field of
twelve, Fred Reinfeld of the Marshall Chess Club of New
York City recaptured the New York State championship at
the annual midsummer meeting of the New York State
Chess Association, held at Syracuse under the auspices of
the Syracuse Chess Club, August 21–26, and duplicated his
performance at Rome, two years ago. As in 1931, Reinfeld
went through the eleven rounds without losing once. Of the
eleven games contested by him at Syracuse, he won eight
and drew the other three. Arnold S. Denker of the Manhattan and Empire City Chess Clubs, lost only to the leader
and was placed second. Reuben Fine and A. E. Santasiere
divided the third and fourth prizes and David S. Polland
took the fifth. Roy T. Black, now a resident of Buffalo, was
placed sixth, half a point ahead of Walter Muir of Albany.
Other contestants were R. J. Guckemus of Utica, Professor
G. H. Perrine of Clinton, Prof. C. K. Thomas of Ithaca,
Arthur W. Wood of Syracuse and Charles H. Bourbeau of
New York City." In his memoirs, Walter Muir recalled that
the players had to play three games on three of the days (all
three of his losses, including the one to Fine—in the fifth

hour of play—came in the evening round). Combining these
reports suggests that rounds one and two were held on 22
August, three, four and five on the 23rd, six, seven and
eight on the 24th and nine, ten and eleven on the 25th.
Muir also gives the first ten moves of the game Guckemus–Fine, apparently he too fell into this line, and escaped
with a draw.

		1	2	3	4	5	6	7	8	9	10	11	12	
1	Reinfeld	*	1	½	½	1	1	1	1	½	1	1	1	9½
2	Denker	0	*	1	1	1	½	½	1	1	½	1	1	8½
3	Fine	½	0	*	0	½	1	1	1	1	1	1	1	8
4	Santasiere	½	0	1	*	½	½	1	½	1	1	1	1	8
5	Polland	0	0	½	½	*	1	½	1	1	1	1	1	7½
6	Black	0	½	0	½	0	*	½	1	1	1	1	1	6½
7	Muir	0	½	0	0	½	½	*	½	1	1	1	1	6
8	Guckemus	0	0	0	½	0	0	½	*	½	1	½	½	3½
9	Perrine	½	0	0	0	0	0	0	½	*	½	½	1	3
10	Thomas	0	½	0	0	0	0	0	0	½	*	½	1	2½
11	Wood	0	0	0	0	0	0	0	½	½	½	*	½	2
12	Bourbeau	0	0	0	0	0	0	0	½	0	0	½	*	1

(119) SANTASIERE, A—FINE

New York State Chess Association, Syracuse, 1933 (Aug.)
Queen's Indian Defence [A30]

1. c4 Nf6 2. Nf3 e6 3. g3 b6 4. Bg2 Bb7 5. 0–0
c5 6. Nc3 Be7 7. d4 cxd4 8. Nxd4 Bxg2 9. Kxg2
0–0 10. e4 d5 11. cxd5 exd5 12. e5 Ne4 13. Qg4
Qd7 14. Nf5 g6 15. Nxd5! Bg5 16. Qxe4 gxf5
17. Qf3 Bd8 18. Nb4 a5 19. Qxa8 axb4 20. Bh6
Re8 21. Racl Be7 22. Rfdl Qe6 23. Bf4 Bc5
24. Qb7 Qc6+ 25. Qxc6 Nxc6 26. Rd5 Ra8
27. Be3 Bxe3 28. fxe3 Ne7 29. Rd7 Ng6 30. e6
fxe6 31. Rcc7 Nf8 32. Rg7+ Kh8 33. Ra7 1–0 Fiala
QCH3 1999, 462–3 from *Brooklyn Daily Eagle*, 31 August,
1933.

(120) GUCKEMUS, R—FINE

New York State Chess Association, Syracuse, 1933 (Aug.)
Sicilian Defence [B40]

1. e4 c5 2. Nf3 e6 3. c3 d5 4. e5 Nc6 5. Na3
Nge7 6. Bb5 Bd7 7. Qa4 a6 8. 0–0 axb5?? (Black
stands better in this position. It is a fatal error to allow the
knight to arrive at b5. Simply 8 ... d4 would confirm the second player's superior game. AW) 9. Nxb5 Ng6 10. Qxa8
Bc8 , but Fine went on to win. 0–1 Muir, 1997.

34th Western Open, Detroit, September 23–October 1, 1933

"Maintaining the best traditions of the Western Chess
Association, the unbroken record of which was mentioned

in the last issue of the *Bulletin*, the local committee, representing the Auto City Chess & Checker Club, put on and managed the fourth annual meeting in Detroit in such a way as to reflect credit upon one and all who in any way participated. From September 23, when the business meeting took place and the first round of the championship tournament was contested, until the finals were played on October 1, the Egyptian Room of the Hotel Tuller, facing Grand Circus Park, was the scene of constant activity, noon and night." "Fourteen entered the competition for the coveted title of Western Champion, held by Reuben Fine of New York in consequence of his win in Minneapolis 1932. Necessarily, the schedule, which called for thirteen rounds on nine days, was rather severe on some of the players and certainly no child's play for any of them. Nevertheless, every one, with a fine spirit of good fellowship, faced the music cheerfully and the net result was perfect harmony. The fact that not a single game was allowed to go by default, although some of them left before the last day, speaks volumes for the healthy enthusiasm that permeated the sessions of the congress." "Interest in the fortunes of the players in the championship tournament never lagged from the first round to the very last. Fine led from the start and his early games showed that he was at his best. A freshness of imagination and a will to win seemed to inspire his tactics. It was not long before the struggle resolved itself into a duel between him and Samuel Reshevsky, champion in 1931 and his chief rival at Minneapolis. They clashed in the sixth round at a time when Fine had a clean score and Reshevsky had been drawn but once (by Factor). This might well have been the turning point, but the invincibility of Fine in all of his other encounters tipped the balance in his favor and eventually he emerged in triumph with the grand total of 12–1." (ACB 1933)

		1	2	3	4	5	6	7	8	9	10	11	12	13	14	
1	Fine	*	0	1	1	1	1	1	1	1	1	1	1	1	1	12
2	Reshevsky	1	*	½	1	½	1	1	½	1	1	1	½	1	1	11
3	Dake	0	½	*	1	1	1	0	0	1	1	1	1	1	1	9½
4	Willman	0	0	0	*	1	1	1	1	0	½	1	1	1	1	8½
5	Factor	0	½	0	0	*	0	1	0	1	1	1	1	1	1	7½
6=	Stolcenberg	0	0	0	0	1	*	½	½	½	1	1	½	1	1	7
6=	Eastman	0	0	1	0	0	½	*	½	1	½	1	1	½	1	7
6=	Margolis	0	½	1	0	1	½	½	*	1	0	0	½	1	1	7
9	Fox	0	0	0	0	0	½	0	0	*	1	1	½	1	1	5
10	Michelsen	0	0	0	1	0	0	½	1	0	*	0	1	0	1	4½
11	Opsahl	0	0	0	½	0	0	0	1	0	1	*	½	0	1	4
12	Barnes	0	½	0	0	0	½	0	½	½	0	½	*	1	0	3½
13	Palmer	0	0	0	0	0	0	½	0	0	1	1	0	*	1	3½
14	Streeter	0	0	0	0	0	0	0	0	0	0	0	1	0	*	1

(121) BARNES, G—FINE

Western Chess Association, Detroit, 1933 (Sept.)

This gamescore is unavailable. **0–1**

(122) FINE—MARGOLIS

Western Chess Association, Detroit, 1933 (Sept.)
van't Kruijs Opening/English Opening [A00]

1. e3 d5 2. Nf3 Nf6 3. b3 g6 4. Bb2 Bg7 5. c4 c6
6. Be2 0–0 7. 0–0 Bg4 8. d3 Nbd7 9. Nbd2 Qa5
10. Qc2 Rac8 11. Rfe1 Rfe8 12. Racl e5 13. e4 dxe4
14. dxe4 Nh5 15. a3 Rcd8 16. b4 Qc7 17. h3 Be6
18. c5 h6 19. Nc4 Bxc4 20. Bxc4 Nf8 21. Rcd1 Nf4
22. Nd2 N8e6 23. Bxe6 Nxe6 24. Nc4 Kh7
25. Nd6 Rg8 26. Qc4

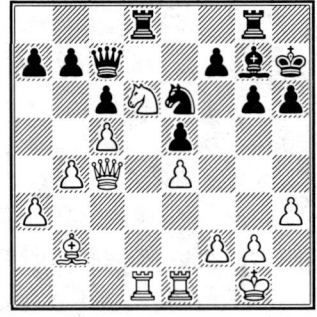

*Position after
White's 26th move*

26 ... b6 27. Bc3 Qe7 28. Rd2 Rd7 29. Red1 Rgd8
30. g3 f6 31. Nc8 Qe8 32. Nd6 Qe7 33. Nc8 Qe8
34. Rxd7 Rxd7 35. Rxd7 Qxd7 36. cxb6 Qxc8
37. bxa7 Nd8 38. b5 Qb7 39. b6 Bf8 40. Bb4
Bxb4 41. Qxb4 Kg8 42. Qd6 Qxb6 43. a8Q 1–0
New York Sun, 1933.

(123) FINE—PALMER, M

Western Chess Association, Detroit, 1933 (Sept.)
Nimzowitsch-Indian Defence, Rubinstein Variation [E43]

1. d4 Nf6 2. c4 e6 3. Nc3 Bb4 4. e3 b6 5. Bd3
Bb7 6. f3 c5 7. Nge2 d5 8. cxd5 exd5 9. 0–0
Nc6 10. Qe1 cxd4 11. exd4 0–0 12. g4 Ne7 13. Bg5
Ng6 14. h4 Re8 15. h5 Nf8 16. Qh4 Be7 17. Qh3
Nxh5 18. Bd2 Nf6 19. Kg2 Bc8 20. Rh1 Be6
21. Nf4 g6 22. Qh6 Bxg4 23. fxg4 Nxg4 24. Qh3
Nf6

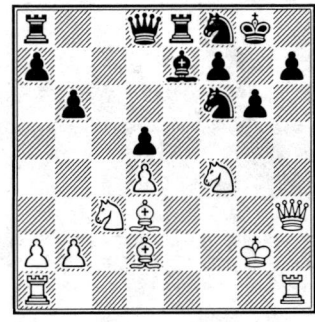

*Position after
Black's 24th move*

25. Qf3 Ne6 26. Nxe6 fxe6 27. Qh3 Kf7 28. Rae1
Qd6 29. Nb5 Qd7 30. Nc7 Qxc7 31. Qxe6+ Kg7
32. Rxh7+ Kxh7 33. Qf7+ Kh8 34. Rh1+ 1–0 *Fiala*

QCH3 1999, 463 from *Brooklyn Daily Eagle*, 28 September, 1933.

(124) FINE—STREETER, W

Western Chess Association, Detroit, 1933 (Sept.)
Queen's Gambit Declined [D36]

1. d4 Nf6 2. c4 e6 3. Nc3 d5 4. Bg5 Nbd7 5. cxd5 exd5 6. e3 c6 7. Bd3 Bd6 8. Qc2 Be7 9. Nge2 h6 10. Bf4 0–0 11. 0–0–0 Nb6 12. h3 Be6 13. g4 Rc8

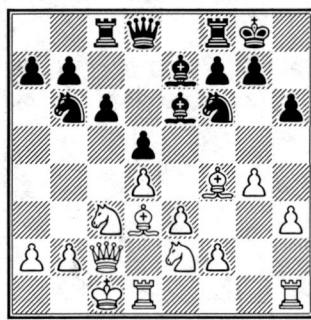

Position after Black's 13th move

14. g5 hxg5 15. Bxg5 c5 16. Rdg1 cxd4 17. exd4 Ne4 Fine reckoned that this was unsound. He preferred 17 … Qd7, but then 18 Bh6 Ne8 19 Bb5 wins an exchange. **18. Bxe7 Qxe7 19. Bxe4 dxe4 20. Qxe4 Rc7 21. Kb1 Qf6 22. Qf4 Qxf4 23. Nxf4 Bf5+ 24. Ka1 Rd8 25. h4 a6 26. Rg5 Bc2 27. Rhg1 Rxd4 28. Rxg7+ Kh8 29. Ne6 1–0** Black resigned. ACB 1933, 130.

(125) MICHELSEN, E—FINE

Western Chess Association, Detroit, 1933 (Sept.)
Sicilian Defence, Scheveningen Variation [B83]

1. e4 c5 2. Nf3 Nf6 3. Nc3 d6 4. d4 cxd4 5. Nxd4 e6 6. Be2 Be7 7. 0–0 0–0 8. Be3 a6 9. Qd2 Qc7 10. Rad1 b5 11. Bf3 Bb7 12. a3 Nbd7 13. Bg5 Ne5

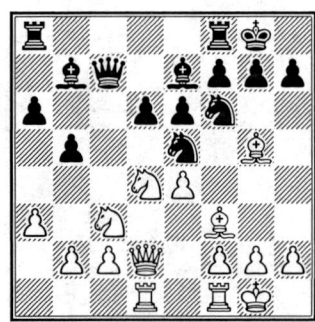

Position after Black's 13th move

14. Bxf6 Bxf6 15. Be2 Rfd8 16. f3 Rac8 17. Kh1 Qb6 18. Na2 d5 19. f4 Nc4 20. Bxc4 dxe4 21. Bb3 Rxd4 22. Qe2 Rcd8 23. c3 Rxd1 24. Bxd1 e3 25. Qg4 Rd2 26. Bf3 Rf2 27. Rxf2

exf2 28. Be2 Qe3 29. Bf1 Bd5 30. Nb4 Bc4 0–1 Fiala QCH3 1999, 463–4 from *Brooklyn Daily Eagle*, 28 September, 1933.

(126) FACTOR, S—FINE

Western Chess Association, Detroit (4), 1933 (Sept.)
Nimzowitsch-Indian Defence, Classical Variation [E34]

1. d4 e6 2. c4 Nf6 3. Nc3 Bb4 4. Qc2 d5 5. e3 A very tame, move which allows Black to equalize quickly. **5 … 0–0 6. Nf3 c5 7. dxc5 Nc6 8. cxd5** Better is 8 Bd3. After the text, Black obtained the initiative. **8 … exd5 9. Bd3 d4 10. exd4 Bg4 11. Be3** 11 Qd1 Bxf3 12 Qxf3 Qxd4 and 11 Ng5 Nxd4 12 Bxh7+ Kh8 13 Qd3 Qe7+ 14 Be3 Rad8 both favour Black. AW **11 … Bxf3 12. gxf3 Nxd4 13. Bxd4 Qxd4 14. 0–0–0**

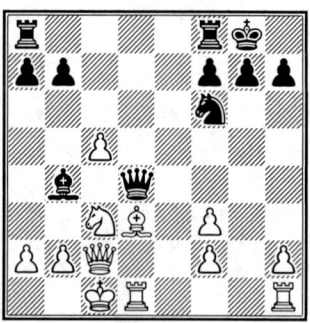

Position after White's 14th move

14 … Bxc3 15. Bxh7+ 15 Qxc3 Qxc3 16 bxc3 would leave Black with a much better endgame. **15 … Nxh7 16. Rxd4 Bxd4 17. b4 a5 18. Rd1 Bf6 19. b5 Ng5 20. Rd7 Rad8 21. Rxb7 Nxf3** Now White cannot play 22 c6 because of 22 … Rfe8 23 Qc4 Ne5 and wins. **22. Qf5 Nd4 23. Qg4 Rd5 24. c6 Rc5+ 25. Kd2 Nxb5 26. a4 Nd4 27. c7 Ne6 28. Rb8 Rxc7 29. Rxf8+ Kxf8 30. Qe4 Bc3+ 31. Kd1 g6 32. f4 Rc5 33. h4 Kg7** White resigned. **0–1** Fine, *ACB* 1933, 130.

(127) FINE—FOX, M

Western Chess Association, Detroit (5), 1933 (Sept.)
Queen's Gambit Declined [D51]

1. d4 Nf6 2. c4 e6 3. Nc3 d5 4. Bg5 Nbd7 5. e3 c6 6. a3 dxc4 7. Bxc4 Qa5 8. Bh4 Ne4 9. Nge2 g5 This advance is pointless and only serves to weaken Black's kingside. **10. Bg3 h5 11. b4 Nxc3 12. Nxc3 Qd8 13. h4 Nb6 14. Bd3 Nd5 15. Nxd5** Simpler is 15 Ne4. White would probably have won the game more quickly in that case, since it is dangerous for Black to castle on either side. **15 … exd5 16. Be5 Rh6 17. hxg5 Qxg5 18. Qf3 Qg4 19. Qxg4 hxg4 20. Rxh6 Bxh6 21. Kd2 Be6 22. f4** 22 Rh1 Bf8 23 Rh8 Kd7 24 Bg7 Ke7 leads to nothing. **22 … gxf3 23. gxf3 0–0–0 24. Rh1 Bf8 25. f4**

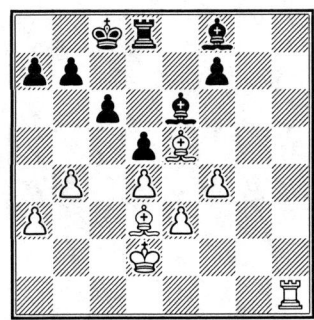

Position after White's 25th move

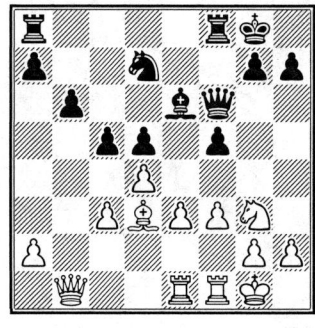

Position after Black's 16th move

25 ... Be7 This loses a pawn. Relatively best is 25 ... Bd6 26 f5 Bxe5 27 fxe6 Bd6 28 exf7 with some drawing chances for Black. **26. Rh7 Rf8 27. f5 Bd7 28. f6 Bd8 29. Bd6 Rg8 30. Rxf7 Be6 31. Rh7 Rg2+ 32. Ke1 Bxf6 33. Rh6 Bxd4 34. exd4 Kd7 35. Be5 Ra2 36. Rh7+ Kc8 37. Rc7+ Kd8 38. Rxb7 Rxa3 39. Bg6 Bd7 40. Bd6 Rf3 41. Bh5 Re3+ 42. Kd2 Re4 43. Bg6** Black resigned. He cannot prevent 44 Rb8+ followed by 45 Bf5. **1–0** Fine, ACB 1933, 132.

(128) RESHEVSKY, S—FINE

Western Chess Association, Detroit (6), 1933 (Sept.)
Queen's Indian Defence [E16]

1. d4 Nf6 2. c4 e6 3. Nf3 Bb4+ 4. Bd2 Bxd2+ 5. Qxd2 b6 6. g3 Bb7 7. Bg2 0–0 8. Nc3 Qe7 9. 0–0 d6 10. Qc2 c5 11. dxc5 bxc5 12. Rad1 Nc6 13. e4 Rfd8 14. Rd2 Ng4 15. Rfd1 Nge5 16. Nxe5 Nd4 I was afraid that after 16 ... dxe5 17 Rxd8+ Rxd8 18 Rxd8+ Qxd8 my opponent's drawing chances would be too great. RF **17. Ng6 hxg6 18. Qd3 e5 19. Rf1 Bc6 20. f4 Rab8 21. f5 Qg5 22. f6 Rb7 23. Rdf2 gxf6 24. b3** 24 Rxf6 is bad because of 24 ... Rxb2 25 Rxf7 Rd2. RF **24 ... f5** This leads to the loss of the game. After 24 ... a5 25 Rxf6 Kg7 Black has the better chances. RF **25. exf5 Bxg2 26. Kxg2 gxf5 27. Rxf5 Nxf5 28. Rxf5 Qh6** Although Black is the exchange ahead, in the middle game the white knight is stronger than a black rook. RF **29. Qe4 Re7 30. Qg4+ Kf8 31. Rh5 Qg7** Not 31 ... Qd2+ 32 Kh3 Re6 33 Qh4 Rde8 34 Rh8+ Kg7 35 Qh7+ Kf6 36 Ne4+. **32. Qh4 Ke8 33. Nd5 f5 34. Nxe7** Black resigned. **1–0** Fine, ACB 1933, 131.

(129) FINE—WILLMAN, R

Western Chess Association, Detroit (7), 1933 (Sept.)
Queen's Gambit Declined, Lasker Variation [D53]

1. d4 d5 2. c4 e6 3. Nc3 Nf6 4. Bg5 Be7 5. e3 Ne4 6. Bxe7 Qxe7 7. cxd5 Nxc3 8. bxc3 exd5 9. Qb3 c6 10. Bd3 0–0 11. Ne2 A more usual idea for White is 11 Nf3. The text seems, however, to be very promising. **11 ... b6 12. 0–0 Be6 13. Rae1** I was playing for a break in the centre; that is, e4 as soon as possible. The alternative is a queenside advance; a2-a4-a5. **13 ... Nd7 14. Ng3 f5 15. f3 c5 16. Qb1 Qf6**

17. e4 dxe4 If 17 ... cxd4 18 exd5 Bxd5 19 Nxf5 and White wins a pawn. **18. fxe4 cxd4 19. e5 Qh4** If 19 ... Nxe5 Black loses immediately by 20 Bxf5 or, still better (as my opponent pointed out after the game) 20 Nh5. **20. Bxf5 Nc5 21. Bxe6+ Nxe6 22. Nf5 Qg5 23. Qb3 Rae8 24. Nd6 Rxf1+ 25. Rxf1 Qe3+ 26. Kh1 Qe2 27. Rg1 Re7 28. cxd4 Kh8** Now Black's game is hopeless. 28 ... g6 should have been tried. **29. Qd5 h6 30. Nf5 Re8 31. Qd7 Rf8 32. Qxe6 Qg4 33. d5 Qxf5 34. Qxf5 Rxf5 35. Re1 Kg8 36. Kg1** If now 36 ... Kf8 37 Rf1 and if 36 ... Rg5 37 d6 Kf8 38 Rc1 Ke8 39 e6 and wins. **36 ... Rf8 37. e6 Rb8 38. d6 Kf8 39. Rf1+ Ke8 40. Rf7** Black resigned. **1–0** Fine, ACB 1933, 132.

(130) EASTMAN, G—FINE

Western Chess Association, Detroit (8), 1933 (Sept.)
French Defence, Chatard-Alekhine Attack [C13]

1. e4 e6 2. d4 d5 3. Nc3 Nf6 4. Bg5 Be7 5. e5 Nfd7 6. h4 c5 7. Bxe7 Kxe7 8. Qg4 Kf8 9. dxc5 Nc6 10. Nf3 Ncxe5 11. Nxe5 Nxe5 12. Qg3 Nc6 13. Bb5 White gets into trouble later because of the exposed position of this bishop. 13 0–0–0 or 13 Bd3 is more logical. **13 ... Qe7 14. 0–0–0 Bd7 15. Rhe1 Qxc5 16. Qc7 Be8 17. Qxb7 Rb8**

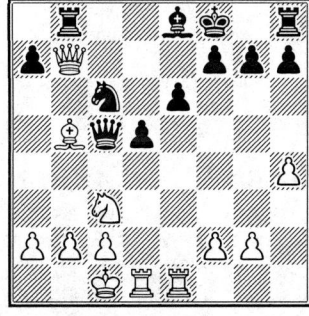

Position after Black's 17th move

18. Qc7 The sacrifice is now forced for after 18 Qa6 Nb4 Black comes out a piece ahead with a very easy defence. **18 ... Rxb5 19. Rxd5 Qxf2 20. Rdd1** Here White should at any rate win the black queen for two rooks and a piece. 20 Re2 Qxe2 21 Nxe2 Rxd5, although Black should win in any case. **20 ... Rb8 21. Qd6+ Kg8 22. Nd5 Qxh4 23. Nc7 Qb4 24. b3 Qxd6 25. Rxd6 Ne7 26. Nxe8 Rxe8 27. Rd7 a5 28. c4 h5 29. Re5 h4**

30. Rxa5 Nf5 31. c5 Rc8 32. b4 g5 33. Raa7 f6
34. Rf7 Rh6 35. Kd2 g4 36. b5 h3 37. gxh3 gxh3
38. b6 h2 39. b7 Rd8+ 40. Rd7 Rxd7+ 41. Kc3
Rxb7 White resigned. 0–1 ACB 1933, 133.

(131) FINE—DAKE, A

Western Chess Association, Detroit (10), 1933 (Sept.)
Grünfeld Defence [D70]

1. d4 Nf6 2. c4 g6 3. f3 d5 4. cxd5 Nxd5 5. e4
Nb6 6. Be3 Bg7 7. Nc3 0–0 8. Qd2 e5 Better seems
8 ... Nc6 9 Rd1 e5 10 d5 Nd4!, Alekhine–Bogolyubov, Bled
1931. 9. d5 c6 10. a4 But this is not good. I overlooked
the possibility of Black's 11th move. Correct, in my opinion,
is 10 0–0–0! Black is then underdeveloped; White's attack is
easier and should succeed first. 10 ... cxd5 11. exd5
Qh4+ 12. Bf2 Qb4 13. a5 Nc4 14. Bxc4 Qxc4
15. Nge2 Na6 16. 0–0 Nc5 17. Bxc5 Qxc5+ 18. Kh1
Rd8 19. Qg5 f6 20. Qh4 g5 Black's last two moves have
only succeeded in blocking the diagonal of his king's bishop.
Now the white knights are superior to the black bishops.
21. Qa4 Bf5 22. Rfd1 Rac8 23. Ng3 Bg6 24. Nge4
Qc4 25. Qa3 Bf8 26. d6 Kg7 27. Rd5 If 27 Rd2 f5!
28 Nxg5 h6 29 Nh3 Rc6 30 Rad1 Qe6 31 Nb5 (31 Qb4 Rd7
32 Nb5 a6 33 Nf4! preserves White's advantage. AW) a6. 27
... Bf7 28. Rd2 Rc6 Threatening ... Ra6 followed by ...
b6. To this manoeuvre, however, White has an adequate
reply. Safer is the exchange of queens; 28 ... Qb3, after
which Black has a slight advantage because of White's weak
pawns. 29. Rad1 Ra6 30. Qa1 b6 This is not good as
the continuation of the game shows. If 30 ... f5 31 b3! Qxb3
32 Nd5+. Relatively best was 30 ... h6. 31. Qc1 Rxa5

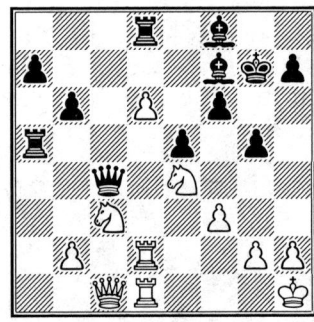

*Position after
Black's 31st move*

32. Nxf6!! Kxf6 33. Ne4+ Kg7 34. Rc2! The point:
the roads are now opened for the white pieces. 34 ... Qa4
He must keep an eye on White's rook. On 34 ... Qe6 there
could follow simply 35 Qxg5+ and 36 Qxd8. 35. Qxg5+
Bg6 36. Rc7+ Kg8 The text allows mate in three, but Black
is lost in any case. If 36 ... Rd7 37 b3! Qb5 38 Qf6+ Kg8 39
Qe6+ Rf7 40 d7 and wins. Also good is 37 Nc3. 37. Qxg6+!!
He resigns right before mate: 37 ... hxg6 38 Nf6+ Kh8 39
Rh7 mate. 1–0 Fine 1958, 23; Fine, ACB 1933, 131.

(132) OPSAHL, E—FINE

Western Chess Association, Detroit (11), 1933 (Sept.)
French Defence, Advance Variation [C02]

1. e4 e6 2. d4 d5 3. e5 c5 4. Qg4 The Nimzowitsch
Variation 4 ... cxd4 5. Nf3 Nc6 6. Bd3 Qc7 7. Bf4
Nge7 8. Qh3 f6 9. 0–0

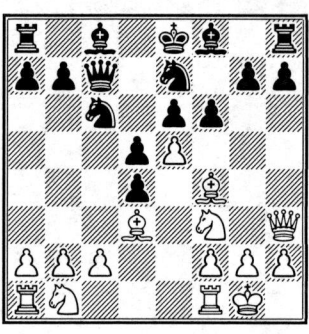

*Position after
White's 9th move*

9 ... Bd7 After this move Black's game is inferior. Better
was 9 ... fxe5 10 Nxe5 Nxe5 11 Qh5+ g6 12 Bxe5 gxh5 13
Bxc7 with a slight advantage for Black. (Simply 12 Qxe5
Qxe5 13 Bxe5 Rg8 14 Bxd4 looks equal. AW) 10. Re1
0–0–0 11. Bg3 fxe5 12. Nxe5 Nxe5 13. Bxe5 Qb6
14. Nd2 Nc6 15. Nf3 h5 16. a3 Be7 17. Bxg7 Rhg8
18. Be5 Qxb2 This is apparently risky, but is in reality
much safer than, say 18 ... Rg6 19 b4. 19 b4 must be prevented. 19. Reb1 The wrong rook. After 19 Rab1 Qc3 20
Rb3 Qa5 21 Reb1 White has a promising attack. 19 ... Qc3
20. Rb3 Qxa1+ White resigned. 0–1 Fine, ACB 1933,
130.

(133) STOLCENBERG, L—FINE

Western Chess Association, Detroit (13), 1933 (1 Oct.)
King's Indian Defence [E94]

1. d4 Nf6 2. Nf3 g6 3. c4 Bg7 4. Nc3 0–0 5. e4
d6 6. Be2 Nbd7 7. 0–0 e5 8. a3 Qe7 9. dxe5
dxe5 10. Qc2 c6 11. b4 a5 12. Rb1 Nh5 13. Re1 Re8
14. c5 Nf8 15. Na4 axb4 16. axb4 Bg4 17. Nb6
Rad8 18. Nc4 Ne6 19. Nd6 Rf8 20. Ra1

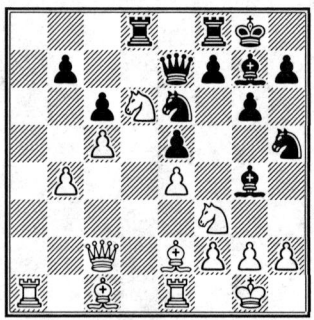

*Position after
White's 20th move*

20 ... Rxd6 An interesting sacrifice. Black obtains, to be
sure, only one pawn for the exchange but White's other
pawn on the queenside is weak. With the white pieces tied
up in the defence of the b-pawn, Black has good attacking
chances on the kingside. 21. cxd6 Qxd6 22. Be3 Nhf4
If 22 ... Qxb4 23 Reb1 Qe7 24 Ra7 winning back the pawn
with the better game. 23. Bc5 Nxc5 24. bxc5 Qe7
25. Ra7 Ne6 26. h3 Bxf3 27. Bxf3 Rd8 28. Rc1

Bh6 29. Rb1 N×c5 30. g3 Rd2 31. Qc4 Bf8
32. Kg2 b5 33. R×e7 b×c4 34. Re8 c3 35. Bd1 c2
36. B×c2 R×c2 37. Rbb8 Ne6 38. g4 g5 39. h4 h6
White resigned. 0–1 Fine, ACB 1933, 133.

17th Marshall Club Championship, New York, 1933/4

"For the third time, Reuben Fine holds the proud distinction of being the champion of the Marshall Club of New York. Without losing one game in eleven, this talented young graduate of the College of the City of New York went through victoriously and finished with a total of 9½–1½. Fine also holds the Western title and, being a member of last year's triumphant United States team at Folkestone, he ranks very high among America's greatest exponents of the game." (ACB 1934)

		1	2	3	4	5	6	7	8	9	10	11	12	
1	Fine	*	1	½	1	1	1	½	½	1	1	1	1	9½
2=	Kevitz	0	*	1	½	0	1	½	1	1	1	1	1	8
2=	Reinfeld	½	0	*	1	0	1	1	1	1	½	1	1	8
4=	Polland	0	½	0	*	1	0	1	1	1	1	1	1	7½
4=	Santasiere	0	1	1	0	*	½	1	1	0	1	1	1	7½
6	Simonson	0	0	0	1	½	*	1	½	1	1	1	1	7
7	Costa-Rivas	½	½	0	0	0	0	*	1	1	1	1	0	5
8	Hamermesh	½	0	0	0	0	½	0	*	½	1	½	1	4
9	Chernev	0	0	0	0	1	0	0	½	*	½	½	1	3½
10	Dunst	0	0	½	0	0	0	0	0	½	*	½	1	2½
11	Grossman	0	0	0	0	0	0	0	½	½	½	*	½	2
12	Frere	0	0	0	0	0	0	1	0	0	0	½	*	1½

(134) CHERNEV, I—FINE

Marshall CC championship 1933/4, New York, 1933
Queen's Gambit Declined [D30]

1. d4 e6 2. Nf3 d5 3. c4 Nf6 4. Bg5 Nbd7 5. e3 c6 6. a3 Be7 7. Nc3 0-0 8. Qc2 a6 9. Bd3 h6 10. Bh4 b5 11. c×d5 c×d5 12. 0-0 Bb7 13. Rac1 Rc8 14. Qb1 Nb6 15. Ne5 Nc4 16. B×c4 d×c4 17. f4 Nd5 18. B×e7 Q×e7 19. N×d5 B×d5

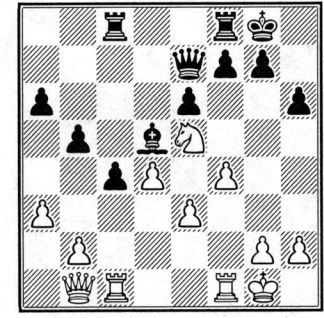

Position after Black's 19th move

20. f5? Qg5 21. Nf3 Q×e3+ 22. Kh1 Be4 23. Qa1 B×f5 24. Rc3 Bd3 White resigned. 0–1 ACB 1933, 173.

(135) DUNST, T—FINE

Marshall CC championship 1933/4, New York, 1933
Modern Defence [A48]

1. e3 g6 2. d4 Bg7 3. Nf3 Nf6 4. Bd3 0-0 5. 0-0 d6 6. e4 Nbd7 7. Be3 e5 8. d×e5 d×e5 9. h3 Qe7 10. Qd2 Rd8 11. Rd1 Nf8 12. Nc3 c6

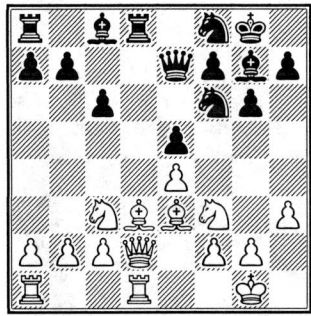

Position after Black's 12th move

13. Bh6 Nh5 14. B×g7 K×g7 15. Qe3 Qf6 16. Bf1 Be6 17. Kh2 b6 18. g3 h6 19. Be2 Kh7 20. b3 Ng7 21. Na4 g5 22. Nb2 Ng6 23. Rd3 Qe7 24. a4 f5 25. e×f5 N×f5 26. Qe4 Nd6 27. R×d6 R×d6 28. Bd3 Bd5 29. Q×e5 Re6 30. Qc3 Rf8 White resigned. 0–1 ACB 1934, 10.

(136) FINE—GROSSMAN, N

Marshall CC championship 1933/4, New York, 1933
Queen's Gambit Declined, Marshall Variation [D50]

1. d4 Nf6 2. c4 e6 3. Nc3 d5 4. Bg5 Bb4 5. e3 5 Qa4+ is also good. 5 ... c6 Too passive—5 ... c5 should have been tried. 6. Qb3 B×c3+ 7. b×c3 Nbd7 8. c×d5 To avoid the exchange of queens which would be necessary after 8 Bd3 d×c4 9 B×c4 Nb6 10 Bd3 Qd5. 8 ... c×d5 8 ... e×d5 is better, but my opponent was relying on the open c-file. 9. Bd3 0-0 10. Ne2 Qa5 A weak sortie which allows White to build up a steamroller attack by f3 and e4. 11. f3 b6 12. 0-0 Ba6 13. Qc2 B×d3 14. Q×d3 Rfc8 15. Bh4 b5

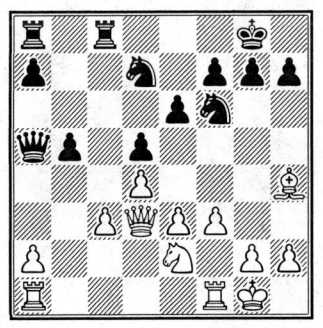

Position after Black's 15th move

16. e4 The fun is about to begin. 16 ... Rc4 Advance for advance, as a famous Hebrew grandmaster remarked thousands of years ago. 16 ... b4 was correct. 17. e5 Ne8 18. f4 g6 19. g4 Qb6 20. Kh1 Ng7 21. f5 There is no time to

lose, since Black threatens to set up an unassailable position. **21 ... exf5 22. gxf5 Nxe5** In the event of 22 ... Nxf5 23 Rxf5 gxf5 24 Nf4 Fine only considered 24 ... Kh8 and 24 ... Nf8, each leading to a win for White, the first after 25 Qxf5 Qc6 26 e6 and the second after 25 Rg1+ Ng6 26 Qxf5 Rxc3 27 Bf6 Qc6 28 Nxg6. However, Black also has 24 ... Nxe5!!, removing the crucial e-pawn, hitting the queen, and the knight by X-ray and seemingly turning the tables: 25 Qxf5 (25 dxe5 Rxf4) Ng6 26 Nxd5 Qc6 27 Rg1 Re8 28 Qf3 Re2! 29 Ne7+ Rxe7 30 Qxc6 Rxc6 31 Bxe7 Rxc3 32 d5 Rd3 33 d6 f5, and only Black should be able to win. AW **23. Qh3 Nc6 24. Bf6 Nh5 25. fxg6 hxg6** Black seems to have escaped with a whole skin, but this is only an optical illusion. His king will soon begin to moult.

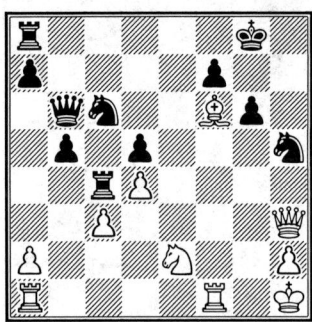

Position after Black's 26th move

26. Nf4! The object of this sacrifice is to sacrifice so as to sacrifice with the purpose of sacrificing with the object of carrying out a swindle. **26 ... Nxf6 27. Nxg6!** ... to sacrifice ... **27 ... Kg7 28. Rg1!** ... so as to sacrifice ... **28 ... fxg6 29. Rxg6+!!** ... with the purpose of sacrificing ... **29 ... Kxg6 30. Qe6!!** ... with the object of swindling the opponent, who, it should be mentioned, had about four minutes for the remaining eleven moves. The swindle is not too flagrant, and might be regarded as a little superior to the average swindle, since Black can only manage to draw if he finds as obscure defensive manoeuvre.

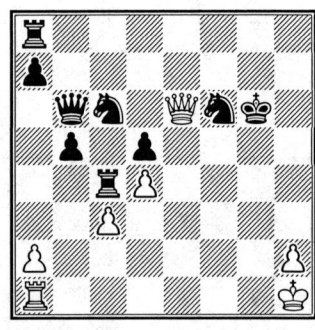

Position after White's 30th move

30 ... Nxd4? "It's better to be lucky than good," has been Capablanca's motto for a long time. Black can escape with a draw only by returning both knights and a rook. The correct move is 30 ... Ne5!. Then 31 Rg1+ Kh6! 32 Qxe5 gives Black time to get his pieces over to the kingside: 32 ... Rg8! 33 Qe3+ Kh7 34 Qh3+ Nh5! 35 Qxh5+ Qh6 36 Qxh6+ Kxh6 37 Rxg8 the ending is a simple draw. Another line here is 32 ... Rc7 33 Qg5+ Kh7 34 Qh4+ Nh5 35 Qxh5+ Qh6 36 Qf5+ Kh8 37 Qe5+ Rg7 38 Rxg7 Qxg7 39 Qh5+ with a draw by

perpetual check, for if 39 ... Kg8 40 Qxd5+ followed by Qxa8 wins. **31. Rg1+ Kh6 32. Qe3+ Kh7 33. Qe7+ Kh6 34. Qg7+** Black resigned. **1–0** Fine in *Chess* 1938–9, 50–1.

(137) FINE—POLLAND, D

Marshall CC championship 1933/4, New York, 1933
Queen's Gambit Declined [D64]

1. d4 Nf6 2. c4 e6 3. Nc3 d5 4. Bg5 Nbd7 5. e3 Be7 6. Nf3 0–0 7. Rc1 c6 8. Qc2 Re8 9. a3 dxc4 10. Bxc4 Nd5 11. Bf4 Nxf4 12. exf4 Nf8 13. 0–0 b6 14. Rfe1 g6 15. Rcd1 Bb7 16. Ne5 Bf6 17. Ne4 Qe7 18. Ba6 Bxe5 19. Bxb7 Qxb7 20. fxe5 Red8 21. Nd6 Qc7 22. Rc1 c5 23. dxc5 bxc5 24. Qxc5 Qxc5 25. Rxc5 Nd7 26. Rc6 Rab8 27. b4 Rb6 28. Rxb6 Nxb6 29. Rc1 f6 30. f4 fxe5 31. fxe5 Nd7 32. Rc7

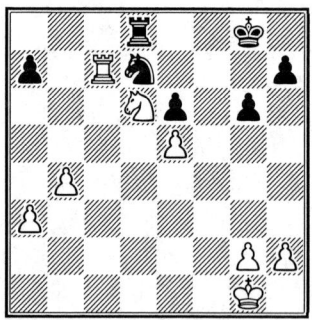

Position after White's 32nd move

32 ... Nxe5 33. Ne4 Ng4 34. g3 Rd4 35. h3 Rxe4 36. hxg4 a6 37. Ra7 Re3 38. Rxa6 Rxg3+ 39. Kf2 Rb3 40. g5 h5 41. gxh6 Kh7 42. Ra5 Kxh6 43. b5 g5 44. a4 g4 45. Ra8 g3+ 46. Kg2 Kg5 47. Kh3 Kf4 48. Rg8 Ra3 49. b6 Rb3 50. a5 Black resigned. 1–0 ACB 1933, 173.

(138) FRERE, W—FINE

Marshall CC championship 1933/4, New York, 1933 (Nov.)
French Defence, Exchange Variation [C01]

1. e4 e6 2. d4 d5 3. Nc3 Nf6 4. exd5 exd5 5. Bd3 Bd6 6. Nf3 0–0 7. 0–0 Bg4 8. Bg5 c6 9. Ne2?! Bxf3 10. gxf3 Nbd7 11. c3 Qc7 12. Kg2 h6 13. Be3 Nh5 14. Qd2 f5 15. Bxh6?! gxh6 16. Qxh6 Ng7 17. Rg1 Rf6 18. Qh4 Re8 19. Kh1 Ree6 20. Bxf5 Rxf5 21. Qg4 Bf8! 22. Qxf5 Rxe2 23. Rg6 Nb6 24. Rag1 Qd7 25. Qh5

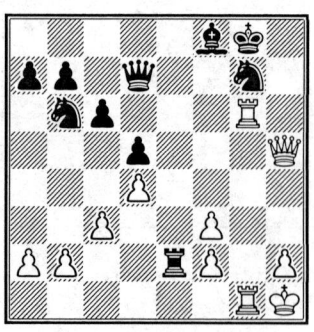

Position after White's 25th move

25 ... Re6 26. R6g4 Qe8 27. Qh3 Re1 28. Rh4 Rxg1+ 29. Kxg1 Qg6+ 30. Kh1 Qf5 31. Rh8+ Kf7 32. Qg3 Nc4 33. Qc7+ Be7 34. Qb8 Qxf3+ 35. Kg1 Qg4+ 36. Kh1 Nd6 37. Qg8+ Kg6 38. h3 Qf3+ 39. Kg1 Ndf5 40. Qh7+ Kf6 41. Rg8 Qd1+ 42. Kg2 Qe2 43. Kg1 Qe1+ 44. Kg2 Qe4+ 45. Kg1 Qb1+ 0–1 *Brooklyn Daily Eagle*, 29 November, 1933.

(139) KEVITZ, A—FINE

Marshall CC championship 1933/4, New York, 1933
English Opening, Flohr-Mikenas Variation [A18]

1. c4 Nf6 2. Nc3 e6 3. e4 d5 4. e5 d4 5. exf6 dxc3 6. bxc3 Qxf6 7. d4 b6 8. Nf3 Bb7 9. Be2 h6! 10. 0–0 Bd6 11. Qa4+ Bc6 12. Qc2 0–0 13. Be3 Nd7 14. Rad1 Rad8 15. Nd2 e5 16. d5 Bb7 17. Qa4 Qg6 18. Qxa7 Bc8 19. Nb3 Nf6 20. Kh1 Bd7 21. c5 Ra8 22. Qb7

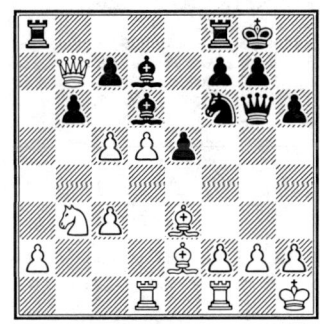

Position after White's 22nd move

22 ... bxc5 23. Bd3 e4 24. Nxc5 Rfb8 25. Qxb8+ Rxb8 26. Nxd7 Nxd7 27. Bb1 Qh5 28. g3 Nf6 White resigned. 0–1 *ACB* 1933, 173.

Before leaving New York to spend Christmas in Havana, José Raúl Capablanca took part in one of the Marshall Chess Clubs weekly rapid transit tournaments. He captured first place with nine straight wins. Fine, who reportedly had a long sequence of victories in the event to his credit, scored 7–2 and shared second to fourth places with Hanauer and Reshevsky.

New York Metropolitan League, February–April, 1934

Fine, playing on board 4 for the Marshall Chess Club, drew with Isaac Kashdan in the decisive match with the Manhattanites. The Manhattan Club won all 11 of their matches, whereas the Marshalls, in addition to their loss, were held to a draw by the Stuyvesant Chess Club. This game was recorded in the numeric notation. Another game, with Jaffe (Stuyvesant), recorded in English descriptive, Fine lost on time on the 59th move in a roughly equal position. A further game, not recorded in the notebooks, has been supplied by Erik Osbun. Empire City and West Side were among other teams contesting the event.

Fine	1	Hellman	0
Jaffe	1	Fine	0
Kashdan	½	Fine	½

(140) FINE—HELLMAN, G

Metropolitan Chess League, New York, 1934
Evans Gambit [C51]

1. e4 e5 2. Nf3 Nc6 3. Bc4 Bc5 4. b4 Bxb4 5. c3 Bc5 6. d4 exd4 7. cxd4 Bb4+ 8. Kf1 Qe7 9. Bb2 Qxe4 10. Nbd2 Qg6 11. d5 Nd8 12. Qb3 a5 13. a3 Be7 14. Re1 d6

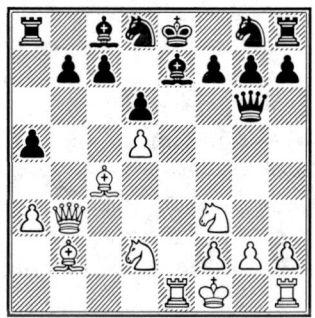

Position after Black's 14th move

15. Qc3 Kf8 16. Bd3 Qf6 17. Qc2 Qf4 18. Ne4 f5 19. Ng3 Nf6 20. Qe2 Ne4 21. Bxg7+ Kg8 22. Qb2 Nf7 23. Bxe4 Bf8 24. Nh5 fxe4 25. Nxf4 1–0 Gamescore provided by Erik Osbun.

(141) JAFFE, C—FINE

Metropolitan Chess League, New York, 1934 (Feb.)
King's Indian Defence [E94]

1. d4 Nf6 2. Nf3 g6 3. c4 Bg7 4. Nc3 0–0 5. e4 d6 6. Be2 Nbd7 7. 0–0 e5 8. h3 Re8 9. d5 Nh5 10. Bg5 f6 11. Bd2 Nf4 12. Bxf4 exf4 13. Nd4 Ne5 14. Qd2 Bh6 15. Rfe1 Bd7 16. b3 Qe7 17. Bf1 Qg7 18. f3 Bg5 19. Kh1 h5 20. Qf2 a6 21. Rad1 Bh6 22. Nce2 Kh7 23. g3 g5 24. Nf5 Bxf5 25. exf5 g4 26. fxg4 fxg3 27. Qxg3 hxg4 28. Nd4 Rg8 29. Ne6 Qf7 30. Bg2 Rac8 31. Qh4 Rh8 32. Rd4 gxh3 33. Qxh3 Kg8 34. Rh4 Qh7 35. Bf3 Nf7 36. Bh5 Ng5 37. Qg4 Qd7 38. Bg6 c6 39. Nf4 Bg7 40. Re2 b5 41. Rxh8+ Bxh8 42. Qg2 bxc4 43. dxc6 Qxc6 44. Nd5 Kf8 45. Rc2 Qb5 46. Ne3 Qe5 47. Nxc4 Qe1+ 48. Kh2 Qh4+ 49. Kg1 Qd4+ 50. Kh2 d5 51. Ne3 Rd8 52. Qg3 Qe4 53. Qc7 Qe5+ 54. Qxe5 fxe5 55. Kg2 e4 56. Rc7 d4 57. Nd1 Bg7 58. b4 Bh6 59. a4 Black overstepped the time limit in playing 59 ... d4-d3. 1–0

(142) FINE—KASHDAN, I

Metropolitan Chess League, New York, 1934 (21 April)
Petroff Defence [C42]

1. e4 e5 2. Nf3 Nf6 3. Nxe5 d6 4. Nf3 Nxe4
5. Qe2 Qe7 6. d3 Nf6 7. Bg5 Qxe2+ 8. Bxe2 Be7
9. Nc3 h6 10. Bh4 Bd7 11. 0–0–0 Nc6 12. d4
0–0–0 13. Rhe1 Rde8 14. Bc4 Nd8 15. d5 g5
16. Bg3 Nh5 17. Be2 f5 18. Nd4 Nxg3 19. fxg3 Bf6
20. Rf1 Be5 21. Bb5 f4 22. Bxd7+ Kxd7 23. Nce2
fxg3 24. hxg3 Rhf8 25. c3 Bg7 26. Kd2 Draw
agreed. ½–½

Match with Al Horowitz,
June?–June 27, 1934

In his autobiography Fine wrote "In the early thirties ... tournaments in the United States were so few and far between that
many more matches were arranged than is the case today. In
the course of the years I met most of the leading masters in
matches, Dake, Steiner, Denker, Horowitz, and others.
Although my tournament results were a little more spotty,
in matches I always succeeded in winning [sic], and I have
since wondered about the discrepancy. A similar occurrence, frequently much more marked, has occurred many
times in chess history .... The only explanation for these
continual upsets must be the psychological factor, which
plays a much greater role in master chess than is generally
realized. A tournament many times resolves into a struggle
between the two top contenders, in which the outcome
depends on what happens with other players, rather than
on what goes on between them. In a match of course the
reverse is true." Games three to eight of this match were
recorded in the numeric notation, games one and two are
not in the notebooks.

	1	2	3	4	5	6	7	8	9	
Fine	1	1	½	½	1	½	0	½	1	6
Horowitz	0	0	½	½	0	½	1	½	0	3

(143) HOROWITZ, I—FINE

Match (1), 1934 (June)
Dutch Defence [A98]

1. d4 f5 2. Nf3 Nf6 3. g3 e6 4. Bg2 Be7 5. 0–0
0–0 6. c4 Note that, in accordance with modern technique, this advance is effected after castling, thus denying
the opponent the relieving sally ... Bb4+. T&dM 6 ... d6
The strategy of the restricted centre. The stonewall formation is also admissible: 6 ... d5 7 Nc3 c6. Playable too is 6 ...
Ne4. T&dM 7. Nc3 Qe8 A regrouping, conforming to the
spirit of the defence, which from the first foreshadows
expansion on the kingside. T&dM 8. Qc2 At the crossroads. White prepares the advance of his e-pawn, which
could also be effected by 8 Re1, or even indirectly by 8 Bg5
(with a view to 9 Bxf6 Bxf6 10 e4). Useless would be the
diversion 8 Nb5 Bd8, but a sound, constructive idea is 8 b3,
for after 8 ... Qh5 9 Qc2 Nbd7 10 Ba3, the counter-thrust 10
... e5 is still impeded. T&dM 8 ... Nc6 9. a3? Excessively
cautious. As 9 e4 would be neutralized by 9 ... e5, he would

do well to harass his opponent by 9 d5 (9 ... Nd8 10 Nd4 or
9 ... Nb4 10 Qb3). T&dM 9 ... e5 Thus Black has achieved
his central advance ahead of his opponent. T&dM 10. d5
Nd8 11. b4 He underestimated the action preparing on
the opposite wing. Better would be, now or on the next
move, Bg5. T&dM 11 ... Bd7 12. Nd2 Qh5 The direct
attack. 13. f3 Nf7 14. e4 A dead point which virtually
immobilizes six (!) of his pieces. He should have tried 14
Rf2, for example, 14 ... f4 15 Nf1. T&dM 14 ... f4 15. g4
Qh4 16. Nb3 Hoping, not so much for action on the
queenside, as for relief, by blocking as far as possible the
critical sector after 17 Qf2 Qh6 18 h4 g5 19 h5. But Black's
strong reply maintains his advantage. Best therefore would
be at once 16 Rf2, with 17 Nf1. T&dM 16 ... h5 17. gxh5
Compulsory. If 17 h3 Ng5. T&dM 17 ... Qxh5

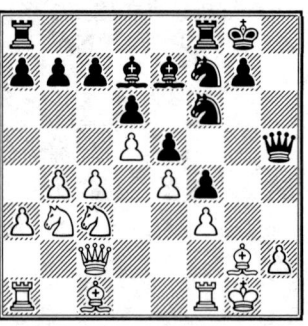

*Position after
Black's 17th move*

18. Rf2 Ng5 19. Nd2 Kf7 Initiating a very instructive
phase, in which Black's artillery exploits the h-file and
thence overruns the adjacent open file. T&dM 20. Nf1
Rh8 21. Ne2 Qh4 22. Qd2 Nh5 23. Nc3 Rh6
24. Re2 Rg6 25. Kh1 Rh8 Now things happen with a
rush. Black's preceding move threatened 25 ... Nxf3+; now
he threatens 26 ... Ng3+. T&dM 26. Rf2

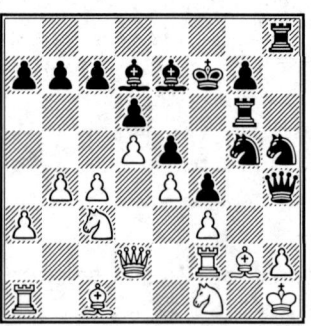

*Position after
White's 26th move*

26 ... Ng3+! 27. Kg1 A tottering king. He hopes to hold
out after 27 ... Nxf1 28 Kxf1 Qxh2 29 Ke2. T&dM 27 ...
Nh3+! 28. Bxh3 Ne2+ White resigned. 0–1 Tartakower
& du Mont 1952, 553–4.

(144) FINE—HOROWITZ, I

Match (2), 1934 (June)
Slav Defence [D18]

1. d4 d5 2. c4 c6 3. Nc3 Nf6 4. Nf3 dxc4 5. a4
Bf5 6. e3 Na6 7. Bxc4 Nb4 8. 0–0 e6 9. Qe2 Be7

10. Rd1 0–0 11. e4 Bg4 12. Bb3 Qa5 13. h3! Bxf3
14. Qxf3 Rad8 15. Be3 Rd7 16. g4 Rfd8 17. g5 Ne8
18. h4 c5 19. d5 e5 20. h5 Bd6 21. Kg2 a6 22. Rh1
Nd3 23. g6 c4 24. Bc2 Nf4+ 25. Bxf4 exf4 26. e5
Bxe5 27. Bf5 Re7 28. gxf7+ Kxf7 29. Rae1! Bxc3
30. Be6+ Kf8 31. bxc3 Nf6 32. Rh4! Rxd5
33. Rxf4 Rg5+ 34. Kf1 Ke8 35. Rxf6 gxf6
36. Qxf6 Rgg7 37. h6 1–0 Hilbert & Lahde, 33–4.

(145) HOROWITZ, I–FINE

Match (3), 1934 (9 June)
Queen's Gambit Declined [D48]

1. d4 Nf6 2. c4 e6 3. Nc3 d5 4. Nf3 Nbd7 5. e3
c6 6. Bd3 dxc4 7. Bxc4 b5 8. Bd3 a6 9. a4 b4
10. Ne4 c5 11. 0–0 Bb7 12. Ned2 a5 13. Bb5 Be7
14. dxc5 Bxc5 15. b3 0–0 16. Bb2 Qe7 17. Rc1
Rfd8 18. Qe2 Bb6 19. Nc4 Bc7 20. Nd4 Rab8
21. Bc6 Ba6 22. Nb5 Bxb5 23. axb5 Nc5 24. Qc2
Nd3 25. Rcd1 Nxb2 26. Qxb2 Nd5 27. Ra1 Nc3
28. Nxa5 Nxb5 29. Bf3 Bxa5 30. Rxa5 Nc3
31. Rfa1 g6 32. g3 Qd6 33. Ra7 Rd7 34. R1a6 Qe7
35. Rxd7 Qxd7 36. Qa1 Qd2 37. Ra8 Rxa8
38. Qxa8+ Kg7 39. Qa6 e5 40. Qc4 e4 41. Bxe4
Nxe4 42. Qxe4 Qd1+ 43. Kg2 Qxb3 Draw agreed.
½–½

(146) FINE–HOROWITZ, I

Match (4), 1934 (16 June)
Queen's Gambit Accepted [D27]

1. d4 d5 2. c4 dxc4 3. Nf3 Nf6 4. e3 e6 5. Bxc4
a6 6. 0–0 c5 7. Nc3 b5 8. Bd3 Bb7 9. a4 b4
10. Nb1 Nc6 11. dxc5 Bxc5 12. Qe2 0–0 13. Nbd2
Qe7 14. Nb3 Bd6 15. a5 Ng4 16. e4 Nce5 17. Nxe5
Nxe5 18. Bc2 Rfc8 19. f4 Ng6 20. Bd3 e5 21. f5
Nf4 22. Bxf4 exf4 23. Nd2 Bc5+ 24. Kh1 Be3
25. Rae1 g5 26. fxg6 hxg6 27. Nc4 Rxc4 28. Bxc4
Qxe4 29. Rd1 Qf5 30. Rd6 Kg7 31. Bxa6 Qh3
32. Rf3 Bxf3 33. Qxf3 Qf5 34. g4 Qe5 35. Rxg6+
fxg6 36. Qa8 Qxa5 37. Qe4 Qa1+ 38. Kg2
Qxb2+ 39. Kh3 Qc3 40. Bc4 Qf6 Draw agreed.
½–½

(147) HOROWITZ, I–FINE

Match (5), 1934 (20 June)
Queen's Indian Defence [E16]

1. d4 Nf6 2. c4 e6 3. Nf3 b6 4. g3 Bb7 5. Bg2
Bb4+ 6. Nbd2 0–0 7. 0–0 Bxd2 8. Qxd2 Qe7
9. b3 d6 10. Bb2 Nbd7 11. Nh4 Ne4 12. Qc2 f5
13. Rad1 d5 14. Nf3 a5 15. cxd5 Bxd5 16. Nd2
Nxd2 17. Rxd2 Bxg2 18. Kxg2 Nf6 19. Qc6 Rad8
20. Rc2 Nd5 21. a3 Rf6 22. Re1 e5 23. Qb7 e4
24. Rec1 Rf7 25. e3 Qd7 26. Qc6 f4

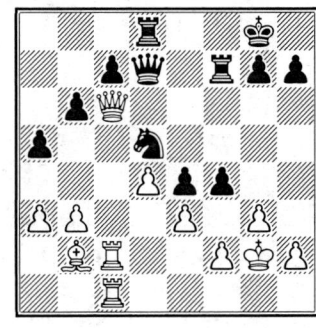

*Position after
Black's 26th move*

27. Qxd7 f3+ 28. Kf1 Rdxd7 29. Rc6 Rf6 30. a4
Rdd6 31. Rxd6 Rxd6 32. Ba3 Rh6 33. Kg1 Kf7
34. h4 Ke8 35. Kh2 Kd7 36. Kh3 Rc6 37. Kg4
Rxc1 38. Bxc1 Nb4 White resigned. 0–1

(148) FINE–HOROWITZ, I

Match (6), 1934 (23 June)
Queen's Gambit Declined [D51]

1. d4 d5 2. c4 c6 3. Nf3 Nf6 4. Nc3 e6 5. Bg5
Nbd7 6. a3 h6 7. Bxf6 Nxf6 8. e3 Be7 9. Bd3
0–0 10. 0–0 b6 11. Qe2 Bb7 12. e4 dxe4 13. Nxe4
c5 14. dxc5 bxc5 15. Rab1 Qb6 16. b4 cxb4
17. axb4 Rfd8 18. Rfc1 Qc7 19. Nxf6+ Bxf6
20. Be4 Rab8 21. Bxb7 Rxb7 22. c5 Rd5 23. Qc4
Draw agreed. ½–½

(149) HOROWITZ, I–FINE

Match (7), 1934 (24 June)
Spanish Game, Modern Steinitz Defence [C73]

1. e4 e5 2. Nf3 Nc6 3. Bb5 a6 4. Ba4 d6 5. Bxc6+
bxc6 6. d4 exd4 7. Nxd4 Bd7 8. Nc3 Nf6 9. Qf3
c5 10. Nf5 Bxf5 11. exf5 Ra7? 12. 0–0 Be7 13. Bg5
0–0 14. Rae1 Re8 15. Re2 h6 16. Bh4 Qa8 17. Qd3
Bd8 18. Rfe1 Rxe2 19. Rxe2 Qb7 20. b3 Ra8
21. Bxf6 Bxf6 22. Nd5 Be5 23. f6 g6 24. Ne7+
Kh7 25. Nxg6 Bxf6 26. Ne7+ Kg7 27. Qg3+ Kh8
28. Qf4 Bg7 29. Qxf7 Qb4 30. Nf5 Qc3 31. Qxg7+
Qxg7 32. Nxg7 Kxg7 33. Re7+ Kf6 34. Rxc7 a5
35. Kf1 a4 36. Ke2 axb3 37. axb3 Ra1 38. Rh7 Rc1
39. Rxh6+ Ke5 40. Kd2 Rf1 41. Ke3 Re1+ 42. Kd3
Rd1+ 43. Kc3 Black resigned. 1–0

(150) FINE–HOROWITZ, I

Match (8), 1934 (25 June)
Queen's Gambit Declined, Semi-Slav [D49]

1. d4 d5 2. c4 e6 3. Nf3 Nf6 4. Nc3 Nbd7 5. e3
c6 6. Bd3 dxc4 7. Bxc4 b5 8. Bd3 a6 9. e4 c5
10. e5 cxd4 11. Nxb5 axb5 12. exf6 Qb6 13. 0–0
gxf6 14. Be4 Bb7 15. Bxb7 Qxb7 16. Nxd4 Rg8
17. f3 Ne5 18. Nb3 Rd8 19. Qe2 Rd5 20. Bf4 Ng6
21. Bg3 h5 22. Rad1 Rxd1 23. Rxd1 h4 24. Qd2

Be7 25. Bd6 Qb6+ 26. Qd4 Qxd4+ 27. Rxd4 Draw agreed. ½–½

(151) HOROWITZ, I—FINE

Match (9), 1934 (27 June)
Caro-Kann Defence, Exchange Variation [B13]

1. e4 c6 2. d4 d5 3. exd5 cxd5 4. Bd3 Nc6 5. Nf3
Nf6 6. h3 g6 7. c3 Bg7 8. 0–0 0–0 9. Re1 Bf5
10. Bxf5 gxf5 11. Nbd2 Ne4 12. Nf1 Qc7 13. Bd2
e6 14. Qc1 Rfc8 15. Bh6 Qe7 16. Bxg7 Kxg7
17. Qf4 Qf6 18. Ng3 Qh6 19. Ne2 Qxf4 20. Nxf4
b5 21. Nd3 a5 22. Nfe5 Nxe5 23. dxe5 Rc4
24. Kf1 Nc5 25. Ke2 Nxd3 26. Kxd3 a4 27. b3
Rc6 28. f4 h5 29. Rg1 Kf8 30. Rab1 h4 31. g4
hxg3 32. Rxg3 axb3 33. axb3

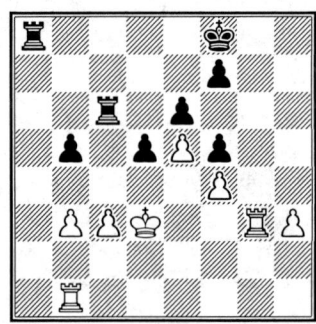

*Position after
White's 33rd move*

33 ... d4 34. Rc1 Ra3 35. Kxd4 Rxb3 36. Rd3
Rc4+ 37. Ke3 b4 38. Rd8+ Ke7 39. Rd3 Rbxc3
40. Rcd1 b3 41. Ra1 Re4+ 42. Kd2 Rxd3+
43. Kxd3 Rxf4 44. Ra7+ Kf8 45. Rb7 Rf3+
46. Kc4 Rxh3 White resigned. 0–1

Match with Arnold Denker,
?June/July, 1934

Writing in Edward Winter's column "Chess Notes" (*New in Chess* 2000/7, 96) Denker recalled playing a match with Fine just before the Western Open of 1934 (I assume a date in June or July to fit in with this memory, but it is possible that it was earlier in the year. Fine also says in his biography that he played a match with Denker but gives no details. I found no mention of the match in *ACB* or *The Chess Review*. AW). The winner was to be the first to win three games, Fine won the first two games, the next two were drawn, Denker won the fifth game and went on to win a further two and draw two to take the stake of $50 put up by James R. Newman. Denker was an exchange up in the ninth game at the adjournment, Fine, apparently, did not turn up for the resumption of play. Denker states that he had the Indian sign on Fine after that, but according to my records the score between them in tournament games after that was four wins to Fine (Fine actually won their very next game at Chicago) two to Denker and three draws. However,

Denker's draws in the first and third U.S. Championship tournaments, coupled with his losses to Reshevsky, were part of the reason for Fine's inability to win those tournaments. Denker, of course, also won their decisive 1944 U.S. Championship encounter. Denker eventually overcame his problems against Reshevsky, winning in two training games of 1948 and again in the United States Championship of 1959/60.

	1	2	3	4	5	6	7	8	9	
Fine	1	1	½	½	0	0	½	½	0	4
Denker	0	0	½	½	1	1	½	½	1	5

Gamescores unavailable.

35th Western Open, Chicago,
Preliminaries, July 21–22, 1934

"All of the thirty-two played two preliminary rounds, after which they were separated into four sections of eight each, according to the merits of the scores." (ACB 1934) After losing, to Henry Woods of Virginia Beach, Virginia, in the first preliminary round, Fine recovered in the second preliminary round, the play-off of 16 losers, to defeat Kirk D. Holland of Chicago, devisor of the seeding system used in the event, and so gain a place in Section C. The game with Woods is recorded in English descriptive notation, whereas the game with Holland is in German algebraic.

Fine	0	Woods	1
Fine	1	Holland	0

(152) FINE—WOODS, H

ACF Open, preliminaries Chicago (1), 1934 (21 July)
Queen's Gambit Declined, Lasker Variation [D55]

1. d4 d5 2. c4 e6 3. Nc3 Nf6 4. Bg5 Be7 5. e3
0–0 6. Nf3 Ne4 7. Bxe7 Qxe7 8. Bd3 Nxc3
9. bxc3 dxc4 10. Bxc4 b6 11. 0–0 Bb7 12. Qe2
Nd7 13. e4 Rfd8 14. Rad1 c5 15. Bb3 Rac8 16. Rfe1
cxd4 17. cxd4 Nf6 18. Bc2 g6 19. Bb1 Rc7 20. Qe3
Kg7 21. Qf4 Rdc8 22. d5 exd5 23. exd5 Qd8
24. d6 Rd7 25. Nd4!? 25 Ne5 Rxd6 26 Rxd6 Qxd6 27
Nxg6! Qxf4 28 Nxf4. 25 ... Rc5 26. Nf5+ Rxf5?!
27. Bxf5 gxf5 28. Qg5+? Kh8 29. Re7?? Qxe7
White resigned. 0–1

(153) FINE—HOLLAND, K

ACF Open, preliminaries Chicago (2), 1934 (22 July)
English Opening [A13]

1. c4 e6 2. Nf3 Nf6 3. b3 Be7 4. g3 c6 5. Bg2 d5
6. 0–0 b5 7. Bb2 Bb7 8. d4 bxc4 9. bxc4 dxc4
10. Ne5 Nd5 11. Nxc4 Nd7 12. e4 Ba6 13. exd5
Bxc4 14. dxc6 Nb6 15. Re1 Bd5 16. Nc3 Rc8
17. Nxd5 Nxd5 18. Bxd5 Qxd5 19. Re5 Qxc6

20. d5 Qc2 21. dxe6 Qxb2 22. Qd7+ Kf8 23. Qxc8+
Black resigned. 1–0

35th Western Open, Chicago, Preliminary Section C, July 22–26, 1934

The tournament used the Kirk Holland system of group qualification in which Section A, which contained the highest scorers from the preliminary games, sent four players through to the finals, Section B three, Section C two and Section D, the low scorers, just one. By winning his first six games in his section Fine made sure that he would progress to the final. In the final round the talented, but occasionally overaggressive, Mexican Champion Captain J. J. Araiza threw everything into his attack, Fine fumbled and so another meeting between the pair was set for the first round of the championship tournament. The first six rounds are recorded in German algebraic form but the last round in English descriptive.

	1	2	3	4	5	6	7	8	
1 Fine	*	0	1	1	1	1	1	1	6
2 Araiza	1	*	1	½	0	1	1	1	5½
3 Grigorieff	0	0	*	1	1	1	1	1	5
4 Jefferson	0	½	0	*	1	1	1	1	4½
5 Barnes	0	1	0	0	*	0	1	½	2½
6= Friedman	0	0	0	0	1	*	½	0	1½
6= Nash	0	0	0	0	0	½	*	1	1½
6= Lew	0	0	0	0	½	1	0	*	1½

(154) FINE–GRIGORIEFF, W

ACF Open, preliminaries section C, Chicago (1), 1934 (22 July)
Nimzowitsch-Indian Defence [E24]

1. d4 Nf6 2. c4 e6 3. Nc3 Bb4 4. a3 Bxc3+
5. bxc3 d6 6. f3 Nc6 7. e4 Ne7 8. Bd3 e5 9. Ne2
Ng6 10. 0–0 Nh5 11. f4 exf4 12. Nxf4 Nhxf4
13. Bxf4 0–0 14. Bg3 Qg5 15. Qc1 Qxc1 16. Raxc1
b6 17. c5 bxc5 18. dxc5 dxc5 19. Bc4 Be6
20. Bxe6 fxe6 21. Bxc7 Rxf1+ 22. Rxf1 Rc8
23. Bd6 c4 24. Rb1 Rc6 25. Rb8+ Kf7 26. e5 Rb6
27. Rc8 Rb5

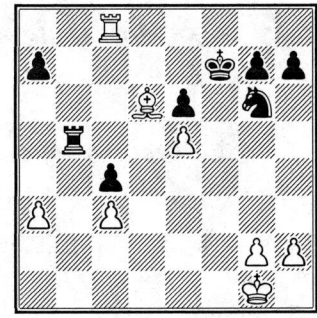

*Position after
Black's 27th move*

28. Rxc4 Nxe5 29. Rc7+ Kf6 30. Rxa7 Ng4
31. Bb4 Rd5 32. Kf1 Nxh2+ 33. Ke2 Ng4 34. a4
Ne5 35. a5 Nc6 36. Ra6 Nxb4 37. cxb4 Ke7
38. Rb6 Kd7 39. a6 Kc7 40. Rb7+ Kc8 41. b5 Rd4
42. b6 Ra4 43. Rc7+ Kb8 44. a7+ Black resigned.
1–0

(155) NASH, E—FINE

ACF Open, preliminaries section C, Chicago (2), 1934
(23 July)
Sicilian Defence [B80]

1. e4 c5 2. Nf3 Nf6 3. Nc3 d6 4. d4 cxd4 5. Nxd4
e6 6. Bd3 Be7 7. 0–0 Qc7 8. h3 a6 9. Qe1 e5
10. Nb3 Be6 11. Kh1 0–0 12. f4 Nbd7 13. f5 Bc4
14. Bxc4 Qxc4 15. Nd2 Qc6 16. Nf3 h6 17. Be3
Rfe8 18. Nd2 b5 19. Qg3 Kh8

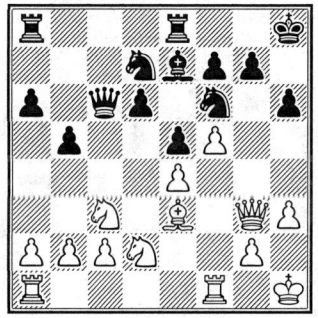

*Position after
Black's 19th move*

20. Qh4 b4 21. Nd1 Qxc2 22. Bxh6 gxh6
23. Qxh6+ Nh7 24. f6 Ndxf6 25. Nf3 Rg8
26. Ne3 Qxe4 27. Ng4 Nxg4 28. hxg4 Qxg4
29. Rf2 Rg6 30. Qh2 Qg3 31. Qxg3 Rxg3 32. Re1
f5 33. Nxe5 dxe5 34. Rxe5 Bd6 35. Rd5 Rg6
36. Rdxf5 Rc8 37. Kg1 Bg3 White resigned. 0–1

(156) FINE—JEFFERSON, B

ACF Open, preliminaries section C, Chicago (3), 1934
(23 July)
Queen's Gambit Declined [D30]

1. d4 d5 2. Nf3 e6 3. c4 c6 4. e3 b6 5. Nc3 Bb7
6. cxd5 exd5 7. Bd3 Nf6 8. Ne5 Bd6 9. f4 Nbd7
10. 0–0 c5 11. Qf3

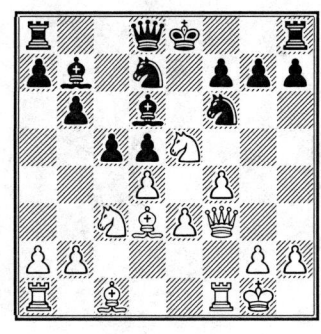

*Position after
White's 11th move*

11 ... cxd4 12. exd4 Bb4 13. Qh3 Bxc3 14. bxc3
Rc8 15. Ba3 Rxc3 16. Bb4 Rc7 17. Bb5 a6 18. Rfe1
Ne4 19. Qf5 Qf6 20. Bxd7+ Kd8 21. Nxf7+ Qxf7
22. Qxf7 Rxd7 23. Qe6 Black resigned. 1–0

(157) BARNES, G—FINE

ACF Open, preliminaries section C, Chicago (4), 1934
    (24 July)
*Queen's Gambit Declined, Cambridge Springs Defence–Yugoslav
Variation [D52]*

1. d4 e6 2. Nf3 Nf6 3. Bg5 d5 4. c4 Nbd7 5. Nc3
c6 6. e3 Qa5 7. cxd5 Nxd5 8. Qb3 Bb4 9. Rc1 h6
10. Bh4 e5 11. Bd3 exd4 12. exd4 Nf4 13. Bc4
Bxc3+ 14. Rxc3 0–0 15. 0–0 Nb6 16. Bg3 Qf5
17. Bxf4 Qxf4 18. Re1 Nxc4 19. Rxc4 Qd6 20. Qb4
Qxb4 21. Rxb4 Rd8 22. h3 Kf8 23. Rb3 Rb8
24. Rd3 Be6 25. b3 Rbc8

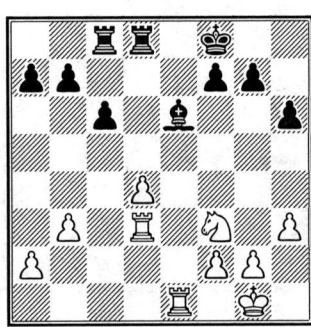

*Position after
Black's 25th move*

26. Red1 a5 27. R3d2 Ra8 28. Ne1 a4 29. b4 a3
30. f4 Ra4 31. Rb1 Rd5 32. g4 Rb5 33. Nd3 Bc4
34. Ne5 Rbxb4 35. Rxb4 Rxb4 36. Nxc4 Rxc4
37. Kf2 Rb4 38. Ke3 Rb2 39. Kd3 Rxd2+
40. Kxd2 Ke7 White resigned. 0–1

(158) FINE—LEW, H

ACF Open, preliminaries section C, Chicago (5), 1934
    (25 July)
Sicilian Defence, Dragon Variation [B33]

1. e4 c5 2. Nf3 Nc6 3. d4 cxd4 4. Nxd4 Nf6
5. Nc3 a6 6. a4 d6 7. Be2 h5 8. 0–0 g6 9. h3 Bg7
10. Be3 Bd7 11. f4 Nxd4 12. Bxd4 Qc8

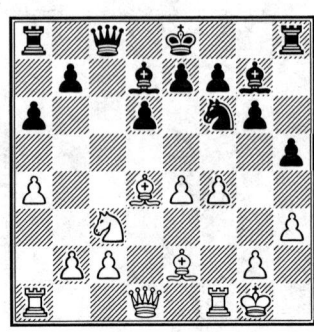

*Position after
Black's 12th move*

13. e5! 0–0 14. exf6 exf6 15. Bd3 f5 16. Be2
Bxd4+ 17. Qxd4 Bc6 18. Bc4 Re8 19. Qxd6 Bxg2
20. Qxg6+ Kh8 21. Qxh5+ Black resigned. 1–0

(159) FRIEDMAN, S—FINE

ACF Open, preliminaries section C, Chicago (6), 1934
    (25 July)
Dutch Defence [A81]

1. d4 f5 2. g3 Nf6 3. Bg2 e6 4. Nh3 Be7 5. 0–0
0–0 6. Nd2 Nc6 7. c3 d6 8. e4 fxe4 9. Nxe4 e5
10. Nxf6+ Bxf6 11. d5 Ne7 12. Ng5 Bf5 13. Ne6
Bxe6 14. dxe6 d5 15. f4 Qd6 16. f5 e4 17. Bf4 Be5
18. Bxe5 Qxe5 19. g4 g6

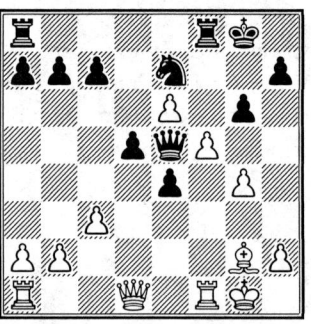

*Position after
Black's 19th move*

20. Qd4 Qxd4+ 21. cxd4 gxf5 22. Rf4 fxg4
23. Rxg4+ Kh8 24. Rf1 Rxf1+ 25. Kxf1 Rf8+
26. Ke2 Rf6 27. Bh3 Rxe6 28. Rg8+ Kxg8
29. Bxe6+ Kg7 30. Ke3 Kf6 31. Bxd5 Nxd5+
32. Kxe4 Ke6 33. a3 h5 White resigned. 0–1

(160) FINE—ARAIZA, J

ACF Open, preliminaries section C, Chicago (7), 1934
    (26 July)
English Opening, Flohr–Mikenas Variation [A18]

1. c4 Nf6 2. Nc3 e6 3. e4 d5 4. e5 d4 5. exf6
dxc3 6. bxc3 Qxf6 7. d4 Nd7 8. Nf3 h6 9. Bd3
Bd6 10. 0–0 0–0 11. Re1 c6 12. Qe2 Re8 13. Ne5
Qh4 14. g3 Qh3 15. f4 Nf6 16. Rb1 c5 17. Ba3 b6
18. dxc5 bxc5 19. Qf3 Bd7 20. Nxd7 Nxd7 21. Bf1
Qf5 22. Qc6 Bxf4 23. gxf4 e5 24. Rbd1 Nf6
25. Bg2 Rac8 26. Qf3 exf4 27. Bh3 Qg5+ 28. Kh1
Qh4 29. Rxe8+ Rxe8 30. Bxc5 Ne4 31. Bd7 Re5
32. Bg1 Ng3+ 33. Kg2 Rg5 34. Qa8+ Kh7
35. Kf3? 35 Qf3 Ne2+ 36 Kh1 Ng3+. 35 ... Qh5+
36. Kf2 Qe2 Mate. 0–1

*35th Western Open Finals,
Chicago, July 27–August 1, 1934*

"With thirty-two competing in the preliminary and
qualifying rounds and ten in the final, making a total of
eighteen rounds for those going through to the finish, there

was supplied chess aplenty, even for the most avid, by the thirty-fifth annual tournament of the Western Chess Association held at the Victor Lawson YMCA, under the auspices of the Professional Men's Chess Club and allied clubs in Chicago from July 21 to August 1." (ACB) After a strong start Fine was pegged back by old rival Arthur Dake in round five. Three further wins left Reuben equal with the undefeated Sammy Reshevsky in the final round. By move twenty a position had arisen which was slightly in White's, Reuben's, favour, Black having potentially weak pawns on the queen's rook and queen's bishop files. Deciding that discretion would be the better part of valour, the leading players agreed the peace and shared the prize money. The games are recorded in English descriptive in the notebook.

		1	2	3	4	5	6	7	8	9	10	
1=	Fine	*	½	0	1	1	1	1	1	1	1	7½
1=	Reshevsky	½	*	1	½	1	½	1	1	1	1	7½
3	Dake	1	0	*	½	1	½	1	1	1	½	6½
4	Denker	0	½	½	*	0	1	1	½	1	1	5½
5=	Eastman	0	0	0	1	*	½	1	1	½	½	4½
5=	Kashdan	0	½	½	0	½	*	1	1	½	½	4½
7	MacMurray	0	0	0	0	0	0	*	1	1	1	3
8	Araiza	0	0	0	½	0	0	0	*	1	1	2½
9	Belson	0	0	0	0	½	½	0	0	*	1	2
10	Engholm	0	0	½	0	½	½	0	0	0	*	1½

(161) FINE—ARAIZA, J

American Chess Federation Open, finals, Chicago (1), 1934 (27 July)
Nimzowitsch-Indian Defence, Sämisch Variation [E24]

1. d4 Nf6 2. c4 e6 3. Nc3 Bb4 4. a3 Bxc3+ 5. bxc3 Ne4 6. Qc2 f5 7. e3 b6 8. Bd3 Bb7 9. Ne2 Qh4?! 10. 0–0 0–0 11. f3 Rf6?! 12. g3 Rg6 13. Nf4 Rxg3+ 14. hxg3 Nxg3 15. Qg2 Nxf1 16. Bxf1 Nc6 17. Bd2 g5 18. Qh3 Qxh3 19. Nxh3 h6 20. e4 fxe4 21. fxe4 Na5 22. Nf2 Ba6

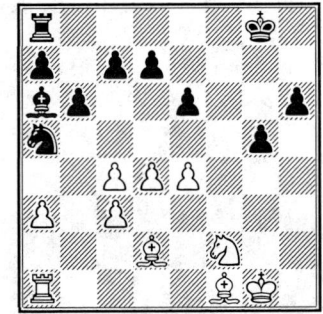

Position after Black's 22nd move

23. c5 Bxf1 24. Rxf1 bxc5 25. Rb1 cxd4 26. cxd4 Nc4 27. Bc1 Nb6 28. Rb3 Kg7 29. Kg2 Kg6 30. Rf3 h5 31. Nh3 g4 32. Nf4+ Kh7 33. Rc3 h4 34. Rxc7 Rc8 35. Nxe6 Rxc7 36. Nxc7 Kg6 37. Nb5 a6 38. Nd6 Kf6 39. Bf4 Ke6 40. Nb7 Kf6 41. Nc5 d5 42. e5+ Kf5 43. e6 Black resigned. 1–0

(162) FINE—DENKER, A

American Chess Federation Open, finals, Chicago (2), 1934 (27 July)
Sicilian Defence, Pin Variation [B40]

1. e4 c5 2. Nf3 e6 3. d4 cxd4 4. Nxd4 Nf6 5. Nc3 Bb4 6. e5 Qa5 7. exf6 Bxc3+ 8. bxc3 Qxc3+ 9. Qd2 Qxa1 10. c3 Qb1 11. Bd3 Qb6 12. fxg7 Rg8 13. Qh6

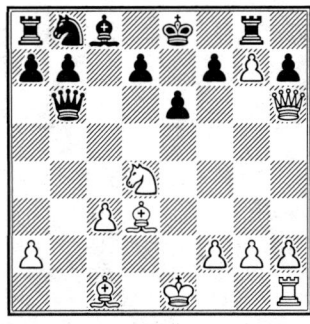

Position after White's 13th move

13 ... Nc6 14. Bxh7 Nxd4 15. Bxg8 Nc2+ 16. Kd1 Qxf2 17. Bh7 Black resigned. 1–0

(163) KASHDAN, I—FINE

American Chess Federation Open, finals, Chicago (3), 1934 (28 July)
Dutch Defence [A90]

1. d4 f5 2. c4 Nf6 3. g3 e6 4. Bg2 Bb4+ Taking advantage of White's second move to exchange a piece which might otherwise be quite useless. 5. Bd2 Bxd2+ A good alternative seems 5 ... Qe7 6 Nh3 0–0 7 0–0 Bxd2 8 Qxd2 d6 9 Nc3 e5. 6. Qxd2 0–0 7. Nc3 d6 8. 0–0–0 In order to prevent ... e5, but White's king is not well placed now; the same object could have been achieved more simply by 8 Rd1, and if 8 ... Qe7 9 Nf3 e5? 10 dxe5 dxe5 11 Nd5! with advantage. 8 ... d5 Changing his plan—evidently with a view to opening a file on the queenside. 9. Nf3 c6 10. Ne5 Nfd7 11. cxd5 Nxe5 12. dxe5 cxd5 13. Kb1 Nd7? A blunder which loses a pawn; 13 ... Nc6 was necessary, although after 14 f4 a6 (to prevent Nc3-b5-d6) 15 h3 Ne7 (15 ... Bd7 or 15 ... b5 would be answered by 16 Nxd5) 16 e3 followed by Nc3-e2-d4, Black would have had a difficult game. 14. Nxd5 Nxe5 Of course if 14 ... exd5 15 Qxd5+ and 16 e6. 15. Qc3! Nc6 There is nothing better in view of the threatened Nc7. 16. Nb4 Qa5 The exchange of queens is Black's only chance. 17. Nxc6 The alternative 17 Bxc6 bxc6 18 Nxc6 (not 18 Qxc6 Qxb4 19 Qxa8 Bb7 20 Qxa7 Bxh1 21 Rxh1 Qe4+) Qxc3 19 bxc3 Bb7 20 Rd6 Rf7 21 Rhd1 Rc7 would also involve some difficulties. 17 ... Qxc3 18. bxc3 bxc6 19. Bxc6 Rb8+ 20. Ka1 Ba6 21. Rd2 Better was 21 e3, now the rook is tied up. 21 ... Kf7 22. Ba4 Rfc8 23. Rc1 Rc5 24. Bb3 Rb6 25. e3 Kf6 26. Rd4 The ending has become extremely difficult now; 26 f4 was probably best. 26 ... g5 27. Rd7 Rb7 28. Rxb7 Bxb7 29. Kb2 And again f4 was in order. 29 ... g4 Creating a very slight chance for himself, now that the h-pawn

and the f-pawn are fixed. **30. Rd1 Rc7 31. Rd6 Bc8 32. Rd4 Rg7** Obviously aiming at Rg7-g6-h6. **33. Ka3**

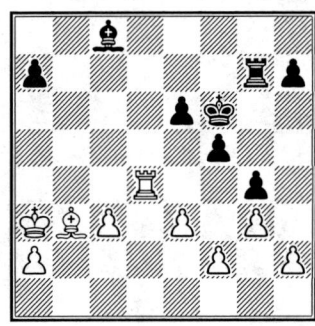

Position after White's 33rd move

33 ... Ke7 34. c4 e5 35. Rd5 e4 36. c5 Rg6 37. Ba4 Rh6 In his last moves Fine has skillfully combined attack with defence. **38. c6 Rxh2 39. c7 Rxf2 40. Rd8 Bb7 41. Bc6** The game is lost: if 41 Rb8 Ba6 42 Bb5 Rc2 43 Bxa6 Rxc7 44 Rb7 Rxb7 45 Bxb7 h5! 46 Ba6 h4 47 gxh4 g3 48 Bf1 f4 49 exf4 e3 and wins. **41 ... Rc2 42. Re8+ Kf7 43. c8Q Bxc8 44. Rxc8 Rc3+ 45. Kb2 Rxe3 46. Rc7+ Kf6 47. Rxa7 Rxg3 48. a4 Rg2+ 49. Kb3 Rg1 50. Ra8 e3 51. Re8 f4 52. a5 Rc1 53. Bg2 Kg5 54. Kb2** White's game is hopeless in any event. **54 ... f3 55. Bxf3 gxf3 56. Rg8+ Kh6 57. Kxc1 f2** White resigned. A weird finish to an interesting but by no means perfect game. The twenty-year-old [*sic*] Fine showed plucky and resourceful play. 0–1 Reinfeld, *BCM* 1934, 424–5.

(164) BELSON, J—FINE

American Chess Federation Open, finals, Chicago (4), 1934 (29 July)

Nimzowitsch-Indian Defence, Classical Variation [E34]

1. d4 Nf6 2. c4 e6 3. Nc3 Bb4 4. Qc2 d5 5. e3 c5 6. cxd5 exd5 7. Nf3 Nc6 8. Bd3 0–0 9. 0–0 cxd4 10. exd4 Bg4 11. Ne5 Nxd4 Black can afford to take the pawn because of a combination involving a mate threat. **12. Qa4 Bxc3** Here Fine wrote "He cannot afford to play simply 12 ... Bc5, then 13 Be3 regains the pawn, since Black must reply 13 ... Bd7 to avoid the loss of a piece." Both 13 ... Qe8 and 13 ... Qb6, however, seem to be to Black's advantage, he certainly doesn't lose a piece. AW **13. Nxg4** Under the impression that he is winning a piece. On 13 bxc3 Ne2+, Black comes out a healthy pawn to the good. (It actually looks slightly tricky for Black to extricate himself after 14 Bxe2 Bxe2 15 Re1. AW) **13 ... Nxg4 14. bxc3 Qc7 15. g3 Qxc3 16. Ba3 Qxd3 17. Bxf8 Qe4** White resigned. 0–1 Fine 1953, 152.

(165) DAKE, A—FINE

American Chess Federation Open, finals, Chicago (5), 1934 (30 July)

Spanish Game, Exchange Variation [C68]

1. e4 e5 2. Nf3 Nc6 3. Bb5 a6 4. Bxc6 The exchange variation in which White has the better pawn formation, but which is supposed to be offset by Black's two bishops. **4 ... dxc6 5. d4 exd4 6. Qxd4 Qxd4 7. Nxd4 Bd7 8. Nc3 0–0–0 9. Be3 Bd6 10. 0–0–0 b6 11. Nde2 c5 12. Bf4 Bc6 13. f3 f6 14. Rd2 Bxf4 15. Nxf4 Ne7 16. Rhd1 Rxd2 17. Kxd2 f5 18. Ke3 Re8 19. g4 fxg4 20. fxg4 Bd7 21. h3 Rf8** A good move, the threat being 22 ... Nc6, followed by 23 ... Ne5 and 24 ... g5. White's next move is the only way to prevent the loss of a pawn. **22. Rd2 Nc6 23. Rf2 Ne5 24. Nd3 Nc4+ 25. Ke2 Re8 26. Rf7 Rg8 27. e5 Be8 28. Rf4 Na5 29. Nd5 Nc6 30. e6 Kb7** Black has played well up this point. He should play 30 ... Kd8, with a good game. Black thought after 31 e7, he could play 31 ... Bg6 and win the pawn, but if 31 ... Bg6 32 Ne5! and Black is lost. **31. e7 Nd4+ 32. Ke3 Ne6 33. Re4 Ng5 34. Re5 Nf7 35. Rf5 c6 36. Nc3 Kc7 37. Ne5 Nh6 38. Rf4 g6 39. Rf8 Kd6 40. Nc4+ Kxe7 41. Rxg8 Nxg8 42. Nxb6 Nf6 43. Ne4 Nxe4 44. Kxe4 Bf7 45. Ke5 Bxa2 46. g5 Bb1 47. c3 Bc2 48. Nc4 Kd7** After this move I took more than half an hour to analyze, for he threatened to march his king over to White's queen-side pawns, and it was a question as to who would queen first. **49. Ne3 Bd3 50. Ng4 Kc7 51. Nf6 Kb6 52. Nxh7 Kb5 53. Nf8 Kc4 54. Kf6 Kb3 55. Nxg6 Kxb2 56. Ne5 Be4 57. h4 Kxc3 58. h5 a5 59. h6 a4 60. Ng6** The winning move, as Black cannot queen his pawn without losing. A hard game. **60 ... a3 61. h7 a2 62. h8Q Kc2 63. Qh2+ Kb1 64. Qb8+ Kc2 65. Qe5 Bxg6 66. Qa1** Black resigned. 1–0 Dake, *ACB* 1934, 124–5.

(166) EASTMAN, G—FINE

American Chess Federation Open, finals, Chicago (6), 1934 (30 July)

French Defence, Alekhine-Chatard Attack [C13]

1. e4 e6 2. d4 d5 3. Nc3 Nf6 4. Bg5 Be7 5. e5 Nfd7 6. h4 c5 7. Qg4 Kf8 8. Nf3 Nc6 9. 0–0–0 cxd4 10. Nxd4 Ndxe5 11. Bxe7+ Qxe7 12. Qg3 Nxd4 13. Rxd4 Nc6 14. Rd1 Bd7 15. f4 Rc8 16. a3 f5 17. Qf2 h5 18. Bb5 a6 19. Bd3 b5 20. Rhe1 Qf7 21. Qb6 Ra8

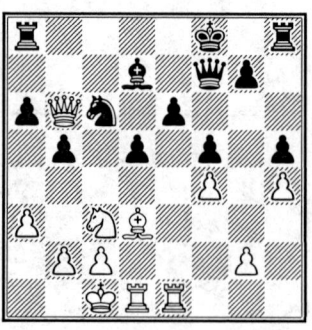

Position after Black's 21st move

22. Bf1 Kg8 23. g3 Kh7 24. Bg2 Rhb8 25. Qf2 b4
26. axb4 Rxb4 27. Bxd5 exd5 28. Nxd5 Rb7 White
resigned. **0–1**

(167) FINE—ENGHOLM, N

American Chess Federation Open, finals, Chicago (7), 1934
   (31 July)
King's Indian Defence [A42]

1. c4 e5 2. Nf3 d6 3. Nc3 g6 4. d4 Nd7 5. e4
Bg7 6. Bg5 f6 7. Be3 Nh6 8. h3 Nf7 9. Qc2
exd4 10. Nxd4 Nde5 11. 0–0–0 Nc6 12. h4
Nfe5

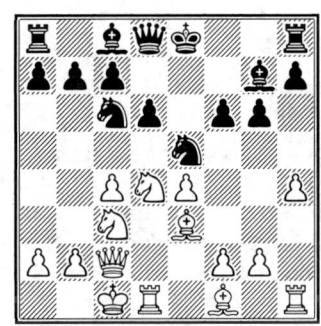

*Position after
Black's 12th move*

13. c5 Nxd4 14. Bxd4 0–0 15. h5 Be6 16. hxg6
hxg6 17. f4 Ng4 18. f5 Bf7 19. Be2 Ne5 20. Bxe5
fxe5 21. Qd3 Qg5+ 22. Kb1 dxc5 23. Qh3 Rfd8
24. Rdf1 Rd6 25. Nd5

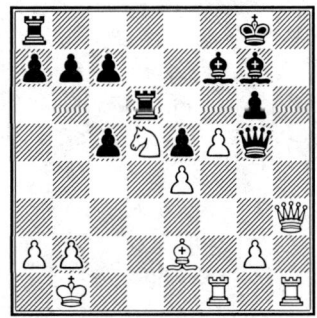

*Position after
White's 25th move*

25 ... Re8 26. Rf2 c6 27. Qh7+ Kf8 28. fxg6 Qxg6
29. Qxg6 Rxg6 30. Bh5 Black resigned. **1–0**

(168) FINE—MACMURRAY, D

American Chess Federation Open, finals, Chicago (8), 1934
   (31 July)
Colle System [D05]

1. d4 d5 2. Nf3 Nf6 3. e3 e6 4. Bd3 c5 5. c3 Nc6
6. 0–0 Bd6 7. Nbd2 0–0 8. Qe2 e5 9. dxc5 Bxc5
10. e4 d4 11. Nb3 Bb6 12. cxd4 Bxd4 13. Nbxd4
Nxd4 14. Nxd4 Qxd4 15. Be3 Qb4 16. Racl b6
17. f4 Ng4

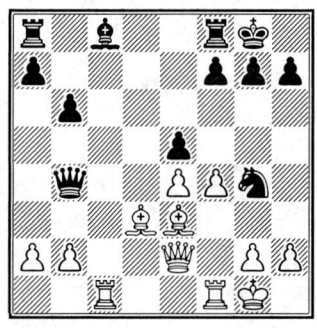

*Position after
Black's 17th move*

18. Bd2 18 Rxc8 Raxc8 19 Qxg4. 18 ... Qxb2 19. h3
Nf6 19 ... Qd4+ 20 Kh1 Rd8. 20. fxe5 Qxe5 21. Bc3
Qg5 22. e5 Nd5 23. Bd2 Qd8 24. Rc4 g6 25. Bh6
Re8 26. Qf3 Be6 27. Rd4 Rc8 28. Bb5 Rc3
29. Qf2 Re7 30. Qf6 Black resigned. **1–0**

(169) FINE—RESHEVSKY, S

American Chess Federation Open, finals, Chicago (9), 1934
   (1 Aug.)
Nimzowitsch-Indian Defence [E22]

1. d4 Nf6 2. c4 e6 3. Nc3 Bb4 4. Qb3 Nc6 5. e3
a5 6. a3 a4 7. Qc2 Bxc3+ 8. Qxc3 Qe7 9. Bd3 e5
10. Ne2 d5 11. c5 0–0 12. 0–0 Bd7 13. Ng3 Rfb8
14. Bd2 b6 15. cxb6 Rxb6 16. dxe5 Nxe5 17. Be2
Nc4 18. Bxc4 Rc6 19. Qb4 Qxb4 20. Bxb4 Draw
agreed. **½–½**

More International
Experience, 1934–1935

   In the later part of 1934 Fine took part in two international tournaments and a brief match against Mexico's
strongest player of the pre-modern era. At Syracuse Reshevsky was outstanding, winning practically all of his games
from the lower two thirds of the table. Kashdan, like Reshevsky, did not lose a game and therefore outscored Fine and
Dake by half a point.

   Towards the end of the year Reuben paid an extended
visit south of the border. He gave many exhibitions, and
encountered Carlos Torre, who had been a mighty force in
American and European chess from 1924 to 1926. When
Torre had retired from professional chess at the age of
twenty-one he had already established himself among the
best in the world. Nine years later, however, he was evidently out of practice, only managing to draw one of the
two games played. At the Mexico City tournament over
Christmas and New Year Fine was one of three United
States players who shared first place, defeating all of the
Mexican representatives.

Syracuse, August 13–25, 1934

		1	2	3	4	5	6	7	8	9	10	11	12	13	14	15	
1	Reshevsky	*	½	1	½	½	1	1	1	½	1	1	1	1	1	1	12
2	Kashdan	½	*	½	½	½	1	½	1	1	½	1	½	1	1	1	10½
3=	Dake	0	½	*	½	½	1	½	1	1	1	0	1	1	1	1	10
3=	Fine	½	½	½	*	½	0	1	1	1	1	0	1	1	1	1	10
5	Kupchik	½	½	½	½	*	0	½	½	1	½	1	1	1	1	1	9½
6	Horowitz	0	0	0	1	1	*	½	0	½	1	1	1	½	1	1	8½
7	Steiner	0	½	½	0	½	½	*	½	1	1	0	1	½	1	1	8
8	Monticelli	0	0	0	0	½	1	½	*	½	1	0	½	½	1	1	6½
9=	Reinfeld	½	0	0	0	0	½	0	½	*	½	1	1	½	½	1	6
9=	Santasiere	0	½	0	0	½	0	0	0	½	*	1	1	½	1	1	6
11=	Denker	0	0	1	1	0	0	1	1	0	0	*	0	½	0	½	5
11=	Seitz	0	½	0	0	0	0	0	½	0	0	1	*	1	1	1	5
13	Araiza	0	0	0	0	0	½	½	½	½	½	½	0	*	½	1	4½
14	Tholfsen	0	0	0	0	0	0	0	0	½	0	1	0	½	*	1	3
15	Martin	0	0	0	0	0	0	0	0	0	0	½	0	0	0	*	½

"As Syracuse, the ancient city of Sicily, will ever be associated with the name of Archimedes, so will that of its namesake in Onondaga County, in the State of New York, be identified, in the thoughts of chess lovers, with valorous deeds and eventual triumph at the Jubilee Congress of the New York State Chess Association of Samuel Reshevsky, erstwhile chess prodigy, subsequently Western Champion and now, matured, advanced by common consent to the rank of Grandmaster. As one of fifteen who entered the international masters tournament, held at the Hotel Onondaga from August 13 to 25 Reshevsky came through unscathed, winning first prize by a comfortable margin in advance of Isaac I. Kashdan, Arthur W. Dake, Reuben Fine and Abraham Kupchik, the other prize winners. For the benefit of local visitors it was decided to hold evening sessions from 7 to 11 o'clock, with a time limit of 36 moves in the first two hours and 18 moves an hour thereafter. After a slight delay, due to the belated arrival of clocks, play began at 7.30 P.M. on August 13, with the BULLETIN'S publisher as tournament director and Malcolm Sim, chess editor of the Toronto *Telegram*, as associate.

"The grand ballroom, ablaze with light, offered the best accommodations for a competition of this sort that have ever been available for the purpose in this country. Eight giant chessboards hung on the wall immediately back of the row of contestants, affording all spectators ample view of the progress of the games, the moves of which were promptly reproduced thereupon by a corps of tellers. David Polland of New York was the winner of the solving contest for prizes donated by Alain C. White of Litchfield, Conn., international authority. Polland solved the eight problems submitted in thirty-seven minutes. The other prize winners were Reuben Fine, New York, Second; Professor C. K. Thomas, Ithaca, third; Harold D. Grossman, New York, fourth; George N. Cheney, Syracuse, fifth. Announcement

was made by Captain Jose J. Araiza that an international tournament will be held in Mexico City, and during November. In addition to eight Mexicans, including himself and Carlos Torre, those to be invited are Reuben Fine, Arthur W. Dake, Herman Steiner, Fred Reinfeld, Arnold S. Denker, Dr. Adolf Seitz and Dr. S. T. Tartakower. Fine will make a tour of the leading Mexican chess centers." (ACB 1934)

The games are recorded in English descriptive up to the game with Denker. The notebooks then change to the numeric notation, with the exception of the game with Reshevsky which is in English descriptive again.

(170) FINE—SEITZ, A

Syracuse (1), 1934 (13 Aug.)
Dutch Defence [A89]

1. d4 f5 2. g3 Nf6 3. Bg2 g6 4. Nf3 Bg7 5. 0–0 0–0 6. c4 d6 7. Nc3 Nc6 8. b3 e5 9. dxe5 dxe5 10. Ba3 Re8 11. Qc2 e4 12. Rfd1 Nd7 13. Ne1 Nd4 14. Qd2 c6 15. Bb2 Ne6 16. Na4 Qe7 17. Bxg7 Qxg7 18. Nc2 Ndf8 19. Ne3 Bd7 20. c5 Nc7 21. Nc4 Nd5 22. Nd6 Reb8 23. f3 e3 24. Qb2 f4 25. Qxg7+ Kxg7 26. gxf4 Nxf4 27. Nc3 Bf5 28. Bf1 Bc2 29. Rdc1 Bf5 30. Rd1 Bc2 31. Rdc1 Bf5 32. Nd1 Nd5 33. Rc4 Ne6 34. Rac1 a5 35. h4 Ra7 36. Kh2 Kf6 37. Kg3 Ng7 38. Ne4+ Ke7 39. Nec3 Be6 40. Re4 Kf6 41. Kh2 Rd8?! 42. Nxe3 Nxe3 43. Rxe3 Nf5 44. Re4 Raa8 45. Bh3 Rd2 46. Bxf5 Bxf5 47. Ra4 Kg7 48. Kg3 Rdd8 49. Kf2 h6 50. Rd1 Rxd1 51. Nxd1 Rd8 52. Ne3 Kf6 53. Nxf5 gxf5 54. Ke3 Re8+ 55. Kd3 Ke5 56. Rd4 Re6 57. f4+ Kf6 58. Rd7 Re4 59. e3 Rb4 60. Rd6+ Kg7 61. h5 a4 62. Rd4 Rb5 63. b4 b6 64. cxb6 Rxb6 65. Kc4 Rb7 66. Kc5 Black resigned. **1–0**

(171) HOROWITZ, I—FINE

Syracuse (2), 1934 (14 Aug.)
Spanish Game, Steinitz Defence Deferred [C74]

1. e4 e5 2. Nf3 Nc6 3. Bb5 a6 4. Ba4 d6 5. c3 f5 The Siesta Variation. **6. exf5! Bxf5 7. d4 e4 8. Ng5!** Much stronger than either 8 Qe2 Be7 9 Nfd2 Nf6 10 h3 d5 11 Nf1 b5 12 Bc2 Na5 13 Ne3 Bg6 14 Nd2 0–0 with an even position; or 8 Bg5 Be7 9 Nh4 Be6 10 Bxe7 Ngxe7! 11 Qh5+ g6 12 Qh6 Ng8 13 Qf4 Nf6 14 Nd2 0–0 15 0–0 d5 and Black stands slightly better, E. Steiner–Capablanca, Budapest 1928. A game H. Steiner–Capablanca, New York 1931, continued 8 d5 exf3 9 b5 10 Qxf3 Bxb1! 11 Bb3 Bg6 12 0–0 Nf6 13 Bg5 Be7 14 Rfe1 Kf8 15 Re3 h6 16 Bxf6 Bxf6 17 Qd5 h5 18 g3 Qc8 19 Re6 Qd8 20 Re3 Qc8 21 Re6 Qd8 with a draw by repetition of moves, MCO 275. **8 ... d5** Better than 8 ... h6 9 d5 b5 10 Bc2, or 8 ... Nf6 9 f3 d5 10 0–0 Qd7 11 c4!, or 8 ... Be7 9 0–0! Bxg5 10 Qh5+ Bg6 11 Qxg5 Qxg5 12 Bxg5

Nge7 13 Nd2 b5 14 Bb3 d5 15 Rae1 Kd7 16 f3 exf3 17 Rxf3 Szabo–Znovsko-Borovsky, Tata–Tovaros 1935, MCO. **9. f3 e3?** 10. f4 White has a distinct superiority, MCO. **10 ... Bd6 11. Qf3 Qd7 12. Qxe3+ Nge7 13. Nf3 0–0 14. Ne5 Nxe5?! 15. Bxd7 Nd3+ 16. Kd1 Bxd7 17. Qxd3 Bg4+ 18. Ke1 Rae8 19. Kf2 Bxf4 20. Bxf4 Rxf4+ 21. Kg3 g5 22. h3 Be2 23. Qd2 Nf5+ 24. Kh2 Re3 25. Re1 Rfe4 26. Na3 g4 27. Nc2 1–0** *New York Times*, 19 August, 1934.

(172) SANTASIERE, A—FINE

Syracuse (4), 1934 (15 Aug.)
English Opening [A12]

1. c4 Nf6 2. Nf3 c6 3. g3 d5 4. b3 Bf5 5. Bg2 e6 6. 0–0 Bd6 7. Bb2 0–0 8. d3 Qe7 9. Nbd2 e5 10. Nh4 Be6 11. e4 d4 12. Nf5 Bxf5 13. exf5 Ba3 14. Bxa3 Qxa3 15. Qc1 Qe7 16. a3 a5 17. Re1 Nbd7 18. h3 Rfe8 19. Qc2 g6 20. fxg6 hxg6 21. Rec1 Nc5 22. Rab1 Kg7 23. b4 axb4 24. axb4 Na4 25. Re1 Nc3 26. Rb2 Ra3 27. Nb1 Nxb1 28. Rbxb1 Rc3 29. Qe2 Nd7 30. b5 cxb5 31. Rxb5 Nc5 32. Bd5 Qd6 33. Reb1 Re7 34. Rb6 Qd7 35. Kg2 Qc8 36. Qf3 Qf5 37. Qxf5 gxf5 38. Kf1 Rxd3 39. Bxb7 Rd2

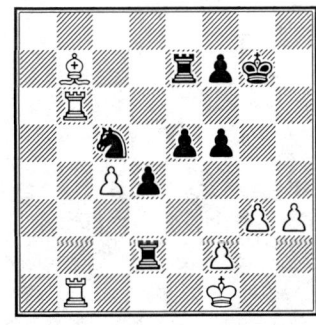

Position after Black's 39th move

40. g4 fxg4 41. hxg4 e4 42. R6b5 Nd3 43. Rg5+ Kf8 44. Bc6 Re6 45. Rb8+ Ke7 46. Re8+ Kf6 47. Rf5+ Kg6 48. Bxe4 48 Bd5! e3 49 Bxe6 e2+! 50 Kg2 fxe6 51 Rxe6+ Kg7. **48 ... Rxe8 49. Re5+ f5 50. Rxe8 fxe4 51. Rxe4 Nc1 52. Ke1 Nb3 53. f4 Rc2 54. Re6+ Kf7 55. Rd6 Rc3 56. Ke2 d3+ 57. Kf2 d2 58. Ke2 Rc1 59. Rxd2 Nxd2 60. Kxd2 Rxc4 61. Ke3 Ke6** White resigned. **0–1**

(173) FINE—KUPCHIK, A

Syracuse (5), 1934 (16 Aug.)
French Defence [C11]

1. e4 e6 2. d4 d5 3. Nc3 Nf6 4. Bg5 dxe4 5. Nxe4 Be7 6. Bxf6 Bxf6 7. Nf3 Nd7 8. Bd3 Nf8 9. c3 Ng6 10. g3 Bd7 11. Qe2 Bc6 12. 0–0–0 Bxe4 13. Bxe4 c6 14. Nd2 Ne7 15. f4 Qc7 16. Bg2 0–0–0 17. Ne4 Nf5 18. Rhe1 Nd6 19. Nc5 Kb8 20. Qc2 Be7 21. Qb3 Qb6 22. Kc2 Nc8 23. Nd3

Qxb3+ 24. axb3 Kc7 25. Ne5 Nd6 26. Nc4 Nxc4 27. bxc4 Bf6 28. Re2 g6 29. Ree1 h5 30. h4 Rd7 Draw agreed. **½–½**

(174) MONTICELLI, M—FINE

Syracuse (6), 1934 (17 Aug.)
Caro-Kann, Classical Defence [B18]

1. e4 c6 2. d4 d5 3. Nc3 White's most promising line against the Caro-Kann Defence is undoubtedly 3 exd5 cxd5 4 c4 Nf6 5 Nc3 Nc6 6 Bg5! (first played in the match Botvinnik–Flohr). **3 ... dxe4 4. Nxe4 Bf5 5. Ng3 Bg6 6. Nf3** 6 h4 h6 is not to be feared by Black. **6 ... e6 7. Bc4** The bishop is not effectively placed here; 7 Bd3 was better. **7 ... Nf6 8. Qe2 Nbd7 9. Ne5 Nxe5 10. dxe5 Nd7** Already Black is threatening ... Qa5+ winning a pawn. **11. f4** After this Black has undoubtedly the better game. 11 0–0 was necessary; the position would then be even. **11 ... Bc5 12. Bb3** That White's game is already difficult can be seen from the fact that upon 12 Bd2 Black can reply ... Bxc2 with perfect safety, while if 12 Be3 Qb6! 13 Bxc5 Qxb2 White has nothing for the pawn. As Monticelli pointed out after the game if 12 f5 exf5 13 e6 0–0! 14 exd7 Qxd7 Black has a winning attack. However, 12 c3 was slightly better than the text. **12 ... a5!** An excellent move to which there is no satisfactory reply; for example, if 13 Bd2 a4 14 Bc4 Bxc2; or 13 Be3 Qb6 14 Bxc5 Nxc5. **13. a4** (It would seem that 13 c3 a4 14 Bd1 0–0 15 Ne4 would have been better. AW) **13 ... Qb6** The attractive 13 ... Bb4+ 14 c3 (if 14 Bd2 Nc5 15 Bc4 Qxd2+ 16 Qxd2 Bxc2) Nc5 15 Bc2 Nd3+ 16 Kf1 Bc5 is refuted by 17 f5! (But then 17 ... Nxc1 18 Rxc1 Qg5!. AW) **14. Bd2 0–0–0 15. Nf1** If 15 0–0–0 Bd4 followed by ... Nc5 leaves White defenceless. **15 ... Bb4! 16. 0–0–0** 16 c3 is bad because of 16 ... Bxc3!. Relatively best is 16 Bxb4 Qxb4+ 17 Qd2 Nc5 18 Qxb4 axb4, although Black's game remains manifestly superior. **16 ... Nc5!** If now 17 Bxb4 Rxd1+ 18 Qxd1 Nxb3+ 19 cxb3 Qxb4 and White is lost. **17. Qe3**

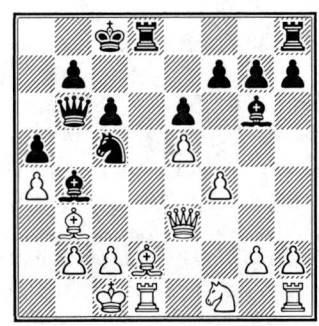

Position after White's 17th move

17 ... Rd3! 18. cxd3 Nxb3+ 19. Kc2 If 19 Kb1 Nxd2+ 20 Ka2 Qxe3 21 Nxe3 Bxd3 and wins. **19 ... Bc5 20. Qh3** Or 20 Qe1 Nd4+. **20 ... Nd4+ 21. Kc1** If 21 Kb1 Qb3, threatening both rook and d-pawn, wins quickly. **21 ... Qb3** White resigned. For if 22 Ne3 Qxd3 and mates in two. **0–1** Fine, BCM 1934, 463-4.

(175) FINE—REINFELD, F

Syracuse (7), 1934 (18 Aug.)
Queen's Gambit Accepted [D24]

1. d4 d5 2. c4 dxc4 3. Nf3 Nf6 4. Nc3 a6 5. a4
Bg4 6. Ne5 Bh5 7. f3 e6 8. g4 Bg6 9. h4 h6
10. Nxg6 fxg6 11. e3 c5 12. dxc5 Qxd1+ 13. Kxd1
Bxc5 14. Bxc4 Ke7 15. Ke2 Nc6 16. Bd2 Ne5
17. Bb3 g5 18. Rac1 b6 19. a5 Rhd8 20. hxg5 hxg5

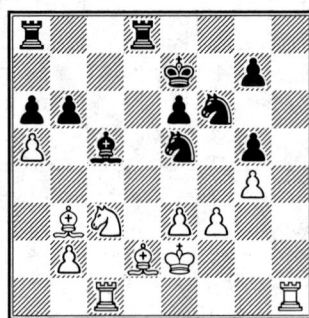

*Position after
Black's 20th move*

21. Na4 Nxf3 22. Bc3 Nh4 23. Nxb6 Ne4 24. Be1
Rab8 25. Rxc5 Nxc5 26. Bb4 Rdc8 27. Rc1 Kd6
28. Ba2 Black resigned. 1–0

(176) DENKER, A—FINE

Syracuse (8), 1934 (19 Aug.)
Semi-Slav Defence, Meran Variation [D48]

1. d4 c6 2. c4 d5 3. Nc3 Nf6 4. Nf3 e6 5. e3
Nbd7 6. Bd3 dxc4 7. Bxc4 b5 8. Bd3 a6 9. 0–0
c5 10. a4 cxd4 10 ... b5 should be played. The text leads
to complications in which Black may find himself at a disadvantage because of his inferior development. **11. Nxd4!?** 11
exd4 was simpler, but in this tournament I was always looking for complications! (11 exd4 b4 12 Ne4 Bb7 13 Bg5 Be7
looks fine for Black. AW). Black's best practical chance now
may well have been 11 ... Nc5. **11 ... b4 12. Qf3! Rb8** Giving up the exchange immediately will not do: 12 ... bxc3 13
Qxa8 Qc7 (13 ... Nc5 14 Bc4!) 14 Bxa6 Nb6 15 Bb5+ and
wins. **13. Nc6 Qc7** He could have preserved material
equality with 13 ... Bb7 14 Ne4! (not 14 Nxd8 Bxf3 15 gxf3
bxc3 16 Nc6 cxb2) Bxc6 15 Nxf6+ gxf6 16 Qxc6 Rb6. But
after 17 Qc2 the combination of Black's retarded development and weak pawn structure will spell trouble for him.
(one might continue this line 17 ... b3 18 Qe2 Nc5 19 Bc4
Rg8 20 Bd2 Qa8. White certainly holds the long term
trumps, but Black is still struggling. AW) **14. Nxb8 Ne5**
The move on which Fine relied. White is momentarily a
rook ahead, but he has four pieces *en prise.* **15. Qa8! Nxd3**
If 15 ... Bb7 16 Nxa6+! Bxa8 17 Nxc7+ with an easy win.
**16. Nxa6 Qb7 17. Nb5! Qxa8 18. Nac7+ Kd7
19. Nxa8 Kc6 20. Na7+ Kb7 21. Nxc8 Kxc8
22. Nb6+ Kb7 23. Nc4 Be7 24. Na5+ Kb6
25. Nb3 Ne4 26. f3 Nec5 27. Nxc5 Bxc5 28. Bd2
Rd8 29. b3 Nb2 30. Rf2 Nd3 31. Re2 Nf4 32. Kf1!**

Nxe2 33. Kxe2 Kc6 34. Rc1 Kd6 35. Rc4 Rb8
36. Kd3 e5 37. e4 g6 38. Be3! Bxe3 39. Kxe3 f5
As soon as Black's pawn moves are exhausted, he will be in
Zugzwang. If his king moves, Rc4-c5-b5 wins easily. If his
rook moves on the file, White wins with Rc4-c8 followed by
Ke3-d3-c4. **40. Ke2 f4 41. Kd2 g5 42. h3 h5 43. Ke2
Kd7 44. Rc5 Kd6 45. Rd5+! Ke6 46. Rb5 Rc8** If 46
... Rxb5 47 axb5 Kd6 48 Kd3 Kc5 49 b6 Kxb6 50 Kc4 and
wins. **47. Rxb4 Rc2+ 48. Kf1 Ra2 49. Rb6+ Kf7
50. Kg1 Ra1+ 51. Kh2 Ra2 52. Rh6 Rb2** Or 52 ... h4
53 Rb6 Ra3 54 Rb5 Ke6 55 a5 followed by b4 and Rb6+
and so on. **53. Rxh5 Kg6 54. Rh8 Rxb3 55. a5 Ra3
56. Ra8 Kf7 57. a6 Kg7 58. a7 Ra1 59. h4** Black
resigned. 1–0 Denker, 51–5.

(177) FINE—DAKE, A

Syracuse (9), 1934 (20 Aug.)
Queen's Gambit Declined [D63]

1. d4 Nf6 2. c4 e6 3. Nf3 d5 4. Nc3 Be7 5. Bg5
0–0 6. e3 Nbd7 7. Rc1 c6 8. a3 a6 9. Qc2 h6
10. Bh4 Re8 11. Bd3 dxc4 12. Bxc4 b5 13. Ba2 c5
14. dxc5 Nxc5 15. Rd1 Qb6 16. b4 Ncd7 17. Bb1
Nf8 18. Bxf6 Bxf6 19. Ne4 Be7 20. 0–0 Bb7
21. Ne5 Rad8 22. Qe2 f6 23. Nf3 Rxd1 24. Rxd1
Rd8 25. Nd4 f5 26. Nd2 Bf6 27. N2b3 Bd5
28. Nc5 Bc4 29. Qc2 Bd5 30. Qe2 Bc4 Draw agreed.
½–½

(178) FINE—STEINER, H

Syracuse (10), 1934 (21 Aug.)
Spanish Game, Worrall Attack [C86]

1. e4 e5 2. Nf3 Nc6 3. Bb5 a6 4. Ba4 Nf6 5. 0–0
Be7 6. Qe2 d6 7. c3 0–0 8. d4 Bd7 9. Bc2 Bg4
10. Rd1 Nd7 11. h3 Bh5 12. g4 Bg6 13. d5 Ncb8
14. Nbd2 h5 15. Nh2 hxg4 16. hxg4 Bg5 17. Ndf1
Bf4 18. f3 Qg5 19. Qg2 f6 20. Ng3 Be8 21. Ne2
Be3+ 22. Bxe3 Qxe3+ 23. Qf2 Qxf2+ 24. Kxf2 g6
25. f4 exf4 26. Nxf4 Ne5 27. Kg3 Bd7 28. Rh1 a5
29. Nf3 Kg7 30. Nd4 Rc8

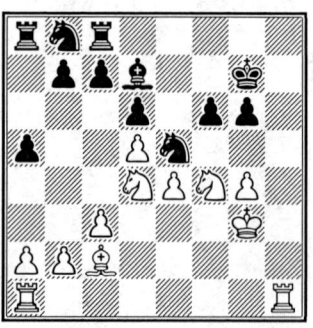

*Position after
Black's 30th move*

31. Nfe6+ Bxe6 32. Nxe6+ Kg8 33. Rh6 Nbd7
34. Rah1 Nf8 35. Rh8+ Kf7 36. Nxf8 Rxf8
37. R1h7+ Black resigned. 1–0

(179) THOLFSEN, E—FINE

Syracuse (11), 1934 (21 Aug.)
Grünfeld Defence [E61]

1. d4 Nf6 2. Nf3 g6 3. c4 Bg7 4. Nc3 0-0 5. g3
d5 6. Bg2 dxc4 7. 0-0 Nd5 8. e4 Nxc3 9. bxc3 c5
10. h3 cxd4 11. cxd4 Nc6 12. Be3 b5 13. Rb1 a6
14. d5 Ne5 15. Nxe5 Bxe5 16. f4 Bg7

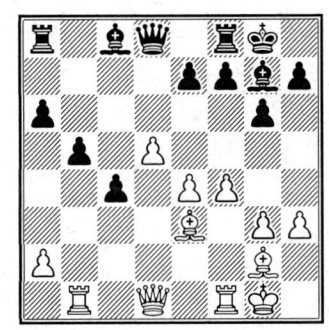

*Position after
Black's 16th move*

17. g4 Bd7 18. e5 Rc8 19. Bd4 e6 20. d6 f6
21. exf6 Bxf6 22. g5 Bxd4+ 23. Qxd4 c3 24. h4
Rc4 25. Qe3 Qc8 26. Qg3 Qc5+ 27. Kh2 b4
28. h5 c2 29. Rbc1 Qxd6 30. hxg6 hxg6 31. Rf2
Ba4 32. Bh3 Rcxf4 33. Rxf4 Rxf4 34. Bxe6+ Kg7
White resigned. 0-1

(180) FINE—KASHDAN, I

Syracuse (13), 1934 (23 Aug.)
Queen's Gambit Declined [D49]

1. d4 Nf6 2. c4 e6 3. Nc3 d5 4. Nf3 Nbd7 5. e3
c6 6. Bd3 dxc4 7. Bxc4 b5 8. Bd3 a6 9. e4 c5
10. e5 cxd4 11. Nxb5 Nxe5 12. Nxe5 axb5 13. 0-0
Qd5 14. Qe2 Rb8 15. Bf4 Bd6 16. Rac1 0-0
17. Nc6 Rb6 18. Bxd6 Qxd6 19. Na7 Bb7
20. Nxb5 Qd5 21. f3 Qxa2 22. Bc4 Qa5 23. Nxd4
Rd8 24. Qf2 Rbd6 25. Nb3 Qf5 26. Rfe1 h5
27. Qg3 Nd5 28. Nc5 Ba8 29. Ne4 Rb6 30. Qh4
Rdb8 31. Bxd5 exd5 32. Ng3 Qg6 33. Qxh5 Qxh5
34. Nxh5 Rxb2 35. Rcd1 Ra2 36. Ra1 Rbb2
37. Rxa2 ½-½ *New York Sun*, 31 August, 1934.

(181) FINE—RESHEVSKY, S

Syracuse (14), 1934 (24 Aug.)
Spanish Game, Worrall Attack [C86]

1. e4 e5 2. Nf3 Nc6 3. Bb5 a6 4. Ba4 Nf6 5. 0-0
Be7 6. Qe2 b5 7. Bb3 d6 8. c3 Na5 9. Bc2 c5
10. d4 Qc7 11. Rd1 0-0 12. h3 White improved by 12
Bg5 Bg4 13 dxe5! dxe5 14 Nbd2 Rfd8 15 Nf1 Nh5 16 h3!
Be6 17 Ne3 f6 18 Nh2! g6 19 Bh6, Alekhine–Keres, Salzburg
1942, PCO 363. **12 ... cxd4 13. cxd4 Bd7 14. dxe5
dxe5** The position is even, *PCO*. **15. Nc3 Rac8 16. Bb1
Be6 17. Bg5** 17 Nd5!? **17 ... Rfd8 18. Bd3 h6**

19. Bxf6 Bxf6 20. Nd5 Bxd5 21. exd5 g6 22. Kh1
Kh8 23. Kg1 Kg8 24. Kh1 Kh8 25. Kg1 Kg8
26. Kh1 Kh8 Draw agreed. ½-½

(182) ARAIZA, J—FINE

Syracuse (15), 1934 (24 Aug.)
French Defence, Advance Variation [C02]

1. e4 e6 2. d4 d5 3. e5 c5 4. Qg4 cxd4 5. Nf3 Nc6
6. Bd3 Qc7! 7. Qg3 f6 8. Bf4? If 8 exf6 Qxg3 9 f7+
Kxf7 10 hxg3 e5! and Black stands better, MCO 70. **8 ...
g5 9. Bd2 Nxe5 10. Nxe5 Qxe5+** (This is as far as the
entry in MCO goes. 11 Qxe5 fxe5 12 Bxg5 e4 would seem to
be the most logical continuation. AW) **0-1**

Marshall CC—Mercantile Library CA,
Philadelphia, October 21, 1934

"Entertaining twenty-two players from the Marshall
Chess Club of New York at the Ben Franklin Hotel in
Philadelphia on October 21, the Mercantile Library Chess
Association of that city made a gallant attempt to square
accounts with the New Yorkers for the defeat sustained away
from home in 1933. The home team failed only by a narrow margin. How well the Philadelphians fought may be
judged from the final score, which was 11½-10½. A particularly fine showing was made by the Mercantile players at
the first eight boards, where they scored at a rate of 6-2.
Frank J. Marshall captained the team and was held to a
draw by Jacob Levin." (ACB 1934) On boards three to six
Reinfeld, Tholfsen, Santasiere and Smirka lost to Drasin,
Regen, Winkelman and Sharp.

Fine	½	Weiner	½

(183) FINE—WEINER, G

Marshall CC vs. Mercantile Library CC, Franklin Hotel,
 Philadelphia, 1934 (21 Oct.)
French Defence, Winawer Variation [C17]

1. e4 e6 2. d4 d5 3. Nc3 Bb4 4. e5 c5 5. Bd2
cxd4 6. Nb5 Bxd2+ 7. Qxd2 Nc6 8. Nf3 Nge7
9. Nd6+ Kf8 10. Qf4 Nf5 11. Nxf7 Kxf7 12. g4
Qa5+ 13. Kd1 Re8 14. Rg1 Re7 15. Bd3 Ke8
16. gxf5 exf5 17. Qh4 g6 18. Qf6 Qc5 19. a3 a5
20. Kd2 Rb8 21. h4 Rf7 22. Qg5 Qe7 23. Bb5
Qc5 24. Bd3 Qe7 25. Rae1 Qxg5+ 26. Nxg5 Re7
27. f4 Kf8 28. h5 Bd7 29. hxg6 hxg6 30. Rh1 Rg7
31. Nf3 Ke7 32. Reg1 Rbg8 33. Rg2 Nd8 34. Nxd4
Ne6 35. Nxe6 Bxe6 36. Ke3 Bd7 37. Rg5 Be6
38. Kd4 Rc8 39. Rhg1 Kf7 40. Rh1 Ke7 Draw
agreed. ½-½ ACB 1934, 161.

Match with Carlos Torre Repetto, Monterrey, November, 1934

"Having accepted an invitation to play in the international tournament beginning at the *Club de Ajedrez "Mexico"* in Mexico City on December 27, Reuben Fine sailed from New York on board the steamship Orizaba of the Ward Line on November 7. His first exhibition took place at that club on November 16 and the youthful expert encountered strong opposition. Of a total of 33 games, he won 24, drew 4 and lost 5. This compares favorably with Dr. Alekhine's performance against 40 at the same club, where the world champion also drew 4 and lost 5. Fine's second performance was at the Carlos Torre Chess Club in Mexico City on November 22. There he played 20 games, winning 18 and drawing 2, the highest percentage obtained by any master in Mexico. Subsequently, while visiting Monterrey, not far from the section of the country where Carlos Torre resides, Fine contested two games with Torre under a time limit, winning the first and drawing the second." (ACB 1934).

	1	2	
Fine	1	½	1½
Torre	0	½	½

(184) TORRE REPETTO, C—FINE

match Monterrey (1), 1934 (Nov. ?)
Caro-Kann Defence [B12]

1. e4 c6 2. d4 d5 3. f3 An idea developed by Dr. Tartakower. It prevents the early development of the queen's bishop, which is Black's desire in this opening. IK **3 ... e6** If 3 ... dxe4 4 fxe4 e5 5 Nf3 exd4 6 Bc4! White has a splendid attack. The text leads to positions of the French Defence. IK **4. Nc3 Nf6 5. Be3 Be7 6. e5 Nfd7 7. f4 c5 8. Nf3 Nc6 9. Bb5** This leads to the exchange of the bishop, which should be an important weapon of attack. 9 g3, followed by Bg2, or Bh3, is more in the spirit of the game. IK **9 ... Qb6 10. 0–0 0–0 11. Kh1 a6** With an even position, MCO 22. **12. Bxc6 bxc6!** **13. Na4** On the surface, White seems well off, as the black queen's bishop is apparently out of play. This is only a temporary difficulty, however, as Black will soon demonstrate. IK **13 ... Qa5 14. c3 cxd4 15. cxd4 c5 16. Rc1** Allowing Black to establish a strong pawn chain. 16 dxc5 Nxc5 17 Nxc5 Bxc5 18 Nd4 would give White more play. IK **16 ... c4 17. g4?!** A tempting advance, but White's pieces are not well placed for attack, and the effect is only to weaken the kingside. IK **17 ... f6 18. Rf2 fxe5 19. fxe5 Bb7 20. Qc2** Had White seen what was coming, he would have played 20 Kg1, an essential defensive measure. But the long diagonal looks securely closed at this point. IK **20 ... Bc6! 21. Nc3**

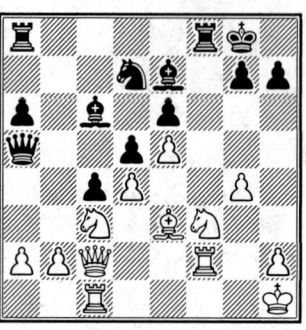

Position after White's 21st move

21 ... Nc5!! A brilliant conception. If 22 dxc5 d4 23 Bxd4 Bxf3+ 24 Kg1 Rad8 and White is helpless against the enemy threats. And if the knight is not captured, it can penetrate with deadly effect. IK **22. Rcf1 22 ... Nd3 23. Rg2 Nxe5!!** Breaking out in a new spot. Now the knight must be taken, and White is worse off than ever. IK **24. dxe5 d4 25. Ne4** 25 Bxd4 Bxf3 would lose the exchange, but the text is hardly better. IK **25 ... dxe3 26. Kg1** If 26 Qxc4, 26 ... Qd5 27 Qxd5 Bxd5 wins at least a piece. There is no longer an adequate defence. IK **26 ... Qd5 27. Nc3 Qd3** The quickest method of finishing matters. IK **28. Qxd3 cxd3 29. Rg3 e2 0–1** White resigned. Kashdan, ACB 1934, 156–7.

(185) FINE—TORRE REPETTO, C

match Monterrey (2), 1934 (Nov. ?)
Queen's Gambit, Slav Defence [D18]

1. d4 d5 2. c4 dxc4 3. Nf3 Nf6 4. Nc3 c6 5. a4 Bf5 The weakness of this system is that this bishop cannot be maintained against the eventual e3-e4. In both games Torre shows a slight inaccuracy in his opening play, which may be due to his long absence from the chess arena. **6. e3 Na6 7. Bxc4 Nb4 8. 0–0 e6 9. Qe2 Bg4** 9 ... Nbd5 would delay the intended e3-e4, but White would continue 10 Ne5, followed by f2-f3, and so on. **10. Rd1 Be7 11. Bb3 0–0 12. e4 Re8 13. h3 Bxf3 14. Qxf3 Rc8 15. Be3 Qa5 16. d5** White simplifies far too soon, perhaps under the influence of the Christmas spirit of peace and good will. 16 g4 would lead to a promising attack, as Black's movements are seriously hampered by the strong centre pawns. **16 ... exd5 17. exd5 cxd5 18. Nxd5 Nbxd5 19. Bxd5 b6** If 19 ... Nxd5 20 Rxd5 Qa6 21 Rd7 would be very strong. White still has the advantage but it proves insufficient for a win. **20. Bc6 Red8 21. Bb5 Qb4 22. Qb7 Bc5 23. Bxc5 Qxc5 24. Rdc1** Draw agreed. There is still good play after 24 ... Qxc1+ 25 Rxc1 Rxc1+ 26 Kh2 h5. ½–½ Kashdan, ACB 1934, 157.

Mexico City, December 27, 1934–January 15, 1935

"As at Hastings, a triple tie for the first three places was the outcome of Mexico's second international masters tournament held at Mexico City from December 27 to January 16. These honours came to three youthful representatives of the United States, who received invitations to match wits with the leading experts of our neighbour to the south. The successful trio were Reuben Fine of New York, Arthur W. Dake of Portland, Oregon, and Herman Steiner of Los Angeles. Each of them lost one game. Fine winning from Steiner, Dake from Fine and Steiner from Dake. There was no play-off and the three prizes were shared in equal proportions. Among others, Carlos Torre had been invited, but for reasons of health it was deemed best that he should not participate. The tournament was conducted in somewhat leisurely fashion at the *Club de Ajedrez "Mexico,"* San Juan de Letran, No. 10, the regular sessions of play being from 8 P. M. until midnight." (ACB 1935). The games from this tournament are recorded in either the Spanish descriptive form or English descriptive in the notebooks.

	1	2	3	4	5	6	7	8	9	10	11	12	13	
1= Dake	*	1	0	1	1	1	1	1	1	1	1	1	1	11
1= Fine	0	*	1	1	1	1	1	1	1	1	1	1	1	11
1= Steiner	1	0	*	1	1	1	1	1	1	1	1	1	1	11
4 Araiza	0	0	0	*	0	1	1	1	1	1	1	1	1	8
5 Soto-Larea	0	0	0	1	*	½	1	1	1	1	½	1	½	7½
6 Glicco	0	0	0	0	½	*	½	1	1	1	1	1	1	7
7= Perez	0	0	0	0	0	½	*	½	½	1	½	1	½	4½
7= Medina	0	0	0	0	0	0	½	*	½	½	1	1	1	4½
7= Rojo	0	0	0	0	0	0	½	½	*	½	1	1	1	4½
10 Lamego	0	0	0	0	0	0	0	½	½	*	0	1	1	3
11= Aguirre	0	0	0	0	½	0	½	0	0	1	*	0	½	2
11= Solares	0	0	0	0	0	0	0	0	0	0	1	*	1	2
13 Tejada	0	0	0	0	½	0	½	0	0	0	½	0	*	1½

(186) FINE—STEINER, H

Mexico City (1), 1934 (27 Dec.)
English Opening, Classical Defence [A27]

1. c4 e5 2. Nc3 Nc6 3. Nf3 f5 4. d4 e4 5. Nd2 Nf6 6. e3 Bb4 7. Qb3 0–0 8. d5 Bxc3 Forced now, of course, but parting with this bishop makes Black partially vulnerable on the long diagonal leading to the king's position. **9. Qxc3 Ne7 10. b3 d6 11. Bb2 Ng6 12. 0–0–0 Qe7 13. Be2 a5 14. Rde1** Intending, possibly, 15 Bd1 in reply to 14 ... a4, and also to discourage ... exf3 when the f-pawn advances. **14 ... c6 15. dxc6 bxc6 16. f4 Rf7 17. h3 Nf8 18. Reg1 Ne6** The ensuing complications are favourable to White. 18 ... d5 was the natural continuation. **19. g4**

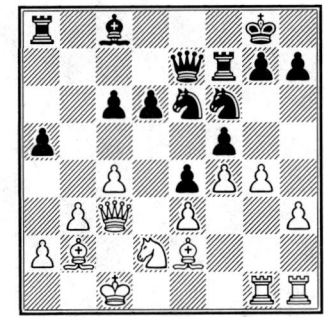

Position after White's 19th move

19 ... d5 20. gxf5 d4 21. Qc2 d3 All this is somewhat laboured and really gets him nowhere. **22. Qc3 Nxf4 23. exf4 dxe2 24. Qe5 Ra7** The annotator in ACB now states "If 24 ... Qxe5 25 fxe5 Nh5 26 Nxe4 Nf4 27 Kd2, and Black's position will soon become untenable.". 27 e6 would be stronger as things are not so clear after 27 ... Bxf5 28 Nd6 Rd7. Indeed Black can similarly play 26 ... Bxf5 27 Nd6 Rff8 28 Kd2 Nf4. Therefore, this should, perhaps, have been preferred to the text. AW **25. Rh2 Qd8 26. Rxe2 Rae7 27. Qc5 e3** 27 ... Qd3 would be met by 28 Re3. Instead, 27 Re8 came into consideration. **28. Rxe3 Rxe3 29. Qxe3 Bxf5 30. Nf3 Ne4 31. Nd4 Qd7 32. Rd1 Bg6 33. Ba3 h6 34. h4 c5 35. Nf3 Qh3 36. Re1 Qf5 37. Ne5 Nf2** A brave attempt at recovery, but White meets him at every point. **38. Nxg6 Nd3+ 39. Kd2 Nxe1 40. h5 Nf3+** The knight cannot get away on account of the threat of Qe8+. If 40 ... Qxh5 41 Qe8+ Kh7 42 Nf8+ Kg8 43 Nd7+ Kh7 44 Qe4+ Kg8 45 Ne5 Rxf4 46 Qxf4 Qxe5 47 Qxe5 Nf3+ 48 Ke3 Nxe5 49 Bxc5 and still White has the better of it. **41. Qxf3 Rd7+ 42. Kc3 Kh7 43. Ne5 Rd4 44. Bxc5 Rxf4 45. Qd3 Qxd3+ 46. Kxd3 Rh4** The copy of the score in Fine's papers actually reads 46 ... RxP 47 P-B5, and so on. **47. Bd6 Rxh5 48. c5 Rh1 49. c6 Rd1+ 50. Ke4 1–0** Black resigned. ACB 1935, 13.

(187) AVILES SOLARES, J—FINE

Mexico City (2), 1934 (28 Dec.)
French Defence, Steinitz [C11]

1. e4 e6 2. Nc3 d5 3. d4 Nf6 4. e5 Nfd7 5. Nce2 c5 6. c3 Nc6 7. f4 Be7 8. Nf3 Qb6 9. dxc5 Nxc5 10. Ned4 f6 11. Bb5 0–0

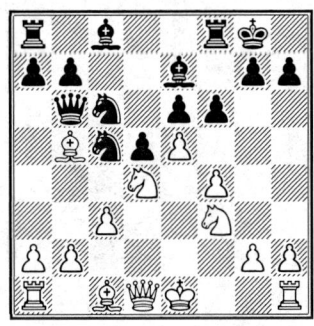

Position after Black's 11th move

12. c4 Ne4 13. Qd3 fxe5 14. fxe5 Nxd4 15. Nxd4 Nf2 16. Qf1 Nxh1 17. Be3 Qc7 18. Qd3 Qxe5 19. 0–0–0 Nf2 White resigned. **0–1**

(188) FINE—MEDINA, J

Mexico City (3), 1934 (29 Dec.)
Queen's Gambit Declined, Exchange Variation [D35]

1. d4 Nf6 2. c4 e6 3. Nc3 d5 4. Bg5 Nbd7 5. cxd5 exd5 6. e3 c6 7. Bd3 Bd6 8. Qc2 Nf8 9. 0–0–0 Ne6 10. Bh4 h6 11. Nf3 g5 12. Bg3 Qe7 13. Kb1 Bd7 14. Ne5 Ng7 15. e4 dxe4 16. Nxe4 Nxe4 17. Bxe4 0–0 18. h4 g4 19. Rde1 Bxe5 20. Bxe5

Be6 21. Qd2 f5 22. Bc2 Kh7 23. f3 Qf7 24. b3 gxf3 25. g4 Bd5 26. Rhg1 Be4

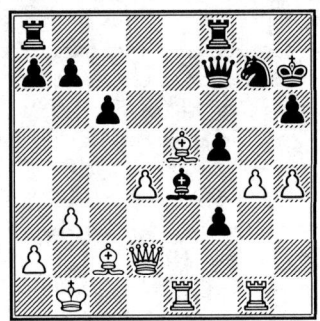

*Position after
Black's 26th move*

27. Rxe4 f2 28. Rf1 fxe4 29. Bxe4+ Kg8 30. Qxh6 Qd7 31. Qh7+ Kf7 32. Rxf2+ Black resigned. 1–0

(189) PEREZ, A—FINE

Mexico City (4), 1935 (2 Jan.)
Sicilian Scheveningen [B84]

1. e4 c5 2. Nf3 Nf6 3. Nc3 d6 4. d4 cxd4 5. Nxd4 e6 6. Be2 a6 7. 0–0 Qc7 8. f4 Be7 9. Kh1 b5 10. a3 Nearly 60 years later a game Massimi–Vernadet, Paris 1993, continued 10 Bf3 Bb7 11 a3 Nbd7 12 Qe1 1–0 (40). The position after Black's ninth move did not appear in my databases from the time of the text until 1985. AW 10 ... 0–0 11. Bf3 Bb7 12. Be3 Nbd7 13. Nb3 Rac8 14. Qe2 Nb6 15. Na5 Ba8 16. Qf2

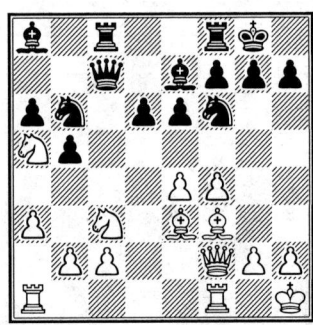

*Position after
White's 16th move*

16 ... Na4! 17. Nxa4 bxa4 18. Bb6 Qxc2 19. Qxc2 Rxc2 20. e5 Ne4 21. Rfe1 Nf2+ 22. Bxf2 Rxf2 23. Re2 Rxf3 White resigned. 0–1

(190) FINE—DAKE, A

Mexico City (5), 1935 (3 Jan.)
English Opening, Classical Defence [A28]

1. c4 e5 2. Nf3 Nc6 3. Nc3 Nf6 4. e4 A favourite move of Nimzowitsch. AW 4 ... Bb4 5. d3 d6 6. Be2 0–0 7. 0–0 Bxc3 8. bxc3 Qe7 9. Ne1 Ne8 10. Nc2 f5 11. exf5 Bxf5 12. Ne3 Be6 13. d4 Bf7 The position is even, MCO 36. 14. Ba3 Nf6 15. Re1 Rfe8 16. Bf3 Qd7 17. Qd2 Bh5 18. dxe5 Rxe5 19. Bxh5 Rxh5 20. f4 Rf8 21. Nd5 Qf7 22. Rad1 Nxd5

23. cxd5 Na5 24. Qd4 24 Bc1 should have been played. SR 24 ... Qxf4 25. Qxf4 Rxf4 26. Re7 Nc4 27. Rxc7 If 27 Bc1 Rf7 28 Re8+ Rf8 29 Re7 Rc8 and Black should win. SR 27 ... Nxa3 White is reported to have been under time pressure. SR 28. Rxb7 Nc4 29. Rxa7 Ne3 30. Rb1 Rxd5 31. a4 Rd1+ 32. Rxd1 Nxd1 33. a5 Nxc3 34. g3 Rf7 35. Ra6 Rd7 36. Rb6 Nd5 37. Rb8+ Kf7 White resigned. 0–1 Reshevsky, ACB 1935, 14.

(191) LARDO DE TEJADA, J—FINE

Mexico City (6), 1935 (4 Jan.)
Queen's Pawn Game [D04]

1. d4 Nf6 2. Nf3 d5 3. e3 c5 4. c4 cxd4 5. Nxd4 g6 6. Nc3 dxc4 7. Bxc4 Bg7 8. 0–0 0–0 9. Qb3 a6 10. a4 Nbd7 11. Nf3 Qc7 12. Bd2 Nb6 13. Be2 Be6 14. Qb4 Nfd5

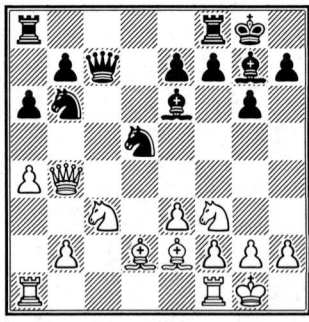

*Position after
Black's 14th move*

15. Nxd5 Nxd5 16. Qh4 h6 17. Racl Qb6 18. e4 g5 19. Qg3 Nf6 20. Qc7 Qxc7 21. Rxc7 Nxe4 22. Rxb7 g4 23. Bb4 Rfb8 24. Bxa6 gxf3 25. Bxe7 fxg2 26. Re1 Bd5 White resigned. 0–1

(192) FINE—GLICCO, M

Mexico City (7), 1935 (7 Jan.)
Spanish Game, Worrall Attack [C86]

1. e4 e5 2. Nf3 Nc6 3. Bb5 a6 4. Ba4 Nf6 5. 0–0 b5 6. Bb3 Be7 7. Qe2 d6 8. c3 Na5 9. Bc2 c5 10. a4 b4 11. d4 Qc7 12. cxb4 cxb4 13. b3 Be6 14. d5 Bd7 15. h3 Nb7 16. Be3 0–0 17. Bd3 a5 18. Nbd2 Rfb8 19. Rac1 Nc5 20. Bxc5 dxc5 21. Nc4 Bd6 22. Nxd6 Qxd6 23. Qe3 Rc8 24. Nd2 Nh5 25. Qg5 Nf4 26. Nc4 Qg6 27. Qxg6 hxg6 28. Rfd1 f5 29. Bf1 Ra7 30. g3 Nh5 31. Nb6 Rd8 32. exf5 gxf5 33. Rxc5 e4

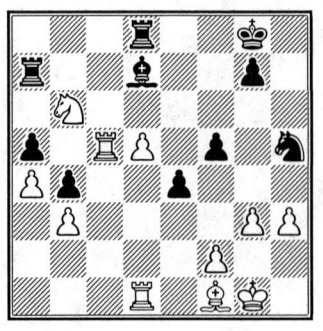

*Position after
Black's 33rd move*

34. N×d7 Rd×d7 35. d6 g6 36. Bb5 Rd8 37. d7
Kf7 38. Rc8 Ke7 39. Rd5 Nf6 40. Re5+ Kd6
41. R×d8 K×e5 42. Re8+ Black resigned. 1–0

(193) AGUIRRE, A—FINE

Mexico City (8), 1935 (8 Jan.)
Nimzowitsch-Indian Defence, Spielmann Variation [E22]

1. d4 Nf6 2. c4 e6 3. Nc3 Bb4 4. Qb3 c5 5. a3
B×c3+ 6. b×c3 0–0 7. Bg5 h6 8. B×f6 Q×f6 9. e3
e5 10. d×e5 Q×e5 11. Nf3 Qf6 12. Rd1 Nc6 13. Be2
b6 14. 0–0 Rd8 15. Rd2 Na5 16. Qc2 Ba6 17. Rfd1
d6 18. Qe4 Re8 19. Qg4 Rad8 20. Rd5 Q×c3
21. Nd2 Qc2 22. Bd3 Bc8

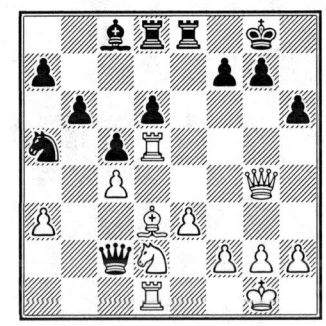

*Position after
Black's 26th move*

23. Qh5 Qa4 24. Bf5 B×f5 25. R×f5 g6 26. Qg4
Qd7 27. Rf4 Q×g4 28. R×g4 d5 29. Rc1 d×c4
30. N×c4 h5 White resigned. 0–1

(194) FINE—LAMEGO, S

Mexico City (9), 1935 (9 Jan.)
Alekhine's Defence, Four Pawns Attack [B12]

1. e4 c6 2. d4 Nf6 3. e5 Nd5 4. c4 Nc7 5. f4 d6
6. Nf3 Bf5 7. Be2 e6 8. Nc3 Nd7 9. 0–0 d5
10. c×d5 N×d5 11. N×d5 c×d5 12. Bd3 g6 13. b3
B×d3 14. Q×d3 Be7 15. Ng5 h6 16. N×e6 Qb6
17. Nc5 N×c5 18. d×c5 B×c5+ 19. Kh1

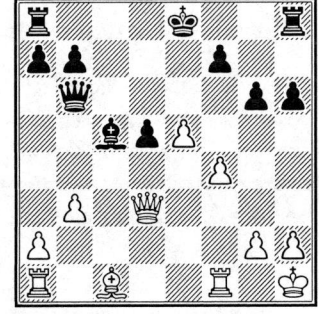

*Position after
White's 19th move*

19 ... 0–0–0 20. Bb2 Rhe8 21. f5 d4?! 22. f×g6
f×g6 23. Rf6 Qa5 24. e6 Bb6 25. R×g6 Qe5
26. Rf1 R×e6 27. Qc4+ Bc7 28. Q×e6+ Q×e6
29. R×e6 Black resigned. 1–0

(195) FINE—SOTO LARREA, M

Mexico City (10), 1935 (11 Jan.)
Double Fianchetto [A13]

1. Nf3 Nf6 2. c4 e6 3. b3 g6 4. g3 b6 5. Bg2 Bb7
6. 0–0 c5 7. Bb2 Bg7 8. d4 c×d4 9. N×d4?! B×g2
10. K×g2 0–0 11. Nb5 d5 12. Ba3 Ne4?! 13. B×f8
B×a1 14. Bh6 a6

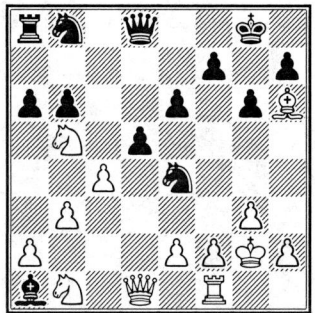

*Position after
Black's 14th move*

15. N1c3! B×c3 16. N×c3 N×c3 17. Qd4 f6 18. Q×c3
d4 19. Rd1 Nc6 20. Qf3 Rc8 21. e3 d3 22. Qe4 Ne5
23. Bf4 Rc5 24. B×e5 R×e5 25. R×d3 Qc8 26. Qd4
Qc6+ 27. f3 Kf7 28. Qd8 Black resigned. 1–0

(196) ARAIZA, J—FINE

Mexico City (11), 1935 (13 Jan.)
French Defence, Classical Variation [C14]

1. e4 e6 2. d4 d5 3. Nc3 Nf6 4. Bg5 Be7 5. e5
Nfd7 6. B×e7 Q×e7 7. Qd2 0–0 8. f4 c5 9. Nf3
Nc6 10. g3 f6 11. e×f6 N×f6 12. d×c5 Q×c5 13. Bd3

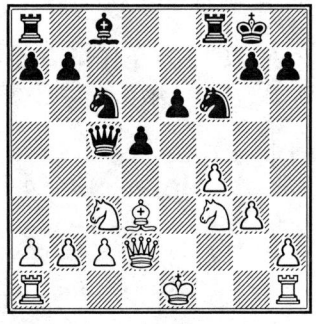

*Position after
White's 13th move*

13 ... e5 14. N×e5 N×e5 15. f×e5 Ng4 16. Rf1 R×f1+
17. B×f1 d4 18. Ne2 Ne3 19. N×d4? Q×d4 20. Q×d4
N×c2+ White resigned. 0–1

(197) FINE—GONZALES ROJO, E

Mexico City (12), 1935 (15 Jan.)
Queen's Gambit Declined, Exchange Variation [D36]

1. d4 d5 2. c4 e6 3. Nc3 Nf6 4. Bg5 Nbd7 5. c×d5
e×d5 6. e3 c6 7. Bd3 Be7 8. Qc2 h6 9. Bf4 0–0
10. 0–0–0 b5 11. Nf3 Re8

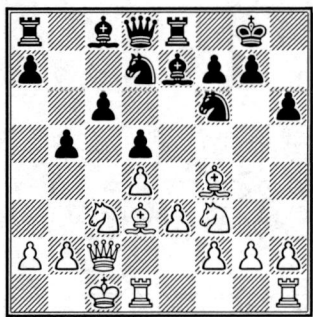

*Position after
Black's 11th move*

12. Nxb5 Ne5 13. dxe5 cxb5 14. exf6 Bxf6 15. Qc7
Bxb2+ 16. Kxb2 Qf6+ 17. Be5 Qe6 18. Bxb5 Rf8
19. Bc6 Rb8+ 20. Qxb8 Qxc6 21. Rc1 Qa6 22. Nd4
Bb7 23. Qd6 Qd3 24. Rhd1 Qe4 25. f3 Qxe3
26. Bxg7 Re8 27. Qxh6 Black resigned. 1–0

Open Champion
Once More

Fine's trip to Mexico from November 1934 to January
1935 meant that he was unable to defend his title at the 18th
Marshall Club Championship of 1934/5. In his absence the
title was won by Fred Reinfeld, ahead of Hanauer, Santasiere and Polland, among others (others including a player
by the name of Byrne). Once again there seems to have been
little activity in the first half of the year, but when the Western open came around this time Reuben went undefeated
through the three stages to win a fourth championship
ahead of a strong field in the final.

Marshall CC—Brooklyn Chess League,
June 8, 1935

"The Marshall C.C., headed by Reuben Fine and
including F. J. Marshall himself, who both won their games,
defeated a picked team from the Brooklyn Chess League by
8½–5½." (BCM 1935). Fine recorded this game in his notebook in numeric notation.

Gustaffson   0   Fine   1

(198) GUSTAFSON, T—FINE

Brooklyn League v Marshall CC, New York, 1935 (8 June)
French Defence, Advance Variation [C02]

1. e4 e6 2. d4 d5 3. e5 c5 4. c3 Nc6 5. Bb5 A mistaken conception, 5 Nf3 is correct. AW **5 ... Qb6
6. Bxc6+ bxc6 7. Ne2** The knight should go to f3 as
Black shows by his next move. AW **7 ... Ba6 8. 0–0
cxd4 9. cxd4 Bxe2 10. Qxe2 Qxd4 11. Rd1 Qb6**
Black has won an important central pawn and although he

is behind in development this is not critical as the position
is closed. AW **12. Nc3 Ne7 13. Be3 Qc7 14. f4 Nf5
15. Bf2 Be7 16. Rac1 0–0 17. g4 Nh6 18. h3 Qb7**

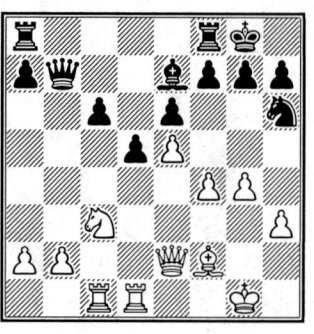

*Position after
Black's 18th move*

19. b3 19 Na4 might have been better here and on the next
move. AW **19 ... Kh8 20. Qc2 Ba3 21. Rb1 Bb4
22. Na4 Ng8 23. Nc5 Qe7 24. Nd3 Rfc8**

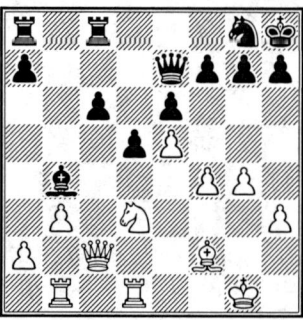

*Position after
Black's 24th move*

25. Nc5 25 Nxb4 Qxb4 26 Rd4 Qe7 27 Rc1 would have
given White some chances. AW **25 ... f6 26. Qc1 fxe5
27. fxe5 Rf8 28. Nd3 Rf3 29. Kg2 Raf8 30. Bg3**
White would be under intense pressure after 30 Qxc6 Qf7.
AW **30 ... Ba3 31. Qd2 Qf7 32. Qe2 Qg6 33. b4 a5
34. bxa5 h5 35. Rb3 Be7 36. Nf2 R3f7 37. Qd3 Qh6
38. Rb2 Bc5 39. gxh5 Ne7 40. Rf1 Qxh5 41. Rc2
Rf3 42. Ng4 Rxd3 43. Rxf8+ Kh7 44. Rxc5 Nf5
45. Rxf5 Qxf5 46. Kh2 Rd2+** White resigned. 0–1

36th Western Open, Milwaukee,
Preliminaries, Group A, July 21–25, 1935

The American Chess Federation was founded in 1934
as a successor to the Western Chess Association, itself
founded in 1900. In its first incarnation the Association had
held an unbroken series of annual tournaments whose winners had included Showalter, Edward Lasker, Kostich, Torre,
Kashdan, Reshevsky and Fine. The officers of the newly
formed Federation were Arpad Elo, Kirk D. Holland and
Ernest Olfe, and the directors included Fine, Reinfeld, Kashdan, Factor and several other notable American players of
the time. The tournament book formed the first volume of
the long running series of Yearbooks of the American Chess
Federation and the later United States Chess Federation.
The tournament had to be brought forward from its

intended start date to allow time for the departure of the players who were to make up the United States team in the team tournament in Warsaw. Because of the degree of interest the tournament had to be moved to larger quarters provided by the Hotel Schroeder. Thirty players started the event. Fine was seeded into section A along with Ruth, Factor and Morton. The seeds in section B were Kashdan, Santasiere, Belson and Winkelman and in section C Dake, Simonson, Eastman and Elison. Nine unseeded Milwaukee players were divided between the sections and then the remaining, local, players distributed by lot.

		1	2	3	4	5	6	7	8	9	10	
1	Fine	*	½	½	1	1	½	1	1	1	1	7½
2	Ruth	½	*	½	1	0	1	1	1	1	1	7
3=	Factor	½	½	*	0	1	1	½	1	1	1	6½
3=	Morton	0	0	1	*	1	1	1	1	½	1	6½
5	Towsen	0	1	0	0	*	1	½	1	1	1	5½
6	Dahlstrom	½	0	0	0	0	*	1	½	1	1	4
7	Kraszewski	0	0	½	0	½	0	*	1	1	½	3½
8	Drummond	0	0	0	0	0	½	0	*	½	1	2
9	Nash	0	0	0	½	0	0	0	½	*	½	1½
10	Kreznar	0	0	0	0	0	0	½	0	½	*	1

(199) NASH, E—FINE

American Chess Federation Open, preliminaries, Milwaukee (1), 1935 (21 July)
Sicilian Defence, Scheveningen Variation [B84]

1. e4 c5 2. Nf3 d6 3. d4 cxd4 4. Nxd4 Nf6 5. Nc3 e6 6. Be2 a6 7. 0–0 Qc7 The main alternative to this line is 7 ... Nbd7 8 f4 b5 9 Bf3 Bb7 10 e5 Bxf3 11 Nxf3 Ng4 12 Qe2 b4 13 Na4 Qa5 14 b3 Qb5 15 Qe1 dxe5 (15 ... Nc5 16 h3 gives White a clear plus—Kasparov) with an unclear position or, after 7 ... Nbd7, 8 a4 b6 9 f4 Bb7 10 Bf3 Qc7 11 Qe2 e5 12 Nf5 g6 13 fxe5 Nxe5 14 Nh6 Bg7, intending ... Nfd7, when White stands a little better. S. Abramov, EMCO 1996. **8. Kh1 b5 9. a3 Bb7 10. f3** White's last three moves have been somewhat overcautious and now the equalizing advance d6-d5 is in the air. **10 ... Be7 11. Be3 0–0 12. Qe1**

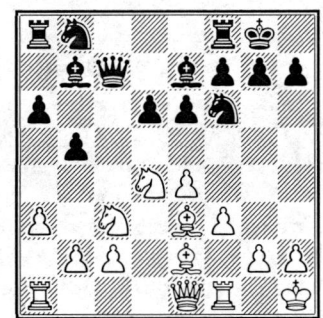

*Position after
White's 12th move*

12 ... d5! Black waited until he had safely tucked his king away to play this move, White no longer has any trace of his

first-move advantage. AW **13. exd5 Nxd5 14. Nxd5 Bxd5 15. Bd3 Nd7 16. c3 Rfc8 17. Qf2 Ne5**

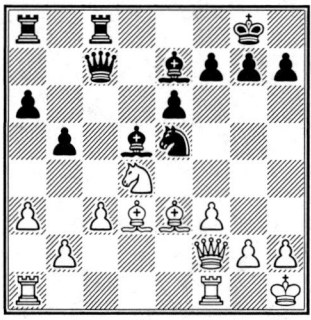

*Position after
Black's 17th move*

18. Qc2? White has just been fiddling around apparently without any particular plan, but this is a gross oversight losing an exchange, after which Fine soon mops up. AW **18 ... Nxd3 19. Qxd3 Bc4 20. Qc2 Bxf1 21. Rxf1 Qc4 22. Rd1 a5 23. Qb3?** Overlooking another neat tactic. AW **23 ... Qxb3 24. Nxb3 Bxa3 25. Bb6 Bxb2 0–1** Lahde 2001, 40.

(200) FINE—TOWSEN, A

American Chess Federation Open, preliminaries, Milwaukee (2), 1935 (22 July)
Queen's Gambit Declined, Tartakower Variation [D58]

1. d4 Nf6 2. c4 e6 3. Nc3 d5 4. Bg5 Be7 5. e3 h6 6. Bh4 0–0 7. Nf3 b6 8. cxd5 exd5 9. Bd3 Be6 10. 0–0 c5 11. Rc1 c4 This weakens the formation, particularly as the supporting b5 cannot yet be played. **12. Bb1 Nfd7 13. Bg3 a6 14. e4 dxe4 15. Bxe4 Ra7 16. d5 Bg4 17. Qd4** Winning the pawn as b5 is still prevented. **17 ... f5 18. Bb1 Bxf3 19. gxf3 Bc5 20. Qxc4 b5 21. Qd3 Qg5 22. Rce1 b4 23. Na4**

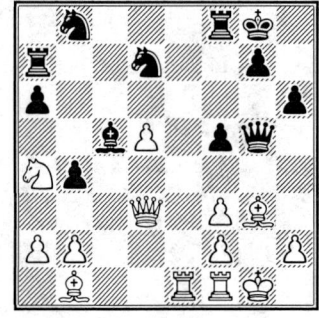

*Position after
White's 23rd move*

23 ... f4 Too risky, though perhaps the only chance for counterplay. **24. Qh7+ Kf7 25. Nxc5 Nxc5 26. h4 Qf6 27. Bxf4** An interesting sacrifice, but it should only have led to a draw. More accurate is 27 Bh2 and White's attack, if slower, would be very hard to meet. **27 ... Qxf4 28. Qg6+ Kg8 29. Re8 Qf6** Black's 29th is missing from the text, but this seems to fit in with the finale. He could have put up much stiffer resistance by 29 ... Nbd7. AW **30. Qh7+ Kf7 31. Rxf8+ Kxf8 32. Qh8+ Kf7 33. Qxb8 Re7 34. d6 Rb7 35. Qc8** If the reconstruction is right however 35 ... Qxd6 would be much better. **35 ... Qxf3 36. Re1 Qd5 37. Qe8+ 1–0** Kashdan in *American Chess Federation Yearbook 1935, 37–8.*

(201) KREZNAR, S—FINE [B50]

American Chess Federation Open, preliminaries, Milwaukee (3), 1935 (22 July)
Sicilian Defence

1. e4 c5 2. Nf3 d6 3. c4 e5 4. Nc3 f5 5. d3 Nf6 6. Be2 Be7 7. Bd2 0–0 8. Qc2 Nc6 9. Nd5 fxe4 10. Nxf6+ Bxf6 11. dxe4 Bg4 12. Bc3 Qd7 13. h3 Bh5 14. g4 Bg6 15. g5 Be7 16. 0–0–0

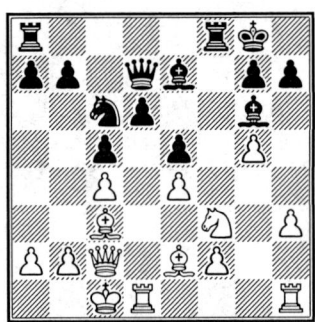

Position after White's 16th move

16 ... Nd4! 17. Bxd4 exd4 18. h4 Rf4 19. Nd2 Rxf2 20. Bf3 Rf8 21. Qd3 Qe6 22. Rdf1 Rxf1+ 23. Rxf1 Qh3 24. Rh1 Qg3 25. Be2 Qe3 26. Rh3 Qxd3 27. Bxd3 Bh5 28. Rh2 h6 29. gxh6 gxh6 30. Nf1 Bf6 31. Kd2 Bf3 32. h5 Bg5+ 33. Ke1 Rf4 34. Nd2 Bg4 35. Be2 Kf7 36. Bxg4? Rxg4 37. Ke2 Bxd2 38. Kxd2 Rxe4 39. Rf2+ Ke6 40. Rf8 Rh4 41. Rb8 Rh2+ 42. Kc1 b6 43. Rb7 d3 44. Rxa7 Rc2+ 45. Kd1 Ke5 46. Re7+ Kd4 47. Re6 Rxb2 48. Rxd6+ Kc3 49. Rd8 Rb1 mate 0–1 Lahde 2001, 40.

(202) FINE—DRUMMOND, F

American Chess Federation Open, preliminaries, Milwaukee (4), 1935 (23 July)
King's Indian Defence [E60]

1. d4 Nf6 2. c4 g6 3. f3 Bg7 4. e4 e6?! 5. Ne2 Nh5?! 6. d5?! d6 7. Nbc3 Nd7 8. Be3 a5 9. Qd2 b6 10. 0–0–0 Nc5 11. Bh6 Nd3+ 12. Qxd3 Bxh6+ 13. Kb1 f5 14. Qc2 Bd7 15. Ng3 Qh4 16. Bd3 0–0 17. exf5 g5

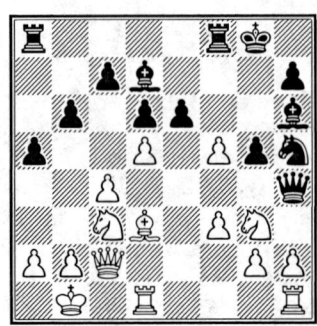

Position after Black's 17th move

18. Nxh5 White could have won by the simple 18 fxe6 Be8 19 Bxh7+ Kh8 20 Nf5. AW **18 ... Qxh5 19. g4 Qh3 20. Be4 Rf6 21. Rdg1 Bf8 22. Rg3 Qh6 23. h4 Qg7 24. hxg5 Qxg5 25. Rgh3 h6 26. Bd3 Bg7 27. Ne4 1–0** Lahde 2001, 40–1.

(203) MORTON, H—FINE

American Chess Federation Open, preliminaries, Milwaukee (5), 1935 (23 July)
French Defence, Exchange Variation [C01]

1. d4 e6 2. e4 d5 3. exd5 exd5 4. Bd3 Bd6 5. Nc3 Ne7 6. Nge2 Nbc6 7. Nb5 The exchange involves loss of time, but it still seems justified. **7 ... Bf5 8. Nxd6+ Qxd6 9. Bxf5 Nxf5 10. 0–0 0–0–0 11. c3 Rde8**

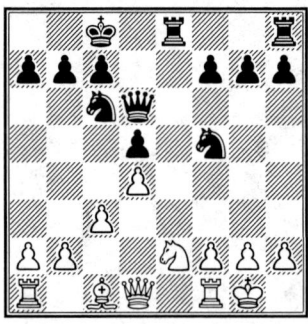

Position after Black's 11th move

12. Nf4 A pointless move, which is the cause of most of his trouble. Either 12 Bf4 or 12 Ng3 is preferable. **12 ... Re4 13. Nd3 Rhe8 14. Bg5** The bishop is far too exposed here. **14 ... Qg6 15. f3?** An oversight by White. He had to try 15 Bd2. AW **15 ... Re2!** Correct, greatly adding to Black's threats. White may have thought this move was prevented. **16. Qc1** If 16 Nf4 Qxg5 17 Nxe2 Ne3 wins. **16 ... Ne3!** Winning a piece, as the bishop evidently cannot move. **17. Rf2 Rxf2 18. Nxf2 Qxg5 19. Ng4 h6 20. h4 Qe7 0–1** Kashdan, *American Chess Federation Yearbook 1935, 38.*

(204) FINE—KRASZEWSKI, C

American Chess Federation Open, preliminaries, Milwaukee (6), 1935 (24 July)
Alekhine's Defence [B02]

1. e4 Nf6 2. e5 Nd5 3. c4 Nb6 4. d4 d6 5. exd6 Qxd6 Seemingly introduced by Grünfeld in 1925, when he essayed it in games with von Gottschall (which he won) at the DSB Congress and Zubarev (which ended in a draw) at the Moscow International Tournament. Of the other three occasions on which it was played the leaders of the black forces were Flohr, Mikenas and Fine himself against Kashdan in 1945. The queen is somewhat exposed on this square, therefore 5 ... cxd6 or 5 ... exd6 are more common. AW **6. Nf3 c5 7. Be3 Bf5** This too might be considered a mistake, since the bishop is forced to move again when a white knight takes on d4. AW **8. Nc3 cxd4 9. Nxd4 Bd7 10. Ndb5 Qc6**

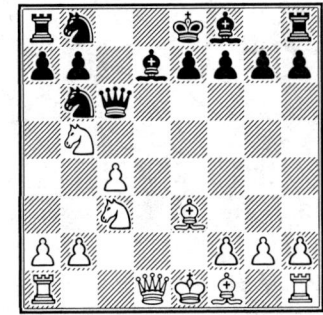

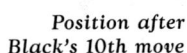

Position after Black's 10th move

11. Qd4 Making it difficult for Black to develop his kingside. AW **11 ... Na6 12. Be2 Qxg2?! 13. 0-0-0 Rd8 14. Rhg1 Qxh2 15. Bf4 Qh4 16. c5 Na8 17. Qe3** Setting up a trap of a well-known kind. AW **17 ... Qf6 18. Nd6+** 1-0 Lahde 2001, 41.

(205) FACTOR, S—FINE

American Chess Federation Open, preliminaries, Milwaukee
   (7), 1935 (24 July)
Giuoco Piano [C54]

1. e4 e5 2. Nf3 Nc6 3. d4 exd4 4. Bc4 Bc5 5. c3 Nf6 6. cxd4 Bb4+ 7. Bd2 Bxd2+ 8. Nbxd2 d5! 9. exd5 Nxd5 10. Qb3 Nce7 11. 0-0 0-0 12. Rfe1 c6 13. Ne4 Qb6 14. Qxb6 14 Nc3 Qxb3 15 Bxb3 gave White some advantage in Bogolyubov–Euwe, 7th match game, Carlsbad 1941. **14 ... axb6 15. Nc3 Ra5 16. a4! Be6 17. Ng5 Bg4 18. b4! Ra7 19. Nxd5 Nxd5 20. a5! h6 21. Ne4 Rd8 22. f3 Bf5 23. Bxd5 Rxd5 24. axb6 Rxa1 25. Rxa1 Bxe4! 26. fxe4 Rxd4 27. Ra7 Rxe4 28. b5! Rb4 29. Rxb7 Rxb5 30. Rb8+ Kh7 31. b7** ½ Hilbert & Lahde, 54–5.

(206) RUTH, W—FINE

American Chess Federation Open, preliminaries, Milwaukee
   (8), 1935 (25 July)
Semi-Slav [D45]

1. d4 Nf6 2. Nf3 d5 3. c4 c6 4. e3 e6 5. Nc3 Nbd7 6. Qc2 Be7 7. Bd2 0-0 8. Rc1 a6 9. a3 b5 10. cxd5 cxd5 11. a4 b4 12. Na2 a5 13. Bd3 Ne4 14. 0-0 Bb7 15. Qc7 Rb8 16. Bb5 Ndf6 17. Qxd8 Rfxd8 18. Rfd1 Rdc8 19. Rxc8+ Rxc8 20. Rc1 ½-½ Lahde 2001, 41.

(207) FINE—DAHLSTROM, B

American Chess Federation Open, preliminaries, Milwaukee
   (9), 1935 (25 July)
Spanish Game, Exchange Variation [C68]

1. e4 e5 2. Nf3 Nc6 3. Bb5 a6 4. Bxc6 dxc6 5. d4 exd4 6. Qxd4 Qxd4 7. Nxd4 Nf6 8. f3 Be7 9. Bf4 Bd6 10. Be3 0-0 11. Nd2 h6 12. Kf2 Bd7 13. Nc4 Rfe8 14. Rad1 Rad8 15. Rd2 Bc8 16. Rhd1 Bc5

17. Nb3 Rxd2+ 18. Rxd2 Bxe3+ 19. Nxe3 g6 20. Nd4 c5 21. Ne2 Be6 22. b3 Kf8 23. Nf4 Ke7 24. e5 Nd7 25. Nfd5+ Kd8 26. f4 Kc8 27. Kf3 Bxd5+ 28. Nxd5 c6 29. Ne3 b6 30. Rd6 Re6 31. Rxe6 fxe6 32. Ng4 h5 ½-½ Lahde 2001, 41.

36th Western Open Finals, Milwaukee, July 26–August 1, 1935

The top three finishers from each section played in the Master's final and the remaining players gained entry to the Consolation Masters or Class A tournament. Because of ties and a lack of time for play-offs, eleven players ended up in the Masters Tournament. Ten days of grueling play with two games daily had a telling effect on the quality of play. First prize was $250, second $150, third $100, fourth $75 and fifth $50. The biographical sketches at the back of the Yearbook recorded "REUBEN FINE—in winning the 1935 tournament of the American Chess Federation and going undefeated, once more demonstrated that he is the foremost tournament player in America today. In the finals he took the lead from the start and was never seriously threatened from then on. He played to the score as would Capablanca and utilized the psychological elements of play as would Dr. Lasker. At the age of 20 he exhibits the technique of a veteran master. He learned chess at the age of twelve [*sic*] and made his debut in the chess world in intercollegiate competition while representing his school, City College of New York." (ACF 1935)

		1	2	3	4	5	6	7	8	9	10	11	
1	Fine	*	½	½	1	1	1	1	½	1	½	1	8
2	Dake	½	*	½	½	½	½	1	1	1	1	1	7½
3	Kashdan	½	½	*	½	½	½	½	½	1	1	1	6½
4=	Chevalier	0	½	½	*	½	0	½	½	1	1	1	5½
4=	Factor	0	½	½	½	*	1	½	1	½	½	½	5½
4=	Simonson	0	½	½	1	0	*	½	½	½	1	1	5½
7	Santasiere	0	0	½	½	½	½	*	½	½	1	1	5
8	Morton	½	0	½	½	0	½	½	*	½	0	1	4
9	Belson	0	0	0	0	½	½	½	½	*	½	½	3
10	Elo	½	0	0	0	½	0	0	1	½	*	0	2½
11	Ruth	0	0	0	0	½	0	0	0	½	1	*	2

(208) BELSON, J—FINE

American Chess Federation, Open Milwaukee (1), 1935
   (26 July)
English Opening, Mikenas-Flohr Variation [A18]

1. c4 Nf6 2. Nc3 e6 3. e4 d5 4. e5 d4 If 4 ... Nbd7; 5 d4 is favourable to White. The text leads to a drawish position. **5. exf6 dxc3 6. fxg7** 6 bxc3 is more promising for White. AW **6 ... cxd2+ 7. Qxd2 Qxd2+ 8. Bxd2 Bxg7 9. 0-0-0 c5 10. Be3 b6 11. Be2 Nc6 12. Bf3 Bd7**

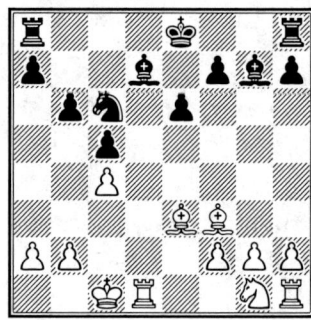

*Position after
Black's 12th move*

13. Rd6 A tempting attack but the rook is not well placed here, and soon gets into trouble. **13 ... Rc8 14. Ne2** Overlooking the force of Black's reply. The rook should have retreated to d2. **14 ... Nd4! 15. b3** If 15 Nxd4 cxd4 16 Bxd4 Rxc4+ 17 Bc3 Bxc3, and Black wins a pawn. **15 ... Ke7** 15 ... Be5 would win the exchange without difficulty. The text allows more chances. **16. Bf4 e5** Not 16 ... Nxf3 17 gxf3 e5 18 Rhd1 and White escapes. **17. Rxd7+ Kxd7 18. Nxd4 cxd4 19. Bg4+ Kd6 20. Bxc8 Rxc8 21. Bg3 b5** Now Black will have a strong passed pawn ahead, which proves sufficient. **22. Rd1 Ke6 23. c5 Rxc5+ 24. Kb1 Kd5 25. f3 f5 26. Rc1 Rxc1+ 27. Kxc1 e4 28. Kd2 Bh6+ 29. f4 Bf8 0–1** Kashdan, ACF 1935, 8.

(209) FINE—RUTH, W

American Chess Federation, Open Milwaukee (2), 1935
    (27 July)
English Opening, Classical Defence [A27]

1. c4 e5 2. Nf3 Nc6 3. Nc3 f5 4. d4 e4 5. Nd2 Nf6 Not 5 ... Nxd4 6 Ndxe4 as this opens up the game for White. **6. e3 d6** Here Black should develop the kingside ready for castling, and we prefer the continuation 6 ... g6! 7 Be2 Bg7 8 0–0 d6 9 f3 exf3 10 Nxf3 0–0. **7. Be2 Bd7 8. a3 g6** White's last prepares to "biff" the knight. Black should have frustrated this by 8 ... a5! **9. b4 a5 10. b5 Ne7 11. g4 fxg4 12. Ndxe4 Neg8 13. Ng3 Qe7 14. Qc2 Bg7 15. e4 Bh6 16. Bb2 Bf4 17. Bd3 Nh6**

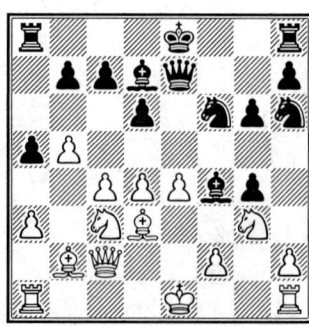

*Position after
Black's 17th move*

18. Nge2 Bg5 18 ... g5 seems best, as White could not immediately play e4-e5. **19. e5 Nh5 20. Nd5 Qf7 21. Nxc7+ Kd8 22. Nxa8 g3 23. Nxg3 Nf4 24. Be4**

Bg4 25. f3 Bh3 26. 0–0–0 Nd5+ 27. Kb1 Ne3 28. Qc3 Nxd1 29. Qxa5+ Ke8 30. Nc7+ 1–0 G. H. Hastings, *Australasian Chess Review* 1935, 341–2.

(210) ELO, A—FINE

American Chess Federation, Open Milwaukee (3), 1935
    (27 July)
French Defence, Exchange Variation [C00]

1. e4 e6 2. d4 d5 3. Bd3 Bd6 4. exd5 exd5 5. Qe2+ Ne7 6. Nf3 Nbc6 7. c3 Bg4 8. 0–0 Qd7 9. Be3 0–0–0 10. Nbd2 f5 11. Bg5 Rde8 12. Bxe7 Rxe7 13. Qd1 Re6 14. Qc2 Qf7 15. h3 Qh5? Fine embarks on an unsound combination. 15 ... Bxf3 would leave White with a positional advantage. AW **16. hxg4 fxg4 17. Bf5 Nd8 18. Rfe1** Here 15 Ne5 Bxe5 19 dxe5 Rf8 20 Bxe6+ Nxe6 and White should win. BDE **18 ... Rf8 19. Bxe6+ Nxe6 20. Rxe6 gxf3 21. Nxf3 Rxf3 22. Rxd6 Rf4 23. Rxd5** Here 23 g3! would win. AW **23 ... Qxd5 24. Qxh7 b6 25. Qxg7 Rf5 26. Qg4 Kb8 27. Re1 Rf8 28. Qg6 Qxa2 29. Re8+ Rxe8 30. Qxe8+ Kb7 31. Qe2 a5 32. f4 a4 33. g4 Ka7 34. Kf2 Qa1 35. Qc2 Qh1 36. Qe2 Qh2+ 37. Ke3 Qg1+ 38. Ke4 Qb1+ 39. Kf3 Qh1+ 40. Kg3 Qg1+ 41. Kh4 Qh1+ 42. Kg5 Qc1 43. Kf5 Qb1+ 44. Kf6 Qh7 45. Qb5 a3 46. Qa4+ Kb7 47. Qxa3 Qg8 48. g5 Qh8+ 49. Kf5 Qc8+ 50. Ke5 Qe8+ 51. Kf6 Qh8+ 52. Kg6 Qe8+ 53. Kg7 Qd7+ 54. Kh6 Qh3+ 55. Kg6 Qe6+ 56. Kg7 Qd7+ 57. Kg8 Qe6+ 58. Kg7 Qd7+ ½–½** Lahde 2001, 51 (*Brooklyn Daily Eagle*, August 22, 1935).

(211) FINE—CHEVALIER, F

American Chess Federation, Open Milwaukee (4), 1935
    (28 July)
Nimzowitsch-Indian Defence, Spielmann Variation [E23]

1. d4 Nf6 2. c4 e6 3. Nc3 Bb4 4. Qb3 c5 5. dxc5 Nc6 6. Nf3 Ne4 7. Bd2 Nxc5 8. Qc2 f5 9. a3 Bxc3 10. Bxc3 0–0 11. b4 Ne4 12. Bb2 b6

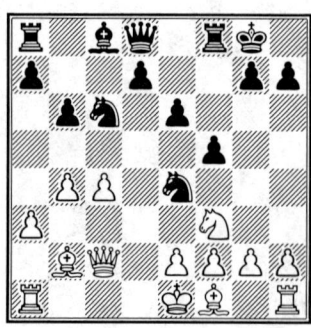

*Position after
Black's 12th move*

13. g4 An interesting idea, but risky in view of White's still backward development. **13 ... Ng5** Losing ground. Black has nothing to fear after 13 ... fxg4 14 Qxe4 gxf3 15 b5 (or 15 Rg1 Rf7 16 exf3 d5) d5 16 Qg4 e5 with a good game. (In the main line here White may retain some advantage by 17 Qg3. AW) **14. gxf5 Nxf3+ 15. exf3 Rxf5** Now White gets the attacking formation he wants. But 15 ... exf5 is little better. **16. Bd3 Rh5 17. 0–0–0 Qf8 18. Be4** A strong move, making it impossible for Black to develop properly. **18 ... Rb8 19. Rhg1 e5 20. Rg3 h6?** Creating a bad weakness, after which it is quickly over. The best chance was 20 ... Ne7 21 Rdg1 g6, but the position is too weak for long resistance. **21. Bd5+ Kh8 22. Qg6 Qf4+** This amounts to resignation. If 22 ... Rh4 23 Rdg1 wins. But not 23 Bxc6 Rxc4+. **23. Rd2 1–0** Kashdan, ACF 1935, 14.

(212) FINE—SIMONSON, A

American Chess Federation, Open Milwaukee (5), 1935 (28 July)
Stonewall Defence [D31]

1. d4 d5 2. c4 e6 3. Nc3 c6 4. e3 Nd7 Black avoids the complications of the Meran Variation. If he wishes, however, to reach the Stonewall formation, he does better to play ... f5 at once, to be able to capture with the e-pawn later. RF **5. Nf3 Bd6 6. Bd3 f5** Transposing into the "Stonewall Defence." JHB **7. cxd5 cxd5** Now this weakening reply is forced. RF **8. Bd2!** Exact timing is necessary here. With the text, White gains a vital tempo because of the threat, 9 Nb5. On 9 ... Bb8, 10 Bb4 secures the dark squares; and, on 9 ... Be7, 10 Rc1 gains entry to c7. Thus, the reply is forced. RF **8 ... a6 9. 0–0 Qf6** The annotators all condemn this move, preferring instead 9 ... Nf6 followed by ... Qe8 or ... Qe7. Fine believed that White would have a substantial advantage after, for example, 9 ... Nf6 10 Qb3 0–0 11 Ne2 Qe7 12 a3, intending 13 Bb4. AW **10. Re1!** Preparing the sacrifice. If now 10 ... Ne7, White has 11 e4! fxe4 12 Bxe4! as, on 12 ... dxe4 13 Nxe4 regains the piece at once. RF **10 ... Bb8** If 10 ... Ne7 11 e4 fxe4 12 Bxe4 dxe4? 13 Nxe4 wins. But the text loses too much ground. 10 ... Qe7, followed by 11 ... Ngf6, was still preferable. IK **11. Rc1 Ne7 12. e4!** Thanks chiefly to Black's 9th move White is so well ahead in development that he feels able to afford a piece for two pawns to break up Black's centre. JHB **12 ... fxe4 13. Bxe4!** A bold sacrifice, based on positional considerations. Black will be unable to castle, and his pieces are already badly misplaced. IK **13 ... dxe4** Black has no good way of declining the sacrifice: 13 ... 0–0? 14 Bxh7+! Kxh7 15 Rxe6! and White wins as both 15 ... Qf7 and 15 ... Qxe6 are met by 16 Ng5+. RF **14. Nxe4 Qf8** Black aims to keep the king's knight protected. There is no good alternative, for example, 14 ... Qg6 15 N4g5 Nf6 16 Qb3 and Black is lost: 16 ... 0–0 17 Nxe6 Bxe6 18 Qxe6+ Rf7 19 Ng5. RF **15. Qb3 h6** Black is move-tied. If 15 ... Nf6 White wins with 16 Rxc8+ Nxc8 17 Qxb7, but 16 Rxc8 now fails with ... Nb6 at the end. RF **16. Qxe6** Now White threatens Rxc8+ and, on 16 ... Kd8 17 Ba5+ is ruinous. RF **16 ... Nc5**

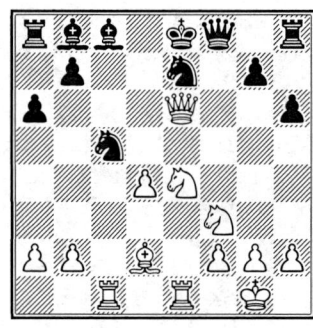

Position after Black's 16th move

17. Nf6+! The point. If the knight is taken, White regains the piece, and if 17 ... Kd8 18 Ba5+ Bc7 19 Qd6+ and mate next move. IK **17 ... Qxf6 18. Qxc8+ Kf7 19. Qxc5** Not 19 Qxh8 because of 19 ... Bxh2+. White is now two pawns ahead, with all the better of the position besides. IK **19 ... Rd8 20. Qb4 Bd6 21. Qb3+ Kf8 22. Re6 Qf5 23. Rce1 Nd5 24. Qxb7 Rab8 25. Rxd6!** White has of course a sure win here by commonplace methods; but that is not the young American player's way, and he reduces Black to helplessness with a few vigorous strokes. JHB **25 ... Rxb7 26. Rxd8+ Kf7 27. Ne5+ Ke7** If 27 ... Ke6 28 Nc4+ wins the queen. IK **28. Rxd5 Qc2 29. Bc3 Rc7 30. Nf3+ Kf7 31. Rde5 Qa4 32. h3** Black resigned. **1–0** Fine 1958, 43–6; J. H. Blake, BCM 1936, 34–5; Kashdan, ACF 1935, 17–8.

(213) FINE—FACTOR, S

American Chess Federation, Open Milwaukee (6), 1935 (29 July)
Nimzowitsch-Indian Defence, Spielmann Variation [E23]

1. d4 Nf6 2. c4 e6 3. Nc3 Bb4 4. Qb3 c5 5. dxc5 Nc6 6. Nf3 Bxc5 Black gains more ground by the usual 6 ... Ne4 7 Bd2 Nxc5. **7. Bf4 Nh5 8. Bg5 Qb6 9. Qxb6 Bxb6 10. a3 h6 11. Bh4** 11 Bd2 would have avoided the exchange of this piece, and maintained the better game, due to Black's backward d-pawn. **11 ... f5** More consistent is 11 ... g5 12 Bg3 Nxg3 13 hxg3 g4, with a fair position. **12. e3 e5?** Threatening to win the piece, but as there is a simple defence, this only weakens the pawns. **13. Be2 0–0** If 13 ... g5 14 Nxe5 is to White's advantage. **14. Nd2 Nf6 15. Bxf6 gxf6 16. 0–0–0 d6** This soon leads to the loss of a pawn but he must begin to develop the queenside. **17. Nb3 f4 18. Nd5 fxe3 19. Nxb6 axb6 20. fxe3 Rd8 21. Rhf1 Kf7 22. Nd2 Ke7 23. Ne4 Be6** If 23 ... f5 24 Nc3 Be6 25 Nd5+ Bxd5 26 cxd5 and the f-pawn falls. **24. Nxf6 Rac8 25. Kb1 Na5 26. Nd5+ Bxd5 27. cxd5**

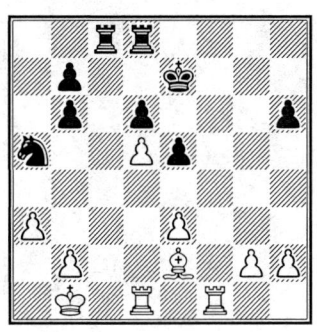

Position after White's 27th move

27 ... Nb3 28. Bg4 Rb8 29. Ka2 Nc5 30. b4 Na6
31. Rf3 Rf8 32. Rc1 R×f3 33. B×f3 Rf8 34. Rc4
Kf6 35. Kb3 Rf7 36. Rh4 Kg7 37. Rg4+ Kf6
38. Be4 Rg7 39. R×g7 K×g7 40. Bf5 Nc7 41. e4 b5
42. Bc8 b6 43. Bd7 Now the knight will remain tied up,
and the White king can enter on the kingside with the aid
of the extra pawn. 43 ... Kf6 44. Kc3 Kg5 45. g3 h5
46. h4+ Kf6 47. Kd3 Kg6 48. Ke3 Kf6 49. Kf3
Kg6 50. g4 Kh6 51. g×h5 K×h5 52. Kg3 Kh6
53. Kg4 Kg6 54. h5+ Kf6 55. Kh4 Ke7 56. Kg5
Black resigned, for if 56 ... K×d7 57 h6 and White must
queen, and if 56 ... Kf7 57 h6 Kg8 58 Kf6 wins. **1–0** Kashdan, ACF 1935, 21–2.

(214) FINE—SANTASIERE, A

American Chess Federation, Open Milwaukee (7), 1935
    (29 July)
Benoni Defence, Blockade Variation [A44]

1. d4 c5 2. d5 e5 An old system, which is not very
favourable to Black, as the pawn at d5 limits the mobility of
his pieces. **3. e4 d6 4. f4** (In MCO, 211, Fine offered the
line 4 Nc3 Be7 (4 ... f5 5 Bb5+ Kf7! merits consideration)
5 Bd3 Bg5 6 Nf3 B×c1 7 Q×c1 Nh6 8 h3 f5 9 Qg5! 0–0 10
Q×d8 R×d8 11 Ng5 g6 12 f4! with advantage, as in Alekhine–
Tartakower, Dresden 1926.) **4 ... e×f4 5. B×f4 Ne7 6. Nf3
Ng6 7. Bg3 Nd7 8. Nbd2 Be7** 8 ... Nde5 9 Nc4 f6 would
have been a more effective formation. **9. Nc4 Nb6** Well-nigh
forced, since if 9 ... Qc7 10 e5 is very powerful. **10. Ne3 0–0
11. Bd3** (White stands slightly better, MCO) **11 ... Bf6 12. c3
Bg5** The bishop should not have been given up. 12 ... Re8,
followed by ... Ne5 was in order. **13. N×g5 Q×g5 14. Qd2
Ne5 15. Bc2 Bd7 16. a4 Rae8 17. a5 Nc8 18. 0–0
Qd8 19. h3** White's next moves are a quiet consolidation,
preparing for the eventual breakthrough. Black can already do
little but mark time. **19 ... f6 20. c4 Qc7 21. b3 Ne7
22. Kh2 N7g6 23. Nf5 Nf7 24. Qc3 Nge5 25. Be1
g6 26. Ng3 Kg7 27. Qe3 h6 28. Bc3 Ng5 29. Rf2
Qc8 30. Ne2 Qd8 31. Qg3 Qe7 32. Nf4 Kh7 33. Raf1
Qg7 34. Kg1 Ngf7 35. Ne2 Nd8 36. Qe3 Rf7 37. Bb2**
Making room for the knight, which is to be placed at d2 to
protect the c-pawn and thus prepare for b3-b4. **37 ... Bc8
38. Nc3 Bd7 39. Nb1 Qf8 40. Nd2 Bc8 41. b4**
Finally. This creates new weaknesses in Black's game, and it
proves difficult for his pieces to shift to the defense. **41 ...
b6 42. a×b6 a×b6 43. Qa3 Nb7**

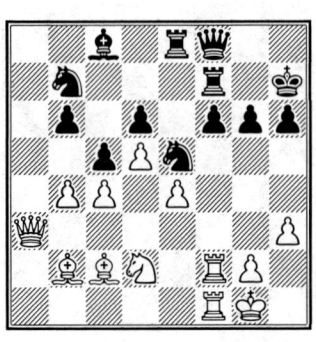

*Position after
Black's 43rd move*

Miscalculating the effect of Qa3-a7, to which Black believed
he had a sufficient counter. **44. Qa7 Na5 45. R×f6** A pretty
retort which forces the win. Of course, if 45 Q×b6 Na×c4,
and Black is all right. **45 ... Ree7 46. R×f7+ N×f7
47. Q×b6** Remaining two pawns up, and with a strong
attack still to come. **47 ... Nb7 48. e5 Qg7 49. e×d6
Q×b2 50. d×e7 Nfd6 51. e8Q N×e8 52. Q×g6+** and
Black resigned. **1–0** Kashdan, ACF 1935, 24–5.

(215) KASHDAN, I—FINE

American Chess Federation, Open Milwaukee (8), 1935
    (30 July)
Spanish Game, Chigorin Variation (without h3) [C90]

**1. e4 e5 2. Nf3 Nc6 3. Bb5 a6 4. Ba4 Nf6 5. 0–0
Be7 6. Re1 b5 7. Bb3 d6 8. c3 Na5 9. Bc2 c5 10. d4**
10 h3 would transpose into the normal variations of the Chigorin Defence. Black does not take advantage of White's
omitting this move either here or on the next move. AW **10
... Qc7 11. Nbd2 Nc6?! 12. d5 Nd8 13. Nf1 0–0
14. h3 Ne8 15. g4 g6 16. Ng3 Ng7 17. Be3 f6 18. Qe2
Nf7 19. Kh2 Ng5 20. Ng1 Bd7** ½–½ Lahde 2001, 55.

(216) DAKE, A—FINE

American Chess Federation, Open Milwaukee (10), 1935
    (31 July)
Petroff Defence [C42]

**1. e4 e5 2. Nf3 Nf6 3. N×e5 d6 4. Nf3 N×e4
5. Qe2** A drawish variation. 5 d4 d5 6 Bd3 is more enterprising. **5 ... Qe7 6. d3 Nf6 7. Bg5 Q×e2+ 8. B×e2
Be7** Black is behind in development, but the game is too
balanced to work out any advantage. **9. Nc3 h6 10. B×f6**
This gives Black the better chances. 10 Bd2 is preferable. **10
... B×f6 11. d4 Bf5 12. 0–0–0 0–0 13. h3 Nc6
14. Bd3 B×d3 15. R×d3 Rae8 16. Nd5 Bd8 17. Re1
R×e1+ 18. N×e1 Re8** Soon exchanging this piece as well,
after which the draw is assured. 18 f7-f5 and g7-g5 might still
have made things interesting. **19. Nf3 Re2 20. Rd2
R×d2 21. K×d2 Kf8** ½–½ Kashdan in ACF 1935, 31.

(217) MORTON, H—FINE

American Chess Federation, Open Milwaukee (11), 1935
    (1 Aug.)
Grünfeld Defence

The score of this game is not available. ½–½

The Warsaw Olympiad
and Łódź, 1935

On his second trip to Europe with the United States
team Fine was selected to head the American contingent,

which was captained once more by Frank Marshall. Kashdan and Reshevsky, who was subject to the Polish draft by reason of his place of birth, were not available to the American team. Nevertheless, a strong unit headed east, Reuben being joined by players of the calibre of Marshall, Dake, Kupchik and Horowitz, and the U.S. duly completed a hat trick of wins at Olympiads. Poland, who had been amongst the favourites at the team tournament, consoled themselves with a win for their team captain in a subsequent tournament to which several of the visiting masters had been invited. There were quite a number of draws in the event, as little as one and a half points separated the top six players and the Estonian-born Lithuanian International Master Vladas Mikenas was relegated to last place. In such an evenly matched field, Fine's second, behind one of the strongest players of the time, was no bad result.

Warsaw Olympiad,
August 16–31, 1935

"America once again triumphant and for the third time in succession! It is almost too good to be true, but an accomplished fact nevertheless. The average chessplayer in this country, upon reading the news with which we were promptly supplied, probably rubbed his eyes and took another look to make sure he saw right. Europeans were slightly stunned when, in 1931, our American boys came away with the Hamilton-Russell trophy which no one over there dreamed would ever cross the Atlantic. The result was laughed off good-naturedly. They were taken by surprise, off their guard, so to speak, but it would never happen again. However, two years later, in another breathtaking finish, the wonderful performance was repeated. Poland and Sweden had been passed in a final brilliant spurt. Great Britain was the last hurdle to be overcome. Our boys expected a good fight, but won 2½–1½. The key ticked off the totals: United States, 54; Sweden, 52½; Poland 52. As at Prague and Folkestone, the Americans and the rest of the contenders had been kept in suspense until the last day. The crowning achievement was saved for the final round and once more they survived the nerve-taxing strain with credit to themselves and honour for their country. A review of their work shows that they won seventeen of the matches and lost two. Strangely enough, they started out with a 3–1 victory over Czechoslovakia, which must have surprised them as much as their opponents on that auspicious day. But what is truly most remarkable is the fact that it was the Czech's only defeat in the entire tourney, and yet they did not win the cup! Next in a close match our team disposed of Argentina, which by its showing in other matches, furnished one of the surprises of the meeting. Thereupon, sudden disaster came upon the arms of the North Americans. They lost to Hungary, 1–3, and, on the same day, to Sweden, 1½–2½. A trifle discouraging, one would say, but if there

was any dismay in the United States camp, it did not show in the subsequent play. One after another fifteen countries lowered their colours to the all-conquering lads from across the sea. The points continued to pile up until, at last, in the semifinal round, the ultimate victors were seen to be ahead. And then the crisis—our boys did not fail. Marshall, owing to lack of practice, was slow in finding his form, but performed splendidly from the eleventh round on. Likewise, Reuben Fine, victor at Milwaukee, who carried the heavy burden of playing at the top board, had a minus total in the first ten rounds, after which his score comprised two wins and five draws." (ACB 1935)

In *Meet the Masters* Euwe reported that Fine's poor start at Warsaw was attributed to seasickness as a result of the poor crossing.

> Flohr (Czechoslovakia) ½ Fine
> Grau (Argentina) 0 Fine 1
> Fine 0 Lajos Steiner (Hungary) 1
> Ståhlberg (Sweden) ½ Fine
> Fine 1 Count Sacconi (Italy) 0
> Reilly (Ireland) 1 Fine 0
> Alekhine (France) ½ Fine
> Petrovs (Latvia) 0 Fine 1
> Fine 1 Professor Nägeli (Switzerland) 0
> Vidmar (Yugoslavia) 1 Fine 0
> Fine ½ Tartakower (Poland)
> Andersen (Denmark) ½ Fine
> Fine rested in Round 13 (U.S.A.–Austria)
> Böök (Finland) ½ Fine
> Fine ½ Mikenas (Lithuania)
> Keres (Estonia) ½ Fine
> Fine 1 Foerder (Palestine) 0
> Fine rested in Round 18 (U.S.A.–Romania)
> Fine 1 Winter (BCF) 0

(218) Flohr, S—Fine

Warsaw Olympiad (1), 1935 (16 Aug.)
Queen's Gambit Declined [D61]

1. d4 Nf6 2. c4 e6 3. Nc3 d5 4. Bg5 Nbd7 One would expect Flohr's favourite 5 cxd5. FR **5. e3 Be7 6. Nf3 0–0 7. Qc2 c6 8. a3 a6 9. Rc1 Re8 10. Bd3 h6** So that if 11 Bh4, b5! with a good game. FR; This weakens the kingside position. Best is probably 10 ... dxc4 11 Bxc4 Nd5. IK **11. Bf4** 11 Bh4 dxc4 12 Bxc4 b5 13 Ba2 c5 14 dxc5 (14 Rd1 cxd4 15 Nxd4 Qb6 16 Bb1 Bb7! 17 0–0 Rac8 is better for Black, Grünfeld–Alekhine, Carlsbad 1923) Nxc5 15 Bb1 (15 0–0 Qd3) Ncd7! 16 0–0 Nf8 17 Rfd1 Qb6 with equality. RF **11 ... dxc4 12. Bxc4 b5** This and the following advance is risky, as will soon be seen. But if 12 ... Nd5 13 Bg3, with a strong game. This variation if played on Black's 10th move would have forced White to exchange this bishop. IK **13. Ba2 c5** This premature move is the cause of Black's difficulties. 13 ... Bb7, which was played in an earlier game in the Olympiad, is simpler. FR **14. d5 exd5 15. Nxd5 Ra7!**

Also playable is 15 ... Rf8; 16 N×f6+ N×f6 17 Qg6 c4 (but not 15 ... N×d5 16 B×d5 Ra7 17 Qg6!). The text had to be calculated carefully, in view of the possibility of 16 N×f6+ B×f6 17 B×h6 g×h6 (17 ... Ne5! might be even stronger. AW) 18 Qg6+. But Black has 18 ... Bg7 19 B×f7+ Kf8 20 B×e8 Q×e8 with a clear advantage. Black's bishops are powerful and his queenside pawns menacing, while White's kingside pawns will be immobile. FR **16. N×e7+ Q×e7** Again White can sacrifice: 17 B×h6 g×h6 18 Qg6+ Kh8 (18 ... Kf8 19 Q×h6+ Kg8 20 Ng5 Ne5 21 Bb1 N5g4 22 Bh7+ Kh8 23 Qh4 Kg7 24 h3 N×e3! is a possibility and would force White to take a draw with 20 Qg6+) 19 B×f7 Rf8 20 Q×h6+ Nh7 but, despite the four connected passed pawns, White is at a disadvantage, as the extra piece should tell in the middle game. FR **17. 0–0 Bb7 18. Rfd1 Be4 19. Qe2 c4 20. Ne1 Nd5 21. Bg3 Nc5** Fine has defended himself skillfully and managed to neutralize whatever disadvantage he laboured under previously. FR **22. Rd4 Rd7 23. Rcd1 Red8 24. h3 Bd3 25. N×d3 N×d3**

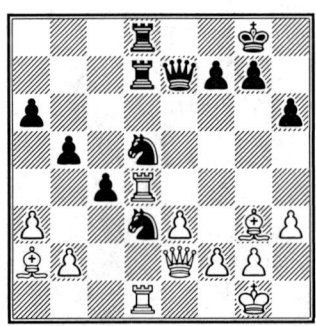

Position after Black's 25th move

26. Kh2 Nb6 27. R×d7 R×d7 28. Bb1 Qd8 White's two bishops are of slight value, as they are not coordinated and have little scope. Thus 29 e4 would be answered by 29 ... Na4! 30 B×d3 R×d3 31 R×d3 Q×d3 32 Q×d3 c×d3 and wins (White could avoid the queen exchange in this line by playing 32 Qg4, but simply 31..c×d3 does win. AW). Flohr therefore decides to rid himself of the weak b-pawn. FR **29. b3 Nc5 30. R×d7 Q×d7 31. b×c4 N×c4 32. Qc2 g6 33. Qc3 Qe7 34. Qb4** Threatening a3-a4, which Black's reply guards against. IK **34 ... Qf8 35. Qc3 Qe7 36. Qb4 Qf8 37. Qc3 Qd8 38. Bc2 Qe7 39. a4** Forcing a further simplification. The only remaining chance for play was 39 e4! If then 39 ... N×e4 40 Qe1 f5 41 f3 wins a piece. But 39 ... Ne6 40 a4 Qa3 would be sufficient to equalize. IK **39 ... Ne4 40. B×e4 Q×e4 41. a×b5 a×b5 42. Qb4 Qd5 43. Qe7 ½–½** Kashdan in *The Chess Review* 1935, 355; Reinfeld 1936, 21–2; Litmanowicz, 86–7.

(219) GRAU, R—FINE

Warsaw Olympiad (2), 1935 (17 Aug.)
Nimzowitsch-Indian Defence [E20]

1. d4 Nf6 2. c4 e6 3. Nc3 Bb4 4. g3 B×c3+ In modern chess the fianchetto has come to be regarded as a cure-all for every problem; but this exchange is a definite refutation of White's last move, since it enables Black to

exploit the unprotected state of White's c-pawn. However, the exchange need not be hurried; an excellent (and less dogmatic) mode of procedure would be 4 ... 0–0 5 Bg2 d5! 6 Qd3 c5 7 a3 B×c3+ 8 b×c3 Qa5 9 Bd2 Qa4! (Vukovics–Johner, Debreczin 1925). **5. b×c3 0–0 6. Bg2 d6 7. Nf3 Nc6** A strangely inconsistent move. If Black wishes to justify his 4th move by attacking the weak c-pawn, he must fix it by 7 ... c5. As played White is able to rid himself of the weakling later on. **8. 0–0 Na5 9. Qd3 Qe7 10. Nd2 e5** If 10 ... c5 11 Nb3! with a good game. **11. Rb1 Rb8 12. Ba3** With a slight advantage to White, MCO 217. **12 ... b6 13. c5! Rd8** After the foregoing advance, White's position is decidedly superior. The most energetic continuation would now be 14 c6! followed by Bb4 or d5, leaving Black with a fearfully cramped game. White selects a quieter course. **14. c×d6 c×d6 15. d×e5 Q×e5 16. f4 Qh5?** 16 ... Qe7 is better, for after 17 e4 Bb7 Black would still have a playable game: 18 Rfe1 Qc7 followed by ... Rbc8; or 18 e5? d×e5! 17. **e4 Bg4 18. Rfe1 Nb7 19. Qa6! Nc5** So that if 20 Q×a7? Rb7. **20. Qf1 Bc8?!** The point of White's finesse is that the black queen is now cut off from the queenside, so that he must guard against h3 and g4. **21. Bf3 Qh6 22. B×c5! d×c5 23. Rbd1 Bb7 24. c4 Nd7 25. e5 B×f3 26. Q×f3 Qe6** Finally Black has managed to bring his queen into play again; but meanwhile White has been able to monopolize the centre. **27. f5! Qe7 28. Qf4 Nf8** Allowing the entry of the knight at e4, but what is he to do? If for example 28 ... f6 29 e×f6 Q×f6 30 Ne4 Qe5 31 R×d7! or 30 ... Qh6 31 Q×h6 g×h6 32 R×d7 and wins. **29. Ne4 R×d1 30. R×d1 Rd8 31. Rd5!** Qe8? Losing outright, although 31 ... R×d5 would not hold out long. Fine is unrecognizable in this game. **32. Qg5 Nd7 33. R×d7! 1–0** Reinfeld 1936, 28–9.

(220) FINE—STEINER, L

Warsaw Olympiad (3), 1935 (18 Aug.)
Sicilian Defence, Pin Variation [B40]

1. e4 c5 2. Nf3 e6 3. d4 c×d4 4. N×d4 Nf6 5. Nc3 Bb4 6. Bd3 Nc6 7. Nde2 0–0 8. 0–0 Ne5 9. h3?! a6 10. Bf4 Qc7 11. Kh1 d6 12. Bh2 Bd7 13. f4 N×d3 14. Q×d3 Bc6 15. a3 Bc5 16. Ng3 Rfd8 17. Rad1 b5 18. Qe2 b4 19. a×b4 B×b4 20. Rd3 Qb7 21. e5 Ne8 22. f5 d×e5 23. f×e6 f6 24. Nf5 R×d3 25. c×d3 Kh8 26. d4 g6 27. d×e5 g×f5 28. e×f6 N×f6 29. R×f5 Rg8 30. Rf2 Rg6 31. Be5 Be7 32. Qd2 Kg8 33. Kh2 Ne8 34. Qf4 Bf6 35. e7 Q×e7 36. Qc4+ Qf7 37. Q×c6 B×e5+ White resigned **0–1** . Litmanowicz, game 87.

(221) STÅHLBERG, G—FINE

Warsaw Olympiad (4), 1935 (18 Aug.)
Queen's Gambit Declined [D66]

1. d4 d5 2. c4 e6 3. Nf3 Nf6 4. Nc3 Nbd7 5. Bg5 Be7 6. e3 0–0 7. Rc1 c6 8. Bd3 Re8 9. 0–0 a6

10. Qc2 h6 11. Bh4 dxc4 12. Bxc4 b5 13. Be2 Bb7 14. Rfd1 Qb6 15. Ne5 Rad8 16. Nxd7 Rxd7 17. Bxf6 Bxf6 18. Ne4 Be7 19. Nc5 Bxc5 20. Qxc5 Qxc5 21. Rxc5 Kf8 22. f4 Ke7 23. Rdc1 Rd6 24. Kf2 Kd7 25. Bh5 Re7 26. Bf3 Kc7 27. g4 f6 28. h4 Kb6 29. Kg3 Re8 30. g5 hxg5 31. hxg5 Rh8 32. Rh1 Rxh1 33. Bxh1 f5 34. Bf3 Rd8 35. Bh5 Kc7 36. Rc1 Kd6 37. Bf3 Rh8 ½–½ (Fine's Archive–Whyld).

(222) FINE—SACCONI, A

Warsaw Olympiad (5), 1935 (19 Aug.)
Semi-Slav, Meran Variation [D48]

1. d4 d5 2. c4 c6 3. Nc3 e6 4. e3 Nf6 5. Nf3 Nbd7 6. Bd3 dxc4 7. Bxc4 b5 8. Bd3 a6 9. 0–0 c5 10. a4 b4 11. Nb1 Bb7 12. Nbd2 Be7 13. Qe2 0–0 14. a5 Re8 15. Nc4 Nf8 16. Rd1 Qc7 17. Bd2 cxd4 18. Nxd4 Nd5 19. Racl Bc5 20. Nb3 Nf6 21. Nb6 N8d7 22. Nxd7 Nxd7 23. Nxc5 Nxc5 24. Bxb4 Qc6 25. f3 Nxd3 26. Rxc6 Nxb4 27. Rb6 1–0 (Fine's Archive–Whyld)

(223) REILLY, B—FINE

Warsaw Olympiad (6), 1935 (20 Aug.)
Dutch Defence [A98]

1. d4 e6 2. Nf3 f5 After having been refuted "once and for all," this defence has been enjoying quite a vogue for the past few years. Now that critical opinion seems to be turning against it once more, it will doubtless disappear—and bob up again a few years later! FR 3. g3 Nf6 4. Bg2 Be7 5. c4 d6 6. Nc3 0–0 7. 0–0 Qe8 8. Qc2 Nbd7 Herzog–Flohr, Liebwerda 1934, continued 8 ... Nc6 9 e4 fxe4 10 Nxe4 e5 11 dxe5 dxe5 with a good game for Black. Fine's move, however, is better; for 8 ... Nc6 can be answered advantageously by 9 d5! Nd8 10 Nd4! or 9 ... exd5 10 cxd5 Ne5 11 Nd4 g6 12 Ncb5. FR 9. e4 Nh5? The corollary of his last seems to be 9 ... fxe4 10 Nxe4? Nxe4 and 11 ... Nf6; but White would play 10 Ng5, obtaining complete control of the square e4; that is not to Black's liking. JHB 10. exf5 exf5 11. Rel Ndf6 12. Ng5! c6 13. d5! c5 14. Bd2 Ng4 As the queen's bishop must take the white knight when it goes to e6 he does not want to waste a tempo by moving the bishop before that. The text-move aims at ... Ne5 later, and incidentally clears the air a little by forcing on White's Ng5-e6. JHB 15. Nb5 Qd8 A very unwelcome necessity, as expert practitioners of this defence attach much importance to the sortie of the black queen on the king's wing as opportunity serves. JHB 16. Ne6 Bxe6 17. Rxe6 a6 18. Rae1 Rf7 Neither Reinfeld nor the annotator in *B.C.M.* make any comment about this move. The logical consequence of Black's previous was surely 18 ... axb5 19 Rxe7 Ne5 20 Bg5 Qa5, which looks like quite a reasonable try. AW 19. Nc3 Ne5 20. Nd1 f4 Giving White e4 for his pieces; but against other moves, White plays f2-f4 with a stranglehold on the e-file. FR (20 ... b5 does not allow 21 f4, instead after 21 Bc3 Bf6 22 cxb5

Fine makes a move. A portrait from around 1935.

axb5 Black would gain some activity. AW) 21. Be4! White has no ground for uneasiness at the retreat of his king's rook being cut off, as he stands to get a passed pawn and an enhanced attack by its capture. JHB 21 ... g6 Unavoidably weakening the long diagonal, on which White now trains his guns. FR 22. Bc3 Ng7 Winning the exchange, but White has ample compensation since he obtains d5 for his pieces, while the powerful pawn at e6 paralyses Black's game. FR; The policy of grasping at the exchange is not well considered; he should seek rather to consolidate his position by 22 ... Nd7 23 b3 Qf8 etc. JHB (In the event of 22 ... Nd7 White could start a dangerous attack by 23 Bxg6 hxg6 24 Qxg6+ Ng7, for example 25 gxf4 Bf6 26 Rxd6 Bxc3 27 Nxc3 Rxf4 28 Qg3 Rf7 29 Ree6 b5 30 Ne4 and wins. AW) 23. Bxe5 dxe5 24. Nc3! This and the next show fine position judgment; after the exchange is taken a few hammer strokes place White in complete control. JHB 24 ... Rf8 Now might have been a good time to take the material: 24 ... Nxe6 25 dxe6 Rf6! 26 Bxb7 Rb8 27 Bd5 fxg3 28 hxg3 Qb6 with chances for Black. AW 25. Rd1! fxg3 26. hxg3 Nxe6 He should still postpone the capture of the rook and play 26 ... Kh8;White's later move of Bd5 would then be much less potent. JHB 27. dxe6 Qe8 28. Rd7 Bf6 29. Bd5 Kh8 30. Ne4 Bg7 There is no good defence: if 30 ... Be7 31 Qc3 wins. FR 31. Nd6 Qb8 32. e7! Re8 33. Nf7+ Kg8 34. Nxe5+ 34 Rxb7 wins the queen, but White sees his way to something still more decisive, for which the elimination of this pawn is necessary.

JHB 34 ... Kh8 35. Nf7+ Kg8 36. Nd6+ Kh8 37. Qe4! Much stronger than 37 Bf7 Rxe7 38 Rxe7 Qxd6. **RF** 37 ... Bd4 38. Kg2 A needless precaution: 38 Rd8 would win easily. **FR** 38 ... Bf6 39. Qe6 Bxe7 40. Qe5+ Obviously Fine has not done himself justice; but that does not detract from the Irish master's admirable play. **FR** 1–0 J. H. Blake in *BCM* 1935, 481–2; Reinfeld 1936, 60–1.

(224) FINE—ALEKHINE, A

Warsaw Olympiad (7), 1935 (21 Aug.)
Colle System [A43]

1. d4 c5 2. e3 2 d5 is stronger, as it restrains Black's game for some time. After the text, Black gets the initiative. **IK 2 ... d5 3. Nf3 Nc6 4. c3 Bg4** Obtaining the initiative, since White does not want to cope with the difficulties of 5 dxc5 e5 6 b4 against an attacking player of Alekhine's calibre. **FR 5. Nbd2 cxd4 6. exd4 e6** The opening has now transposed into a Queen's Gambit Declined with colours reversed. Fine does not seem to have noticed this at the moment since his next move loses a tempo. **FR 7. Bd3** The bishop belongs on e2. White is really playing the defensive side of the opening, and his plan should be 0–0, Re1 and eventually Ne5. **IK 7 ... Bd6 8. 0–0 Qc7 9. h3 Bh5 10. Re1 Nge7 11. Be2 Bg6 12. Nh4 0–0–0 13. Nxg6 Nxg6** Probably the best method of recapture, since the king's rook file would be of no great value after 13 ... hxg6. **FR;** The older masters would invariably have retaken with the h-pawn, but Alekhine's idea is to advance his pawns, try to exchange them, and thus open more than one file. The h-file would not be very useful at this point. **IK 14. Bf1 Kb8 15. Nf3 h6 16. Qd3 Nge7** Preparing to advance; a counter by White is indicated, so that the game soon takes an exciting turn. **FR 17. b3 g5 18. c4 Rdg8 19. c5 Bf4 20. b4!?** While this sacrifice is rather speculative, it is not to be condemned, since after 20 a3 (or Rb1) Bxc1 21 Rexc1 g4 22 hxg4 Rxg4 23 b4 Qf4 24 Rd1 Nf5 White would lose a pawn under far less advantageous circumstances (23 ... Nf5 is more accurate since in the line given White can just play 25 Nh2. AW). Black's best reply to the text was doubtless 20 ... Bxc1 and 21 ... Nxb4, gaining a tempo as against the actual continuation. **FR 20 ... Nxb4 21. Qb3 Nbc6 22. Bxf4 gxf4 23. Rab1 Ka8 24. Rb2 Nf5 25. Reb1 Rb8** White's sacrifice has had the effect of slowing down his opponent's attack, but if Black is able to perfect his defence, he will threaten to advance strongly in the centre. **FR 26. Qa4 f6 27. Bd3 Nfe7 28. Rb6!**

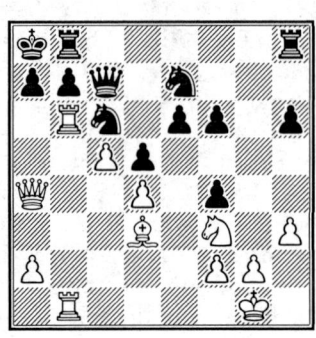

Position after White's 28th move

28 ... Rhg8 28 ... e5 looks natural here, but after 29 dxe5 fxe5 30 R1b3 White would have some dangerous threats; 30 ... e4 31 Nd4 Nxd4? 32 Qxa7+! Kxa7 33 Ra3 mate; or 31 ... exd3 32 Nb5 (Reinfeld). Now play might go 32 ... Qe5 33 Nxa7 Qe4 34 R6b4 Qe1+ 35 Kh2 Nxb4 36 Rxb4 Qxb4 37 Qxb4 with unclear complications. **AW 29. Bb5 Rg7 30. Rb3 Rbg8** Leads to a series of exchanges which are somewhat unfavourable for Black because of the exposed position of his king. Again ... e5 seems in order, but after 31 dxe5 fxe5 all of Black's pieces are tied to their posts (with the exception of the king's rook, which cannot appreciably improve its position), while the formidable looking centre pawns are really useless (... e4 is always met by Nd4). **FR 31. Kf1 Rxg2 32. Bxc6 Nxc6** Not 32 ... bxc6? 33 Qa6 followed by Rb7. **FR 33. Rxb7 Qxb7 34. Rxb7 Kxb7 35. Qc2 R2g7** Since Black cannot avoid the loss of a pawn (after Qd2 or Qh7+) he decides to lose it in such a way as to obtain a compensating d-file. **FR 36. Qd2 e5 37. dxe5 fxe5 38. Qxd5 Rd8 39. Qb3+ Kc7 40. Qe6 Rd1+ 41. Ke2 Rgd7** Fortunately Black has enough tactical threats to keep his opponent occupied (42 Nxe5?? Nd4+ and Black comes out a piece ahead). **FR 42. Qxh6 Rc1** Not 42 ... e4? 43 Qxf4+ Kb7 44 Qxe4 Re7 45 Qxe7+. **FR 43. Qf8 Re7 44. Ng5 Nd4+ 45. Kd2 Rc2+ 46. Kd3 Rd7 47. Ne4! Rc1** Avoiding 47 ... Ne6 48 Qd6+! with good winning chances for White. **FR 48. Kd2 Nb3+ 49. Ke2 Nd4+ 50. Kd2 Nb3+** An extremely difficult game, very ably handled on both sides, with the exception of Fine's inexact play in the opening. **FR** ½–½ Kashdan, *The Chess Review* 1935, 254–5; Reinfeld 1936, 69–71.

(225) PETROVS, V—FINE

Warsaw Olympiad (8), 1935 (21 Aug.)
Queen's Gambit Declined [D65]

1. d4 d5 2. Nf3 Nf6 3. c4 e6 4. Bg5 Nbd7 5. e3 Be7 6. Nc3 0–0 7. Rc1 c6 8. Qc2 a6 9. cxd5 exd5 10. Bd3 h6 11. Bh4 c5 Black decides that his winning chances will be slim after the orthodox continuation 11 ... Re8 and ... Ne4. He therefore prefers to take some risks (isolated d-pawn), in return for play on the c- and e-files, and free development for his other pieces. **12. dxc5 Nxc5 13. 0–0 Be6** Here and later, Black avoids the dubious benefit of obtaining two bishops by ... Nxd3, for (1) simplification always facilitates the attack against an isolated pawn; (2) the exchange would be counter to his aim of creating complications; (3) the queen will be awkwardly placed on the c-file after Black's next move. **14. Nd4 Rc8 15. Rfd1 b5 16. a3 Ne8 17. Bxe7 Qxe7 18. b4** White has weakened his position and ceded c4 to Black, who energetically exploits this circumstance by applying pressure to the knight on the c-file. Now 18 ... Nxd3 would not be so good, because the d-pawn would not be so dangerous as in the game. **WL 18 ... Na4 19. Qd2 Nxc3 20. Rxc3 Nd6 21. Nb3 Nc4 22. Bxc4 dxc4** Black's excellent play has been rewarded with this protected passed pawn; but now the knight takes up a fine post at d4, and it is difficult to see how White could have come to grief if he had maintained a "stand-pat" policy at move 25. **23. Nd4 Qf6** If 23 ... Rfd8 24 Nc6! wins the exchange. **24. Qe2 Rfd8 25. f4? Bd5!**

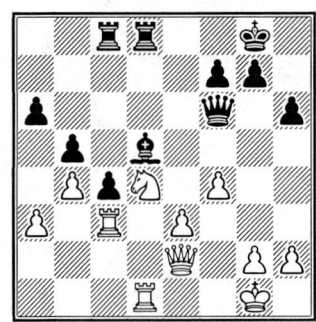

Position after Black's 25th move

Now the aspect of the game has changed completely: the occupation of d3 by the bishop, coupled with the attack on the e-pawn, will give Black a very strong game. **26. Rd2 Be4 27. Qf2 Rd7 28. Qg3 Re8 29. Qf2** White has a difficult game. If 29 Re2 Bd3 30 Re1 Rxd4! 31 exd4 Qxd4+ and wins. **29 ... Bd3** And now White's best chance of a long resistance would be with Rxd3. (In that case White probably wouldn't last long as the black major pieces can infiltrate via the c-file, when his position would soon collapse. AW) **30. Rc1 Rde7** There is no satisfactory reply (31 Re1 Qxd4!). **31. Nf3 Rxe3 32. Ne5 Qb6!** If now 33 Nxd3 (33 Re1?? Rxe1 mate) cxd3 34 Rxd3? Re1+. **33. h3 f6 34. Nxd3 cxd3 35. Kh2 Qd6 36. Rcd1 R8e4** White resigns, for if 37 g3? Re2 wins; or 37 Kg1 Qd4! and so on. An excellent game by Fine. 0–1 Reinfeld 1936, 75–6; Litmanowicz, 83–4.

(226) FINE–NAEGELI, O

Warsaw Olympiad (9), 1935 (22 Aug.)
King's Indian Defence [E68]

1. d4 Nf6 2. c4 g6 3. Nc3 Bg7 4. e4 d6 5. Nf3 Nbd7 6. g3 0–0 7. Bg2 e5 8. 0–0 Re8 9. Re1 exd4 10. Nxd4 Nc5 11. b3 Bg4 12. f3 Bd7 13. Bb2 Qc8 14. Qd2 Re7 15. Nc2 a5 16. Ne3 Bc6 17. Rad1 Qf8 18. Qc2 b6 19. Ne2 Nh5 20. Nd4 Bb7 21. Nd5 Bxd5 22. cxd5 Ree8 23. f4 Nf6 24. Re2 h5 25. Rf1 Nfd7 26. a3 Kh7 27. e5 Qh8 28. Nc6 f5 29. Rfe1 Nb8 30. Nxb8 Raxb8 31. b4 axb4 32. axb4 Na6 33. Qb3 Re7 34. e6 Bxb2 35. Qxb2 Qxb2 36. Rxb2 1–0 (Fine's Archives–Whyld)

(227) VIDMAR, M–FINE

Warsaw Olympiad (10), 1935 (23 Aug.)
Queen's Gambit Declined [D68]

1. d4 Nf6 2. c4 e6 3. Nf3 d5 4. Bg5 Nbd7 5. e3 Be7 6. Nc3 0–0 7. Rc1 c6 8. Bd3 dxc4 9. Bxc4 Nd5 10. Bxe7 Qxe7 11. 0–0 Nxc3 12. Rxc3 e5 13. Qc2 13 e4 exd4 14 Qxd4 b5 15 Bb3 c5 with some

advantage for White, Alekhine–Breyer, Scheveningen 1913. **13 ... e4 14. Nd2 Nf6 15. Rc1** 15 f4 Bf5 16 Bb3 g6 17 h3 h5 is unclear, Weenink–Maróczy, match 1930; but White gained some advantage by 15 Bb3 Bg4 16 Re1 Rfe8 17 h3, Zvyagintsev–Adelman, New York 1997. AW **15 ... Bg4?** Not a particularly productive idea. Trifunović proposes 15 ... Bf5 16 f4 Rfd8, whereas Asztalos suggested the prophylactic 15 ... a5!. **16. b4!** The minority attack. **16 ... a6** Trifunović's suggestion of 16 ... Qxb4 17 Nxe4 Nxe4 18 Qxe4 Bh5 19 Rb3 Qd2, with a slight advantage for White, actually looks suicidal after 20 Qb1 Bg6 21 Bd3! AW. **17. Qb1 Rad8 18. a4 Rd6** 18 ... Nd5 19 Bxd5 cxd5 20 Rc7 Rd7 would minimize White's advantage. **19. b5** White has a clear plus, MCO 134. **19 ... axb5 20. axb5 Bd7 21. bxc6 Bxc6** Now both b7 and e4 are weak. **22. Bb5 Bd5 23. Be2 h6 24. Qb4 Re6 25. Qa5 Qd8 26. Qxd8 Rxd8 27. Bc4! Bxc4 28. Rxc4 Rb6 29. Rc8 Rxc8 30. Rxc8+ Kh7 31. Kf1 Rb2 32. Ke1 Ra2 33. Rc5** Asztalos suggested 33 Rc7 Ra1+ 34 Ke2 Nd5 35 Rc5, intending Rb5. This would however allow Black counterplay by 33 ... Nd5 34 Rxb7 Nc3. AW **33 ... Ra1+ 34. Ke2 Ra2 35. h3** To prevent 35 ... Ng4 and 36 ... Nxf2. **35 ... Nd7 36. Rb5!** Not 36 Rc7 Nb6 37 Rxb7? Nc4! **36 ... b6 37. Kd1 g6 38. Nxe4 Kg7** In the event of 38 ... f5, simply 39 Nd2. **39. g4! Ra1+ 40. Ke2 Rh1 41. Kf3! Kf8** Not 41 ... Rxh3+ 42 Kg2 Rh4 43 f3 and Black is helpless. **42. Kg2 Rc1 43. h4 Ke7 44. g5! hxg5 45. hxg5 Kd8 46. Kf3 Kc7 47. Rb3 Kc6 48. Ke2 Kd5 49. Kd3 Rd1+ 50. Nd2 Kc6 51. Rc3+ Kb7** If 51 ... Kb5 52 Rc7. **52. Kc2 Ra1 53. Ne4 b5 54. Nd6+ Kb6 55. f4** Trifunović gives this an exclamation mark and queries 55 Nxf7, citing 55 ... Ra2+ 56 Kd3 Rxf2. If however White were to play 56 Kb3! Rxf2 57 Nd8 he would win fairly easily, for example: 57 ... Nf8 58 Rc6+ Ka7 59 Kb4 Rf5 60 e4 Rf4 61 Kxb5 Kb8 62 Ne6 Nxe6 63 Rxe6. **55 ... b4 56. Rc4 Ra2+ 57. Kb3 Ra3+ 58. Kxb4 Rxe3 59. Nxf7 Re4 60. Ne5** 1–0 Based on notes by Trifunović in Trifunović *et al*, 227–8.

(228) FINE–TARTAKOWER, S

Warsaw Olympiad (11), 1935 (24 Aug.)
King's Indian Defence [E85]

1. d4 Nf6 2. c4 g6 3. f3 Bg7 4. e4 d6 5. Nc3 e5 The modern main line is 5 ... 0–0 (keeping his options open), when the most frequent reply is 6 Be3, though 6 Bg5 is also possible. **6. Nge2** In NCO Joe Gallagher marks this as an interesting move, but offers no examples or analysis. He notes that 6 dxe5 leads to equality by 6 ... dxe5 7 Qxd8+ Kxd8 8 Be3 Be6 9 0–0–0+ Nfd7, but suggests 6 d5 Nh5 7 Be3 f5 8 Qd2 Qh4+ (or 8 ... 0–0) 9 Bf2 Qf4 10 Qxf4 exf4 11 exf5 Bxf5 Nge2 with a slight plus for White. **6 ... Nbd7** In the tournament at Łódź, after the Olympiad, Appel varied with 6 ... Nc6. **7. Be3 0–0 8. Qd2** 8 ... c6 9 0–0–0 with approximate equality. JG **8 ... Ne8!** White gained a promising position after 8 ... Re8 9 d5 Nb6 10 b3 Bd7 11 g4 Qe7 12 Ng3 c6 13 h4 cxd5 14 cxd5 Rac8 15 Rc1

Rc7 16 h5 Rec8 17 g5, Belavenyets–Pogrebissky, U.S.S.R. championship, Leningrad 1939. **9. dxe5?** In PCO Fine suggests 9 g3 as leading to a clearly better game for White, it would however lead to a fairly overextended pawn centre. 9 Bg5 could be tried. **9 ... Nxe5! 10. Nd4 Be6 11. b3** Now Black equalizes easily by dissolving the centre and leaving White with a host of dark-square weaknesses. White could play for the advantage by 11 Nxe6 fxe6 12 0-0-0. **11 ... c6 12. Be2 d5! 13. cxd5 cxd5 14. exd5** Perhaps here was Fine's best chance to play for the advantage: 14 Nxe6 fxe6 15 exd5 Qh4+ (or 15 ... Qa5 16 Rc1) 16 Bf2 Qb4 17 Rc1 Rc8 18 0-0 Nxf3+ 19 Bxf3 Bxc3 20 Qe3 Ng7. **14 ... Bxd5! 15. Nxd5** If White wished for more than a draw he could try 15 Ndb5, for example: 15 ... Bc6 16 Nxa7 Qa5 17 Nxc6 Nxc6 18 Rc1. **15 ... Qxd5 16. 0-0 Nd6 17. Rad1 Rfe8 18. Nb5 Qxd2 19. Bxd2 Nxb5 20. Bxb5 Nc6** ½-½ Fine, apparently not in his best form, seems to have been content with a draw in this his eleventh game in nine days. The fact that Fine played this same opening less than two weeks later, against a player who would be familiar with it, suggests he was confident of improving his play. Game source Litmanowicz, 120.

(229) ANDERSEN, E—FINE

Warsaw Olympiad (12), 1935 (25 Aug.)
London System/East Indian Defence [A48]

1. d4 Nf6 2. Nf3 g6 3. Bf4 Bg7 4. Nc3 0-0 5. e4 d6 6. Qd2 Nbd7 7. Bh6 c5 8. Bxg7 Kxg7 9. 0-0-0 cxd4 10. Nxd4 Nc5 11. f3 Be6 12. g4 The pawn configuration is now the same as that which would arise in the Rauzer/Yugoslav Variation of the Dragon Sicilian. **12 ... Qa5 13. Nxe6+ Nxe6 14. h4 Rac8 15. f4 Rxc3 16. Qxc3 Qxc3 17. bxc3 Nxg4 18. Rg1 Nf2 19. Re1 h5 20. f5 Nc5 21. e5 Ng4 22. exd6 exd6 23. fxg6 fxg6 24. Be2 Nf6 25. Bd3 Ng4 26. Re7+ Kh6 27. Be2 Ne5 28. Rg5 Rf4 29. Bd1 Re4** ½-½ (54) Game sources: VI Olimpiada Szachowa, game 332, and www.games-of-chess.de. According to Litmanowicz the game ended as a draw on move 54. The final moves were 54 Kb6xa6 Re8-b8 and the final position was—White: Ka6, Pb7; Black: Kf7, Rb8.

(230) BÖÖK, E—FINE

Warsaw Olympiad (14), 1935 (26 Aug.)
French Defence, Exchange Variation [C01]

1. e4 e6 2. d4 d5 3. exd5 exd5 4. Bd3 Bd6 5. Ne2 Nf6 6. 0-0 Nc6 7. c3 0-0 8. Bf4 Bxf4 9. Nxf4 Qd6 10. Qf3 Bg4 11. Qg3 Ne7 12. h3 Bf5 13. Nd2 Be4 14. Bxe4 Nxe4 15. Nxe4 dxe4 16. Rae1 f5 17. f3 e3 18. Kh2 Nd5 19. Nxd5 Qxd5 20. Qf4 Qxa2 21. Rxe3 Rf7 22. Rfe1 Raf8 23. Re7 Qc4 24. Qg5 h6 25. Qg6 b6 26. Re8 Qd5 27. Rxf8+ Rxf8 28. Qe6+ Qxe6 29. Rxe6 f4 30. Kg1 Rf6 31. Re8+ Rf8 32. Rxf8+ Kxf8 Most weak pawn positions

are not permanently inferior, unless there is an indissoluble doubled pawn or a succession of isolated pawns. Usually pawn inferiority is relative to the amount of time available to straighten out the pawns and bring up the king. This position is a case in point. **33. Kf2** If White were an obliging fellow and went to sleep for a while, Black could set up his pawns at c6, b5 and a5, his king at d5, when his opponent's game in turn is hopelessly lost. But making one move at a time Black must defend his f-pawn and prevent the entrance of the king on the queenside—an impossible task. **33 ... Kf7 34. Ke2 Kf6** Or 34 ... Ke6 35 Kd3 b5 36 Ke4 g5 37 d5+ Kd6 38 b4 c6 39 dxc6 Kxc6 40 h4 Kb6 41 h5! a5 42 bxa5+ Kxa5 43 Kf5 and White queens when Black's pawn is on the sixth. **35. Kd3 Kf5 36. Kc4 c6 37. d5 cxd5+ 38. Kxd5 Kg5 39. Ke5?** Here there is a routine win by 39 c4 Kh4 40 b4 but White is bedazzled by the fact that he can win a pawn. **39 ... b5! 40. b4 g6!!** This draws—the point will soon be seen. **41. Ke4 Kh4! 42. Kxf4 h5 !!!** (It was essential to have this pawn protected.) **43. Ke5 Kg3 44. Kf6 Kxg2 45. Kxg6 Kxh3! 46. f4** On 46 Kxh5 Kg3 White would lose. **46 ... h4** and White could do nothing in the queen and pawn ending. **47. f5 Kg3 48. f6 h3 49. f7 h2 50. f8Q h1Q 51. Qb8+ Kg4 52. Qc8+ Kg3 53. Qc7+ Kg4 54. Qd7+ Kg3 55. Qd6+ Kf2 56. Qd2+ Kg3 57. Qg5+ Kf2 58. Qxb5 Qe4+ 59. Kf6 Qf3+ 60. Ke6 Qxc3 61. Qc5+ Qe3+** ½-½ Fine 1941, 66.

(231) FINE—MIKENAS, V

Warsaw Olympiad (15), 1935 (27 Aug.)
Slav-Grünfeld [D95]

1. d4 Nf6 2. c4 g6 3. Nc3 d5 4. Nf3 Bg7 5. e3 0-0 6. Qb3 e6 7. Bd2 c6 8. Bd3 Nbd7 9. 0-0 Nb6 10. cxd5 exd5 11. a4 a5 12. Rfc1 Ne8 13. Nd1 Nd6 14. Ne5 f6 15. Nf3 Re8 16. Be1 Bf8 17. Qc2 Nbc4 18. Nc3 Bf5 19. Bxf5 Nxf5 20. e4 dxe4 21. Nxe4 Nb6 22. Qb3+ Nd5 23. Nc3 Qb6 24. Qc4 Rad8 25. Nxd5 Rxd5 26. Bc3 Nd6 27. Qd3 Nf7 28. Nd2 Qd8 29. Nb3 Bd6 30. Re1 Rxe1+ 31. Rxe1 Bf8 32. Qe2 Kg7 33. h3 Ng5 34. Qe8 Qc7 35. Nc5 b6 36. Ne6+ Nxe6 37. Rxe6 Bd6 38. g3 Rf5 39. d5 cxd5 ½-½ (Fine's Archives–Whyld)

(232) KERES, P—FINE

Warsaw Olympiad (16), 1935 (28 Aug.)
French Defence, Advance Variation [C02]

1. e4 e6 2. d4 d5 3. e5 c5 4. Nf3 Nc6 5. dxc5 Bxc5 6. Bd3 Qc7 7. Bf4 Nge7 8. Bg3 Ng6 9. 0-0 Bd7 10. Nc3 a6 11. Re1 Nge7 12. a3 Nd4 13. Nxd4 Bxd4 14. Qg4 Bxc3 15. bxc3 Ng6 16. h4 h5 17. Qg5 18. Qe3 Nxh4 19. Bf4 Ng6 20. Bxg6 fxg6 21. Bg5 Qc8 22. Qd3 0-0 23. Qxg6 Qe8 24. Qd3 Bb5 25. Qg3 Qg6 26. Rac1 Rac8 27. Re3 Rc4 28. f4

Ba4 29. Qf2 Rfc8 30. Qd2 Qf5 31. Rg3 Kh7
32. Rh3 Be8 33. Rf1 Bg6 34. Rf2 d4 35. cxd4
Rxc2 36. Qe3 Rc1+ 37. Kh2 Qb1 38. Qf3 Qa1
39. f5 Rh1+ 40. Kg3 Rxh3+ 41. Kxh3 Bxf5+
42. Kh2 Qxd4 43. Qxh5+ Kg8 44. Re2 b5 45. Qh4
Qxh4+ 46. Bxh4 Rc4 47. Be7 Be4 48. Rf2 Bd5
49. Bd6 Kh7 50. Kh3 Kg6 51. g3 Be4 52. Rf4 a5
53. Rf2 Bc6 54. Rf4 Be4 55. Rf2 Rc3 56. Rf4 Bf3
57. Be7 Bd5 58. Rg4+ Kf7 59. Bd6 Rc1 60. Rf4+
Kg6 61. Rg4+ Kh7 62. Rh4+ Kg8 63. Rf4 Ra1
64. Kg4 b4 65. axb4 a4 66. Kg5 Rg1 67. g4 a3
68. Kg6 Be4+ 69. Rxe4 a2 70. Rf4 Rxg4+ 71. Rxg4
a1Q 72. Kg5 Qb2 73. Kf4 Qf2+ 74. Kg5 Qe3+
75. Kh4 Qf3 76. Rg3 Qf1 77. Rg4 Kh7 78. Kg3
Qg1+ 79. Kf3 Qf1+ 80. Ke3 Kh6 81. Rf4 Qe1+
82. Kd3 Qd1+ 83. Ke3 g5 84. Rf6+ Kh5 85. Rf8
Kg4 86. Rb8 Qc1+ 87. Kd3 Qb1+ 88. Kc4 Qe4+
89. Kc5 Qd5+ 90. Kb6 Kf3 91. b5 g4 92. Kc7
½–½ Litmanowicz, Aneks, game 6b.

(233) FINE—FOERDER, H

Warsaw Olympiad (17), 1935 (29 Aug.)
Nimzowitsch-Indian Defence, Sämisch Variation [E27]

1. d4 Nf6 2. c4 e6 3. Nc3 Bb4 4. a3 Bxc3+ 5. bxc3
0–0 6. f3 Nc6 7. e4 e5 8. Be3 Re8 9. d5 Na5
10. Bd3 b6 11. c5 bxc5 12. Bxc5 d6 13. Be3 c6
14. c4 Ba6 15. Rc1 Rb8 16. Ne2 Rb3 17. dxc6 d5
18. Bc5 dxe4 19. Bc2 Qxd1+ 20. Rxd1 Rb2 21. Ba4
Nxc4 22. Nc3 Rxg2 23. c7 Nb2 24. Bxe8 Nxd1
25. Bb5 Bc8 26. Kxd1 exf3 27. Kc1 f2 28. Rd1 Rg1
29. Rxg1 fxg1Q+ 30. Bxg1 a6 31. Bc6 g5 32. Na4
Nd7 33. Bxd7 Bxd7 34. Nb6 Be6 35. c8Q+ Bxc8
36. Nxc8 Kg7 37. Nd6 Kg6 38. Nb7 f5 39. Nc5 f4
40. Nxa6 g4 41. Nc5 h5 42. a4 h4 43. a5 g3
44. hxg3 1–0 Fiala, QCH3 507.

(234) FINE—WINTER, W

Warsaw Olympiad (19), 1935 (31 Aug.)
Queen's Gambit Declined, Exchange Variation [D35]

1. d4 d5 2. c4 c6 3. Nf3 Nf6 4. Nc3 e6 5. Bg5
Nbd7 6. cxd5 The Exchange Variation has been a
favourite with many American masters since Pillsbury.
Reshevsky is particularly fond of it. RF 6 ...
exd5 Of
recent years the alternative 6 ... cxd5 has been played extensively. 7. e3 Be7 8. Bd3 h6 Black ought to avoid any
weakening moves in such positions. The best is 8 ... 0–0, 9
... Re8 and an early ... Ne4. RF 9. Bf4 White now has a
target at which to aim on Black's kingside. RF 9 ... 0–0
10. 0–0 With 10 h3 White can hold onto his queen
bishop, but the text variation is equally satisfactory. RF 10
... Nh5 It is difficult to suggest a better continuation, since
if 10 ... Re8 11 h3 Nf8 12 Ne5 Bd6 13 Bg3 followed by f4 is
better for White. Black plays for the two bishops, but meanwhile his opponent gains time and entrenches his knight at

e5. FR 11. Be5 Nxe5 12. Nxe5 Nf6 13. f4 The classical
attacking position of the Queen's Gambit has been reached.
If Black does nothing, White proceeds with Kh1, g2-g4-g5
and the opening of the g-file. RF 13 ... c5 Counterplay:
Black threatens 14 ... cxd4 15 exd4 Qb6 attacking two
pawns. FR 14. Kh1 Qb6 Or 14 ... c4 15 Bc2 a6 16 a4 or
14 ... cxd4 15 exd4 Qb6 16 Rb1 followed in either case by
g2-g4. So long as Black keeps the centre liquid, White does
not have time for a kingside assault. RF; Colourless. If 14 ...
cxd4 15 exd4 Qb6 16 Qd2 (16 ... Qxd4? 17 Bh7+. This
explains White's 14th move). Better was 14 ... c4 15 Bc2 Bb4
with the idea of ... Bxc3 and the advance of the queenside
pawns. White could prepare to storm the kingside with
g2-g4 and so on having a ready made target in .Black's..h6.
Still this plan would require careful execution, else White's
king might become exposed. FR 15. Na4! Qa5 16. dxc5
White secures a strongpoint. RF 16 ... Bd7 Reinfeld writes
"Fine expected 16 ... Bxc5 17 Nxc5 Qxc5 18 Qd2 with a
clear advantage for White.". Whereas Fine states that Black
was "understandably reluctant to give up his king bishop"
because "sooner or later the weakness on the black squares
will prove fatal." 17. Nxd7 Nxd7

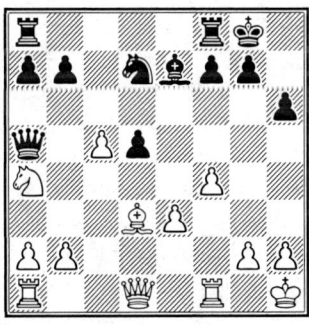

*Position after
Black's 17th move*

18. Bc2! Nxc5 19. Nc3! Decisive. Black had hoped
instead for 19 Qxd5? Rad8 20 Qf5 g6 21 Qe5 Bd6 22 Qc3
Qxc3 23 Nxc3 Rfe8 after which the opposite-coloured
bishops offer excellent drawing chances. RF 19 ... Bf6 The
unexpected retreat of the knight is embarrassing for Black. If
19 ... Rad8 then simply 20 Nxd5. The text is cleverly refuted
by White, who is not misled by the mirage of 20 b4 Qxb4?
(20 ... Qa6! but not 20 ... Qd8 21 bxc5 Bxc3 22 Qd3!) 21
Nxd5 Qb2 22 Rab1 Qxa2 23 Nxf6+ gxf6 24 Qg4+ Kh8 25
Qf5. FR 20. Nxd5! Bxb2 21. Rb1 Bc3 The bishop seeks
a hiding place. He tries naturally to avoid going to f6 because
of the resultant disruption of the kingside pawns, but White
can make excellent use of the threat. RF; Not 21 ... Qxa2?
22 Rf2 Rfd8 23 Rxb2! Qxd5 24 Rd2!! FR (With all White's
pawns on the kingside, this would at least ensure a long
technical struggle with some hope of salvation. As the game
goes White wins by a direct attack in only ten more moves.
AW) 22. Qe2! a6 White threatened to win a piece with
Rb5 and Qc4 (or in reverse order). After the text he finds a
brilliant finesse which gains two valuable tempi. FR 23. Rfc1!
Bd2 Else Nxc3 and Bh7+. FR 24. Rd1 Bc3 25. Qc4 Now
the retreat to f6 can no longer be avoided; for if 25 ... Bd2,
White wins a piece with 26 Qd4. 25 ... Bf6 26. Nxf6+
gxf6 27. Rd6! Ne6 Or 27 ... Kg7 28 Qd4 Ne6 29 Rfd8

(or 29 ... Rfe8 30 Qh7+ Kf8 31 Rd7) 30 Rxe6! fxe6 31 Qxb7+, and White wins. RF (29 ... f5, although obviously better, only leads to a lost ending. AW) **28. Rxe6! fxe6 29. Qxe6+ Kh8 30. Qh3 Kg7** If 30 ... h5 then either 31 Bg6 (Fine) or 31 Bf5 (Reinfeld) will win. **31. Qg4+ Kh8 32. Qg6 1–0** Fine 1958, 48–50; Reinfeld 1936, 169–70.

Łódź, September 3–13, 1935

"Poland, disappointed in failing to finish first at Warsaw, had some compensation when the tournament at Łódź, September 3–13, ended in the success of her gallant team captain, Dr. Savielly Tartakower. The victory was the more satisfying in that Reuben Fine, No. 1 on the champion U.S. team, finished in a tie for second place. The latter, too, had reason to be elated, for he played nine games without losing one." (*ACB* 1935) Fine won three of his five games with black but could not make any headway with the white pieces. Meanwhile Tartakower showed his superior class in combinational and endgame play, shrugging off his fourth round loss to Winter he amassed sufficient points to head Fine by half a point going into their last round encounter. In *Chess*, 14 October, 1935, Winter reported "The tournament took place at the headquarters of the Łódź Chess Club (Klub Szachowy), the best club in Poland, and was conducted under ideal conditions. Soft carpets eliminated the noise of spectators' footsteps which had been a terrible nuisance in Warsaw, and even a sham air-raid, in which all electric light was cut off, did not seriously incommode the players." The organizers had tried to tempt Alekhine, Flohr and Vidmar, Eliskases, Lilenthal, Pirc and Ståhlberg to play, but they all declined the invitation, apparently the prizes were too low.

		1	2	3	4	5	6	7	8	9	10	
1	Tartakower	*	½	1	½	1	0	1	1	½	1	6½
2	Fine	½	*	½	½	½	1	1	½	½	1	6
3	Kolski	0	½	*	1	1	½	1	½	1	½	6
4	Opočenský	½	½	0	*	1	1	½	½	1	½	5½
5	Steiner	0	½	0	0	*	½	1	1	1	1	5
6	Winter	1	0	½	0	½	*	1	½	½	1	5
7	Frydman	0	0	0	½	0	0	*	1	1	1	3½
8	Appel	0	½	½	½	0	½	0	*	½	½	3
9	Regedziñski	½	½	0	0	0	½	0	½	*	1	3
10	Mikenas	0	0	½	½	0	0	0	½	0	*	1½

(235) REGEDZIÑSKI, T–FINE

Łódź (1), 1935 (3 Sept.)
Nimzowitsch-Indian Defence, Classical Variation [E37]

1. d4 Nf6 2. c4 e6 3. Nc3 Bb4 4. Qc2 d5 5. a3 Bxc3+ 6. Qxc3 Ne4 7. Qc2 Nc6 8. Nf3 e5 9. e3 Bf5 10. Bd3 exd4 11. exd4 dxc4 12. Qxc4 0–0 13. 0–0 Nd6 14. Qc3 Ne7 15. Re1 Nd5 16. Qc2 Bxd3 17. Qxd3 Qd7 18. Bd2 Rfe8 19. Re5 c6 20. Rae1 f6 21. Rxe8+ Rxe8 22. Rxe8+ Qxe8 23. h3 Qe6 24. a4 g5 25. Kf1 Kg7 26. b3 Ne4 27. Be3 a5 28. Bd2 b6 29. Kg1 h6 30. Qe2 Qf5

31. Qc4 Qd7 32. Qe2 Nd6 33. Qd3 Nf5 34. Qe4 Nfe7 35. Ne1 Qd6 36. Nc2 f5 37. Qe2 Qf6 38. Qc4 f4 39. Qd3 Qf5 40. Qxf5 Nxf5 41. Kf1 Kf7 42. Ke2 Ke6 43. Kd3 Nde7 44. b4 axb4 45. Bxb4 Ng6 46. a5 ½–½ Lahde 2001.

(236) FINE–APPEL, I

Łódź (2), 1935 (4 Sept.)
King's Indian Defence, Sämisch Variation [E85]

1. d4 Nf6 2. c4 g6 3. f3 Bg7 4. e4 d6 5. Nc3 e5 6. Nge2 Nc6 7. d5 Ne7 8. Be3 0–0 9. Qd2 Ne8 Now Black is threatening to get a highly satisfactory game with ... f7-f5. DS **10. 0–0–0** White should play g4 in order to restrain Black from advancing (as Holmov did against Tsvetkov at Moscow 1947, going on to win in 50 moves. AW). However, such as sharp position is not to Fine's taste. DS **10 ... f5** (This was the earliest occurrence of this position in my databases.) **11. exf5** (Modern players prefer to avoid making this exchange—11 Kb1, 11 h3, 11 c5 being more common. AW) **11 ... Nxf5 12. Bg5 Qxg5 13. Qxg5 Bh6 14. Qxh6 Nxh6** In the mistaken belief that he stands better in the ending, Fine now tries to win, spurning two drawing opportunities and undertaking a risky combination which brings him to the brink of defeat. DS **15. Ng3 b6 16. Nge4 Nf5 17. Bd3 Nh4 18. Rd2 Bd7 19. b4 a5 20. a3 axb4 21. axb4 Nf6 22. Kb2 Nxe4 23. fxe4 g5 24. Kb3 Ng6 25. Rc1 Nf4 26. Bf1 Nh5 27. Rdc2** White continues to prepare for the breakthrough c4-c5, but it never happens. DS **27 ... Nf6 28. Bd3 Kg7 29. Rf1 h6 30. Rcf2** White dreams up a combination, unfortunately it is entirely incorrect. DS **30 ... Ng4 31. Rxf8 Rxf8 32. Ra1** 32 Rxf8 was correct. DS **32 ... Nxh2 33. Ra7 Rf7** It would be a mistake to try to protect the pawn by 33 ... Rc8 because of 34 c5 bxc5 35 Ba6. DS **34. Rxc7** Allowing Black to win the exchange by 34 ... Ba4+. However, this would reveal the point of White's combination: after 35 Kxa4 Rxc7 36 Kb5 White's pair of connected passed pawns gives him winning chances. DS **34 ... h5!** Black avoids the trap and advantageously activates his kingside. DS **35. b5 h4 36. Rb7 g4 37. Ne2** (If 37 Rxb6 h3! 38 gxh3 (or 38 Rxd6 hxg2 39 Ne2 Nf3 40 Kb4 Nd4! 41 Ng1 Rf1 42 Rxd7+ Kf6 43 Rd6+ Kg5! 44 b6 Rxg1 45 b7 Rb1+ 46 Bxb1 g1Q 47 Rb6 Nc6+) gxh3 39 Rxd6 Nf3 40 Ne2 Ne1 41 Kc3 Bg4 42 Ng3 Nxd3 43 Kxd3 Rf3+ wins. AW) **37 ... Nf1 38. Ng1 Ne3 39. Rxb6 Nxg2 40. Rxd6**

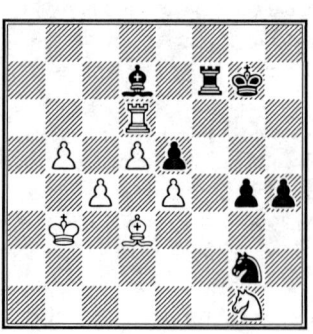

Position after White's 40th move

40 ... Nf4 The two black pawns seem to decide the issue, but White finds something. RF (*De Schaakwereld* indicates that 40 ... h3 would have won.) **41. Bf1** The sealed move. Everyone had already given up my game as lost. RF **41 ... h3** An endgame problem. On 41 ... g6 42 Rxd7! Rxd7 43 c5, the White pawns will win. Now there is no time for this sacrifice. RF **42. Nxh3** Forced, as is White's following move. DS **42 ... gxh3** If 42 ... Nxh3 again 43 Rxd7! Rxd7 44 c5 Kf6, and now it is Black who can just manage to draw by giving back his rook. Black did not foresee what happens; but he can hardly be blamed for thinking that he must win with two pieces ahead. RF **43. Bxh3 Nxh3** Reaching an ending rarely seen in practice. With three connected passed pawns for two minor pieces White has definite drawing chances. DS **44. b6 Bc8 45. Rc6 Bg4!** On the alternative 45 ... Bb7 46 Re6 wins the e-pawn, and White's four pawns will then at least draw as at least one piece must be given back to stop them. RF **46. Kb4 Nf2 47. Kb5 Nxe4 48. Ka6 Be2 49. b7 Rxb7 50. Kxb7 Bxc4!** Now 51 Rxc4 fails to 51 ... Nd6+ and 51 d6 loses to 51 ... Bd5 52 d7 Nc5+ followed by ... Nxd7. DS **51. Rc7+ Kg6 52. Kc6 Nf6** Black's last is seemingly sufficient in view of 53 d6 Be6 (54 Re7 Kf5 55 Kc5 Bd7. DS) and the advance of Black's pawn. RF **53. Re7!** The saving move: White gives up his own pawn but can hold back the enemy pawn. RF **53 ... Kf5** Still hoping for 54 d6 Be6. RF **54. Kd6! e4 55. Kc5! Bxd5 56. Kd4! Kf4 57. Re5** The mobility of White's rook keeps the pawn from advancing. RF **57 ... Bb3** The bishop is trying to make for f3. DS **58. Rb5! Bc2** If 58 ... Be6 59 Rb6 Kf5 60 Rb1. RF **59. Rb2!** An important zwischenzug. White will pin the Nf6 on f7 or f8 when ... Bf3 is played; the king is forced to go back and Black cannot make any progress. On the immediate 59 Rb7 Black has the tactical finesse 59 ... e3! 60 Rf7 e2 61 Rf1 Bf5 and wins. DS **59 ... Bd1** Or 59 ... Bd3 60 Rf2+ (RF) or on 59 ... Bd3, 60 Rd2, with the threat of Rxd3, can follow (DS). **60. Rb7!** 60 Rb1 Bf3 61 Rf1 Ng4 loses. Now, if 60 ... e3 61 Rf7. RF **60 ... Bh5 61. Re7! Bg6** There is no good alternative. RF **62. Re6! Kg5** The try, 62 ... Kf5 63 Re5+ is no better. RF **63. Ke5 Ng4+ 64. Kd4 Nf2** Black allows a quick draw, but 64 ... Nf6 65 Ke5 accomplishes nothing. RF **65. Rxg6+!** If 65 ... Kxg6 66 Ke3 is a draw. RF; With so little material remaining the quality of Black's bishop was a significant factor. As long as the pawn was on e5, the bishop was "good," after ... e5-e4 it became "bad" introducing a weakness of the dark squares (actually but one square: d4) and this allowed White the chance to activate his king and save this difficult ending. DS ½–½ Based on notes from *De Shaakwereld* (with additional translation by Bernard de Bruycker), 1/22, 8–9; Fine 1941, 455; Fine 1958, 50–2.

(237) OPOČENSKÝ, K—FINE

Łódź (3), 1935 (5 Sept.)
English Opening, Flohr-Mikenas Variation [A18]

1. c4 Nf6 2. Nc3 e6 3. e4 d5 4. e5 d4 5. exf6 dxc3 6. bxc3 Qxf6 7. d4 b6 8. Nf3 Bb7 9. Be2 h6

10. Ne5 Bd6 11. Qa4+ Kf8 12. Bf3 Bxf3 13. Nxf3 Ke7 14. 0–0 Nd7 15. Re1 Rhd8 16. Nd2 Kf8 17. Re3 Qg6 18. Ba3 Nf6 19. Rg3 Qf5 20. Rf3 Qg5 21. Nf1 c5 22. Rd1 Kg8 23. Qc2 Rac8 24. Bc1 Qh4 25. Qe2 Qe4 26. Re3 Qg6 27. d5 exd5 28. cxd5 c4 29. Rf3 Qh5 30. Re3 Qxe2 31. Rxe2 Bc5 32. Red2 Rd7 33. Ne3 Bxe3 34. fxe3 Ne4 35. Rc2 Nf6 36. d6 Ne4 37. Rd4 f5 38. Ba3 h5 39. g3 Kf7 40. Kg2 Ke6 41. Kf3 Nxd6 42. Rcd2 Rcd8 43. Bxd6 Rxd6 44. Rb2 Rc8 45. Rb5 g6 46. h4 Rc7 47. a4 Rdc6 48. Rbd5 a6 49. Rd8 Rb7 50. Rg8 Kf6 51. e4 fxe4+ 52. Rxe4 b5 53. Rf4+ Ke5 54. Re8+ Kd5 55. a5 Kc5 56. Re5+ Kd6 57. Ke4 Rd7 58. Rd5+ Kc7 59. Rxd7+ Kxd7 60. Kd5 Rd6+ 61. Kc5 Rc6+ 62. Kd5 Rd6+ 63. Kc5 Rd3 64. Kb4 Kc6 65. Rf8 ½–½ Lahde 2001.

(238) FRYDMAN, P—FINE

Łódź (4), 1935 (6 Sept.)
Sicilian Defence [B84]

1. e4 c5 2. Nf3 e6 3. Nc3 d6 4. d4 cxd4 5. Nxd4 Nf6 6. Be3 a6 7. Be2 Qc7 8. a4 b6 9. 0–0 Bb7 10. f3 Be7 11. Qe1 0–0 12. g4 Nc6 13. g5 Nd7 14. f4 Nxd4 15. Bxd4 e5 16. Be3 exf4 17. Bxf4 Bxg5 18. Rd1 Bxf4 19. Rxf4 Nc5 20. Qf2 Rfd8 21. Bf1 Qc5 22. Nd5 Bxd5 23. Rxd5 Qxf2+ 24. Rxf2 Kf8 25. Kg2 Ke7 26. Rfd2 a5 27. Kf2 Rac8 28. Ke3 Rc5 29. Be2 g6 30. c3 Ke6 31. Kf4 h6 32. Bg4+ Nxg4 33. Kxg4 f5+ 34. Kf3 fxe4+ 35. Kxe4 Rxd5 36. Rxd5 Rf8 37. Rd2 g5 38. b3 Rf4+ 39. Kd3 Rh4 40. Rf2 Ke5 41. Rb2 Kd5 42. Re2 Rh3+ 43. Kd2 g4 44. Rg2 h5 45. Re2 Rf3 46. Kc2 h4 0–1 Lahde 2001.

(239) FINE—STEINER, L

Łódź (5), 1935 (7 Sept.)
Nimzowitsch-Indian Defence, Sämisch Variation [E24]

1. d4 Nf6 2. c4 e6 3. Nc3 Bb4 4. a3 Bxc3+ 5. bxc3 c5 6. f3 d5 7. e3 0–0 8. Bd3 Qc7! 9. cxd5 cxd4! 10. Qc2 dxe3 11. dxe6 Bxe6 12. Bxe3 Bc4! 13. Ne2 Bxd3 14. Qxd3 Nc6 15. 0–0 Rad8 16. Qc4 Rfe8 17. Bf2 Qe7 18. Ng3 Ne5 19. Qh4 Qc7 20. Bd4 Ng6 21. Qg5 h6 22. Qc5 Qxc5 23. Bxc5 b6 24. Bd4 Nd5 25. a4 Ne3 26. Rf2 Nc4 27. Nh5 f6 28. f4 Kf7 29. f5 Nge5 30. Nf4 Rd6 31. h3 Nc6 32. Ne6 Nd8 33. Nxd8+ Rdxd8 34. Kf1 Rd5 35. g4 Re4 36. Re2 Rxe2 37. Kxe2 Ra5 38. Kd3 Nb2+ 39. Kc2 Nxa4 40. Ra3 Kg8 41. Kb3 Nc5+ 42. Bxc5 Rxc5 43. Rxa7 b5 44. Rb7 h5 45. Kb4 Rc4+ 46. Kb3 Rc5 ½–½ Lahde 2001.

(240) MIKENAS, V—FINE

Łódź (6), 1935 (8 Sept.)
Queen's Gambit Declined, Exchange Variation [D36]

1. d4 Nf6 2. c4 e6 3. Nc3 d5 4. cxd5 exd5 5. Bg5
Be7 6. e3 0–0 7. Qc2 c6 8. Bd3 Nbd7 9. Nf3 Re8
10. h3 Nf8 11. 0–0–0 b6 12. g4 Bb7 13. Kb1 Ne4
14. Bxe7 Nxc3+ 15. Qxc3 Qxe7 16. Rhg1 c5
17. dxc5 bxc5 18. Bc2 Nd7 19. g5 Rab8 20. h4
Nb6 21. h5 g6 22. h6 d4 23. exd4 Nd5 24. Qd2
Qe2 25. Ne5 Qxd2 26. Rxd2 cxd4 27. Ng4 f5
28. gxf6 Bc8 29. Bb3 Bf5+ 30. Kc1 Rxb3 31. axb3
Nf4 32. Kd1 d3 33. Ne3 Be4 34. Ke1 Kf7 35. Rg4
Ng2+ 36. Kf1 Nxe3+ 37. fxe3 Kxf6 38. Rf2+ Ke5
39. Ke1 Rc8 40. Kd1 Bd5 41. Rff4 Rc2 42. Rg5+
Ke6 43. Rd4 Bf3+ 44. Ke1 Re2+ 45. Kf1 d2
46. Ra5 Rh2 47. Rxa7 d1Q+ 48. Rxd1 Bxd1
49. Rxh7 Bxb3 50. Kg1 Rh5 51. e4 Bc2 52. Rh8
Bxe4 53. b4 Kf7 54. Kf2 g5 55. b5 Kg6 56. Re8
Bh1 57. Re6+ Kf5 58. Rd6 Ke5 59. Ra6 Bd5
60. Kg3 Be6 61. Ra5 Rh3+ 62. Kg2 Rxh6 63. b6+
Bd5+ 64. Kg3 Rxb6 65. Kg4 Rg6 66. Rb5 Rg8
67. Ra5 Kd6 68. Ra6+ Bc6 0–1 Lahde 2001.

(241) FINE—KOLSKI, J

Łódź (7), 1935 (9 Sept.)
Queen's Gambit Declined, Exchange Variation [D36]

1. d4 Nf6 2. c4 e6 3. Nc3 d5 4. Bg5 Nbd7 5. cxd5
exd5 6. e3 Be7 7. Bd3 c6 8. Qc2 0–0 9. Nge2 Re8
10. h3 Nf8 11. 0–0–0 b5 12. Kb1 a5 13. g4 a4
14. Ng3 Qa5 15. Nce2 b4! 16. Qd2 Ne4! 17. Nxe4
dxe4 18. Bxe7 Rxe7 19. Bc4 Nd7 20. Rc1 Nb6
21. Ng3 Nxc4 22. Rxc4 Be6! 23. Rc5 Qb6
24. Rhc1 Bd5 25. Nh5 Rd7 26. Nf4 Rdd8 27. Qe2
g6 28. g5 Qb8 29. h4 Qd6 30. Qg4 Ra7 31. h5
Qd7 32. Nxd5 cxd5 33. Rc8! gxh5!! 34. Rxd8+
Qxd8 35. Qf5! Rc7 36. Rh1 b3 37. axb3 axb3
38. Rxh5 Rc1+! 39. Kxc1 Qc7+ 40. Kd2 Qc2+
41. Ke1 Qb1+ 42. Ke2 Qd3+ ½–½ Lahde 2001.

(242) WINTER, W—FINE

Łódź (8), 1935 (10 Sept.)
Nimzowitsch-Indian Defence, Three Knights Variation [E21]

1. d4 Nf6 2. c4 e6 3. Nc3 Bb4 4. Nf3 Bxc3+
5. bxc3 b6 6. Bg5 Bb7 7. Nd2 d6 8. f3 e5 9. e4
Nc6 10. Nb3 h6 11. Be3 0–0 12. Bd3 Qe7 13. 0–0
Nd8 14. Qd2 Ne6 15. d5 Nc5 16. Nxc5 bxc5
17. Rab1 Rfb8 18. Rb3 Nd7 19. f4 exf4 20. Bxf4
Bc8 21. Rf3 Ne5 22. Rg3 Kh7 23. Qe2 Qf6
24. Bc1 Kg8 25. Rb2 Rxb2 26. Qxb2 Qh4 27. Qb5
c6 28. dxc6 Nxd3 29. Bd2 Ne5 30. c7 Kh7
31. Qe8 Qxe4 32. Qf8 Ng4 0–1 Lahde 2001.

(243) FINE—TARTAKOWER, S

Łódź (9), 1935 (11 Sept.)
Queen's Gambit Declined, Lasker Variation [D55]

1. d4 d5 2. c4 e6 3. Nc3 Nf6 4. Bg5 Be7 5. e3
0–0 6. Nf3 Ne4 7. Bxe7 Qxe7 8. Qc2 Nxc3
9. Qxc3 c6 10. Bd3 dxc4 11. Bxc4 b6 12. 0–0 Bb7
13. Ne5 c5 14. dxc5 Qxc5 15. Rac1 Nd7 16. Nxd7
Qc6 17. Nf6+ gxf6 18. f3 b5 19. Be2 Qxc3
20. Rxc3 a6 21. Rc7 Bd5 22. b3 Rfc8 23. Rfc1
Rxc7 24. Rxc7 e5! 25. Kf2 Be6 26. Ke1 Rc8
27. Rxc8+ Bxc8 28. Kd2 Bd7 29. Kd3 f5 ½–½
Lahde 2001.

The Grandmaster Title, 1935–1936

An invitation to participate in the annual Christmas tournament at Hastings was Fine's prize for his success over the preceding year. At the time, this was an excellent proving ground, recent winners included Tartakower, Capablanca, Euwe, Flohr and Lajos Steiner. Fine's victory in this event was considered proof that he had joined the ranks of the strongest international masters, and therefore paved the way for further invitations to European events, an essential factor in making a success as a chess professional. Fine capitalized on his good fortune in saving a lost position against the man who had won for the three previous years, all of his other wins coming against the home contingent.

Hastings, December 28, 1935– January 6, 1936

"Following in the footsteps of Morphy, Pillsbury, Marshall, Capablanca, Kashdan and Reshevsky, who crossed the Atlantic Ocean in search of European chess honours and came back with first prizes, Reuben Fine of New York, No. 1 for the victorious United States team at Warsaw, journeyed to Hastings, England for the annual Christmas Congress at St. Leonard's Chess Club, held from December 27 to January 4, finished in first place after surviving nine rounds of the international tournament undefeated, and came back crowned with the victor's laurels and with new responsibilities on his youthful shoulders. Fine drew three games with Dr. Tartakower, Koltanowski and Alexander, and defeated all the rest. The pivotal game really was with Flohr, and this happened to be scheduled for the opening day. It was a fine exhibition of wide-open chess, in which Flohr, the attacking party, overreached himself after missing his chance. The young American kept his head under strong pressure. After once gaining the lead, he never relinquished it." (ACB 1936, 2) Fine annotated all of his games for the *Bulletin* and included two in his collection of his own games. He recalled in his autobiography "In the winter of 1935–36 I received my first invitation to play in an important European tournament, at Hastings. Although it was a small one, with ten players, this annual event was considered one of the high-lights of world chess events." (Fine 1958) The *Glasgow Herald* made this comment: "Fine is a New Yorker of 21 years who hardly looks his age. His particular mannerism consists in walking to and fro across the floor of the hall behind the chess tables, while his opponent studies the game." "Like Capablanca, Fine takes his chess easily and lets his opponents do most of the worrying. If you know how, it's a good way to conserve your energies." (ACB 1936, 6)

		1	2	3	4	5	6	7	8	9	10	
1	Fine	*	1	½	½	½	1	1	1	1	1	7½
2	Flohr	0	*	½	1	1	1	1	½	1	½	6½
3	Tartakower	½	½	*	½	1	½	½	½	1	1	6
4	Koltanowski	½	0	½	*	1	½	½	1	1	½	5½
5	Alexander	½	0	0	0	*	0	1	1	½	1	4
6	Golombek	0	0	½	½	1	*	½	0	½	½	3½
7	Thomas	0	0	½	½	0	½	*	1	½	½	3½
8	Tylor	0	½	½	0	0	1	0	*	½	½	3
9	Michell	0	0	0	0	½	½	½	½	*	1	3
10	Winter	0	½	0	½	0	½	½	½	0	*	2½

(244) FLOHR, S—FINE

Hastings 1935/6 (1), 1935 (28 Dec.)
Queen's Gambit Declined [D61]

1. d4 e6 2. c4 Nf6 3. Nc3 d5 4. Bg5 Nbd7 5. e3 Be7 6. Nf3 0–0 7. Qc2 Flohr's favourite, which I was prepared for. RF **7 ... c6** This cramping move, necessary after 7 Rc1, is not so here. In the eighth match game Alekhine v. Capablanca, there occurred 7 ... c5 8 cxd5 cxd4 9 Nxd4 Nxd5 10 Bxe7 Qxe7 11 Ncxd5 exd5 12 Bd3 Qb4+ 13 Qd2 Ne5 14 Be2 Qxd2+ 15 Kxd2 Bd7 with equality. JHB **8. a3 Re8 9. Rd1 dxc4** Inadvisable. Instead 9 ... a6 and, if then 10 Bd3, dxc4 would have led to equalisation. ACB **10. Bxc4 Nd5 11. Bxe7 Qxe7 12. 0–0 Nxc3 13. Qxc3 c5** A little more preparation is needed for this move; 13 ... b6 and 14 ... Bb7 would be better. JHB **14. d5! exd5 15. Rxd5 b6** If 15 ... Nf6 16 Re5 Qf8 17 Ng5 winning; or 15 ... Nb6 16 Re5 Qf8 17 Ba2 and so on. If, however, Black had played 9 ... a6 he could have continued with 15 ... b5 16 Ba2 c4, with fair prospects. ACB **16. Rfd1** Black is in a bad way. On the natural 16 ... Nf6 17 Re5 is murderous, for if 17 ... Qc7 18 Rxe8+ Nxe8 19 Ng5 Nd6 20 Qd3 wins. RF **16 ... Rf8!** To avoid the alternative threats of 17 Bb5 or 17 Ng5. JHB **17. b4!** A timely advance which exerts strong control over the queenside. ACB **17 ... cxb4 18. axb4 Nf6 19. Re5 Qc7** Threatening ... Be6. RF **20. Ng5** White does not give his opponent any time. The text prepares 21 Bxf7+ Rxf7 22 Qxc7 Rxc7 23 Rd8+ and mate. RF **20 ... Bb7 21. Ne6!** Initiating what should have been a winning combination. JHB **21 ... Qc6** To take the knight would cost the queen. RF **22. f3 Ba6** He still cannot take the pawn because of 23 Rxe6; and it is necessary to prevent b4-b5. JHB **23. Rd4** If 23 Nxf8 Bxc4 24 Nd7

Nxd7 25 Rxd7 Qxd7 26 Qxc4, with a draw as the likely result. ACB **23 ... Rfc8**

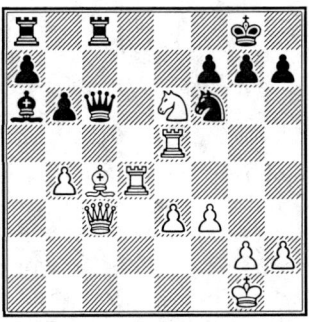

Position after Black's 23rd move

24. Nd8? Throwing away the win. But this is a very tricky position which has caused problems for analysts right up to the present day. In 1958 Fine wrote that his opponent "had considered only 24 Rg5, which fails to 24 ... Qxe6." In fact this line doesn't work out too badly for White after 25 Rd8+ Rxd8 26 Bxe6 Rd1+ 27 Kf2 Kh8 28 Bxf7. J. H. Blake in BCM however wrote that the players' post-mortem (with Alexander and Winter) produced the correct idea: 24 ... fxe6 when White should continue 25 Rxg7+ (perhaps a little better than the players' 25 Rdg4 Kh8+! 26 Rxg7 e5, and Black wins) Kxg7 26 Rg4+ Kf7 27 Rf4 Qxc4 28 Qxf6+ Ke8 29 Rxc4 Bxc4, though Black should still win after 30 Qh8+ Kd7 31 Qxh7+ Kc6! 32 Qe4+ Kb5. In 1958 Fine gave 24 Rg4 as the winning move. Now 24 ... Nxg4 loses to 25 Rg5 f6 26 Rxg7+ Kh8 27 Qd3!, as pointed out by Alexander, and 24 ... Qxc4 is refuted by 25 Rxc4 Rxc4 26 Qa3!. Fine therefore continues 24 ... Bxc4 25 Rxg7+ Kh8 26 Rh5 Qxe6 27 Rgh7+ Kg8 28 Rh8+ Kg7 29 R5h7+ Kg6 30 Qc2 Ne4 31 Rh6+ Kg7 32 R8h7+ (The Belgian master Bernard de Bruycker points out that this is one check too far: 32 Rxe6 Bxe6 33 Rxc8 Rxc8 34 Qxe4 wins more simply.) Kg8 33 Rxe6, and wins. But here de Bruycker suggests 33 ... Bxd3 and the struggle will continue, though probably in White's favour. Yet another possibility, suggested by IM Michael Jadoul, is 24 ... fxe6 25 Rxe6 Qxc4 (alternatively 25 ... Kh8! 26 Rxc6 Rxc6 27 Rd4 b5 28 Qd3 bxc4 29 Rd8+ Rxd8 30 Qxd8 Ng8 31 Qe8 Bb5. de Bruycker) 26 Rxc4 Rxc4 when Black has nothing to fear. I believe White should prefer 25 Reg5! Kh8 26 Rxg7 e5 (forced) 27 Qxe5 Re8 28 Rxh7+! Kxh7 29 Qf5+ Kh8 30 Rg6 Re7! 31 Rh6+ Rh7 32 Qxh7+ Nxh7 33 Rxc6 Bxc4 34 Rxc4 a5 35 bxa5 bxa5 36 Ra4 and a draw should result. All of which shows that, whilst White has a dangerous attack, Black has considerable defensive resources. In 1936, however, Fine had analyzed, after 24 Rg4, 24 ... Kh8 as being an adequate defence. He considered that after 25 Rxg7 Qxc4! threatening mate, or 25 Nxg7 Bxc4 the attack would fail. White can play more strongly though, for example 25 b5! Bxb5 26 Rxg7 Qxc4 27 Qxc4 Bxc4 28 Rxf7 Bxe6 29 Rxe6 Rc1+ 30 Kf2 Rc2 31 Kg3 Nd5 32 Rd7 Rg8+ 33 Kh3 Rd2 34 Red6 Rgxg2 35 Rxd5 Rxh2+ 36 Kg4 Rxd5 37 Rxd5 Rg2+ 38 Kf4, with the better of a tricky rook ending for Black. So how about 25 Rc5! bxc5 26 Rxg7 Bxc4 27 Rxf7 Qxe6 28 Rxf6 Kg8 29 Rxe6 Bxe6, when perpetual check looks a distinct possibility for

White. It seems that 24 Rg4 does not win after all. However, Blake tells us that during the post-mortem Winter had found the finesse 24 b5!, with the idea 24 ... B×b5 25 N×g7! K×g7 26 Rg4+, or 25 ... B×c4 26 Nf5. In this second line however there is a saving resource: 26 ... Qa4 27 Re8+! R×e8 28 Rg4+ Kf8 29 Q×f6 Qd1+ 30 Kf2 Qc2+ 31 Kg3 Q×f5! (A point which was missed by the Soviets Blumenfeld, in his contemporary notes, and Kotov, who published supposedly independent, but identical, analysis many years later) 32 Q×f5 Be6 and Black should at least draw, for example, 33 Q×h7 B×g4. So, in place of Nf5, Fine proposed 26 Nh5 Bd3! (rejecting 26 ... Bb5 because of 27 N×f6+ Q×f6 28 Rg4+, but here 28 ... Qg6 is probably better than Fine's 28 ... Kf8) 27 Rd8+ R×d8 28 Q×c6 N×h5 29 R×h5 Bg6 (but 29 ... Rac8 might be better. AW) 30 Rg5, and White should eventually win, though Black's drawing chances should not be underestimated (RF). Therefore for a long time it seemed that White simply did not have a knockout blow in what de Bruycker describes as a "dynamite position". However, as recently as 2001 David Peel pointed out, in Ken Whyld's *BCM* column *Quotes and Queries*, that by 24 N×g7!! Black has nothing better than 24 ... K×g7 25 b5 B×b5 26 R×b5, or 26 Rg4+ transposing to the better line. It seems that after 26 Rg4+ Kh8 27 R×b5 Black might save himself by 27 ... Rd8! (instead of 27 ... Rg8, as given by previous analysts). Therefore White is obliged to play the other line: 26 R×b5 Rd8 27 Rg5+ Kh8 28 Rf5 R×d4 29 Q×d4 Kg7 30 Rg5+ Kf8 31 Bb5 (a line found with the aid of Fritz, and presumably that to which Mr. Peel alludes, but not in any of the sources I have consulted), and wins. **24 ... Qc7 25. Rg4** "Too late" says Fine. Note that the alternative, 25 Rg5 can be met by 25 ... B×c4, winning. Black has the superior position with 25 B×f7 Q×f7 26 Q×c8 R×c8 27 N×f7 K×f7. Nevertheless, this was the best chance for White. Now the white knight is astray in Black's camp. LS **25 ... Q×d8 26. Reg5 Qd1+ 27. Kf2 N×g4+ 28. R×g4 g6** White's attack has fizzled out. LS **29. B×f7+ K×f7 30. Rf4+ Kg8 31. Qf6 Qd7** White resigned. **0−1** Fine 1958, 53−6; Fine in *ACB* 1936, 3−4; J. H. Blake in *BCM* 1936, 91−2; David Peel in *BCM* 2001, 128; Leonid Shamkovich in *Chess Life*, August 1996, 56−7 quoted in Fiala 1999, QCH3, 511−2

(245) TYLOR, T−FINE

Hastings 1935/6 (2), 1935 (29 Dec.)
Sicilian Defence [B50]

1. e4 c5 2. Nf3 d6 3. Nc3 3 d4 is much stronger. RF **3 ... e5 4. Bc4 Nc6 5. d3 Bg4 6. h3 Be6** But not 6 ... Bh5 7 N×e5! and wins. RF **7. Nd5 Be7 8. 0−0 Nf6 9. Ng5 B×d5 10. exd5 Nb8** If 10 ... N×d5 11 B×d5 (or 11 N×f7. WK) B×g5 12 Qh5!. AW **11. Bb5+ Nbd7 12. Ne6 fxe6 13. dxe6 0−0 14. exd7 a6 15. Ba4 b5 16. Bb3 d5 17. c3 Q×d7 18. f4 Bd6 19. f×e5 B×e5 20. Be3** Tylor trusts in the strength of the bishop pair! He also displays a willingness to enter the struggle with his opponent, simply 20 Bf4 would have led to an even position. WK **20 ... c4 21. d×c4 b×c4 22. Bc2 Rab8 23. Rb1 Qd6 24. Bd4 Rfe8 25. b4 B×d4+ 26. Q×d4 Re2 27. Rf2 Rbe8**

28. Rbf1 Qg3 29. Bd1 R×f2 30. R×f2 Re1+ 31. Rf1 Re4 31 ... Qe3+ 32 Q×e3 R×e3 and the c-pawn cannot be defended. Schroeder **32. Qd2 Qe3+ 33. Rf2 Qe1+ 34. Kh2** 34 Q×e1 R×e1+ 35 Rf1 R×f1 36 K×f1 Ne4 would be immediately disastrous for White. RF **34 ... Re3 35. Q×e1 R×e1 36. Bf3 Rc1 37. Rd2 R×c3 38. B×d5+ Kf8 39. a4** A mistake. 39 Bb7 would have drawn. RF **39 ... Rd3 40. R×d3 c×d3 41. Bb3** 41 Bf3 would have made it much more difficult, but after 41 ... d2 42 b5! a×b5 43 a5! b4 44 a6 Nd5 45 a7 Nc7 46 Bd1 Ke7 47 Kg3 Kd6 48 Kf2 Kc5 49 Ke3 Kb6 50 K×d2 K×a7 51 Kd3 Kb6, and although it is not easy, Black should eventually win. RF **41 ... Ne4 42. Kg1 Ke7 43. b5 a5** White resigned. **0−1** *ACB* 1936, 24; Kubel, 3

(246) FINE−MICHELL, R

Hastings 1935/6 (3), 1935 (30 Dec.)
Nimzowitsch-Indian Defence, Spielmann Variation [E23]

1. d4 Nf6 2. c4 e6 3. Nc3 Bb4 4. Qb3 In recent years this continuation has gone out of favour because of the strength of the Zurich Variation 4 ... Nc6 (Introduced by Milner-Barry in 1928−9, and therefore named for him in England, but popularized at Zurich 1934. AW). RF **4 ... c5** Then the usual line. RF **5. d×c5 Nc6** 5 ... Na6 6 a3 B×c5 7 Nf3 b6 8 Bg5 9 e3 Be7 with equality, Eliskases−Botvinnik, Moscow 1936. **6. Nf3 Ne4 7. Bd2 N×d2** On the alternative 7 ... N×c5 8 Qc2 f5, the eventual g2-g4 gives White a strong attack. RF **8. N×d2 B×c5 9. e3 0−0 10. 0−0−0** Threatening to occupy the squares e4 and d6. RF (10 Be2 b6 11 Rd1 f5 12 Nf3 Qf6 with equality (NCO), Christiansen−Speelman, Munich 1992.) **10 ... f5** Black's pawn formation is weakened, and White consequently already has formulated his major plan: to exploit it. Just how this will be done depends on the continuation. RF **11. Be2 Qe7** 11 ... b6 was played in the game Spielmann−Johner, Carlsbad 1929. WK **12. Nf3 a6** Intending an eventual attack by b7-b5; but the move only weakens the queenside. 12 ... d6 was preferable. If instead 12 ... f4 13 Ne4 f×e3 14 f×e3 and Black remains cramped. The text, however, sets up a weakness at b6 which White will soon profit from. RF **13. Kb1 d6 14. Na4 Ba7?** It is only after this move that Black's disadvantage becomes serious. 15 ... Qc7 was called for. RF **15. Nb6** with advantage to White, MCO 186. **15 ... Rb8** To give up the king's bishop would further weaken the d-pawn. **16. Rd2 Qc7** On 16 ... Na5 17 Qb4 follows, for if then 17 ... Nc6 18 N×c8! RF **17. N×c8 Rb×c8 18. Rhd1 Rfd8**

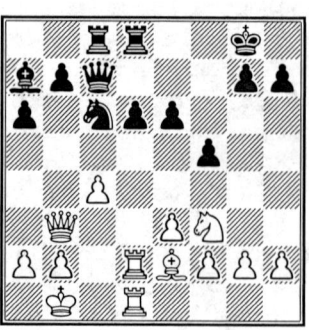

Position after Black's 18th move

The first objective has been reached: to tie down the black pawns. Surprisingly, as will be seen, the next step is to break through—on the kingside! RF **19. a3 Qe7 20. g3** Now that Black's pieces are tied down to the defence of his d-pawn, White can safely proceed to expose the position of the black king. The first step is to play Be2-f1-h3, followed by the eventual g3-g4, opening the g-file or attacking the e-pawn. RF **20 ... Rd7 21. Bf1 Rf8** To hold the white bishop to the defence of the c-pawn. RF **22. Ka2 h6 23. Qa4 Rfd8 24. Bh3!** Preparing the thrust. 24 ... h5 would be too weakening, since White can break through with e3-e4 at his leisure. RF **24 ... Kh7 25. g4 g6** 25 ... fxg4 is no better. RF **26. gxf5 gxf5** On the alternative 26 ... exf4 the square d5 is too weak, not to mention the isolated pawn.

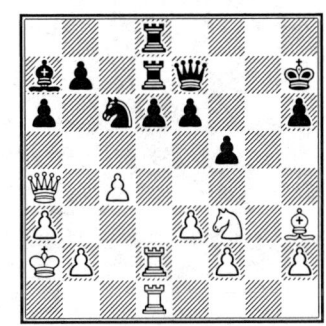

Position after Black's 26th move

White has secured his second objective—a further weakening of the Black position to guard the centre pawn. RF **27. e4!!** Much more elegant than 27 Qc2 first. RF **27 ... f4** The pawn is poison: if 27 ... fxe4 28 Qc2 d5 29 cxd5 and the e-pawn cannot recapture because it exposes the rook. RF Nevertheless, this may have been Black's best chance since now he loses to a rapid attack. AW **28. e5!!** Direct and to the point, Black's king must be exposed. RF **28 ... dxe5 29. Qc2+ Kh8 30. Rxd7 Rxd7 31. Nh4!** **Qf7** Not 31 ... Nd4 32 Ng6+ Kg7 33 Nxe7 Nxc2 34 Rxd7. AW **32. Ng6+ Kg7 33. Rg1 Kf6 34. Nh8 Nd4** This loses, as do the two plausible alternatives, 34 ... Qh7 and 34 ... Qh5. If 34 ... Qh7 35 Rg6+ Ke7 36 Bxe6 Nd4 (or 36 ... Qxh8 37 Bxd7 Kxd7 38 Qf5+) 37 Qe4 Nxe6 38 Qxe5; while if 34 ... Qh5 35 Rg6+ Ke7 36 Bg4 Qxh2 37 Rxe6+ Kd8 38 Qf5, with a winning game in both cases. RF **35. Rg6+ Ke7 36. Qe4 Qe8 37. Qxe5** Black's position now falls apart. RF **37 ... Kd8 38. Rxh6 Bb8? 39. Qxb8+** Black resigned. **1−0** Fine 1958, 57−60; ACB 1936, 25.

(247) KOLTANOWSKI, G—FINE

Hastings 1935/6 (4), 1936 (1 Jan.)
Colle System [D05]

1. d4 Nf6 2. Nf3 e6 3. e3 c5 4. Bd3 Nc6 5. c3 d5 6. Nbd2 Bd6 7. 0-0 0-0 8. Qe2 e5 9. dxc5 Bxc5 10. e4 Bg4 11. exd5 Qxd5 12. Bc4 12 Ne4 is much stronger. RF **12 ... Qd7 13. h3 Bh5 14. Ne4 Nxe4 15. Qxe4 Qc7 16. Nh4** The only move, for 16 ... Bg6 had to be prevented at all costs. RF **16 ... Ne7 17. Bg5 Kh8 18. Bxe7 Bxe7 19. Bd3 g6 20. Nf3 Bd6 21. Qc4**

Well played. White forces an ending of opposite colours. RF **21 ... Qxc4 22. Bxc4 Bxf3 23. gxf3 Rac8 24. Bd5 b6 25. Rad1 Be7 26. Rfe1 Bf6 27. Bb3 Rc7 28. Rd3 Kg7 29. Red1 Re8 30. Rd7 Re7 31. Ba4 Bg5 32. Rxe7 Rxe7 33. Rd7 Rxd7 34. Bxd7 Kf6** 34 ... Bc8, in order to prevent c3-c4 and b2-b4, was probably stronger, although it should not win against best play. RF **35. c4 Bc1 36. b4 Ba3 37. b5 Ke7 38. Bc6 Kd6 39. Bd5 f6 40. Bg8 h6 41. Bf7 g5 42. Kg2 Kc5 43. Kg3 Kd4 44. Kg4 Kd3 45. Kf5 Ke2 46. Kxf6 Bb2** If 46 ... Kxf3 47 Kxe5 Kxf2 48 Kd5 and White, after giving up his bishop for Black's eventual passed g-pawn, will have all the winning chances with his pawns, on the queenside. RF **47. Bh5** After this accurate move, Black no longer has any winning chances. RF **47 ... Kd3 48. Kf5 Kxc4 49. Be8 Kd3 50. Bd7 Ke2 51. Ke4 Kxf2 52. Be6** Draw agreed. ½−½ ACB 1936, 24−5.

(248) FINE—THOMAS, G

Hastings 1935/6 (5), 1936 (2 Jan.)
Queen's Gambit Declined [D64]

1. d4 d5 2. c4 e6 3. Nc3 Nf6 4. Bg5 Be7 5. e3 Nbd7 6. Nf3 0-0 7. Rc1 c6 8. Qc2 Nh5 Unusual but nevertheless playable. RF **9. Bxe7 Qxe7 10. Bd3 Nhf6 11. 0-0 dxc4 12. Bxc4 e5 13. e4 exd4 14. Nxd4 Nb6 15. Be2 Rd8 16. Rfd1 Bg4 17. h3 Bxe2 18. Qxe2 Qe5 19. Nf3 Qe7 20. g3** Preparing e4-e5, which at present would be inferior because of the continuation 20 e5 Nfd5 21 Ne4 Nf4. RF **20 ... Rxd1+ 21. Rxd1 Rd8 22. Rxd8+ Qxd8 23. e5 Nfd5 24. Ne4 Nc8 25. Nd4 Qd7** Kubel suggested 25 ... Nf4, which he believed would lead to an equal game. It is certainly an interesting idea, the continuation might be: 26 Qg4 Ng6 27 e6 Nd6 28 Nf5 Nxe4 29 Nxe4 Ne7 30 exf7+ Kxf7 31 Nxe7 Qxe7 32 Qxh7. Queen endings are notoriously difficult. Fine would at least have had the opportunity to torture the distinguished gentleman for some time. AW **26. Qh5 h6** 26 ... g6 27 Qh6 Qe7 28 Ng5 f6 29 exf6 Nxf6 was better for Black than the text. RF **27. Nf5 b6** The only move was 27 ... Nce7, still after 28 Nfd6 Ng6 29 f4 White retains a slight advantage. RF **28. Qg4** By going 28 Qg4! White organizes a double attack on g7 and poses a mating threat ... At the same time White has set up another threat, that is a second double attack by 29 Nh6+, threatening the king and attacking the unprotected queen at d7 with his queen ... Being unable to defend himself, Black resigned. YuA **1−0** Fine, ACB 1936, 5; Kubel, 7: Averbakh 1984a, 197.

(249) WINTER, W—FINE

Hastings 1935/6 (6), 1936 (3 Jan.)
Queen's Gambit Declined, Vienna Variation [D39]

1. d4 Nf6 2. c4 e6 3. Nf3 d5 4. Bg5 Bb4+ 5. Nc3 dxc4 6. e4 c5 7. dxc5 Not considered by NCO. Burgess gives 7 e5 cxd4 8 Qa4+ Nc6 9 0-0-0 Bd7 10 Ne4 Be7 11

Considering a position from around the time of Hastings 1935-1936, the time of his "Becoming a Grand Master."

exf6 gxf6 12 Bh4 Rc8 Kb1 Na5 as unclear, or 7 Bxc4 cxd4 8 Nxd4 Bxc3+ 9 bxc3 Qa5 10 Bb5+ Nbd7 11 Bxf6 Qxc3+ 12 Kf1 gxf6 13 h4 a6 as slightly better for White. The text was first played in the game Pleci–Kostich, Warsaw 1935. AW **7 ... Qa5 8. Bxf6 gxf6 9. Qd4 Nd7** But not 9 ... e5 10 Nxe5 Bxc5 11 Nxc4 and wins. RF **10. Bxc4** Not good. After 10 c6 bxc6 11 Bxc4 e5 12 Qe3 Nb6 13 Be2 Be6 (13 ... Na4!?—AW) the position is approximately even. RF **10 ... Bxc3+ 11. bxc3 Qxc5 12. 0–0 e5 13. Qd5 Qxd5 14. Bxd5 Nc5 15. Nd2 Be6 16. f4 Ke7 17. Nc4**

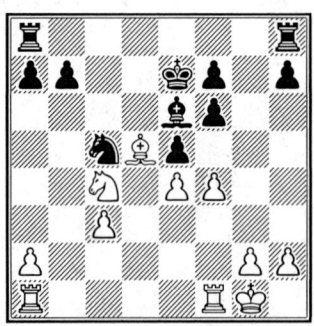

Position after White's 17th move

17 ... exf4! Black could have won a pawn here by 17 ... Nxe4 18 Bxe4 Bxc4. Possibly Fine thought his chances would be better if he retained the tension. AW **18. Rxf4 Rac8 19. Ne3 Nd3 20. Nf5+ Kd7 21. Rf3** If 21 Bxe6+ Kxe6 22 Ng7+ Ke5 23 Rf5+ Kxe4 24 Rxf6 Rxc3 25 Rxf7 Rhc8 26 h3 R8c7 27 Rxc7 Rxc7 28 Nh5 Ke5! and Black should win the ending. RF (This doesn't look very clear to me, in any case wouldn't White do better by

26 Re7+ Kd5 27 Rd1 Kc6 28 Nf5? AW) **21 ... Ne5 22. Rg3 Bxf5 23. exf5 b6 24. c4** The commencement of a plan which turns out badly for the Englishman. The attack on the queenside is too slow and does not cause Black any real problems. AW **24 ... Ke7 25. Ra3 Rc7 26. Ra6 Rd8 27. a4** This loses quickly, but if instead 27 Rb1 Rdd7 28 Rb4 Kd6 29 Ra3 Kc5 30 Rb5+ Kd4 with a very superior position. RF (In that case White's 28th move would be a blunder in view of 28 ... Rxd5 29 cxd5 Rc1+ 30 Kf2 Nd3+, picking up the exchange. If instead 28 Re1 Kf8 29 Re4, Black's advantage is not apparent, indeed that also is the case in the line quoted after 31 Rh3. AW) **27 ... Nd3 28. a5 b5 29. Rc6 Rxc6 30. Bxc6 bxc4 31. Rb1 c3 32. Ba4 Rd5** Resigns. For White must eventually give up a piece for the passed c-pawn. **0–1** *ACB* 1936, 4; *Chess* 1936, 236–7; *Shakhmatny Ezhegodnik* 1937, 255–6.

(250) FINE—GOLOMBEK, H

Hastings 1935/6 (7), 1936 (4 Jan.)
Nimzowitsch-Indian, Classical Variation [E34]

1. d4 Nf6 2. c4 e6 3. Nc3 Bb4 4. Qc2 d5 5. cxd5 Qxd5 6. e3 c5 7. Bd2 Bxc3 8. bxc3 Nc6 I prefer 8 ... cxd5, which prevents White from obtaining strong centre pawns. **9. Nf3 Bd7 10. c4 Qd6 11. Bc3 Rc8** (Incorrectly given as 11 ... a6 in some sources) **12. Be2 cxd4 13. exd4 0–0 14. 0–0 Rfd8 15. Rad1 Be8 16. Rfe1 b6 17. Bf1 Ne7 18. Ne5 Ng6 19. Qc1 Bc6 20. Nxc6** 20 f4 Ba4 gives White a dangerous attack, but Black has excellent counterchances. **20 ... Qxc6 21. Qa3 Ne4 22. Bb2 Nd6**

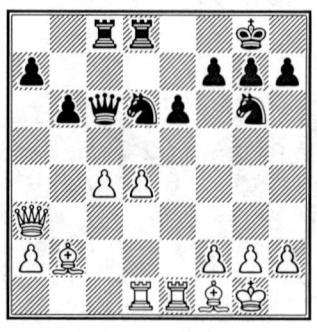

Position after Black's 22nd move

23. d5 exd5 24. Rxd5 a5 Better was 24 ... Nxc4 25 Qc3 Nce5 26 Rxd8+ Rxd8 27 Rxe5 Qxc3 28 Bxc3 Nxe5 29 Bxe5, with a very unclear endgame, apparently in White's favour. **25. Qd3 Nb7 26. g3 Qc7 27. Qd4 f6 28. Bg2 Nc5 29. Qe3 Rxd5 30. Bxd5+ Kf8 31. Ba3 Qd6** A mistake under time pressure. But even after the best move, 31 ... Ne7 32 Be6 Rd8 33 Qe2 White's position is vastly superior. **32. Qe6 Qxe6 33. Rxe6 Rb8 34. Rxb6** Black resigned. **1–0** Fine in ACB 1936, 6.

(251) TARTAKOWER, S—FINE

Hastings 1935/6 (8), 1936 (5 Jan.)
Italian Game, Canal Variation [C50]

1. e4 e5 2. Nc3 Dr Tartakower has always been partial to the Vienna Game. RF **2 ... Nf6 3. Bc4 Bc5** 3 ... Nxe4 4 Qh5 is considered inferior for Black. RF **4. Nf3 Nc6 5. d3 d6 6. Bg5 h6 7. Bxf6!** The Canal Variation, which Dr Tartakower has called "Making something out of nothing". RF **7 ... Qxf6 8. Nd5 Qd8 9. c3** White obtains the initiative but Black can equalize by judicious exchanges. RF **9 ... Ne7!** Rubinstein's move, which I chose because Rubinstein has drawn very easily with it against Dr Tartakower at Budapest 1929. Indeed only a draw was needed in this game to make sure of first prize. RF **10. d4 Nxd5 11. dxc5** Or 11 Bxd5 exd4 12 Nxd4 0-0 13 Qd3 Bxd4 14 cxd4 c6 15 Bb3 Qa5+ 16 Qd2 Qxd2+ 17 Kxd2 with an early draw, as occurred in the above-mentioned game. RF **11 ... Nf4** Simpler is 11 ... Nf6. RF **12. Bb5+** If instead 12 0-0 0-0 followed by ... Qf6 and Black would obtain a strong attack. RF **12 ... Bd7 13. Bxd7+ Qxd7 14. g3 Ne6 15. cxd6 Qxd6** With equality, MCO, 79. **16. Qa4+** The critical moment of the game. The text apparently leaves Black with a cramped position, but this superficial judgment proves deceptive. However, since the alternatives 16 Qd5 Qxd5 17 exd5 e4! with equality and 16 Qxd6 cxd6 17 0-0-0 Ke7 18 Rd2 Rhc8 19 Rhd1 Rc6 followed by ... b5 with a promising minority attack are both unsatisfactory for the first player, the move chosen must be considered best. RF **16 ... c6 17. Rd1 Qc7 18. Qa3 Ng5 19. Nh4** Apparently White now has a strong game, for if 19 ... g6 20 0-0 followed by f2-f4-f5 gives him a promising attack. RF **19 ... Qe7!** The only move, but a difficult one to make since its consequences had to be carefully calculated. RF **20. Qxe7+ Kxe7 21. Nf5+ Kf6 22. Rd6+** If 22 Nd6 b7 23 f4 exf4 24 gxf4 Ne6 25 e5+ Ke7, and White has only succeeded in weakening his pawns. RF **22 ... Ne6 23. Ke2** 23 Rd7 Nc5 leads to nothing. RF **23 ... Rhd8 24. Rhd1 h5** Preparing g7-g6. RF **25. b3 g6** Here I proposed a draw, which Dr Tartakower declined. RF **26. Ne3 Rxd6 27. Rxd6 Rd8 28. Rxd8 Nxd8 29. f4 exf4 30. gxf4 g5!** The most direct; 30 ... Ne6 31 Kf3 would still have offered Black some difficulties. RF **31. e5+ Ke6 32. fxg5 Kxe5 33. Kf3 Ne6 34. Nc4+ Kd5 35. h4 Nf8 36. Ne3+ Ke5 37. Nc4+ Kd5 38. Ne3+** Drawn. As Dr Tartakower remarked after the game, with one additional

tempo either side could win. White because his king would get to f5 without leaving the h-pawn *en prise*; Black because his king would penetrate to the queenside. RF ½–½ Fine in *Chess 1935-6*, 282-3; ACB 1936, 5.

(252) FINE—ALEXANDER, C

Hastings 1935/6 (9), 1936 (6 Jan.)
Petroff Defence [C42]

1. e4 e5 2. Nf3 Nf6 3. Nxe5 d6 4. Nf3 Nxe4 5. Qe2! The best move ... when half a point is all that is required! Kubel **5 ... Qe7 6. d3 Nf6 7. Bg5 Qxe2+ 8. Bxe2 Be7 9. Nc3 h6 10. Bh4 Bd7 11. 0-0-0 Nc6 12. d4 0-0-0 13. Bc4 Rhf8 14. Rhe1 Bg4 15. Re3 d5 16. Bb5 Ng8 17. Bxe7 Ngxe7 18. h3 Be6 19. Bxc6 Nxc6 20. Ne5 Nxe5 21. Rxe5 c6 22. Rde1 Rde8 23. Nd1 Bd7 24. Rxe8+ Rxe8 25. Rxe8+ Bxe8 26. Ne3 Bd7 27. Kd1 Kc7 28. c3 Kd6 29. Kd2 Be6 30. Ke2 Ke7** A routine draw, justified by the score. RF ½–½ ACB 1936, 5.

The First United States Championship Tournament, 1936

Returning to the States Fine took up his place as a seed in the first modern United States Chess Championship, for which he was one of the favourites. The tournament turned out to be a struggle between Samuel Reshevsky and Albert C. Simonson, with the former showing his best fighting qualities to capture the first of four successive titles. Fine would certainly not have believed that he was destined never to win the laurels in this pre-eminent event of the United States.

New York Metropolitan League, February–March, 1936

Following his return to the United States, and in the build up to the first U.S. Championship, Fine played several games in the Metropolitan League. Taking the black pieces, in all of the games recorded in the notebooks, he scored four points in as many games. On the leap day he defeated Rubin of the Williamsburg Chess Club, the leader of the white forces playing very passively in response to a Sicilian. A week later Fine neatly exploited some inaccurate opening play by George Treysman to gain victory against the Stuyvesant Chess Club, and on March 14 another rather unusual Sicilian brought Fine the point in the match against the Empire City Chess Club representative Simchow. In the match which usually decided the title around this time, the Marshall Chess Club against the Manhattan Chess Club, Fine downed Al Simonson, the man who was nearly to win the United States Championship title in the first of the modern tournaments. The rest of the team did not fare so well however; Horowitz defeated Dake on the top board and Willman, Cohen and Denker beat respectively Santasiere, Polland and Hanauer; Sidney Bernstein won his game with MacMurray, but Reshevsky and Marshall only drew. The Manhattan Club, therefore, won the title for the third consecutive year. Games were played on Saturdays.

Rubin	0	Fine	1
Treysman	0	Fine	1
Simchow	0	Fine	1
Simonson	0	Fine	1

(253) RUBIN, A—FINE

Metropolitan Chess League, New York, 1936 (29 Feb.)
Sicilian Defence [B20]

1. e4 c5 2. d3 Nc6 3. Be3 Nf6 4. Nc3 e6 5. Nf3 d5 6. Bg5 d4 7. Ne2 h6 8. Bh4 Qb6 9. b3 Bd7 10. Nd2 Qa5 11. Bxf6 gxf6 12. Ng3 h5 13. Nxh5 0-0-0 14. Nxf6 Bh6 15. g3 Qc3 16. f4 Nb4

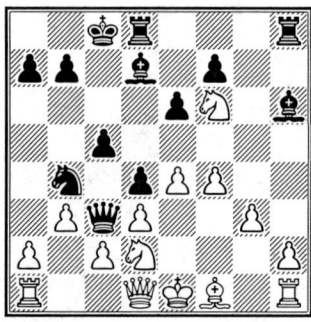

Position after Black's 16th move

17. Ke2?! Bb5 18. Kf2 Bg7 19. e5 Bxf6 20. exf6 Bc6 21. Bg2 Bxg2 22. Kxg2 Nxc2 23. Nc4 Nxa1 24. Qxa1 Qc2+ 25. Kf3 Qxd3+ 26. Kf2 Qc2+ 27. Kf3 Rxh2 28. Rxh2 Qxh2 29. Ne5 d3 30. Qd1 Qh5+ 31. g4 Qh3+ 32. Kf2 Qh2+ 33. Kf3 Rd4 34. Qc1 Qxf4+ 35. Qxf4 Rxf4+ White resigned. 0-1

(254) TREYSMAN, G—FINE

Metropolitan Chess League, New York, 1936 (7 March)
Spanish Opening [C77]

1. e4 e5 2. Nf3 Nc6 3. Bb5 a6 4. Ba4 Nf6 5. c3 b5 6. Bc2 d5 7. exd5 Qxd5 8. d3 Bg4 9. a4 Rd8 10. axb5 axb5 11. Be3 Be7 12. Ra6 0-0 13. Nbd2 Qd7 14. 0-0 Nd5 15. h3 Bh5

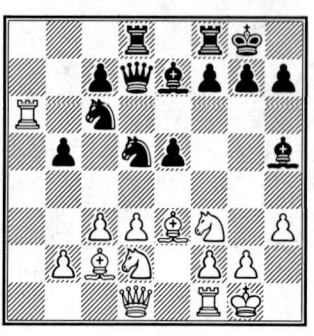

Position after Black's 15th move

16. Ne4 Nb8 17. Ra1 f5 18. Ned2 Kh8 19. g4 fxg4 20. Nxe5 Qd6 21. d4 Nxe3 22. fxe3 Qh6 23. hxg4 Qxe3+ 24. Kg2 Be8 25. Rxf8+ Bxf8 26. Ne4 Nc6 27. Qf1 Be7 28. Re1 Qh6 29. Qf5 Nxe5 30. Qxe5 Qh4 31. Ng3 Bc6+ 32. d5? 32 Be4! 32 ... Rxd5 White resigned. 0-1

(255) SIMCHOW, A—FINE

Metropolitan Chess League, New York, 1936 (14 March)
Sicilian Defence [B50]

1. e4 c5 2. Nf3 d6 3. Nc3 e5 4. Bc4 Nc6 5. d3 Be7 6. Ng5 Bxg5 7. Qh5 g6 8. Qxg5 Nd4 9. Qxd8+ Kxd8 10. Kd1 Bg4+ 11. f3 Be6 12. Nd5 b5 13. Bb3 Nxb3 14. axb3 Bxd5 15. exd5 Kc7 16. Ra6 Ne7 17. c4 Rhb8 18. b4 cxb4 19. Bd2 Rb6 20. Rxb6 axb6 21. Kc2 Nf5

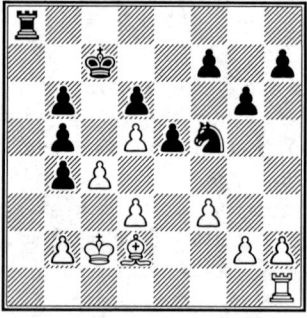

Position after Black's 21st move

22. Bxb4 bxc4 23. dxc4 Ne3+ 24. Kb3 Nxg2 25. Bd2 Nh4 26. Rf1 Nf5 27. Kc3 f6 28. Re1 g5 29. Be3 Nxe3 30. Rxe3 Ra1 31. f4 gxf4 32. Rh3 e4 33. Rxh7+ Kd8 34. Rf7 e3 35. Kd3 Rd1+ 36. Ke2 Rd2+ 37. Ke1 f3 38. Rxf6 f2+ 39. Kf1 Rd1+ White resigned. 0-1

(256) SIMONSON, A—FINE

Metropolitan Chess League, New York, 1936 (28 March)
Queen's Gambit Declined [D30]

1. d4 Nf6 2. Nf3 d5 3. c4 e6 4. e3 Rather timid, for Black equalizes at once. 4 Nc3 is at present considered best. RF 4 ... c5 Getting an isolated pawn, but trusting to the greater freedom of his pieces as compensation. IK 5. cxd5

exd5 6. dxc5 Bxc5 7. a3 a5 8. Nc3 0–0 9. Be2 Nc6 10. Nb5 To prevent the liquidation of the centre by d5-d4, and to establish his knight eventually at d4. IK 10 ... Qe7 11. b3? This move is quite illogical. Nimzowitsch would have said that White has committed three positional blunders with one move, namely: 1 he has weakened his a-pawn; 2 he has restricted the scope of his queen and 3 he has permitted Black to develop his light-squared bishop at f5. To move either knight to d4 would have been far superior to the text. RF 11 ... Bf5 12. 0–0 Rfd8 13. Bb2 Ne4 14. Nfd4 Bg6 15. Rc1 Nxd4 In spite of considerable reflection, I could find no satisfactory alternative to this move. If instead 15 ... Rac8, 16 Bg4 forces the rook to return to a8; whilst 13 ... f5 would have left me with a dangerously exposed position. RF 16. Bxd4 Rac8 If 16 ... Bxa3, 17 Rc7 is favourable to White. IK 17. f3 Bxd4 Again Black must exchange although he would have preferred to complicate the position. If, for example, 17 ... Nf6 18 Bxc5 Rxc5 19 Qd4 and Black's knight is not well posted. RF 18. Qxd4 Nc5 19. Rc3 Ne6 20. Qd2 Rxc3 21. Qxc3 d4!? A tempting but hazardous sacrifice. 21 ... Qc5 would have been safer but drawish. On the other hand, 21 ... Nf4 22 exf4 Qxe2 23 Nd4 Qd3 24 Rc1 is decidedly in White's favour. RF 22. exd4 Nf4 23. Bc4 h5! If 23 ... Qg5 24 g3 h5 25 Kh1. But not 24 Qb2 Re8, threatening Re2! IK 24. Qe1 This and the next move get the queen into a weak position, and lead to trouble. It is a case of over-anxious defense, where there was actually little danger. Simplest was 24 Qd2 Qg5 25 Kh1 h4 (if 25 ... Re8 26 g3) 26 Re1, threatening d4-d5, and so on. IK 24 ... Qg5 25. Qg3 Qf6

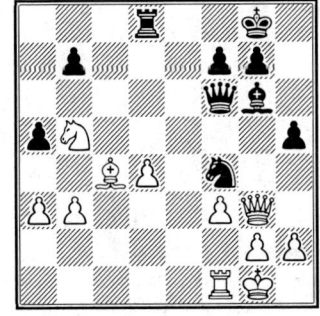

Position after Black's 25th move

26. h4? Overlooking the sharp threat involved in Black's reply. 26 a4 was best to secure the bishop, or 26 Qe1 was preferable to the text. IK 26 ... a4! 27. Rf2 If 27 bxa4 Rc8 wins, as the bishop cannot move because of ... Ne2+. Black must now regain the pawn with a superior position. IK 27 ... axb3 28. Bxb3 Bd3 29. Nc3 Qxd4 30. Qg5 Re8 31. Nd5 This loses, but there is no good defense. If 31 Ne4 Rxe4! 32 fxe4 Ne2+ 33 Kh2 Qxf2 34 Qd8+ Kh7 35 Qxd3 Qg1+, and mate next move. IK 31 ... Nxd5 32. Qxd5 White resigned. If 32 Bxd5 Re1+ 33 Kh2 Qxf2 wins, as Black can easily avoid the checks after 34 Bxf7+ Kxf7. IK 32 ... Re1+0–1 Kashdan, ACB 1936, 80; Fine, *Chess* Volume 1, 342–3.

1st U.S. Championship, New York, April 25–May 16, 1936

"In general the plan is to separate the entries received into sections of not more than ten each and to have all divisions contest complete tourneys to permit those making the best scores to qualify for the finals in which the championship and other prizes will be at stake. It is estimated that about 12 or 16 will be in this final and all important tournament. Entrance fees of $20 for those within 100 miles of New York City, and $10 for those living elsewhere will be required. In addition to consolation money, the following five cash prizes have been offered.: $600, $400, $250, $150 and $100. It is planned to hold the preliminaries at the rooms of various clubs within the Metropolitan area of New York City which, it is expected, will cooperate to that end. After a reasonable interval, the rounds of the main tournament will be staged in some public place yet to be selected. Because of their records, based chiefly upon international performances, the following nine players were listed as exempt from participation in the preliminaries, this year, and will receive invitations to play in the championship final: Arthur W. Dake, Reuben Fine, Israel A. Horowitz, Isaac I. Kashdan, Alexander Kevitz, Abraham Kupchik, Edward Lasker, Samuel Reshevsky and Herman Steiner. The international Chess Code will govern the play. The tentative programme calls for five games a week and the daily sessions of play will last for not less than five hours. On regular week days these will be from 6 P.M. to 11 P.M. On Saturdays and Sundays the play will be from 2 P.M. to 7 P.M. and, if necessary, from 9 P.M. to 1 A.M." (ACB 1936)

Fred Reinfeld wrote an article, published in *Chess* of April 1936, assessing the chances of the main contenders. This is how he described Fine: "The favourite, in my opinion is **Reuben Fine**. Slightly over 21, he has had time to defeat two of the best American players (Dake and Steiner) in match play, to take part in two International Team Tournaments (Folkestone and Warsaw), to win the championship tournament of one of the strongest chess clubs in the world (the Marshall Chess Club: 1931-32, 1932-33, 1933-34), to take four first prizes in the formidable Western Tournaments (St. Paul 1932, Detroit 1933, Chicago 1934 and Milwaukee 1935), and to acquit himself creditably in five International Tournaments (Pasadena 1932, Syracuse 1934, Mexico City 1934-35, Łódź 1935 and Hastings 1935-36)!

The above summary gives the reader some idea of the phenomenal rapidity with which Fine has developed. Equally amazing is the rapidity with which he analyses and sizes up a position. Playing over a game with him gives one the sensation of a cross country race, and it requires considerable mental agility and alertness to keep up with the bewildering stream of comments, improvements, suggestions, variations (and disparagements!) that follow one upon another. Such quickness is usually associated with superficiality or inaccuracy, but this is far from the case with Fine. He is very painstaking and conscientious in analysis, and despite his marvelous skill as a "lightning" player, he has lost several games by overstepping the time limit, and is frequently in time pressure! I have known him to spend days in perfecting and polishing up a recalcitrant variation which famous annotators would have dismissed with a platitude.

As a "rapid transit" and simultaneous expert, Fine has equals but (I believe) no superiors. I recall an instance when he defeated 25 fairly good club players in an hour, achieving a perfect score! Here is an amusing example of his penchant for quick play; in the Western Tournament of 1932, he had an adjourned game with Elison, one of the best Chicago players. Fine was ahead a pawn with rooks and a knight each on the board; however, the position presented considerable technical difficulties, and Fine needed the full point to keep ahead of Reshevsky. Fine spent many anxious hours on the position, finally winning. The following year he gave an exhibition in Chicago, Elison being one of his opponents. But here Fine developed a powerful attack, and won in twenty-odd moves by a brilliant combination!

He is also a first-class blindfold player; thus far he has not played more than eight games simultaneously blindfold, but I have no doubt that he could play many more if his imagination were stimulated by a commensurate financial offer. His rapidity is also in evidence when it comes to playing over games: he has been known to complete a tournament book in one or two evenings! He disdains an ordinary set, which is "too slow," and almost always uses a pocket set. As a result of incessant use, the men are always faded, and I never understand how he can tell a pawn from a knight on his set. But since he is such an excellent blindfold player, perhaps it does not matter much!

His heroes among the great masters are Alekhine, Lasker, Nimzowitsch and (above all) Steinitz. *The International Chess Magazine* is his Bible, and chuckling over Steinitz's vigorous excoriations of his enemies is certainly a good method of relaxation from too much preoccupation with the intricacies of the Indian Defence.

However, Fine is not one of those chess masters who are inarticulate about anything but chess. He is a university graduate, extremely well-read, especially in the fields of philosophy and psychology, and he loves the music of the great masters. His reading tastes are perhaps too austere for most people's taste: he has read all of Dostoyevsky's works with rigorous thoroughness, but he abhors detective stories. By temperament he is a pessimist and believes with Bertrand Russell that only a universal knowledge of the principles of formal logic can save the world from its chronic ills. Of late he has become interested in politics, and peruses assiduously the rantings of the politicians, noting with masochistic relish the logical fallacies in which they abound. He loves to argue, and he is as ruthless in exploiting his adversary's mistakes as he is in unscrupulous in employing sophistries

for his own side. He is often impatient with his intellectual inferiors and his impish humour seldom lacks a target. However, his extensive travels have mellowed him considerably, and in view of the traditional attitude of mutual condescension which exists between Englishmen and Americans, I am happy to report that he cherishes a real affection for England, its customs and people.

Lately he has taken to reading books (very popular in America) which describe in detail the adulteration and vitiation of foods. He has been greatly impressed by this information, so much so that he reveals his knowledge at the most unseasonable time: during a meal. 'You like coca? Very bad, it contains indigestible fats.' I make a wry face, for I am a person who takes a luscious enjoyment in the sight, preparation and consumption of food. 'Milk,' he continues imperturbably, 'is really useless for adults. In fact, it is sometimes even harmful, as it leads to decalcification of their teeth.' He used to have a passion for grapefruit, but he has discovered that it has very little value. Oranges? 'Just advertising.' It is very reassuring to learn, however, that meat is really nourishing, according to the latest investigations."

The lead in the tournament was taken by Kashdan, Dake, Simonson, and Treysman and finally by Reshevsky. Fine lost to Simonson in the tenth round and had to beat Treysman in the final round to tie for third place.

		1	2	3	4	5	6	7	8	9	10	11	12	13	14	15	16	
1	Reshevsky	*	½	½	1	1	½	1	1	0	1	1	1	0	1	1	1	11½
2	Simonson	½	*	1	1	0	½	½	½	1	0	1	1	1	1	1	1	11
3	Fine	½	0	*	1	1	½	½	½	½	½	1	½	1	1	1	1	10½
4	Treysman	0	0	0	*	1	½	1	1	½	1	1	1	½	1	1	1	10½
5	Kashdan	0	1	0	0	*	1	½	½	1	1	1	1	1	0	1	1	10
6	Kupchik	½	½	½	½	0	*	0	1	½	1	½	1	½	½	1	1	9
7	Dake	0	½	½	0	½	1	*	½	½	1	0	1	½	1	1	1	9
8	Kevitz	0	½	½	0	½	0	½	*	1	0	0	1	1	½	1	1	7½
9	Horowitz	1	0	½	½	0	½	½	0	*	1	1	0	½	1	½	0	7
10	Factor	0	1	½	0	0	0	0	1	0	*	1	½	0	1	½	1	6½
11	Steiner	0	0	0	0	0	½	1	1	0	0	*	0	1	½	1	1	6
12	Denker	0	0	½	0	0	0	0	0	1	½	1	*	½	1	½	1	6
13	Bernstein	1	0	0	½	0	½	½	0	½	1	0	½	*	½	0	0	5
14	Hanauer	0	0	0	0	1	½	0	½	0	0	½	0	½	*	½	1	4½
15	Morton	0	0	0	0	0	0	0	0	½	½	0	½	1	½	*	0	3
16	Adams	0	0	0	0	0	0	0	0	1	0	0	0	1	0	1	*	3

(257) DENKER, A—FINE

U.S. Championship, New York (1), 1936 (25 April)
Queen's Gambit Accepted [D26]

1. d4 Nf6 2. Nf3 d5 3. c4 e6 4. Nc3 dxc4 5. e3 c5 6. Bxc4 a6 7. 0–0 Be7 8. dxc5 Qxd1 9. Rxd1 Bxc5 10. a3 Ke7 11. b4 Bd6 12. Bb2 b5 13. Be2 Bb7 14. Nd4 Nbd7 15. Rac1 Rac8 16. Nb1 Nb6 17. Nd2 Na4 18. Ba1 Bd5 19. Bf3 Bxf3 20. N2xf3 Rxc1 21. Rxc1 Ra8 22. Nc6+ Ke8 23. Be5 Bxe5 24. Ncxe5 Nd5 25. Rc6 Ne7 26. Rc7 f6 27. Nc6 Nxc6 28. Rxc6 Kd7 29. Rc2 e5 30. Nd2 Nb6

31. Kf1 a5 32. Rc5 axb4 33. axb4 Ra1+ 34. Ke2 Na4 35. Rc2 Ra2 36. Kd3 Ra3+ 37. Ke2 Nc3+ 38. Kf3 f5 39. g4 g6 40. gxf5 gxf5 41. Kg2 Kd6 42. Nf3 Ne4 43. Nh4 f4 44. Kf3 Rc3 45. Rxc3 Nxc3 Draw agreed. ½–½

(258) FINE—ADAMS, W

U.S. Championship, New York (2), 1936 (26 April)
English Opening, Classical Four Knights [A28]

1. c4 e5 2. Nf3 Nc6 3. Nc3 Nf6 4. e4 Nimzowitsch's move, which is, in my opinion, at least as strong as the more usual 4 d4. **4 … Bc5 5. Be2** The best reply. Black need not fear 5 Nxe5 Nxe5 6 d4 Bb4 7 dxe5 Nxe4 (and White's pawn position will become very weak) 8 Qd4 f5 (8 … Nxc3 9 bxc3 c5 10 Qe3 Ba5 11 Ba3 b6 12 Be2 Ba6 looks unclear. AW) 9 exf6 Nxf6 10 c5 Qe7+ 11 Be3 Bxc3+ 12 bxc3 0–0 with equality, List–Colle, Berlin 1926. **5 … d6 6. 0–0 0–0 7. d3 Bg4** An excellent move, but Black does not follow it up properly. **8. Bg5 h6 9. Be3** After 9 Bh4 g5 10 Bg3 Nh5 Black has the better position. **9 … Bb6** But here Black misses his way. 9 … Bxf3 10 Bxf3 Nd4 was sufficient to equalize. **10. Kh1** Preparing for an eventual f2-f4. **10 … Nh5?** Black decides to break first, but the manoeuvre leaves him with an inferior game. 10 … Bxf3 11 Bxf3 Nd4 was still best. **11. Nd5 f5 12. exf5 Bxf5** Now he sees he is forced to allow d3-d4, for if instead 12 … Rxf5? 13 Bxb6 axb6 14 Ne3 wins. **13. d4** With a clear advantage for the first player, *PCO* 42. **13 … exd4 14. Nxd4 Nxd4 15. Bxd4 Bxd4 16. Qxd4**

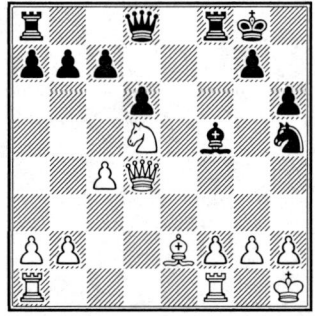

Position after White's 16th move

16 … Nf6 The position now seems simplified, but the weakness of Black's queenside proves fatal. **17. Bf3 Kh8 18. Ne3** 18 Nxf6 Qxf6 19 Qxf6 Rxf6 20 Bxb7 Rb8 leads to no advantage for White. **18 … Bc8 19. Rad1 Qe7 20. Rfe1 Qf7 21. Nd5 Nxd5** Practically forced, if instead 21 … Be6 22 Nxc7! wins. **22. Bxd5 Qg6** The alternative 22 … Qxf2 can best be met by 23 Re8!! Qf5 24 g4 Qxd5+ 25 cxd5 or even more simply (since Black has counterchances in the above variation) 23 Qxf2 Rxf2 24 Re8+ Kh7 25 Kg1! Rf6 (25 … Rxb2 26 Rf1 threatening Be4+ is even worse) 26 Rdel with a winning position. **23. Re7 c6 24. Bf3** White feels that his position should yield him more than a pawn in the long run. 24 Be4 Bf5 25 Bxf5 Rxf5 26 Rxb7 Rf7 is too simplifying and gives Black too many drawing chances. **24 … Rf6** If 24 … Bh3!?

25 Qxd6 Rf6 26 Qg3 wins. **25. Rde1 Kh7** But here Black's only hope was 25 … Bh3 with the continuation 26 Be4 (best) Bf5 27 f3 White must eventually win a pawn but the ending with queen and two rooks on each side would be difficult. **26. Bh5! Qg5** Not 26 … Qxh5? 26 Qxf6. **27. h4 Qf4** If 27 … Qf5 28 Be2 Qg6 29 h5 Qg5 30 Re8 and the threat of Bd3+ will decide quickly. **28. Qxf4 Rxf4**

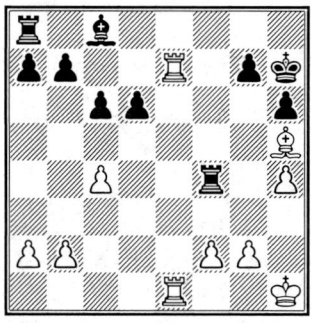

Position after Black's 28th move

29. g3! The point to White's manoeuvre: Black must either retreat, in which case simply doubling the rooks on the seventh rank wins easily, or capture one of the bishop's pawns, as actually occurred. **29 … Rxc4** 29 … Rxf2 is no better: after 30 Re8 b6 31 Kg1! (more precise than either 31 Rd8 or 31 R1e7 c5! 32 Rc7 Bf5 and so on) 31 … Rf6 (or 31 … Rxb2 32 R1e7 Rxa2 33 Bf3 Kg6 34 Rf8! and wins, since 34 … Bb7 allows a mate in two.) 32 R1e7 and again the threat of Bh5-e2-d3+ is decisive. **30. Re8 b6 31. Bf7 Rg4 32. h5 Bb7 33. Rxa8 Bxa8 34. Re8** Black resigned.
1–0 Fine in *Chess* 1936, 471–2; Hilbert & Lahde, 99–100.

(259) HANAUER, M—FINE

U.S. Championship, New York (3), 1936 (27 April)
Grünfeld Defence, Exchange Variation [A34]

1. c4 Nf6 2. Nf3 c5 3. Nc3 d5 4. cxd5 Nxd5 5. e4 Nxc3 6. bxc3 g6 7. Bc4 Bg7 8. 0–0 0–0 9. d4 cxd4 10. cxd4 Nc6 11. Be3 Bg4 12. Rb1 Rc8 13. Be2 Bxf3 14. Bxf3 b6 15. d5 Na5 16. Bd4 Bxd4 17. Qxd4 Rc4 18. Qd2 Qc7 19. Rfc1 Rc8 20. Rxc4 Qxc4 21. e5 Qc2

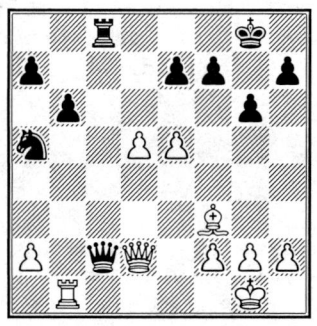

Position after Black's 21st move

22. Qe1 22 Qxc2 Qxc2 23 d6. **22 … Qxa2 23. e6 Nb7 24. exf7+ Kf8 25. Ra1 Qb2 26. Rxa7 Qc3 27. Qxc3 Rxc3 28. h4 Nd6 29. Bg4 Kxf7 30. Be6+ Kf6**

31. f4 h5 32. Ra8 b5 33. Rf8+ Kg7 34. Rg8+ Kh7 35. Rb8 Rc4 36. g3 Rc2 37. Kf1 Rb2 38. g4? h×g4 39. B×g4 Rb4 40. Kg2 R×f4 41. Kg3 Rd4 42. Be6 Kg7 43. Kh3 Kf6 44. Rf8+ Kg7 45. Rg8+ Kh7 46. Rb8 b4 47. Kg3 Kg7 48. Kh3 Kf6 49. Rf8+ Ke5 50. Rg8 b3 51. R×g6 b2 52. Rg1 Rb4 53. Rb1 Ne4 54. h5 Kf6 55. h6 Kg6 56. Bf5+ K×f5 57. h7 Ng5+ White resigned. **0–1**

(260) FINE—KEVITZ, A

U.S. Championship, New York (4), 1936 (29 April)
Budapest Defence [A52]

1. d4 Nf6 2. c4 e5 3. d×e5 Ng4 4. Bf4 Rubinstein's Variation. **4 ... Bb4+ 5. Nc3 Nc6 6. Nf3 Qe7 7. Qd5 f6 8. e×f6 B×c3+ 9. b×c3 N×f6 10. Qd3 d6 11. e3 Ne4 12. Nd4 Nc5 13. Qd2 0–0 14. Be2** White has a clear advantage, PCO 291. **14 ... Ne4 15. N×c6 b×c6 16. Qd4 Bb7 17. 0–0 c5 18. Qd3 g5 19. Bg3 Rae8 20. Rac1 Qc6 21. Rfc1 N×g3 22. h×g3 g4 23. Rf1 Rf6 24. Rce1 Rh6 25. e4 Q×e4 26. Q×e4 R×e4 27. Bd3 R×e1 28. R×e1 Rf6 29. Re8+ Kg7 30. Re7+ Rf7 31. R×f7+ K×f7 32. B×h7** Wherever a sacrifice or an exchange is contemplated it is essential to calculate the resulting pawn against bishop ending with great precision. A case in point, with a blockaded pawn position, is this ending. **32 ... Ba6 33. Bd3 d5 34. Kf1 Kf6 35. Ke2 d4!** 35 ... d×c4 would leave Black with a hopeless tripled pawn, while 35 ... B×c4 36 B×c4 d×c4 37 Ke3 Ke5 38 f3 is an easily won king and pawn ending. **36. Kd2 Bb7 37. Be2 Bc8** The exchange of the g-pawns would clearly be inadvisable, since White would then have two connected passed pawns. **38. f3 Be6 39. a3 Bd7 40. Kc2 Bf5+ 41. Bd3 Be6** Again the exchange of bishops would be a hopeless loss. **42. Kb3 a5 43. c×d4 c×d4 44. f4** Here 44 Ka4 leads to a simple win because of a finesse in the pawn ending: 44 ... c5 (if 44 ... Bf5 45 B×f5 K×f5 46 c5! Ke5 47 Kb3 Kd5 48 c6!! Kc5 49 a4 Kd5 50 f×g4 and it is all over.) 45 K×a5 Bf5 46 Be2 (46 B×f5 K×f5 47 Ka4 is simpler, but 46 Be2 is more systematic.) Bc2 47 f×g4! d3 48 Bf3 d2 49 Kb5 d1Q 50 B×d1 B×d1 51 K×c5 B×g4 52 Kb6 and the bishop cannot hold the three isolated pawns, for example, Ke7 53 c5 Kd8 54 c6 Kc8 55 a4 Kb8 56 a5 Bf5 57 a6 Be4 (57 ... Bd3 58 a7+ Ka8 59 g4!) 58 g4! B×g2 59 g5 Be4 60 a7+ Ka8 61 c7 Bf5 62 g6 and wins. **44 ... Bf5 45. Be2 Ke6 46. Ka4 Bc2+ 47. K×a5 Kf5 48. Kb5 d3 49. B×d3+ B×d3** This might be called a normal position in this type of ending—the three pawns draw against the bishop. **50. Kc6 Ke4 51. K×c7 B×c4 52. a4 Kd5** It would be a blunder to play 52 ... Ke3 53 a5 Kf2 54 f5 K×g2 55 f6 K×g3 56 a6, when one of the pawns queens. A&Ch **53. a5 Ke6** 53 ... Kc5 54 Kd7 Kb5? 55 f5 K×a5 56 f6 Kb5 57 K×e7 loses for Black. **54. Kb7 Bd5+! 55. Kc7** 55 Kb6 Kd6 56 a6 B×g2 57 a7 Bc6 leads to a draw. A&Ch **55 ... Bc4** and the game was called a draw. That every pawn played its part here, even the despised doubled pawn, is shown by the fact that if we remove the white pawn at g2 after move 49, White will lose.

For after 1 Kc6 B×c4 2 K×c7 Ke4 3 a4 Kf3 4 f5 K×g3 5 f6 Kf4 6 a5 Ke5 7 a6 K×f6 8 a7 Bd4 the pawn is stopped and Black will soon queen. ½–½ Hilbert & Lahde, 117–8; Fine 1941, 136–7 and 153–4; Averbakh & Chekhover 50.

(261) FACTOR, S—FINE

U.S. Championship, New York (5), 1936 (30 April)
Sicilian Defence, Scheveningen [B85]

1. e4 c5 2. Nf3 d6 Interestingly in MCO Fine treats this move order essentially as a sideline, though he does call it the "modern" variation, and says it is usually adopted to avoid the Richter Attack. His main variations begin either 2 ... Nc6 or 2 ... e6. **3. d4 c×d4 4. N×d4 Nf6 5. Nc3 a6 6. a4 e6** Transposing from what we know as the Najdorf into the Scheveningen Variation. **7. Be2 Be7 8. 0–0 0–0 9. Kh1 Nc6 10. Be3 Qc7 11. f4 Na5** More recently Bd7 (Cherta–Najdorf, Barcelona 1946), Re8 or Rd8 (Grechkin–Rudakovsky, U.S.S.R.-sf Kiev 1940 and Yanofsky–Kotov, Saltsjobaden izt 1948) have been played here. This move however had been seen before. **12. Qd3 e5** An earlier game, Palau–Pulcherio, Mar del Plata 1928, continued 12 ... Bd7 13 Nb3 Bc6 14 N×a5 Q×a5 15 Bf3 Nd7 16 Qd2 Qc7 17 Rad1 Rac8 with an even position. **13. Nb3 N×b3 14. c×b3 Be6 15. f5 Bd7 16. g4 Bc6 17. g5 N×e4! 18. N×e4 d5 19. f6 d×e4 20. Qc3 Bd6 21. f×g7 K×g7 22. Qe1 Qe7 23. Rc1 f5 24. g×f6+ R×f6 25. R×f6 Q×f6 26. Qg3+ Kh8 27. Rg1 b6?! 28. Rg2 Bc5?? 29. Bc4? h6 30. B×h6 Q×h6 31. Q×e5+ Kh7 32. Qf5+ Kh8** Draw agreed. **½–½**

(262) FINE—KUPCHIK, A

U.S. Championship, New York (6), 1936 (2 May)
Queen's Gambit Declined, Semi-Slav [D46]

1. d4 Nf6 2. c4 e6 3. Nc3 d5 4. Nf3 c6 5. e3 Nbd7 6. Bd3 Bb4 7. 0–0 0–0 8. a3 B×c3 9. b×c3 c5 10. Qc2 b6 11. c×d5 e×d5 12. c4 d×c4 13. B×c4 c×d4 14. N×d4 Bb7 15. Bb2 Nc5 16. Rad1 Qc7 17. Nb5 Qe7 18. Nd6 Be4 19. N×e4 Nc×e4 20. Rd4 Rac8 21. Qd3 Rfd8 22. Rd1 R×d4 23. Q×d4 h6 24. h3 Qc5 25. Ba6 Re8 26. f3 Q×d4 27. B×d4 Nc5 28. B×c5 b×c5 29. e4 g5 30. Rd6 Re6 31. Rd8+ Re8 32. Rd1 Re7 33. Kf2 Kg7 34. Ke3 Nh5 35. Bc8 Rc7 36. Bf5 Rb7 37. Rd7 Rb2 38. Rd2 Rb3+ 39. Rd3 Rb2 40. Rd2 Draw agreed. **½–½**

(263) KASHDAN, I—FINE

U.S. Championship, New York (7), 1936 (3 May)
Nimzowitsch-Indian Defence, Spielmann Variation [E23]

1. d4 Nf6 2. c4 e6 3. Nc3 Bb4 4. Qb3 Then still popular, though rarely seen nowadays. **4 ... c5** This variation has been somewhat discredited of late, but without adequate reason, in my opinion. *Chess* **5. dxc5 Nc6 6. Nf3** The game Winter–Capablanca, Hastings 1929/30 now proceeded 6 ... 0–0 7 Bg5 h6 8 Bh4 g5 9 Bg3 Ne4 10 e3 Qa5 11 Rc1 f5 with a complicated position. **6 ... Bxc5** Although this move is not often seen, it is much stronger than the customary 6 ... Ne4 7 Bd2 when neither 7 ... Nxc5 nor 7 ... Nxd2 is wholly satisfactory for Black. *Chess* **7. e3** It is characteristic of Kashdan's style that when confronted with an unfamiliar opening he chooses the safest line. However, neither 7 Bg5 h6 8 Bxf6 Qxf6 9 Ne4 Bb4+! nor 7 Bf4 (recommended by Grünfeld) d5! gives White any advantage. *Chess* **7 ... 0–0 8. Be2 b6** White can no longer prevent the liberating d7–d5, but Black need not be in a hurry about it. **9. 0–0 Bb7 10. a3 Qe7** 10 ... e5 (to play for a kingside attack) would be refuted by 11 Qc2 Qe7 12 Nd5. *Chess* **11. Rd1 Rad8 12. Bd2?** But this timid move is definitely weak. 12 Qc2 and if 12 ... d5 13 cxd5 exd5 14 b4 Bd6 15 Bb2 transposing to a Queen's Gambit Accepted with colours reversed was essential. *Chess* **12 ... d5** Black stands a little better, MCO 187. **13. cxd5 exd5 14. Be1** This bishop moves around like a sore thumb. Black has a strong initiative. **14 ... d4 15. exd4 Nxd4 16. Nxd4 Bxd4** Already threatening to win a piece with ... Bxc3 and ... Qxe2. **17. Bf1** Threatening 18 ... Ng4 19 g3? Qxe1! and also preventing White from playing 18 Nb5, since the b-pawn would then be *en prise*. *Chess* **17 ... Qe5 18. h3 h5**

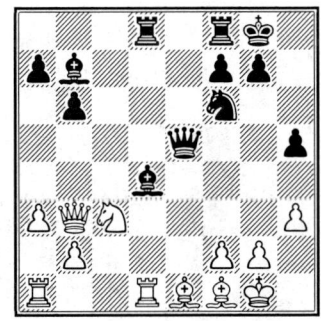

*Position after
Black's 18th move*

19. Rd2 Crossing Black's plan, since he would double rooks on the d-file, which would pin Black's bishop. **19 ... Bc5** In view of the threat of Rad1 Black's bishop is forced to relinquish his strong central post. 19 ... Bxc3 would be answered by 20 Rxd8+ Rxd8 21 Bxc3. *Chess* **20. Rxd8** White's best bet is to head for an endgame. Black, on the other hand, wants to force some permanent weakness before that is reached. **20 ... Rxd8 21. Rd1 Rxd1** Black exchanges rooks to gain a tempo for the attack. If 21 ... Re8 22 Qa4 prevents h4. *Chess* **22. Qxd1 Bd6** The alternative 22 ... h4 would be adequately met by 23 Qe2. *Chess* **23. g3 Bc5 24. Kh2 h4 25. Qd8+** With the object of misplacing Black's knight, but the knight goes to d6 where it is even more strongly posted than at f6. *Chess*; White must defend with utmost care. If, instead, 25 f4, Qe3 is immediately decisive. An interesting try is 25 b4 but 25 ... Bd4! 26 Nb5 Qe4 then wins: after 25 b4, it would be a mistake to play 25 ... Bxf2 26 Bxf2 Qxc3 27 Qd8+ Kh7 28 gxh4 with drawing

chances, for if 28 ... Qf3 29 Qd3+. **25 ... Ne8** After 25 ... Kh7 26 Qd2 Ne4 27 Nxe4 Bxe4 28 Bd3 White would have been able to simplify too much. *Chess* **26. Qd2** The only reply. If, for example, 26 Bb5?? hxg3+ 27 fxg3 Bg1+! and mates in three. *Chess* **26 ... Nd6** Now he must defend against Ne4. **27. f4** If instead 27 Bg2 Bxg2 28 Kxg2 hxg3 29 fxg3 (better than 29 Bd4 as Fine suggested in *Chess*. AW) Nc4 30 Qc1 (or 30 Qd8+ Bf8) is decisive. **27 ... hxg3+ 28. Bxg3 Qe3** Black has forced a fatal weakening of the white pawns, and is now content to shift to the endgame. **29. Qxe3 Bxe3**

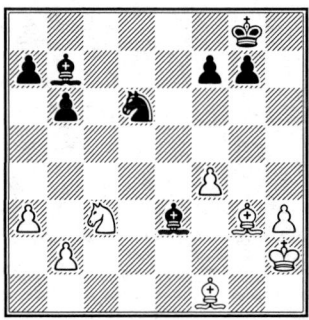

*Position after
Black's 29th move*

He already threatens to win a pawn with ... Bc1. **30. a4 Bc1 31. b3 Bd2 32. Nb5** Hoping for salvation in exchanges, but he cannot avoid a further weakening of his pawns. On 32 Nd1 (or 32 Ne2) Bd5 wins a pawn. **32 ... Nxb5 33. Bxb5 g6** At first sight this looks like a mistake, since White can now reply 34 Bc4. But if 33 ... Bd5 at once 34 Bc4 Bxc4 35 bxc4 g6 36 Kg2 Kg7 37 Kf3 Kf6 38 Ke4 and White prevents the Black king from getting to the vital f5 square, and can probably draw. RF; White has defended himself very coolly. 33 ... Be3 here would not be sufficient for Black, since White could then reply 34 f5. *Chess* **34. Kg1** A much more difficult problem is posed with 34 Bc4 at once. Black can still win, but it is not so easy. The correct line is 34 ... Kg7 35 Kg1 Kf6 36 Kf2 Bc8! 37 h4 Be6 38 Bxe6 Kxe6 39 Ke2 and Black's king gets to f5 after all, when the f-pawn will eventually go. **34 ... Bd5 35. Bc4 Bxc4 36. bxc4** The split of the pawns on the queenside is not by itself so important: what counts is that the black king can get to f5 and win the f-pawn. **36 ... Kg7 37. Kf2 Kf6 38. Ke2 Bc1 39. Kd1** 39 Kf3 offered better drawing chances, but even after 39 Kf3 Ke6 40 Bf2 f6! (40 ... f5 41 Be3 is a draw) Black has some winning chances left. *Chess* **39 ... Ba3 40. Ke2 Kf5 41. Kf3**

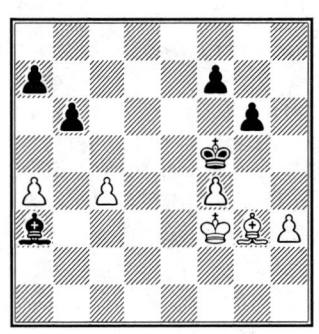

*Position after
White's 41st move*

41 ... Bd6 The decisive position, which Black had been building up to. White is in *Zugzwang* because of his need to protect the f-pawn. If 42 Ke3 g5 and 42 h4 f6, merely postpones the inevitable. **42. Bh2 g5 43. Bg1** 43 Bg3 of course loses, but Black must avoid a pretty trap: 43 ... Bxf4 44 Bxf4 gxf4 45 h4 f6? 46 a5 Ke5?? 47 axb6 axb6 48 h5 Kf5 49 h6 Kg6 50 Kxf4 Kxh6 51 Kf5 Kg7 52 Ke6 Kg6 53 Kd6 f5 54 Kc6 f4 55 Kxb6 f3 56 c5 f2 57 c6 f1Q 58 c7 and the position is a well-known draw. But Black can play 45 ... a5 46 h5 Kg5 47 h6 Kxh6 48 Kxf4 Kg6 and win without any trouble. *Chess* **43 ... Bxf4 44. c5** The only hope. RF **44 ... bxc5 45. Bxc5 a6 46. Bb6** The ending still requires precise handling. RF **46 ... Bd6 47. Bd8 Be5 48. Ba5 Bf6** Black wishes to play f7-f5. To do this he must first have the g-pawn protected. *Chess* **49. Bb6 Be7 50. Ba5 Ke6 51. Kg4 f5+ 52. Kf3 Kd5** The first step in winning the ending is to force White's a-pawn to a5, where it can be attacked by Black's bishop. *Chess* **53. Bc7 Kc5 54. Ba5 Kc4 55. Bc7 Kb4 56. a5** The pawn, of course, cannot be held, but the problem is to win it without giving up a pawn on the other side. The next step is to force the White bishop to a less favourable position. RF **56 ... Kc5!** If, instead, 56 ... Kb5 57 Bb6 Bb4? 58 Bd8 Bxa5 59 Bxg5 the ending is drawn. RF **57. Bb6+ Kc6 58. Be3 Bd8 59. Bd2** Now White's access to the kingside can soon be barred with f4. RF **59 ... Kb5 60. Kf2**

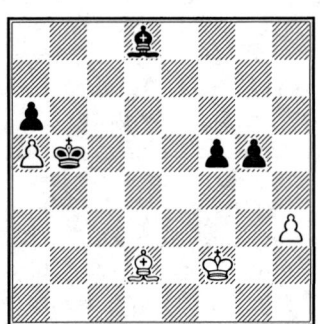

Position after White's 60th move

60 ... f4 Black has accurately calculated that he wins by one tempo. It is interesting to note that an alternative win succeeds by the same tempo, that is, Black can play his king to h5, his bishop to c7, his pawn to g4, then again play the king to the queenside. White's defence would be to exchange the pawns (a-pawn and g-pawn), play his king to f2, the bishop to d2, eventually give up the h-pawn, and win the g-pawn. The ending would then be exactly the same as the one which actually occurred. *Chess* **61. Bc3** The best defensive chance, for if now 61 ... Bxa5? 62 Bf6 at least draws. *Chess* **61 ... Kc4! 62. Bd2** The bishop remains on the diagonal e1-a5, for if 62 Bg7 Kb4 wins at once. *Chess* **62 ... Be7!** Threatening ... Bb4, against which there is no defence. RF **63. h4 gxh4 64. Bxf4 Bd8 65. Bd2 Kb5 66. Kg2** Or 66 Kg1 Bxa5 67 Bg5 h3. RF **66 ... Bxa5 67. Bg5** Black must remain careful since the h-pawn is tied to the bishop of the wrong colour. RF **67 ... Bb6** 67 ... Be1 would be a mere waste of time: White replies 68 Bd8 and Black must then manoeuvre his bishop to b6, since after 68 ... a5??

69 Bxa5 the game is a well-known draw. *Chess* **68. Bxh4** Or 68 Bd2, Bb6-c5-b4. *Chess* **68 ... a5 69. Kf3 a4 70. Ke2** Or 70 Be7 Bc5. RF **70 ... a3 71. Bf6** Or 71 Kd3 Bd4! and Black queens. RF **71 ... Kc4 72. Kd2 Kb3 73. Kc1 a2** Resigns, for Black plays Bc5-a3+-b2 and queens his pawn. *Chess* **0–1** This game shared the prize for Best Played Game with Kashdan's own win over Kupchik. Principal annotations from Fine 1958, 61–6; Hilbert & Lahde, 132–6; Fine 1941, 145–6, 151 and 168; *Shakhmatny Ezhegodnik* 1938, 144–6; ACB 1936, 141.

(264) FINE—MORTON, H

U.S. Championship, New York (8), 1936 (4 May)
Budapest Defence [A52]

1. d4 Nf6 2. c4 e5 3. dxe5 Ng4 4. e4 h5 5. Be2 Nxe5 6. Nf3 Nbc6 7. Be3 Ng4 8. Bg5 f6 9. Bf4 Bc5 10. Bg3 f5 11. exf5 Qf6 12. Nc3 Qxf5 13. 0-0 d6 14. Nd5 Qd7 15. Nh4 0-0 16. h3 Nge5

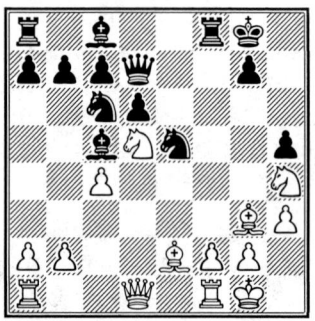

Position after Black's 16th move

17. Bxh5 Nxc4 18. Rc1 18 Nxc7 Qxc7 19 Qd5+ wins easily. **18 ... b5 19. Ng6 Re8 20. b3 Nb6 21. b4 Nxb4 22. Nxb4 Bxb4 23. Qb3+ Nc4 24. Qxb4 c5 25. Qb3 Bb7 26. Nf4 Re7 27. Rfe1 a6 28. Bg4 Rxe1+ 29. Rxe1 Qc6 30. Be6+ Kh8 31. Qd1 g6 32. Nxg6+ Kg7 33. Nf4 Ne5 34. Rxe5 dxe5** Black resigned. **1–0**

(265) RESHEVSKY, S—FINE

U.S. Championship, New York (9), 1936 (6 May)
French Defence, Exchange Variation [C01]

1. e4 e6 2. d4 d5 3. exd5 exd5 4. Bd3 Bd6 5. Ne2 Ne7 6. c3 0-0 7. Qc2 h6 8. Nd2 b6 Attempting to infuse some life into an unusually dull variation. **9. b4 Nd7 10. Nb3 c5** But this leads to a series of exchanges and a hopelessly even position. More enterprising was 10 ... c6, followed by ... Qc7 and a careful preparation of the break. **11. bxc5 bxc5 12. dxc5** With an equal game, MCO 62. **12 ... Nxc5 13. Nxc5 Bxc5 14. 0-0 Qc7 15. Rb1 Bd7 16. Bf4 Bd6 17. Bxd6 Qxd6 18. Qd2 Rab8 19. Qf4** After this further exchange there is practically no play left for either side. **19 ... Qxf4 20. Nxf4 Rfc8 21. Rxb8 Rxb8 22. Rb1 Rxb1+ 23. Bxb1 g6 24. Bc2 Kg7 25. Bb3 Bc6 26. Ne2 Kf6 27. f4 Ke6**

28. Nd4+ Kd6 29. Nf3 Bd7 30. Kf2 f6 31. Ke3 g5
32. Nd4 Kc5 33. fxg5 fxg5 34. Bc2 Draw agreed.
½–½ ACB 1936, 88–9.

(266) FINE—SIMONSON, A

U.S. Championship New York (10), 1936 (7 May)
Queen's Gambit Declined, Exchange Variation [D53]

1. d4 Nf6 2. Nf3 d5 3. c4 e6 4. Nc3 Be7 5. Bg5
Nbd7 6. e3 a6 If this is played at all, it should be delayed
until White plays Rc1, a move which does not fit in with the
Carlsbad System. 7. cxd5 exd5 8. Bd3 0-0 9. Qc2 c6
10. 0-0-0?! The direct opposite of the Carlsbad System,
but not necessarily illogical. For White still seeks to utilize
his "bind" on Black's queenside, in the following wise: as
White intends a kingside attack, Black must advance on the
queenside, but c6-c5 will give him an isolated d-pawn, and
b7-b5 a backward c-pawn. In this system, however, White's
king's knight is now usually developed at e2, with Ng3-f5 in
view. 10 ... Re8 11. Kb1 This is always necessary at some
stage after queenside castling in the Queen's Gambit, so it is
best to play it at once. 11 ... Nf8 12. Ka1? Cautious to the
point of recklessness. This is not the Fine we know! White
should immediately proceed with h2-h3 and so forth, with
at least equal chances. 12 ... Be6 13. h3 Qa5 14. Bf4
Stopping 14 ... Ne4! 14 ... Rac8 15. Nd2 b5 Compulsory
boldness. Black shows he can stand the backward c-pawn,
but White's lost tempo may have made all the difference
between victory and defeat. 16. g4 N6d7 17. Nb3 Qd8
18. Ne2 a5 19. Nc5 Nxc5 20. dxc5 a4 21. Nd4 Qa5
22. Rc1? To protect the c-pawn when b5-b4 comes, but this
looks like another waste of tempo. 22 Bd6, although probably leaving Black better, looks essential. AW 22 ... b4
23. Rhd1 Qa7! 24. Qd2 A pawn goes, and the game
with it, but b4-b3 was threatened. (Again Bf4-d6 looks the
only way to play. AW) 24 ... Bxc5 25. Kb1!? Kh8
Threatening Bxd4. 26. Be2 Bd7 27. Ba6 Rcd8 28. Bf1
Ne6 29. Bh2 Ng5 30. Qc2 Bxd4 31. exd4 b3
32. Qd3 Ne4 33. Qa6 It was equally hopeless to permit
a4-a3! 33 ... Qxa6 34. Bxa6 Nxf2 35. Rf1 Nxh3
36. Rxf7 Ng5 37. Rff1 Bxg4 38. Bc7 Rd7 39. Rxc6
Nf3 40. Rd1 Nxd4 41. Rxd4 Re1+ 42. Rc1 Rxc1+
White resigned. 0–1 Notes from *Australasian Chess Review*,
quoted in Hilbert & Lahde, 154–6. Compare with Fine-
Kolski, Łódź 1935 and several other games under the ECO
code D36. This was Simonson's only win over Fine, he lost
seven times and drew once.

(267) DAKE, A—FINE

U.S. Championship, New York (11), 1936 (9 May)
Queen's Gambit Declined, Tarrasch Variation [D40]

1. d4 Nf6 2. Nf3 e6 3. c4 d5 4. Nc3 c5 5. Bg5
cxd4 If Black wishes to avoid an isolated d-pawn, he can do
so by 5 ... dxc4 first. ACR 6. Qxd4 Be7 6 ... Nc6? 7 Bxf6
gxf6 8 Qh4 dxc4 9 Rd1 Bd7 10 e3 Ne5 11 Nxe5 fxe5

12 Qxc4 with a clear advantage for White, Pillsbury–Lasker,
Cambridge Springs 1904. 7. cxd5 7 0-0-0? is a mistake: 7
... Nc6 8 Qh4 Qa5 9 e3 Bd7 10 Kb1 h6, Pillsbury–Lasker, St
Petersburg 1895/6. 7 ... exd5 8. e3 Nc6 9. Bb5! 0-0
Black has compensation for the slight weakness, in that
White's queen must move, and has no good square. ACR
10. Qa4 Bd7 With an equal game, MCO 150. 11. 0-0 a6
12. Be2 Better seems 12 Bxc6 Bxc6 (or 12 ... bxc6 13 Ne5)
13 Qb3. RF 12 ... h6 13. Bxf6 Bxf6 14. Qb3 Bad for
White is 14 Nxd5? Bxb2 15 Rab1 (15 Rae1! b5 16 Qb3 Be6
17 e4 considerably improves the variation for White. AW)
Nd4 16 Qd1 Nxe2+ Bb5 and Black wins the exchange. RF
14 ... Be6 15. Rfd1 But now he could and should have
played 15 Qxb7 Na5 16 Qb4 Rb8 17 Qa3 Be7 18 Qa4 Rxb2
19 Bxa6 when Black must fight for a draw. RF 15 ... Na5
16. Qb4 Rc8 17. Rac1 Be7 18. Qd4 Nc6 Not 18 ...
Nc4 because of 19 Nxd5. RF (Presumably the line Fine
intended here was 19 ... Qxd5 20 Qxd5 Bxd5 21 Rxd5,
however in this position Black has the trick 21 ... Nxe3!
22 Rxc8 Nxd5 equalizing. AW) 19. Qd2 Qb6 20. Nxd5
Bxd5 21. Qxd5 Qxb2 22. Bc4 Qf6 23. Qe4 Ba3
24. Rb1 b5 25. Bd5 Ne7 26. Bb3 Bd6 27. Qd4
Qxd4 28. Rxd4 Bc5 29. Rd7 g6 30. Ne5 Kg7
31. Kf1 a5 A bold attempt to free his position. The point
appears several moves later. RF 32. Rb7 Rb8! Well calculated. ACR 33. Rxb8 Rxb8 34. Bxf7 Not 34 Nxf7,
because of 34 ... a4 winning. RF (This isn't too clear after
35 Bxa4 Kxf7 36 Bxb5. AW) 34 ... Bd6 35. Nd7 Kxf7
36. Nxb8

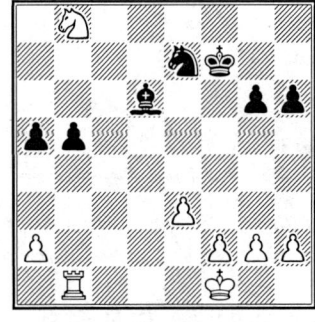

*Position after
White's 36th move*

36 ... b4!! The point. After 36 ... Bxb8 37 Rxb4 Bc7, Black
can only hope for a draw at best. With the text move he risks
losing in order to try to win. RF 37. Nd7 Nd5 38. Rb2
a4 39. e4 White misses the strongest continuation, which
was 39 Rd2 Ke6 40 e4 Nc3 41 Nb6 and White's knight gets
to c4 with tempo. RF 39 ... Nc3 40. e5
40 Nb6 was better, but this was hard to foresee. ACR 40 ...
Be7 41. Nb6 a3 If instead 41 ... b3 42 a3! Bxa3 43 Nxa4!
and again White has all the winning chances. RF (After
43 Bxb2 44 Nxb2 Ke6 45 f4 g5 Black should be fine. AW)
42. Rc2 Nxa2 43. Rxa2 b3 44. Rxa3 Bxa3 45. Nc4
Bc1 46. g3 Ke6 47. Ke2 b2 48. Na3 Simpler was
48 Nxb2 Bxb2 49 f4. White can exchange Black's g-pawn
and since Black's bishop is of the wrong colour the game is
drawn. RF 48 ... Kxe5 49. Kd3 Kd5 50. Nb1 Kc5
51. Kc3 h5 52. h4 Kd5 53. f3 Ke5 54. Na3 Kf5

55. Kc2 Be3 56. Nc4 Bf2 57. Nd6+ Ke5 58. Ne4 Be1 Leading to an immediate draw. 58 ... Bd4 still offered some winning chances. RF 59. Kxb2 Kd4 60. Kc2 Ke3 61. Kd1 Bb4 62. Ng5 Be7 63. g4 hxg4 64. fxg4 Draw agreed. ½–½ Fine in ACB 1936, 91; *Australasian Chess Review* quoted in Hilbert & Lahde 159–60; Bush, 76–7.

(268) FINE—BERNSTEIN, S

U.S. Championship New York (12), 1936 (10 May)
Queen's Gambit Declined, Chigorin Defence [D07]

1. d4 d5 2. c4 Nc6 This defence is not quite playable, and is for that reason not often seen. (Nevertheless Morozevich had reasonable success with this variation in the mid–1990s. AW) 3. Nf3 Bg4 4. cxd5 Bxf3 5. gxf3 Qxd5 6. e3 e5 7. Nc3 Bb4 8. Bd2 Qd7 But more in the spirit of the opening is 8 ... Bxc3 9 bxc3 exd4 10 cxd4 Nge7 when White's a- and h-pawns may become a serious weakness. 9. d5 Nce7 10. Bb5 c6 11. dxc6 bxc6 12. Bc4 Rb8 13. a3 Bd6 14. Nc4 Nf6 15. Nxd6+ Qxd6 16. Bb4 Qxd1+ 17. Rxd1 Ned5 18. Bd6 Rxb2 19. Bxe5 Rc2 20. Bb3 Rc5 21. Bd6 Rc3 22. Ba2 Rc2 23. Bb1 Rb2 24. Bd3 Rb7 25. 0–0 Kd7 26. Be5 Ke6 27. Bd4

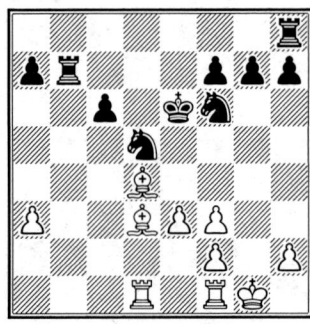

Position after White's 27th move

27 ... Rd8 Black has at last developed all his pieces, but his weak pawn position and the strength of White's two bishops prove fatal. 28. Rc1 Rc7 29. Rc2 Nd7 30. Bc4 Ne5 31. Be2 g5 32. Rfc1 Rd6 33. Kg2 h5 Somewhat better was 33 ... f6, but then after 34 h4, opening the h-file, Black still has serious problems to solve. 34. h4 gxh4 35. f4 Ng6 36. Bc5 Rd8 37. Kh2 Not 37 Bxh5 Nxf4+!. 37 ... Nge7 38. Bxh5 Rh8 39. Bf3 Rhc8 40. f5+ Kd7 41. Rd2 Ke8 42. Rc4 Rd7 43. Rxh4 Kd8 44. e4 Nf6 45. Rb2 Rdc7 Adjourned; Black resigned without resuming play. 1–0 ACB 1936, 91–2; Hilbert & Lahde 167–8.

(269) STEINER, H—FINE

U.S. Championship New York (13), 1936 (11 May)
Spanish Game, Berlin Defence [C66]

1. e4 Nc6 2. Nc3 e5 3. Nf3 Nf6 4. Bb5 d6 5. d4 exd4 6. Nxd4 Bd7 7. 0–0 Be7 8. h3 0–0 9. Nxc6 bxc6 10. Bd3 Re8 11. b3 Bf8 12. Bg5 h6 13. Bxf6

Qxf6 14. Ne2 d5 15. exd5 cxd5 16. Qd2 Bd6 17. Rae1 Re5 18. Ng3 Rg5 19. c4 c6 20. Bb1

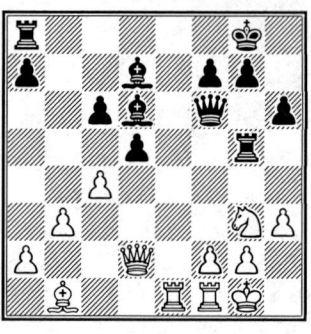

Position after White's 20th move

20 ... g6 21. Qd3 Qf4 22. Re3 Bc5 23. Rf3 Qd4 24. Qxd4 Bxd4 25. Rd3 Bb6 26. Ne4 dxe4 27. Rxd7 Re8 28. b4 c5 29. a3 Rge5 30. g3 f5 31. Kg2 e3 32. fxe3 Rxe3 33. Bd3 Rd8 34. Rxd8+ Bxd8 35. Rf3 Re6 36. h4 h5 37. Bf1 Be7 38. Rb3 Kg7 39. Rd3 cxb4 40. axb4 Bxb4 41. Rd5 a5 42. Kf3 Re1 43. Bd3 a4 44. c5 Rc1 45. Rd7+ Kf8 46. Rd4 a3 47. Rxb4 a2 48. Ra4 a1Q 49. Rxa1 Rxa1 50. Ke3 Ke7 51. Kd4 Rg1 52. Kd5 Rxg3 53. Bc4 Kd7 White resigned. 0–1

(270) FINE—HOROWITZ, I

U.S. Championship New York (14), 1936 (13 May)
Queen's Gambit Declined, Semi-Slav [D46]

1. d4 Nf6 2. c4 e6 3. Nc3 d5 4. Nf3 c6 5. e3 Nbd7 6. Bd3 Be7 7. 0–0 0–0 8. e4 dxe4 9. Nxe4 b6 10. Qe2 Bb7 11. Ng3!? 11 Rd1 Qc7 12 Bg5 c5 is unclear, Burgess. 11 ... c5! 12. Be3 cxd4 13. Nxd4 Ne5 14. Bc2 Neg4 15. Rad1 Nxe3 16. fxe3 Qc7 17. Rf2 Qe5 18. Rdf1 Ne4 19. Nxe4 Bxe4 20. Bxe4 Qxe4 21. Qf3 Qd3 22. b3 Bc5 23. Rd1 Qg6 24. Nc6 Qg5 25. Re2 a5 26. g3 f5 27. Kg2 Qf6 28. e4 f4 29. e5 Qg6 30. g4 h5 31. h3 hxg4 32. hxg4 Rac8 33. Nd4 Rcd8 34. Red2 Rd7 35. Nc6 Rxd2+ 36. Rxd2 Qb1 37. a4 Qg1+ 38. Kh3 Qe3 39. Rd3 Qxf3+ 40. Rxf3 g5 41. Rd3 f3 42. Rd8 f2 43. Rxf8+ Kxf8 44. Kg2 Ke8 45. Na5 Bd4 46. Nc8 Bc5 47. Na7 Bd4 48. Nb5 Bxe5 49. Kxf2 Kd7 50. Ke3 Bb2 51. Nd4 Bxd4+ 52. Kxd4 Kd6 53. Ke4 Kc5 54. Ke5 Kb4 55. Kf6 Kxb3 56. Kxg5 Kxa4 57. Kh5 Kb4 58. g5 a4 59. g6 a3 60. g7 a2 61. g8Q a1Q 62. Qxe6 Qd4 63. Kg6 Kc3 64. Qc6 Kd3 65. Qb5 Qc5 66. Qb3+ Kd4 67. Kg7 Qc6 68. Qb4 Qc7+ 69. Kf6 Qc5 70. Qb3 Qc6+ 71. Ke7 Kc5 72. Kd8 Qf6+ 73. Kc8 Draw agreed. ½–½

(271) TREYSMAN, G—FINE

U.S. Championship New York (15), 1936 (16 May)
Spanish Game, Worrall Attack [C86]

1. e4 Treysman opened with 1 d4 five times, but 1 e4 only thrice, in this competition. AW 1 ... Nc6 For the second

time in successive games with Black Fine offers the Nimzo-witsch Defence, and for the second time his opponent prefers to go into an Open Game. Fine did end up in a Nimzowitsch against van Doesburgh in the Bussum tournament of 1936, and won. AW **2. Nf3 e5** Of course, Black need not play this way, but this is a very common response in this position. AW **3. Bb5 a6 4. Ba4 Nf6 5. 0–0** In round 7 Treysman had played 5 c3 against Horowitz. AW **5 ... Be7 6. Qe2 b5 7. Bb3 0–0 8. c3** Probably better was 8 a4! b4 9 d4 Nxd4 10 Nxd4 exd4 11 e5! GH (8 c3 is the main line in *EMCO 1994*. AW) **8 ... d5!? 9. exd5** Since White does not intend accepting the pawn offered, he should play 9 d3 immediately. RF **9 ... Nxd5 10. d3** White can take the proffered pawn, when, after 10 Nxe5 Nf4 11 Qe4 Nxe5!, he must play 12 d4!, and it seems doubtful whether Black has a sufficiently strong attack. WS (Following on from this line *EMCO 1994* gives 12 ... Bb7 13 Qf4 Nd3 14 Qf5 Nxc1 15 Rxc1 g6 16 Qg4 Bg5 17 Rd1 with some advantage to White.) **10 ... Bf6 11. Ng5!?**

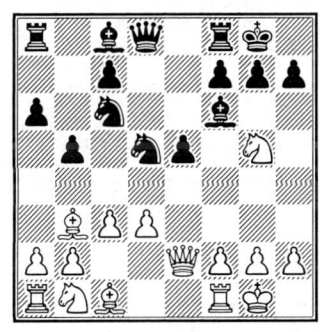

*Position after
White's 11th move*

A bold, but unsound move, which should have given White a definite disadvantage. RF **11 ... Nf4!** It is curious that during the game neither side saw that here 11 ... Nxc3 wins a pawn without any compensation for White (After 11 ... Nxc3 12 Nxc3 Bxg5 13 Bd5 Nd4 14 Qh5 White does seem to have some compensation. AW). With the text, Black sacrifices a pawn for possibilities of a kingside attack. The alternative 11 ... g6 is bad because of 12 Qe4 Nde7 13 Qh4 h5 14 Nxf7! and wins. RF; Deeply calculated. WS **12. Bxf4 exf4 13. Nxh7** Accepting Black's bid for complications. Nevertheless the simple reply 13 Ne4 followed by d3-d4, would have given him a much superior position. RF **13 ... Kxh7 14. Qe4+ g6 15. Qxc6 Rb8**

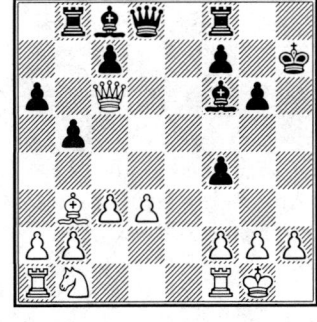

*Position after
Black's 15th move*

Black has adequate counterplay for the pawn. WS **16. Qd5** Exchanging queens is bad because Black is already almost

fully developed, while White has only one piece in the game. Correct was 16 Qf3 g5 17 Nd2 Kg7 with good attacking possibilities for the second player. RF; Probably best. White does not have time for 16 d4, since Black would obtain an extremely dangerous attack, for example 16 d4 Bb7 17 Qc5 Be7 18 Qe5 (in view of the practically forced nature of the ensuing variation it would seem that White must play 18 Qa7 f3 19 d5. AW) Bd6 19 Qe1 f3 20 g3 Qd7 21 Kh1 Rbe8 22 Qd1 Qh3 23 Rg1 Kg7! 24 Qf1 Qxh2+! 25 Kxh2 Rh8+ 26 Qh3 Rxh3+! 27 Kxh3 Bc8+ 28 Kh4 Be7 mate. WS **16 ... Qxd5 17. Bxd5 Rd8! 18. Be4** This loses the pawn, but if instead 18 Bxf7 Rxd3 19 Na4 b4. RF **18 ... c5 19. Nd2 Bg7** Superior to the alternative 19 ... Be7 20 Rfe1 Bf8 21 Nb3 f5 22 Bf3 Rxd3 23 Re8 with pressure for White. RF **20. Nb3 f5 21. Bf3 c4! 22. dxc4 bxc4 23. Na5 Rxb2 24. Nxc4 Rc2 25. Rfc1 Rxc3** Black has found an attractive way of recovering the pawn. The following ending provides a splendid illustration of the strength of the bishop pair. WS **26. Rxc3 Bxc3 27. Rc1 Bg7 28. Kf1 Be6 29. Bb7 a5!**

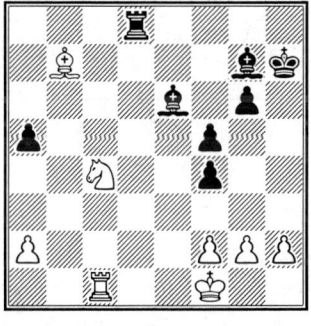

*Position after
Black's 29th move*

30. a4 Better was 30 Nxa5 Rd2 31 Nb3 Rxa2 32 Nc5 Bg8 33 Nd3 Bd4 34 Bc6 Rd2 35 Bb5. GH **30 ... Rd4 31. Ba6** 31 Nxa5 Rxa4 32 Nc6 is better. WS **31 ... Bf8 32. Bb5 Bb4 33. Ne5 Kg7 34. h4 Kf6 35. Nf3 Rd6 36. Ng5 Bb3 37. Nf3** Better was 37 Rc6. Now the black bishops are very powerful. GH **37 ... Rd1+ 38. Rxd1 Bxd1 39. Bc6 Bc3 40. Be8 Ke7! 41. Bb5** His best drawing chance. If 41 Bxg6? Bxa4 42 Bxf5 Bb3 43 Bb1 a4 44 h5 a3 45 h6 Bc4+ and Black wins by marching his king to b2. RF **41 ... Kd6 42. Ne1** White goes after the a-pawn, overlooking the deep-laid trap of his opponent. GH **42 ... Bf6 43. Nd3 f3! 44. gxf3** White's best chance would seem to be 44 Nf4 fxg2+ (44 ... Bxh4 45 g3 followed by Nxg6) 45 Kxg2 g5 (45 ... Bxh4 46 Nxg6) 46 hxg5 Bxg5 47 Kg3 Bc2. AW **44 ... Bxh4 45. Nb2** If 45 Kg2, then Be2!, but 45 f4 is no better for White. WS **45 ... Bxf3 46. Nc4+ Kc5 47. Nxa5** But this blunder loses at once. Correct was 47 Ne5 but after 47 ... Be4 48 Nxg6 Bf6 it would not have been easy for White to draw. RF (It seems to me that White has some drawing chances in this variation after 49 Ke2. AW) **47 ... Bd5! 48. Ba6 Bd8! 49. Nb7+ Kb6** White resigned. Black wins a piece, for after 50 Nxd8 Kxa6 his knight cannot escape. A nicely played game by Fine. GH **0–1** G. H. Hastings from *Australasian Chess Review*, September 1936 in Hilbert & Lahde, 187–9; Fine in *ACB* 1936, 90; Notes from *Wiener Schachzeitung* (WS) taken from *Shakhmatny Ezhegodnik* 1938, 154–5; Denker & Parr, 129–30.

After the tournament had finished *Chess* reported that Fine and Kashdan had accepted invitations to a tournament in Puerto Rico (Reshevsky, who had professional commitments as an accountant, turned down the offer), in which the Spanish Champion Rey Ardid was to compete.

A Return to Europe, 1936–1937

Fine's third trip to Europe turned out to be an extended visit. He stayed for a year and a half, basing himself in the Netherlands, but roaming widely around the continent. During this period he won eleven first prizes, two second and one third, but towards the end of his stay he became fatigued and suffered two of the very few poor results in his whole career. The initial six months was, however, almost entirely successful. Fine started with a victory in an event where the opposition was largely of master class, in fact the majority of players were recognized as grandmasters (a far rarer animal in those days than now). He came a full point ahead of World Champion Max Euwe. At Nottingham he was only half a point behind joint winners Botvinnik and Capablanca. The top seven placed in this event, along with Paul Keres, were later to form the field for arguably the strongest tournament of all time just two years later. A small tournament in Norway provided an opportunity for Fine to finish ahead of Salo Flohr once more, after which a return to Holland brought a shared first place with the World Champion ahead of once-and-future king Alexander Alekhine. The annual Hastings tournament, however, found the Russian back to his best, he not only won the event but defeated the American in their personal encounter.

Zandvoort, July 18–August 1, 1936

"New European chess laurels have come to the United States as a result of the most recent American victory abroad—the triumph of Reuben Fine of New York City in the international masters tournament held at Zandvoort in the Netherlands from July 18 to August 1. Notwithstanding the presence of Dr. Max Euwe of Amsterdam among the twelve competitors, this twenty-two year old [*sic*] champion from across the Atlantic came through with flying colours, with the Stars and Stripes leading all the rest. To this we are becoming pretty well accustomed. Fine's victory, by a full point over Dr. Euwe, who was second in a well-contested race, may properly be regarded as a decisive one. Through eleven rounds he played with the steadiness of a veteran, winning six of his games and drawing the remaining five. Three of these wins were at the expense of fellow prize winners. With two sessions of play daily, afternoon and evening, play progressed steadily, excepting on July 21, 24 and 31, which were set apart for adjourned games or rest. Awards of prizes were made at a formal dinner arranged in honour of the masters on the evening of August 2." (*ACB* 1936)

		1	2	3	4	5	6	7	8	9	10	11	12	
1	Fine	*	½	1	1	½	1	½	½	1	½	1	1	8½
2	Euwe	½	*	½	1	0	1	1	½	½	1	½	1	7½
3	Tartakower	0	½	*	½	½	½	½	½	1	½	1	1	6½
4	Keres	0	0	½	*	1	0	½	½	1	1	1	1	6½
5	Bogoljubow	½	1	½	0	*	½	0	1	0	½	1	1	6
6	Maróczy	0	0	½	1	½	*	½	½	1	½	1	½	6
7	Grünfeld	½	0	½	½	1	½	*	½	½	½	½	½	5½
8	Spielmann	½	½	½	½	0	½	½	*	½	½	½	1	5½
9	Landau	0	½	0	0	1	0	½	½	*	1	1	1	5½
10	Van Doesburgh	½	0	½	0	½	½	½	½	0	*	0	1	4
11	Becker	0	½	0	0	0	0	½	½	0	1	*	½	3
12	Prins	0	0	0	0	0	½	½	0	0	0	½	*	1½

(272) FINE—MARÓCZY, G

Zandvoort (1), 1936 (18 July)
Queen's Gambit Declined [D66]

The game which follows took a fairly quiet course. Queens came off early, and there were no combinations of note. Fine played pretty keenly withal: in the very beginning he conceded the "minor exchange" and the pawn majority on the queen's wing, convinced that his superior mobility on other fronts would count for more. Keen and efficient play is required, in a case like this, to make the abstract advantage turn the scale against the concrete. Fine succeeds convincingly. ME **1. d4 e6 2. c4 Nf6 3. Nc3 d5 4. Nf3 Be7 5. Bg5 Nbd7 6. e3 0–0 7. Rc1 c6 8. Bd3** More aggressive is 8 Qc2. At the time, however, my knowledge of the openings was still not what it might have been. RF **8 ... h6** Weakening. Better is the immediate 8 ... dxc4 9 Bxc4 Nd5. RF **9. Bf4** 9 Bh4 is more usual; the text move is "sharper" in so far as it permits Black to exchange off White's queen's bishop for a knight. The resulting situation is difficult to assess, White's command of greater terrain being balanced against Black's retention of his two bishops. Fine often makes moves in the opening which sharpen, or rather could sharpen, the conflict. He does not go in for direct attack, but strives after some positional aim in a more or less provocative way. If his opponent takes up the gauntlet, a lively game quickly ensues, in which it usually becomes evident that Fine has seen far more deeply into the position than his opponent. ME **9 ... dxc4?** Black would better have played 9 ... Nh5 at once if he is going to play it at all, for example, 10 Be5 Nxe5 11 dxe5 g6 12 0–0 Bd7 13 Qd2 dxc4 14 Bxc4 Qc7 15 Ne4 Rad8 16 Qc3 Bc8 17 g4 f5!, with good play for Black (Thomas–Lasker, Nottingham, 1936). ME **10. Bxc4 Nh5** Once Black has given up the centre,

10 ... Nd5 deserves preference. The point is that then, after the attacked bishop moves, 11 ... N×c3 can be played, White having to capture with the pawn, since otherwise he would lose the exchange by ... Bb4. The blocking of the c-file thus produced would ease Black's task considerably, and for this reason White does best, after 10 ... Nd5, to allow Black to capture his queen's bishop by continuing 11 0–0. ME **11. Be5! N×e5** Consequential, but bad. 11 ... Nhf6 (undoing the mistake) is better. BB **12. d×e5** Threatening to win a piece by 13 g4. We now perceive the important distinction between the continuations 10 ... Nd5 and 10 ... Nh5; the first allows Black to play 11 ... N×e5 and concentrate unhindered on the task of bringing his queen's bishop into play, whilst the second, adopted here, leaves his knight most awkwardly placed, so that he has to postpone the important job of getting out the bishop until he has attended to its security. ME **12 ... Q×d1+** His best course. On 12 ... g6 White avoids the exchange of queens with 13 Qc2 and develops a strong attack. RF **13. R×d1 g6** Black has the two bishops and the better pawn position. His preponderance on the queenside is a clear advantage in itself, since one of White's pawns on the other wing is doubled; whilst the bishop pair is a certain guarantee for the future. All these factors are not quite enough to counterbalance his difficulties in developing, however, as Fine has foreseen. ME **14. g4** Blumenfeld considered this to be a mistake, intended to prevent the advance of the f-pawn, and recommended the immediate 14 0–0 with the continuations 14 ... b5 15 Be2, with the threat of 16 Nd4 and 17 Bf3, or 14 ... b6 15 Ne4. AW **14 ... Ng7**

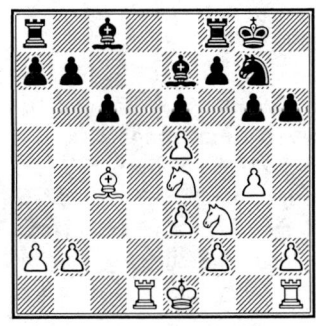

Position after Black's 14th move

15. Ne4 Cancelling out one of Black's advantages already; White can now play Nf6+ whenever he chooses, as good as forcing the reply ... B×f6, so that Black's better bishop disappears. ME **15 ... a6** The only way he can develop his queen's bishop. RF **16. h4** Preparing what follows, for if at once 16 Nf6+ B×f6 17 e×f6 Ne8 Black wins a pawn. RF **16 ... b5 17. Be2** The logical reply—to keep the queen's file open for White's rook. GK **17 ... c5** Here Maróczy had no doubt considered the alternative 17 ... f6 to avoid the bind which ensues now. However, after 17 ... f6 18 e×f6 B×f6 19 N×f6+ R×f6 20 Ne5 White again has a won game. On the defensive 17 ... Ne8 18 g5 would be the reply. RF **18. 0–0** Very well played. Superficially it might seem good to forego castling, leaving the rook at h1 and playing for a kingside attack, for example with h4-h5 in mind (which

would induce Black to play ... g5 so that White could then break through by f2-f4). Fine does the job more simply and safely. He prefers to base his operations on the queen's file, and his judgment is speedily vindicated. ME **18 ... Bb7 19. Nf6+ B×f6** Forced, because of the threat of Rd7. GK **20. e×f6 Ne8 21. g5 Bd5** Black has nothing better in face of the threat of 22 Rd7. ME **22. Ne5** Threatening to win the exchange with Nd7. RF **22 ... Nd6** Hoping to build up some counterplay. However, 22 ... Nc7 was safer. RF **23. f3!** Threatening to win a piece by 24 e4. If 23 ... Rfd8 24 e4 Bb7 (24 ... B×a2? 25 Nc6 Rd7 26 e5 and wins) 25 Rd2 Ne8 26 Rfd1 R×d2 27 R×d2 and wins easily through his possession of the queen's file. Black is at a loss for a satisfactory reply. ME **23 ... Nc4** Black has already had to give back the minor exchange, and now he sees his pawn majority on the queenside disappear. The ensuing exchanges leave his pawns badly scattered, and soon one of them must go. ME; Blumenfeld here thought the best practical chance was 23 ... Nf5 and if 24 Kf2 then simply 24 ... B×a2, or if 24 e4 Ng3 25 e×d5 N×e2+ 26 Kf2 Nf4!. An interesting idea, but White would surely still have excellent winning chances with 27 d6! AW **24. B×c4 B×c4 25. N×c4 b×c4 26. Rc1 Rab8 27. Rf2 Rb4**

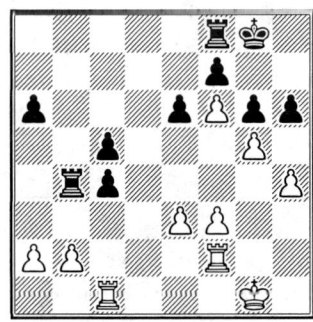

Position after Black's 27th move

28. a3! Driving the rook to an inferior square. ME **28 ... Ra4 29. Rc3** To prevent the freeing ... c3. RF **29 ... Rd8 30. Rfc2** Winning the pawn on c4. ME **30 ... Rd5** 30 ... Rb8 or 30 ... Rd8+ 31 Kg2 Rb8 would be no better. White would not capture the pawn at once, but would first bring his king to g3. ME **31. f4 e5 32. R×c4 R×c4 33. R×c4 e×f4 34. e×f4 h×g5 35. h×g5** Black can now regain the pawn temporarily, but not the game; if 35 ... Rd1+ 36 Kf2 Rd2+ 37 Kg3! R×b2 38 R×c5 Rb3+ 39 Kg4 R×a3 40 Rc8+ Rh7 41 Rf8 and wins. RF **35 ... Rd2 36. R×c5 R×b2 37. Rc8+ Kh7 38. Rf8 Rb7** According to Euwe, Black played this move and then immediately resigned. **39. Kf2** Black resigned. At this point an amusing interlude occurred. Bogolyubov came over and suggested 39 ... a5 40 a4?? Rb2+ 41 Ke3 Rb3+ 42 Kd4 Rd3+!! with a draw by perpetual check, since Black is stalemated. Maróczy replied that he was sure I would have seen through such an elementary trap. Actually I had not noticed the stalemate position, but after 39 ... a5 40 Ra8 White avoids it and wins easily. RF **1–0** Fine 1958, 67–70; George Koltanowski in *BCM* 1938, 163–4; Euwe 1945, 205–10; Beniamin Blumenfeld in *Shakhmatny Ezhegodnik* 1938, 184–8.

(273) SPIELMANN, R—FINE

Zandvoort (2), 1936 (19 July)
Queen's Gambit Declined, Ragozin System [D38]

1. d4 Nf6 2. c4 e6 3. Nc3 Bb4 4. Nf3 d5 Unusual, but nevertheless quite playable. Against 4 ... Bxc3+ 5 bxc3 b6 6 Nd2! Bb7 7 f3 0–0 8 e4 is quite strong for Black. ACB **5. Qa4+** A doubtful manoeuvre. Simplest and safest is 5 e3, but White then has little hope of obtaining an advantage. RF **5 ... Nc6 6. Ne5** Energetic, but questionable. 6 a3 was preferable. RF **6 ... Bd7 7. Nxd7** An interesting alternative was 7 Nxc6 Bxc3+ 8 bxc3 Bxc6 9 Qb3 dxc4 10 Qxc4 Ne4! (necessary, since f3 followed by e4 must be prevented) 11 Bf4! Nd6! 12 Qd3 Be4 13 Qd1!, with a slight advantage for White. RF **7 ... Qxd7 8. e3** 8 a3 Bxc3+ (not the tempting 8 ... Nxd4, as given by Fine, because of 9 axb4. AW) 9 bxc3 e5 10 e3 is better. Alekhine **8 ... e5 9. dxe5** Best. In a game between Colle and Alekhine, Hastings 1925/6, the continuation was 9 a3 exd4 10 axb4 dxc3 11 bxc3 0–0 12 Be2 dxc4 with advantage to Black. RF **9 ... d4!** Grünfeld here recommends 9 ... Ne4 10 Qc2 Nxe5 (but not 10 ... d4, because of 11 a3! Bxc3+ (11 ... Nc5 looks interesting. AW) 12 bxc3 Nxc3 13 Bb2) 11 cxd5 Bxc3+ (again if 11 ... Qxd5 12 Qa4+ Nc6 13 Qxb4 Nxb4 14 Nxd5 Nxd5 15 f3) 12 bxc3 Qxd5 but after the simple 13 Be2 Black's pieces will be unable to maintain themselves in their advanced posts. RF **10. a3!** The only reply, but a sufficient one. RF **10 ... Bxc3+ 11. bxc3 dxe3!** The point to Black's previous play. If now 12 exf6 exf2+ 13 Kxf2 Qf5+ 14 Ke1 0–0–0, and Black's attack is irresistible. RF **12. Bxe3 Ng4** Better than the immediate capture at e5, since Black now forces the exchange of one of White's bishops. RF **13. Bd4 Ngxe5 14. f4** An excellent move which leads to a tenable endgame. RF **14 ... Nxd4** With equality, MCO 149. **15. Qxd7+ Kxd7 16. 0–0–0 Nec6** Not 16 ... Ng4 because of 17 Be2! with advantage to White. HK **17. cxd4 Rad8 18. d5** Again played with profound insight. White sacrifices the square c5 in order to obtain a satisfactory development for his bishop. In point of fact, after 18 Kc2 Kc8 19 Kc3 Rhe8, Black has much the better of it. RF **18 ... Na5 19. Bd3 Kd6** Black is striving to obtain the position with king at c5 and knight at d6, but White cleverly prevents this formation. RF **20. Rhe1** If now 20 ... Kc5 21 Re7. RF **20 ... Rde8 21. Kc2 b6** Again 21 ... Kc5 was useless, because of 22 Kc3 b6 23 Re5 and Black's king must return, for if 23 ... Nb7 24 d6+ Rxe5 25 fxe5 cxd6 26 Be4, with the better position. RF **22. Kc3 g6** Black has the advantage on the queenside as the pawn position restricts the white bishop. In order to exploit this advantage he must exchange rooks, for which purpose his king must redeploy to d7. This cannot be achieved without further preparation since a bishop check on f5 could cause problems. However, the consequent weakening of the kingside gives White the advantage on that side of the board, thus evening the chances overall. HK **23. g3 Nb7 24. Kd4** Once the king has reached this square, a draw is the natural result. RF **24 ... Nc5 25. Bc2 Kd7 26. h4 Rxe1**

27. Rxe1 Re8 28. Re5! Very good. Clearly Black himself cannot exchange rooks. He must force his opponent to make the exchange, but in doing so he further weakens his kingside. HK **28 ... f6 29. Rxe8 Kxe8 30. h5!** Strongly played. Now the significance of the weakness of Black's kingside becomes apparent. HK **30 ... f5 31. hxg6 hxg6 32. Ke5 Ke7 33. Kd4 Kd6 34. Bd1!** A last-minute trap. If 34 ... Ne4 35 g4 Nf2 36 gxf5 Nxd1 37 fxg6 Ke7 38 f5 or 38 c5 (Fine just writes 38 P-B5 and either looks possible. AW), and Black must play carefully to hold the draw. RF **34 ... Nd7** Draw agreed. ½–½ Kmoch 1936, 17–9; Fine in ACB 1936, 108–9.

(274) FINE—TARTAKOWER, S

Zandvoort (3), 1936 (20 July)
Queen's Indian Defence [E14]

1. d4 d5 2. Nf3 Nf6 3. c4 e6 4. Nc3 Be7 5. e3 An invitation to the Meran, which he refuses. RF **5 ... 0–0 6. Bd3** Simpler is 6 ... dxc4 7 Bxc4 c5, transposing to a variation of the Queen's Gambit Accepted. RF **6 ... b6 7. 0–0 Bb7 8. b3** An almost symmetrical position is now set up, which is not so easy for Black as would appear. RF **8 ... c5 9. Bb2 Nc6 10. Rc1 Rc8 11. Qe2 Qc7?** The crucial position. Black cannot capture the d-pawn, for after 11 ... cxd4 12 exd4 dxc4 13 bxc4 Nxd4?? 14 Nxd4 Qxd4 15 Nd5! Qc5 16 Bxf6! gxf6 (or 16 ... Bxf6 17 Qe4) 17 Qg4+ Kh8 18 Qh4 wins. However he can equalize with 11 ... cxd4 12 exd4 Nb4! for if 13 Bb1 dxc4 and 14 ... Bxf3. RF **12. cxd5 exd5** This loses quickly. Better is 12 ... Nxd5 13 Nxd5 exd5 14 dxc5 bxc5 15 Ba6 (or 15 Rfd1. AW) with a superior game for White (similar to Euwe–Winter, Nottingham, 1936), but with lots of play left. RF **13. Nb5 Qb8** 13 ... Qd8 is no improvement: after 14 dxc5 Bxc5 (if 14 ... bxc5 15 Bxf6) 15 Rfd1 White has much the better of it. RF **14. dxc5 bxc5 15. Bxf6 Bxf6** The alternative of ... gxf6 would invite disaster through 16 Nh4. ACB **16. Rxc5 Nb4 17. Rxc8 Rxc8 18. Nbd4 Nxd3 19. Qxd3** As Fine is a past master in the art of handling knights, he is not disturbed by the fact that the adversary has kept his two bishops. ACB **19 ... Qd6**

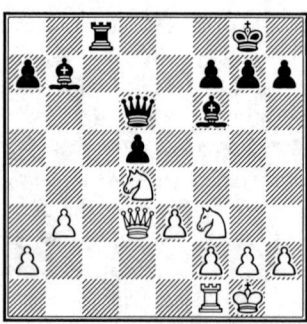

Position after Black's 19th move

20. Qd2 Qa3 21. h3 g6 22. Rb1 Preparing to dislodge the queen with Qb2. RF **22 ... Be7 23. Qb2 Ba6** 23 ... Qxb2 24 Rxb2 Rc1+ would mean nothing, for White continues with 25 Rc2. RF **24. Qxa3 Bxa3 25. Rd1 Kf8**

26. Ne1 Now White threatens to win a pawn with N4-c2. RF **26 ... Bb7 27. Nd3** Threatening Nb5. RF **27 ... a6 28. Rd2 Ke7 29. Rc2** After the exchange of rooks the rest is relatively easy. RF **29 ... Kd6 30. Kf1 Rc7 31. Rxc7 Kxc7 32. b4!**

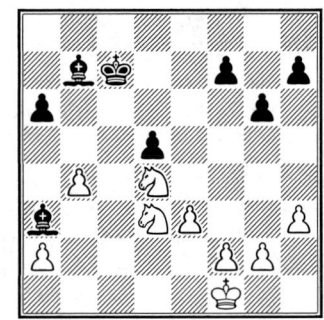

Position after White's 32nd move

32 ... Bc6 So that if 33 Nc2? Bb5. RF **33. Ke2 Kb6?** His last chance to extract the bishop lay in 33 ... a5. Failing to take it spells finis for Black. ACB **34. Nc2 d4 35. Nxa3 Bxg2 36. Nf4 dxe3 37. Nxg2** Black resigned. **1–0** Fine 1958, 71-4; ACB 1936, 107-8.

(275) KERES, P–FINE

Zandvoort (4), 1936 (22 July)
Réti Opening [A09]

1. Nf3 d5 2. c4 dxc4 3. e3 Nf6 4. Bxc4 e6 5. 0-0 c5 6. b3 More energetic is 6 d4. ACB **6 ... Nc6 7. Bb2 a6 8. a4 Be7** Black has already equalized. RF **9. Ne5 Na5 10. d4** If 10 Be2 Qb6 is strong. ACB **10 ... Nxc4 11. Nxc4 0-0 12. Nbd2 Bd7 13. Ne5** Insufficient would have been 13 dxc5 Bxc5 14 Bxf6 gxf6 15 Ne4 Be7 16 Qg4+ Kh8 17 Rfd1, and now simply 17 ... Rg8. ACB **13 ... Be8 14. Rc1 cxd4 15. Bxd4 Nd7** Equalizes. Bad, however, would have been 15 ... Nd5, because of 16 Qg4. ACB **16. Nxd7 Bxd7 17. Nc4** Hoping to make something of the hole at b6, but it has no real meaning. RF **17 ... Rc8 18. Qf3** Only apparently good. Best was 18 Ne5. ACB **18 ... b5 19. Qg3** Stronger is 19 Nb6, when Black's best is the sharp 19 ... Rxc1 20 Rxc1 e5! 21 Nxd7 Qxd7 22 Bxe5 bxa4 (if 23 Rc7? Qe6) with equality. RF **19 ... f6 20. Bb6** Loses a pawn in exchange for bishops of opposite colours. Now 20 Nb6? fails altogether against 20 ... Rxc1 21 Rxc1 e5. RF **20 ... Qe8 21. Nd6** After 21 axb5 Bxb5, White's position is bad. ACB **21 ... Bxd6 22. Qxd6 bxa4 23. bxa4 Bxa4 24. Bc5 Rf7** White's initiative soon peters out. RF **25. Ba3** 25 Qxa6 loses the exchange. ACB **25 ... Rd8 26. Qb6** Not 26 Qxa6 Bb5. RF **26 ... h6 27. Rc5 Bb5 28. Rfc1 Rfd7 29. h3 Rb8** (*see diagram*) **30. Qxb8** Fine thought this ending was only a draw, but in his notes he makes a strange oversight at move 46. The notes in *Lessons from My Games* occasionally suffer from having been written many years after the events they describe. AW **30 ... Qxb8 31. Rc8+ Qxc8 32. Rxc8+ Kh7 33. Bb4!** Prevents the advance of the pawn. To try to get the king over to the

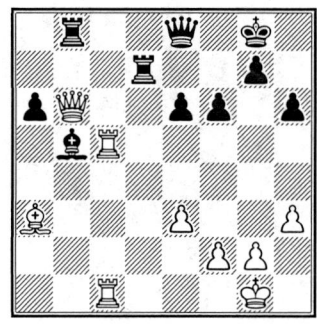

Position after Black's 29th move

queenside would be futile, since Black cannot cross the c-file. Nor can Black attempt to advance the a-pawn by Rd7-d1+-a1, for White would then reply Rc7 and get a dangerous counterattack against the black king position. Consequently the only chance is to secure some advantage on the kingside. *BCE* **33 ... h5 34. h4** He must prevent h5-h4. ACB **34 ... Kg6 35. Kh2 e5 36. Kg3 Bd3 37. Rc6 Rb7 38. Bc3** Threatening 39 Bxe5. RF **38 ... Bb5 39. Rc8 Kf7 40. f3** To allow the king to get to the queenside if rooks are exchanged. Black, however, now sees a possibility on the seventh rank. RF **40 ... Bd7 41. Ra8 Bb5** Not 41 ... Rb3, because of 42 Ra7. ACB **42. Rc8 Rd7 43. Kf2 Rd1 44. Rc7+ Kg8**

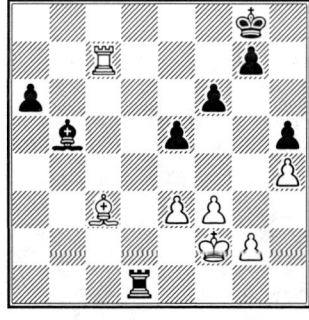

Position after Black's 44th move

45. g4! Curiously this is the strongest defence, although even if it weren't it would suit Keres' temperament best. If, instead, 45 Rc8+ Kh7 46 Rc7 with the idea of playing Bc3-b4-f8, Black has a neat win in 46 ... Rc1 47 Ba5 Rf1+ 48 Kg3 Ra1 49 Bb4 Ra2 50 Bf8 Kg8 51 Bxg7 Bf1 52 Rc1 Rxg2+ 53 Kh3 Rxg7+ 54 Rxf1 Ra7 with a won rook and pawn ending. RF **45 ... Rf1+ 46. Kg2** Fine called this the fatal mistake and recommended 46 Kg3 with the idea 46 ... e4 47 fxe4! hxg4 48 e5! Rf3+ (why not 48 ... f5?) 49 Kxg3 Be2 50 exf6!! gxf6 51 Kh5 with a draw. However, all this ignores 46 ... Be2, mopping up the white pawns, which seems to give Black a clearly winning position. AW **46 ... e4! 47. fxe4** Or 47 g5 exf3+ 48 Kg3 Be2 49 gxf6 gxf6 50 Bxf6 Rg1+ 51 Kf2 Rg2+ 52 Ke1 Bb5 and wins. RF **47 ... hxg4 48. e5** After this blunder, White is clearly lost. Correct was 48 Kg3 Rf3+ 49 Kxg4! Be2 50 e5! and Black has no effective discovered check. ACB **48 ... Rf3!** The decisive manoeuvre: White is now caught in a mating trap. RF **49. exf6** No better is 49 e6 Rxe3 50 e7 f5 and the black pawns march on. RF **49 ... gxf6 50. Kg1**

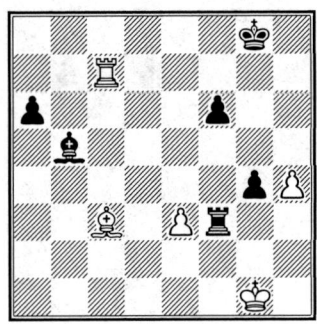

*Position after
White's 50th move*

50 ... Bf1! Threatening ... g3, ... Bh3 and ... Rf1 mate so that White must beat a hasty retreat. The game would still be a draw with the rooks off the board, but now Black has a mating attack. *BCE* **51. Rc6 Kf7 52. e4** After the exchanges 52 Rxf6+ Rxf6 53 Bxf6 Kxf6 54 Kxf1 a5 Black queens first. RF **52 ... g3 53. e5 fxe5 54. Bxe5 Bh3 55. Rc1** Forced; the white rook is now immobilized. RF **55 ... a5** The most precise winning line. Black still had to be careful; for instance: if 55 ... Kg6 56 Ra1 draws at once. *ACB* **56. Kh1** There is no defence. If, for instance, 56 h5 a4 57 Rb1 a3 58 Rb7+ Ke6 59 Bxg3 Rxg3+ 60 Kh2 Rc3 61 h6 Bf5 62 Ra7 Ke5 63 h7 Bxh7 64 Rxh7 Kd4 and wins. *ACB* **56 ... a4** The tempting 56 ... Rf1+ fails because 57 Rxf1 is check. And if 56 ... Ke6 57 Bxg3 (not 57 Bd4 Rf1+ 58 Rxf1 g2+) Rxg3 58 Ra1! and draws. RF **57. Bd4** Or 57 Rg1 h7+ 58 Kh2 Rf1 59 Bd4 a3 60 Kxh3 Rxg1 61 Bxg1 a2, and one of the black pawns must queen. *ACB* **57 ... a3 58. Rc2** If 58 Rc7+ Ke6 59 Ra7 Rf1+ 60 Bg1 Rf2! is the simplest. *ACB* **58 ... Rb3 59. h5 Rb1+ 60. Bg1 Rb2 61. Rc7+ Ke6 62. Bd4** The threat was ... Bg2 mate. **62 ... Rb1+ 63. Bg1 a2** White resigned. **0–1** Fine 1958, 75–8; *BCE* 1941, 444–5; *ACB* 1936, 109–10.

(276) FINE—EUWE, M

Zandvoort (5), 1936 (23 July)
Queen's Gambit, Slav Defence [D10]

1. d4 d5 2. c4 c6 3. Nc3 dxc4 4. a4 Curiously enough this move seems to be a mistake, although of course I did not realize it at the time the game was played. But since 4 e3 b5 gives Black an even game at once, 3 Nf3 must be considered preferable to 3 Nc3. RF (Alekhine introduced the innovation 4 e4 against Euwe in 1937. AW) **4 ... e5! 5. dxe5** Relatively best. After 5 e3 exd4 6 exd4 Be6 the second player already has a strategically won game. RF **5 ... Qxd1+ 6. Kxd1 Na6 7. e3 Be6 8. Nf3 0–0–0+ 9. Bd2 Nh6** Quite strong, but Black could have maintained his advantage more simply by 9 ... Bb4 10 Nd4 (10 Ne4! AW) Nc5 11 Nxe6 fxe6 12 Bxc4? Bxc3 13 bxc3 Ne4 and wins. RF **10. Ke1** After 10 h3 Black has again the opportunity to enter the variation given in the note above. RF **10 ... Nb4 11. Rc1 Nd3+ 12. Bxd3 Rxd3!** Stronger than 12 ... cxd3 13 Nd4. RF **13. h3** If at once 13 Nd4 Ng4 wins a pawn. RF **13 ... Be7 14. Nd4** In order to obtain some counterplay. But the quieter continuation 14 Ke2 was preferable. RF **14 ... Rd8 15. Nxe6 fxe6**

16. Rc2 Nf7 17. f4 g5 18. Ke2! gxf4 19. exf4 Rg3! 20. Ne4! Rxg2+ 21. Kf3 Rdg8 22. Rxc4 Probably better was 22 Ng5 Bxg5 23 Kxg2 Bxf4+ 24 Kf3 Bxd2 25 Rxd2 Nxe5+ 26 Ke4 with good drawing chances. But I was not yet convinced that my position was hopelessly lost. RF **22 ... Nh6 23. Rcc1 Nf5 24. Bc3 Bc5!!** A crushing rejoinder, which I had not foreseen when I made my 22nd move. I had only taken 24 ... Bd8 into consideration, when 25 a5 is an adequate reply. Naturally, capturing the bishop would allow mate in two moves. RF **25. Ng5** Loses the exchange. Relatively best was 25 h4 Be3 26 Rce1 R8g4 27 Rxe3 R4g3+ 28 Nxg3 Rxg3+ 29 Kf2 Rxe3 30 Rg1 and although Black's position is decidedly superior no immediate win is visible. Both players were already in time pressure. RF **25 ... Rf2+ 26. Ke4 Ng3+** Fine felt that 26 ... Rd8 would be well answered by 27 Rcg1. In that case play might continue 27 ... Re2+ 28 Kf3 Bxg1 29 Rxg1 Re3+ 30 Kf2 and now 20 ... Rdd3 looks like a powerful move for Black. AW **27. Kd3 Nxh1 28. Rxh1 Rxf4 29. Nxe6 Rg3+ 30. Kc2 Rf2+** Returning the exchange was not necessary, but by no means bad. RF **31. Kb1 Be7 32. Be1 Rgg2 33. Bxf2 Rxf2 34. Nd4 c5?** After this mistake Black can no longer win. Correct was 34 ... Rf4 35 Rd1 Re4 winning a pawn. White's best chance to save the game would then have been 36 Nf5 Rxe5 37 Nxe7+ Rxe7 38 Rd6, but the ending is not to be held against best play. RF **35. Nb5 a6 36. Nc3 Kd7 37. Nd5! Bd8 38. Rc1** Simpler was 38 Rg1, since now 38 ... Rf5 still offered Black some winning chances. RF **38 ... Rf3 39. Rxc5 Rxh3 40. e6+! Kd6** Of course not 40 ... Kxe6? 41 Nf4+ Kd6 42 Rd5+ and wins. RF **41. Rc8 Kxd5 42. Rxd8+ Kxe6 43. Rb8 Rd3** No win is possible. If 43 ... Rb3 44 Rh8 Rh3 45 Rb8. RF **44. Rxb7 Rd7 45. Rb8 Kf5 46. Kc2** Draw agreed. **½–½** Fine in *Chess* 1935–6, 457–8.

(277) GRÜNFELD, E—FINE

Zandvoort (6), 1936 (25 July)
Nimzowitsch-Indian Defence, Classical Variation [E37]

1. d4 Nf6 2. c4 e6 3. Nc3 Bb4 4. Qc2 d5 5. a3 Bxc3+ 6. Qxc3 Ne4 7. Qc2 Nc6 8. Nf3 e5 9. e3 Bf5 10. Qa4 According to Fine 10 Qb3 was stronger, preserving some advantage for White. **10 ... 0–0 11. cxd5 Qxd5 12. Qb5 Qxb5 13. Bxb5 Na5 14. Ba4** White must prevent ... Nb3. **14 ... exd4 15. Nxd4** From this point on there follows some intricate knight-play. **15 ... Nc5 16. Bd1 Nd3+ 17. Ke2 Bg6 18. b4 Nc4 19. Bc2 Nde5 20. Bxg6 hxg6 21. Bd2 Rad8 22. Bc3 Rfe8 23. h3 Nb6 24. Rhd1 Nd5 25. Be1 Nc4 26. Kf3 c6 27. a4 Rd6 28. Nc2 Rf6+ 29. Kg3 Nd6 30. Kh2** On 30 ... Ne4 White will reply with 31 Kg1. **30 ... Nc4** Draw agreed. **½–½** Kmoch 1936, 59.

(278) FINE—BECKER, A

Zandvoort (7), 1936 (26 July)
Nimzowitsch-Indian Defence, Classical Variation [E33]

1. d4 Nf6 2. c4 e6 3. Nc3 Bb4 4. Qc2 Nc6 5. Nf3 d6 6. a3 And not 6 Bg5 h6 7 Bh4? g5 8 Bg3 g4 followed by ... Nxd4. The text allows White to obtain two bishops against bishop and knight, considered by the modern players as an advantage. K&R **6 ... Bxc3+ 7. Qxc3 Qe7** Here Black should have played 7 ... a5, to forestall the push of the b-pawn. K&R; Or 7 ... 0–0 8 b4 Re8! 9 e3 e5 10 dxe5, MCO 185. **8. b4!** The most energetic continuation. After 8 e3 e5 Black has a good game. RF **8 ... 0–0** As a result of his inexact play, Black is unable to play 8 ... e5, which is the point of the plan begun with 4 ... Nc6, since after 8 ... e5 9 b5 Nxd4 10 Nxd4 exd4 11 Qxd4 White is clearly better. K&R **9. Bb2 Re8** Black keeps trying to force e6-e5 while White plays to prevent it. K&R **10. b5** Preventing the move e6-e5. **10 ... Nb8 11. g3 b6 12. Bg2 Bb7 13. 0–0 Nbd7 14. a4 a6 15. Ba3** Continuing to hold up the e-pawn. K&R **15 ... Ra7** 15 ... e5 was better. Now White gains a decisive advantage. RF **16. Ne5!** Initiating a series of exchanges leading to a clear advantage to White, MCO. **16 ... Bxg2 17. Kxg2** Threatening to win a rook by the double attack 18 Nc6. K&R **17 ... Nxe5 18. dxe5 Ne4 19. Qe3 Nc5 20. Rfd1 Rea8** Or 20 ... Nxa4 21 exd6 cxd6 22 Bxd6 Qb7+ 23 f3 Nb2 24 Rd4 with a winning position. RF **21. Bxc5! dxc5** If 21 ... bxc5 then 22 Rab1 axb5 23 axb5 dxe5 24 Qxe5 wins. RF **22. Rac1 axb5 23. axb5 Ra2 24. Rd3 Rd8 25. Rcd1 Rxd3 26. Rxd3 g6** Providing a bolthole for the king in case of an eventual invasion of the eighth rank. K&R **27. h4!**

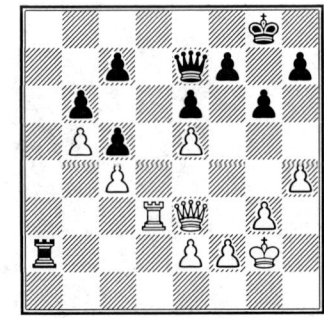

Position after White's 27th move

27 ... h5 White threatened h4-h5-h6. RF **28. Qf3!** With the threat Qc6. RF **28 ... Qe8 29. Qf6** An extremely interesting position would have arisen if White had nevertheless played 29 Qc6. It is then bad for Black to exchange of c6, since after 29 ... Qxc6 30 bxc6 Rxe2 31 Rd7 the passed pawn at c6 is decisive and passive defence by 30 ... Kf8 31 Rd7 Ra7 likewise proves insufficient. In that case the white rook on d7 is effectively protected by the pawn and cannot therefore be driven away by the black king. White improves the position of his king and wins easily by a pawn breakthrough on the kingside. Black would answer 29 Qc6 with 29 ... Qc8! 30 Rd7 Ra7. White is then hardly in a position to strengthen his hold on the game, for example, 31 Re7 Kf8 32 Qd7 Qxd7 33 Rxd7 Ke8, and the white rook is forced to retreat. The difference between the position in which the white pawn is on c6 and this one, where it still stands on b5, is very striking and demonstrates how impor-

tant it is to control the squares via which the rook can invade the enemy camp. LP **29 ... Ra8** 30 Rd8 is threatened, and because of that the black rook is pushed back on to the defensive. LP **30. g4!!** Since White cannot exploit the d-file directly, he opens a file on the kingside by a pawn breakthrough combination (the threat is 31 gxh5 gxh5 32 Rg3+). LP **30 ... hxg4 31. h5!** **Qf8** Desperation. If 31 ... gxh5 then 32 Qg5+ Kf8 33 Qxh5 and White wins without particular difficulty. The main variations are 33 ... f5 (or 33 ... c6 34 Rd1!! cxb5 35 Qh8+ Ke7 36 Qf6+ Kf8 37 Rh1 Qc6+ 38 f3 gxf3+ 39 exf3 Ke8 40 Rh8+ Kd7 41 Qxf7 mate; neither is 33 ... Qc8 34 Qxg4 Ra1 35 Qf4 Qa8+ 36 Rf3 any help) 34 Qh8+ Kf7 35 Qh7+ Kf8 36 Rd7 and Black must give up his queen. RF **32. hxg6 Qg7 33. Rd8+ Rxd8 34. Qxd8+ Qf8 35. gxf7+ Kxf7 36. Qf6+** This is one of those pleasant positions in which all roads lead to victory. RF **36 ... Kg8 37. Qxe6+ Kh7 38. Qd7+ Kh6 39. e6 Qa8+ 40. Qd5 Qe8 41. Qe5 Qe7 42. Kg3** Black resigned. My best game from Zandvoort. RF **1–0** Fine in *Chess* 1935–6, 458–9; Kahn & Renaud, 57–8; Pachman, 42–3.

(279) FINE—LANDAU, S

Zandvoort (8), 1936 (28 July)
Queen's Indian Defence [E14]

1. d4 d5 2. c4 e6 3. Nc3 Nf6 4. Nf3 Be7 5. e3 0–0 6. Bd3 b6 Black plays into one of the American's favourite variations. By continuing 4 ... c5 or 6 ... dxc4, followed by ... c5, he could have taken the game along a different path. **7. 0–0 Bb7 8. b3 Nbd7 9. Bb2 c5 10. Qe2 Ne4** (10 ... dxc4 11 bxc4 cxd4 12 exd4 Rc8 13 Ne5 a6 14 Rad1 and White stands slightly better, Reshevsky–Feigins, Kemeri 1937.) **11. Rad1 Qc7 12. Nb5 Qb8 13. cxd5 Bxd5 14. Ne5 Nxe5?** After this mistake White gets a strong attack, which he pursues relentlessly. 14 ... Rd8, with a difficult but not a lost game, was essential. **15. dxe5 f5** White was threatening to win a piece with 16 f3. **16. exf6** (White has a distinct superiority, but there is no question of a forced win, MCO 158.) **16 ... Nxf6**

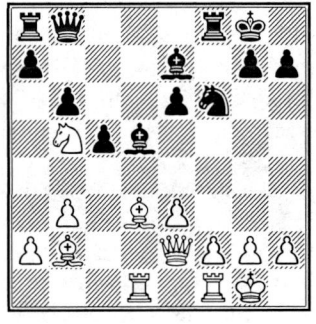

Position after Black's 16th move

17. e4! Black has no defence to this thrust. **17 ... Bc6 18. e5 Nd5 19. Qh5** White makes chess look so simple! **19 ... h6** On 19 ... g6 White simply sacrifices. **20. Qg6 Nf4 21. Qh7+ Kf7 22. Nd6+ Bxd6 23. exd6 Rg8**

24. Bc4! Threatening 25 Qf5+. **24 ... Qf8 25. Rfe1 Bd7 26. Re4 Ng6 27. Rg4** Winning a piece. **27 ... Ke8 28. Qxg6+ Kd8 29. Bxg7** Black resigned. **1–0** Kmoch 1936, 78–9.

(280) BOGOLJUBOW, E–FINE

Zandvoort (9), 1936 (29 July)
Queen's Gambit Accepted [D27]

1. Nf3 d5 2. c4 dxc4 3. e3 Nf6 4. Bxc4 e6 5. d4 c5 6. 0–0 a6 6 ... cxd4 7 exd4 a6 8 Qe2 b5 9 Bd3 Bb7 10 a4! b4 11 Nbd2 Be7 12 Nc4 a5 13 Bf4 0–0 14 Rfd1 and White has the freer game, Landau–Reshevsky, Kemeri 1937. **7. Bd3 Nc6 8. Nc3 Be7 9. a3 cxd4 10. exd4 0–0 11. Bc2 b5 12. Be3 Bb7 13. Qe2 Rc8 14. Rac1 Na5 15. Ne5** White stands a little better, MCO 132. **15 ... Nc4 16. Nxc4 bxc4** On 16 ... Rxc4 White has a strong reply in 17 a4. After the text the play revolves around whether the pawn on c4 is weak or strong. HK **17. Bb1 Qd7 18. Ba2 Bd5 19. Bf4 Qb7 20. Nxd5 cxd5 21. Rc3 Rfc8 22. Be5 Ne4 23. Re3 Bg5!** To induce f2-f4 and thereby establish his knight more strongly on e5. However, it costs a pawn. ACB **24. f4 Bf6 25. Bxc4! dxc4** Or 25 ... Rxc4, then equally 26 Rxe4. If 26 ... Bd8 27 Re3 f6 28 Bxf6! (28 Bc7 wins outright. AW) Rxe3 29 Qxe3 gxf6 30 Qe8+ recovering the piece. ACB **26. Rxe4 Bd8!** Even in time pressure Fine defends well in a critical situation. He threatens 27 ... f6, and moreover, plans to transfer his bishop to the strong square b6. HK **27. Re1 Ba5! 28. Bd6!** The only way to avoid getting into a poor position. HK **28 ... Rxe4 29. Qxe4 Qd7 30. Qe7** This leads to a completely equal position, whereas 30 Bb4 would offer some winning chances in view of the strong passed pawn. HK **30 ... Qxe7 31. Rxe7 Bb6! 32. Bc5 Bxc5 33. dxc5 f6!** It is important to prevent 34 Re5. HK **34. Re6 Rxc5 35. Rxa6 Rb5 36. Rc6 Rxb2 37. Rxc4 Rb1+ 38. Kf2 Rb2+ 39. Kf1 Rb1+ 40. Ke2 Rb2+ 41. Kd3** White takes a chance to avoid a draw, but it is not to be. ACB **41 ... Rxg2 42. Rc2 Rxc2** Only a player wholly sure of himself would venture upon this all-important exchange. The subsequent play is most instructive. ACB **43. Kxc2 Kf7** The king enters into the "quadrangle" with the pawn, which means that he will arrive in time to prevent his queening. ACB **44. Kd3 Ke6 45. Ke4 g6!** Highly necessary of course. ACB **46. Kd4 Kd6 47. Kc4 h6** Masterly inactivity, but it all has a meaning, as presently will be seen. ACB **48. Kd4 Kc6 49. Ke4 Kb5** Having taken all the necessary preliminary steps, the Black king now departs upon the long journey which the average player would hesitate to embark upon. ACB **50. Kd5 g5 51. fxg5** Nothing is to be gained by 51 f5, as the Black h-pawn will advance. ACB (I'm not sure what specific line the annotator had in mind here, there is a rather interesting possibility: 51 f5 h5 52 Ke6 g4 53 Kd5! h4 54 Ke4 Kc5 55 Kf4 g3 56 hxg3 h3 57 Kf3 and White wins. AW) **51 ... fxg5 52. Ke5 Ka4 53. Kf5 Kxa3 54. Kg6 Kb4 55. Kxh6 g4** Draw agreed. A neat finish. Because White must stop to capture the pawn, the Black king will

reach f8 and there be in a position either to stop the hostile passed pawn, or to oppose the other king, should he go to h7, and thereby also draw. ACB ½–½ Kmoch 1936, 83–4; ACB 1936, 106–7; Fine 1941, 46.

(281) FINE–PRINS, L

Zandvoort (10), 1936 (30 July)
Grünfeld Defence [D95]

1. Nf3 Nf6 2. c4 g6 3. Nc3 Bg7 4. d4 d5 5. e3 0–0 6. Qb3 e6 By 6 ... c6 Black could reach a normal position from the Alapin-Schlechter variation of the Queen's Gambit Declined. The position being more often reached through the Grünfeld Defence. **7. Be2 Nc6 8. cxd5** Otherwise ... Na5 could be unpleasant. The text is, however, hardly likely to unsettle Black, since now the light-squared bishop can develop freely. **8 ... exd5 9. 0–0 b6** Why the hurry? The natural continuation was 9 ... Ne7 with ... c6 to follow. The development of the Bc8 would then be a simple matter after either ... Qb6 or Ne7-f5-d6. There was no need for Black to be so hasty since White's queen's bishop cannot emerge for some time. **10. Rd1 Na5 11. Qc2 Bf5 12. Bd3 Bxd3 13. Qxd3** If Black thought that this exchange would be to his advantage then he was mistaken. The weakness of his kingside is now shown in a starker light. **13 ... Re8 14. b3 Ne4** Another dubious attempt to exchange pieces. HK **15. Bb2 Qd7 16. Rac1 Rad8**

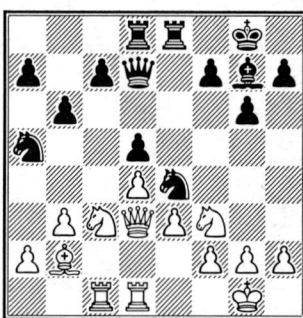

Position after Black's 16th move

17. Ne5! White stands considerably better than his opponent and simply continues with calm development. Obviously 17 ... Bxe5 18 dxe5 Rxe5 would fail to 19 Nb5, attacking both c7 and e5. **17 ... Qf5 18. f3 Nxc3 19. Bxc3 f6 20. Ng4 Qxd3 21. Rxd3** White has a decisive advantage now. His opponent's next move already costs him a pawn. **21 ... h5** (Bernard de Bruycker indicates that Black could still defend by 21 ... Nb7.) **22. Bxa5 hxg4 23. Bd2 Rd7 24. fxg4 a5** Too hasty. Firstly the bishop should have been transferred to d6, freeing one of the rooks. After the text White has a comfortable win, as Black's pieces are all tied up. **25. Rc6 Kf7 26. Rdc3 Ree7 27. Kf2 Ke8 28. Kf3 Rf7 29. Be1 Rde7 30. h4 Kd8 31. Bg3 Bh6 32. Ke2 Bg7 33. Bf4 Bh8 34. g5 fxg5 35. Bxg5 Bxd4 36. Rd3 Kd7 37. Rxg6** Black resigned. **1–0** Kmoch 1936, 97–8.

(282) van Doesburgh, G—Fine

Zandvoort (11), 1936 (1 Aug.)
French Defence, Exchange Variation [C01]

1. e4 e6 2. d4 d5 3. exd5 After this move Fine could already be congratulated on his first prize. **3 ... exd5 4. Bd3 Bd6 5. Ne2 Ne7 6. c3 0–0 7. Qc2 h6 8. Be3 b6 9. 0–0 c5 10. c4 cxd4 11. Nxd4 Nbc6 12. Nxc6 Nxc6 13. cxd5 Nb4 14. Qb3 Nxd5 15. Bc4 Nxe3** (Of course, Fine was guaranteed first place, but perhaps he should have been thinking about winning the game. The text is in some ways typical of Fine, he simplifies and at the same time saddles his opponent with a weak pawn. Black might instead have tried to build up pressure on the white position, for example, 15 ... Bb7 16 Bxd5 Bxd5 17 Qa4 Qc7 18 Qh4 Be5 19 Rc1 Qb7 gives Black a clear superiority. AW) **16. fxe3** The position is completely lifeless now and the game does not last much longer. **16 ... Qe7** (Even here 16 ... Qc7 looks more active. AW) **17. Nd2 Be6** (A clear indication that Fine had no interest in trying to win. 17 ... Bb7 still looks more comfortable for Black. AW) **18. Bxe6 Qxe6 19. Qxe6 fxe6 20. Nb3 Rxf1+ 21. Rxf1 Rc8 22. Rc1 Rxc1+ 23. Nxc1 Kf7 24. Kf2 Ke7 25. Kf3 Kd7 26. g3 Ke7 27. Nd3 Kf7 28. Ke4 Kf6 29. a4 h5 30. Kd4 h4** Draw agreed. ½–½ Kmoch 1936, 103.

Nottingham, August 10–28, 1936

The tournament was held to mark the 50th anniversary of the Nottingham Tournament of 1886. The participants included Euwe, the then World Champion, Lasker, Capablanca and Alekhine, who between them had held the title from 1894 to 1935, Flohr, Botvinnik, Reshevsky and Fine, the upcoming generation (but sadly not Keres, whose strength was not yet fully appreciated), Vidmar, Bogolyubov and Tartakower, all experienced grandmasters, and Thomas, Tylor, Winter and Alexander, the home contingent. The venue for the tournament was the Great Assembly Hall of the University of Nottingham (early rounds were held in smaller accommodation, which proved inadequate in view of the popularity of the event). (Watts (ed) 1962) "Several of the masters were provided with private retiring rooms for their own use and convenience. A lounge for the use of the players and visitors, where analysis and friendly games and conversation could be indulged in, was also available. Fine shows himself to be a most ingenious player. He was one of two unbeaten ones (Botvinnik was the other) and the reputation he has so quickly won will be enhanced by his play in this tournament." (Watts (ed) 1962, xiii) The joint winners shared the 1st and 2nd prizes of £200 and £150 ($1,000 and $750 according to *ACB* 1936, 9), whilst Euwe, Fine and Reshevsky shared the 3rd and 4th prizes of £100 and £75 ($500 and $375). (Watts (ed) 1962) This was the first of several tournaments around this time to which the principal candidates for world championship honours were invited. Keres' rise to fame had been so sudden, and he was so young (though in fact not much more than a year younger than Fine) that, unfortunately, the organizers did not see fit to secure his participation.

		1	2	3	4	5	6	7	8	9	10	11	12	13	14	15	
1	Capablanca	*	½	½	1	½	1	0	½	1	½	½	1	1	1	1	10
2	Botvinnik	½	*	½	½	½	½	½	½	1	1	1	1	1	1	½	10
3	Fine	½	½	*	½	½	½	½	1	½	½	1	1	1	½	1	9½
4	Reshevsky	0	½	½	*	0	1	½	1	1	½	1	1	1	1	½	9½
5	Euwe	½	½	½	1	*	0	½	0	1	1	½	1	1	1	1	9½
6	Alekhine	0	½	½	0	1	*	1	½	½	1	1	½	1	½	1	9
7	Flohr	1	½	½	½	½	0	*	1	1	½	1	0	0	1	1	8½
8	Lasker	½	½	0	0	1	½	0	*	½	½	1	1	1	1	1	8½
9	Vidmar	0	0	½	0	0	½	0	½	*	½	1	½	1	½	1	6
10	Tartakower	½	0	½	½	0	0	½	½	½	*	½	0	0	1	1	5½
11	Bogoljubow	½	0	0	0	½	0	0	0	0	½	*	1	1	1	1	5½
12	Tylor	0	0	0	0	0	½	1	0	½	1	0	*	½	½	½	4½
13	Alexander	0	0	0	0	0	0	1	0	0	1	0	½	*	½	½	3½
14	Thomas	0	0	½	0	0	½	0	0	½	0	0	½	½	*	½	3
15	Winter	0	½	0	½	0	0	0	0	0	0	0	½	½	½	*	2½

(283) Fine—Lasker, Em

Nottingham (1), 1936 (10 Aug.)
Queen's Gambit Declined [D37]

1. d4 d5 2. c4 e6 3. Nf3 Nf6 4. Nc3 Be7 5. e3 A harmless continuation as Black can now enter on a variation of the Queen's Gambit Accepted with a tempo more. More aggressive, if White does not want to play the usual 5 Bg5, is even 5 Bf4. AA **5 ... 0–0 6. Bd3 dxc4 7. Bxc4 c5 8. 0–0 a6** Black is obviously not content to equalize by 8 ... Nc6 9 dxc5 Qxd1 and so on. AA **9. Qe2** Of doubtful value. More correct was 9 Bd3, with the intention of answering 9 ... b5 by 10 dxc5, thus forcing the position that occurred in the actual game. AA **9 ... b5 10. Bd3** The opening has transposed into a kind of Meran Variation in which Black has played 5 ... 0–0 in place of the more usual 5 ... Nbd7. dM&G **10 ... Bb7?** Rather tame. Better is either 10 ... cxd4, or more aggressively, 10 ... b4, a variation frequently tried in the Alekhine–Bogolyubov match of 1934 with little success for White. RF; 10 ... Nbd7 in order to recapture with this knight in case of dxc5 was more promising by far. After the text White gets a slight positional advantage, which however does not endanger Black's game. AA **11. dxc5!** Obtaining a strong initiative. RF **11 ... Bxc5 12. e4! Nbd7** Intending to answer 13 e5 with 13 ... Bxf3 14 gxf3 Nd5 (or Atkins suggests 14 ... Nh5 15 Qe4 (15 Rd1!? AW) g6 16 Bh6 Re8 17 Rfd1) with welcome complications. AA **13. Bg5 h6** Black is already uncomfortable. If he wishes to avoid this weakening move, and chooses, instead, 13 ... Be7 at once, 14 Rfd1 continues the pressure, for if, for example, 14 ... Qb6? 15 e5 wins at once. RF **14. Bh4 b4** So as to force this knight to a relatively undesirable spot. RF **15. Na4 Be7 16. Rfd1 Nh5** A natural freeing manoeuvre. RF **17. Bxe7 Qxe7**

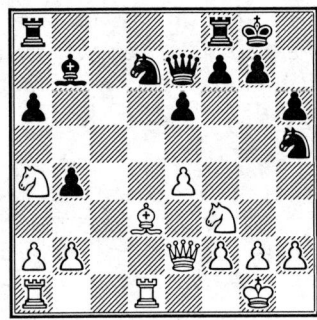

Position after
Black's 17th move

18. Rac1 Maintains the pressure. The idea is that if now
18 ... Nf4 19 Qe3 N×d3 20 Rc7! (not 20 R×d3 Nf6) and
Black is lost, for example, 20 ... N×f2 21 Rd×d7, or 20 ...
Bc6 21 R×c6 N3e5 (Alekhine suggests 21 ... N7e5 22 N×e5
N×e5 23 Rc5 23 Rfd8 when Black would emerge from his
difficulties.) 22 Rc7! (22 ... Rac8 looks good enough for
Black here. AW), or 20 ... Bc8 21 R×d3 and Black is immobilized. RF **18 ... Ndf6** He wishes to stop Rc7 at all cost. If,
instead, 18 ... Rfc8 (the a-pawn must be protected) 19 R×c8+
B×c8 20 Qc2 continues the pressure. RF; The final phase,
not altogether difficult, is played by Fine with his usual accuracy. AA **19. g3 a5** To be able to oppose rooks. If 19 ...
Rfc8 20 Nb6 wins, for example, 20 ... R×c1 21 R×c1 Ra7
(21 ... Rd8 AW) 22 Nc8 B×c8 23 R×c8+ Kh7 24 e5+. RF
20. Nc5 Rfc8 Alekhine believed that 20 ... g6, consolidating the knight, would give some hope. Whereas 20 ... Bc6
would lose to 21 Nd4! AW **21. N×b7 Q×b7 22. Ne5!**
Tieing the black knights down. Eventually White will now
win one of the weakened queenside pawns. RF; Intending
an eventual Nc6 and e5. dM&G **22 ... R×c1** Also 22 ... g6
23 Nc4 Qe7 24 e5, followed by Be4, would not help. AA
23. R×c1 Rc8 On 23 ... a4 there would follow 24 Qc2, for
example, 24 ... b3 25 a×b3 a×b3 26 Qc7 and White should
win. RF **24. R×c8+ Q×c8**

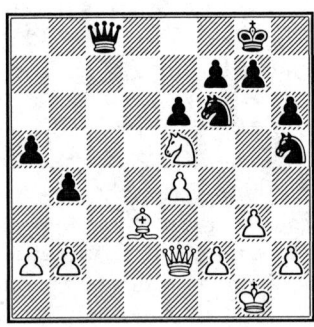

Position after
Black's 24th move

25. Qc2! A very strong move; if now 25 ... Q×c2 26 B×c2
threatening Nc6 and the loss of a pawn cannot be avoided.
If 25 ... Qb8 26 Qc5 threatening Nc6. HEA **25 ... Qb7** If
25 ... Qd8, as suggested by Alekhine, 26 Nc6 looks very
strong. AW **26. Qc6! Qa7** This loses at once, but Black
has no move; if 26 ... Qe7 26 Qa8+ (HEA); or if, instead
26 ... Qb8 27 Qc5 a4 28 Nc6 wins (RF). **27. Qc8+ Kh7
28. Nc6 Qc5 29. e5+ g6 30. e×f6 N×f6 31. Qb7
Kg8 32. Be2** To play Kg2. RF; Preventing Black's ... Ng4.
If Black now checks and takes the b-pawn then White's Nd8

wins easily. A very interesting example of positional play.
HEA **32 ... Nd5 33. Ne5** Black resigned. **1–0** Fine 1958,
79–82; Alekhine 1937, 33–5; H. E. Atkins in *BCM* 1936,
427; de Marimon & Ganzo 13–4.

(284) BOTVINNIK, M—FINE

Nottingham (2), 1936 (11 Aug.)
Réti Opening [A09]

1. Nf3 d5 2. c4 d×c4 The motif of the Queen's Gambit
Accepted, to which opening Flohr, Reshevsky and Fine are
partial. ME **3. Na3** Réti's original plan—White intends to
recapture on c4 with his knight to increase the pressure on
e5, but this is now considered too artificial. RK; It was also
possible to take the game into the paths of the Queen's
Gambit Accepted by 3 e3, which would have been a better
idea than the text which leads to no particular advantage.
RF **3 ... c5 4. N×c4 Nc6 5. b3 f6** A logical counter-
measure. Black overprotects e5 and prepares to build up
a barrier on the centre to reduce the activity of White's
pieces. RK **6. Bb2 e5** Black has gained the upper hand in
the centre, but on the other hand White is the better developed. It promises to become a difficult, lively struggle. ME
7. g3 White's position must be handled with care. If 7 Qc2?
Bg4 8 Rc1 Qd7 9 Ne3 Be6 10 Qb1? Nh6 11 h3 Nd4 12 d3
Be7 13 Nd2 0–0 14 Ne4 Rfc8 and Black has a clear advantage, Réti–Nimzowitsch, Semmering 1926. **7 ... Nge7
8. Bg2 Nd5** As the game shows, in this position 8 ... Nf5
would have been better, since the text interferes with the
operation of the bishop. RF; 8 ... Nf5! 9 0–0 Be7 10 Rc1
(10 Ne1 Be6 11 Nd3 Bd5 12 Bh3 Nfd4 13 Rc1 is unclear.
AKh) Be6 11 d3 0–0 12 Nfd2 Qd7 would have given Black
the better game, MCO 222. **9. 0–0 Be7 10. Nh4!** The
Maróczy Bind, with colours reversed; the standard method
of undermining such central formations is the flanking blow
f4. RK **10 ... 0–0 11. Qb1!** A strong move. The main
threat is 12 Be4, which would put Black into grave difficulties since 12 ... h6 would lose to 13 Bh7+, and 12 ... g6 to
13 B×g6 h×g6 14 Q×g6+ Kh8 15 Qh6+ Kg8 16 Ng6, followed
by f4 and so on. ME **11 ... Rf7** Now the sacrifice on g6
(after 12 Be4 g6!) would not be quite sound. ME **12. Nf5**
This was the second idea behind 11 Qb1. ME **12 ... Be6**
Many a player would have played 12 ... Bf8 more or less
automatically here, but this would have lost the exchange
(13 Nfd6! B×d6 14 B×d5). ME **13. f4!** Much stronger than
exchanging on e7; eliminates Black's e-pawn and re-estab-
lishes equality in the centre. It now becomes very difficult
for Black, but Fine defends coolly and painstakingly. ME
13 ... e×f4 14. g×f4 Nb6! Excellently played. He threatens to win a pawn on c4 or d2. White cannot play 15 d3,
because that would leave the king's knight unprotected; to
exchange on b6 or e7 would weaken his attack. ME **15. Be4**
With this fine move White sustains his attack. ME; 15 B×c6
b×c6 would not lead to any advantage for White in view of
the resultant weakness of the light squares on the kingside.
RF **15 ... B×c4!** Again the best. After 15 ... B×f5 or 15 ...
h6 Black would soon go downhill. Nor would 15 ... N×c4 be

very good, because of 16 bxc4 Bxc4 17 Ne3! recovering the pawn in favourable circumstances, since 17 ... Bxe2 would fail against 18 Rf2 Qxd2 (Why not 18 ... Bh5? AW) 19 Nf1. ME **16. bxc4 Nxc4** Khalifman assesses 16 ... Qxd2 17 Qd3 Qxd3 18 exd3 Bf8 as slightly in Black's favour. AW **17. Bc3!!** Protecting the d-pawn and threatening 18 Qxb7. Black cannot continue with 17 ... Nxd2 on account of 18 Bxd2 Qxd2 19 Qxb7 and wins. 17 ... Bf8 is also unsatisfactory, for example, 18 Ne3! Nxe3 (18 ... Nxd2 18 Bxh7+ Kh8 20 Qg6!, threatening 21 Qh5) 19 Bxh7+ Kh8 20 dxe3 and White's attack should win; 21 Qg6 and 21 Rf3 are among immediate threats. ME; The best move. 17 Nxe7+ Nxe7 18 Bxh7+ Kf8 would leave White defenceless against Black's many threats. In the event of 17 Ne3 there would follow 17 ... Nxd2 18 Bxh7+ Kf8 19 Qg6 Nxf1 20 Rxf1 Qd2 21 Bc1 Qxe2 White would have no compensation for the sacrificed material. RF **17 ... Nd4!** Both sides play finely. Whereas White can continually choose from among all sorts of safe continuations, Black is fighting for the draw all the time, and repeatedly has to find the one and only good move, which makes his task much more difficult than his opponent's and his achievement in this game a greater one. ME **18. Nxd4** After 18 Bxd4 cxd4 19 Nxe7+ Rxe7 20 Bxh7+ Kf8 (20 ... Kh8 21 Qf5!) 21 Qb3 Qd5 22 Bg6 (threatening 23 Qh3) White's attack could hardly be stopped (Black's position looks quite resilient after 22 ... Rxe2, and if 23 Qh3 Nxd2. AW). But Black has better, namely 18 Bxd4 Nxd2!. Now the White queen is *en prise*, and 19 Nxe7+ Rxe7 20 Bxh7+ Kh8 would not essentially alter the situation. Hence the text which, however, allows Black to capture the d-pawn with gain of time. ME; The critical position! White could play 18 Qd3 Nxf5 19 Bxf5 Qxd3 20 exd3 Nb6 21 Be6 Rd8 winning an exchange, which advantage would, however, prove difficult to convert. RF **18 ... cxd4 19. Bxh7+ Kf8!** Not 19 ... Kh8, because of 20 Bg6 (20 ... dxc3 21 Qf5 and wins). ME **20. Bb4 d3!!** The magnificent idea behind Black's last few moves. Black threatens to check from b6 and win the bishop, so that White has no time to go for the exchange by 21 Bg6. Black thus forces a simplification in which he sheds a pawn but gets a dead drawn position. ME **21. Bxe7+** There is nothing better; let us examine, for instance, the consequences of 21 Bxd3 Qb6+!- (a) 22 Kg2? or 22 Kh1? Bxb4 23 Bxc4 Qc6+ followed by 24 ... Qxc4 and Black has won a piece; (b) 22 Rf2 Qxb4 23 Qxb4 Bxb4 24 Bxc4 Rc7 and White cannot save his d-pawn, since 25 d3 is refuted by 25 ... Bc5; (c) 22 e3 Qxb4 23 Qxb4 Bxb4 24 Bxc4 Re7! 25 Rf2 Rd8 26 Rd1 Rxe3 27 dxe3 Rxd1+ with a drawn game. ME **21 ... Rxe7 22. Qxd3** The pawn cannot be captured in any other way because of 22 ... Nxd2. ME **22 ... Qxd3 23. exd3** Or 23 Bxd3 Nxd2 with an equal game. The text move gains a pawn (since 23 ... Nxd2 would lose the knight through 24 Rf2); but what a pawn it is! Black's position amply counterbalances such a small material advantage. ME **23 ... Nb6 24. Be4 Rd8 25. Rac1 Nd5 26. a3 Red7 27. Kg2 b6 28. Kf3 Nc7!** So as to bring the knight to the beautiful square c5. White must now play carefully so as not to fall behind. ME **29. Ke3 Na6 30. Rc3 Nc5!** Despite the extra pawn, White cannot win.

dM&G **31. Rf2 Rd4 32. f5 Ra4 33. Rg2 Rad4 34. Rf2** The game has come to a dead end. Neither player can undertake anything effective. ME **34 ... Ra4 35. Rg2 Rad4 36. Rc4** Khalifman suggests here that White could try to squeeze more out of the position by 36 h4! Kf7 37 h5 R4d7 38 Rh2 intending h6, with some initiative. AW **36 ... R4d6** Draw agreed. A splendid example of intrepid defence and at the same time a new illustration of Fine's skill in the handling of critical positions. ME ½–½ Euwe 1945, 222–8; Keene, 11–2; Khalifman in Soloviov 2000, 248; Fine in *64* 30 August 1936 game 475; de Marimon & Ganzo 24–5.

(285) FINE—THOMAS, G

Nottingham (3), 1936 (12 Aug.)
Queen's Indian Defence [E16]

1. d4 Nf6 2. Nf3 b6 3. c4 Bb7 4. g3 e6 5. Bg2 Bb4+ 6. Bd2 Qe7 As Black has to take the bishop anyhow, he should do so at once and develop the queen at a more opportune moment. The sequence of moves which prevents White taking control of e4 at this phase of the game is 6 ... Bxd2+ 7 Qxd2 d6 (not 7 ... 0–0 8 Nc3! as in the game Euwe–Reshevsky from round 1) 8 0–0 0–0. AA **7. 0–0 Bxd2 8. Qxd2 d6** 8 ... 0–0 9 Re1 d5 10 Ne5 Ne4 11 Qc2 f6 12 cxd5 exd5 13 Nd3 Nc6 14 Qa4 and White stands slightly better, Euwe–Spielmann, match 1932, MCO 192. **9. Qc2!** Of course not 9 Nc3 because of the simplifying Ne4. The queen's manoeuvre is very subtle. AA **9 ... Be4 10. Qb3 Bb7** Black cannot, of course, allow the eventual exchange of his bishop for a knight. AA **11. Nc3 Nbd7 12. Qc2 Rc8 13. e4** Thus definitely acquiring an advantage in space, which cannot however be easily increased as d6 (after c7-c5) can be protected without much difficulty. AA **13 ... 0–0 14. Rfe1 c5 15. b3 cxd4 16. Nxd4 Ne5 17. Rad1 Rfd8** As the opponent's rook is never a pleasant vis-à-vis for the queen she would be better placed on c7; and 17 ... a6 preparing for this would be a better positional move. AA **18. Qb2** With the obvious intention of playing Qa3 eventually, and besides, another very obvious threat which Black actually overlooks. AA **18 ... a6** Comparatively better was 18 ... Ne8 followed eventually by ... Nc6 in order to simplify matters. AA **19. f4 Nc6?** Loses a pawn. 19 ... Ned7 would also be a mistake because of 20 e5, but 19 ... Ng6 (20 f5 Nf8) could still be tried. AA **20. Nd5!!** This combination, which often occurs in different forms in the so-called "Scheveningen" variation of the Sicilian Defence should in the present position be decisive, as after a few exchanges Black must lose a pawn. AA **20 ... Nxd5** If 20 ... exd5 21 exd5 Ne5 22 Nf5 or 22 fxe5. **21. exd5 Nxd4 22. Qxd4 b5** Under the circumstances the best move. AA **23. cxb5 axb5 24. dxe6 Bxg2 25. exf7+ Qxf7 26. Kxg2 Rc2+ 27. Rd2 Qb7+ 28. Kg1 Rxd2 29. Qxd2 d5 30. Qd4** White has now, as well as the material advantage, the far better position and his win should only be a question of technique. AA **30 ... h6 31. Re5** White was probably short of time, as this and the next moves are certainly not the best. For instance: 31 f5 (threatening f6) Qc6 32 g4 (threatening Re7) was natural and strong. AA **31 ... Kf7 32. f5 Qc6 33. Kg2 Rd7** Of course not 33 ... Qc2+ 34 Kh3 Qxa2 35 Rxd5 and wins. AA **34. Qg4** This almost looks like an oversight, as it is hard to understand what advantage White can expect by permitting the advance of Black's free pawns. By simply playing 34 Re2 (in order to prevent the pin after ... Qf6) followed by the advance g3-g4, h2-h4 and so on, he would make the win certain. AA **34 ... d4+ 35. Kh3 Kf8! 36. Re6** If 36 f6 then simply 26 ... gxf6 37 Re6 (or 37 Qg6 Rg7) Rd6. The White position looks stronger than it actually is. AA **36 ... Qd5 37. Qg6 Rf7 38. Kg4** The last attempt to reach a decision in the middle game. AA **38 ... d3! 39. Rd6** Black need not fear 39 Qh7 Re7 40 Qh8+ Kf7 41 Rxe7+ Kxe7 42 Qxg7+ Kd8, as his strong passed pawn would secure a draw in the queen ending. AA **39 ... Qe4+ 40. Kh3 Qxf5+ 41. Qxf5 Rxf5 42. Rxd3 Ke7** Unfortunately for White the advance 43 a4 bxa4 44 bxa4 Ra5 45 Ra3 would not be sufficient to win, as in such positions the pawn has to be at least on the fifth rank in order to exert a decisive pressure. As it is, White in order to profit by his advantage on the queenside must here bring the king across and Black will find the necessary time to create sufficient counter-chances on the other wing. Sir George Thomas's play in the whole endgame is of a high class. AA **43. Kg2 Ke6 44. Rd2** According to Fine in *Basic Chess Endings* he missed a win here by 44 a4! bxa4 45 bxa4 Ra5 46 Ra3 Kd5 47 Kf3 Kc5 48 h4 Kb4 49 Ra1 Kb3 50 Rb1+! Kc4 51 Rb7! g5 52 hxg5! hxg5 53 Re7 Kd5 54 Kg4 Rxa4+ 55 Kxg5 Ra8 56 g4 Rg8+ 57 Kf5 Rf8+ 58 Kg6 Rg8+ 59 Rg7. **44 ... Rc5 45. Kf3 Ke5 46. Rd7 g6 47. Re7+ Kf5 48. Re2 Rc3+ 49. Kf2 h5 50. Ke1 Kg4 51. Kd2 Rc5 52. Kd3 g5 53. Rc2 Rf5 54. Kc3 h4 55. gxh4 gxh4 56. Kb4 h3 57. a4 bxa4** Or 58 bxa4 Rf4+ 59 Kb3 (after 59 Rc4 Rxc4+ the pawn ending is drawn) Rf3+ 60 Kb2 Rf4 61 a5 Ra4 62 Rc5 Kf3 63 Rg5 Kf4 64 Kb3 Ra1 with equality. AA **58. Kxa4 Kf3 59. b4 Rg5 60. b5** Draw agreed. ½–½ Alekhine 1937, 62–6; Fine 1941, 358; de Marimon & Ganzo 31.

(286) RESHEVSKY, S—FINE

Nottingham (4), 1936 (13 Aug.)
Catalan System [E03]

1. d4 Nf6 2. c4 e6 3. Nf3 d5 4. Nc3 dxc4 5. Qa4+ In this position the check is stronger than at the 4th move. For instance, after 1 d4 d5 2 c4 dxc4 3 Nf3 Nf6 because Black cannot here force the exchange of queens by 5 ... Qd7 followed by Qc6. AA; Weaker than the usual 5 e4. RF **5 ... Nbd7 6. Qxc4?** White should of course wait until Black forces him to take the pawn by threatening to protect it. The correct move was 6 g3 with the better prospects. AA **6 ... a6 7. g3** 7 Bf4 could be simply answered by 7 ... Bd6. AA **7 ... b5 8. Qd3** 8 Qb3 would have been weaker of course since the d-pawn would have been inadequately defended. RF **8 ... Bb7 9. Bg2** White's strategic plan lies in the advance e2-e4. Black tries to prevent this. RF **9 ... c5 10. 0-0 c4!** A bold advance, which finally proves advanta-

geous in spite of the belated development of the king's rook; with 10 ... Be7 Black could obtain an excellent game without taking any chances. AA; Black with this move offers White a difficult and complicated struggle. If alternatively 10 ... cxd4 11 Nxd4 Bxg2 12 Kxg2 Nc5 13 Qe3 and White's development is slightly superior. RF **11. Qc2 b4** This move must obviously be played at once if at all for if, for example, 11 ... Be7 12 a3, preventing it and preparing 13 e4. RF **12. Nd1 Rc8 13. Bg5 Qa5** Threatening to win a piece by 14 ... Bxf3, and thus bringing about a helpful exchange. RF **14. Bxf6 Nxf6 15. Ne3 c3** Black stands slightly better (MC0 228). If 15 ... Be4 then 16 Nxc4. RF **16. Ne5 Bxg2 17. Kxg2 Qb5!** Preventing 18 Nc4. White has no compensation for the pawn majority on the queenside. AA **18. bxc3 Rxc3 19. Qb2 Be7?** 19 ... Bd6 would have been better. At the time it seemed to me that the variation 19 ... Bd6 20 a3 Rxa3 21 N5c4 Qc6+ 22 d5 would have been good for White. In point of fact, 22 ... Nxd5 would have given Black a won game. RF **20. Rfc1 Rxc1 21. Rxc1 0-0 22. f3 Bd6** This bishop's manoeuvre is not convincing. As White does not threaten anything, the simple advance 22 ... a5 was indicated. AA **23. N5c4 Bb8 24. a3! Nd5** Alekhine reckoned that Black's advantage had gone, but that this was the best under the circumstances. Abrahams on the other hand thought Black's best was 24 ... bxa3 25 Qxb5 axb5 26 Nxa3 b4, but Fine points out that then 27 Nb5 soon wins a pawn. **25. axb4 Nxe3+ 26. Nxe3 Bd6 27. Rb1** White does not take advantage of the tactical opportunity 27 d5! (27 ... exd5 28 Nf5 and wins). Black would then have to fight for a draw (27 ... Bxb4 28 dxe6 fxe6 may well be tenable. AW). AA **27 ... Rb8 28. Qa2 a5?** Both players were very short of time and do not play as well as they might have. Necessary was 28 ... Bxb4 29 d5 exd5 30 Nxd5 a5 and Black has an equal, if not slightly superior, position. RF **29. Nc4! Bxb4** Or 29 ... Bc7 30 Na3 Qa4 31 Qc2 with a clear advantage. AA **30. Nxa5 Qa6** If 30 ... Ra8 then 31 Qc4 holding everything. RF **31. Kf1?** But this move throws away the best part of his winning chances; the correct move was 31 Rb2 protecting both the queen and the e-pawn. AA **31 ... Rb6 32. Ra1 Bc3 33. Rc1** The only way to keep the material advantage. If now 33 ... Bxa5 34 Qxa5 or if 33 ... Bxd4 34 Nb3 winning. AA **33 ... Bb2 34. Rc2?** Leads to a queen ending which gives White only very slight winning hopes. After 34 Rc4 (even at the next move) h6 35 Ra4 White would keep his extra pawn and have an advantageous middle game. AA **34 ... g6?** Instead 34 ... h6 would lead to a difficult queen ending. The text-move should lose, as will be shown. AA **35. Rxb2 Rxb2 36. Qxb2 Qxa5 37. Qb8+ Kg7 38. Kf2?** It was certainly not easy to calculate, even having plenty of time as White had at that moment (the control being at the 36th move—Fine makes it clear that neither player was aware that they had passed the time control as they had ceased to record their moves. AW), that the pawn ending resulting from 38 Qe5+ Qxe5 39 dxe5 could be won; but still it was by no means impossible. The winning procedure consisted in the advance of the h-pawn in order to weaken the opponent's pawn position. The main variation is the following: 39 ... Kf8 40 h4 Ke7 41 Kg2 Kd7 42 h5 after which Black would have three continuations:- A. 42 ... Kc6 43 h6 (Fine gave 43 h×g6 f×g6) (after 43 ... h×g6 44 f4 Kd5 45 Kf3 White's king reaches f6) 44 f4 Kd5 45 Kf3 Kd4 (by activating his king, Black complicates his opponent's task) 46 g4 g5 47 f×g5 K×e5 48 Ke3 Kd5 49 Kf4 Kd4 50 g6! h×g6 51 Kg5 Ke3 52 K×g6 and White wins) Kd5 44 f4 Ke4 45 Kh3 Kf5 46 Kh4 g5+ 47 f×g5 K×e5 48 g6 f×g6 49 Kg5 and wins. B. 42 h2 h6 43 h×g6 f×g6 44 f4 Kc6 45 Kf3 Kd5 46 Ke3 g5 47 Kd3 followed by e4+ and f5 winning. C. 42 ... g×h5 43 Kh3 Kc6 44 Kh4 Kd5 45 f4 Ke4 46 K×h5 Ke3 47 Kh6 (or 47 Kg5 K×e2 48 g4 Kf3 49 f5 and White wins RF) Kf2 48 K×h7 K×g3 49 e3! and wins. This last one is the only variation where White would have any technical difficulties. As played in the text, Black has a comparatively easy defence; by bringing his king into the centre he will stop the free d-pawn and the necessarily exposed position of the white king will give him an opportunity for counter-attack. AA 38 ... Qa1 39. Qe5+ Kg8 40. Kg2 Qe1 41. Qb8+ Kg7 42. Qb2 Kg8 43. Qc2 Qb4 44. Qd3 Kf8 Now White has attained the position he has been aiming for. Against White's threats to gain a passed pawn by e4 and d5 Black has two possible lines of defence, namely 1. to bring the king out to stop the passed pawn or 2. to stop the pawn with the queen. The disadvantage of the latter would be that the queen would lose her mobility. RF 45. Kh3 Qa5 46. e4 Qh5+ If Black should play 46 ... Ke7 then 47 Qc4 Kd7 48 d5 e×d5 49 e×d5 Kd6 50 Qc6+ and wins. RF 47. Kg2 Qa5 Because now 48 Qc4 would have been answered with 48 ... Qd2+ with perpetual check. RF 48. d5! Ke7 49. Qd4! e×d5! In connection with the following move an exactly calculated transaction which leads to a clearly drawn position in a few moves. AA 50. e×d5 Kd6! 51. Qf4+ Alekhine, in the tournament book, records the game continuation as 51 Qf6+ K×d5 52 Q×f7+, which would cut out the possible defences mentioned in the next note. BCM 1936, 437 and Fine's notebooks and subsequent writing on the ending, however, proceed as in the text. AW 51 ... K×d5 This loses, whereas after 51 ... Ke7 (51 ... Kc5 also looks possible AW) 52 Qe5+ Kd7 it would have been no easy matter to win the ending. Averbakh et al 52. Q×f7+ Kd4 53. Q×h7? Black's king is cut off from his pawns, and by 53 Qd7+! Ke3 54 Qe7+ Kd3 (54 ... Kd4 55 Qe4+, exchanging queens) 55 h4! White could have easily realized his advantage. Averbakh et al 53 ... Qa2+ 54. Kh3 Qe6+ 55. g4 Ke3 56. Qb7 Kf2 Threatening 57 ... Qf6. White has to give up his f-pawn. RF 57. Qb8 K×f3 58. Qf8+ Ke2 59. Qf4 Qd5 The game is broken off here in the tournament book. AW 60. Qg3 A dead drawn position, and the further course of the game has nothing of interest to offer. Reshevsky did not agree to a draw, however, until the 85th move. RF 60 ... Qg5 61. Qc3 Kf2 62. Qc2+ Kf3 63. Qd3+ Kf2 64. Qc2+ Kf3 65. Qg2+ Ke3 66. Qf1 Qh6+ 67. Kg2 g5 68. Qf2+ Ke4 69. Qf5+ Kd4 70. Qc2 Ke3 71. Qc3+ Ke4 72. h3 Kd5 73. Qd3+ Kc5 74. Kf2 Qf6+ 75. Ke2 Qb2+ 76. Kf3 Qb7+ 77. Ke3 Qe7+ 78. Kd2 Kc6 79. Qa6+ Kd5 80. Qa8+ Ke5 81. Qa4 Qd6+ 82. Ke2 Kf6 83. Qa1+

Kg6 84. Qb1+ Kh6 85. Qd3 Qh2+ Draw agreed. ½–½ Alekhine 1937, 83–6; Notes by Fine from 64 translated by Dr. Lloyd Storr-Best for Chess 1936–7, 136–7; Fine 1941, 57–8 and 548; Abrahams, 157–8; Averbakh & Maizelis, 207–8; Averbakh et al, 115 & 117;Fine's notebooks.

(287) FINE—VIDMAR, M

Nottingham (5), 1936 (14 Aug.)
Queen's Gambit Declined, Semi-Slav, Meran Variation [D48]

1. d4 d5 2. c4 c6 3. Nf3 Nf6 4. e3 e6 5. Nc3 Nbd7 6. Bd3 d×c4 7. B×c4 b5 8. Bd3 a6 9. e4 b4 Thus avoiding the main variation of the Meran Defence which continues 9 ... c5. The move seems to give Black quite a playable game, especially in connection with his strong 14th move. **10. Na4 c5 11. d×c5** 11 e5 Nd5 12 0-0 c×d4 13 Re1 Nc5 14 Bg5! Qa5 15 N×c5 B×c5 16 Rc1 h6 17 Bh4 with advantage to White, Ragozin–Levenfish, Moscow 1935. **11 ... B×c5 12. 0-0 Bb7 13. Qe2 Be7** Black could even castle at once as the variation 13 ... 0-0 14 e5 B×f3 15 g×f3 Nd5 16 N×c5 N×c5 17 B×h7+ K×h7 18 Qc2+ Kg8 19 Q×c5 Qh4 20 Qc2 f5 was certainly not to his disadvantage. **14. Rd1 Qa5** This is more convincing than Lasker's stratagem in a similar position in the first round (after 0-0, Bg5) viz h6 followed by Nh5. **15. b3 0-0** The game is equal, MCO 162. **16. Bg5 Rfd8 17. Nb2 Nc5** The simplest; if now 18 Nc4 Qc7 19 e5 N×d3 and if 20 e×f6 (20 R×d3 R×d3 21 Q×d3 Rd8 22 Qe2 Nd5 23 Nd6 looks more challenging. AW) g×f6 with a good game. **18. e5 N×d3 19. R×d3** Definitely eliminating any danger; if 19 e×f6 then 19 ... N×b2 20 Q×b2 B×f3 21 R×d8+ B×d8 or 20 f×e7 R×d1+ 21 R×d1 N×d1 winning in either case. **19 ... R×d3** Not 19 ... Nd5 20 R×d5!. **20. N×d3 Nd5 21. B×e7 N×e7 22. Nf4 Rd8** Black had some slight chances in the middle game owing to his well-placed bishop; but the text which allows the opponent to exchange rooks facilitates White's task. A good move was 22 ... Rc8 threatening B×f3 eventually. **23. Rd1! Nd5 24. N×d5** Drawn. The game has some theoretical interest. ½–½ Alekhine 1937, 104–5.

(288) EUWE, M—FINE

Nottingham (6), 1936 (15 Aug.)
Queen's Gambit Declined [D67]

1. d4 Nf6 2. c4 e6 3. Nf3 d5 4. Nc3 Be7 5. Bg5 Nbd7 6. e3 0-0 7. Rc1 c6 8. Bd3 d×c4 9. B×c4 Nd5 10. B×e7 Q×e7 11. Ne4 Dr. Euwe seems to like this invention of mine, which I, on the contrary, no longer adopt, chiefly because of the possibility of the Capablanca defence 11 ... N5f6, followed by Qb4+, which leads to a comparatively easy draw. **11 ... N5f6 12. Ng3 c5** But this, I think, is more risky than the queen check, or even Lasker's move, e6-e5. White could play now 13 e4, and if 13 ... c×d4, either 14 e5 (14 ... Qb4+ 15 Qd2 Q×d2+ 16 K×d2 Ng4 17 Rhf1, followed by h3) or—even simpler—14 Q×d4 Qb4+ 15 Ke2, followed by Rhd1, and after an exchange of queens

White's prospects for the endgame would be excellent. **13. 0–0 a6 14. Ne5** At this moment 14 e4 would be less promising, as Black could protect himself against e5 by playing ... b5 and ... Bb7, keeping command over d5. **14 ... cxd4** This opening up of the central files looks very risky, but, as Black's next excellent move shows, was very correctly calculated. **15. exd4 Qd6** Protecting the squares c7, c6 and d5. **16. Qe2 b5** Not 16 ... Qxd4, because of 17 Nxf7! Rxf7 18 Bxe6 (18 Qxe6? Ne5!), followed by Rfd1, with a winning position for White. **17. Bb3 Bb7 18. Rfd1 Rac8** This plausible occupation of the open file has also to be carefully calculated. **19. Rxc8 Rxc8** The champion here offered a draw, which was naturally accepted as Black saw that it could be forced by 20 Nf5 exf5 21 Nxf7 Qc7 22 Qe7 Nb6 Nh6+. But White would not have had any winning chances in this variation. ½–½ Alekhine 1937, 120–1.

(289) FINE—WINTER, W

Nottingham (7), 1936 (17 Aug.)
Queen's Gambit Declined, Slav Defence [D12]

Now follows a game which illustrates above all Fine's combinative intrepidity. **1. d4 d5 2. c4 c6 3. Nf3 Nf6 4. e3** White wants to make it as difficult for his opponent as he can, hence avoids 4 Nc3, which is the strongest according to theory but has also been most analyzed. **4 ... Bf5 5. Nc3** 5 cxd5 cxd5 6 Qb3 gives White some initiative on the queenside. After his next move Black has no further opening difficulties. Alekhine **5 ... e6 6. Nh4** To avoid all chance of the game becoming drawish and to produce a difficult game, White submits to a slight delay in development to win the "minor exchange." **6 ... Be4** If, instead 6 ... Bg4 7 Qb3 followed by h3 and g4 gives White some pressure. **7. f3 Bg6 8. Nxg6 hxg6 9. g3!** Because he is so strong in defence, Fine can permit himself the luxury of many variations which are superficially risky and only produce a satisfactory game with the most accurate handling. With this hardly obvious move, White forestalls all dangers along the open h-file; after 9 Bd3, for instance, the reply 9 ... Nh5 would have been rather troublesome. **9 ... Bd6 10. f4** The logical consequence of his preceding move. The threat was 10 ... Bxg3+, and 10 Bg2? would be faulty owing to 10 ... Rxh2 11 Rxh2 Bxg3+. **10 ... Ne4** 10 ... Nbd7 merited preference, whilst 10 ... Nh5 followed by 11 ... f5 and ... Nf6 was also worth considering. **11. Nxe4** An important exchange. Any other move would allow Black to get a very strong position by 11 ... f5. **11 ... dxe4** White has now got a mobile centre—the d-pawn being blocked no longer—and this circumstance enhances the significance of his two bishops. The ensuing operations on each side are dictated by the pawn situation: White must work in the centre and on the queen's wing, Black on the king's wing—which incidentally offers him few chances, as White naturally does not castle on that side. **12. Bd2 Qe7** Probably so as to be able to play 13 ... Bb4 and exchange off one of the White bishops. 12 ... Nd7 would have been better, however. (Fine reckoned that in the event of 12 ... Nd7 he would win a pawn by 13 Qc2 f5

14 c5 Bc7 15 Qb3.) **13. a3!** One of those little moves which mark a great master. White prevents both 13 ... Bb4 and 13 ... c5, which latter would now be very strongly met by 14 dxc5 Bxc5 15 b4. In answer to the more obvious 13 Qb3, Black would have been able to play 13 ... c5, and continue possibly with ... Nc6 with much better chances. **13 ... Nd7 14. Qb3** Now this move is made with gain of time. (Fine points out that Black cannot play 14 ... b6 in view of 15 Qa4, when 15 ... Nb8 would be forced, in order to protect the pawn, after which there comes 15 b4 and Black finds himself in a lost position.) **14 ... Rb8** The pawn was too difficult to protect. Obviously 14 ... 0-0-0 would be too dangerous. 14 ... Nf6 was not quite satisfactory either, since Black could then only with difficulty play ... f5, a move which is required to protect the pawn on e5. Black's queen's rook is not very beautifully placed now. **15. Qa4 a6 16. Be2 g5** This attempt to open up the kingside is, to say the least, premature. Black should have castled. **17. 0-0-0 f5** Black persists in his risky tactics, advancing his pawns before completing his development. **18. fxg5** The precursor to some pretty little combinations. **18 ... Qxg5** Yet again 18 ... 0-0 would have been better. (Fine suggested the pawn sacrifice 18 ... b5 19 Qxa6 bxc4 with a strong attack for the sacrificed material.) **19. c5 Bc7** Had Black divined his opponent's intentions, he would certainly have retreated to e7 instead, for example, 19 ... Be7 20 Qb3 Qf6 21 Bc4 Kf7 (21 ... Nf8? 22 Bxa6); but even then his situation would not have been pleasant.

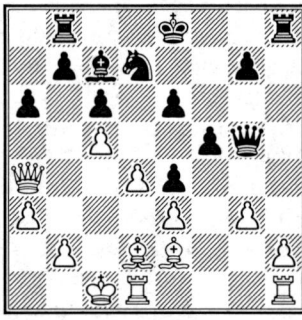

*Position after
Black's 19th move*

20. Bxa6! A fine and surprising move. White gets several pawns for his piece, together with a strong kingside. **20 ... bxa6** The real beauty of White's combination would have been disclosed by 20 ... Ra8 21 Qb3! bxa6 (21 ... Rxa6 22 Qxb7 regaining the piece) 22 Qxe6+ (22 Qb7 Qd8) followed by 23 Qxc6. **21. Qxc6** Attacking the bishop, so that Black is compelled to leave his e-pawn in the lurch. **21 ... Kd8** There is no better continuation. In this way Black at any rate avoids the pawn's being captured with a check. **22. Qxe6** White has already got three pawns for his piece, among them two united passed pawns. Another of Black's pawns is in the air at a6, and his king is badly placed. Clearly White has an overwhelming game. **22 ... Qf6 23. Qd5** Even the exchange of queens would have been good; but the text move is much stronger, as it keeps the kingside attack going. The main threat now is 24 c6, regaining the piece sacrificed. **23 ... Ke7** On 23 ... Kc8 there follows 23 Rdf1 Rf8 24 g4 g6 25 h4 and White will win yet another pawn. RF **24. Bb4!** Threatening 25 c6+ (25 ... Rxb4 26 Qxd7+). **24 ... Rhc8** 25 c6+ would now be answered, rather neatly, by 25 ... Bd6!, with a promising game. (Fine indicated 24 ... Nf8 as the only way to defend, but believed that White would nevertheless win in the end.) **25. Kb1** Threatening c5-c6 once again. **25 ... Nf8 26. g4!** White continually finds the strongest line. **26 ... a5** Not 26 ... fxg4? 27 Rhf1 with crushing effect, for example, 27 ... Qe6 28 Qg5+. **27. Bc3 g6 28. gxf5 Qxf5** Or 28 ... gxf5 29 Rdf1. **29. Qc4 Ne6** Black is up against an impossible task, and it already matters little how he plays. **30. Rhf1 Qh5 31. d5 Nxc5** Desperation! RF **32. d6+** A pretty finish. Black resigns; mate in a few moves is inevitable (32 ... Bxd6 33 Qf7+). A charming little game. Here again Fine lays his foundations in the very opening, but by methods quite different from Alekhine's. Not attack, but some concrete advantage—a pair of bishops— is his primary aim. To achieve this he even submits to being placed on the defensive, relying on being able to hold his own until he is able to pass over to the attack himself—and his confidence is vindicated. **1–0** Euwe 1945, 216–22.

(290) ALEXANDER, C—FINE

Nottingham (8), 1936 (18 Aug.)
English Opening, Flohr-Mikenas Variation [A18]

A game which impressively illustrates two features of the art of the contemporary technician: in rounding off the corners in the most complicated openings, and in exploitation in an inexorable endgame of the slightest weakness in the enemy camp. T&dM **1. c4 Nf6 2. Nc3 e6 3. e4 d5 4. e5 d4** 4 ... Ne4 used to be condemned by theory because of 5 Nxe4 dxe4 6 Qg4, however this gambit has turned out to be quite playable, having been used by Petrosyan and Ehlvest. AW **5. exf6 dxc3 6. bxc3** After 6 fxg7 cxd2+ 7 Qxd2 Qxd2+ 8 Bxd2 Bxg7 Black would have a satisfactory position for the coming endgame. The variation chosen leads to a complicated game in which White in compensation for his somewhat spoilt pawn position, has a certain advantage in space. AA **6 ... Qxf6 7. d4 b6 8. Nf3 Bb7 9. Be2 h6** The continuation 9 Nd7 was played in the well-known game Flohr–Kashdan, Folkestone 1933. AW **10. Ne5! Bd6** He has nothing better. If 10 ... Bxg2 11 Qa4+ c6 12 Rg1 Be4 13 f3 Qh4+ 14 Kd1 Qxh2 15 Re1 and wins. AA **11. Qa4+** The temptation to prevent Black's castling is great. If 11 0-0 Bxe5 12 dxe5, Black would do well to decline the offer of a pawn (12 ... Qxe5 13 Bf3) and to consolidate his base by 12 ... Qe7. A simplified position results from 11 Bf3 Bxf3 12 Qxf3 Qxf3 13 Nxf3. T&dM **11 ... Ke7 12. Bf3** Now this is practically forced, and White gets a worse pawn position and no real attacking chances. AA **12 ... Bxf3 13. Nxf3 Rd8 14. 0-0 Kf8** Artificial castling! Now all is safe. T&dM; The position is in equilibrium, White dominates more space but his pawn position is fractured. dM&G **15. Re1 Nd7 16. Qc6!?**

Alekhine recommends 16 Qd1, and if 16 ... e5, then 17 a4, eliminating at least one weakness in his position, whereas Tartakower & du Mont prefer 16 Qc2. **16 ... e5** A strategically sound move, which frees Black's game but contains also the threat of 17 ... exd4 (18 cxd4 Bxh2+). Tactically, the text is made possible because after 17 Qe4, White cannot gain material by 18 dxe5 Nxe5 19 Nxe5 Bxe5 20 Qxe5 Qxe5 21 Rxe5, because of 21 ... Rd1+. T&dM **17. Qe4 Kg8 18. Bb2!?** Fine reckoned that 18 Qg4! (to stop 18 ... Qe6 AA) would have been quite strong here (MCO, 41), while Tartakower and du Mont propose 18 Be3. **18 ... Re8 19. Re2**

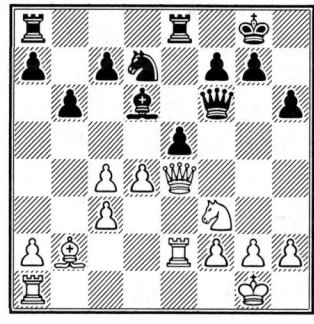

Position after White's 19th move

19 ... Qe6! The exchange of queen for two rooks after 19 ... exd4 would be a good transaction for White. But now Black threatens not only 20 ... Qxc4, but also 20 ... f5, thus getting an advantage in the centre. White therefore decides to relieve the tension; but the ensuing endgame cannot be saved against correct play by Black. AA **20. dxe5?** 20 Nd2 (T&dM) or 20 Rae1 look like better bets. **20 ... Nxe5 21. Nxe5 Qxe5 22. Qxe5 Rxe5 23. Rxe5 Bxe5** The following part of the game is only interesting from the technical point of view. Black's choice of a winning line comes to the exploitation of his opponent's queenside weakness, merely as a means of keeping the White pieces busy on this side of the board. In the meantime he opens a file on the other wing and wins through intrusion of his rook. Simple but instructive! AA **24. Rd1** If 24 Re1 then Rd8 with ... Bf6 to follow. dM&G **24 ... Re8 25. Kf1** If 25 Rd7 Bd6!, entombing the rook and threatening both Re8+ and Re7. dM&G **25 ... Re6 26. Re1 Kf8 27. g3 g5 28. Re4 Ke7 29. Ke2 f5 30. Re3 Kf6 31. Kd3 Rd6+ 32. Kc2 f4!** An energetic move which considerably restricts the action of the white rook. dM&G **33. Re2** If 33 gxf4 Bxf4. dM&G **33 ... h5 34. Bc1 Rc6 35. Kd3 b5!** The endgame crisis begins. White's reply is unavoidable, as his 38th move shows. AA **36. gxf4 gxf4** Cool, calm and collected! If 36 ... bxc4+, then not 37 Ke4 Bxf4 38 Bxf4 Re6+ 39 Kf3 g4+ winning the exchange; but 37 Kc2 gxf4 38 f3 and the "dead points" in Black's position prevent the full deployment of his forces. T&dM **37. Re4 Kf5 38. f3 Rd6+ 39. Kc2** If 39 Ke2, then 39 ... Rg6 40 Kf2 Rc6, forcing an entrance into the hostile camp. AA **39 ... bxc4 40. Rxc4 Rg6** A salient point. Although the forces are balanced, and all eight pawns equally weak, Black's prospective passed pawn proves more dynamic than its counterpart. T&dM **41. Ra4 Rg2+ 42. Bd2 Rxh2 43. Rxa7 h4 44. Ra8** If 44 a4 h3 45 a5 Rxd2+ 46 Kd2 h2. dM&G **44 … h3 45. Rf8+ Ke6 46. Rb8 Rh1 47. Re8+ Kd6** White resigned. The rook cannot prevent the h-pawn from queening. A superbly played ending by Fine! dM&G **0–1** Alekhine 1937, 151–3; Tartakower & du Mont 1952, 632–4; de Marimon & Ganzo 76–7.

(291) FINE—BOGOLJUBOW, E

Nottingham (10), 1936 (21 Aug.)
Dutch Defence [A98]

1. d4 f5 2. g3 Nf6 3. Bg2 e6 4. Nf3 Be7 5. 0–0 0–0 6. c4 d6 I believe that 6 … Ne4—introduced by me against F. Sämisch, Dresden, 1936, and played also in the present tournament against J. R. Capablanca—offers Black comparatively better fighting chances. It is generally in the interests of the second player to delay as long as logically possible the advance of his d-pawn in this opening, so as to keep the choice between the two points, d6 and d5. **7. Nc3 Qe8 8. Qc2** Alternatives are 8 Re1 Qh5 9 e4 fxe4 10 Nxe4 Nxe4 11 Rxe4 Nc6 12 Bf4 Bf6 13 h4 h6 14 Rc1 a6 15 c5! with some advantage for White, Winter–Mikenas, Łódź 1935; or 8 b3 Qh5 9 Ba3 Nbd7 10 Qc2 Ng4 11 Rad1 a6 12 Rfe1 Rb8 13 e4 fxe4 14 Nxe4 b6 15 h3 with a clear advantage, Alexander–Tartakower, Nottingham 1936. **8 … Nc6?** An obvious positional error, which enables White to get control of that important square, d5. The logical move was 8 … Qh5; for Black has no reason to fear 9 e4 fxe4 10 Nxe4 Nc6. **9. d5! Nb4 10. Qb3 Na6 11. dxe6 Nc5 12. Qc2 Bxe6 13. b3** Intending to play 14 Nd4; a threat which should be met by 13 … Ng4, followed by … Bf6. The passive line adopted by Black in the next moves leads to an almost hopeless situation for him. **13 … Qh5? 14. Nd4 Bc8** Obstructing the development of the queen's rook. dM&G **15. b4 Na6** The position of this knight turns out to be a little unfortunate. dM&G **16. Rb1 Kh8** He could not play 16 … Nxb4 17 Rxb4 c5 on account of 18 Nd5. **17. Nd5**

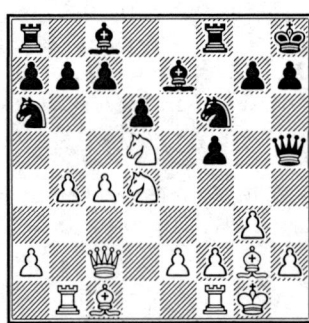

Position after White's 17th move

17 … Qf7? An oversight which loses a pawn without compensation. After 17 … Nxd5 18 cxd5 it would take White some time to transform his positional into material advantage. **18. b5 Nc5** If 18 … Nxd5 19 bxa6 Nb6 20 axb7 wins a piece. dM&G **19. Nxc7 Rb8 20. Nd5 Ne6?!**

21. Nxf5 Nxd5 22. cxd5 Ng5? Losing two more pawns. He might as well resign. **23. Nxd6 Bxd6 24. Bxg5 Bd7 25. e4 Qh5 26. Be3 Rf3 27. Rb3 Rbf8 28. Bc5 Rxb3 29. Bxd6 Rf6 30. axb3 Rxd6 31. Qc7 Rh6 32. Qb8+ Be8 33. g4 Qf7 34. Rc1 Kg8 35. Rc7 Qf8 36. Rc8** Black resigned. **1–0** Alekhine 1937, 186–8; de Marimon & Ganzo 95–6.

(292) TARTAKOWER, S—FINE

Nottingham (11), 1936 (22 Aug.)
Queen's Pawn Game, Tartakower Variation [D03]

1. Nf3 Nf6 2. d4 d5 3. Bg5 e6 4. e3 By renouncing the attack on the centre through c2-c4 White can only hope to get an even game. In fact Black has not the slightest trouble in developing his pieces efficiently. **4 … c5 5. Nbd2 Nbd7** In harmony with the subsequent development of queen and bishop. **6. c3 Qb6 7. Qc2 Bd6 8. Bd3 h6 9. Bh4 0–0 10. 0–0 Qc7 11. Bg3 a6** Black intended to continue the development of his queen's bishop with a pawn advance on the queenside. Otherwise he could as well play here 11 … Bxg3 12 hxg3 b6 and if 13 e4 dxe4, followed by … Bb7. **12. Rad1 b5 13. dxc5?** Slightly better was 13 Bxd6 Qxd6 14 dxc5 Nxc5 15 e4. But the text move was good enough for equality. **13 … Bxg3 14. hxg3 Nxc5** Black has a slight advantage, MCO 180. **15. Nb3?** It is difficult to explain why the "routinier" (as Dr. Tartakower calls himself) yields to his opponent the full control of the centre, with no compensation. The course indicated was 15 e4 Nxd3 (Black need not take the bishop immediately 15 … Bb7 looks more dangerous to White) 16 Qxd3 dxe4 17 Nxe4 Nxe4 18 Qxe4 Bb7 19 Qe3, with an even game. **15 … Nxd3 16. Qxd3 e5 17. Nh2 Rd8** Black's advantage was overwhelming, and the most natural way to exploit it was a "minority attack," starting with a6-a5. It is surprising that Fine, here as well as in the next few moves, appears not to think of this. His play in the following part of the game is not exactly weak, but lacks a definite plan. Tartakower, on the contrary makes the utmost of his inferior position, and finally succeeds in saving half a point. **18. Rfe1 Be6 19. Qe2 Ne4** This knight manoeuvre cannot be commended. He could still play Rab8, followed by a6-a5. **20. Rc1 Rac8 21. Red1 Qc4 22. Qe1 Qc7** Admitting by this that his last move was useless. **23. Qe2 Nd6 24. Nd2 Qb6 25. a3 Nc4 26. Nxc4 bxc4 27. Rd2 Bf5** Black is still slightly superior and might try to get up an attack on the b-pawn with … Rb8 and so on. The text allows his alert opponent to obtain further simplification. **28. Qh5! Qg6** If 28 … Qf6, then 29 Nf3 and eventually g3-g4. **29. Qxg6 Bxg6 30. f4!** Just at the right moment, as 30 … f6 would now be inferior because of 31 fxe5 fxe5 32 Ng4. **30 … exf4 31. gxf4 Rb8 32. Rcd1 Be4 33. Ng4** Practically forcing the exchange of the remaining minor pieces, with an unavoidable draw. **33 … Rb6 34. Nf2 Rdb8 35. Nxe4 dxe4 36. Rd8+ Rxd8** Draw agreed. **½–½** Alekhine 1937, 203–5.

(293) Fine—Alekhine, A

Nottingham (12), 1936 (24 Aug.)

Queen's Gambit Declined [D53]

1. d4 Nf6 2. c4 e6 3. Nc3 d5 4. Nf3 This method of development, whereby the second knight is brought into play before the queen's bishop, has recently come into fashion. When Fine plays it he has in mind the definite possibility of following up with e3 and the development of the queen's bishop on b2, an opening system which has already brought him several fine successes (for example, his victory over Lasker). **ME 4 ... Be7** Less committal than 4 ... Nbd7, after which Fine is inclined to play e3 at once. **ME 5. Bg5** If now 5 e3 then Black can very successfully transpose into the Queen's Gambit Accepted 5 ... 0–0 6 Bd3 dxc4 7 Bxc4 c5 and if White selects the standard continuation he gets into difficulties, for he is a move behind, having taken two moves with his bishop to reach c4, instead of one, as in the normal Queen's Gambit Accepted. **ME 5 ... h6** Probably no better and no worse than the usual 5 ... Nbd7. As White plays in the present game, however, Black gets almost immediately a perfectly satisfactory game. **AA 6. Bxf6?** This in conjunction with the next move would be rather promising, were Black's c-pawn already at c6; but, as it is not, the logical move was 6 Bh4. **AA 6 ... Bxf6 7. e4 dxe4 8. Nxe4 Nc6** Forcing the exchange that follows. **AA 9. Nxf6+ Qxf6 10. Qd2** White must do something at once against the threat of ... 0–0 and ... Rd8. **AA 10 ... 0–0 11. Qe3!** After 11 0–0–0 e5 (and if 12 d5 e4) Black's game would be preferable. **AA 11 ... Rd8?** This superficial move spoils Black's chances, which would be excellent after 11 ... Nb4! 12 Qd2 c5 13 dxc5 Na6, followed by Nxc5. **AA 12. 0–0–0 Ne7** As White's d-pawn is now sufficiently protected, Black must think seriously how he can meet an attack against his king, beginning with the simple advance h2-h4, g2-g4 and so forth. The knight's manoeuvre in the text is enough for that purpose, but allows White through the exchange of queens to obtain a slightly superior endgame. **AA 13. Bd3 Nf5 14. Qe5!** Securing a clear pull in the endgame. 14 Bxf5 would not have been so good for the reply 14 ... Qxf5 would have brought the queen into strong play, commanding crucial squares in the white king's field. **ME 14 ... Qxe5** Forced, for 15 Qxf6 followed by 16 Bxf5, giving Black ugly tripled pawns, was threatened. 14 ... Qe7? would have lost a piece through 15 Bxf5 and 14 ... Nxd4? the exchange through 15 Qxf6 gxf6 16 Nxd4 Rxd4 17 Bh7+ followed by 18 Rxd4. **ME 15. dxe5 Bd7 16. Be4** Forcing Black's reply, after which the mobility of his bishop will for a time be very limited. **AA 16 ... c6 17. Rd3 Be8 18. Rhd1** Obtaining control of the open d-file, but that is about all. It is not easy to see how a more tangible advantage is to be gained for there exists no convenient point at which White can break through (he cannot get either a rook to d7 or a knight to d6). **ME 18 ... Rxd3 19. Rxd3 Kf8 20. Kc2 h5** In order to play Ke7, at present impossible on account of 21 g4. **AA 21. Bxf5** White hopes to take advantage of the weakness of the black squares of his opponent's king-side; but this hope is destined to prove illusive, as the bishop soon becomes active again. After the exchange chances may be considered about even. **AA 21 ... exf5 22. Ng5 Ke7 23. b3?** This allows Black to profit by the fact that the white king and rook are posted on the same diagonal, and so to obtain even winning prospects. Simpler and better was 23 Kc3, in which case, after 23 ... c5 24 h4, Black would not continue as in the actual game, but would make a diversion on the queenside with 24 ... b5 25 b3 Rb8, when his prospects would be satisfactory. **AA 23 ... c5 24. h4** Hoping to play quietly Ng5-h3-f4, obtaining an "ideal" position. **ME 24 ... Bc6 25. f3** The consequences of the inaccurate 23rd move now become obvious: White, to guard against the threat of ... Be4, has to place yet another of his pawns on a light square, where it will henceforth be far more vulnerable to Black's bishop than on a dark. **ME 25 ... f4!** With this strong move (which White overlooked when he played 23 b3) Black obtains a definite pull, which he maintains until the end. By Fine's accurate defence, however, the advantage is not allowed to become enough for winning purposes. **AA 26. Kc3** He has nothing better. 26 Nh3 would lose, for then 26 ... Bd7!, with the double threat of ... Bxh3 and Bf5. **AA** (Is White really losing after 26 Nh3 Bd7 27 Rd5! Bxh3 28 gxh3?) **26 ... Re8** Threatening with ... Kf8 to win the e-pawn. **AA 27. Rd6! Kf8 28. e6 f6!** With a series of fine moves Alekhine has now set on foot a far-seeing plan to obtain a dangerous passed pawn on the kingside. **ME 29. Nh3 Ke7 30. Rd2 Kxe6 31. Nxf4+ Kf7 32. Nxh5 Rh8** It was to keep this move in hand that Black captured the pawn at e6 with his king, instead of playing to protect the h-pawn and pick up the e-pawn by a multiple attack at his leisure. **ME 33. Nf4 Rxh4** The last few moves for both sides were practically forced. In the next part of the endgame the bishop proves slightly superior to the knight. **AA 34. Nd5 Rh5 35. Nf4 Re5 36. a4 g5 37. Nd3 Re3 38. Ra2!** Fine defends himself excellently in his compromised position. The threat is now 39 Kd2 followed by Nxc5 and if Black defends the pawn by ... b6 then the way has been subtly prepared for the white rook to support an effective attack by a5! **ME 38 ... g4! 39. Kd2 Re7 40. fxg4 Bxg2 41. Nxc5 Bf3! 42. Kc3 Bxg4** The remaining portion of the endgame is instructive on account of the clever way in which White prevents the passed pawn being brought as far as f4. He succeeds in this mainly because Black's bishop does not command (see note to move 56) the queening square of his a-pawn; and White can speculate therefore in many variations on a sacrifice of the knight for the passed pawn. **AA 43. Rf2 f5** If 43 ... a5 44 b4 with a draw. **FR 44. a5 Kf6 45. b4 Kg5 46. Nd3!** The square f4 now becomes a Rubicon which Black is never able to cross. **ME 46 ... Kh4 47. Rf4! Kg3 48. Rd4 Bf3 49. Rd8!** So as to reply to 49 ... f4 with 50 Rf8 Re4 51 a6 bxa6 (51 ... b6 52 c5) 52 Rxf4!! Black then would remain a whole bishop to the good but would be unable to win since his only remaining pawns would queen on a square of opposite colour to his bishop. **ME 49 ... Be2 50. Rg8+ Kf3 51. Rf8 Ke3** The rook ending after 51 ... Bxd3 would also be a draw only. ME **52. Ne1 Ke4 53. Ng2 Bh5** Threatening 54 ... Rg7 and so on. But White, as several times before, has again the saving move. AA (If 53 ... Rg7 54 Re8+ Kf3 55 Nh4+ wins for White. JN) **54. Rd8! Kf3 55. Nh4+ Kg4 56. Rd4+! Kg5** If 56 ... f4, then 57 Ng2 Rf7 58 a6!, followed by R×f4+, with a draw. AA **57. Ng2 Bf3 58. Nf4 Be4 59. Nd5 Re5 60. Rd1! Bf3** If 60 ... f4 now, 61 Kd4. AA **61. Rg1+ Bg4 62. Kd4 Re4+ 63. Kd3 Re6 64. Ne3 Rd6+ 65. Kc3 Rd8 66. b5 Re8** Draw agreed. ½–½ Euwe in *Chess* 1936–7, 50–3; Alekhine 1937, 205–9; Reinfeld and Nunn in *Encyclopaedia of Chess Endings: Rook Endings*.

(294) Flohr, S—Fine

Nottingham (13), 1936 (25 Aug.)
English Opening, Classical Defence [A28]

1. c4 Nf6 2. Nc3 e5 3. Nf3 Nc6 4. e3 The experience of the last few years has proved that the variation 4 d4 e×d4 5 N×d4 Bb4 is quite satisfactory for Black. But also with the text-move White cannot hope for any advantage. **4 ... Bb4 5. Qc2 0–0 6. Be2 Re8 7. 0–0 d6** Black intends to play ... d5 only after having finished his development. This is a good logical plan, which at any rate secures him a balanced position. But still more promising was, I think, first 7 ... Bf8, to prevent the exchange of this bishop, which in the actual game became practically forced. **8. Ne1** Obviously to avoid the opening of files after 8 ... B×c3 and 9 ... e4. **8 ... Be6 9. a3 B×c3** Comparatively better than 9 ... Ba5 10 b4 Bb6 after which he would lose the chance of playing d5. **10. Q×c3 a5 11. b3 Qd7** Instead of this unnecessary preparatory move he should play at once 11 ... d5, which would either force an exchange or allow next move ... d4, without giving White the opportunity (which he had in the actual game) of blocking the centre by e3-e4. In either case White would have to deal with more difficult problems than after the queen's move. **12. d3 d5 13. Qc2!** With an equal game, MCO 37. **13 ... Rad8 14. Bb2 Bg4** Hoping to get rid of one of White's pair of bishops. Flohr meets this strategical threat most energetically. **15. c×d5 Q×d5 16. Nf3** The further weakening of the pawn position is in this particular case without much importance. **16 ... B×f3 17. g×f3 Nd7 18. Rac1 Nf8 19. Qc4** Draw agreed. Although the chances are in fact about even, this premature decision, after the interesting opening play, is regrettable. ½–½ Alekhine 1937, 227–8.

(295) Fine—Capablanca, J

Nottingham (14), 1936 (27 Aug.)
Queen's Gambit Declined, Slav Defence [D19]

1. d4 d5 2. c4 c6 3. Nf3 Nf6 4. Nc3 d×c4 5. a4 Bf5 6. e3 e6 7. B×c4 Bb4 8. 0–0 0–0 9. Qe2 Ne4 10. N×e4 B×e4 11. Rd1 Nd7 12. Bd2 This seems to give Black even less trouble than 12 Bd3, played by Dr. Lasker in the 6th round, as he can exchange by force almost

all the minor pieces. AA **12 ... B×f3** An equal position is also reached after 12 ... Bd6 13 Bd3 Nf6 14 B×e4 N×e4. AKh **13. Q×f3 Qa5** If 13 ... B×d2 14 R×d2 Ne5 15 Qe2 Nc4 16 Qc4, White retains a small advantage. AKh **14. Qe2 B×d2 15. Q×d2 Q×d2 16. R×d2 a5 17. g3 Nb6 18. Bb3 Rfd8 19. Rc2 Nd5 20. B×d5 R×d5** Draw agreed. ½–½ Alexander Khalifman in Soloviev 1997, 227; Alekhine 1937, 243–4.

(296) Tylor, T—Fine

Nottingham (15), 1936 (28 Aug.)
Sicilian, Dragon Variation [B73]

1. e4 c5 2. Nf3 d6 3. d4 c×d4 4. N×d4 Nf6 5. Nc3 g6 6. Be2 Bg7 7. Be3 0–0 8. Qd2 This move is as good as the more usual 8 0–0, and in the present game proves so far a success that it induces Black to prepare a tempting, but strategically unjustifiable, exchange. **8 ... Nc6 9. Rd1** With the threat of an eventual N×c6, followed by e5. Although Black gets the two bishops, his position will remain slightly inferior, because of White's strength in the centre and his ability to protect easily the vulnerable squares on the c-file. The normal 9 ... Bd7, followed by ... a6, ... b5, is better. **9 ... Ng4 10. B×g4 B×g4 11. f3 Bd7 12. 0–0 Rc8 13. Rf2** Protecting c2 and thus making ready for Nd5. **13 ... Ne5 14. b3 f5?** This weakens his central squares without real compensation and White's advantage becomes quite obvious. Black should try for some kind of initiative on the queenside by 14 ... a6, and if 15 a4 Rb8, eventually followed by b5. **15. e×f5 g×f5 16. Nce2 Nf7 17. f4** After this Black's position in the centre becomes unsound, and will be very difficult to improve. **17 ... Qe8 18. h3** But this is overcautious. He could quietly play first 18 c4 and only in the case of 18 ... e5? 19 f×e5 N×e5 20 h3 and wins. **18 ... Kh8 19. Qa5 Nd8 20. c4** 20 Q×a7? e5 would be in Black's favour. **20 ... Qg6?** Now, however, Black had no earthly reason to leave his a-pawn *en prise.* 20 ... a6 was indicated. **21. Q×a7 Rg8** The open file is rather harmless to White, and would have been more so if he had not played the useless h3. **22. Qb6 Bf6 23. Nc3!** In connection with the following move, one of simplest ways to break Black's attempts at attack. White gives his extra pawn back, but eliminates one of the hostile bishops, so forcing a distinctly superior endgame. **23 ... Bc6 24. Nd5 B×d5 25. c×d5 Qh5 26. Nf3 Q×h3 27. Bd4 Qh6**

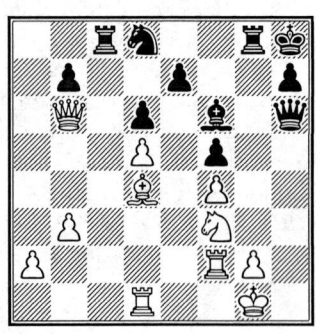

Position after
Black's 27th move

28. Bxf6+? White is too anxious to exchange queens. With 28 Re1 (threatening Rxe7) he could gain a very valuable, probably decisive, tempo, since the middle-game after 28 ... Qxf4 29 Bxf6+ exf6 30 Nd4 would be scarcely defensible by Black. **28 ... Qxf6 29. Qd4 Kg7!** The king comes in time to prevent catastrophe. **30. Re2 Qxd4+ 31. Nxd4 Kf6** The ensuing endgame is slightly in White's favour, as Black has some compensation for his obvious weakness on the e-file, through possession of the open c-file. But a loss for White by accurate play is of course out of the question. **32. Kf2 Rc5 33. Nf3 h6 34. Rd4 Re8 35. b4 Rc3 36. Re3?** Much simpler was 36 a4, when it would be Black who must look for drawing variations. **36 ... Rc2+ 37. Rd2 Rxd2+ 38. Nxd2 e5** Clearly a great relief for Black. **39. dxe6 Nxe6 40. g3?** Here and in what follows White plays decidedly too passively. By making a counter-attack he would have an easy draw—for example, 40 Rd3 Ke7 41 Rd5 Nxf4 42 Rxf5 Nd3+ 43 Kf3 Nxb4 44 Rb5. **40 ... Rc8 41. Rd3 Ke7 42. Ke3 Rc2 43. a4 Nc7 44. Rb3?** Better was 44 Nb3 Ra2 45 a5. **44 ... Ra2 45. a5 Nb5 46. Rb1 Kf6 47. Kd3 d5 48. Nb3** As this combination, rightly carried out, offered good drawing chances, it is not to be condemned. Otherwise White would have had to tackle a number of technical difficulties. **48 ... Rg2 49. Nc5 Rxg3+ 50. Kd2 Nd6**

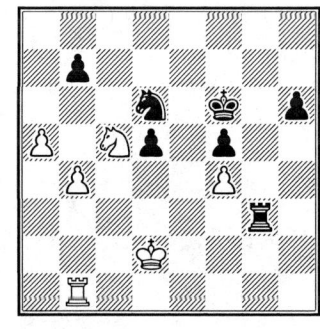

Position after Black's 50th move

51. Nxb7 A desperate sacrifice in a situation where it was not as yet necessary. As a matter of fact, it is very doubtful whether Black would have had any real winning chances after 51 Ke2, threatening both 52 b5 and 52 Rd1. 51 ... Ne4 in reply would not be sufficient, because of 52 Nxb7 Nc3+ 53 Kf2. **51 ... Nxb7 52. a6 Nd6 53. b5 Ra3 54. b6 Rxa6 55. b7 Nxb7 56. Rxb7 Ke6?** A grave mistake, which almost threw away the win. The correct—and simple—line was 56 ... Kg6 57 Rd7 Ra5 58 Rd6+ Kh5 59 Kc3 Ra3+, followed by Kg4 and so on. **57. Rh7! Ra2+ 58. Kd3 Rh2 59. Ra7 Rh4 60. Ra6+ Kf7 61. Kd4?** After this it is all over. The right continuation was 61 Ke3! and if ... h5 or ... Kg7, then 62 Rd6. Or if 61 ... Ke7, then 62 Kd4. **61 ... Rxf4+ 62. Kxd5 Kg7 63. Ke5 Rf1 64. Ra2 Kg6 65. Rg2+ Kh5 66. Kf6 Kh4 67. Rg6 h5 68. Rg5 f4 69. Kf5 Ra1 70. Rg2 f3** White resigned. **0–1** Alekhine 1937, 261–5.

Oslo, September 13–21, 1936

"Reuben Fine of New York placed still another success to his credit by emerging from a masters tournament at the Oslo Chess Club with a winning total of 6½ points out of a possible seven. With the exception of one draw, the New Yorker made a clean sweep. Fine's chief rival was Salo Flohr of Czechoslovakia, with whom he drew. Flohr drew one other game with Myhre, one of four Oslo representatives, in consequence of which the famous Czechoslovakian was placed second in the prize list. H. Pedersen, a schoolmaster of Vejen, Denmark, finished third with a score of 4–3. Myhre tied Jens Enevoldsen of Copenhagen for fourth and fifth." (ACB 1936) Oslo 1936, organized by Sjakkutvalget i Arbeidernes Idrettsforbund, AIF, was the first international tournament to be held in Norway. It was arranged to protest the decision of the Norsk Sjakkforbund sending a team to the unofficial Olympiad, Munich 1936 (17 August–1 September). Botvinnik and Capablanca were also invited, but did not attend. Play took place in the Banquet Hall and National Theatre in the Norwegian capital. Fine's play was on the whole steady and effective. However, he had to show great courage to fend off attacks by Heiestad and Myhre in the final rounds. Flohr struggled with Myhre for 116 moves before their draw was agreed.

	1	2	3	4	5	6	7	8	
1 Fine	*	½	1	1	1	1	1	1	6½
2 Flohr	½	*	1	1	½	1	1	1	6
3 Pedersen	0	0	*	0	1	1	1	1	4
4 Enevoldsen	0	0	1	*	½	1	0	1	3½
5 Myhre	0	½	0	½	*	1	½	1	3½
6 Johnsen	0	0	0	0	0	*	1	1	2
7 Knudsen	0	0	0	1	½	0	*	0	1½
8 Heiestad	0	0	0	0	0	0	1	*	1

(297) FINE—KNUDSEN, J

Oslo (1), 1936 (13 Sept.)
Nimzowitsch-Indian Defence [E40]

1. d4 Nf6 2. c4 e6 3. Nc3 Bb4 4. e3 Ne4 5. Qc2 f5 6. Bd3 Bxc3+ 7. bxc3 Nf6 8. Ne2 d6 9. 0–0 0–0 10. Ba3 Nbd7

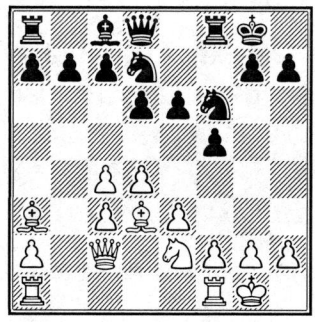

Position after Black's 10th move

11. c5 dxc5 12. Nf4 Re8 13. Qb3 c4 14. Bxc4 Nf8 15. Bxf8 Kxf8 16. Nxe6+ Bxe6 17. Bxe6 Qd6 18. Bxf5 g6 19. Bd3 Kg7 20. Rae1 Ng4 21. g3 h5 22. e4 h4 23. e5 Black resigned. **1–0**

(298) PEDERSEN, H—FINE

Oslo (2), 1936 (14 Sept.)
Budapest Defence [A52]

1. d4 Nf6 2. c4 e5 3. dxe5 Ng4 4. e4 h5 5. Be2
Nxe5 6. f4 Ng4 7. Bxg4 Qh4+ 8. g3 Qxg4 9. Qxg4
hxg4 10. Nc3 Bc5 11. Nd5 Na6 12. Be3 Bxe3
13. Nxe3 Nc5 14. Nxg4 Nxe4 15. Nf2 Nd6

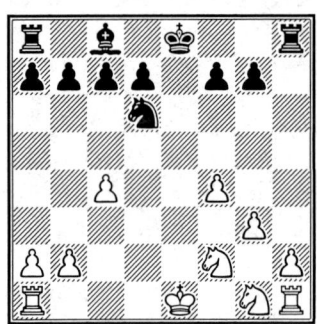

*Position after
Black's 15th move*

16. b3 b5! 17. c5 Nf5 18. Ngh3 Bb7 19. 0–0 Nd4
20. Rae1+ Kf8 21. Ng5 f6 22. Nfe4 fxg5 23. fxg5+
Kg8 24. h4 Kh7 25. h5 Rhf8 26. Nf6+ gxf6
27. Re7+ Kg8 28. g6 Rae8 29. Rxd7 Re2 30. Rd1
Nf5 White resigned. **0–1**

(299) FINE—JOHNSEN, E

Oslo (3), 1936 (15 Sept.)
English Opening, Classical Four Knights [A28]

1. c4 Nf6 2. Nc3 e5 3. Nf3 Nc6 4. e4 Bb4 5. d3
d6 6. Be2 0–0 7. 0–0 Bxc3 8. bxc3 Ne8 9. Rb1
b6 10. d4 Qe7 11. Re1 Bb7 12. Ba3 Nf6 13. Bd3
Nd7 14. Qd2 Kh8 15. Qe3 f6 16. Nd2 Nd8 17. c5
dxc5 18. dxc5 Bc6 19. Bc4 Nb7 20. Bd5 Bxd5
21. exd5 Ndxc5 22. Ne4 Rfd8 23. c4 Rac8
24. Nxc5 Nxc5 25. Bxc5 bxc5 26. Rb7

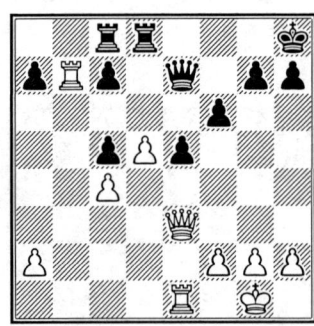

*Position after
White's 26th move*

26 ... Rb8 27. Rxa7 Ra8 28. Qa3 Rxa7 29. Qxa7
Qd6 30. Qb7 Qb6 31. Qxb6 cxb6 32. Rb1 Rd6
33. a4 Kg8 34. g3 Kf7 35. Rb5 f5 36. a5 bxa5
37. Rxa5 e4 38. Rxc5 Kf6 39. h4 g6 40. Rc7 h6
41. Rh7 h5 42. Rc7 Ke5 43. Re7+ Kf6 44. Re8 Rd7
45. Re6+ Kf7 46. Rc6 Ra7 47. c5 Ra1+ 48. Kg2
Rd1 49. Rc7+ Kf6 50. Rd7 Black resigned. **1–0**

(300) ENEVOLDSEN, J—FINE

Oslo (4), 1936 (17 Sept.)
Queen's Gambit Declined [D38]

1. d4 Nf6 2. c4 e6 3. Nf3 d5 4. Nc3 Bb4 5. e3 c5
6. dxc5 0–0 7. Be2 Ne4 8. Qc2 Nxc3 9. bxc3
Bxc5 10. 0–0 dxc4 11. Bxc4 Nc6 12. Rb1 Na5
13. Bd3 h6 14. Nd4 Qc7 15. Qe2 Bd7 16. c4 Rfc8
17. Nb3 Rab8 18. Bd2 Nxb3 19. axb3 Bd6

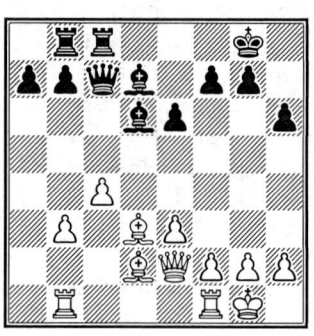

*Position after
Black's 19th move*

20. f4 e5 21. Bc3 exf4 22. exf4 Re8 23. Qf2
Bc5 24. Bd4 Bxd4 25. Qxd4 Rbd8 26. Rbe1
Be6 27. Qc3 Bf5 28. Bxf5 Qc5+ 29. Rf2 Qxf5
30. Rxe8+ Rxe8 31. g3 h5 32. Qf3 h4 33. g4 Qc5
34. Qd3 g6 35. Kf1 Re3 36. Qd8+ Kg7 37. f5?
Rxb3 38. fxg6 Qxc4+ 39. Kg1 Qxg4+ 40. Rg2
Rb1+ White resigned. **0–1**

(301) FINE—FLOHR, S

Oslo (5), 1936 (18 Sept.)
Benoni [A44]

1. d4 c5 2. d5 e5 3. dxe6 fxe6 4. e4 Nc6 5. Nc3
Nf6 6. Bc4 Ne5 7. Be2 d5 8. exd5 exd5 9. Bg5 d4
10. Ne4 Qa5+ 11. Qd2 Qxd2+ 12. Nxd2 Bf5
13. 0–0–0 Bd6 14. Ngf3 0–0–0 15. Nxe5 Bxe5
16. Bd3 Bd7 17. Rde1 Rde8 18. Nf3 Bd6 19. Bxf6
gxf6 20. Rxe8+ Bxe8 21. Re1 Bd7 22. Nh4 Bf4+
23. Kb1 Kd8 24. g3 Bg5 25. Nf3 Bh6 26. Nh4
Bg5 27. Nf3 Bh6 28. Nh4 Bg5 Draw agreed. **½–½**

(302) HEIESTAD, S—FINE

Oslo (6), 1936 (19 Sept.)

The score of this game is not available. **0–1**

(303) FINE—MYHRE, E

Oslo (7), 1936 (21 Sept.)
Caro-Kann Defence [B19]

1. e4 c6 2. d4 d5 3. Nc3 dxe4 4. Nxe4 Bf5 5. Ng3
Bg6 6. h4 h6 7. Nf3 Nd7 8. Bc4 e6 9. Qe2 Bd6
10. h5 Bh7 11. Ne4 Bxe4 12. Qxe4 Ngf6 13. Qe2
0–0 14. Bd2 Qc7 15. 0–0–0

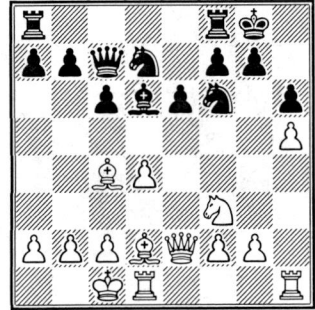

Position after White's 15th move

15 ... b5 16. Bd3 a6 17. g4! Nd5 18. g5 Nf4 19. Qe4 f5 20. Qe3 Kh8 21. Rdg1 Nb6 22. Nh4 Nbd5 23. Qe1 Kh7 24. Ng6 Rfe8 25. Rh4 Nxd3+ 26. cxd3 c5! 27. dxc5 Qxc5+ 28. Kb1 Rac8 29. gxh6 Qc2+ 30. Ka1 gxh6 31. Rh3 a5?! 32. Ne5 Bxe5?! 33. Qxe5 Rg8 34. Rhg3 Rg5 35. Qxe6 Nb4 36. Bxg5 hxg5 37. Qg6+ Black resigned. **1–0**

Bussum Section 1, September 26–29, 1936

"Fine was invited to play in a tournament in celebration of the 25th anniversary of the Chess Club at Bussum in Holland." (ACB 1936). Players from the club played in sections against the masters. Dr. Tartakower was the other master to take a section. Crosstable unavailable.

(304) Fine—Dekker, C

Bussum (1), 1936 (26 Sept.)
Queen's Gambit Declined [D36]

1. d4 d5 2. c4 e6 3. Nc3 Nf6 4. Bg5 Nbd7 5. cxd5 exd5 6. e3 Be7 7. Bd3 c6 8. Qc2 0-0 9. Nge2 Re8 10. 0-0-0 Nf8 11. h3 Ne4 12. Bxe7 Qxe7 13. Bxe4 dxe4 14. g4 Be6 15. Qxe4 Qb4

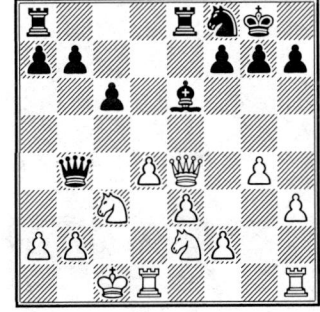

Position after White's 15th move

16. Qc2 a5 17. Nf4 a4 18. d5 cxd5 19. Rd4 Qd6 20. Nfxd5 Bxd5 21. Rxd5 Qc6 22. a3 b5 23. Rhd1 b4 24. Nb5 Qh6 25. axb4 Qxh3 26. Nc7 Rac8 27. Rc5 Red8 28. Nd5 Rxc5?! 29. bxc5 Ne6 30. c6 Kf8 31. c7 Rc8 32. Qc6 Black resigned. **1–0**

(305) Mulder, E—Fine

Bussum (2), 1936 (27 Sept.)
Nimzowitsch-Indian Defence, Spielmann Variation [E23]

1. d4 Nf6 2. c4 e6 3. Nc3 Bb4 4. Qb3 The best continuation is Flohr's preferred move 4 Qc2. RF **4 ... c5 5. dxc5 Nc6 6. Nf3 Bxc5** This strong move is seldom seen, but is probably the most satisfactory way to gain equality. The modish continuation of 1930–34, 6 ... Ne4 is not to be commended in view of the sequence 7 Bd2 Nxc5 8 Qc2 0-0 9 a3 Bxc3 10 Bxc3 f5 11 b4 Ne4 12 Bb2 b6 13 g3!. RF **7. Bg5** Now Black has adequately solved his opening problems. The tame move 7 e3 is less good, and on 7 Bf4 Black can satisfactorily reply 7 ... d5. RF **7 ... h6 8. Bh4** In the second game of the match Alekhine–Bogolyubov, 1929, 8 Bxf6 was played, there followed 8 ... Qxf6 9 Ne4 Bb4+ 10 Qxb4 Nxb4 11 Nxf6+ gxf6 with equality. RF **8 ... Qa5 9. e3?** White had to play 9 Bxf6. After the text his position can already be considered as lost. RF; White could have avoided the spoiling of his pawn formation by 9 Nd2. TKNS **9 ... Ne4** White cannot prevent Black from doubling his pawns on the c-file. On 10 Rc1 there follows 10 ... Nxc3 11 Rxc3 Bb4. RF **10. Be2 0-0 11. 0-0 Nxc3 12. bxc3 e5** The bishop on h4 is shut out of the game and at the same time the white knight is denied the square d4. RF **13. g4** White's position is strategically so poor that this risky attempt to control the f5-square is his only practical counter-chance. RF **13 ... d6 14. Nd2** The pressure on c4 is starting to mount. RF **14 ... Qc7 15. Bf3 Be6 16. Qc2 Na5 17. Bd5!** The point of White's plan. Now on 17 ... Bxg4? there follows 18 Qg6 Be6 19 Bxe6 fxe6 20 Qxe6+ Qf7 21 Qd5 with an even game. RF **17 ... Qd7!**

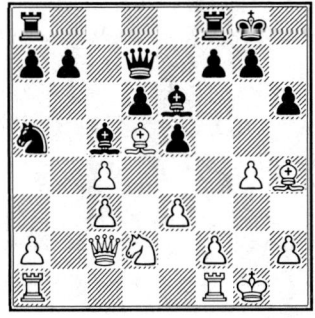

Position after Black's 17th move

18. Kh1? Consequent, but weak! The intention is clear: 18 ... Bxd5+ 19 cxd5 Qxg4 20 Bf6! Qg6! 21 Ne4 with attacking chances. Had White tried 18 h3 instead, however, he might well have had an inferior position, but he would probably have been able to defend himself for longer after 18 ... Bxd5 19 cxd5 f5 20 gxf5 Rxf5 21 Bg3!. RF **18 ... Nxc4** Winning a pawn without any risk. RF **19. Bxc4 Bxc4 20. Nxc4 Qxg4 21. Be7 Qf3+ 22. Kg1 Rfe8 23. Nxe5 Qh5** Good, but 23 ... dxe5 24 Bxc5 Rac8 25 Ba3 Re6 was simpler. RF **24. Qd1** If 24 Bxd6 Bxd6 25 f4 Bxe5 26 fxe5 Rxe5 White is not only a pawn to the bad, but also suffers from an exposed king on g1. RF **24 ... Qxe5 25. Bh4 Qxc3 26. Rc1 Qe5 27. Bg3 Qe6**

28. Qa4 a6 29. Rfd1 b5 30. Qa5 h5 With the white queen "out of the loop," Black begins an assault on the kingside. RF **31. h4 Qg4 32. Kh2 Re6 33. Rd5 Bxe3** The quickest route to the win. RF **34. fxe3 Rxe3 35. Rg5** If 35 Rg1 Black can win by 35 ... Re2+ 36 Rg2 Rxg2+ 31 Kxg2 Qe4+. RF **35 ... Re2+ 36. Kg1 Qf3 37. Bxd6** In time trouble White allows a quick mate, but even after 37 Be1 Qe3+ 38 Kf1 Rae8 39 Qc3 Qf4+ 40 Kg1 f6 41 Rg3 Qxc1 he can happily resign. RF **37 ... Qe3+ 38. Kf1 Qf2 Mate. 0–1** *Tijdschrift van den Koninklijken Nederlandschen Schaakbond* 1936, game 509; Fine, *De Schaakwereld* 1936, 3–4.

(306) FINE—MULLER, W

Bussum (3), 1936 (28 Sept.)
Old Indian Defence [A53]

1. d4 Nf6 2. c4 d6 3. Nc3 Bf5 4. f3 h6 5. e4 Bh7 6. Bd3 e5 7. Nge2 Be7 8. Be3 c5 9. d5 g5 10. Ng3 Nbd7 11. Qd2 Bg6 12. 0–0–0 Nb6 13. Kb1 Qd7 14. Rc1

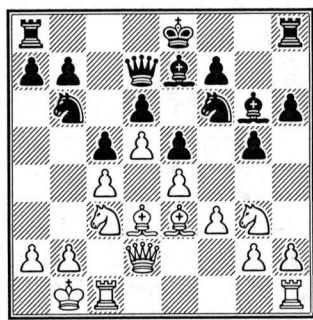

Position after White's 14th move

14 ... Na4? 15. Nb5 Threatening 16 Qa5. **15 ... Bd8** Not 15 ... a6 16 Qa5!. The text prevents the threatened queen incursion, but c5 is weak now. **16. Qc2 Nb6 17. b4!** cxb4 Forced, on 17 ... Be7 White wins a pawn by 18 Nxd6+ Bxd6 19 bxc5. **18. c5! dxc5** If 18 ... Rc8 there would follow 19 Nxa7 or 19 Nxd6+, and on 18 ... Nc8 19 c6!. **19. Bxc5 Be7 20. Bxb6 0–0 21. Nxa7 Rxa7 22. Bxa7 Ra8 23. Bf2 b3 24. Qxb3 Ra3 25. Qb5 Qd8 26. Rhd1 Qa8 27. Nf5 Bxf5 28. exf5 Kg7 29. Bc4** Black resigned. **1–0** *De Schaakwereld* 1936, 4–5.

(307) VAN DOESBURGH, G—FINE

Bussum (4), 1936 (29 Sept.)
Nimzowitsch Defence [B00]

1. e4 Nc6 2. d4 d5 3. e5 Bf5 4. Nf3 Qd7 5. Bd3 Be4 6. Nc3 Qg4 7. 0–0 Bxf3 8. Qxf3 Qxf3 9. gxf3 Nxd4 10. Nxd5 0–0–0 11. Be4 f5 12. exf6 exf6 13. c3 Ne2+ 14. Kh1 Nxc1 15. Raxc1 g6 16. Rcd1 f5 17. Bc2 Bd6 18. Rfe1 c6 19. Ne3 Nf6 20. Nc4 Bc5 21. Kg1 Rxd1 22. Rxd1 Re8 23. Kf1 Nh5 24. b4 Bf8 25. Bb3 Kc7 26. Ne3 Bd6 27. Bf7 Rf8 28. Be6 Ng7 29. Nc4 Nxe6 30. Rxd6 Nf4 31. Rd4 Nd5 32. Rd3 Rd8 33. Nb2 Rd7 34. a3 b5 35. Ke1 Re7+ 36. Kf1

Nf4 37. Rd4 g5 38. Rd2 Re6 39. c4 Rh6 40. Kg1 Rh3 41. cxb5 cxb5 42. Nd3 Rxf3 43. Nxf4 Rxf4

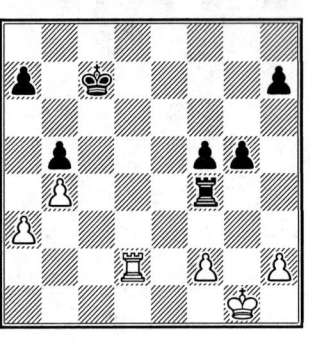

Position after Black's 43rd move

44. Rd5 Kc6 45. Rc5+ Kb6 46. Re5 a5 47. Re6+ Kc7 48. bxa5 Ra4 49. Re5 Kc6 50. Rxf5 Rxa3 51. Rxg5 b4 52. Rh5 b3 53. Rh6+ Kc5 54. Rb6 Kc4 55. a6 Kc3 56. f4 b2 57. Kf2 Kc2 58. f5 b1Q 59. Rxb1 Kxb1 60. a7 Rxa7 61. Ke3 Re7+ White resigned. **0–1**

ASB Jubilee, Amsterdam, October 5–7, 1936

Immediately prior to the international tournament in Amsterdam, Fine played in an event organized by the Amsterdam Chess League, in which over six hundred players participated in groups of four, winning all of his games. In Group A Alekhine and Landau came in joint first, Group C was won by Grünfeld, and Group D by Kmoch. That there are no further games recorded in the notebooks suggests that there was no play-off, indeed there was hardly any time available for such. In any case, the newspapers (*Algemeen Handelsblad* and *Nieuwe Rotterdammer Courant*) published no reports after the last round games of the group stage.

(308) WITTENSON, P—FINE

Amsterdam Jubilee (1), 1936 (5 Oct.)
Sicilian Defence [B51]

1. e4 c5 2. Nf3 d6 3. c3 Nf6 4. Bb5+ Nbd7 5. e5 dxe5 6. Nxe5 a6 7. Qb3 e6 8. Nxd7 Nxd7 9. Bxd7+ Qxd7 10. c4 b5 11. d3 Bb7 12. 0–0 Rd8 13. cxb5 axb5 14. a4

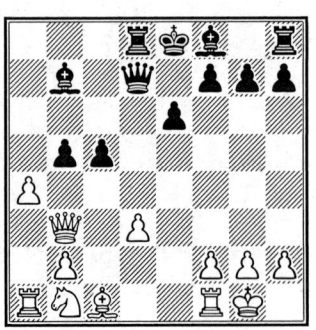

Position after White's 14th move

14 ... b4 15. a5 Ba6 16. Nd2 Qxd3 17. Re1 Qxb3
18. Nxb3 Rd3 19. Nd2 Be7 20. Nf3 Bf6 21. Be3
Bxb2 22. Rad1 c4 23. Bc5 Bc3 24. Rxd3 cxd3
25. Rb1 Kd7 26. Bd4 Rc8 27. Ne5+ Ke8 White
resigned. **0–1**

(309) FINE—MULDER, E

Amsterdam Jubilee (2), 1936 (6 Oct.)
Nimzowitsch-Indian Defence, Classical Variation [E33]

1. d4 Nf6 2. c4 e6 3. Nc3 Bb4 4. Qc2 Nc6 5. Nf3
d6 6. a3 Bxc3+ 7. Qxc3 a5! 8. b3 0–0 9. g3 Re8
10. Bg2 e5 11. d5 Ne7 12. Nd2 Bd7 13. 0–0 b6
14. e4 Ng6 15. Bb2 Qc8 16. f4 Bh3 17. Bxh3 Qxh3
18. f5 Nf8 19. Rae1 Ng4 20. Nf3 f6 21. Qc2 Nd7
22. Qe2 Nc5 23. Kh1 Nh6 24. Ng1 Qg4 25. Rf3
Qh5 26. Bc1 a4 27. b4 Nb3 28. Qg2 Kh8 29. h3
Nd4 30. Rc3 Qf7 31. Be3 Nb3 32. g4

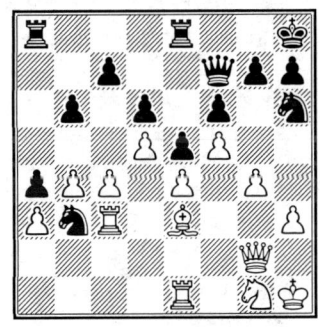

*Position after
White's 32nd move*

32 ... Ng8 33. Nf3 Qd7 34. g5 Ne7 35. Rg1 Rg8
36. Qg4 Qe8 37. Qh4 Qf8 38. Rg4 Black resigned.
1–0

(310) VAN SCHELTINGA, T—FINE

Amsterdam Jubilee (3), 1936 (7 Oct.)
Grünfeld Defence [D85]

1. Nf3 Nf6 2. c4 c5 3. Nc3 d5 4. cxd5 Nxd5
5. d4 Nxc3 6. bxc3 g6 7. e4 Bg7 8. Bc4 0–0
9. h3 Nc6 10. Be3 Qa5 11. 0–0 Qxc3 12. Rc1 Qa3
13. dxc5 Rd8 14. Qb3 Qxb3 15. axb3 Bd7 16. Rfd1
Na5 17. Bd5 e6 18. Bd2 Nc6 19. Bc4 h6 20. b4
Be8

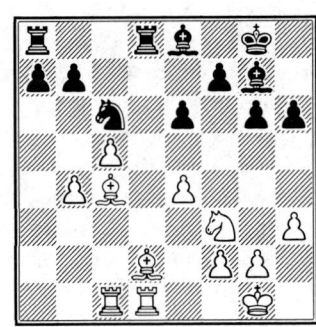

*Position after
Black's 20th move*

21. Be1 a6 22. Rb1 Na7 23. Bb3 Bc6 24. Bc2 Nb5
25. Rxd8+ Rxd8 26. Rb3 Nd4 27. Rd3 Ne2+ 28. Kh2
Rxd3 29. Bxd3 Nc1 30. Bb1 Bb5 31. Bd2 Nd3 32. Bxd3
Bxd3 33. e5 Be4 34. Bc3 Bxf3 35. gxf3 Kf8 36. Kg3
Ke8 37. Kf4 Kd7 38. Ke4 Kc6 39. Kd4 Kb5 40. Bd2
h5 41. f4 Bf8 42. f3 a5 White resigned. **0–1**

De Arbeiderspers International,
Amsterdam/The Hague/Rotterdam,
October 10–18, 1936

"Returning to Holland soon after the conclusion of the
congress at Nottingham, Reuben Fine took part in an
important tournament of eight players, beginning at Amsterdam on October 10. But for the fact that he lost in the
first round to Hans Kmoch of Vienna, it might well have
been another triumph for the American. As it was, he tied
for first place with Dr. Max Euwe, both finishing half a
point ahead of Dr. Alexander Alekhine. Dr. Euwe was not
defeated, but drew four of his games. He won from Dr.
Alekhine, however. Fine, on the other hand, played drawn
games with his two chief rivals and won four times. Insofar
as these three masters were concerned, it was practically a
repetition of their experiences at Nottingham, except that,
in the Euwe–Alekhine game, the result was reversed." (*ACB*
1936) "In October 1936, the Amsterdam Socialist newspaper *Het Volk* arranged a small tournament of eight masters
in conjunction with the celebration of the 10th anniversary
of the Amsterdam Chess Club. Five of the games were to
take place in Amsterdam, with the 4th round played at the
Hague and the 6th round in Rotterdam." (Fine 1937, 5)

Lodewijk Prins was in the initial line-up but withdrew
after playing two rounds. Koltanowski, writing in *Chess*,
claimed that this was because he was reprimanded for turning up late for his second round game with Fine. *BCM* however reported that Prins objected to the substitution of the
stronger van Scheltinga for van den Bosch, when the latter
fell ill. On his withdrawal, Prins was replaced by the apparently recovered van den Bosch. In a Dutch newspaper article Euwe observed: "In the Amsterdam tournament Fine lost
his first game to Kmoch. It was a short tournament, and in
order to finish in a high position it was now essential that he
win practically all of his remaining games. Most players would
have succumbed to the temptation to "mix things" a bit, to
take risks in order to avoid the draw and seek critical positions. But Fine did nothing of the sort. On the contrary, he
simply intensified the accuracy and mathematical rhythm of
his positional play—and scored win after win with surprising persistence, ultimately to tie with me for first place."
Because of the peculiarities of the draw and Prins' decision
to drop out of the tournament Fine had the unusual experience (for an individual tournament) of playing with the
black pieces five times in the first six games. The rate of
play was forty moves in two-and-a-half hours.

	1	2	3	4	5	6	7	8	
1= Euwe	*	½	1	½	½	1	½	1	5
1= Finc	½	*	½	1	1	1	0	1	5
3 Alekhine	0	½	*	½	1	½	1	1	4½
4= Grünfeld	½	0	½	*	½	½	½	1	3½
4= Landau	½	0	0	½	*	½	1	1	3½
4= Van den Bosch	0	0	½	½	½	*	1	1	3½
7 Kmoch	½	1	0	½	0	0	*	1	3
8 Van Scheltinga	0	0	0	0	0	0	0	*	0

(311) KMOCH, H—FINE

Amsterdam AP (1), 1936 (10 Oct.)

Queen's Gambit Declined, Manhattan Variation [D51]

1. d4 Nf6 2. c4 e6 3. Nc3 d5 4. Bg5 Nbd7 5. e3 Bb4 6. cxd5 exd5 7. Bd3 c5 8. Nge2 If White hopes to obtain an advantage, he must play his knight to f3. After the text move Black can equalize with 8 ... cxd4; for example 9 exd4 0–0 10 0–0 Nb6 11 Rc1 h6 12 Bxf6 Qxf6, Sämisch–Marshall, Brunn (Brno) 1928. During the game I feared the reply 9 Nxd4 (after 8 ... cxd4) but the continuation of a game Pleci–Marshall, Liege 1930 showed that here, too, Black can obtain a good game: 9 ... h6 10 Bh4 0–0 11 0–0 Bxc3 12 bxc3 Nc5 13 Bc2 Re8 14 Rc1 b6 and White's c-pawn is just as weak as Black's d-pawn. **8 ... c4?** Black hopes to get more than equality and the result is an uncomfortably cramped position. Correct, as explained in the previous note, is 8 ... cxd4. **9. Bc2 h6** The object of this move is to prevent Nf4 later, but it weakens the kingside appreciably. Therefore it would have been better to avoid this advance and to drive the bishop only when the white knight had already played to f4, for Black can always defend his d-pawn adequately. **10. Bh4 0–0 11. 0–0 Be7 12. f3!** White pursues the proper plan: formation of a strong pawn centre. **12 ... b5?** A miscalculation which loses a pawn. The black position is not good, but this blunder was not yet necessary. Best is 13 ... a6 14 a4 b6 15 Bg3 (not 15 e4 because of Nxe4! and Black equalizes: 16 Bxe7 Nxc3 17 Nxc3 Qxe7 18 Nxd5 Qd6) Bb7 16 e4 dxe4 17 fxe4 Ng4 and Black has counterplay. **13. Nxb5 Rb8** 13 ... Qb6 14 Ba4 is no better. **14. Nxa7** The simple move Black had overlooked. **14 ... Rxb2 15. Nc6 Qe8 16. Nxe7+** Simpler was 16 e4, which in the future Black is able to prevent. After 16 e4 dxe4 17 fxe4 g5 18 Bg3 Ba3 19 Nc3 Bb7 20 d5, and the black position is hopeless. **16 ... Qxe7 17. Qc1** If 17 e4 g5 wins a pawn. **17 ... Rb6** Of course not 17 ... Qa3? 18 Be1 winning at once. **18. Nc3 Bb7 19. Qd2** More direct would have been 19 a4, after which the black pieces are tied to the defence against the a-pawn. **19 ... Re8 20. Rfe1** Again threatening e4. **20 ... Qa3 21. Rab1 Rxb1 22. Rxb1** Here, too, it would have been better to recapture with the knight and follow with a4. **22 ... Bc6 23. Bf2 Kh8** To prevent Qc1. Black loses time but his position is such that no promising swindle is visible. **24. Bd1 Kg8 25. Qb2 Qa5 26. Qb4 Qa7 27. Bc2** Again he should have taken advantage of the opportunity to advance the a-pawn, if then 27 ... Rb8 28 Nb5. But White was already in time pressure. **27 ... Rb8 28. Qd6 Rxb1+ 29. Bxb1 Qb7 30. Qa3** An inroad of the black queen must be prevented. **30 ... Nb6 31. Qb4 Qa7 32. Bc2 Nfd7 33. Bg3 Nb8 34. Qd6** White does not fall into the trap 34 Qc5? Qb7 35 Bxb8? Nd7 36 Qa7 Qb2! with strong counterplay. **34 ... N6d7 35. Qb4 Nb6 36. h3 g6 37. Qc5 Qb7 38. Qb4** Again 38 Bxb8 would have been inferior owing to 38 ... Nd7 39 Qa7 Qb2. **38 ... Na6 39. Qd6 Nd7 40. Qa3 Nb4 41. Bd1** After 41 Qb2 Nxc2 42 Qxc2 Nb6 Black has some drawing chances because of the bishops of opposite colours. (I think that here, and elsewhere in other games, Fine overestimates the drawing possibilities associated with opposite-coloured bishops while there are other pieces still on the board. AW) **41 ... Nd3 42. Bd6?** This move deserves a question mark, not because it is bad, but because after 42 Qd6, Black has no good moves at his disposal. White had feared the reply 42 ... Qb2 but then would follow 43 Qxc6 Qxc3 44 Qxd7 Qc1 45 Qa4! Qxe3+ (the point is that after 45 ... Nb2 46 Qe8+ leads to mate) 46 Kh2 Qxd4 47 Qe8+ Kg7 48 Bc2 and Black can resign. After 42 Qd6, if Black should wait with, for example ... h5, there would follow 43 Bc2, followed by e4 and d5. Again here, if 43 ... Qb2 (42 Qd6 h5 43 Bc2) 44 Bxd3 Qxc3 45 Qxc6 Qxd3 46 Qxd7 wins easily. **42 ... h5 43. Kf1** Simpler was 43 Kh2, followed by Bg3 and Qd6, transposing to the note above. **43 ... Nb6 44. Qa5 Kh7 45. Bc2 Nc8 46. Ba3** Again to prevent ... Qb2 but Black has now materially improved his position. **46 ... Na7 47. Ke2 Nb5 48. Nxb5** If 48 Bxd3 Nxc3+ 49 Qxc3 cxd3+ 50 Kxd3 Bb5+ 51 Kd2 Bf1 and Black can draw the ending. **48 ... Bxb5 49. Bd6 Ba6 50. Qa3 c3?** Seduced by White's time pressure, Black allows himself an unsound combination. After the correct 50 ... Bb5, White would have experienced some difficulties, although the position is won with perfect play. **51. Qxc3** Avoids the trap 51 Bxd3?? Qb2+ 52—Bxd3 and Black—of all things—wins! (This is not completely obvious after 52 Kf1 Bxd3+ 53 Kg1 Qd2 54 Qa7 Qxe3+ 55 Kh2. AW) **51 ... Nc1+ 52. Kf2 Qb5** Another oversight. 52 ... Nxa2 still gave a fighting chance. **53. Bxg6+ Kxg6 54. Qxc1 Qe2+ 55. Kg1 Qxa2 56. Qe1** The last move before the time control; instead, 56 Qc6 would have been immediately decisive. At this point Black overstepped the time limit and lost the game. With best play the position is lost for Black, but after the best move 56 ... f6 (on 56 ... Kh7, with the object of answering 51 Qg3 with ..Qb1+ and ... Qg6, the reply 51 e4 cannot be satisfactorily met) White will still be faced with practical difficulties. My overstepping the time limit was quite accidental, since I had five minutes for my last move. But Kmoch had been in fearful time pressure, and, after making his 56th move, he remarked to the tournament controller "The time control is over." I unfortunately heard this remark and was under the mistaken impression that it applied to us both. **1–0** Fine, 1937 12–6.

(312) PRINS, L—FINE

Amsterdam AP (2), 1936 (11 Oct.)
Colle System [D05]

1. d4 Nf6 2. Nf3 d5 3. e3 c5 4. c3 e6 5. Bd3 Nc6 6. 0–0 Bd6 7. Nbd2 e5 8. dxe5 Nxe5 9. Nxe5 Bxe5 10. f4?! Bc7 11. e4 c4 12. Bc2 0–0 13. h3?! Bb6+ 14. Kh1 Ng4! 15. Nf3 Nf2+?! 16. Rxf2 Bxf2 17. exd5 Re8 18. Qf1 Bb6 19. Qxc4

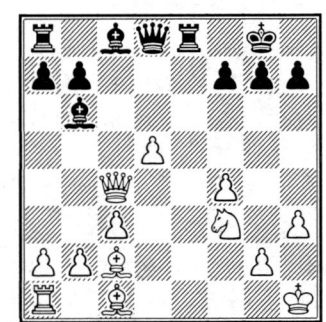

Position after White's 19th move

19 ... Qf6 20. Ba4 Re7 21. Bd2 Bf5 22. Be1 Re4 23. Qb3 Bxh3 24. Bg3 Bf5 25. Re1 Rxe1+ 26. Nxe1 Be4 27. c4 Qd4 28. Bh2 Qf2 White resigned. 0–1 *Christian Science Monitor*, 1 December 1936.

(313) VAN SCHELTINGA, T—FINE

Amsterdam AP (2), 1936 (15 Oct.)
Queen's Gambit Declined [D38]

1. d4 Nf6 2. c4 e6 3. Nf3 d5 4. Nc3 Bb4 I have recently had considerable success with this rather unusual move. **5. Bg5 c6 6. cxd5 exd5 7. Qb3** A pointless excursion since 7 e3 Qa5 8 Qb3 Ne4 9 Rc1 is in White's favour. **7 ... Be7 8. e3 Qb6 9. Bd3** Allowing the exchange of queens only furthers Black's plans. Best was 9 Qc2 Bf5! 10 Bd3. **9 ... Qxb3 10. axb3 a5** Better was 10 ... Nbd7. White should have now continued with 11 Bxf6 Bxf6 12 b4 with an even game, for if 12 ... Bd8 13 0–0 followed by doubling rooks on the a-file. **11. 0–0 Nbd7 12. Rfc1 Nb6 13. Bf4 Kd8**

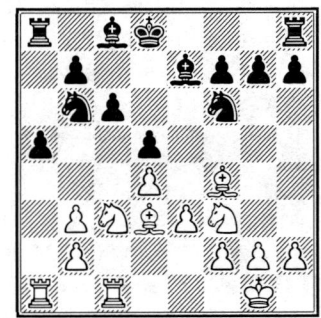

Position after Black's 13th move

14. Nb5? A serious loss of time. Correct was the simple 14 h3, when Black would have continued with ... Nf6-e8-d6, but White would have two tempi more. **14 ... Ne8**

15. Nc3 Threatening Nf3-g5, which would now have been answered by 15 ... Bxg5 16 Bxg5+ f6 and wins a piece. **15 ... f6 16. Na4 Nxa4 17. Rxa4** After this inferior recapture Black has a definite advantage. 17 bxa4 would have equalized. **17 ... Bd7 18. Be2?** White cannot find a proper plan, but this continuous loss of time must eventually prove fatal. If 18 Rca1 b6 19 b4, the reply 19 ... c5 is too strong, but White, with Ne1-c2 could have prepared the eventual b3-b4 or f2-f3 and e3-e4, with good counterplay. **18 ... b6 19. Raa1 Kc8 20. Ne1 Kb7 21. Bf3 Nd6 22. Nd3?** At least he should have prevented his opponent from obtaining the two bishops with 22 h3. **22 ... Bf5 23. Be2 g5 24. Bg3 Ne4 25. Rd1 h5 26. f3 Nxg3 27. hxg3 Rae8 28. Kf2 Bd6 29. g4** Probably based on the feeling that symmetry is a virtue, but 29 Rh1 was more to the point. **29 ... hxg4 30. fxg4 Be4 31. Rh1 Rh4 32. Rxh4 gxh4 33. Nf4**

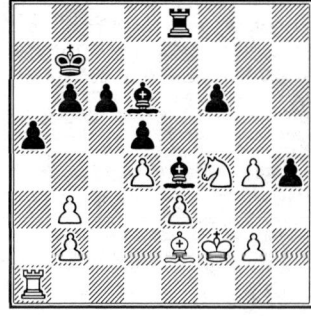

Position after White's 33rd move

33 ... c5 With 33 ... Bxf4 34 exf4 Bxg2 35 Kxg2 Rxe2+ 36 Kh3 Rxb2 37 g5 Rxb3+ 38 Kxh4 fxg5+ 39 fxg5 White's passed pawn would have been too dangerous. **34. Bb5** He could have made it far more difficult with the problematical manoeuvre 34 Bf3 cxd4 35 Nxd5 Bxg3+ 36 Kf1! (But not 36 Ke2? Kc6 37 Nxf6 Bxf3+ and wins) dxe3! (If now 36 ... Kc6? 37 Nxf6 and White wins!) 37 Ke2! Bxf3+ 38 gxf3—but even here with 38 ... Be5! 39 Rb1 Kc6 Black would have eventually won in view of the weakness of White's pawns. **34 ... Rg8 35. dxc5** There is nothing better. If 35 Be2, then 35 ... cxd4. **35 ... Bxf4 36. c6+ Kc7 37. exf4 Rxg4 38. b4** Desperation: if 38 Rg1 Rxf4+ 39 Ke3 Rg4. **38 ... Rxg2+ 39. Ke3 Rxb2 40. bxa5 Rb3+** The bishop could also have been captured at once, but the variations are the same after the text move. White resigned, for if 41 Kd4 Rxb5 42 a6 Rb3; and if 41 Kd2 Rxb5 42 a6 d4 43 a7 Bxc6; winning easily in both cases. 0–1 Fine 1937, 27–9.

(314) FINE—GRÜNFELD, E

Amsterdam AP (3), 1936 (13 Oct.)
Queen's Gambit Declined, Vienna Variation [D39]

A feature of this fine game is a positional queen's sacrifice on the 13th move, an unusual occurrence. T&dM **1. d4 d5 2. Nf3 Nf6 3. c4 e6 4. Nc3 dxc4 5. e4 Bb4** The so-called Vienna Variation which should really be called the Grünfeld Variation since it was he who discovered it and investigated it most extensively. Since Grünfeld had had no time to prepare himself for the tournament—he took Maroczy's place at the last moment—he was unaware that a refutation had been discovered in Germany and in off-hand games at Nottingham during the past summer. RF **6. Bg5 c5 7. e5** Accepting the challenge. After 7 dxc5 Black could either simplify by 7 ... Qxd1+ 8 Rxd1 Nbd7, remaining with an extra pawn, or complicate matters by 7 ... Qa5. Useless would be 7 d5 (7 ... h6 8 Bxf6 gxf6), or the exchange 7 Bxf6 (7 ... Qxf6 8 Bxc4 cxd4 9 Qxd4 Nc6 10 Qxf6 gxf6). Therefore the simplest is 7 Bxc4 cxd4 8 Nxd4. T&dM **7 ... cxd4 8. Qa4+** Well timed! 8 Nxd4 Qa5 9 exf6 Qxg5 would be weak. After 8 exf6 gxf6 9 Bh4 (if 9 Qxd4 Qxd4 10 Nxd4 fxg5, and if 9 Qa4+ Nc6 Bd2 dxc3, with even chances) 9 ... Nc6 (and here clearly not 9 ... dxc3 10 Qxd8+ Kxd8 11 Bxf6+ Kc7 12 bxc3) 10 Nxd4 Nxd4 11 Bxc4, White has some compensation for the pawn. T&dM **8 ... Nc6 9. 0–0–0 Bd7 10. Ne4!** The difference between the text and the usual continuation is that White delays capturing on f6, and thereby gains time to post his queen's knight strongly in the centre. RF **10 ... Be7!** If 10 ... h6 11 Nxf6+ gxf6 12 Bxf6 and wins. That is why Black intends to give up a piece for three pawns, which plan White will soon thwart by an orgy of sacrifices. T&dM **11. exf6 gxf6 12. Bh4! Nb4** (In 1948 Fine suggested the alternative 12 ... Na5 13 Qc2 e5 14 Nxd4 exd4 15 Rxd4 and if now 15 ... Qb6? 16 Rd6! and White's game is distinctly superior (PCO 201), though perhaps it is not so clear after 16 ... Qb4. Instead of 15 ... Qb6, a game Van der Sterren–Sosonko, Wijk aan Zee 1988 continued 15 ... Nc6 16 Rxd7 Qxd7 17 Nxf6+ Bxf6 18 Bxf6 Rg8 19 Bxc4, ending in a draw after 30 moves.) **13. Qxb4!** A striking, even though compulsory, sacrifice of the queen. 13 Qa3 looks a possible expedient (13 ... Nd3+ 14 Rxd3 Bxa3 15 Nxf6+, and White sacrifices his queen in a far more sustained manner) but— Black would reply 13 ... Nd5 with advantage. T&dM **13 ... Bxb4 14. Nxf6+ Kf8** On account of the insecure black king, the minor piece player here has a very favourable game, if not an outright win. ME **15. Rxd4!** Another finesse. He refrains from recovering his queen by 15 Nxh7+ Rxh7 16 Bxd8 Rxd8 17 Rxd4 b5, and if anything Black has the best of it. T&dM **15 ... Qa5** This escape succeeds but partially. The best course is 15 ... Be7 (as later occurred in Greenfeld–Korchnoi, Beersheva 1988, which continued 16 Ne5 Bb5 17 Rxd8+ Rxd8 18 Be2 Kg7 19 Nf5+ and soon drawn. AW) 16 Nxd7+ (not 16 Rxd7 Bxf6) Kg7 (Black should play 16 ... Ke8 17 Nf6+ Bxf6 18 Rxd8+ Bxd8. AW) 17 Rg4+ Kh6 18 N7e5 (White now wins after the forced 18 ... Rf8 19 Bg3! Kh5 20 Bf4. AW), the battle is in full swing. T&dM **16. Nxd7+ Ke8 17. Nf6+ Kf8 18. Bxc4** The simplest. In the game Gereben–de Groot, Munich 1936, White played 18 Ne5 with the continuation 18 ... h5 19 Ned7+? Kg7 with good counter chances. Again after 19 Bxc4 Rc8 20 Kb1 Be7 21 Rhd1 Kg7 22 N5d7 Rhd8 the tables are suddenly turned and White's pieces are all tied up. The object of White's manoeuvring now is to exchange as little as possible, so that Black will have no chance of increasing his mobility. RF **18 ... Rc8 19. Kb1**

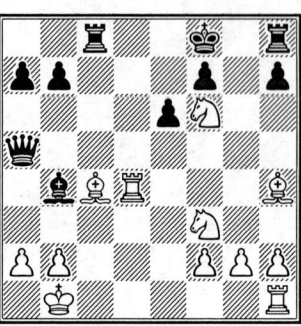

Position after White's 19th move

19 ... h5 20. Rhd1 Be7 21. Nd7+ Although White's position is clearly superior, a direct win is not to be seen. White therefore decides to prevent Black from coordinating his pieces. Black was threatening not only ... Bxf6 and ... Qf5+ winning a piece, but also to free himself with ... Kg7 and ... Rhd8. 21 Ne5 was seductive but bad, for Black replies 21 ... Kg7 22 Ned7 Rhd8 and suddenly White is again in difficulties. RF **21 ... Ke8 22. Bg3** Maintaining the pressure. 22 Bxe7 Kxe7 23 Nde5 Rhd8 would only develop Black's game. ME **22 ... Rg8 23. h3** To prevent ... Rg4. **23 ... Rg7** It is difficult for Black to form a good plan. With the text move he hopes eventually to play ... f6 and ... e5. RF **24. a3** Clears a2 for the king. White wishes to post a piece at f6 without having to fear ... Qf5+. Black now realizes his position is critical and attempts to obtain counterplay. RF **24 ... b5 25. Bb3 b4** Better was 25 ... Qa6 26 Be5 Rxg2 27 Nf6+ Kf8 28 Nxh5—and although Black is lost with best play he has good practical chances. RF **26. axb4**

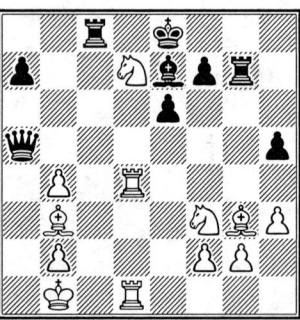

Position after White's 26th move

26 ... Bxb4 To 26 ... Qb5 follows 27 R1d3, and to 26 ... Qa6 27 Nc5, while after 26 ... Qf5+ 27 Ka2 Rc6 28 Nc5 and White has a clearly won game. RF **27. Be5** Not 27 Rxb4 at once against 27 ... Rxg3. To 27 ... Rg6 follows 28 Nh4. RF **27 ... Rxg2 28. Rxb4** A complementary sacrifice. T&dM **28 ... Qxb4 29. Nf6+ Ke7 30. Rd7+ Kf8 31. Bd6+ Qxd6 32. Rxd6 Rxf2 33. Rd3** Although White, with three pieces for a rook, has a won game he must still play carefully. RF **33 ... Ke7 34. Nxh5 Rf1+ 35. Bd1** Not 35 Ka2 since 35 ... Rc5. RF **35 ... Rg8 36. Nd4 e5 37. Nc6+ Ke6 38. Ka2 Rxd1** Getting two pieces for the rook, but as his pawns become doubled, the transaction is a poor one. T&dM **39. Rxd1 Rg5**

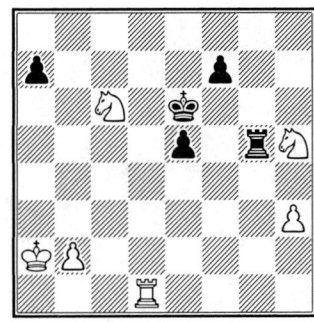

40. Nf4+ The simplest. RF **40 ... exf4 41. Nd4+ Kf6 42. Rf1 Ra5+ 43. Kb1** Avoiding the last trap: 43 Kb3 Rh5 44 Rf4+ Ke5 45 Ne2 Rxh3+ 46 Kc2 Rh2 draws! RF **43 ... Ra4 44. Nf3 Re4 45. Re1 Re6** Or 45 ... Rc4 46 Re5. RF **46. Rxe6+ fxe6** On the surface, Black has improved his pawn formation and has better prospects, but the white king, arriving in time, decides the issue. T&dM **47. Kc2 e5 48. Kd3 Kf5 49. Nd2 Kg5 50. Ke4 Kh4 51. Kxe5 Kxh3 52. Kxf4** Black resigned. A magnificent game. T&dM **1–0** Fine 1937, 33–6; Tartakower & du Mont 1952, 500–1; Euwe & Kramer 1964, 50–2.

(315) EUWE, M—FINE

Amsterdam AP (4), 1936 (14 Oct.)
Queen's Gambit Declined [D60]

1. d4 Nf6 2. c4 e6 3. Nf3 d5 4. Bg5 Be7 5. e3 0–0 6. Nc3 Nbd7 7. Bd3 c5 Better is 7 ... dxc4 8 Bxc4 b6, as occurred, for example, in the game Euwe–Becker, Zandvoort, 1936. **8. 0–0 a6?** A strategical error, after which Black has to fight for a draw. Necessary was 8 ... cxd4 9 exd4 dxc4 10 Bxc4 Nb6—although the game Botvinnik–Vidmar, Nottingham 1936, shows that Black's troubles have only begun. **9. cxd5 Nxd5 10. Bxe7 Qxe7 11. Nxd5 exd5 12. Qc2 g6** Stronger than 12 ... h6, as in the game Schlechter–Süchting, Prague 1908, with the continuation 13 dxc5 Nxc5 14 Nd4 Be6 15 Qe2 Ne4 16 Bc2 Rc8 17 Rad1 Rc7 18 f4! **13. dxc5 Nxc5 14. Rac1 b6** An unusual continuation in this type of position, but it seems to be superior to the customary plan of ... Nc5-e4 and ... Bc8-e6. **15. Nd4 Bb7 16. Be2 Rac8 17. Bg4** Since Black would have had to continue with ... f7-f5 in any case, he could have spared this move. Probably best was 17 Rfd1 so that if 17 ... Ne4 18 Qb3. After 17 Rfd1 Black had intended 17 ... Rc7, when the position still seems tenable. **17 ... f5 18. Bf3 Ne4 19. Qd3 b5** Further weakening his pawns, but Black must obtain some counterplay on the c-file—he now threatens ... Rc4 followed by ... Rfc8. Bad would have been 19 ... Qb4 because of 20 Nb3 and if 20 ... Rc4? 21 Bxe4 fxe4 22 Qd2, with a clear advantage. **20. Nb3 Qf6 21. Qd4 Qxd4 22. Nxd4 Kf7 23. Nb3 Rxc1 24. Rxc1 Rc8 25. Rxc8 Bxc8** Although the white pawn formation is so much more favourable, Black's knight at e4 is so strongly placed that White cannot turn his advantage to account. If White exchanges the d-pawn recaptures, Black will then have rid

himself of his weakness and with ... Bc8-e6 will be able to post his bishop on a good diagonal. If White does not capture, his king can never occupy the vital square d4, since it is tied to the defence of f2. **26. Be2 Ke7 27. Kf1** If 27 f3 Nd6, with the threat of ... Nc4. **27 ... Kd6 28. Ke1 Nc5 29. Nc1 Ne6 30. Nb3 Nc5 31. Nd4 Ne6 32. Nc2** In order to avoid trouble Black must now rid himself of his weak d-pawn. If 32 ... f4 33 Bg4 followed by Bxe6, with a strong knight against a weak bishop, which would be decidedly in White's favour. **32 ... d4 33. exd4 Bb7** Drawn, for if 34 f3 Kd5; and if 34 Bf3 Bxf3 35 gxf3 Kd5 36 Nb4+ Kc4; while if 34 Kd2, not 34 ... Bxg2 because of 35 f3, but first 34 ... Be4 35 Bd3 Bxg2 when the bishop cannot be shut in. Black has equality in all cases. **½–½** Fine 1937, 39–41.

(316) LANDAU, S—FINE

Amsterdam AP (5), 1936 (16 Oct.)
Queen's Gambit Declined [D61]

1. d4 d5 2. c4 e6 3. Nc3 Nf6 A word about the opening: one of the chief reasons for the continued popularity of 1 d4 among the masters is that a completely satisfactory defence has yet to be found. In every defence Black is in difficulties and rarely obtains more than an equal position. Recently I have come to the conclusion that the Orthodox is the best of all possible defences not because it gives Black the better game—this is of course not true—but because it gives Black a solid position which though a bit cramped has—more important—no organic weaknesses. **4. Bg5 c6 5. e3 Nbd7 6. Nf3 Be7 7. Qc2 0–0** It is often maintained that this position is decidedly in White's favour and that therefore the reply 7 ... c5 is best against 7 Qc2 in the Orthodox Defence. Although the position has been reached here by transposition, so that Black never had the opportunity to play ... c5, I believe that against 7 Qc2 the reply 7 ... c6 is at least as good as 7 ... c5. **8. Rd1** The best move, since it prevents the well known freeing manoeuvre 8 ... dxc4 9 Bxc4 b5 and eventually ... b4. **8 ... Re8 9. a3** The attentive reader has probably noticed that the present position also arose in my game with Flohr at Hastings last year where I replied 9 ... dxc4 10 Bxc4 Nd5 and soon obtained a lost position. **9 ... a6** This variation of the Queen's Gambit has rightly been called "the struggle for a tempo." After considering my game with Flohr carefully I came to the conclusion that my mistake there consisted in losing a tempo by exchanging c4 before playing my a-pawn to a6. The difference is that Black can play eventually ... c5 and still maintain his hold on the b5 square, the importance of which can be seen in the following variation: 10 Bd3 dxc4 11 Bxc4 Nd5 12 Bxe7 Qxe7 13 0–0 Nxc3 14 Qxc3 c5: this position arose in my game with Flohr with the all-important difference that my a-pawn was still at a7. The result was that he could play 15 d5! exd5 16 Rxd5! b6 17 Rfd1 Rf8 and Black's position is not agreeable. Had I, however, already had my pawn at a6, on 15 d5 exd5 16 Rxd5 I could have replied 16 ... b5 17 Be2 Bb7 and Black's game is wholly satisfactory, since the queenside majority may prove a deadly weapon in the endgame. **10. c5?** Premature, since Black's breakthrough in the centre is too strong. Best is probably 10 h3, but even then 10 ... dxc4 11 Bxc4 Nd5 gives equality. (A game Eliskases–Landau, Noordwijk 1938, continued 10 Bd3 dxc4 11 Bxc4 Nd5 12 Bxe7 Qxe7 13 Ne4 N5f6 14 Bd3! Nxe4 15 Bxe4 h6 16 0–0 c5 17 Ne5 with a slight advantage to White, MCO 139) **10 ... e5 11. b4** A strategical error, after which Black's position is far superior. Necessary was 11 dxe5 Ng4 12 Bf4 Bxc5 13 Be2 Ngxe5 14 Nxe5 Nxe5 15 Nxd5 Bf8! and both sides can be satisfied with a draw. For the sake of those chess lovers who are interested in historical parallels, I record here that a similar strategical error occurred in a match game between Zukertort and Steinitz in the World Championship Contest in 1886. **11 ... e4 12. Nd2 Nh5 13. Bxe7 Qxe7 14. Ne2** Now White realizes the weakness of 11 b4. After the natural 14 Be2 Qg5 15 0–0 Ndf6 16 Kh1 Ng4 Black has an overwhelming attack. A more doubtful defence is, however, 14 g3 followed by Bg2, 0–0, Re1, and eventually f3. That he must already think of defending himself shows the inferiority of his eleventh move. **14 ... g6** Black intends to storm the position with f7-f5 and, after due preparation, f5-f4. For this purpose it is, of course, essential that the knight should return to g7 rather than f6. **15. Ng3 Ng7 16. Be2 f5**

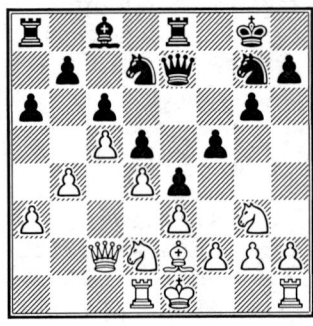

*Position after
Black's 16th move*

17. h4 White feels compelled to alter his previous scheme of passive resistance and instead to undertake more aggressive measures. After 17 0–0 Qh4, followed by ... Nd7-f6, ... g6-g5, and ... f5-f4—Black's attack is indeed practically irresistible. The opening of the h-file really gives White some counter-chances, but with precise play Black can ensure his attack has little sting. **17 ... Nf6** Black must proceed slowly and surely. Here 17 ... f4 comes into consideration with the continuation 18 exf4 e3; but the reply 19 Nf3 shatters Black's hopes. The text threatens 18 ... f4 19 exf4 e3 20 Nf3 Ng4. White's reply meets this threat adequately. **18. Qc3 Ne6 19. h5 f4 20. exf4** Loses a pawn, but if 19 Ngf1 g5 and White will soon run out of moves. **20 ... Nxf4 21. hxg6 hxg6 22. Ndf1!** A desperate defence in which he speculates on the possibility of a kingside attack later. Despite its appearance, however, the move is objectively the best and makes it considerably more difficult for Black to win. If, for example, 22 Kf1 (the same remarks apply to 22 Rg1) 22 ... e3 23 fxe3 Qxe3 24 Qxe3 Rxe3 25 Bf3 (or 25 Nf3 Ne4 26 Nxe4 dxe4 27 Ng1 Nxe2 28 Nxe2 Bg4

29 Rd2 Rf8+ 30 Ke1 Rxa3 and wins) Rxa3 and the ending is largely a question of the proper digestion of White's pawns. **22 ... Nxg2+ 23. Kd2 Ng4 24. Rg1 e3+!** Forced, but forcing. If instead 24 ... Nf4 25 Ne3 Nxe3 26 fxe3! Nxe2 27 Nxe2—White suddenly has a powerful attacking position. **25. Kc2** After considerable reflection White decides to stake everything on the middle game. His judgment is justifiable, since after 25 fxe3 N2xe3 26 Nxe3 Qxe3 (seductive but fruitless is 26 ... Nxe3 27 Rde1 Qg5 28 Ne4! Nf1+! 29 Kd1! Qxg1, and now White should insert 30 Nf6+ Kh8, since after Fine's suggested 30 Rxf1, and White again has an attack which is not so easy to meet, Black can continue 30 ... Qxf1 and 31 ... Bg4+ followed by 32 ... Rxe4. AW) 27 Qxe3 Nxe3 28 Rde1 Nf5—Black's remaining difficulties are purely technical. **25 ... Nf4**

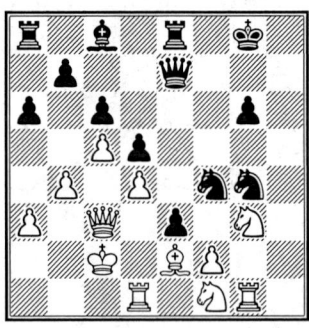

*Position after
Black's 25th move*

26. f3! An excellent move which again confronts Black with serious problems. The idea is simple: if 26 ... Nf6 27 Re1 and eventually Bd1 regaining the pawn with a strong attack. To defend himself against this threat Black evolves the following curious series of knight moves, the object of which is to place his knights at g2 and f4 without loss of time. **26 ... Nf2 27. Re1 N2h3! 28. Rh1 Ng2 29. Rc1 Nhf4** The manoeuvre is completed and one may well ask: What has Black accomplished? First of all the pawn at e3 is adequately defended. Secondly the blockader of the pawn, the bishop at e2, is attacked or to put it more precisely the square e2 is under Black's control. Third the reserve blockade square (to use Nimzowitsch's terminology) is likewise controlled by Black which, incidentally, prevents White from attacking the pawn. All the strategy hinges about the passed pawn's "lust to expand" by advancing. **30. Kb2 Bd7** Black has now time to proceed with his development! It is interesting to note that here and for the next few moves the attempt to obtain an attack by ... a6-a5 is refuted by 31 bxa5 Qd8 32 a6! and White has counterchances on the open b-file. **31. Rc2 Kg7** Defends the g-pawn and prepares the possibility of the occupation of the h-file by a rook. **32. Rg1** White is anxious to rid himself of Black's knights which maintain such a stranglehold on the position. **32 ... Rf8** Against purely passive play Black will eventually win the f-pawn. With the following rather surprising combination White succeeds in re-establishing material equality, but his position remains lost. **33. Bd1 Bh3** 33 ... Ne1? is, because of 32 Rh2, pretty but useless. **34. Ne2** Loses the exchange but White hopes to settle the knight at e5 and thereby obtain an attack. **34 ... Bf5** Also good, but less convincing, was 34 ... Nxe2 35 Rxe2 Rxf3 36 Rexg2 Bxg2 37 Bxf3 Bxf3 38 Nxe3 Be4 39 Ng4. **35. Nxf4 Nxf4 36. Nxe3** Of course if 36 Rh2, 36 ... e2 is immediately decisive. **36 ... Bxc2 37. Bxc2 Rae8!** The simplest road to victory. **38. Nf5+ Rxf5 39. Bxf5 Qe2+ 40. Qc2** There is nothing better, since if 40 Bc2 Re3 and if 40 Kc1 Qf2; while if 40 Ka1 Qf2 41 Rg4 Re3 42 Qb2 Qxf3 and the double threat of 43 ... Rxa3+ 44 Kb1 and 43 ... Re1+ wins at once. **40 ... Qe3 41. Bxg6** If instead 41 Rg4 Qxf3 42 Bxg6 Re2 43 Bh5+ Kh6! and wins, for if 44 Rg6+ Kxh5! At this point the game was adjourned but since, after the text, 41 ... Re6! wins a piece, Mr. Landau resigned without further play. **0–1** Fine in *Chess* 1936–7, 100–2.

(317) FINE—ALEKHINE, A

Amsterdam AP (6), 1936 (17 Oct.)
Dutch Defence [A92]

1. d4 e6 2. c4 Although certain that the Dutch Defence would be played, White allows his opponent to exchange his king's bishop, for although this used to be considered favourable, the experience of the last few years shows that with the exchange Black weakens himself on the dark squares. **2 ... f5 3. Nf3 Nf6 4. g3 Be7** For some time Alekhine considered it better to play ... Bb4+ and then return to e7, now he is of the opinion that Black must play ... Nf6-e4 as quickly as possible and should not lose a tempo, for after 4 ... Bb4+ 5 Bd2 Be7 White can play 6 Nc3 at once. **5. Bg2 0–0 6. 0–0 Ne4** Preventing Nc3 and preparing ... Bf6, ... d6, and eventually ... e5. The former system of 6 ... d6 7 Nc3 Qe8, is considered to be refuted by 8 Qc2, for example, 8 ... Nc6 9 d5 Nb4 10 Qb3 Na6 11 dxe6 Nc5 12 Qc2 Bxe6 13 b3, Fine–Bogolyubov, Nottingham 1936. **7. Nbd2** This prevents ... d6 and ... e5, since after the following move ... d5 is forced, but Black still obtains counterplay. (Reshevsky–Suesman, New York 1938, continued 7 d5 Bf6 8 Qc2 a5 9 Nbd2 Nc5 10 e4 Nxe4 11 Nxe4 fxe4 12 Qxe4 exd5 13 Qxd5+ Kh8 14 Ng5 Qe8 15 Bf4 with a slight advantage to White, MCO 212) **7 ... Bf6 8. Qc2 d5 9. b3 c5!** Black must play energetically. After 9 ... c6 10 Ba3 Rf7 11 Ne5 White has a marked advantage. **10. Bb2 cxd4 11. Nxd4 Nc6 12. Nxe4!** If instead 12 N2f3 Nb4 13 Qb1 e5 14 Nc2 Nxc2 15 Qxc2 d4 is good for Black. **12 ... fxe4!** The best reply. To 12 ... Bxd4, White must not play 13 cxd5? Nb4, but simply 13 Nd2 with positional advantage. **13. Rad1** White's position now seems decidedly better. He threatens not only Nxc6 and Bxe4, but chiefly Nb5 and eventually Nc3 or Nd6. To 13 ... Nxd4 White replies 14 Bxd4 Bxd4 15 Rxd4 Qf6 16 e3. Still Dr. Alekhine finds a resourceful defence. **13 ... Qb6!** And suddenly White sees that his supposed advantage will disappear in thin air. Capturing at c6 or advancing c5 would only strengthen the black centre. The following playable alternatives came into consideration: A. 14 Nb5 Bxb2 15 Qxb2 dxc4 16 Nd6! cxb3 17 Qxb3 Nd4! and Black has a good position; B. 14 e3 Nb4 15 Qe2 Kh8 and the square d3 is

seriously weak. **14. Qd2 Bd7!** Again the only move. If, for example, 14 ... dxc4 15 Nxc6 Qxc6 16 bxc4 Bxb2 17 Qxb2 Qxc4 18 Rd4 and White regains his pawn with an overwhelming position. **15. Nxc6** Simplifying, but White no longer has a continuation that is really good. If, for example, 15 Nb5 Ne7. **15 ... Bxc6** Not 15 ... bxc6? against 16 Bxf6 Rxf6 17 Bxe4. **16. Bxf6 Rxf6 17. cxd5 exd5 18. Qd4 Qxd4 19. Rxd4 Re8 20. Rc1 Kf7 21. f3 Rfe6 22. Rf1 Rf6 23. Rc1 Rfe6 24. Rf1 Rf6** Draw agreed. **½–½** Fine 1937, 58–60.

(318) FINE—VAN DEN BOSCH, J

Amsterdam AP (7), 1936 (18 Oct.)
Nimzowitsch-Indian Defence, Zurich or Milner-Barry Variation [E33]

1. d4 Nf6 2. c4 e6 3. Nc3 Bb4 4. Qc2 Nc6 5. Nf3 d6 6. a3 Bxc3+ 7. Qxc3 0–0 On 7 ... a5 the best reply is 8 b3 (but if 8 Bg5 h6 9 Bxf6 Qxf6 with equality, Lasker–Alekhine, Nottingham 1936), for example, 8 ... 0–0 9 g3 Re8 10 Bg2 e5 11 d5 Ne7 12 Nd2 with advantage to White, Fine–Mulder, Amsterdam Jubilee Tournament 1936. **8. b4 e5!?** An interesting pawn sacrifice, typical of van den Bosch's dashing style: the sacrifice had been played before but Black had found a valuable strengthening of the attack. **9. dxe5 Nxe5** 9 ... Nc4 10 Qb2 (10 Qc3 Fine Alexander, Margate 1937) dxe5 11 Nxe5 Nxe5 12 Qxe5 Re8 13 Qb2 Qh4 14 g3 with a slight advantage to White, MCO 185. **10. Nxe5 dxe5 11. Qxe5 Re8 12. Qb2** On other moves 12 ... Ne4 is strong, but now it would be answered by 13 Bf4 Bf5 14 f3 g5 15 Bc1, with a clear advantage, Flohr–Milner-Barry, London 1932. **12 ... Qd3!** An innovation. White has now two defensive systems at his disposal: 1. 13 Bg5 (as in the game) and 2. 13 e3 Qg6 14 f3 Bf5 15 Kf2 Bd3 (in MCO Fine continues this line 16 Be2! with the clearly better game); or 15 ... Rad8. Judging from the experience of this game, the second system must be considered preferable. **13. Bg5 Ng4 14. e3 Qf5 15. Bh4 Qe4!** Suddenly the position seems to be critical for White: Black now threatens 15 ... Nxe3; and if 16 Bg3 Nxe3! 17 fxe3 Qxe3+ 18 Be2 Bg4 with a winning game. **16. 0–0–0** The only defence for if now 16 ... Nxe3 17 Rd4 wins. **16 ... c5** Again threatening 16 ... Ne3 and therefore forcing White to allow his pawn position to be ruined. **17. Bg3 cxb4 18. Qxb4 Be6?** But this plausible continuation of the attack is not the most forceful. Best was 18 ... Bf5! 19 Bd3 Qe6 20 Rhe1 (not 20 e4 Bxe4 21 Rhe1 Qh6+) Bxd3 21 Rxd3 Rac8 and in view of White's exposed king position and his weak pawns Black has sufficient compensation for the pawn. **19. Rd4 Qf5** If 19 ... Qc6 20 Qd6. **20. Be2! Ne5** Or 20 ... Nf6 21 Bf3, when White has a pawn plus the attack. 20 ... Nxf2? would have been a blunder because of 21 Rf1. The position again seems critical for White, Black's principal threat being 21 ... Nc6. But fortunately White can force the exchange of queens, which of course puts an end to the attack. **21. Qb5! Bd7** Or 21 ... f6 22 Qb1 Qg5? 23 f4 and the piece can safely be captured. **22. Qb1 Qf6?** The exchange of queens could not have been avoided but, after 22 ... Nc6 23 Qxf5 Bxf5,

White's problems are not yet completely solved. However, after 24 Rd2 Rac8 25 Kb2 Be6 26 Rc2! Na5 27 c5 White should eventually win the ending. **23. Bxe5 Qxe5 24. Rxd7 Qc3+ 25. Kd1 Red8 26. Rd5 b5** Black's attack has no force. If 26 ... Rxd5 27 cxd5 Rd8 28 Bd3! (28 Bf3 is also good) Rxd5 29 Ke2 and Black may resign. **27. Qc1 Qb3+ 28. Ke1 Rdc8 29. Rd4 Rab8 30. Bd1 Qa2 31. Rd2 Qxc4 32. Qxc4 bxc4 33. Bc2 c3 34. Rd4 Rb2 35. Kd1 Ra2 36. Re1 g6 37. e4 Rb8 38. Re3** Black resigned. **1–0** Fine 1937, 66–8.

V.A.S. Winter Tournament, November, 1936

Fine managed only a single win in three games in a four-player event held on consecutive Wednesdays at the Verenigd Amsterdams Schaakgenootschap (United Amsterdam Chess Association). Crosstable unavailable.

(319) FINE—VAN LAAFSVELT

V.A.S. Winter Tournament, Amsterdam (1), 1936 (4 Nov.)
Italian Game [C53]

1. e4 e5 2. Nf3 Nc6 3. Bc4 Bc5 4. c3 Nh6 5. d4 exd4 6. cxd4 Bb4+ 7. Nc3 Bxc3+ 8. bxc3 Qf6 9. 0–0 0–0 10. e5 Qd8 11. Bg5 Qe8 12. Re1 Nf5 13. Qc2 Nfe7 14. Bd2 d6 15. exd6 cxd6 16. Bd3

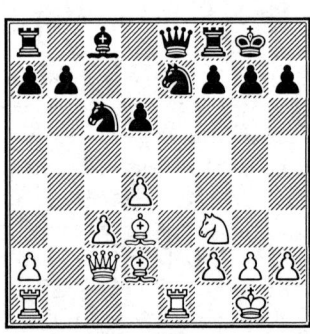

Position after White's 16th move

16 ... Qd7 17. Bxh7+ Kh8 18. Bd3 Nd5 19. Bc4 Nf6 20. Bg5 Qf5 21. Bd3 Qd5 22. Bxf6 gxf6 23. Re4 Kg7 24. Rh4 f5 25. Qd2 Kf6 26. Re1 Rg8 27. Qh6+ Rg6 28. Qh8+ Black resigned. **1–0**

(320) STORK—FINE

V.A.S. Winter Tournament, Amsterdam (2), 1936 (11 Nov.)
Petroff Defence [C42]

1. e4 e5 2. Nf3 Nf6 3. Nxe5 Qe7 4. Nf3 Nxe4 5. Be2 d5 6. 0–0 Qd8 7. Nc3 Nxc3 8. dxc3 Bc5 9. Bb5+ c6 10. Re1+ Be7 11. Bd3 0–0 12. Ne5 Nd7 13. Qe2 Nxe5 14. Qxe5 Bf6 15. Qh5 g6 16. Qf3 Bg7 17. Be3 Re8 18. Bc5 Bd7 19. Re2 Rxe2

20. Qxe2 Qc7 21. Re1 Be6 22. h4 b6 23. Bd4 Bxd4 24. cxd4 h5? 25. Bxg6 fxg6 26. Qxe6+ Kh7 27. Qf6 Black resigned. **1–0**

(321) FINE—VAN FOREDEN, R

V.A.S. Winter Tournament, Amsterdam (3), 1936 (18 Nov.)
French Defence [C00]

1. e4 e6 2. d4 d5 3. Bd3 dxe4 4. Bxe4 Nf6 5. Bd3 Nc6 6. c3 Bd6 7. Nf3 b6 8. 0–0 Bb7 9. Bg5 0–0 10. Re1 h6 11. Bh4 Ne7 12. Bxf6 gxf6 13. Nbd2 f5 14. Bc2 Kh7 15. Nc4 Rg8 16. Nxd6 Qxd6 17. Nh4 Ng6 18. Nxg6 Rxg6 19. f3 Rag8 20. g3 Rxg3+ White resigned. **0–1**

Hastings, December 28 1936–January 6, 1937

"The 17th annual series of tournaments organized by the Hastings and St. Leonards C.C. was carried through with the usual success from Monday, December 28 to Wednesday, January 6. The premier section soon resolved itself into a match for first place between Alekhine and Fine. In the first round Fine got a half-point more than the game was worth against Eliskases, who in trying to win a drawn game got into trouble, and getting short of time, and generally 'rattled', as he admitted, drifting into a mating position with Fine's rooks on the seventh and eighth. Alekhine drew a sensational game with Eliskases in round 3, and both masters won all their games up to round 8, when the two met. Then a magnificent effort by the ex-champion in a Lopez game brought him a win and he passed Fine with 7½ to 7. Both had a tight squeeze in the last round, but each scored a draw and they maintained the same order." (*BCM* 1937)

		1	2	3	4	5	6	7	8	9	10	
1	Alekhine	*	1	½	1	1	1	1	½	1	1	8
2	Fine	0	*	1	½	1	1	1	1	1	1	7½
3	Eliskases	½	0	*	½	½	1	1	½	½	1	5½
4	Vidmar	0	½	½	*	0	½	½	1	½	1	4½
5	Feigins	0	0	½	1	*	0	1	1	½	½	4½
6	Tylor	0	0	0	½	1	*	½	0	½	1	3½
7	Winter	0	0	0	½	0	½	*	1	1	½	3½
8	Koltanowski	½	0	½	0	0	1	0	*	½	½	3
9	Menchik	0	0	½	½	½	½	0	½	*	0	2½
10	Thomas	0	0	0	0	½	0	½	½	1	*	2½

(322) ELISKASES, E—FINE

Hastings 1936/7 (1), 1936 (28 Dec.)
Nimzowitsch-Indian Defence, Classical Variation [E34]

1. d4 Nf6 2. c4 e6 3. Nc3 Bb4 4. Qc2 d5 5. cxd5 Qxd5 6. e3 c5 7. Nge2 Here Euwe against Botvinnik at

Nottingham played 7 a3 B×c3 8 b×c3. EZB **7 ... c×d4 8. N×d4 Nc6 9. Nf3** If 9 N×c6 Q×c6 and there must be some delay before White can develop his king's bishop. Or if 9 Nb5 Qd8 threatening ... a6. DB **9 ... Ne4** If instead 9 ... 0–0 10 Bd2. DB **10. Bd2 B×c3 11. B×c3 N×c3 12. Q×c3 Qa5** After 12 ... 0–0 13 Be2 Black cannot develop his queen's bishop because of Rd1. DB **13. Q×a5 N×a5 14. Bb5+ Bd7** If 14 ... Ke7 15 Rac1. DB **15. B×d7+ K×d7**

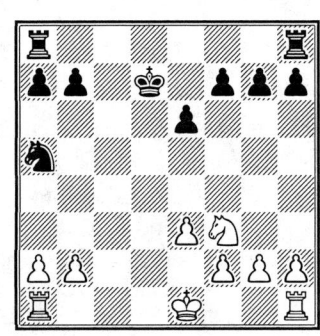

Position after Black's 15th move

16. Ne5+ Now it is certainly a drawn position, and one does not quite understand how it can be lost by anyone. White seems to fear Black's single threat ... Na5-c4 too much. 16 Ke2 was surely better to bring the rooks into play as soon as possible. EZB **16 ... Ke7 17. 0–0** Here still 17 Ke2 would be better. EZB **17 ... Rac8 18. Rac1 Rhd8** Now one of Black's rooks threatens to enter on the seventh rank. EZB **19. g3** Perhaps 19 Nf3 would be better; if 19 ... Nc4 then 20 Rc2, but not 20 b3 Nd2 21 N×d2 R×c1 22 R×c1 R×d2. EZB **19 ... f6 20. b4** Now 20 Nf3 would be bad because of 20 ... Nc4 21 Rc2 Ne5. EZB **20 ... f×e5 21. b×a5 Rc6 22. Rb1** Now White's position is most difficult; if he exchanges the rooks he is a pawn down, for instance: 22 R×c6 b×c6 23 Rb1 c5 24 Rb7+ Rd7 25 a6 Kd6 and wins. EZB **22 ... Rd7 23. Rb5**

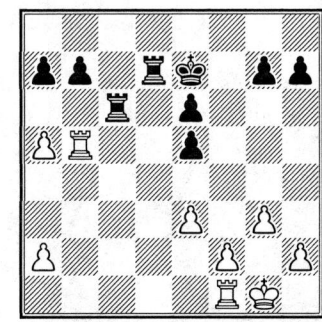

Position after White's 23rd move

23 ... a6! A very good move. Black offers two pawns in order to be able to post his rooks on the 7th rank. DB **24. R×e5** If 24 Rb2 Kd8 25 Rfb1 Kc8 26 Rb6 Rdc7 27 R×c6 R×c6 28 Rb2 Rc5 29 Rb6 R×a5 30 R×e6 R×a2 31 R×e5 b5 and Black wins. RF **24 ... Rc2!** A simple, but beautiful stroke. It required a very exact analysis to adventure the sacrifice of the second pawn. But two rooks on the seventh rank must force the win. EZB **25. Rb1 Rdd2 26. R×b7+ Kf6 27. Re4 R×f2 28. Rb6** This loses.

Instead, White should force an exchange of rooks by 28 Rf4+ R×f4 29 e×f4 R×a2 30 Ra7 R×a5 31 Kg2, and although he is a pawn down, the good position of his rook behind the passed pawn would probably enable him to draw with best play. Both players were very short of time at this stage of the game and the moves up to and including Black's 34th were made at express speed. DB **28 ... Rg2+ 29. Kf1 Rcf2+ 30. Ke1 R×a2 31. Rb×e6+** 31 Kf1 would prolong, not save, the game. DB **31 ... Kg5 32. R6e5+** If 32 R4e5+ Kg4 33 Re4+ Kh5 34 R4e5+ g5 and wins. DB **32 ... Kh6 33. Rh4+ Kg6 34. Kf1 Rgb2 35. Rg4+ Kf6** White resigned. **0–1** Brandreth (ed), 4–5; Eugene Znosko-Borovsky in *BCM* 1937, 55–6; Fine in *De Schaakwereld* 27, 2–3.

(323) FINE—WINTER, W

Hastings 1936/7 (2), 1936 (29 Dec.)
Semi-Tarrasch Defence, Pillsbury Variation [D40]

The most interesting game of the tourney: superbly played by Fine, and ably defended by Winter. FR **1. d4 Nf6 2. c4 e6 3. Nf3 d5 4. Nc3 c5 5. Bg5** This leads to very lively play. A more prosaic continuation is 5 c×d5 N×d5 6 e4 N×c3 7 b×c3 c×d4 8 c×d4 Bb4+ 9 Bd2. PSMB **5 ... c×d4 6. N×d4 e5 7. Ndb5** The sequence 7 Nf3! d4 8 Nd5 Nc6 9 e4 Be7 10 B×f6 B×f6 11 b4!, is correct, as occurred in the 4th Euwe–Alekhine exhibition game, Rotterdam 1937. Grekov & Maizelis **7 ... d4** For the correct 7 ... a6 see Fine–Yudovich, Moscow 1937. **8. Nd5** It would be safer to precede this by 8 B×f6 g×f6, since after the following exchanges the position is by no means necessarily in White's favour. PSMB **8 ... N×d5!** In *Practical Chess Openings*, Fine suggested the interesting alternative 8 ... Na6 9 Qa4 Bd7 10 B×f6 g×f6 11 b4 with a clear positional advantage. It is not so clear that Black is so badly off after, for example, 11 ... Nc6. Another possible plan of development for White would be 11 g3 and 12 Bg2. AW **9. B×d8 Bb4+ 10. Qd2 B×d2+ 11. K×d2 K×d8 12. c×d5** White has a clear positional advantage, *PCO* 189. **12 ... b6?** The cause of all the trouble. It was essential to dislodge the knight. A possible continuation would be 12 ... a6 13 Nd6 Ke7 14 Nc4 Nd7 15 a4 (to stop ... b5) Nc5! 16 Ra3 Ne4+ 17 Ke1 Bd7!; if now 18 N×e5 Rac8 and Black has a splendid game, while to 18 f3 the reply is still 18 ... Rac8. PSMB **13. g3! Ba6 14. a4! Nd7 15. Bg2 B×b5** The exchange is forced. 15 ... Nc5 is answered by 16 Ra3, with the following sample variations: I. 16 ... N×a4? 17 Nd6 Ke7 18 R×a4 winning; II. 16 ... Kd7 17 b4! Nb7 (17 ... N×a4? 18 Bh3+! Kd8 and once again 19 Nd6) 18 d6! B×b5 (19 Nc7 was threatened) 19 a×b5 Rhb8 20 Rha1 K×d6 21 Be4, and Black is totally paralyzed; III. 16 ... B×b5 17 a×b5 a5 18 b×a6 R×a6 19 R×a6 N×c6 20 Ra1 Nb8 21 Ra7 with a clear advantage. W. Sch. **16. a×b5 f5 17. Ra3 Re8** 17 ... e4 might be tried, since 18 g4, suggested by Milner-Barry, fails to 18 ... Ne5!, and 18 Rha1 Re8 19 R×a7 R×a7 20 R×a7 Re5, as suggested by Smith in a note to the next move, also looks playable. AW **18. g4! f×g4** After 18 ... g6 19 g×f5 g×f5 20 Bh3 White's rook will break through on the g-file. W. Sch **19. Rha1 Nf6 20. Kd3!** Much better than 20 R×a7 R×a7 21 R×a7, for Black could then offer the exchange with 21 ... Re7. PSMB **20 ... Re7 21. d6 e4+ 22. K×d4 Rd7 23. Ke5!**

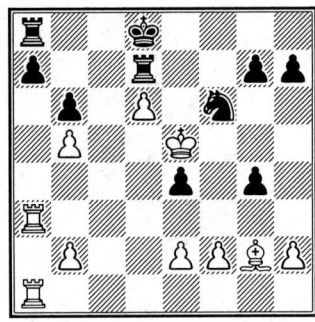

Position after White's 23rd move

Mr. Fine is a disciple of Steinitz. PSMB **23 ... Ke8** The last hope of freeing himself lay in ... Rad8, and after ... Kf7(f8) following up with ... Re8+ or ... Ne8. W. Sch. **24. B×e4** White simplifies the position, transforming it into a rook ending, but he comes up against stubborn resistance from his opponent. W. Sch. **24 ... N×e4 25. K×e4 R×d6 26. R×a7 R×a7 27. R×a7 Rd2** In the very interesting rook endgame which follows White has good prospects owing to the unfavourable position of Black's king. Winter, however, makes a great fight of it. PSMB **28. Ke3 R×b2 29. R×g7 h5** 29 ... R×b5 30 R×h7 would be weaker, since the black king would remain cut off from the action. W. Sch. **30. Rg5 Rb3+ 31. Kf4 Rh3 32. Rg6 R×h2 33. Kg3 Rh3+ 34. Kg2 Rb3** Once again Black finds a defence. If now 35 R×b6, then 35 ... Kf7, and White cannot win, for example, 36 e3 h4 37 Rh6 g3! 38 R×h4 g×f2 39 K×f2 R×b5 and so on. W. Sch. **35. Rg5 Rh3** Black would, of course, lose after 35 ... h4 36 R×g4 R×b5 37 R×h4. W. Sch. **36. f3!** Exploiting the poor position of the opponent's rook. W. Sch. **36 ... Kd7?** After the game, Fine pointed out that with 36 ... Kf7 (preventing Rg6) Black can draw: 37 f×g4 h×g4 38 R×g4 Rh5 39 Rb4 Ke6 and although White is a pawn ahead, he cannot win. GES **37. Rg6 Kc7 38. Rc6+ Kd7?** By very ingenious play White has bottled up the black rook, and the only means of releasing it is to give up the b-pawn. None the less 38 ... Kb7! seems to have been the best chance, since the win still has to be proved. 39 Rh6 Rh4 (40 Rh7+ Kc8 41 f4 Rh3. W. Sch.) does not lead to much; nor 39 Rc4 Rh4 40 f×g4 h×g4 41 Kg3 Rh5 42 Rb4 Re5 43 e4 Rg5. The most promising line appears to be 39 Rg6! Rh4 40 f×g4 h×g4 41 Rg7+ Kc8 42 Rg5! followed by 43 Kg3. This wins a pawn but not necessarily the game. PSMB **39. R×b6 g×f3+! 40. e×f3 Rh4 41. Rh6 Kc7 42. b6+ Kb7 43. Kg3 Rd4** After 43 ... Rb4 44 f4 Black cannot play 44 ... R×b6? because of 45 R×b6+ K×b6 46 Kh4 followed by K×h5 and Kg6. Black could win a tempo, in comparison with the game, by 43 ... Rb4 44 f4 Rb5 45 Rf6 Kc8 46 Kh4 Kd8 47 f5 Ke7 48 Kg5 h4, however it would not save the game: 49 Kg6 h3 50 Rf7+ Ke8 51 b7 h2 52 Rh7 R×b7 53 R×h2 and wins. W. Sch. **44. f4 Rd5 45. Rf6** White is accurate to the end: 45 Kh4? Rf5. W. Sch. **45 ... Rb5 46. Kh4 Kc8 47. f5 Kd8 48. K×h5 Ke7 49. Kg6 Rb1 50. Re6+ Kf8 51. Rc6** Black resigned. An extraordinarily interesting game, and not without theoretical importance. W. Sch. **1–0**

Fred Reinfeld and G. E. Smith in Brandreth (ed), 12–3; P. S. Milner-Barry in BCM 1937, 106–7; notes from *Wiener Schachzeitung* in *Shakhmatny Ezhegodnik* 1938, 195–7.

(324) MENCHIK, V—FINE

Hastings 1936/7 (3), 1936 (30 Dec.)
Semi-Tarrasch Defence [D40]

1. d4 Nf6 2. Nf3 d5 3. c4 e6 4. e3 This tame move does not answer the needs of the position. If White wishes to play the gambit without developing her queen's bishop for some time, she should first play 4 Nc3, thereby forcing Black to disturb the symmetry of the position. **4 ... c5** The difference between this move and the Tarrasch Defence (2 or 3 ... c5) is that White no longer has the Schlechter-Rubinstein attack 5 c×d5 e×d5 6 g3 at her disposal. **5. Nc3 a6 6. d×c5** To avoid moral disgrace. After 6 Bd3 d×c4 7 B×c4 b5 8 Bd3 c×d4 Black would be playing with colours reversed without having lost a tempo with his king's bishop. **6 ... B×c5 7. Be2 0–0 8. 0–0 Nc6 9. a3** Imitation, it has been said (though by someone who may not have been a chessplayer) is the sincerest form of flattery. **9 ... Bd6** Losing a tempo to avoid simplification. At this point White should not have hesitated to play 10 c×d5 e×d5 when a normal Queen's Gambit with colours reversed would have ensued. The text, it should be noted, prevents White from playing the logical 10 b4, for then 10 ... d×c4 11 B×c4 Qc7 wins a pawn (12 Qb3 Ne5). **10. Re1** Preparing the later advance of the e-pawn; but more logical was, as indicated above, 10 c×d5. **10 ... d×c4 11. B×c4 b5 12. Ba2 Bb7** Black is now most promisingly developed. **13. e4 Ng4** A centralization manoeuvre. The square e5 is to be used as a pivot for the black forces. The first step is to occupy the square with a knight which will keep an eye on the squares c4, d3 and f3. **14. h3** Repelling the dangerous beast, but driving him where he wants to go. White need not have been in such a hurry, in fact the reply 14 Bg5 would have been far better; for 14 ... B×h2+ is unsound because of the simple reply 15 N×h2. And if 14 ... Qc7 15 h3 Nge5 16 Rc1 with a fair position. **14 ... Nge5 15. Be3**

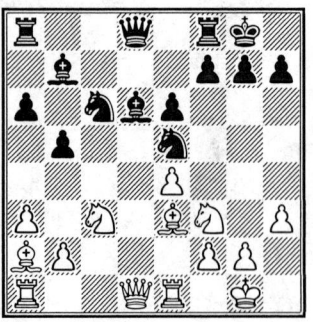

Position after White's 15th move

15 ... Rc8 Threatening to win a pawn by 16 ... N×f3+ 17 Q×f3 Ne5 followed by 18 ... B×a3. **16. Rc1** White appears to have missed a chance here: 16 Ng5! Nc4 (16 ... h6? 17 N×e6!) 17 B×c4 b×c4 18 Qh5. AW **16 ... N×f3+** Avoiding the trap. 16 ... Nd3 apparently wins the exchange for nothing, for if then 17 Q×d3! Bh2+ 18 K×h2 Q×d3; but here White replies 19 Red1 and Black's queen is beyond good and evil. **17. g×f3** Unfortunately this unwanted weakness cannot be avoided. If 17 Q×f3 Ne5 does win the exchange although Black's knight must go through some tortuous movements. There are two main variations: I. 18 Qe2 Nd3 19 Rcd1 (or 19 Q×d3 Bh2+ 20 K×h2 Q×d3 21 Red1 R×c3! and wins) N×e1 20 Bf4 (or 20 e5 N×g2!) Rc6 21 e5 N×g2! and wins; II 18 Qd1 Nd3 19 Rc2 N×e1 20 Rd2 Nc2! 21 Ba7 N×a3 with a winning advantage. **17 ... Ne5 18. Kg2** A better defence was 18 f4 Ng6 19 Qg4 with some attacking chances on the g-file. Now the white pawns are completely blocked. **18 ... Ng6 19. Rh1 Qe7 20. Rc2 Rfd8 21. Rd2 Nf4+ 22. Kf1** The alternative is equally cheerless: 22 B×f4 B×f4 23 R×d8+ R×d8 24 Qe1 Qg5+ 25 Kf1 Rd2 with a crushing position. **22 ... Be5 23. Bb6** Both players were already in time trouble, but White's position suffers chiefly from the fact the blockade of her kingside pawns has immobilized her king and king's rook, which makes it certain that a pawn will fall on the queenside. With the text, White at any rate deprives Black of control of the d-file. **23 ... R×d2 24. Q×d2 g6** Black cannot undertake any direct decisive action but must quietly build up his position certain that eventually the b-pawn will fall. Mating attacks such as 24 ... Qg5 are refuted by simply 25 Rg1 threatening, among other things, Qd7. **25. Bb3** An inaccuracy which further cramps her game. But even after 25 Be3 Rd8 followed by ... Nd3 or 25 Ba5 Qc5 26 Bb4 Qb6 White's difficulties are for practical purposes insurmountable. **25 ... b4** Because of her last move, the pawn cannot be captured by White for then 26 ... Q×b4 wins at once. **26. Nb1 Qd6** An inconsistency which does not, however, spoil the position effectively. Correct was the energetic 26 ... a5 when against the threat of ... Ba6+ followed by ... Qg5+ or ... Nd6+ the white player has no defence. **27. Q×d6 B×d6** Not attempting 27 ... Rc1+ 28 Qd1 and wins. But now the check is threatened. **28. Be3 a5 29. Ba4** In bad time pressure, both players were swimming; but White is practically stalemated. **29 ... Be5 30. a×b4 a×b4 31. b3** Thus saving the b-pawn, but her bishop is now out of play and Black gains absolute control of the 7th rank. **31 ... Rc2 32. Ke1** The only chance was 32 Bb5, but then 32 ... Rb7 wins at least a pawn. **32 ... Ng2+ 33. Kd1 N×e3+ 34. f×e3 Rf2** If now 35 f4 B×e4. **35. Nd2 Bc3** White resigned; for after 36 Nc4 R×f3 37 Nd6 Ba6 38 Nc4 Rf2 (to choose the simplest line) White's position is so weakened that further resistance is obviously useless. **0–1** Fine in Brandreth (ed), 17–9.

(325) FINE–THOMAS, G

Hastings 1936/7 (4), 1936 (31 Dec.)
Queen's Gambit Declined [D46]

1. d4 Nf6 2. c4 e6 3. Nc3 d5 4. Nf3 Nbd7 5. e3 c6 6. Bd3 Bd6 The Meran Variation 6 ... d×c4 7 B×c4 b5 gives more prospects for Black. BCM **7. 0–0 0–0 8. e4 d×e4** Johner–Capablanca, New York 1911, continued 8 ... d×c4 9 B×c4 e5 10 Bg5 h6 11 Bh4 e×d4 (Hort suggested 11 ... Qc7 12 d5 g5!? 13 Bg3 Nb6 instead) 12 Q×d4 Bc5 13 Qd3 Nb6 and now, instead of 14 Q×d8, Khalifman proposes 14 e5! Q×d3 15 B×d3 Nfd5 16 Ne4 and White retains some advantage. **9. N×e4 N×e4 10. B×e4 Qc7** Black is now hard put to free his game because ... e5 always runs into trouble. If at once 10 ... e5? 11 d×e5 N×e5 12 N×e5 B×e5 13 B×h7+ K×h7 14 Qh5+ winds up with White a pawn ahead. RF (In view of the fact that Black can never safely play ... e5, 10 ... Nf6 might be better than the text. AW) **11. Qe2!** If now 11 ... e5 12 c5 Be7 13 N×e5! wins a pawn: 13 ... N×e5 14 d×e5 B×c5 15 B×h7+ K×h7 16 Qc2+ and 17 Q×c5. RF; Vidmar against Spielmann, New York, 1927, played 11 Bc2 h6 12 b3 b6 13 Bb2 Bb7 13 Qd3 f5 with an equal game. BCM **11 ... Bf4** Fine suggested that perhaps 11 ... b6 might have worked out better. After the text White could simply have won a pawn by 12 B×h7+ and 13 Qe4+. **12. B×f4 Q×f4 13. Rad1 Rb8** It becomes now very difficult for Black to develop his queen's bishop, and through this he loses the game. BCM **14. Rd2 Nf6** Inconsistent, though 14 ... c5 does not lead to real freedom. RF **15. Bc2 Qc7** Not only is the aim to play ... b6 and ... Bb7, but White threatens also Ne5, and the queen is in difficulties. BCM **16. Rfd1 c5**

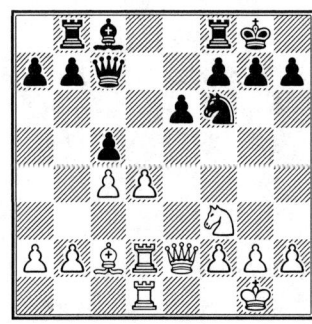

Position after Black's 16th move

17. Qe5! Q×e5 18. d×e5 Ne8 19. Ng5! g6 20. Rd8! b5 21 Ba4 was threatened, and 20 ... h6 is answered by 21 Ne4 b6 22 Ba4 Nc7 23 Nf6+ Kg7 24 R×f8 R×f8 25 Rd7!. **21. c×b5 Nc7 22. Ne4** The simplest win, as pointed out by Reinfeld, was 22 N×h7!. **22 ... Nd5 23. Nf6+ Kg7** Or 23 ... N×f6 24 e×f6 Bb7 25 R×b8 R×b8 26 Rd7. FR **24. R×f8 K×f8 25. N×d5 e×d5 26. R×d5 Be6 27. R×c5 B×a2 28. b3 Ke8 29. Kf1 Kd7 30. Ke1 Rb6 31. Kd2 a6 32. b×a6 R×a6 33. Kc3** Black resigned. **1–0** Fine 1958, 96–9; Fred Reinfeld in Brandreth (ed), 22–3; BCM 1937, 61.

(326) TYLOR, T–FINE

Hastings 1936/7 (5), 1937 (1 Jan.)
Queen's Gambit Declined [D38]

1. Nf3 d5 2. d4 Nf6 3. c4 e6 4. Nc3 Bb4 Fine follows the path of the modern Vienna Variation, doubtless preparing a novelty. 5. e3 Refusing to cope with the theoretical problems of 5 Bg5 dxc4 6 e4 c5. Now Black has no more opening difficulties. 5 ... c5 6. Bd2 0-0 7. Qc2 After this too careful move, Black gives White an isolated d-pawn and develops a concentrated attack on it. It would have been better to play 7 a3 or 7 cxd5. 7 ... cxd4 8. exd4 If 8 Nxd4, e5 is unpleasant. 8 ... dxc4 9. Bxc4 Nc6 10. Be3 Bd7 11. 0-0 Rc8 12. Bd3 Bd6 13. Qe2 Nb4 14. Ne4 Nxe4 15. Bxe4 Bc6 16. Bxc6 Rxc6 17. a3 Nd5 18. Rac1 Rxc1 19. Rxc1 h6 20. Ne5 Qe7 21. g3 Rd8

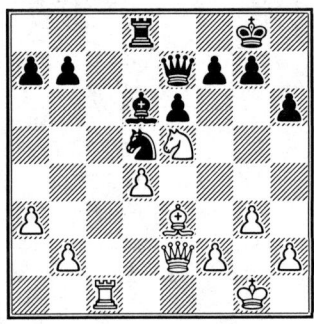

*Position after
Black's 21st move*

22. Bd2 In order to free the queen from the defence of e3; for if the queen had moved, then 22 ... Nxe3 23 fxe3 Bxe5 24 dxe5 Qg5 attacking the weak pawns. The manoeuvre which now follows will be ineffective, however, because of Black's exact play. 22 ... Qe8 23. Nc4 Bc7 24. Ne3 Bb6 25. Qc4 Ne7 The pressure on the d-pawn is gradually accentuated. 26. Bc3 Qc6! 27. Qxc6 Loses quickly; still after 27 Rd1 Qf3 28 Qf1 Nc6, Black would win the d-pawn. 27 ... Nxc6 28. d5 exd5 White resigned. His game has no prospects. 0-1 Notes by Ragozin in Brandreth (ed), 27-8.

(327) FEIGINS, M—FINE

Hastings 1936/7 (6), 1937 (2 Jan.)
Nimzowitsch-Indian Defence, Classical Variation [E37]

1. d4 Nf6 2. c4 e6 3. Nc3 Bb4 Fine has an extraordinarily deep knowledge of this line of play, which has conceded him many a useful win. To my mind, his great strength lies in his ability to preserve tactical chances in the most widely differing types of position; this ability has an excellent field for practice in the difficult and complicated variations of the Nimzowitsch-Indian Defence, particularly against play by his opponent which errs a little, perhaps on the side of solidity. ME 4. Qc2 d5 5. a3 Bxc3+ 6. Qxc3 Ne4 7. Qc2 Nc6 8. e3 e5 9. cxd5 Qxd5 10. Bc4 White has a less sharp, but also dangerous, alternative in 10 Nf3. AW 10 ... Qa5+ 11. b4 Nxb4 12. Qxe4 Nc2+ 13. Ke2! Qe1+ 14. Kf3 Nxa1 15. Bb2 In *Lessons from My Games* Fine says that he realized at this point that he had fallen into a prepared variation. Neither here nor in his works on the openings does he show any awareness of the precedent Rauzer–Konstantinopolsky, Kiev 1932. Euwe too, writing in *Chess*, seemed to think that this was an innovation. AW 15 ... Be6! Fine's over the

board inspiration! The main line is considered to be 15 ... 0-0 16 Kg3 Bd7 (16 ... Kh8 was refuted in Atalik–Sax, Maróczy Memorial 1997) 17 Nf3 Qxh1 18 Ng5 g6 19 Qxe5 Rae8 20 Qf6, when Fine gives 20 ... Rxe3+ 21 fxe3 Qe1+ 22 Qf2 and White has a distinct superiority (MCO 184). At the end of this line, however, 22 ... Nc2! seems to give Black chances. In place of 17 Nf3, 17 Bd3 may be viable. AW 16. d5

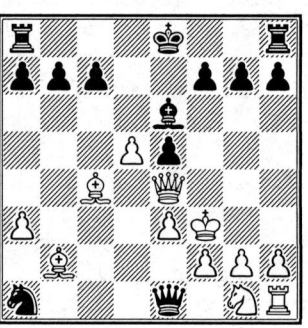

*Position after
White's 16th move*

16 ... 0-0-0 The attacked bishop must not retreat for then 17 Qxe5+ would be drastic. With the piece sacrifice involved in the text, however, Black's attack is mightily augmented. ME 17. dxe6 fxe6 18. Kg4!? In 1958 Fine showed that it is not all over after the recommended 18 g3! because of the continuation 18 ... Rd2! 19 Bxe5 h5! 20 Bxe6+ Kb8 21 Kg2 Qxf2+ 22 Kh3 Nc2. Another try is 19 Bxe6+ (instead of 19 Bxe5) Kb8 20 Bxe5, when there is the fascinating line 20 ... Rxf2+ 21 Kg4 Qd1+ 22 Kh4 Qd8+ with unclear complications. A second try at refutation was 18 Kg3 and then Fine, in MCO, proposed 18 ... Rhf8 19 Bxe6+ (a game Bogatirev–Golovko, 5th U.S.S.R. Correspondence Chess Championship 1960–63 proceeded 19 Bxe5 Qxf2+! 20 Kh3 and Black may have done better by 20 ... Nc2!, rather than 20 ... Rd1) Kb8 20 Bxe5 Rde8 with excellent counterchances (and not 20 ... Rxf2 21 Kh3 Rf1 22 Bg4!, Winter–Reynolds, Birmingham 1937, but possibly 20 ... Qxf2+ 21 Kh3 Nc2!). The latest theoretical volume (Lalić 2001) makes the critical line 18 Bxe5 Rhf8+ 19 Kg4 Rxf2 20 Nh3 (Lazarev–A. Sokolov, French Team Tournament 1998), which is probably a genuine improvement. AW 18 ... Qxf2! 19. Bxa1? White's 18th move is usually awarded a question mark on the basis that "After 19 Bxe5 Nc2 Black would have had just as easy a task." according to Euwe. However, it does not seem so clear cut should White then play 20 Bxe6+ Kb8 21 Nh3 Nxe3+ (probably better than 21 ... Qxe3, 21 ... Qe2+ or 21 ... Qd2) 22 Kg5 Qxg2+ 23 Qxg2 Nxg2 24 Rc1. AW 19 ... h5+ 20. Kh3

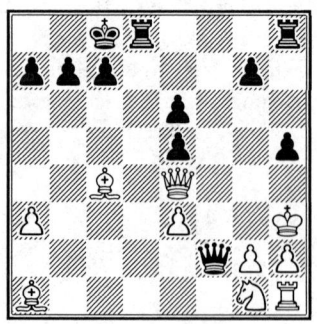

*Position after
White's 20th move*

20 ... g5! White's king is too exposed, and the win becomes easy for Black. RF **21. Bxe6+ Kb8 22. Nf3 g4+ 23. Bxg4 hxg4+ 24. Kxg4 Qxg2+ 25. Kf5 Rh5+ 26. Kf6 Rf8+ 27. Ke6 Qg8+** Black resigned. An excellent example of Fine's capabilities in razor sharp positions. AW **0–1** Fine 1958, 100–2; Euwe in *Chess*, 14 January, 1937, 165–7.

(328) Fine—Koltanowski, G

Hastings 1936/7 (7), 1937 (4 Jan.)
King's Indian Defence [E72]

1. d4 Nf6 2. c4 g6 3. Nc3 Bg7 Having played the Grünfeld Defence (3 ... d5) with little success against Vidmar in round 3, Koltanowski returns to his favourite variation. **4. e4 d6 5. g3 0–0 6. Bg2 Nc6 7. Nge2** He develops the knight in this way instead of at f3 so as not to impede the advance of the f-pawn or allow ... Bg4. **7 ... e5 8. d5 Ne7** If 8 ... Nb8, intending ... a5 and ... Nb8-d7-c5, White's strategy would be to dislodge the knight by b3, a3, Be3 and b4; then to bring the king's knight to d3, followed by c4-c5 with strong queenside pressure which can only be offset by aggressive tactics on the other wing by Black. (For a classic example of play for both sides in this variation, see Rubinstein–Réti, London 1922.) **9. 0–0 Nd7 10. Be3 f5 11. Qd2 Nf6 12. f3 Kh8** 12 ... fxe4 13 Nxe4 Nxe4 14 fxe4 would yield the f-file to White, but Black might have tried 12 ... Rf7 in order to preserve his king's bishop. **13. Bh6 Bxh6 14. Qxh6 fxe4 15. fxe4 Bd7 16. h3 Neg8 17. Qe3 h5** The open f-file favours White here, for in the long run the exchange of rooks is inevitable, and this will reduce Black's chances of a kingside attack. White's chances, on the other hand, consist of a pawn-storm against Black's base (the d-pawn) and this operation will not be hindered by the exchange of rooks. ME **18. Nc1 Qc8** Waste of time. Black should still play ... a5 and ... b6. White's chances would then be minimized by the necessity of exchanging off at b4 and c5 (after the respective moves b2-b4 and c4-c5), and Black would have some counterplay by placing his rooks at a8 and b8; although White would of course still maintain the upper hand strategically. Black's aimless meanderings are in contrast to Fine's admirably methodical attainment of objectives. **19. Kh2 Kg7 20. Nd3 Nh6** Threatening ... Ng4+. **21. Qd2** The text parries the threat and allows White to go ahead undisturbed on the queenside. Fine now goes straight for his target. ME **21 ... Qe8 22. c5 Qe7 23. b4 Nh7 24. Qe3 Qg5?** Considerably lightening Fine's task, as he is now able to turn his entire attention to the queenside. More promising, though in the long run insufficient, was 24 ... g5 followed by ... h5, establishing a potential post for Black's knights at f4. **25. Qxg5 Nxg5 26. b5 Rxf1 27. Rxf1** *(see diagram)* **27 ... Rf8** Or 27 ... b6 28 c6. Fine's concluding play is a marvel of precision and artistry. **28. Rxf8** All according to schedule. ME **28 ... Kxf8 29. c6 Bc8** If 29 ... bxc6 30 bxc6 Bc8 31 a4! (not 31 Nb5 Ba6 and White must play 32 a4 after which 32 ... Bxb5 draws. In this line 32 Nxc7? would be unsound, as the

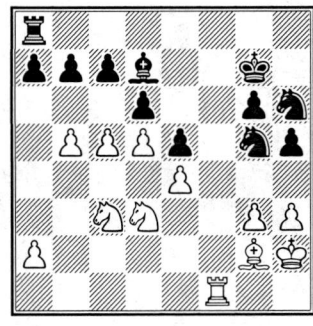

Position after White's 27th move

c-pawn is easily stopped), Ke7 (if 31 ... a5 32 Nb2 Ba6 33 Kg1! followed by 34 h4 and 35 Bf1) 32 a5 Ba6 33 Nb4 Bc4 34 Kg1 Kd8 35 h4 Nh7 36 Bf1 Bxf1 37 Kxf1 Kc8 38 Nb5 Kb8 39 Na6+ wins (39 ... Ka8 40 N5xc7 mate!). **30. Nb4** It is as good as over. If 30 ... b6 31 Na6 Bxa6 32 bxa6 and 33 Nb5. ME **30 ... Ke8 31. cxb7 Bxb7 32. Nc6 a6** On 32 ... Bxc6 there is a neat win by 33 bxc6 Kd8 34 Nb5 a6 35 Na3 Ng8! (not 35 ... Kc8 36 h4 Ng4+ 37 Kg1 and 38 Bf1) 36 h4 Nf7 37 Nc2 Kc8 38 Nb4 a5 39 Nd3 Kb8 40 Nb2 Ka7 41 Nc4 Ka6 42 a4 Nf6 43 Bf1 Ka7 44 Bd3 and so on. **33. Bf1 axb5 34. Bxb5 Bxc6** On 34 ... Kc8 35 a4 Nf3+ 36 Kg2 Nd4 White wins by the simple 37 a5. **35. Bxc6+ Kd8 36. Kg2 Ng8 37. h4 Nf7 38. a4 Ne7** Equally hopeless would be 38 ... Kc8 39 Nb5 Ne7 40 Be8: I. 40 ... Nd8 41 g4 hxg4 42 Kg3 and the entrance of the king is decisive: Nb7 43 Kxg4 Nc5 44 Nc3 Kd8 45 Bf7; II. 40 ... Nh6 41 Na7+ Kd8 42 Bb5 Nc8 43 Nc6+!. **39. Bb7 Kd7 40. a5 Nd8 41. a6 Nc8 42. Nb5 Nb6 43. Na7!** Black resigned, because 44 Nc6 is decisive. **1–0** Sidney Bernstein in Brandreth (ed), 38–9; Euwe & Kramer 1964, 179–80.

(329) Alekhine, A—Fine

Hastings 1936/7 (8), 1937 (5 Jan.)
Spanish Game, Chigorin Variation (without h3) [C90]

Fine described this as the best game he ever lost, including it in his tribute to Alekhine in *The Chess Review* and in his own collection of his games. **1. e4 e5 2. Nf3 Nc6 3. Bb5 a6 4. Ba4 Nf6 5. 0–0 Be7 6. Re1 b5 7. Bb3 d6 8. c3 Na5 9. Bc2 c5 10. d4 Qc7 11. Nbd2 0–0** The more exact move is 11 ... Nc6 in order to force White to a decision in the centre. The reply 12 Nf1 would then be rather doubtful because of 12 ... cxd4, with temporary gain of a pawn, as in the 3rd and 5th games of the Lasker–Tarrasch Match 1908. AA **12. Nf1 Bg4** The continuation of this game proves convincingly that the early exchange of this bishop gives White promising attacking opportunities on the kingside—but a fully satisfactory plan is not easy to find. The comparatively most logical method seems 12 ... Bd7 followed by ... Rfc8 and ... Bf8. AA **13. Ne3** A safer line would have been 13 d5 followed by Ne3 with at least a tempo more than in the usual variation. The text carries with it a promising pawn sacrifice. AA **13 ... Bxf3 14. Qxf3 cxd4 15. Nf5** Alekhine considered this move to be risky, recommending instead 15 cxd4! expecting 15 ... Nc6 (or 15 ... exd4 16 Nf5

Q×c2 17 N×e7+ Kh8 18 Nf5! with decisive advantage according to Alekhine, but there appears to be no direct win after 18 ... d3! 19 N×g7 Nd7! 20 Bh6, although White certainly stands better) 16 d5 Nd4 17 Qd1 N×c2 18 N×c2 a5 19 Bd2. **AW 15 ... d×c3 16. Q×c3!** The first point of the sacrifice, White gets rid of the pressure on the c-file without loss of time. **AA 16 ... Rfc8 17. Qg3 Bf8 18. Bd3 Nc6 19. Bg5 Ne8** Black's position is theoretically equal, but the defence offers great practical difficulties, MCO 255. **20. Rac1** After 20 Rad1! followed by Bb1, a3 and Ba2, Black would have a very difficult game. The text proves to be the loss of a valuable tempo. **AA 20 ... Qb7 21. a3** The manoeuvre intended here, Bd3-b1-a2-d5 induces Black to start a counter demonstration on the queenside, and, in order to do so, he must first force the exchange of the white knight. **AA 21 ... g6** Spielmann recommends doubling rooks on the c-file. **AA 22. Nh6+ B×h6 23. B×h6 Nd4 24. Rcd1 b4 25. f4!** e×f4 Alekhine considered that this was best, believing that 25 ... b×a3 26 f×e5 would lead to an advantageous position for White. Black, however, seems to be able to make things difficult by 26 ... a×b2 27 e×d6 Rc3! **AW 26. Q×f4 b×a3 27. b×a3 Rc3 28. Qf2 Ne6** Alekhine notes that Fine had planned the drawing combination 28 e5 R×d3! 29 R×d3 Ne2+ 30 R×e2 Qb1+ 31 Kf2 Q×d3 32 e6! Qf5 33 Q×f5 g×f5 34 e7 f6 35 Ke3, but Alekhine needed to win the game to pass Fine in the tournament standings. Fine believed that he would have had winning chances after 28 ... Nc6 29 Bb1 Ne5 30 Ba2 Rac8 as did Alekhine after 28 ... Nc6 29 Bc1! Ne5 30 Bf1, though here the Russian reckoned that his bishop pair would have almost counterbalanced the extra pawn. Brandreth recommends instead 28 ... Nc6 29 a4 and Tartakower 28 ... Nc6 29 e5 d×e5 30 Be4. It is difficult to find a clear win for either side, the position would probably remain in dynamic equilibrium after 28 ... Nc6. **AW 29. a4!** This insignificant-looking pawn will henceforth support White's threats in a very efficient way. **AA 29 ... Rac8 30. Rf1 R3c7** Spielmann considers that 30 ... R8c7 offered a better defence. **AA 31. Rb1 Qc6 32. a5! Nc5 33. Bc4 Qd7 34. Qa2!** This reply was overlooked by Black and leaves him completely defenceless. **AA 34 ... N×e4 35. R×f7 Q×f7 36. B×f7+ R×f7 37. Qe6** Black resigned. **1–0** Alekhine et al, 245–8; Alekhine in *Chess* 1937, 164–5; Fine 1958, 103–6; Brandreth (ed), 43–5; Tartakower & du Mont 1952, 99–100.

(330) FINE—VIDMAR, M

Hastings 1936/7 (9), 1937 (6 Jan.)
Catalan System [D34]

1. d4 d5 2. c4 e6 3. Nf3 c5 4. c×d5 e×d5 5. g3 Nc6 6. Nc3 Nf6 7. Bg2 Be7 8. 0–0 0–0 9. d×c5 Facing the Rubinstein Variation of the Tarrasch Defence requires Black to make a critical choice, he can play a gambit with 9 ... d4 or enter into a difficult positional struggle after 9 ... Bc5. The gambit variation happens to suit my style best. **MV 9 ... d4 10. Na4** At Sliac I myself played 10 Nb5 against Maróczy. **MV 10 ... Bf5** A well-known form of the Tarrasch Defence in which, by means of a pawn sacrifice, Black has pushed his isolated pawn to the 5th rank. According to Tarrasch, Black's space advantage is now ample compensation for the lost pawn. **ME 11. Nh4** White himself later suggested 11 Bf4 here, and applied it in his play. It is to be observed that 11 a3 Ne4 12 b4 Nc3 13 N×c3 d×c3 14 Q×d8 Rad8 15 Bg5 B×g5 16 N×g5 Nd4 gives Black satisfactory counterchances. **ME 11 ... Bg4!** The usual move here is 11 ... Be4, however, Black can happily try to induce h2-h3 from White. **MV 12. a3 Nd5 13. Qb3** If 13 Nf3, Bf6 with a good game. **VR 13 ... Be6! 14. Nf5!** White cannot very well take the b-pawn: 14 Q×b7 Na5 15 Qa6 Nb3 16 Rb1 B×h4. **ME 14 ... Nb6! 15. N×e7+ Q×e7 16. Qd1** White concedes that his opening has not been a complete success. **MV 16 ... N×a4 17. Q×a4 Q×c5** Black has recovered his pawn and stands well. **ME 18. Bf4 Qb6** Threatening ... Bb3. **MV 19. b4 Bc4 20. Qc2 Qa6 21. Rfe1 Rfe8 22. Be4 h6 23. Bh7+** A good idea: as he intends to play for the ending, he removes the king from the centre. **VR 23 ... Kh8 24. Bd3 B×d3 25. Q×d3 Q×d3 26. e×d3 a6** The pressure which Black exerts on the open e-file is almost bound to give rise to this sort of endgame. It would be going too far for us to discuss it in any detail; suffice it to say that Black's position is certainly not inferior. In fact, he had a chance later on of seizing the advantage. **ME 27. Kf1 Kg8 28. Rac1 f6 29. Bc7** This bishop is heading for b6, from where it attacks the weakest black pawn. **MV 29 ... Kf7 30. Re4 g5 31. Rc5 R×e4 32. d×e4 Re8 33. f3 Re7! 34. Bb6 g4!** Thus Black gains the advantage. **MV 35. f×g4** Not 35 Ke2 g×f3+ 36 K×f3 Ne5+ 37 Ke2 Nd7! winning the exchange. **VR 35 ... R×e4 36. Rc4** The pawn is lost: 36 h3 Re3. **MV 36 ... R×g4 37. a4 Rg5** In this way he retains the extra pawn. **VR 38. Ke2 Rd5 39. Rc5 d3+** 39 ... Ke6 40 b5 a×b5 41 a×b5 Ne5 would have been simpler, but the text should also have won. **MV 40. Kd2 Rd7 41. b5 a×b5 42. a×b5 Nd4 43. Rc7 R×c7? 43** ... Nf3+ 44 Ke3 R×c7 45 B×c7 d2 46 Ke2 h5 was better. **ME 44. B×c7 N×b5 45. Bf4 h5 46. K×d3** The upshot is that White still remains a pawn minus, but the strong position of his king assures the draw. **VR 46 ... Ke6 47. h3 f5 48. Kc4 Nd6+ 49. Kc5 Nc8 50. Bb8 Kd7 51. Bf4 Ne7 52. Bg5** Naturally White does not play 52 Kb6 Nd5+ 53 K×b7 N×f4 54 g×f4 Kd6. **MV 52 ... Nc6 53. Kd5 b5 54. Bd2** Black can make no more progress since White can give up his bishop to secure the draw, for example, 54 ... b4 55 B×b4! N×b4+ 56 Ke5 and so on. **MV ½–½** Vidmar 562–6; Ragozin in Brandreth (ed), 50–1; Euwe & Kramer 1964, 255–6.

Swedish Punch, 1937

Fine started 1937 by spending a month in Sweden. Forewarned by the experience of his former team captain Frank Marshall, Fine was suitably wary of the hospitality of his hosts, being sure not to overindulge in the alcoholic local punch, and thereby keeping his head clear for exhibitions. He allowed just two draws in a tournament containing the strongest Swedish players, then a considerable force at team tournaments. A hard fought match with the number one Swedish player, which he won by two clear points, was excellent preparation for a tough schedule against two lesser lights of the local scene, against whom he allowed but a single draw in six games.

Stockholm, January 16–24, 1937

After Hastings Fine headed straight for Sweden, where he stayed for about two months. His visit started with him giving exhibitions of simultaneous play on January 13 and 14. Following a day of rest he participated in a tournament, held to celebrate the 20th Jubilee of the Wasa Chess Club in Stockholm, which included the Dutch number two Salo Landau, the principal players of the Swedish team—Ståhlberg, Lundin, Stoltz, and Danielsson, against whom he scored three out of four, and four other Swedish masters, Nils Bergkvist, Bertil Sundberg and Gösta Holm of Stockholm and John Collet of Uppsala.

		1	2	3	4	5	6	7	8	9	10	
1	Fine	*	½	½	1	1	1	1	1	1	1	8
2	Ståhlberg	½	*	½	½	½	½	1	1	1	1	6½
3	Stoltz	½	½	*	½	½	½	½	1	1	½	5½
4	Danielsson	0	½	½	*	½	1	1	½	½	1	5½
5	Bergkvist	0	½	½	½	*	½	½	½	1	1	5
6	Lundin	0	½	½	0	½	*	1	½	½	1	4½
7	Sundberg	0	0	½	0	½	0	*	1	½	1	3½
8	Landau	0	0	0	½	½	½	0	*	½	1	3
9	Holm	0	0	0	½	0	½	½	½	*	0	2
10	Collett	0	0	½	0	0	0	0	0	1	*	1½

(331) FINE—STÅHLBERG, G

Stockholm (1), 1937 (16 Jan.)
Queen's Gambit Declined [D63]

1. d4 d5 2. c4 e6 3. Nc3 Nf6 4. Bg5 Be7 5. Nf3 Nbd7 6. e3 0–0 7. Rc1 c6 8. a3 Ne4 9. Bxe7 Qxe7 10. Qc2 A couple of years later, at Kemeri-Riga 1939, Bogolyubov played 10 Bd3 Nxc3 11 Rxc3 dxc4 12 Rxc4 e5 13 Qc2 against the selfsame Ståhlberg, obtaining an advantageous position which he successfully converted into a winning position. **10 ... Nxc3** 10 ... f5 also comes into consideration. **11. Qxc3 Re8 12. Rd1 dxc4 13. Bxc4 b6** Black cannot free his game by 13 ... e5 since after 14 dxe5 Nxe5 15 Nxe5 Qxe5 16 Qxe5 Rxe5 White will mate on e8. However Ståhlberg finds another way to equalize the game. **14. 0–0 Bb7 15. e4 c5!** Black has equalized, MCO 137. **16. Bb5** The immediate 16 Rfe1 would have been better. **16 ... Red8 17. Bxd7 Qxd7!** White threatened 18 dxc5 weakening

Black's queenside, but now after exchanging his queen it would be Black who would gain the advantage. **18. Qc2 Qc6 19. Rfe1 cxd4 20. Qxc6 Bxc6 21. Nxd4 Ba4! 22. b3 e5 23. bxa4 exd4 24. e5 Rac8 25. g3 Kf8?** Here Ståhlberg allowed his advantage to slip and White happily grabbed his chance to escape. After the game Ståhlberg indicated that in the event of 25 ... Rc4 White would not be able to hold out for too long, for example, 26 a5 bxa5 27 Re4 Kf8 28 Rd3 Rc3 29 Rxc3 dxc4 30 Rc4. Though 25 ... Rc3 followed by d3 seems stronger. **26. e6! fxe6 27. Rxe6 Rc3 28. a5 bxa5 29. Re4 d3 30. a4 Rd5** On 30 ... d2 there would follow not 31 Re2 because of 31 ... Rc1 but 31 Kf1 Rc1 32 Ke2 and so on. **31. Kg2 Kf7 32. Kf3 Rc2 33. Ke3 g5 34. Rxd3 Rxd3+ 35. Kxd3 Rxf2 36. Re5 Kg6 37. Rxa5 Rxh2 38. Ke3! Kh5 39. Kf3 Ra2 40. Rxa7 Ra3+ 41. Kg2 Kg4 42. Rxh7 Ra2+ 43. Kf1 Kxg3 44. Ra7 g4 45. a5 Ra1+ 46. Ke2 Kg2 47. Kd3 g3 48. Kc4** Draw agreed. ½–½ Jonasson, 15–7.

(332) SUNDBERG, B—FINE

Stockholm (2), 1937 (17 Jan.)
Queen's Pawn Game [D04]

1. d4 Nf6 2. Nf3 d5 3. e3 c5 4. b3 Nc6 5. Bb2 Bg4 6. Be2 e6 7. Nbd2 Rc8 8. 0–0 Bd6 9. h3 Bf5 10. a3 cxd4 11. exd4 0–0 12. Re1 Ne4 13. Bd3 Nxd2 14. Qxd2 Qf6 15. Bxf5 Qxf5 16. c4 dxc4 17. bxc4 Rfd8

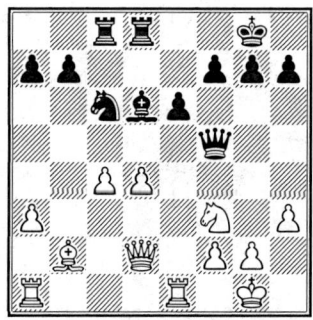

Position after Black's 17th move

18. Qc3 Be7 19. Rad1 h5 20. d5 Bf6 21. Qd2 b6 22. Bxf6 Qxf6 23. Qe2 Na5 24. Ne5 g6 25. d6 Nc6 26. Nf3 e5 27. Qd2 Nd4 28. Nxe5 Rxd6 29. Qe3 Rcd8 30. Rd2 Qf5 31. Rxd4 Rxd4 32. Nc6 R4d7 33. Nxd8 Rxd8 34. Qe7 Rd2 35. Qe3 Rd3 36. Qe8+ Kg7

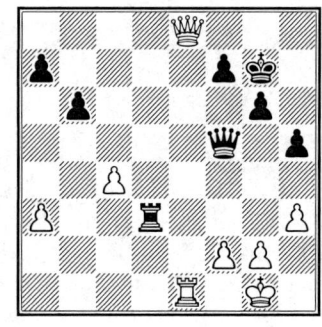

Position after Black's 36th move

37. a4 Qf4 38. Qe7 Rd2 39. Rf1 a5 40. Qa7 Qd4
41. Qe7 Rc2 42. Qe3 Rxc4 43. Rb1 Qxe3 44. fxe3
Rb4 45. Ra1 Kf8 46. Kf2 Ke7 47. Kf3 Kd6 48. Ke2
Kc5 49. Kd3 Rb3+ 50. Ke4 Kb4 51. g4 Rb2
52. gxh5 gxh5 53. Kd4 Rd2+ 54. Ke5 Rd3 55. Ke4
Ra3 56. Rb1+ Kc5 57. Rb5+ Kc6 58. Rxh5 Rxa4+
59. Kd3 Ra3+ 60. Kd4 Ra1 White resigned. 0–1

(333) FINE—DANIELSSON, G

Stockholm (3), 1937 (18 Jan.)
Nimzowitsch-Indian Defence, Classical Variation [E37]

1. d4 Nf6 2. c4 e6 3. Nc3 Bb4 4. Qc2 d5 5. a3
Bxc3+ 6. Qxc3 Ne4 7. Qc2 0–0 8. e3 Nd7 In the
3rd match game Bogolyubov–Euwe 1929 8 ... b6 9 Bd3 Ba6
was played, and White, recognizing the danger of 10 Bxe4
dxe4 11 Qxe4 Bxc4 12 Qa8 Bd5 13 Qxa7 Bxg2 played
instead 10 Ne2 but without obtaining satisfactory compensation for Black's freer game. 9. Bd3 f5 10. Ne2 c6
11. 0–0 Nd6 Black forces the c-pawn forward, after which
he can carry out the counter ... e6-e5, which could only be
prevented by f2-f4, untroubled by the prospect of cxd5. But
Black's does not hamper White's chances of an advance in
the centre. 12. c5 Ne4 13. b4 White stands slightly
better, MCO 184. 13 ... a6 14. f3 Nef6 15. Bd2 g6
16. Ng3 e5 17. e4! f4 Black cannot allow the centre to
be opened up as it would simply open up the diagonals for
White's bishops. 17 ... fxe4 would have been bad because of
18 fxe4 exd4 followed by Bg5 and Rae1. 18. Ne2 g5 After
18 ... dxe4 Bc4+ Kg7 20 fxe4 g5 21 d5 White is certainly
better, but he has no immediate win. 19. exd5 cxd5
20. Bc3 e4 This pawn sacrifice breathes some life into
Black's game, but White finds a clear path through to victory. 21. fxe4 Nxe4 22. Bxe4 dxe4 23. Qa2+! Kg7
Or 23 ... Rf7 24 Nxf4! 24. d5+ Kg6 25. Qc2 Qe8 Or
25 ... Nf6 26 Bxf6 Qxf6 27 Qxe4+ Bf5 28 Qd4 and so on.
26. Rae1 Rf5

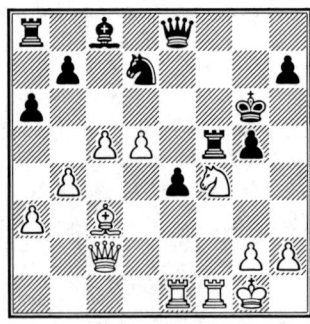

*Position after
Black's 26th move*

27. Nxf4+!! An example of Fine's great strength. After a
game of positional manoeuvring he is quick to spot the
chance for a lightning strike against the black king. 27 ...
gxf4 28. Rxe4 Qf7 29. Rexf4 Ne5 30. Bxe5 h5
31. Qd3 Black resigned. White threatens to win the bishop
by 32 Qg3+ Kh6 33 Rxf5 Bxf5 32 Rxf5, when the queen
cannot capture on f5 because of mate on g7. 1–0 *De Shaakwereld* 30, 3–4; Jonasson, 23–4, after *TfS* and *DSZ*.

(334) BERGKVIST, N—FINE

Stockholm (4), 1937 (19 Jan.)
Nimzowitsch-Indian Defence, Classical Variation [E33]

1. d4 Nf6 2. c4 e6 3. Nc3 Bb4 4. Qc2 Nc6 5. Nf3
d6 6. e3 A weak continuation. White must proceed as
energetically as possible, by forcing the exchange of the black
king's bishop. After 6 a3 Bxc3+ 7 Qxc3 0–0 (on 7 ... a5
played by Dr. Alekhine against Dr. Lasker at Nottingham
1936, White does best to avoid all complications with 8 b3
0–0 9 g3 and with the two bishops he maintains a slight
advantage) 8 b4! and the experience of recent master tournaments proves that White's game is somewhat preferable.
6 ... 0–0 7. Bd3 e5 8. d5 Nb8 9. Bd2 Black was
threatening 9 ... Bxc3+, when the undesirable reply 10 bxc3
would have been forced, for if 10 Qxc3 e4 would win a
piece. 9 ... Qe7 10. a3 White is losing much time, but
he wishes to force b2-b4 as quickly as possible. 10 ... Bxc3
11. Bxc3 Nbd7 Not 11 ... e4? because of 12 Bxf6. Now ...
e4 is threatened. 12. Be2 Still hoping to obtain an advantage with the eventual b2-b4. But White has moved back
and forth so much that Black now seizes the opportunity to
obtain a strong initiative. Better than the text was 12 e4 Nc5
13 0–0 a5 when White's position would have been tenable.
12 ... b5! 13. cxb5 The alternative, 13 b3 bxc4 14 bxc4
Nc5 after which Black's knight at c5 cannot be dislodged, is
obviously unsatisfactory. 13 ... Nxd5 14. Ba5 Bb7!

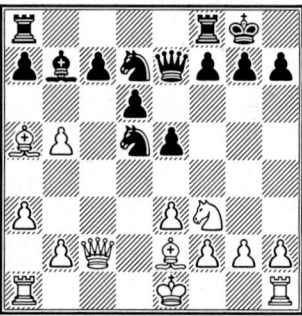

*Position after
Black's 14th move*

15. Rd1 White does not care to accept the pawn offered.
Since after 15 e4 Nf4 16 Qxc7 (not 16 Bxc7? Rac8) Bxe4
17 Bb4 Rfc8 18 Qxd6 Qxd6 19 Bxd6 Rc2 Black has a very
strong attack, White's judgment was quite right. 15 ... Nc5
16. Bc3 After 16 b4 Ne6 White's queen's bishop would be
entirely out of play. 16 ... Kh8 17. b4 In his eagerness to
preserve his two bishops White forgets to castle. 17 ... Ne6
18. Bb2 f5 19. Bc4? This ecclesiastical perpetual motion
is obviously quite faulty. He should simply have castled,
when Black's attack, though strong, is far from decisive.
19 ... Nb6 20. Be2 Back again! Bad would have been
20 Bxe6 Qxe6 21 Qxc7 Bd5 22 Qc3 Bc4 when White cannot castle; but 20 Ba2 was somewhat better than the text.
20 ... Rac8 21. Qd2? Fearing c7-c6, which Black had
never intended. 21 ... f4 22. Bc1 22 0–0 would have been
bad because of ... e4 followed by ... f3. White's position is
now lost and Black proceeds to the execution. 22 ... Ng5!
23. 0–0 Nxf3+ 24. Bxf3 Bxf3 25. gxf3 Qg5+

26. Kh1 Qh5 27. Qe2 Rf6 28. Rg1 Rh6 29. Rg2 e4 White resigned. **0–1** *Chess* 1936–7, 217–9; Jonasson, 27–8.

(335) FINE–HOLM, G

Stockholm (5), 1937 (20 Jan.)
Queen's Gambit Declined [D46]

1. d4 d5 2. c4 e6 3. Nc3 Nf6 4. Nf3 Nbd7 5. e3 c6 6. Bd3 Bd6 7. 0-0 0-0 8. e4 dxe4 9. Nxe4 Nxe4?! 10. Bxe4 Qc7 11. Qe2 Re8 12. Re1 Nf8? Now Black encounters difficulties. The knight must stay on d7 to maintain control over c5 and e5. Black should have completed his development by ... b6, ... Bb7 and ... c5. **13. Bd2 Bd7 14. Bc3 Rac8 15. Rad1** White has such an overwhelming position that Black can no longer hope for much from the game. **15 ... Ng6 16. Ne5 f5** Hastening the end. **17. Bc2 Nxe5 18. dxe5 Be7**

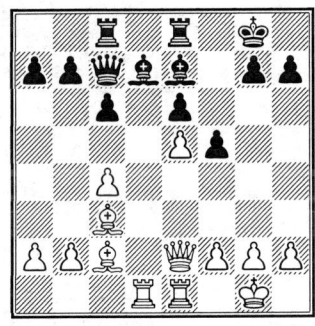

Position after Black's 18th move

19. g4! With this forceful move White decided the struggle in his favour. Black cannot play 19 ... fxg4 because of 20 Qd3! **19 ... Rf8 20. gxf5 exf5 21. e6 Be8 22. Rd7! Qf4!** 22 ... Bxd7? would have cost the bishop on e7. In reply Black sets a little trap, 23 Rxe7? would allow the reply ... Qg5+, a pitfall Fine easily avoids. **23. Qe3 Qh4 24. Qg3! Qxg3+ 25. hxg3 Bf6 26. Bxf6 Rxf6 27. Rxb7 c5 28. Rxa7 Bc6 29. Ba4 Be4 30. e7** Black resigned. **1–0** Fine in *De Shaakwereld* 32, 3; Jonasson, 30.

(336) LUNDIN, E–FINE

Stockholm (6), 1937 (21 Jan.)
Nimzowitsch-Indian Defence, Rubinstein Variation [E53]

1. Nf3 d5 2. d4 Nf6 3. c4 e6 4. Nc3 Bb4 Bringing about a kind of Nimzowitsch-Indian Defence. The position can also arise by way of 1 d4 Nf6 2 c4 e6 3 Nc3 Bb4 4 Nf3 d5, as occurred, for example, in the game between Ståhlberg and Sundberg in the previous round. However, the bishop move here is just a waste of time as it is later forced to retreat from b4 (but see note to move 10. AW). **5. e3 c5 6. Bd3 0-0 7. 0-0 a6 8. a3 cxd4 9. exd4 dxc4 10. Bxc4** Apart from the Nimzowitsch-Indian and Queen's Gambit, this position can also arrive by way of the Caro-Kann Defence. AW **10 ... Be7** Lev Psakhis has played 10 ... Bxc3 with success, and, in further outings by Kharitonov and Bareev, White has been unable to win a game.

AW **11. d5!** White won after 11 Ba2 b5 12 d5! in the game Dolmatov–Larsen, Amsterdam 1980, but Black took the half point with 11 ... Bd7 instead of 11 ... b5, Yuneev–Novik, St. Petersburg 1994. AW **11 ... Qc7** It is my impression that Fine leaves ... exd5 until it is too late. He would have gained better chances than in the game by taking the pawn either on this move or the next. AW **12. Qe2 b5 13. Bb3 exd5**

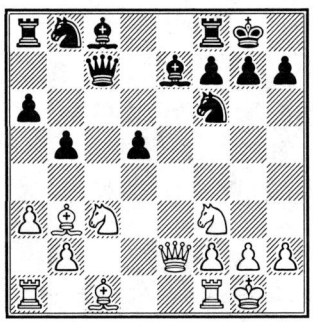

Position after Black's 13th move

14. Bg5 14 Nxd5 Nxd5 15 Bxd5 Bb7 16 Bf4! is also strong, for example, 16 ... Qd7 17 Bxb7 Qxb7 18 Rac1. After the text Lundin, for his pawn, has a slightly better position with many excellent variations to choose from. **14 ... Be6 15. Rac1 Qd6 16. Rfd1 Nbd7 17. Bh4** A small inexactitude, but it takes more than this for Fine to turn the situation round. If White had exchanged on d5 he could have reached an advantageous ending: 17 Bxd5 (17 Nxd5 may be more accurate. AW) Bxd5 (Black can apparently play 17 ... Nxd5 18 Rxd5 Bxd5 19 Bxe7 Qf4! 20 Rd1 Bxf3 21 Qf3 Qxf3 22 gxf3 Ne5 with the better ending. AW)18 Nxd5 Nxd5 19 Bxe7 Qxe7 Nxe7 21 Rxd7 (the advantage seems fairly minimal after 21 ... Ng6. AW) **17 ... Rfe8 18. Bg3?** Now White's game is going downhill. This was the last chance to exchange on d5: 18 Bxd5 Nxd5 (18 ... Bxd5! 19 Nxd5 Nxd5 20 Bxe7 Qf4 21 Qd3 N7f6 22 Bxf6 Nxf6. AW) 19 Nxd5 Bxd5 20 Bxe7 Rxe7 21 Rxd5! and White can look forward to a favourable ending. **18 ... Qb6 19. Qf1** It is no longer possible to take on d5, because after 19 Nxd5 Nxd5 20 Bxd5 Bxd5 21 Rxd5 Black has the resource 21 ... Bg5! **19 ... Qb7 20. Nxd5?** A completely erroneous combination after which Black wins material. **20 ... Bxd5 21. Rc7 Qxc7! 22. Bxc7 Bxb3 23. Rc1 Rac8 24. Ba5 Bc4 25. Qd1 Nc5 26. Nd4 Nd3 27. Rb1 Bc5 28. b3 Bxd4 29. bxc4 bxc4** White resigned. **0–1** *Tijdschrift van den Nederlandschen Schaakbond* 1937, 52; Jonasson 33–4.

(337) FINE–STOLTZ, G

Stockholm (7), 1937 (22 Jan.)
Queen's Gambit Declined [D60]

1. d4 d5 2. c4 e6 3. Nf3 Nf6 4. Nc3 Be7 5. Bg5 0-0 6. e3 Nbd7 7. Bd3 a6 8. cxd5 Nxd5 9. Bxe7 Qxe7 10. Nxd5 exd5 11. 0-0 c6 12. Qb1 White plans a rapid advance by b2-b4 and a2-a4, but Black finds a way of solving the problems which arise by transferring his knight to d6. **12 ... g6 13. b4 Nf6 14. a4 Ne4** 14 ... Ne8, after which White cannot play Bxe4!, is more precise since without the support of a knight on d6 the black queenside would become very weak. **15. Qb2 Bd7 16. Rfc1 Nd6!** **17. Qc3 Rfc8 18. Qc5 Rab8 19. Qb6 Qd8** In the ending which now arises the saviour knight on d6 prevents Stoltz from losing the game. **20. Qxd8+ Rxd8 21. Nd2 Rbc8 22. Nb3 Be8 23. f3 f5! 24. Kf2 Bf7 25. Nc5 Rc7 26. Rc3 Re7 27. Bf1 Rde8 28. Racl Kg7 29. h3 h5 30. Rb1 Rc7** Draw agreed. On 31 b5 there would follow 31 ... axb5 32 axb5 Ree7 33 bxc6 bxc6 34 Rb6 Re8!. ½–½ Jonasson, 37.

(338) FINE—LANDAU, S

Stockholm (8), 1937 (23 Jan.)
Queen's Gambit Declined, Slav Defence [D18]

1. d4 d5 2. c4 c6 3. Nf3 Nf6 4. Nc3 This variation was out of fashion for a long time but of late it has been proved fully playable. RF; To make this capture is to "abandon" the centre and allow White to place his centre pawns in their ideal positions at e4 and d4 respectively without difficulty. Ordinarily the centre should never be abandoned without compensation. The compensation here is that White must play 5 a4, leaving a "hole" for a black piece, bishop or knight, at b4. If White omits 5 a4, Black protects the extra pawn by 5 ... b5 and, even if he does not retain it, it can make a threatening queenside pawn advance, incommoding White's queenside pieces as in the 23rd Alekhine–Euwe match game. As long as White's forced 5 a4 is considered adequate compensation for the loss of the centre, so long will this variation continue to be played. *Chess* **4 ... dxc4 5. a4 Bf5 6. e3 e6 7. Bxc4 Bb4** The idea of utilizing this square for the queen's knight (brought there by way of a6) was introduced by Lasker, and experimented with for a while but found inferior owing to White's grip on the centre, for example, 6 ... Na6 7 Bxc4 Nb4 8 0–0 e6 9 Qe2 Be7 10 e4. *Chess* **8. 0–0 0–0** Now 9 Qe2 would allow Levenfish's move 9 ... Ne4, and Black has fully equalized. RF **9. Ne5 Qe7** In the game between Capablanca and Euwe at Nottingham, 1936 there followed 9 ... c5! and after 10 Na2 Ba5 11 dxc5 Qxd1 12 Rxd1 Bc2 Black can be shown to have sufficient compensation for his sacrificed pawn. RF **10. Qe2** If 10 f3 Rd8 11 e4? Rxd4. RF **10 ... c5** Quite playable. On the other hand, if 10 ... Ne4 11 Nxe4 Bxe4 12 f3 White would stand better. *Chess* **11. e4** An attempt to get something out of the position. Otherwise White must continue with 11 dxc5 Qxc5 12 Nf3 after which Black has, if anything, the better position. RF **11 ... Bxc3 12. exf5 Bxd4 13. fxe6 fxe6 14. Nf3 Nc6 15. Ng5** An attempt at attack which is not the best line. White should have contented himself with 15 Qxe6+ Qxe6 16 Bxe6+ Kh8 17 Nxd4 Nxd4 18 Bc4 with the eventual outcome probably a draw. RF **15 ... Ne5!** Very committal but strong. RF **16. Ba2** Here *Chess* and Jonasson have 16 Nxe6 Nxc4 17 Qxc4 Qf7 18 Qa2 Rfe8 19 Nxd4 Qxa2 20 Rxa2 cxd4 with a winning ending for Black. This, however, overlooks 19 Nc7. If instead 18 ... Rfc8 Black looks slightly better, but not necessarily winning. AW **16 ... Kh8!**

A fine move which gives Black the advantage. 16 ... Nd5 would be bad: 17 Qe4 Nf6 18 Qh4 and so on. *Chess* **17. Nxe6 Nfg4!!**

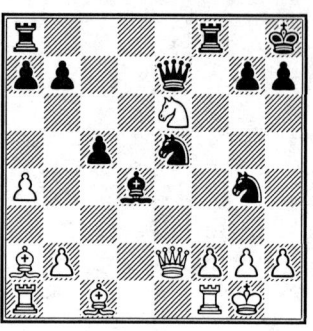

Position after Black's 17th move

18. h3 Ought to have lost the game. The only playable continuation was 18 Nxd4 cxd4 (threatening 19 ... Nf6+) 19 f4 d3 20 Qe1. The offer of the exchange could not be safely accepted 18 Nxf8 Rxf8 19 Be3 Qd6 (19 ... Nxh7 20 Rfe1 is less clear, the threat is now ... Nf3+ again) 20 g3 Nf3+ 21 Kh1 Nfxh2 and Black should win. *Chess* **18 ... Bxf2+ 19. Kh1 Qh4 20. Bf4 Rxf4** Perfectly correct. *Chess* **21. Nxf4 Rf8?** But this is a mistake. Nor would 21 ... Qg3 do, for 22 hxg4 Nxg4 23 Qxg4 Qxg4 24 Rxf2 would leave White with a clear win. But 21 ... Bd4 g3! Qh6 23 h4 (23 Bd5!? seems to hold. AW) Ne3 24 Rf2 (24 Ne6!? is perhaps more stubborn. AW) g5 25 Ng2 gxh4 26 gxh4 N5g4 would have given Black, apparently a winning attack. *Chess* **22. Be6! Rxf4 23. Bxg4** Now it is all over, for 23 ... Nxg4 would allow 24 Qe8 mate. *Chess* **23 ... Ng6 24. Bf3 Bg3 25. Bxb7 Rxf1+ 26. Rxf1 Qxa4 27. Qe6** Black resigned. 1–0 Fine (from *TfS*) in *Chess* 1936–7, 251–2; *De Shaakwereld* 30, 4–5; Jonasson, 39–41.

(339) COLLETT, J—FINE

Stockholm (9), 1937 (24 Jan.)
Queen's Gambit Declined [D30]

When there is an unequal distribution of pawns, without any doubled pawns, both sides either have passed pawns or potential passed pawns. In such cases the potential passed pawn away from the king position confers an advantage. Since most players generally castle on the kingside, this means that the majority of pawns on the queenside is an advantage. It is of course an endgame advantage, that is, one that is best exploited in the endgame. The following game is a model for the use of the pawn majority. **1. d4 Nf6 2. c4 e6 3. Nf3 d5 4. Bg5 Nbd7 5. e3 c6 6. Nbd2 Be7 7. Bd3 0–0 8. 0–0 c5 9. cxd5 exd5 10. Rc1 c4!** With this move Black sets up the queenside majority. Since he has an endgame advantage, the next step is to exchange pieces. White unwisely conforms to Black's plan. **11. Bf5 b5 12. a3 Re8 13. Qc2 g6 14. Bh3 Nb6 15. Bxc8 Rxc8 16. Ne5 Nfd7 17. Bxe7 Qxe7 18. Nxd7 Qxd7 19. Nf3 Qd6 20. h4** White's only chance is an attack. **20 ... a5 21. h5 Nd7** Black must take some steps to safeguard the king. **22. g3 Qe6 23. Kg2** Intending to double on the h-file. **23 ... Qe4 24. Qxe4** The exchange is not favourable, but alternatives are worse. **24 ... dxe4 25. Nd2 Nb6**

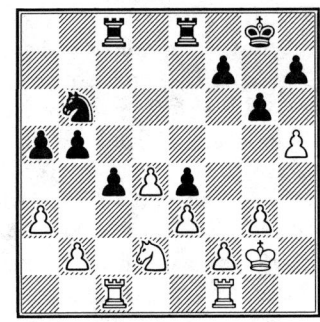

Position after Black's 25th move

Black has reached the favourable ending he was looking for. The next step is to get a passed pawn on the queenside, or to force entry that leads to a passed pawn. **26. hxg6 hxg6 27. Rc2 f5 28. f3** Hoping to get some air. **28 ... Nd5 29. Re1 Kg7 30. fxe4 fxe4 31. a4** Desperation: on other moves the slow methodical advance decides. **31 ... bxa4 32. Rxc4 Rxc4 33. Nxc4 Rc8 34. Na3** If 34 Nxa5 Rc2 forces the passed pawn. **34 ... Kf6 35. Re2 Ke6 36. Kh3 Rh8+ 37. Kg2** Not 37 Kg4 Rh5 and mates. **37 ... Rb8 38. Kh3 Rb3 39. Nc4 a3 40. bxa3 a4** Threatening ... Rc3. **41. Rc2 Nxe3 42. Nxe3 Rxe3 43. Rc6+ Kd5 44. Rxg6 Rxa3**

Position after Black's 44th move

Black has achieved his goal; a passed a-pawn. Now the two passed pawns decide. **45. Kg2 Ra2+ 46. Kf1 a3 47. g4 Rb2** White resigned. **0–1** Fine 1953, 261–3.

Match with Gideon Ståhlberg, Stockholm, January 30–February 7, 1937

Following the tournament in Stockholm Fine played alongside the other competitors from the Jubilee tournament in a Blitz tournament on January 25, which he once again won with 8 points ahead of Lundin on 6½, Ståhlberg on 6 and Stoltz on 5½, and gave exhibitions in Örebro on January 26 and 27. Fine then returned to the capital where an eight game match had been arranged with the number one Swedish player. The match was extremely hard fought, with six of the eight games being decisive and only two

draws, neither of which was perfunctory. If Ståhlberg had not missed a tactic in the fifth game things might have been even more tense. It is noteworthy that Ståhlberg drew a similar match with Keres just over a year later, each player scoring two wins and four draws.

	1	2	3	4	5	6	7	8	
Fine	1	0	1	1	½	½	1	0	5
Ståhlberg	0	1	0	0	½	½	0	1	3

(340) FINE—STÅHLBERG, G

Match, Stockholm (1), 1937 (30 Jan.)
Nimzowitsch-Indian Defence, Classical Variation [E37]

1. d4 Nf6 2. c4 e6 3. Nc3 Bb4 4. Qc2 d5 5. a3 Bxc3+ 6. Qxc3 Ne4 It may be old-fashioned to talk about moving the same piece twice in the opening or about the inadvisability of an attack as a defence to the Queen's Gambit, but it is well to remember that old-fashioned virtues are rather fundamental after all—in any event, after a series of brilliant moves, Black manages to emerge with a poor game—thanks to White's calm, conservative play. **7. Qc2 Nc6 8. Nf3 e5 9. e3 Bf5** You will soon see how White wins bishop for a rook; curiously enough, exactly the same material was won in a game, Horowitz–Dake, which went (instead of 9 ... Bf5) 9 ... exd4 10 cxd5 Qxd5 11 Bc4 Qf5 12 Bd3 Qa5+ 13 b4 Nxb4 14 axb4 Qxa1. **10. Qb3** Alternatively 10 Qa4 0-0 11 cxd5 Qxd5 12 Qb5 Qxb5 13 Bxb5 Na5 14 Ba4 exd4 15 Nxd4 Nc5! with an equal game (MCO 184), or 10 Bd3 exd4 11 0-0 Bg6 12 exd4 0-0 13 b4 Re8 14 c5 a6 15 Bb2 Ng5 again with equality, Lautier-Timman, Moscow Olympiad 1994. AW **10 ... 0–0?** If 10 ... Na5! 11 Qa4+ c6 12 cxd5 Qxd5 13 b4 Qb3 leads to equality, MCO. **11. cxd5 Na5 12. Qa2**

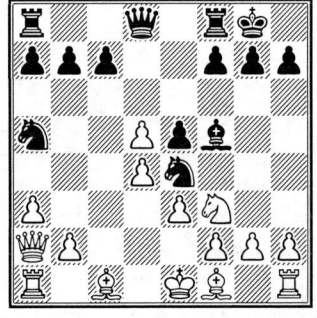

Position after White's 12th move

12 ... c6 Black must pay the penalty for his superficial play. After his loss of material, he remains with the initiative due to the limited scope of the white bishops. Fine strives rather strenuously to bring them into play, but only succeeds after his opponent's attack has petered out. **13. b4 Nc3 14. Qd2** White has a distinct superiority, MCO. **14 ... Nb3** *(see diagram)* **15. Qxc3 Nxa1 16. Qxa1 e4 17. Ng1 cxd5 18. Ne2 Rc8 19. Ng3 Bg6 20. Be2 h5 21. h4 Rc6 22. Bd2 f5 23. Bd1 a6 24. Qa2 Kh7 25. Nxh5 Bxh5 26. Bxh5 Rh6 27. Be2 g5 28. g3 gxh4**

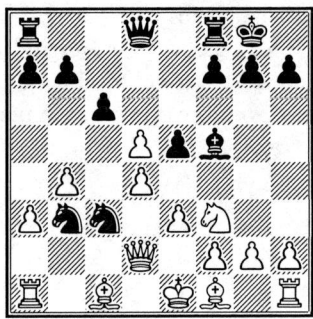

Position after Black's 14th move

29. gxh4 Rg8 30. h5 Rd6 31. a4 Qc7 32. Qb3 Qg7 33. b5 axb5 34. Qxb5 Qc7 35. a5 Rgd8 36. Rg1 Rc6 37. Bd1 Rd7 38. Rg5 Rg7 39. Rxg7+ Qxg7

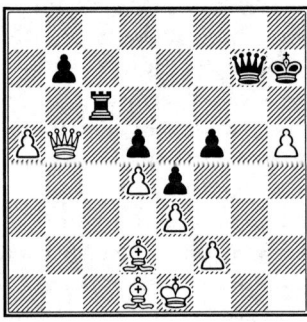

Position after Black's 39th move

40. Be2 Qf7 41. Qa4 Qg8 42. Kd1 f4 43. exf4 Qg1+ 44. Be1 e3 45. Qb4 A good thrust, having an eye to defence and attack—after which Black must acknowledge the inevitable. 45 ... Rc7 46. Bd3+ Kg8 47. fxe3 Qxe3 48. Qd2 Qe8 49. Qg2+ Kh8 50. Qxd5 Re7 51. Bc3 Qc8 52. Qf5 Black resigned. 1–0 A. E. Santasiere in *ACB* 1937, 5.

(341) STÅHLBERG, G—FINE

Match, Stockholm (2), 1937 (31 Jan.)
Queen's Gambit Declined, Slav Defence [D12]

The match between Ståhlberg and Fine, interesting on its own account, became still more interesting when Ståhlberg, following his loss in the first game, won the second. Both games brought valuable contributions to opening theory. ME **1. d4 d5 2. c4 c6 3. Nf3 Nf6** In this position White is on the horns of a dilemma. Is he to play 4 Nc3, allowing Black to accept the gambit quite profitably at once; or is he to adopt the move chosen in this game, which shuts in his own queen's bishop? The move 4 Nc3 has more adherents. Since it has been shown, however, that after 4 ... dxc4 5 a4 Bf5! White has few prospects of obtaining an appreciably better game, the possibilities of 4 e3 are once again being explored. The crucial question is whether Black can reply to it with 4 ... Bf5. The game Landau–Euwe supplied a partial answer in the negative sense, for White discovered a new resource for the attack. Ståhlberg, after following this game for a while, branches off into an even stronger line. Although he seizes the initiative and ultimately wins the game, I cannot

regard this opening problem as satisfactorily solved as yet. ME **4. e3 Bf5** 4 ... e6 5 Nc3 would have led into the Meran Variation, not nowadays considered any too favourable for Black. Up to a short while ago, the text was considered to merit an exclamation mark; but whether it will preserve this distinction for long is a question for the future to decide. It would be going too far to condemn it as doubtful on the evidence of two games. ME **5. cxd5** The only way of making things difficult for Black. If the capture is delayed for as much as one move , it loses all its force, for Black can play 5 ... e6 and recapture with the e-pawn instead of the c-pawn. As the game Lasker–Euwe, Nottingham 1936, showed, Black has then a clear advantage. His queen's bishop is developed, White's not; and if he attempts to bring it out by advancing his e-pawn (the only effective way) then Black plays ... dxe4 leaving him with an isolated pawn. ME **5 ... cxd5** The move 4 ... Bf5 stands or falls by this follow-up. Should 5 ... cxd5 be proved bad, then 4 ... Bf5 must also be condemned. For 5 ... Nxd5 (though played for a long time) is unsatisfactory because of 6 Bc4 followed by 0–0, Qc2 and e4. White must guard (after 5 ... Nxd5) against the temptation of developing his queen's knight in too great a hurry, however, as in the game between Bogolyubov and Tylor at Nottingham. ME **6. Qb3** Attacking the square b7 weakened by the early development of the black queen's bishop. ME **6 ... Qc8 7. Na3** As played by Landau in a game against Dr. Euwe, which resulted in a draw. AS **7 ... e6 8. Bd2 Ne4** Black must try to "rattle" his opponent somehow. The text has in mind 9 ... Nxd2 giving White only the choice between sacrificing the possibility of castling by recapturing with the king or undeveloping his king's knight by recapturing with that. ME **9. Rc1 Nc6 10. Bb5** Atkins writes that "10 Ne5 is not as strong as it looks since Black can play 10 ... Nxd2 11 Kxd2 Bb4+ 12 Kd1 0–0 13 Nxc6 Bxa3 14 Ne7+ Bxe7 15 Rxc8 Rfxc8 and White has a difficult game". If, in place of the check on move fourteen, however, White were to simply retreat by 14 Ne5, he would win a piece. Black should, therefore, prefer 12 ... Bd6 (or perhaps even better 11 ... Bd6), when 13 Ba6! bxa6 14 Rxc6 Qd8 15 Rxa6 0–0, with unclear complications, seems best. AW **10 ... Nxd2 11. Nxd2** The move adopted by Landau, 11 Kxd2, also gives relatively good chances. The text, though it looks quieter, is actually, when considered in connection with the ensuing pawn sacrifice, a more incisive continuation. GS **11 ... Bd6** Probably overlooking White's reply. 11 ... Be7 followed by 12 ... 0–0 is better. HEA **12. e4!** The commencement of a strong attack which Black has to handle with the greatest care. The main idea of the text is to decoy the black d-pawn away from its command of c4, over which White's queen's knight wishes to pass. The ultimate aim is to make things thoroughly uncomfortable for the pinned knight before Black can complete his development. ME **12 ... dxe4** To capture with the bishop would have been more prudent. After 12 ... Bxe4 13 Nxe4 dxe4 14 Nc4 could then come 14 ... Qd8; whilst 14 d5 exd5 15 Qxd5 could be answered by 15 ... Bxa3 which, through the threat of ... Bb4+, gives White no time for combinations against the pinned knight. ME **13. Nac4** The push 13 d5 would only have freed Black's game. Now Black has difficulty in completing his development, for after 12 ... Bc7 13 Qa3 would prevent his castling. GS **13 ... Qd8 14. Nxd6+ Qxd6 15. Nc4 Qf4** By this manoeuvre Black seems to emerge from his worst difficulties. White could certainly recover his pawn by castling at once, exchanging on c6 twice and playing Ne5, but his advantage would then be very slight. GS **16. Qe3** White therefore elects to bring about an endgame in which he is sure to regain his pawn speedily and remain with a pawn majority on the queenside (always a potent factor in an endgame because the opposing king has difficulty in getting over to hinder their advance) and with a knight whose aggressive position is in sharp contrast to that of the black bishop. GS **16 ... Qxe3+ 17. fxe3 Ke7 18. Bxc6 bxc6 19. Na5 Rhc8 20. Rxc6 e5!? 21. Kd2** Fine tries to free his game. After 21 dxe5 Rxc6 22 Nxc6+ Ke6 he would have obtained good counterplay. White finds a much stronger move than 21 dxe5 however, one which finally consolidates his advantage and therefore Fine might well have gone at once for the draw by 20 ... Rxc6 21 Nxc6+ Kd6 22 Na5 Rc8. White's strongest continuation would then be 23 Kd2, for example, 23 ... e5 24 dxe5+ Kxe5 25 Rc1 and, though drawing chances are better than after the text, Black is still in great danger in spite of the reduced material after an exchange of rooks. GS **21 ... Bd7** 21 ... exd4 22 exd4 Rxc6 appears to give a fairly level position. HEA **22. Rc5 Rxc5 23. dxc5 Be6 24. Kc3! Rc8 25. b4! Bxa2 26. Ra1 Bd5 27. Nc4 Rc7 28. Nxe5 f6 29. Nc4 Bxc4 30. Kxc4 Kd8** 30 ... Ke6 is met by b4-b5, c5-c6, Kc4-c5, b5-b6 winning easily. HEA **31. Kd5 f5 32. c6 Kc8 33. b5 Kb8 34. Rf1 Rf7** Forced as, after 34 ... g6 35 g4 fxg4 36 Rf8+ Rc8 37 Rxc8+ Kxc8 38 Kxe4 Kc7 39 Kf4 White would win the pawn ending easily. AS **35. g4 f4** Black has no choice; if 35 ... g6 36 Ke6. HEA **36. exf4 e3 37. f5 h5 38. h3 hxg4 39. hxg4 Kc7** For, after 39 ... e2 40 Re1 Re7 41 Kd4, followed by 42 Kd3, would be decisive. AS **40. Re1 Re7 41. Re2 Kb6 42. g5 Kxb5 43. f6 gxf6 44. gxf6 Rc7 45. Rxe3 a5 46. Re7** Black resigned. 1–0 Euwe and Ståhlberg (from *Tidskrift för Schack*) in *Chess* 1936–7, 242–5; H. E. Atkins in *BCM* 1937, 216–7; Dr. A. Seitz in *ACB* 1937, 5–6.

(342) FINE—STÅHLBERG, G

Match, Stockholm (3), 1937 (2 Feb.)
Queen's Gambit Declined [D62]

1. d4 Nf6 2. c4 e6 3. Nc3 d5 4. Nf3 Be7 5. Bg5 Nbd7 6. e3 0–0 7. Qc2 This continuation of Flohr's has recently come to the fore in place of Rubinstein's 7 Rc1. DS **7 ... c5 8. cxd5 cxd4 9. Nxd4 Nxd5 10. Bxe7 Qxe7 11. Nxd5 exd5** The standard position in this variation. Play against the isolated pawn gives White the initiative, but if Black handles the defence with absolute accuracy it is not enough to win. RF **12. Bd3 Qb4+** So as not to lose a tempo in defending h7. ME; This whole plan is poorly conceived; Black exchanges knights, and is left with the bad bishop. Better is 12 ... Nf6 13 0–0 Be6 14 Rac1 Rac8. RF

13. Qd2 Ne5 The game Flohr–Capablanca, Moscow 1935, continued 13 ... Nc5 14 Bb5!, eventually ending in a draw after 52 moves. AW **14. Be2** Obviously not 14 Qxb4, because of 14 ... Nxd3+ and 15 ... Nxb4. ME **14 ... Qb6** Following the rule that the weakness of an isolated pawn is less serious in the middle game than in an ending. But this rule holds good only in so far as one's extra freedom of movement can be utilized in a kingside attack. In the present game Black will not be able to mount an assault on the king, so that the text must be classed as faulty. After 14 ... Qxd2+ 15 Kxd2, the ending is admittedly in White's favour, but it is very much open to question whether the advantage is sufficient for a win. ME **15. b3 Nc6 16. Rd1** Obviously White is not going to allow his opponent to make the pawn position symmetrical by exchanges on d4. ME **16 ... Be6 17. 0–0 Rac8** Better would have been 17 ... Nxd4. AS **18. Qb2 Nxd4** In order to double rooks on the c-file. ME **19. Rxd4 Rc5 20. Rfd1 Rfc8 21. R4d2 h6 22. Bf3** White has the advantage. His opponent has no compensation for the weakness of his pawn formation. DS **22 ... Qc6 23. h3** In view of an eventual ... Rc1 by Black, a flight square is necessary for the king. ME **23 ... Rc7**

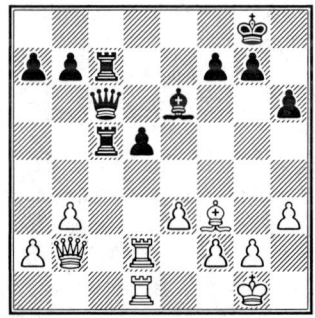

Position after Black's 23rd move

Black is marking time, but it soon appears that the rook is not well placed at c7. It is very difficult, however, to find any freeing manoeuvre. After 23 ... Rc2 24 Qd4 Rxd2 25 Rxd2, the isolated pawn would be indefensible, for 25 ... Rd8 is answered by 26 e4. ME **24. Qe5!** Threatening to win a pawn. In itself that is of no consequence, but Black is forced to weaken his position. RF **24 ... f6 25. Qf4 Rc8** This is where the unfortunate side of 23 ... Rc7 shows itself. White threatened to win a pawn by 26 Bxd5 Bxd5 27 Rxd5 Rxd5 28 Rxd5 Qxd5 29 Qxc7. Black's move parries this threat, but now danger comes from another quarter. ME **26. e4!** Leading to a liquidation which is very much in White's favour. ME **26 ... dxe4 27. Rd6!** The point. If Black now protects the attacked bishop by 27 ... Qe8, White plays 28 Qxe4, with a double attack on the bishop and the b-pawn. ME **27 ... exf3** Hoping for chances of a draw in the endgame, but Black is deceived. ME **28. Rxc6 R5xc6 29. Qxf3 Rc1 30. Rxc1 Rxc1+ 31. Kh2 Rc6 32. Qf4!** White evolves a plan: to weaken the queenside pawns and march his king in. RF **32 ... a6 33. Qb8+ Bc8 34. b4** More correct is 34 a4. RF **34 ... Kh7** Essential was 34 ... b5, when White can no longer break through. RF **35. a4 f5 36. Qe5 Rf6 37. Qc7 Rc6 38. Qe7 Rg6 39. f3**

Rc6 40. b5! a×b5 41. a×b5 Now the black rook will have to abandon the third rank, which initiates a new phase. RF 41 ... Rc4 42. h4 Rc2 43. h5 Rc4 44. Qf7 Rc5 45. Kg3! Rc2 46. Qg6+ Kh8 47. Qe8+ Kh7 48. Kf4 Rc1 49. Qg6+ Kg8 50. Ke5 Bd7 51. Qb6 Bc8 52. Kd6 Kh8 53. Qe3 Black resigned. 1–0 Fine 1958, 107–10; Dr. A. Seitz in *ACB* 1937, 6; *De Shaakwereld* 1937, 34 10–11; Euwe & Kramer 1964, 249–50.

(343) STÅHLBERG, G—FINE

Match, Stockholm (4), 1937 (3 Feb.)
Semi-Slav, Anti-Meran Variation [D43]

1. d4 Nf6 2. c4 e6 3. Nc3 d5 A chorus of groans from ye hypermoderns. 4. Nf3 c6 5. Bg5 5 d×c5 is a good alternative. 5 ... h6 6. B×f6 Q×f6 7. e4 d×e4 8. N×e4 Bb4+ 9. Nc3 0–0 10. Bd3 This move gives Black the initiative. 10 Qc2 and , if 10 ... c5, 11 a3 and so on is preferable. Also 10 c5 is an interesting idea. 10 ... c5 11. 0–0 c×d4 12. Nb5 Nc6 13. Nb×d4 N×d4 14. N×d4 Rd8 15. Nf3 b6 16. Qe2 Bb7 17. Be4 Beginning a sacrificial combination which nets him exactly one pawn for two—almost always equivalent to resignation against a player of Fine's strength. After the alternative of 17 Ne5, while I prefer Black's game, I fail to see any definitely winning continuation. (White's game looks very dicey to me after 17 Ne5 Bd6 18 Ng4 Qf4. AW) 17 ... B×e4 18. Q×e4 Q×b2 19. Rab1 Qa3 20. Rb3 Qa4 21. c5 A good move; it restricts the defensive potentialities of the bishop. 21 ... b×c5 22. Qc4 Santasiere suggested the apparently more aggressive 22 Ne5 instead. The text, however, is likely a little trap, as 22 Ne5 could be answered by 22 ... Q×a2, which would be a mistake after the text in view of 23 R×b4! AW 22 ... Qd7 23. Ne5 Qc7 24. Qe4 Rd5 25. Nd3 There's a lot of humour in this retreat. What's become of the glorious kingside assault for which White yielded two pawns a few moves ago? 25 ... Rc8 26. N×b4 Rd4 27. Qb1 c×b4 28. R×b4 R×b4 29. Q×b4 Qc4 30. Qb7 a6 31. h3 Qc6 32. Qb3 Qc4 33. Qb6 Qe2 34. a4 Rc2 35. Rb1 Qd2 36. g3 a5 37. Qa7 Qd5 38. Qb8+ Kh7 39. Qf4 f6 40. Qe3 Rc4 41. Re1 e5 42. Qb3 Rd4 43. Qc2+ e4 White resigned. Since Black's threat (... Qc4) will leave him little to hope for. In both the first and fourth games Fine won because of unwise aggressiveness on the part of his opponent. Fine's play impresses me as being sound, keen and clever in a psychological sense, but it is only very rarely, if at all, inspired or brilliant, experimental or profound. 0–1 A. E. Santasiere in *ACB* 1937, 7.

(344) FINE—STÅHLBERG, G

Match, Stockholm (5), 1937 (4 Feb.)
Queen's Gambit Declined [D60]

1. Nf3 d5 2.d4 Nf6 3. c4 e6 4. Bg5 Be7 5. e3 Nbd7 6. Nc3 0–0 7. Bd3 d×c4 8. B×c4 c5 9. d×c5

Burgess (NCO 420) gives 9 0–0 a6 10 a4 c×d4 11 e×d4 Nb6 12 Bb3 Bd7 13 Ne5 Bc6 14 Re1 Nfd5 with an equal game. 9 ... N×c5 10. 0–0 a6 11. a4 Nce4 12. N×e4 N×e4 13. B×e7 Q×e7 14. Qd4 Nf6 15. Rfd1 Bd7 16. Ne5? This move is an unobvious error. White's best was probably 16 Bd3. AW 16 ... Bc6? The point is that Black could have played 16 ... B×a4!, since 17 R×a4 would be answered by 17 Rad8! AW 17. Qd6 Q×d6 18. R×d6 Bd5 19. B×d5 N×d5 20. e4 Draw agreed. ½–½ Ironically Santasiere's only comment about this game in *ACB* was "This wasn't a chess game; it was a little (memorized) exercise on how to avoid weakness. At move nine, Fine might have accepted an isolated pawn for a promising initiative—but horrors! an isolated pawn is like the kiss of Judas!—never, never have an isolated pawn!" *ACB* 1937, 7.

(345) STÅHLBERG, G—FINE

Match Stockholm (6), 1937 (5 Feb.)
Queen's Gambit Accepted [D28]

1. d4 d5 2. c4 d×c4 3. Nf3 Nf6 4. e3 e6 5. B×c4 c5 6. 0–0 a6 7. Qe2 Nc6 8. d×c5 Bad; at least wait until the king's bishop has moved; even with the possible isolated pawn, White would have a good game 8 a4 or 8 Rd1 should have been played. 8 ... B×c5 9. a3 b5 10. Bd3 0–0 11. b4 Bd6 12. Bb2 Bb7 13. Nbd2 Qe7 14. Rfd1 Rfd8 15. Ne4 N×e4 16. B×e4 Rac8 17. Rac1 Na7 18. B×b7 Q×b7 19. Nd4 Bf8 20. Qf3 Q×f3 21. g×f3 R×c1 22. R×c1 Rc8 23. R×c8 N×c8 24. Kf1 Nb6 25. Ke2 Nc4 26. Bc1 Bd6 27. f4 Kf8 28. Kd3 Ke8 29. f5 B×h2 30. f×e6 Be5 31. e×f7+ K×f7 32. a4 B×d4 33. K×d4 g5 34. e4 Kg6 35. a×b5 a×b5 36. f4 g×f4 37. B×f4 h5 38. Kc5 Na3 39. Kd6 h4 40. Bh2 Nc2 41. Kc5 Na3 42. Kd6 Nc2 43. Kc5 Na3 44. Kc6 h3 45. Kd6 Nc2 46. Kc5 Na3 47. Bf4 Kf7 48. Kc6 Ke6 49. Bh2 Ke7 Draw agreed. ½–½ Santasiere in *ACB* 1937, 8.

(346) FINE—STÅHLBERG, G

Match Stockholm (7), 1937 (6 Feb.)
King's Indian Defence, Fianchetto Variation [E72]

This game is characteristic of the winner's methods—simple means, both discreet and logical, bring about the collapse of the hostile position with almost elemental force. T&dM 1. d4 Nf6 2. c4 c5 A bold reply. T&dM 3. d5 The only continuation likely to give White any advantage in the opening. T&dM 3 ... e5 The merits of 3 ... b5 or 3 ... e6 were not fully appreciated at the time. AW 4. Nc3 d6 5. e4 g6 Awkward, but after 5 ... Be7 9 g3 0–0 7 Bg2 White has the better chances. T&dM 6. g3 Bg7 7. Bg2 0–0 8. Nge2! Nbd7 9. 0–0 White has treated the opening simply and powerfully, and can already boast of a superiority in territory. T&dM 9 ... Ne8 10. Be3 a6 Black recognizes that the thrust 10 ... f5 would be useless, as after 11 Qd2 this pawn's further progress would be stopped. On the other hand 11 ... fxe4 12 Nxe4 would be in favour of White. That is why Black seeks to get his queen's rook into play. T&dM **11. Qd2 b6 12. Rae1 Ra7 13. f4** A well-prepared advance. T&dM **13 ... exf4** This exchange is assuredly unfavourable. Normally exchanges can only benefit the better-developed side. 13 ... f6 would therefore have been better, followed by a regrouping of forces by ... Nb8 and ... Raf7. T&dM **14. gxf4 f5** Continuing the faulty strategy of expansion, instead of prudently resigning himself to 14 ... f6. T&dM **15. exf5 gxf5**

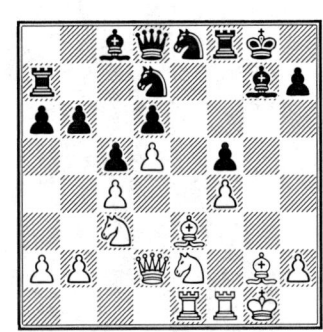

Position after Black's 15th move

16. Ng3 Ndf6 17. Bh3 This unpretentious looking move plays a decisive part in the attack. Black's reply is forced, after which White's troops penetrate victoriously into the enemy camp. T&dM **17 ... Ng4 18. Bxg4 fxg4 19. f5** With the twofold function of opening the way for White's bishop and preventing 19 ... Bf5, which would have tended to consolidate Black's position. T&dM **19 ... Raf7 20. Bg5!** An excellent *Zwischenzug*, since the bishop is really aiming for h6; its object, to force the queen from a good diagonal; if, in answer, 20 ... Bf6, then 21 Nce4, followed, if necessary, by Nh5, must win. AES **20 ... Qc7 21. Bh6!** Kh8 Black might consider returning with the queen: 21 ... Qd8 22 Nce4 Bxf5. AW **22. Nce4! Bxh6** Neither 22 ... Bxf5 23 Ng5, nor 22 ... Nf6 23 Bxg7+ would be of any help. AW **23. Qxh6 Kg8 24. f6 b5 25. Nh5 g3 26. Re3 gxh2+ 27. Kxh2 Kh8 28. Ng5** Black resigned. The most interesting game of the match; Fine was at his best—this may or may not be the reason why Ståhlberg's play seemed futile, haphazard and not deeply thought out. AES **1–0** A. E. Santasiere in *ACB* 1937, 8; Tartakower & du Mont, 565–6.

(347) STÅHLBERG, G—FINE

Match Stockholm (8), 1937 (7 Feb.)
Queen's Gambit Declined [D68]

1. d4 Nf6 2. c4 e6 3. Nc3 d5 Another Queen's Gambit! I have just finished playing the eight games of this match (six Queen's Gambits and two Queen's Pawn) and I was never more bored with any set of eight chess games. Why do they stick to the Queen's Gambit?—not because it is sounder than any other opening or more advantageous for White—certainly not because it is more interesting, but simply because they have thoroughly memorized the first sixteen moves (and all variations leading therefrom) and if the opponent, having

done his lessons well, defends a la mode, then the game starts at move seventeen (clock time having been conserved; also, I suspect, the necessity for thinking), but if there is the slightest slip up in memory and the opponent falls for one of the thousand (and very well known) inferior variations, then he is very promptly gobbled up and the point is scored. They play the Queen's Gambit because they fear the unknown and, therefore, their own judgments on it. Here is the mystery and romance, but they will have nothing of it, for it involves uncertainty and risk and they're the "play safe" boys. My theory of the opening is simply this—that there is no opening, that the middle game begins with move 1—that's the kind of game chess can be and ought to be—a grand struggle, where you stand ready to give and take—knowing no restraint, no fear. AES **4. Bg5 Be7 5. Nf3 Nbd7 6. e3 0–0 7. Rc1 c6 8. Bd3 dxc4 9. Bxc4 Nd5** Fine not only plays the Queen's Gambit almost invariably, but even resorts to a defence, of which Capablanca himself has tired. AES **10. Bxe7 Qxe7 11. 0–0 Nxc3 12. Rxc3 e5 13. Bb3** The usual continuation is 13 dxe5 Nxe5 14 Nxe5 Qxe5 15 f4 Qf6 16 e4 Be6. In this variation, has the following Bogolyubov innovation been refuted? 15 ... Qe4 16 Qe2 Rd8 17 Bd3 Bg4! AES **13 ... e4** 13 ... exd4 14 exd4 Nf6 15 Re1 Qd6 would have been more cautious, for example, 16 h3 Bf5 17 Re5 Be4! GS **14. Nd2 Nf6** Ståhlberg has the move order 14 ... Kh8 15 Qc2 Nf6 with the comment "After 15 ... f5?, comes 16 f3 Nf6 (Why not 16 ... exf3? AW) 17 fxe4 fxe4 18 Rc5! with advantage to White." However, ACB and Fine's notebooks give the order in the text. AW **15. Qc2** Instead 15 Qb1 would make Bc2 and even the attack by b2-b4 possible. AES **15 ... Kh8** Neither good nor necessary; 15 ... Re8, followed by ... Bf5 (overprotection) was the correct plan. AES **16. h3 Be6 17. Bxe6 Qxe6 18. Rb3 Qe7** 18 ... b6 is simpler and better. GS **19. Rc1 Rfe8 20. Qc5!** White is aiming for an ending in which Black's position will be slightly uncomfortable. GS **20 ... a5?** A weakening of Black's pawn formation which makes White's plan all the stronger. GS **21. Ra3! Qxc5 22. dxc5** White has a distinct superiority, MCO 134. **22 ... Nd7 23. Rc4 f5 24. Nb3 Ne5 25. Rca4 Rad8** Black can no longer hold onto the pawn, so he looks for compensation elsewhere. GS **26. Nd4 f4! 27. Rb3! fxe3 28. fxe3 Nd3 29. Rxa5 h6** White can parry 29 ... Rxd4 30 exd4 e3 31 Rxd3 e2 by 32 Re3! GS **30. Ne2 Rd7 31. Rb6 Re5 32. Ra7!** The introduction to a simplifying manoeuvre which breaks Black's resistance. GS **32 ... Rxc5 33. Rbxb7 Rxb7 34. Rxb7 Rc2 35. Nd4 Rd2** White wins easily after 35 ... Rxb2 36 Rxb2 Nxb2 37 Nxc6 Nd1 38 a4. GS **36. a4! c5 37. Ne6 g5 38. a5 Rd1+ 39. Kh2 Ra1 40. Ra7 c4 41. Kg3** Now the white king decides the struggle. GS **41 ... Nxb2 42. Kg4 c3 43. Kh5 Nc4 44. Kxh6 Rxa5 45. Rc7 Nd6 46. g4 Ra6 47. Kxg5 Nb5** Or 47 ... Ne8 48 Re7. GS **48. Rc8+ Kh7 49. Kf6** Black resigned. Ståhlberg played the endgame well. Fine played, on the whole, indifferently. Doubtless he was influenced by the score of the match. But just there is his greatest weakness—the score is almost everything, the game is only a necessary medium. AES **1–0** Ståhlberg, 95–6; Santasiere in *ACB* 1937, 9.

Matches with Eric Jonsson and E. Larsson, Göteborg, February 8–13, 1937

Fine played two other short matches during his stay in Sweden. Jonsson was the Swedish reserve for the team tournament later in the year. According to Koltanowski (*Chess*, 14 February, 1937), Fine was feeling homesick and made a dash back to New York. This seems quite incredible as there would have been little over two weeks from the end of his stay in Sweden to the beginning of his stay in the Soviet Union. Bearing in mind the sailing times in that era it actually looks highly unlikely.

	1	2	3			1	2	3	
Fine	1	1	1	3	Fine	1	1	½	2½
Larsson	0	0	0	0	Jonsson	0	0	½	½

(348) LARSSON, E—FINE

Göteborg (1), 1937 (8 Feb.)
Sicilian Defence, Scheveningen Variation [B84]

1. e4 c5 2. Nf3 d6 3. d4 cxd4 4. Nxd4 Nf6 5. Nc3 e6 6. Be2 Qc7 7. 0-0 a6 8. Be3 b5 9. a3 Bb7 10. Bf3 Nbd7 11. Nb3 Ne5 12. Nd2 Nxf3+ 13. Qxf3 Be7 14. Qg3 0-0 15. Rac1 Rfd8 16. f3 Rac8 17. Ne2 d5 18. e5 Nh5 19. Qh3 d4 20. Nxd4 Rxd4 21. Bxd4 Nf4 22. Qg4 Ne2+ 23. Kh1 g6 24. Nb3 h5 25. Qh3 Nxc1 26. Rxc1 Bg5

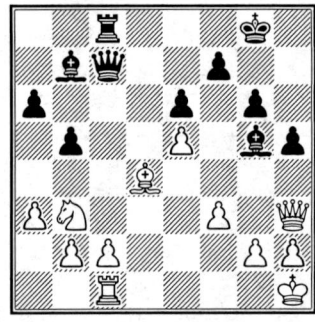

Position after Black's 26th move

27. Rg1 Qxc2 28. Qg3 Be7 29. Na1 Qd3 30. Qf2 Rc4 31. Bb6 Qf5 32. Re1 Bh4 33. g3 Qxf3+ 34. Qxf3 Bxf3+ 35. Kg1 Bg5 36. Be3 Bxe3+ 37. Rxe3 Bd5 38. Kf2 g5 39. Re2 Kg7 40. Nc2 Kg6 41. Ne3 Re4 42. Rc2 Rxe5 43. Rc7 f5 44. Ra7 f4 45. gxf4 gxf4 46. Nxd5 Rxd5 47. Kf3 Kf5 48. Rxa6 e5 49. h4 Rd2 White resigned. **0–1**

(349) FINE—JONSSON, E

Göteborg (2), 1937 (9 Feb.)
Grünfeld Defence, Russian Variation [D96]

1. d4 Nf6 2. c4 g6 3. Nc3 d5 4. Qb3 dxc4 5. Qxc4 Bg7 6. Nf3 c6 7. e4 0-0 8. Be2 b5 9. Qb3 Qa5 10. e5 Be6 11. Qc2 Nd5 12. Bd2 Nxc3 13. Bxc3 b4 14. Bd2 Qb6 15. Bc4 Bg4 16. Qe4 Bxf3 17. gxf3 Nd7 18. h4 c5 19. h5 cxd4

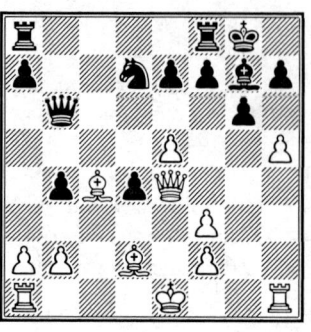

Position after Black's 19th move

20. e6 Ne5 21. exf7+ Nxf7 22. Be6 g5 23. Bxg5 Rad8 24. h6 Rd6 25. Bb3 Bf6 26. Bf4 Kh8 27. Bxf7 Rxf7 28. Bxd6 Black resigned. **1–0**

(350) FINE—LARSSON, E

Göteborg (3), 1937 (10 Feb.)
Queen's Gambit Declined [D61]

Fine is a great specialist in exploiting small positional advantages. The game below, the second of a short match, draws our attention to the manner in which the American Grandmaster transforms a greater freedom of mobility into a winning position. **1. Nf3 e6 2. c4 Nf6 3. d4 d5 4. Nc3** A well-known variation of the Orthodox Queen's Gambit has come about by a transposition of moves. **4 ... Be7 5. Bg5 0-0 6. e3 Nbd7 7. Qc2** Because theory has come to see the position after 7 Rc1 as not so favourable for White, the text has become increasingly popular. **7 ... c6** After 7 ... c5 8 cxd5 Nxd5 9 Bxe7 Qxe7 10 Nxd5 exd5 11 Bd3 g6 12 dxc5 Nxc5 13 0-0 (as in a game Flohr–Vidmar) White will be able to build up pressure against the isolated d-pawn. On the other hand, the text restricts the mobility of the black forces. **8. a3** This move restrains the knight from leaping to e4: 8 ... Nxe4 9 Bxe7 Qxe7 10 Nxe4 dxe4 11 Qxe4 and now Black does not have the reply 11 ... Qb4+. **8 ... b6 9. Rd1!** An extremely strong move, directed against an eventual ... c6-c5. **9 ... Bb7 10. Bd3 dxc4 11. Bxc4 Nd5** With White holding up ... c5 Black attempts to free his game another way. **12. Bf4 Nxc3** 12 ... Nxf4 13 exf4 would provide White with an open e-file and a strong square for the knight on e5. **13. Qxc3 h6** A precautionary measure. **14. 0-0 Re8 15. e4** White has completed his development and has absolute control over the centre. In contrast the position is difficult for his opponent, it will not be easy for him to find suitable posts for his pieces. **15 ... Rc8** Black is greatly handicapped by his cramped position, in particular the queen is uncomfortable on the d-file. The text initiates a new plan: to transfer the Be7 to f8, allowing the queen to vacate the d-file. **16. Rfe1 Bf8 17. Rd3** The preparation for a flank attack. **17 ... Qe7 18. Ne5** Clearing a path for the rook on d3. **18 ... Nxe5 19. Bxe5 f6** Rendering the threat of Rg3 followed by d5 harmless. **20. Bg3 Kh8** The final preparation for ... c6-c5. The immediate 20 ... c5 would be answered by 21 d5, and if 21 ... e5 22 d6+. **21. b4!** White can no longer prevent ... c5, but the text prepares for an advance on the queenside following

Black's pawn break. **21 ... c5** At last! **22. dxc5 bxc5 23. b5** White has a clear advantage by reason of his greater freedom of movement. Now he sets up the creation of a passed pawn on the queenside. **23 ... Red8 24. f3 Rxd3 25. Qxd3 Rd8 26. Qb3 Bc8 27. Rd1!**

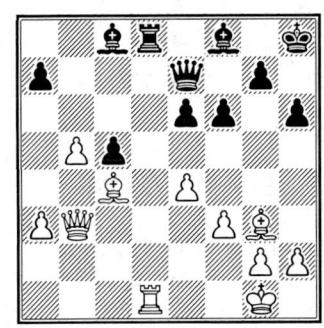

Position after White's 26th move

27 ... Rxd1+ 28. Qxd1 Kg8 29. a4 Mobilizing the pawn majority. **29 ... Kf7 30. a5 Qb7** To hold up the advance b5-b6. **31. Qd3** Preparing his next move. The immediate 31 Bd6 would be answered by 31 ... Qd7. **31 ... Ke8 32. Bd6 Be7 33. e5 f5** Preventing Qg6+. **34. Qa3** Now Black must lose the pawn on c5. **34 ... Bxd6 35. exd6 a6** Hastening the end. **36. Qxc5 axb5 37. a6!** An attractive final move which forces Black's capitulation. Black resigned in view of 37 ... Qa8 38 Bxb5+. **1−0** Based on notes by Dr. Max Euwe in *De Shaakwereld* 1e Jaargang game 37, 4–5.

(351) JONSSON, E—FINE

Göteborg (4), 1937 (11 Feb.)
Double Fianchetto Defence [A47]

1. d4 Nf6 2. Nf3 b6 3. g3 Bb7 4. Bg2 c5 5. 0−0 cxd4 6. Qxd4 g6 7. Bd2 Bg7 8. Bc3 0−0 9. Nbd2 d5 10. Qh4 Nbd7 11. Rad1 Qc7 12. e3 e5 13. g4 Rac8

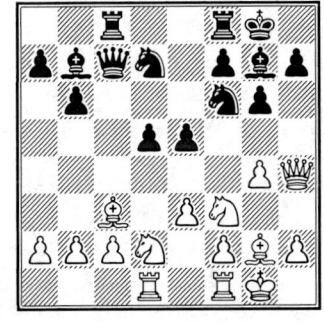

Position after Black's 13th move

14. Bh3 d4 15. exd4 Nd5 16. Bg2 Nf4 17. dxe5 Nxg2 18. Kxg2 Nxe5 19. Rfe1 Nxf3 20. Nxf3 Bxc3 21. bxc3 Qxc3 22. Re3 Qxc2 23. Rd7 Qc6 24. Rde7 Rc7 25. Rxc7 Qxc7 26. Qf6 Qc6 27. Qf4 Re8 28. Rxe8+ Qxe8 29. Kg3 Qc6 30. Ne5 Qg2+ 31. Kh4 f6 32. Nxg6 hxg6 33. Qxf6 Qxh2+ 34. Kg5 Qc7 35. f4 Qg7 36. Qd8+ Kh7 37. Qd6 Qh6+ 38. Kf6 g5+ White resigned. **0−1**

(352) LARSSON, E—FINE

Göteborg (5), 1937 (12 Feb.)
Sicilian Scheveningen [B85]

1. e4 c5 2. Nf3 Nf6 3. Nc3 d6 4. d4 cxd4 5. Nxd4 e6 6. Be2 a6 7. a4 Qc7 8. 0−0 b6 9. f4 Bb7 10. Bf3 Be7 11. Kh1 0−0 12. Be3 Nc6 13. Nb3 Nd7 14. Ne2 Nc5 15. Nxc5 dxc5 16. Qe1 Nb4 17. Rc1 Rad8 18. Qg3 Rd7 19. Qh3 f5 20. Ng3 g6 21. Be2 Kg7

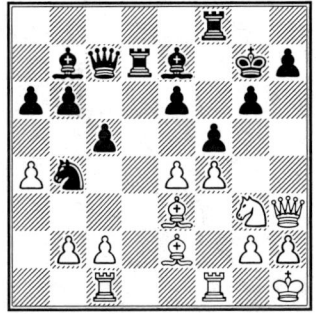

Position after Black's 21st move

22. Rf3 fxe4 23. Nh5+ gxh5 24. Rg3+ Kh8 25. Bxh5 Nd5 26. Bg6 Bf6 27. Qh6 Qd8 28. Re1 Nxe3 29. Rgxe3 Kg8 30. Rg3 hxg6 31. Rxg6+ Bg7 32. h4 Rf6 33. Qg5 Rxg6 34. Qxg6 Qxh4+ White resigned. **0−1**

(353) FINE—JONSSON, E

Göteborg (6), 1937 (13 Feb.)
Queen's Gambit Declined, Semi-Slav Defence [D46]

1. Nf3 Nf6 2. d4 e6 3. c4 d5 4. Nc3 c6 5. e3 Nbd7 6. Bd3 Be7 7. 0−0 0−0 8. b3 Re8 9. Bb2 b6 10. Qe2 Bb7 11. Rfd1 Qc7 12. e4 dxe4 13. Bxe4 c5 14. dxc5 Nxe4 15. Nxe4 Bxe4 16. Qxe4 Nxc5 17. Qg4 Bf8 18. Nd4 Rad8 19. Qf3 Qe5 20. Re1 Qg5 21. Rad1 e5 22. Nc6 e4 23. Qe3 Rxd1 24. Rxd1 Qg4 25. Rd5 Nd3 26. h3 Qc8 27. Nxa7 Qa8 28. Bc3 Bc5 29. Qg5 f6 30. Qf5 Nxf2 31. b4 Nd1+ 32. bxc5 Nxc3 33. Rd7 Ne2+ 34. Kf2 e3+ 35. Kxe2 Qxg2+ 36. Ke1 Qg1+ ½−½ (Presumably Black thought the best he could do was to give perpetual check. However he missed a chance to cover himself in glory: 37 Ke2 (37 Qf1 Qg3+ 38 Kd1 e2+) Qh2+! 38 Ke1 e2! and wins. AW) Gamescore supplied by Peter Lahde from Fine's notebooks.

A Trip to Soviet Russia, 1937

During the 1930s Soviet chess organizers were keen to test the development of their players against western talent. This led to their arranging several tournaments, most notably the great Moscow tournaments of the mid–1930s, with the express aim of pitting the up-and-coming masters of Soviet chess against foreign masters. Players such as Lasker, Capablanca, Euwe, Flohr, Spielmann, Lilienthal and Pirc all tested this emerging force of world chess. Much of the strength of Soviet chess was still based in the traditional centres, Moscow and Leningrad, though there was a significant number of notable practitioners in Ukraine too. Fine was invited to compete in short tournaments in both of the major cities during March of 1937. Although Reuben ultimately showed his superiority over the Soviet masters, there was considerable evidence of the strength of this developing chess power.

Moscow, March 7–16, 1937

	1	2	3	4	5	6	7	8	
1 Fine	*	1	½	1	½	0	1	1	5
2 Kan	0	*	½	½	1	1	1	½	4½
3 Panov	½	½	*	½	1	½	½	½	4
4 Belavenyets	0	½	½	*	0	1	1	½	3½
5= Alatortsev	½	0	0	1	*	0	1	½	3
5= Yudovich	1	0	½	0	1	*	0	½	3
7= Bondarevsky	0	0	½	0	0	1	*	1	2½
7= Lilienthal	0	½	½	½	½	½	0	*	2½

"In March of 1937 I was invited to visit Russia, as an official guest of the Soviet Union. I played in two tournaments, one in Moscow and one in Leningrad, in which the strongest Soviet players of the day, except Botvinnik, participated. Botvinnik acted as a reporter for the Leningrad tournament; he continually complained that my play was very bad, which convinced me that he looked upon me as a dangerous opponent." (Fine 1958, 111)

Fine started well in the Moscow tournament, winning four games on the trot. He was held to a draw in the fifth round by Panov. In the sixth round he was caught in some opening preparation by Yudovich and had a lost game by move eight (Ed Tassinari pointed out, in Winter's *Chess Notes* 966, that Chernev had noted in 1951 that Fine reversed the colours in MCO, 6. It seems to have escaped the notice of Chernev, Tassinari and Winter that this error had already been corrected by Fine in 1948 in *PCO*). In the final round a tough struggle with Alatortsev ended in a draw in mutual time-trouble. In spite of his loss Fine still won the tournament comfortably. The up-and-coming player Bondarevsky was apparently a replacement for the Ukrainian former U.S.S.R. Champion Fedor Bohatirchuk, whose participation in the tournament had been announced in the journal *64*. The time control was set at 32 moves in 2 hours followed by 16 moves an hour thereafter, hours of play to be 5.30 until 11.30 in the evening, except on 12 March when play was from 12 noon to 6 o'clock in the evening. The first adjournment session, when Fine presumably finished his first round adjourned game with Belavenyets, took place on 11 March, no hours of play indicated. The tournament was to be held in the "House of Teachers" on Putechny Street. The tournament committee comprised Zubarev, Golts, Lisitsyn and Snegiryov.

(354) FINE—BELAVENYETS, S

Moscow (1), 1937 (7 March)
Queen's Gambit Declined [D66]

1. d4 Nf6 2. c4 e6 3. Nc3 d5 4. Nf3 Be7 5. Bg5 0–0 6. e3 h6 7. Bh4 Nbd7 8. Rc1 c6 9. Bd3 dxc4 10. Bxc4 b5 11. Bd3 a6 12. a4! bxa4 The best reply. If, instead 12 ... b4 13 Ne4 Nxe4 14 Bxe7 Nxf2! 15 Bxd8 Nxd1 16 Kxd1 Rxd8 17 Rxc6 and White should win the endgame. RF **13. Nxa4 Qa5+ 14. Nd2 Bb4 15. Nc3 c5** At least he has been able to move the c-pawn—but at a price in development. RF **16. Nc4** In *NCO*, Burgess gives 16 Nb3 Qd8 17 0–0 cxd4 18 Nxd4 Bb7 19 Be4 with a slight advantage to White. **16 ... Qc7** If instead 16 ... Qd8 17 Qf3 Rb8 18 0–0 Bb7 19 Qh3 with a strong attack. RF **17. Bg3 Qb7 18. 0–0 cxd4 19. exd4 Rd8**

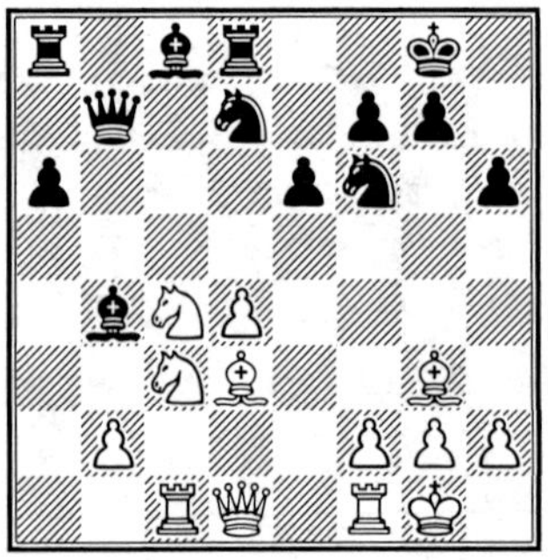

Position after Black's 19th move

The position has cleared somewhat. White has an isolated pawn, but Black's position is out of alignment. RF **20. Na4 Nd5 21. Be4** White stands slightly better, MCO 135. **21 ... N7f6 22. Bf3 Bd7 23. Nc5 Qa7 24. Nd6 Bb5** Creates a target, at the price of some freedom. RF **25. Nxb5 axb5 26. Qd3 Qb6 27. Be2! Ne7 28. Rfd1 Nc6 29. Nb3 e5?** I have often had occasion to observe that the Russian players, though brilliant on the attack, are poor in defence. Much more resistance could have been put up with 29 ... Ra2! for if then 30 Qxb5 Qxb5 31 Bxb5 Rxb2 with sufficient counterplay. After 29 ... Ra2 30 Bf3 Nd5 White still has lots of pressure but no clear cut win. RF **30. Qxb5 Qxb5 31. Bxb5 Nxd4 32. Nxd4 Rxd4** If instead, 32 ... exd4 the pawn can be won in a variety of ways, for example, 33 Bc7, or 33 Rc4. Mate is prevented by the possibility of Bf1. RF **33. Bxe5 Rxd1+ 34. Rxd1 Ra5 35. Rd8+ Bf8 36. Bd6 Rxb5 37. Bxf8 Kh7 38. Ba3 Nd5 39. Kf1 Kg6 40. g3 Nb4 41. Rc8 Nd3 42. Rc2 Re5 43. Rd2 Re1+ 44. Kg2 Ne5 45. Bb4 f6 46. Bc3 Rb1 47. Rd4 Kf5 48. h3** *(see diagram)* **48 ... g5** Hastening defeat. But on the more stolid 48 ... Kg6 49 f4 Nf7 50 Rd7 is decisive. RF (The quoted hours of play indicate that this must have been the last move before adjournment. AW) **49. Rd6 h5 50. f4! gxf4 51. gxf4**

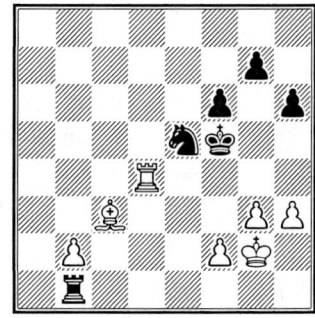

Position after White's 48th move

Nc4 52. Rxf6+ Ke4 53. Kg3 Rg1+ 54. Kh4 Rg2 55. Kxh5 Nxb2 56. Bxb2 Rxb2 57. h4 Kf3 58. Kg5 Rg2+ 59. Kf5! Rh2 60. Ra6! Ke3 61. Ke5 Kf3 62. f5 Kg4 63. Kf6 Kxh4 64. Kg7 Black resigned. 1–0 Fine 1958, 111–6.

(355) KAN, I—FINE

Moscow (2), 1937 (9 March)
King's Fianchetto Opening [D02]

1. Nf3 d5 2. g3 c5 3. Bg2 Nc6 4. d4 Bf5 5. 0–0 e6 6. c3 Nf6 7. Nbd2 h6 8. a3 a5 9. Qb3 Qc7 10. dxc5 Bxc5 11. Qb5 Ba7 12. c4 Rd8 13. c5 e5 14. b4

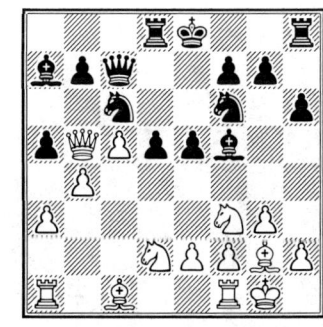

Position after White's 14th move

14 ... Bd7 15. bxa5 e4 16. Ne1 Nxa5 17. Qb1 Bxc5 18. Nb3 Nxb3 19. Qxb3 Bc6 20. Nc2 0–0 21. Bb2 d4 22. Nb4 Bb5 23. Rfe1 Qb6 24. Bf1 d3 25. e3 Rfe8 26. Rab1 Qe6 27. Qxe6 Rxe6 28. Bxf6 Rxf6 29. Nd5 Rxd5 30. Rxb5 Bxe3 31. Rxd5 Bxf2+ 32. Kg2 Bxe1 33. Rd4 Rf2+ 34. Kg1 d2 White resigned. 0–1

(356) FINE—BONDAREVSKY, I

Moscow (3), 1937 (10 March)
Dutch Defence [A90]

1. d4 e6 2. Nf3 f5 3. g3 Nf6 4. Bg2 d5 5. 0–0 Bd6 6. c4 c6 7. b3 0–0 8. Bb2 On other occasions I have also been successful with Ba3. I felt, however, that he would try too hard for the attack. 8 ... Nbd7 9. Nbd2 Qe8 10. Ne5 Qh5 11. e3! Certain that he would not exchange, although 11 ... Qxd1 leaves White with an advantage in any case. 11 ... Qh6 In similar positions Botvinnik

has generally retreated ... Qe8, with a complicated position. 12. Qe2 Ne4? A fatal mistake, which gives White the chance to open up the position. Best is probably 12 ... Bc7 and if 13 f3 Nxe5 14 dxe5 Nd7 with counterplay. 13. Nxe4! fxe4

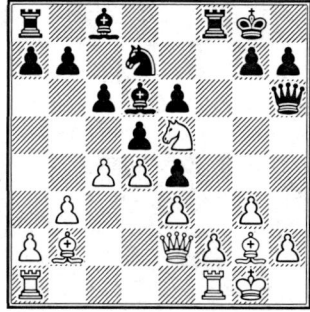

Position after Black's 13th move

14. Ng4! Qg5 15. f3! The last three moves have opened up so many lines for White that Black is already lost. 15 ... exf3 16. Bxf3 h5 Another characteristic error: at least he should have developed with ... Nf6 and ... Bd7. 17. Nf2 h4 18. Nh3 Qd8 Black is faced with a choice of evils. If 18 ... Qh6 19 g4 b6 20 e4 with continued pressure.

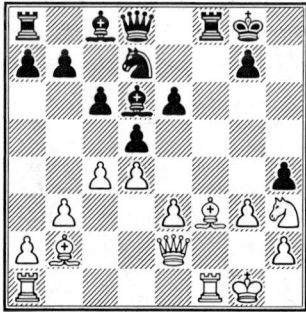

Position after Black's 18th move

19. e4! dxe4 20. Qxe4 e5 Hoping for 21 dxe5? Nxe5! 22 Bxe5 Bxe5 23 Qxe5 Bxh3 with equality. 21. Bg2! hxg3 The alternative 21 ... exd4 is refuted by 22 Qe6+, while if 21 ... Nf6 22 Qxh4 exd4 23 Ng5 wins. 22. dxe5 gxh2+ 23. Kh1 Be7 24. Qg6 Rxf1+ 25. Rxf1 Nf8 26. Qf7+ Kh8 27. e6 Nxe6 28. Be4 Black resigned. 1–0 Fine 1958, 117–20.

(357) FINE—LILIENTHAL, A

Moscow (4), 1937 (12 March)
Grünfeld Defence, Russian Variation [D95]

A purely positional game in which, each move is the result of deep and exact calculation. The finish after 30 Rd3, in which White, in spite of being a pawn down, seeks liquidation—relying on the paralysis of the opposing queenside—is a revelation. T&dM 1. d4 Nf6 2. c4 g6 3. Nc3 d5 4. Qb3 A Russian idea; its chief merit is that it is fashionable, as its main idea, pressure against the point d5, can be met satisfactorily. T&dM 4 ... c6 A passive reply. A far more independent treatment is 4 ... dxc4 5 Qxc4 Be6

6 Qd3 (if 6 Qb5+ Nc6 7 Nf3 Nd5 not without danger for White) Nc6 7 Nf3 a6 8 e4 Nb4 9 Qd1 Bg4 and Black contests the initiative. T&dM **5. Nf3** Instead of playing impulsively 5 Bg5 or 5 cxd5 cxd5 6 Bg5, White speeds up his kingside development. T&dM **5 ... Bg7 6. e3 0–0 7. Bd2** Fight for the tempo (7 Bd3 dxc4 8 Bxc4). Again, if 7 cxd5 cxd5 8 Bd3 Nc6 Black's development becomes easier, and his queen's knight is better placed at c6 than d7. T&dM **7 ... e6?** The only alternative worth considering is 7 ... dxc4 8 Bxc4 Nbd7 9 0–0 Nb6 10 Bd3 Be6 11 Qc2 Bc4, likewise leaving White with a slight advantage. RF **8. Bd3 Nbd7 9. 0–0 Nb6** An artificial idea. If—a. 9 ... Re8 10 Rfd1 Qe7 11 Rac1, and the white forces are better placed; b. 9 ... dxc4 10 Bxd4 b5 11 Be2 a6, in order to effect the freeing advance ... c6-c5; c. 9 ... b6 (Fine–Mikenas, Kemeri 1937), followed by ... Bb7, deferring any trenchant decision. T&dM **10. Rfd1!** A reply both deep and unexpected. White allows his king's bishop to be exchanged for a knight, because he foresees his increasing mastery of the centre. T&dM **10 ... dxc4 11. Bxc4 Nxc4 12. Qxc4 Nd7** In order to play ... e5. RF **13. e4 Qc7** But now Black satisfies himself that 13 ... e5 would not be good because of 14 Bg5 and if 14 ... Qc7 15 Nd5 Qb8 16 Ne7+ Kh8 17 Nxc8 Qxc8 18 Be7 winning a pawn. Or if 14 ... Qb6 (14 ... Qa5 15 b4 Qb6) 15 d5 with complications advantageous for White. Thus Black's whole opening strategy has been discredited. RF **14. e5!** With a lasting pressure and, incidentally, providing a powerful support for a knight at d6 or f6. T&dM; Preventing the intended ... e5 or ... c5, for instance 14 ... c5 15 Bg5 b6 16 Be7 Re8 17 Bd6 Qc6 18 d5 exd5 19 Nxd5. RF (What did Fine intend after 19 ... Nxe5?) **14 ... Nb6** Or else (after 14 ... b6) 15 Nb5 followed by Nd6. T&dM **15. Qe2 f5** Eliminating an adverse strong point, but at the cost of a serious weakness. More steady would be 15 ... Bd7, followed by ... Rad8. T&dM; A nervous move. 15 ... Nd5 would have been more solid. RF **16. exf6 Rxf6 17. Ne4**

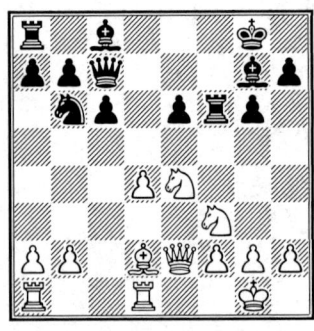

Position after
White's 17th move

17 ... Rf5 More exact would be 17 ... Rf8 18 Bb4 Rd8. T&dM **18. Bb4! Rd5 19. Ne5!** Very astute. Black begins to lack breathing space. T&dM **19 ... Rd8** For if 19 ... Bd7 20 Nc3 winning the exchange. On the other hand, after 19 ... Bxe5 20 dxe5, neither 20 ... Rxe5 21 Bd6, nor 20 ... Qxe5 21 Bc3 is playable. T&dM **20. Rac1 Nd5 21. Ba3 Ne7** If 21 ... Bd7 22 Bd6, and if 21 ... Bxe5 22 dxe5 Qxe5 23 Be7 with the double threat 24 Bxd8 or 24 Nf6+. T&dM **22. Qf3 Nd5** After 22 ... Rf8 23 Qh3, there are many

threats such as 24 Bd6 or 24 Ng5. More enterprising would be 22 ... Nf5 (According to Fine this is a mistake which would be punished by 23 g4!). T&dM **23. Qg3 Bh6** 23 ... Bf8 at once offered better chances. RF **24. Rc2 Bf8** The weakness of d6 still prevents him from getting his queen's bishop into play. Black's game generally suffers from weakness on the dark squares. T&dM; If 24 ... Bf4, then simply 25 Nf6+ with a decisive attack. RF **25. h4! Bxa3 26. Qxa3 Rf8** He must fortify his kingside. If 26 ... Bd7 27 h5. T&dM **27. h5**

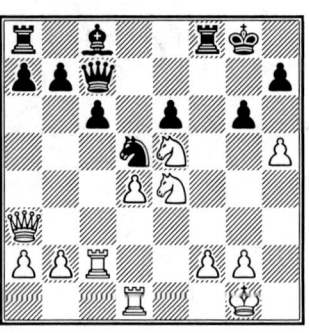

Position after
White's 27th move

27 ... Rf4 If 27 ... gxh5 28 Rd3 with a quick win. RF **28. Re2 gxh5 29. Qg3+ Qg7 30. Rd3!** A curious position, in which White can afford to exchange queens when a pawn down. T&dM **30 ... h4 31. Qxg7+ Kxg7**

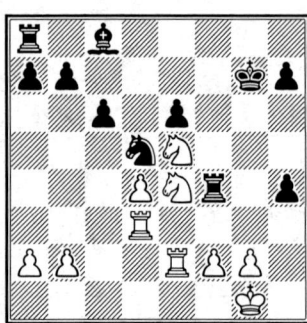

Position after
Black's 31st move

32. g3! hxg3 33. Rxg3+ Kf8 34. f3! The second rook is called into play. T&dM **34 ... Nf6** There is nothing to be done. If 34 ... Ne7 35 Reg2 followed by Rg7. RF **35. Rh2 Rxe4** A despairing sacrifice. If 35 ... Nxe4 36 fxe4 Rxe4 37 Rxh7 Rxd4 38 Rgg7 forcing a speedy mate. T&dM **36. fxe4 Nxe4 37. Rg4 Nf6** Losing a piece. But after 37 ... Nd6 38 Rxh7, there is no hope for Black. T&dM **38. Rf2** Black resigned. Triumph of the positional combination. T&dM; Alekhine was staying in Nice when this game was played. When he was shown it he exclaimed "That is the game of a true Grandmaster." K&R **1–0** Fine 1958, 121–5; Tartakower & du Mont 1952, 583–4; Kahn & Renaud, 61–2; Fine in *The Chess Review* 1938, 76.

(358) PANOV, V—FINE

Moscow (5), 1937 (13 March)
French Defence, Chatard-Alekhine Attack [C13]

1. e4 e6 2. d4 d5 3. Nc3 Nf6 4. Bg5 Be7 5. e5 Nfd7 6. h4 c5 7. Bxe7 Kxe7 8. f4 Nc6 9. Nf3 cxd4 10. Nxd4 Qb6 11. Nb3 a5 12. a4 Qb4 13. Qd2 Nb6 14. Nb5 Nxa4 15. Qxb4+ axb4 16. Nc7 Ra7 17. Nb5 Ra8 18. Nc7 Draw agreed. ½–½

(359) FINE—YUDOVICH, M

Moscow (6), 1937 (14 March)
Queen's Gambit Declined [D40]

1. d4 d5 2. c4 e6 3. Nc3 Nf6 4. Nf3 4 Bg5 is more energetic but Fine always plays this, keeping the option of 5 e3 if suitable, developing the bishop perhaps at b2. MY **4 ... c5** Against this defence White's usual plan is to isolate the black d-pawn by an immediate cxd5 and a subsequent dxc5, and concentrate his attack on it. *Chess* **5. Bg5** A favourite variation of Fine's. MY **5 ... cxd4 6. Nxd4 e5** The first, fourth and sixth moves were played by Mikhail Yudovich Sr. after several minutes' thought, or after pretended hesitation. He wished to create a certain psychological impression on his opponent. JP&MS **7. Ndb5?!** So far it had been held that 7 ... d4 8 Nd5 Nxd5 9 Bxd8 Bb4+ 10 Nc3 dxc3 gives Black a good game. Fine had already played this position (against Winter, Hastings 1936-7), and strengthened the variation: 10 Qd2 Bxd2† 11 Kxd2 Kxd8 12 cxd5 b6 13 g3!. Now on the basis of his opponent's longer deliberations, he believed that Yudovich did not know the improvement. JP&MS **7 ... a6!! 8. Nxd5??** One must assume that the psychological ploy worked and that Fine did not give this move much thought. In the post-mortem, former World Champion Emanuel Lasker suggested 8 Qa4! Bd7 9 e4! (Fine's 9 cxd5 Qb6 10 Bxf6 gxf6 11 e4 Ra7, from MCO 6, 150, may also be worth a try, for example 12 Qb3 axb5 13 Bxb5 and either 13 ... Rg8 14 0-0 Bc5 15 Bxd7+ Nxd7 16 Qc2 Bd4, or 13 ... Bxb5 14 Nxb5 Ra5 15 a4 Na6 16 0-0 Bc5 17 Qf3 leave Black with work to do) dxc4 10 Bxc4 axb5 11 Bxf7+ Kxf7 12 Qxa8 Bc6 13 0-0 Qc7 14 Qa7 Nbd7 and White has a rook and pawn for two pieces. Przewoznik and Soszynski propose the alternative 8 Na3! d4 9 Nd5 (9 Bxf6!? AW) Nxd5 10 Bxd8 Bb4+ 11 Qd2 Bxd2+ 12 Kxd2 Nb4!. AW **8 ... axb5 9. Nxf6+** Expecting 9 ... gxf6 10 Qxd8+ Kxd8 11 Bxf6+. According to an article on the internet, the story of this game and the innovation is recounted in a Soviet chess book, where the author of the novelty is identified as Ragozin. He apparently showed the idea to Yudovich with the intention to use it against Fine, who had otherwise scored very well against the Soviet players, much to Krylenko's annoyance. AW **9 ... Qxf6!!** Black's ninth move reappeared in Shakarova–Zankovich, Simferopol 1989. JP&MS **10. Bxf6 Bb4+ 11. Qd2 Bxd2+ 12. Kxd2 gxf6 13. cxb5** White has just two pawns for a piece and his only chance, creating a passed pawn on the queenside, proves insufficient to trouble Black. Yudovich cannot have had any time problems since the variation had been prepared in advance, not found over the board. Perhaps Fine thought his opponent would slip up, or perhaps he simply could not bear to resign so early and played on through inertia. AW **13 ... Be6**

14. a3 Ke7 15. e4 Rd8+ 16. Ke3 Nd7 17. Be2 Nb6 18. Rhc1 Rac8 19. Rxc8 Rxc8 20. a4 Nc4+ 21. Bxc4 Rxc4 22. a5 Rb4 23. a6 bxa6 24. bxa6 Rb3+ 25. Kd2 Rxb2+ 26. Kc3 Rb3+ 27. Kc2 Rb8 28. a7 Ra8 29. Kc3 Kd6 30. Kb4 Kc6 31. g3 Kb6 32. f4 exf4 33. gxf4 f5 34. exf5 Bxf5 35. Ra5 Bg6 36. h4 Rxa7 37. Rxa7 Kxa7 38. Kc5 Kb7 39. Kd6 Kb6 40. Ke5 Kc5 41. Kf6 Kd5 42. f5 Bh5 43. Kg5 Ke5 White resigned. 0–1 Yudovich (from 64) in *Chess* 1936-7, 294-5; Przewoznik & Soszynski, 64; *64* 1937, No 15.

(360) ALATORTSEV, V—FINE

Moscow (7), 1937 (16 March)
Tarrasch Defence, Rubinstein Variation (MCO 6, 151); Catalan Variation (Linder & Linder)[D34]

1. Nf3 d5 2. g3 c5 3. Bg2 Nc6 4. d4 Nf6 In the game with Kan I played 4 ... Bf5, but after 5 0-0 e6 White can reach an attacking position with good prospects by 6 c4!. **5. 0-0 e6 6. c4!** A very good move. On 6 c3 Qb6 White is playing a Grünfeld Defence with a move in hand, but in spite of this he cannot hope for any advantage. **6 ... Be7** Taking the game into the Schlechter–Rubinstein System of the Tarrasch Defence, which is considered to be advantageous for White. 6 ... dxc4, and on 7 Qa4 cxd4 8 Nxd4 Qxd4 9 Bxc6+ Bd7 10 Rd1 Bxc6 11 Qxc6+ bxc6 12 Rxd4 Rd8, is undoubtedly more reliable. **7. cxd5 exd5 8. Nc3 0-0 9. dxc5 d4** A risky gambit variation, which does however give Black reasonable chances. **10. Na4 Bf5 11. Bf4!** With the intention to play Ne5. This move is stronger than the usual 11 Nh4, on which Black gets the better game by 11 ... Bg4! 12 a3 Nd5 13 Qb3 Be6, Fine–Vidmar, Hastings 1936/7. **11 ... Ne4** In order to answer 12 Ne5 with ... Bf6. **12. b4!** Again a very strong move. Black must take the pawn, for b5 is threatened. **12 ... Nxb4 13. Nxd4** 13 Qxd4, so as to answer 13 ... Qa5 with Qe5! and the game turns in White's favour, or after 13 ... Qxd4 to play 14 Nxd4 Bg6 15 Rfb1, was more advantageous. **13 ... Bg6 14. Rb1 a5** In the event of 14 ... Nc6 15 Nxc6 bxc6 16 Rb7 Black's position is practically hopeless. **15. Rb2** By 15 a3 Nxc5 (or 15 ... Nc6 16 Nxc6 bxc6 17 Rb7, PCO) 16 Nxc5 Bxc5 (16 ... Bxb1 17 Nxb7) 17 Nb3 Na6 (17 ... Bxb1 18 Qxb1) 18 Bxb7 Bxb1 19 Qxb1 Bxa3 20 Bxa8 Qxa8 21 Nxa5, true White would win a pawn, but he would be faced with greater technical difficulties. **15 ... Qe8** Here both partners found themselves in terrible time trouble until the final move of the game. **16. a3 Nd5**

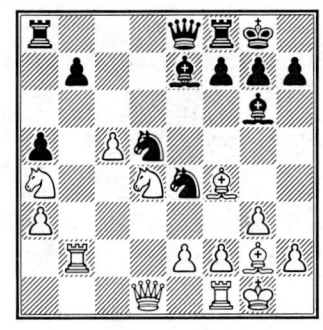

Position after Black's 16th move

17. Bc1 (By excellent play White has achieved a won position. Only the great time trouble can explain why he played 17 Bc1?. After 17 Rb7 with the threat to advance the c-pawn and promote to a queen his opponent could not have found a satisfactory defence. This was forced, as Fine also realized. Linder & Linder) 17 Rxb7 Rd8 18 Bxe4 (18 c6! AW) offered greater chances, but then Black would have a lasting, dangerous and unpleasant attack, especially under pressure of time. This was however undoubtedly better, since after the text Black gains the upper hand. **17 ... Rd8 18. e3 Nxc5** The game is equal, MCO. **19. Nxc5 Bxc5 20. Rxb7 Nc3 21. Qd2 Bxd4 22. exd4 Ne2+ 23. Kh1 Be4 24. Ra7 Nxd4** Now Black obviously stands better. **25. Qe1** On 25 Qxa5 there would follow 25 ... Qc6. **25 ... Bxg2+ 26. Kxg2 Qc6+ 27. f3 Rfe8 28. Re7 Rxe7 29. Qxe7 Re8 30. Qg5 h6** By 30 ... f6 or even 30 ... Re2+ 31 Kh3 f6 Black could quite likely even win, however, in view of the strong mutual time-trouble the opponents agreed to a draw. ½–½ (All the same the columnists took note: Fine had reached an objectively lost position and should have been vanquished. Ilya Kan, for example, wrote "Master V. Alatortsev completely outplayed the Grandmaster but, only in conditions of mutual time-trouble with the guest, failed to win.") Linder & Linder, 281–3.

Leningrad, March 19–25, 1937

Fine had a relatively easy time in Leningrad, winning thrice and drawing twice. In the final round, however, he got into a bad position against Alexander Budo, but the Soviet player was unable to crown his attack and he was eventually worn down by Fine's excellent technical play. Among Fine's victims was Grigory Levenfish who won the 9th and 10th Soviet Championships (1934/5 and 1937), and who was to draw a match with Botvinnik later that year, and hence retain his national title and add to it the Soviet Grandmaster title.

		1	2	3	4	5	6	
1	Fine	*	1	½	½	1	1	4
2	Levenfish	0	*	1	½	1	½	3
3	Rabinovich	½	0	*	½	½	1	2½
4=	Rauzer	½	½	½	*	0	½	2
4=	Budo	0	0	½	1	*	½	2
6	Ilyin-Zhenevsky	0	½	0	½	½	*	1½

(361) FINE—RABINOVICH, I

Leningrad (1), 1937 (19 March)
Queen's Gambit Declined [D68]

1. d4 d5 2. c4 e6 3. Nc3 Nf6 4. Bg5 Be7 5. e3 Nbd7 6. Nf3 0-0 7. Rc1 c6 8. Bd3 dxc4 9. Bxc4 Nd5 10. Bxe7 Qxe7 11. 0-0 Nxc3 12. Rxc3 e5 13. Bb3 e4 14. Nd2 Kh8 15. Qh5 f5 16. f3 Nf6 17. Qh4 Be6 18. fxe4 fxe4 19. Rc5 Bd5 20. Bxd5

cxd5 21. Rfc1 Qe6 22. Qg3 Qa6 23. h3 Rg8 24. a3 Raf8 25. Nf1 Qe2 26. R5c2 Qb5 27. Qg5 h6 28. Qg6 Nd7 29. Nh2 Rf6 30. Qg3 Rgf8 31. Ng4 R6f7 32. Kh2 Kh7 33. Qd6 h5 34. Ne5 Nxe5 35. dxe5 Re8 36. e6 Rf6 37. Rc5 Qxb2 38. Qxd5 Rexe6 39. Qxh5+ Rh6 40. Qf5+ Rhg6 41. Qh5+ Rh6 42. Qf5+ Rhg6 43. R1c2 Qf6 44. Qxf6 Rgxf6 45. Rc7 Ra6 46. Rxb7 Draw agreed. ½–½

(362) LEVENFISH, G—FINE

Leningrad (2), 1937 (20 March)
Queen's Gambit Declined, Exchange Variation [D51]

1. d4 Nf6 2. c4 e6 3. Nf3 d5 4. Nc3 Nbd7 5. Bg5 c6 6. cxd5 This is certainly not a particularly energetic continuation, and causes Black no great difficulties. 6 Qc2! would have been much stronger. If Black tries to win a pawn he will find himself in a disadvantageous situation: 6 Qc2 dxc4 7 a4! (after which, the black knight, having already left b8, cannot head for b4 without a loss of time, hence the quite expedient move a4) Bb4 8 e4 and White has an excellent game. In the event of 6 Qc2 Black cannot safely aim for the Cambridge Springs Defence, since after 6 ... Qa5 7 cxd5! Nxd5 8 e4! Nxc3 9 Bd2 White gains the advantage. This variation occurred in the match game Capablanca–Alekhine, Buenos Aires 1927 (9), with the difference that the Cuban lost a tempo by playing 5 e2-e3 followed by 8 e3-e4, having left his knight on g1. **6 ... cxd5** A move typical of Fine's style. In the event of 6 ... exd5 the game would take on a more quiet character and, perhaps, end up as a draw. Having given the matter some consideration, Fine decides to enter into the tactical complications. The text has been recommended and used by Bogolyubov. **7. e3 a6 8. Bd3 Be7 9. 0-0 0-0 10. Rc1 b5 11. Ne5 Bb7** The continuation 11 ... Nxe5 12 dxe5 Nd7 (but not 12 ... Ne4 13 Bxe7 Nxc3? 14 Bxh7+ and White wins) 13 Bxe7 (13 Bf4 Bb7 14 Ne2 Qb8 15 Nd4 and White stands a little better, Euwe–Bogolyubov, match 1928, is also possible. AW) Qxe7 14 f4 f6 (Otherwise White would have brought the knight to d4 with an advantageous position), bringing the draw closer, was also possible. **12. f4 h6 13. Bh4 Nxe5 14. fxe5** (Better than 14 dxe5 Ne4 15 Bxe7 Qxe7 with equality, Eliskases–Fine, Semmering/Baden, 1937. AW) **14 ... Ne4 15. Bxe7 Qxe7 16. Bxe4 dxe4 17. Qg4 Qg5**

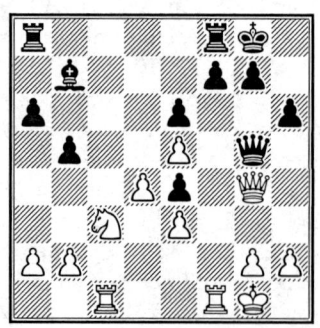

Position after Black's 17th move

18. Qxg5 After this Black gets a strong initiative in the endgame. White should have considered 18 Rf4 Qxg4 19 Rxg4 Rac8! 20 Rb1! b4 21 Nxe4 Bxe4 22 Rxe4 Rc2 23 Rf4 (23 d5 exd5 24 Rxb4 Re8 25 Rb6 Rxe5 26 Rxa6 Rxe3) with an approximately equal game. **18 ... hxg5 19. Ne2** After this unsuccessful try Black assumes the advantage. 19 Rc2 (with a distinct superiority for White, MCO 146) Rc8 20 Rfc1 f6 would have been better. **19 ... Bd5 20. b3 b4!** An excellent move, fixing the pawns on a2 and b3 and threatening to increase Black's advantage by the advance of the a-pawn. **21. h4** The continuation 21 Rc5 a5 22 Rfc1 a4 23 Rb5 axb3 24 axb3 Rfb8 25 Rxb8+ Rxb8 26 Rb1 leads to a clearly lost position. **21 ... gxh4 22. Nf4 Rfc8 23. Rc5 Rxc5 24. dxc5 Rc8 25. Rc1 Kh7 26. Kh2 Kh6 27. g4 hxg3+ 28. Kxg3 Kg5 29.Rh1 Kf5**

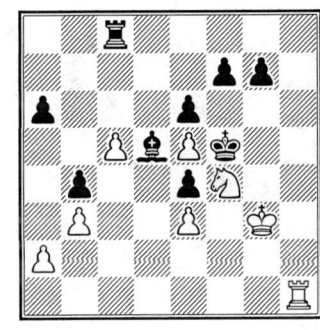

Position after Black's 29th move

30. Rh7 White would gain nothing from 30 Rh5+ g5 31 Nh3 Kxe5 32 Rxg5+ f5. **30 ... Kxe5 31. Rxg7 Rxc5 32. Rxf7 Rc2 33. Ng6+ Kd6 34. Rf2 Rxf2 35. Kxf2 a5 36. Nf4 a4 37. Ne2**

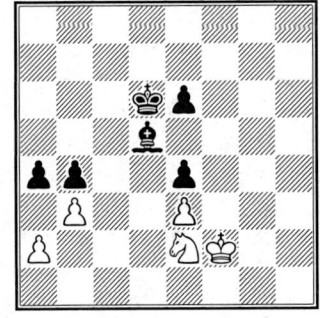

Position after White's 37th move

37 ... Bxb3! 38. axb3 On 38 Nc1 there follows 38 ... Bxa2 and Black wins. **38 ... axb3 39. Ng3! Kd5 40. Nf1 Kc4 41. Ke2** If 41 Nd2+ Kc3 42 Nxe4+ Kc2. RF **41 ... Kc3 42. Kd1 b2 43. Nd2 Kd3 44. Nb1 Kxe3 45. Kc2 Kf2** White resigned. **0–1** Fine demonstrated his impressive endgame technique. B. Ya. Ratner in *Shakhist*, 1937; Fine 1941, 94.

(363) Fine—Ilyin Genevsky, A

Leningrad (3), 1937 (22 March)
Queen's Gambit Declined, Tarrasch Defence [D40]

1. d4 Nf6 2. c4 e6 3. Nc3 d5 4. Nf3 c5 5. e3 Nc6 6. a3 cxd4 7. exd4 dxc4 8. Bxc4 Be7 9. 0–0 0–0 10. Be3 Nd5 11. Bxd5 exd5 12. Qb3 Na5 13. Qxd5 Be6 14. Qe4 Bc4 15. Rfe1 f5 16. Qf4 h6 17. h4 Bd6 18. Ne5 Qf6 19. Qh2 Rad8 20. Bf4 Bb3 21. Re3 Bc7 22. Nf3 Bb6 23. Be5 Qc6 24. Rae1 Nc4 25. R3e2 Nxb2

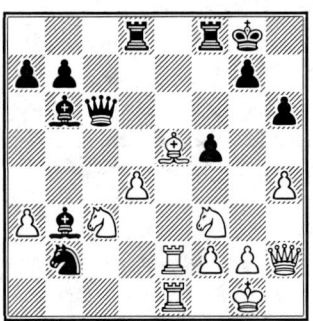

Position after Black's 25th move

26. d5! Bxd5 27. Nxd5 Rxd5 28. Bxb2 f4 29. Qh3 Rd6 30. h5 Qc5 31. Qg4 Rf7 32. Ne5 Rc7 33. Ng6 Black resigned. **1–0**

(364) Rauzer, V—Fine

Leningrad (4), 1937 (23 March)
Alekhine's Defence [B03]

1. e4 Nf6 2. e5 Nd5 3. d4 d6 4. c4 Nb6 5. f4 The ultra-sharp Four Pawns Attack. **5 ... dxe5 6. fxe5 Nc6 7. Be3 Bf5 8. Nc3 e6 9. Be2** Alekhine introduced this defence into tournament play in September 1921 at Budapest (having already tried it out in a consultation game a fortnight earlier), but this soon became established as one of the main lines, for example, 9 Nf3 Bb4 10 Bd3 Bg4 11 Be2 Bxf3 12 gxf3 Qh4+ with a satisfactory position, Lasker–Tarrasch, Maehrisch Ostrau 1923. **9 ... Be7** At the Vienna tournament of 1922 Bogolyubov found himself in a difficult situation against H. Wolf after 9 ... Nb4 10 Rc1 c5 11 Nf3 cxd4 12 Nxd4 Bg6 13 a3 Na6 14 Ndb5 Nd7 15 Nd6+. **10. Nf3** In EMCO 1996a, Bagirov gives 9 Nf3 Be7 10 Be2 as the preferred move order. After 9 ... Qd7 is reckoned, like 9 ... Be7, to lead to an even game. Instead of 10 Be2, after 9 Nf3 Be7, 10 d5 exd5 11 cxd5 Nb4 12 Nd4 Bd7 13 e6 fxe6 14 dxe6 Bc6 15 Qg4 Bh4+ 16 g3 Bxh1 is unclear. **10 ... 0–0 11. 0–0 f6 12. exf6** 12 Qe1 Nb4 13 Rd1 Nc2 14 Qf2 Nxe3 15 Qxe3 c6!? is another suggestion of Bagirov. **12 ... Bxf6 13. Qd2 Qe7 14. Rad1 Rad8 15. Qe1** Or 15 Qc1 h6 16 Kh1 Kh8 17 h3 Bh7 18 Bg1 Rfe8 19 Rfe1 Qf7 20 c5 Nd5 21 Bb5 Nbd4 22 a3 a6 with equality, Hecht–Timman, Wijk aan Zee 1971. **15 ... Nb4 16. a3!** Nc2 17. Qf2 Nxe3 18. Qxe3 Nd7 18 ... c6 with an even game, MCO 2. **19. c5!** White has a distinct superiority, MCO. **19 ... Nb8** Fine regroups his knight in order to counter White's coming queenside advance and put pressure on the centre. **20. Bc4 Kh8 21. Ne4 Bxe4 22. Qxe4 Nc6 23. b4 a5! 24. Bb5?!** White does not achieve

anything by doubling Black's pawns on the c-file. Further play in the centre by 24 Rfe1 may have been better. **24 ... axb4 25. Bxc6 bxc6 26. axb4 Rd5 27. Rfe1** Draw agreed. ½–½

(365) FINE—BUDO, A

Leningrad (5), 1937 (25 March)
Nimzowitsch-Indian Defence, Classical Variation [E32]

1. d4 Nf6 2. c4 e6 3. Nc3 Bb4 The Nimzowitsch Defence is frequently employed in international tournaments, despite its often being overrated. The basic idea of Black's play is to generate piece pressure on the centre, (which can be suitably increased by the striking at the centre with the pawn advances ... d7-d5 or ... c7-c5), or even in some cases by the thrust e7-e5 (after suitable preparation). **4. Qc2** The most attractive method for White. Less dangerous for Black is 4 Qb3, which has often been played by Bogolyubov. **4 ... 0–0** 4 ... d5 is also good for Black, for example 5 cxd5 Qxd5! 6 Nf3 c5 7 a3 Bxc3+ 8 bxc3 Qe4! as was played in the game Ryumin–Alatortsev at the tournament of young masters in Leningrad. **5. a3** A move very much in Fine's style. Trying to avoid the opening complications, White obtains a quiet position, while retaining the bishop pair. 5 e4 would be more risky in view of 5 ... c5! when Black obtains a good game in all variations. **5 ... Bxc3+ 6. Qxc3 d6** (The moves 6 ... b5, 6 ... Ne4 and 6 ... b6, the main line, are also possible in this position. AW) **7. Nf3** (An earlier game of Fine's, against Arthur Dake, New York 1933, had continued 7 e3 Nbd7 8 Bd3 e5 9 Ne2 Re8 10 0–0. The main line given by Emms in NCO is 7 Bg5 Nbd7 8 e3 h6 9 Bh4 Re8 with slight advantage to White. Had Black now continued 7 ... Nbd7 followed by 8 g3 b6 9 Bg2 a position would have been reached which Emms assessed as roughly equal. AW) **7 ... a5!** A strong move, typical for this kind of position. Black threatens to play 8 ... a4, causing White great difficulties in arranging his force on the queenside, and also prevents the immediate 8 b4 in view of 8 ... axb4 9 axb4 Ne4! 10 Qb2 Rxa1 11 Qxa1 c5! with the more attractive position for Black, mainly in view of his pressure against White's undeveloped king's flank. **8. b3 Qe7 9. g3 Re8 10. Bg2 e5 11. 0–0 Nc6** Black has equalized, PCO 248. **12. d5** Black's active play against White's centre has caused great problems for his opponent, so Fine decides to close the centre. White would not achieve any great success by opening the centre, for example: 12 dxe5 dxe5 13 Bb2 Ne4! followed by transferring the knight to c5 and eventually developing play against the queenside, which is very promising. **12 ... Nb8** 12 ... Nd4 13 Nxd4 exd4 14 Qxd4 Qe2 15 Bg5 Qe5 would not have given any advantage either. **13. Nd2 Nbd7 14. b4** A mistake, having closed the centre by 12 d5, White could more reasonably have been expected to secure it and only then commence active play on the queen's flank. 14 e4! was correct, after which White can calmly commence operations on the queenside. Black's opening up the game in the centre with ... f7-f5 (naturally, after suitable preparation), was

harmless to White because of the opposing bishop pair. After the text Black assumes the initiative. **14 ... axb4 15. axb4 Rxa1 16. Qxa1 e4 17. e3** (The alternative 17 Qd4 allows 17 ... e3! when, after 18 Nf3 exf2+ 19 Rxf2 b5! 20 Bb2 bxc4 21 Qxc4 Nb6 22 Bxf6 Nxc4 23 Bxe7 Rxe7, the ending with four pawn islands against two is disadvantageous for White. AW) **17 ... b5!** A tremendous move which ruins the white centre. **18. cxb5 Nb6 19. Qd4 Bb7** 19 ... Nbxd5 is not possible because of the reply 20 Nxe4. **20. Bb2 Bxd5 21. g4?!** This risky move, completely out of keeping with Fine's style, should have led to a loss for White. It was essential to play the immediate 21 Rc1, in order to win the weak pawn on c7 and increase the influence of the two bishops. The text considerably weakens White's kingside, allowing his opponent to organize an attack there. **21 ... h6 22. Rc1 Qd7! 23. h3 Re5 24. Ba1**

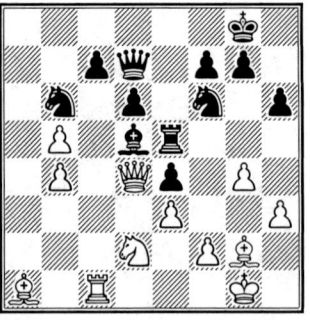

Position after White's 24th move

24 ... Rg5 This is not the strongest way of continuing the attack, since it allows White time to bring up his reserves in defence. The immediate 24 ... h5! was essential, for example, 25 gxh5 Rg5! 26 Nf1 Nxh5, or 25 Nf1 hxg4 26 h4 Rh5 27 Qd1 Ne8!. In either case Black would have excellent winning chances. The text, as soon becomes clear, will very quickly prove to be a waste of time. **25. Nf1 h5** At once this move is not so strong and does not lead to any advantage for Black. Meanwhile he had the opportunity to carry out an interesting combination, though with accurate defence White would have been able to hold the draw even so: 25 ... Nxg4 26 hxg4 Qxg4 27 Ng3 h5! 28 Qd1 (The only move. Anything else would be bad, for example, 28 Rxc7 h4 29 Qxb6 hxg3 and White is unable to evade the numerous threats) Qxd1+ 29 Rxd1 h4 30 Rc1! (the strongest move is) 30 ... Nc4! 31 Rxc4 (31 Bxe4 Bxe4 32 Rxc4 f5 33 Rxc7 hxg3 34 f3!. Bxf3 35 b6 Rh5 36 Rxg7+ Kf8 37 Rxg3 looks an easier path for White to draw. AW) Bxc4 32 Nxe4 Rxb5 with a probable draw. With the exception of the main line, where White has some chances, the variations are all favourable to Black. **26. Qd1!** The strongest manoeuvre, containing a deal more poison than it would seem at first glance. **26 ... hxg4 27. h4 Rh5?** The turning point of the game. Black makes a grave error, most probably explicable by serious time-trouble. It was, undoubtedly, worthwhile to fall back to g6 with the rook. In which case the struggle might have continued with approximately even chances. After the text Black's position rapidly descends into ruins.

28. Bxf6 gxf6 29. Rxc7! Qe6 All the same, it would have been better to take the rook, for example, 29 ... Qxc7 30 Qxg4+ Rg5 31 hxg5 fxg5 32 Qxg5+ Kf8 33 Ng3 and Black would have some, though modest, chances of a draw. **30. Qd4 Nc4 31. Ng3 Rxh4**

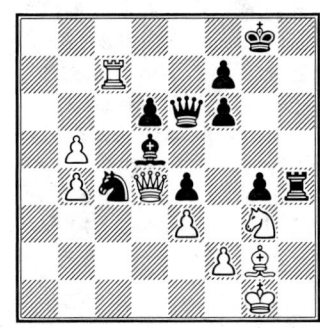

Position after Black's 31st move

32. Ne2! From this point until the end of the game Fine's play is of the highest order. There is no defence to the threat of 33 Nf4. **32 ... Qe5 33. Rxc4 Bxc4 34. Qxc4 f5 35. Qc8+ Kg7 36. Ng3 Rh8** There is no satisfactory way of defending the f-pawn, for example 36 ... Kg6 37 Qg8+ Kh6 38 Qxf7 Kg5 39 Qg8+ Kh6 40 b6 winning easily. **37. Qxf5 Qxf5 38. Nxf5+ Kf6 39. Nxd6 Rb8 40. Nxe4+ Ke5 41. Nc3 f5 42. Bc6 f4 43. exf4+ Kxf4 44. Kg2** Black resigned. 1−0 Black had conducted the game in exemplary fashion until move 24, unfortunately he failed to finish off his opponent and suffered the consequence. B. Goldenov in *Shakhist*, 1937.

Sharing the Honours with Keres, 1937

Fine continued his winning ways on his return from the Soviet Union, but he had to share honours in his next two tournaments with rising star Paul Petrovich Keres of Estonia. Returning to England he placed ahead of former World Champion Alekhine once more at the traditional Easter congress at another of Britain's south coast resort towns—Margate, a tournament won two years previously by Reshevsky ahead of Capablanca. From there both young men crossed the North Sea to Belgium, where they shared first to third with the Swiss player Grob.

Margate, March 31–April 9, 1937

The third of the annual Easter meetings at Margate was held from Wednesday, March 31 to Friday, April 9, in the ballroom of the Grand Hotel. The time limit was 34 moves in the first two hours and 17 per hour thereafter. There were prizes of £12, £8, £4 and £2. "The anticipated duel between Alekhine and Fine gave way to a struggle for first place between Fine and Keres ... Keres led near the end,

but was only able to draw (a little fortunately) in the eighth round against Foltys, when Fine won and caught him up. The game between Fine and Keres in the last round showed Keres to advantage, and Fine instead of winning, as at one stage he expected, had hard work to draw. Only Fine and Keres went through the tournament unbeaten." (*BCM* 1937)

		1	2	3	4	5	6	7	8	9	10	
1=	Fine	*	½	1	1	1	½	1	½	1	1	7½
1=	Keres	½	*	1	½	½	1	1	1	1	1	7½
3	Alekhine	0	0	*	1	1	1	1	1	0	1	6
4	Foltys	0	½	0	*	1	½	1	1	1	½	5½
5	Milner-Barry	0	½	0	0	*	1	½	1	1	1	5
6=	Alexander	½	0	0	½	0	*	½	½	1	1	4
6=	Menchik	0	0	0	0	½	½	*	1	1	1	4
8	Thomas	½	0	0	0	0	½	0	*	1	1	3
9	Berger	0	0	1	0	0	0	0	0	*	1	2
10	Tylor	0	0	0	½	0	0	0	0	0	*	½

(366) FINE—TYLOR, T

Margate (1), 1937 (31 March)
King's Indian Defence, Fianchetto Variation [E72]

1. d4 Nf6 2. c4 g6 3. Nc3 Bg7 4. e4 d6 5. g3 The move 5 f4 which was very popular some years ago, is now considered not quite satisfactory. Instead, there is played generally nowadays 5 Nf3 with h2-h3, Bc1-e3 and so on to follow, but 5 f3, 6 Nge2, 7 Be3, 8 Qd2 is also very desirable. **5 ... 0−0 6. Bg2 Nbd7** In the game Réti–Yates, Hastings 1927, 6 ... Nc6 7 d5 Nb8 8 0−0 Nbd7 was played. **7. Nge2 e5 8. 0−0 exd4 9. Nxd4 Ne5** Black intends to put the queen's knight at c6. It appears to be not well placed there, and it was better to play it to c5, as in the game Grünfeld–Havasi, Debrecin 1925, after a7-a6 or a7-a5. **10. b3 Bd7 11. Bb2 Nc6 12. Nc2 Qc8 13. Re1 Bh3 14. Bh1 Ng4 15. f3 Nh6 16. Qd2 f5 17. Ne3 Qd7** If 17 ... f4, then 18 gxf4 Rxf4 19 Ncd5, or if 17 ... fxe4, then 18 Nxe4 Bxb2 19 Qxb2 Ne5 20 f4 Neg4 21 Nd5 with a superior game. **18. f4 fxe4 19. Nxe4**

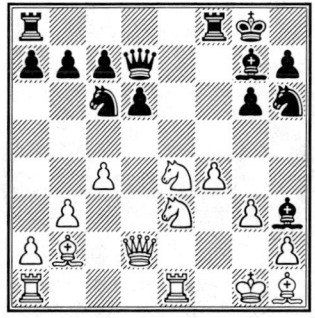

Position after White's 19th move

19 ... Ng4 A curious mistake which brings an unexpected and quick end. White's position is much superior, but with 19 ... Bf5 or even 19 ... Bxb2 20 Qxb2 Qg7 Black could still hold the game. (19 ... Bf5 looks unconvincing after 20 Nxf5

Qxf5 (20 ... Rxf5 21 Ng5!, while 20 ... Nxe5 and 20 ... gxe5 lose to 21 Nc5!) 21 Bxg7 Kxg7 22 Ng5, whereas the more promising 19 ... Bxb2 20 Qxb2 Qg7 would produce the kind of situation Fine reveled in after 21 Qxg7 Kxg7 22 c5! AW) **20. Nc5 Qc8 21. Bd5+ Kh8 22. Bxg7+ Kxg7 23. Ne6+** Black resigned. He only loses the exchange, but is threatened with mate, for instance: 23 ... Kh6 24 Nxg4+ Bxg4 25 f5+, or 23 ... Kh8 24 Nxg4 Bxg4 25 Qc3+. **1–0** Eugene Znosko-Borovsky, BCM 1937, 236.

(367) FINE—MENCHIK, V

Margate (2), 1937 (1 April)
Queen's Gambit Declined [D37]

1. d4 Nf6 2. c4 e6 3. Nc3 d5 4. Nf3 Nbd7 5. e3 a6 6. c5 c6 7. Bd2 e5 Black of course gets the pawn back, but possibly 7 ... Qc7 first would have led to an easier game. **8. dxe5 Ng4 9. Na4 Nxc5** If 9 ... Ngxe5 10 Nxe5 Nxe5 11 Bc3 Nd7 12 b4 and Black's game is difficult. If 12 ... Nf6 13 Nb6 followed by Bc5 and Qd4. **10. Nxc5 Bxc5 11. h3 Nh6 12. Bd3 Qe7** Evidently not 12 ... Bf5 at once as then 13 Bxf5 Nxf5 14 Qc2. 12 ... f5 is just a little tempting, as after 13 exf6 Qxf6 14 Qc2 Bd6 15 Bxh7 Rxh7 17 Qxh7 17 Qh8+ Bf8 18 Bc3 Qe7 and Black castles queenside and gets some attack for the exchange; but unfortunately the simple move 15 Bc3 first wins the pawn without trouble. **13. a3** An important move, not only preventing the exchange of bishops, but threatening the line of play Qc2, Rc1 and Bb4. **13 ... Bf5 14. Bxf5 Nxf5 15. Qc2 g6** This leaves a permanent weakness. 15 ... Nh6 is better, though Black's game is very trying. **16. 0–0**

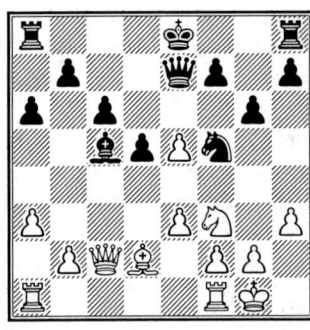

*Position after
White's 16th move*

16 ... Ng7 An alternative is 16 ... Ba7, if then 17 e4 dxe4 18 Bg5 Black could play 18 ... Nd4 with some improvement in position. White however could play 18 Qxe4 with a much superior game. Possibly 16 ... 0–0–0 is Black's best chance, if then 17 e4 Nd4. **17. e4 dxe4** 17 ... Ne6 is no worse. **18. Bg5 Qc7** 18 ... Qf8 would hold out a good deal longer; but there is not much hope of anything beyond delay. **19. Qxc5 exf3 20. Bf6 fxg2 21. Rfe1 Ne6 22. Qe3 Rg8** Evidently 22 ... 0–0 would be useless against 23 Qh6 and 24 Re4. **23. Rad1 g5 24. Rd6 Nf4 25. Bxg5 Rxg5 26. Qxf4 Qe7 27. e6 f6 28. Rd7 Qc5 29. Rxh7 Qa5 30. b4** Black resigned. **1–0** H. E. Atkins, BCM 1937, 274–5.

(368) THOMAS, G—FINE

Margate (3), 1937 (2 April)
Spanish Opening, Steinitz Defence Deferred [C73]

1. e4 e5 2. Nf3 Nc6 3. Bb5 a6 4. Ba4 d6 5. Bxc6+ bxc6 6. d4 f6 7. Be3 Ne7 8. Qd2 f5 9. dxe5 fxe4 10. Ng5 Bf5 11. Nc3 dxe5 12. Qe2 Nd5 13. Qc4 Qd7 14. 0–0 Nxc3 15. Qxc3 Bd6 16. Qc4 h6 17. Nxe4 Be6 18. Qe2 0–0 19. Rad1 Bd5 20. f3 Qf7 21. b3 Qg6 22. Bf2 Bxe4 23. Qxe4 Qxe4 24. fxe4 Rf4 25. c4 Raf8 26. g3 Rxe4 27. c5! Be7 28. Rd7 Bg5 29. h4 Be3 30. Bxe3 Rxe3 31. Rxf8+ Kxf8 32. Rxc7 Rxg3+ 33. Kf2 Rc3 34. Rxc6 a5 35. Rc8+ Draw agreed. **½–½**

(369) MILNER BARRY, P—FINE

Margate (4), 1937 (4 April)
Sicilian Defence, Dragon Variation [B72]

1. e4 c5 2. Nf3 d6 3. d4 cxd4 4. Nxd4 Nf6 5. Nc3 g6 6. Be2 Bg7 7. Be3 0–0 8. 0–0 a6 9. f4 Qc7 10. Bf3 Nc6 11. Nb3 Na5 12. Nxa5 Qxa5 Both players have handled the opening in a normal fashion. White has his chances on the kingside and in the centre, while Black has counterplay on the queenside. White's best continuation now would be 13 Qd2 threatening the standard Nd5. In this way White could have won an important tempo. The move he actually makes is a little hasty. **13. g4 Be6**

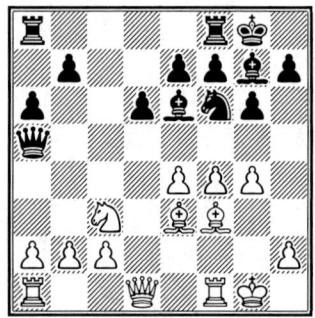

*Position after
Black's 13th move*

14. Bd4? A mistake, after which Black wins a pawn in an attractive manner. The continuation 14 Nd5, after which White still has a decent game, was more in keeping with the situation on the board. **14 ... Bxg4!** This well-known tactic from a similar position has a particularly attractive point here. **15. Bxg4** On 15 Bxf6 naturally there follows 15 ... Bxf3. **15 ... Nxg4** This is the point of Black's combination. On 16 Bxg7 there follows 16 ... Qh5! threatening mate and simultaneously protecting the knight on g4. **16. Nd5 Bxd4+ 17. Qxd4 Qd8 18. h3 Nf6!** After 18 ... Nh6 White could develop a dangerous kingside attack with 19 f5. **19. Nxf6+ exf6** It might seem that Black's extra pawn has little significance. In a material sense this is indeed true, but in a positional sense it has a serious consequence, simply because the white kingside is weakened. Fine excellently exploits this last circumstance. The remainder of the game is therefore highly instructive. **20. Rad1** Apparently leading to the recovery of the lost pawn. **20 ... Qc8!** By counterattacking c2 and h3, the enemy's threat is parried indirectly. **21. Qd3 Re8 22. Rfe1 Qc5+ 23. Kg2 Qc6** Black keeps his opponent busy with threats. He intends to follow the text with 24 ... f5, so the white king must immediately remove itself form the critical diagonal. **24. Kg3 Rac8** With a counter-threat once more. **25. c3 Qa4 26. Qd5 Rc4!** Excellently played. Black continually finds ways to preserve his pawn while increasing his advantage. The text yields him a decisive attack. **27. Q×b7** The pawn on e4 can no longer be saved, since on 27 Kf3 27 ... f5 decides. **27 ... Rcxe4 28. Rxe4** If 28 b3 Black replies 28 ... Re3+.

The participants at Margate 1937, the first of three tournaments in which Fine shared first place with Paul Keres. Standing (left to right): Buerger, Alexander, Foltys, Keres, Milner-Barry; seated (left to right): Tylor, Menchik, Alekhine, Fine, Sir George Thomas.

28 ... Rxe4 29. Rf1 Once again 28 b3 is answered by 28 ... Re3+. **29 ... Qc4 30. Rf2 d5 31. Qb6 Kg7 32. a3 h5 33. Rf3 h4+ 34. Kg2** After this move it is all over rather quickly. He had to try 34 K×h4. **34 ... Re2+** White resigned. **0–1** *Tijdschrift van den Nederlandschen Schaakbond* 1937, 145.

(370) FINE—ALEKHINE, A

Margate (5), 1937 (5 April)
Dutch Defence [A90]

Fine provides a magnificent specimen of positional play in the following game which differs from the last (Fine–Maróczy, Zandvoort 1936. AW) in that it his opponent who first seizes the initiative. The way in which Fine not only parries but punishes these attempts, gains the upper hand, and eventually consolidates the win is indeed memorable. ME **1. d4 e6 2. c4 f5 3. g3 Nf6 4. Bg2 Bb4+ 5. Bd2 Be7** One of Alekhine's favourite variations. RF (He had also played 5 ... B×d2+: 6 Q×d2 0–0 7 Nc3 d5! (7 ... d6 8 Nf3 Nc6 9 Rd1 Ne7 10 0–0 Ng6 11 Qc2 c6 12 e4 with a clear plus for White, Euwe–Alekhine, match game 10, 1927) 8 Nf3 Nc6! 9 cxd5 exd5 10 Ne5 Ne7 11 0–0 c6 12 Rac1 Qe8 with an even game, Ståhlberg–Alekhine, Zurich 1934. AW) **6. Nc3 Nc6!?** According to the "books" the Dutch Defence is inferior, only the Stonewall formation, which Black could now set up by 6 ... d5, offering prospects of equality. Experience teaches, however, that it is not easy for

White to maintain an opening advantage in practice, since the play usually becomes very involved and Black can threaten all sorts of dangerous attacks; the play suits Alekhine's style, and he has indeed won many beautiful games with this opening. Alekhine typically rejects the quiet 6 ... d5 in favour of the complications implied by the text. This time he learns a little lesson! ME **7. d5! Ne5 8. Qb3 0–0 9. Nh3 Ng6** Black's pieces are crowded and cramped, but he threatens to free himself with ... e5. RF **10. dxe6!** Simple but strong. White simultaneously opens the d-file and the long diagonal with the result that his pieces are able to co-operate harmoniously. Experience shows that in this opening it is to Black's benefit entirely for the centre to remain closed. ME **10 ... dxe6 11. Rd1** If 11 B×b7, Black would play for attack by 11 ... B×b7 12 Q×b7 Rb8 13 Q×a7 R×b2. This is stronger than 11 ... Rb8 12 B×c8 R×b3 13 B×e6+ Kh8 14 a×b3, with rook, bishop and two pawns for the queen. ME **11 ... c6 12. 0–0 e5** Far too risky. Black should have played 12 ... Kh8 or 12 ... Qc7, after which, though he does have the worse of it, he retains chances of equalizing. Alekhine thinks he can permit himself aggressive tactics and thus gives Fine the opportunity of displaying his skills in positional play and defence. ME **13. c5+** An attacking move with positional aims, which necessitated accurate reckoning of its consequences. ME **13 ... Kh8 14. Ng5** White has a distinct superiority, MCO 214. **14 ... Qe8 15. Ne6 Bxe6 16. Qxe6 Bxc5** Black has no satisfactory means of protecting his f-pawn, for both 16 ... Qc8 17 Q×c8 Q×c8 18 Bh3

Nd7 19 b4 (threatening 20 e4), and 16 ... Nd7 17 b4 a5 18 a3 would have given White an overwhelming game. ME **17. Q×f5**

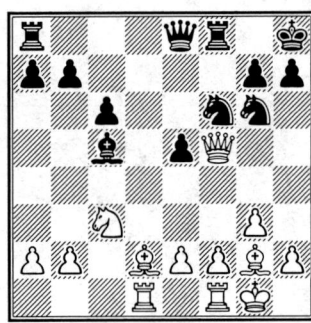

Position after White's 17th move

This is the position White envisaged when playing 13 c5+. He has two bishops and the better pawn formation (his pawns are in two groups, his opponent's in three). The isolated pawn is not weak in itself, but cannot be employed for attack, and consequently Black is denied his normal chances in this opening, which consist in direct attacks on the kingside. As compensation, he has the pawn majority on the queen's wing, but the sequel shows he cannot exploit this owing to the power of the white bishops. ME **17 ... Rd8 18. Qc2 Qe6 19. Na4** 19 Ne4 was also to be considered, but White does not want to exchange off either of the black knights—they are not mobile anyway. ME **19 ... Be7 20. a3** Preparing a minority attack against the queenside, and defending the a-pawn. The immediate threat is Nc5, which cannot be played right away because the a-pawn is loose after 20 Nc5 B×c5 21 Q×c5 Q×a2. RF **20 ... Rd4** Averting White's threat finely. Now if 21 Nc5?, then 21 ... B×c5 22 Q×c5 Rfd8 23 Qc2 Qd7, and Black wins a piece. ME **21. h3** A restraining move: White wishes to play Be3, and to do that he prevents ... Ng4. RF **21 ... b5** Since 22 Nc5? would still lose a piece and the knight must therefore return to c3, Black considers the time ripe to start evaluating his majority on the queenside; but this advance, as becomes apparent later, only weakens his position still further. One or other of the quieter continuations such as 21 ... Qc4 or 21 ... Rfd8 would have been better. ME **22. Nc3 a5** Here Dr. Alekhine suggests he should have played 22 ... Qc4, and if 23 Be3 Nd5. BCM **23. Be3 R×d1 24. R×d1 b4** Black persists in his aggressive tactics, and quickly succumbs as a result. The less pretentious 24 ... Rd8 merited preference, but in any case White has now the better of the game. ME **25. a×b4 a×b4 26. Na4** The pressure against Black's queenside now leads to the loss of a pawn. RF **26 ... Nd5 27. Bc5!** The two bishops no longer mean a lot. ME **27 ... Qf7** Black's only hope lies in the counterattack against f2, but it is insufficient. RF **28. e3 Rc8** Losing a pawn; but Black was already at a loss for a satisfactory continuation. If, for instance, 28 ... Rd8, then 29 B×e7 winning material just the same (29 ... Ng×e7 30 e4, or 29 ... Q×e7 30 Q×c6). Black's position is full of holes—this must prove fatal in the long run. ME **29. Qc4!**

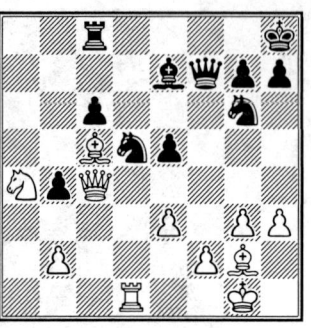

Position after White's 29th move

Threatening principally 30 e4, winning a piece. Several black pawns are in danger, too. ME **29 ... Qf8** Nothing is much good by now, for example, 29 ... B×c5 30 N×c5 Rf8 31 Rd2 and Black must lose a pawn; or 29 ... Rf8 30 Rd2. ME **30. B×e7 Ng×e7** Not 30 ... Q×e7, because of 31 B×d5. 30 ... Nd×e7 would be answered by 31 Qb4. ME **31. e4! Nf6 32. Qb4** White has picked up a pawn and still has an overwhelming position into the bargain. The job of pushing home these big advantages we can leave to Fine. ME **32 ... Rd8 33. R×d8 Q×d8 34. Nc5 Qd6 35. Qc3 h6 36. Nd3 Nd7 37. h4 Ng6 38. Bh3 Ngf8 39. b4 h5 40. Nc5 Nf6 41. Qc4 Qe7** The pawn might be held by playing a knight over to b8. BCM **42. Nb3! Qd6 43. Na5 Qd2 44. N×c6 Qe1+ 45. Bf1 N×e4 46. Qe2!** This settles it. ME **46 ... Q×e2 47. B×e2 g6 48. N×e5 Nc3 49. Bd3 Kg7 50. f4 Nd5 51. b5 Kf6 52. Kf2** With the entry of the king, Black might as well resign, his own king being tied to the g-pawn. BCM **52 ... Nb6 53. Ke3 Na4 54. Kd4 Ne6+ 55. Kd5 Nc7+ 56. Kc6 Ne6 57. b6 Nd8+ 58. Kd7 Ne6 59. b7 Nac5+ 60. Kc8** Black resigned. A model performance in the realm of logical positional play. After acquiring a small advantage in the opening, White continually exhausted his opponent of good moves. There are few direct threats, but in spite of all Black's efforts, his situation steadily deteriorates. He missed the best line once or twice, but he was never permitted the least chance to get back on level terms. ME **1–0** Fine 1953, 275–8; Euwe 1945, 210–6; Euwe 1965, 298–9; BCM 1937, 300.

(371) FINE—ALEXANDER, C

Margate (6), 1937 (6 April)
Nimzowitsch-Indian Defence, Zurich or Milner-Barry Variation [E33]

1. d4 Nf6 2. c4 e6 3. Nc3 Bb4 4. Qc2 Nc6 5. Nf3 d6 6. a3 B×c3+ 7. Q×c3 0–0 8. b4 Probably best; it was played for the first time by Flohr against Milner-Barry, London 1932. **8 ... e5** A most interesting pawn sacrifice, which is very characteristic of the whole variation. **9. d×e5 Ne4** This intermediate move, introduced by Milner-Barry in his game against Miss Menchik, Cambridge 1932, is much superior to that of taking the pawn: 9 ... N×e5 10 N×e5 d×e5 11 Q×e5 Re8 12 Qb2, as he played against Flohr. **10. Qe3** This is better than 10 Qb2 (10 ... d×e5 11 N×e5 N×e5 12 Q×e5 Re8 13 Qb2 Qh4 (13 ... Be6 14 c5 Wheatcroft-

Alexander) 14 g3, with advantage to White, MCO 185), as Wheatcroft played against Alexander at Chester 1934. **10 ... f5 11. Bb2 Nxe5 12. Nxe5 dxe5 13. g3** Winter against Alexander, Hastings 1936, accepted the pawn sacrifice: 13 Bxe5 Qe7 14 f4 Be6 15 g3 Bxc4, and lost the game. **13 ... Be6 14. f3** With this move White wins the e-pawn. **14 ... Nd6** Other moves are no better: 14 ... Qg5 15 Qxg5 Nxg5 16 Bxe5 Bxc4 17 Bxc7; or 14 ... Nf6 15 Qxe5 Bxc4 16 Qxf5. **15. Qxe5 Qe7 16. e3** White stands a little better, MCO 185. **16 ... Qf7 17. c5 Nc4 18. Bxc4 Bxc4** Black now has a bishop of different colour with a great chance of a draw. **19. Kf2 Bb3** In order not to allow White's rook to occupy the d-file. **20. Bd4 Rae8 21. Qf4 Bd5 22. Be5** A mistake that costs a pawn and leads White to a bad position. 22 Kg2, Rhf1 and Rae1 would be the right plan. **22 ... Bxf3!** A nice combination. If 23 Kxf3, then 23 ... Qd5+ and 24 ... Qxe5. If instead 23 Qxf3, then 23 ... Rxe5 24 Qxb7 Rxe3 25 Kxe3 (25 Rhe1 f4) Qb3+ and Black has at least perpetual check. **23. Bxg7 Bxh1 24. Bxf8 Rxf8 25. Rxh1 Qa2+ 26. Kf1** If 26 Kf3, then Qd5+. Now a draw seems inevitable. **26 ... Qxa3 27. Kg2 Qb2+ 28. Kh3 Qe2 29. Rf1 Qg4+ 30. Kg2 Re8 31. Qxf5 Qxb4 32. Rf4 Qd2+ 33. Kh3 Qxe3 34. Qd7 Qe7** Draw agreed. ½–½ Eugene Znosko-Borovsky, BCM 1937, 304.

(372) FOLTYS, J—FINE

Margate (7), 1937 (7 April)

Spanish Game, Steinitz Defence Deferred [C73]

I am particularly fond of certain games in which I hauled myself out of seemingly hopeless situations, pulled even, and at times even won. One such is the following, against the Czech master Foltys. RF **1. e4 e5 2. Nf3 Nc6 3. Bb5 a6 4. Ba4 d6 5. Bxc6+ bxc6 6. d4 f6 7. Be3** This is now considered the best continuation. Its main idea is to stop Black's development— ... g6, ... Ng8-h6-f7—by playing Be3 and Qd2. EZB **7 ... Ne7 8. Nc3 Be6** If 8 ... Ng6 9 h4 h5, MCO 270. **9. Qd2 Ng6** Alekhine's idea for Black's development is ... Ne7-c8-b6, ... Be7 and so on. EZB **10. h4** 10 b3? d5 11 0-0 dxe4 12 Nxe4 Bd5 13 Ng3 Bxf3 14 gxf3 Nh4 with an excellent game for Black, Sir George Thomas–Capablanca, Nottingham 1936. **10 ... h5 11. d5! cxd5 12. Nxd5**

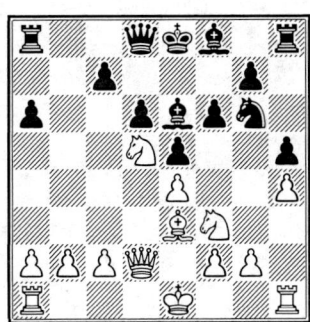

Position after White's 11th move

12 ... Be7 A mistake, which loses a pawn; I had simply overlooked the reply. 12 ... Qd7 is necessary, and if then 13 Qa5 Bxd5 14 Qxd5 c6. RF **13. Qa5!** This new idea temporarily wins a pawn and Black will have great difficulty regaining it. Perhaps Tartakower's move 8 ... a5 is to be advised, avoiding this unexpected attack. EZB **13 ... Rc8!** I realized that I had to lose a pawn, and looked around for the best way to get compensation. RF **14. Qxa6 c6!** **15. Nxe7 Qxe7** Black has excellent counterplay for the sacrificed pawn, MCO. **16. Qa7** Loses a pawn in the long run. However, Black already has counterplay: for example, 16 Qe2 Bg4 and castling either side is dangerous. RF **16 ... Qxa7 17. Bxa7 c5 18. a4 Kd7 19. Bb6 Rb8 20. a5 Ne7** Threatening 21 ... Nc8. RF **21. 0-0-0 Kc6 22. Rd2 Nc8 23. Rhd1** Still holding the pawn by virtue of the counterthreat against the d-pawn. RF **23 ... Re8 24. Ng1** White cannot stop Black regaining the pawn. Perhaps the manoeuvre Nf3-h2-f1-e3 with f2-f3 and g2-g4 to follow would be better. EZB **24 ... Re7! 25. Ne2 Rd7** Now the bishop can be taken. RF **26. Nc3 Nxb6 27. axb6 Rxb6**

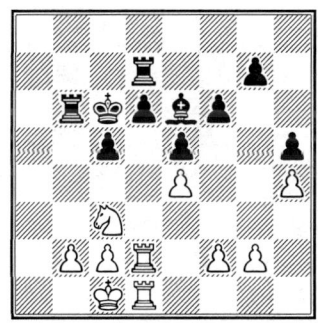

Position after Black's 27th move

28. f3 Rb4! With even pawns the ending looks drawish, but Black's pieces are more aggressively placed, and he has winning chances. The text is played with the intention of blocking the d-file with ... Rd4. If 29 Ne2 Bc4. RF **29. Nd5** Hoping that another exchange will help. RF **29 ... Bxd5 30. Rxd5 f5!** This move gives Black the advantage. The weakness of White's h-pawn allows Black subtle manoeuvres. EZB **31. c3** If now 31 exf5 Rxh4 followed by ... Rf4 will win a pawn for Black. RF **31 ... Ra4 32. Re1 fxe4 33. fxe4 Ra1+!** Not 33 ... Rxe4 34 Rxd6+. RF **34. Kd2 Rxe1 35. Kxe1 Rf7**

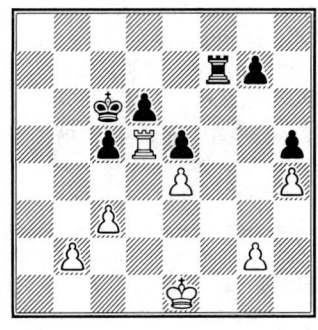

Position after Black's 35th move

36. Ke2 Rf4 37. Ke3 Rxh4 Black at last wins a pawn, and now follows a very difficult ending. EZB **38. Rd2 Rg4**

39. Kf3 Rf4+ 40. Ke3 h4 41. Rd1 g5 42. g3 Desperation. But against passive play he loses as follows: 42 Rd2 Rg4 43 Kf3 Rg3+ 44 Kf2 c4! 45 Rd1 Rd3! 46 R×d3 e×d3 47 Ke3 g4 48 K×d3 h3 and queens. RF **42 ... h×g3 43. Rg1 g4 44. R×g3 c4 45. Rg1 Kb5 46. Rh1 g3 47. Rg1 Rf2 48. R×g3 R×b2 49. Rg8** The only way to hold for a while the c-pawn. If 49 Kf3 Rd2 and if 50 Kg4 Rd3. EZB **49 ... Rc2 50. Rb8+ Ka6 51. Ra8+ Kb7 52. Ra3**

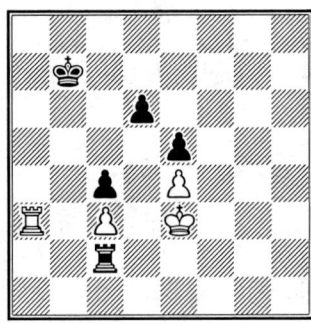

Position after White's 52nd move

52 ... Kc6 White's rook is now tied to the defence of the c-pawn; the winning idea is to bring the black king in via the kingside. RF **53. Ra6+ Kd7 54. Ra3 Ke6 55. Kf3 Kf6 56. Kg3 Kg5 57. Kf3 Kh4** A pretty *Zugzwang* position has been reached: after 58 Ke3 Kg3 there is no direct threat, but the white rook must move and abandon the defence of the c-pawn. RF **58. Ra6 R×c3+ 59. Ke2 Rd3 60. Rc6 Rd4 61. Ke3 Kg3 62. Rc8 Rd3+ 63. Ke2 Kf4** White resigned, for if 64 R×c4 Re3+ 65 K- R×e4 and the ending is elementary. After the game my opponent made a remark rarely heard among chessmasters. He said "You play better than I do." RF **0–1** Fine 1958, 131–5; 1941, 359; Eugene Znosko-Borovsky, BCM 1937, 305–6.

(373) BUERGER, V—FINE

Margate (8), 1937 (8 April)
Queen's Gambit Declined, Vienna Variation [D39]

1. d4 Nf6 2. Nf3 e6 3. c4 d5 4. Bg5 Bb4+ 5. Nc3 d×c4 6. Qa4+ With transposition of moves the game has now reached the Vienna Variation of the Queen's Gambit. White's move is surely bad. The most interesting line is 6 e4 with a very complicated game after 6 ... c5. **6 ... Nc6 7. e4 Bd7 8. Qc2 h6 9. Bh4?** A mistake which loses a second pawn. White had the choice between 9 Be3, 9 Bd2 and 9 B×f6. **9 ... g5 10. Bg3 g4 11. 0–0–0** White decides to sacrifice a piece, as the game is obviously lost after 11 Ne5 N×d4 12 Qd1 (12 Qd2 Ba4) Nb5 13 Qd2 N×e4 14 Qf4 Ned6. However the sacrifice does not give any chance, and White could quietly resign. 11 e5 does not save anything: 11 ... Nd5 12 Nd2 N×d4. **11 ... g×f3 12. d5 e×d5 13. e×d5 Ne7 14. B×c4 Bd6 15. Rhe1 f×g2 16. Rd3 Kf8 17. Rf3 Ng6 18. Rfe3 Kg7 19. f4 N×f4 20. Qf2 Ng4** White resigned. **0–1** Eugene Znosko-Borovsky in BCM 1937, 309.

(374) KERES, P—FINE

Margate (9), 1937 (9 April)
French Defence, Tarrasch Variation [C05]

1. e4 e6 2. d4 d5 3. Nd2 The freshness and variety of Keres' ideas are most amazing. As White against the French Defence he has infused new life into a number of doubtful variations, notably the controversial Steinitz–Nimzowitsch line 3 e5. The text is rather unusual, but the Russian analysts have recently shown that it is one of White's strongest lines against the French Defence. **3 ... Nf6** Whether this move is better than 3 ... c5 is still an open question. After 3 ... c5 4 e×d5 e×d5 5 Bb5+ Bd7 (or 5 ... Nc6 6 Qe2+ Be6 7 Nf3 and White has a strong initiative) 6 Qe2+ Qe7 7 B×d7 N×d7 8 d×c5 (Bondarevsky–Yudovich, Moscow 1937) Black has little compensation for his isolated pawn. (Both 3 ... c5 and 3 ... Nf6 are still theoretically important. AW) **4. Bd3 c5** Now this move is not at all dangerous, since White has lost a tempo with his king's bishop. **5. e5 Nfd7 6. c3 Nc6 7. Ne2 f6!?** It would have been better to defer this move for a while and play instead 7 ... c×d4 8 c×d4 Qb6 9 Nf3 Bb4+ 10 Bd2 0–0 11 0–0 f6. **8. Nf4 Qe7 9. Nf3 f×e5 10. N×e5** A weak move which allows Black to gain an easy equality. Correct was 10 Ng6! h×g6 (10 ... Qd8 11 d×e5! wins) 11 B×g6+ Kd8 12 Bg5 Nf6 13 d×e5 with a clear advantage for White. **10 ... Nd×e5 11. d×e5 g6** Wins the pawn at e5. The sacrifice 12 B×g6+ h×g6 13 N×g6 Qh7 14 N×h8 is unsound because Black can afford to reply 14 ... N×e5. **12. 0–0 N×e5 13. Re1 Bg7** If 13 ... N×d3 14 Q×d3 the black d-pawn is doomed. **14. Bb5+!** The best continuation. If instead 14 N×d5 e×d5 15 f4 0–0 16 f×e5 Be6 the white pawn at e5 will be lost in the long run. **14 ... Bd7 15. Qa4** But this is decidedly inferior to 15 B×d7+ Q×d7 16 N×d5 e×d5 (16 ... 0–0–0 17 Ne3 Nd3 looks interesting. AW) 17 Bf4 0–0 18 B×e5 with an even ending. **15 ... a6 16. B×d7+ Q×d7 17. Q×d7+** A better chance was 17 Qb3 Kf7 (the only move to keep the pawn [I don't understand this. AW]) 18 Be3 Rac8 19 Rad1 with considerable advantage in development. **17 ... K×d7 18. Be3 b6** The black position is now won, but Black, impressed by this fact proceeds to allow himself the luxury of a series of weak moves. 18 ... Rac8 was preferable to the text. **19. a4 Nc4** And here 19 ... a5 was simpler. **20. Nd3 e5** Fine awarded this natural move with a question mark, and proposed 20 ... N×e3 or 20 ... a5, leading to a win for Black, instead. It is not, however, clear that this is really a mistake. AW **21. a5 d4** Here Fine writes that 21 ... e4 22 Nf4 Kc6 23 a×b6 N×b6 24 Ra5 Bf8 25 Rea1 Kb7 26 b4 would be difficult for Black, which is not really obvious after 26 ... d4. However, 23 ... N×b2 might be better than 23 ... N×b6. AW **22. Bg5 N×a5** Here Fine gives 22 ... d×c3 23 b×c3 N×a5 24 N×c5+ Kd6 (24 ... b×c5 25 R×a5 c4 is probably better) with good winning chances, so his 20th cannot have been so bad. AW **23. c×d4 Nb3** And here Fine writes "If 23 ... c×d4 24 f4 regaining the pawn with a good position." This is an interesting line which might continue 24 ... h6 25 Bh4 g5 26 f×g5 Nc6! 27 Bg3 Kd6 28 g×h6 R×h6 with a promising position for Black. AW **24. Rad1**

Nxd4 **25. b4 Kc6 26. bxc5 bxc5 27. Be7** Inferior is
27 Nxe5+ Bxe5 28 Rxe5 Rhe8 29 Be7 Nb3 30 Rd3 c4 and
wins. **27 ... Nb3 28. Nxc5! Nxc5 29. Rd6+ Kc7** If
29 ... Kb7? 30 Rb1+ Ka7 31 Rc6 Nb7 32 Bc5+ Kb8 (32 ...
Nxc5 33 Rc7+ Nb7 34 Rxb7 mate) 33 Bd6+ Ka7 34 Rc7
Rab8 35 Rxg7. **30. Rc1 Rac8 31. Rd2 Kb7 32. Bxc5
Bf8** Fine here considered 32 ... Rhd8 more precise, since
33 Rb2+ Ka8 34 Ra1 Rc6 35 Bb6 e4! 36 Rxa6+ Kb7 37 Ra7+
Kc8 38 Ra8+ Kb7! forces a draw by perpetual check. In this
line the surprising 37 ... Kb8! seems to lead to a winning
position for Black since White has no useful discovery, for
example, 38 Bd4+ Kc8 39 Ra8+ Kc7! 40 Ra7+ Kd6. AW
33. Rb1+ Ka8 34. Bxf8 Rhxf8 35. Rd6 Ka7 36. Ra1
After 36 Rd7+ Ka8 37 Rxh7 perhaps Black should try 37 ...
Rc2, rather than 37 ... Rfe8, which Fine considered to be
forced but passive. AW **36 ... Rc2 37. f3 e4!** Black must
obtain counterplay at all costs. **38. fxe4 Rff2** But this is
premature and should have lost. Correct was 38 ... Re2 and
if then 39 Re6 Rff2 with an easy draw. **39. Raxa6+ Kb7
40. Rdb6+ Kc7 41. Rc6+ Kd8 42. Rxc2 Rxc2
43. Ra7?** And now White revenges himself for Black's last
blunder! Correct was 43 Ra8+ Ke7 44 Ra7+ Kf6 45 Rxh7
Re2 46 Rh4 Kg5 47 g3 with a winning ending. **43 ... Rc4
44. Rxh7 Rxe4 45. Kf2 Ke8 46. Kf3 Ra4 47. g3
Kf8** Now that the black king is near the pawns a win is no
longer possible. The remaining moves require no comment.
**48. Rd7 Rb4 49. Ke3 Ra4 50. h3 Rb4 51. Rd4
Rb5 52. Kf4 Kg7 53. Re4 Kf6 54. h4 Ra5 55. g4
Rb5 56. Ra4 Rc5 57. Ra6+ Kf7 58. Rd6 Ra5
59. Rc6 Rb5 60. g5 Rb4+ 61. Ke5 Rxh4 62. Rc7+
Kg8 63. Kf6 Ra4 64. Re7 Rb4** Draw agreed. ½–½
Fine, BCM 1937, 330–2.

Ostend, April 11–19, 1937

Fine immediately traveled, along with Keres, to a tournament held at the Kursaal Casino in Ostend. In *Chess* it
was reported that the competitors were given duplicate
score-sheets, secured one above the other by means of spring
clips, with carbon paper between, apparently an innovation
at the time. "A very active group of chess amateurs of
Ostend organized the 2nd international tournament from
11 April to 19 April 1937. It was a great success. We must
pay tribute to the gentlemen J. Vi, R.P. and R.B., respectively President, Vice-President and Secretary of the said
club. Before sanctioning the results, we must honour the
press who regularly distributed, day after day, the results for
the chess chronicles and the specialized journals all over
the world. It was thus that our Belgian beach of Ostend
became known elsewhere and remembered by former visitors. The Belgian Newspaper *Le Soir* wrote about this important competition: 'We have seen one of the most sensational
tournaments ever in Belgium. If we have already had some
in the past where the quality was not inferior, never have
we hosted a competition where there were so many surprising occurrences! Certainly, if the same ten players were

to meet again, the final result would be completely different.
At least twenty of the forty-five games could well have had
a completely different result. At the end we saw three players in first place with less than 70 percent scores. This was
not caused by any lack of courage, which would have
resulted in a wealth of draws, but on the contrary to games
lost by the leaders to the lesser players. Fine and Keres have
confirmed their dead heat of Margate, and we wait with
impatience for a third contest to separate them. Fine (who
is 22 years old) has more experience and technique, but
Keres (at 21 years of age) has a pure style not seen for a long
time amongst masters of the game. It is remarkable to see
how he constructs mating attacks with such innocent-look-
ing moves. In a number of openings he makes deeply calculated pawn sacrifices which bring to mind the classical
Evans Gambit and Max Lange Attack. When he analyzes
his games he sees many combinational ideas. Both Fine and
Keres are very promising and surely one of them will become
World Champion. Therefore, it is a great honour for Master Grob to share first place with them, but more than that
he managed to defeat them. His greatest quality (he nearly
won the tournament last year) is his tenacious play. He plays
on in endings where others would concede the draw. Grob
was assuredly the hardest worker in the tournament.'"
(Diemer, translation by de Bruycker)

"A triple tie among Reuben Fine, Paul Keres and Henry
Grob (Switzerland) was the outcome of an international
tournament at Ostend in Belgium from April 11 to 19. Off
to a bad start by losing to Keres on the first day, Fine sustained two additional losses to Grob and Reynolds of
England, but defeated all his other opponents." (ACB 1937)
"This tournament [Margate] represented the culmination,
for the time being, of his success; months of play without
a moment's respite had begun to sap his powers, and in a
tournament at Ostend which immediately followed Margate, he received a serious warning. In the middle of this
tournament he rushed over to London to give a simultaneous display, returning to complete his schedule of games
at high pressure. In the circumstances he did well to share
the final first place with Grob and Keres; but in doing so
he lost no fewer than three games, a result the more per-
turbing, as the chess world had become accustomed to seeing him lose only on the rarest occasions." (Euwe, 1940)

		1	2	3	4	5	6	7	8	9	10	
1=	Grob	*	1	1	0	1	½	0	½	1	1	6
1=	Fine	0	*	0	1	1	1	1	1	1	0	6
1=	Keres	0	1	*	1	0	½	½	1	1	1	6
4=	List	1	0	0	*	½	1	½	1	0	1	5
4=	Tartakower	0	0	1	½	*	½	½	½	1	1	5
4=	Landau	½	0	½	0	½	*	1	½	1	1	5
7	Koltanowski	1	0	½	½	½	0	*	½	½	1	4½
8	Dunkelblum	½	0	0	0	½	½	½	*	½	½	3
9	Dyner	0	0	0	1	0	0	½	½	*	½	2½
10	Reynolds	0	1	0	0	0	0	0	½	½	*	2

The participants at Ostend 1937 in a casual pose (from left to right): Grob, Fine, Koltanowski, Keres, Dunkelblum, Landau, Tartakower, Reynolds, Dyner, Mrs. List, List. Fine (six wins, three losses and no draws) shared first with Paul Keres and Henry Grob.

(375) KERES, P—FINE

Ostend (1), 1937 (11 April)

Queen's Gambit Declined, Semi-Tarrasch Defence [D41]

1. Nf3 d5 2. d4 Nf6 3. c4 e6 4. Nc3 c5 5. cxd5 Nxd5 6. e4 This advance results in a simplification of the position, as compared with the alternative 6 e3. With 6 e3 White maintains the tension in the centre and the game takes on the character of a Queen's Gambit Accepted, whereas 6 e4 permits Black to simplify the position by a long and forced variation. PK **6 ... Nxc3 7. bxc3 cxd4 8. cxd4 Bb4+** It is advantageous for Black to exchange off as many pieces as possible, since in the first place, White's chances of a kingside attack are thereby lessened, and in the second place Black gets nearer to his eventual objective—the endgame. PK **9. Bd2 Bxd2+** Black might have forced the exchange of queens by 9 ... Qa5, and from a dogmatic point of view this would have been in his favour (queenside pawn majority). Yet this "advantage" is only theoretical, as was demonstrated in Rubinstein–Schlechter, San Sebastian 1912: 10 Rb1! Bxd2+ 11 Qxd2 Qxd2+ 12 Kxd2 0–0 13 Bb5!! (forcing the weakening of the b6 square) a6 14 Bd3 Rd8 15 Rhc1 with a winning advantage. EV **10. Qxd2 0–0 11. Bc4** Here the bishop stands every bit as well as on d3 and it can support the advance d4-d5 in some eventualities. PK **11 ... Nd7** At the time the reply 11 ... Nc6 was considered adequate in view of the sequence 12 0–0 b6 13 Rfd1 Bb7 14 Qf4 Rc8 (or 14 ... Qf6! Reshevsky–Fine, Hastings 1937/8) 15 d5 exd5 16 Bxd5 Qe7 17 Ng5 Ne5 as in Alekhine–Euwe, match game 18, 1937. In the mid–1960s Polugaevsky and Spassky

discovered the strength of 13 Rad1! Bb7 14 Rfe1 (the same arrangement of rooks as Keres–Fine). Their joint analysis led to individual victories over World Champions Tal and Petrosyan respectively. AW **12. 0–0 b6 13. Rad1** Placing a rook on the c-file would serve no purpose and would lead sooner or later to further exchanges. White places his rooks behind the two centre pawns and is always threatening either d5 or e5, so that Black has to pay great care to his defence. **13 ... Bb7 14. Rfe1 Rc8 15. Bb3 Nf6** Many commentators have criticized this move and recommended that Black should bring his knight to f8 to protect his kingside. Such passive play is not to everyone's taste and therefore Fine's choice is not to be censured, especially since Black arrives at a tenable position with it. By posting his knight on f6 Black is adequately protected against the thrust d5 and is also ready, in the event of e5, to play ... Nd5. PK **16. Qf4 Qc7 17. Qh4 Rfd8 18. Re3** In the event of 18 Ne5 Nunn suggests Black initiate play on the queenside by 18 ... b5 (not 18 ... Qc3 19 Re3 Qxd4? 20 Red3). Keres explained that, after long thought in this position, he would like to be able to play d5 and if ... exd5, continue that attack by e5. But, on the immediate 18 d5 exd5 19 e5, Black can reply 19 ... Ne4, when the exchange sacrifice 20 Rxe4 dxe4 leaves the rook on d1 *en prise*. Therefore, White first removes the rook from the d-file. This plan should have been insufficient to win and so Keres later proposed the improvement 18 e5 Nd5 19 Ng5 h6 20 Ne4 Nc3 21 Nf6+. Nunn, however, pointed out that Black can defend by 21 ... Kh8! 22 Rd3 Ba6 and White cannot continue his attack because of the weakness of his back rank. Vuković suggested (instead of Keres' 21 Nf6+) 21 Nxc3 Qxc3 22 Re3 Qb4 23 Rg3 Kh8 24 Qg4 Qf8 25 h4 Rc7 26 f4, intending f4-f5 followed, after exchanges, by e6. In this line 26 ... Be4 (not analyzed by Vuković) would at least hold up f5 and transfer a piece to defensive duties on the kingside. AW **18 ... b5!** A very strong move that not only prepares the advance of the queenside pawns but also gives the queen the important square b6. PK **19. Rde1 a5** 19 ... h6 would have been more prudent, practically putting an end to White's hopes on the kingside. PK **20. a4 b4** While this is positionally attractive, it allows the initiative to slip out of Black's hands, with the result that White comes back into the game with prospects which are worth a draw at least. Black should have played 20 ... bxa4 21 Bxa4 h6, when White's attack would have petered out. VV **21. d5! exd5 22. e5 Nd7** On 22 ... Ne4! Keres had planned 23 e6 fxe6 24 Rxe4 dxe4 25 Ng5 with a strong attack, but, after the game analysts showed that 25 ... Qc3! would be an adequate reply, since, in the event of White continuing his attack by 26 Qxh7+, the king could escape to the queenside. Therefore Keres later proposed 26 Bxe6+ Kf8 27 Rf1, threatening Qf4+ followed by Qf7+ and Qxb7, or simply 28 Bxc8. However, Nunn points out that Black can meet the twin threats with 27 ... Rb8. After 28 Qf4+ Ke7 29 Qf7+ Kd6 White would have to play 30 Qf5 to prevent the king escaping, and Black can at least draw by 30 ... Ke7. Because of the lack of a decisive continuation after 25 Ng5, Vuković reckoned White's best line was to force the draw by 25 Bxe6+ Kh8 26 Ng5 h6 27 Nf7+ Kh7 28 Ng5+. AW **23. Ng5** Because of the possibility of a defence to this mode of attack, Vuković reckoned that 23 Nd4!. Nf8 24 Bc2 Ng6 25 Bxg6 fxg6 26 Ne6 Qd7 27 Nxd8 Qxd8, winning the exchange for inadequate compensation, was best. AW **23 ... Nf8?** Keres wrote "This is a fatal error. By 23 ... h6! Black could have resisted. White would then continue 24 e6! (Vukovic's suggestion 24 Nxf7 Kxf7 25 e6+ Kg8 26 exd7 Rxd7 does not seem to work— AW) hxg5 25 exf7+ Kxf7 26 Re7+ after which the following continuations could arise: 1) 26 ... Kg6 27 Qh3! (Nunn's improvement over 27 Qd4 Qc3 28 Bc2+ Kh5 29 Qd1+, when 29 ... g4 30 Bf5 Nf6! 31 Rxb7 Re8, rather than 29 ... Kh6 R1e3 winning the queen, is unclear), when Black cannot meet the threats based on Qd3+ and R1e6+. 2) 26 ... Kg8 27 Qxg5 (after 27 Qh5 Black has the good defence of 27 ... Qf4! and 28 Qd4 is answered by 28 ... Qc3, or according to Vuković 28 Rxd7 by 28 ... Rxd7 29 Re8+ Qf8 30 Rxf8+ Kxf8) Qc3 28 h4! (this seems even stronger than 28 Bxd5+ Bxd5 29 Qxd5+ Kh8 30 Qh5+)," and now Keres believes that 28 ... Qf6 is forced, when 29 Bxd5+ Bxd5 30 Qxd5+ Kh8 31 Rxd7 gives winning chances. FRITZ, however, does not find anything wrong with 28 ... Rc5. AW **24. Nxh7!** This typical knight sacrifice is speedily decisive, since the black kingside, so bereft of its own pieces cannot resist the ensuing attack. Acceptance of the sacrifice is more or less forced, as 24 ... Ng6 25 Qh5 Nf4 26 Qf5 would grant White a powerful attack with level material. PK **24 ... Nxh7 25. Rh3 Qc1 26. Qxh7+ Kf8 27. Rhe3 d4 28. Qh8+ Ke7 29. Qxg7 Rf8 30. Qf6+ Ke8 31. e6** Black resigned. After the forced line 31 ... dxe3 32 exf7+ Rxf7 33 Bxf7+ Kd7 34 Qe6+, he either loses his queen or is mated. PK **1–0** Notes based on Keres 1996, 59–65; Keres in *Chess* 1936-7, 331–2; Vuković, 230-6; Varnusz, 1994 37–8. I have only quoted the principal variations of this fascinating struggle, the game is analyzed in much greater detail by both Keres and Vuković. There has been a recent edition of *Art of Attack*, which I have not seen, and which may or may not have been updated to clarify certain lines. In any case this game is well worth further investigation. AW

(376) FINE—TARTAKOWER, S

Ostend (2), 1937 (12 April)
Nimzowitsch-Indian Defence, Classical Variation [E37]

1. d4 Nf6 Seldom played by Tartakower, who prefers 1 ... d5. **2. c4 e6 3. Nc3 Bb4** Again one is led to observe how

seldom Tartakower is to be found playing the Nimzowitsch-Indian Defence. **4. Qc2 d5** According to the very latest theory, this move is insufficient. The Milner-Barry Variation 4 ... Nc6, followed as quickly as possible by ... e5 is possibly the best continuation, offering Black good chances of early equality. Tartakower naturally knows all this, but he has a novelty up his sleeve. **5. a3** For long condemned as a waste of time, this moved is now looked upon as very strong. **5 ... Bxc3+** Grünfeld once tried (against Ahues) 5 ... Be7 and obtained a satisfactory game. In spite of this the retreat with the bishop must be regarded as suspect: White transposes back into a normal Queen's Gambit in which he has received as a present the move a3, often very useful (for example enabling the king's bishop, after capturing on c4 at a later stage, to retreat to a2 and possibly support the queen in a mating attack from b1). **6. Qxc3** Much stronger than the recapture with the pawn. **6 ... Ne4 7. Qc2 0–0** The "normal" variation follows the Vidmar–Alekhine game at San Remo, 1930: 7 ... Nc6 8 e3 e5. In this very line, however, several improvements in White's play have been discovered. **8. e3 Nd7 9. Bd3 e5** This is the novelty to which we previously referred. One cannot condemn it altogether, in spite of the result of the game, since White obtains "only" the slightly better game which seems to be all that any other continuation for Black brings. The switch into a "Stonewall" formation which Danielsson tried against Fine at Stockholm a few weeks ago (9 ... f5) proved perfectly satisfactory for White. **10. cxd5** The best. After 10 Bxe4 dxe4 11 Qxe4 Black would have far better counterplay, for example, 11 ... Nc6 12 Qxe5 Re8 13 Qf4 Re4 14 Qg3 Qxd4. **10 ... Nef6 11. e4 Re8 12. Nf3** White does not bother himself for a moment with any attempt to retain his extra pawn such as 12 dxe5 Nxe5 13 Be2. It soon becomes obvious how excellent his plan is. **12 ... Nxd5** Cleverly conceived. After 13 exd5 e4 14 Bxe4 f5 Black would have a most promising game. **13. 0–0!** But White does not oblige, proceeding to pile up a superiority in development which soon becomes dangerous. **13 ... N5b6** Difficulties already! The knight cannot retreat to f6; 13 ... N5f6 because of the reply 14 Nxe5 Nxe5 15 dxe5 Rxe5 16 f4 Re8 17 e5 and White not only picks up the h-pawn but retains his positional advantage. The knight stands badly at b6 and makes White's advantages (the two bishops, the centre) even more easily evaluated. **14. a4** Threatening 15 a5 and the knight has nowhere to go. **14 ... a5**

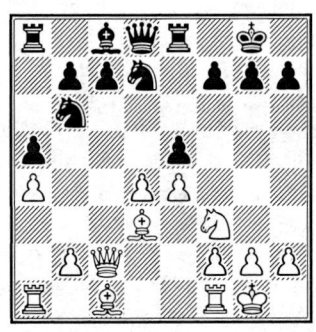

Position after
Black's 14th move

15. Rd1 Again with a threat: 16 Nxe5 Nxe5 17 dxe5 Rxe5 18 Bf4 followed by Bxc7 for 18 ... Re7 comes to grief on

19 Bg5 f6 20 Bc4+. **15 ... exd4** Parrying the threat but yielding to White complete control of the centre. **16. Nxd4 Ne5 17. Be2 Qe7 18. b3** Another knock. 19 Ba3 is threatened and would win at least the c-pawn. **18 ... c6 19. Be3** Now that through the threat of going to a3 this bishop has forced c6, it now stands better on e3, where it bears on the knight at b6 thus rendered unprotected. **19 ... Qf6 20. h3** Prepares for f4; this threat engulfs Black in fatal difficulties. **20 ... g5** Very venturesome but under the circumstances conceivable, for Tartakower is never afraid of taking a risk. The only other move worth consideration is 20 ... Ng6 after which there could follow 21 Nf5 Nd5 22 Nh6+ gxh6 23 exd5 with an overpowering position for White. So perhaps bold measures were necessary. **21. Rac1 Ng6** An oversight. 21 ... Nbd7 was necessary. **22. Nf3!** Decides the game, for it wins the important g-pawn. **22 ... Nd7 23. Bxg5 Qg7 24. Nd4** Allowing Black the opportunity, if he care to take it, of recovering the pawn. 24 Be3 as an alternative was simple and good. **24 ... Qe5 25. Nf5 Nf6** Black perceives that the e-pawn cannot be taken: there would follow 26 Bd3 and the resulting attack would be unstoppable. **26. Bc4** Threatening Nh6+ followed by Nxf7. **26 ... Be6 27. f3** The e-pawn has got to be protected sooner or later. **27 ... Bxf5** The knight is too strong to be allowed to stay there forever. All the same, this move yields White the conclusive advantage of two bishops against two knights and, in conjunction with the preceding move by Black represents a waste of time. **28. exf5 Nf4**

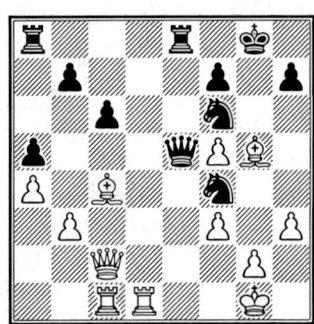

Position after Black's 28th move

29. Re1 Forcing a simplification very useful for White—the text had to be carefully calculated, though. **29 ... Qd4+** Black realizes that both 29 ... Qxe1+ and 29 ... Nxh3+ would lead to a mere worsening of his already compromised position, for example, 29 ... Qxe1+ 30 Rxe1 Rxe1+ 31 Kf2 and White wins a piece or 29 ... Nxh3+ 30 Kh1 (not 30 gxh3 because of 30 ... Qg3+ nor 30 Kf1 because of 30 ... Qh2) Qxe1+ (if 30 ... Qg3 31 Rxe8+ followed by 32 gxh3) 31 Rxe1 Rxe1+ 32 Kh2 Nxg5 33 Qd2 and White wins since not only the rook but both knights are attacked, so that such moves as 33 ... Rae8 fail to prevent the loss of at least a piece. **30. Qf2** Forcing the exchange of queens. **30 ... Qxf2+** After 30 ... Qd6 White would win a piece by 31 Bxf6 followed by Qg3+. **31. Kxf2** His two bishops and well protected majority on the kingside ensure White a safe win in the endgame. **31 ... N4d5 32. g4 Kg7 33. Bd2 h6** Overanxious attention to the threat of g5 costs a second pawn. 33 ... b6 would have

been better. **34. Rxe8 Rxe8** Or 34 ... Nxe8 35 Bxd5 exd5 36 Rc5. **35. Bxa5 Nf4 36. Kg3 N6d5 37. Re1 Rxe1 38. Bxe1 Kf6 39. Bd2 Ke5 40. a5 h5 41. h4 f6 42. Bc1 c5 43. Bd2 hxg4 44. fxg4 Ke4 45. Bxf4 Nxf4 46. h5 Nxh5+ 47. gxh5 Kxf5 48. Kh4** Black resigned. **1–0** Euwe in *Chess* 1936–7, 329–31.

(377) FINE—LANDAU, S

Ostend (3), 1937 (14 April)
Queens Indian Defence [E15]

My style has usually been described as more of a defensive than an offensive character. To my own way of thinking this has not been accurate; my chief objective was always precision, wherever that would take me. In the following game I was able to take advantage of a weak opening move on my opponent's part to launch a speculative but promising attack. RF **1. Nf3 Nf6 2. g3 b6 3. d4 Bb7 4. c4 e6 5. Bg2 Qc8** 5 ... Be7 6 0–0 0–0 7 Nc3 (7 Qc2 Be4 was fine for Black in Capablanca–Alekhine, A.V.R.O. 1938) Ne4 8 Qc2 Nxc3 9 Qxc3 f5 10 Be3 Bf6 11 Qd2 d6 12 d5 Alekhine–Botvinnik, A.V.R.O. 1938. **6. 0–0 c5 7. d5!?** Introduced in this game, but originally analyzed by Chekhover and Rabinovich. 7 b3 had been the usual move in practice. **7 ... exd5 8. cxd5 Bxd5** 8 ... Nxd5 9 e4 (9 Ne5 Nf6 10 Qb3 d5 11 Nc3 preserves the pressure) Nc7 10 Nc3 Be7 is better, MCO 193. **9. Nc3 Bc6 10. e4 Be7** Of course the pawn may not be taken because of the pin on the e-file. RF **11. e5 Ng8** Trying to hold onto his advantage. If 11 ... Ne4 12 Nd5 and Black's game is far from easy. RF **12. Re1 Qb7** Preventing 13 Ne4. **13. Qd3 Na6 14. Ne4 Nc7** To get to e6. If, instead, 14 ... Nb4 15 Nd6+ Bxd6 16 exd6+ Kf8 17 Qf5 is very strong. An intriguing continuation here is 17 ... g6 18 Qe5 f6 19 Bh6+!! Kf7 20 Ng5+! and mates, or here 19 ... Nxh6 20 Qxf6+ Nf7 21 Ng5 wins. RF (In this line 17 ... h6 looks harder to break down, for example: 18 a3 Nd5 19 Ne5 Ngf6, however after 20 b3 Re8 21 Bb2 Qa8 22 Rad1 Kg8 23 Nxc6 dxc6 24 Rxe8+ Qxe8 25 Bxf6 Nxf6 26 d7 Qd8 27 Bxc6 White is in control. Perhaps Black can improve on this though. AW) **15. Nh4!** With the very powerful threat of Nf5. Black had hoped, instead, for the weaker 15 Nd6+ Bxd6 16 exd6 Ne6. RF **15 ... Kf8** He has only a choice of evils. If 15 ... 0–0–0 16 Nf5, and if 15 ... g6 16 Bg5 are both hard to meet. RF **16. Nd6 Bxd6 17. Qxd6+ Ke8** If, instead, 17 ... Ne7 18 Bg5 Re8 19 Bxe7+ Rxe7 20 Nf5 wins. RF **18. Nf5!!**

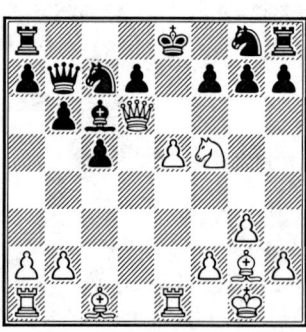

Position after White's 18th move

18 ... Bxg2 19. Nxg7+ Kd8 20. e6!! The point: White has all kinds of mating threats. RF 20 ... Nxe6 On the alternative 20 ... fxe6 White wins with 21 Rxe6! Bh1 (or 21 ... Nxe6 22 Nxe6+ and Qf8 mate) 22 Qf8+ Ne8 23 Rxe8+ Kc7 24 Bf4+. RF 21. Rxe6! Nh6 22. Rxh6 Bh1 23. f3! The simplest road to victory. RF 23 ... Qxf3 24. Qf6+ Kc7 25. Qxf3 Bxf3 26. Rf6 Played a little carelessly, though it is still sufficient. More exact was 26 Bf4+ Kb7 27 Rd6 (better yet 27 Nf5! AW) Bc6 28 Nh5. RF 26 ... Bd5 27. Bf4+ Kb7 28. Rf5 Kc6 29. b3 Rhg8 30. Rd1 Bxb3 31. axb3 Rxg7 32. Rd6+ Kb5 33. Rxd7 a5 34. Rfxf7 Rxf7 35. Rxf7 h5 36. Rf6 Black resigned. 1–0 Fine 1958, 136–9.

(378) LIST, P—FINE

Ostend (4), 1937 (15 April)
English Opening, Symmetrical Variation [A34]

1. Nf3 Nf6 2. c4 c5 3. Nc3 d5 4. cxd5 Nxd5 5. d4 Nxc3 6. bxc3 g6 7. e3 Bg7 8. Bb5+ Nd7 9. 0–0 a6 10. Be2 0–0 11. a4 b6 12. Ba3 Qc7 13. Qb3 Bb7 14. Rab1 Rab8 15. Rfd1 e6 16. Rd2 Rfc8 17. Rc1 This amounts to a loss of time. The correct move was 17 Qd1! with Rb2 to follow. EJD 17 ... b5!

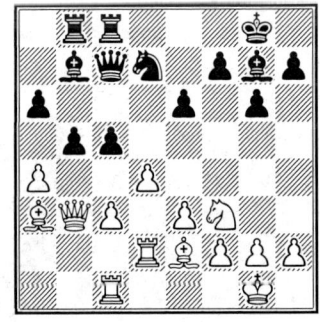

Position after Black's 17th move

18. axb5 axb5 19. Ne1 Bd5 20. Qd1 Qa5 21. Bb2 cxd4 22. cxd4 White could put up more resistance by 22 exd4. EJD 22 ... Bb3 23. Ra1 Qb4 24. Nd3 Bxd1! 25. Nxb4 Bxe2 26. Rxe2 Bf8 27. Nd3 Nb6 28. f3 Nc4 29. Kf2 Ra8 30. Rxa8 Rxa8 31. Ne5 Nxe5 32. dxe5 b4 33. Bd4 b3 34. Rb2 Ra2 35. Ke2 Ba3 36. Rxa2 bxa2 37. Kd3 Bc5! 38. Ba1 Kg7 39. g4 39 Kc4 Bxe3 40 Kb3 Kh6 41 Kxa2 Kg5 42 Kb3 Bg1 43 Kc4 Bxh2 44 Kd3 Kf5 is also lost. RF 39 ... h5 40. h3 Kf8 Now entry via h6 and g5 is not feasible, since White can play f3-f4. RF 41. e4 Bf2 Again threatening ... Kf8-g7-h6-g5 if White's king should go after the a-pawn. RF 42. Ke2 Bg3 43. Ke3 Ke7 44. Kd4? Simplifying Black's task! After the text, the Black king cannot be prevented from penetrating the white position. EJD; A mistake. But on 44 Kd3 Kd7 45 Kc4 Kc6 46 Bc3 Kb6! 47 Kb3 Kc5 48 Kxa2 Kc4 49 Kb2 Kd3 White is also lost. RF 44 ... f6! 45. exf6+ Kxf6 46. g5+ Else 46 ... Be5. RF 46 ... Kxg5 White resigned. A magnificent demonstration of Fine's exemplary technique! EJD 0–1 Diemer, 28; Fine 1941, 158; *Encyclopaedia of Chess Endings: Minor Piece Endings* 468–9.

(379) GROB, H—FINE

Ostend (5), 1937 (15 April)
Giuoco Piano [C50]

1. e4 e5 2. Nf3 Nc6 3. Bc4 Nf6 4. d3 Bc5 5. Nc3 d6 6. Bg5 The Canal Variation. EJD 6 ... h6 Either 6 ... Be6 or even 6 ... Na5 would be better. EJD 7. Bxf6 Qxf6 8. Nd5 Qd8 9. c3 Ne7 9 ... Be6 is weak in view of 10 d4! EJD 10. d4 exd4 11. cxd4 In the well-known game Canal–Johner, Carslbad 1929, there followed 11 Nxd4 Nxd5 12 Bxd5 0–0 13 Qd3 Qf6 14 Bb3 Re8 15 0–0 Be6 16 Bc2 g6 17 Kh1 Rad8 18 f4 and White won quickly. EJD 11 ... Bb6 12. Nxb6 (12 0–0 Nxd5 13 Bxd5 0–0 14 h3 c6 with equality Golombek–Michell, Hastings 1935/6.) 12 ... axb6 13. Qb3 0–0 14. 0–0 Nc6 15. Qc3 Na5?! 16. Bd3 d5?! Fine gets carried away and overplays his hand with this double-pawn offer, but his attack does not last. EJD 17. exd5 Qxd5 18. Qxc7 Nc6 19. Qxb6 Bg4 20. Be2 Rfe8 21. Bd1! Re7 22. Ne5!! Nxe5 23. dxe5 Bxd1 24. Rfxd1 Qxe5 25. h3 Ra6 26. Qd4 Qxd4 27. Rxd4 The game has entered a double-rook ending of a kind not as yet known to chess literature; it actually requires fairly delicate handling. EJD 27 ... Re2 28. Rb4 Rf6 29. Rf1 b6 30. g4 White's conduct of this ending can be taken as a model. The combination 30 ... Rd6 does not work now; 31 a4 Rdd2 32 Rxb6 Rxb2 33 Rxb2 Rxb2 34 Ra1 and wins. RF 30 ... Kf8 31. Kg2 Ke8 32. Kg3 Lifting the pin. The threat is now f3 and Rb3 followed by Rf2. RF 32 ... Rd6 33. a4 33 f3? Rdd2, threatening mate. RF 33 ... g5 34. Kf3 Rc2 35. Kg2 Kd7 36. Rb5 Kc6 37. Rf5! Liberating the other rook. RF 37 ... Rxb2 38. Rc1+ Kb7 39. Rxf7+ Ka6 40. Rc8 Ka5 41. Rc4 Again threatens mate. RF 41 ... Ka6 42. Re4 The ending now enters its second phase: White has succeeded in freeing both rooks and his next objective is to set up a passed pawn on the kingside. RF 42 ... Ra2 43. h4! gxh4 44. Kh3 Rd1 45. Kxh4 Rh1+ Black has no real counterplay: he can only harry his opponent. RF 46. Kg3 h5 Rather exchange than lose it for nothing. RF 47. gxh5 Rxh5 Now we have an ending which is quite simple with only one rook, but the extra pieces produce complications. RF 48. Kg4 Rh1 49. f4 Rg1+ 50. Kf5 Rga1 51. Rf8 Rc1 If instead 51 ... Kb7 52 Re7+ Kc6 53 Rf6+ Kc5 54 Re5+ Kd4 55 Rxb6 Rxa4 56 Re4+ Kd5 57 Rxa4 Rxa4 58 Kg5 with an elementary win while on 51 ... Rxa4 52 Rxa4+ Rxa4 53 Ra8+ Kb5 54 Rxa4 Kxa4 55 Ke4 (Fine actually gives 55 Ke6 55 b5 56 f5 White queens first and wins Black's queen by checking at a8 and b8, but readers can easily determine for themselves that this is in error. AW) b5 56 f5 b4 57 f6 b3 58 Kd3 (and wins. AW). RF 52. Rfe8 Rca1 53. Rb4 Kb7 54. Re7+ Kc6 55. Rc4+ 55 Re6+ is not so clear. RF 55 ... Kd5 56. Rc8 Threatening mate. RF 56 ... Kd4 57. Rd8+ Kc3 58. Rc7+ Kb3 59. Rb8 Rxa4 60. Rxb6+ The rest is routine, but requires a little more care than the corresponding ending with one pair of rooks. RF 60 ... Ka3 61. Rc3+ Ka2 62. Re6 Rf1 63. Re4 Ra5+ 64. Ke6 Rh1 65. Re5 Rh6+ 66. Kf5 Rh5+ 67. Kf6 Ra6+ 68. Kg7 Rh1

69. f5 Rb1 70. Re2+ Ka1 71. Re6 Rg1+ 72. Kf7 Ra7+ 73. Re7 Ra6 74. Rce3 Black resigned. The march of the pawn cannot be halted. RF **1–0** Diemer, 31–2; Fine 1941, 435.

(380) FINE—DUNKELBLUM, A

Ostend (6), 1937 (16 April)
Queen's Gambit Declined [D37]

1. Nf3 Nf6 2. c4 e6 3. d4 d5 4. Nc3 Be7 5. e3 0–0 6. Bd3 c5 7. 0–0 dxc4 8. Bxc4 a6 9. Qe2 b5 10. Bd3 Nbd7!? 11. a4! b4 12. Ne4 Bb7 13. Ned2 cxd4 14. exd4 a5 15. Nc4 Nb6 16. Nce5 Nbd5 17. Be3 Qb6 18. Nc4 Qd8 19. Rad1 Nd7 This leads to an unnecessary weakening of the kingside. **20. Nfe5 N7b6 21. Nxb6 Nxb6**

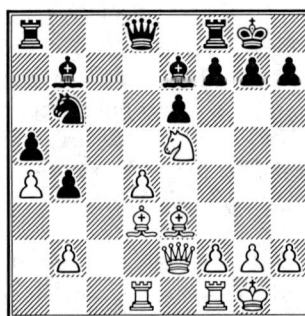

Position after Black's 21st move

22. Qh5! f5 23. Bb5 Nd5 24. Rfe1 Nf6 25. Qe2 Bd5 26. Nc6 Qd6 27. Nxe7+ Qxe7 28. Bf4 Rfc8 29. Rc1 Ne4 30. Bc4 Qd7 31. Bxd5 exd5 32. Qb5! Nf6 33. Rxc8+ Qxc8 34. Re7 Qf8 35. Rc7 Re8 36. Be5 Re7 37. Qxa5 Rxc7 38. Qxc7 Ng4 39. Qb8 Qxb8 40. Bxb8 Nf6 41. a5 Black resigned. Routine play and apparently insignificant mistakes can lead to a swift loss against Fine. **1–0** Diemer, 35.

(381) DYNER, I—FINE

Ostend (7), 1937 (17 April)
Queen's Gambit Declined, Vienna Variation [D39]

1. d4 Nf6 2. Nf3 d5 3. c4 e6 4. Nc3 Bb4 5. Bg5 dxc4 6. e4! The sharpest continuation. **6 ... c5!** Maroczy's move. **7. Bxc4 cxd4 8. Bxf6** In *NCO* Burgess's main line is 8 Nxd4 Bxc3+ (Diemer gave 8 ... Qa5 9 Bd2 Qc5! 10 Bb5+ Bd7) 9 bxc3 Qa5 10 Bb5+ Nbd7 11 Bxf6 Qxc3+ 12 Kf1 gxf6 13 h4 a6 14 Rh3 Qa5. AW **8 ... Qxf6 9. Qxd4 Qxd4** 9 ... Nc6! 10 Qxf6 gxf6 11 Rc1 Bd7 12 0–0 Rc8 as in the game Chekhover–Lasker, Moscow 1935, is more promising. **10. Nxd4 a6 11. a3 Be7 12. Rc1 Bd7 13. 0–0 Nc6 14. Nxc6 Bxc6 15. g3 Bf6 16. Rfe1 Bd4 17. Rcd1** From here on White is swimming, it is no wonder that the decisive mistake is not long in coming. **17 ... 0–0–0 18. Rc1 Kb8 19. Bf1 Rd7 20. Bg2 Rc8 21. h4 Rdc7 22. Red1 Bf6 23. Re1 Be5 24. Re3 Bd7 25. Rd1** A decisive loss of tempo. The white king must move off the

dark-squared diagonal, in order to allow him to play f2-f4 to drive the bishop from e5 or force it to take on c3 immediately. **25 ... Be8 26. Rc1 Rc6 27. Rd3 Rb6 28. f4 Bxc3 29. bxc3 Rb3 30. e5 Bb5 31. Re3 Rxa3 32. Be4 Bc6 33. Bxc6 Rxc6 34. Kf2 b5 35. h5 Rb3 36. h6 gxh6 37. g4 Rc4 38. Rf3 b4 39. f5 Rbxc3 40. Rfxc3 Rxc3 41. fxe6 fxe6 42. Rh1 b3** White resigned. **0–1** Diemer, 37–8.

(382) FINE—REYNOLDS, A

Ostend (8), 1937 (18 April)
Nimzowitsch-Indian Defence, Classical Variation [E33]

1. d4 Nf6 2. c4 e6 3. Nc3 Bb4 4. Qc2 Nc6 A rare line akin to Milner-Barry's idea against 4 Qb3. **5. Nf3 0–0** He could even play 5 ... d6 at once, for example 6 Bd2 e5. A different and less flexible, although playable line is 5 ... d5. T&dM **6. Bd2** If 6 e4, then 6 ... e5 and if 7 dxe5 Ng4 8 Bf4 Qe7 9 a3 Bxc3+ 10 Qxc3 Re8 regaining the pawn with a level game. 6 a3 at once is often played, when follows 6 ... Bxc3+ 7 Qxc3 Ne4, with a fairly good game. HEA; A consolidating manoeuvre. Either 6 Bg5 Re8 7 e3 d6 8 Be2 e5, or 6 e4 e5, or 6 g3 Re8, or 6 a3 Bxc3+ 7 Qxc3 Ne4 8 Qc2 f5 and Black contests mastery of the centre. T&dM; This natural move, a product of the present Russian school, was not unexpected by me, since Fine has recently played in two Russian tournaments. AR **6 ... d6 7. a3 Bxc3 8. Bxc3 Re8** If 8 ... Qe7 9 g3 (9 e3 e5 10 d5 Nb8 11 Bd3 (11 Nd2! Sokolov) Nbd7 12 Ng5 g6! 13 Ne4 Nxe4 with an equal game, Euwe–Alekhine, match game 22, 1935) e5 10 d5 Nd8!? (10 ... Nb8 Sokolov) and White won in 26 moves, M. Gurevich–Timman, Rotterdam 1990. **9. Rd1 Qe7** An unfortunate necessity, this square being very useful for the queen's knight in many variations of the defence. AR **10. e3** If 10 e4 e5 11 d5 Nd4. T&dM **10 ... e5 11. d5 Nb8 12. Nd2?!** Fine does not play this opening with his customary accuracy. Without a doubt it is this move which causes him difficulties and leads to the ultimate loss of the game. 12 Be2 is right and then if 12 ... e4 13 Nd4 followed by b4 and pressure on the queenside. The text initiates a faulty idea which only leads to the opening of favourable lines to the opponent. AR **12 ... Nbd7 13. e4?** If 13 g3 e4 14 Bg2 Nc5 15 0–0 Bg4, with a strong attack. If 16 Bxf6 Bxd1. HEA **13 ... Nh5!** With this move Black seizes the initiative and with a few bold strokes obtains the better game. AR **14. g3 f5!** Evidently this possibility had been overlooked by my opponent when he played 12 Nd2. AR **15. exf5 e4** Black stands a little better, MCO 186. **16. Be2 Ndf6** Not the tempting 16 ... e3? because of 17 0–0! and White wins. AR **17. 0–0** If 17 Bxf6 Nxf6 18 g4 e3 19 fxe3 (White might do better to brave 19 Nf1. AW) Nxg4 20 Bxg4 Qh4+. T&dM; Any attempt to hold the pawn would be speedily fatal: 17 g4 Nf4 (17 ... e3! seems clearer, since at the end of Reynolds variation 22 Nf1 defends the mate. AW) 18 g5 Nd3+ 19 Kf1 Bxf5! 20 gxf6 Bh3+ 21 Ng1 gxf6 and mate follows. AR **17 ... Bxf5** The first phase of the game is now over with Black in the ascendancy. The second part of the game now centres around the fight for Black's strong (weak?) pawn on e4. AR **18. Rfe1 Qf7!** Just sufficient. AR **19. Nf1 Ng4** Threatening 20 ... e3 or 20 ... N×f2. T&dM **20. Ne3 N×e3 21. f×e3 Qg6 22. Bf1** After 22 B×h5 Q×h5 the bishops of opposite colours would render White's defence more difficult, as Black's bishop would become practically inexpugnable. T&dM **22 ... Bg4 23. Rd4 Bf5** If 23 ... Bf3 24 Bg2 with a little more hope. HEA **24. Bg2 Nf6** The initiation of the knight manoeuvre which decides the game. AR **25. Rf1** This might have been a good time to remove the rook from d4. AW **25 ... Ng4 26. Bd2 Ne5 27. Rf4** Evidently if 27 B×e4 White loses the exchange. HEA **27 ... Nd3** Just in time! The pawn at e4 is now proved to be a strong pawn and helps materially to decide the game. AR **28. Rf1 h5!** Black's evolutions are animated by a praiseworthy spirit of aggression. T&dM **29. Bc3 Re7 30. Qe2 Rf8 31. Qd2 Ref7 32. Rf4** White must give up something. The queen's rook and queen's bishop are both out of play and ... h5-h4 followed by ... Bh3 and ... Rf2 is threatened. HEA **32 ... N×f4 33. e×f4 h4 34. Qe3 h×g3 35. h×g3 Re7 36. Rd2 Bg4 37. Rf2 Rfe8 38. Kh2 Qf5 39. Bd4 g6** He skillfully provides his rooks with an effective base of action. T&dM **40. Bc3 Rh7+ 41. Kg1 Kf7 42. c5 Bf3** This threatens ... Qf5-h5-h1+. HEA **43. B×f3 e×f3 44. Q×f3 Qh3** Threatening ... Re8-e3. IIEA **45. Bd2 Reh8** Black now changes off and wins easily. A very interesting game. HEA **46. f5 Qh1+ 47. Q×h1 R×h1+ 48. Kg2 R8h2+ 49. Kf3 R×f2+ 50. K×f2 g×f5 51. c6 b×c6** White resigned. A jewel of aggressive chess. T&dM **0–1** Atkins in *BCM* 1937, 381–2; Tartakower & du Mont 1952, 617–8; Reynolds in *Chess* 1936-7, 322.

(383) KOLTANOWSKI, G—FINE

Ostend (9), 1937 (19 April)
Colle System [D04]

1. d4 Nf6 2. Nf3 d5 3. e3 c5 4. c3 Nbd7! 5. Nbd2 Qc7! 6. Qa4! g6! 7. d×c5 As is well known, the correct continuation is 7 c4! Bg7 8 c×d5 N×d5 and now, not 9 Qb3 N5b6 10 a4 c×d4! 11 e×d4 a5 with equality, as in the game Alekhine–Reshevsky, Nottingham 1936, but, 9 e4!! N5b6 10 Qc2! Qd6 11 a4!! and White won quickly, Colle–Rubinstein, Rotterdam 1931. **7 ... Q×c5 8. Bd3** 8 c4! is still the right move. **8 ... Bg7 9. 0–0 0–0 10. e4 Qc7!**

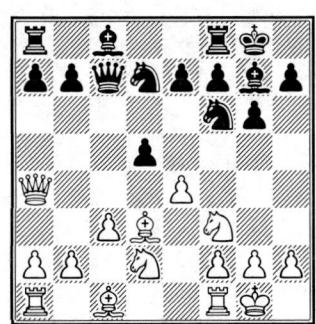

Position after Black's 10th move

11. e×d5 And here 11 Qc2! Nc5 12 Re1!. **11 ... Nc5 12. Qc2 N×d5 13. Ne4 N×d3 14. Q×d3 Rd8 15. Qe2 b6 16. Ng3 Bb7 17. Re1** Here White might try 17 Bg5!?. **17 ... e5! 18. Bd2 Rac8 19. Rad1 Re8**

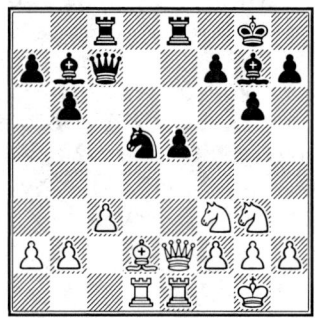

Position after Black's 19th move

20. Nd4 White might have preferred 20 Qf1 to this introduction to a curious counterattack. **20 ... Qb8!** If 20 ... e×d4 21 Q×e8+!. **21. Ndf5** If 21 Nf3 Nf4 with ... N×g2! to follow. **21 ... g×f5 22. N×f5 Re6 23. Qh5 Qc7 24. Re4 Rg6 25. Bg5 Nf6 26. B×f6 B×f6! 27. Rg4 Rd8** White resigned. **0–1** Diemer, 43–4.

A Drop in Form, 1937

Fine did not include a single game, out of about sixty available, from the next six events in his own published collection. Unfortunately neither does he discuss his drop in form, which was generally attributed by other writers to staleness, or possibly distraction caused by his imminent announcement of his engagement. His results in this period seem to be the source of his reputation as a drawing master and for his low estimation by many commentators writing in advance of the A.V.R.O. tournament. In the summer of 1937, following almost two months off from serious competition, Fine had perhaps the worst result of his whole career. He lost five games in a tournament and only just managed to stay above the fifty percent mark. His play was patchy throughout the event, no sooner would he pick up a point than he would drop it again. He did not manage to win a single game against the grandmasters in the field.

V. A. S. Tournament, April 24–May 1, 1937

Fine took part in another four-player tournament in the spring of 1937. On this occasion his play was far superior to the hesitant display of the equivalent event of six months earlier. Crosstable unavailable.

(384) FINE—SPINHOVEN, F

V.A.S. Tournament, Amsterdam (1), 1937 (24 April)
English Opening, Classical Variation [A28]

1. c4 e5 2. Nf3 Nc6 3. Nc3 Nf6 4. e4 Bc5 5. Be2 d6 6. 0–0 Nd4 7. d3 Nxe2+ 8. Qxe2 a5 9. Be3 Qe7 10. d4! This advance has been made possible by Black's sixth and seventh moves. White now has an excellent game. **10 ... exd4 11. Nxd4 0–0 12. f3 Re8 13. Rae1 a4 14. Qc2 a3 15. b3 Bb4 16. Re2 c6 17. Rd1 Qc7 18. Kh1 Nd7 19. Qc1 Ne5 20. Na4 c5?** A grave blunder. (20 ... Qa5. Fritz) **21. Nb5 Qc6** Now White wins the queen. **22. Rxd6** Black resigned. **1–0** *De Shaakwereld* 43, 10

(385) POLAK, J—FINE

V.A.S. Tournament, Amsterdam (2), 1937 (25 April)
Nimzowitsch-Indian Defence, Spielmann Variation [E23]

1. d4 Nf6 2. c4 e6 3. Nc3 Bb4 4. Qb3 c5 5. Nf3 Nc6 6. dxc5 Ne4 7. e3 Here 7 Bd2 is normal. After the move played White is saddled with doubled isolated pawns on an open file which the American Grandmaster exploits in expert fashion. **7 ... Nxc3 8. bxc3 Bxc5 9. Bd3 0–0 10. 0–0 b6 11. Qc2 h6 12. Nd4 Bb7**

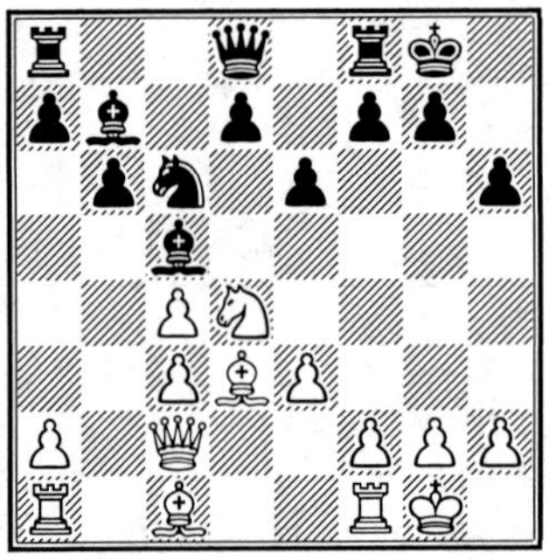

Position after Black's 12th move

13. f4 Intended to prevent ... Nc6-e5. **13 ... Rc8 14. Qe2 Ba6** Commencing operations against c4. **15. Bb2** The bishop is condemned to inactivity on b2; 15 Rf3 would have been better. **15 ... Re8** Preparing ... e6-e5, after which the weakness of e3 will be exposed. **16. Rad1 Na5 17. Nb5** Black threatened to win a pawn by taking on d4 followed by ... Bxc4. **17 ... e5 18. Bf5 exf4 19. Kh1** Not 19 Bxd7, as after 19 ... Rxe3 Black has a nasty discovered check. **19 ... Rxe3 20. Qg4 Nxc4** Black is attacking both the knight and the bishop. **21. Rxd7 Qg5! 22. Nxa7 Qxg4 23. Bxg4 Nxb2** White resigned. **0–1** Notes based on those in *Tilburgse Courant*, 5 June, 1937.

(386) VOS, F—FINE

V.A.S. Tournament, Amsterdam (3), 1937 (1 May)
Sicilian Defence, Scheveningen Variation [B85]

1. e4 c5 2. Nf3 d6 3. d4 cxd4 4. Nxd4 Nf6 5. Nc3 e6 6. Be2 a6 7. a4 Qc7 8. 0–0 Nc6 9. Kh1 Be7 10. f4 0–0 11. Nb3 Na5 12. Nxa5 Qxa5 13. Bf3 Qc7 14. Qe2 Bd7 15. Rd1 Bc6 16. Be3 Nd7 17. Rd2 Bf6 18. Rad1 Bxc3 19. bxc3 Nc5 20. e5 dxe5 21. Bxc5 Bxf3 22. gxf3 Qxc5 23. Qxe5 Rac8 24. Rb1 Qxc3 25. Qxc3 Rxc3 26. Rxb7 Rc4 27. a5 Rc5 28. Ra7 Rxa5 29. c4 Rc5 30. Rd4 a5 31. Kg2 g6 32. Kg3 Rfc8 33. Rdd7 Rf5 34. Rd4 Rb8 35. Rdd7 Rb3 36. c5 g5 37. c6 gxf4+ 38. Kh4 Rc3 39. c7 Kg7 40. Rd8 Rfc5 41. Rd7 Kg6 42. Rxf7 Draw agreed. ½–½

Kemeri/Riga, June 15–July 10, 1937

"Decidedly disappointing was the showing of Reuben Fine. The 23-year-old [*sic*] American master, whose engagement to Miss Emmy Keesing of Amsterdam has just been announced, has developed an impenetrable armour much like that of Flohr's. At Kemeri, he actually lost five games, which his friends found difficult to understand. The mystery is partially cleared up by the interesting news from Holland. Evidently, the brilliant young New Yorker had not rested sufficiently after his strenuous efforts in Europe during the past year. Nevertheless it is good to know that he can join the United States team at Stockholm." (*ACB* 1937) "A two months' rest ensued [after Ostend], apparently not long enough, for his performance at Kemeri in June 1937 was a debacle; he finished ninth out of eighteen, and—what was even more painful—could only amass a single point against the seven leaders, Flohr, Petrovs, Reshevsky, Alekhine, Keres, E. Steiner and Tartakower. Was staleness alone to blame for this setback? The historian gropes in the dark; he can only record that a month afterwards Fine announced his engagement to Miss Keesing. Within another month he was married and had gone off to take part in the very strong tournament at Semmering-Baden, where he really threw himself into the fray." (Euwe, 1940)

		1	2	3	4	5	6	7	8	9	10	11	12	13	14	15	16	17	18	
1	Reshevsky	*	1	½	0	1	1	½	1	½	1	0	0	1	½	1	1	1	1	12
2	Petrovs	0	*	½	½	½	½	½	1	1	0	1	1	1	1	1	1	1	½	12
3	Flohr	½	½	*	½	½	½	½	½	½	½	1	1	½	1	1	1	1	1	12
4	Alekhine	1	½	½	*	½	1	½	1	½	0	½	½	½	½	1	1	1	1	11½
5	Keres	0	½	½	½	*	1	½	½	0	1	1	1	½	1	½	1	1	1	11½
6	Steiner, E	0	½	½	0	0	*	1	1	0	1	½	1	1	1	1	1	½	1	11
7	Tartakower	½	½	½	½	½	0	*	1	½	0	1	1	1	½	½	1	½	1	10½
8	Fine	0	0	½	0	½	0	0	*	½	½	½	1	1	1	1	½	1	1	9
9	Ståhlberg	½	0	½	½	1	1	½	½	*	0	0	1	½	½	0	1	½	½	8½
10	Mikenas	0	1	½	1	0	0	1	½	1	*	0	0	0	0	1	1	0	1	8
11	Rellstab	1	0	0	½	0	½	0	½	1	1	*	0	½	1	0	0	1	½	7½
12	Böök	1	0	0	½	0	0	0	0	0	1	1	*	½	1	1	0	1	½	7½
13	Apšenieks	0	0	½	½	½	0	0	0	½	1	½	½	*	0	1	1	½	1	7½
14	Bergs	½	0	0	½	0	0	½	0	½	1	0	0	1	*	0	1	1	½	6½
15	Feigins	0	0	0	0	½	0	½	0	1	0	1	0	0	1	*	0	½	1	5½
16	Landau	0	0	0	0	0	0	0	½	0	0	1	1	0	0	1	*	1	1	5½
17	Hazenfuss	0	0	0	0	0	½	½	0	½	1	0	0	½	0	½	0	*	0	3½
18	Ozols	0	½	0	0	0	0	0	0	½	0	½	½	0	½	0	0	1	*	3½

(387) LANDAU, S—FINE

Kemeri/Riga (1), 1937 (16 June)

Queen's Gambit Declined, Marshall Variation [D50]

1. d4 Nf6 2. c4 e6 3. Nc3 d5 4. Bg5 Bb4 A defence well thought of by Marshall, who has frequently adopted it. *ACB* **5. Qa4+ Nc6 6. e3** Best. If 6 Nf3 d×c4 7 e3 (7 e4 h6!) Qd5! 8 B×f6 g×f6 9 Nd2 B×c3 10 b×c3 b5 11 Qc2 Bb7 12 Rb1 (if 12 Be2 Q×g2! 13 Bf3 N×d4!) Rb8 13 e4 Qd7! 14 Be2 (not 14 R×b5 N×d4) Ne7 15 0–0 0–0 with a good game for Black. *SB* **6 ... 0–0 7. Nf3** If 7 Bd3 e5! 8 d×e5 B×c3+ followed by 9 ... N×e5. *SB* **7 ... h6 8. Bh4 Be7** In order to answer 9 Bd3 with 9 ... Nb4! *SB* **9. Rd1** 9 Rc1 seems more logical, leaving d1 for the king's rook. *SB* **9 ... Ne4** Black reluctantly goes in for simplification. If 9 ... a6 10 Ne5! *SB* **10. B×e7 N×c3 11. Qc2** If 11 B×d8 N×a4 12 B×c7 N×b2 13 Rc1 N×c4 14 B×c4 d×c4 15 R×c4. *dM&LE* **11 ... N×e7 12. Q×c3** Both players have manoeuvred skillfully to avoid doubled pawns—beautiful negative chess! *ACB* **12 ... d×c4** This seems unnecessary; 12 ... b6 immediately is better. *ACB* **13. B×c4 b6** Weakens the queenside, but it is hard to find a better move. *KB* **14. e4 Bb7 15. Qe3 Ng6 16. 0–0 Qf6! 17. Rd2 Rfd8 18. Rc1 Rac8 19. Bd3** If 19 Bb5 c6! 20 Bc4 (or 20 Ba4 e5 21 d×e5 N×e5 22 R×d8+ R×d8 23 N×e5 Q×e5 and Black's c-pawn cannot be captured) Rd7 followed by 21 ... Rcd8 and an eventual advantageous break by ... c5 or ... e5. *SB* **19 ... e5** White was threatening 20 e5! *KB* **20. d5 c6 21. d×c6 R×c6 22. R×c6 Q×c6 23. Bc4!** The best move. On 23 Rc2 Black would answer 23 ... Qd6 with the superior game. *KB* **23 ... Rc8** Fruitless would be 23 ... R×d2 24 N×d2 b5 25 Bd5 Qc1+ 26 Nf1. *SB* **24. Rc2! Kh7** 24 ... Qd7 would have been somewhat better. *KB* **25. Bb3!** Shows up the weakness of Black's 23rd and 24th moves. It is obvious that f7 has been weakened by moving the e-pawn. *KB* **25 ... Q×c2** Very surprising and probably not sound; 25 ... Qd7 26 R×c8 B×c8 and the game is even. With the more speculative continuation Fine strives desperately to avoid a draw. *ACB* **26. B×c2 R×c2 27. h4** The following line of play, while an improvement on Landau's play, by no means exhausts the possibilities of this interesting position: 27 g3 R×b2 28 a3 f6 29 Kg2 Nf8 30 Nh4 Ne6 31 Nf5 Nc5 32 Nd6 Rb3 33 Qe2 with initiative on the light squares (Qe2-g4). *ACB* (This would appear to favour Black after 33 ... Bc6 34 Qg4 Bd7. *AW*) **27 ... f6 28. g3 R×b2 29. h5 Nf8** Cleverly played, as is shown by White's ensuing futile effort to win a piece. *SB* **30. Qa3 Rb1+ 31. Kg2 B×e4** A key defensive manoeuvre. The White knight is removed from the attack. *dM&LE* **32. Q×f8 Rd1! 33. Qb4 f5!** Or 33 ... Rd4 34 Qe1! f5 35 Qc3! drawing easily. *SB* **34. g4** 34 Qe7 was also good. *SB* **34 ... Rd4 35. Qe7 f×g4 36. Q×e5 B×f3+ 37. Kg3 Rd5 38. Qc7 Rd3 39. Kf4** 39 Q×a7 Be2+ 40 Kf4 R3+ 41 Ke5 b5 also leads to an even position. *AW* **39 ... Rd4+ 40. Kg3 Rd3 41. Kf4 Rd4+ 42. Kg3 Bd1 43. Qc3 Rd8 44. Qe3 Bc2** Yielding a pawn, but assuring a powerful position for the rook. *ACB* **45. K×g4 Rd5 46. f3 Ra5 47. a3 Bb1 48. Qb3 Bf5+ 49. Kg3 Kh8 50. Qe3 Kh7 51. Qe7**

Kg8 52. Kh4 Draw agreed. ½–½ Betins, 48–50; *ACB* 1937, 48; Sidney Bernstein in Reinfeld & Bernstein 67–8; de Marimon & Lopez Esnaola, 18–9.

(388) FINE—FEIGINS, M

Kemeri/Riga (2), 1937 (17 June)

Queen's Gambit Declined [D47]

1. d4 d5 2. Nf3 Nf6 3. c4 c6 4. e3 The modern continuation, by which White avoids the Czech Defence. *KB* **4 ... e6** Black transposes to the Orthodox Defence. In this position 4 ... Bf5 also suffices (5 c×d5 c×d5 6 Qb3 Qc8 7 Nba3 e6 8 Bd2 Nc6 9 Bb5 Nfd7 with equality). *KB* **5. Nc3 Nbd7 6. Bd3 d×c4 7. B×c4 b5 8. Bd3 b4** In order to avoid the complications resulting from 8 ... a6 9 e4 c5 10 e5 c×d4 11 N×b5 N×e5 12 N×e5 a×b5 13 Qf3! (as in the game Reshevsky–Petrovs from the 1st round. *AW*) *SB* **9. Ne4 c5 10. Qa4! c×d4 11. N×d4 Bb7 12. N×f6+ g×f6** This leads to a most difficult game for both sides. Black's king will be insecure and subject to all kinds of tactical menaces; by way of compensation, he will have excellent play for his pieces. *SB* **13. 0–0 Rg8**

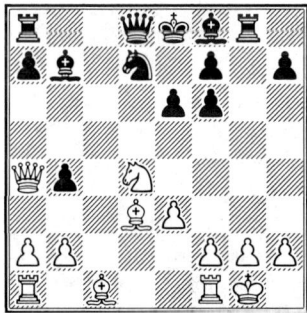

Position after Black's 13th move

14. e4!? The square g2 is difficult to defend. If 14 f3, 14 ... Bd6 exploits the weakening of h2, for example, 15 Nb5 Be5 16 Q×b4 Qb8 17 h3 Bh2+ 18 Kh1 R×g2. 14 g3!—less weakening of the kingside—offered more defensive chances, but would not have secured the better game, for 14 ... f5 15 Bb5, with Bc6 to follow, gives Black a satisfactory position. *KB* **14 ... f5! 15. Bf4** Protecting the e-pawn is impossible, if 15 f3? then 15 ... Bc5 with ... Qb6 to follow, or if 15 Rfe1 Bc5 16 Nb3 Bf2+ 17 K×f2 Qh4+ 18 Kf1 Q×h2. *KB* **15 ... f×e4 16. Bb5 e3! 17. Bc6** If 17 f3 a6!. *AW* **17 ... e×f2+** If now 18 R×f2 Bc5. *AW* **18. Kh1** White is temporarily two pawns down, but he has a certain amount of pressure which compels Black to play with great care. *SB* **18 ... B×c6 19. Q×c6 Rc8 20. Qa4 Rc4!** Counterplay. *SB* **21. Rad1 Qb6 22. R×f2!** If 22 ... R×d4? 23 R×d4 Q×d4 24 Rd2! *SB* **22 ... Qb7! 23. Bg3 Rg5!** According to Bernstein 23 ... Bc5 was more promising, and White has nothing better than 24 Rfd2 (if 24 Nf5 e×f5 25 Rfd2 Rd4 26 R×d4 B×d4 27 R×d4 Rg4!) and Black obtains a good attack by 24 ... B×d4 25 R×d4 R×d4 26 R×d4 Rg5 27 R×b4 Rc5 28 h3 Qc6 29 Q×a7 Rc1+ 30 Kh2 Rc2 31 Qg1 Nf6. Unfortunately, after 32 Rb8+ Ke7 33 Qa7+ Nd7 34 Qa3+ Nc5 35 Bh4+ f6

36 Qg3 it is White who has the attack. AW **24. Rfd2 Rd5 25. h3 Bc5!?** Although this was awarded an exclamation in the tournament books, 25 ... e5 looks to lead to an excellent ending for Black: 26 Bxe5 Rxe5 27 Nf3 Re7 28 Rxd7 Rxd7 29 Rxd7 Qxd7 30 Qxd7 Kxd7 31 Ne5+ Ke6 32 Nxc4 and, with pawns on both sides of the board and an active king, Black has good chances. AW **26. Nf3 Rxd2 27. Rxd2 Rc1+ 28. Kh2**

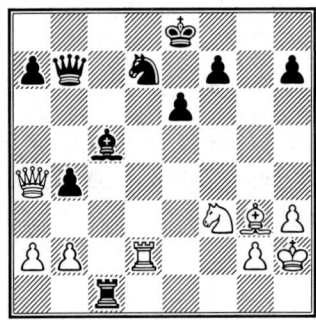

Position after White's 28th move

28 ... f6? With his last move Black threw away a well-deserved victory! Black can escape from all of the complications and emerge with an extra pawn by means of 28 ... Ke7!. After 28 ... Ke7 White's attempt to complicate matters can be seen to lead to an advantage for Black: 29 Bf4 Nb6 30 Qb5 Qe4 31 Bb8 (31 Bc7 Nd5!) Be3!, with ... Bf4+ to follow, and Black wins, or 29 Bh4+ f6, or 29 Qb3 Qe4. Clearly then Black's victory should simply have been a matter of time. After the text tricky complications arise and now Black must fight for a draw. KB **29. Qb3!** Attacking e6 directly and h7 (by Qd3) indirectly. KB **29 ... Qb6!** Threatening 30 ... Qg1+ and 31 ... Be3. dM&LE **30. h4!** The only defence against the threat of 30 ... Bg1+. KB **30 ... Ke7** Leads to a lost game. Correct was 30 ... Qc6 and it is not clear how White can continue the attack. If 31 Nd4 Bxd4 32 Rxd4 Rc2! SB (30 ... Bg1+ 31 Nxg1 Qxg1+ 32 Kh3 Qb6 (but not 32 ... Nc5 33 Qf3 Qh1+ 34 Bh2 Kf7 35 Qh5+ Kg7, as given by the German language tournament book, because of 36 Qg4+ Kf7 37 Rd8 and, in an amusing echo of Black's play, White gets in round the back. AW) **31. Bf4** Both players were in time trouble. After the natural 31 Qd3 Black can reply 31 ... Nf8!, and everything is covered. The text is a gross trap, which Black fails to notice. KB **31 ... Qb5?** Black would still have drawing prospects after 31 ... Bg1+ 32 Nxg1 Qxg1+ 33 Kh3 Qh1+ 34 Bh2. What follows is simply the result of time trouble. KB **32. Rxd7+ Kxd7 33. Bxc1 Bd6+ 34. Kg1 Qe2 35. Qe3 Qa6 36. Qh6 Qd3 37. Qd2 Qb1 38. b3 Ke7 39. Qb2 Qe4 40. Qf2 Bb8 41. Qc5+ Kf7 42. Bh6 Qb1+ 43. Kf2 Qxa2+ 44. Nd2 Kg6 45. Qc8 Qa5 46. g4 Qb6+ 47. Be3** Black resigned. If 47 ... Bg3+ White can even play 48 Kxg3 Qxe3+ 49 Nf3. SB **1–0** Betins, 66–8; Sidney Bernstein in Reinfeld & Bernstein 76–7; de Marimon & Lopez Esnaola, 31–3.

(389) FLOHR, S—FINE

Kemeri/Riga (3), 1937 (19 June)
Catalan System [E03]

1. d4 Nf6 2. c4 e6 3. g3 d5 4. Bg2 White's third and fourth moves avoid the Nimzowitsch-Indian Defence. KB **4 ... dxc4** Black transposes the game into a form of the Queen's Gambit Accepted with bishops fianchettoed on g2 and b7. KB **5. Qa4+ Nbd7 6. Nf3 a6 7. Qxc4 b5 8. Qc2** 8 Qd3 transposes to Reshevsky–Fine, Nottingham 1936. AW **8 ... Bb7 9. a4 b4 10. 0–0 c5** If Black can safely play this freeing move then he has completely equalized the game. KB **11. dxc5 Bxc5 12. Nbd2 Rc8 13. Qd3 0–0** The position is even, MCO 228. **14. Ne1** White would also achieve very little with 14 Nb3. Black would then reply 14 ... Be7! with excellent play on the light squares. The text leads to simplification. KB **14 ... Qc7 15. Bxb7 Qxb7 16. Qf3 Qxf3 17. Nexf3 e5 18. Nb3 Be7 19. Rd1 Rc2 20. Kf1 Rfc8 21. Ne1 R2c7 22. Nf3 Rc2 23. Ne1 R2c7** Draw agreed. ½–½ Betins, 79–80.

(390) FINE—RESHEVSKY, S

Kemeri/Riga (4), 1937 (20 June)
Grünfeld Defence, Fianchetto Variation [D73]

1. Nf3 d5 2. g3 Nf6 3. Bg2 g6 4. d4 Bg7 5. c4 c6! 6. cxd5 The exchange in this position is not to be recommended. 6 0–0 is better. KB **6 ... Nxd5!?** 6 ... cxd5 7 0–0 0–0 8 Nc3 Ne4 (8 ... Nc6 is also good enough: 9 Ne5 Nxe5 10 dxe5 Ng4 11 Nxd5 Nxe5 12 Qb3 Nc6 13 Be3 e6 14 Nc3 Nd4 with a perfectly level position, Sämisch–Grünfeld, Carlsbad 1923) 9 Qb3 Nxc3 10 bxc3 Nc6 11 Nd2 e6 12 Ba3 Re8 with equality, Rabinovich–Botvinnik, Moscow 1935. **7. e4?!** At the Semmering/Baden tournament, Keres improved on this against Flohr by 7 0–0 (as suggested by Reshevsky in his notes to this game) 0–0 8 Nc3 Nxc3 9 bxc3 c5 10 Ba3 cxd4 11 Nxd4! Qc7 12 Qb3, winning in just twenty-four moves. AW **7 ... Nb6 8. 0–0** 8 h3 is to be considered. Black then intended to play 8 ... c5. If 9 dxc5 Qxd1+ 10 Kxd1 Na4 regaining the pawn with a good position. If 9 d5 e6 10 d6 Nc6 and White will have great difficulty retaining the d-pawn. SR **8 ... Bg4 9. Be3 c5! 10. e5** If 10 dxc5 Qxd1 11 Rxd1 Na4 12 Bd4 e5 13 Bc3 (13 Be3 Nxb2) Nxc5 and Black has a slight edge. SR **10 ... Nc6! 11. dxc5 Qxd1 12. Rxd1 Nc4** Black has a clear advantage, MCO 201. **13. Nbd2 Nxe3!** Black does not hurry to regain the pawn. Instead he weakens White's pawn formation. KB **14. fxe3 0–0–0 15. Nc4 Be6!** Black is not in a hurry to regain the pawn as that can always be done. SR **16. Bf1 Bd5 17. Be2 Kc7 18. Kf2** 18 Rac1 was better. KB **18 ... Rhf8 19. Nd6** More promising was 19 Nd4 Nxe5 20 Nxe5 Bxe5 and White still has a playable game. SR **19 ... Bxf3 20. Nb5+ Kb8 21. Bxf3 Nxe5 22. Be2** Black threatens ... Nd3+. 22 Nd4 may have offered better prospects. On 23 ... Nxf3 24 Kxf3 Rd5 24 Rac1 Rfd8 25 c6!. KB **22 ... Nc6** This is why Black went in for the exchange. Now White must lose a pawn or get into a lost endgame. He chooses the latter. SR **23. Nc3 Bxc3 24. bxc3 Kc7 25. e4 Ne5 26. Rd5 Nd7 27. Bb5 Nf6 28. Rxd8 Rxd8 29. Ke3 Nd7 30. Bxd7** If 30 Kd4 a6 31 Bxd7 (31 Be2 Nb6+ 32 Ke3 Na4) Rxd7+ 32 Kc4 Rd2. SR **30 ...**

Rxd7 31. Rf1 e6 32. g4 Kc6 33. g5 Kxc5 34. Rf4 Kd6 As a last resort White tries to win the pawn on h7 and to play h2-h4-h5 and g5-g6. SR 35. Rh4 f6! 36. gxf6 Ke5 37. Rf4 Rf7 38. Rf1 Rxf6 39. Rb1 Rf7 40. Rb5+ Kd6 41. Ra5 a6 42. Rg5 Rf1 White resigned. 0–1 Reshevsky, *Chess 1936-7*, 415–6; Betins, 93–6.

(391) TARTAKOWER, S—FINE

Kemeri/Riga (5), 1937 (21 June)
French Defence, Exchange Variation [C00]

1. e4 e6 2. Ne2 d5 3. exd5 exd5 4. Ng3 Nf6 5. d4 The sum total achieved by White's second move is a mere transposition to the Exchange Variation of the French Defence, so that one cannot claim that it has revolutionized opening theory. SGT 5 ... Bd6 6. Bd3 0–0 7. 0–0 Re8 A promising complication seems 7 ... Ng4, for example, 8 h3 Nxf2 9 Kxf2 Qh4 10 Qf3 f5!. But White would reply 9 Rxf2 Bxg3 10 Bxh7+ Kxh7 (surely 10 ... Kh8 not allowing the fork is better. AW) 11 Qd3+ Kg8 12 Qxg3. SGT 8. Nc3 Nc6 Developing his minor pieces, rather than attempting to make his position solid and secure by 8 ... c6, and also refraining from the free fight that might result from 8 ... Ng4. SGT 9. Nf5 Ne4? Black rejects the simpler lines 9 ... Bf8, or 9 ... Bxf5 10 Bxf5 Nc7. SGT 10. Nxd6 Qxd6 Not 10 ... Nxd6 11 Nxd5, nor 10 ... Nxc3 11 Bxh7+. SGT 11. Nb5! Qd8 12. Bf4 Re7 Black's position has become uncomfortable, but is still defensible. SGT 13. f3 Methodical play. After 13 c4 dxc4 14 Bxe4 Rxe4 15 Bxc7 Qg5 Black has an adequate defence. SGT 13 ... Nf6 14. Re1 Ne8 15. Qd2 a6 16. Nc3 Rxe1+ 17. Rxe1 Be6 The storm has died down; but it might rise again if Black were to venture on 17 ... Nxd4 18 Nxd5!. SGT 18. Ne2 Qd7 19. g4! Completing the idea formed on White's second move which consists in a fight for control of f5. SGT 19 ... Nd6 20. c3 Re8 21. Ng3 One might think that—like a phoenix—this was the same knight that assumed command of this square at the very beginning of the game. SGT 21 ... f6 A weakness that will provoke another. This should have been avoided by 21 ... Ne7 22 h4 Ng6 23 h5 Nf8, when it would not be easy to loosen Black's position. SGT 22. Qc2 h6 After 22 ... g6, the sacrifice 23 Bxg6 is promising. SGT 23. Qd2! Nd8 24. Bxh6!! gxh6 25. Nh5! This intermediary move is decisive; whereas after 25 Qxh6 Qg7 26 Qf4 Qg5 Black beats back the attack. SGT 25 ... Rf8 26. Qxh6 f5 27. Qg6+ Kh8 28. Nf6 Black resigned. 1–0 Tartakower 89–90.

(392) FINE—OZOLS, K

Kemeri/Riga (6), 1937 (22 June)
Nimzowitsch-Indian Defence, Classical Variation [E37]

1. d4 Nf6 2. c4 e6 3. Nc3 Bb4 4. Qc2 d5 5. a3 The customary continuation here is 5 cxd5 Qxd5 6 e3 c5 7 a3 Bxc3 8 bxc3 b6 9 Nf3 Nbd7 or even 9 ... Nc6 with a completely equal game. See, for example, the match games

Levenfish–Botvinnik 1937 and Alekhine–Euwe 1937. KB 5 ... Bxc3+ 6. Qxc3 Ne4 7. Qc2 0–0 The theoreticians prefer 7 ... c5. dM&LE 8. e3 Nd7 In order to support the plan to maintain the Ne5. Nevertheless 8 ... b6! 9 Bd3 Ba6 10 Ne2 Nd7 11 0–0 c5 leads to an equal game. dM&LE 9. Bd3 f5 10. Ne2 c6 11. 0–0 Ndf6 (11 ... Nd6 Fine-Danielsson, Stockholm 1937.) 12. f3 Qc7 An erroneous conception at a crucial moment. Black presumably overlooked White's 15th move. 12 ... Nd6! is the only satisfactory solution to the problems. dM&LE 13. cxd5 exd5 14. fxe4 fxe4 15. Bb5 Bd7 Black could quietly resign. 16. Ng3 h5 17. Be2 g6 18. Rb1 Rf7 19. Bd2 g5 20. b3 g4 21. Rf4 a5 22. Rbf1 Raf8 23. b4 b6 24. bxa5 bxa5 25. Qc5 Nh7 26. Nxh5 a4 27. Bd1 Rxf4 28. Rxf4 Rxf4 29. Nxf4 Qc8 30. Qe7 g3 31. hxg3 Be8 32. Bg4 Black resigned. 1–0 Betins, 123–4; de Marimon & Lopez Esnaola 76–7.

(393) STÅHLBERG, G—FINE

Kemeri/Riga (7), 1937 (23 June)
Queen's Gambit Declined [D41]

1. d4 Nf6 2. c4 e6 3. Nc3 d5 4. Nf3 c5 Not a continuation to be recommended, as now White has the happy choice between forcing a middle game in which Black cedes the centre and playing an ending in which Black is burdened with a weak pawn on d5. The usual moves, 4 ... Nbd7, 4 ... Be7 and 4 ... c6, secure Black a satisfactory game. 5. cxd5 Nxd5 6. e4 Nxc3 7. bxc3 cxd4 8. cxd4 Bb4+ 9. Bd2 Bxd2+ 10. Qxd2 0–0 11. Bd3 Nc6 12. e5!? Accepting weakness in the centre, but in return White gains a useful outpost for his pieces on e4—both the knight and the bishop, together with pressure along the diagonal c6-a8, even without considering the attacking chances he gains on the kingside. 12 ... Qa5! The point of Black's system of defence. The exchange of queens draws the king out of shelter on the kingside and provides Black with a queenside pawn majority. White, however does retain the greater freedom and central control. 13. Rc1 Bd7 14. Rc5 Qxd2+ 15. Kxd2 The king centralizes and proves to be a useful defender of d4. 15 ... Rfd8 16. Be4 Be8 17. Ke3 Rab8 18. Rb1 Up to this point Ståhlberg has played excellently, but now he fails to find the correct path—the pressure on Black's position reduces and the game simplifies to a draw. The correct strategy was to exchange the centralized bishop for the knight-c6, use the e4-square as a base for the knight and king, and, in the Nimzowitschian manner, exchange off the blockading pieces. With 18 Rhc1 White occupies the c-file and threatens the minority attack a2-a4-a5-a6; on the reply 18 ... Rdc8 White should exchange pieces in the centre by 19 Ng5 h6 20 Bxc6 Bxc6 21 Ne4, with excellent prospects in the endgame—either the knight will reach d6 or, after an exchange on e4, the strong centralized position of the white king in the rook ending would probably tip the balance. 18 ... Kf8 19. a4 Rdc8 20. Rbc1 Too late. 20 ... Ne7 21. Rxc8 Rxc8 22. Rxc8 Nxc8 23. Bxb7 Nb6 24. d5 exd5 25. a5 Nc4+ 26. Kd4

Nxa5 27. Bxd5 Nc6+ 28. Kc5 Ne7 29. Be4 Although White has the superior position—more active pieces and the weak black a-pawn—the reduced material guarantees Black a draw. 29 ... a5 30. Nd4 a4 31. f4 a3 32. Bb1 Ba4 33. g3 g6 34. Ba2 Ke8 35. Kb4 Nc6+ 36. Nxc6 Bxc6 37. Kxa3 Ke7 38. Kb4 f6 39. Kc5 Bd7 40. Bb1 h6 41. Be4 Ba4 42. Kd4 Bd7 43. Bd5 Ba4 44. Bc4 Be8 Draw agreed. ½–½ Betins *et al*, 138–9.

(394) FINE–BÖÖK, E

Kemeri/Riga (8), 1937 (25 June)
Queen's Gambit Declined, Lasker Defence [D55]

1. d4 d5 2. c4 e6 3. Nc3 Nf6 4. Bg5 Be7 5. e3 0–0 6. Nf3 Ne4 7. Bxe7 Qxe7 8. cxd5 Nxc3 9. bxc3 exd5 10. Qb3 Rd8 This strengthening of the Lasker Defence is a discovery of H. Wolf. Recently Dr. Bernstein has recommended 10 ... Qd6, so as to answer 11 c4 with 11 ... dxc4 12 Bxc4 Nc6 with a view to ... Na5. HK 11. c4 Black equalized after 11 Bd3 c5 12 Qa3 b6 13 0–0 Nc6 14 Bb5 c4 15 Qxe7 Nxe7, Marshall–Treybal, Folkestone Team Tournament 1933. AW 11 ... Nc6 12. c5 Fine assessed the main continuation 12 cxd5 Qb4+ 13 Nd2 Qxb3 14 Nxb3 Nb4 15 Rc1 Nxd5 16 e4 Re8 17 f3 f5 18 Bc4 c6 19 Bxd5+ cxd5 20 e5 b6 as equal, MCO 147. AW 12 ... b6 Ståhlberg recommends 12 ... Bg4 threatening ... Bxf3 and then Nxd4. If 13 Qxb7 Bxf3 14 Qxc6 (forced), then 14 ... Be4 with a difficult game for White, for if 15 f3 Bxf3! Meanwhile Black threatens f7-f5-f4. The text gives White a very promising game. HK 13. Bb5 Bd7 14. Bxc6 Bxc6 15. 0–0 bxc5 16. Qa3! In MCO, Fine considered that White had already gained a clear advantage in this position. 16 ... Re8 17. dxc5 Bb5 18. Rfb1 a6 19. Nd4 Although White has an excellent game, there seems little possibility of measurably strengthening his position. HK 19 ... Qd7 20. Rb3 h6 21. Rab1 Bc6 If 21 ... c6 22 Qa5 followed by 23 a4. dM&LE 22. Qa5 Kh8 23. h3 Kg8 Black is limited to waiting moves. HK 24. R1b2 Kh8 25. Rd2 Kg8 26. Rb1 Red8 27. Qc3 Qe8 28. Nf5 f6 29. Nd4 Kh8 30. Qa5 Qd7 31. a3 Kh7 32. Rc1 Kg8 33. Rb1 Kh7 34. Rbd1 Finally a threat: 35 e4! dxe4 36 Nxc6 and wins. HK 34 ... Ba4

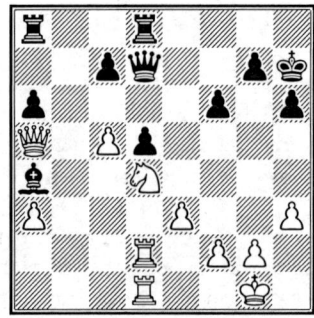

Position after Black's 34th move

35. c6! This simplification helps White to increase his advantage. New lines are opened for his pieces, so that they become dangerously effective. HK 35 ... Bxc6 36. Rc1!

Bb5 37. Rxc7 Qe8 38. Qc3 Rd7 39. Qc2+ Kh8 40. Rc5 Bc4 41. Qf5 The sealed move. Analysis revealed that while White still has the better game, the realization of his advantage would be most laborious. HK 41 ... Qe7 The first move on resumption is a grave blunder, which leads to a speedy defeat. The correct move was 41 ... Rc8. HK; Or 41 ... Rb7 with counterplay. dM&LE 42. Rxc4! dxc4 43. Nc6 Rxd2 On other moves White would come out a piece ahead, with an easier win. HK 44. Nxe7 c3 45. Qc5! Just in time to render the passed pawn harmless. HK 45 ... c2 46. Kh2 Re8 On 46 ... Rxf2 there follows 47 e4 and 48 Nf5. HK 47. Nf5 Re5? Overlooking the mate in two, but his game was lost in any case. HK 48. Qc8+ Black resigned. 1–0 Hans Kmoch in Reinfeld & Bernstein 66–7; de Marimon & Lopez Esnaola 96–7.

(395) PETROVS, V–FINE

Kemeri/Riga (9), 1937 (26 June)
Alekhine Defence, Four Pawns [B03]

Another catastrophe for Fine against 1 e4. "Up to the 35th move, this is a well-played, exciting game, which shows the fighting spirit of the Latvian Champion in the most favourable light." ME 1. e4 Nf6 2. e5 Nd5 3. d4 d6 4. c4 Nb6 5. f4 The main variation of the opening, although rarely played, seems to be the surest way of maintaining the advantage. ME (John Nunn opined in one of his books that ultra-sharp, forcing variations tend to equality, and that may be the case here. According to Bagirov, in EMCO 1996a, the theoretical status of the Alekhine Defence against the Four Pawns is satisfactory. The positional treatment 4 Nf3 is more popular nowadays. AW) 5 ... dxe5 6. fxe5 Nc6 The ultra-sharp 6 ... c5 was the subject of much interest in the 1970s. 6 ... Bf5 is answered by 7 Nf3. AW 7. Be3 Bf5 8. Nc3 e6 9. Nf3 Nb4 The oldest method of playing this variation, the idea being to gain time for 10 ... c5. Originally it was thought that this move was absolutely necessary, but later it was discovered that 9 ... Qd7 (as given by Fine in MCO. AW) followed by 10 ... 0–0–0, was quite playable. ME 10. Rc1 c5 11. Be2 Be7 12. 0–0 0–0–0 The usual continuation here is 12 ... cxd4 13 Nxd4 Bg6. KB 13. a3 Bagirov's main line, in EMCO 1996, is 13 dxc5 Nd7 14 a3 Nc6 15 b4 Ndxe5 16 Nb5 Bd3 with a clear advantage for the first player. Fritz suggests 16 ... Qb8 with an even game. AW 13 ... cxd4 Important, for 13 ... Nc6 14 d5 is not good for Black. The text amounts to a temporary sacrifice of a pawn, with critical complications as a result. ME 14. Nxd4 Nc6 15. Nxf5 exf5 16. Rxf5 g6 Regaining the pawn. However, the text weakens the kingside a bit, and White at once tries to exploit this. ME 17. Rf1 Bg5! This intermediate move is essential, for after 17 ... Nxe5 18 Qxd8 followed by 19 Nb5 gives White the better game. ME 18. Bc5! A promising offer of the exchange, which is based on the general consideration that after 18 ... Bxc1 19 Qxc1 (not 19 Bxf8? Be3+), Black's kingside is badly weakened, which, in combination with White's two bishops, offers him very promising attacking possibilities. ME (Bagirov includes the text as a footnote, with the conclusion, White stands better, Estrin–Kopylov, corr 1971. The soon-to-be 7th World Correspondence Chess Champion had a lost position just a few moves later, Kopylov eventually scoring the full point. Apart from this game, which seems to be the stem game, the line had already occurred in Keres–Sajtar, Prague 1943 and two earlier correspondence chess games before 1971. AW) **18 ... Re8** Black rightly declines this dubious transaction. ME **19. Qxd8** The game Estrin–Nikolai Kopylov continued 19 Ne4 Rxe5! 20 Nxg5 Qxg5 21 Bd6 Qe3+ with a winning position for Black (0–1, 48). AW **19 ... Raxd8 20. Rcd1** The position is similar to the one that would have arisen after 17 ... Nxe5—with the difference that all of Black's pieces have been developed. ME **20 ... Rd2!** A good move which gives Black adequate counterplay. Note that he still does not capture on e5. ME (Sajtar did play 20 ... Nxe5 against Keres and held the draw. AW) **21. Rxd2** Altogether too dangerous would be 21 b4 Rc2 and so on. ME **21 ... Bxd2 22. Bd6!** Preventing the immediate 22 ... Nxe5, which would be answered by 23 Ne4. This is better than 22 Ne4 Rxe5 and Black has good play for his pieces. ME **22 ... Bxc3 23. bxc3 Nxe5** At last. We now have a very interesting struggle in view, White having the two bishops and Black the better pawn position. The position is about even, but Black must play very cautiously to prevent his opponent from getting any attacking chances—in which case the two bishops will reveal their power. ME **24. c5 Nd5?! 25. Rc1** Not the immediate 25 c4 because of 25 ... Nc5!. KB **25 ... Re6 26. Bf1** White prefers to sacrifice the pawn-c3 and retain control of the f1-a6 diagonal. KB **26 ... a6** Black overestimates his position and commits a decisive mistake. He wishes to adopt an active policy, but he overlooks that he is playing into his opponent's hands. 26 ... Ne3 should have been played with almost an even game. ME **27. Rb1 b5** Forced—but this is just what Black intended, ME; After 27 ... Nxc3 28 Rxb7 the passed c-pawn will soon decide. KB **28. cxb6!!** A deeply calculated endgame combination, allied to a piece offer, and the only correct reply. KB **28 ... Rxd6 29. b7 Nc6** Not 29 ... Nd7? because of 30 Rd1 then c4. KB **30. c4!** Evidently Fine had reckoned only on 30 b8Q+, and even then, to be sure, Black would have had nothing better than a draw. The text however is much stronger. ME **30 ... Ne3 31. Rb6!** Threatening 32 Rxc6 as well as 32 b8Q+. Black can just manage to parry these threats. ME **31 ... Rd1** Threatens mate. ME **32. Kf2 Rxf1+** 32 ... Nxf1 33 Rxc6 or 32 ... Nb8 33 Be2 lose outright. ME **33. Kxe3 Nb8 34. Rd6** Betins *et al* question this move and propose 34 Ke2 Rf5 35 Rd6 Re5+ 36 Kd3 Re8 37 c5 and wins. Instead of 36 ... Re8, however, 36 ... Kf8! seems good for Black. AW **34 ... Re1+ 35. Kd4** Euwe awarded this move a question mark. He believed that White would obtain a winning position by 35 Kd2 Re8 36 c5 Kg7 37 Kc3! (not 37 c6 Re7! and Black gets both passed pawns for the knight). Now White threatens to march his king to b6, and, according to the World Champion 37 ... Re7 can be answered by 38 Rb6. However after 38 ... Re6 Black wins after both 39 Rxe6 fxe6 followed by Nc6(+), and all entry points on the fifth rank can be covered, and 39 Kc4

Rxb6 40 cxb6 Kf6!. AW **35 ... Kf8?** Black misses his opportunity and is compelled to resign a few moves later. The indicated move was 35 ... Kg7! which would have involved White in difficulties. For he cannot play 36 Rd8? because of 36 ... Rd1+; nor can he play 36 Kc5 Rb1! and Black wins the b-pawn (37 Rb6 Nd7+). Hence he must play 36 c5, but then comes 36 ... Re7! 37 c6 Nxc6+ 38 Rxc6 Rxb7 39 Rxa6 Rb2 and Black has winning chances. ME **36. Rd8+ Re8 37. Rc8!** Fine had not considered this move. He now finds himself in a hopeless situation. ME **37 ... Ke7 38. Kd5 Rd8+ 39. Rxd8 Kxd8 40. Kd6** Black resigned. **1–0** Euwe in Reinfeld & Bernstein 32-4; Betins *et al* 164-7.

(396) FINE—KERES, P

Kemeri/Riga (10), 1937 (27 June)
Colle System [D05]

1. d4 d5 2. Nf3 Nf6 3. e3 c5 4. Nbd2 Nbd7 5. c3 e6 6. Bd3 Bd6! The best. 6 ... Be7 is less good as Black cannot play ... e5. **7. 0–0 0–0 8. Re1 Qb6!** Increasing the pressure in the centre, and also eventually against b2. It would seem that the text is better than 8 ... Qc7, since on b6 the queen is safer and possesses a greater sphere of influence. The principal objective is to prevent the immediate advance e3-e4, after which there would follow: 9 e4 cxd4 10 Nxd4 (10 cxd4 exd4 11 Nxe4 Nxe4 12 Bxe4 Bf6 and White has no particular initiative to compensate for the weakened central pawn-d4) Nc5! 11 Bc2 Nce4 12 Nxe4 Nxe4 13 Bxe4 dxe4 14 Rxe4 e5 and Black has the two bishops and an overwhelming game. **9. b3!** Best. **9 ... e5! 10. e4! cxd4 11. cxd4 dxe4 12. Nxe4 Nxe4** With an equal game, MCO 216. **13. Bxe4 exd4 14. Bb2 Nf6 15. Bxd4 Bc5 16. Bxc5 Qxc5** Following the massacre on the central files, the games has become absolutely even. Both players continue to find accurate moves and the peace is soon concluded. **17. Rc1 Qa5 18. Qd2 Qb6 19. Qe3 Qa5 20. Qd2 Qb6 21. Qe3 Qa5** Draw agreed. In this game Black demonstrated an excellent method of play against the Colle System. **½–½** Betins, 170.

(397) HAZENFUSS, V—FINE

Kemeri/Riga (11), 1937 (28 June)
Closed Sicilian [B23]

A first class game by Fine despite the abominable form in which he found himself in this tourney. R&B **1. e4 c5 2. Nc3** An old idea of Chigorin's intending g3 and Bg2. KB **2 ... Nf6** Played a tempo, Fine only reckoned on the usual Nf3, d4 and so forth. The move in fact donates a free tempo to his opponent. The normal continuation here is 2 ... Nc6 with ... g6, ... Bg7, ... e6!, ... Nge7 and ... d5 to follow as in the game Alexander–Botvinnik, Nottingham 1936. KB **3. e5 Ng8** This manoeuvre is a loss of time which turns out to be harmless, in view of White's subsequent listless play. Ordinarily Black plays 2 ... d6 or 2 ...

Nc6. SB **4. f4** This routine move spoils White's chances of obtaining any advantage from the opening. He should have borne in mind that the tempi gained are only of value if used to further his piece development. In a closed position White will gain no benefit from his extra tempi. He should have played instead 4 Nf3 Nc6 5 Bc4 followed by 0–0, when White's quicker development would have brought him a perceptible result. KB **4 ... Nc6 5. Nf3 d5! 6. g3** He should try to open up the position to profit by his edge in development: 6 exd6 Qxd6 (6 ... exd6 7 d4 Bg4 8 Bb5) 7 Bc4! Qxf4 (if 7 ... Be6 8 Nb5 or 7 ... e5 8 fxe5 Nxe5 9 Qe2) 8 d3 followed by 9 0–0 with a tremendous attack. SB **6 ... e6 7. Bg2** 7 Bh3 at once would have saved time. SB **7 ... Nh6 8. Ne2 Be7 9. d4** After this Black obtains a favourable variation of the French Defence, but 9 d3 would have left White with a cramped game anyway. SB **9 ... Nf5 10. c3 Qb6 11. Bh3** 11 0–0 loses a pawn: 11 ... cxd4 12 cxd4 Ncxd4 13 Nxd4 Bc5 or 12 Nxd4 Bc5. SB **11 ... cxd4 12. Nexd4 Ncxd4 13. cxd4 0–0 14. 0–0** Interesting would be 14 g4 Bb4+ (14 ... Nh4!? AW)15 Kf2 Nh6 (not 15 ... Ne7? 16 a3) 16 Qg3! with a complicated game. SB **14 ... h5** Black not only occupies the open c-file and applies pressure to the weak d-pawn, he also has a superior position on the kingside thanks to the knight on f5. KB **15. Rf2 Bd7 16. Bxf5 exf5** White has relieved the pressure somewhat; but later on, the weakness of the light squares will be painful. SB **17. Be3 Rac8 18. Rc1 Qa6!** A strong continuation highlighting the opponent's weakness on the light squares and inducing further weakness on the queenside. KB **19. b3 Bb5 20. Rxc8 Rxc8 21. Ne1** Threatening Bb5-d3-e4. KB **21 ... Qg6 22. Rg2 Qg4**

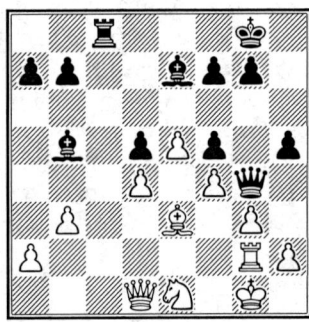

Position after Black's 22nd move

23. Qxg4 Going into a quite inferior ending, but even worse would be 23 Qd2 Ba3 24 Nd3 (or 24 Qa5 Bc1! 25 Qxb5 Bxe3+ 26 Kf1 Rc1 27 Qe2 Bxd4. If 25 Bf2 in this variation, then 25 ... Qe2 26 h3 Bd2) Bxd3 25 Qxd3 Qf3 26 Qe2 Qe4 27 h3 (if 27 Rf2 Bc1) Rc3 and wins. SB **23 ... fxg4 24. a4 Bd7 25. Rc2 Rxc2 26. Nxc2 Bf5 27. Ne1 Bb1! 28. Bd2 Kh7 29. Kf2 Kg6 30. Ke3 Kf5** (*see diagram*) **31. a5** If 31 Nd3 Bc2 32 Nc1 g5! (but not 32 ... Ba3 33 a5 Bxc1 34 Bxc1 Bxb3 35 Ba3 with an easy draw) 33 fxg5 Bxg5+ 34 Ke2 Bd8! 35 Ke3 (Black's king must not be allowed to reach e4) h4!! and White is in *Zugzwang*. If now 36 Nd3 Bg5+ 37 Ke2 Bxd3+ 38 Kxd3 Bxd2 39 Kxd2 Ke4 40 Kc3 Ke3 and wins. SB **31 ... g5!** Setting up a potential outside passed pawn. RF **32. Nd3 Bc2 33. Nc5** Or

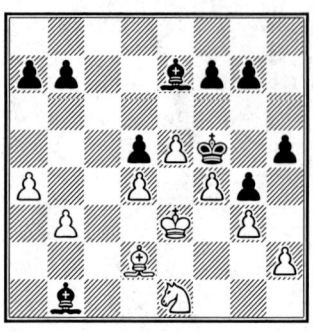

Position after Black's 30th move

33 b4 Bxd3 34 Kxd3 gxf4 35 gxf4 Bf8 followed by 36 ... Bh6 and wins. SB **33 ... gxf4+ 34. gxf4 b6** Bernstein suggests Black could also have won the opposite-coloured bishop ending after 34 ... Bxc5 35 dxc5 Bxb3 36 Kd4 h4 37 Kxd5. He does not, however, consider the interpolations 36 a6! or 37 a6! which would, at the very least, make things difficult. AW **35. axb6 axb6 36. Nd7 b5 37. b4 h4 38. Nc5 g3 39. hxg3 hxg3 40. Kf3 Bh4 41. Be3 Bd1+** Black's bishops co-operate ideally. The g-pawn can be stopped, but in the process White's king is forced away from other sectors. SB **42. Kg2 Kg4 43. Bd2 Bf3+ 44. Kg1 Kf5 45. Be3 Be4 46. Bd2 g2** Threatening to bring the king to f3 followed by ... Bf2+. SB **47. Nxe4 Kxe4 48. Kxg2 Kxd4 49. Kh3** Or 49 Kf3 Kd3 50 Be3 (if 50 Bc1 Kc3 51 Ba3 Kb3) d4 51 Bc1 Be7 52 Ba3 Kc2. SB **49 ... Be7 50. Kg4 Kd3** And the d-pawn decides. RF **51. Be1 Ke2 52. Bc3 Ke3 53. f5 d4 54. Be1 Ke2 55. f6 Bf8 56. Bg3 d3** White resigned. Superb endgame play by Fine. SB **0–1** Betins *et al*, 192–4; Bernstein in Reinfeld & Bernstein 29–31; Fine 1941, 259.

(398) RELLSTAB, L–FINE

Kemeri/Riga (12), 1937 (1 July)
Spanish Game, Steinitz Defence Deferred [C71]

1. e4 e5 2. Nf3 Nc6 3. Bb5 a6 4. Ba4 d6 5. c4! The idea of this move is to seize control of the d5 square. It would seem that if this move were correct Black's whole system of defence would be refuted. **5 ... Bd7 6. Nc3 g6 7. d4** Forced, otherwise the square d4 would be under Black's control after 7 ... Bg7. **7 ... Bg7 8. dxe5** 8 Be3 Nf6 9 dxe5 dxe5 10 Bc5 Nh5 11 Nd5 Nf4 12 Nxf4 exf4 13 0–0! (L. Steiner's suggestion) Ne7 14 Bxd7+ Qxd7 15 Qb3 and White has a clear advantage, MCO. **8 ... dxe5 9. Nd5 Nf6 10. Nxf6+?** A completely incomprehensible mistake which deprives White of the fruits of his excellent opening play. With 10 Bg5! h6 11 Bxf6 Bxf6 12 Qd2 with 0–0–0 to follow, or 10 Qe2 or even 10 Bc2, White could retain his positional advantage. Moreover, the foolish exchange promotes Black's development. **10 ... Qxf6 11. h3 h6 12. Be3 0–0–0 13. Qe2 Qe7 14. 0–0–0 f5** (Black stands slightly better, MCO 271.) **15. Rd5 Rhe8 16. Bc5 Qf7 17. Rhd1 Nd4** With this well-calculated move, Black achieves equality. **18. Bxd7+ Rxd7 19. Qd3** On 19 Nxd4 exd4 the white pawn-e4 hangs. **19 ... fxe4 20. Qxe4**

Red8 21. Nxd4 exd4 22. Rxd7 (22 ... Bxd4 is fatal because of 22 ... c6 23 Rxd7 Qxd7 (not 23 ... Qxc4+ 24 Kb1 Rxd7 25 Qe8+ Rd8, as given by the tournament book, because of the simple 24 Bc3.) 24 Qxg6 Bxd4. AW) 22 ... **Qxc4+ 23. Kb1 Rxd7 24. Qe8+ Rd8 25. Qxg6 Qxc5 26. Qxg7 Qf5+ 27. Kc1 Kb8?!** (Surely Black stands better after 27 ... Qxf2 28 Qxh6 Qxg2—an extra pawn and the safer king position. AW) **28. Rd2 Rd6 29. b3 Qe4 30. Kb2 d3 31. f3?** (Dr. Richard Cantwell points out the line 31 Qh8+ Ka7 32 Qc3 and White should draw.) **31 ... Qe1 32. Qf8+ Ka7 33. Qf4 Qf1?** (Here Cantwell points out that 33 ... c5! wins outright. [The rook cannot be taken because White is mated after 34 ... Qxd2+, meanwhile 34 ... Rf6, forcing the white queen to unprotect the rook, is threatened]) **34. Qe5 Qg1 35. Qf4 Qc5 36. Qc4 Qe3 37. Qc3 h5 38. h4 Qe1 39. Qc5+ Kb8 40. Qg5 Re6** Now Black must force the draw, otherwise White can realize the material advantage on the kingside with 41 ... g4. **41. Qd8+ Ka7 42. Qxd3 Qxh4 43. g4 Qf6+ 44. Qd4+ Qxd4+ 45. Rxd4 Re2+ 46. Ka3 b5 47. gxh5** Draw agreed, as on 47 ... a5 White plays 48 b4 and the pawn-f3 must go. ½–½ Betins *et al*, 194–5.

(399) FINE—BERGS, T

Kemeri/Riga (13), 1937 (2 July)
English Opening, Classical Defence [A20]

1. c4 e5 2. Nf3 Nc6 3. d4 exd4 4. Nxd4 Bb4+ 5. Bd2 Bxd2+ 6. Qxd2 Nge7! 7. g3 0–0 8. Bg2 Ne5! Black is well prepared for the equalizing move ... d5! KB **9. b3 d5! 10. cxd5 Nxd5 11. Nc3 Nxc3 12. Qxc3 c6 13. 0–0** 13 e4 would be answered by 13 ... c5! with Nd3+ to follow. KB **13 ... f5!** This seems risky, but is not only necessary, but even good. Black must take measures to restrain the white e- and f-pawns. KB **14. f4** White has a distinct superiority, MCO 37. **14 ... Ng4 15. e4 fxe4 16. Bxe4 Qb6 17. Rfe1 Bf5 18. Bf3 Rad8 19. Rad1 Bc8?** Black should have preferred 19 ... Rfe8. **20. Kg2 c5??** In making this gross error Black overlooks the loss of a piece. Instead 20 ... Nf6 preserves the equilibrium. KB **21. Qc4+ Kh8 22. Ne6 Rxd1 23. Bxd1** Black resigned. If 28 ... Bxe6 24 Rxe6 wins a piece. If the rook moves then 24 Bxg4 with the same result, and if 23 ... Qc6+ 24 Bf3. dM&LE **1–0** Betins, 218; de Marimon & Lopez Esnaola 182–3.

(400) STEINER, E—FINE

Kemeri/Riga (14), 1937 (3 July)
Spanish Game, Steinitz Defence Deferred [C74]

1. e4 e5 2. Nf3 Nc6 3. Bb5 a6 4. Ba4 d6 An old line of play which is now very fashionable. Alekhine, for example, has often adopted it and achieved some very fine successes with it. The interpolation of 3 ... a6 gives a wholly different character from that of the Steinitz Defence (3 ... d6). This is due to Black's being able to banish the pin by ...

b5, which robs d2-d4 of much of its strength. ME **5. c3** White cannot gain any opening advantage from 5 d4, as may be seen from the game Stoltz–Alekhine, Bled 1931: 5 d4 b5 6 Bb3 Nxd4 7 Nxd4 exd4 8 Bd5 (8 Qxd4 loses a piece after 8 ... c5 9 Qd5 Be6 10 Qc6+ Bd7 11 Qd5 c4) Rb8 9 Bc6+ Bd7 9 Bxd7 Qxb7 10 Qxd4 Nf6 and Black obtains a good game without any trouble. Much more difficult, however, is another mode of attack whereby White first interpolates the exchange 5 Bxc6+ bxc6 and then 6 d4. If Black plays 6 ... exd4, we have the Steinitz Defence, the addition of 3 ... a6 if anything being disadvantageous to Black. A better reply is 6 ... f6, holding the centre. White then has a superior development and more mobility, while Black has two bishops, and it is difficult to judge the position. After 7 Nc3 g6 8 Be3 Nh6! 9 Qd2 Nf7 followed by ... Bg7 and ... 0–0, Black has an eminently satisfactory position; but with 7 Be3, in order to answer 7 ... g6 with 8 Qd2, thus preventing ... Ng8-h6-f7, White seems to get the better game. The quiet text avoids all these problems. ME **5 ... Nf6 6. Qe2** An old continuation, but in recent times little used. The idea is to protect e4 with the queen in order to play Rfd1 and d4. KB **6 ... Bd7 7. 0–0 Be7 8. Rd1 0–0 9. d3** In conjunction with White's previous move, this comes as a surprise: White has prepared for d2-d4 and now plays d2-d3, an obviously illogical proceeding. But the continuation shows that White's plan is a deep one: he avoids d4 for the time being, so as to induce his opponent to take measures against d3, whereupon the advance d3-d4 follows with more effect than ever. ME **9 ... Ne8** Preparing for f7-f5, which is the best method of playing against the pawn formation c3, d3 and e4. ME **10. Bb3 Kh8** Consistent but not best, as it permits White to carry out his plan. Counterplay on the queenside (10 ... Na5 11 Bc2 c5) was preferable. ME **11. d4** Just at the right moment. White now secures a lasting initiative. ME **11 ... Qc8** An elastic method of removing the chains on the d-file and preparing for ... f5. KB **12. Ng5 Nd8 13. h3 Ne6 14. Nxe6 Bxe6 15. Nd2** White does not play Bc2, for Black's queen's bishop (his "good" bishop) is at least as useful as White's king's bishop. ME **15 ... Bxb3 16. Nxb3 f5!?** Black carries out the objective of his last few moves, but this only leads to a slight weakening of his pawn position—an isolated e-pawn. It was therefore worth considering an alternative plan: operating in the centre and on the queenside, a good preliminary to this being ... c7-c5. ME; Black has good compensation in the open f-file and active piece play. KB **17. dxe5 dxe5 18. exf5 Qxf5 19. Be3 Nd6 20. Nc5** White has successfully weakened the black e-pawn and follows up by inducing weakness on the queenside too. In contrast Black has to generate counterplay on the kingside. dM&LE **20 ... Rf6 21. a4 Rg6 22. Kh1 a5 23. Qd3** White wants to exchange queens, as this will simplify the utilization of his superior pawn position. ME **23 ... e4!?** It soon becomes clear that the pawn is extremely weak on this square. But in any event Black is confronted with onerous problems. Equally inadequate, for example, was 23 ... Qxd3 24 Rxd3 Nc4 25 Rd7 Nxe3 26 Rxe7 Nxg2 27 Rg1 Nf4 28 Rxg6 Nxg6 29 Rxc7 and the complications have been favourable to White. ME **24. Qd5** Attacking the b-pawn and thus forcing the exchange of queens. ME **24 ... Qxd5 25. Rxd5 b6 26. Nd7!** Directed against 26 ... Nc4 which is to be answered by 27 Ne5, winning at least a pawn. ME **26 ... Re6 27. Re5! Rxe5 28. Nxe5 Bf6** Black is determined to play 29 ... Nc4 even if it means weakening his pawn position. On other continuations White would strengthen his game with Rd1 and (at the proper moment) b3. ME **29. Ng4 Nc4** Allowing White to exchange his knight for a bishop, after which the bishop is able to set to work against the weak pawns. 29 ... Be7 would have been better. dM&LE **30. Nxf6 gxf6 31. Bf4!** This simple move, which is extremely powerful, indicates the considerable extent of White's advantage. He threatens above all 32 b3 (if 32 Bxc7 Rc1!) Nd6 33 Rd1 soon winning a pawn. The bishop shows himself distinctly superior to the knight in this ending. ME **31 ... Nxb2** He has nothing better. ME **32. Bxc7 Ra6** Preparing for a combination which is incorrect and leads to a speedy defeat. Correct was 32 ... Nc4 followed by 33 ... Rc8 with some drawing chances. ME **33. Kg1 Kg7 34. Kf1 Nc4 35. Bf4** Leaving the black knight with hardly a leap. dM&LE **35 ... Ra7 36. Rd1 Kf7 37. Rd4 b5** Beginning unsound combinations. But even without this move the game was lost for Black. ME **38. axb5 Nb2** Black sees too late that the intended continuation 38 ... a4 39 Rxc4 a3 fails because of 40 Bc1 a2 41 Bb2 a1Q+ 42 Bxa1 Rxa1+ 43 Ke2 and White is two pawns to the good. The text is just inadequate, and White wins easily. ME **39. Bc1 Nd3 40. Ba3 Rc7 41. c4 Nb4 42. Bxb4 axb4 43. b6 Rc6 44. c5 Rxc5 45. Rxb4** Black resigned. 1–0 Betins 220–1; Euwe in Reinfeld & Bernstein 11–3; de Marimon & Lopez Esnaola 190–3.

(401) FINE—APŠENIEKS, F

Kemeri/Riga (15), 1937 (4 July)
Queen's Gambit Declined [D51]

1. d4 d5 2. Nf3 Nf6 3. c4 e6 4. Nc3 Nbd7 5. Bg5 c6 6. a3 With this move White prevents the Cambridge Springs Defence, but Black can still play the Lasker Defence, after which White's sixth move will be a loss of tempo. KB **6 ... Be7 7. e3 Ne4!** Now this move is highly favourable, White's sixth move has no significance in this position, meanwhile Black has made the useful move ... Nbd7! and the perhaps yet more important ... c6. This makes it possible for Black to transpose into a favourable version of the Dutch Stonewall Defence. KB **8. Nxe4** Otherwise on 8 Bxe7 Qxe7 9 Bd3 Black can again enter the Dutch a tempo up (again the unfortunate a3). KB **8 ... dxe4 9. Bxe7 Qxe7 10. Nd2 f5 11. c5** Otherwise White can scarcely continue his development. On the solid 11 Be2 e5! 12 dxe5 Nxe5 Black has a powerful centre and the better game. KB **11 ... Nf6** Black fails to carry out the logical plan of forcing through e6-e5, after which he would have the better game. On the immediate 11 ... e5 White can hinder Black's castling by 12 Bc4, when a sharp game arises: 12 ... exd4 13 exd4 b5! (directed against Qb3) 14 Bb3 Nf6 15 a4! Bb7 and Black is overstretched in the centre. But Black can play 11 ... 0–0

12 Qb3 Kh8 with e6-e5 to follow, with a very good game. After the text Black is condemned to a boring defence. KB **12. Nc4 0–0 13. Be2 Nd5 14. Qc2** Hindering ... f4 with counterplay for Black. KB **14 ... b5** This error concedes White a definite advantage. Black should have aimed for counterplay on the kingside by preparing the advance ... f5-f4. dM&LE **15. cxb6 axb6 16. Ne5 Bd7 17. 0–0 Rfc8 18. b4!** In order to fix the weak pawn-c6. True, White's a-pawn is also weak, but it is easy to defend whereas the c-pawn will prove more difficult to protect. KB **18 ... Be8 19. Qd2 Rc7 20. Rfc1 Rca7 21. Qb2 f4** Now there is no justification for this advance, which simply weakens the black pawn formation. dM&LE **22. exf4 Nxf4 23. Bf1 Qd6 24. Re1 Nd5 25. g3** 25 Rxe4 Nxb4! 26 Nc4! is less clear. AW **25 ... Nf6 26. Bg2 Qd5 27. f3!** A well-judged breakthrough. If 27 ... exf3 28 Bxf3 Qd6 29 Nc4 Black would be unable to deal with all of the threats. dM&LE **27 ... c5** Black seeks to rescue himself by simplification, but White's extra pawn ultimately decides matters. What follows is well-crafted and precise endgame play from Fine. KB **28. dxc5 bxc5 29. fxe4 Qb7 30. Nd3 cxb4 31. Nxb4** And the a-pawn must decide. Though admittedly it is another fifty moves before Black throws in the towel. KB **31 ... Bc6 32. Qb3! Qb6+ 33. Qe3 Qxe3+** Simplification only aids White. dM&LE **34. Rxe3 Bb7 35. Nc2 Ra4 36. Rae1 Rc8 37. Nb4 Rca8 38. e5 Bxg2 39. Kxg2 Ne8 40. Nc2 Nc7 41. Rb3 Nd5 42. Rb7?!** A weak move which could have snatched from Fine a well-deserved triumph. dM&LE **42 ... Rc4! 43. Nb4 Rc7** Apšenieks fails to adjust to the altered circumstances. 43 ... Nxb4 44 axb4 Ra2+ 45 Kh1 Rb2 46 b5 Rc5 47 b6 Rc3 48 Rb8+ Kf7 49 b7 Rcc2, and the draw is obvious, was correct. dM&LE **44. Rxc7 Nxc7 45. Nc2 Ra5 46. Kf3 Kf7 47. Ke4 Nd5 48. Ra1 Ra4+ 49. Kd3 Ke7 50. Rb1 Ra5 51. Rb3 Kd7 52. Kc4 Nc7 53. Rd3+ Kc8 54. Re3 Nd5 55. Rb3 Kc7 56. Kd4** Fine has re-established control and does not allow his opponent a second chance. dM&LE **56 ... Ne7 57. Nb4 Ng6** The knight is poorly placed on the opposite side of the board from the theatre of operations. dM&LE **58. Rc3+ Kd7 59. Nd3 Rd5+ 60. Ke4 Ra5 61. Nc5+ Ke7 62. Kd4 h5** ... KB **63. h4 Kf7 64. Rf3+ Kg8 65. a4 Ne7 66. Rc3 Nc6+ 67. Ke4 Kf7 68. Rc4 Ke8 69. Kf4 Ke7 70. Nb7 Ra6 71. a5 Kf8** Naturally not 71 ... Nxa5? 72 Ra4. dM&LE **72. Rc5 Ke7 73. Kg5 Kd7 74. Kxh5 Ra7 75. Nd6 Nxa5 76. Kg6 Nc6 77. Kxg7 Ra3 78. Ne4 Re3 79. Nf6+ Kc7 80. g4 Kb6 81. Nd7+ Kc7 82. Nb8 Rxe5 83. Rxc6+ Kxb8 84. g5** Black resigned. 1–0 Betins *et al*, 243–4; de Marimon & Lopez Esnaola 213–5.

(402) ALEKHINE, A—FINE

Kemeri/Riga (16), 1937 (7 July)
Queen's Gambit Accepted [D23]

1. d4 d5 2. c4 dxc4 3. Nf3 Nf6 4. Qa4+ Qd7 This and the next move force the exchange of queens, leading to a simple drawn position, apparently—but it is not quite so simple. ME **5. Q×c4 Qc6 6. Na3 Q×c4** This brings the knight to a very strong position. 6 ... e6 was to be considered. ME **7. N×c4 e6 8. a3!** Played with insight. This move not only forestalls the check by the bishop, which would force further simplification, but it threatens b4, which would cramp Black by preventing ... c5, his freeing move. If Black gets in ... c5 at all, he must therefore play it at once; but this, as we shall see, puts him in trouble otherwise. ME **8 ... c5** Alekhine awarded this move with a question mark and several annotators have slavishly followed his example. If Fine's 14 ... a6 or Euwe's 15 ... a6 are sound then there is nothing wrong with this highly logical move. Although the variation has had a few outings since this game none have followed Alekhine's example, and so his suggestion of 8 ... a5!? 9 Bf4 b5 and 10 ... Bd6 has not yet been tried out in practice. AW **9. Bf4!** **Nc6** Black cannot well avert the threatened 10 Nd6+, which will force off one of the bishops. ME **10. d×c5** Before playing Nd6, White takes the opportunity to gain several moves on his opponent. ME **10 ... B×c5 11. b4 Be7 12. b5!** Alekhine extracts every ounce of advantage from the position. ME **12 ... Nb8 13. Nd6+ B×d6 14. B×d6** The opening is over, and Alekhine, once again, has achieved his primary aim—a favourable position. Again it was not any particular move, but a coherent series of moves, each simple in itself, which brought this about. The apparently innocent 8 a3 forced, as we have seen, the immediate advance of the black c-pawn, creating a weakness at d6 which was shown up by 8 Bf4. Now White has the small advantage of two bishops against bishop and knight, but we shall see that this is not easily retained. ME **14 ... Ne4** Correct now is 14 ... a6 when White's advantage is minimal, *PCO* 161. **15. Bc7!** At this stage, the dark-squared bishop is practically White's only winning chance, and he must play extremely carefully in order to prevent its exchange. Inadvisable would be 15 Bb4 a5! 16 b×a6 N×a6, or 15 Bf4 f6!, followed by 16 ... e5, with approximately equal prospects in both cases. AA **15 ... Nd7** 15 ... a6, fighting for counterplay along the a-file, was the correct move. White could hardly reply 16 b6 to much advantage, because it would give Black's knight a free entry to c6. ME **16. Nd4** Extremely strong; White intends to place his pawns on f3 and e4, denying Black the use of his light squares d5 and e4 for his pieces. He already has a little advantage on the dark squares (e5 and d4) through possessing the only remaining dark-squared bishop. ME **16 ... Nb6 17. f3 Nd5 18. Ba5** If 18 Be5, then 18 ... f6. ME **18 ... Nef6** If 18 ... Nd6 19 e4 Ne3 20 Bb4! would also leave White well on top. ME **19. Nc2** The final preparation for e4, preventing the reply ... Ne3. ME **19 ... Bd7 20. e4 Rc8 21. Kd2** Avoiding simplification, which would favour the defence. dM&LE **21 ... Nb6 22. Ne3** Otherwise comes 22 ... Nc4+. The movements of this knight have been most remarkable; first it went to d4 to prepare f3; then it went to c2 to prepare e4; and now it goes to e3 to prevent Black's winning back the minor exchange by 22 ... Nc4+. ME **22 ... 0–0** 22 ... Na4, followed by 23 ... Nc5 would have been a little better: compare with our note to Black's fifteenth. Alekhine contrasts

with other great masters in the great rarity of such little lapses. After the text White never permits ... Na4 again. ME (22 ... Na4 23 Nc4! is bad for Black. AW) **23. a4!** White, after 23 moves, has now only two pieces in play, yet they are ideally positioned. The beautifully central post of the knight on e3, the solid centre, the attacking formation on the queenside, the mobility of the bishop on a5—these things make it impossible for Black to find good squares for his pieces, whereas White's pieces can develop their maximum combined effect within a few moves. Situations like this are common in Alekhine's games. They draw one's attention to the distinction between "quantitative" and "qualitative" development. Alekhine always follows qualitative precepts, that is to say, he studies the effectiveness far more than the numerical strength of the forces at his command. ME **23 ... Rfd8 24. Bd3 e5** To free his bishop. ME **25. Rhc1 Be6 26. R×c8** Not 26 Bb4 at once, because of 26 ... R×c1 27 R×c1 N×a4. ME **26 ... R×c8 27. Bb4** Preparing to push still further on the queenside. ME **27 ... Ne8 28. a5 Nd7** Not 28 ... Nc4+ because of 29 N×c4 B×c4 30 Rc1 Be6 31 R×c8 B×c8 32 Bc5 a6 33 b×a6 b×a6 34 Kc3 and Black will soon lose his a-pawn. ME **29. Nd5** 29 Rc1 might perhaps have been simpler, but Alekhine avoids exchange of rooks because endgames with only lighter pieces give many more drawing chances. The text gains White a passed pawn which, in conjunction with his two bishops, soon becomes a powerful force. There is one slight flaw in White's tactics: Black obtains control—even though only temporarily—of c5, a factor which undoubtedly gives him some opportunities. ME **29 ... B×d5 30. e×d5 Nc5 ...** KB **31. Bf5! Rd8** The plausible 31 ... Nb3+ would leave Black with a hopeless position after 32 Kd3 Rd8! 33 Re1 Nd4 34 R×e5 N×b5 35 R×e8+ (better still 35 Be7! AW) and wins. FR **32. Kc3!!** **b6** On 32 ... R×d5 Alekhine intended 33 Kc4 Rd4+ 34 K×c5 b6+ 35 a×b6 a×b6+ 36 K×b6 R×b4 37 Ra8 Kf8 38 Bd7. FR **33. a×b6 a×b6 34. B×c5!** As is well known, the force of the bishop-pair often lies in the possibility of exchanging back one of them for a knight at the appropriate moment. By the text, White obtains a second passed pawn, which carries the day. ME **34 ... b×c5 35. b6! Nd6** If 35 ... R×d5 36 b7! dM&LE **36. Bd7!** A beautiful finish. Black is completely helpless against the menace of Bc6, b7 and Ra8. ME **36 ... R×d7 37. Ra8+ Ne8 38. R×e8** Mate. The whole game is a beautiful example of Alekhine's great versatility in attack. Many other attacking players would have more or less lost interest when queens disappeared so early, but not Alekhine! He keeps up the fight right into the endgame, creating initiatives anew all the time. ME **1–0** Alekhine *et al* 252–4; Euwe 1945, 47–54; Reinfeld in Reinfeld & Bernstein 53–4; Heidenfeld 1983, 40–2.

(403) FINE–MIKENAS, V

Kemeri/Riga (17), 1937 (8 July)
Grünfeld Defence, Russian Variation [D95]

1. d4 Nf6 2. c4 g6 3. Nc3 d5 4. Qb3 This move is currently recommended as best against the Grünfeld. **4 ...**

The United States team won the Hamilton-Russell cup for the fourth, and last, time at the Stockholm Olympiad of 1937. Marshall (far right and this time on fourth board) was present on each occasion. Fine (second from right, second board), Horowitz (third from the right, reserve) and Kashdan (fourth from the right, third board) had all played on three of the teams, whereas it was the debut appearance for U.S. champion Reshevsky (second from the left, first board). Fritz Brieger stands at the far left.

c6 **5. Nf3 Bg7 6. e3** But this continuation is too quiet, White should play either 6 Bf4 or even 6 Bg5 if he wishes to seize the initiative. **6 ... 0–0 7. Bd2 e6** This is not good. In any event it does not turn out well for Black. Since he is planning to develop the bishop on b7 he ought to play the immediate 7 ... b6. On 8 Bd3 Bb7 an attempt by White to play the desirable break e4 is not possible: 9 e4 dxe4 10 Nxe4 c5! 11 Nxf6+ Bxf6 12 dxc5 Na6! with advantage to Black. **8. Bd3 Nbd7 9. 0–0 b6** (For 9 ... Nb6 see Fine–Lilienthal, Moscow 1937) **10. cxd5 exd5 11. e4! dxe4 12. Nxe4 c5!** In the event of 12 ... Nxe4 13 Bxe4 Bb7 14 Racl Rac8 15 Qa4 White retains the advantage. **13. Nxf6+ Nxf6 14. dxc5 bxc5 15. Rfd1 Be6 16. Qa3 Nd5!** (Black's weak pawn position is sufficiently counterbalanced by the aggressive placement of his pieces, MCO 203.) **17. Qxc5 Bxb2 18. Rab1** The following tactics involve Black in the loss of a pawn, but the superior co-ordination of his pieces guarantees him a draw. **18 ... Qf6 19. Be4! Rac8** 19 Rfd8 is inadequate on account of 19 ... Bg5. **20. Qxa7 Ra8 21. Qb7 Rfb8 22. Qc6 Rc8 23. Qb5 Rab8 24. Qe2** Having won a pawn the queen returns home. **24 ... Nc3! 25. Bxc3 Qxc3 26. Rd2 Bc4 27. Bd3 Bxd3 28. Qxd3 Qa5 29. Rc2** Draw agreed. A sharp tussle with a peaceful conclusion. ½–½ Betins, 271.

The Stockholm Team Tournament, 1937

With the United States chess champion Samuel Reshevsky making his debut in the team, Fine was relegated to second board for his third appearance at the international team tournament. His form seemed to have improved considerably in the three weeks since the end of the great Latvian tournament. Kashdan and Horowitz were also in tremendous form which, coupled with Reshevsky's solid plus three on top board, led to the most comfortable of the United States' four consecutive wins in official Olympiads.

Stockholm Olympiad, 31 July–15 August, 1937

The Swedish team had performed excellently in the previous two Olympiads, placing third behind the United States and Czechoslovakia at Folkestone, 1933, and second only to the Americans in Warsaw, 1935. For Fine this was a return to a city where he had enjoyed considerable success earlier in the year. Fine took the second board behind the U.S. champion Reshevsky, playing in his first international team tournament. Cozens remarks: "With nineteen nations competing, the Stockholm event was, with Prague 1931, the second largest contest for the Hamilton-Russell Cup—just one short of Warsaw 1935." Hungary had won every match in the interim Munich tournament of 1936, in which several teams including the United States had declined to participate, and Poland had been the most consistent team over the years, never failing to place in the top three, and so they, along with the returning Americans, were considered to be the favourites, and so it turned out.

Back to Cozens: "The playing schedule was fierce. Six times during the fifteen days two rounds had to be played in one day. The other days, which had only one round, had to see adjourned games from the previous three rounds cleared up. Playing hours were 10.30–15.30 and 17.30–22.30. This crushing routine meant, for many players, ten hours play out of twelve, day in, day out." The time control was set at 50 moves in 2½ hours and Cozens observed that: "... the fact that there was no adjournment after 40 moves treacherously encouraged players to take things easy for three or four hours, only to find themselves having to play difficult endgames at lightning speed in the 5th hour."

The programme was: Saturday July 31 the draw and round 1, Sunday August 1 rounds 2 and 3, Monday round 4 and adjournments, Tuesday rounds 5 and 6, Wednesday round 7 and adjournments, Thursday rounds 8 and 9, Friday round 10 and adjournments, Saturday August 7 rounds 11 and 12, Sunday free day, Monday round 13 and adjournments, Tuesday rounds 14 and 15, Wednesday civic reception, Thursday rounds 16 and 17, Friday round 18 and adjournments, Saturday August 14 round 19 and adjournments, Sunday Prizegiving. The U.S.A. had the bye in round

7, but by the end of round 11 they had taken the lead, with a match in hand over their main rivals who had not yet sat out a round. In the end the Americans won comfortably with 54½ out of 72, 6 points ahead of the second placed Hungary and a further 1½ ahead of Poland in third. Fine's score of nine wins, five draws and one loss, an exciting game with Apšenieks, was the best percentage score on board 2 (76.7 percent). Although Fine naturally did not play against the strongest opponents, he did meet players of the calibre of Lundin, Pirc, Szabó, O'Kelly, Foltys, Najdorf, Apšenieks and Paul Schmidt. A blitz tournament was held after the team tournament had finished. No details of whether Fine competed, and if so how he fared, are available. According to the *American Chess Bulletin* a sum of $2,251.00 was collected to pay expenses for the team at Stockholm. It was distributed, in part, as follows: Frank Marshall $425; Samuel Reshevsky $545; Reuben Fine, $275; Isaac Kashdan $425; Israel Horowitz $425. Reshevsky received $120 to compensate him for loss of earnings, and all the players with the exception of Fine, who was already in Europe, received $150 for traveling expenses. (In fact Reshevsky did not travel from the States, since he spent the second half of 1937 in Europe anyway. AW)

Vaitonis (Lithuania)	0	Fine	1
Fine	½	Lundin (Sweden)	
Kavli-Jørgensen (Norway)	0	Fine	1
Pirc (Yugoslavia)	½	Fine (Board 1)	
Szabo (Hungary)	½	Fine	
Fine	1	Grau (Argentina)	0

U.S.A. had the bye in round 7
Fine did not play in the match with Finland

Fine	1	O'Kelly (Belgium)	0
Foltys (Czechoslovakia)	0	Fine	1
Fine	½	Najdorf (Poland)	
Fine	1	Sørensen (Denmark)	0

Fine did not play in the match with the Netherlands

Apšenieks (Latvia)	1	Fine	0
Fine	½	Schmidt (Estonia)	

Fine did not play in the match with England

Fine	1	Riello (Italy)	0
Gudmundsson (Iceland)	0	Fine	1
Fine	1	Montgomerie (Scotland)	0

(404) VAITONIS, P—FINE

Stockholm Team Tournament (1), 1937 (31 July)
Queen's Gambit Accepted [D28]

1. Nf3 d5 2. c4 dxc4 3. e3 c5 4. Bxc4 Nf6 5. Nc3 Nc6 6. d4 e6 7. 0–0 a6 8. Qe2 cxd4 9. Rd1 Be7

10. exd4 Nd5 11. Qe4 f5 12. Qe2 0–0 13. Bb3 Bf6 14. Nxd5 exd5 15. Ne5 Re8 16. Qf3 Be6 17. Nxc6 bxc6 18. Bf4 Bf7 19. Rac1 Rc8 20. Qg3 Bh5 21. Rd2

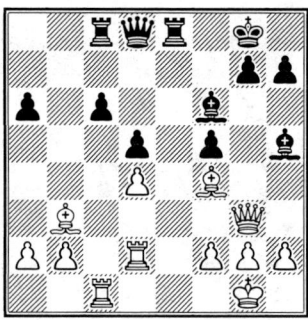

Position after White's 21st move

21 ... Re4 22. Be5 Bxe5 23. dxe5 f4 24. Qh3 Rxe5 25. Qc3 Qd6 26. Qa5 Rce8! Fine is not concerned about his straggling queenside pawns; it's straight for the king. 27. h3 f3 28. g3 Bf7 29. Qxa6 Qh6 30. Rdc2 Qxh3 31. Qf1 On which Vaitonis had been relying. 31 ... Re1!! White resigned. After 32 Rxe1 Rxe1, mate on g2 is inevitable. **0–1** Cozens, 207.

(405) FINE—LUNDIN, E

Stockholm Team Tournament (2), 1937 (1 Aug.)
Sicilian Defence, Moscow Variation [B54]

1. e4 c5 2. Nf3 d6 3. d4 cxd4 4. Nxd4 Nf6 5. f3 e6 6. c4 Be7 7. Nc3 0–0 8. Be2 Nc6 9. Nc2 a6 10. 0–0 Qc7 11. Kh1 b6 12. f4 Bb7 13. Ne3 Na7 14. Bf3 b5 15. cxb5 Nxb5 16. Nxb5 axb5 17. Qd3 Bc6 18. Nc2 Qb7 19. Re1 d5 20. e5 Ne4 21. Be3 b4 22. Nd4 Nc5 23. Qe2 Bd7 24. b3 Qa6 25. Qxa6 Rxa6 26. Rec1 Rc8 27. Rc2 Raa8 28. Rac1 g6 29. Kg1 Kf8 Draw agreed. **½–½**

(406) KAVLI-JØRGENSEN, O—FINE

Stockholm Team Tournament (3), 1937 (1 Aug.)
Grünfeld Defence [D70]

1. d4 Nf6 2. c4 g6 3. f3 A logical attempt to build a broad centre but on principle it would be prudent to develop some pieces first. 3 ... d5! Fine strikes at the centre, Grünfeld fashion, though the absence of the knight from c3 makes quite a difference. 4. cxd5 Nxd5 5. e4 Nb6 6. Be3 Bg7 7. Nc3 0–0 8. Rc1 White is in difficulties with the development of his kingside, chiefly on account of the obstruction caused by the pawn on f3. 8 Bd3 loses the d-pawn, while 8 Be2 further obstructs the king's knight. Now follows a systematic demolition job against the white centre. 8 ... f5! 9. Qd2 Nc6 10. d5 (Already White loses his way over the protection of his centre. 10 Rd1 would have been better than the text. DS) 10 ... Ne5 (With the unpleasant threat of ... Nc4. DS) 11. Bxb6 This unnecessary opening of the a-file—which he will shortly have cause

to regret—is part of White's plan to establish a really crushing pawn-centre by f4 followed by e5. There is a tactical snag, however, which has escaped his notice, on which his strategy will founder. (If 11 f4 Nec4 12 Bxc4 Nxc4 13 Qe2 Nxe3 14 Qxe3 fxe4 15 Qxe4 Bf5 16 Qc4. DS) 11 ... axb6

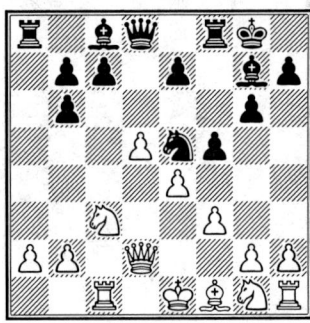

Position after Black's 11th move

12. f4 Now if the knight retreats 13 e5 will give White a dangerous territorial superiority. **12 ... Bh6!** A deadly interpolation. **13. g3 fxe4** And there goes White's centre, leaving him with incurable light-square weaknesses. **14. Nxe4 Bg4!** With the nasty threat of ... Bf3. **15. Be2 Bxe2!** The disappearance of this bishop leaves the white squares defenceless, as well as shifting the king. 16 Qxe2 would now lose the d-pawn (for the f-pawn has not been unpinned). 16 Nxe2 is worse (16 ... Nf3+), so there is nothing for it but: **16. Kxe2 Qd7!** Onto the light squares. White does not know whether he is going to be hit from right or left. **17. Rc3 Qb5+ 18. Kf2 Rxa2** The rook comes in for the knockout down the file which White's eleventh move obligingly opened. **19. Ne2** Development! (If 19 Rc2 Rxb2 20 Rxb2 Qxb2 21 Qxb2 Nd3+. DS) **19 ... Rxb2 20. Rc2 Ng4+** The white squares! **21. Kf3 Qb3+ 22. Rc3** Else the rook goes. **22 ... Ne5+ 23. Kf2 Qb4!** White resigned. Queen and knight are both attacked, and 24 Qe3 runs into one light-square disaster by 24 ... Ng4+ while 24 Rc2 runs into another by 24 ... Qxe4 25 Rxb2 Qxh1. The f-pawn has stood pinned for more than half the game. 0–1 Cozens, 205–6; *De Schaakwereld*, 1937 107–8.

(407) PIRC, V—FINE

Stockholm Team Tournament (4), 1937 (2 Aug.)
Queen's Gambit Declined, Exchange Slav [D13]

1. d4 d5 2. Nf3 Nf6 3. c4 c6 4. cxd5 cxd5 5. Nc3 Nc6 6. Bf4 e6 7. e3 Be7 8. Bd3 0–0 9. Rc1 Nh5 10. Be5 f6 11. Bg3 Nxg3 12. hxg3 g6 13. a3 Bd7 14. Nd2 Rf7 15. 0–0 Be8 16. b4 Bf8 17. Nb3 Rc7 18. Nc5 Bf7 19. Ne2 e5 20. Qa4 Ne7 21. Bb1 Nc8 22. Ba2 Nb6 23. Qd1 a5 24. Qd2 Nc4 25. Bxc4 dxc4 26. Qc3 b6 27. Ne4 axb4 28. axb4 f5 29. Nd2 e4 30. Ra1 b5 31. g4 Rxa1 32. Rxa1 Qe7 33. Rb1 Ra7 34. Qc2 Be8 35. Nc3 Qg5 36. Qd1 Bd6 37. Nd5 Bc6 38. f4 Qh4 39. Nc3 Qg3 40. Nf1 Qxg4 41. Qxg4 fxg4 42. d5 Bd7 43. Nxe4 Bf5 44. Nfg3 Bf8 45. Nxf5 gxf5 46. Nc3 Ra3 47. Nxb5 Rxe3 48. d6 Rd3 49. Rc1 c3 50. Rxc3 Rxc3 51. Nxc3 Bxd6 52. b5 Kf7 53. Na4 Ke6 54. g3 Kd5 55. Kg2 Kc4

56. Nb6+ Kxb5 57. Nd5 Bc5 58. Nf6 h5 59. Ng8 Bf8 60. Nf6 Bb4 61. Ng8 Draw agreed. ½–½

(408) SZABÓ, L—FINE

Stockholm Team Tournament (5), 1937 (3 Aug.)
Queen's Gambit Declined, Semi-Tarrasch [D41]

1. Nf3 d5 2. d4 Nf6 3. c4 e6 4. Nc3 c5 5. cxd5 Nxd5 6. e4 Nxc3 7. bxc3 cxd4 8. cxd4 Bb4+ 9. Bd2 Bxd2+ 10. Qxd2 0–0 11. Be2 b6 12. 0–0 Bb7 13. Qe3 Nc6 14. Rfd1 Rc8 15. Rac1 Qe7 16. Rc2 Nb4 17. Rb2 Rfd8 18. Bb5 Nc2 19. Qe2 Na3 20. Bd3 b5 21. h3 a6 22. Rb3 h6 23. Qb2 Nc4 24. Qe2 Nb6 25. Bb1 Na4 26. Qd2 Rc7 27. Ne5 b4 28. Rg3 Nc3 29. Re1 f6 30. Ng4 h5 31. Nh6+ Kh7 32. Bc2 gxh6 33. Qf4 Bc8 34. Qh4 e5 35. Qxh5 Qf7 36. Qh4 Rxd4 37. f4 Rd2 38. Bb3 Be6 39. fxe5 Bxb3 40. exf6 Ne2+ 41. Rxe2 Rxe2 42. axb3 Qe8 43. Qf4 Rec2?! 44. e5 R2c6 45. Qe4+ Kh8 46. Rg6 Qf8 47. Kh2 Rc5 48. Qf4 Kh7 49. Qe4 Kh8 50. Qf4 Kh7 51. Qe4 Draw agreed. ½–½

(409) FINE—GRAU, R

Stockholm Team Tournament (6), 1937 (3 Aug.)
Queen's Gambit Declined, Grau Variation [D06]

1. d4 d5 2. Nf3 Bf5 3. c4 e6 4. Qb3 Nc6 5. c5 Rb8 6. Nc3 Be7 7. Bf4 g5?! 8. Bg3 g4 9. Ne5 Bf6 10. Qa4 Nge7 11. Nxc6 bxc6 12. b3 0–0 13. e3 Qd7 14. Be2 Ng6 15. 0–0 Bg5 16. Qa5 e5 17. dxe5 Rfe8 18. Rad1 Be6 19. Ne4 Qe7 20. Nxg5 Qxg5 21. Qxc7 Rec8 22. Qa5 Nxe5 23. Ba6 Rd8 24. Qc7 Black resigned. 1–0

(410) FINE—O'KELLY DE GALWAY, A

Stockholm Team Tournament (9), 1937 (5 Aug.)
English Opening [A12]

1. c4 Nf6 2. Nf3 c6 3. b3 d5 4. Bb2 Bf5 5. g3 e6 6. Bg2 Nbd7 7. 0–0 Bd6 8. d3 0–0 9. Nbd2 e5 10. Qc2 h6 11. e4 dxe4 12. dxe4 Bh7 13. Rad1 Qc7 14. Nh4 Rfe8 15. Nf5 Bf8 16. Rfe1 Rad8 17. Nf3 Bg6 18. h3 Bc5 19. Kh2 Bh5 20. N5h4 Bxf3 21. Nxf3 Nh7 22. h4 f6 23. Re2 Ndf8 24. Bh3 Ne6 25. Rxd8 Qxd8 26. Rd2 Qe7 27. Qd1 Nhf8

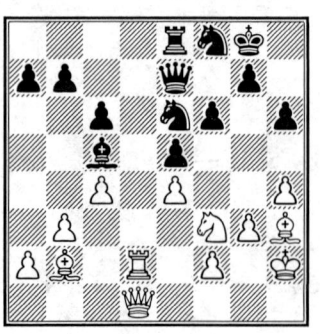

Position after Black's 27th move

28. h5 Bb4 29. Rd3 Nc5 30. Re3 Rd8 31. Qc2
Nce6 32. Rd3 Rxd3 33. Qxd3 Bc5 34. Kg2 Qd6
35. Qxd6 Bxd6 36. Nh4 Kf7 37. Nf5 Bc5 38. Bg4
Nd7 39. Nxg7 Nxg7 40. Bxd7 Bd4 41. Bxd4 exd4
42. c5 Nxh5 43. Kf3 Ke7 44. Bg4 Ng7 45. Ke2 b6
46. b4 bxc5 47. bxc5 Black resigned. 1–0

(411) FOLTYS, J—FINE

Stockholm Team Tournament (10), 1937 (6 Aug.)
Queen's Gambit Declined, Tarrasch Defence [D40]

1. d4 Nf6 2. Nf3 e6 3. e3 c5 4. c4 d5 5. Nc3 Nc6
6. a3 Ne4 A recommendation of Alekhine. 7. Qc2 Qa5
8. dxc5!? An insufficiently energetic counter. 8 ... Bxc5
9. cxd5 exd5 10. Bd3 Nxc3 11. bxc3 h6 12. 0–0
0–0 Black has equalized, MCO 154. 13. Nd4 Qc7
14. Nxc6 White mistakenly believed he could relieve his
game through exchanges. But this simply removes the well-
placed knight. 14 ... Qxc6 15. c4 Be6 16. Bb2 Rac8
17. Rac1 Rfd8 18. cxd5 Bxd5 19. Qc3 Bf8 20. Qd4
Qe6 21. Rxc8 Qxc8 22. Rc1 Bc6 23. Qc4 Qd7 24. Rd1
Perhaps the decisive mistake. 24 Bb1 is better. 24 ... Qe7
25. Bc2 Rxd1+ 26. Bxd1

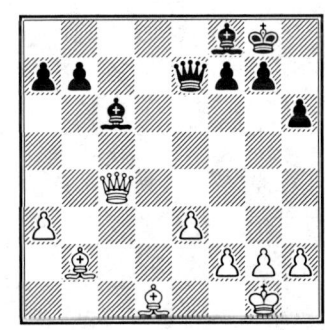

*Position after
White's 26th move*

26 ... Qg5 27. g3 Qf5 28. h4 a6 29. a4 Be7 30. Qc2?
Be4 31. Qe2 Qh3 White resigned. 0–1 Foltys, 76.

(412) FINE—NAJDORF, M

Stockholm Team Tournament (11), 1937 (7 Aug.)
Nimzowitsch-Indian Defence, Classical Variation [E37]

1. d4 Nf6 2. c4 e6 3. Nc3 Bb4 4. Qc2 d5 5. a3
Bxc3+ 6. Qxc3 Ne4 7. Qc2 c5 8. dxc5 Nc6 9. e3
Qa5+ 10. Bd2 Nxd2! 11. Qxd2 dxc4! 12. Qxa5
Nxa5 13. Rc1 b5! 14. cxb6 Bb7 15. Nf3 0–0 16. bxa7
Rxa7 17. Nd2 Ba6 18. Rc3 g6 19. Nxc4 Bxc4
20. Bxc4 Rb8 21. Bd3 Rxb2 22. 0–0 Kf8 23. g3
Nb7 24. Rb1 Rd2 25. Bb5 Nd6 26. Bc6 Nf5 27. Rb7
Ra5 28. a4 Nd6 29. Rb4 e5 30. Rb8+ Ke7 31. Ra8
Rxa8 32. Bxa8 Ra2 33. Bc6 f5 34. Kg2 e4 35. h4
Rd2 36. a5 Ra2 37. Rc5 Ra3 38. Bd5 Ne8 39. Bc4
Kd6 40. Rc8 Nc7 41. Bg8 h6 42. Bh7 Rxa5 43. Bxg6
Nd5 44. Rh8 Ke5 45. Bf7 Nf6 46. Rxh6 Ra7
47. Bh5 Ra2 48. Rh8 Nd5 49. Kg1 Ra1+ 50. Kg2
Ra2 51. Re8+ Kf6 52. Kg1 Ra1+ 53. Kh2 Ra2

54. g4 Nxe3 55. g5+ Kg7 56. Re7+ Kf8 57. Rb7
Rxf2+ 58. Kg3 Rf1 59. Rf7+ Kg8 60. Rf6 Kg7
61. Be2 f4+ 62. Rxf4 Nf5+ Draw agreed. ½–½

(413) FINE—SØRENSEN, E

Stockholm Team Tournament (12), 1937 (7 Aug.)
Queen's Gambit Declined [D51]

1. d4 Nf6 2. c4 e6 3. Nc3 d5 4. Bg5 Nbd7 5. e3
c6 6. a3 Be7 7. Qc2 0–0 8. Nf3 Re8 9. Rd1 a6
10. h3 Nh5 11. Bxe7 Qxe7 12. Bd3 Nhf6 13. 0–0
b5 14. cxb5 cxb5 15. a4 b4 16. Na2 Bb7 17. a5
Rab8 18. Rc1 Ne4 19. Qa4

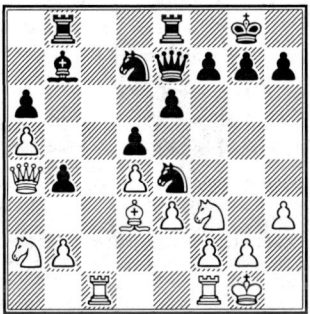

*Position after
White's 19th move*

19 ... e5 20. Nxb4 exd4 21. exd4 Qd6 22. Rc2
Ndf6 23. Rfc1 Bc8 24. Nc6 Ra8 25. Nce5 Be6
26. Rc6 Qd8 27. Rxa6 Rb8 28. Qc2 Rc8 29. Rc6
Nh5 30. Rxc8 Qxc8 31. Qxc8 Rxc8 32. Rxc8+ Bxc8
33. a6 Nhf6 34. a7 Bb7 35. Bb5 Black resigned. 1–0

(414) APŠENIEKS, F—FINE

Stockholm Team Tournament (14), 1937 (10 Aug.)
Four Knights Game [C49]

1. e4 e5 2. Nf3 Nc6 3. Nc3 Nf6 4. Bb5 Bb4
5. 0–0 0–0 The Double Ruy Lopez is alleged to be the
most drawish of openings; there are, however, many ways of
breaking the symmetry and reaching dynamic positions. The
masters of the early 20th century played the Four Knights
with aggressive intent and extracted some fine wins from it.
6. d3 Qe7 Fine chooses this moment to vary, going into
Metger's System, which protects the e-pawn and proposes to
redevelop the queen's knight via d8 to e6, where it will pose
an awkward question to the white queen's bishop. 7. Bg5
Bxc3 8. bxc3 Nd8 9. d4! Black has delayed moving his
d-pawn and Apšenieks takes a second bite at the centre.
9 ... d6 10. d5! Spiking the Metger plan: the black queen's
knight now has no move. 10 ... h6 11. Bh4 c6 12. Ba4
Bg4 13. Qd3 cxd5 14. exd5 Rc8? A fateful move.
Black is hurrying to get his pieces into action, but his lines
of communication are cut by the knight still held immobile
on d8 by the white pawn on d5. The undefended position
of the rook on c8 ultimately permits a combination which
loses the game for Black. 15. Bb3 Kh8 16. Qe3 White
clearly stands better, PCO. 16 ... Bxf3? More to the point

would be 16 ... b6, screening the a-pawn and preparing to get the knight to c5 via b7. Fine has in mind an aggressive kingside advance. **17. Qxf3 g5?!** Not only rather wild on principle but tactically quite unsound; in short a clanger. Fine has forgotten the undefended rook. **18. Bxg5! hxg5 19. Qh3+ Kg7 20. Qxc8** Apšenieks has won the exchange and a pawn. He has hooked his fish and just needs to reel it in. What he has at the end of his line, however, is a man-eating shark. Fine now has the h-file at his disposal and it is the white pieces that are out of play. In less than no time, Black has a powerful attack on the white king. **20 ... Ne6!!** In an instant the out-of-play knight becomes the ringleader of the attack. **21. Qc4 Nf4! 22. Rad1 Qd7 23. Rfe1 Qg4 24. Qf1 Rh8** What a transformation! For all his extra material, White will now be hard-pressed to survive. One beautiful conclusion to the game would be 25 Re3 (the likeliest-looking defence) Nh3+! 26 Kh1(?) Qxd1!! 27 Qxd1 Nxf2+. (26 Rxh3 obviously wins for White. AW) **25. Rd3** The one and only saving move [sic], returning the exchange. **25 ... Qh4** Is this the best? It looks as though Fine could force the game by 25 ... Nxd3 26 cxd3 Rxh2!!? 27 Kxh2 Qh4+ 28 Kg1 Ng4 with mate to follow. The mate is not forced, however, for instead of accepting the rook on h2 White could play 27 Re3! Qh4 28 Rh3 but then, after 28 ... Rxh3 29 gxh3, White could hardly hope for more than a draw. It was probably Black's best line, for now Apšenieks holds on to the win. **26. h3 Nxd3 27. cxd3 g4?** Carried away by his remarkable recovery—now only a pawn down—Fine goes all out to force the game. **28. Re3** The rook on the third rank suddenly imperils both the black queen and king. Moreover, the bishop is now threatening to re-enter the game at d1. **28 ... gxh3?** Black could still have kept some hopes alive with 28 ... Rh6. AW **29. Rg3+!!** Fine must have expected only 29 Rxh3. This interpolated check is a killer, for if the king goes to the h-file 30 Rxh3 wins the queen, while if 29 ... Kf8 the same move wins the rook. **29 ... Ng4 30. gxh3 f5 31. Qg2! Qh6 32. Qf3 Kf8 33. Rxg4** Black resigned. A thrilling game. **1–0** Cozens, 106–8.

(415) FINE—SCHMIDT, P

Stockholm Team Tournament (15), 1937 (10 Aug.)
Queen's Gambit Declined, Slav Defence [D12]

1. d4 d5 2. c4 c6 3. Nf3 Nf6 4. e3 Bf5 5. Nc3 The Landau Variation, cxd5, Qb3 and Na3, has been shown not to be dangerous. **5 ... e6 6. Nh4 Be4** Reinfeld played 6 ... Bg4 against Fine in this position, New York 1938. AW **7. f3 Bg6 8. Qb3 Qc7 9. Bd2 Be7** Here the bishop is certainly better placed than on the more normal d6, since in that case White would immediately advance with f4 and g3. **10. Nxg6 hxg6 11. 0-0-0 Nbd7 12. Be2** Now White will be unable to maintain his bishop pair, the immediate g3 was better. Thanks to the bishop move Black will be able to play Nd7-b6! **12 ... dxc4 13. Bxc4 Nb6 14. g3** White stands slightly better, MCO. **14 ... Nxc4 15. Qxc4 Nd5** Easing his position, as 16 Ne4 would be answered by 16 ...

e5. **16. e4 Nxc3 17. Bxc3 0-0-0 18. Kb1 Rh5** Preventing the advance d5. **19. f4 Rdh8** A trap. On 20 Rd2 b5 21 Qb3 b4 22 Bxb4 Rb5 Black wins a piece. The immediate implementation of the plan 19 ... b5 would fail against 22 Bxe7 followed by 23 Bxd8. **20. d5!?** This merely leads to equality; on 20 h4 Black had planned to answer 20 ... g5! with wild complications. **20 ... cxd5 21. Qa4! Qc6?** The usual consequence of a surprise; Black makes a mistake. 21 ... Qc4 was correct when White must immediately, or after 22 Qxa7 Bc5 23 Qa8+ Kc7 24 Qa5+ (not 24 Be5+ Kb6!) Bb6, swap queens. Black had overlooked 25 Qa5+!! A case of chess blindness. **22. Qxa7 Bc5 23. Qa8+ Kd7** On 23 ... Kc7 there would follow 24 Be5+ and so on. **24. exd5!** A very powerful move. **24 ... exd5 25. Qa5 d4!** Counterplay! On 25 ... Rxh2 26 Rhe1! the game would already be decided. **26. Bxd4** Forced. **26 ... Qe4+ 27. Ka1 Bxd4 28. Qb4!** A very fine move, which above all prevents 28 ... Rd5. 28 Qa4+ Kc8 29 Qxd4 offers good prospects of a draw (after 29 ... Qxd4 30 Rxd4 Rxh2 31 Rc1+ Kb8. AW). **28 ... Kc8 29. Rhe1 Bxb2+ 30. Qxb2 Qf5** It is indeed surprising that the black king can hold out. **31. Re5** Played after a long think; on 31 Qxg7 there follows 31 ... Rxh2, threatening to sacrifice on a2 and also on 31 Re7 Qf6 32 Qxf6 gxf6 33 Rxf7 Rxh2 34 Rxf6 Rg2 it is hardly possible for White to win the game, since he is unable to protect the pawn on a2. **31 ... Qf6 32. Rc1+ Kb8 33. Rb1 b6!** Forced. On 33 ... Qc6, 34 Re7 is decisive. **34. Qd4 Ka7 35. Re7+** Otherwise on 35 Qa4+ Kb7 36 Qd7+ Ka6 and so on. **35 ... Ka6** Of course not 35 ... Qxe7 36 Qxb6+ Ka8 37 Qa6+ Qa7 38 Qc6+ followed by mate. **36. Qxf6 gxf6 37. Rxf7 Rf5 38. Re7** 38 h4 also affords White but little chance of winning. Both players were now getting into terrible time trouble. **38 ... Rxh2 39. Re6 Ra5 40. Rexb6+ Ka7 41. Rb7+** At this point Schmidt's record differs slightly from Fine's. He continues 41 R6b2 Rh7 (Black relies on the strength of the two rooks to bring the draw and so refrains from 41 ... Rxb2) 42 Rb3 Ka6 43 a3 (Not 43 Rb6+ Ka7 44 Rxf6 Rh2 with perpetual check) g5 44 fxg5 Rxg5 45 Rb4 Rhg7 46 R1b3 R7g6 47 Kb2 Rg4 48 Rxg4 Rxg4 and we reach the same position as that after move 49 in the text. AW **41 ... Ka8 42. R7b2 Rh7 43. Rb3 Ka7 44. a3 g5 45. fxg5 Rxg5 46. Rb4 Ka6 47. R1b3 Rhg7 48. Kb2 Rg4 49. Rxg4 Rxg4 50. Rf3 Rg6?** Time trouble! Black could force the draw by the simple ... f5 or ... Kb7. **51. Kc3 Kb7 52. Kd4 Kc7 53. Kd5** On 53 Ke4 Rg5. **53 ... Kd7 54. a4 Rg5+ 55. Kc4 Kc8** Black must take care to maintain the opposition. **56. Ra3 Kb7 57. a5 Kc6! 58. Rf3 Rxa5 59. Rxf6+ Kd7 60. Kd4 Ke7 61. Rf3 Ke6** Draw agreed. **½–½** Paul Schmidt from an unidentified Czech column.

(416) FINE—RIELLO, M

Stockholm Team Tournament (17), 1937 (12 Aug.)
Catalan System [E09]

1. d4 d5 2. Nf3 Nf6 3. c4 e6 4. g3 Nbd7 5. Bg2 c6 6. Nbd2 Be7 7. 0-0 0-0 8. Qc2 Qc7 9. e4

dxe4 10. Nxe4 Nxe4 11. Qxe4 Nf6 12. Qe2 c5
13. Bf4 Qb6 14. dxc5 Bxc5 15. Ne5 Bd7 16. Rab1
Rfd8

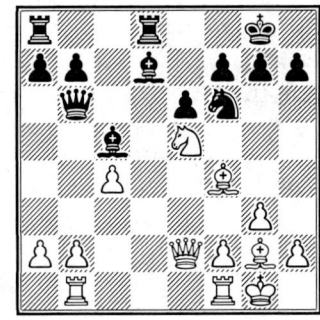

*Position after
Black's 16th move*

17. b4! Be7 18. Nxd7 Rxd7 19. c5 Qd8 20. c6!
bxc6 21. Bxc6 Nd5 22. Bxd7 Nxf4 23. Qf3 Nh3+
24. Kg2 Ng5 25. Qd3 e5 26. Rfd1 Qb6 27. h4 Ne6
28. Qe4 Rd8 29. Bxe6 Qxe6 30. Rxd8+ Bxd8
31. Rd1 Black resigned. 1–0

(417) GUDMUNDSSON, J—FINE

Stockholm Team Tournament (18), 1937 (13 Aug.)
Grünfeld Defence [D93]

1. d4 Nf6 2. Nf3 g6 3. c4 Bg7 4. Nc3 d5 5. Bf4 c6
6. e3 0–0 7. Qb3 Qa5 8. Bd3 dxc4 9. Bxc4 c5
10. 0–0 cxd4 11. exd4 Qf5 12. Bd2 Nc6 13. Nb5
Ne4 14. Be1 Bd7 15. Bd3 Qf4 16. Nc3 Nxc3 17. bxc3
b6 18. Bd2 Qd6

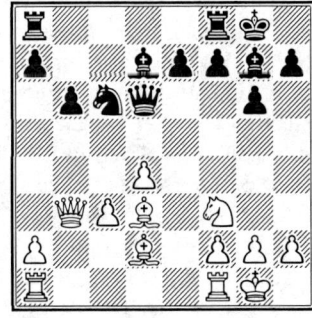

*Position after
Black's 18th move*

19. Rfe1 Rac8 20. Qd1 Rfe8 21. Ba6 Rcd8
22. Qc1 e5! 23. dxe5 Nxe5 24. Nxe5 Bxe5 25. f4
Bf6 26. Rxe8+ Bxe8 27. Be1? b5 White resigned.
0–1

(418) FINE—MONTGOMERIE, J

Stockholm Team Tournament (19), 1937 (14 Aug.)
English Opening, Classical Variation [A20]

1. c4 e5 2. Nf3 Nc6 3. d4 exd4 4. Nxd4 Bc5
5. Nb3 Be7 6. g3 Nf6 7. Bg2 0–0 8. 0–0 d6
9. Nc3 Ne5 10. Nd2 Rb8 11. b3 Ng6 12. e4 Ne8
13. Nd5 f5 14. f4 Bf6 15. Nxf6+ Nxf6 16. Bb2

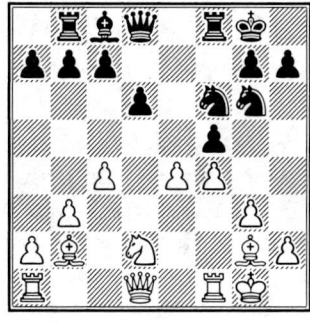

*Position after
White's 16th move*

16 ... Be6 17. Re1 Qc8 18. Qc2 Kh8 19. Qc3 Qd7
20. Re2 Qf7 21. Rae1 c6 22. exf5 Bxf5 23. Ne4
Bxe4 24. Bxe4 Rbe8 25. Qd4 d5 26. cxd5 cxd5
27. Bf3 a6 28. Qc5 Rc8 29. Qa5 Rfd8 30. f5 Nf8
31. Re7 Qg8 32. Rxb7 Black resigned. 1–0

Reuben Fine was married to Miss Emma Thea Keesing
in Amsterdam on September 1st. The reception was at the
Hotel de l'Europe. Few figures of the chess world were present, Messrs. Schelfout and Kmoch being exceptions. A correspondent describes Miss Keesing as 20 years of age, small,
dark, kind, good-humoured, very pretty. She has been a
journalist for *Het Volk* where somebody described her as
being "something between Shirley Temple and Mae West."
(*Chess*, 14 September, 1937, 3)

*During a busy 1937, Fine married for the first time. The bride, Emma
Keesing, a reporter for* Het Volk, *was the daughter of the Dutch publisher of Chess Archives.*

More Poor Form and a World Championship, 1937–1938

By now firmly established as one of the leading players in the world, Fine was a natural for invitations to the strongest tournaments. At the time there was considerable discontent in the chess world about the manner in which contenders for the world title were chosen by the champion. Euwe had promised to allow the International Chess Federation (FIDE) to organize future matches should he retain the title in his return match with Alekhine, as he was expected to do by many commentators. Tournament committees were therefore keen to invite the acknowledged candidates to their events and several were described as Candidates Tournaments, though as far as I am aware the only one that approached that in official terms was the A.V.R.O. event. Fine's result at one of these events, Semmering/Baden, looked better than it really was. He struggled to win games and rode his fortune to second place, a whole point behind Keres. At the end of year Hastings event he once more failed to defeat any of the grandmasters and had to settle for fourth place.

Fine certainly took on a greater volume of tournament and match games during 1937. Since 1931 his total number of games played per year had been as follows (counting events that span December and January in the earlier year): 1931–49; 1932–48; 1933–69; 1934–58; 1935–54 and 1936–77. During 1937, however, he played in total 111 games or about twice the average number of games for his most active years. This was clearly too many; in the next two years he reduced his activity to 33 games in 1938 and 25 games in 1939, then increased it again to 59 games in 1940 and 42 games in 1941 (the increase being largely as a result of his participation in the Marshall Chess Club Championship). From 1942 onwards it was rare for Fine to participate in more than a single event (he never contested the Marshall Club Championship again, even when he was resident in New York). This is reflected in the number of games played in those years: 1942–9; 1943–0; 1944–22; 1945–15; 1946–2; 1947–6; 1948–10; 1949–9 (these nine and nine of the previous year being played within a five week period); 1950–2 and 1951–17.

Semmering-Baden, "Candidates Tournament," September 8–27, 1937

"No less than five of the world's leading masters, generally acknowledged to be entitled to consideration in connection with any possible world championship negotiations, were found in the list of eight competitors invited to participate in the double round tournament arranged by the management of the Hotel Panhans at Semmering, under the auspices of the Austrian Chess Federation. The chief prizes were in fact divided among this quintet. The games of the tournament were divided between Semmering, Sept. 8–12 (4 rounds) and Baden, near Vienna, Sept 14–27, at the Hotel Gruner Baum. Dr. Max Euwe undertook the task of directing the tournament, but gave way to Rudolph Spielmann a week before the end, as he was obliged to go home. The time limit was 40 moves in 2½ hours, the innovation of Capablanca, several years ago. The four regular prizes consisted of 2,500, 2,000, 1,500, and 1,200 shillings. A fund of 600 shillings was distributed among the non–prize-winners." (ACB)

		1	2	3	4	5	6	7	8	
1	Keres	**	½½	½½	10	½1	10	½1	11	9
2	Fine	½½	**	½½	½½	½½	½½	1½	1½	8
3=	Capablanca	½½	½½	**	½½	1½	½0	½1	½½	7½
3=	Reshevsky	01	½½	½½	**	½½	11	½0	10	7½
5	Flohr	½0	½½	0½	½½	**	1½	½½	1½	7
6=	Eliskases	01	½½	½1	00	0½	**	½1	0½	6
6=	Ragozin	½0	0½	½0	½1	½½	½0	**	1½	6
8	Petrovs	00	0½	½½	01	0½	1½	0½	**	5

(419) CAPABLANCA, J—FINE

Semmering-Baden (1), 1937 (8 Sept.)
Slav Defence [D19]

1. d4 d5 2. c4 c6 3. Nf3 Nf6 4. Nc3 dxc4 5. a4 Bf5 6. e3 e6 7. Bxc4 Bb4 8. 0–0 0–0 9. Qe2 Bg4 10. Rd1 Qe7 11. h3 Bh5 12. e4 Nbd7 13. e5 Practically forced, else Black frees himself with ... e5. ME **13 ... Nd5 14. Ne4 f6** Thus far the game has been identical with the Nottingham encounter between Bogolyubov and Euwe, with the exception—favourable to White—of the 11th move for both sides as played in the present game. ME **15. exf6 gxf6** 15 ... N7xf6 would lead to difficulties after 16 Ng3 Bf7 17 Ne5. ME **16. Ng3 Bf7 17. Bh6** White has managed to obtain a very promising position. In earlier times Capablanca would surely have turned it into a winning position. JH **17 ... Rfe8 18. Ne1!** Despite the complicated character of the position, Capa realizes the pre-eminent strategical importance of the square f4. ME **18 ... Kh8 19. Nd3 Bd6 20. Qf3 Rg8 21. Nf4 Nxf4 22. Bxf4 Bxf4 23. Qxf4** The disappearance of the minor pieces has somewhat eased Black's position. JH **23 ... Nb6 24. Bb3 Rad8** Black fixes the weak d-pawn as the object of counterplay. JH **25. Re1** White has manoeuvred with great care, and has some advantage in view of the decided weakness of the e-pawn and f-pawn, while his own d-pawn is safe enough. ME **25 ... Nd5 26. Qh4!** A very powerful move which threatens to win at once with 27 Nf5 followed by 28 Bxd5 and 29 Qxf6+. ME **26 ... Bg6 27. Ne4 f5** Black is forced to make this unfavourable move, for after 27 ... Bxe4 28 Rxe4, the e-pawn would soon become untenable. ME **28. Qxe7 Nxe7 29. Nc5 Rxd4 30. Rxe6 Nd5** The following moves were played in rapid succession, both players being in severe time pressure. ME **31. N×b7** The material advantage which results from his excellent position play. **31 ... Bh5 32. B×d5** Black threatened 32 ... Nf4. However this exchange was not absolutely forced. White could have played instead 32 R×c6 (unmasking the bishop vis-à-vis the rook on g8) Bf3 33 g3 Rd2 34 Rc2! R×c2 35 B×c2 Nb4 36 Bb3 B×b7 37 B×g8 K×g8 with rook and two pawns against bishop and knight. AW **32 ... R×d5 33. Nd6 Rb8** If 33 ... Bf3 34 Nf7+ Kg7 35 Ng5. ME (In this line 35 Nh6, with an attack on both rook and bishop, may be slightly better because Black has the tricky 35 ... B×g2 36 K×g2 h6 recovering the piece. AW) **34. Rc1 Rd1+ 35. R×d1 B×d1 36. Re7 B×a4! 37. R×a7 Bc2 38. Rc7 R×b2 39. R×c6** After considerable blood-letting, White has retained the plus-pawn. ME **39 ... Kg7 40. Nc4 Ra2 41. Ne3 Be4 42. Re6 Kf7 43. Re5 Kf6 44. Rb5** The first adjournment was taken here. White's extra pawn is enough to win. ME **44 ... Ra6 45. Kh2 Ra2 46. Kg3?** With this all too obvious move, White lets the win slip out of his grasp. He should have played 46 f3 Bd3 47 Rc5 Ra4 48 Nd5+ and then Kg3. ME **46 ... Ra4** Threatening ... f4+ and thus forcing the king to retreat. ME **47. Kh2 Rd4 48. f3 Bd3 49. Ra5 Ke6** White can no longer reach the desired position. ME **50. g3 Be2 51. f4 Bd3 52. Re5+ Kf6 53. Nd5+ Kf7 54. g4 f×g4 55. h×g4 Bc4 56. Rf5+ Kg7 57. Ne3 Re4** (The second adjournment was taken here, but the draw is already clearly established. ME) **58. Rg5+ Kf6 59. Rf5+ Kg7 60. Ng2 Rd4 61. Ne1 Rd5 62. R×d5 B×d5 63. Kg3 Kf6 64. Nf3 Be4 65. Ne5 Bc2 66. Kh4 h6 67. Nd7+ Kg7 68. f5 Ba4 69. Nc5 Bd1 70. Kg3 Kf7 71. Kf4 Be2 72. Ne4 Bd1 73. Nc3 Bb3 74. Ke5 Bc4** Draw agreed. ½–½ Reinfeld 1938, 12–3; Soloviev 1997, 229; Wood, 10–1; *Encyclopaedia of Chess Endings: Minor Piece Endings*, 264; Lopez Esnaola & de Marimon, 17–9; Hannak, 39–40; Averbakh 1984b.

(420) FINE—FLOHR, S

Semmering-Baden (2), 1937 (9 Sept.)
Grünfeld Defence, Russian Variation [D81]

1. d4 Nf6 2. c4 g6 3. Nc3 d5 4. Qb3 d×c4 5. Q×c4 Be6 5 ... Bg7 leaves White in command of more space, but this advantage may easily prove to be of ephemeral value 6 e4 0–0 7 Nf3 (A direct transposition into what is now known as the Russian System, a major alternative to the Exchange Variation. Apart from the text, Black can chose between 6 ... c6—common in the 1930s and 1940s, Simagin's 7 ... Nc6, the Hungarian Variation 7 ... a6 (first played by Alekhine in the 12th match game with Euwe in 1935, Euwe won and the move was apparently then ignored until about 1969) Prins' 7 ... Na6 and Smyslov's 7 ... Bg4. AW) b6 8 Bf4 c5! 9 d×c5 Ba6 10 Qd4 (10 Qa4!) Q×d4 11 N×d4 B×f1 12 R×f1 N×e4! is good for Black, Botvinnik–Levenfish, 8th U.S.S.R. Championship, Leningrad 1933. MCO 206 **6. Qa4+** 6 Qb5+ Nc6 7 Nf3 Nd5! 8 e4 (better than 8 N×d5

B×d5 9 e3 e6! 10 Bd2 a6 11 Qa4 Bd6 12 Be2 0–0 13 Qc2 Nb4 which favours Black, Feigins–Flohr, Kemeri 1937) Nbd4 9 Qa4 Bd7 10 Qd1 with the better game. MCO **6 ... Bd7 7. Qb3 Bc6 8. Nf3 Bg7 9. e3 0–0 10. Be2 Nbd7 11. 0–0 Nb6** Black must manoeuvre with some care because White is in charge of the pawn centre. **12. Qc2 Nbd5 13. Ne5** White stands slightly better, MCO. **13 ... Be8 14. Bf3 c6 15. Rd1 Nb6 16. b3** Here White misses a good chance to get a strong initiative with e3-e4. Doubtless fearing that the centre might later prove shaky, Fine adopts a more prudent continuation. **16 ... Nfd5 17. Ba3 f6 18. Nd3 N×c3 19. Q×c3 Bf7 20. Nc5 Qc7 21. Rac1 Rfe8 22. Qa5 Rec8 23. g3 f5 24. Nd3 Nd5 25. Q×c7 R×c7** Draw agreed. ½–½ Reinfeld 1938, 15–6.

(421) KERES, P—FINE

Semmering-Baden (3), 1937 (10 Sept.)
Réti Opening [A09]

A difficult game characterized by small finesses. Such games are not so easy to play as they appear on the surface! FR **1. Nf3 d5 2. c4 d×c4** The Réti Gambit Accepted. **3. Na3** Bad according to Alekhine, who finds 3.e3 "more natural." BW **3 ... c5 4. N×c4 Nc6 5. Nce5** This move, suggested by Hans Mueller, has to be met with care. FR **5 ... N×e5 6. N×e5 Nf6** 7 Qa4 was "in the air." BW **7. e3 e6 8. b3 Nd7 9. Bb5** Stronger seems 9 Bb2, after which Black cannot play out his king's bishop at once, and if 9 ... N×e5 10 B×e5 f6 11 Bb2 Be7 12 Qh5+ g6 13 Qh6 and Black is in difficulties. FR (Black need not play the weakening 10 ... f6. AW) **9 ... Bd6 10. Bb2 0–0 11. N×d7 B×d7 12. Qg4** Simply a developing move, and not a brilliancy. FR **12 ... f6** The game is approximately equal, MCO. **13. Bc4 Qe7 14. a4** To prevent the dislodging of White's light squared bishop from its fine post. BW **14 ... Kh8** 14 ... a6 15 a5 and Black is "no forrarder." BW **15. f4 Rae8** A strong alternative is 15 ... e5 16 f5 g6 followed by ... g×f5 and ... Rg8. FR **16. 0–0 Bc6** Fine's play has been well timed; the text not only gives this bishop a better diagonal, but what is more important, prevents the dangerous manoeuvre Rf1-f3-h3. FR **17. Qh5 Qf7** Accepting the invitation. The ending is however a bit thorny for Black. FR **18. Q×f7 R×f7 19. Rac1** It does not appear that anything can be gained from 19 f5 Bd5 20 f×e6 B×e6 21 Rac1 Rc7. FR **19 ... Rd7 20. d4 c×d4 21. B×d4 a5 22. Bb6 Bc7** 22 ... Bb4 would leave the black rooks too cramped. BW **23. B×c7 R×c7 24. Rfd1 h6** 25 B×e6 was threatened. If now 25 Rd6 Bd5! FR **25. Rd4** If at once 25 Rd6 Bd5! followed by 26 ... Rec8. BW **25 ... Rce7 26. Rd6 f5!** If at once 26 ... e5?, 27 f5 would practically immobilize all Black's pieces. BW **27. Rcd1 e5** The game is still in the balance. **28. Rd8 e×f4 29. R×e8+ R×e8 30. e×f4 Kh7** White still had a slight threat of 31 Bf7 and 32 Bg6, but it's easily scotched. BW **31. Kf2 Re7 32. Rd8 g6 33. g3 Kg7 34. h3 Rc7 35. Ke3?** In bad time trouble he overlooks the simplest threat. Luckily his slip is harmless. BW **35 ... B×a4** Simplifies down to a draw. FR **36. b×a4 R×c4**

37. Rd7+ Kf6 38. R×b7 R×a4 Now Black has an extra pawn, but the position is a simple draw. JH **39. Rb6+ Kf7 40. Rb7+ Ke6 41. Rb6+** Drawn by repetition of moves. ½–½ Reinfeld 1938, 19–20; Wood, 15–6; Fine 1941, 269 and 388; Lopez Esnaola & de Marimon, 26–7; Hannak, 44.

(422) RAGOZIN, V—FINE

Semmering-Baden (4), 1937 (12 Sept.)
Queen's Gambit Declined [D51]

1. d4 d5 2. c4 e6 3. Nc3 Nf6 4. Bg5 c6 5. e3 Nbd7 6. Qc2 Qa5 Black has a Cambridge Springs pawn-formation but White holds back his king's knight so that it can come if necessary to e2, rendering Black's Bb4 innocuous. White's next move is prompted by the possibility of 7 ... d×c4 opening the queen's line onto the bishop. BW **7. Bh4 c5** If 7 ... Bb4 8 Bd3 Ne4 9 Ne2 followed by f2-f3. FR **8. Nf3 a6** Or 8 ... c×d4 9 e×d4 Ne4 10 Bd3 Ndf6. BW **9. Be2 d×c4 10. 0–0** A temporary sacrifice to gain time. If now 10 ... b5 11 a4 b4 Ne4 with an attack. FR **10 ... Qc7 11. Rfd1 c×d4 12. e×d4 Bd6 13. d5!** If 13 ... e×d5 14 N×d5 N×d5 15 R×d5 0–0 16 Rad1 Bf4 17 Qe4! with a very powerful position. FR **13 ... e5** White's passed pawn should now have won the game. BW **14. a4** White is planning now to recapture on c4 with the king's knight; but it is necessary to safeguard against the possibility of 14 ... b5 in the meantime. BW **14 ... 0–0 15. Nd2** With some advantage to White, MCO 144. **15 ... b6 16. N×c4 Bb7 17. Qf5 Rfe8 18. Rac1 Bc5 19. Bf3 g6** Wood rejects 19 ... B×f2+ 20 B×f2 Q×c4 on the basis of 21 Nb5, winning the exchange (21 ... Q×a4 22 Nc7). However after 21 ... a×b5! 22 R×c4 b×c4 Black has rook, knight and pawn, with possibly a second pawn (d5) to come, and the initiative for the queen. Plenty of compensation surely. Even in the intended variation, 22 ... e4 23 N×a8 B×a8 is not so clear. AW **20. Qd3 Qb8** The idea behind this curious looking move is simply that he can now answer d6 with ... e4. BW; The position of the queen on the c-file was too exposed. FR **21. Bg3 Nf8** What this achieves it is difficult to say. BW **22. b4** In reply to 22 Re1 or 22 Qe2 Black has 22 ... Bd4. JH **22 ... B×b4** If 22 ... Bd4 23 Q×d4 wins a pawn. FR **23. N×b6 Ra7 24. Nc4 N8d7 25. Rb1 a5 26. Nb5** Stronger than 26 Na2, which is answered by 26 ... Ba6. FR **26 ... Ra6**

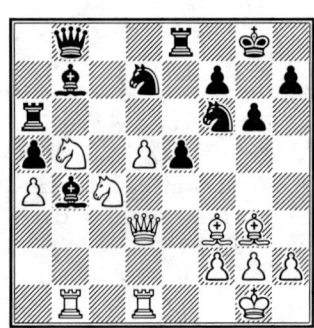

Position after Black's 26th move

27. Qe3 Qd8 28. Ncd6 Plunging into complications: the exchanges free Black's game a little. BW; 28 d6! was far

stronger. FR **28 ... B×d6 29. N×d6 R×d6 30. R×b7 Qc8 31. Rb5 Qc2 32. Qa3 Rb6!** Black defends well in a difficult position. If now 33 R×a5 e4 34 Rc1 e×f3! FR **33. Rc1 Qd2 34. Rd1 Qc2 35. Rc1** 35 Qd6 would be a risky winning attempt in view of the reply 35 ... e4. AW **35 ... Qd2** The influence of time pressure is apparent. Yet as soon as the control is passed White makes a fatal blunder. BW **36. R×b6 N×b6 37. d6?? e4 38. Bd1** Again 38 Rd1 would be answered by 33 ... f×e3. FR **38 ... Qe1** Mate. 0–1 Reinfeld 1938, 24; Wood, 17–8; Lopez Esnaola & de Marimon, 32–4; Hannak, 47.

(423) FINE—PETROVS, V

Semmering-Baden (5), 1937 (14 Sept.)
Owen's Defence [A50]

1. d4 Nf6 2. c4 b6 While this move is perfectly satisfactory after 2 Nf3, it is not good after 2 c4, as White is on the way to building up a strong centre. FR (Daniel King's preferred move orders to reach the English Defence are 1 d4 e6 2 c4 b6! or 1 c4 b6 2 d4 e6, so that White cannot play with a d4/e4 centre with the c-pawn on its original square. AW) **3. f3!? Bb7** Hannak, Reinfeld and Wood recommend 3 ... d5, Black might also consider 3 ... e6. **4. e4 e5?** Wood remarks "The sacrificial raft on which Black now embarks has presumably been thoroughly examined in advance but its timbers begin to creak under the impact of Fine's transatlantic squalls.". While Fine writes that 4 ... d6 is necessary, but White retains the superior position (MCO 197). **5. d×e5 N×e4** This sacrifice of a piece is incorrect. JH **6. f×e4 Qh4+ 7. Kd2! Qf4+ 8. Kc2 B×e4+ 9. Bd3 B×d3+** If 9 ... Qf7+ 10 Qe2! holds everything. FR **10. Q×d3 Qf2+ 11. Nd2!**

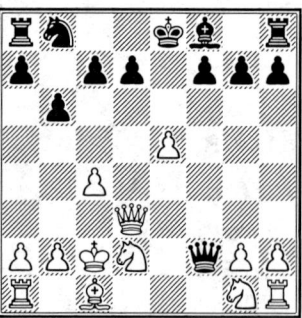

Position after White's 11th move

Fine used this game as his first example in Chapter VI Material Advantage in his treatise on the middle game: "[Play from the diagram] illustrates the winning procedure with an extra piece. As a result of an unsound opening sacrifice, Black has only one pawn for the piece. He can gain another pawn (g2) only at the cost of an exchange of queens (11 ... Q×g2 12 Qf3). Hence he cannot take, but must speculate on the attack." **11 ... Nc6** If 11 ... Q×g2 12 Qe4! FR **12. Qe4 0–0–0** Under ordinary circumstances, a player would not castle into an attack in this manner, but Black is desperate. RF **13. a3 Re8 14. Ngf3 Bd6 15. Re1** Holding the pawn by a combination. RF **15 ... Q×g2** There might have been more in 15 … B×e5 16 N×e5 R×e5 17 Q×e5 N×e5 18 R×e5 Q×g2 leaving White with rook, knight and bishop for queen and two [*sic*] pawns. BW (Reinfeld also gives this line and opines that White has more than enough material for the queen, but Sidney Bernstein (in the Errata) feels that Black would have his chances here. I concur, however, the clearer consolidating line 16 Re2 Qc5 17 Nb3 (or 17 Qd5, forcing the exchange of queens, as given by Fine in 1953) Qd6 18 Bg5, threatening Rad1, was more in Fine's style, and would give him an obviously better game. AW) **16. Qf4 Qg6+** The game is virtually over. White has the better development and control of the centre. Black's two pawns for the sacrificed piece hardly count, for all his pawns except one stand on their original squares. BW (Comparing Black's compact pawn mass with White's loose structure I would have thought this was an advantage and not the reverse. AW) **17. Kb3 Bc5 18. Ka2 Qc2?!** Black would like to play Qc2-a4 to pressurize the white king's fortifications. White's next move prevents this. In fact 19 Nb3 would also be effective against the computer's suggestion of 18 … d6. AW **19. Nb3** Now he threatens both 20 Q×f7 and 20 N×c5 b×c5 21 Be3. Black, as so often in these cases, becomes desperate. RF **19 … g5** Meaningless. Black's attack is over. FR **20. N×g5 f6** For the e-pawn is pinned. RF **21. Qe4** The position permits of combinations. If now 21 … Q×h2 22 Bf4 Qa5 23 N×c5 b×c5, and now White can win in two ways: 24 e6 f×g5 25 e×d7+ K×d7 26 Qf5+ Kd8 27 B×g5+ and 24 Rh1 Qg6 25 Q×g6 h×g6 26 e×f6. RF **21 … Q×e4** The simplest. If now 21 … Qf2 22 Nf3 f×e5 23 N×c5 Q×c5 24 Be3. FR **22. N×e4 R×e5 23. Bf4 Rf5** Here we see an example of the principle that a material advantage leads to even more material. The rook must defend either the bishop or the f-pawn. To hold both it gets into an uncomfortable position, which costs material later on. RF **24. Rf1 Be7 25. Ng3** Now the rook has no more moves. RF **25 … R×f4 26. R×f4** Black resigned eight moves later (do it now!). FR **26 … h5 27. Rh4** Again a pawn goes; it's two against one at every turn. RF **27 … f5 28. R×h5 Rf8 29. R×f5 Rh8 30. Rh5 Rg8 31. Rd1 a5 32. Nd4** Exchanges! RF **32 … Nd8 33. Ndf5 Bd6 34. R×d6** Black resigned. More material goes; on 34 … c×d6 35 Ne7+ follows. **1–0** Reinfeld 1938, 27–8; Wood, 24–5; Fine 1953, 172–5; Lopez Esnaola & de Marimon, 38–9; Hannak, 49–50.

(424) ELISKASES, E—FINE

Semmering-Baden (6), 1937 (16 Sept.)
Queen's Gambit Declined [D51]

1. d4 d5 2. c4 e6 3. Nc3 Nf6 4. Bg5 c6 5. e3 Nbd7 6. c×d5 c×d5 Now that White has avoided the Cambridge Springs Defence, Black in turn avoids the Orthodox Defence proper. For all that the variation has a rather barren character. FR **7. Nf3 Be7 8. Bd3 0–0 9. 0–0 a6 10. Rc1 b5 11. Ne5 Bb7 12. f4 h6** As his opponent threatens to achieve a formidable kingside pawn formation, Black must play to simplify. One can already foresee that

Black's queen's bishop will be of little value, as there are too many black pawns on white squares. FR **13. Bh4 N×e5 14. d×e5** This unusual mode of capture is explained by his 17th move. FR **14 … Ne4 15. B×e7 Q×e7 16. B×e4 d×e4 17. Qd6** In his desire to simplify the game White does not chose the best continuation. JH **17 … Q×d6 18. e×d6 Rad8 19. Rfd1 b4!** This eventually results in the gain of a pawn, but the position becomes so simplified (removal of all the queenside pawns) that the win is thereafter impossible. FR **20. Na4 Bd5 21. Rd4 a5 22. Rc5 R×d6 23. R×a5 Rc8 24. Rc5** If 24 Rb5 Rc1+ 25 Kf2 Rc2+ 26 Kg3 Re2, or 24 R×b4 Rc1+ 25 Kf2 Bc4 with a powerful attack. BW **24 … R×c5 25. N×c5 Rc6 26. Nb3** If 26 N×e4 Rc1+ 27 Kf2 Rc2+ 28 Kg3 f5 or 28 Nd2 R×b2 and so on. JH **26 … Rc2 27. R×b4 R×b2 28. Rb8+ Kh7 29. Rc8 R×a2** Despite his material gain, the game cannot be won by Black, as it is impossible to undouble the e-pawn advantageously. FR **30. Nd4 g5 31. g3 Kg6 32. Rc2! Ra3** On the exchange of rooks the game would be a simple draw. JH **33. Kf2 Kh5 34. Nb5 Rd3 35. Nd6** Black will have to watch out for this wandering knight. JH **35 … Bb3 36. Rc6 Rd2+ 37. Ke1** In the event of 37 Kg1 Black could penetrate the White position by … Bb3-d1-f3, after securing f7. JH **37 … R×h2 38. N×f7 Kg4 39. f×g5 h×g5 40. Rc8** Threatening 41 Rg8. JH **40 … Ra2 41. Ne5+!** Very well played; if 41 Rg8 Kf3! wins. Whereas if now 41 … K×g3 42 Rg8 Kh4 (but perhaps 42 … Ra1+ 43 Kd2 Bd1 44 R×g5+ Kf2. AW) 43 Rh8+ draws. FR **41 … Kf5 42. Nc6 Kf6 43. Nd4 Bd5 44. Rc2 Ra6 45. Rc5 Kg6 46. g4 Ra2 47. Rc2 Ra8 48. Kf2 Rf8+ 49. Kg2 Rf7 50. Rc5 Rd7 51. Kg3 Kf6 52. Rc8 Ra7 53. Rf8+ Kg7 54. Rc8** The game is an obvious draw. BW **54 … Ra3 55. Kf2 Ra6 56. Rc5 Kf6 57. Kg3 Ba2 58. Rc1 Rb6 59. Rc5 Rb1 60. Rc2 Bd5 61. Kg2 Bb7 62. Rc5 Ra1 63. Rc7 Bd5 64. Rc8 Ra7 65. Rf8+ Kg7 66. Rc8 Rd7 67. Rc5 Kf6 68. Rc8 Rd6 69. Rf8+ Kg7 70. Rc8 Rb6 71. Rc7+ Kf6 72. Rc8 e5 73. Nf5 Be6 74. Rc2** Draw agreed. Of course, if 74 … B×f5 75 Rf2. FR **½–½** Reinfeld 1938, 33; Wood, 26; Lopez Esnaola & de Marimon, 50–1; Hannak, 55.

(425) FINE—RESHEVSKY, S

Semmering-Baden (7), 1937 (17 Sept.)
Spanish Game, Rubinstein Variation [C79]

A hard fought battle of a novel character. Reshevsky's lion-hearted tenacity rescues a seemingly lost game. FR **1. e4 e5** The only "open game" of the whole tournament. BW **2. Nf3 Nc6 3. Bb5 a6 4. Ba4 Nf6 5. 0–0 d6 6. Qe2** From the view point of those who consider having a knight against a bishop a crime or a cosmic misfortune, it would have been more precise to play 6 c3. FR; EMCO 1994 only considers B×c6 (as played by Simonson against Fine in the third U.S. championship), d4, Re1 and c3 in this position. 6 Qe2 seems to have been introduced by Sir George Thomas in 1923, and subsequently played by him on at least two more occasions. The move scores well in my database, 17 points out of 22! AW **6 … b5 7. Bb3 Na5** Since

White has refrained from playing c2-c3, Black correctly hurries to eliminate the bishop. JH **8. d4 N×b3 9. a×b3 Nd7 10. Nc3 Bb7 11. d×e5 d×e5** White preserves the advantage of the move in spite of the fact that Black holds him in the centre. He has definitely the better development and two files along which to work. As slight compensation Black retains two bishops. BW **12. Rd1 Bd6** At the moment, it seems that the d-file is reserved exclusively for White's use; but after Black completes his development and consolidates his position—a laborious process, to be sure—he will revise this state of affairs. FR **13. Bg5** With the aim of forcing Black to weaken his pawn formation in advance of an offensive by White. E&M **13 ... f6 14. Be3 0–0** Decidedly inferior would be 14 ... b4 15 Nd5 c6 (if 15 ... 0–0 17 Qc4!) 16 Nb6! with a clear advantage. FR **15. Nh4** Inducing a further weakening of the black position. E&M **15 ... g6 16. Qg4** White's attack has commenced. Black can only wait for an opportunity for counter-attack. E&M **16 ... Kh8 17. Qg3 Qe8 18. Nd5 Qf7 19. Nf3 Nc5** Forcing White to concede his second bishop for a knight since otherwise his e-pawn would be lost. BW, Fine seems to be able to bear up under the catastrophe of having two knights against two bishops. FR **20. B×c5 B×c5** An important moment. Black has gained the bishop pair while White has the two knights. Perhaps if Reshevsky had had more time for reflection the game would not have ended in a draw, as it turns out the clock becomes his greatest enemy. E&M **21. Ne1 Rfd8 22. Nd3 Bf8** 22 ... Ba7, with good prospects, was also possible. E&M **23. c4 c6 24. Ne3 Rd4** The position has definitely turned in Black's favour. Not only has he repulsed the attack, but now he also has an active plan of his own. E&M **25. Qf3 Qe6 26. Ne1 Rad8 27. N1c2 R4d7 28. R×d7 R×d7 29. Rd1 Kg7 30. Qe2 Kf7 31. h3 Bc8** He hopes to post this bishop on the more useful square e6. FR **32. Rd2 Be7 33. Qe1 R×d2 34. Q×d2 Qd6**

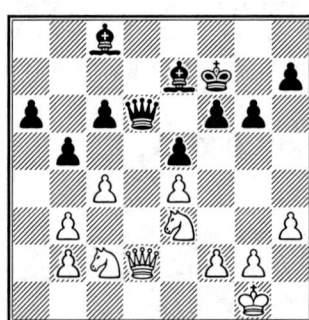

Position after Black's 34th move

35. Qc3 After the exchange of queen's the win for Black would merely be a matter of technique. JH (Is this true? 35 Q×d6 B×d6 36 b4 f5 37 e×f5 g×f5 38 c5 Bc7. AW) **35 ... b4** Of doubtful value as it merely splits up his own pawns on the queen's side. Reshevsky was in very bad time-trouble at this stage—as usual—and lets a won game slide away. BW **36. Qe1 Qd3!** There is no time for 36 ... a5, for then 37 Qe2 prevents the invasion of Black's queen. FR **37. N×b4 Q×e4** This looks promising, but White has counterchances, of which Fine cleverly avails himself. FR **38. Qc3 Bb7**

39. Nbc2 c5 Necessary to give the queen's bishop some scope; but it gives White his chance. FR **40. b4! c×b4** The time-control is a thing of the past—but so is Black's advantage! BW **41. N×b4 f5** Seemingly very formidable, as he threatens to win a piece with 42 ... B×b4 43 Q×b4 f4. FR **42. Nd3** Unexpectedly, The knights have become as strong as the bishops all of a sudden. JH **42 ... Ke6** Judging by the sequel it would have been better to play 42 ... Bd6. FR **43. Qb3 f4 44. c5+ Bd5** With the departure of one of the bishops White begins to have even a chance of a win. *L'Echiquier* gives as an alternative 44 ... Kf6 45 Ng4+ Kg7 46 f3 Qd4+ 47 Kh2 Bd5 48 Qc2 Bf6 (48 ... e4 49 N×f4 e×f3 50 N×d5 Q×d5 may be better. AW) 49 c6. BW **45. N×d5 Q×d5 46. Qb6+ Kf5!** Best under the circumstances. There are some pretty points in the position, not readily apparent to people who inveigh dogmatically against the dullness of modern chess: if 46 ... Kd7 47 c6+! wins; or if 46 ... Kf7 47 Q×a6 B×c5 48 Qc4! and wins. FR **47. Q×a6 e4!** Reshevsky gives up a pawn to increase his advantage. Fine must avoid allowing his king to get into trouble. E&M **48. Qc8+!** The same move would have followed 48 ... B×c5? with somewhat greater effect! BW **48 ... Kg5** Black continues to find the best defence: if 48 ... Kf6 49 N×f4 Q×c5 50 Qe6+ should win. FR **49. Qg4+ Kh6 50. Q×f4+ Kg7**

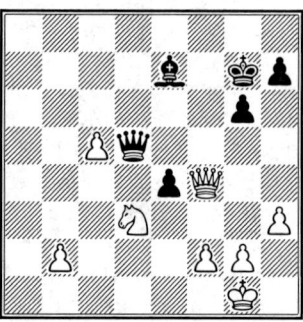

Position after Black's 50th move

51. Qe5+ Shereshevsky explains that Fine had the choice here of playing immediately for the minor piece ending, or of retaining the queens, bearing in mind the well-known strength of the queen and knight combination. He proposes the continuation 51 Nb4 (not 51 Ne5!? B×c5 52 Ng4? Qd1+ 53 Kh2 Bd6) Q×c5 52 Na6 Qc6 (or 52 ... Qc2 53 Nc7 Q×b2 54 Ne6+ Kg8 55 Q×e4 Kf7 56 Nf4) 53 Nc7 Kg8 (53 ... Bd6 54 Q×d6) 54 Qe5 Bd6 55 Qd5+ Q×d5 56 N×d5 Kf7 57 Nc3 Be5 58 Kf1 h5 (58 ... Ke6 59 N×e4) 59 Ke2 Bd4 60 f3! e×f3 61 K×f3 Ke6 62 Ke4 with excellent winning chances. **51 ... Q×e5 52. N×e5 B×c5** Fine has come out of the extended complications a pawn to the good. It is extraordinary that Reshevsky should have managed to save this game. BW; The ending which follows is most instructive—and very difficult. The bishop is well placed. White's winning chances suffer from the fact that his king cannot reach the important squares e3 and c4; and furthermore, the f-pawn requires watching. FR **53. b3 Bd4 54. Nc6** While one naturally feels hesitant about criticizing the play of an endgame expert of Fine's calibre, it seems to me that here (and later on) he misses the only chance which promises a win—at least on logical considerations. The idea is: 54 Nc4 Kf6 55 Kf1 Ke6 56 Ke2 Kf5 57 Nd2 Kf4 58 g3+ Ke5 59 f3 exf3+ 60 Kxf3. Now White has eliminated his weak f-pawn, his king is in play, and he can proceed along the following lines: (1) He centralizes his king at e4, threatening to advance to the kingside to menace Black's pawns, or to support his passed pawn. If Black tries to prevent the centralizing manoeuvre, then it stands to reason that White's king will be able to invade the kingside. (2) Once Black's king is committed to one side or the other, White can use his knight on the other side: thus, if Black's king goes to the kingside, the knight can support the advance of the b-pawn; if the king goes to the queenside, the knight can attack the weakened kingside pawns. Of course it is possible that the position would be too simplified for a win to result; but, as I have already indicated, this plan seems the most logical at White's disposal. FR **54 ... Bb6 55. Nb4 Kf7 56. Nd5 Bd4 57. Kf1 Ke6 58. Ne3 Bc5** Black has succeeded in fully activating all of his forces, and the win becomes difficult, if at all possible. MSh **59. Ke2 h5 60. Nc2 g5** Reshevsky places a pawn on the kingside on the same colour as his bishop, so as to make it difficult for his opponent to create a second weakness. An interesting decision. MSh **61. b4 Bd6 62. g3 Ke5 63. b5 Bc5 64. Ne3 Kd4 65. Nf5+ Ke5 66. Ng7! h4** The pawns have been forced onto Black squares—very bad for the defender. For if he uses his bishop to defend, the b-pawn can advance; if he uses the king to defend, then White's king can take a hand in the proceedings. Hence Reshevsky decides on a bold plan. FR **67. g4 Bb6** Reshevsky's precision in this ending is a marvel to behold. It looks like the product of a laboratory. E&M **68. Nf5 Bc5 69. Ne3 Kd4!** He is to cut the Gordian knot by at once removing the dangerous pawn even though something must be lost on the kingside. a deep and courageous plan! FR **70. Nf5+** In Fine's own opinion he could have won by 70 f3! Bb6 71 Nf1! Ke5 72 Nd2 exf3+ 73 Kxf3 Kf6 74 Nc4. However, Reshevsky showed that after 71 ... exf3+! 72 Kxf3 Kd3! (but not 72 ... Kc4 73 Ke4) 73 Nh2 (perhaps 73 Kg2, preserving the protection of e3, might be better, but it would probably still lead to the same result. AW) Be3 24 Kg2 Kc4 Black achieves the draw. MSh **70 ... Kc4! 71. Nh6 Kxb5! 72. Nf7 Kc4!** The only way to achieve the drawing position Reshevsky has envisaged, it would be an inexactitude to defend the g-pawn with 72 ... Be7, since the simple 73 Ke3 wins the e-pawn and with it the game. E&M **73. Nxg5 Kd5 74. f3** White seems just about to win, but he was never further from victory! There was nothing else in the position, for example 74 Nh7 Ke5 75 g5 Kf5 76 Nf6 Be7 and so on. FR **74 ... exf3+ 75. Nxf3 Ke4!! 76. Nxh4 Kf4 77. Nf5** This move is forced ... otherwise Black with ... Kg3 wins a pawn and can always sacrifice a bishop for the remaining pawn. Nevertheless, after the text, White comes into a position where neither his knight nor his pawns can move. The only hope of winning was to play his king up the board so as ultimately to arrive via f7 and g6 at h5, in which case the game would be won. Black can, however, easily prevent this manoeuvre by playing at the right time Kg5 and the game is, therefore, drawn. BW **77 ... Bb6 78. Kd3 Bd8 79. Kd4**

Bf6+ **80. Kd5 Bh8 81. Kd6 Be5+ 82. Ke6 Ba1 83. Ke7 Bb2 84. Kf7 Kg5!** Draw agreed. ½–½ Reinfeld 1938, 40–3; Reshevsky, 115–7; Wood, 29–30; Shereshevsky, 272–3; Fine 1941, 203 and 215–6; Lopez Esnaola & de Marimon, 54–7; Hannak, 57–9; Averbakh 1984b, 49 & 103.

(426) FINE—CAPABLANCA, J

Semmering-Baden (8), 1937 (18 Sept.)
Slav Defence [D17]

1. d4 Nf6 2. c4 c6 3. Nf3 d5 4. Nc3 dxc4 5. a4 Bf5 6. Ne5 Nbd7 The popular Kmoch continuation aiming at a direct and early ... e5. BW **7. Nxc4 Qc7 8. g3 e5 9. dxe5 Nxe5 10. Bf4 Nfd7 11. Bg2 f6 12. 0–0 Rd8** This refinement introduced by Euwe in his first match against Alekhine and which drives the white queen to a less advantageous square. Both players ignore the "surprise" move 13 Ne4 which brought Euwe a win in the first game of the 1937 match. BW **13. Qc1 Be6 14. Nxe5 Nxe5 15. a5! a6** Otherwise the White pawn gets to that square with effect. BW **16. Ne4 Bb4 17. Bd2 Bxd2!** In the next round (actually round 10, AW), against Eliskases, Capablanca enigmatically played the less forceful 17 ... Qe7. BW **18. Nxd2 0–0 19. Qc3 Qd6 20. Nc4 Qd4 21. Nc5 Bc8 22. Qb3+ Qc4** Draw agreed. Prematurely of course. BW ½–½ Wood, 33–4; Soloviev 1997, 235.

(427) FLOHR, S—FINE

Semmering-Baden (9), 1937 (19 Sept.)
Queen's Gambit Accepted [D27]

1. d4 d5 2. c4 dxc4 3. Nf3 Nf6 4. e3 e6 5. Bxc4 c5 6. 0–0 a6 7. a4 Nc6 8. Qe2 Be7 9. Rd1 Qc7 10. Nc3 0–0 11. h3 Rd8 12. d5 exd5 13. Nxd5 Nxd5 14. Bxd5 Nb4 Leaving the bishop no useful square of retreat. BW **15. e4** The ensuing exchanges ensure White a passed pawn but it is isolated and useless, and Black's two bishops even give him the advantage. BW **15 ... Nxd5 16. exd5 Bf5 17. Bg5** Reshevsky improved on this in the last round with 17 Bf4! FR **17 ... Bxg5 18. Nxg5 Qf4 19. Qd2 Qxd2 20. Rxd2 h6 21. Nf3 Rd6 22. Rc1 Rad8 23. Rxc5 Be4 24. Rc3 Rxd5 25. Rxd5 Bxd5** 25 ... Rxd5 would also secure a simple draw. BW **26. Rd3 Kf8 27. Nd4 g6** Not 27 ... Be4, 28 Ne6+. BW **28. f3 Ke7 29. Kf2 Bc4 30. Rd2 Be6** Draw agreed. ½–½ Reinfeld 1938, 48; Wood, 37.

(428) FINE—KERES, P

Semmering-Baden (10), 1937 (22 Sept.)
Grünfeld Defence, Grünfeld Gambit [D93]

A most interesting game. First Keres makes something out of nothing, then he makes nothing out of something! FR **1. d4 Nf6 2. c4 g6 3. Nc3 d5** Keres' catholicity of taste in the opening is remarkable. He plays every opening under the sun, for instance in spite of his predilection for the king's pawn he frequently tries 1.d4 for a change. BW **4. Bf4 Bg7 5. e3 0–0 6. Qb3 c6 7. Nf3 dxc4** The opening has become a normal Slav Defence. BW **8. Bxc4 Nbd7 9. 0–0 Nb6 10. Be2 Be6 11. Qc2 Nfd5** 11 … Nbd5 12 Be5 Bf5 13 Qb3 Qb6 with an equal game, Capablanca–Flohr, Semmering-Baden 1937. **12. Bg3 Rc8 13. e4 Nc7 14. Rfd1** White has a very fine game. JH **14 … h6** Without playing so picturesquely as Black perhaps, White has more than maintained the advantage of the first move. Black's king's position has been weakened by the moves of the g- and h-pawns whereas White's king's position is intact; White has command of the centre and occupies it and his development is much more harmonious than that of Black, whose knights are none too well placed. Black's next few move demonstrate how cramped his position is. BW **15. Ne5 Qe8 16. a4** Black's game gets steadily more uncomfortable. JH; This position is clearly in White's favour, PCO 283. **16 … f6 17. Nd3 Nd7** Guarding against 18 Nc5. BW **18. a5 f5!** This move, by plunging the game into complications, gives Keres many chances. It seems surprising that Fine should have left it on (his reply is forced, since his d-pawn is attacked as well). BW; Black's only chance is to create complications, or as the saying goes, fish in troubled waters. JH **19. exf5** 19 Bxc7 Rxc7 20 Nf4 Bf7 21 e5 g5 22 e6 gxf4 23 Nd5! Rc8 24 Nxf4, suggested by Fritz, looks extremely dangerous, so Wood's previous comment is incorrect. Perhaps Fine also believed the reply was forced. He was often ingenious in defence but seems to have avoided unclear attacking possibilities, preferring a controlled build-up. AW **19 … gxf5 20. a6** Very subtly calculated; but it leaves Keres with more chances of counterplay than Fine perhaps realized. BW; Again Black seems headed for trouble but Keres is already on the lookout for counterplay. JH **20 … bxa6 21. Nf4 Bf7 22. Bxa6 Rb8** Threatening 23 … Bb3 whether White plays 23 Qxf5 or not. 23 b4 would now have been a better reply than the one Fine adopts but his d-pawn is precarious in any case; 23 Qe3 [sic] Rb4 24 Ra4 Nxa6! etc. BW **23. Re1?** Fine missed a great opportunity here, as pointed out in the Spanish booklet. He could have played 23 Ng6!! and after 23 … f4 24 Nxf8 fxg3 25 Nxd7 Qxd7 his position would clearly be better. AW **23 … Bxd4 24. Bd3** 24 Nfe2, not mentioned by the tournament books, retains White's advantage. AW **24 … Bb3 25. Qe2?** Taking away the retreat square from the knight on f4. 25 Qd2 would have preserved the balance of position. AW **25 … e5!** The players have reversed roles, as Black institutes a telling counter-attack. JH **26. Bc4+ Bxc4 27. Qxc4+ Qf7 28. Qxc6** Possibly 28.Qxf7+ followed by 29.N4e2 might have been a better defence (for defence is White's problem now!). But Black would have held his extra pawn in the end-game. However, White gets a lot of play now. BW **28 … exf4 29. Bh4** If 29 Bxf4 Rxb2. JH **29 … Ne5** A simple and opportunistic move which wins an important tempo, and simultaneously saves the knights from becoming caught in their own camp by the king's rook, thereby refuting the combination begun by Fine

on his 28th move. E&M **30. Qd6 Qd7** It is very likely that 30 … Qg7! would have decided the day in Black's favour, for the threat of … Nf3+ is well-nigh irresistible. JH **31. Qxh6 Qg7** One move too late. JH **32. Qxg7+ Kxg7 33. Ne2** From henceforth White goes all out for simplifications which will leave on the board inadequate material for a decisive result. Keres seems not to realize the danger until too late. BW **33 … Bxb2 34. Rxa7 Rf7 35. Nxf4** Reducing the number of pawns on the board and thereby increasing the likelihood of a draw. E&M **35 … Re8 36. Kf1** 36 … Nf3+ was threatened again. AW **36 … Ne6** Black should have avoided this simplification, especially the double exchange of rooks. Now the game, which has been so exciting, tapers off to a draw. JH **37. Nxe6+ Rxe6 38. Rxf7+ Kxf7 39. Bg3 Kf6 40. f4** Forcing off the second Black rook and thus removing the only piece which could give mate aided by king alone. BW **40 … Ng4 41. Rxe6+ Kxe6 42. h3** Draw agreed. One has the impression that Keres was in great time difficulties from the 30th move on; but this is not the first lost position from which Fine extricated himself in the manner of a Houdini. FR ½–½ Dr. J. Hannak in Reinfeld 1938, 55–6; Wood, 38–9; Lopez Esnaola & de Marimon, 70–2.

(429) FINE—RAGOZIN, V

Semmering-Baden (11), 1937 (23 Sept.)
Catalan System [E06]

Fine again extricates himself from a ticklish situation! **1. d4 Nf6 2. c4 e6 3. g3 d5 4. Nf3 c6 5. Qc2 Be7 6. Bg2 0–0 7. 0–0 b6 8. Ne5 Ba6 9. Rd1 Nfd7 10. cxd5 Nxe5 11. d6! Bf6** After 11 … Ng6 12 dxe7 Qxe7 White would build up a strong centre. JH **12. dxe5 Bxe5 13. Nc3! Nd7** If 13 … Bxd6? 14 Ne4. JH **14. Be3 Rc8 15. Rd2 Bc4! 16. Ne4 Bd5 17. f4 f5 18. fxe5 fxe4 19. Qc3 Qe8!** Black takes the initiative now. JH **20. Rf1 Qh5 21. Bf4 g5 22. Be3 Rxf1+ 23. Bxf1 Rf8 24. Bg2 Qg4** If … Rf5 25 h3 with numerous counter-threats. JH **25. b3 h5** Hannak wrote "If 25 … Rf5 26 Bxb6 axb6 27 h3 Qh5 28 g4. Or 25 … Qf5 26 h3 Nxe5 27 g4 Qf6 28 Bd4.". But in the first line 27 … Rf3!! 28 exf3 Qxg3 looks good for Black. White could play 26 Bd4, with a roughly equal game, instead. In the second line 26 … g4!! also turns out well for Black. AW **26. Rd1 h4** 26 … Qf5 would be answered by 27 Rf1 Qxe5 28 Qxe5 Nxe5 29 Bxg5. JH **27. Rf1 hxg3 28. Rxf8+ Kxf8 29. h3 Qxe2 30. Qd2 Qxd2 31. Bxd2 Nxe5 32. Bxg5** The upshot of the foregoing play is that Black is two pawns ahead, and even if he loses the g-pawn. he should still be able to win. But the result is different. JH **32 … Ke8 33. Bf4 Nf7** 33 … Nd3! 34 Bxg3 e3! looks very promising. AW **34. Bxg3 Kd7** Now this partisan finally falls, and what is to prevent Black from winning? JH **35. h4** At once seizing his only chance. JH **35 … Nxd6 36. h5 Nf5 37. Bf4 Ke7 38. Bh3!** In order to get bishops of the opposite colour. JH **38 … Nd4 39. Kf2 Kf6 40. Bb8 a6 41. Ba7** White must now win a pawn, and the remaining extra pawn is doubled and compensated for by the h-pawn. Hence the draw. Fine's play has been extremely cold-blooded! JH ½–½ Hannak in Reinfeld 1938, 58; Lopez Esnaola & de Marimon, 77–8; Wood, 42.

(430) PETROVS, V—FINE

Semmering-Baden (12), 1937 (24 Sept.)
Catalan System [E02]

1. d4 d5 2. Nf3 Nf6 3. c4 e6 4. g3 dxc4 5. Qa4+ Nbd7 6. Bg2 a6 7. Nc3 Bd6!? The only example I can find of this move in ChessBase or Megacorr 2. The book line is 7 ... Rb8 8 Qxc4 b5 9 Qd3 Bb7 10 0–0 c5 11 dxc5 Bxc5 12 Bf4 Rc8 13 Rad1 0–0 14 Ne5 Bxg2 15 Kxg2 Nxe5 16 Bxe5 Be7 with equality, Burgess (NCO 444). **8. 0–0 0–0 9. Qxc4 b5 10. Qd3 Bb7 11. Rd1 Qe7** The black pieces are well-placed for the liberating moves ... c5 or ... e5. **12. Ne5?!** Black has no difficulties after this move. 12 e4 would be interesting. **12 ... Bxg2 13. Nxd7 Qxd7 14. Kxg2 b4 15. Nb1 Rfd8 16. Nd2 e5 17. Ne4 Nxe4 18. Qxe4 exd4 19. Rxd4 Qb5 20. Qf3 Be5 21. Re4 Bf6 22. a4** Draw agreed. If 22 ... bxa3 23 Rxa3. ½–½

(431) FINE—ELISKASES, E

Semmering-Baden (13), 1937 (26 Sept.)
Sicilian Defence, Moscow Variation [B54]

1. e4 c5 2. Nf3 d6 3. d4 cxd4 4. Nxd4 Nf6 5. f3 5 Nc3 is more usual. JH **5 ... e5!** (5 ... Nc6 6 c4 g6 7 Nc3 Bg7 8 Be3 Nd7 (8 ... 0–0 9 Qd2 Qa5!? 10 Nb3 Qb4 11 Qc2 Nd7 12 Bd2 Nc5 13 Nxc5 Qxc5 with chances for both sides, Keres–Capablanca, Semmering-Baden 1937) 9 Qd2 Nxd4 10 Bxd4 Bxd4 11 Qxd4 0–0 12 Nd5 Nb6 with equality, Keres–Landau, Noordwijk 1938.) **6. Nb5 a6 7. N5c3 Be6 8. Nd5** Out of eight moves, this knight has made five, but now he jumps to an early grave. FR (8 Bg5 Be7 9 Bxf6 Bxf6 10 Nd5 11 Bg5 with an equal game, Spielmann–Landau, first match game, 1938.) **8 ... Nxd5 9. exd5 Bf5 10. Bd3 Bg6 11. 0–0 Be7 12. c4 Nd7** The position is even, MCO 295. **13. Nc3 0–0** As a result of White's numerous knight moves, Black has completed his development quickly and effortlessly. FR **14. Be3** None of the annotators explains why White does not prefer 14 Bxg6. AW **14 ... Bg5 15. Bxg5 Qxg5 16. Bxg6 Qxg6 17. Qd2 Rac8 18. b3 f5 19. f4 e4 20. Ne2 Nc5 21. Rac1 Rfe8 22. Rc3 Qf6 23. Qd4** Draw agreed. Eliskases' position is certainly preferable. However, in view of the barricaded pawn structure, a long and arduous positional struggle would have been inevitable. But with the tourney nearing its close, neither player had any real desire for this. Hence the decision. FR; What a fierce struggle! Fine in making certain of second place missed a possible first, in view of Keres' lapses. BW (Wood is evidently being ironic, but his failure to annotate does not enlighten the reader as to how the game might have been sharpened.)½–½ Reinfeld 1938, 66–7; Wood, 47; Hannak, 79–80. (Some of Reinfeld's notes

read like Hannak's, but my photocopies do not indicate why.)

(432) RESHEVSKY, S—FINE

Semmering-Baden (14), 1937 (27 Sept.)
Queen's Gambit Accepted [D27]

Fine has to work hard for the necessary half-point. FR **1. Nf3 d5 2. d4 Nf6 3. c4 dxc4 4. e3 e6 5. Bxc4 c5 6. 0–0 a6 7. Qe2 Nc6 8. a4** 8 Rd1 is the ordinary move. The text move is less usual, but Eliskases got a won game with it against Reshevsky himself. The latter has learnt his lesson and does the same against Fine. BW/HK; The customary reply is 8 Nc3. White not only hinders ... b5, but also incidentally prepares the advance d4-d5. JH **8 ... Be7 9. Rd1 Qc7 10. Nc3 0–0 11. h3 !** (Hannak) In order to deny Black's queen's bishop the use of the square g4. JH **11 ... Rd8** If 11 ... Nb4 12 e4! cxd4 13 Nxd4 with the better game for White, as Black is unable to prevent the e-pawn from charging on. JH **12. d5 exd5 13. Bxd5! Nb4 14. e4 Nfxd5 15. exd5 Bf5** The position is even, MCO 131. **16. Bf4!** Very troublesome for Black. It seems that Black has been a bit hasty in playing 13 ... Nb4 and 14 ... Nfxd5. BW/HK (Fine evidently did not believe this. See his analysis at move 17.) **16 ... Qxf4** 16 ... Bd6 would have been a more cautious approach. JH **17. Qxe7 b6?** Black could have improved on this by 17 ... Bxh3 18 Ne2 Qg4 19 Ng3 Nxd5 20 Qxb7 Qc8 21 Qxc8 Bxc8 22 Ne4 c4, MCO 131. **18. a5 Re8?** Here White cannot retain any advantage by replying to 18 ... Bxh3 by 19 Qe3, as suggested by Dr. Hannak, because of 19 ... Qg4 20 Ne1 Bxg2 21 Nxg2 Nc2. AW **19. Qh4! Qxh4 20. Nxh4 Bc2 21. Rd2 bxa5 22. Rxa5** White stands slightly better, MCO. **22 ... Rac8 23. Na2** Obtaining decisive advantage. BW/HK **23 ... g6 24. Nxb4 cxb4 25. Rxa6 Re1+ 26. Kh2 b3** Threatens ... Rb1 followed by ... Rxb2, but Black is given no time to carry out this threat. HK; The immediate 26 ... Rb1 is answered by 27 Rc6. BW **27. Nf3 Rb1 28. d6! Rd8** If 28 ... Rxb2 29 d7 wins. JH (29 ... Rd8 30 Nd4 Rxd7 31 Ne6! AW) **29. d7 Bf5** Necessary! HK **30. Nd4!** If 30 ... Rxd7 31 Nxf5, or if 30 ... Bxd7 31 Nxb3. BW/HK **30 ... Rc1 31 Nxf5** 31 Nxb3 was also very good. HK **gxf5 32. Rad6** 32 Kg3 was stronger. Reshevsky, being in time pressure, makes some inferior moves hereabouts. BW/HK **32 ... f4! 33. h4 Kg7 34. g3** If 34 Kh3 h5 threatening mate (BW/HK) but 34 h5 h6 35 Kh3 should win (JH). **34 ... fxg3+ 35. fxg3 Rc2 36. Kg2 Kf8 37. Kf3 Ke7 38. Rxc2 bxc2 39. Rc6 Rxd7 40. Rxc2 Rd3+ 41. Kf4 Rb3** The game is a dead draw now. BW **42. Rg2 Kf6 43. g4 Rb4+ 44. Ke3 h5! 45. gxh5 Rxh4 46. Kd3 Rxh5 47. Kc4 Ke5 48. b4 Kd6 49. Rc2 f5 50. Kb5 f4+ 51. Ka6 Ke5 52. b5 Ke4 53. b6 f3 54. Rf2 Rh3 55. Ka7 Ke3 56. b7 Rh7 57. Ka8 Rxb7** Draw agreed. Reshevsky probably missed a win at one stage, just as Fine must have missed the win somewhere in their first encounter. BW ½–½ Reinfeld 1938, 69–70; Wood, 49–50; Gordon, 54; Lopez Esnaola & de Marimon 91–2; Hannak, 81–2.

That there is now a break in Fine's almost non-stop playing is explained by the fact that he was acting as Euwe's second, and writing reports for a Dutch newspaper, in his return match against Alekhine, which ran from October 5 to December 16. Fine was hospitalized after the second game of the match (7 October) and underwent an operation for appendicitis. The newspaper articles were eventually turned into a match book, to which Reshevsky, who also acted as a reporter on the match, also contributed (notes to games 3 to 8, played between 10 October and 21 October. Fine's notes to the 9th game, October 24, onwards making up the remainder of the book). During the period which Fine was unavailable, Euwe lost three games and won only one. In the section about Euwe in *Meet the Masters* we read "From October until December he acted as 'second' to Euwe in the return match for the world's title, and we need make no secret of the fact that— in spite of his principal's disappointing result—he discharged this task nobly. That after these weeks of exertion and tension he could only tie for fourth and fifth places with Flohr in the Christmas tournament at Hastings was hardly surprising."

"Early reports said that Euwe intended to challenge again at once; but with characteristic grace he has signified that he will stand aside for at least four years, to give younger players such as Flohr, Keres, Reshevsky and Fine a chance." (*Chess* 14 December, 1937) *Chess* of 14 November, 1937 reported: "A writ claiming damages for alleged libel has been issued by Ernst Klein, the Austrian chess master now living at Clarnicarde Gardens, Bayswater, London, against Dr. Alekhine, Miss Menchik, G. Koltanowski, E. Cox, L. Prins, Reuben Fine, W.A.T. Schelfout, S. Landau and G. van Doesburgh. The writ was served on Koltanowski ... Most of the other masters named are in Amsterdam at the moment. The action is concerned with a document prepared at Margate during the Easter congress in which certain allegations were made concerning Mr. Klein's desirability as an opponent." A later edition of the same periodical (*Chess* 14 April, 1938) recorded that: "Ernst Klein has withdrawn his libel action against Alekhine, Miss Menchik, Prins and a group of other masters, having obtained an apology, with indemnification for costs. He states that 'his honour has now been vindicated.'"

Hastings, December 28 1937– January 6, 1938

Playing the traditional Christmas tournament for the third year in a row Fine got off to a slow start but eventually pulled himself up the table with three wins in a row. In the final round Fine was unable to catch the leaders and a fairly short draw was agreed with Flohr. Reshevsky, who placed first, and Alexander, tieing with Keres for second half a point behind, were in excellent form.

		1	2	3	4	5	6	7	8	9	10	
1	Reshevsky	*	½	½	½	½	1	1	1	1	1	7
2	Alexander	½	*	½	½	½	1	½	1	1	1	6½
3	Keres	½	½	*	½	½	1	1	½	1	1	6½
4	Fine	½	½	½	*	½	1	½	½	1	1	6
5	Flohr	½	½	½	½	*	0	1	1	1	1	6
6	Mikenas	0	0	0	0	1	*	1	1	1	1	5
7	Thomas, G	0	½	0	½	0	0	*	½	½	1	3
8	Tylor	0	0	½	½	0	0	½	*	1	½	3
9	Fairhurst	0	0	0	0	0	0	½	0	*	½	1
10	Thomas, A	0	0	0	0	0	0	0	½	½	*	1

(433) THOMAS, G—FINE

Hastings 1937/8 (1), 1937 (28 Dec.)
Alekhine's Defence [B05]

In the opening White hesitated for a moment over c2-c4, after which the opposing knight was able to deploy to f5 by way of e7. From that point on the knight stood more aggressively than it would have on b6. With 16 d5 White opened up the game and eventually created pressure against the bishop on d6. He could have won a pawn, but was unable to prevent the game ending in a draw. It is doubtful whether he could have achieved more by 24 Rxd6 Qxd6. ML **1. e4 Nf6 2. e5 Nd5 3. d4 d6 4. Nf3 Bg4 5. Be2 e6 6. c4** EMCO 1996 has only 6 0-0 here. **6 ... Ne7 7. Nc3 Nf5** 7 ... dxe5 would equalize quite simply. **8. h3 Bxf3 9. Bxf3 Nc6** Fine assesses this as equal in PCO, however White has a more comfortable position. **10. Bxc6+ bxc6 11. Bf4 Be7 12. 0-0 0-0 13. Ne2 f6 14. Qc2 Qe8 15. exd6 cxd6 16. d5 Qd7 17. dxe6 Qxe6 18. Rfe1 Qd7 19. Rad1 Rfe8 20. Nd4 Nxd4 21. Rxd4 Bf8 22. Red1 Rad8 23. Bxd6 Bxd6 24. Qd3 c5 25. Rxd6 Qxd6 26. Qxd6 Rxd6 27. Rxd6 Re1+ 28. Kh2 Re2 29. Rd8+ Kf7 30. Rd7+ Kg6 31. Rxa7 Rxb2 32. Kg3 Rb4 33. Kf3 Rxc4 34. Ke3 Rc2 35. g3 h5 36. a4 Ra2 37. a5 Kf5 38. a6 Ra3+ 39. Kd2 g5 40. Ra8 g4 41. hxg4+ Kxg4 42. a7** Agreed a draw. (42 ... Kf3 43 Rf8, or 42 ... Kh3 43 Rh8, or 42 ... Kf5 43 Rc8.) ML ½–½ Lachaga 1975, 1.

(434) FINE—ALEXANDER, C

Hastings 1937/8 (2), 1937 (29 Dec.)
Catalan System [E01]

The unusual handling of the opening by White (the omission of 5 cxd5), brought him nothing. A minor piece ending arose on the 28th move. Fine undertook a winning attempt and thereby lost two pawns. He still managed to draw, as the black king was tied to the defence of his extra pawns. ML **1. Nf3 d5 2. c4 e6 3. d4 Nf6 4. g3 c5 5. Bg2 cxd4 6. 0-0 Bc5 7. cxd5 Nxd5 8. Nxd4 0-0 9. a3** 9 Nb3 is better: Bb6 10 Bd2 Nc6 11 Na3 Qe7 Best. (If instead 11 ... a6 12 Nc4 Ba7 13 Nca5 Nxa5 14 Bxa5 Qe7 15 Rc1 Bd7 16 e4 is better for White, Simonson–Fine,

New York 1938.) 12 Nc4 Bc7 13 e4 Nbd4 with equality, MCO 228. **9 ... Bb6 10. Nc2 Nc6 11. e4 Nc7 12. Nc3 e5 13. Na4 Ne6 14. Qxd8 Bxd8 15. Be3 Ncd4** and now Black has the better game, MCO, 228. **16. Nb4 Ba5 17. Rfd1 Bd7 18. Nc3 Rfd8 19. Rac1 Rac8 20. Nbd5 Rxc3 21. bxc3 Ne2+ 22. Kh1 Nxc1 23. Rxc1 b6 24. c4 Ba4 25. h3 Kf8 26. c5 Rc8 27. cxb6 Rxc1+ 28. Bxc1 axb6 29. h4 Nd4 30. Kh2 Bd1 31. f4 Nf3+ 32. Kh1 exf4 33. Bxf4 Ne1 34. Bc7 Bc2 35. Bxb6 Nxg2 36. Bxa5 Nxh4 37. Nc3 Nf3 38. Kg2 Nd2 39. e5 Nc4 40. Bc7 Ke8 41. a4 Kd7 42. Bb8 Kc8 43. Ba7 Nxe5 44. Bc5 Kb7 45. Bf8 g6 46. Kf2 Ka6 47. Ke3 Nd7 48. Bb4 Bxa4 49. Ne4 h6 50. Be7 Kb6 51. Nf6 Nc5 52. g4 Ne6 53. Ng8 h5 54. gxh5 gxh5 55. Nh6 Be8 56. Ke4 Kc6 57. Ke5 Kd7 58. Bh4 Nc5 59. Ng8** Draw agreed. ½–½ Lachaga 1975, 6–7.

(435) Reshevsky, S—Fine

Hastings 1937/8 (3), 1937 (30 Dec.)
Queen's Gambit Declined, Semi-Tarrasch [D41]

1. d4 Nf6 2. c4 e6 3. Nf3 d5 4. Nc3 c5 5. cxd5 Nxd5 6. e4 Nxc3 7. bxc3 cxd4 8. cxd4 Bb4+ 9. Bd2 Bxd2+ 10. Qxd2 0–0 11. Bc4 Nc6 11 ... Nd7 Keres–Fine, Ostend 1937. **12. 0–0 b6 13. Rfd1 Bb7 14. Qf4 Qf6** 14 ... Rc8 15 d5 exd5 16 Bxd5 Qe7 17 Ng5! Ne5! 18 Bxb7 Ng6 19 Qf5 Qxb7 20 Rd7 Qa6! with equality, Alekhine–Euwe, match game 18, 1937. **15. Qe3 Rfd8 16. e5 Qh6** Despite the possible doubled pawn on the h-file Black offers the exchange of queens, because it would paralyze his opponents centre. ML **17. Rac1 Qxe3** Equalizing, MCO 6, 150. **18. fxe3 Rac8 19. Nd2 h6 20. Bb3** Planning Nc4. Not 20 Ne4? on account of 20 ... Nxe5. ML **20 ... Na5 21. Bc2 Bd5** Draw agreed. ½–½ Lachaga, 6–7.

(436) Fine—Tylor, T

Hastings 1937/8 (4), 1937 (31 Dec.)
Schlechter Variation [D11]

A well-played game by Tylor, in which White's pressure on the queenside was countered by a kingside initiative leading to perpetual check on the 30th move. ML **1. d4 d5 2. c4 c6 3. Nf3 Nf6 4. Qc2 g6 5. Nc3 Bg7 6. e3 0–0 7. Bd3 Na6 8. a3 c5 9. 0–0 cxd4 10. exd4 dxc4 11. Bxc4 Nc7 12. Qb3 a6 13. a4 b5 14. Be2 Be6 15. Qa3 Rb8 16. axb5 axb5 17. Qc5 Bd7 18. Ra7 Rc8 19. Qa3 Nfd5 20. Nxd5 Nxd5 21. Qb3 Nc7 22. Bd2 Bg4 23. Ba5 Qd5 24. Qa3 Ne6 25. Bc3 Ng5 26. Qxe7 Nxf3+ 27. Bxf3 Bxf3 28. gxf3 Qxf3 29. Qe3 Qh5 30. Re1 Rce8 31. Qxe8 Qg4+ 32. Kf1 Qh3+ 33. Kg1 Qg4+** Draw agreed. ½–½ Lachaga 1975, 14.

(437) Keres, P—Fine

Hastings 1937/8 (5), 1938 (1 Jan.)
Vienna Game, Falkbeer Variation [C26]

Interesting opening play. With 15 h4, White maintained his attack, which Black countered with an attack on the Bd3, if 16 Bxf4 exf4 17 Qxf4 Nc5. The position remained in equilibrium and the game soon ended peacefully. ML **1. e4 Nf6 2. Nc3 e5 3. Bc4 Bc5 4. d3 d6 5. Na4 Bb4+ 6. c3 d5 7. exd5 Bd6 8. Be3 0–0 9. Nc5 b6 10. Ne4 Bb7 11. Bg5 Nbd7 12. Qf3 Be7 13. Ng3 Bxd5 14. Bxd5 Nxd5 15. h4 Nf4 16. Bxe7 Qxe7 17. N1e2 Qe6 18. 0–0 Nxe2+ 19. Nxe2 Rad8 20. Rfe1 Rfe8 21. Nd4 Qf6 22. Qxf6 Nxf6 23. Nc6 Rxd3 24. Nxe5 Rd2 25. Nc4 Rdd8 26. Rad1 h5 27. Ne3 Kf8**

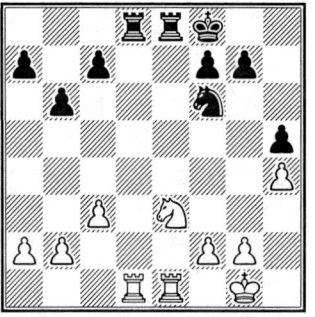

Position after Black's 27th move

28. g3 g6 29. Kg2 Draw agreed. ½–½ Lachaga 1975, 19.

(438) Fine—Mikenas, V

Hastings 1937/8 (6), 1938 (3 Jan.)
Nimzowitsch Defence [B00]

1. d4 Nc6 2. Nf3 d6 3. e4 Bg4 4. Bb5 a6 5. Ba4 b5 6. Bb3 Nf6 7. c3 e6 The pawn structure greatly resembles a Spanish, though with the black king's pawn on e6. AB **8. Qe2 Be7 9. 0–0 0–0 10. Nbd2 Bh5 11. a4** White stands slightly better, MCO 85. **11 ... Qd7 12. Re1** Not immediately 12 axb5 because of 12 ... axb5 13 Rxa8 Rxa8 14 Qxb5 Bxf3 (15 gxf3 Nxd4!). AB **12 ... Na5 13. Bc2 Rfb8 14. Bd3 c6 15. Ra2** The start of a plan to put pressure on the a-pawn, which he eventually wins on the 35th move. AB **15 ... Nb7 16. b3 Qc7 17. Bb2 c5 18. Rea1 bxa4 19. Rxa4 a5 20. Nc4**

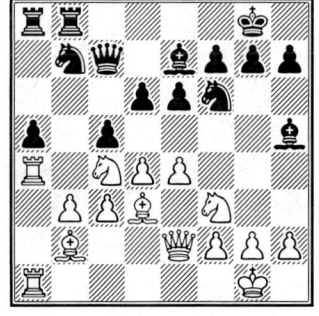

Position after White's 20th move

20 ... d5 21. exd5 Nxd5 22. Qe5 Bxf3 23. Qxc7 Nxc7 24. gxf3 Nd5 25. Be4 Ra6 26. Kf1 cxd4 27. cxd4 g6 28. Ne3 Nb6 29. R4a2 f5 30. Bd3 Raa8 31. Bc3 Nd5 32. Nxd5 exd5 33. b4 Rc8

34. Be1 Bf6 35. bxa5 Bxd4 36. Rd1 Ba7 The
d-pawn is untenable. If, for example, 36 ... Bb6? 37 Rb2, or
36 ... Bc3 37 a6 Nd6 38 Bxc3! (not 38 Be2 d4 39 Bxc3
dxc3!) Rxc3 39 Ra5. AB 37. Ba6 Rc7 38. Rxd5 Nc5
39. Bc4 Ne6 40. Rc2 Kg7 41. Bc3+ Kh6 42. Be5
Rc5 43. Rxc5 Nxc5 44. Bd4 Rc8 45. Kg2 Rc7
46. Ba2 Rc8 47. Rc4 Kg5 48. f4+ Kg4 49. Be3 As a
result of Fine's excellent handling of the bishop pair, Black
is powerless against the threat of Ba2-b3-d1+. AB 49 ...
Rd8? 50. Bxc5 Black resigned. 1−0 Albert Becker in
Lachaga 1975, 24.

(439) FAIRHURST, W—FINE

Hastings 1937/8 (7), 1938 (4 Jan.)
King's Indian Defence [E60]

White played against his opponent's isolated d-pawn, but for
this he had to give up his Bb2. Approaching approximate
equality he made the gross blunder 28 Nf3 (28 Be3 is to be
preferred) and so lost a piece and the game. ML 1. d4 Nf6
2. c4 g6 3. d5 Bg7 4. g3 0−0 5. Bg2 e6 6. Nf3
exd5 7. cxd5 c6 8. Nc3 Nxd5 9. Nxd5 cxd5
10. Qxd5 d6 11. 0−0 Nc6 12. Rd1 Qb6 13. Be3
Qxb2 14. Qxd6 Bf5 15. Rac1 Rad8 16. Qc5 Qxe2
17. Rd2 Rxd2 18. Nxd2 Rc8 19. Qa3 h5 20. Bf1
Qg4 21. Rc4 Nd4 22. Rxc8+ Bxc8 23. Qxa7 Kh7
24. h3 Qd7 25. Bg2 Nf5

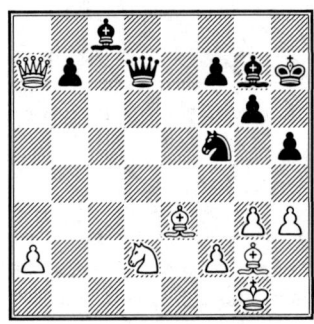

*Position after
Black's 25th move*

26. Bf4?! h4 This should not have been successful.
Instead 26 ... Nxg3! 27 Bxg3 Qxd2 28 a4 Bd4 29 Qb8 Qc1+
30 Kh2 b6 would have won a pawn, but the ending would
be difficult to win. AW 27. g4?! A mistake. 27 Qb8 is fine
for White. AW 27 ... Nd4 28. Nf3?? Ne2+ White
resigned. 0−1 Lachaga 1975, 27.

(440) FINE—THOMAS, A

Hastings 1937/8 (8), 1938 (5 Jan.)
English Opening, Classical Variation [A20]

1. c4 e5 2. Nf3 Nc6 3. d4 exd4 4. Nxd4 Nf6 5. g3
Qe7 Instead of developing his bishop by 5 ... Bb4+ or 5 ...
Bc5 Black makes a premature attempt to win a pawn by 6 ...
Qb4+; he is duly punished. 6. Bg2 Qb4+ 7. Nc3 Qxc4
8. Ndb5 Nb8

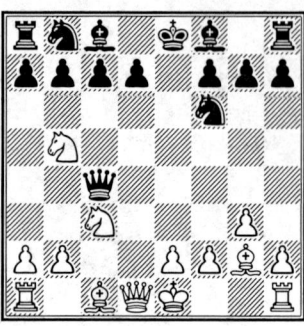

*Position after
Black's 8th move*

9. b3 White could have turned the game into an ultra-
miniature by 9 Bd5! when the black queen is trapped in the
middle of the board and the queen's rook in the corner,
while 9 ... Nxd5 is prevented by the family fork on c7. AW
9 ... Qb4 10. Nxc7+ Kd8 11. N7b5 Qa5 If 11 ... a6
then 12 Ba3 Qa5 13 Bxf8 axb5 14 b4 Qc7 15 Nxb5 Qc4
16 Bxg7 and wins. 12. Bf4 Ne8 13. a3 a6 14. b4 Qb6
15. Be3 Qg6 16. Nd4 Good enough, but 16 Nd5 axb5
17 Bb6+ Nc7 18 Bxc7+ Ke8 19 Nb6 is more forcing. AW 16
... Nd6 17. Qb3 Be7 18. Nd5 Bf6 19. Rd1 Bxd4
20. Bxd4 Black resigned. 1−0 George Koltanowski, BCM
1938, 164.

(441) FINE—FLOHR, S

Hastings 1937/8 (9), 1938 (6 Jan.)
Réti Opening [A09]

1. Nf3 d5 2. c4 d4 3. e3 Nc6 4. exd4 Nxd4 5. Nxd4
Qxd4 6. Nc3 Bg4 7. Be2 Another, though not necessarily better, possibility is 7 Qa4+ and then, either 7 ... Bd7
8 Qb3 Bc6 9 d3, or 7 ... c6 8 d3 followed by Be3. ML 7 ...
Bxe2 8. Qxe2 e6 9. 0−0 Nf6 10. d3 c6 11. Be3
Qh4 12. g3 Qh3 13. f3 Be7 14. Rad1 0−0 15. d4
Qf5 16. Bf2 Rfd8 17. Rd3 Rd7 18. Rfd1 Rad8
19. Ne4 Qa5 20. b3 h6 21. Kg2 Kh7 22. Qc2 Kg8
23. Qe2 Kh7 24. Qc2 Draw agreed. ½−½ Lachaga
1975, 36.

The Second United States
Championship Tournament,
1938

In January, 1938 Fine sailed back to New York, arriving home on 7 February, and returned to complete his
mathematical studies; but in the meantime he competed in
the United States Championship. The 1938 Championship
tournament turned out to be a close affair, but Reshevsky
was always ahead and Fine was unable to come up with an
opening idea which would give him genuine winning
chances in their decisive final round encounter.

New York Metropolitan League, March, 1938

Fine played in two matches, as usual taking the black pieces and, also as usual, winning his games, the first against Nathan Beckhardt of the Bronx Chess Club. In the crucial Marshall–Manhattan match, on the next Saturday, the Marshall Club fielded an extremely strong side including Fine (#1), Reshevsky (#2), Bernstein (#3), Hanauer (#4), Marshall (#5), Santasiere (#6), Polland (#7), Green (#8), Reinfeld (#9) and Seidman (#10).

| Beckhardt | 0 | Fine | 1 |
| Kashdan | 0 | Fine | 1 |

(442) Beckhardt, N–Fine, R

Metropolitan Chess League, New York, 1938 (5 March)
Sicilian Defence, Dragon Variation [B74]

1. e4 c5 2. Nf3 d6 3. d4 cxd4 4. Nxd4 Nf6 5. Nc3 g6 6. Be2 Bg7 7. 0–0 0–0 8. Be3 Nc6 9. Nb3 Be6 10. Qd2 Rc8 11. Bh6 Ne5 12. Bxg7 Kxg7 13. Rad1 Qb6 14. Qd4 Qxd4 15. Rxd4 Bc4 16. Re1 Bxe2 17. Rxe2 Nc4 18. Nd1 e5 19. Rd3 Rfd8 20. Nd2 Nb6 21. Nc3 Ng8 22. f3 Ne7 23. Nf1 Nc4 24. Nd1

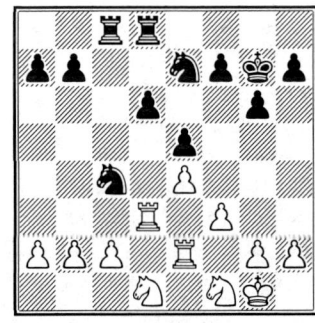

Position after White's 24th move

24 ... d5 25. b3 Na3 26. exd5 Nxc2 27. Rxe5 Kf6 28. f4 Nb4 29. Rf3 Rc1 30. Nde3 Nexd5 31. Ng4+ Kg7 32. f5 Nc6 33. f6+ Nxf6 White resigned. 0–1

(443) Kashdan, I–Fine

Metropolitan Chess League, New York, 1938 (12 March)
Grünfeld Defence [D80]

1. d4 Nf6 2. c4 g6 3. Nc3 d5 4. Bg5 Alekhine first tried this in a game against Grünfeld and lost. But in 1933 Lundin successfully revived it against Spielmann. Although it has rarely been seen since then, the consensus of opinion is that the white prelate would do better to confine himself to his own diocese. 4 ... Ne4 Never move the same piece twice in the opening—except when necessary! Black cannot afford to see his pawn position ruined. 5. cxd5 The bishop is ready to die for the cause, but all to no avail. Lundin's improvement against Spielmann consisted in exchanging knights and developing quickly: 5 Nxe4 dxe4 6 Qd2.

Subsequently, however, it was shown that by replying 6 ... Bg7 and ... c5 as soon as possible, Black could weather the crisis satisfactorily. 5 ... Nxg5 Grünfeld played instead 5 ... Nxc3 6 bxc3 Qxd5 and also obtained a good game. The reason for choosing the text was purely psychological—it deprives White of ecclesiastical support. 6. h4 Ne4 7. Nxe4 Qxd5 8. Nc3 Qa5 Black is playing for an attack. He intends to get his queen's knight and queen's bishop out of the way, play ... 0–0–0 quickly, and then concentrate on the d-pawn. 9. h5 Leads to practically nothing. 9 Qb3 appears to be more logical, but after 9 ... Bg7 10 0–0–0, Black can change his intentions and castle on the kingside, since his attack will be even stronger than White's. 9 ... Bg7 10. Qd2 Nc6 11. e3 Too passive, for Black now builds up a strong attack. 11 hxg6 hxg6 12 Rxh8+ Bxh8 and only now 13 e3 was better. 11 ... Bf5 An invitation to the wars. 11 ... Bd7 was also good, but less exciting. 12. h6 Calling the bluff, but Black has some high cards up his sleeve. If at once 12 e4 Bd7, and if 13 d5 Nd4 is quite strong. However, the sacrifice 12 ... Nxd4 would then have been less advantageous, since White obtains counterplay on the h-file. 12 ... Bf6 All the bishops are in a sacrificial mood. But 12 ... Bf8 would be like being sent to a concentration camp. 13. e4?! Nxd4 No surprise for 13 ... Bd7 14 e5 would lose a full piece for nothing. 14. exf5 0–0–0 Better than 14 ... Nb3 at once, for then Black could not castle and unite his rooks quickly. 15. Bd3 15 Qc1 would be refuted by 15 ... Qxf5. Better than the text seems 15 Rd1 (but not 15 0–0–0 Nb3+ 16 axb3 Rxd2 17 Rxd2 Bxc3 18 bxc3 Qa1+ with a rich harvest) Nf3+ 16 Nxf3 Rxd2 17 Nxd2 gxf5 18 Rh3 when the game would still be a hard fight. 15 ... Nb3 16. axb3 Qxa1+ 17. Ndl e5 A difficult decision. The alternative was 17 ... Rd6 18 Ne2 Rhd8 19 Rh3 (No pasaran!) but then I saw no way in which Black could continue the attack. And if 17 ... Bg5 18 Qe2 (not 18 Qxg5 Rxd3 19 Qg4 gxf5 20 Qxf5+ Rd7 21 Qf3 Rhd8 and wins) the "brilliant" 18 ... Rxd3 19 Qxd3 Rd8 20 Qe2 Rd2 21 Qxd2! leaves White with a solid position.

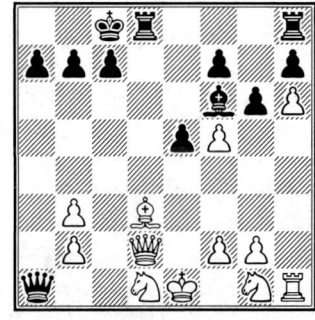

Position after Black's 17th move

18. fxe6 Also a difficult decision. True, 18 fxg6 e4 19 g7 Rhe8 would have been immediately disastrous. But he might well have tried 18 f3, for example, 18 ... e4 19 fxe4 gxf5 20 exf5 Bg5 21 Qc2 Rhe8+ 22 Ne2 Re3 23 Bc4 or 18 ... Rd6 19 Ne2 Rhd8 20 Nc1. In both cases Black's attack seems to come to a standstill. Black's best continuation would have been 18 ... Bg5 19 Qc2 Rd6 20 Nh3 (forced now) Rhd8 21 Nhf2 Be3 22 Ke2 Qxf2 23 Nxf2 Qa5 although the

outcome would then have been unclear. **18 ... Rhe8
19. Ne2 Rxe6 20. Rh3** Castling is bad, for on 20 0–0
Red6 21 Nc1 Qa6! wins. It is difficult to see now just how
Black can strengthen his position. **20 ... Be7** Threatening
... to threaten. **21. Qc2?** 21 Re3 Bg5 22 f4 Rxe3 23 Qxe3
Bxh6 24 Qh3+ f5 would have been good for Black. But
21 Kf1 seems to be a satisfactory defence. If then 21 ... Bb4
22 Nc3 Bxc3 23 bxc3 Ra6 24 Ke1 and White can still hold
the position. **21 ... Bb4+ 22. Kf1 Rc6 23. Nec3 Bxc3
24. bxc3**

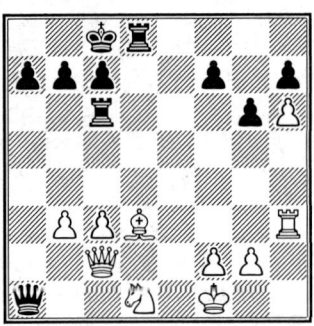

*Position after
White's 24th move*

24 ... Rxc3 White had not included this in his calculations.
If now 25 Bf5+ gxf5 26 Rxc3 Qxd1+, while if 25 Qxc3
Qxd1+ 26 Qe1 Rxd3, with a winning ending in both cases.
**25. Qe2 Rxb3 26. Rf3 Qd4 27. Bc2 Rxf3 28. Qxf3
Qc4+ 29. Qe2 Qh4** The simplest way to win was 29 ...
Qxe2+ followed by the advance of the queenside pawns. But
Black wanted to clean up the kingside first. **30. Qf3 Qxh6
31. Qxf7 Qh1+ 32. Ke2 Qxg2 33. Ne3 Qh3 34. Bb3
Qh5+ 35. Kf1 a6** Losing one of his pawns. More precise
was 35 ... Kb8, for if then 36 Qe7 Qh3+ 37 K moves Qd7 and
White's position is ripe for resignation. **36. Qe7! Qb5+
37. Bc4 Qe8 38. Qxh7 Kb8 39. Qh4 Rd6 40. Qf4
Qd8 41. Kg2 Rd4** Here the game was adjourned. **42. Qf7**
Black undoubtedly has a win, but the technical process requires care and patience. The most important point to bear
in mind is that White by exchanging queens would only sign
his own death warrant, for the queenside pawns would then
decide. As a result, however, Black can build up an attack on
White's king. **42 ... Qg5+ 43. Kf3** Or 43 Kf1 Rf4. **43 ...
Rd6** Black's winning plan can be divided into two parts: a)
first he wishes to tie White's queen to the defence of the
f-pawn; b) then he will advance the a-pawn. In the absence
of the white queen this advance should prove decisive.
Because of White's inability to exchange queens, this plan
cannot be crossed. **44. Ke2** Or 44 Nd5 Rc6. **44 ... Rf6
45. Qe8+ Ka7 46. Qe4** Or 46 Nd5 Qg4+ 47 Kd3 Rf3+
48 Ne3 Qf5+ and wins. **46 ... Qf4 47. Qg2 Rb6** There is
no hurry. First Black wishes to paralyze as many white pieces
as possible. **48. Bd3 Rb2+ 49. Bc2** Or 49 Nc2 Qe5+
50 Kd5 g5. **49 ... g5 50. Qd5 g4** The escape of the black
king via f3 is now impossible. White must lose so much time
to release the pin, that his game cannot be saved. **51. Qg2**
Or 51 Qc5+ Kb8 (or even 51 ... b6 52 Qc3 Rb5). **51 ... a5
52. Kd3** If 52 Qd5 b6. **52 ... Qd6+ 53. Ke2 Qd4
54. Qg3 c6 55. Qc7 Qb4 56. Kd3 a4 57. Nd1 a3!**

58. Nxb2 a2! 59. Nc4 a1Q White resigned. **0–1**
Reuben Fine in *The Chess Review* 1938, 94–5.

2nd U.S. Championship New York, April 2–24, 1938

Ten players—Reshevsky, Fine, Kashdan, Horowitz,
Dake, Simonson, Polland, Kupchik, Treysman and Morton—were seeded into the finals. They were joined by qualifiers from three preliminary groups. From Section A (fatally
for Fine's chances, as it would turn out): Hanauer, Cohen
and Santasiere (there was a tie for 2nd and 3rd place in this
group, both players being allowed through to the final),
from Section B: Bernstein and Suesman, and from Section
C: Reinfeld and Shainswit. Hence the final was contested
by one more player than in 1936. It is noticeable in the final
table that the top half is occupied by the seeds and the bot-
tom by the qualifiers, with hardly any exceptions.

This time Reshevsky started well and after 13 rounds,
including a bye, both he and Fine had scored 10 points out
of 12, at which time Kashdan had nine and a half points
(he, however, had a bye and four losses in the last five
rounds) as did Simonson (who lost twice in the closing
rounds). Fine had lost a well-played game to Santasiere in
the 7th round, but had won nine games to Reshevsky's
eight. In the 14th round Fine overlooked a tactical point in
a won position, eventually going down to Milton Hanauer.
Meanwhile Reshevsky was winning again. Fine took both
points in rounds 15 and 16, while Reshevsky only drew in
the penultimate round. In the last round Fine had to beat
his rival to win the championship. He found an interesting
sacrifice to disrupt his opponent's central pawn formation,
but Reshevsky defended well and a draw was agreed when
the defending champion reached a favourable position. First
prize was $600, second $400, third $250, fourth $150 and
sixth $100. Consolation money was distributed amongst the
non-prizewinners at $8 per point.

		1	2	3	4	5	6	7	8	9	10	11	12	13	14	15	16	17	
1	Reshevsky	*	½	1	½	1	1	1	½	½	1	1	1	½	½	1	1	1	13
2	Fine	½	*	½	1	1	½	1	1	1	0	1	0	1	1	1	1	1	12½
3	Simonson	0	½	*	1	½	½	½	0	1	½	1	½	1	1	1	1	1	11
4	Horowitz	½	0	0	*	½	½	1	½	1	0	1	1	1	1	½	½	1	10
5	Kashdan	0	0	½	½	*	1	0	1	1	1	1	½	0	1	1	1	0	9½
6	Polland	0	½	½	½	0	*	0	1	½	½	0	1	1	½	1	1	1	9
7	Dake	0	0	½	0	1	1	*	0	½	1	½	½	½	½	1	1	1	9
8	Kupchik	½	0	1	½	0	0	1	*	½	½	½	½	1	1	½	0	1	8½
9	Bernstein	½	0	0	0	0	½	½	½	*	½	1	1	½	½	0	1	1	7½
10	Santasiere	0	1	½	1	0	½	0	½	½	*	0	½	0	½	½	½	1	7
11	Treysman	0	0	0	0	0	1	½	½	0	1	*	1	1	½	1	0	½	7
12	Hanauer	0	1	½	0	½	0	½	½	0	½	0	*	½	0	1	½	1	6½
13	Cohen	½	0	0	0	1	0	½	0	½	1	0	½	*	0	½	1	1	6½
14	Reinfeld	½	0	0	0	0	½	½	0	½	½	½	1	1	*	0	½	1	6½
15	Shainswit	0	0	0	½	0	0	0	½	1	½	0	0	½	1	*	1	½	5½
16	Morton	0	0	0	½	0	0	0	1	0	½	1	½	0	½	0	*	1	5
17	Suesman	0	0	0	0	1	0	0	0	0	0	½	0	0	0	½	0	*	2

(444) KUPCHIK, A—FINE

U.S. Championship, New York (1), 1938 (2 April)
Grünfeld Defence, Fianchetto Variation [D75]

When I first joined the Manhattan Chess Club in 1929, Kupchik was the best rapid-transit (ten seconds per move) player around, and used to win all the "pots." His method consisted of winning a pawn, and then pressing the advantage home by flawless technique. In the following game I used his own style to defeat him. **1. d4 Nf6 2. c4 g6 3. g3 Bg7 4. Bg2 d5 5. c×d5 N×d5 6. Nf3** 6 e4 Nb4 (or 6 ... Nb6 7 Ne2 Bg4 8 f3 Bd7 9 Nbc3 Qc8 10 0–0 Bh3 11 Be3 Réti–Euwe, Kissingen 1928) 7 a3 N4c6 8 d5 Nd4 9 Ne2 Bg4 10 Nbc3 e5 11 0–0 Qf6 12 f3 Bd7 13 Be3 c5 14 d×c6 Nb×c6 15 Nd5 and White stands slightly better, Rubinstein–Réti, Semmering 1926. **6 ... 0–0** Kasparov–Hübner, Cologne 1992, continued 6 ... Nb6 7 0–0 Nc6 8 e3 e5 9 d×e5 Q×d1 10 R×d1 N×e5 11 N×e5 B×e5 12 Nd2 c6 13 Nf3 Bg7. AW **7. 0–0 c5!** White has handled the opening tamely and Black now takes the initiative. RF 1938 **8. d×c5** Perhaps hoping to win a pawn (we are back to "Kupchik's pawn"). Preferable, however, is 8 Nc3, with fairly speedy equality. RF; In the game Alekhine–Mikenas, Kemeri 1937, Alekhine tried 8 e4 Nf6 9 e5 Nd5 and then 10 d×c5 ... also without success. RF 1938 **8 ... Na6 9. c6** Fine reckoned that after 9 Qc2, Black would have a strong reply in 9 ... Qa5, but 10 c6! then seems to keep the extra pawn. AW **9 ... b×c6 10. a3 Rb8 11. Qc2** White continues passively. Better was 11 e4 which would at any rate have made the following excursion less effective. RF 1938 **11 ... Qa5!** Black stands slightly better, MCO 220. **12. Nbd2** The pawn is taboo. If 12 Q×c6 Nab4 13 Qc4 Ba6 14 Qe4 (or 14 Qh4 Nc2) Nf6! and the decisive ... Nc2 cannot be prevented (things don't look completely clear after 15 Q×e7 Nc2 16 b4! Qb6 17 Be3 AW). Of course, on 12 Q×c6 B×b2 is also strong. **12 ... Qc5!** Hammering away at the defences of the b-pawn. **13. Qd3! Nac7!** Dr. O. Bernstein once made the astute observation that a pawn is often won at the cost of the initiative. That is the case here, for example, 13 ... B×b2 14 B×b2 R×b2 15 Rfc1 with all kinds of counterplay. **14. Ne4 Qb5** White's queen is his only active piece, while Black's queen, although equally active is constantly subject to attack by White's minor pieces. This explains why White is so reluctant to exchange queens hereabouts. RF 1938 **15. Qc2 Ba6 16. Re1** 16 Nc5 Q×e2 17 Nd2 Rfd8 is bad for White. RF 1938 **16 ... Ne6 17. Bf1**

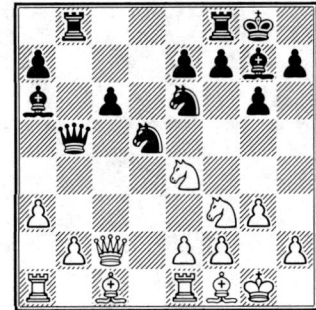

Position after White's 17th move

17 ... Qc4! Now the exchange of queens can no longer be avoided. 17 ... Qb6 18 Nfd2 followed by e4 would finally allow White to develop his pieces. RF 1938 **18. Q×c4 B×c4 19. Ned2 Bb5 20. Ra2** A clumsy but unavoidable move. If, instead 20 Rb1 Ba4 penetrates. RF 1958; If instead 20 e4 Nb6 (not 20 ... B×f1?? 21 e×d5 and wins) 21 B×b5 c×b5 followed by ... Na4 and White's pieces are still tied down. RF 1938 **20 ... a5 21. b3 a4!** After 22 b×a4 B×a4 White's pieces are still hopelessly isolated. **22. b4 c5 23. b×c5 Rfc8** If 23 ... Nc3 first then 24 Rc2 Rfc8 25 Bb2 R×c5 26 B×c3 (not 26 Rec1! N×e2+ 27 B×e2 B×b2! and wins) R×c3 27 R×c3 B×c3 28 Rb1 and White is not so badly off. RF 1938 **24. Bb2 N×c5** Not 24 ... B×e2? 25 B×g7 B×f1 26 Be5 and wins. RF 1938 **25. B×g7 K×g7**

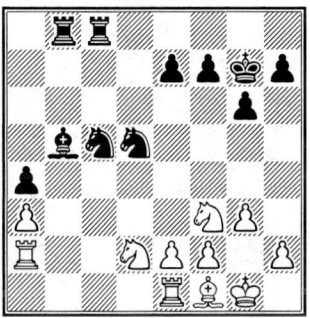

Position after Black's 25th move

26. Rc2 26 Rb2 (as suggested by Fine in 1938) seems adequate, for example, 26 ... Nc3 27 Nd4! AW **26 ... Nb3! 27. Rb2** The attempt to free himself with 27 R×c8 R×c8 28 N×b3 a×b3 29 Rb1 ends disastrously after Ba4 30 Nd4 Nc3 31 Rb2 Nd1! 32 Rb1 b2!. Now he has a threat for once, which Black must handle. **27 ... Be8 28. e3 Nc3 29. Nd4 N×d2 30. R×d2 e5 31. Nf3** If 31 Nc2, Rb2 is decisive. **31 ... f6** White has succeeded in freeing himself to a certain extent, but the weak a-pawn will prove fatal. RF 1938 **32. Rc2 Nb5! 33. Ra2** Somewhat better was 33 R×c8 R×c8 34 B×b5 B×b5, although the Black rook cannot be prevented from penetrating to the seventh rank. **33 ... Rc3 34. B×b5** The toughest defence would seem to be 34 Rb1 Rb3, as given by Fine, and then 35 Nd2 R×b1 36 N×b1 Nd4! 37 Nc3 Nf3+ 38 Kg2 Bc6 39 Bc4 when Black is not home and dry yet. AW **34 ... R×b5 35. Nd2 Bc6 36. Nb1 Rcb3 37. Ra1** If, instead, 37 Nd2 Rb2 38 R×b2 R×b2 39 Nc4 Rc2 40 Nb6 (or 40 Na5 Bf3) Kf7! and suddenly the knight is trapped. **37 ... Rc5 38. Ra2 Bd5** Threatening ... R×b1. RF 1938 **39. Ra1 Rc2** Now the struggle is over; both black rooks get to the seventh rank. **40. Rd1 Be6** But not 40 ... Bf3? 41 Rd7+ Kh6 42 Nd2 and White's troubles are over. The position is now hopeless for White. RF 1938 **41. Nd2 Rbb2 42. Ne4 Bf5 43. Nd6 R×f2 44. N×f5+ g×f5 45. Rab1 Rg2+ 46. Kf1 Rbf2+ 47. Ke1 Ra2 48. Kf1 R×h2 49. Kg1 Rhc2** White resigned. **0–1** Fine 1958, 140–4; *The Chess Review* 1938, 114–5.

(445) FINE—SHAINSWIT, G

U.S. Championship, New York (2), 1938 (3 April)
Classical English [A20]

1. c4 e5 2. Nf3 e4 3. Nd4 Nc6 4. Nc2 d5! 5. cxd5
Qxd5 6. Nc3 Qe5 7. d4 exd3 8. Qxd3 Nb4 9. Nxb4
Bxb4 10. Qc4 Bxc3+ 11. Qxc3 Qxc3+ 12. bxc3 Be6

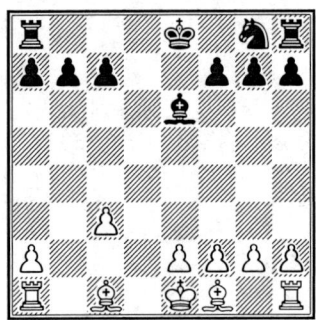

*Position after
Black's 12th move*

13. e4 Nf6 14. f3 Nd7 15. Be3 Nb6 16. Be2 f6
17. Kf2 Nc4 18. Bf4 0–0–0 19. Rhb1 c5 20. a4
Na5 21. Rb5 b6 22. Rab1 Nc4 23. Ra1 Na5 24. h4
h6 25. h5 Kd7 26. Be3 Ke8 27. Rab1 Bd7 28. R5b2
Bxa4 29. Bxc5 Nc6 30. Be3 Ne5 31. Ra1 Bd1 32. Bb5+
Kf8 33. Bd4 Black resigned. 1–0

(446) SUESMAN, W—FINE

U.S. Championship, New York (3), 1938 (4 April)
Queen's Gambit Declined, Ragozin Variation [D38]

1. d4 Nf6 2. c4 e6 3. Nf3 d5 4. Nc3 Bb4 5. cxd5
Qxd5 6. e3 c5 7. a3 Bxc3+ 8. bxc3 0–0 9. c4 Qd6
10. Bd3 b6 11. 0–0 Bb7 12. Bb2 cxd4 13. exd4 Rd8
14. h3 Qf4 15. Ne5 Nbd7 16. Nxd7 Rxd7 17. Qe2
Be4 18. Rfe1 Bxd3 19. Qxd3 Rc8 20. Rac1 h6

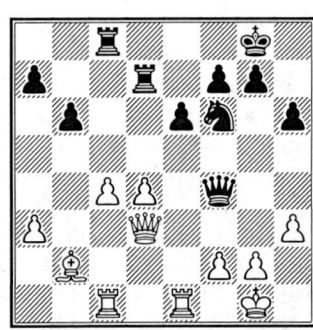

*Position after
Black's 20th move*

21. a4 Qd6 22. Qb3 Qf4 23. Qb5 Rdc7 24. Rc2 Rc6
25. a5 bxa5 26. c5 Qf5 27. Rce2 Nd5 28. Qxa5 Nf4
29. Rd2 Qg5 30. g3 Nxh3+ 31. Kf1 Qd5 32. Re5
Qh1+ 33. Ke2 Ng1+ 34. Kd3 Nf3 White resigned. 0–1

(447) FINE—REINFELD, F

U.S. Championship, New York (5), 1938 (7 April)
Queen's Gambit Declined, Slav Defence [D12]

1. d4 d5 2. c4 c6 3. Nf3 Nf6 4. e3 Bf5 5. Nc3 e6
6. Nh4 Bg4 7. Qb3 Qb6 8. h3 Bh5 9. g4 Bg6
10. Nxg6 hxg6 11. Bg2 Bb4 12. Bd2 Nbd7 13. 0–0–0
Bxc3 14. Bxc3 Qxb3 15. axb3

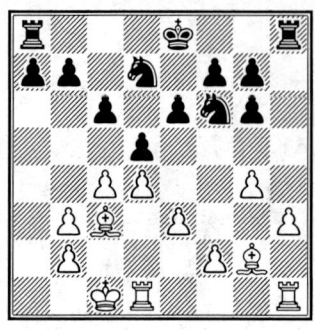

*Position after
White's 15th move*

15 ... Nb6! 16. c5 Nc8 17. Kc2 Kd7 18. f3 Ne7
19. h4 Rh7 20. Be1 Rah8 21. Bg3 Ne8 22. Rhe1 f5
23. g5 f4 24. Bxf4 Rxh4 25. Bf1 Nf5 26. Kc3 Rf8
27. Be5 Rh5 28. Ra1 a6 29. Bxa6 bxa6 30. Rxa6
Nc7?! 31. Bxc7 Kxc7 32. Ra7+ Kd8 33. Rea1 Ne7
34. Ra8+ Nc8 35. Rxc8+ Kxc8 36. Ra8+ Kd7
37. Rxf8 Ke7 38. Rg8 Kf7 39. Rc8 Rh3 40. Rxc6
Rxf3 41. Kd3 Black resigned. 1–0

(448) FINE—HOROWITZ, I

U.S. Championship, New York (6), 1938 (9 April)
Catalan System [E06]

1. d4 d5 2. c4 e6 3. Nf3 Nf6 4. g3 Be7 5. Bg2
0–0 6. 0–0 Ne4 7. Nfd2 f5 8. Nxe4 dxe4 9. Nc3
c5 10. d5 e5 11. f3 exf3 12. Bxf3 e4 13. Bg2 a6
14. Be3 Bd6 15. Bf4 Qe7 16. g4!? g6 17. Qe1 Nd7
18. Qg3 Bxf4 19. Rxf4 Kh8 20. Raf1 Nf6 21. Nxe4
Nxe4 22. Bxe4 g5 23. Qc3+ Kg8

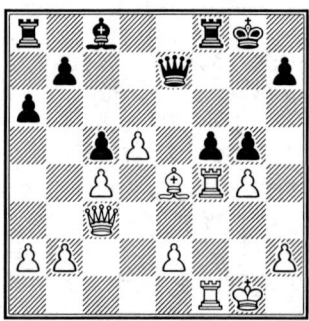

*Position after
Black's 23rd move*

24. d6 Qf6 25. Bd5+ Kg7 26. R4f2 Qxc3 27. bxc3
f4 28. e3 Bxg4 29. exf4 Bh3 30. Rb1 gxf4 31. Rxb7+
Kh8 32. Be4 Rae8 33. Rxh7+ Kg8 34. Re7 Rxe7
35. dxe7 Re8 36. Rxf4 Rxe7 37. Kf2 Kg7 38. Bd5
Bc8 39. Re4 Rxe4 40. Bxe4 Kf6 41. h4 Black
resigned. 1–0

(449) SANTASIERE, A—FINE

U.S. Championship, New York (7), 1938 (10 April)
King's Indian Attack [A07]

1. Nf3 d5 2. g3 Nf6 3. Bg2 c5 4. d4 e6 4 ... Bf5 5 c4
and White stands slightly better, for if 5 ... dxc4 6 0–0 Nc6
(or perhaps 6 ... cxd4!? 7 Nxd4 Be4 8 Qa4+ Nbd7. AW)

7 Qa4 cxd4 8 Nxd4 Qxd4 9 Bxc6+ Bd7 10 Rd1 Qxd1+ (10 ... Bxc6?! 11 Qxc6+ bxc6 12 Rxd4 with the better ending) 11 Qxd4 Bxc6 12 Nc3 and White should win, MCO 230. **5. 0–0 Qb6** Better than 5 ... Nc6 when 6 c4 would follow; if then 6 ... dxc4 7 Qa4 cxd4 8 Nxd4 Qxd4 9 Bxc6+ Bd7 10 Rd1 and so on. **6. e3** White counters Black's pressure on his d-pawn and b-pawn with his invention, a quiet system which he had already tried, with colours reversed, in games against Polland and Bernstein. **6 ... Nc6 7. b3 Be7 8. Bb2 cxd4 9. exd4 0–0 10. Nbd2 Bd7 11. c4** Voluntarily accepting an isolated pawn; far too much stress has been laid on the negative aspects of "isolani"—do chess masters realize (as Tarrasch certainly did) that an isolated pawn has its own peculiar advantages, affording open files and, as here a strong post for a knight at either e5 or c5? Isn't it about time that we discarded the isolated pawn fear complex in favour of a policy of positive realism? How full of irony chess (like everything else) can be—Fine, who is always super-careful about isolated pawns, sees to it here that his opponent gets one. Nevertheless, as the game progresses, not only does that opponent's isolated pawn become transformed into a husky e5 variety, but lo and behold! Fine, himself, is saddled with an isolated pawn and it is a strong factor in his downfall! **11 ... dxc4 12. Nxc4 Qa6** 12 ... Qc7 looks better. AW **13. Nfe5 Rfd8 14. Nxd7** The black queen's bishop, though temporarily obscured, is definitely an asset; hence, the exchange. **14 ... Nxd7** Not 14 ... Rxd7 15 Bxc6. **15. Qf3 Nf6** 15 ... Nb6 would equalize, MCO. **16. Rfd1 Nd5 17. a4** A powerful restrictive move with the strong threat of Bg2-f1. **17 ... b5?!** Possibly too bold; 17 ... b6 may have been better. **18. Ne5 Nxe5** Forced, to meet the double threat of 19 Bf1 and 19 Qxf7+. **19. dxe5 b4 20. Bf1 Qa5 21. Rac1** Fine took a long time in considering this position. He was obviously ill at ease and, to prove the point, he managed to spill a whole cup of coffee over the chessboard, causing general consternation among the spectators, and a heart attack on the part of our genial schoolmaster and tournament director. Well, the march of time was halted; the cleaning department did its level best and Fine immediately made his next move. **21 ... Rac8 22. Rxc8 Rxc8 23. Bc4** This is the point of the exchange. White threatens to win a pawn and 23 ... Nc3 is bad because of 24 Rd7 which should win. **23 ... Rd8 24. Bxd5** Seeing that Black has no knight to put on e4, White (a little regretfully breaking up his two bishops combination) takes this opportunity of giving Black an isolated pawn, going on the general principle that knights are better than bishops anyway. **24 ... Rxd5** A surprise to me; I never expected Fine to exchange the major artillery, as I felt the resulting endgame was definitely in my favour. However, with queens and rooks on the board, White still has pressure on the d-pawn and also more roaming space which should enable him to bring forth favourable kingside complications. (24 ... exd5 25 e6! fxe6 26 Qg4 Bf8 27 Qxe6+ Kh8 28 Qf7 would be disastrous for Black. AW) **25. Rxd5 Qxd5 26. Qxd5 exd5 27. Bd4 a6 28. f4 f6** A good try which not only enables a quick king approach, but also invites 29 e6 or 29 exf6, both offering Black better chances.

On 29 exf6 gxf6!, for instance Black gets his king on e6 and bishop on d6, whence if the white f-pawn move on, he can take up a strong post on e5. **29. Kf2 Kf7 30. Ke3 fxe5 31. Bxe5 g6 32. Kd4 Ke6 33. g4 Bd8** Since this move permits the entrance of the white king, 33 ... Bf8 was probably better. In that case White wins as follows: 33 ... Bf8 34 Bb8 Be7 (he must wait) 35 Ba7 Bf8 36 Bc5 Bg7+ 37 Kd3 Bc3 38 Bd4! Be1 (the exchange results in a won king and pawn ending) 39 Ke2 Bh4 40 Bc5 Be7 (forced) and the exchange of bishops again results in a won king and pawn endgame. Also, on 39 ... Bc3 (instead of 39 ... Bh4) 40 Bxc3 again results in a winning endgame, White obtaining two distant passed pawns. **34. Kc5 Be7+**

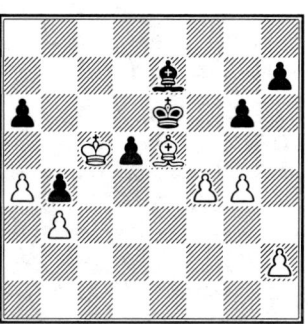

Position after Black's 34th move

35. Kd4 There was an immediate win with 35 Kb6, but I examined this line, 35 Kb6 Bd6 36 Ka5? Bxe5 37 fxe5 Kxe5 38 Kxb4 d4, and found a win for Black! It never occurred to me that White could exchange bishops—that is: 35 Kb6 Bd6 36 Bxd6! Kxd6 37 Ka5 Kc5 38 f5! d4 39 f6 d3 40 f7, and queens with check. The text again permits ... Bf8, but Fine's eye was more on the clock than on the board. **35 ... Bd8 36. f5+ gxf5 37. gxf5+ Kxf5 38. Kxd5 Kg4 39. Bd6 a5 40. Kc6 Kh3** The last move under a time limit, and according to some annotators (including Fine), a blunder. But many hours of analysis prove that term an exaggeration, for, while 40 ... h5 is doubtless somewhat better than the text, it leaves him only slim chances of a draw. The analysis: 40 ... h5! 41 Kd7 Bb6 42 Be7 Bg1! 43 h4! Bf2 44 Bd8 Bxh4 45 Bxa5 Bg3 (best). Now White may follow two different plans: (A) 46 Bd8 h4 47 Bxh4 Bxh4 48 Kc6 Kf5 49 Kb5 winning the pawn (doesn't Black draw this by 49 ... Ke6 50 Kxb4 Kd7? AW) or (B) 46 Bb6 h4 47 a5 h3 48 Bg1 Bf2 49 Bh2 Kf3 50 a6 Kg2 51 Bc7 h2 52 Bxh2 Kxh2 53 Kc8 Kg3 54 Kb7 Kf4 55 a7 Bxa7 56 Kxa7 Ke5 57 Kb6 Kd6 58 Kb5 Kc7 59 Kxb4 Kb6 and draws. In over the board play this latter analysis would have been very difficult, if not impossible, for Black to work out, the pitfalls being numerous. **41. Kd7** The sealed move and best; of course not 41 Bc7, when Black would queen first, control White's queening square and win. **41 ... Bb6 42. Be7 Kxh2 43. Kc6 Bf2 44. Kb5 Kg3 45. Kxa5 Kf4 46. Kxb4 Ke5 47. Bc5** After this important move, Black is without hope. **47 ... Be1+ 48. Kb5 Ke6 49. Kc6 h5 50. b4 h4 51. b5 Bg3 52. Bg1 h3 53. a5 Kf5** He might have tried the sly "swindle" 53 ... Bf2! 54 Bh2 Bd4 55 b6 (the only winning move—on such slender threads hang "easily won" games) Be5 and 56 Bxe5 is possible because White queens with a check. **54. b6 Ke4 55. a6 Kf3 56. a7 Kg2 57. Bc5 h2 58. a8Q h1Q 59. Kd7+ Kh2 60. Qxh1+ Kxh1 61. Bd6** Black resigned. Fine had not lost a game at Nottingham, Semmering or Hastings; his score in this tournament was 5–0 before this game; as for the game itself, there is one curious fact which proves that it was conducted on a high standard by the winner, and that is that, in all these notes, not once have I pointed out the losing move! (Aside from Black's 40th, after he had a definitely lost game.) Was there no losing move? **1–0** Santasiere in ACB 1938, 36–7.

(450) BERNSTEIN, S—FINE

U.S. Championship, New York (8), 1938 (11 April)
Queen's Gambit Declined [D43]

1. d4 Nf6 2. c4 e6 3. Nf3 d5 4. Bg5 h6 5. Bxf6 Qxf6 6. Nc3 c6 7. Qb3 Nd7 8. g3 Bd6 9. Bg2 0–0 10. 0–0 Rd8 11. Rac1 dxc4 12. Qxc4 Qe7 13. Rfd1 e5 14. Ne4 Bc7 15. dxe5 Nxe5 16. Qc5 Rxd1! 17. Rxd1 Qxc5 18. Nxc5 Nxf3+ 19. Bxf3 Kf8 20. Rd3 Bb6 21. Nd7+ Ke7 22. Nxb6 axb6 23. a3 Bf5 24. Rb3 b5 25. Kg2 Kd6 26. Rc3 Ra4 27. b4 Ra8 28. e4 Be6 29. Be2 Ke5 30. Kf3 g5 31. Ke3 g4

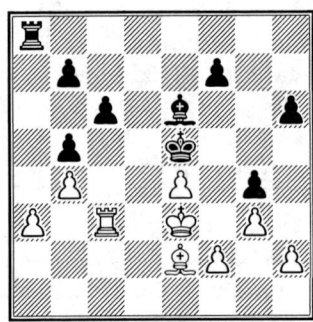

*Position after
Black's 31st move*

32. f4+?! gxf3 33. Bxf3 Bc4 34. Kd2 Rd8+ 35. Kc2 Rd6 36. Bg2 Rf6 37. Bf3 Kd4 38. Kd2 Rd6 39. Bg2 Ke5+ 40. Kc2 Rd4 41. Re3 b6 42. Bh3 c5 43. bxc5 bxc5 44. Bf5 b4 45. axb4 cxb4 46. Rf3 Rd8 47. g4 Ra8 48. Rh3 Ra2+ 49. Kc1 b3 50. Bh7 f6 51. Bf5 Rf2 52. Bh7 Kd4 53. e5 fxe5 54. Rxh6 e4 White resigned. **0–1**

(451) SIMONSON, A—FINE

U.S. Championship, New York (9), 1938 (13 April)
Catalan System [E01]

1. Nf3 d5 2. d4 Nf6 3. c4 e6 4. g3 c5 5. cxd5 Nxd5 6. Bg2 cxd4 7. 0–0 Bc5 8. Nxd4 0–0 9. Nb3 Bb6 10. Bd2 Nc6 11. Na3 a6 12. Nc4 Ba7 13. Nba5 Nxa5 14. Bxa5 Qe7 15. Rc1 Bd7 16. e4 Nf6 17. Bc7 Ne8 18. Bb6 Bxb6 19. Nxb6 Rd8 20. Qc2 Qb4 21. Qc5 Qxc5 22. Rxc5 Bb5 23. Rfc1 Rd6 24. Nc8 Rd2 25. e5 f6 26. f4 Rxb2 27. Bxb7 Rxa2 28. Nd6 Nxd6 29. exd6 Rd2 30. f5 Bd7 31. fxe6 Bxe6

32. Rc6 Rd8 33. Re1 Bd5 34. Rc7 Bxb7 35. Rxb7 R2xd6 36. Ree7 g5 37. Rg7+ Kf8 38. Rxh7 Kg8 39. h4 gxh4 40. gxh4 Rc6 Draw agreed. **½–½**

(452) FINE—MORTON, H

U.S. Championship, New York (10), 1938 (14 April)
Grünfeld Defence [D93]

1. d4 Nf6 2. c4 g6 3. Nc3 d5 4. Bf4 Bg7 5. e3 0–0 6. Qb3 c6 7. Nf3 b6 8. Be2 Bb7 9. 0–0 e6 10. Rfd1 Re8 11. Ne5 Nbd7 12. Bf3 Qe7 13. h3 Nxe5 14. Bxe5 Nd7 15. Bg3 Rac8 16. cxd5 exd5 17. e4 Nf6 18. exd5 Nxd5 19. Bxd5 cxd5 20. Nb5 Red8 21. Nxa7 Rc4 22. Nb5 Bc6 23. Na3 Rxd4 24. Qxb6 Rxd1+ 25. Rxd1 Ba8 26. Nc2 d4 27. Ne1 Re8 28. Qb5 Qe2 29. a4 d3 30. Qxd3 Qxb2 31. Qb5 Rc8 32. Nd3 Qd4 33. Re1 Bc6 34. Qa6 Qd8 35. Rc1 Bd7 36. Rxc8 Bxc8 37. Qa8 h6 38. Ne5 Bxe5 39. Bxe5 Kh7 40. a5 Qe8 41. Bc3 Qe6 42. Qb8 f6 43. Qc7+ Kg8 44. Bxf6 Qd7 45. Qg3 Kf7 46. Bc3 h5 47. Qf4+ Qf5 48. Qd4 Qb1+ 49. Kh2 Qf5 50. Bb4 Qf6 51. Qc5 Ba6 52. Qc7+ Ke8 53. Bd6 Qe6 54. Qc6+ Black resigned. **1–0**

(453) COHEN, S—FINE

U.S. Championship, New York (11), 1938 (16 April)
Caro-Kann Defence [B18]

1. e4 c6 2. d4 d5 3. Nc3 dxe4 4. Nxe4 Bf5 5. Ng3 Bg6 6. Nh3 Based on Russian analysis which is superficially attractive. The good old 6 Nf3 is better. **6 ... Nd7 7. Nf4 e5 8. Nxg6 hxg6** White has the famous two bishops, but in the process of obtaining them has given Black a useful open file and has left himself with a poorly placed knight which will play no part in the coming struggle. **9. dxe5 Qh4 10. e6** White could maintain the pawn with 10 f4 but after 10 ... 0–0–0 11 Bd2 Nh6 Black has used his open file to give him a strong attack. The text looks attractive, but the ultimate result is that it gives Black another open file. **10 ... fxe6 11. Qe2 0–0–0 12. Bd2** White can hardly go in for 12 Qxe6 Ngf6 13 Be2 Bb4+ followed by ... Rhe8 with an enormous lead in development for Black. **12 ... Ngf6 13. 0–0–0 Bc5 14. Be3?!** After this the game is lost by force. 14 f3 would still leave White with a playable game. **14 ... Ng4! 15. Bxc5 Nxc5** Already threatening 16 ... Qg5+ 17 Kb1 Rxd1+ 18 Qxd1 Nxf2. **16. c3**

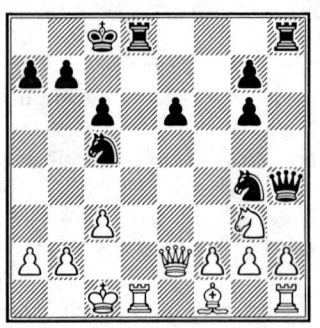

*Position after
White's 16th move*

16 ... Rxd1+ Up to this point the game followed L. Steiner–Opočenský, Łódź 1935. The latter was concluded in the following manner [at this point Reinfeld quoted moves 16–40 of a completely different game, beginning with 16 ... Rad8] 16 ... Qg5+ 17 Kc2 Rxd1 18 Kxd1 Rf8! 19 f4 Rxf4 20 Ke1 Rf2 21 Qd1 Qe3+ 22 Be2 Rxe2+ 0–1. Fine also competed in this tourney, which explains his familiarity with this line of play. The method chosen by him is somewhat less forceful—but quite adequate. (correction by Peter Lahde) 17. Kxd1 Rd8+ 18. Kc2 Nxf2 19. b4 If 19 Qxf2 Qa4+ 20 b3 Qxa2+ 21 Ke1 Nxb3 mate. 19 ... Nxh1 20. Nxh1 Ne4 21. Qe3 Qg4 22. Kb2 Qd1! 23. Qxe4 Rd2+ 24. Ka3 Qc1+ 25. Kb3 Qb2+ White resigned. The conclusion would be 26 Kc4 Qxa2+ 27 Kc5 Rd5+ with mate on the next move. 0–1 Reinfeld, *CCLA Bulletin*, May-June 1938 in Lahde 2001, 43–4.

(454) POLLAND, D—FINE

U.S. Championship, New York (12), 1938 (17 April)
Queen's Gambit Declined, Semi-Tarrasch [D41]

1. c4 c5 2. Nf3 Nf6 3. d4 e6 4. Nc3 d5 5. cxd5 Nxd5 6. e4 Nxc3 7. bxc3 cxd4 8. cxd4 Bb4+ 9. Bd2 Bxd2+ 10. Qxd2 0–0 11. Bc4 Nc6 12. 0–0 b6 13. Rac1 Bb7 14. Qe3 Qe7 15. Rfd1 Rfd8 16. Bd3 Rac8 17. h3 h6 18. Bb1 Rc7 19. Rc3 Rcd7 20. a3 b5 21. Kh2 a5 22. e5 Na7 23. Be4 b4 24. axb4 axb4 25. Rb3 Bxe4 26. Qxe4 Nb5 27. Rd2 Nc3 28. Qg4 Ra7 29. Rdb2 Nd5 30. Ne1 Qg5 31. Qxg5 hxg5 32. Nc2 Rb7 33. Ne3 Ne7 Draw agreed. ½–½

(455) FINE—KASHDAN, I

U.S. Championship, New York (13), 1938 (18 April)
Catalan System [E06]

The preparation of MCO led to a considerable deepening of my knowledge of openings, which I put to particularly good use in the A.V.R.O. tournament. In the United States championship of 1938 I was able to obtain a winning advantage against Kashdan fairly easily because of his faulty opening play. 1. d4 Nf6 2. c4 e6 3. Nf3 d5 4. g3 The Catalan System, which was one of my favourites in the period 1938–42. In effect White is playing a Grünfeld Defence in reverse. There are so many transpositional possibilities that it requires a very thorough knowledge of the openings to play it properly. 4 ... Be7 More aggressive is 4 ... c5; but Kashdan was always a cautious player. 5. Bg2 0–0 6. 0–0 c5 6 ... b6 7 cxd5 Nxd5 8 e4 Nf6 9 Nc3 Bb7 10 Ne5 c5 11 d5! with advantage to White, Ragozin–Rabinovich, Leningrad 1934, MCO 227. 7. cxd5 Nxd5 7 ... exd5 is weak, since it transposes into the disadvantageous Tarrasch Defence in the Queen's Gambit Declined, MCO. 8. e4 Nb6 It is difficult to find a thoroughly satisfactory square for this knight; on 8 ... Nf6 9 Nc3 Nc6 10 d5 Nb4 11 Ne5 is strong. 9. Nc3 cxd4

If, instead, 9 ... Nc6 (as he may have originally intended) 10 dxc5 Qxd1 11 Rxd1 Bxc5 12 Nb5 Bd7 13 Nd6 with a strong initiative, for example, 13 ... Rab8 14 Bf4. 10. Nxd4 Bf6 In MCO Fine suggested 10 ... Nc6! 11 Nxc6 (11 Be3? Nc4!) bxc6 12 Qe2 e5 13 Be3 Be6 14 Rfd1 Qc7 15 Racl Qb7 with an even game. AW 11. Ndb5! Because 11 Be3 can be met by 11 ... Nc4. 11 ... Nc6 12. Be3 White must play accurately, otherwise his advantage will slip away. 12 ... Nc4 13. Bc5 Qxd1 14. Raxd1 Rd8 He cannot afford to play 14 ... Nxb2 15 Rb1 Rd8 (or 15 ... a6 16 Nc7) 16 Rxb2 a6 because of 17 Nc7. 15. Rxd8+ Bxd8 16. b3 White has a distinct superiority, MCO. 16 ... Bb6 If 16 ... Nb6 17 Rd1 and Black is all tied up. 17. Na4! Bxc5 18. Nxc5 N4e5 19. f4 Nd7 As is natural, he seeks exchanges. 20. Nxd7 Bxd7 21. Rd1

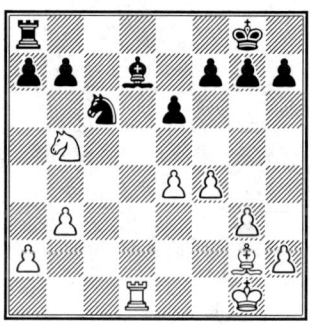

*Position after
White's 21st move*

21 ... Be8 It was essential to foresee that this move would be forced. If, instead, 21 ... Rd8 22 e5 (threatening 23 Bxc6) a6 23 Bxc6 bxc6 24 Na7 winning just about everything. 22. Nd6 Rb8 There is no way to avoid this purely defensive move. If 22 ... Rd8 23 Bf3 b6 24 Nxe8 Rxe8 25 e5 is decisive. 23. e5 Kf8 24. a3 Ke7 25. b4 a6 26. Rc1 Threatening to win a pawn with Nxe8 and Bxc6 (after preparation). 26 ... f6 27. Rc5! Not immediately 27 Nxe8 Rxe8 28 Bxc6 because of 28 ... Rc8. 27 ... fxe5 28. fxe5 Black cannot now save his pawn. If 28 ... Nxe5 29 Nxe8 Nd7 30 Nxg7 wins. 28 ... Bd7

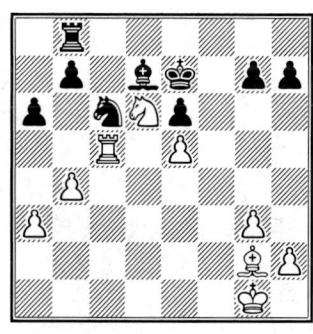

*Position after
Black's 28th move*

29. Nxb7! With the loss of this pawn Black's whole position collapses. 29 ... Rxb7 30. Bxc6 Rc7 Hoping for 31 Bxd7 Rxc5 32 bxc5 Kxd7 and White actually loses. But the trap is easily avoided. 31. Be4 Rxc5 32. bxc5 h6

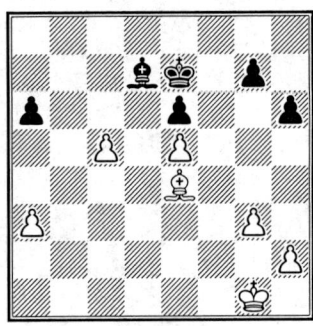

*Position after
Black's 32nd move*

33. Kf2 It seems impossible for White's king to break through to the black pawn on the queenside, but it is this plan that leads to a win. The readers of *Shakhmaty v SSSR* found an alternative winning plan: 33 c6 Bc8 34 a4 a5 (otherwise 35 a5) 35 Bd3! Kd8 36 Kf2 Kf7 37 Bb5 Kb6 38 Ke3 Kc5 39 Ke4. A&Ch **33 ... Kd8 34. Ke3 Kc7 35. Kd4** The king has been centralized, but that is not the aim of its journey. It has to approach the black a-pawn. A&Ch **35 ... a5** After 36 Kd4 Black would all the same have been forced to play this, in view of the threat of 37 Kb4. A&Ch **36. Bd3** White begins improving the position of his bishop, which has to help the king penetrate to b5. A&Ch **36 ... Be8 37. Bc4 Bd7 38. Bb3!** This forces Black's reply, since on 38 ... Kb7 there follows 39 c6+! Bxc6 (39 ... Kxc6 40 Ba4+ Kc7 41 Bxd7 Kxd7 42 Kc5, with a won pawn ending) 40 Bxe6 Kc7 41 Kc5, with an easy win. A&Ch **38 ... Bc8 39. Ba4! Bb7** Averbakh and Chekhover demonstrate that Black could have put up greater resistance by 39 ... Ba6! when White must sacrifice his passed pawn to free a path for his king: 40 c6! Kb6! 41 c7! Bc8 42 Be8 Kxc7 43 Kc5 ("By the pawn sacrifice White has improved further the position of his king") Ba6 44 Ba4 g5 45 Bb3 Bc8 46 Kb5 Bd7+ 47 Kxa5 ("Thus White has achieved his aim: he has exchanged his c-pawn for the a-pawn. The way for the white king is open, and the rest does not cause any difficulty.") Kb7 48 Ba4 Bc8 49 Kb5 Bd7+ 50 Kb4 Bc8 51 Kc5 Kc7 52 Bb3 Bd7 53 a4 Bc8 54 a5 Bd7 55 a6 Bc8 56 Bc4 Bd7 57 Bb5 Bc8 and wins. **40. Kc4 Ba6+ 41. Bb5 Bb7 42. Kb3** Black resigned. The a-pawn must fall and there is no ghost of counterplay. **1–0** Fine 1958, 145–9; Fine 1941, 151; Averbakh & Chekhover 88–9.

(456) HANAUER, M–FINE

U.S. Championship, New York (14), 1938 (20 April)
English Symmetrical Opening, Rubinstein Variation [A34]

1. c4 Nf6 2. Nf3 c5 3. g3 The better course here is to play 3 d4 and allow the game to transpose in a queen pawn opening. MH **3 ... d5 4. cxd5 Nxd5 5. Bg2 Nc6 6. 0–0 e5** Turning the game into a Dragon Variation with colours reversed. Query: is White's extra move of value? MH **7. Nc3 Nc7 8. d3 Be7 9. Be3 0–0 10. Rc1 Be6 11. a3** Seemingly strong for it threatens 12 Na4 b6 13 b4! But Black plays to the point. MH **11 ... b6 12. Nh4 Nd5 13. Nf5 Bf6 14. Be4 Rc8 15. Qd2** A pretty collection

of pieces in the centre!—but this move is not accurate. MH **15 ... Nd4 16. Bxd4 exd4 17. Nxd5 Bxd5 18. Qf4** Trap: 18 ... Bg5? 19 Qe5. MH **18 ... Re8** Trap: 19 Nd6 Be5 and neither 20 Bxh7+ Kf8! nor 20 Qf5 Qxd6 amounts to anything for White. MH **19. Rc2?** More in keeping with the play thus far was 19 Qg4. MH **19 ... Bxe4** With this move Black emphasizes his control of the centre and begins play on the kingside. His only difficulty is clock trouble (15 minutes left for 20 moves), which explains to some extent his 24th move. MH **20. dxe4 Rc6 21. Rd1 Rce6** Black forces f3 so that White cannot retreat Nf5-e3 because of ... Bg5. MH **22. f3 g6 23. Nh6+ Kg7 24. h4 Qb8?!** A stunning lapse of concentration. Black can win at least two pawns with 24 ... Be5. White is lost after either 25 Qxf7+ Kxh6 26 f4 R8e7 or 25 Nxf7 Bxf4 26 Nxd8 Be3+!. Following the game, Fine explained that he failed to notice the elementary capture 25 ... Kxh6. AD **25. Qxb8 Rxb8 26. Ng4 Be7 27. Nf2 Bd6 28. f4 Be7 29. Kg2 Rd8 30. Kf3 Rc6 31. e3 dxe3 32. Rxd8 Bxd8 33. Kxe3 b5?!** White's king is about to become very active, and a more circumspect move is 33 ... Kf6. AD **34. e5 c4 35. Kd4! c3!** Black is fighting for a draw. AD **36. bxc3 Be7 37. Ne4 Bxa3 38. Ra2 Rc4+ 39. Kd3 Ra4 40. Nd6 a6 41. Kc2** The sealed move. Everyone expected 41 c4, but after 41 ... Bb4 Black has chances because of the fact that White's kingside pawns are on dark squares and White's king can't leave the a-pawn too soon. MH **41 ... Kf8 42. g4** Off dark squares. MH **42 ... f6** A better try is 42 ... h5!. AD **43. Nc8** Threatens 44 Nb6 Ra5 45 Kb3. MH **43 ... Bc5?** The last chance to put up a tough fight was 43 ... Rxf4 44 Rxa3 fxe5 45 Rxa6 b4 46 cxb4 Rxb4 47 Ra7. AD **44. Rxa4 bxa4 45. exf6 Be3 46. c4 Bxf4 47. c5 g5!?** Black cannot run after the h-pawn: 47 ... Bg3 48 c6 Bxh4 49 c7 Bg3 50 Nd6. MH **48. hxg5 Bxg5 49. c6 Bf4 50. Ne7 Kf7 51. Nd5 Bh2 52. g5 Be5 53. Kb1 Bh2 54. Kb2 Bd6 55. Ka2 Kg6** Zugzwang! If 55 ... Ke6 56 c7 and White recaptures with check, thereby spoiling Black's plan of ... Bxc7 and ... h6 dissolving all the pawns. MH **56. Ne7+ Kf7 57. Nf5 Bc7 58. Ka3 Kg6 59. Kxa4 Kf7** The knight is immune because of 60 f7 Bd6 61 c7. MH **60. Kb3** Now the king comes over to the kingside and the end is near. Strangely enough, Black can never play ... h5 while the knight is on f5 because of gxh6 *en passant*, Kxf7 h7! MH **60 ... a5 61. Ka4 Bd8 62. Kb5 Ke6 63. Kc4 Kf7 64. Kd5 Bb6 65. Nd6+ Kf8 66. Ke6 a4 67. Nc4 Bc7 68. Ne5** Black resigned. If 68 ... a3 69 Nd7+ K moves 70 f7+. If 68 ... Bxe5 White queens a move earlier with check. MH **1–0** Milton Hanauer in *The Chess Review* 1938, 137–8; Denker & Parr, 123–4; Fine 1941, 252.

(457) FINE–TREYSMAN, G

U.S. Championship, New York (15), 1938 (21 April)
Bogolyubov Indian Defence [E11]

1. d4 Nf6 2. c4 e6 3. Nf3 Bb4+ Bogolyubov's move, which is in some disrepute as a result of the generally unfavourable results achieved with it. No matter how Black plays, he seems to run into a position which is not very promising, except from a strictly defensive point of view. **4. Bd2 Bxd2+ 5. Qxd2** As is known, this is far more effective than taking with the queen's knight. This is due to the fact that at c3 the queen's knight commands d5, and may often be planted there effectively after Black has played ... d6 and ... e5. **5 ... 0–0** It would be more accurate to play the moves in the following order: 5 ... b6 6 g3 Bb7 7 Bg2 d6 (if 7 ... 0–0 8 Nc3 Ne4 9 Qc2 Nxc3? 10 Ng5!) 8 0–0 (if 8 Nc3 Ne4 9 Qc2 Nxc3 is quite playable) 0–0 9 Nc3 Ne4 10 Qc2 Nxc3 (if now 11 Ng5 Nxe2+). The point of the above is that Black's chief problem is control of e4, at least in such a way he can exchange and thus free his cramped position a bit; Black's last move is irrelevant to this problem. **6. Nc3** If now 6 ... b6 7 g3 Bb7 8 Bg2 and because of his premature castling, Black already finds himself in an inferior variation, since 8 ... Ne4 9 Qc2 is not good for him (see the previous note). **6 ... d6 7. g3 b6** At his previous move Black may have been thinking about playing 7 ... Nc6 8 Bg2 e5. This was doubtless his best chance of obtaining a playable game. **8. Bg2 Bb7 9. Qc2** Preventing 9 ... Ne4 and at the same time preparing e2-e4. **9 ... Nbd7 10. 0–0 Re8 11. e4 e5 12. Rad1** Now we are in a position to appraise the effects of Black's opening play. None of his pieces are placed effectively, and there is no possible plan available which offers a constructive goal. **12 ... exd4** The above considerations lead Black to take the only course remaining in such positions: giving up the centre in order to be able to post his knights on the pre-empted squares. But his lack of terrain makes it impossible for him to maintain these pieces at their new posts. **13. Nxd4 Ne5 14. b3 Nfd7 15. Nd5** Compare the note to White's fifth move. This knight can be removed only by ... c6, which weakens Black's pawn position and obstructs his bishop's diagonal, or by exchange for a black piece—whereupon White retakes with his c-pawn, exerting pressure along the c-file on the backward c-pawn. **15 ... a5** See the note to Black's 12th move. The text inaugurates an abortive attempt to maintain a knight at c5. **16. a3 Nc5 17. f4 Ng4 18. Rfe1 c6** The significance of this move has already been made clear. The qualitative difference between the two positions is well expressed in the fact that whereas Black's last move is weakening, White's 17th move (which has precisely the same function!) greatly strengthens his game. **19. Nc3 Qc7 20. h3 Nf6 21. b4** All according to schedule. **21 ... Ne6**

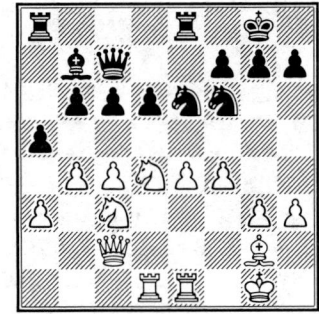

Position after Black's 21st move

22. Ndb5! A fine sacrifice based on positional considerations. **22 ... cxb5 23. Nxb5 Qe7 24. Nxd6** The probable results of the sacrifice are already beginning to make themselves noticeable. White has two pawns for the piece, and can win the exchange if he wants to. He has a pawn preponderance in the centre and on the queenside, and the helpless black pieces offer convenient targets for the steady advance of the pawns. **24 ... Nh5 25. f5 Nf8 26. Qf2** White is content to increase the pressure, rather than collect immediate dividends. **26 ... Bc6 27. b5?** A transposition of moves that might have had fatal results. Correct was 27 Nxe8! with the following possibilities: (a) 27 ... Bxe8 28 g4 Nf6 29 e5, (b) 27 ... Qxe8 28 b5 Bb7 (or d7) 29 g4 Nf6 30 e5, (c) 27 ... Rxe8 28 g4 Nf6 29 e5. In every variation White wins a piece, remaining with a winning advantage. **27 ... Red8 28. g4 Rxd6 29. Rxd6 Qxd6 30. e5 Qxa3?** For now Black could have played 30 ... Qh6! 31 Bxc6 Nf4 or 31 bxc6 Nf4 retaining his piece to the good. **31. bxc6 Ng3 32. e6!** The most accurate move. AW **32 ... fxe6 33. fxe6 Ng6 34. Qf7+ Kh8 35. e7 Qc5+ 36. Qf2!** Immediately decisive. **36 ... Qxf2+ 37. Kxf2 Re8 38. c7** Black resigned. **1–0** Fred Reinfeld, *BCM* 1938, 368–70.

(458) FINE—DAKE, A

U.S. Championship, New York (16), 1938 (23 April)
Catalan System [E02]

1. d4 Nf6 2. c4 e6 3. Nf3 d5 4. g3 dxc4 The most usual reply. **5. Qa4+ Nbd7 6. Bg2 a6 7. Nc3** Better than recapturing the pawn at once, since Black must now wait some time before he can play ... b5. **7 ... c5 8. 0–0 Be7 9. dxc5 Bxc5** If 9 ... 0–0 10 c6 b5 11 Qc2 Nc5 12 Rd1 Qb6 13 a4 b4 14 a5 with a distinct advantage, MCO 228. **10. Qxc4 b5 11. Qh4 Bb7 12. Bg5** Up to this point the game is identical with the sixteenth game of the recent Alekhine–Euwe match, the famous Comedy of Errors. **12 ... b4** Euwe played 12 ... 0–0 but 13 Rad1 gave Alekhine a strong attack. Dake's move is a novelty. **13. Na4 Be7 14. Rfd1 Qa5** If instead 14 ... 0–0 15 Ne5! Bxg2 16 Nxd7 Bd5 17 Ndb6 Rb8 18 e4 and wins. **15. b3 Rd8** And now 15 ... 0–0? would have been refuted by 16 Rxd7. **16. Nb2 Nb6** The alternative 16 ... 0–0 was safer, even though Black's position would have remained cramped. **17. Rxd8+ Bxd8 18. Nd3** White stands slightly better, MCO. **18 ... Be7 19. Bd2 Ne4?!** This loses a pawn, but there were no attractive alternatives, for example, if 19 ... Nfd5 20 Qd4 0–0 21 a3 bxa3 22 b4 (now 22 ... Qb5 threatening ... Bf6, ... Rc8 and ... Na4 looks alright for Black. AW) and if 19 ... Nbd5 20 a3 Nc3 21 Bxc3 bxc3 22 Qc4. Relatively best was 19 ... Bxf3. **20. Qxe7+ Kxe7 21. Bxb4+ Qxb4 22. Nxb4 Nc3 23. Nd4 Nbd5** (see diagram) **24. Bxd5** The simplest. If 24 ... Bxd5 25 Rc1 Rc8 26 Nc6+ wins easily. **24 ... Nxd5 25. Nxd5+ Bxd5 26. Rc1 Kd6 27. f3 f5 28. Kf2 Rb8 29. Ke3 g6 30. f4 Rg8 31. Nf3 Ra8 32. Ng5 a5** Or 32 ... Ra7 33 Kd4 h6 34 e4! **33. Nxh7 a4 34. bxa4 Rxa4 35. Nf8 Rxa2 36. Nxg6 Ra8**

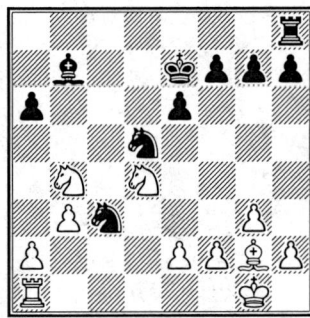

*Position after
Black's 23rd move*

37. Ne5 Ra3+ 38. Kf2 Ra7 39. h4 Rh7 40. Rc8
Black resigned. **1–0** Fine in *The Chess Review* 1938, 139–40.

(459) FINE—RESHEVSKY, S

U.S. Championship, New York (17), 1938 (23 April)
Nimzowitsch-Indian Defence, Spielmann Variation [E22]

1. d4 Nf6 2. c4 e6 3. Nc3 Bb4 4. Qb3 Nc6 5. Nf3
5 e3 a5 6 Bd2 (6 a3 Fine–Reshevsky, 1934) e5 7 d5 Ne7
8 Bd3 d6 9 Nge2 Nd7 10 Qd1 Nc5 11 Bc2 Bg4 with an even
game, Ståhlberg–Nimzowitsch, match game 7, 1934. **5 ... a5**
A new idea in the Milner-Barry Variation of the Nimzowitsch Defence. Its point is that it takes advantage of the vulnerable position of the queen on b3 to establish an outpost
for the knight. BCM; 5 ... d5 6 Bg5 h6 7 Bxf6 Qxf6 8 e3
dxc4 9 Bxc4 0–0 10 0–0 Qe7 11 Qc2 Bd6 12 Rad1 Kh8
with equality, Emms, NCO 471. **6. a3 a4 7. Qc2 Bxc3+
8. Qxc3 h6 9. d5** A vigorous continuation; but the
simpler 9 Qc2 threatening e2-e4 and preventing ... Nc6-a5
would have given White a more lasting hold on the position. BCM **9 ... exd5 10. cxd5 Na5 11. d6** An interesting temporary pawn sacrifice. If instead 11 e4 0–0 and Black
will get the better game by ... Re8. BCM **11 ... cxd6 12. Bf4
0–0 13. Rd1** Not 13 Bxd6 because of 13 ... Ne4. BCM
13 ... Re8 14. e3 Ne4 Black has equalized the game,
MCO 187. **15. Qc2 Nb3 16. Bc4 Qa5+** A strong move
which prevents White from castling. BCM **17. Kf1 b6
18. Kg1 Ba6 19. Rd5 Nbc5 20. h3** Fine deliberated for
three quarters of an hour. He was obviously in a quandary
and was seen frequently to shake his head, loosening the
hair on his forehead. When he made his 20th move he had
1 hour 53 minutes on his clock with 21 moves to go before
reaching the time control. 21 moves in 7 minutes! Reshevsky
had 30 minutes to spare. Asked what he thought of the
game Marshall said "Fine's all right—if he finally gets his
rook out." Simonson said Fine had a lost game. *Chess* **20 ...
Bxc4 21. Qxc4 b5! 22. Qd4** Simonson gave 22 Qe2 at
once. The sequence of moves now came in rapid fire order,
Fine played sometimes with one hand on the clock and the
other moving the pieces. *Chess* **22 ... Nb3 23. Qd3
Nbc5 24. Qe2 b4** Now Black has definitely the better
position. White has to spend a tempo getting his rooks
united and in addition Black has a menacing position on
the queenside. However, White will get some compensation
in the eventual isolation of the d-pawn. BCM **25. axb4**

**Qxb4 26. Bxd6 Nxd6 27. Rxd6 Rab8 28. Rd2
Ne4 29. Rc2 Rec8 30. Kh2 Rxc2 31. Qxc2 d5**
Reshevsky offered a draw since this was sufficient to win
the championship, but he has something very like a
winning position! BCM; Reshevsky said afterwards he
might have played for a win. Fine, who still had nine
moves to make in a single minute before reaching the time
control, remarked he had got everything possible out of the
pawn sac. There was no win he said. After 32 Ra1 White
probably has to shed a pawn but preserves good fighting
chances of a draw. *Chess* ½–½ *Chess* 1937-8, 320; BCM
1938, 246–7.

Marshall CC—Manhattan CC,
May 21, 1938

The two premiere clubs of New York had finished their
Metropolitan League schedules tied for first place, so a
return match was arranged to decide the outcome of the
contest. Unfortunately I have seen no report of the result
of the match.

Horowitz   0   Fine   1

(460) HOROWITZ, I—FINE

Manhattan–Marshall return match, New York, 1938 (21 May)
Spanish Game, Worrall Attack [C86]

**1. e4 e5 2. Nf3 Nc6 3. Bb5 a6 4. Ba4 Nf6 5. 0–0
Be7 6. Qe2 d6 7. c3 0–0 8. d4 Bd7 9. Bb3 exd4
10. cxd4 Na5 11. Bc2 Bb5 12. Bd3 Bxd3 13. Qxd3
d5 14. e5 Ne4 15. Nc3 Nxc3 16. Qxc3 Nc6 17. Be3
Qd7 18. Rac1 Rac8 19. Qd3 f5 20. Qb3 Nd8
21. Bg5 Bxg5 22. Nxg5 h6 23. e6 Qe7 24. Nh3
Nxe6 25. Qxb7 Qd7 26. Qb4 Rb8 27. Qc3 Qa4
28. Rfe1 Rf6**

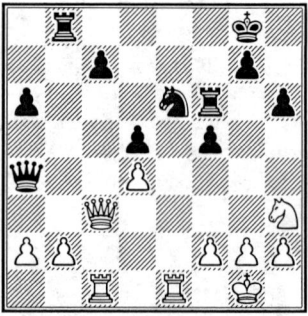

*Position after
Black's 28th move*

**29. b3 Qxa2 30. Re3 f4 31. Rd3 Qa3 32. Ra1 Qd6
33. f3 c5 34. dxc5 Nxc5 35. Rdd1 Nxb3 36. Rab1
Rb5 37. Nf2 Qb6 38. Qc8+ Rf8 39. Qc3 Nd4
40. Qd3 Ne2+ 41. Kf1 Nc3 42. Rxb5 Qxb5 43. Ra1
Rb8 44. g3 fxg3 45. hxg3 a5 46. Qxb5 Rxb5
47. Nd3 a4 48. Ke1 d4 49. Kd2 a3 50. Kc2 a2
51. Nc1 Rb1 52. Nb3 Rxa1 53. Nxa1 h5 54. Kd3
Kf7 55. Nb3 g5** White resigned. **0–1**

At the time of the A.V.R.O. tournament of 1938

Chess 14 June, 1938, 337, announced that Flohr had arranged practice matches with Keres and Ryumin as part of his training for a match for the World Championship, for which contracts had been signed—the event to have taken place in autumn of 1939. It was to be a peripatetic match in Czechoslovakia.

The Great A.V.R.O. "Candidates" Tournament, 1938

Fine's fourth, and final, European expedition as a professional chess player was undertaken in order to fulfill a contract with the Dutch broadcasting company A.V.R.O. In fact Fine wanted to pull out of the event but he was prevented from doing so. His long lay off from chess seemed to have done him a great deal of good, and his decision to switch from his usual queen-pawn opening to the king's

pawn turned out to be an excellent choice at the beginning. Following a couple of reverses against Keres and Reshevsky, however, he switched back to 1 d4 against Euwe, and promptly lost from a position he knew well. Nevertheless, his second place, on tiebreak, ahead of the strongest players in the world was well deserved.

Practice Game with Max Euwe, Bergen-aan-Zee, October 30, 1938

A week before the start of what was to be one of the strongest tournaments ever held, Fine played a warm-up game with the man for whom he was working as a second exactly a year earlier. The former World Champion held off a strong attack to register the win.

Euwe   1   Fine   0

(461) EUWE, M—FINE

Practice game, Bergen-aan-Zee, 1938 (30 Oct.)
Grünfeld Defence [D96]

1. d4 Nf6 2. c4 g6 3. Nc3 d5 Fine had only rarely used the Grünfeld before, though it was part of his armoury earlier in the year in the Metropolitan League and in the U.S. Championship. 4. Nf3 Bg7 5. Qb3 c6 6. cxd5!? cxd5 7. Bg5 Assessed by Khalifman as "slight advantage to White" in *Mikhail Botvinnik Games I 1924-1948* Soloviov (ed) 2000.
7 ... Nc6 8. e3 e6 9. Be2 0–0 10. 0–0 h6 11. Bh4 g5 12. Bg3 Nh5 13. Na4 f5 14. Ne1 Nxg3 15. hxg3 A game Keres–Frydman, Buenos Aires Olympiad 1939, developed along similar lines, with the difference that White's light-squared bishop stood on d3. 15 ... f4 16. gxf4 gxf4 17. Nf3 Qd6 18. Nc5 b6 19. Nd3 fxe3 20. fxe3 Bd7 21. Nf4 Rxf4! 22. exf4 Qxf4 23. Kh1 Rf8?! 23 ... Nxd4!? 24 Nxd4 Qxd4 25 Rac1 with an obscure position. 24. Bb5 Na5 25. Qd3 Bxb5 26. Qxb5 Nc4 26 ... Bxd4!? 27 Rae1 is unclear. 27. Qd7 Ne3?! 27 ... Qe4!? 28 Rae1 Ne3 again is unclear. 28. Qxe6+ Kh8 29. Ne5 Qh4+ 30. Kg1 Rxf1+ 31. Rxf1 Qe4 32. Nf7+ Kg8 33. Nxh6+ Kh7 34. Qxe4+ dxe4 35. Nf5 Nxf1 36. Kxf1 Bf6 37. Ke2 Kg6 38. g4 Bg5 39. Nd6 Bc1 40. b3 Kg5 41. Nxe4+ Kxg4 42. Kd3 Bf4 43. Kc4 Kf3 44. Nc3 Bh2 45. b4 Bc7 46. b5 Bd6 47. Nd5 Ke4 48. Nf6+ Ke3 49. Kd5 Be7 50. Ng4+ Kd3 51. Ne5+ Kc3 52. Nc6 Bf6 53. a4 Bg7 54. Kd6 Black resigned. 1–0

A.V.R.O., "Candidates Tournament," November 6–27, 1938

The culmination of Fine's career in Europe was the great tournament organized by the Dutch organization Algemeene Vereeniging voor Radio Omroep (General Association for Radio Broadcasting). The event brought together

In nine meetings with Alexander Alekhine (World Champion 1927–1935 and 1937–1946) Fine won three times and lost twice. This win with the black pieces took him to a score of 5½ in the first 6 rounds at A.V.R.O. 1938. The official FIDE challenger Salo Flohr looks on.

Ian eight strongest players of the day for a double-round, peripatetic tournament. The company planned to use the tournament to determine a challenger for a World Championship title match in 1939 or 1940. Alekhine declared at the time that he would not be bound by the result of the event, but was willing to meet any master of the required standing with financial backing. Nevertheless, the winner would be the most credible candidate, and would have the necessary financial and logistical backing, in what was an extremely close-matched group at the time. Such was the determination of the A.V.R.O. to ensure that a match would take place that they not only organized the event and promised to provide the purse, but they also decided that a tie-break system would be put into operation in the event of two or more players ending on the same highest score. This way there would be no delay caused by the necessity to hold a play off. Play was from 6 P.M. to 11 P.M. each week day, and from mid-day to 5 P.M. each Sunday. Adjourned games being allocated to the eight vacant dates. According to *Chess Life* October 1984, Fine shared the first prize of $1,200 with Keres.

The first cycle began in Amsterdam, the opening round seeing Fine take the sole lead immediately. He defeated Botvinnik, who later wrote that Fine played superbly, varying from his normal queen's pawn opening. All the other games in this round were drawn. The second round, at 's-Gravenhage, was highly significant for Reuben: he won his first game from American rival Reshevsky, to retain his lead, while Dr. Euwe moved up to second by defeating the unfortunate Salo Flohr. (The night of the 9 and 10 November 1938, the night of the rest day after the second round, was Kristallnacht.) The action moved to Rotterdam for round 3, Capablanca drew from a lost position, but Reuben retained the lead as Euwe was beaten by the World Champion. Round 4, Groningen, and Fine faced his friend Dr. Euwe; excellent defence in a slightly inferior position

led to a favourable ending, and another full point for the American. At Zwolle Fine demolished Flohr in an energetically conducted game. "At the end of the fifth round Dr. Tartakower, who reported the tournament in *De Telegraaf*, asked Fine to reveal the "secret of his success" in obtaining 4½ points out of a possible 5. Reuben ascribes his remarkable results to:

"1. The theoretical knowledge obtained through his work on a new textbook on the openings which will shortly be published.

"2. Abstinence from tournament play during the last 6 months. He felt he had too much of it in the previous 2 years.

"3. Forcefully withdrawing himself from the enchantment of chess, thus regaining inner restfulness. Earlier this year he had decided to give up chess as a profession and complete his studies in mathematics. Last May he had asked the A.V.R.O. committee to release him, but was forced to live up to his contractual agreement to play. (The same thing happened to Spielmann at Semmering in 1926. He really did not care to play but won first prize!)

"4. Playing 1 e4 in the first game against Botvinnik. This was selected more by intuition than by reason, and was psychologically in line with the above because it forced him to deal with new and less familiar situations and thus removed overrating and under-estimation of both himself and his opponent from his calculations.

"5. *He had much less to lose than his opponents and this he believes is the main reason for his success.*" (Translated by J. B. Snethlage for *The Chess Review*)

Haarlem, round 6, and Reuben played an astute psychological battle with Dr. Alekhine, who eventually over-reached himself, allowing Fine to move to 5½ out of 6 against the cream of the world's chess talent. It was clear that Leiden's seventh round meeting between the two youngest players, who were leading the competition, would be crucial. Even a draw would have left Fine one and a half points clear at the end of the first cycle. Unfortunately for Reuben his opponent showed his great knowledge of the open game and his talent in finding tactical solutions. Reuben retained the lead in the tournament, but it was only by the narrowest margin.

The second cycle began in Utrecht with a solid draw against Botvinnik, who appeared to have no particular idea in the open game he encountered. In round 10, Arnhem, disaster struck for Fine in the adjournment session. In the opening session Reshevsky had refuted Fine's opening play and generated a significant advantage on the queenside, making a strong advance with an a-pawn on the fortieth move. Reshevsky had two other adjourned games to continue before resuming against Fine. Having completed these games the tournament committee scheduled the third, and summoned Fine from his afternoon rest. Prins, writing twelve years later ('Time Trouble!', BCM 1950, 399) recalled that Fine "turned up sleepy and infuriated and proceeded to struggle exasperatedly against the man who had been his arch-rival for years. In the end, both sides running utterly short of time, he managed to hold his own in an apparently critical position and was in the act of making the move that would secure the draw when both flags appeared to have dropped. 'You are too late' hissed Fine before the management could interfere. 'You are' the other snarled back. The referee had witnessed Fine's flag drop first and proclaimed his decision accordingly: win for Reshevsky." It would be interesting to read a direct contemporary account of this incident, after all if both flags were down and Fine had not struck his clock having made the last move, then Reshevsky cannot have completed his previous move. Did Fine press the button on the clock and then both hands fall practically simultaneously? Whatever the case Fine must have come within a split second of a likely undivided first place. In any event, following round 10 in Breda, another hair-raising game with Capablanca, in which it was the Cuban's turn to miss the win, Fine found himself tied with Keres a full point ahead of Botvinnik and a further half point ahead of Alekhine, Capablanca and Reshevsky. Round 11, Rotterdam, and Fine dropped out of first place, he lost to Euwe, Keres drew with Reshevsky and Botvinnik won a famous victory over Capablanca. In the next round, held at 's-Gravenhage, Keres and Fine drew, with Alekhine and Flohr respectively, but the Soviet player was knocked back by a loss to Euwe. In the penultimate round, in Leiden, Fine made up lost ground when he became the only player to inflict a 2–0 defeat on any of his opponents, no less a player than World Champion Alekhine, while the other games were all drawn. Going into the final round at Amsterdam, a draw would be sufficient for the two youngest players to divide first prize. After eleven moves by White a critical position arose. Fine solved his opening problems efficiently (though knowing the tie-break would favour Keres perhaps he should have tried a Sicilian) and peace was soon concluded. The first and second prizes were shared, but in accordance with the agreed tie-break system Keres was declared the winner of the event.

		1	2	3	4	5	6	7	8	
1	Keres	**	1½	½½	½½	1½	½½	1½	½½	8½
2	Fine	0½	**	1½	10	10	11	½½	1½	8½
3	Botvinnik	½½	0½	**	½0	1½	1½	½1	½½	7½
4	Euwe	½½	01	½1	**	0½	0½	01	1½	7
5	Reshevsky	0½	01	0½	1½	**	½½	½½	1½	7
6	Alekhine	½½	00	0½	1½	½½	**	½1	½1	7
7	Capablanca	0½	½½	½0	10	½½	½0	**	½1	6
8	Flohr	½½	0½	½½	½0	0½	½0	½0	**	4½

(462) FINE—BOTVINNIK, M

A.V.R.O., The Netherlands (1), 1938 (6 Nov., Amsterdam)
French Defence, Winawer Variation [C17]

1. e4 Before this tournament I was known as a 1 d4 player, hence my first move must have come as somewhat of a surprise to Botvinnik. RF 1976 **1 ... e6 2. d4 d5 3. Nc3 Bb4** This old continuation was originally tried in a game Steinitz–Winawer, Paris 1867 and revived by Nimzowitsch. It is considered stronger than the classical 3 ... Nf6. CR **4. e5 c5 5. dxc5** In later rounds Fine used Bogolyubov's 5 Bd2. Bohatirchuk also had success in this line against Botvinnik with 5 Qg4, but the main line is 5 a3. The text was tried by Bogolyubov against Alekhine at Bad Nauheim 1937. Baturinsky reckoned that Fine had chosen this rarely played line in order to avoid theory well known to Botvinnik. AW **5 ... Ne7** Alekhine had played 5 ... Nc6, on which there followed 6 Nf3 f6 7 Bb5 Bxc5 8 0–0 Bd7 9 Re1 fxe5? 10 Nxe5, to White's advantage. AW **6. Nf3** It was later recognized that 6 Qg4 is stronger in this position. VB **6 ... Nbc6** The development of the queen's knight to d7 and the king's knight to c6 deserves consideration here, as played by Ståhlberg against Keres. CR **7. Bd3** White does not allow ... d4 by choice. However, on 7 Bd2 there follows 7 ... Bxc5 8 Bd3 Ng6, and support for the e-pawn is a concern. ME **7 ... d4!** Accepting the complications. On 7 ... Bxc5 8 0–0, White's game is freer. RF 1976 The best move, after which Black has at least equalized. VB **8. a3 Ba5** The continuation 8 ... dxc3 9 axb4 cxb2 10 Bxb2 Nxb4 11 Nd4 Nxd3+ 12 Qxd3 Bd7 13 0–0, with a small advantage to White, was suggested by Belavenyets. In place of 11 Nd4, Euwe suggested 11 Be4, when White's bishop pair gives him the better game. AW **9. b4** A complex setup, requiring an accurate forecast arrived at during prepared analysis or in over-the-board play. For the most part, the fragmented details of diverse lines fall into an apparently uniform pattern only *a posteriori*. In practice, the seemingly compact course of a grandiose game is a synthesis of many factors. Fine could not foresee what defence Botvinnik would adopt. He kept a memory bank of responses, suitable against individual styles, but one cannot mentally computerize all and sundry permutations. The final analysis is left to the occasion. Else, why ponder, with the clock ticking? WK **9 ... Nxb4 10. axb4 Bxb4** Now White could simply play 11 0–0 (as occurred in Hodgson–Arkell, London 1988), but the text was apparently part of the pre-game preparation (contrary to Korn's assumption). **11. Bb5+**

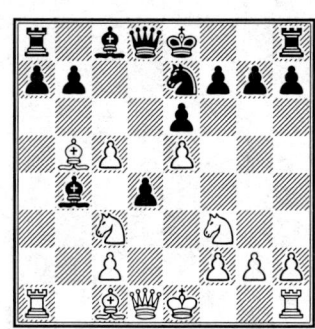

*Position after
White's 11th move*

11 ... Nc6? After this move White gets a bind on the position. Most analysts suggested the improvement 11 ... Bd7! to exchange the bad light-squared bishop: 12 Qxd4 Bxc3+ 13 Qxc3 Bxb5 with and approximately equal game (PCO 86). **12. Bxc6+! bxc6 13. Ra4!** An unexpected reply which Botvinnik had not foreseen. White recovers his pawn with the better game. VB **13 ... Bxc3+** If 13 ... a5 then 14 Rxb4. Botvinnik **14. Bd2** Suddenly Black discovers that he is lost. The bishop is hopelessly shut in, and it is only a question of time before White's superior development makes itself felt. RF 1976 **14 ... f6** A second mistake, after which Black is unable to save the game. 14 ... a5, introducing the bishop into the game, offered greater chances. VB (Belavenyets proposed the line 14 ... a5 15 Bxc3 dxc3 16 Qa1! Ba6 17 Rxa5 Qc8 with a minimal edge for White. It seems, however, that 17 ... Qd5, in place of 17 ... Qc8 would force perpetual check by 18 Rxa6 Qe4+ 19 Kd1 Rd8+ 20 Kc1 Qf4+ 21 Kb1 Qb4+. AW) **15. 0–0 0–0 16. Bxc3 dxc3 17. Qe1 a5** In order to place the bishop on the commanding diagonal a6–f1. Offhand Black would seem to have the better position, but shortly the potential strength of White's forces will become apparent. CR **18. Qxc3 Ba6 19. Rfa1 Bb5**

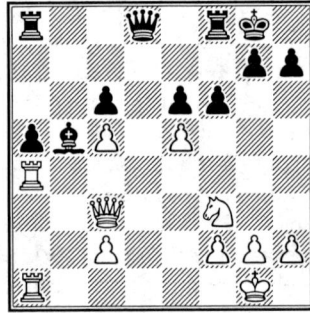

Position after
Black's 19th move

20. Rd4! Ordinarily, one would take what's up for grabs by 20 Rxa5. But Fine's positional instinct tells him that to occupy d6 with a tempo, and to dominate the centre, is better strategy, as the a-pawn can be blocked at will if necessary. There is a drop of poison in the future World Champion's bait of 20 Rxa5 Rxa5 because 21 Qxa5 Qxa5 23 Rxa5 reduces to a possible draw, whereas 21 Rxa5 Qd1+ 22 Ne1 Qe2 spells disaster for White. WK **20 ... Qe7 21. Rd6 a4** If 21 ... fxe5 22 Nxe5 Rf5 23 Qe1! Raf8 24 f3 Qg5 25 Rxe6 R5f6 26 Rxf6 Qxf6 27 c4! **22. Qe3!** White's advantage resides in his possession of a good knight against a bad bishop coupled with the absence of any counterplay for his opponent. VB **22 ... Ra7**

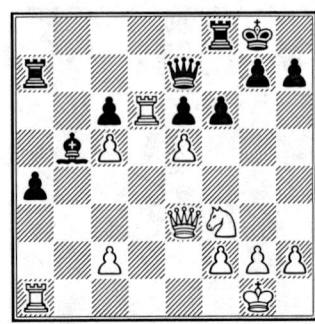

Position after
Black's 22nd move

23. Nd2!! The point: the poor bishop will be driven away. RF 1976 **23 ... a3** The pawn goes anyhow. RF 1976 **24. c4 Ba4 25. exf6! Qxf6 26. Rxa3** Now the bishop is pinned and everything is under attack. RF 1958 **26 ... Re8 27. h3** After this quiet move Black might as well resign. RF 1976 **27 ... Raa8 28. Nf3 Qb2** Botvinnik had just 9 minutes to make his remaining 12 moves. **29. Ne5 Qb1+ 30. Kh2 Qf5 31. Qg3!** Black resigned. Botvinnik's resignation here was somewhat of a surprise to me, but the position is hopeless. White threatens Ra3-f3-f7 and Rd6-d7, to which there is no defence. RF 1958 **1–0** Fine 1958, 150–4; 1976, 224–8; Euwe 1938, 14–6; notes from *Haagsche Courant* translated by J. B. Snethlage for *The Chess Review* 1938, 281–2; Baturinsky, 518; Soloviov 2000, 292–3; Korn 167–9.

(463) RESHEVSKY, S—FINE

A.V.R.O., The Netherlands (2), 1938 (8 Nov., 's-Gravenhage)
Catalan System [E02]

The technique for handling the unbalanced position is markedly different from that for the balanced. When the pawns are unbalanced, mechanical simplification can be almost suicidal, while the preservation of the tension may be the only way to keep chances even. To maintain equality, we must maintain the dynamic forces in equilibrium, rather than the material situation as such. In practice this means that each side must exploit his chances as effectively as possible. Another way of looking at it is that there should be simultaneous attack and counterattack. RF 1953 **1. d4 Nf6 2. c4 e6 3. Nf3 d5 4. g3** Very fashionable, though not necessarily superior to Bg5 or Nc3. ME **4 ... dxc4 5. Qa4+ Nbd7 6. Bg2 a6 7. Nc3** Recommended by Alekhine, who himself replies to this move with 7 ... Rb8. AES **7 ... Be7** Not 7 ... b5 8 Nxb5! SSC **8. Ne5** Black would also be slightly better after 8 Qxc4 b5 9 Qd3 Bb7 10 0–0 0–0 11 Bf4 c5 12 dxc5 Nxc5 13 Qxd8 Rfxd8, PCO 316. **8 ... Rb8 9. Qxc4 b5 10. Qb3** The normal 10 Qd3 is not good here because he has placed a knight on e5. AES **10 ... Nxe5 11. dxe5 Nd7 12. Bf4** White is at a theoretical disadvantage, with two pawns to three on the queenside. He must accordingly play for the attack, which is not Reshevsky's strong point. RF 1958; This method of supporting the e-pawn is risky as it restricts the activity of the bishop. 12 f4 is more elastic. ME **12 ... c5** If instead 12 ... g5 13 Be3! SSC; Black has more than equalized; he has a queenside pawn majority which he at once starts rolling and White's pawn on e5 is none too secure, though it cramps Black's game somewhat. AES **13. 0–0 Qc7**

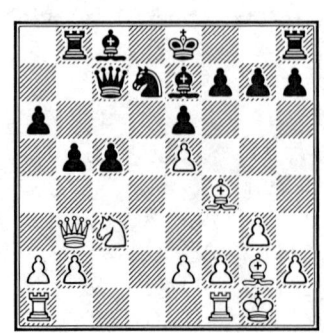

Position after
Black's 13th move

14. a4! An ingenious defence. If now 14 ... Nxe5 15 axb5, and if 14 ... b4 15 Ne4 (15 Nd5 exd5 16 e6 Ne5 17 exf7+ Kxf7 18 Qxd5+, Euwe, and it appears Black survives after 18 ... Kf6. AW) Nxe5 16 Rac1 0–0 17 Qe3 and the initiative has passed to White; the pawn can easily be regained. RF 1958 **14 ... 0–0 15. axb5 axb5 16. Ne4** After 16 Nxb5, 16 ... Qb6 does not win a piece as Fine wrote, there might then follow, for example, 17 Rfd1! Rd8 (17 ... Qxb5 18 Qxb5 Rxb5 19 Bc6 Rxb2 20 Bxd7 c4 21 Bc1 Rxe2 22 Bb5 Rxe5 23 Bxc4 Rd8 24 Be3 Rd1+ 25 Rxd1, and it will not be easy to convert the extra pawn. AW) **16 ... Bb7** In this position White with one pawn to two on the queenside has a theoretically lost endgame. His chances lie on the kingside and in the centre, in a possible attack. But he chose to simplify mechanically Which led to his downfall. RF 1953 **17. Ra7?** Inconsistent; he should have played for the attack by 17 Qe3. RF 1958 **17 ... Qb6** Naturally not 17 ... Ra8? at once because of 18 Rxb7 and 19 Nf6+. RF 1953 **18. Rfa1 Ra8 19. Rxa8 Rxa8 20. Rxa8+ Bxa8**

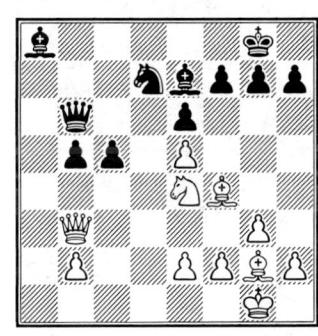

Position after Black's 20th move

21. Qd3 Fine reckoned that on 21 Nf6+ Bxf6 22 Bxa8 Bxe5 Black would win quite simply, but White seems to cause great difficulties by 23 Qd3. Instead of 22 ... Bxe5, 22 ... Nxe5 23 Be4 c4 might be better. AW **21 ... Bc6 22. Ng5** Reshevsky had to make the last 18 moves in 8 minutes. Santasiere suggested the alternative 22 Nd6 Bxg2 23 Kxg2 c4 24 Qe4, threatening 25 Nc8 or 25 Qa8+. Black can defend the twin threats by 24 ... Qa6, when Reshevsky would still be slightly worse with 16 moves yet to make. AW **22 ... Bxg5 23. Bxg5 Qb7** Naturally not 23 ... Nxe5? 24 Qd6! RF 1958 **24. f3** According to Fine 24 Bxc6 Qxc6 would leave White with a hopeless ending after 25 f4 (Santasiere proposes 25 Bf4 h6 26 h4 c4 27 Qc3 Qc5!) c4 26 Qd2 Kf8. Even if this were true White seems to have a better move in 25 Be7!, envisaging 25 ... c4 26 26 Qd6 Qxd6 27 exd6 b4 28 Bg5. These positions certainly don't seem to be trivial wins. AW **24 ... h6 25. Be7 c4 26. Qc3 Nxe5!** Finally the pawn can be taken. The rest is elementary. RF 1958 **27. Bc5 Nd7 28. Bd4 e5!** To be able to advance the queenside pawns. RF 1953 **29. Bxe5 b4 30. Qd4 Nxe5 31. Qxe5** *(see diagram)* **31 ... c3!** Now 32 bxc3 would be met by 32 ... b3. The rest is simple. ME **32. b3 Qb6+ 33. Kf1 c2 34. Qb2 Qc5 35. Qc1 Bd5 36. f4 Bxg2+ 37. Kxg2 Qd5+** White resigned. The first time Fine has ever won from Reshevsky, who here over-reached himself and met with flawless technique. AES **0–1** S. S. Cohen in *The Chess Review* 1938, 287–8; Fine

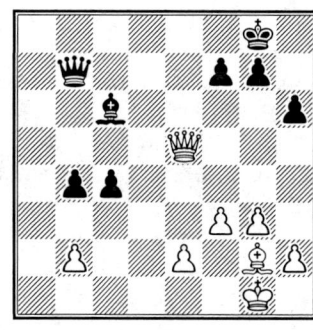

Position after White's 31st move

1958, 155–8; 1953, 406–8; Euwe 1938, 19–21; Santasiere in *ACB* 1938, 122.

(464) FINE—CAPABLANCA, J

A.V.R.O., The Netherlands (3), 1938 (10 Nov., Rotterdam)
French Defence, Winawer Variation [C17]

1. e4 e6 2. d4 d5 3. Nc3 Bb4 4. e5 c5 5. Bd2 Varying from 5 dxc5 which he played against Botvinnik, probably expecting a prepared line of play. Instead of the text 5 a3 seems preferable. AES **5 ... cxd4** A draw resulted from 5 ... Nc6 6 Nb5 Bxd2+ 7 Qxd2 Nxd4 8 Nxd4 cxd4 9 Nf3 Ne7, Lasker–Bohatirchuk, Moscow 1935. **6. Nb5 Bxd2+** Also playable is 6 ... Nc6, but not 6 ... Bc5 7 Qg4! with a strong attack. SSC **7. Qxd2 Nc6 8. Nf3 f6** Fine–Weiner, Marshall Club versus Mercantile Library, 1934 continued 8 ... Nge7 9 Nd6+ Kf8 10 Qf4 Nf5 11 Nxf7!?, and the second player held off the attack to gain a draw. **9. Qf4** A rather daring sortie, since on 9 ... Qa5+ he intends 10 Kd1. The text threatens 10 exf6 and 11 Nc7+. AES **9 ... Nh6 10. Nd6+** If now 10 exf6 then 10 ... 0–0. AES **10 ... Kf8** The time consumed by both players up to this point was: Fine, 47 minutes—Capablanca 1 hour. SSC **11. Bb5 Nf7!?** In *PCO* Fine wrote that Capablanca suggested 11 ... Nxe5! 12 Nxe5 Ke7! 13 Nxc8+ Rxc8 regaining the piece satisfactorily. Simagin, had he reached this position in a U.S.S.R. Correspondence Chess Championship, intended 11 ... Kg8 when Khalifman and Yudasin analyse 12 Bxc6 bxc6 13 0–0 c5 14 Rfe1 with an unclear game. **12. Nxf7 Kxf7 13. Bxc6** This opens a diagonal for the bishop but the removal of the black knight was essential. AES **13 ... bxc6 14. exf6** Withholding this exchange would lead to a more complex type of game with better winning chances for both players; that is, White castles and puts pressure on the e-file. AES **14 ... gxf6** After 14 ... Qxf6 White plays 15 Qc7+, and then, after 15 ... Qe7, continues with 16 Ne5+ Kf8 17 Qxe7 Kxe7 18 Nxc6+ and 19 Nxd4, with a won endgame, Black having no compensation for the lost pawn. ME **15. Ne5+ Kg7** Or 15 ... Ke8 16 Nxc6 Qd7 17 Nxd4. Or 15 ... Kg8 16 Qg3+, running into the game continuation. Black always comes out a pawn short. ME **16. Qg3+ Kf8** Now the time read: Fine, 1 hour 25 minutes—Capablanca, 1 hour 33 minutes. SSC **17. Nxc6 Qd7** There is no choice for the queen cannot be allowed in at d6. After 17 ... Qb6 18 Qd6+ Kf7 19 0–0–0 e5 20 f4! the white attack gathers decisive strength. ME **18. Nxd4 e5** A pawn down and with an insecure king, Black must be considered lost. In the circumstances passive play would be quite hopeless; the only chance is to adopt an active policy. Here, as in so many cases, the best method of defence is attack! ME **19. Nb3 Qf5 20. Qd3 d4** It seems surprising here that Black makes no attempt to avoid the exchange of queens. The point is that, with the queens off, the exposure of the black king would be less serious, while White's other advantage, the extra pawn, would become problematical since in an endgame the far-striding bishop would be more than a match for the white knight. ME **21. 0–0 Rg8** The exchange of the white queen on d3 would produce a closed type of position, with White's d-pawn more or less blocking the black centre. This closed formation would favour the white knight. ME **22. f4** At first sight this seems premature but, as the following variation shows, the black king will take up a dominating position behind a passed pawn with 22 Q×f5 B×f5 23 f4 Bh3! 24 Rf2 Ke7 25 Re1 Kd6 and 26 ... Kd5. AES **22 ... Bb7!** With this pretty resource, Black almost equalizes. AES **23. Rf2 Be4 24. Qd2 Kf7!**

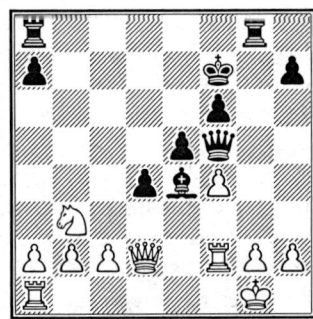

*Position after
Black's 24th move*

25. Re1! In the tournament book Euwe wrote that 25 f×e5 would be answered by 25 ... R×g2+ 26 R×g2 B×g2 27 N×d4 Q×e5 28 K×g2 Rg8+ 29 Kf1 Qe4 30 Re1 Qg4! which is no more favourable to White, but Fritz reckons that the White king will escape after 31 Kf2! Qh3 32 Re2 Rg2+ 33 Kf1 R×h2+ 34 Rg2 Rh1+ 35 Kf2 Qh4+ 36 Ke3. The text, however, should have led to a much clearer win, as shown in the note to White's next move. **25 ... Rg4! 26. Nc5?** Here Euwe pointed out 26 f×e5!, with the point that 26 ... R×g2+ now fails to 27 R×g2 B×g2 28 e6+!, so Black must play 26 ... Q×e5, on which White has 27 h3!, forcing 27 ... Rh4 28 Q×d4 Q×d4 29 N×d4 B×g2 30 Nf5 and wins. **26 ... B×g2!** A pretty combination which turns the tables. ME **27. R×g2 Rag8!! 28. Ree2 e×f4** Threatening the knight as well as ... f4-f3. AES **29. Nb7! Qd5!** Preventing 30 Nd6+, and maintaining both threats. ME **30. R×g4 R×g4+ 31. Rg2 R×g2+ 32. Q×g2 f3! 33. Qh3!** Holds the piece because of the threat (Q×h7+) but he cannot steer his king into a safe port and continue to hold the piece. AES **33 ... Qg5+! 34. Qg3 Qc1+ 35. Kf2 Qe3+ 36. Kf1 Qe2+ 37. Kg1 Qd1+ 38. Kf2 Q×c2+** A queer turn of events; Capablanca is actually refusing the draw, and with some reason. AES **39. K×f3** 39 Kf1 acquiescing to the draw is safer. Fine must have been in great time trouble. **39 ... Qc6+ 40. Ke2 Q×b7** From move 29 right down to here, every move was forced. The success achieved by Black in this phase shows that even in apparently lost positions

there may still be chances in practical play—a fact which provided Lasker with many of his wins. ME **41. b3 Qe4+ 42. Kd2 Qe5?!** 42 ... f5! would have been very strong. ME **43. Qh3 Qg5+** With 43 ... Qe4 Black could still have tried for a win. ME **44. Kd3!** Draw agreed. It is indeed a rare pleasure to see Capablanca work—for a draw! But, to tell the truth, he put up a great fight—he had to! Fine's play was aggressive, as well as sound, as enterprising as he was subtle. AES ½–½ S. S. Cohen in *The Chess Review* 1938, 289; Khalifman and Yudasin in Soloviev 1997, 249–50; Euwe 1938, 32–4; Santasiere in *ACB* 1938, 125; Euwe & Kramer 1965, 131–3.

(465) EUWE, M—FINE

A.V.R.O., The Netherlands (4), 1938 (12 Nov., Groningen)
Queen's Gambit Declined [D30]

1. d4 e6 2. c4 Nf6 3. Nf3 d5 4. Bg5 h6 With this move Black gains the pair of bishops, however in return he burdens himself with some development problems. ME **5. B×f6** Not 5 Bh4 Bb4+! 6 Nc3 d×c4! and the gambit pawn can be held. CR **5 ... Q×f6 6. Qb3** Or 6 Nc3 c6 7 Qb3 d×c4 8 Q×c4 Nd7 9 e4 e5 10 d5 Nb6 with equality, Petrovs–Ståhlberg, Kemeri 1937. **6 ... c6 7. Nbd2** Here the knight is more effectively placed than on c3, since White has N×c4 as a reply to ... d×c4. ME **7 ... Nd7 8. e4!** Euwe, in line with expectations, has advanced in the centre and forced his opponent to yield the centre. AES **8 ... d×e4 9. N×e4 Qf4!** More challenging than the routine 9 ... Qd8. A review of the position is in order. White's development is somewhat superior. In exchange, Black has the two bishops. The crucial question now is whether White can build up an attack or not. RF **10. Bd3 e5** Black's game is cramped, hence this bid for freedom. Its timing is a brave gesture because of the risks inherent in his lack of development. AES (10 ... Nf6! 11 N×f6+ Q×f6 12 0–0 Bd6 13 Rfe1 0–0 14 c5 Bc7 15 Be4 Rd8 16 Rad1 Rb8 17 Ne5 Bd7, Ståhlberg–Capablanca, Buenos Aires 1939 is better.) **11. 0–0! Be7** 11 ... f5 12 Ng3 e4 would be risky, as the following continuation shows: 13 Rfe1 Kd8 (13 ... Be7 14 B×e4 f×e4 15 R×e4 with Rae1 to follow leads to the recovery of the sacrificed material) 14 N×e4 f×e4 15 R×e4 Qf6 16 Rae1 Kc7 17 Re8 and White has practical attacking chances. ME **12. Rfe1** White has some advantage, MCO 157. **12 ... e×d4** 12 ... 0–0 is no good: 13 Ng3 Bd6 14 Nf5 and Black has insuperable difficulties. ME **13. N×d4** 13 Bc2 intending Qd3 came into consideration. ME **13 ... 0–0 14. Bc2 Nf6 15. Rad1** Euwe has retained his lead in development, but Fine has two bishops. AES **15 ... g6** (*see diagram*) **16. N×f6+** Releases the tension too soon. Correct is 16 Qc3!, with good attacking prospects. RF **16 ... B×f6 17. Re4 Qc7 18. Qe3 Kg7 19. h4** A determined attempt to keep the attack going, which only increases Black's chances, since White's pawn formation turns out to be suspect. White would do better to consolidate his position by b3 and g3. ME **19 ... h5 20. Rf4** Threatening 21 R×f6 K×f6 22 Qc3 Qe5 23 f4. RF **20 ... Re8!** With this clever

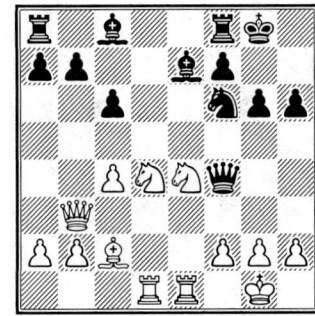

*Position after
Black's 15th move*

reply he eliminates the dangerous white rook. AES **21. Qxe8** 21 Qd2 was better, but Black's position is preferable now anyway. ME **21 ... Qxf4 22. Nf3** According to Fine, Euwe considered 22 Ne6+ Bxe6 23 Qxa8, after which Black would retain some advantage by 23 ... Bd4 (not 23 ... Bxh4 because of 24 Qxa7, protecting f2). Chekhover suggested 22 Bxg6! Kxg6 23 Qg8+ Bg7 24 Nf3. If we continue this line by 24 ... f6 we see that White is actually in trouble, for example, 25 Rd8 Be6! 26 Qe8+ Bf7 27 Ne5+ fxe5 28 Rd6+ Kh7 29 Qxa8 e4! and Black will win. The soundest move would seem to be 22 g3. AW **22 ... Rb8** A very fine move, preparing the development of the light-squared bishop, and threatening first of all ... Be6. ME **23. Qe4** This simplification is forced. ME **23 ... Qxe4 24. Bxe4 Bg4** Best. On 24 ... Bxb2 25 Rb1 Bf6 26 Bxc6! CR **25. Rd2 Re8!** The only way to win. 25 ... Bxf3 26 Bxf3 Bxh4 would only draw because of opposite-coloured bishops. CR **26. Bd3 Rd8!** **27. b3 Bxf3 28. gxf3 Bxh4** White's broken pawn structure and Black's outside passed pawn now permits the win in spite of opposite bishops. SSC **29. Kg2**

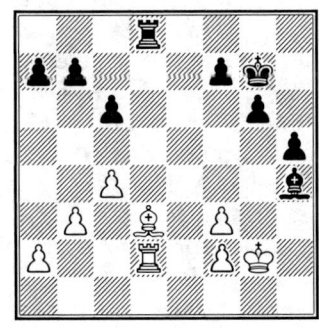

*Position after
White's 29th move*

29 ... Bg5 30. Rd1 Bf4 31. Kf1 h4 32. Kg2 f5 **33. Kh3 Kf6!** **34. Kg2** Naturally not 34 Kxh4 Rh8 mate. ME **34 ... Rd4 35. Kh3 g5 36. Bc2 Rxd1 37. Bxd1** Black now wins on the queenside because the white king is immobilized on the other wing. RF **37 ... Bd6! 38. Bc2 Ke5** The strong centralization of the king makes the win comparatively simple. AES **39. Kg2 Bc5 40. Bd3 a5!** **41. Bc2 f4!** Since the entrance of the king on the queenside is assured. AES **42. Bg6 Kd4 43. Bf5 Kc3 44. Bc8 Kb2** White resigned. The finish could be: 45 Bxb7 Kxa2 46 Bxc6 Kxb3 47 Kf1 a4 and White must give up his bishop. RF **0–1** S. S. Cohen in *The Chess Review* 1938, 290–1; Fine 1958, 159–62; Euwe 1938, 41–3; Anthony E. Santasiere in *ACB* 1938, 129.

(466) FINE—FLOHR, S

A.V.R.O., The Netherlands (5), 1938 (13 Nov., Zwolle)
French Defence, Winawer Variation [C17]

1. e4 e6 2. d4 d5 3. Nc3 Bb4 4. e5 c5 5. Bd2 Ne7 **6. Nf3 Nf5?** A mistake which is drastically punished. Correct is 6 ... Nbc6 or 6 ... 0–0, with theoretical equality. RF 1958 **7. dxc5! Bxc5 8. Bd3** Threatening to split Black's pawns. RF 1953 **8 ... Nh4 9. 0–0 Nc6 10. Re1 h6** In order to castle. On 10 ... 0–0? at once White wins with the sacrifice 11 Bxh7+ Kxh7 12 Ng5+ Kg6 13 Qg4. White is now in danger of losing the initiative, so he thinks of something. RF **11. Na4! Bf8** Falls in with White's plan, but he had no choice. On 11 ... Be7 12 Nxh4 Bxh4 13 Qg4 compels a weakening move because 13 ... 0–0? is refuted by 14 Bxh6. After the text he hopes to be able to play ... g6 and ... Bg7, which would allow him to castle, but White has other intentions. RF 1953 **12. Rc1** Preparing to bring this rook into the game. RF 1953 **12 ... Bd7** With the threat of ... Nxf3+ and ... Nxe5. RF 1953 **13. Nxh4** This exchange was unavoidable, but it also has the advantage of forcing Black's queen to an unfavourable square. RF 1953 **13 ... Qxh4**

*Position after
Black's 13th move*

14. c4! White has a clear positional advantage, PCO 84. **14 ... dxc4 15. Rxc4 Qd8** Black is now threatening 16 ... b5. To answer this White masses his forces against the enemy king. RF 1953 **16. Qh5** Hitting the weak point on f7. On 16 ... b5? now 17 Rf4 is decisive, while 16 ... g6 is refuted by 17 Bxg6. RF 1953 **16 ... Ne7** To reply to 17 Rf4 with 17 ... g6. He is also threatening ... Bxa4. RF 1953 **17. Rd4!** White has a terrific lead in development. It is not surprising that the denouement is swift. ME **17 ... g6** **18. Qf3 Qc7 19. Nc3 Nf5** If 19 ... Bc6, 20 Nb5!. ME **20. Nb5** The queen remains harassed. On 20 ... Qc6 White wins with 21 Qxc6 bxc6 22 Nc7+ Kd8 23 Bxf5 Kxc7 24 Ba5+ Kc8 25 Red1. RF 1953 **20 ... Qb6**

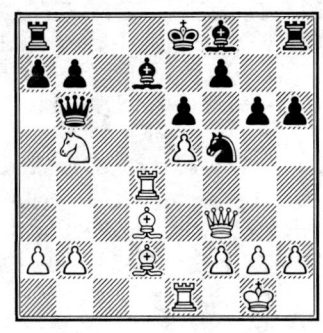

*Position after
Black's 20th move*

White has come as far as he can with purely positional means; now the king must be driven out into the open with a sacrifice. RF 1953 **21. Rxd7!** A fluent resolution. White secures the point with the offer of the exchange leading to a winning attack. ME **21 ... Kxd7 22. g4 Nh4** An attempt to counterattack. After 22 ... Ne7 23 Qxf7 White's pressure is irresistible. RF 1953 **23. Qxf7+ Be7 24. Bb4 Rae8** With the threat of 25 ... Rhf8. RF 1953 **25. Bxe7 Rxe7 26. Qf6! a6** Hoping for 27 Qxh8 Nf3+. But White has a speedier decision in mind. RF 1953 **27. Rd1! axb5 28. Be4+** Black resigned. **1–0** Fine 1958, 163–5; Fine 1953, 343–6; Euwe 1938, 48–50.

(467) ALEKHINE, A—FINE

A.V.R.O., The Netherlands (6), 1938 (14 Nov., Haarlem)
Spanish Game, Open Defence [C83]

1. e4 e5 2. Nf3 Nc6 3. Bb5 a6 4. Ba4 Nf6 5. 0–0 Nxe4 The Open Variation, a favourite of Tarrasch, provides more chances for active piece play for Black than 5 ... Be7 or 5 ... d6. AES **6. d4 b5 7. Bb3 d5 8. dxe5 Be6 9. c3 Be7 10. Nd4** In this well-known and critical position, many moves have been tried, each developing countless variations of more or less interest. 10 Re1 (concentrates on the e-file, after dislodging the knight, not so intent on f4 and so on); 10 Nbd2 (a conservative non-committal developing move, though challenging the black knight); 10 Be3 (pointing to a positional type of game, that is, holding back the c-pawn or otherwise profiting from the queenside pawn structure); 10 Qe2 (reserves the possibility of f4—an altogether routine move); 10 a4 (an aggressive continuation difficult to defend); and 10 Nd4 (the text—speculative and rarely played). AES **10 ... Nxe5** Black courageously accepts the pawn. An alternative was 10 ... Qd7 11 f4 Nxd4 12 cxd4 c5 13 Be3, maintaining pressure on both sides of the board. SGT **11. f3** Stronger than Qe2. SGT **11 ... Nf6** The best square for the knight for defensive purposes. If 11 ... Nc5 12 Bc2 and the knight is out of play. SGT; 11 ... Nc5 12 Bc2 Bd7 13 b4 Na4 14 Re1 Nc4 15 Qe2 Kf8 16 Nd2 Bf6 (16 ... Nxc3 17 Qd3 Na4 18 Bxa4 bxa4 19 Nxc4 and White has improved his prospects, MCO 250) 17 Nxc4 bxc4 18 Bxa4 Bxa4 with equality, Engels–Kieninger, Barmen 1938. **12. Qe2** If instead 12 f4, Black plays 12 ... Bg4! SGT; On 12 Re1 Nc4 is again best. Black gets a slight advantage by offering to return the pawn, PCO 345. **12 ... Nc4** Black prefers to return the pawn rather than seek for complications with 12 ... Qd6 13 Bf4 Nfd7 14 Re1. SGT **13. Bc2** After twenty-five minutes of thought, Alekhine decides to maintain the pressure rather than give Black relief through 13 Nxe6 fxe6 14 Qxe6 Qd7! SGT **13 ... Qd7 14. b3 Nb6** (see diagram) **15. Re1** True to his best style, Alekhine has seized the initiative regardless of the cost in minor material loss; here he can regain his pawn, but then Fine will at least equalize; again in his best tradition Alekhine refuses the offer of material and prefers to keep the pot boiling. AES **15 ... 0–0** The black king wants no part in the fight. SGT **16. Bg5** Alekhine disdains the recovery of the sacrificed

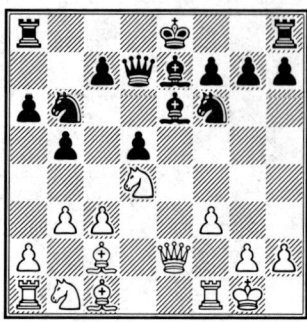

Position after Black's 14th move

pawn by 16 Nxe6. Chess **16 ... Rfe8 17. Nd2 Nh5** Well-played; he poses the question on the diagonal and reserves the possibility of ... Nf4. AES; On 17 ... Bc5 follows 18 Qd3 with the threat of 19 Bxf6. SGT **18. Bxe7 Rxe7** Black has a distinct superiority, MCO. **19. Qe5 g6** Santasiere reckoned this was forced in view of 19 ... Nf6 20 Nf5 and Nxg7!, but this line is unsound because of the attack on the queen on e5, for example, 19 ... Nf6 20 Nf5 Bxf5! 21 Qxf5 (21 Qxe7 Bxc2) Rae8!. 20 Bf5, after 19 ... Nf6, would be answered by 20 ... Rae8, with a satisfactory position for Black. Tartakower remarked that the weakening of the dark squares is unimportant since White no longer has his queen's bishop. AW **20. g4** When you survive an Alekhine attack, you realize what an elemental force you have encountered—like a Tornado in the south. AES **20 ... Ng7** Both of Black's knights are awkwardly placed. SGT **21. b4** To prevent ... c5: a liberating move. SGT **21 ... Rae8 22. Qf4 Na4** A clever rejoinder; the knight becomes a nuisance but his removal (tempting) means an end of the white attack. AES **23. Re3 Qd6** Another sly dig; if 24 Qh6 Bd7 and Black for choice. AES; Black is not unwilling to risk isolated doubled pawns (through the ensuing exchange of queens) because he will be enabled to exert pressure on White's c-pawn along the newly opened file. Chess **24. Qxd6** The exchange is forced. After 24 Qh6 c5! Black has nothing to fear. SGT **24 ... cxd6** Black's extra pawn is doubled and isolated, therefore Alekhine's risky treatment of the opening has not thrown away the draw. SGT **25. Rae1 Rc7 26. Nb1** Preferable would seem 26 Bxa4 first; then, this troublesome knight can aim for d4 via b1, a3, c2, the other going to e2 and f4; so much for the ideal, but Fine would be sure to be on hand with the sad world of realities. AES **26 ... Bd7 27. Rxe8+ Bxe8 28. Bb3!** By 28 Bxa4 Alekhine could have smashed up his opponent's pawn position still further; he wants more—but he does not get it! Still, the text forces Fine somewhat on the defensive, whereas, after 28 Bxa4 bxa4 there is threatened 29 ... Ne6 followed by ... Bb5 as soon as the white knight is moved or exchanged. Chess **28 ... Nb6** Not 28 ... Nxc3 29 Rc1! SGT **29. Kf2 Kf8 30. Rd1 Ne6 31. Ne2 Bc6 32. Na3 Ke7** Both players manoeuvre for a purpose, and ingeniously. SGT **33. Nc4 Nc4 34. Ne3** Thus he regains his pawn, but Fine remains with the superior endgame, his pawn position is more sound and his rook, more effective. AES **34 ... h6 35. h4** Renders White's kingside a little too easily attacked (Black's 38th and 43rd moves) and might well have been rejected in favour of 35 h3. *Chess* **35 ... Nb6 36. Bxd5 Bxd5 37. Nxd5+ Nxd5 38. Rxd5**

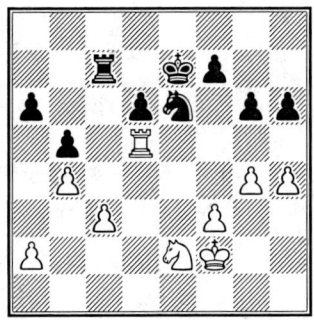

Position after White's 38th move

38 ... Rc4 In order to simplify further with ... Nf4. SGT **39. Ke3 Kd7** A draw is acceptable to Fine, but Alekhine still nurses the delusion that he may coax a win out of a draw; in situations of this kind Fine is particularly dangerous; he awaits the push of the kingside pawns with equanimity, realizing well that aggression may breed over-expansion, with loose ends hanging (for the rooks to gobble up). AES **40. f4 Kc6** Here the game was adjourned. Alekhine has the slightest advantage in space, but fights on and on trying to win long after the position has become fully equalized. He was a little upset by having (by the time the game was resumed) let slip wins against Reshevsky and Keres in turn. It is a little easier for White to open the game (Rf1 and f5; or Ra1 and h5), but his weakness at c3 is a lasting one. *Chess* **41. Rd1** The sealed move. ME **41 ... Kd7 42. Rf1** This shifting of the battle scene took twenty minutes of thought by the world champion. Apparently, he does not care to draw by repetition: 42 Rd5 Kc6 43 Rd1. SGT **42 ... Ke7 43. Kd3** To relieve the knight from its duty of protecting the c-pawn. SGT **43 ... g5!** Black starts a sharp counter-offensive. SGT **44. hxg5 hxg5 45. f5** Now Black is in command. AES **45 ... Nf8 46. f6+** From bad to worse; this weakens this pawn also, whilst also letting in the black knight at once. AES **46 ... Kd7 47. a4! Ng6!** If 47 ... Rxg4, Tartakower gave 48 axb5 axb5 49 Rf5 recovering the pawn with a fine game. *Chess* **48. axb5 Ne5+ 49. Kd2 axb5 50. Nd4 Nxg4 51. Nxb5** Both horses have been fed, and the battle is somewhat simplified. SGT **51 ... Ne5**

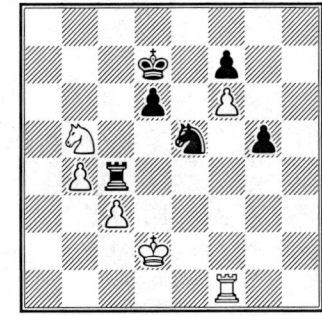

Position after Black's 51st move

52. Nd4 g4 53. Kc2 A bad move, again due to his insane desire for a win (which is excusable) and to his mis-appraisal of his prospects in this ending (which is

surprising). He doesn't seem to realize how dangerous Black's passed pawn is. It was essential to keep the king near the kingside, so that he could approach via the centre squares, should Black's king abandon the c-file. His more immediate moves could be Rf2-g2-g3-g2 and so forth. Fine could hardly prove a win. AES; Of course not 53 Rg1, due to 53 ... Rxd4+ 54 cxd4 Nf3+! SGT **53 ... Rc8 54. Nf5 Rg8 55. Ng3 Rh8** 55 ... Ke6 is also good, threatening 56 ... Rg6. Alekhine is now on the defensive; Fine has played the endgame with perfection throughout. Presumably Alekhine considered his united passed pawns stronger than Black's—which are really disunited—but the outstanding feature of the position is the advanced passed g-pawn. *Chess* **56. Rf2 Nf3 57. Re2** Even here a purely defensive attitude might hold the day; for example 57 Kd1 Rh3 58 Rg2 Ke6 59 b5 or first Kd1-e2-e3 and then b5 strongly. But Alekhine, sensing that he is losing his grip, wavers between offence and defence and this inconsistency costs him the game. Fine's conduct of this endgame has been and is masterful and perfect; he misses none of his chances and, where he has hardly any, manufactures them out of thin air. AES **57 ... Rh3 58. Nf5** Deserving of consideration was 58 Re7+ followed by Nf5. SGT **58 ... Ne5! 59. b5** 59 Rd2 gets nowhere: 59 ... Ke6 60 Nxd6? Nf3! *Chess* (59 Rf2, Euwe, is presumably met by 59 ... g3 60 Re2 Ke6, but is this a win? AW) **59 ... Rf3** The encircling movement of this rook in pursuit of a knight is charming and conclusive. AES **60. Nd4 Rxf6 61. b6** After ten minutes thought, White gives his free pawn—his sole hope—a little shot in the arm. SGT **61 ... Kc8 62. Nb5 g3!** The only move against the threatened 63 Nxd6+, which is now refuted by 63 ... Rxd6 64 Rxe5 Rxb6 65 Rg5 Rg6. *Chess* **63. Kb3** White had only four minutes left for nine moves, but the position was hopeless. 63 Nxd6+ Rxd6 64 Rxe5 Rg6! 65 Re1 f5 66 Kd3 f4 67 Kc2 Rc6+ 68 Kd2 Rxe1 69 Kxe1 Kb7 followed by 70 ... Kxb6 and wins. SGT **63 ... Rg6 64. Rg2 f5 65. Ra2** Order, counter-order, disorder! Purposeless also would be 65 Nxd6+ Rxd6 66 Rxg3 Rxb6+ 67 Kc2 f4! White had only two minutes left. SGT **65 ... Kb7 66. Rd2 f4 67. Nxd6+ Rxd6 68. Rxd6 g2** White resigned. For after 69 Rd1 f3 70 Rg1 f2 71 Rxg2 f1Q there is no saving miracle left in this position. This was the most sensational result of the first half of the tournament. SGT **0–1** *Chess* 1938–9, 144; Euwe 1938, 63–5; Tartakower, translated by J. B. Snethlage from *De Telegraaf*, *The Chess Review* 1939, 9–10; Santasiere in *ACB* 1938, 131–2.

(468) FINE—KERES, P

A.V.R.O., The Netherlands (7), 1938 (15 Nov., Amsterdam)
Spanish Game, Worrall Attack [C86]

1. e4 e5 2. Nf3 Nc6 3. Bb5 a6 4. Ba4 Nf6 5. 0–0 Be7 6. Qe2 There has been quite a vogue in this recently; the advantage over the usual 6 Re1 lies chiefly in its comparative novelty. Also the rook may now go to d1. AES **6 ... b5 7. Bb3 d6** Better than 7 ... 0–0 (Kashdan–Horowitz, match 1938) when, after the further moves 8 c3 d6 9 d4

White obtained a strong initiative. AES **8. a4** Not so bad in itself, but here it is the prelude to a campaign of aggression designed to gain material; this particular strategy has been proven superficial and unwise. AES **8 ... Bg4** More aggressive than 8 ... Rb8 as played by Euwe against Alekhine in their 1927 match. CR/BCM **9. c3** On 9 axb5 follows 9 ... Nd4! CR **9 ... 0–0 10. axb5** 10 d3, when the black queen's bishop is not well placed, was more to be recommended. ME **10 ... axb5 11. Rxa8 Qxa8 12. Qxb5?! Na7!** Up to this point the opening has been identical with that of a game Böök–Alexander, Margate 1938. The text is much better than Alexander's 12 ... Na5 to which White replied 13 Bc2 Nxe4 14 Nxe5 Rb8 15 Bxe4 Rxb5 16 Bxa8 Rxe5 17 d4, and Black has no compensation for the pawn sacrifice. BCM **13. Qe2** Keres believed during the game that he had introduced a new move. He found out later, however, that this had already occurred in the 1935 game Rogmann–Rellstab, which continued 13 Qa5 Qxe4 14 Qxa7 Bxf3 15 gxf3 Qxb1 16 Qxc7 Qg6+ 17 Kh1 Qd3 18 Kg1 Nh5 (Fine gave only 18 ... Qg6+ with a draw by perpetual check, in *PCO*, 362) 19 Qc4 Qxf3 20 Bd1 and now, rather than the game continuation 20 ... Qf4 21 Qxf4 Nxf4 with an eventual draw, 20 ... Qf5 keeps the tension. AW **13 ... Qxe4 14. Qxe4 Nxe4 15. d4** White must allow the weakening of his kingside pawn structure and complete his development as soon as possible. For example, 15 Bd1 Nc5 could be very troublesome for him. PK **15 ... Bxf3 16. gxf3 Ng5 17. Kg2** The annotator in *BCM* was of the opinion that White's best chance was 17 Bxg5 Bxg5 18 dxe5 dxe5 19 Re1 Bf4 20 Re2 Rd8 21 Na3, Fine on the other hand considered that White's game would still be quite difficult. AW **17 ... Rb8 18. Bc4 exd4 19. cxd4 Ne6 20. d5?!** White hopes that by retaining the bishop pair and cramping Black's game he will generate counterplay. *The Chess Review* suggests the alternative 20 Re1 Bf6!. Now Keres continues with 21 Bxe6 fxe6 22 Rxe6 Bxd4 with difficulties for White, perhaps instead of the exchanges White could play 21 d5. AW **20 ... Nc5 21. Nc3 Nc8** Keres later felt he should immediately have challenged the enemy bishop by 21 ... Rb4, with the idea of 22 Re1 Kf8 23 Bf1 f5 intending 24 ... Bf6. AW **22. Re1 Kf8** Now some annotators recommended 23 Ne4, in answer to which Keres intended 23 ... Rb4! with advantage to Black. The Estonian Grandmaster considered that 23 Nb5 Nb6 24 b3 Nxd5 might have been the best chance. AW **23. Re2 f5?** Dissipating his advantage. Keres explains that now was the time for 23 ... Rb4. AW **24. Nb5! Nb6 25. b3 Nxd5! 26. Nd4** Fine felt that 26 Nxd6 Bxd6 27 Bxd5 Nxb3 28 Rb2 Ba3 29 Rxb3 Rxb3 30 Bxb3 Bxc1 should be drawn, whereas Keres felt he had, at least, practical winning chances. In fact, Fine even felt he was starting to get some winning chances himself. AW **26 ... Nb4 27. Bd2?** Here White should simply play 27 Nxf5 Bf6 28 Bf4 with good prospects of equality. Apparently White was convinced that after the text Black would have nothing better than to transpose into this variation by 27 ... Bf6 28 Nxf5, but now comes a cruel surprise. PK **27 ... d5!!** Black had placed all of his hopes on this thrust. The ensuing complications are more or less forced and even-

tually lead to a position where Black is the exchange down, but his passed pawns on the queenside ensure him a decisive advantage. PK **28. Bxb4 Rxb4 29. Nc6 dxc4! 30. Nxb4 cxb3 31. Nd5 Nd3! 32. Rd2 b2 33. Rd1 c5 34. Rb1 c4 35. Kf1 Bc5 36. Ke2 Bxf2! 37. Ne3 c3! 38. Nc2 Ne1! 39. Na3 Bc5 40. Kxe1** The best chance was 40 Rxe1 Bxa3 41 Kd3 Bb4, when the black bishop is rather awkwardly placed. Best then is 42 Kc2 Kf7 43 Re5 Bd6! 44 Rxf5+ Kg6 45 Rb5 Bxh2 46 Kxc3 Be5+! 47 Kd3 Kf5 48 Ke3 g5. Black wins by manoeuvering the two passed pawns on the opposite wings; the fact that the bishop is of the wrong colour does not matter here. RF **40 ... Bxa3 41. Kd1 Bd6 42. Kc2 Bxh2 43. Rh1 Be5 44. Rxh7 Kf7 45. Rh1 g5 46. Re1 Kf6 47. Rg1 Kg6 48. Re1 Bf6 49. Rg1 g4! 50. fxg4 f4! 51. g5 Bd4 52. Rd1 Be3 53. Kxc3 Bc1 54. Rd6+ Kxg5 55. Rb6 f3 56. Kd3 Kf4 57. Rb8 Kg3** Black resigned. Another interesting game more deeply annotated by Keres in his collection. **0–1** Keres, 1996 128–35; *The Chess Review* 1939, 12–3; Fine 1976, 237–42; BCM 1939, 32–3; Anthony E. Santasiere in *ACB* 1939, 10–1.

(469) BOTVINNIK, M—FINE

A.V.R.O., The Netherlands (8), 1938 (17 Nov., Utrecht)
Four Knights Game [C48]

1. e4 e5 2. Nf3 Nf6 In the footsteps of Marshall. ME; Bearing in mind his position as leader of the tournament, Fine does not strive for a sharp game, but selects an opening which comparatively quickly leads to simplification. VB (In fact, Fine noted in MCO that this variation had been used as a counterattacking weapon by the American masters Pillsbury and Marshall. It is Botvinnik's insipid play which produces the early draw. AW) **3. Nc3** White does not take up the gauntlet. The Russian game is a complicated system requiring a good knowledge of theory. ME (Botvinnik did try 3 Nxe5 against Smyslov, Leningrad–Moscow 1941, but only drew. AW) **3 ... Nc6 4. Bb5 Nd4!** Yet another challenge. can you refute the Rubinstein Variation of the Spanish Four Knights? ME (Botvinnik had lost a game, with Black, to Bohatirchuk, Moscow 1935, after 4 ... Bb4. AW) **5. Ba4 Bc5 6. d3** The continuation 6 Nxe5 0–0 7 Nd3 Bb6 8 e5 offers more prospects. VB **6 ... 0–0 7. 0–0** White refuses to yield Black the initiative. If 7 Nxe5 or 7 Be3 Black answers with 7 ... d5! Also on 7 Nxd4 exd4 8 Ne2 d5! CR; Now though in the event of 7 Nxe5 d6 8 Nf3 Bg4 (Ryumin) Black would gain a strong initiative for the pawn. VB **7 ... d6 8. h3 c6 9. Nxd4** Otherwise 9 ... b5 10 Bb3 a5 11 a3 Nxb3 with advantage to Black. VB **9 ... Bxd4 10. Ne2 Bb6 11. Ng3 Ne8** Initiating the manoeuvre ... Ne8-c7-e6, strengthening his position. VB (11 ... Nd7 Botvinnik–V. Makogonov, 13th U.S.S.R. Championship, Moscow 1944, also ended in a draw.) **12. Bb3 Nc7 13. Be3 Ne6 14. c3 g6** Black's position is slightly more comfortable, *PCO* 67. **15. Bxe6 Bxe6 16. d4 d5** Forcing further simplification. VB **17. dxe5! Bxe3 18. fxe3 Qg5 19. Qf3** 19 Rf3 would be refuted by 19 ... Bxh3! VB **19 ... Qxe5** Draw since White has the good move 20 Qf4 at his disposal. ME ½–½ Euwe 1938, 84–5; *The Chess Review* 1939, 39; Baturinsky, 529–30; Soloviov 2000, 362.

(470) FINE—RESHEVSKY, S

A.V.R.O., The Netherlands (9), 1938 (19 Nov., Arnhem)
Spanish Game, Chigorin Defence [C97]

1. e4 e5 2. Nf3 Nc6 3. Bb5 a6 4. Ba4 Nf6 5. 0–0 Be7 6. Re1 b5 7. Bb3 d6 8. c3 Na5 9. Bc2 c5 10. d4 Qc7 11. h3 Reshevsky reckoned that if White intended to play a2-a4 he should have done so at once, for example, 11 a4 b4 (11 ... Rb8 12 Nbd2 Nc6 13 axb5 axb5 14 h3 0–0 15 d5 Nd8 16 Nf1 Ne8 17 g4 and White went on to win in 58 moves, Stoltz–Asztalos, Bled 1931) 12 cxb4 cxb4 13 h3 0–0 14 Nbd2 Be6 15 Nf1 Rfc8 16 Ne3 g6 17 b3 Nh5 18 Bb2 Bf6 19 Rc1 exd4 20 Nxd4 Qd7 21 Rb1 and White won in 35 moves, Keres–Reshevsky, Stockholm Team Tournament 1937. In his article "Current Trends in the Opening: I(b)—The Ruy Lopez" (BCM 1938, 62–5) Fine gave the line 11 ... Rb8 12 Nbd2 Nc6 13 d5 Nd8 with even chances. **11 ... 0–0** Here Fine preferred 11 ... Nc6 because of the Keres–Reshevsky game. **12. a4** The most usual move here has been 12 Nbd2, introduced at least as early as 1907, when it was played twice by Süchting at Oostende. The same position often arises by way of 11 Nbd2 0–0 12 h3. **12 ... Bd7** After 12 ... b4 and 12 ... Bb7 Lajos Steiner beat Havasi at Ujpest 1934 and Furlani at Ljubljana 1938. **13. Nbd2?!** Reshevsky suggested instead either 13 d5 or 13 axb5, as later occurred in Ban–Barcza, 1st Hungarian Correspondence Chess Championship 1941-2. In that game there followed 13 ... axb5 14 Nbd2 Nc6 15 Rxa8 Rxa8 d5, with a roughly equal game. **13 ... cxd4! 14. cxd4 Rfc8! 15. Bd3** He decides to surrender the a-pawn—a plausible idea, for Black's a-pawn does not give the impression of being very strong, while the alternative 15 axb5 Qxc2 16 Qxc2 Rxc2 17 Rxa5 Bxb5, as in my match with Kashdan (U.S. Championship play-off 1942, drawn in 38 moves. AW), is very promising for Black and allows White only drawing chances at best. SR **15 ... bxa4** Contrary to White's expectations, both a-pawns play a useful role throughout the game! SR **16. Qe2 Nh5!** Reshevsky wrote "A strong move which gives White little choice. Thus if 17 Bxa6 Nf4 18 Qf1 Rxa6! 19 Qxa6 Rb8! and White is helpless against the threat of ... Bb5. If 17 Nf1 Nb3 is a powerful reply; while 17 Nxe5? is refuted by 17 ... Nf4.". In the first line, however, White has the resource 20 b4! at the end. Instead of 18 ... Rxa6, 18 ... Qb6 is good for Black. AW **17. g3! Rcb8** On 17 ... Bxh3 18 Bxa6 followed by 19 Rxa4, Black has succeeded in freeing his game. ME **18. Kg2 g6 19. Ra3** If 19 Bxa6, 19 ... Rxa6 followed by 20 ... Bb5. AW **19 ... exd4 20. Nxd4 Bf6 21. N2f3 Qb6** Black's position is distinctly superior, PCO 352. **22. Qd2** To answer 22 ... Bxd4 23 Nxd4 Qxd4 with 24 Qxa5. Having played the opening quickly both players consumed oceans of time hereabouts. *Chess* **22 ... Nc6** Maintaining the pressure. If instead 22 ... Nb3 23 Nxb3 axb3 24 Bc4 and the b-pawn falls. SR **23. Nc2** Reshevsky

explained that Fine had played this, rather than 23 Nxc6 Bxc6 which he believed would give Black too comfortable a game, in order to introduce complications. After 23 Nxc6 Bxc6 24 Bc2 Bxb2 (or 24 ... Qb4 25 Qd1 Qc5 26 Bxa4 Bxa4 27 Rxa4 Bxb2 28 Bxb2 Rxb2 29 Re2 Rxe2 30 Qxe2, with a good chance of picking up one of the isolated pawns with his more active pieces) 25 Bxb2 Qxb2 26 Rc3 Rc8 27 Rb1 Qa1 White's game seems to have more prospects than the text. **23 ... Qa5** Reducing the position to an ending is a much simpler course than 23 ... Bxb2 24 Bxb2 Qxb2 25 g4 Nf6 26 Qf4 Ne8 27 Bc4 Be6 28 Ra2 and the position is rather unclear. SR **24. Qxa5 Nxa5 25. e5** Advancing desperately in order to obtain more room for his pieces, but this works both ways: Black also benefits. SR **25 ... dxe5 26. Nxe5 Be8 27. g4 Ng7** Black is not troubled by this retreat since the knight will soon be posted more advantageously. SR **28. Nd4** Perhaps having played g3-g4 White should have continued in the same –fashion: 28 g5! Bxe5 29 Rxe5 Bc6+ 30 Kh2 Nb3 31 Bf4 Ne6 32 Be3 looks more comfortable than the position reached in the game. AW **28 ... Rd8** White had here three minutes left for twelve moves, Black the almost princely (by comparison) allowance of thirteen. It is time difficulty which loses this game for Fine—twice over! CR **29. Ndf3 Be7 30. Ra2 Ne6 31. Bf1?** The position of the bishop was beginning to get too precarious, but the text is the first of a series of moves which reduce White's mobility to the vanishing point. SR **31 ... Nb3 32. Be3 Bb4** Black's bishops begin to assert themselves. If 33 Re2 Rd1 with the terrible threat of ... Bb5. SR **33. Rb1 a5 34. Kg1** White wants to play Nd3, but this cannot be done at once because of the reply 34 ... Bc6 with a nasty pin. SR **34 ... Kg7 35. Be2 f6 36. Nc4** Reshevsky writes "The alternative 36 Nd3 is answered by 36 ... Bb5 37 Rd1 Rac8 38 Nxb4 Bxe2 39 Rxd8 Nxd8 winning a piece.". White, however, is not obliged to make mistakes on moves 37 and 38, instead he can play 37 Nf4! AW **36 ... Bb5 37. Kf1! Rac8 38. Nb6 Bxe2+ 39. Kxe2 Rc2+ 40. Kf1 a3! 41. bxa3** If instead 41 Nc4 Rxc4 42 bxa3 Nc1! 43 Bxc1 Rd1+ 44 Kg2 Rcxc1 45 Rxc1 Rxc1 46 axb4 axb4 47 Rb2 Nf4+ 48 Kg3 Nd3 and wins. 44 Ke2 would be no better in this variation. SR **41 ... Rxa2 42. axb4 Rd3!** Much stronger than 42 ... a4 43 Nxa4. SR **43. bxa5 Rxa5** 43 ... Ng5, with the continuation 44 Nxg5 Rxe3 45 fxe3 Nd2+, was generally given as a quicker win, but instead of 45 fxe3, 45 Rd1 seems to keep matters in the balance. AW **44. Kg2 Ra2 45. Kg3** With all the pawns on the kingside 45 Nd5 Rxd5 46 Rxb3 might have been a better chance. AW **45 ... Nec5** Threatening 46 ... Ne4+ 47 Kg2 Rxe3!. ME **46. Re1 Ne4+** Fine has taken so much time he has only one minute left to make eight moves. CR **47. Kg2 Rc2 48. Na4 f5 49. gxf5 gxf5 50. Ne5 Rd5 51. Nf3 Kf6 52. Rb1 Ra5?** 52 ... f4! was the move to win. SR **53. Rxb3 Rxa4 54. Rb6+ Ke7 55. Nd4** But as he [Fine] reached towards his clock, the flag fell. Bad luck, for he has more than equalized the game. *Chess* 0–1 *Chess* 1938-9, 151; Reshevsky, 153–5; Euwe 1938, 89–91; *BCM* 1939, 122; *The Chess Review* 1939, 40–1.

(471) CAPABLANCA, J—FINE

A.V.R.O., The Netherlands (10), 1938 (20 Nov., Breda)
Nimzowitsch-Indian Defence, Classical Variation [E34]

1. d4 Nf6 2. c4 e6 3. Nc3 Bb4 4. Qc2 d5 5. cxd5
A typically pragmatic Capablanca decision, avoiding the
heavily analyzed 5 a3. **5 ... Qxd5 6. Nf3 c5** Romanishin's
6 ... Qf5 is currently popular. **7. Bd2 Bxc3 8. Bxc3
Nc6?!** An uncompromising counter. More usual was 8 ...
cxd4 9 Nxd4 for example: 9 ... e5 10 Nf3 (or 10 Nf5 Bxf5
11 Qxf5 Nc6 12 e3 0–0 13 Be2! Qe4 14 Qf3 Capablanca–
Euwe from round 7) Nc6 11 Rd1 Qc5 12 e3 0–0 13 Be2 Bg4
14 0–0 Rac8 with an even game, Levenfish–Botvinnik,
match game 7, 1937. **9. Rd1!** An improvement over 9 e3
cxd4 10 Nxd4 Nxd4 11 Bxd4 0–0 12 Bxf6 gxf6 13 Bd3
Qa5+ 14 Qd2 with a slight edge, Nimzowitsch–Canal, Carlsbad 1929. **9 ... 0–0** Fine thought that it was too dangerous
to take the pawn offered by 9 ... cxd4 10 Nxd4 Nxd4
11 Rxd4 Qxa2 12 e4!, threatening 13 Bc4. After 12 ... Bd7
providing a safe square for the queen on a4, however, things
don't look clear. **10. e3** A few months later the Cuban tried
10 a3 against Najdorf at Margate, that game continued 10 ...
cxd4! 11 Nxd4 Nxd4 12 Rxd4 Qc6 (Khalifman and Yudasin
suggest instead 12 ... Qh5 or 12 ... Qg6) 13 e4 e5!? 14 Rc4
Qe6 15 Rd5 Qg6 17 f3 Nb6! 18 Rxe5 Be6 when, according
to Fine in *PCO*, Black has sufficient compensation for the
pawn. **10 ... b6 11. a3 Bb7 12. dxc5 Qxc5 13. b4
Qh5!** If 13 ... Qe7 then 14 b5! and if 13 ... Qf5 14 Qxf5
exf5 15 Bxf6 gxf6 16 Rd7. Kh & Yu **14. Bxf6** White stands
very well, but not nearly as well as he thinks he does. With
this move and his next Capablanca tries to force a swift decision, but in reality he merely allows his opponent to uncork
a terrific combination. ME **14 ... gxf6 15. Rd7** Capablanca rushes headlong into the attack, meanwhile his right
wing is still paralyzed. The golden rules of chess, however,
also hold for the great masters. ME

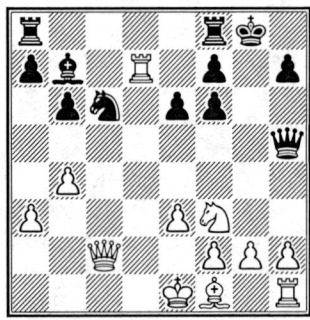

*Position after
White's 15th move*

15 ... Rac8! Indirectly protecting the Bb7. ME **16. Qb2**
If 16 Rxb7 then 16 ... Nxb4 17 Qd2 (or 17 Qb3 Nc2+ 18 Ke2
Na1! 19 Qb1 Rc2+ 20 Ke1 Qa5+ 21 Qb4 Rc1+ 22 Kd2 Nb3+
and 23 ... Qa6+. Heidenfeld) Nc2+ 18 Kd1 Nxa3 19 Rxa7
Nb5 20 Bxb5 Qxb5 21 Ra1 Rfd8 22 Nd4 Qe8!, and it is
Black who is winning. Kh & Yu **16 ... Rfd8! 17. Rxb7** On
17 Rxd8+ Nxd8 18 Qxf6 there follows 18 ... Qd5 19 Qg5+
(19 Qb2 Qe4) Qxg5 20 Nxg5 Rc1+ and 21 ... Ra1 with an
overwhelming position for Black. ME **17 ... Ne5!! 18. Be2**

Capablanca later recommended 18 Nd4 but then Fine would
have played 18 ... Qg6 (keeping the bishop on f1 and threatening ... Qe4 and ... Rxd4 followed by ... Rc2), after which
the game might continue 19 f3 (or 19 Qd2 Qb1+ 20 Ke2 Nc6
21 Kf3 e5 with a strong attack) Nd3+ 20 Bxd3 Qxd3 21 Kf2
Rc3 22 Re1 Rxd4 23 exd4 Qxd4+ 24 Kg3 Rxf3+ 25 Kxf3
Qxb2 followed by advancing the e- and f-pawns. **18 ...
Nxf3+ 19. Bxf3 Qe5!!** The real point. Obviously White
must take the queen. On, for example, 20 Qb1, 20 ... Qc3+
wins. On 19 gxf3 Bxf3 the text would have been even more
effective since 20 Qxe5 leads to mate in three moves: 20 ...
Rc1+ 21 Bd1 Rcxd1+ 22 Ke2 R8d2 mate. ME **20. Qxe5
Rc1+ 21. Bd1** On other moves White cannot escape
perpetual check. ME **21 ... Rcxd1+ 22. Ke2 R1d2+
23. Kf3 fxe5 24. Rxa7** Thus when all is said and done
White has nevertheless won a pawn. Though real enough, this
gain is somewhat offset by the activity of the black
rooks. ME **24 ... e4+ 25. Kg3** Capablanca's excellent
counterplay has preserved a small advantage: Black will have
to worry about the pawn e4. WH **25 ... Ra2 26. Ra6
Rdd2 27. Rf1 Rdb2 28. Rxb6 Rxa3 29. b5 Kg7
30. h4?!** 31 Rd1 would force Black to bail out to a rook-
ending with three pawns against four on the same side: 31 ...
Rab3 32 Rd4 Rxb5 34 Rxb5 Rxb5 35 Rxe4. **30 ... Rab3
31. Kf4 Rxb5 32. Rxb5 Rxb5 33. g4** On 33 Kxe4,
33 ... Rb4+ and 34 ... Rxh4 would follow. ME **33 ... Rb4
34. Rc1 Rb2 35. Kg3 Kf6** Both players were by now in
great time trouble and therefore make some inaccuracies.
35 ... Rb4 was correct. ME (Fine had to make five moves in
thirty-five seconds.) **36. Rc4 Ke5** Here Heidenfeld remarks
"Black had to let go the e-pawn and play the ending with
three pawns against four, even though Capablanca was
famous for his handling of this particular ending." **37. Rc8?!**
Here Euwe suggested 37 g5. I don't see a clear win after
37 ... Rb7 38 Rc8 f6!. AW **37 ... Kf6** Khalifman and Yudasin propose 37 ... Rb7, and if 38 Rh8, 38 ... f6. **38. Rg8!
h6?** And here the Russian analysts suggest 38 ... e5 39 g5+
Kf5 40 Rg7 f6 41 Rxh7 fxg5 42 Rh5 Rb1 43 Rxg5+ Kf6
39. g5+! hxg5 40. Rxg5? And now with the simplest of
simple wins after 40 h5, the "chess-machine" misses it. In
fact, so great was the end-game myth woven around the
Cuban by his contemporaries that at the time nobody seems
to have looked for a missed win, which was pointed out a
good twenty years later by Paul Schlensker in *Schach-Echo*.
WH **40 ... Rb8 41. Kh3 e5 42. Rg1** The sealed move.
On the homeward journey this exciting game was given up
as a draw. ME ½–½ Fine 1958, 166–8; Heidenfeld 1982,
6–8; Khalifman & Yudasin in Soloviev 1997, 256–7; Euwe
1938, 101–3; *The Chess Review* 1939, 65.

(472) FINE—EUWE, M

A.V.R.O., The Netherlands (11), 1938 (22 Nov., Rotterdam)
Queen's Gambit Declined, Vienna Variation [D39]

1. d4 (For the only time in the tournament Fine does not
open with his king's pawn. Around this time Euwe usually
replied to 1 e4 with 1 ... e5, 1 ... e6 or occasionally 1 ... Nf6.)

1 ... Nf6 2. c4 e6 3. Nf3 d5 4. Bg5 Bb4+ (This variation was played and analyzed by the great theoretician Grünfeld (MCO, 157) (Indeed MCO offers his name as an alternative for the variation). In his analysis of the game Vidmar–Bogolyubov in the Nottingham tournament book Alekhine wrote that he considered its popularity undue. It does however still get outings today.) 5. Nc3 dxc4 6. e4 c5 7. e5 The original main line, which after much analysis and practical play has now become a secondary one. 7 Bxc4 is an improvement. T&dM 7 ... cxd4 The logical consequence of the system Black has opted for which, although it loses a piece, yields Black a mighty pawn fortress. The text is in any case stronger than 7 ... h6 8 exf6 hxg5 9 fxg7 Rg8 10 dxc5, leading to an endgame that favours White. ME 8. Qa4+ (8 exf6 gxf6 9 Qa4+ Nc6 led to Black's advantage in Apšenieks–Grünfeld, Folkestone Team Tournament 1933, after 10 0–0–0 Bxc3 11 Bh4 b5!!) 8 ... Nc6 9. 0–0–0 Bd7 With 9 ... h6 Black could hang on to the piece, but then, after 10 exf6 hxg5 11 fxg7 Rg8 12 Nxd4, White starts to dominate the proceedings. ME 10. Ne4! Be7 Masterly play on both sides. White, with consummate virtuosity, has brought his reserve cavalry to the front, while Black adds fuel to the fire by sacrificing a piece, in preference to the less propitious 10 ... h6. T&dM 11. exf6 gxf6 12. Bh4 Rc8 The tempting 12 ... Nb4 is bad in view of 13 Qxb4 Bxb4 14 Nxf6 Kf8 15 Rd4, and White captures three pieces for the queen in a very favourable position that is fairly certain to lead to a win. This is how Fine surprised the great expert of this variation, Grünfeld, in the "Arbeiderspers" eight-player event of 1936. ME (According to *The Chess Review* the text was an innovation by Euwe, though Botvinnik apparently stated that it had been the subject of analysis in the Soviet Union. In MCO Fine also gave the line 12 ... Na5 13 Qc2 e5 14 Nxd4 exd4 15 Rxd4 Qb6 16 Rd6!) 13. Kb1 Also possible was 13 Bxf6 Bxf6 14 Nd6+ Kf8 15 Nxc8 Qxc8 16 Qxc4 e5. White is the exchange ahead but Black has a strong centre and good winning chances. CR 13 ... Na5 14. Qc2 e5 15. Nxd4 The best continuation; as long as the black pawn formation remains intact, White cannot complete his development satisfactorily. ME (BCM preferred 15 Nxe5 fxe5 16 Nd6+, but then 16 ... Kf8, rather than 16 ... Bxd6 17 Bxd8 Kxd8 18 Qd2 as given by the annotator, 17 Bxe7+ Kxe7 18 Nxc8+ Qxc8 leaves Black with a powerful position; while Tartakower and du Mont propose 15 Bg3, with the latent threat Nxe5. AW) 15 ... exd4 16. Rxd4 Qb6 (In MCO Fine assessed the position as being favourable to Black.) 17. Qc3? (A line suggested in *The Chess Review*, 17 Rd6! Rc6 18 Rxc6 (or 18 Bxf6 Rxd6 19 Bxh8 Bf5 20 Be2 dos Santos–Gyimesi ICCF EM/TT/B/02 1998) Qxc6 19 Be2 led to a draw in Komarov–Smagin, Norilsk 1987. Euwe's suggestion of 17 Rxd7 also resulted in sharing of the point (Goldin–Gelfand, Vilnius 1988), and according to Lalić 17 Nxf6+ Bxf6 18 Qe4+ Kf8 19 Bxf6 Qxf6 20 Rxd7 Re8 21 Qd4 Re1+ 22 Kc2 Qxd4 23 Rxd4 Ke7 Kasparov–Ribli, Barcelona 1989, leads to a roughly balanced ending. Khalifman also failed to break down Ribli's resistance after 17 Rd5 Be6 18 Qa4+ Nc6 19 Bxc4 Qb4 20 Qxb4 Nxb4 21 Bb5+ Kf8 22 Rd2 Bxa2+ 23 Ka1 Be6 24 Nxf6 Kg7

25 Nh5+, Groningen 1993.) 17 ... Bf5 An important pin on Ne4, eliminating the threat of Nf6 and Re4. ME 18. g4 Bg6 Black obviously has to maintain the pin on the Ne4. ME 19. f4? (Lalić gives the line 19 Bd3 Rc6 20 Bc2 Re6 21 Rhd1 0–0 22 f4 Bb4 23 Qf3 Bc5 with a satisfactory position for both sides. 19 Bg2 as suggested by BCM, and 19 Kc1 may also be playable.) 19 ... Bc5! Now Black wins at least an exchange. ME 20. Rxc4 Forced as Black could not abandon his cover of the Ne4. ME 20 ... Nxc4 21. f5 21 Qxc4 will no longer work either in view of 21 ... 0–0, with the threat of 22 ... Be3. ME 21 ... Bd4 22. Qb3 22 Nxf6 was impossible in view of 22 ... Bxf6 23 Bxf6 Qxf6! 24 Qxf6 Nd2, and mate. ME 22 ... Qc6 23. Bg2 Qxe4+ The simplest liquidation, which immediately results in a winning endgame. ME 24. Bxe4 Nd2+ 25. Ka1 Nxb3+ 26. axb3 0–0 27. fxg6 hxg6 28. Kb1 28 Bb7 would be met by 28 ... Rc2. 28 ... Rfe8 29. Bd3 Re3 30. Rd1 Be5 White resigned. 0–1 Euwe, from the tournament book, in Münninghoff 2001, 233; BCM 1939, 125; Tartakower & du Mont 1955, 103–4; *The Chess Review* 1939, 67; Lalić 2000, 9.

(473) FLOHR, S—FINE

A.V.R.O. The Netherlands (12), 1938 (24 Nov., 's-Gravenhage)
Zwolle System [E02]

1. d4 Nf6 2. c4 e6 3. g3 d5 4. Bg2 This opening deserves the name Zwolle system, on account of its use in the 14th match game Alekhine–Euwe, Zwolle 1937. It should be borne in mind that the continuation 3 g3 has a particular effect here; White, by not playing 3 Nc3, avoids the Nimzowitsch-Indian Defence (3 ... Bb4), and also, by not playing 3 Nf3, avoids the replies 3 ... b6 (Queen's Indian Defence) and 3 ... d5 (4 Bg5 Bb4+ or 4 Nc3 c5). Any one of these would not be unfavourable for White, but they present the slight psychological burden that it is the player of the black pieces who would initiate the complications. On 3 Nf3 d5 4 g3 the Catalan System, against the Queen's Gambit Declined, would arise. Both systems, the Zwolle and the Catalan, though similar in aim, have their own nuances. 4 ... dxc4 5. Qa4+ Bd7 The simplest way of disrupting White's plan. 6. Qxc4 Bc6! 7. Nf3 Bd5 8. Qc2 8 Qd3 or even 8 Qa4+ would have been better. After the text the white queen will be forced to lose another tempo. 8 ... Nc6 White now has to reckon with the threat of ... Bxf3 followed by ... Nxd4. 9. Qd1 Bb4+ 10. Nc3 0–0 11. 0–0 In order to avoid drifting into a passive position, White offers a pawn. 11 ... Bxf3 12. Bxf3 Qxd4 13. Bxc6 Qxd1 14. Rxd1 bxc6 15. Na4 The game stands approximately equal. White's better pawn formation and Black's extra material balance each other out. ME 15 ... Rfd8 16. Bg5 Rxd1+ 17. Rxd1 Nd5 18. a3 h6 19. Bd2 Draw agreed. ½–½ Euwe 1938, 120–1.

(474) FINE—ALEKHINE, A

A.V.R.O., The Netherlands (13), 1938 (25 Nov., Leiden)
Spanish Game, Steinitz Defence Deferred [C76]

1. e4 e5 2. Nf3 Nc6 3. Bb5 a6 4. Ba4 d6 5. 0–0 Bd7
Or 5 ... b5 6 Bb3 Na5 7 d4 exd4 8 Nxd4 Bb7 9 c4 Nxc4 10
a4 c6 11 Qe2 Ne7 12 Bg5 h6 with equality, Leonhardt–
Schlechter, Ostend 1906. 6. c3 g6 7. d4 Bg7 The fianchetto development is rarely seen nowadays. RF 8. dxe5
Alternatively 8 Be3 Nge7 9 c4! (9 Re1 0–0 10 dxe5 Nxe5
11 Nxe5 Bxe5 12 Bb3 Nc6 13 Nd2 Bg7 with an even game,
Michell–Capablanca, Hastings 1919) exd4 10 Nxd4 0–0
11 Nc3 Nxd4 12 Bxd4 Bxa4 13 Nxa4 Bxd4 14 Qxd4 Nc6
15 Qd2 Qf6 16 Rad1 with a minimal advantage, Yates–Capablanca, Hastings 1929. 8 ... Nxe5 Perhaps better is 8 ...
dxe5 9 Be3 Nge7 10 Bc5, but Black's game is still not easy
(if 10 ... 0–0 11 Bxc6 cripples the Black pawns). RF 9. Nxe5
dxe5 10. f4! New and strong. The usual move is 10 Be3.
BCM 10 ... Bxa4 Much later Romanovsky found an improvement here for Black: 10 ... Bb5! 11 Bxb5+ axb5 12 Qb3
Qd7 13 fxe5 Bxe5 14 Na3 c6. But by 15 Bf4 White still gets
good play. ME 11. Qxa4+ Qd7 A temporary pawn sacrifice
which is practically forced, since 11 ... b5 12 Qb3 would give
White chances, not only on the f-file, but also on the queen's
wing (a2-a4!). ME 12. Qxd7+ Kxd7 13. fxe5 Ke6 14. Bf4
So that the pawn cannot be taken by Black: if 14 ... Bxe5
15 Bxe5 Kxe5 16 Rxf7. RF 14 ... Rf8 14 ... Ne7 was not
much better. There would follow 15 Nd2 Nc6 16 Nf3, and it
would be difficult for Black to meet the twin threats of Nd4+
and Ng5+. CR 15. Nd2 Bxe5 16. Nb3! Threatens 17 Nc5+.
It is clear that the vulnerable position of White's king is still
causing trouble. ME 16 ... Bxf4 A trap. If now 17 Nc5+
Black wins a piece by 17 ... Kd6 18 Nxb7+ Kc6 19 Na5+ Kb5.
ME 17. Rxf4 b6

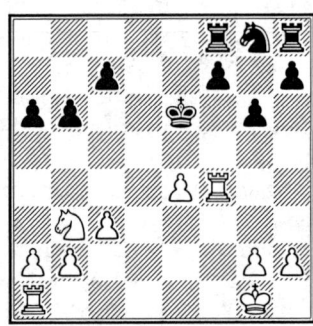

*Position after
Black's 17th move*

18. a4! Threatening 19 a5! to which Black could not reply
19 ... b5 because of 20 Nc5+. BCM 18 ... Ke5 Up and at
'em. Euwe considers this a serious error, but Black is already
lost. If 18 ... a5 (as he suggests) 19 Nd4+ Ke7 20 Rd1 wins;
Black cannot develop. RF 19. g3! Black had underestimated
the force of this simple little move. Apparently he had reckoned only with 19 Raf1, whereupon 19 ... f5 20 g4 Ne7 would
have followed. The advantage of White's actual move is that
his queen's rook remains on its own file—a very important
point in view of the threatened a4-a5. ME 19 ... Nf6
19 ... g5? would have been fatal, for after 20 Rf5+ Kxe4
21 Raf1, the black king is in a mating net. Nor is there time
for 19 ... a5 because of 20 Nd4!, after which 20 ... Nf6 fails
against 21 Nf3+! Ke6 22 Ng5+ Ke5 (or 22 ... Ke7) 23 Raf1,
winning the f-pawn. ME 20. Nd2 Nh5 The knight is out

of play here. 20 ... Nd7 would have been a little stronger.
ME 21. Rf2 Ke6 Black now realizes that 18 ... Ke5 was an
unfortunate choice. 21 ... a5 would have been met by 22 b4.
ME 22. a5! Ra8 Not 22 ... b5 23 Nb3 Kd6 24 Rd1+ Kc6
25 Rdf1 f6 26 g4 and Black's position crumbles to pieces.
BCM 23. Raf1! Rhd8 Black loses a pawn after 23 ... Rhf8
24 g4 Ng7 25 axb6 cxb6 26 Rf6+ Ke7 27 Nc4. BCM 24. Nf3
Threatening not only 25 Ng5+ but also 25 Nd4+. ME 24 ...
Ke7 If 24 ... f6 then 25 g4 Nf4 26 Nd4+ Rxd4 27 Rxf4
Rd2 28 Rxf6+. BCM 25. axb6 cxb6 26. Ng5! Now
26 ... f6 loses to 27 Nxh7 Rd6 28 g4. The loss of a pawn is
no longer to be avoided. ME 26 ... h6 Alekhine was in terrible time straits. Three minutes left for fourteen moves. CR
27. Rxf7+ Kd6 28. Nf3 g5 29. Nd4 The rest is only
a matter of endgame technique. ME 29 ... Re8 30. Rh7
Rh8 31. Rff7 Rxh7 32. Rxh7 Rf8 33. Rxh6+ Nf6
34. Nf3 Kc5 35. Nd2 g4 Fifteen seconds with five
moves to go. CR 36. Rg6 Nd7 37. Rxg4 Ne5 38. Rg5
Kd6 39. Rf5 Rd8 40. Nf3 Nd3 Under the wire in time
to resign. CR 41. Rd5+ Ke7 42. Rxd8 Kxd8 43. b3
Kc7 44. Nd2 a5 45. Kf1 b5 46. Ke2 Black resigned.
1–0 *The Chess Review* 1939, 91–2; Fine 1958, 169–72; Euwe
1938, 133–5; BCM 1939, 160; Euwe & Kramer 1964, 64–5;
Euwe & Kramer 1965, 193–5.

(475) KERES, P–FINE

A.V.R.O. The Netherlands (14), 1938 (27 Nov., Amsterdam)
Spanish Game, Open Variation [C83]

1. e4 e5 2. Nf3 Nc6 3. Bb5 a6 4. Ba4 Nf6 5. 0–0
Nxe4 Considering the circumstances, both players dead-
locked in the final round; the text is to say the least, rather
ambitious. The staid and stolid 5 ... Be7 is less risky. CR (1
minute) 6. d4 (30 seconds) 6 ... b5 7. Bb3 d5 (30 seconds) 8. dxe5 (30 seconds) 8 ... Be6 9. c3 (2 minutes)
9 ... Be7 (1 min 30 seconds) 10. Nbd2 (2 minutes)
10 ... 0–0 (2 minutes) 11. Nd4 Keres hoped to surprise
his opponent with this rare continuation. ME (7 minutes)
11 ... Nxd4 After considerable thought Fine finds the best
answer. The text and the two following moves were a
favourite of Dr. Tarrasch. It would be a mistake to take the
pawn-e5, as is shown by: 11 ... Nxe5? 12 Nxe4 dxe4 13 Bxe6
fxe6 14 Nxe6 Qxd1 15 Rxd1 Rfc8 16 Re1 and White at the
least captures a pawn in favourable circumstances. ME
(13 minutes) 12. cxd4 Nxd2 (24 minutes) 13. Bxd2 c5
A fairly weak isolated d-pawn is the result of the rapid
exchanges. CR 14. dxc5 (2 minutes) 14 ... Bxc5 Black's
d-pawn is isolated, but that is not so important as White is
not in any position to exploit it, as it is difficult for White to
make the advance f2-f4. The game stands about even. ME
15. Rc1 Rc8 (16 minutes) 16. Rxc5 Apparently attractive,
but only leading to simplification. ME (5 minutes) 16 ...
Rxc5 17. Bb4 Qc7 (2 minutes) 18. Qd4! (14 minutes
30 seconds) 18 ... Rc1 (4 minutes 30 seconds) 19. Bxf8
Kxf8 (1 minute 30 seconds) There is nothing left in the
position. Black offered a draw here and White did not need
to think it over for long. So end the battles and the celebra-

tions begin. ME ½–½ *Chess* 1938-9, 162; *The Chess Review* 1939, 113; Euwe 1938, 137-8.

The day after the end of the tournament Keres officially issued a challenge to Alekhine with the backing of the A.V.R.O. committee. Alekhine kept them waiting for a considerable length of time. Keres, however, did not wish to play the match until he had completed his studies in 1940. Botvinnik was also working to get a match in the Soviet Union (He had discussed such a match with the World Champion immediately after the A.V.R.O. event). Flohr was still the official FIDE Candidate, but his sponsorship was insecure as a result of the political situation. Reshevsky (who unlike Fine was not a professional, and who had a sponsor) apparently tried to arrange a match, as did Capablanca. Euwe decided to stand aside for a few years to let one of the younger players have a shot. Fine seems not to have made any effort at all, evidence perhaps that he did not believe chess was to be his career or perhaps he felt that Keres had the moral right to play the match (Fine, of course, knew it was likely to be difficult for him to raise funds in the States).

During the A.V.R.O. tournament several of the participants were invited to take part in an experiment in chess psychology conducted by the player and scientist Adriaan de Groot. De Groot was attempting to determine the thinking processes of players, and how these varied between players of different strengths. Keres, Alekhine, Flohr, Fine and Euwe all agreed. The principal experiment took the form of the presentation of a chess position upon which the players would comment aloud.

De Groot determined that Fine had a tendency to "try out" variations, rather than, for example, conceive a plan and work out all its ramifications as far as was possible, the highly systematic method of Dr. Euwe. Discussing the technique of Fine (and Nico Cortlever), De Groot remarked, "Like Dr. Euwe, these two subjects seem to make relatively little use of intuitive experience while their thought processes are also consciously organized to a high degree, but their attitude is more *inductive* than deductive; they tend to try out and calculate sample variations and to see *empirically* whether an idea has any value rather than to group, to systematize, and to order. Subjects like M2 (*Cortlever*) and G4 (*Fine*) could be called 'empiricists' in thinking. Like G5 (*Euwe*) they do not rely much on intuition, but unlike G5 they do not believe in 'logical' systematization either." (De Groot, 314)

U.S. Open Champion Again, 1939–1941

Back in the United States, with war looming in Europe, with a wife to support and academic obligations,

Fine reduced his activity. He had evidently already decided that professional chess was unlikely to be sufficiently rewarding to keep his attention in the long term, or provide financial stability. During the summer lay off he regained his United States Open title ahead of a strong field, but engaged in little other chess. He then proceeded to recapture the Marshall Club Championship in a rather drawn out tournament.

The 1940 United States Championship turned out to be the closest he would get to the title. In another final round encounter with long-time rival Sammy Reshevsky he returned to the king pawn openings, springing a surprise by renovating the classical Two Knights. Having obtained a winning position, he made an error which allowed his opponent to simplify to an equal ending, and the chance was gone. The Open Championship was another story: Reuben made a clean sweep in the final to win with ease. There followed a trip west and powerful displays in two minor events.

At the beginning of 1941 he retained his Marshall Chess Club title, but it was to be the last time he would play in the event. At the United States Open tournament in Saint Louis, he allowed two draws (contrary to his recollection when discussing Fischer's 11–0 victory in the U.S. Championship. His suggestion that this, and his clean sweep the year before, were perhaps qualitatively equivalent to the feat of the greatest American player looks unconvincing when the quality of opposition, particularly in the lower half of the table, is considered.). The New York State Chess Association meeting at Hamilton that year attracted a strong entry. Fine's draw with Reshevsky was somewhat fortunate, though perhaps he was due some luck against this opponent, but in the end he came out a clear winner ahead of three other grandmasters.

The years 1940 and 1941, highly successful competitively, were the last in which Fine undertook multiple events. He only exceeded twenty games in a year on one more occasion, and then by but a single game. In effect Fine gave up his professional career as a chessplayer at the age of 26 at the height of his powers. Had he been able to continue playing professionally, he would almost certainly have improved further—most players reach their peak some time around their mid-thirties. Instead, in late 1941, he moved away from the centres of gravity of American chess to the capital where he was to undertake work for the government.

New York Metropolitan League, March, 1939

Fine's return to chess in the States was marked by his now familiar successful outings in the Metropolitan League. On 18 March he defeated Simchow of the Rice Progressive Chess Club, the following Saturday he was successful in the match between the Marshall Club and their main rivals the Manhattan Chess Club.

Simchow   0   Fine   1
Kupchik   0   Fine   1

(476) SIMCHOW, A—FINE

Metropolitan Chess League, New York, 1939 (18 March)
Alekhine's Defence [B02]

**1. e4 Nf6 2. e5 Nd5 3. Bc4 e6 4. d4 d6 5. Nf3 c5!?
6. 0–0 Nb6 7. Bb5+ Bd7 8. Bxd7+ N8xd7 9. dxc5
Nxc5 10. Nc3 dxe5 11. Nxe5 Qxd1 12. Rxd1 Rc8
13. Be3 f6 14. Bxc5 Bxc5 15. Nd3 Be7 16. Re1 Kf7
17. Re2 Rhd8 18. Rae1 Rc6 19. Nf4 e5 20. Nd3
Nc4 21. Nd1 Bf8 22. f3 Nd6 23. N1f2 Nf5 24. c3
Rcd6 25. Rd2 R6d7 26. Redl Kg8 27. b4 Ne3
28. Re1 Nd5 29. Rc2 Rc7 30. Recl Rdc8 31. Ne4**

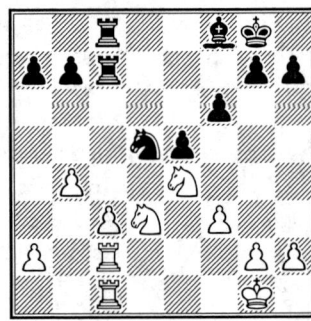

*Position after
White's 31st move*

**31 ... Nxb4 32. Nxb4 Bxb4 33. g4 b6 34. h4 Be7
35. h5 Kf7 36. Kf1 g6 37. hxg6+ hxg6 38. Ke1 f5
39. gxf5 gxf5 40. Nf2 Ba3 41. Rd1 Rxc3 42. Rxc3
Rxc3 43. Rd7+ Ke6 44. Rxa7 Rxf3 45. Ke2 e4
46. Ra4 Bc5 47. Nd1 Rh3 48. Rc4 Rh2+** White
resigned. **0–1**

(477) KUPCHIK, A—FINE

Metropolitan Chess League, New York, 1939 (25 March)
Sicilian Defence, Four Knights Variation [B45]

**1. e4 c5 2. Nf3 e6 3. Nc3 Nc6 4. d4 cxd4 5. Nxd4
Nf6 6. Be2** Emms main line in this position begins
6 Ndb5, with White retaining some advantage. AW **6 ...
Bb4** Fine reckoned that Black had at least equalized now.
AW **7. Nxc6** An unusual reply, but probably safest. After
7 0–0 Bxc3 8 bxc3 Nxe4 White has nothing for the pawn
sacrificed. **7 ... dxc6** 7 ... bxc6 8 e5 Nd5 9 Bd2 is in
White's favour. **8. Qxd8+ Kxd8 9. f3** Too passive. 9 Bg5
h6 10 Bxf6+ gxf6 11 0–0–0+ was relatively best. **9 ... e5
10. Bd2** Since the exchange of bishop for knight was not to
be feared, 10 Be3, occupying the important diagonal was
indicated. **10 ... Be6 11. 0–0–0 Nd7 12. a3** Driving the
black bishop where he wants to go. 12 Be2 was still preferable. **12 ... Bc5 13. Rhe1** Preparing to challenge Black's
command of the g1-a7 diagonal. **13 ... Kc7 14. Bf1 Bf2
15. Re2 Bd4** Preventing 16 Be3, which would be met now
by 16 ... Bc4 17 R2e1 Bxf1 18 Bxd4 exd4 and wins. **16. Ree1
a5 17. Be3 Bxe3+ 18. Rxe3 Nc5** White is now burdened

with a hopelessly passive position: the best he can do is wait
for Black to make a break. **19. a4** Sealing the queenside, but
creating another weakness. **19 ... g5 20. b3 g4 21. fxg4
Bxg4 22. Be2 Be6**

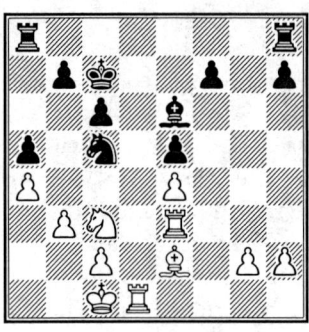

*Position after
Black's 22nd move*

23. Rf1 An inconsistent manoeuvre which only makes
White's position worse. The counterattack on Black's f-pawn
will fail and Black will have a chance to occupy the vital
d-file. The most logical defence policy was 23 Rg3, provoking the exchange of one pair of rooks, followed by g3 and
just sitting tight. Although Black's position is preferable no
matter what White does, this policy would still reduce his
winning chances to a minimum. **23 ... Rhg8** Preventing
the occupation of the g-file. **24. Rf2 Rad8 25. Bh5 Rd4
26. Ref3 Rg7 27. h3** If 27 Rf6 Kd8! 28 Rh6? Bxb3! and
Black should win. **27 ... Kd8 28. Kb2 Ke8** Better than
28 ... Ke7, when 29 Bg4 gives White strong counterplay.
29. Re3 Rd4 30. Be2 Ke7 31. Bf1 White can hardly
do anything but mark time. **31 ... Rg8 32. Kc1 Rgd8
33. Rfe2 Rb4 34. Re1?** This loses immediately. 34 Rd2
is refuted by 34 ... R8d4, threatening both ... Bxb3 and ...
Nxe4, while 34 Nb2 fails because of 34 ... Rb6 35 Nc3 Rd4.
The only playable defence was 34 Kb2. **34 ... Bxb3!
35. cxb3 Nxb3+** Or 36 Kb1 Rd2 37 Nb2 Rb6 38 Rxb3
Rxb3+ 39 Ka1 Ra3 40 Bc4 Rxa4 and wins. **36. Kb2 Rd2+
37. Ka3 Nd4** White resigned. **0–1** Fine, *The Chess Review*
1939, 81–2.

Chess, 14 May, 1939, 312, announced that there was to
be no Keres–Alekhine match for the world title. Alekhine,
with good reasons outlined in an article for the *Manchester
Guardian*, refused to take part in a peripatetic match (even
though that was apparently the plan for the Alekhine–Flohr
match), and did not answer a letter addressed to him from
the A.V.R.O. committee after the conclusion of the tournament in November 1938. Fine had returned to college on
returning from his extended sojourn in Europe and obtained an M.S. degree in education in 1939. The Alekhine–
Flohr match apparently fell through after the occupation
of Czechoslovakia led to the loss of funding for the event.

North American Championship Preliminaries, New York, July 17–20, 1939

"The fortieth annual congress of the American Chess
Federation opened at New York City in the beautiful colo-

nial room of the George Washington Hotel, on Tuesday, July 18, 1939. The field of twenty-eight aspirants for the Open Chess Championship of the Federation includes for the first time both the names of the United States champion and the American Federation titleholder, as U.S. Champion Reshevsky makes a bid to hold both titles simultaneously. Chief obstacles in his path loom as Reuben Fine, jointly with Keres, the A.V.R.O. conqueror, and I. A. Horowitz, winner at Philadelphia in 1936. The unbroken record of the Federation—a tournament every year for forty years—was preserved as the players banded together under the guidance of Milton L. Hanauer and Fred Reinfeld, to stage a Tournament of the Players. No funds were guaranteed. Prizes will be provided from entry fees, special contributions and gate receipts. The entrants represent a wide geographical area, with Pinkus doing the ambassadorial honours from the tropics, Ulvestad and Yanofsky [sic] the Far West, and the North being ably represented by the Canadian trio, Rauch, Kitces and Blumin. Twenty-eight entrants are divided into four sections of seven contestants each. The top three scorers in each group will qualify for the twelve-man North American Championship Finals. Fine's score [in the preliminaries] might indicate he qualified the easy way, with a mixture of draws and wins. But his many time-pressure troubles were nerve-singeing, Fine withstood them better than the gallery! Unfortunately, a triple tie for the third qualifying post had to be decided on a coin toss. Yanofsky didn't let his poor showing as a coin-tosser mar his triumph at chess in the Consolations." (*U.S.C.F. 5*, 1939 reprinted from *The Chess Review*) Fine qualified ahead of Seidman on four points and Friend and Hellman on three and a half. His address was given as Forest Hills, L.I.

		1	2	3	4	5	6	7	
1	Fine	*	½	½	1	½	1	1	4½
2	Seidman	½	*	1	½	1	½	½	4
3=	Friend	½	0	*	0	1	1	1	3½
3=	Hellman	0	½	1	*	0	1	1	3½
3=	Yanofsky	½	0	0	1	*	1	1	3½
6	Garfinkel	0	½	0	0	0	*	1	1½
7	Peckar	0	½	0	0	0	0	*	½

(478) FINE—YANOFSKY, D

U.S.C.F. Open, preliminaries, New York (1.1), 1939 (17 July)
Sicilian Defence, Accelerated Dragon Variation [B37]

1. Nf3 Nf6 2. c4 c5 I took a bit of time over this move as this was the first time I had given serious thought to this opening. Not knowing better, I copied Fine's move which may (and does) allow White to obtain a favourable variation of the Sicilian Defence. Nowadays I would consider 2 ... e6 or 2 ... d6. DAY **3. d4 cxd4 4. Nxd4 Nc6** This enables White to play e4 presently and is, therefore, not to be recommended; correct is 4 ... e6, with a pin of White's queen's knight by ... Bb4 and a contesting of the centre by ... d5.

ACB **5. Nc3 g6** Better would be 5 ... e6 as after 6 e4, 6 ... Bb4 is quite satisfactory and 6 Nxc6 dxc6 7 Qxd8+ Kxd8 is very drawish. DAY **6. e4 Bg7 7. Nc2** White has obtained one of the ideal positions against the Sicilian as it is very difficult for Black to play ... d5 or ... b5 and these are the best chances Black has in the Sicilian of opening files for his rooks particularly as long as White keeps the c-file valueless. DAY **7 ... 0–0 8. Be2 d6** White should have played 8 Be3 and after 8 ... d6 9 Be2 Nd7 10 Qd2 when I probably would still have tried 10 ... Nc5 11 f3 and eventually ... f5. DAY **9. 0–0 Nd7 10. Qd2** Intending, of course, a fianchetto of the bishop; but it seems to me that White gains by adopting the normal line: Be3, f4, Bf3 and Qe2, or even, instead of f4, f3 and Qd2. ACB **10 ... Nc5 11. f3 a5 12. b3 f5** A surprise! Although this leaves him weak along centre files, passive play in this position is tantamount to resignation. ACB **13. exf5** This reserves his f-pawn to dislodge a knight which may be posted at e5. ACB **13 ... Bxf5 14. Bb2 Bxc2** Seizing an opportunity to simplify. ACB **15. Qxc2 Nd4 16. Qd2 a4! 17. Nxa4** The obvious 17 b4 loses to 17 ... a3! 18 bxc5 (18 Bc1 Nxe2+) axb2 19 Rab1 (19 Rad1 Nxe2+ 20 Nxe2 Rxa2 21 cxd6 exd6 22 Qxd6 Qxd6 23 Rxd6 Ra1 24 Rdd1 Rfa8 and the pawn queens) Nxe2+ 20 Nxe2 Rxa2 21 Nc3 Ra3. DAY **17 ... Nxe2+ 18. Qxe2 Nxa4 19. Bxg7 Kxg7 20. bxa4 Rxa4** Simpler to draw would be 20 ... Qc7 21 Qb2+ Kg8 22 Rb1 Rxa4 23 Qxb7 Rxc4. DAY The net result of Black's courageous play is that he has created two weak pawns in the white camp (a- and c-pawns) as compensation for his own weak spots (b-, e- or d-pawns). ACB **21. Qb2+ Rf6 22. Qxb7 Rxc4 23. Rfe1 Rc7 24. Qb2** Fine tries to tie Black's pieces to the defence of the backward e-pawn before advancing the passed pawn. DAY **24 ... Kf7 25. Re4** By not going to e2, he finds it necessary to double his rooks to protect the second rank. But with 25 Re2, this rank is secure, the queen's rook may remain on a1 (where it belongs) behind the a-pawn which can advance at once. ACB **25 ... Qc8 26. Rae1 Qb7 27. Qd2 Kg8 28. h3 Rf5 29. Re6 Kg7** Black nonchalantly bides his time until Fine gives up the idea of winning. DAY **30. Qd4+ Kg8 31. Kh2 Rf7 32. Qh4 Rc2!** This abrupt counter brings White's previous manoeuvres to naught. DAY **33. R6e2** On 33 Rxe7, 33 ... Qxf3! gives Black an easy draw. DAY **33 ... Rxe2 34. Rxe2 Kf8 35. a4** White's only winning chance, but no win! DAY **35 ... Qd5 36. Qb4 Qc5 37. Qxc5 dxc5 38. Rc2 Rf5 39. a5 c4 40. Ra2 Rc5 41. a6 Rc8** His defence is precise and good enough for a draw; on 42 a7, he plays ... Ra8 and pushes his c-pawn. ACB **42. Kg3 c3 43. a7** Hoping for 43 ... c2 44 Rxc2! DAY **43 ... Ra8** Draw agreed. Introducing you to a highly talented sixteen-year-old [sic] Canadian, who impresses one with his intelligence, nerve and fighting qualities. ACB ½–½ Yanofsky, 18–9; ACB 1939, 89–90.

(479) FINE—GARFINKEL, B

U.S.C.F. Open, preliminaries, New York (1.2), 1939 (18 July)
Nimzowitsch-Indian Defence [E40]

1. d4 Nf6 2. c4 e6 3. Nc3 Bb4 4. e3 Bxc3+ 5. bxc3
b6 6. Bd3 Bb7 7. f3 c5 8. Ne2 Nc6 9. e4 d6
10. 0–0 Qd7 11. Be3 0–0–0 12. Nc1 Na5 13. Nb3
Qa4 14. Qe2 Ba6 15. Nxa5 Qxa5 16. Rfb1 Qa4
17. Bc1

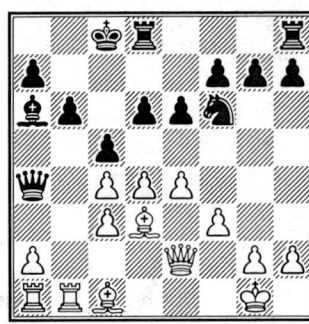

*Position after
White's 17th move*

17 ... Nd7 18. Rb3 Qc6 19. a4 Kc7 20. a5 Ra8
21. Rba3 Rab8 22. d5 Qa8 23. axb6+ Black resigned.
1–0

(480) PECKAR, M—FINE

U.S.C.F. Open, preliminaries, New York (1.3), 1939 (19 July)
Sicilian Defence [B20]

1. e4 c5 2. Ne2 e6 3. g3 d5 4. Bg2 dxe4 5. Bxe4
Nf6 6. Nbc3 Nxe4 7. Nxe4 Nc6 8. c3?? f5 White
resigned. 0–1

(481) FINE—HELLMAN, G

U.S.C.F. Open, preliminaries New York (1.4), 1939 (19 July)
Spanish Opening [C84]

1. e4 e5 2. Nf3 Nc6 3. Bb5 a6 4. Ba4 Nf6 5. 0–0
Be7 6. d4 exd4 7. e5 Ne4 8. Re1 Nc5 9. Bxc6 dxc6
10. Nxd4 Ne6 11. Nf5 Qxd1 12. Rxd1 Bd7 13. Nc3
Rd8 14. Be3 Bc8 15. Ne4 b6 16. f4 h6 17. Nxe7
Kxe7 18. f5 Rxd1+ 19. Rxd1 Rd8 20. Rxd8 Nxd8
21. g4 c5 22. c3 Bb7

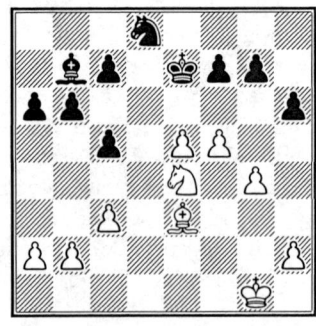

*Position after
Black's 22nd move*

23. f6+ Kf8 24. fxg7+ Kxg7 25. Nf6 Ne6 26. Kf2
Bc6 27. Kg3 Nf8 28. h4 Ne6 29. h5 Bb7 30. Kh4
Bc6 31. g5 hxg5+ 32. Bxg5 Nxg5 33. Kxg5 b5
34. a3 a5 35. h6+ Kh8 36. Kf5 Bg2 37. Ne8 c6

38. Kf6 Bd5 39. Nd6 Kg8 40. Nxf7 Bxf7 41. h7+
Resigns. 1–0

(482) FRIEND, B—FINE

U.S.C.F. Open, preliminaries, New York (1.5), 1939 (20 July)
Grünfeld Defence [D70]

1. d4 Nf6 2. c4 g6 3. f3 d5 It is interesting to note that
Fine prefers this to 3 ... d6, for this variation is a great
favourite of his—with the White pieces! 4. cxd5 Nxd5
5. e4 Nb6 6. Nc3 Bg7 7. Be3 Nc6 The idea of exerting pressure along the long diagonal is one of the cardinal
points of this defence. 8. Bb5 The usual course 8 d5 Ne5
9 Bd4 gives White a fine game. The deviation in the text
also has its points, though not quite so strong as the book
line. 8 ... 0–0 Proceeding on the theory that after 9 Bxc6
bxc6 the possibilities of ... Nc4 and ... Ba6, coupled with
pressure on the d-pawn and the general effectiveness of the
two bishops, will compensate for the weakness of the doubled c-pawn. 9. Nge2 Bd7 10. a3 To prevent ... Nb4.
10 ... a6 11. Bd3 Be8 12. d5 Ne5 13. Bxb6! Surprising and original play. White is not afraid to part with a
bishop, as he is left with a strong centre which gives him
good chances. 13 ... cxb6 14. Qd2 b5 15. 0–0 Qb6+
16. Kh1 b4 17. axb4 Qxb4 18. Ra2 The b-pawn is safe
for the moment, as Black was not really threatening to win
the pawn with ... Nxd3 and ... Qxb2?—for then Rfb1 would
win the queen. But eventually the b-pawn would have to be
guarded directly. Incidentally, the peculiar position of the
rook at this square could have been put to good use later on
by White! 18 ... Rc8 19. Rd1 Bd7 20. h3 Qb6 21. f4
Nc4 22. Bxc4 Rxc4 23. e5! g5?! Fine has played in
good positional style, but the power of White's centre pawns
has become even more evident. Since the vaunted two bishops cut a sorry figure against the knights, Fine adopts a vio-
lent method (doubtless based on underestimation of his
youthful opponent!) of putting the centre pawns in their
place. But they become stronger than ever! 24. Qd3! Rfc8
25. d6! e6 Leaving White with a powerful passed d-pawn,
but Nd5 had to be ruled out of order. 26. Qg3! The shift
to the kingside has been executed very cleverly. Black finds
himself in a miserable position now; for example 26 ... gxf4
27 Nxf4 Kh8 28 Nh5 Rg8 29 Rf1 with a winning position.
Fine therefore adopts the tried and true method of "swindling." To appreciate his artistry in this respect, it should be
borne in mind that he had already consumed all but a
minute or so of his time, and his next 14 moves were made
so rapidly that he looked like Liszt playing a cadenza! 26 ...
Kh8?! 27. Qxg5 Qf2?! 28. Rd3? Although White has
more time, he is also infected by the fever, and misses his
chance for immortality. Correct was the subtle 28 b3! Rb4
(if 28 ... Rb5? 29 Ne4. If 28 ... R4c6? 29 Nd4. If 28 ... Rxc3?
29 Rxc3. Who said knights are weak against bishops?)
29 Qe7! Bc6 30 Rg1 and White wins at least another pawn
to start with, leaving Black in a hopeless state. 28 ... Rg8
29. Rg3 Bc6 30. Kh2 h6 31. Qh4? White is evidently
rattled by his opponent's time pressure! 31 Qg4 would have

kept up the pressure on Black's position. **31 ... B×g2!** Saved! Fine is all eyes and fingers, and greedily clutches the g-pawn. Simplification spells salvation. **32. Rg4 Qxh4 33. Rxh4 Bc6 34. Rg4 Rc8 35. Rg3 f6 36. Re3 fxe5 37. fxe5 Rf8 38. Kg1 Rc5 39. Nd4 Rxe5** Black might even have won. If 39 ... Bxe5 40 Nxc6 (or 40 Nxe6 Bxc3! 41 bxc3 Rg8+), he should play 40 ... Bxd6! with a decisive advantage, and not 40 ... bxc6 41 Kg2 with a draw the likely result (Reinfeld). AW **40. Rxe5 Bxe5 41. Nxc6 bxc6 42. Ne4 Rd8** If 42 ... Rf4 43 d7! Bc7 44 Nc5! (not 44 Rxa6—Reinfeld—44 ... Rxe4 45 Rxc6 Ba5!). AW **43. Rxa6 Bxb2 44. Rxc6 Kg7 45. Rc7+ Kg6** Draw agreed. ½–½ Reinfeld, *U.S.C.F.* 1939, 42–4.

(483) SEIDMAN, H—FINE

U.S.C.F. Open, preliminaries, New York (1.7), 1939 (20 July)
Symmetrical English, Rubinstein Variation [A34]

1. c4 Nf6 2. Nc3 c5 3. Nf3 d5 4. cxd5 Nxd5 5. g3 Nc6 6. Bg2 Nc7 7. 0–0 e5 8. d3 Be7 9. Be3 0–0 10. Rc1 Rb8 11. Nd2 Nd4 12. Nc4 f6 13. a4 Be6 14. f4 Nf5 15. Bd2 Draw agreed. ½–½

North American Championship Finals (40th U.S. Open), New York, July 21–29, 1939

"Transferred somewhat belatedly from the Pacific coast, where it was originally intended to hold it somewhere in California, the annual meeting of the American Chess Federation was held from July 17 to 29 in New York City at the Hotel George Washington, Lexington Avenue and East 23rd Street. Doubtless the change in program and the little time left for preparation accounted for the comparatively small attendance of competitors. Nevertheless twenty-eight entered the four groups of seven players each in the preliminaries of the championship tournament, including Samuel Reshevsky and Reuben Fine. These were the favourites and they won the chief prizes. Reversing the order in the last United States championship tournament of the National Chess Federation, U.S.A., Fine finished first, half a point ahead of his great rival, and earned custody of the Kirk D. Holland trophy." (ACB 1939) "Reuben Fine had one tremendous advantage over the other aspirants and his win of the Federation championship was due entirely to this fortuitous, but not unique 'break' in the schedule. Reuben Fine did not have to play Reuben Fine! Everybody else did. If his form and time-gauging were uncertain in the preliminaries, his superlative play in the finals banished all memory of it, for he scored the 'money games' with sureness and regularity. His middle-of-the-road tactics evidenced a ready willingness to cope with the 'pet openings' of his adversaries, all of which he left in crumpled heaps along the road to the title." (*U.S.C.F. Yearbook 5*) Pandolfini records that the first prize in this event was $100. The time limit

was forty moves in the first two hours. The dating of Fine's games is open to question, they are misdated in his notebooks. The dates provided here are based on the assumption that the majority of dates were correct.

		1	2	3	4	5	6	7	8	9	10	11	12	
1	Fine	*	½	1	1	1	1	1	1	1	1	1	1	10½
2	Reshevsky	½	*	1	½	1	1	1	1	1	1	1	1	10
3	Horowitz	0	0	*	½	1	½	1	1	1	1	1	1	8
4	Pinkus	0	½	½	*	0	½	1	1	1	1	1	1	7½
5=	Santasiere	0	0	0	1	*	½	½	1	0	1	1	1	6
5=	Seidman	0	0	½	½	½	*	½	0	1	1	1	1	6
7=	Green	0	0	0	0	½	½	*	½	½	0	1	1	4
7=	Hellman	0	0	0	0	0	1	½	*	1	½	0	1	4
9=	Adams	0	0	0	0	1	0	½	0	*	0	1	1	3½
9=	Ulvestad	0	0	0	0	0	0	1	½	1	*	1	1	3½
11	Blumin	0	0	0	0	0	0	0	1	0	1	*	1	3
12	Jaffe	0	0	0	0	0	0	0	0	0	0	0	*	0

Jaffe forfeited six games, including one to Fine, but was defeated by Reshevsky.

(484) FINE—SANTASIERE, A

U.S.C.F. Open Championship, New York (1), 1939 (21 July)
Spanish Game, Worrall Attack [C86]

1. e4 e5 2. Nf3 Nc6 3. Bb5 a6 4. Ba4 Nf6 5. 0–0 Be7 6. Qe2 b5 7. Bb3 d6 8. a4! Bg4 9. c3 Rb8 10. h3 Bxf3 11. Qxf3 Na5 12. Bc2 c5 13. d3 Nc6 14. Qe2 Nd7 15. f4 Bf6 16. Be3 0–0 17. fxe5 Ndxe5 18. axb5 axb5 19. Nd2 Ng6 20. Nf3 Nce5 21. Rad1 Nxf3+ 22. Qxf3 Rc8 23. Bb1 Bg5 24. Bf2 Qf6 25. Qg4 Ne5 26. Qe2 Qh6 27. Ba2 Ng6 28. Bg3 Ne5 29. Kh1 Rc7 30. Rf5 g6 31. Rff1 Rd8 32. d4 cxd4 33. Rxd4

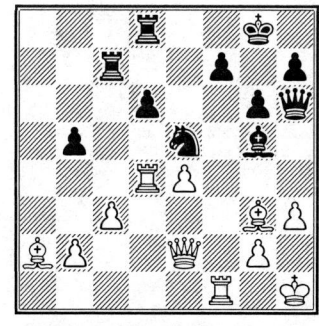

Position after White's 33rd move

33 ... Qf8 34. Qxb5 Rb8 35. Qe2 Rb6 36. Rdd1 Kg7 37. Rf2 h5 38. Rdf1 Rbb7 39. Bd5 Ra7 40. Qd1 h4 41. Bh2 Qe8 42. Qd4 f6 43. Bf4 Bxf4 44. Rxf4 Qd8 45. Qb6 Rd7 46. Qxd8 Rxd8 47. Rxf6 Rb8 48. b3 Rc7 49. Rxd6 Rxc3 50. Re6 Nd3 51. Rff6 Ne5 52. Rf4 Nd3 53. Re7+ Kh6 54. Rxh4+ Kg5 55. Rg4+ Kh6 56. Kh2 Nc5 57. Rc7 Nxe4 58. Rxg6+ Black resigned. **1–0**

(485) SEIDMAN, H—FINE

U.S.C.F. Open Championship, New York (2), 1939 (21 July)
Semi-Tarrasch [D41]

1. c4 Nf6 2. Nc3 c5 3. Nf3 d5 4. cxd5 Nxd5 5. d4 e6 By transposition we have reached a position in the Queen's Gambit Declined where the usual continuation is 6 e4 Nxc3 7 bxc3 cxd4 8 bxd4 Bb4+ 9 Bd2 Bxd2+ 10 Qxd2 0–0 with about even prospects; White has a preponderance in the centre and some attacking chances, while Black fianchettos his bishop and has good endgame possibilities with his queenside majority and play on the c-file. **6. e3** A move introduced by the Russians to avoid the somewhat hackneyed line just mentioned. Some excellent results have been achieved with it but Black should equalize with a little care. **6 ... Be7 7. Be2** A strangely timid move, 7 Bc4 being called for. Black is then in some embarrassment about his knight at d5, and White is in a position to obtain a normal development with Qe2, 0–0 and Rd1. In the A.V.R.O. Tournament, Botvinnik won a notable game from Alekhine, the continuation after 6 e3 being 6 ... Nc6 7 Bc4 cxd4 8 exd4 Be7 9 0–0 0–0 10 Re1 b6? (better 10 ... Nxc3 followed by 11 ... b6) 11 Nxd5 exd5 12 Bb5 Bd7 13 Qa4 and White has distinctly the better of it. **7 ... 0–0 8. 0–0 b6 9. Qb3** White would have done better to play for simplification with 9 Nxd5 Qxd5 10 dxc5. **9 ... Bb7 10. Rd1 Nd7** Black has equalized, PCO 193. **11. Ne5?** Another mistake, and this time one which contributes in large part to the loss of the game. After the ensuing exchange, Black has a queenside pawn majority, while White's doubled e-pawn is worthless, requires the attention of his pieces and thus prevents their most effective deployment. 11 Bd2 followed by Rac1 would have been better. **11 ... Nxe5 12. dxe5 Qc7 13. Nxd5** Not 13 e4? Nxc3 and Black wins a pawn. **13 ... Bxd5 14. Qc3**

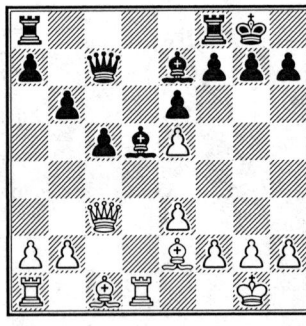

Position after White's 14th move

14 ... Rfd8 15. b3 Rd7 16. Bb2 Rad8 17. Qc2 If 17 Bb5 Bc6 18 Rxd7 Qxd7 19 Bxc6 Qxc6 and Black retains control of the c-file. **17 ... Qb7 18. f3** A final inexactitude, after which White's game goes steadily downhill. Proceeding from the view that Black's bishops are far more effective than are White's, the logical procedure was 18 Bb5 Bc6 19 Rxd7 Qxd7 20 Bxc6 Qxc6 21 Rd1 with a far more bearable position than the text. **18 ... b5!** Now the queenside pawns get in motion, and White is left with both ineffectual bishops. **19. Rac1 Qb6 20. e4 Bc6 21. Rxd7**

Rxd7 22. Rd1 c4+ 23. Kf1 Or 23 Kh1 cxb3 24 axb3 Qf2 and White is helpless. **23 ... cxb3 24. axb3 Rxd1+ 25. Qxd1**

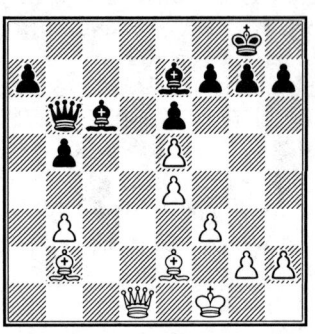

Position after White's 25th move

25 ... Bc5! Black's queen will eventually reach f2 with decisive effect. **26. Bc3 a5 27. Qd3 h6** Freeing his queen for action. **28. Ke1 b4 29. Bb2 Bg1 30. h3 a4!** The interesting attack on both wings leaves White without resource. **31. bxa4 Bxa4 32. Kd2 Kh7 33. g4** If 33 Bf1 Bh2 followed by ... Bf4+ with a winning position. **33 ... Qf2** Putting White in *Zugzwang*, 34 Kc1 being answered by 34 ... Qe1+. **34. Ba1**

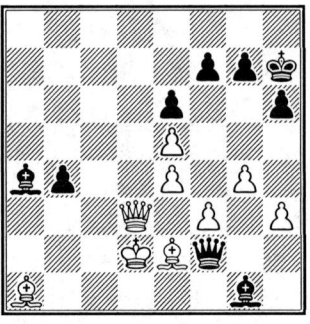

Position after White's 34th move

34 ... Qh2! 35. Bd4 There was no longer any sufficient defence: if 35 Qa6 Qf4+ wins; or 35 Ba1 Qf4+ 36 Ke1 Be3!. The text allows a conclusive simplifying manoeuvre. **35 ... Bxd4 36. Qxd4 Bb5 37. Qe3 b3** White resigned. Fine's excellent play, with his clever utilization of the queenside pawns and the two bishops, is analogous to his treatment of a similar position in one of his A.V.R.O. games against Reshevsky. **0–1** Reinfeld, BCM 1939, 405–7.

(486) FINE—ADAMS, W

U.S.C.F. Open Championship, New York (3), 1939 (22 July)
Albin Counter Gambit [D08]

1. Nf3 Nc6 2. c4 e5 3. d4 d5 4. dxe5 d4 5. a3 a5 6. g3 Be6 7. Nbd2 Bc5 8. Bg2 Nge7 9. 0–0 0–0 10. Qc2 Ng6 11. Nb3 Ba7 12. Bg5 Qd7 13. Rad1 Ngxe5 14. Nxe5 Nxe5 15. c5 d3! 16. exd3 Qa4 17. Na1 Qxc2 18. Nxc2 Bb3 19. d4 (see diagram) **19 ... Bxc2 20. Rd2 Bb3?! 21. dxe5 Bxc5 22. Rc1 Bb6 23. Bxb7 Rae8 24. Bf4 Rd8 25. Be4 Rxd2 26. Bxd2 Re8 27. Bc3 f6 28. Re1 fxe5 29. Bf3 Rf8**

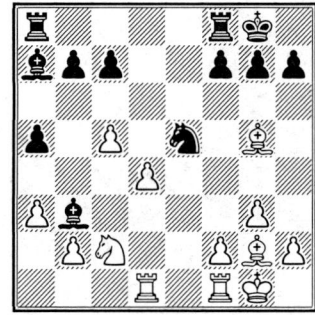

Position after White's 19th move

30. Kg2 Bxf2? 31. Kxf2 Bd5 32. Rxe5 Bxf3 33. Bxa5 c6? 34. Bb4 Black resigned. 1–0

(487) BLUMIN, B—FINE

U.S.C.F. Open Championship, New York (4), 1939 (23 July)
Nimzowitsch-Indian Defence, Classical Variation [E33]

1. d4 Nf6 2. c4 e6 3. Nc3 Bb4 4. Qc2 Nc6 5. Nf3 d5 6. e3 0–0 7. a3 Bxc3+ 8. Qxc3 Bd7 The course of the game provides an explanation of this, at first sight, mysterious move. Black wishes to exchange this bishop for White's king's bishop in order to come out with a knight against a bad bishop. 9. Bd3 a5 10. b3 a4 The sequel to the foregoing will soon become clear. 11. b4 11 Nd2 Re8 12 0–0 e5 13 dxe5 (13 Bb2 e4 14 Be2 Na5) Nxe5 14 Bb2 axb3 15 Nxb3 Ne4 Kotov–Botvinnik, Moscow 1939. Botvinnik claimed that 16 Qc2 was now forced since, after 16 Bxe4 dxe4, Black would play 17 ... Qg5 to his advantage. After 17 Nc5 Qg5, however, either 18 Nxe4 or 18 Nxd7 look playable. AW 11 ... dxc4 12. Bxc4 Na7 The point! White cannot prevent ... Bb5 (if 13 Qd3 Qe8) and this practically forces the desired exchange. 13. Ne5 Bb5 14. Bb2 Bxc4 15. Qxc4 Qd5

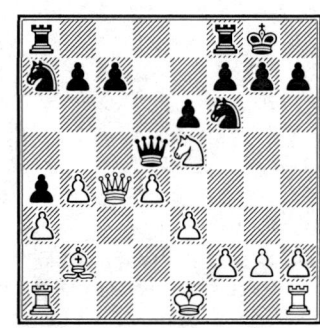

Position after Black's 15th move

The verdict of theory that Black has the better game, now needs no explanation; it is the preponderance of the knight over the "bad bishop." 16. Qxd5 exd5 17. Rc1 Nb5 Blockade of the pawns on dark squares. 18. 0–0 Ne4 19. Rc2 Ned6 20. Bc1 Rfe8 21. Rd1 f6 22. Nd7 A blunder, which costs a piece. He should have played 22 Nd3, after which, however, 22 ... Nc4 follows with a definite advantage to Black. 22 ... b6 Cutting off the knight's retreat. 23. Rc6 Re7 24. Nc5 bxc5 25. Rxc5 Rc8 26. f3 f5 27. Rd3 c6 28. Kf2 Nc4 29. g4 fxg4

30. e4 dxe4 31. fxe4 Ncd6 32. Re5 Rf8+ 33. Ke2 Rxe5 34. dxe5 Nxe4 35. Re3 Nec3+ 36. Ke1 Rf3 White resigned. 0–1 Euwe, BCM 1949, 268.

(488) FINE—ULVESTAD, O

U.S.C.F. Open Championship, New York (5), 1939 (23 July)
Dutch Defence, Stonewall Variation [D30]

1. d4 d5 2. c4 c6 3. Nf3 e6 4. e3 Bd6 4 ... f5 5 Bd3 Nf6 6 Nbd2 Ne4 7 Ne5 Qa5 with equality, PCO 214. 5. Bd3 f5 The Stonewall formation has one fancied advantage and two very real disadvantages. It is thought to give attacking chances, but these rarely materialize because of Black's generally cramped game and the nature of his pawn position, which simultaneously weakens his dark squares and condemns his queen's bishop to inactivity. 6. 0–0 Qf6 7. Nc3 Nh6 8. b3 0–0 9. Bb2 Nd7 10. Qc1! Very good! White intends to bring about the exchange of his queen's bishop (his "bad" bishop, as it is hemmed in by White pawns on dark squares) for Black's king's bishop (his "good" bishop). 10 ... Qe7 11. a4 Rf6 12. Ba3! Nf7 13. Bxd6 Qxd6 14. Qa3! Qxa3 15. Rxa3

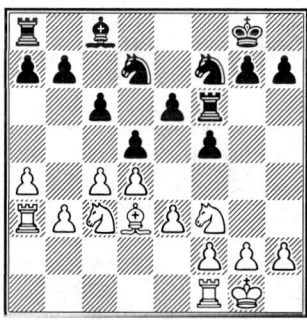

Position after White's 15th move

15 ... a5 Else White gains further terrain with b4. The foregoing exchanges have obviously favored White, who is left without his ineffectual bishop. The following play is an instructive lesson in the skilful utilization of greater terrain. 16. Rc1 Kf8 17. Ra2 Ke7 18. Nd2! Preparing for a big "push" in the centre, for White's superior mobility gives him greater opportunity to profit by the resulting open lines. 18 ... Nd6 19. f3 Ne8 20. e4! e5 This meets White half-way in opening up the game, but it is difficult to see how Black is to free his game altogether if he does not have recourse to the text. 21. cxd5 exd4 22. Ne2 cxd5 23. Nxd4 dxe4 24. fxe4 Ne5 25. Bb5 f4 White's e-pawn soon becomes very formidable; but if instead 25 ... Nd6 26 Rc5! 26. Rac2 Be6 27. Rc5 Nd7 Not 27 ... Kd6? 28 Rxe5! Kxe5 29 N4f3+ Kd6 30 e5+. 28. e5! Rg6 29. Nxe6 Rxe6 30. Bxd7 Kxd7 The exchanges have greatly simplified matters for White, whose inroads into the hostile position become steadily more menacing until the desired result is achieved. 31. Nc4 b6 32. Rd1+ Ke7 33. Rcd5 Ra7 Guarding the second rank from White's depredations, but the last rank will serve equally well. 34. Rd8 Rc7 35. Rb8 Rcc6 36. Rb7+ Rc7 37. Rb8

Rcc6 38. Rd5! 38 ... Nc7 On other moves, 39 Rb5 wins easily. **39. Rd6 Kf7 40. Rb7** Strengthening the pressure instead of winning the pawn at once. **40 ... Ke7 41. h4 Ke8** Loses at once; but the position was of course untenable. **42. Rxc7!** Black resigned. **1–0** Reinfeld, U.S.C.F. 1939, 62–3.

(489) RESHEVSKY, S—FINE

U.S.C.F. Open Championship, New York (6), 1939 (24 July)
Nimzowitsch-Indian Defence, Rubinstein Variation [E56]

1. d4 Nf6 2. c4 e6 3. Nc3 Bb4 4. e3 d5 5. Nf3 c5 6. Bd3 0–0 7. 0–0 dxc4 8. Bxc4 Nc6 9. a3 Ba5! 10. Ne2 cxd4 11. Nexd4 Nxd4 12. exd4 Qd6 13. Bg5 Nd5 14. Rc1 Bd8 15. Bd2 Bb6 16. Qe2 Bd7 17. Qe5 Qxe5 18. Nxe5 Rfd8 19. Bg5 Nf6 20. Nxd7 Rxd7 21. Bxf6 gxf6 22. d5 exd5 23. Bd3 Re7 24. Rfd1 Re5 25. g3 Kg7 26. Kg2 Rd8 27. Rc2 Draw agreed. **½–½**

(490) FINE—GREEN, M

U.S.C.F. Open Championship, New York (7), 1939 (25 July) (25 July)
Queen's Gambit Accepted [D23]

1. d4 d5 2. c4 dxc4 3. Nf3 Nf6 4. Qa4+ c6 5. Qxc4 g6 6. g3 Bg7 7. Bg2 0–0 8. 0–0 Nbd7 9. Qc2 Nb6 10. Nc3 Nbd5 11. e4 Nxc3 12. bxc3 c5 13. Ba3 cxd4 14. Nxd4 a6 15. Qb3 Qc7 16. f4 Ng4 17. Rae1 Rd8 18. h3

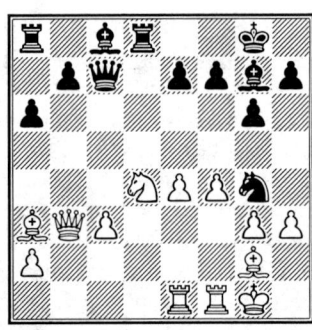

Position after White's 18th move

18 ... Rxd4 19. cxd4 Bxd4+ 20. Kh1 Be6 21. Qf3 Nf6 22. Rc1 Qd7 23. Rfd1 Bxh3 24. Rc4 Bg4 25. Rcxd4 Black resigned. **1–0**

(491) HELLMAN, G—FINE

U.S.C.F. Open Championship, New York (8), 1939 (25 July)
Sicilian Defence, Modern Paulsen Variation [B45]

1. e4 c5 2. Nf3 e6 3. d4 cxd4 4. Nxd4 Nf6 5. Nc3 Nc6 6. Be2 Bb4 7. Bf3 0–0 8. 0–0 Ne5 9. Qe2 a6 10. Nd1 b5 11. a4 bxa4 12. Rxa4 a5 13. b3 Bb7 14. c3 Bc5 15. Re1 Qb6 16. Nb2 Nxf3+ 17. Qxf3 Nxe4 18. Qh5

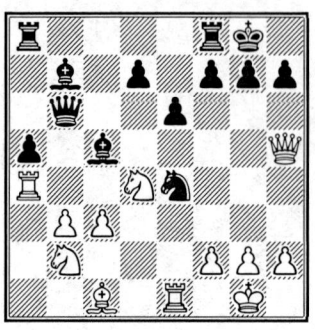

Position after White's 18th move

18 ... g6 18 ... Nxc3! 19. Qh4 d5 20. Nd3 Bd6 21. Re3 Rfe8 22. Rh3 h5 23. Bg5 Nxg5 24. Qxg5 Qd8 25. Qh6 Bf8 26. Qf4 Bg7 27. Ne5 Qf6 28. Ndf3 Qxf4 29. Rxf4 Re7 30. g4 hxg4 31. Rxg4 Rc7 32. Rf4 Rf8 33. Rfh4 Rxc3 34. Nd7 Rd8 35. Nfe5 Rxh3 36. Rxh3 Bc8 37. Rf3 Bxd7 White resigned. **0–1**

(492) FINE—HOROWITZ, I

U.S.C.F. Open Championship, New York (9), 1939 (26 July)
Queen's Gambit Declined, Tarrasch Defence [D34]

1. Nf3 d5 2. d4 c5 3. g3 Nf6 After 3 ... cxd4 4 Nxd4 e5 5 Nb3 the issue resolves itself into a contest to maintain the centre against direct and wing threats. IAH **4. Bg2 e6 5. 0–0 Nc6 6. c4 Be7** A commentary on the evil of rote! Intent on the speculative Tarrasch, Black neglects a line of play offering better prospects: 6 ... dxc4 7 Qa4 Bd7 8 Qxc4 Qb6! IAH **7. cxd5 exd5 8. Nc3 0–0 9. dxc5 d4 10. Na4 Bf5 11. Bf4!** As previously played in Alatortsev-Fine. The underlying idea of the move becomes apparent as the game progresses. IAH **11 ... Ne4 12. b4! Bf6** In his notes to this game in *Lessons from My Games* Fine writes "Of course not 12 ... Nxb4 13 Nxd4," but he does not mention that this is exactly what he had played against Alatortsev! Fine's title for the chapter in which the game appears is "I refute an old variation," even though it was not his refutation. Horowitz in his notes seems to be aware of the game from Moscow, but Fine claims that he won the game because, as a result of his continuous playing, he was aware of variations unknown to his competitors. MCO 6, although finished by January or February 1939, was not published until the summer (being reviewed in *BCM* August 1939). However, Fine's series "Current Trends in the Opening," covered the Tarrasch Defence, and mentioned this variation, up to White's twelfth, in *BCM* May 1939. AW **13. b5 Ne7 14. Be5** The point of White's 11th move. IAH **14 ... Bxe5 15. Nxe5 Qd5** If 15 ... Qc7, not 16 Qxd4? as 16 ... Rfd8 nets a piece, but 16 Nf3 and White maintains his pawn plus. IAH **16. Nd3 Rad8 17. Qc1** Sharper is 17 Qc2, which threatens to gain a piece by 18 g4 and 19 Nf4. IAH **17 ... Qe6** Releasing the pin, and exiting from a square which might be better occupied by the knight. IAH **18. Re1 Rfe8** For pressure against White's backward e-pawn. This, in a measure, compensates for Black's pawn minus. IAH **19. Qb2** Thinking to prevent

... Nd5. IAH **19 ... Nd5!** For the d-pawn may not be captured: 20 Q×d4 N5c3 21 Qb4 N×a4 22 Q×a4 Nc3, followed by ... N×e2+. IAH **20. Rac1 Bh3** Attempting to penetrate the invulnerable king position. 20 ... N5c3, exerting more pressure on the e-pawn was in order: 21 N×c3 N×c3 22 Nf4 Qc4. Of course the d-pawn is still immune to capture: 21 Q×d4 B×g2 22 K×g2 N5c3 23 Qb4 N×a2 wins the exchange. Or if 21 B×h3 Q×h3 22 Q×d4 N5f6 (not 22 ... Nf4 23 N×f4!) followed by 23 ... Ng4! IAH **21. Bh1 Qf5** Again expending effort to get at the king, who, nevertheless, remains safely ensconced. IAH **22. c6!** The extra pawn! White correctly ignores the d-pawn for the third, successive time: 22 Q×d4 Ndc3 23 Qc4 (23 Q×d8! R×d8 24 N×c3 N×c3 25 R×c3 and White is clearly better. AW) R×d3! wins. IAH **22 ... b×c6 23. b×c6 Ndc3** To blockade the pawn with 23 ... Nc7 would be a tacit admission of defeat, at least insofar as Black's plans are concerned. Nevertheless, a stouter resistance might have been offered with that move. IAH **24. N×c3 N×c3 25. Nf4 Bg4 26. e3!** Accurate and delicate calculation which banishes the last vestige of counterplay on the e-pawn. IAH **26 ... g5 27. e×d4 Nd1** No better is 27 ... R×e1+ 28 R×e1 Nd1 29 c7 Rc8 30 R×d1 g×f4 (30 ... B×d1 31 Nd5) 31 f3 wins. IAH **28. Qd2 R×e1+** 28 ... g×f4 29 c7 Rc8 30 R×e8+ R×e8 31 Bb7 Qb5 32 c8Q wins. IAH **29. Q×e1 g×f4 30. c7 Rc8 31. Bb7 f×g3 32. h×g3 Bf3 33. B×c8 Q×c8 34. Qe7!** Black resigned. **1–0** Horowitz, *The Chess Review* 1939, 176.

(493) JAFFE, C–FINE

U.S.C.F. Open Championship, New York (10), 1939 (26 July)

Defaulted **0–1**

(494) FINE–PINKUS, A

U.S.C.F. Open Championship, New York (11), 1939 (28 July)
Zukertort Opening [D37]

1. Nf3 d5 2. d4 Nf6 3. c4 e6 4. Nc3 Nbd7 5. e3 Be7 6. Bd3 0–0 7. b3 c5 8. 0–0 c×d4 9. e×d4 b6 10. Bf4 Bb7 11. Qe2 a6 12. Rad1 Re8 13. Ne5 Nf8 14. Be3 Rc8 15. Na4 d×c4 16. b×c4 Bd6 17. Rb1 Bc7 18. Rfd1 Rb8 19. Rb3 Ba8 20. Bg5

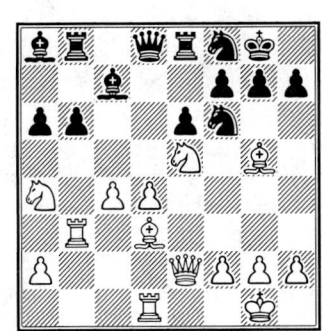

Position after White's 20th move

20 ... b5 21. c×b5 Qd5 22. Nf3 Qd6 23. Ne5 Qd5 24. Qf1 a×b5 25. Nc3 Qd6 26. N×b5 R×b5 27. B×b5 Rb8 28. Bf4 Nd5 29. Bg3 Qd8 30. Nc6 B×c6 31. B×c6 R×b3 32. a×b3 B×g3 33. h×g3 Black resigned. **1–0**

Unfortunately the newly formed U.S.C.F. was unable to gather sufficient funds to send a team to defend the Hamilton-Russell Trophy at the final International Team Tournament of the 1930s, held in Buenos Aires in August and September 1939. Fine and Reshevsky therefore missed their chance to compete again with the best players of Europe and South America, and incidentally to try to tempt Alekhine into a match. Fine, of course, never played in a tournament abroad again (though he played in Moscow in the U.S.A.–U.S.S.R. match of 1946), while Reshevsky had to wait until 1948. In 1939 the *Chess Archives* project was started by Keesing & Sons of Amsterdam and New York for a subscription of $8 per year. A binder for 1939–44 was supplied with an initial collection of 471 games. Hans Kmoch was editor in chief, Fine the American editor. The binder was inscribed in gold lettering with the names of all eight participants of the A.V.R.O. tournament, suggesting that they had evolved the idea together. Fine's address was given as 1347 Bristow Street, New York.

"Scoring 9½ points out of a possible ten in the weekly rapid transit tournament at the Marshall Chess Club on September 19, Hermann Helms carried off the first prize, with Reuben Fine as runner-up. Fine lost only to Helms and finished with a score of 9–1. With the exception of a draw with Tobias Stone, Helms downed all opposition. Stone was third with 7½–2½. The fourth prize was won by Matthew Green, 6–4, and the fifth by K. Darby, 5½–4½.

Two weeks later, Fine was again a competitor and this time he finished first with a score of 11–0. Other prize winners were Matthew Green, 8½–2½; Sidney Bernstein, 8–3, and Milton Hanauer, 7½–3½." (ACB 1939). "Reuben Fine was again invincible in the weekly lightning tourney at the Marshall C.C., in which he won a total of 14 points. Matthew Green 13½–1½, and Frank J. Marshall 12½–2½ were second and third respectively. Fourth Prize went to Olaf I. Ulvestad 10–5." (ACB November-December 1939)

23rd Marshall Club Championship, New York, November 1939–March 1940

"Scoring 14 points out of a possible 16, Reuben Fine is again champion of the Marshall Chess Club in consequence of his finishing first in the annual tournament for that honour. He lost only one game—to Matthew Green—and drew with Frank J. Marshall and David S. Polland. Second prize went to Milton Hanauer (13–3) who, a year ago,

shared the honours of first place with Sidney Bernstein."
(*ACB* 1940) Play took place on Sundays.

		1	2	3	4	5	6	7	8	9	10	11	12	13	14	15	16	17	
1	Fine	*	1	½	½	1	1	1	0	1	1	1	1	1	1	1	1	1	14
2	Hanauer	0	*	½	0	1	1	1	1	1	½	1	1	1	1	1	1	1	13
3	Marshall	½	½	*	1	½	1	0	0	1	1	½	1	1	1	1	1	1	12
4	Polland	½	1	0	*	½	0	½	1	½	½	½	1	1	1	1	1	1	11
5=	Seidman	0	0	½	½	*	1	½	1	½	0	1	½	1	1	1	1	1	10½
5=	Lasker	0	0	0	1	0	*	½	1	1	½	1	½	1	1	1	1	1	10½
7	Reinfeld	0	0	1	½	½	½	*	½	½	1	½	1	1	1	1	0	1	10
8	Green	1	0	1	0	0	0	½	*	½	½	½	½	1	1	1	1	½	9
9=	Bernstein	0	0	0	½	½	0	½	½	*	½	1	0	1	1	1	1	1	8½
9=	Donovan	0	½	0	½	1	½	0	½	½	*	0	½	1	1	½	1	1	8½
11	Collins	0	0	½	½	0	0	½	½	0	1	*	0	½	1	1	1	1	7½
12	Santasiere	0	0	0	0	½	½	0	½	1	½	1	*	½	1	½	0	1	7
13	Goldwater	0	0	0	0	0	0	0	0	0	0	½	½	*	0	½	1	1	3½
14	Rogosin	0	0	0	0	0	0	0	0	0	0	0	0	1	*	1	½	1	3½
15	Knorr	0	0	0	0	0	0	0	0	0	½	0	½	½	0	*	1	½	3
16	Heal	0	0	0	0	0	0	1	0	0	0	0	1	0	½	0	*	0	2½
17	Howard	0	0	0	0	0	0	0	½	0	0	0	0	0	0	½	1	*	2

(495) FINE—ROGOSIN, H

Marshall CC championship 1939/40, New York (1), 1939
   (26 Nov.)

Nimzowitsch-Indian Defence, Rubinstein Variation [E47]

**1. d4 Nf6 2. c4 e6 3. Nc3 Bb4 4. e3 0–0 5. Bd3
Nc6 6. Nge2 e5 7. d5 e4 8. Bb1 Ne5 9. Qb3 Qe7
10. 0–0 Bd6 11. Ng3 Neg4 12. h3 Bxg3 13. fxg3
Nh6 14. Qc2 Qe5 15. Qf2 d6 16. g4 Nhxg4
17. hxg4 Nxg4 18. Qf4 Qxf4 19. Rxf4 f5
20. Nb5 Bd7 21. Nd4 g6 22. Bc2 Ne5 23. b3 c6
24. dxc6 bxc6 25. Bd2 d5 26. cxd5 cxd5 27. Bd1
Rac8**

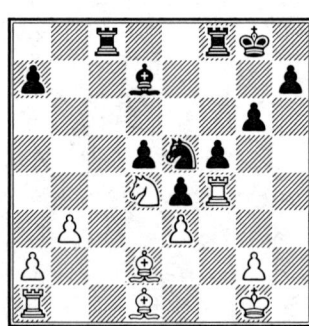

*Position after
Black's 27th move*

**28. Be2 Nc6 29. Bc3 Ne5 30. Bb2 Nd3 31. Bxd3
exd3 32. Rd1 g5 33. Rf2 f4 34. Rxd3 Bf5 35. Nxf5
Rxf5 36. exf4 gxf4 37. Rdf3 Rcf8 38. Bc1 Rc8
39. Bxf4 d4 40. Rd3 Rd5 41. Rfd2 Rc1+ 42. Kf2
Ra1 43. Kf3 h5 44. Ke4 Rd8 45. Rxd4 Re1+ 46. Kf5
Rf8+ 47. Kg6 Rf1 48. Bg5 R1f7 49. Rd7** Black resigned. **1–0**

(496) KNORR, T—FINE

Marshall CC championship 1939/40, New York (2), 1939
   (3 Dec.)

Sicilian Defence, Scheveningen [B45]

**1. e4 c5 2. Nf3 e6 3. d4 cxd4 4. Nxd4 Nf6 5. Nc3
Nc6 6. Ndb5 d6 7. Be2 Be7 8. Bg5 0–0 9. Bxf6
Bxf6 10. 0–0 Qa5 11. Qe1 Rd8 12. Rd1 Be7 13. a3
Rd7 14. Kh1 a6 15. Nd4 Qc7 16. f4 Bf6 17. Nb3
Rd8 18. Rd3 b5 19. Rh3 b4 20. Nd1 a5 21. Bd3 e5
22. f5**

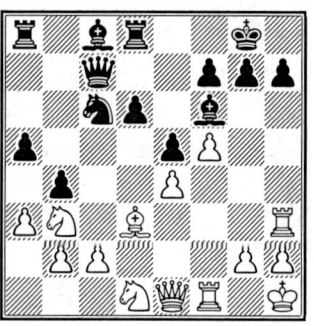

*Position after
White's 22nd move*

**22 ... d5 23. Ne3 dxe4 24. Bxe4 Ba6 25. Rff3 Rac8
26. Nd5 Qd6 27. Rfg3 Bc4 28. Nb6 Nd4 29. Nxc8
Rxc8 30. Nxd4 exd4 31. b3 Bd5 32. Bxd5 Qxd5
33. axb4 axb4 34. Qd1 Qe4 35. Rd3 Rxc2 36. Rhe3
Qxg2** Mate. **0–1**

(497) GREEN, M—FINE

Marshall CC championship 1939/40, New York (4), 1939
   (10 Dec.)

Queen's Gambit Declined, Ragozin Variation [D38]

1. d4 Nf6 2. c4 e6 3. Nf3 d5 4. Nc3 Bb4 Fine has
had great success with this variation. My reply is an attempt
to transpose into the Exchange Variation of the Queen's
Gambit Declined (which I believe gives White a slight advantage). **5. cxd5 Nxd5** 5 ... Qxd5 would transpose into
the Nimzowitsch-Indian Defence, as for example in Fine's
game against Suesman in the U.S. Championship Tournament of 1938. Fine claims that the text line has never been
played before. **6. Bd2 0–0 7. e4 Nxc3 8. bxc3 Be7
9. Bd3 c5 10. 0–0 b6 11. Qe2 Bb7 12. Rfd1 Nc6
13. dxc5** 13 d5 is met cleverly by 13 ... exd5 14 exd5 Qxd5
15 Bg5 Nd4! 16 cxd4 Bxg5 17 dxc5 Qxc5 and Black has a
pawn plus without too much discomfort—enough for Fine!
bxc5 In subsequent analysis Fine and I decided that 13 ...
Bxc5 was quite playable. For if 14 e5 Be7 (the move which
Fine says he failed to consider; without it the kingside attack
is hard to counter, which explains the text) 15 Bh6 gxh6
16 Bxh7+ (16 Qe4! seems to win fairly simply. AW) Kxh7
17 Rxd8 Black gets too much for his queen. **14. e5 Qc7
15. Rab1 Rad8 16. Bf4 Na5 17. Be4 Bc6 18. Qc2
g6?!** The only move that can really be criticized. 18 ... h6 is

necessary, as will be seen later on in the game. **19. h4!** (The version given by Green continued 19 Rxd8 Rxd8 20 Re1 [Not only following Nimzowitsch's idea of over-protection, but having in mind the possible utilization of this rook later on (see move thirty).] Qb7 [At this point I realised that I had somewhat the better of it—but how to continue? I had already consumed an hour and three quarters to Fine's hour (forty moves in two hours being the time limit), and I felt that after this last move he was going to put the pressure on, and turn the game in his favour—as he so often does in such positions!] 21 h4! Nc4 transposing to Fine's note-books.) **Nc4 20. Rxd8 Rxd8 21. Re1 Qb7 22. Bxc6 Qxc6 23. h5 Nb6?!** This move doesn't look right. Yet it threatens the exchange of queens and a winning endgame. **24. Bg5! Bxg5** Alas! If only 18 ... h6 had been played. **25. Nxg5 Qa4 26. Qc1! Qh4** If 26 ... Qxa2 27 Qf4 Rf8 28 Ne4 wins. **27. Ne4 Kg7** Forced. He can't permit Qh6. **28. Nf6! h6?!** 29 Re4, winning the queen, was threatened. **29. hxg6 fxg6 30. Re4 Qg5 31. Qa3! Rd1+** A last stab. It's all rapid transit from now on. **32. Kh2 Qc1 33. Qxc5** Even stronger than Qxa7+. **Kf7** If 33 ... Rh1+ 34 Kg3 Qg5+ 35 Rg4 and that's all. **34. Qc7+ Nd7 35. Nxd7 Rh1+ 36. Kg3 Qg5+ 37. Rg4 Qe7 38. Rf4+ Kg7 39. Qd6 Qe8 40. Qf8+** It's a check and the fortieth move! A victory over a Grandmaster is not conducive to modesty—I hope this explanation excuses the personal nature of the comments! **Qxf8 41. Nxf8** Black resigned. Based on notes by Green from *Chess Review*, April 1940 (Hilbert 2002, 81). **1–0**

(498) FINE—HOWARD, K

Marshall CC championship 1939/40, New York (5), 1939 (17 Dec.)
Queen's Gambit Declined [D30]

1. d4 d5 2. c4 c6 3. Nf3 e6 4. e3 Nd7 5. Bd3 Ngf6 6. 0–0 Bd6 7. Nc3 e5 8. cxd5 cxd5 9. e4 dxe4 10. Nxe4 Nxe4 11. Bxe4 0–0 12. dxe5 Nxe5 13. Nxe5 Bxe5 14. Bxh7+ Kxh7 15. Qh5+ Kg8 16. Qxe5 Re8 17. Qg3 Bf5 18. Bf4 Re6

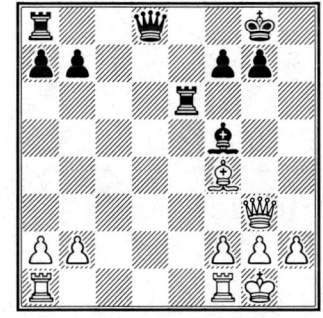

Position after Black's 18th move

19. Rfe1 Rxe1+ 20. Rxe1 Qa5 21. f3 Qxa2 22. Be5 Bg6 23. h4 Qa5 24. Kh2 Kh7 25. h5 Rh8 26. hxg6+ Kg8+ 27. Kg1 Qc5+ 28. Qf2 Rh1+ 29. Kxh1 Qxf2 30. Bg3 Black resigned. **1–0**

(499) FINE—HEAL, E

Marshall CC championship 1939/40, New York (6), 1939 (28 Dec.)
English Opening [A12]

1. Nf3 d5 2. c4 c6 3. g3 Bf5 4. Bg2 e6 5. 0–0 Nf6 6. b3 Nbd7 7. Bb2 Be7 8. d3 0–0 9. Nc3 Rc8 10. Re1 h6 11. e4 dxe4 12. dxe4 Bg4 13. e5 Nh7 14. Qd4 Bxf3 15. Bxf3 Ng5 16. Bg2

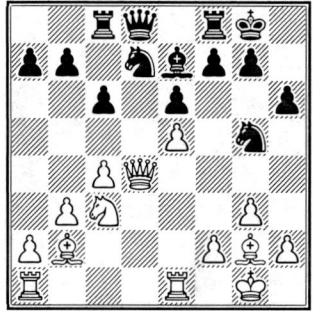

Position after White's 16th move

16 ... Qc7 17. h4 Nh7 18. Ne4 b6 19. Nd6 Rcd8 20. Qg4 c5 21. Rad1 a6 22. f4 h5 23. Qxh5 Bxd6 24. Rxd6 g6 25. Qh6 Nb8 26. h5 gxh5 27. Be4 f6 28. exf6 Rxd6 29. Qg6+ Black resigned. **1–0**

(500) GOLDWATER, W—FINE

Marshall CC championship 1939/40, New York (7), 1939 (30 Dec.)
Sicilian Defence [B40]

1. e4 c5 2. Nf3 e6 3. d4 cxd4 4. Nxd4 Nf6 5. Bd3 Nc6 6. Be3 e5 7. Nxc6 bxc6 8. 0–0 Be7 9. Nd2 0–0 10. f4

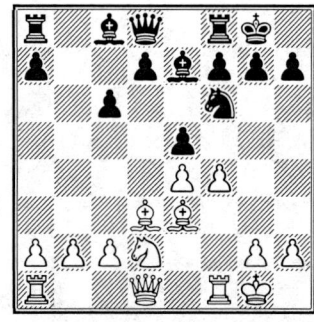

Position after White's 10th move

10 ... d5 11. fxe5 Ng4 12. Qe2 Nxe3 13. Qxe3 Bg5 14. Qf2 Bxd2 15. exd5 Qg5 16. Qf3 Qe3+ 17. Kh1 Qxf3 18. Rxf3 cxd5 19. Bb5 Be6 20. Rd3 Bf4 21. Bc6 Rac8 22. Bxd5 Rxc2 White resigned. **0–1**

(501) FINE—HANAUER, M

Marshall CC championship 1939/40, New York (8), 1939
(23 Dec.)

Caro-Kann Defence, Charousek Variation [B19]

**1. e4 c6 2. d4 d5 3. Nc3 dxe4 4. Nxe4 Bf5 5. Ng3
Bg6 6. h4 h6 7. Nf3 Nd7 8. Bd3 Bxd3 9. Qxd3
Ngf6 10. Bd2 e6 11. 0-0-0 Qc7 12. Kb1 0-0-0
13. c4 Bd6 14. Ne4 Nxe4 15. Qxe4 c5 16. Bc3 Nf6
17. Qe2 a6 18. Ne5 Bxe5 19. dxe5 Nd7 20. Rd6
Nb8 21. Rhd1 Nc6 22. h5**

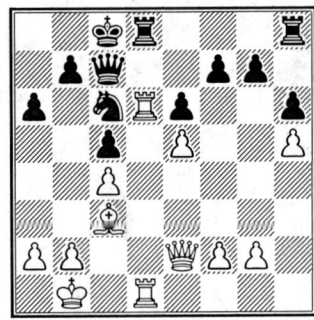

*Position after
White's 22nd move*

22 ... Rhg8 23. Qe3 Nd4 24. Rxd8+ Rxd8 25. Bxd4
cxd4 26. Rxd4 Rxd4 27. Qxd4 Qa5 28. g4 Qe1+
29. Kc2 Qe2+ 30. Kb3 Kb8 31. Kb4 Qe1+ 32. Ka4
Qe2 33. Ka5 Qf3 34. Qc5 Qe2 35. b4 Qd2 36. Qd6+
Qxd6 37. exd6 g6 38. Kb6 Kc8 39. c5 gxh5 40. gxh5
e5 41. d7+ Black resigned. **1-0**

(502) REINFELD, F—FINE

Marshall CC championship 1939/40, New York (9), 1940
(7 Jan.)

Queen's Indian Defence [E16]

**1. d4 Nf6 2. c4 e6 3. Nf3 b6 4. g3 Bb7 5. Bg2
Bb4+ 6. Bd2 Be7 7. Nc3 0-0 8. 0-0 d5 9. Ne5 c5
10. dxc5 bxc5 11. Qb3 Qb6 12. Bg5 h6 13. cxd5
Qxb3 14. axb3 hxg5 15. d6 Bxg2 16. dxe7 Bxf1
17. exf8R+ Kxf8 18. Kxf1 a5 19. Na4 Nfd7 20. Nxd7+
Nxd7 21. Rd1 Ke7 22. Rxd7+ Kxd7 23. Nb6+ Kc6
24. Nxa8 Kb7 25. Ke1 Kxa8** (*see diagram*) **26. Kd2**
Although weak pawns are a serious danger, they are not

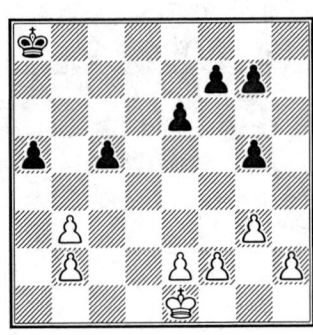

*Position after
Black's 25th move*

necessarily fatal unless they are combined with an inferior
king position. In [this position] White could have held the
draw because his king is not badly placed. **26 ... Kb7
27. Kc3 Kc6 28. Kc4 g4 29. f3 f5 30. f4** Now
Black does not have an extra tempo. **30 ... Kb6
31. Kd3 Kc7 32. Kc3 Kd6 33. Kc4 Kc6 34. Kd3
Kd5** 34 ... Kb4 35 Kc3 is useless. Black will first try to get
a pawn at e4, to deprive the white king of the square d3.
35. Kc3 e5 36. Kd3 Not 36 fxe5 g5 37 e3 Kxe5 38 Kc4
Ke4 with a simple win. **36 ... e4+ 37. Kc3 Kd6** To
answer 38 Kc4 with 38 ... Kc6. **38. Kd2 Kc6 39. Kc2?**
This inaccuracy in time pressure loses. It is clear that Black
must have two pawn tempi to win, one to drive the king
from c3, the other to drive it from c2. After 39 e3! Black
would have only one tempo and so could only draw.
Attempts such as ... a4 or ... c4 lead to nothing. **39 ...
Kb5! 40. Kd2** Or 40 e3 Kb4, or 40 Kc3 e3! 41 Kd3 Kb4
42 Kc2 g6. **40 ... Kb4 41. Kc2** Now Black must not play
41 ... g6 42 e3 c4 43 bxc4 Kxc4 44 b3+ Kb4 45 Kb2 with a
draw. **41 ... e3!** White resigned, for if he goes after the
e-pawn, the Black a-pawn will queen in at most six moves.
0-1 Fine 1941, 65-6.

(503) FINE—SANTASIERE, A

Marshall CC championship 1939/40, New York (10), 1940
(14 Jan.)

Sicilian Defence, Moscow Variation [B54]

**1. e4 c5 2. Nf3 d6 3. d4 cxd4 4. Nxd4 Nf6 5. f3
Nc6 6. c4 e6 7. Nc3 Be7 8. Nc2 0-0 9. Ne3 a6
10. Be2 Qc7 11. 0-0 Rd8 12. Kh1 Bd7 13. f4 Bf8
14. g4 Be8 15. g5 Nd7 16. b3 Nc5 17. Bb2 Rab8
18. Rc1 a5 19. Bf3 Na7 20. Ne2 b5 21. Ng3 bxc4
22. Nxc4 Nc6 23. Qe2 Nb4 24. e5 d5 25. Nd6
Nxa2 26. Bd4 Nxc1 27. Rxc1 Rxd6 28. exd6 Bxd6
29. Nh5 Bb5 30. Qg2 Bd3 31. Nxg7 Rxb3 32. Ne8
Qc6 33. Nxd6 Qxd6**

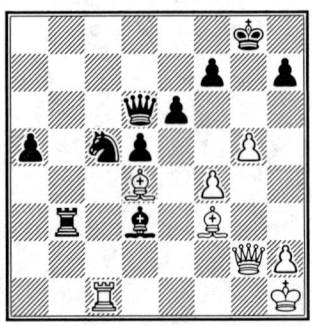

*Position after
Black's 33rd move*

34. g6 Bxg6 35. Qg5 f6 36. Qxf6 Qf8 37. Qxf8+
Kxf8 38. Bxc5+ Kf7 39. Kg2 Rb2+ 40. Kg3 Rb3
41. Kg2 Rb2+ 42. Kg1 Rb3 43. Bd1 Rb2 44. Bd4
Rb4 45. Be5 d4 46. Ra1 d3 47. Kf2 Rb5 48. Ke3
Rd5 49. Kd2 Rb5 50. Bc3 Rf5 51. Be5 Bh5 52. Bb3
Be2 53. Rxa5 Rh5 54. Ra7+ Ke8 55. Bxe6 Rxh2

56. f5 Rg2 57. f6 Bf1+ 58. Kc3 Rc2+ 59. Kd4 Black resigned. **1—0**

(504) BERNSTEIN, S—FINE

Marshall CC championship 1939/40, New York (11), 1940
(21 Jan.)
Italian Game [C50]

**1. e4 e5 2. Nf3 Nc6 3. Bc4 Nf6 4. d3 Bc5
5. Nc3 d6 6. Bg5 Na5** (6 ... h6 7 Bxf6 Qxf6 8 Nd5
Qd8 (8 ... Qg6!? Foltys–Keres, Munich 1936) 9 c3 a6
(9 ... 0–0!?) 10 d4 is the other main continuation here.)
7. Bb3?! (7 Nd5 Nxc4 8 dxc4 c6 9 Nxf6 gxf6 10 Be3
Qb6 11 Qd2 Bxe3 12 fxe3 Qxb2 13 0–0 Qa3 14 Nh4 Be6!
15 Rxf6 0–0–0 is unclear according to Estrin.) **7 ... c6
8. 0–0 h6 9. Be3 Qe7 10. Qe1 Nxb3 11. axb3 Bg4
12. Na4?!** (The weakened kingside pawn formation turns
out to be a major contributing factor to White's loss.
12 Bxc5 dxc5 13 Nd2 is probably about equal.) **12 ... Bxf3
13. gxf3 0–0 14. Nxc5 dxc5 15. f4 Ng4 16. f3
Nxe3 17. Qxe3 f5 18. Rae1 Rae8 19. exf5 Rxf5
20. fxe5 Rxe5 21. Qxe5 Qxe5 22. Rxe5 Rxe5
23. Kf2 Kf7 24. Ra1 a6 25. Ra4 Kf6 26. Re4 g5
27. Rxe5?!** (The king and pawn ending turns out to be
lost; 27 Kg3 or 27 h4 should be tried.) **27 ... Kxe5
28. Ke2**

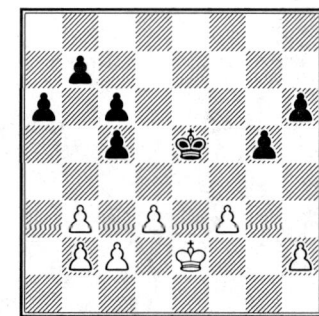

*Position after
White's 28th move*

The complexity of the conversion of a better king position
into one where one has the opposition is illustrated in this
game. The first winning plan which comes to mind consists
of manoeuvring against the weak kingside pawns. Thus,
for example, 28 ... Kf4 29 Kf2 g4 30 fxg4 Kxg4 31 Kg2 h5
32 Kf2 Kh3 33 Kg1 h4 34 Kh1 but now Black has reached a
dead end. However, instead of 29 ... g4, 29 ... h5 might have
been tried: 30 Ke2 g4 31 fxg4 hxg4 32 Kf2 Kg5 33 Kg3 b6
34 Kf2 Kh4 35 Kg2 b5 36 Kg1 Kh3 37 Kh1 g3 38 hxg3 Kxg3
39 Kg1. Thus the variation would result in a draw but it fur-
nishes a valuable hint for a winning scheme: if White's
pawns on the queenside were weakened, that is, if his
c-pawn were at c3 the king could march over (after 39 Kg1)
and gobble up a pawn. Consequently Black's first effort is
to induce a pawn advance on the queenside. **28 ... Kd4
29. Kd2 a5** Clearly Black can only force White to push
his c-pawn at the point of a gun: so instead the reverse of
the first plan will be tried; weaken White's queenside pawns,
force the white king to stand guard over them, exchange and

finally shift over to the other wing. Why the a-pawn had to
move will soon be seen. **30. Ke2 b5 31. Kd2 c4** If the
a-pawn were still at a6, 32 dxc4 bxc4 33 b4 would draw.
32. bxc4 With this a draw can just be squeezed out (But
see the possible correction to analysis at move 35. AW).
How the alternatives lose is instructive: A 32 c3+ Kd5
33 bxc4+ bxc4 34 d4 (34 dxc4+ Kxc4 35 Kc2 a4) Ke6
35 Ke3 Kf5 36 Kf2 Kf4 37 Ke2 h5 38 Kf2 g4 39 fxg4 hxg4
40 Ke2 Kg5 41 Kf2 Kh4 42 Kg2 a4 43 Kh1 Kh3 44 Kg1 g3
45 hxg3 Kxg3 46 Kf1 Kf3 47 Ke1 Ke3 48 Kd1 Kd3 49 Kc1
a3! 50 bxa3 Kxc3 51 a4 (51 Kb1 Kd2; or 51 Kd1 Kb2) Kb4
52 Kc2 Kxa4 53 Kc3 Kb5. B 32 c3+ Kd5 33 dxc4+ bxc4
34 Kc2 c5 (34 ... cxb3 would only draw) 35 bxc4+ Kxc4
36 b3+ (or 36 Kd2 Kb3 37 Kc1 c4 38 Kb1 a4 39 Kc1 a3
40 bxa3 Kxc3) Kd5 37 Kd3 c4+! 38 Kc2 Kc5 39 Kb2 cxb3
40 Kxb3 a4+ 41 Kxa4 Kc4 42 Ka5 Kxc3 43 Kb6 Kd3. Black
gets there first. C. 32 Ke2 c3 33 bxc3+ Kxc3 34 Kd1 a4 and
again White will have to give up two pawns to stop the
a-pawn. **32 ... bxc4 33. dxc4 Kxc4 34. Ke3 a4
35. Ke4** 35 f4! gxf4+ (or 35 ... c5 36 b3+!) 36 Kxf4 Kd4
37 Kf3! h5! (The only chance: if 37 ... c5 38 Ke2 c4 39 Kd2
c3+ 40 Kc1! RF) 38 Ke2 Ke4 39 Kf2 Kf4 40 Ke2! (Fine's
suggestion 40 Kg2, with the continuation Kg4 41 Kf2 Kh3
42 Kg1 h4 43 Kh1 c5 44 Kg1 c4 45 c3 Kg4 46 Kf2 Kf4 47
h3, would lose to 40 ... Ke3. This error is not corrected in
the *Encyclopaedia of Chess Endings*. AW) Kg4 41 Kf2 Kh3
42 Kg1 c5! (42 ... h4 43 Kh1 Kg4 44 Kg2) 43 Kh1 c4 44 c3
Kh4! 45 Kg1 Kg5 46 Kf1 Kf5 47 Ke2 Ke4 48 h4 Kf4 and
Black wins after all. AW **35 ... c5 36. f4 gxf4 37. Kxf4
Kd4 38. h4 c4 39. c3+ Kd3 40. Kf5 Kc2** White
resigned. **0—1** Fine 1941, 73–5 (from move 28).

(505) FINE—COLLINS, J

Marshall CC championship 1939/40, New York (12), 1940
(23 Jan.)
Queen's Indian Defence [E19]

**1. Nf3 Nf6 2. c4 e6 3. g3 b6 4. Bg2 Bb7 5. 0–0
Be7 6. d4 0–0 7. Nc3 Ne4 8. Qc2 Nxc3 9. Qxc3
f5 10. d5 Bf6 11. Qc2 Na6 12. Rd1 Qe7 13. Nd4
Nc5 14. Be3 Ne4 15. Rac1 Rac8 16. a3 a5 17. Nb5
exd5 18. cxd5 c5 19. Qb3 Ba6 20. a4 d6 21. Rc2
Rfe8 22. Bf4 Rcd8 23. Re1**

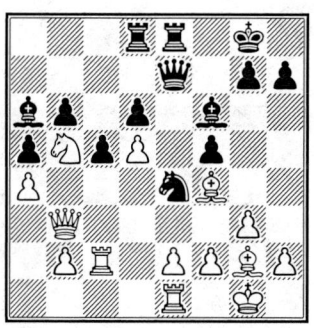

*Position after
White's 23rd move*

**23 ... Rd7 24. f3 Ng5 25. e4 fxe4 26. Rce2 Qf8
27. fxe4 Bc8 28. Nxd6 Bd4+ 29. Kh1 Rxd6 30. Bxg5**

Rg6 31. Bf4 Bg4 32. Rd2 Rf6 33. d6+ Be6 34. Qxb6
Rb8 35. Qc7 Rf7 36. d7 Rd8 37. Bd6 Black resigned.
1–0

(506) SEIDMAN, H—FINE

Marshall CC championship 1939/40, New York (13), 1940
   (20 Jan.)
Bird's Opening [A03]

1. f4 d5 2. e3 Nf6 3. Nf3 g6 4. c4 Bg7 5. Nc3 0–0
6. Qb3 e6 7. d4 c5 8. Be2 Nc6 9. 0–0 Na5 10. Qc2
cxd4 11. Nxd4 Nxc4 12. Bxc4 dxc4 13. Qa4 Qc7
14. Ncb5 Qc5 15. Bd2 a6 16. Na3 b5 17. Naxb5
Bd7 18. Qa3 Qh5

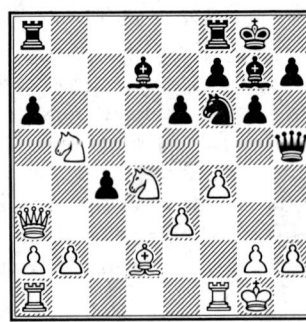

*Position after
Black's 18th move*

19. Nc3 Rfb8 20. b3 e5 21. Nf3 exf4 22. exf4 Bf8
23. Qc1 Bc5+ 24. Be3 Ng4 25. Bxc5 Qxc5+ 26. Kh1
Bc6 27. Nd1 Qh5 28. h3 Re8 29. Kg1 Bxf3 30. hxg4
Bxg4 31. bxc4 Qc5+ 32. Kh1 Rad8 White resigned.
0–1

(507) FINE—DONOVAN, J

Marshall CC championship 1939/40, New York (14), 1940
   (27 Jan.)
Queen's Indian Defence [E18]

1. Nf3 Nf6 2. c4 b6 3. g3 Bb7 4. Bg2 e6 5. 0–0
Be7 6. d4 0–0 7. Nc3 d5 8. Ne5 Qc8 9. Bg5 dxc4
10. e4 Rd8 11. Nxc4 Nbd7 12. Rc1 e5 13. d5 Ba6
14. Bxf6 Nxf6 15. Nxe5 Bxf1 16. Qxf1 Bd6 17. Nc6
Re8 18. Bh3 Qb7 19. Re1 Be5 20. Qd3 b5 21. Nd1
Qb6 22. Kf1 Qc5 23. f4 Bd6 24. b4 Qc4 25. Qxc4
bxc4 26. Nc3

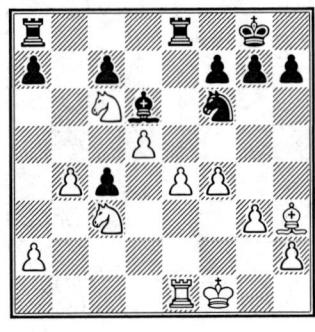

*Position after
White's 26th move*

26 ... a5 27. bxa5 Ra6 28. e5 Rxc6 29. dxc6 Bb4
30. Rc1 Bxc3 31. Rxc3 Ne4 32. Rc2 Ra8 33. Bg2
Nc5 34. Bd5 Rxa5 35. Bxc4 Kf8 36. Kf2 Ke7
37. Ke3 Ra3+ 38. Kd4 Na4 39. Bb3 Nb6 40. Kc5
f6 41. Re2 Nc8 42. Rd2 Nb6 43. exf6+ Kxf6 44. Rd8
h6 45. Rf8+ Kg6 46. Bc2+ Kh5 47. Bd1+ Kg6 48. f5+
Black resigned. 1–0

(508) LASKER, ED—FINE

Marshall CC championship 1939/40, New York (15), 1940
   (16 March)
Grünfeld Defence, 4 Bf4 [D84]

1. d4 Nf6 2. c4 g6 3. Nc3 d5 4. Bf4 Bg7 5. e3
0–0 6. cxd5 Nxd5 7. Nxd5 Qxd5 8. Bxc7 Nc6 8 ...
Na6, which has been played in this position several times,
does not look good to me. 9 Bxa6! Qxg2 10 Qf3 Qxf3
11 Nxf3 bxa6 12 Rc1 (or 12 0–0 Bb7 13 Ne5 f6 14 Nd3 Flohr–
Botvinnik, A.V.R.O. 1938), following this up with Rc5, gives
White a far superior game. Black cannot get his rooks into
action on the d-file or the b-file, as long as White's bishop
remains on c7, and a break-through on the e-file would take
long preparations (... Re8, ... f6 and ... e5), besides giving
White a dangerous passed pawn on the d-file. EL 9. Ne2!
This is the important move which Fine had given in his
analysis as a satisfactory means of stemming the attack Black
obtains in return for the pawn sacrificed. The knight gains a
valuable tempo for White by occupation of c3, which drives
Black's queen from her dominating position. EL (Black
more than equalized after 9 Nf3 Bg4 10 Be2 Rac8 11 Bg3
Qa5+ 12 Nd2 Bxe2 13 Qxe2 e5! Gilg–Helling, Leipzig 1928.)
9 ... Bg4! 10. f3 Rac8 Black could sacrifice the bishop
here with 10 ... Bxf3 11 gxf3 Qxf3 12 Rg1 e5! (or 12 ... Qxe3
13 Bf4 Qe4 14 Bg2 Qf5 15 Qd2 e5 16 Bxc6 exf4 17 Bf3 Rfe8
18 Kf2 Re3 and Black soon won, Safonov–Bohatirchuk,
Moscow 1940. AW), but the White pieces can be brought
into co-operation rather rapidly, and I doubt whether Black's
attack can succeed against best defence. True enough, in a
game with a time limit, White might not be able to find his
way out of trouble. EL **11. Nc3!** 11 Bf4 e5 12 dxe5 Qa5
13 Nc3 Be6 14 Be2 Nxe5 15 0–0 Nc4 16 Bxc4 Bxc4 17 Rf2
Rfd8 with compensation, Keres–Lilienthal, Leningrad–
Moscow, 1939. **11 ... Qe6 12. Bf4** A critical position.
Faced with the double threat of 13 d5 and 13 fxg4, Black is
forced to sacrifice the bishop. EL **12 ... Nxd4 13. fxg4
Rfd8** All of Black's batteries are now unleashed. The immediate threat seemed to be 14 ... Nb5, attacking the queen
and adding a third attack on the knight. However, I decided
I would meet this combination with 15 Bxb5, giving up my
queen for rook and knight, when I would still remain with a
telling advantage in material. With this idea in mind, after
long deliberation, I played 14 Be2, forgetting that I had
rejected this move when I started to analyse the various continuations, which seemed worthy of consideration, such as
Bd3, Rc1 and Qc1. Black can simply exchange the knight for
my bishop and thereby open the diagonal of his bishop on
my insufficiently guarded knight. The correct move would

have been 14 Rc1. After 14 ... h6 15 h4, there is no move by which Black can further increase his pressure. EL **14. Be2** 14 Kf2, suggested by Fine in *PCO*, worked out well for Black in Benko–Laszlo, Budapest 1941, after 14 ... Qb6 15 Qc1 Ne6 16 Bg3 Ng5. 14 Bd3! has, however, turned out to be good for White in practice. **14 ... Nxe2 15. Qxe2**

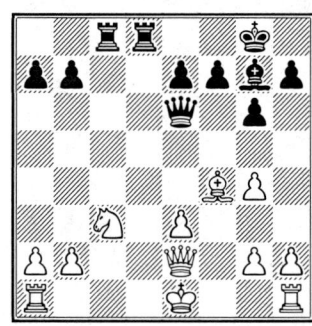

Position after White's 15th move

15 ... Rxc3! Through my blunder Black has regained his piece, and should I castle at this point he would win at least another pawn. 16 0-0 Rcd3 17 Qf3 Rd2 18 Qxb7 Rxb2 19 Qf3 (19 Qxa7? Qe4) Rxa2. I felt that in the long run I would lose this ending, and so I gave up the queen and a pawn for Black's two rooks, hoping that with my rooks I might later regain the pawn. EL **16. bxc3! Bxc3+ 17. Kf2 Rd2 18. Qxd2 Bxd2 19. Rhd1 Ba5 20. Kf3 Qc6+** Khalifman, in Soloviov 1998 (wrongly attributing the game to Emanuel Lasker) suggests 20 ... Bb6!? **21. Kg3 Bb6 22. h3!** Very important, in order to provide a retreat for the king, and also for the bishop. The latter might be attacked by ... e5 or ... g5, after the preparation ... f6. Very bad would have been the attempt to hold the e-pawn with 22 Rac1 Qe4 23 Rc3. Black would have won with 23 ... g5! 24 Rc8+ (24 Bxg5 Qe5+) Kg7 25 Bxg5 Bxe3 26 Bxe3 Qxe3+ 27 Kh4 f5! This threatens, if 28 gxf5, to win the rook by 28 ... Qf4+ and 29 ... Qxf5+, or to checkmate (29 g4 Qxh3+ 30 Kg5 h6 or ... Qh6. I did not mind losing my e-pawn. I was glad to give it up and to exchange bishops, because the queen alone is often unable to force a win against two rooks even with an advantage of two pawns. EL **22 ... Qe4 23. Kh2 Bxe3 24. Bxe3 Qxe3 25. Kh1** A good move to avoid an occasional check with which the queen might simultaneously attack some loose man. Fine, in *Basic Chess Endings*, erroneously recommends 25 Rab1 b6 26 a4. Black would have captured this pawn with the very check on f4 which I avoided with my move. I might have played 25 a4 immediately, and, if 25 ... b6, continued with 26 a5 bxa5 27 Rd5. But the king's move was probably just as good. EL **25 ... Qa3 26. Rd7** A miscalculation. I used up almost all the time I had on the clock, with the following calculation: 26 ... b5 27 Re1 Qxa2 21 Rexe7 a5 29 Rb7 b4 30 Re8+ Kg7 31 R8b8, and I thought I had the pawns effectively stopped in that manner. However there is a flaw in this which I discovered only when it was too late. I should have played 26 Rab1 b6 27 Rd2, and follow this up with Re2 and, if possible, Rb3, in order to double rooks finally on the third rank (with the a-pawn on a3). Then the

black pawns would not have been in a position to advance to their sixth rank. Doubling on the second rank was also to be considered. EL **26 ... b5 27. Re1 Qxa2 28. Rexe7 a5 29. Rd8+ Kg7 30. g5** Now to my horror I saw that my combination was incorrect, for if, 30 Rb7 b4 31 Rdb8, Black can play 31 ... Qd2! 32 Rb5 a4! 33 Rxb4 Qe1+! 34 Kh2 a3. Now the rook on b4 hangs, so that 35 Ra8 is not possible, and if 35 Ra4, the other rook is lost by Qe5+! Neither is 35 Rb1 playable, as 35 ... Qe5+ 36 Kh1 a2 wins a rook. EL **30 ... Qc4 31. Rdd7 a4 32. Rc7 Qf1+ 33. Kh2 Qf4+ 34. Kg1 b4** (Soloviov incorrectly continues the game with 34 ... a3 and then White resigns.) **35. Re1 Qxc7** White resigned. 0–1 Fine 1941, 560; Lasker, 368–74; Soloviov (ed) 1998, 296–7; Fine's notebooks.

(509) FINE–MARSHALL, F

Marshall CC championship 1939/40, New York (16), 1940 (23 March)
Four Knight's Game [C49]

1. e4 e5 2. Nf3 Nc6 3. Nc3 Nf6 4. Bb5 Bb4 5. 0-0 0-0 6. d3 Bxc3 7. bxc3 d5 8. Bxc6 bxc6 9. Nxe5 dxe4 10. dxe4 Qxd1 11. Rxd1 Nxe4 12. Nxc6 Nxc3 13. Re1 Bd7 14. Bd2 Bxc6 15. Bxc3 Rfe8 Draw agreed. ½–½

(510) POLLAND, D–FINE

Marshall CC championship 1939/40, New York (17), 1940 (31 March)
Fianchetto Grünfeld [D75]

1. c4 Nf6 2. d4 g6 3. Nf3 Bg7 4. g3 0-0 5. Bg2 d5 6. cxd5 Nxd5 7. 0-0 c5 8. dxc5 Na6 9. a3 Nxc5 10. Qc2 Qb6 11. e4 Nb3 12. Ra2 Nxc1 13. Rxc1 Nf6 14. Nc3 Be6 15. Raa1 Rac8 16. h3 Bb3 17. Qe2 Bc4 18. Qe3 Qxe3 19. fxe3 Rfd8 20. Nd4 Draw agreed. ½–½

New York Metropolitan League, March–April, 1940

Fine had another highly successful season representing the Marshall Club in the Metropolitan League, defeating Friedman of the Bronx Chess Club, Fajans of the Steinitz Chess Club and finally Moskowitz in the match with perennial rivals the Manhattan Chess Club in the ninth and final round. The representatives of the Marshall Club, including Reshevsky (who lost to Kupchik) and Frank Marshall himself, only needed to draw the match to retain the title. The Manhattan Chess Club, however, won the decisive match by a wide margin, thereby regaining the title from their opponents. The *American Chess Bulletin* reported the match in its March-April issue with the scoreline 11–6 with one game adjourned. Other teams playing in Section

A were Empire City, City College, North Jersey, Queens and West Side Y. M. C. A.

Friedman	0	Fine	1
Fajans	0	Fine	1
Fine	1	Moskowitz	0

(511) FRIEDMAN, S—FINE

Metropolitan Chess League, New York, 1940 (22 March)
Grünfeld Defence [D78]

1. d4 Nf6 2. c4 g6 3. Nc3 d5 4. Nf3 Bg7
5. g3 0–0 6. Bg2 dxc4 7. 0–0 c6 8. Ne5 Be6
9. e4 Nbd7 10. Nxd7 Qxd7 11. d5 cxd5
12. exd5

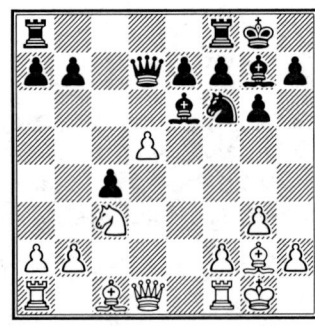

Position after White's 12th move

12 ... Bh3 13. Qf3 Rad8 14. Bg5 Bxg2 15. Kxg2 Nxd5 16. Rad1 Bxc3 17. bxc3 f6 18. Bh6 Rfe8 19. Rd4 b5 20. Rfd1 e6 21. h4 Qf7 22. Rg4 Rd7 23. h5 g5 24. Rdd4 Kh8 25. Qd1 Qxh5 26. Bxg5 fxg5 27. Qe1 e5 White resigned. 0–1

(512) FAJANS, H—FINE

Metropolitan Chess League, New York, 1940 (30 March)
Grünfeld Defence [D94]

1. d4 Nf6 2. c4 g6 3. Nf3 Bg7 4. Nc3 d5 5. e3 0–0 6. Bd2 b6 7. cxd5 Nxd5 8. Rc1 Bb7 9. Bc4 e6 10. Qb3 Ne7 11. Qc2 Nd7 12. Ne4 c5 13. Bc3 cxd4 14. Bxd4 Bxd4 15. exd4 Nf5 16. 0–0 Nf6 17. Ng3

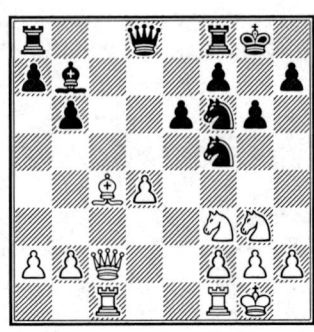

Position after White's 17th move

17 ... Nxd4 18. Nxd4 Qxd4 19. Rfd1 Qf4 20. Qd2 Qxd2 21. Rxd2 Rfd8 22. Rdc2 Rac8 23. f3 Kf8 24. Kf2 Rc7 25. Ne2 Rdc8 26. Nd4 Bd5 27. Bxd5 Rxc2+ 28. Rxc2 Rxc2+ 29. Nxc2 Nxd5 30. a3 e5 31. a4 Ke7 32. Na3 f6 33. g3 Ke6 34. Ke2 Nb4 35. Nb5 a6 36. Nc3 f5 37. Ke3 Nd5+ White resigned. 0–1

(513) FINE—MOSKOWITZ ,J

Metropolitan Chess League, New York, 1940 (20 April)
Spanish Game, Worrall Attack [C86]

1. e4 e5 2. Nf3 Nc6 3. Bb5 a6 4. Ba4 Nf6
5. 0–0 Be7 6. Qe2 b5 7. Bb3 d6 8. a4 Bg4
9. c3 0–0 10. h3 Bh5 11. Rd1 Na5 12. Bc2 Qb8!?
13. d4 c5 14. dxe5 dxe5 15. Bg5 b4 16. Nbd2 bxc3
17. bxc3 Qb2 18. Bd3 Rfd8 19. Bxa6 Qxc3
20. Rdc1 Qb2

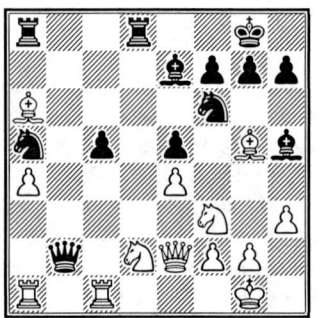

Position after Black's 20th move

21. g4 Bg6 22. Rab1 Qa3 23. Bb5 h6 24. Bh4 Rxd2 25. Nxd2 Qxh3 26. Bxf6 Bxf6 27. Rxc5 Bg5 28. Rd5 Bf4 29. Nf1 h5 30. Bd7 hxg4 31. Bxg4 Qh4 32. Rc5 Rd8? 33. Rxa5 Rd2 34. Ra8+ Kh7 35. Rbb8 Bxe4 36. Qxe4+ Black resigned. 1–0

3rd U.S. Championship,
New York, April 27–May 19, 1940

"By pure chance Reshevsky happened to be paired with Fine in the last round, the result being a dramatic struggle worthy of so tense an occasion. Reshevsky had fought his way to the top and gone into the lead by winning an exceptionally taxing game from Kashdan in 56 moves, defeating Pinkus in a beautiful game, then drawing with Reinfeld, and beating Kupchik in a tenacious battle which went no less than 81 moves; the upshot being that Reshevsky went into the final round a half-point ahead of Fine, needing only a draw to clinch the title. Fine wisely adopted an obscure variation in which Reshevsky seemed unable to find his bearings. It soon became clear that Reshevsky's game was hopeless, and one of the spectators told me later that there were tears in Reshevsky's eyes as he realized he had a lost game. It must have been the most miserable moment of his life! (*What a lucky man if it was, but somehow one doubts it. AW*) But at this point, where most players would have given up all hope, he kept on fighting, and an inexact move by Fine enabled the champion to draw this fateful game. Fine once more justified his great reputation, although he was by no means in his best form. Superior technique and hard plugging had to make up for what was lacking, and he played with almost superhuman determination. In the course of three championship tournaments, it has now become quite clear that it is this element of superb pluck which above all separates Reshevsky and Fine from all their competitors." (*U.S.C.F. Yearbook*)

		1	2	3	4	5	6	7	8	9	10	11	12	13	14	15	16	17	
1	Reshevsky	*	½	1	1	½	1	1	1	½	½	1	1	½	½	1	1	1	13
2	Fine	½	*	½	½	1	0	½	½	1	1	1	1	1	1	1	1	1	12½
3	Kashdan	0	½	*	½	1	1	1	½	½	1	½	0	1	½	1	1	½	10½
4	Pinkus	0	½	½	*	1	½	0	½	½	1	½	½	1	½	1	1	1	10
5	Simonson	½	0	0	0	*	1	½	1	½	½	0	1	1	1	1	1	1	10
6	Kupchik	0	1	0	½	0	*	½	½	½	½	½	1	1	1	½	1	1	9½
7	Denker	0	½	0	1	½	½	*	0	½	0	1	1	1	1	½	1	1	9½
8	Polland	0	½	½	½	0	½	1	*	1	½	0	1	½	0	1	0	½	7½
9	Reinfeld	½	0	½	½	½	½	½	0	*	½	½	½	½	½	½	½	1	7½
10	Shainswit	½	0	0	0	½	½	1	½	½	*	½	½	½	½	½	1	½	7½
11	Bernstein	0	0	½	½	1	½	0	1	½	½	*	0	0	1	0	1	1	7½
12	Adams	0	0	1	½	0	0	0	0	½	½	1	*	0	1	½	1	1	7
13	Seidman	½	0	0	0	0	0	0	½	½	½	1	1	*	½	½	1	1	7
14	Green	½	0	½	½	0	0	0	1	½	½	0	0	½	*	½	1	½	6
15	Hanauer	0	0	0	0	0	½	½	0	½	½	1	½	½	½	*	½	1	6
16	Woliston	0	0	0	0	0	0	0	1	½	0	0	0	0	0	½	*	1	3
17	Littman	0	0	½	0	0	0	0	½	0	½	0	0	0	½	0	0	*	2

(514) ADAMS, W—FINE

U.S. Championship, New York (1), 1940 (27 April)
Sicilian Defence, Pin Variation [B45]

1. e4 c5 2. Nf3 Nc6 3. d4 cxd4 4. Nxd4 Nf6 5. Nc3 e6 6. Be3 Bb4 7. Bd3 0–0 8. 0–0 Ne5 9. Kh1 Nxd3 10. cxd3 e5 11. Nde2 d5 12. Bg5 dxe4 13. dxe4 Be6 14. Qxd8 Rfxd8 15. f4 h6

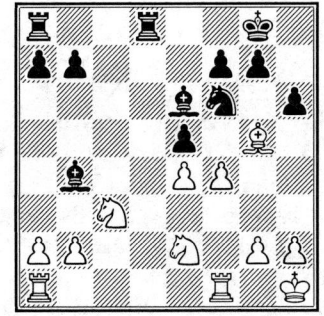

Position after Black's 15th move

16. Bxf6 gxf6 17. f5 Bc4 18. Rfd1 Rac8 19. Ng3 Bxc3 20. bxc3 Kf8 21. Kg1 Rd3 22. Kf2 Rxc3

23. Rd7 Rc2+ 24. Kg1 Ba6 25. Nh5 Rb2 26. Kh1 Rb6 27. h3 Bb5 28. Rd2 Ba4 29. g4 Ke7 30. Kg2 Rc4 31. Re1 Bc6 32. Kf3 Ra6 33. Ng3 Rca4 34. Ree2 Bb5 35. Rf2 Bc4 36. Rc2 b5 White resigned. **0–1**

(515) FINE—KASHDAN, I

U.S. Championship, New York (2), 1940 (28 April)
Slav Defence [D30]

1. d4 d5 2. c4 c6 3. Nf3 Nf6 4. e3 e6 5. Nbd2 Ne4 6. Nxe4 dxe4 7. Nd2 f5 8. f3 Bd6 9. g3 exf3 10. Nxf3 Nd7 11. Qb3 c5 12. Bg2 0–0 13. 0–0 Qe7 14. Bd2 Nf6 15. Rad1 Ne4 16. Bc3 b6 17. Nd2 Nxd2 18. Rxd2 Bb7 19. Qd1 Bxg2 20. Kxg2 Rad8 21. Qf3 Qc7 22. b3 Rf7 23. Rfd1 Bf8 24. a4 Qb7 25. a5 cxd4 26. exd4 Qxf3+ 27. Kxf3 bxa5 28. Bxa5 Rb8 29. Rb1 Bb4 30. Ra2 Bxa5 31. Rxa5 Rfb7 32. Kf4 Kf7 33. Ke5 Rd7 34. b4 Rbd8 35. Rd1 Rb8 36. Rda1 Rbb7 37. b5 Rbc7 38. Ra6 Rxc4 39. Rd6 Rb7 40. Rxe6 Rxb5+ 41. d5 Re4+ 42. Kd6 Rb6+ 43. Kc5 Rbxe6 44. dxe6+ Rxe6 45. Rxa7+ Kf6 46. Kd4 Re2 47. h4 Re4+ 48. Kd3 Rg4 49. Ra6+ Kf7 50. Ke3 h5 51. Kf3 g6 52. Ra7+ Kf6 53. Ra6+ Kg7 54. Ra7+ Kh6 55. Ra6 Re4 56. Ra7 Draw agreed. **½–½**

(516) PINKUS, A—FINE

U.S. Championship, New York (3), 1940 (29 April)
Spanish Game, Open Defence [C83]

1. e4 e5 2. Nf3 Nc6 3. Bb5 a6 4. Ba4 Nf6 5. 0–0 Nxe4 6. d4 b5 7. Bb3 d5 8. dxe5 Be6 9. c3 Be7 10. Nbd2 0–0 11. Qe2 Nc5 12. Nd4 Nxb3 13. N2xb3 13 Nxc6 Nxc1 14 Rac1 Qd7 15 Nxe7+ Qxe7 16 f4 f5 17 exf6 Qxf6 18 Qe3 Bf5 19 Qd4 and White stands slightly better, Janošević–Lukić, Yugoslavia 1955. 13 ... Qd7 14. Nxc6 Qxc6 15. Be3 Bf5 16. f3 16 Rfd1 Qg6 17 Nd4 Bd7 18 b4 Qe4 19 Bd2 Qxe2 20 Nxe2 Rfe8 21 Bf4 c6 22 Nd4 a5 23 a3 axb4 with equality, Mecking–Korchnoi, Augusta 1974. 16 ... Rfe8 17. Rfe1 Bf8 18. Bd4 a5 19. Qf2 Bg6 20. f4 Qd7 21. Rad1 Be4 22. Nc5 Bxc5 23. Bxc5 Qf5 24. Re3 Ra6 25. Rg3 Rg6 26. Rxg6 Qxg6 27. Re1 Re6 28. Re3 Qh5 29. Qe2 Qxe2 30. Rxe2 Rc6 31. Bd4 b4 32. Re3 h5 33. Kf2 Kf8 34. Re1 Ke7 35. Rc1 Ke6 36. Be3 Kf5 37. Bd2 h4 38. cxb4 Rxc1 39. Bxc1 axb4 40. Be3 It is the king position which is usually the decisive factor in these endings. To keep one's own king mobile and to prevent the opponent's king from supporting his pawn majority is often worth a pawn; in many cases a pawn sacrifice is required to make sure that the enemy king does not occupy a dominating position. Black stands better, but his slight superiority will disappear into thin air unless he can get his king to e4. Accordingly he tries **40 ... Bb1**

but after **41. Kf3!!** the best he can do is win a worthless pawn. If White instead makes a routine move such as 41 a3? b×a3 42 b×a3 Ke4 is decisive, for example, 43 a4 d4 44 Bd2 c5 45 a5 Bd3 46 g3 h×g3+ 47 h×g3 Ba6 48 g4 c4 49 Ke1 c3 50 Bc1 d3. **41 ... Be4+ 42. Kf2 Bb1 43. Kf3 B×a2 44. g4+ h×g3 45. h×g3 Bb3 46. g4+ Ke6 47. Bc5 Bd1+ 48. Ke3 b3 49. g5 Kf5 50. Ba7 g6 51. Bc5** The pawn is worthless because the dark squares are effectively blocked. **51 ... Kg4 52. Ba7 Bc2 53. Bc5 Bf5 54. Ba7 Kg3 55. Bd4 Kg2 56. Ba7 Be6 57. Bd4 Kf1 58. Kd2!** Draw agreed. ½–½ Fine 1941, 183.

(517) FINE—REINFELD, F

U.S. Championship, New York (4), 1940 (1 May)
Queen's Gambit Declined, Tarrasch Defence [D40]

1. d4 Nf6 2. c4 e6 3. Nc3 d5 4. Nf3 Be7 5. e3 c5 6. Bd3 d×c4 7. B×c4 Nc6 8. 0–0 0–0 9. a3 a6 10. Bd3 c×d4 11. e×d4 b5 12. Be3 Bb7 13. Qe2 Nd5 14. Ne4 N×e3 15. f×e3 f5 16. Ned2 Bf6 17. Nb3 Qd6 18. Rad1 Rae8 19. Nc5 Bc8 20. b4 Ne7 21. Bc2 Nd5 22. Qd3 g6 23. Bb3 Bg7 24. e4 f×e4 25. N×e4 Qe7 26. Nc5 Qd6 27. Rde1 Rf5 28. Qe2 Nf4 29. Qe4 Nd5 30. Qe2 Nf4 31. Qd2 Rd8 32. Re4 Nd5 33. Rfe1 Re8

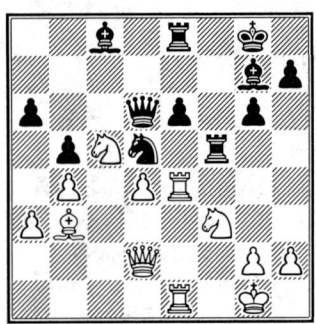

Position after Black's 33rd move

34. B×d5 Q×d5 35. Qe3 Ref8 36. h3 Rd8 37. N×e6 B×e6 38. R×e6 B×d4 39. Q×d4 Q×d4+ 40. N×d4 R×d4 41. R×a6 Rd7 42. Rb6 Kg7 43. Re8 Kh6 44. Rbe6 Rd2 45. Re2 Rd3 46. R8e3 Rd1+ 47. Kh2 Rf7 48. Re5 Ra1 49. R×b5 R×a3 50. Rb2 Rfa7 51. Rd5 Ra2 52. Rdd2 R×b2 53. R×b2 Rb7 54. Kg3 Kg5 55. b5 Rb6 56. Kf3 Kf5 57. Ke3 Ke5 58. Kd3 Kd5 59. Kc3 Kc5 60. h4 h6 61. Rb1 h5 62. Rb2 Kd5 63. Kb4 Rb8 64. Rd2+ Ke5 65. Rd3 Kf5 66. Rb3 Re8 67. b6 Black resigned. **1–0**

(518) KUPCHIK, A—FINE

U.S. Championship, New York (5), 1940 (2 May)
Sicilian Defence [B45]

1. e4 c5 2. Nf3 Nc6 3. d4 c×d4 4. N×d4 Nf6 5. Nc3 e6 This move is played to avoid the Rauzer Attack

which would follow after 5 ... d6 6 Bg5. **6. Be3 Bb4** A favourite continuation with Fine; although his good results with this variation are based on his skill rather than on any particular merit of the variation. FR **7. N×c6 b×c6** 7 ... d×c6 8 Q×d8+ K×d8 is good enough for equality, but Fine won in a game with this line from Kupchik in last year's Manhattan–Marshall match; hence he doubtless feels that after the pitcher oughtn't to go to the well again. FR **8. e5 Nd5 9. Bd2 d6!** Best. Black gets a bad game after 9 ... N×c3 10 b×c3 followed by 11 Qg4. HG **10. N×d5 B×d2+ 11. Q×d2 e×d5 12. e×d6 Q×d6 13. Bd3 0–0 14. 0–0 c5** Black has the better game owing to his possession of the centre. HG **15. Rfe1 Be6?** All Black had to do was play 15 ... Bd7, contest the e-file by ... Re8— and then go to sleep. *Chess* **16. b3** White's main concern of course is to prevent his opponent from safely advancing his d-pawn and c-pawn to the fifth rank, which would give Black excellent prospects. FR **16 ... Rfd8** Black's correct play was 16 ... Rfe8. Purdy **17. Rad1 Rab8 18. Re3** White's counterchances obviously reside in attack on the kingside. HG **18 ... g6** Something of the sort is unavoidable as White intends Rg3 followed by Qh6 or Qg5. FR **19. Bf1** 19 ... c4 is now a serious threat, as the White bishop cannot play 21 B×h7+. *Chess* **19 ... Qb6** Aggressive but compromising; more mobile is 19 ... Qc7, reserving the queen for action on both sides of the board. HG **20. Rde1 c4 21. Re5 a5 22. Qh6! a4 23. b×c4 d×c4 24. h4! Rd6?** Black was now worried by his clock, but in any case he is faced with problems. The best chance was 24 ... Qd6 25 h5 Qf8; but 26 Qf4 retains White's initiative. Purdy **25. B×c4 Rf8?** If 25 ... B×c4 26 Re8 and mate follows. FR (25 ... Qc6!? AW) **26. h5! Bd7? 27. B×f7+** If 27 ... K×f7 28 Q×h7+ and mate next move. If 27 ... R×f7 28 R×e8+ B×e8 29 R×e8+ and mate next move. Pretty, but simple. *Chess*; As Fine resigned, he said ruefully, "This is what comes of trying to win a drawn position." FR **1–0**
Golombek in *BCM* 1940, 273–5; Others quoted from *U.S.C.F.* 6 1940, 46–7.

(519) FINE—SEIDMAN, H

U.S. Championship, New York (7), 1940 (5 May)
Queen's Indian Defence [E17]

1. d4 Nf6 2. c4 e6 3. Nf3 b6 4. g3 Bb7 5. Bg2 Be7 6. 0–0 0–0 7. b3 The more normal move 7 Nc3 permits the simplifying reply 7 ... Ne4; hence Fine decides on another move which may enable him to maintain the tension. **d5 8. Bb2 c5 9. Nbd2 Nbd7** If Black wants to simplify (and why shouldn't he, against Fine?) he can play 9 ... d×c4 10 N×c4 c×d4 11 N×d4 (11 B×d4 Nc6) B×g2 with equality. **10. e3 Rc8 11. Qe2 Qc7 12. Rac1 Qb8 13. c×d5! e×d5 14. Ne5 Rcd8 15. f4 c×d4?** An error which appreciably strengthens White's position; his knight is now more firmly entrenched on e5, the hostile d-pawn becomes more accessible to attack, the hostile king's knight cannot be sunk at White's e4, and in general

White's position acquires more space and manoeuvring elasticity. Black's one compensation is the e-file—or so he hopes. The more patient 15 ... Rfe8, leaving White in some doubt as to the opponent's intentions, was decidedly preferable. If then 15 ... Rfe8 16 Ba3 cxd4 17 Bxe7 Rxe7 18 exd4 Nf8 followed by ... Ne4! with better prospects than after the text. **16. exd4 Rfe8 17. a3!** **Nf8** Black doubtless avoided 17 ... a5 because it would weaken his queenside. White is now able to gain further ground, reserving the eventual possibility of bringing his queen to b3 and his queen's knight to e3. First he settles the problem of the e-file. **18. b4 Bd6 19. Qd3 Qa8** Vainly angling for ... Ne4, which if played at once would lead to 19 ... Ne4 20 Nxe4 dxe4 21 Bxe4 Bxe4 22 Qxe4 f6 23 Qd5+ with a winning game. **20. Rce1 a5 21. b5 Re7 22. Re2 Rde8 23. Rfe1**

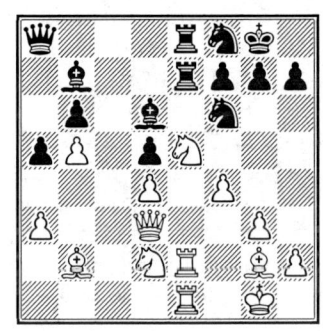

Position after White's 23rd move

N6d7 24. Nf1! f6 25. Nxd7 Nxd7 26. Rxe7 Rxe7 27. Rxe7 Bxe7 If Black expected any relief from the foregoing exchanges, he is soon undeceived, as White now reaches the position outlined in the note to Black's seventeenth move **28. Ne3 g6** Or 28 ... a4 29 Qf5 and so on. The d-pawn is untenable. **29. Qb3 Kf8 30. Nxd5 Qc8 31. a4 f5 32. Nxe7 Kxe7 33. Ba3+ Kf6 34. Qe3 Kg7 35. d5 Nc5 36. Qe7+ Kh6** If 36 ... Kg8 37 Bxc5 Qxc5+ 38 Qxc5 bxc5 39 d6 Bc8 40 b6 Kf8 41 d7 and wins. **37. Bb2** (In view of unavoidable mate, Black resigned.) **1–0** Based on notes by Reinfeld in *Chess Review*, May-June 1940 (Hilbert 2002a, 126-7).

(520) SIMONSON, A—FINE

U.S. Championship, New York (8), 1940 (6 May)
Spanish Game, Steinitz Defence Deferred [C73]

1. e4 e5 2. Nf3 Nc6 3. Bb5 a6 4. Ba4 d6 5. 0–0 Nf6 6. Bxc6+ Not now 6 d4? b5 7 Bb3 Nxd4 8 Nxd4 exd4 and then White can play neither 9 Qxd4??, nor Bd5. Purdy **6 ... bxc6 7. d4 exd4** CONCEPTION OF A PLAN—By the text Black resorts to a fashionable stratagem: exposure of White's e-pawn with a view to immobilizing and attacking it later on. Though as a rule sound policy, in this particular case it is not practicable, because Black's own pawn formation will hinder his free development. In that light Black's plan is too ambitious. The alternative 7 ... Nxe4 8 dxe5 d5

favoured by Reshevsky is somewhat risky to judge by the game Keres–Reshevsky, A.V.R.O. 1938. Comparatively best is probably 7 ... Nd7 8 b3 and now the consequential 8 ... c5 forcing simplification in the centre. EK **8. Qxd4** Both players are tired of routine but the straight and narrow path is often best. 8 Nxd4 was superior to the text. AES **8 ... c5 9. Qd3 Be6 10. c4 Be7 11. Nc3** More to the point is 11 b3, in order to flank the queen's bishop. The worst that could happen then is the exchange of it against Black's king's bishop. As it is, the bishop remains idle throughout the game. EK **11 ... 0–0 12. h3** Almost meaningless—why not continue substantially, either with 12 Bg5 or 12 b3 and 13 Bb2? AES **12 ... Nd7 13. b3** White would like to play 13 Bf4 at once, but is evidently deterred by 13 ... f5, with a masked attack on the bishop. If then 14 e5? dxe5 15 Nxe5 Nxe5 16 Qxd8 Raxd8 17 Bxe5 Bxc4. Hence the protection of the c-pawn in advance. Purdy **13 ... Bf6 14. Bf4!** If instead 14 Bb2, then 14 ... Bxc3 at once. EK **14 ... Qe7 15. Rfe1 Bxc3** The threat was 16 Nd5. AES; In execution of his plan Black does not shirk splitting his pair of bishops. EK **16. Qxc3 f6! 17. Bg3** Preparing to hit the knight with f4, but that move will weaken as well as strengthen White. Purdy **17 ... Qf7 18. Nh4 Ne5 19. f4 Nc6 20. Nf3 Rad8!** Played with excellent positional judgment. One would logically expect, instead, 20 ... a5-a4 but this plan is here too slow—White replying simply 21 Rad1 and 22 e5. AES **21. Rad1 h6 22. Rd2 Rfe8** The crucial position—what shall White undertake now? There are three possibilities—a) the continuation chosen, which, I believe, is entered upon prematurely and developed rashly; b) a dawdling line (Kh2) safe, and deadly; c) the idea Bh4 and g4-g5—risky, but interesting. AES **23. Red1 Qf8 24. e5** Demonstrating that Black has failed in his chief aim. EK **24 ... f5** Though Black has the satisfaction of guarding a central square. EK **25. exd6 cxd6 26. Bf2 Bf7** Much better was 26 ... Bc8 followed by 27 ... Bb7, when Black could combine consolidation of his weakish queen's wing with play in the centre. In that case the game would have been even. The text apparently contains the threat of 27 ... Bh5. EK **27. g4?** THE CRISIS—He succumbs to the fascination of the threat, thereby not only foregoing a first-class chance to win the game, but actually making good Black's failing. 27 Qb2 would have confronted Black with a difficult problem, for if 27 ... Bh5, then 28 Qa3 Bxf3 29 gxf3 a5 30 Qa4 Rc8 31 Kf1! Red8 32 Bxc5 dxc5 33 Qxc6, or 29 ... Nb4 30 Qa5, winning a pawn in either case. The text weakens White's position and Black obtains the advantage. EK **27 ... fxg4 28. hxg4 Re4 29. Bg3 Rde8!** *(see diagram at top of next page)* **30. Rxd6** White elects to exchange a rook for a piece and two pawns, but a deficiency in fighting force will tell against him in view of the open files and exposed king. Purdy **30 ... Nd4! 31. R6xd4 cxd4 32. Rxd4 Re3 33. Rd3 Qc5 34. Bf2 Rxd3 35. Qxd3 Qa3 36. Qc2 Qd6 37. Ne5 Be6** With the intention of dislodging the knight by an eventual ... g5. EK **38. Kg2 Bc8 39. Kg3** With the counter-intention of holding on tenaciously to his central outpost. (39 ... g5 40 Be3 gxf4+ 41 Bxe4, and the knight stands fast, for 41 ... Rxe5 fails on account of

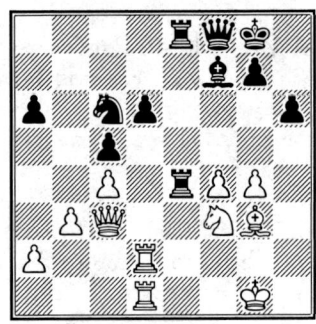

*Position after
Black's 29th move*

42 Qc3.) EK **39 ... Rxe5** FINALE—Here Black shows
accomplishment. He surrenders his material plus and
obtains the initiative owing to the exposure of White's
king. This initiative serves him as a means of advancing
his own pawns quickly while those of his opponent are
easily arrested. The last part of the game is attractive as it
is convincing. EK **40. fxe5 Qxe5+ 41. Kg2 Bxg4** Here
bishops on opposite colours are a big winning factor! the
attacking bishop can never be challenged. Purdy **42. Qd3
Bf5 43. Qd2 Qe4+ 44. Kh2 Qg4 45. c5 Be4
46. Be3 Kh7 47. b4 Bc6 48. Bf4 Qf3 49. Kg1
g5 50. Bb8 Kg6 51. Qc2+ Kh5 52. Qh2+ Kg4
53. Qd2** Resigned—but not resigning—not yet. AES **53 ...
Qh1+ 54. Kf2 Qg2+ 55. Ke3 Qxd2+ 56. Kxd2 Kf3
57. Ke1 g4** White resigned. The black pawns are definitely
on the gold standard. AES **0–1** Purdy quoted in *U.S.C.F.* 6
1940, 51–3; E. Klein, *BCM* 1941, 55–6; Santasiere, *ACB*
1940, 64–5.

(521) FINE—WOLISTON, P

U.S. Championship, New York (9), 1940 (8 May)
Grünfeld Defence, 4 Bf4 [D93]

**1. d4 Nf6 2. c4 g6 3. Nc3 d5 4. Bf4 Bg7 5. e3
0–0 6. Rc1 c6 7. Nf3 dxc4 8. Bxc4 Nbd7 9. 0–0
b5 10. Be2 a6 11. a3 Qb6 12. b4 Qb7 13. Nd2
Nb6 14. Nb3 Be6 15. Na5 Qd7 16. Nb1 Bd5
17. Nd2 Qe6 18. Bc7 Na4 19. Be5 Rfd8 20. Qc2
Rac8 21. Rfe1 Bh6 22. Bf3 c5**

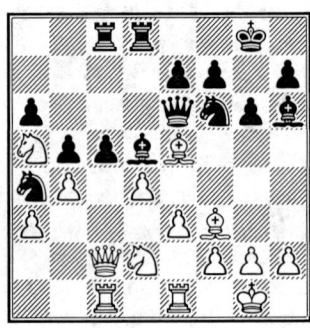

*Position after
Black's 22nd move*

**23. Nb7 Rf8 24. Nxc5 Nxc5 25. bxc5 Nd7
26. Bg3 f5 27. Bxd5 Qxd5 28. Qb3 e6 29. Qxd5**

exd5 **30. Nb3 Nf6 31. Be5 Nh5 32. Rc2 Rfe8
33. f3 Bg7 34. Bxg7 Kxg7 35. Kf2 Nf6 36. Nc1
Re6 37. Nd3 Nd7 38. Nf4** Black resigned. **1–0**

(522) GREEN, M—FINE

U.S. Championship, New York (10), 1940 (9 May)
Nimzowitsch-Indian Defence, Classical Variation [E33]

1. d4 Nf6 2. c4 e6 3. Nc3 Bb4 4. Qc2 Nc6 Not preferred today. The consensus favours 4 ... c5. Fine chose the
Nimzowitsch moves. **5. Nf3 d6 6. g3 0–0 7. Bg2 e5
8. dxe5** Moderately attractive is 8 d5 Nd4 9 Nxd4 exd4
10 a3 Ba5 11 b4 Bb6 12 Na4. **dxe5 9. 0–0 Bg4 10. e3
Re8 11. h3 Bh5 12. Nh4 Qd7 13. Nd5 Nxd5
14. cxd5 Ne7 15. e4 f6 16. Be3 Bd6 17. Nf5** What is
wrong with 17 g4? Nothing radically, except that White must
transfer his pieces to the queenside. **Nxf5 18. exf5 Rad8
19. Be4 Qb5 20. Bd3** A cheap trap (20 ... Qxd5??
21 Bc4). Black returns his queen and White resumes his
post on e4. **Qd7 21. Be4 b6 22. Rac1 Re7 23. f3 Bf7
24. Rfd1 Qb5 25. Rd3 Red7 26. Rcd1 Bf8** Black now
has four attackers to White's three defenders. White brings
a fourth defender with his next move, but in doing so allows
doubled pawns. **27. Qb3 Qxb3 28. axb3 g6!** This forces
White to play g4, and the second set of doubled pawns is
too much. **29. g4 gxf5 30. gxf5 Bh5 31. Kf2 h6**
Would you believe this move is almost brilliant? The plan is
to double rooks on the g-file and leave the black bishop free.
**32. Ke2 Kh7 33. Kf2 Bb4 34. Ke2 Rg7 35. Rg1
Rxg1 36. Bxg1 Rg8 37. Bf2**

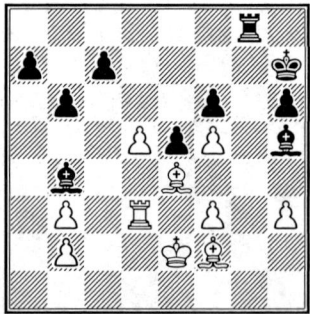

*Position after
White's 37th move*

Be8 Whoops! **38. Rd1** Forced, and White is destined to
eat dust. **Rg2 39. Kf1 Rh2 40. Kg1 Rxh3 41. Ra1 a5
42. d6** The plan was to sacrifice the pawns in such a manner that White would escape with a draw. **Bxd6 43. Rd1
b5 44. b4** The last effort. If 44 ... Bxb4, White's rook penetrates, causing trouble. Fine of course did not allow this,
and White lost. **axb4 45. Ra1 Rh5 46. Be3 Bd7
47. Kg2 Bxf5 48. Rh1 Bxe4 49. Rxh5 Bd5
50. Rxh6+ Kg7 51. Rh1 f5 52. Rc1 Kf7 53. Kf2 f4
54. Ba7 Ke6 55. Bc5 Bxc5+ 56. Rxc5 c6 57. Rc1
Kd6 58. Rc2 c5 59. Rc1 c4 60. Ke2 b3** Notes by
Green written in 1996 (Hilbert 2002, 143). White resigned.
0–1

(523) FINE—DENKER, A

U.S. Championship, New York (11), 1940 (11 May)
Sicilian Dragon, Fianchetto Variation [B70]

**1. e4 c5 2. Nf3 Nc6 3. d4 cxd4 4. Nxd4 Nf6
5. Nc3 d6 6. Nde2** Beginning a manoeuvre which from the theoretical point of view is extremely interesting. White intends to fianchetto his king bishop so that it will bear down on d5 and support the occupation of that vital square by one of the knights, with a strong centralized position. The idea is attractive but it has a practical fallacy: so many moves are required for its execution that Black gets time to complete his development favourably and build up counter-play on the queenside. **6 ... g6 7. g3 Bg7 8. Bg2 0—0 9. 0—0 Be6** Both sides have finished preliminary deployment of their pieces. White aims for occupation of d5, Black for occupation of c4. **10. Nd5** If instead 10 Nf4 Bg4 11 f3 (provoking this advance gives Black useful tactical possibilities) Bd7 and, as in the actual text continuation, Black has ample counterplay on the queenside. **10 ... Rc8 11. c3** 11 c4? is a mistake because of 11 ... Na5 and if 12 b3 Nxe4. **11 ... Ne5 12. Nd4 Bg4 13. f3 Bd7 14. f4 Nc6** But not 19 ... Nc4 15 b3 Nb6 16 Bb2 and White is well on the way to completing his development favourably. **15. Nc2** Black was threatening 16 ... Nxd5 17 exd5 Nxd4 18 cxd4 Qb6 and wins. White's elaborate manoeuvres have not had much effect. **15 ... Na5 16. Nce3 Nc4 17. Nxf6+ Bxf6 18. Nd5 Bg7** White has achieved nothing in the opening. His well-placed knight is about to be driven away, and his queen bishop and queen rook are still waiting to be developed. Black has a promising game. **19. a4** Else ... b5 is strong. But the text creates a target for Black to aim at. **19 ... e6 20. Ne3 Qb6 21. Qe2 Na5 22. Kh1 Nb3** Not the best. Simply 22 ... Rc7 followed by 23 ... Rfc8 assures a lasting advantage. **23. Ra3 a5** Planning to sacrifice the exchange next move. **24. Nc4 Qa6** Getting cold feet at the last moment. I should have gone in for 24 ... Rxc4! 25 Qxc4 Nxc1 26 Rxc1 Qxb2 27 Raa1 Rc8 28 Qf1 Bxc3 29 Rab1 Qa3 30 Rxb7 Bxa4. During the game I felt that this continuation leaves White too many drawing chances; but as a matter of fact, it is difficult to see any good line for him. **25. Rxb3 Rxc4 26. Rxb7! Qxb7** It is true that the text is worthwhile, for despite the loss of a pawn, Black retains the initiative; but 26 ... Bxa4 was stronger. **27. Qxc4 Rc8 28. Qd3 Bf8 29. Qc2 Rb8** The value of White's extra pawn is considerably minimized by the fact that he cannot play out his queen's bishop. **30. f5** Beginning a new phase which is dangerous for both players. The remaining play took place under severe time pressure. **30 ... Qc6** Not 30 ... exf5 31 exf5 attacking Black's queen (31 ... Bxf5 32 Rxf5!). (Denker's record of the game has 30 ... Qa6 at this point, whereas Fine's notebook reads 30 ... Qc6. AW) **31. Qf2 exf5 32. exf5 Qc4** Black's f7 requires additional protection. **33. fxg6 hxg6 34. Be3** The bishop finally joins the fray! **34 ... Bg7 35. Bf4 Bc6!** Threatening 36 ... Rxb2! when the rook would be immune to capture (37 Qxb2?? Qxf1 mate). **36. Bxc6 Qxc6+ 37. Kg1 Rb7 38. Qe2**

d5 **39. Qg2 Qb6+ 40. Kh1** If 40 Rf2 (trying to hold the pawn), then 40 ... d4! actually gives Black winning chances. (A line worth further investigation: 41 c4 d3 42 c5! Qb4 43 c6 Re7 44 c7. AW) **40 ... Qxb2 41. Qxd5 Qe2** Draw agreed. My battle with the clock was hectic. ½—½ Denker 117–21.

(524) BERNSTEIN, S—FINE

U.S. Championship, New York (12), 1940 (12 May)
Nimzowitsch-Indian Defence, Classical Variation [E33]

1. d4 Nf6 2. c4 e6 3. Nc3 Bb4 4. Qc2 Nc6 5. Nf3 d5 A seemingly inconsistent move introduced by Botvinnik. The idea is that after 6 a3 Bxc3+ 7 Qxc3 a5 8 e3 a4 White has weak squares on the queenside. **6. cxd5 exd5 7. Bg5 h6 8. Bf4** Gives Black a chance. Simple enough is 8 Bxf6 Qxf6 9 a3 with equality. **8 ... Ne4! 9. e3 g5! 10. Be5 f6 11. Bg3 h5 12. h3 Nxg3 13. Qg6+ Kf8 14. fxg3 Qd6!** The point is that Black wins a pawn. Paradoxically the white king is even more exposed than the black. **15. 0—0—0** If instead 15 Kf2 Ne7 16 Qc2 Bxc3 17 Qxc3 Nf5 and White is lost. **15 ... Bxc3 16. bxc3 Ne7 17. Qb1 Qa3+**

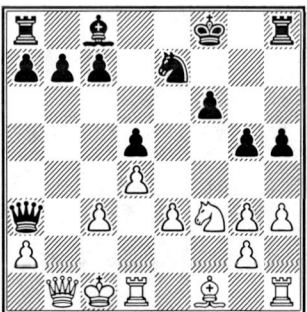

Position after Black's 17th move

18. Kd2 On 18 Qb2 Qxb2+ 19 Kxb2 Nf5 and the pawn goes. White cannot find any real compensation. **18 ... Nf5 19. Bd3 Nxg3 20. Rhe1 Kg7 21. h4 g4 22. Ng1 b5!** A vigorous breakthrough helps to consolidate Black's advantage. If in reply 23 Bxb5 Rb8 and if 23 Qxb5 Qxa2+ 24 Kc1 (24 Bc2 Ne4+) Be6 followed by ... Rab8, with a winning advantage. **23. Rc1** To play 24 Qxb5 and if 24 ... Qxa2+ 25 Rc2. **23 ... Bd7 24. Qb4 Qxb4 25. cxb4 c6 26. a4 bxa4! 27. Rc5** Or 27 b5 Rhc8. **27 ... Rhb8 28. Kc3 Re8 29. Kd2 Rab8 30. Rb1 Re7 31. Ra5 Be8 32. Ne2 Nxe2 33. Bxe2 Reb7 34. Rxa4** Or 34 Kc3 Bg6 35 Rb2 Re7 36 Kd2 Rbe7, winning the e-pawn. **34 ... c5 35. b5 c4 36. e4 Bxb5 37. Rab4 a5 38. R4b2 Ba6 39. Rxb7+ Rxb7** (*see diagram at top of next page*) **40. Re1** Or 40 Rxb7+ Bxb7 41 exd5 Bxd5 42 g3 a4 and White is helpless. **40 ... Re7 41. exd5 c3+ 42. Kxc3 Rxe2 43. Ra1** On 43 d6 Kf7 the black king catches the pawn. **43 ... Re3+ 44. Kc2 Re7 45. Rxa5 Bb7 46. Kd3 f5 47. d6 Be4+ 48. Ke3 Rd7 49. Kf4 Kf6** White resigned. **0—1** Fine 1958, 179–82.

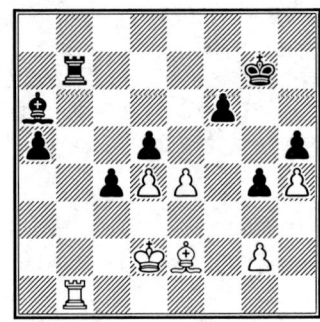

*Position after
Black's 39th move*

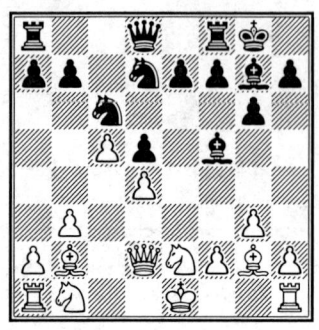

*Position after
Black's 12th move*

(525) FINE—SHAINSWIT, G

U.S. Championship, New York (13), 1940 (13 May)
Catalan System [E01]

1. d4 d5 2. c4 e6 3. Nf3 Nf6 4. g3 c5 5. Bg2 Nc6
6. cxd5 Nxd5 7. 0–0 Nb6 8. dxc5 Qxd1 9. Rxd1
Bxc5 10. Nc3 0–0 11. Bf4 f6 12. Ne4 Be7 13. Bd6
Bxd6 14. Nxd6 Rd8 15. Ne1 Rd7 16. Rac1 Nd8
17. Rd3 Rb8 18. a4 Nc6 19. Bxc6 bxc6

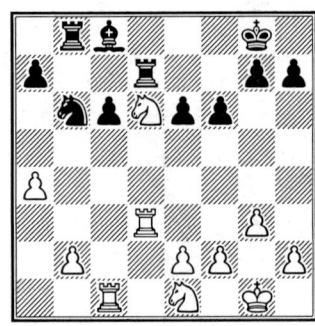

*Position after
Black's 19th move*

20. a5 Ba6 21. axb6 Bxd3 22. bxa7 Ra8 23. Rxc6
Bxe2 24. Rc8+ Rd8 25. Rxd8+ Rxd8 26. Nc2 Bf3
27. Nd4 Ba8 28. N4b5 Kf8 29. f4 Ke7 30. Nc4
Bc6 31. Nc7 Kd7 32. a8Q Bxa8 33. Nxa8 Rxa8
34. Nb6+ Kc7 35. Nxa8+ Kb7 36. Kf2 Kxa8
37. Ke3 Black resigned! 1–0

(526) LITTMAN, G—FINE

U.S. Championship, New York (14), 1940 (15 May)
Alekhine's Defence [B03]

1. e4 Nf6 2. e5 Nd5 3. d4 d6 4. c4 Nb6
5. exd6 cxd6 6. b3 g6 7. Bb2 Bg7 8. g3 Nc6
9. Bg2 Bf5 10. Qd2 0–0 11. Ne2 d5 12. c5 Nd7
(see diagram at top of next column) 13. Bxd5 Nxc5
14. Nf4 Nd3+ 15. Nxd3 Qxd5 16. 0–0 Nxd4
17. Bxd4 Qxd4 18. Nb4 Qxa1 19. Nd5 Bxb1
20. Nxe7+ Kh8 21. h4 Qe5 22. Re1 Be4 White
resigned. 0–1

(527) FINE—HANAUER, M

U.S. Championship, New York (15), 1940 (16 May)
Hanauer-Daikeler Defence [A45]

1. d4 Nf6 2. g3 e5!? 3. dxe5 Ng4 4. e4 Nxe5
5. f4 Nec6 6. Be3 d5?! 7. exd5 Nb4 8. Bb5+
Bd7 9. Bxd7+ Qxd7 10. Nc3 Qf5 11. Rc1 Bd6
12. Nf3 0–0 13. 0–0 Re8 14. Bf2 Nd7 15. a3
Na6 16. Nd4 Qg6 17. Qd3 Qxd3 18. cxd3 Nac5
19. Rfd1 Nf6 20. b4 Ncd7 21. Ndb5 a6 22. Nxd6
cxd6

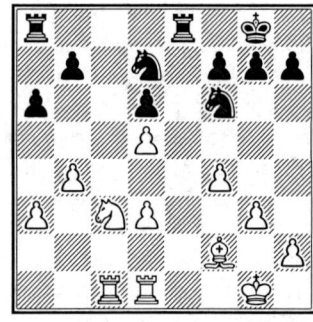

*Position after
Black's 22nd move*

23. Rd2 h5 24. Kg2 Kh7 25. Kf3 Rac8 26. Rdc2
g5 27. fxg5 Ne5+ 28. Ke2 Nfg4 29. Ne4 Rcd8
30. Bg1 Kg6 31. Rf1 Nd7 32. h3 f5 33. hxg4 fxe4
34. gxh5+ Kxh5 35. Rf4 exd3+ 36. Kxd3 Ne5+
37. Kd2 b5 38. Bd4 Kxg5 39. Rc7 Kg6 40. Ke2
Rc8 41. Rxc8 Rxc8 42. Bxe5 dxe5 43. Rf3 Rc2+
44. Ke3 Rc4 45. Rf2 Rg4 46. d6 Rxg3+ 47. Ke4
Rg1 48. Kxe5 Rd1 49. Ke6 Re1+ 50. Kd5 Rd1+
51. Kc6 Rc1+ 52. Kb6 Rd1 53. Kxa6 Rd3 54. Kxb5
Rxa3 55. Rd2 Ra8 56. d7 Rd8 57. Kc6 Black resigned.
1–0

(528) POLLAND, D—FINE

U.S. Championship, New York (16), 1940 (18 May)
Catalan System [E02]

1. d4 Nf6 2. c4 e6 3. Nf3 d5 4. g3 dxc4 5. Qa4+
Bd7 6. Qxc4 Bc6 7. Bg2 Bd5 8. Qa4+ Qd7
9. Qxd7+ Nbxd7 10. Nc3 Bc6 11. 0–0 Bd6 12. h3
a6 13. Re1 0–0 14. e4 Bb4 15. Nd2 Nb6 16. a3

Be7 17. b4 Na4 18. Nxa4 Bxa4 19. Bb2 a5
20. Rec1 axb4 21. Rxc7 bxa3 22. Bc1 Bb4
23. Rxb7 Rfb8 24. Rxb8+ Rxb8 25. Nb1 Bc2
26. Nxa3 Bc3 27. Ra2 Bxe4 28. Nb5 Bb4
29. Bxe4 Nxe4 30. Ba3 Bxa3 31. Rxa3 h5 32. Nc3
Nf6 33. Kg2 Rc8 34. Kf3 Kf8 35. Ne4 Nxe4
36. Kxe4 Rc2 37. Ke3 Ke7 38. Ra5 h4 39. Ra3
g5 40. gxh4 gxh4 41. Kf3 Rd2 42. Ke3 Rd1 43. Rd3
Rg1 44. d5 exd5 45. Rxd5 Rh1 46. Kf3 Rxh3+
47. Kg4 Draw agreed. ½–½

(529) FINE—RESHEVSKY, S

U.S. Championship, New York (17), 1940 (19 May)
Two Knights Defence [C59]

1. e4 e5 2. Nf3 Nc6 3. Bc4 Nf6 That this opening,
which was considered an antique until very recently, should
be adopted in this crucial game, is an indication of how
sharply opening theory has veered. However, Fine knows
what he is about: he is adopting a line of play with which
he is thoroughly familiar, in the hope of exploiting
Reshevsky's unfamiliarity with it. And so it turns out. FR
4. Ng5 d5 5. exd5 Na5 6. Bb5+ c6 7. dxc6 bxc6
8. Be2 h6 9. Nf3 e4 10. Ne5 Bd6 11. f4 Qc7
An inexactitude. For almost a century this variation was
considered unfavourable for White, who got into hot water
by trying to retain the pawn won on move five. Dr. Lasker
was the first, I believe, to popularize the idea of returning
the pawn in return for compensating strategical advantages.
Had Reshevsky known of this idea, he would have played
the more accurate 11 ... 0–0 12 0–0 Bxe5 13 fxe5 Qd4+
14 Kh1 Qxe5 and Black is a vital tempo to the good in
comparison to the line of play which actually occurs. This
would have prevented, for example, White's later powerful
sacrifice of the exchange. FR 12. 0–0 0–0 13. Nc3
Bxe5 14. fxe5 Qxe5 15. d4 exd3 16. Qxd3 Ng4
17. Bf4 17 Rf4 Qc5+ 18 Qd4 Qxd4+ 19 Rxd4 with a
much superior endgame, PCO 446. 17 ... Qc5+ As White
has so considerable an advantage in development, Black
sees no plausible alternative to the gain of the exchange. FR
18. Kh1 Nf2+ 19. Rxf2 Qxf2 20. Rf1 Qh4 The queen
is anything but comfortable here, and the queenside is left
in dire need of reinforcements. But after 20 ... Qb6 21 Qg3!
threatening Bh6 or Bc7 (and in some instances Ne4) Black
would be in a bad way. 21. Qd6 Bg4? Reshevsky soon has
cause for bitter regret after this additional loss of time, for
Fine's reply makes the stranded knight whisper a feeble
SOS. 21 ... Be6 had to be played. FR 22. Ba6! Bc8
23. Bd3! Be6 24. Qb4 Qh5 If instead 24 ... Qd8
25 Qe4 g6 or 25 ... Re8 26 Qh7+ Kf8 27 Ne4 Nb7
28 Qh8+ with a devastating attack. FR 25. Bc7! Nc4
This could almost be called desperation. The knight has
been encircled and only tactics can rescue it. According to
witnesses, Reshevsky was in tears as he considered the hope-
lessness of the situation. Reinfeld, his good friend, called it
the most miserable moment in Sammy's life. AS 26. Bxc4
Qh4

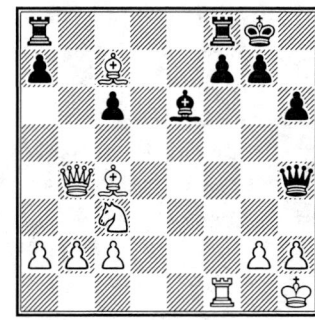

Position after Black's 26th move

Now 27 Rf4 will win Fine a United States championship.
Black may get some counterplay from 27 ... Qg5 28 Bxe6
fxe6 but Fine had consolidated much more difficult
positions in his career. However, Fine sees a more intricate
winning try, involving three forcing moves followed by an
apparent killer. After weighing the two alternatives, he
decides against 27 Rf4! AS 27. Bf4? "A miracle
happened"—Reshevsky. "I must confess that I was
overcome by the fantastic feeling that nothing could
possibly win for me."—Fine (AS) 27 ... Bxc4 28. Qxc4
g5 29. g3 Qg4 Soltis explains "All foreseen by Fine. Now
he intended the knockout blow, 30 Ne4, which threatens
31 Nf6+ and relieves the pin on the fourth rank. That
would permit White to keep his two minor pieces for a
rook under circumstance more favourable than after 27 Rf4,
but ... 30. Qxc6 ... before he could play 30 Ne4, Fine saw
to his horror that Black has 30 ... Qe6!! as an answer. After
31 Qxe6 fxe6, for example, there is a new pin, this time
on the f-file. And on 31 Qd4 Black plays 31 ... f5! 32 Nc5
Qe2 33 Rf2 Qe1+ 34 Kg2 gxf4. Fine had miscalculated.
The win was gone." 30 ... gxf4 31. Rxf4 Qe6 32. Qf3
f5 33. Qd5 Rae8 34. Kg2 Qxd5+ 35. Nxd5 Re2+
36. Rf2 Rxf2+ 37. Kxf2 Kf7 As Black needs only a
draw to hold the title, he has little to fear from this ending.
White will eventually secure two passed pawns on the
queenside, but Black, by keeping his king near the pawns
and posting his rook on the 7th and 8th ranks, will draw
easily. FR 38. c4 a5 39. b3 Re8 40. a3 Rc8 41. Nc3
Ke6 42. Ke3 Ke5 43. Kd3 Rb8 44. Nb5 Rd8+
45. Kc2 h5 46. b4 axb4 47. axb4 h4 48. c5 hxg3
49. hxg3 Kd5 50. Kd3 Rg8 51. Nc3+ Kc6 52. Ne2
Rg4 53. Kc3 Kd5 54. Nf4+ Kc6 55. Kc4 Rxg3
56. b5+ Kd7 57. Kd5 Rg1 58. Nd3 Rd1 59. Kc4
Rb1 60. Nf4 Rb2 61. Nd5 Rb1 62. Nb6+ Kc7 The
game was drawn after seven hours of play. AS ½–½ Reinfeld *The Chess Review*, May 1940; Soltis and McCormick,
56–9.

U.S.C.F. Championship Preliminary Section 2, Dallas, August 19–23, 1940

"The 1940 Open Tournament of the United States
Chess Federation was held in Dallas, Texas, from August
19th to the 28th. The games were played in the beautiful

Adolphus Hotel which placed at our disposal for the tournament a large room on the twenty-first floor, high above the city. From the windows we enjoyed a magnificent view of the city of Dallas and the surrounding country, and contrary to the pessimism of many of our friends who predicted nothing but suffocating heat in Dallas in August, I found the climate truly delightful—warm but not humid and with fresh breezes which kept the air circulating most of the time. Twenty-seven players entered the tournament. Ten States and Canada were represented. Three sections were formed of nine players in each section. Reuben Fine, famous internationalist from New York City, was seeded in one section; Herman Steiner of Los Angeles in another; and Adams of Dedham, Massachusetts, in the third. Two games were scheduled on each day, afternoon and evening. Adjourned games were completed on the following morning. During the course of the tournament many splendid games were played. In the preliminaries Thompson, Albert Roddy of Tulsa and Arpad Elo of Milwaukee each succeeded in drawing their games with Fine who did not actually lose a game during the tournament." (*U.S.C.F. Yearbook*) Crosstable not available.

(530) FINE—RAUCH, J

U.S.C.F. Open, preliminaries, Dallas (1), 1940 (19 Aug.)
English Opening, Classical Variation [A20]

1. c4 e5 2. Nf3 Nc6 3. d4 exd4 4. Nxd4 Nxd4
5. Qxd4 Nf6 6. Nc3 Be7 7. g3 0–0 8. Bg2 c6
9. 0–0 d6 10. Rd1 Qb6 11. Qxb6 axb6 12. Be3 Be6
13. b3 Nd7 14. Rd2 Nc5 15. Rad1

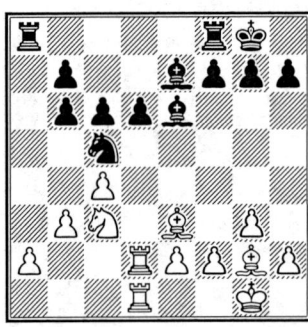

*Position after
White's 15th move*

15 ... g5 16. Ne4 Nxe4 17. Bxe4 f5 18. Bf3 Ra6
19. a4 f4 20. Bd4 g4 21. Bh1 f3 22. exf3 gxf3
23. Re1 Bg5 24. Be3 Bxe3 25. Rxe3 Bg4 26. Rxd6
b5 27. cxb5 cxb5 28. Rxa6 bxa6 29. a5 b4 30. h3
Bxh3 31. Bxf3 Bd7 32. Bd5+ Kh8 33. Re7 Bf5
34. Bc4 Rd8 35. Bxa6 Rd5 36. Bc8 Bxc8 37. Re8+
Kg7 38. Rxc8 Rd3 39. a6 Rxb3 40. a7 Black
resigned. 1–0

(531) RODDY, A—FINE

U.S.C.F. Open, preliminaries, Dallas (2), 1940 (20 Aug.)
Queen's Gambit Declined, Ragozin Variation [D38]

1. d4 Nf6 2. c4 e6 3. Nf3 d5 4. Nc3 Bb4 5. Qb3
c5 6. Bg5 Nc6 7. dxc5 0–0 8. e3 h6 9. Bh4 g5
10. Bg3 Ne4 11. Be2 Qf6 12. Rc1 h5 13. h4 g4
14. Nd4 Nxd4 15. Qxb4 Nxg3 16. fxg3 Nf5
17. cxd5 Nxg3 18. Rg1 exd5 19. Nxd5 Qxh4
20. Qf4 Be6 21. Ne7+ Kh7 22. Bd3+ f5 23. Kd2
Rae8 How is White to salvage the errant knight? He hits on the combination of a lifetime: 24. Rh1!! Nxh1
25. Rxh1 Qxh1 26. Qg5 The point. White's mating threat—forces the draw. 26 ... Qxg2+ 27. Kc3 Rxe7
28. Qxe7+ Rf7 29. Qxe6 Kg7 30. Bc4 Rf6 Drawn. A very creditable game by White, who was not afraid to "mix it" with his formidable opponent. ½–½ *U.S.C.F.* 6 1940, 60–1.

(532) FINE—THOMPSON, J

U.S.C.F. Open, preliminaries, Dallas (3), 1940 (20 Aug.)
Catalan System [E02]

1. d4 Nf6 2. c4 e6 3. Nf3 d5 4. g3 dxc4 5. Qa4+
Bd7 6. Qxc4 Bc6 7. Bg2 Bd5 8. Qa4+ Qd7
9. Qxd7+ Nbxd7 10. Nc3 Bb4 11. 0–0 Bxc3
12. bxc3 0–0 13. Ba3 Rfc8 14. Rfc1 c5 15. Nd2
Bxg2 16. Kxg2 cxd4 17. cxd4 Nb6 18. Kf3 Rxc1
19. Rxc1 Rc8 20. Rc5 Nfd7 21. Rxc8+ Nxc8
22. Nc4 b5 23. Na5 f6 24. Ke4 Kf7 25. Nc6 f5+
26. Kd3 Ndb6 27. Bc5 a6 28. Kc3 Nd5+ 29. Kb3
Ncb6 30. Bxb6 Nxb6 31. Kb4 Nd5+ 32. Ka5 Nc3
33. a3 Nb1 34. Kb4 g5 35. Nb8 a5+ 36. Kxb5
Nxa3+ 37. Kxa5 Nb1 38. Kb4 g4 39. Nc6 Nd2
40. Ne5+ Kf6 41. Nd3 Nf1 42. Nc5 Nxh2 Draw agreed. ½–½

(533) FINE—UNDERWOOD, R

U.S.C.F. Open, preliminaries Dallas (4), 1940 (21 Aug.)
Queen's Gambit Declined [D51]

1. d4 d5 2. c4 e6 3. Nc3 Nf6 4. Bg5 Nbd7 5. e4!?
dxe4 6. Nxe4 Bb4+ 7. Nd2 c5 8. Ngf3 cxd4
9. Nxd4 Qc7 10. a3 Qe5+ 11. Be3 Bxd2+ 12. Qxd2
a6 13. Be2 0–0 14. 0–0 Ne4 15. Qc2 Ndf6 16. Rfe1
Bd7 17. b4 Qc7 18. Bd3 Bc6 *(see diagram at top of next page)* 19. b5 Ng4 20. g3 e5 21. Nxc6 Nxe3 22. Rxe3
bxc6 23. Bxe4 axb5 24. cxb5 Qe7 25. Bxc6 Rac8
26. Rae1 f6 27. a4 Qb4 28. Qb3+ Qxb3 29. Rxb3
Black resigned. 1–0

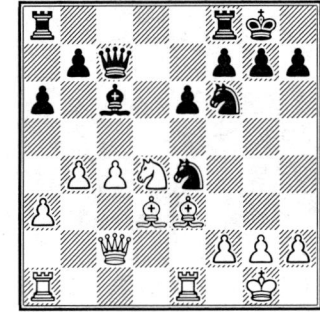

Position after Black's 18th move

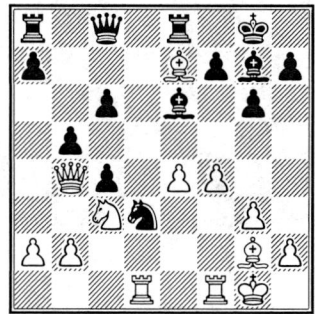

Position after Black's 16th move

(534) HOLLAND, K—FINE

U.S.C.F. Open, preliminaries Dallas (5), 1940 (21 Aug.)
Grünfeld Defence [D94]

1. d4 Nf6 2. c4 g6 3. Nc3 d5 4. e3 Bg7 5. Nf3
0–0 6. Bd3 c5 7. dxc5 Qa5 8. 0–0 dxc4 9. Bxc4
Qxc5 10. Qd4 Qh5 11. Qe5 Qxe5 12. Nxe5
Ne8

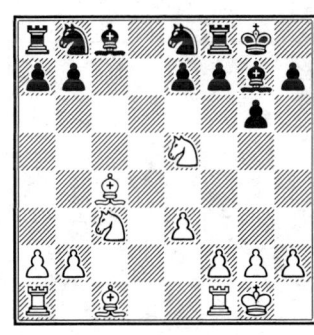

Position after Black's 12th move

13. Nd5 Bxe5 14. Nxe7+ Kg7 15. Nxc8 Nc6 16. f4
Bf6 17. Nxa7 Rxa7 18. e4 Bd4+ 19. Kh1 Nd6 20. Bd5
Nb4 21. Rd1 Bc5 22. a3 Nxd5 23. Rxd5 Nxe4
24. g3 Raa8 25. b4 Bxb4 26. axb4 Rxa1 White
resigned. 0–1

(535) HARTSFIELD, E—FINE

U.S.C.F. Open, preliminaries, Dallas (6), 1940 (22 Aug.)
Fianchetto Grünfeld [D78]

1. d4 Nf6 2. c4 g6 3. Nc3 d5 4. g3 Bg7 5. Bg2 c6
6. Nf3 dxc4 7. 0–0 0–0 8. Ne5 Be6 9. Qa4 Nbd7
10. e4 Nxe5 11. dxe5 Ng4 12. Qb4 b5 13. Bg5 Re8
14. Rad1 Qc8 15. Bxe7 Nxe5 16. f4 Nd3 (*see diagram
at top of next column*) 17. Qd6 Qb7 18. Rxd3 cxd3
19. Bh4 Qb6+ 20. Kh1 Bf8 21. Qe5 Bh3 22. Bxh3
Rxe5 23. fxe5 Re8 24. Bf6 Bg7 25. Bd7 Rxe5
26. Bxe5 Bxe5 27. Be8 f6 28. Nd1 c5 29. a4 a6
30. axb5 axb5 31. Kg2 c4 32. Kf3 Bd4 33. Nc3
Bxc3 34. bxc3 Kf8 35. Bd7 Ke7 36. Bc8 b4
37. cxb4 c3 38. Ra1 c2 White resigned. 0–1

(536) FINE—ALLENTHARP, R

U.S.C.F. Open, preliminaries, Dallas (7), 1940 (22 Aug.)
Queen's Gambit Declined, Marshall Variation [D50]

1. d4 d5 2. c4 e6 3. Nc3 Nf6 4. Bg5 Bb4 5. e3
Bxc3+ 6. bxc3 h6 7. Bh4 g5 8. Bg3 Ne4 9. Qc2
Nxg3 10. hxg3 Qf6 11. Nf3 Nc6 12. Bd3 Bd7
13. e4 dxc4 14. Bxc4 e5 15. d5 Na5 16. Be2 c6
17. c4 c5

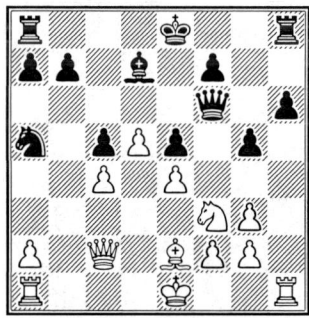

Position after Black's 17th move

18. Qc3 b6 19. Qxe5+ Qxe5 20. Nxe5 f6 21. Bh5+
Kd8 22. Nf7+ Ke7 23. Nxh8 Rxh8 24. Be2 g4
25. Kd2 Kd6 26. f4 gxf3 27. gxf3 f5 28. Rh5
fxe4 29. fxe4 Be8 30. e5+ Kc7 31. Rh4 h5 32. g4
Rf8 33. gxh5 Rf2 34. h6 Bg6 35. Rg1 Bf5 36. h7
Bxh7 37. Rxh7+ Kd8 38. Rg8+ Rf8 39. Rxf8 Mate.
1–0

(537) ELO, A—FINE

U.S.C.F. Open, preliminaries, Dallas (8), 1940 (23 Aug.)
Vienna Game [C27]

1. e4 e5 2. Nc3 Nf6 3. Bc4 Nxe4 4. Qh5 Nd6
5. Bb3 Be7 6. Nf3 Nc6 7. Nxe5 0–0 8. 0–0 Nd4
9. Nd5 Nxb3 10. axb3 Ne8 11. Nxe7+ Qxe7 12. Nc4
Nf6 13. Qh4 d5 14. Ne3 Be6 15. d3 Rfe8 16. Bd2
Ng4 17. Qxe7 Rxe7 18. Nxg4 Bxg4 19. Rfe1 Rxe1+
20. Rxe1 Be6 21. b4 a6 22. f3 Re8 23. Kf2 f6 Draw
agreed. ½–½

U.S.C.F. Championship Finals (41st U.S. Open), Dallas, August 24–28, 1940

"The tournament was won by Fine with a perfect score of 8–0 with Steiner finishing in second place in spite of the fact that he dropped three of his first four games!" (*U.S.C.F. Yearbook*)

		1	2	3	4	5	6	7	8	9	
1	Fine	*	1	1	1	1	1	1	1	1	8
2	Steiner	0	*	0	1	0	1	1	1	1	5
3=	Adams	0	1	*	0	1	1	½	1	0	4½
3=	Marchand	0	0	1	*	1	½	½	1	½	4½
5=	Kendall	0	1	0	0	*	½	1	½	½	3½
5=	Thompson	0	0	0	½	½	*	1	½	1	3½
7=	Elo	0	0	½	½	0	0	*	½	1	2½
7=	Ohman	0	0	0	0	½	½	½	*	1	2½
9	Burdge	0	0	1	½	½	0	0	0	*	2

(538) BURDGE, H—FINE

U.S. Open finals, Dallas (1), 1940 (24 Aug.)
Nimzowitsch-Indian Defence, Classical Variation [E33]

1. d4 Nf6 2. c4 e6 3. Nc3 Bb4 4. Qc2 Nc6 5. Nf3 d6 6. a3 Bxc3+ 7. Qxc3 a5 8. b3 0–0 9. Bb2 Re8 10. Rd1 Qe7 11. e3 e5 12. dxe5 dxe5 13. Be2 Bf5 14. 0–0 Ne4 15. Qc1 Nc5 16. Qc3 f6 17. Ne1 Rad8 18. Nd3 Ne4 19. Qc1 Ng5 20. Qc3 h6 21. c5 Kh8 22. b4 Nd4 23. Bh5 Bg6 24. Bg4 h5 25. exd4 exd4 26. Nf4 Bf7 27. Rxd4 Rxd4 28. Qxd4 hxg4 29. Qc3 axb4 30. axb4 Qe4 31. Bc1 Bc4 32. Rd1 Bb5 33. Bd2 Qf5 34. Be3 Bc6 35. Qd3 Qxd3 36. Rxd3 Kh7 (*see diagram below*) 37. h3 gxh3 38. Nxh3 Nxh3+ 39. gxh3 Ra8 40. Rd1 Ra3 41. Kh2 Rb3 42. Rd4 Rb1 43. h4 Kg6 44. Rg4+ Kf7 45. Kg3 Re1 46. Kh2 Rh1+ 47. Kg3 Rg1+ 48. Kf4 Rf1 49. Kg3 Ke6 50. Kf4 Kf7 51. Kg3 Bd5 52. Rd4 c6 53. b5 Rg1+ 54. Kh2 Rb1 55. bxc6 Bxc6 56. Rg4 Kg8 57. Rd4 Kh7 58. Rg4 Rb3 59. Rf4 Bd7 60. Rf3 Rb1 61. Rf4 Kg6 62. f3 Rb3 63. Bf2 Bc6 64. Kg3 Rd3 65. Bg1 Kf7 66. Bf2 Ke6

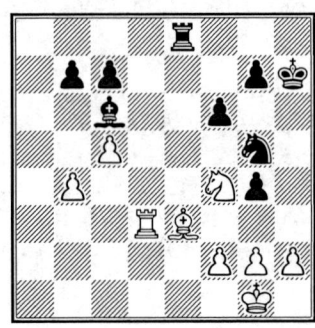

Position after Black's 36th move

67. Kg4 Rd2 68. Kg3 Rc2 69. Be3 Rc3 70. Bd4 Rd3 71. Bf2 Ke7 72. Kg2 Kf7 73. Bg1 Kg6 74. Kg3 Kh5 75. Rf5+ g5 76. hxg5 fxg5 77. Rf8 Bd5 78. Rh8+ Kg6 79. Rf8 Be4 White lost by overstepping the time limit. 0–1

(539) FINE—OHMAN, H

U.S. Open finals, Dallas (2), 1940 (24 Aug.)
Queen's Gambit Accepted [D23]

1. d4 d5 2. c4 dxc4 3. Nf3 Nf6 4. Qa4+ c6 5. Qxc4 Nbd7 6. Qc2 e6 7. g3 Bb4+ 8. Nc3 0–0 9. Bg2 Qe7 10. 0–0 e5 11. e4 exd4 12. Nxd4 Nb6 13. Re1 Bxc3 14. Qxc3 Re8 15. Bf4 Be6 16. a4 Nh5 17. a5

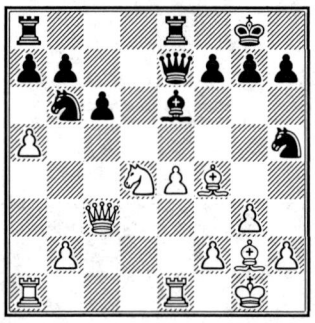

Position after White's 17th move

17 ... Nxf4 18. gxf4 Nc8 19. f5 Bd7 20. a6 Rb8 21. e5 c5 22. e6 cxd4 23. exd7 Qxd7 24. Qxd4 Nb6 25. Qxd7 Rxe1+ 26. Rxe1 Nxd7 27. axb7 Kf8 28. b4 Rd8 29. Rc1 Nb8 30. Rc8 Ke7 31. Bf1 a6 32. Bc4 Rf8 33. Kg2 Rd8 34. Bxf7 Rd7 35. Rxb8 Black resigned. 1–0

(540) ELO, A—FINE

U.S. Open finals Dallas (3), 1940 (25 Aug.)
Sicilian Centre Game [B21]

1. e4 c5 2. d4 cxd4 3. Qxd4 Nc6 4. Qe3 Nf6 5. c4 e6 6. Nc3 Be7 7. Be2 d5 8. cxd5 exd5 9. exd5 Nb4 10. Qd2 Bf5 11. Bb5+ Nd7 12. Ba4 0–0 13. Nge2 Nd3+ 14. Kf1 Bc5 15. Ng3 Bg6 16. Bxd7 Qxd7 17. Nge4 Bxe4 18. Nxe4 Qb5

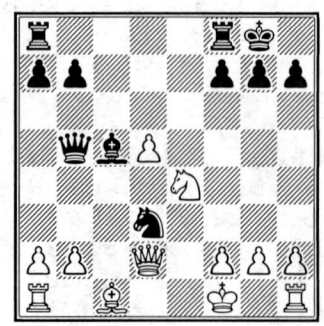

Position after Black's 18th move

19. Nxc5 Nxc1+ 20. Ke1 Nxa2 21. Rxa2 Qxc5
22. Ra3 Rad8 23. Rd3 Rd6 24. Ke2 Re8+ 25. Kf3
Rf6+ 26. Kg3 Rg6+ 27. Kf3 Rf6+ 28. Kg3 Rg6+
29. Kf3 Qc8 30. g3 Qh3 31. Re3 Rf6+ 32. Ke2
Qh5+ 33. Ke1 Rxe3+ 34. Qxe3 g6 35. Qc5 Rc6
White resigned. **0–1**

(541) FINE–STEINER, H

U.S. Open finals, Dallas (4), 1940 (25 Aug.)
Nimzowitsch-Indian Defence, Rubinstein Variation [E49]

1. d4 Nf6 2. c4 e6 3. Nc3 Bb4 4. e3 0–0 5. Bd3
d5 6. a3 Bxc3+ 7. bxc3 c5 8. cxd5 exd5 9. Ne2 b6
10. 0–0 Ba6 11. Bxa6 Nxa6 12. Qd3 Nc7 13. dxc5
bxc5 14. c4 dxc4 15. Qxc4 Qd5 16. Qxd5 Ncxd5
17. f3 Rfe8 18. e4 Nb6 19. Ra2 Rac8 20. Rc2 h6
21. Be3 Nfd7 22. Rfc1 Na4

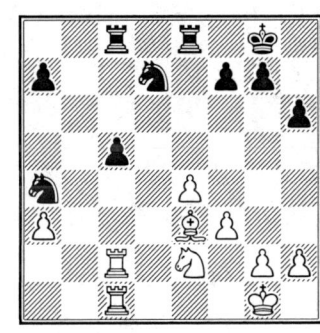

Position after Black's 22nd move

23. Nc3 Nxc3 24. Rxc3 Rb8 25. Bxc5 Nxc5
26. Rxc5 Rb3 27. R1c3 Reb8 28. Rc7 a6 29. h4
Rb2 30. Kh2 g6 31. R3c6 a5 32. Rf6 Rf8 33. h5
gxh5 34. Rxh6 Rb3 35. Rxh5 Rxa3 36. Ra7 a4
37. Rha5 Kg7 38. Rxa4 Re3 39. Ra8 Black resigned.
1–0

(542) ADAMS, W–FINE

U.S. Open finals, Dallas (5), 1940 (26 Aug.)
Bishop's Opening [C24]

1. e4 e5 2. Bc4 Since Adams has written his sensational
book, *White Plays and Wins* he has always played this opening.
Adams is a fine player, and has shown his worth in recent
tournaments, but he ought to know, that it does not pay to
play always the same opening. In this tournament he did not
succeed in winning a single game with White, which in itself
ought to convince him. **2 ... Nf6 3. d3 c6 4. f4 exf4
5. Bxf4 d5** This move gives Black a free game. **6. exd5
Nxd5** Black has a clear advantage, *PCO* 15. **7. Qf3 Be6
8. Nd2 Be7 9. Ne2** White leaves his opponent in doubt,
as to which side he is going to castle. **9 ... 0–0 10. 0–0**
It would probably be too dangerous for White to castle on the
queenside. **10 ... c5** Stops Nd4 for White. **11. Rae1 Nc6
12. Nc3** And this gives Black his chance. 12 Bg3 was best.

12 ... Nxf4 13. Qxf4 Bg5 14. Qf2 Bxd2 15. Bxe6
Qd4! 16. Bb3 Not 16 Bxf7+, because of 16 ... Rxf7. 16 ...
Qxf2+ 17. Kxf2 Bxe1+ 18. Rxe1 Rae8 19. Ne4 Re5
20. Nd6 Rxe1 21. Kxe1 b6 22. Kd2 Na5 23. Ba4 If
23 d4 then 23 ... Rd8. 23 ... Rd8 24. Nf5 g6 25. Ne7+
Kf8 26. Nc6 Nxc6 27. Bxc6 Ke7 28. Bb5 f5 29. Ke3
Kf6 30. a4 Ke5 31. c3 a5 32. Bc6 g5 33. Kd2 As
Fine showed in *Basic Chess Endings*, 33 h3 was essential.
White, however, could not hold the game in the long run.
AW 33 ... Rd6 White resigned. **0–1** Koltanowski, *BCM*
1940, 358; Fine 1941, 478–9.

(543) FINE–MARCHAND, E

U.S. Open finals, Dallas (6), 1940 (26 Aug.)
King's Indian Attack [A07]

1. Nf3 d5 2. g3 Bf5 3. Bg2 c6 4. 0–0 Nd7 5. c4
e6 6. cxd5 exd5 7. Nc3 Be7 8. d3 Ngf6 9. Re1
0–0 10. e4 Be6 11. Nd4 Bg4 12. f3 Bc5 13. Be3
Bh5 14. Kh1 Bb4 15. Bg1 Re8 16. g4 Bg6 17. f4 h5
18. g5 c5

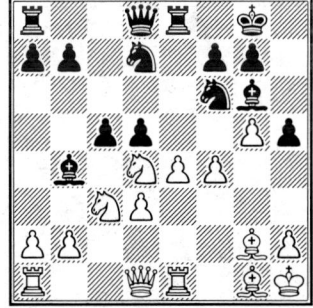

Position after Black's 18th move

19. Nc2 d4 20. Nxb4 dxc3 21. Nc2 cxb2 22. Rb1
Nh7 23. f5 Bxf5 24. exf5 Rxe1 25. Nxe1 Qxg5
26. Rxb2 Qxf5 27. Bxb7 Rd8 28. Be4 Qe5 29. Re2
Qd6 30. Qb3 Nhf6 31. Bg2 Ne5 32. Qc3 Ned7
33. h3 Nd5 34. Qc4 Nb4 35. a3 Ne5 36. Qxc5
Nbxd3 37. Nxd3 Nxd3 38. Re8+ Kh7 39. Qxh5+
Black resigned. **1–0**

(544) KENDALL, W–FINE

U.S. Open finals, Dallas (7), 1940 (27 Aug.)
French Defence, Steinitz Variation [C11]

1. e4 e6 2. d4 d5 3. Nc3 Nf6 4. e5 Nfd7 5. Nce2
White knows what he wants here but Black gives a copy-
book exposition of the correct play against this opening.
**5 ... c5 6. c3 Nc6 7. a3 f6 8. f4 cxd4 9. cxd4
fxe5 10. fxe5 Qh4+ 11. g3?** 11 Ng3 is the only move
worth considering. **11 ... Qe4** Now White must lose a
piece. **12. Kf2 Qxh1** White was apparently hoping to
trap the queen, but there is absolutely no hope of this.
13. Nf3

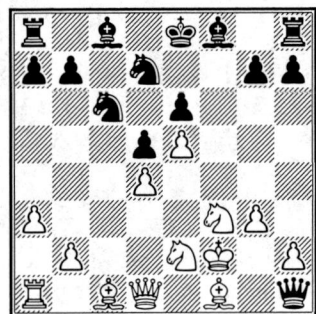

*Position after
White's 13th move*

13 ... Ncxe5! 14. dxe5 Bc5+ 15. Be3 0-0 Now we
see why Fine captured, on move 13, with his queen's knight
instead of with his king's knight (which might seem better
moved, freeing his queen's bishop). His king's bishop is now
protected. **16. Nf4 Bxe3+ 17. Kxe3 Nxe5!** Black resigned. If 18 Nxe5 Qe4+. Merciless execution by Fine! **0-1**
Chess, January 1941; *U.S.C.F.* 6 1940, 65-6.

(545) FINE—THOMPSON, J

U.S. Open finals, Dallas (9), 1940 (28 Aug.)
Spanish Game, Open Variation [C83]

**1. e4 e5 2. Nf3 Nc6 3. Bb5 a6 4. Ba4 Nf6 5. 0-0
Nxe4 6. d4 b5 7. Bb3 d5 8. dxe5 Be6 9. c3 Be7
10. Be3 Na5 11. Nd4 Nxb3 12. axb3**

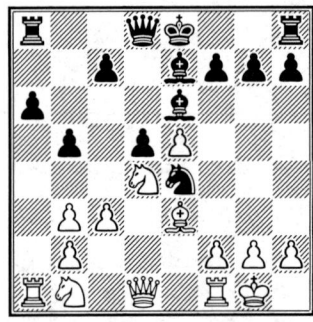

*Position after
White's 12th move*

12 ... c5? 13. Nxe6 fxe6 14. Qg4 Qd7 15. f3 Black
resigned. **1-0**

Utah State Championship,
Salt Lake City, September 1-2, 1940

According to Fine's notebooks he played these seven
games in just two days. This needs clarification. In any case,
he clearly outclassed his opponents, making a clean sweep
of the tournament. Crosstable not available.

(546) FINE—DURHAM

Utah State Championship, Salt Lake City (1), 1940 (1 Sept.)
Nimzowitsch-Indian Defence, Rubinstein Variation [E26]

1. d4 Nf6 2. c4 e6 3. Nc3 Bb4 4. e3 d5 5. a3

**Bxc3+ 6. bxc3 c5 7. Bd3 Nc6 8. Ne2 Qa5 9. 0-0
e5 10. cxd5 Nxd5 11. Bd2 Nde7 12. d5 c4 13. Bxc4
Nxd5 14. Qb3 Be6 15. e4 Nf4 16. Bxf4 Bxc4 17. Qxc4
exf4 18. Nxf4 0-0 19. Nd5 Rac8 20. Qb3 b6 21. Rad1
Rfe8 22. f3 Qc5+ 23. Kh1 Ne7 24. c4 h6 25. Ne3
Nc6 26. Rd5 Na5 27. Qc3 Qc7**

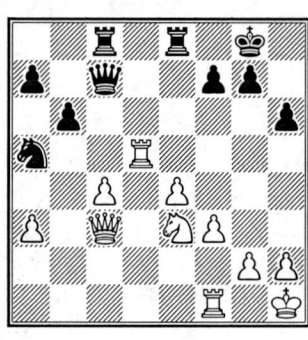

*Position after
Black's 27th move*

**28. Nf5 f6 29. Nd6 Nxc4 30. Nxe8 Rxe8 31. Rc1
Rc8 32. Qd4 a6 33. a4 Qc6 34. Rd8+ Rxd8
35. Qxd8+ Kh7 36. e5 b5 37. axb5 axb5 38. Qd3+
Kg8 39. exf6 Qxf6 40. Qd5+ Kh7 41. Qxb5 Ne5
42. h3 Nf7 43. Qd3+ Qg6 44. Qxg6+ Kxg6 45. Kg1**
Black resigned. **1-0**

(547) GRAHAM—FINE

Utah State Championship, Salt Lake City (2), 1940 (1 Sept.)
Sicilian Defence [B33]

**1. e4 c5 2. Nf3 Nc6 3. d4 cxd4 4. Nxd4 Nf6
5. Nc3 e5 6. Nf3 Bb4 7. Bd2 Bxc3 8. Bxc3 Nxe4
9. Bxe5 Nxe5**

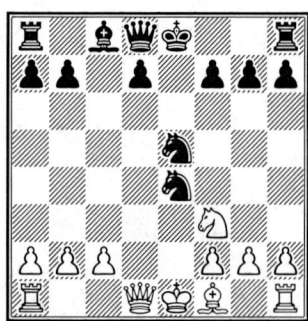

*Position after
Black's 9th move*

**10. Qd5 Nxf3+ 11. gxf3 Nf6 12. Qg5 0-0 13. 0-0-0
h6 14. Qg3 Nh5 15. Qd6 Qf6 16. Qd5 Nf4 17. Qe4
d5 18. Qe1 Bf5 19. Bb5 Rac8 20. c3 d4** White
resigned. **0-1**

(548) MORGAN, D—FINE

Utah State Championship, Salt Lake City (3), 1940 (1 Sept.)
English Opening, Symmetrical Variation [A30]

1. c4 c5 2. Nf3 Nf6 That Black can provocatively indulge
in this symmetry and "get away with it" is a forceful reminder

of Breyer's scepticism about the value of the first move. **3. g3** Any dogmatically theoretical attempt to obtain an opening advantage must presumably begin with 3 d4. **3 ... d5 4. cxd5 Nxd5 5. Bg2 Nc6 6. 0–0 e5** Fine has now transposed into a favourite defence in Réti's Opening (generally starting in the form 1 Nf3 d5 2 c4 dxc4 3 Na3 c5 4 Nxc4 Nc6) which was originated by Nimzowitsch. The variation turns into a clash between the value of White's fianchettoed king's bishop and Black's strong centralization on the squares d5 and d4. Black's chances are the more promising, and only alert and ingenious play (as in the notable encounter Botvinnik–Fine at Nottingham) will generally keep White from having to submit to serious positional disadvantage. **7. d3 Be7 8. Nbd2 0–0 9. Nc4 f6 10. b3 Be6 11. Bb2 Qd7 12. Qd2 Rac8 13. Rac1 Nd4** This suggests another point in Black's favour. The advanced knight is strongly posted, but White can hardly dare to exchange it, for then Black would recapture with the e-pawn, leaving White with a sickly pawn on the half-open e-file. **14. Ne3 Nb4 15. Bc3 Nbc6 16. Nc4** White can hardly be blamed for his indecisive play, as his pieces have reached a dead end. **16 ... Rfd8** Whilst Black remorselessly strengthens his position. **17. Qb2 Bd5!** Threatening serious deterioration of White's pawn position by the capture of the king's knight. **18. Nxd4** The rather unattractive 18 Ne1 was relatively better than this exchange, which submits White's e-pawn to lasting pressure. **18 ... exd4 19. Bd2 Re8 20. Rc2** Here or later on, e4 would be answered by ... dxe3 leaving White with weak centre pawns. **20 ... Bxg2 21. Kxg2 b5 22. Na3** White's positional capitulation is now fully established, but if 22 Na5? Nxa5 23 Bxa5 b4, and the helpless bishop is permanently out of play and in danger of being trapped. **22 ... a6 23. Bf4 Bf8 24. Re1 Nb4 25. Rcc1 Nd5 26. Bd2 Re5** White's pieces are huddled together miserably. Black has achieved magnificent centralization and placed his forces within striking distance of the kingside. **27. Rc2 Rce8 28. Bc1** The previously forecast pressure on the e-pawn adds to White's woes. The game now takes a decisive turn. **28 ... Rh5 29. h4** An unpleasant weakening move; but after 29 Rh1 Qh3+ 30 Kg1 f5, followed by ... Bd6 and ... f4, the end would be nigh.

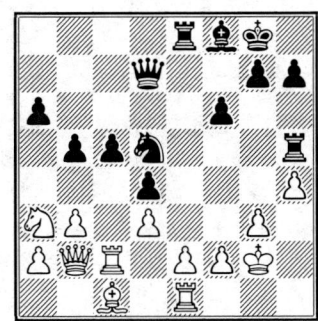

Position after
White's 29th move

29 ... Rxh4! The brilliant finish is all the more impressive after the foregoing fine position play. **30. gxh4 Qg4+**

31. Kf1 Qh3+ 32. Kg1 Re3! A charming sequel. If 33 fxe3 Bd6, and mate follows along well-known lines. White's enormous material advantage being of no consequence!! **33. Bxe3 Nxe3! 34. fxe3 Qg3+** Black resigned. If 35 Kf1 dxe3 or 35 Kh1 Bd6. A convincing example of the finest type of modern positional chess. **0–1** Reinfeld, *BCM* 1941, 197–8.

(549) TAYLOR–FINE

Utah State Championship, Salt Lake City (4), 1940 (1 Sept.)
Queen's Pawn Game [D02]

1. d4 Nf6 2. Nf3 g6 3. g3 Bg7 4. Bg2 0–0 5. 0–0 d5 6. Bf4 c5 7. dxc5 Ne4 8. c3 Nxc5 9. Nbd2 Nc6 10. Be3 Qd6 11. Re1 Rd8 12. Bxc5 Qxc5 13. e4 dxe4 14. Rxe4 Bf5 15. Re2 Rd7 16. Qe1 Rad8 17. Nb3 Qb6

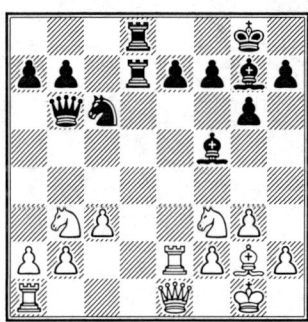

Position after
Black's 17th move

18. Nbd4 Nxd4 19. Nxd4 Bxd4 20. cxd4 Qxd4 21. Rxe7 Qxb2 22. Re3 b5 23. Bf1 a6 24. a4 bxa4 25. Re8+ Rxe8 26. Qxe8+ Kg7 27. Rxa4 Rd1 28. Rxa6 Bh3 White resigned. **0–1**

(550) FINE–GIRARD

Utah State Championship, Salt Lake City (5), 1940 (2 Sept.)
Philidor's Defence [C41]

1. e4 e5 2. Nf3 d6 3. d4 Bg4 4. dxe5 Bxf3 5. Qxf3 dxe5 6. Bc4 Nf6 7. Qb3 Qd7 8. Qxb7 Bc5 9. 0–0 0–0

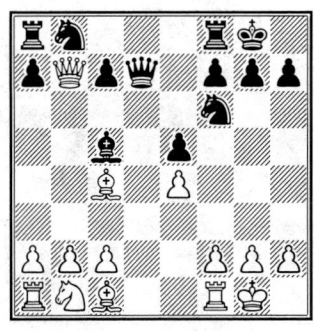

Position after
Black's 9th move

10. Qxa8 c6 11. Nc3 Na6 12. Qxf8+ Bxf8 13. Bxa6 Qg4 14. Be3 Qh4 15. f3 Nh5 16. Ne2 Qd8 17. Bc4

c5 18. Rad1 Qc8 19. Rd3 Nf6 20. Rfd1 Be7 21. Nc3
h6 22. Nd5 Nxd5 23. Rxd5 Qc7 24. Rd7 Qb6
25. Rxe7 Qxb2 26. Bxf7+ Kh7 27. Be6 Qxc2
28. Bf5+ Black resigned. 1–0

(551) FINE—DAVIS

Utah State Championship, Salt Lake City (6), 1940
    (2 Sept.)

Spanish Opening, Møller Defence [C78]

1. e4 e5 2. Nf3 Nc6 3. Bb5 a6 4. Ba4 Nf6 5. 0–0
Bc5 6. c3 b5 7. Bc2 0–0 8. d4 exd4 9. cxd4
Ba7

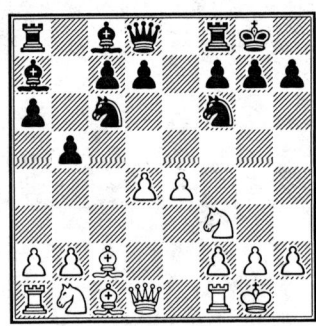

*Position after
Black's 9th move*

10. e5 Ne8 11. Bxh7+ Kxh7 12. Ng5+ Qxg5
13. Bxg5 Nxd4 14. Nc3 Bb7 15. Be3 c5 16. Ne2
Nxe2+ 17. Qxe2 Rh8 18. Qd3+ Kg8 19. Qxd7 Bxg2
20. Kxg2 Kf8 21. Qb7 Black resigned. 1–0

(552) FINE—PAGE

Utah State Championship, Salt Lake City (7), 1940
    (2 Sept.)

Petroff Defence [C42]

1. e4 e5 2. Nf3 Nf6 3. Nxe5 d6 4. Nf3 Nxe4
5. Qe2 Qe7 6. d3 Nf6 7. Bg5 Qxe2+ 8. Bxe2 Nc6
9. Nc3 Bd7 10. 0–0–0 0–0–0 11. d4 Re8 12. Bxf6
gxf6 13. d5 Ne5 14. Nd4 Bh6+ 15. Kb1 f5 16. g3 f4
17. Bb5 c6 18. dxc6 bxc6 19. Be2 Kc7

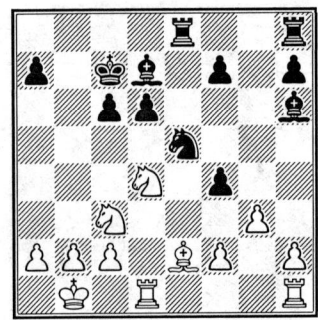

*Position after
Black's 19th move*

20. gxf4 Bxf4 21. Ndb5+ cxb5 22. Nd5+ Kc6
23. Nxf4 Be6 24. Rd4 Rhg8 25. Rhd1 Rd8

26. a4 a6 27. b3 Kc5 28. Kb2 Nc6 29. Re4
Ne5 30. axb5 axb5 31. b4+ Kc6 32. Nxe6 fxe6
33. Ra1 Ra8? 34. Rxa8 Rxa8 35. Rxe5 Black
resigned. 1–0

Hollywood four-cornered tournament, Los Angeles, September 8–13, 1940

Fine had a relatively easy time in this tournament
(which is erroneously dated 1941 in his autobiography, and
hence several other sources). Having scored four wins and
a draw in the first five rounds, he was apparently not even
required to play the final game. Fine gained a double
revenge for his disastrous defeat by Harry Borochow eight
years previously. Crosstable not available.

(553) FINE—BOROCHOW, H

Hollywood 4-cornered tournament, Los Angeles (1), 1940
    (8 Sept.)

English Opening, Mikenas-Flohr Variation [A18]

1. c4 Nf6 2. Nc3 e6 3. e4 Originally an idea of Nimzowitsch. 3 ... d5 4. e5 d4 5. exf6 dxc3 6. bxc3 Qxf6
7. d4 b6 7 ... c5 and 7 ... e5 are the main variations in
ECO, but this was very popular in the 1930s. 8. Be2 Bb7
9. Nf3 Nd7?! 9 ... Bd6 10 Bg5 Qg6 11 c5! Cunningham-
Buerger U.S. Open Championship, Chicago 1994 and
Fabrizi–Shtrickman, BCCA–Israel, correspondence
2000–2002. 10. Qa4 c6 11. Ng5 e5 12. 0–0 Be7
13. Bf3 0–0 14. Be4 exd4 15. Bxh7+ Kh8 16. Bb1
g6 17. Qd1

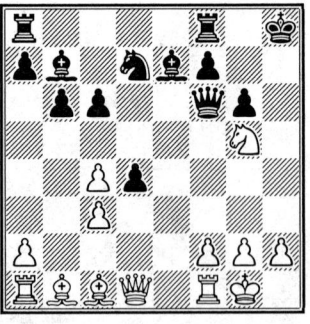

*Position after
White's 17th move*

17 ... c5? 18. Qg4 Because of Black's inexact defence
this move comes with a two-fold threat, to capture on d7
and to mate by Qh4+. 18 ... Rfd8 19. Qh4+ Kg8
20. Qh7+ Kf8 21. Ne6+ Ke8 22. Nc7+ Black
resigned. 1–0

(554) WOLISTON, P—FINE

Hollywood 4-cornered tournament, Los Angeles (2), 1940
(9 Sept.)

Bishop's Opening [C24]

1. e4 e5 2. Bc4 Nf6 3. d3 c6 4. f4 exf4 5. Bxf4
d5 6. exd5 Nxd5 7. Qf3 Be6 8. Nd2 Be7 9. Ne2
0–0 10. 0–0 c5 11. Nc3 Nxf4 12. Qxf4 Bg5
13. Qf2 Bxd2 14. Bxe6 Qd4 15. Qxd4 cxd4
16. Nb5 Nc6 17. Bd5 Rad8 18. Bxc6 bxc6 19. Na3
Be3+ 20. Kh1 f5

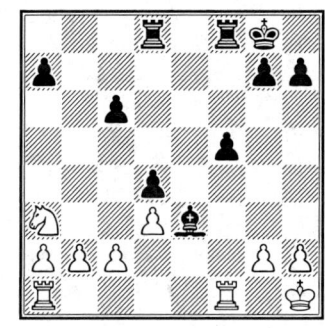

*Position after
Black's 20th move*

21. g3 g5 22. Kg2 f4 23. Nc4 Kg7 24. b4 Rf6
25. g4 h5 26. h3 hxg4 27. hxg4 Rh8 28. Ne5 Rh4
29. Rh1 f3+ 30. Nxf3 Rxg4+ 31. Kh3 Rgf4 32. Nh2
Rh4+ 33. Kg3 Bf4+ 34. Kg2 g4 35. Rae1 Rfh6
36. Nxg4 Rxg4+ 37. Kf3 Rgh4 38. Rxh4 Rxh4
39. Re7+ Kf6 40. Rxa7 Bd6 41. a3 Rh3+ 42. Ke2
Rh2+ 43. Kd1 Rh1+ 44. Ke2 Rc1 45. Ra6 Rxc2+
46. Kd1 Rc3 47. b5 Rxd3+ 48. Ke2 Rxa3 White
resigned. 0–1

(555) STEINER, H—FINE

Hollywood 4-cornered tournament, Los Angeles (3), 1940
(10 Sept.)

Spanish Opening, Exchange Variation [C68]

1. e4 e5 2. Nf3 Nc6 3. Bb5 a6 4. Bxc6 dxc6 5. d4
exd4 6. Qxd4 Qxd4 7. Nxd4 Bd7 8. Bf4 0-0-0
9. Nd2 Bd6 10. Ne2 Ne7 11. 0-0-0 Be6 12. Bxd6
cxd6 13. Nf4 Ng6 14. Nxe6 fxe6 15. Nc4 Rhf8
16. Rxd6 Rxd6 17. Nxd6+ Kc7 18. Rd1 Rxf2 19. Ne8+
Kb6 20. Rd7 Ne5 21. Rd2 Rf1+ 22. Rd1 Rf2 23. Rd2
Rf1+ Draw agreed. ½–½

(556) BOROCHOW, H—FINE

Hollywood 4-cornered tournament, Los Angeles (4), 1940
(11 Sept.)

Sicilian Defence, Pin Variation [B40]

1. e4 c5 2. Nf3 e6 3. d4 cxd4 4. Nxd4 Nf6 5. Nc3
Bb4 6. Bd3 Nc6 7. Nxc6 dxc6 8. e5 Nd7 9. Qg4

Qa5 10. 0–0 Bxc3 11. bxc3 Qxe5 12. Ba3 c5
13. Rad1 0–0 14. Rfe1 Qf6 15. Qh3 g6 16. Bb5 Qe7

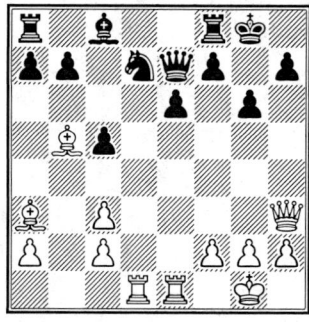

*Position after
Black's 16th move*

17. c4 a6 18. Ba4 Nb6 19. Bb3 Bd7 20. Re5 Na4
21. Bxa4 Bxa4 22. Bxc5 Rfd8 23. Rde1 Qf6 24. Qc3
Bc6 25. Be3 Re8 26. Bg5 Qg7 27. Bc1 Rad8 28. h4
f6 29. Rxe6 Rxe6 30. Rxe6 Rd1+ 31. Re1 Qd7 32. Bb2
Qg4 33. f3 Bxf3 White resigned. 0–1

(557) FINE—WOLISTON, P

Hollywood 4-cornered tournament, Los Angeles (5), 1940
(12 Sept.)

Nimzowitsch-Indian Defence, Rubinstein Variation [E44]

1. d4 Nf6 2. c4 e6 3. Nc3 Bb4 4. e3 b6 5. Nge2 Bb7
6. a3 Be7 7. d5 d6 8. g3

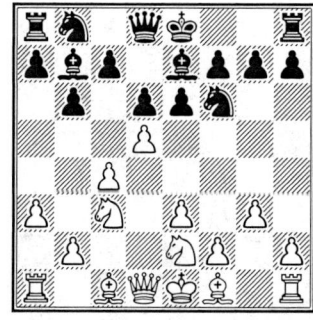

*Position after
White's 8th move*

8 ... c6? 9. dxe6 fxe6 10. Nd4 Qd7 11. Bh3 c5
12. Bxe6 Bxh1 13. Bxd7+ Nbxd7 14. Ne6 Rc8
15. f4 Black resigned. 1–0

(558) FINE—STEINER, H

Hollywood 4-cornered tournament, Los Angeles (6), 1940 (Sept.)

Richard Cantwell believes that this game remained unplayed
as the result of the tournament was already decided. I record
it as a draw, but I don't know whether this was the way it
was scored at the time. ½–½

24th Marshall Chess Club Championship 1940–41, New York, January–May, 1941

For the fifth time Fine won the championship of one
of the premiere clubs in the United States. He cruised

through the field allowing only two draws, the first with runner up Frank Marshall, and the second with Bruno Forsberg in the final round, when victory in the tournament was already assured. Neither of the draws are recorded in the notebooks, which might suggest that they were perfunctory.

		1	2	3	4	5	6	7	8	9	10	11	12	13	14	15	16	
1	Fine	*	½	1	1	1	1	1	1	1	1	1	1	1	½	1	14
2	Marshall	½	*	0	0	½	½	1	1	1	1	1	1	1	1	1	1	11½
3=	Bernstein	0	1	*	½	1	0	1	½	1	½	½	1	1	1	1	1	11
3=	Reinfeld	0	1	½	*	0	1	1	½	1	1	½	1	1	½	1	1	11
5	Seidman	0	½	0	1	*	1	½	½	0	1	1	1	1	1	1	1	10½
6=	Lasker	0	½	1	0	0	*	1	½	0	½	0	1	1	1	1	1	8½
6=	Sussman	0	0	0	0	½	0	*	1	½	½	1	1	1	1	1	1	8½
8=	Green	0	0	½	½	½	½	0	*	1	½	0	1	1	½	1	1	8
8=	Levy	0	0	0	0	1	1	½	0	*	0	1	1	1	1	½	1	8
10=	Halper	0	0	½	0	0	½	½	½	1	*	0	1	1	?	1	?	7½
10=	Santasiere	0	0	½	½	0	1	0	1	0	1	*	0	½	1	1	1	7½
12	Fajans	0	0	0	0	0	0	0	0	0	0	1	*	1	?	1	?	4½
13	Richman	0	0	0	0	0	0	0	0	0	0	½	0	*	1	1	1	3½
14	Cass	0	0	0	½	0	0	0	½	0	?	0	?	0	*	1	½	3
15=	Forsberg	½	0	0	0	0	0	0	0	0	0	0	0	0	0	*	1	1½
15=	Heal	0	0	0	0	0	0	0	0	½	?	0	?	0	½	0	*	1½

Table reconstructed by Jeremy Gaige.

(559) FINE—HALPER, N

Marshall CC championship 1940/41, New York (1), 1941 (1 Jan.)
Dutch Defence, Staunton Gambit [A82]

1. d4 f5 2. e4 fxe4 3. Nc3 Nf6 4. f3 e3 5. Bxe3 d5 6. f4 g6 7. Nf3 Bg4 8. Bd3 c6 9. 0–0 e6 10. h3 Bxf3 11. Qxf3 Nbd7 12. Ne2 Qb6 13. a4 0–0–0 14. a5 Qb4 15. c3 Qe7 16. a6 b6 17. c4 Nb8 18. b3 Rd7 19. Rfc1 Rc7

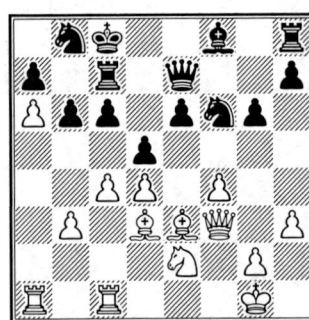

Position after Black's 19th move

20. f5 gxf5 21. Bf4 Rd7 22. cxd5 Nxd5 23. Bb5 Nxf4 24. Nxf4 Qd6 25. Bxc6 Rc7 26. Bb5 Bh6 27. Qb7+ Kd8 28. Qxb8+ Ke7 29. Rxc7+ Black resigned. **1–0**

(560) LASKER, ED—FINE

Marshall CC championship 1940/41, New York (2), 1941 (14 Jan.)
Nimzowitsch-Indian Defence, Ragozin Variation [E52]

1. d4 Nf6 2. c4 e6 3. Nf3 d5 4. Nc3 Bb4 5. e3 0–0 6. Bd3 b6 7. cxd5 exd5 8. 0–0 Bb7 9. Ne5 c5 10. f4 Nc6 11. Ne2 Ne4 12. a3 Ba5 13. Ng3 Ne7 14. Bxe4 dxe4 15. dxc5 f6 16. Nd7 Rf7 17. b4

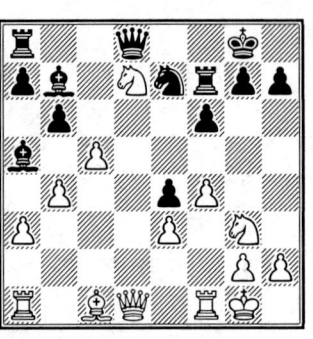

Position after White's 17th move

17 ... Nd5 18. bxa5 Rxd7 19. Qc2 bxc5 20. Nxe4 Qe7 21. Re1 Re8 22. Ng3 Nxf4 23. Qc4+ Ne6 24. Nf5 Qf7 25. Bb2 Bxg2 26. Rad1 Rxd1 27. Rxd1 Bh3 28. Ng3 h5 29. Kf2 Qb7 30. Rd2 Qg2+ 31. Ke1 Qg1+ 32. Nf1 Bxf1 33. Qxf1 Qxe3+ 34. Re2 Qd3 35. Qg1 Kf7 36. Qg2 Qb1+ 37. Kf2 Qf5+ 38. Kg1 White resigned. **0–1**

(561) FINE—BERNSTEIN, S

Marshall CC championship 1940/41, New York (3), 1941 (19 Jan.)
Spanish Game, Worrall Attack [C86]

1. e4 e5 2. Nf3 Nc6 3. Bb5 a6 4. Ba4 Nf6 5. 0–0 Be7 Or 5 ... b5 and 6 ... d6 at once, when 7 Ng5 is refuted by 7 ... d5! **6. Qe2 d6?!** A serious error in this form of the opening. The following exchange is far more advantageous to White with his queen on e2, rather than rook on e1, since d1 is available now for the rook. Black should have played 6 ... b5 first. **7. Bxc6+ bxc6 8. d4 exd4** Necessary, because Chigorin's idea (8 ... Nd7) is not feasible here. The analysis—8 ... Nd7 9 dxe5 dxe5 10 Nbd2 f6 11 Nc4 Nb6 12 Rd1 (since this is possible) Bd7 13 Na5! with the advantage. **9. Nxd4 Bd7 10. c4 0–0 11. Nc3 Re8 12. h3** He intends 13 Qf3 and must, therefore, prevent ... Bg4. **12 ... Bf8** This was the crucial position and this routine tactical manoeuvre, which aims at placing the bishop at g7, is incorrect because it is too slow. Thus we see that the loss of the game can be traced to only two moves—one a routine opening move, and the other a routine middlegame move! Which proves that the chessboard is no place for sleeping! Better than the text was the idea of placing the bishop at f6, not by means of ... h6, and ... Nh7 because White answers Qf3 and e5! but by 12 ... c5 13 Nc2 Bc6 14 any (except Nd5) Nd7 and 15 ... Bf6. **13. Qf3 h6** If 13 ... g6 at once, 14 Bg5. **14. Bf4 Rb8 15. b3 g6 16. Rad1 Qe7 17. Rfe1 Bg7 18. e5 Nh5 19. Bd2 dxe5 20. Nxc6 Bxc6 21. Qxc6 Rb6 22. Qa4 Rd6 23. Nd5 Qd7 24. Qxd7 Rxd7** Now it would seem that Bernstein has, with great ingenuity, overcome the worst; but Fine's next move with its double threat (one of them beginning with g4) makes clear that Black is lost.

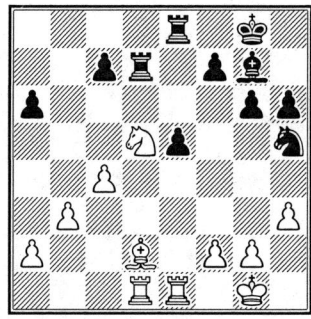

Position after Black's 24th move

25. Ba5 c6 26. Nb4 Rxd1 27. Rxd1 Bf6 28. Nxc6 Nf4 29. Rd6 Kg7 30. Bd2 g5 31. b4 h5 32. b5 axb5 33. cxb5 Ne6 34. b6 Nc5 35. Be3 Na6 36. b7 Black resigned. 1–0 Santasiere, ACB 1941, 15.

(562) SANTASIERE, A—FINE

Marshall CC championship 1940/41, New York (4), 1941 (17 Feb.)

English Opening, Symmetrical Variation [A31]

1. c4 c5 2. Nf3 Nf6 3. d4 cxd4 4. Nxd4 e5 5. Nb5 Bb4+ 6. Bd2 Bc5 7. N1c3 0–0 8. e3 a6 9. Na3 Nc6 10. Nab1 d6 11. Nd5 Nxd5 12. cxd5 Ne7 13. b4 Ba7 14. Nc3 f5 15. Be2 f4 16. exf4 Ng6 17. Bf3 Nxf4 18. 0–0 Qf6 19. Ne4 Qg6 20. Kh1 h5 21. Be3 h4 22. Bxa7 Rxa7 23. Rc1 Bf5 24. Re1 Rf7 25. Rc3 Ra8 26. Rce3 Raf8 27. Rg1 Qh6 28. a4 h3 29. Qd2 Bd7 30. a5 Bb5 31. Qd1 Bc4 32. Rc3 Bb5 33. Re3

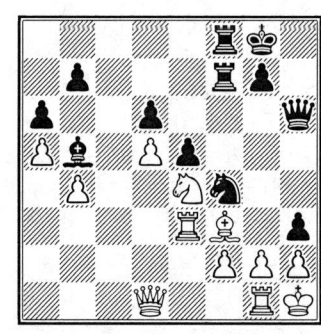

Position after White's 33rd move

33 ... hxg2+ 34. Bxg2 Nxg2 35. Rxg2 Rxf2 36. Rxf2 Qxe3 37. Rxf8+ Kxf8 38. Ng3 Bc4 39. Kg2 Bb3 40. Qf1+ Kg8 41. Qf5 Bxd5+ 42. Kf1 Bc4+ 43. Kg2 Qd2+ 44. Kg1 Qd4+ 45. Kg2 Bd5+ 46. Kh3 Qc4 47. Qg6 Be6+ 48. Kg2 Qc6+ 49. Kg1 Qc1+ 50. Kf2 Qd2+ 51. Kg1 Bf7 52. Qg4 Qc1+ 53. Kf2 Qc2+ 54. Kg1 Qc1+ 55. Kf2 Qf4+ 56. Qxf4 exf4 57. Ne4 Bd5 58. Nxd6 Kf8 59. b5 Ke7 60. Nc8+ Ke6 61. bxa6 bxa6 62. Nb6 g5 63. Na4 Kd6 64. Nc3 Kc5 65. Ne2 Kb4 66. Ng1 Be6 67. Nf3 g4 68. Nd4 Bd7 69. Ne2 f3 70. Nf4 Kxa5 71. Nd5 Kb5 72. Nc7+ Kb6 73. Nd5+ Kc5 74. Nf6 Bf5 White resigned. 0–1

(563) FINE—FAJANS, H

Marshall CC championship 1940/41, New York (5), 1941 (2 Feb.)

Queen's Gambit Accepted [D21]

1. d4 d5 2. c4 e6 3. Nf3 dxc4 4. Qa4+ Nc6 5. e3 Bd7 6. Qxc4 Nf6 7. Be2 Rc8 8. 0–0 Na5 9. Qd3 c5 10. Nc3 c4 11. Qc2 b5 12. Ne5 Be7 13. Rd1 Qc7 14. Nxd7 Qxd7 15. d5

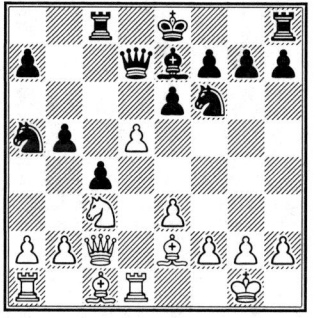

Position after White's 15th move

15 ... e5 16. Bd2 0–0 17. d6 Bd8 18. Ne4 Nb7 19. Bc3 Nc5 20. Nxf6+ Bxf6 21. Rd5 Qe6 22. Rad1 a6 23. d7 Rcd8 24. Rxc5 Rxd7 25. Rxd7 Qxd7 26. Qd1 Qc7 27. Rd5 b4 28. Bc1 Rc8 29. Qc2 Qe6 30. e4 c3 31. bxc3 bxc3 32. Rd3 1–0

(564) GREEN, M—FINE

Marshall CC championship 1940/41, New York (6), 1941 (9 Feb.)

Grünfeld Defence, Fianchetto Variation [D77]

1. d4 Nf6 2. Nf3 g6 3. c4 Bg7 4. g3 0–0 5. Bg2 d5 6. 0–0 Na6 7. cxd5 Nxd5 8. Nc3 Nb6 9. Be3 Nc4 10. Qc1 Nxe3 11. Qxe3 c6 12. Rfd1 Nb4 13. Rac1 Be6 14. a3 Nd5 15. Nxd5? Bxd5 16. Ne5 Bxg2 17. Kxg2 Qd5+ 18. Qf3 Rad8 19. Qxd5 Rxd5 20. Nf3 Rfd8 21. e3

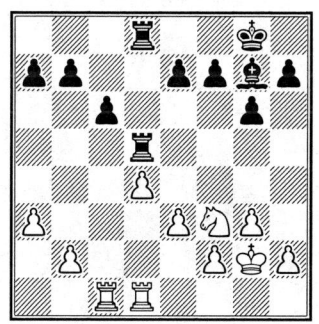

Position after White's 21st move

21 ... e5 22. Re1 exd4 23. exd4 Bxd4 24. Nxd4 Rxd4 25. Re7 R4d7 26. Re2 Rd2 27. Rc2 Rxc2 28. Rxc2 Kf8 29. Re2 Rd6 30. Kf3 Re6 31. Rd2 Ke7 32. h4 Rd6 33. Re2+ Kd7 34. Kf4 h6 35. f3 Rf6+ 36. Kg4 h5+ White resigned. 0–1

(565) FINE—SEIDMAN, H

Marshall CC championship 1940/41, New York (7), 1941
(16 Feb.)
Owen's Defence [A50]

1. d4 Nf6 2. c4 b6 3. f3 e6 4. e4 d5 5. cxd5 exd5
6. e5 Nfd7 7. f4 Bb7 8. Nf3 Bb4+ 9. Bd2 Qe7
10. Bd3 Bxd2+ 11. Nbxd2 c5 12. 0–0 Nc6 13. f5

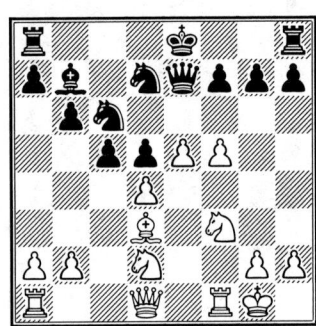

*Position after
White's 13th move*

13 ... 0–0–0 14. Rc1 Kb8 15. Re1 cxd4 16. e6 Nc5
17. Bb5 Nb4 18. Ne5 a6 19. Bf1 f6 20. Nf7 Nbd3
21. Bxd3 Nxd3 22. Nxh8 Rxh8 23. Nb3 Nxc1
24. Qxc1 Re8 25. Nxd4 g6 26. h3 Qd6 27. a3 Bc8
28. Qh6 gxf5 29. Qxf6 f4 30. Rc1 Bb7 31. Qf7
Re7 32. Qf8+ Ka7 33. Nf5 Black resigned. 1–0

(566) FINE—HEAL, E

Marshall CC championship 1940/41, New York (8), 1941
(23 Feb.)
Catalan System [E00]

1. d4 d5 2. c4 e6 3. Nf3 Nf6 4. g3 c6 5. Nbd2
Bd6 6. Bg2 0–0 7. 0–0 Nbd7 8. b3 h6 9. Bb2
Qe8 10. Ne5 Nh7 11. e4 Ndf6 12. f4

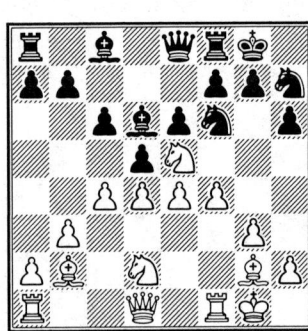

*Position after
White's 12th move*

12 ... dxe4 13. Qe2 Bd7 14. g4 Qe7 15. Rad1 Rad8
16. h4 g6 17. g5 hxg5 18. fxg5 Bxe5 19. dxe5 Nh5
20. Nxe4 Bc8 21. Rd6 Ng7 22. Nf6+ Kh8 23. c5
Nf5 24. Rxf5 Black resigned. 1–0

(567) LEVY, L—FINE

Marshall CC championship 1940/41, New York (9), 1941
(25 Feb.)

Sicilian Defence [B45]

1. e4 c5 2. Nf3 e6 3. d4 cxd4 4. Nxd4 Nf6 5. Nc3
Nc6 6. Be2 Bb4 7. 0–0 0–0 8. Ndb5 a6 9. Nd6 Qe7
10. Bf4 e5 11. Nxc8 Raxc8 12. Bg5 Bxc3 13. bxc3
Rc7 14. Bd3 h6 15. Be3 d5 16. exd5 Nxd5 17. Bh7+
Kxh7 18. Qxd5 Qd7 19. c4 Qg4 20. Qd3+ Qg6 21. Bb6
e4 22. Qg3 Rcc8 23. Rfd1 Nb4 24. Qxg6+ Kxg6
25. Rd6+ f6 26. c3 Nd3 27. Rd4 Rfe8 28. Rb1 Re6
29. f3 f5 30. fxe4 fxe4 31. Rd7 Rxc4 32. Bd4 e3

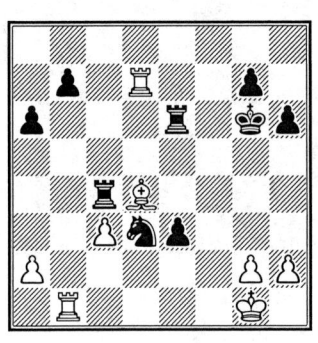

*Position after
Black's 32nd move*

33. Rf1 White should be able to draw by 33 Rxg7+ Kh5 34
Rf1 Nf2 35 Bxe3 Rxe3 36 Rxf2 Re1+ 37 Rf1 Rxf1+ 38 Kxf1
b5. AW 33 ... Ne5 34. Rxb7 e2 35. Rfb1 Rxd4
36. cxd4 Nd3 37. h3 e1Q+ 38. Rxe1 Rxe1+ 39. Kh2
Re2 40. Rb6+ Kf5 41. Rxa6 Ne1 42. Kg1 Nxg2
43. Ra7 g5 44. Rf7+ Kg6 45. Rf2 Nf4 46. Rxe2
Nxe2+ 47. Kf2 Nxd4 48. a4 Nc6 49. Kg3 Kh5
White resigned. 0–1

(568) FINE—REINFELD, F

Marshall CC championship 1940/41, New York (10), 1941
(9 April)
Nimzowitsch-Indian Defence, Rubinstein Variation [E44]

1. d4 Nf6 2. c4 e6 3. Nc3 Bb4 4. e3 b6 5. Nge2
Bb7 6. a3 Be7 7. d5 0–0 8. g3 b5 9. Nf4 bxc4
10. Bxc4 exd5 11. Ncxd5 c6 12. Nc3 d5 13. Be2
Ne4 14. Nxe4 dxe4 15. Qc2 c5 16. 0–0 Bd6 17. Rd1
Qe7 18. Nd5 Qe5 19. Nc3 Rd8 20. b3 Nd7 21. Bb2

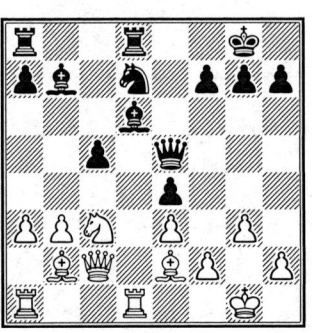

*Position after
White's 21st move*

21 ... Nf6 22. Nb5 Qe7 23. Nxd6 Rxd6 24. Rxd6
Qxd6 25. Rd1 Qe7 26. Bxf6 gxf6 27. Qd2 Rc8
28. Qd6 Rc7 29. Qxe7 Rxe7 30. g4 Kg7 31. Rd8
f5 32. gxf5 Re5 33. Bc4 Kf6 34. Rd7 Re7 35. Rd6+

Kxf5 36. Rh6 Kg5 37. Rxh7 Kg6 38. Rh8 Rd7
39. Kg2 f5 40. Kg3 Bd5 41. Rc8 Bxc4 42. bxc4
Rd3 43. Rc6+ Black resigned. 1–0

(569) MARSHALL, F–FINE

Marshall CC championship 1940/41, New York (11), 1941 (April)

The score of this game is not available. ½–½

(570) RICHMAN, J–FINE

Marshall CC championship 1940/41, New York (12), 1941
  (6 April)

Sicilian Defence [B20]

1. e4 c5 2. g3 d5 3. Bg2 dxe4 4. Nc3 f5 5. f3 exf3
6. Nxf3 g6 7. 0–0 Bg7 8. Qe2 Nc6 9. d3 Nf6
10. Be3 Nd4

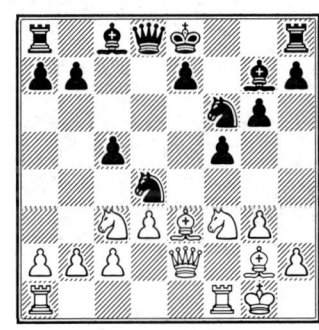

*Position after
Black's 10th move*

11. Qf2 Ng4 12. Qd2 Nxe3 13. Qxe3 Nxc2 14. Qxc5
Nxa1 15. Nb5 0–0 16. Kh1 Qb6 17. Qxb6 axb6 18. Rxa1
Bxb2 19. Re1 Bf6 20. Ne5 Ra5 21. Bd5+ Kg7 22. Bc4
Bxe5 23. Rxe5 Kf6 24. Re2 e5 25. Nc7 Bd7
26. Nd5+ Rxd5 27. Bxd5 Bc6 White resigned. 0–1

(571) FINE–CASS, A

Marshall CC championship 1940/41, New York (13), 1941
  (26 Feb.)

Marshall Defence [D06]

1. d4 Nf6 2. c4 d5 3. cxd5 Nxd5 4. e4 Nf6 5. Bd3
g6 6. Ne2 c5 7. dxc5 Qa5+ 8. Nbc3 Qxc5 9. 0–0
Bg7 10. Nb5 Na6 11. Be3 Qh5 12. f3 Bh6 13. Qd2
Bxe3+ 14. Qxe3 Bd7 15. Nec3 0–0

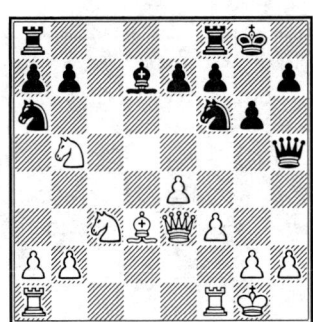

*Position after
Black's 15th move*

16. e5 Ne8 17. Rad1 Bc6 18. Nxa7 Nb4 19. Nxc6
Nxc6 20. f4 f6 21. Qb6 Rb8 22. Bc4+ Kh8 23. Rd7
fxe5 24. Rxb7 Nd6 25. Rxb8 Nxb8 26. Be2 Qh6
27. fxe5 Nf5 28. e6 Rc8 29. Bf3 Nd6 30. a4 Qg5
31. a5 Nc4 32. Qd4+ Kg8 33. Nd5 Nd2 34. h4
Nxf3+ 35. Rxf3 Qc1+ 36. Kh2 Black resigned. 1–0

(572) FINE–SUSSMAN, H

Marshall CC championship 1940/41, New York (14), 1941
  (11 May)

Budapest Defence [A52]

1. d4 Nf6 2. c4 e5 3. dxe5 Ng4 4. e4 Nxe5 5. f4
Nec6 6. Be3 Bb4+ 7. Kf2 d6 8. Nc3 Bxc3 9. bxc3
Nd7 10. h3 Nf6 11. Bd3 Qe7 12. Qc2 0–0 13. Nf3
Re8 14. Rhe1 h6 15. Bd4

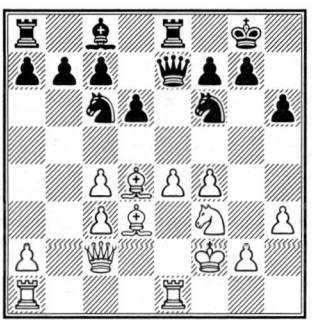

*Position after
White's 15th move*

15 ... Nxd4?! 16. cxd4 c5 17. d5 Nd7?! 18. g4 f6
19. h4 a6 20. g5 h5 21. e5 fxe5 22. Bh7+ Kh8
23. Qg6 Nf8 24. Qxh5 Bg4 25. Qxg4 Nxh7 26. fxe5
dxe5 27. Rxe5 Qxe5 28. Nxe5 Rxe5 29. Rf1 Rae8
30. Kg1 b5 31. d6 Re4 32. Qh5 g6 33. Qxg6 Rg4+
34. Kh2 Rg8 35. Qh5 Rd4 36. d7 Rd2+ 37. Kh1
Black resigned. 1–0

(573) FORSBERG, B–FINE

Marshall CC championship 1940/41, New York (15), 1941 (May)

The score of this game is not available. ½–½

In March 1941 Fine was present at the Manhattan
Chess Club on the day of the election of Maurice Wertheim
as club president. Fourteen players entered a rapid transit
tournament held after the meeting. Horowitz and Fine
scored six straight wins in their preliminary sections. In the
final Horowitz scored 2½–½, Fine 2–1, James R. Newman
1½–1½ and Oscar Tenner 0–3. (ACB 1941)

*New York Metropolitan League,
April–May, 1941*

Fine, taking the white pieces for a change, scored a
win and a rare loss, on board three behind Reinfeld and
Marshall. The win being a game with D. Maisel of the North

Jersey League, the loss being to Al Pinkus of the Manhattan Chess Club. The Manhattanites had won seven straight matches before the final match in May, whereas the players from the Marshall Chess Club had drawn 4–4 with North Jersey. A tight decisive match ended in a win for the Marshall Club by 9½–8½ (+4 –3 =11). Other competing teams were Bronx, Empire City, Steinitz, Queens Chess League (consisting of Astoria, Queens and Forest Park Chess Clubs), Brooklyn College and City College.

| Maisel (North Jersey) | 0 | Fine | 1 |
| Fine | 0 | Pinkus (Manhattan CC) | 1 |

(574) MAISEL, D—FINE

Metropolitan Chess League, New York, 1941 (5 April)
Symmetrical English, Rubinstein Variation [A34]

1. c4 Nf6 2. Nc3 c5 3. Nf3 d5 4. cxd5 Nxd5 5. g3 Nc6 6. Bg2 Nc7 7. b3 e5 8. Bb2 Be7 9. Rc1 f6 10. 0–0 0–0 11. d3 Bc6 12. Nc4 b6 13. Nfd2 Qd7 14. Nc4 Bh3 15. f4 Bxg2 16. Kxg2

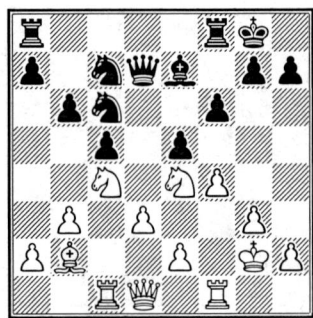

Position after White's 16th move

16 ... f5 17. Ned2 exf4 18. gxf4 Nd5 19. Rf3 Rae8 20. Ne5 Nxe5 21. Bxe5 Bf6 22. e4 Bxe5 23. fxe5 fxe4 24. Nxe4 Qg4+ 25. Ng3 Rxf3 26. Qxf3 Nf4+ 27. Kf2 Qg5 28. Rc2 Rf8 29. Ke1 Qxe5+ 30. Qe4 Qf6 31. Ne2 Nxe2 32. Qxe2 h6 33. Kd1 Qf1+ 34. Qxf1 Rxf1+

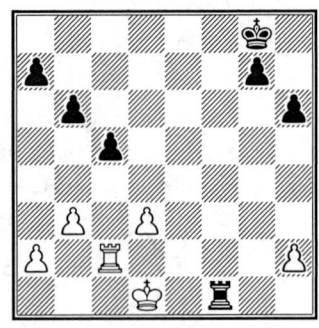

Position after Black's 34th move

35. Ke2 Rf4 36. Ke3 g5 37. Re2 Kf7 38. a3 a5 39. Rg2 Ke6 40. Kd2 g4 41. Ke3 Kf5 42. Kd2 h5 43. Kc3 h4 44. Re2 g3 45. h3 Rf1 46. Kc4 Rh1 47. Kb5 Rxh3 48. Kxb6 Rh2 49. Re1 g2 White resigned. **0–1**

(575) FINE—PINKUS, A

Metropolitan Chess League, New York (8), 1941 (May)
Catalan Opening [E02]

1. d4 Nf6 2. c4 e6 3. g3 d5 4. Bg2 dxc4 5. Qa4+
Nowadays, the preferred move is 5 Nc3, followed by e4. **5 ... Bd7 6. Qxc4 Bc6 7. Nf3 Bd5 8. Qd3 Nc6 9. 0–0 Be4 10. Qd1 Be7 11. Nc3 Bd5 12. Nxd5 exd5 13. Ne5 0–0 14. Bf4** The move, 14 Bg5, which threatens Nxc6 and Bxf6 followed by Rc1, strikes me as stronger. **14 ... Bd6 15. Rc1** Fine is having an off day. He delays too long in playing Nxc6, with the idea of a further Bg5. **15 ... Ne7 16. Bg5 Ne4 17. Bf4 c6 18. f3 Nf6 19. e4 Ne8 20. Rf2?!** White is swimming. More to the point is either 20 Bh3 or 20 Nd3. **20 ... f5!** Excellent. Black challenges the centre and threatens to open the f-file for his rook. **21. Nd3 Bxf4 22. Nxf4 Nc7 23. Qb3 g5 24. Nd3 Rb8 25. Rd1 Kh8!** The threat is ... dxe4, followed by ... Qxd4. **26. exf5 Nxf5 27. Ne5 Qd6 28. Qc3 Rbe8** Black must still take care. On 28 ... Nb5, White picks up material by 29 Qe1 Nbxd4 (if 29 ... Nfxd4, White wins after 30 a4 Rf5 31 f4) 30 g4 Rbe8 31 Nf7+ Rxf7 32 Qxe8+ Rf8 33 Qe1. **29. f4 gxf4 30. Rxf4?** White's last chance was 30 gxf4, though it opens up his king to attack. **30 ... Ne6 31. Rf2 Kg8!** Al was nothing if not thoroughly careful. He guards against such eventualities as 31 ... Nexd4? 32 Rxd4 Qxe5 33 Rdf4 d4 34 Qc2 or 31 ... Nfxd4 32 Nf7+ Rxf7 33 Rxf7. In the latter line, Black cannot play ... Ne2+ because of the pin. **32. Bh3 Nexd4 33. Rxd4 Nxd4 34. Rxf8+ Kxf8 35. Nd7+ Qxd7!** After this fine move, planned long in advance, Black has only a bit of mopping up to do. **36. Bxd7 Ne2+ 37. Kf1 Nxc3 38. Bxe8 Nxa2 39. Bd7 Nb4 40. Ke2 Ke7 41. Bf5 h6 42. g4 Kf6 43. h4 c5 44. Kf3 d4 45. Be4 c4** Bogus generosity, based on having counted the ending. **46. Bxb7 c3 47. bxc3 dxc3 48. Ke3 a5 49. Be4 Ke5 50. g5 h5 51. Bg6 a4** Fine resigned because of 52 Bf7 a3 53 Bb3 a2 54 Bxa2 Nxa2 55 Kd3 Kf4 56 Kc2 Nb4+ 57 Kxc3 Nd5+, when Al picks up both pawns and wins easily. **0–1** Denker in Denker & Parr, 28–30.

U.S.C.F. Championship Preliminaries (42nd U.S. Open), St Louis, July 17–19, 1941

"The 42nd annual congress and Open Tournament of the United States Chess Federation were held July 17–27, 1941, at the Hotel DeSoto in St. Louis, under the auspices of the St. Louis Chess League and Missouri Chess Association. An able committee headed by Erich W. Marchand handled all the arrangements in excellent fashion. There were 16 entrants, divided into three groups for the preliminary play. Of these, 10 qualified for the championship division of the finals." (*U.S.C.F. Yearbook*) Crosstable not available.

(576) Fine—Williams, Mrs. R

U.S. Chess Federation Open, preliminaries, Saint
  Louis (1), 1941 (17 July)
Queen's Gambit Declined [D50]

1. d4 d5 2. c4 e6 3. Nc3 Nf6 4. Bg5 Nc6
5. Nf3 h5 6. e3 Be7 7. Bd3 Bd7 8. Bxf6 Bxf6
9. cxd5 Nb4 10. dxe6 Nxd3+ 11. Qxd3 Bxe6
12. 0–0 c6 13. e4

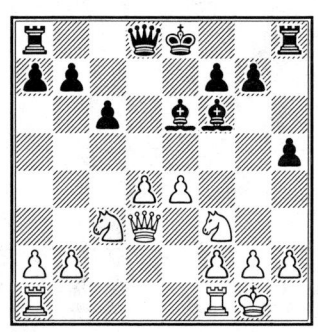

*Position after
White's 13th move*

13 ... h4?! 14. d5 Bxc3 15. Qxc3 cxd5
16. Qxg7 Rf8 17. Rad1 h3 18. exd5 hxg2
19. Rfe1 Qe7 20. dxe6 f6 21. Qg6+ 1–0 *New
York Times, July 20, 1941.*

(577) Fine—Rauch, J

U.S. Chess Federation Open, preliminaries, Saint
  Louis (2), 1941 (18 July)
Sicilian Defence, Dragon Variation [B54]

1. e4 c5 2. Nf3 d6 3. d4 cxd4 4. Nxd4 Nf6
5. f3 g6 6. c4 Bg7 7. Nc3 Nc6 8. Nc2 0–0
9. Be2 Be6 10. 0–0 Na5 11. b3 Nd7 12. Qd2
Rc8 13. Bb2 Qb6+ 14. Rf2 f5?! (14 ... Nxc4! 15
Bxc4 Bxc4 16 Ne3 Be6 17 Ncd5 Bxd5 18 Nxd5 Qd8
19 Bxg7 Kxg7 20 Qd4+ Kg8 and if 21 Qxa7 e6!)
15. Na4 Qc7 16. Bxg7 Kxg7 17. Nd4 Rf6
18. exf5 gxf5 19. Nb5 Qd8 20. Nxa7 Ra8
21. Qd4 Nxc4 22. bxc4

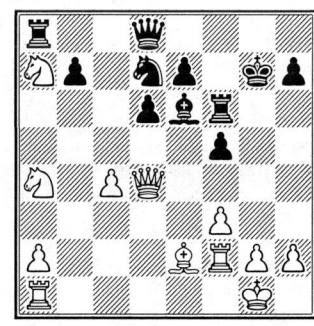

*Position after
White's 22nd move*

22 ... Qa5?! 23. Nb5 Qxa4 24. Nc7 Nc5 25. Nxa8
Qxa8 26. Bf1 Kf7 27. Re1 Qa5 28. Rfe2 Qb4 29. f4
Ne4 30. g4 Qc5 31. Qxc5 Nxc5 32. gxf5 Rxf5

In the summer of 1941, Fine won the United States Open, St. Louis, and the New York State Chess Championship, Hamilton, within the space of a little over five weeks. The State Championship featured such strong local rivals as Reshevsky, Kashdan and Denker.

33. Bh3 Rf6 34. Bxe6+ Rxe6 35. Rxe6 Nxe6 36. Rb1
Nc5 37. Kf2 Kf6 38. Ke3 Kf5 39. Rg1 Ne6 40. Rg8
h6 41. Rb8 Nc5 42. Kf3 h5 43. Rh8 Kg6 44. Rg8+
Kh6 45. f5 Nd3 46. Rg6+ Kh7 47. Re6 Ne5+
48. Rxe5 dxe5 49. Ke4 Kh6 50. h4 Kg7 51. Kxe5
Kf7 52. c5 Black resigned. 1–0

(578) Holland, K—Fine

U.S. Chess Federation Open, preliminaries, Saint Louis (3),
  1941 (18 July)
Budapest Defence [A51]

1. d4 Nf6 2. c4 e5 3. Bg5 h6 4. Bh4 Nc6 5. d5
Nd4 6. e3 Nf5 7. Bxf6 Qxf6 8. Nc3 Bb4 9. Qb3
Bxc3+ 10. Qxc3 0–0 11. Nf3 d6 12. Bd3 Re8

13. Bxf5 Bxf5 14. 0–0 c6 15. Rad1 cxd5 16. cxd5 Rac8 17. Qb4 a5 18. Qa3 Rc5 19. Nd2 Bc2 20. Nb3 Bxb3 21. Qxb3 b5 22. e4 Rec8 23. Qe3 Qg5

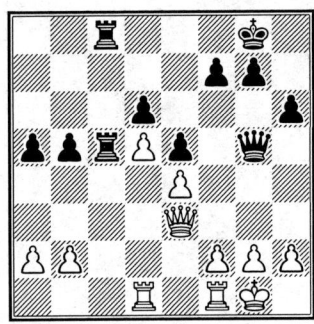

Position after Black's 23rd move

24. f4 exf4 25. Rxf4 Rc2 26. Rd2 Qe5 27. Rf1 Rxd2 28. Qxd2 Qxe4 29. Rf2 Rc5 30. Re2 Rxd5 31. Qe1 Qd4+ 32. Kf1 Rf5+ 33. Rf2 Rxf2+ 34. Qxf2 Qxf2+ 35. Kxf2 f5 36. Ke3 Kf7 37. Kd4 Ke6 38. b3 g5 39. g3 d5 40. Kc5 f4 41. gxf4 gxf4 42. Kd4 b4 0–1 *Los Angeles Times*, 10 August, 1941.

(579) FINE—STEPHENS, L

U.S. Chess Federation Open, preliminaries, Saint Louis (4), 1941 (19 July)
Queen's Gambit Declined, Marshall Variation [D06]

1. d4 Nf6 2. c4 d5?! 3. Nf3?! Bf5 4. Nc3?! e6 5. Bf4 c6?! 6. e3 Bd6 7. Bxd6 Qxd6 8. Bd3?! Bxd3 9. Qxd3 Fine has not really tried to get anything from the opening. With the black bishop on f5, Qb3 at some point would have been more aggressive. AW **9 … Nbd7 10. 0–0 0–0 11. e4!? dxe4 12. Nxe4 Nxe4 13. Qxe4 Nf6 14. Qe2 Rad8 15. Rad1 h6 16. Rd3 Rfe8 17. Rfd1 Qc7 18. b3 Nh5 19. g3** 19 Qe5!? AW **19 … Nf6 20. Kg2** ½–½ *New York Times*, July 20, 1941.

(580) SCHMIDT, B—FINE

U.S. Chess Federation Open, preliminaries, Saint Louis (5), 1941 (19 July)
Spanish Game, Siesta Variation [C74]

1. e4 e5 2. Nf3 Nc6 3. Bb5 a6 4. Ba4 d6 5. c3 f5 The Siesta Variation with which Fine had an unfortunate experience in a well-known game against Horowitz in the Syracuse 1934 tournament. But Schmidt's tame reply (instead of 6 d4) leaves Black with a good game. **6. d3 Nf6 7. 0–0 fxe4 8. dxe4 Nxe4?** A serious blunder, as White immediately demonstrates. **9. Nxe5! dxe5 10. Bxc6+ bxc6 11. Qh5+ Ke7 12. Qxe5+ Kf7 13. Qxe4 Qd5** Black has lost a pawn, and has much the inferior position as well. His situation is a desperate one. **14. Qf4+ Kg8 15. c4** There appears to be no good reason for not taking a second pawn (for example 15 Qxc7 Bf5 16 Bf4 and White has nothing to fear). **15 … Qf7 16. Nc3 Bd6 17. Qxf7+ Kxf7 18. Be3 Be5** Black decides that the bishops of opposite

colours offer the best hope of resistance. **19. Rac1 Bxc3 20. Rxc3 Bf5 21. f3** Beginning an artificial line which soon leaves White's pieces poorly posted. More logical was 21 Bf4 (tying down a rook to the defence of the weak c-pawn) followed by Re1. **21 … Rhb8 22. Rf2 Rd8 23. g4 Bg6 24. Kg2 Rd1 25. Bf4 Re8?!** If 25 … Rc8 26 Re2 and Black's game will soon become hopeless. Hence Fine parts with another pawn. **26. Bxc7 Ree1 27. Kg3 Bd3 28. h4 Rg1+ 29. Kf4 h5 30. Kg5 hxg4 31. fxg4+ Kg8 32. Rf4** With a view to playing Rc3-b3-b8+ followed by R4f8 and mate to follow. Black's plight has become desperate. **32 … Rg2 33. Rb3 Be2** His last hope, preventing the king's rook from leaving f4, and also threatening to double rooks on the g-file. **34. Rb8+?** Plausible though this move is, it throws away the win! Correct was the simple 34 Re3! If then 34 … Kh7 (34 … Re1 35 Kg6 Bxg4 36 Rxe1 Be6+ 37 Kh5 Bf7+ 38 Rxf7); or 34 … Rdg1 35 Ree4 Bd3 36 Rd4 Be2 37 Bb6. **34 … Kh7 35. Bb6 Rf1!** Very good. If now 36 Rxf1 Bxf1 and White has too many pawns *en prise*, with a clear draw in prospect. **36. Re4 Bd3!** If 37 R4f8?? Rf5 mate! **37. Rf4 Rxf4 38. Kxf4** Draw agreed. After 38 … Rxb2, Black regains the other pawn as well. ½–½ Fred Reinfeld, *U.S.C.F. Yearbook 1941-3*, 11–2.

U.S.C.F. Championship Finals (42nd U.S. Open), St Louis, July 20–27, 1941

"Reuben Fine won the tournament by a comfortable margin, maintaining his remarkable record of never finishing out of first place in an Open Tournament. Herman Steiner was second and Weaver W. Adams third. By the luck of the draw, Fine encountered Adams and Steiner in the first two rounds. Victory over these two formidable opponents left him clear sailing the rest of the way. Draws in later rounds with Boris Blumin and Fred Anderson gave him a final score of 8–1." (*U.S.C.F. Yearbook*) First prize was $200. Fine, by scoring 11–0, also won his section of the rapid transit tournament which closed the meeting. Samuel Factor, Chicago, was second with a score of 9–2.

		1	2	3	4	5	6	7	8	9	10	
1	Fine	*	1	1	½	½	1	1	1	1	1	8
2	Steiner	0	*	0	½	1	1	1	1	1	1	6½
3	Adams	0	1	*	0	0	1	1	1	1	1	6
4	Blumin	½	½	1	*	0	1	0	½	1	1	5½
5=	Anderson	½	0	1	1	*	0	0	½	1	1	5
5=	Marchand	0	0	0	0	1	*	1	1	1	1	5
7	Schmidt	0	0	0	1	1	0	*	0	1	1	4
8	Rauch	0	0	0	½	½	0	1	*	1	½	3½
9	Stephens	0	0	0	0	0	0	0	0	*	1	1
10	Sturgis	0	0	0	0	0	0	0	½	0	*	½

(581) ADAMS, W—FINE

U.S. Open finals, Saint Louis (1), 1941 (20 July)
French Defence, Winawer Variation [C17]

1. e4 e6 2. d4 d5 3. Nc3 Bb4 4. e5 c5 5. a3 cxd4
6. axb4 dxc3 7. bxc3 Qc7 8. Qd4 Nc6 9. Bb5 Nge7
10. f4 0-0 11. Qc5 Bd7 12. Bxc6 Nxc6 13. Nf3 b6
14. Qe3 a5 15. Rb1 a4 16. Ra1 Rfc8 17. Ra3 Na7
18. Nd4 Nb5 19. Nxb5 Bxb5 20. Kf2 Qd8 21. Rd1
Rc4 22. Kg1 Qc7

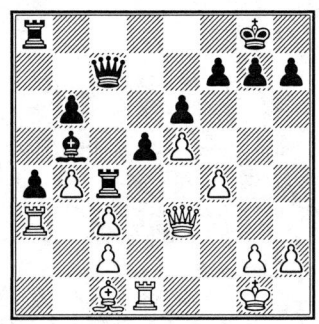

Position after
Black's 22nd move

23. Rd4 Rc8 24. Bd2 Qd8 25. Ra2 R8c6 26. Be1
Qc7 27. Qf2 h6 28. h3 Qd8 29. Ra1 Rc8 30. Qd2
Qc7 31. Ra2 Rxd4 32. cxd4 Qc4 33. c3 Ra8 34. Ra3
Qf1+ 35. Kh2 Bd3 36. Qf2 Qxf2 37. Bxf2 Kf8
38. Be1 Ke7 39. Kg1 Kd7 40. Kf2 Kc6 41. h4 Kb5
42. g4 Kc4 43. g5 b5 44. Ke3 f6 White resigned.
0-1

(582) FINE—STEINER, H

U.S. Open finals, Saint Louis (2), 1941 (20 July)
Bogolyubov Indian Defence [E11]

1. d4 d5 2. c4 e6 3. Nf3 Nf6 4. g3 A favourite continuation with Fine. Black's best course is doubtless 4 ...
dxc4 5 Qa4+ Nbd7 6 Bg2 a6—a defence which Fine himself
prefers. 4 ... Bb4+ A questionable continuation, as the
absence of the dark-squared bishop will make itself felt later
on; the pawn configuration is such that Black's queen's
bishop has slight prospect of being put to good use.
5. Bd2 Qe7 6. Bg2 Nbd7 7. 0-0 c6 If instead 7 ...
0-0 8 Qc2 Bxd2 9 Nbxd2 c5 10 dxc5 Nxc5 11 Rac1 and
Black's position is very uncomfortable. 8. Qc2 0-0
9. Bxb4 Qxb4 10. Nbd2 Re8 11. Rfe1 e5 The crucial
position. If Black can carry out this advance unpunished, he
may be able to equalize. 12. a3! Qb6 12 ... Qf8 would have
been safer, although Black's game would have been cramped.
13. e4!

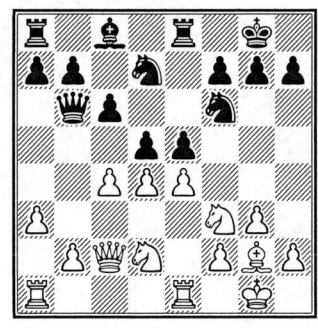

Position after
White's 13th move

13 ... exd4 13 ... dxe4 14 Nxe4 Nxe4 15 Rxe4 f5 looks
plausible, but then comes 16 c5! followed by Qc4+ with
decisive effect (if 16 ... Qb5 17 a4 Qa6 18 Qb3+). 14. cxd5!
cxd5 If 14 ... c5 15 e5! Nxd5 16 Ng5 Qh6 17 Nxf7 with a
winning position. 15. exd5 Rxe1+ Or 15 ... Rd8 16 Nc4
Qc5 17 b4 Qxd5 18 Nfe5 Qe6 (18 ... Qb5 19 Nxf7!) 19 Nc6.
16. Rxe1 Nf8 Of course not 16 ... Nxd5? 17 Re8+. The
superior position of White's pieces must soon lead to a
material advantage. 17. Nc4 Qc5 18. Nfe5!

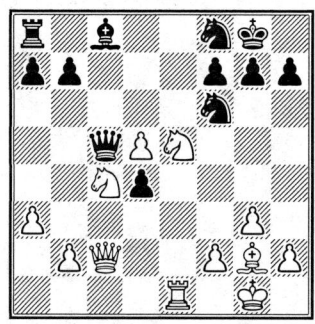

Position after
White's 18th move

18 ... a5 And not 18 ... Nxd5? 19 b4 Qb5 20 Nd6 Qb6
21 Nxc8, while if 18 ... b5 19 b4 Qc7 20 d6 and wins. 19. Qd2!
Ra6 Having in mind the variation 19 ... Nxd5 20 Bxd5 Qxd5
21 Nb6. 20. Rc1! Bf5 The pawn could not be saved: on
20 ... Nxd5? Fine had calculated the following win of a piece
21 Nd3 Qb5 22 a4 Qd7 23 Nce5 Qd8 24 Bxd5 Qxd5 25 Rxc8.
20 ... Qa7 would not help because of 21 Nxf7! 21. Nxf7! Ne4
21 ... Be4 would have held out longer. 22. Qe1! Rf6 23. Nfe5
Qxd5 Losing a piece, but 23 ... Nd6 24 Nxa5 was not
much better. 24. g4 b5 25. gxf5 bxc4 26. Qxe4 Black
resigned. 1-0 Reinfeld, *U.S.C.F. Yearbook 1941-3*, 13.

(583) RAUCH, J FINE

U.S. Open finals, Saint Louis (3), 1941 (22 July)
English Opening, Symmetrical Variation [A30]

1. c4 c5 2. Nf3 Nf6 3. g3 d5 4. cxd5 Nxd5 5. Bg2
Nc6 6. d4 Nf6 7. Be3 e6 8. 0-0 Nd5 9. Nc3 Nxe3
10. fxe3 Be7 11. Na4 cxd4 12. exd4 0-0 13. Rc1 Rb8
14. e3 Bd7 15. Nc5 Be8 16. Qb3 Na5 17. Qc3 Bb5

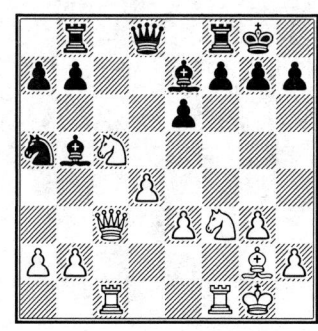

Position after
Black's 17th move

18. b4 Rc8 19. Rfd1 b6 20. bxa5 bxc5 21. dxc5
Qc7 22. Nd4 Ba4 23. Nb3 Bxc5 24. Rd3 Bxb3
25. axb3 Qb8 26. Qb2 Bb4 27. a6 Qb5 28. Rxc8

Rxc8 29. Bf1 Qc5 30. Qd4 Qxd4 31. exd4 Rd8
32. Bg2 Rxd4 33. Rxd4 Bc5 34. Kf2 Bxd4+
35. Kf3 f5 36. Bf1 Kf7 37. g4 Kf6 38. Bc4 g6
39. h3 e5 40. Bg8 e4+ 41. Kf4 g5+ 42. Kg3 f4+
43. Kg2 h6 44. Bh7 Ke5 45. Bg8 f3+ 46. Kf1 e3
White resigned. 0–1

(584) Stephens, L—Fine

U.S. Open finals, Saint Louis (4), 1941 (22 July)
Colle System [A43]

1. d4 c5 2. e3 d5 3. c3 Nd7 4. Nf3 Ngf6 5. Bd3 g6
6. Nbd2 Bg7 7. 0–0 0–0 8. Re1 Re8 9. Bc2 b6 10. e4
cxd4 11. Nxd4 e5 12. N4f3 Bb7 13. exd5 Bxd5 14. Ne4
Bxe4 15. Bxe4 Nxe4 16. Rxe4 Nc5 17. Re1 e4

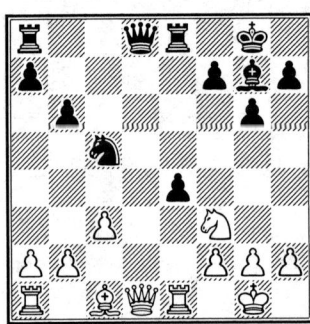

*Position after
Black's 17th move*

18. Nd4 Nd3 19. Re2 Bxd4 20. cxd4 Qxd4 21. Be3
Qd7 22. Qb3 Qg4 23. Rd2 Qe6 24. Qc3 Rac8
25. Qd4 Rc4 26. Rxd3 exd3 27. Qxd3 Rc7 28. Rd1
Qc4 29. Qd6 Rce7 30. h3 Qxa2 31. Kh2 Qe6 32. Qb4
Rd7 33. Rc1 h5 34. Qh4 Qe5+ 35. g3 Qxb2 36. Qg5
Qe5 37. Qxe5 Rxe5 38. Rc8+ Kg7 39. Bc1 Re2
40. Kg2 Rdd2 41. Bxd2 Rxd2 42. Rc7 a5 43. Kf3
a4 44. Ke3 Rb2 White resigned. 0–1

(585) Fine—Blumin, B

U.S. Open finals, Saint Louis (5), 1941 (23 July)
Grünfeld Defence [D93]

1. d4 Nf6 2. c4 g6 3. Nc3 d5 4. Bf4 Bg7 5. e3 0–0
6. Qb3 c6 7. Nf3 Qa5 8. Be2 dxc4 9. Bxc4 b5
10. Be2 Be6 11. Qc2 Nd5 12. Bg3 c5 13. 0–0 Nxc3
14. bxc3 Nd7 15. Rfb1 cxd4 16. Nxd4 Bxd4 17. exd4
Rac8 18. Rxb5 Qxc3 19. Qxc3 Rxc3 20. Ra5 Rfc8
21. Bf4 Nf6 22. Bf3 R3c4 23. Rxa7 Rxd4 24. Be3
Rd7 25. Rxd7 Nxd7 26. a4 Ne5 27. Be2 Ra8
28. a5 Bc4 29. Kf1 Kf8 30. a6 Bxe2+ 31. Kxe2
Ke8 32. a7 Kd7 33. Rd1+ Kc8 34. h4 Nc6 35. Bc5
Kc7 36. Ra1 Kb7 37. Rb1+ Kc7 38. Ra1 Kb7 39. Kf3
Nxa7 40. Bxe7 Re8 41. Bc5 Draw agreed. ½–½

(586) Schmidt, B—Fine

U.S. Open finals, Saint Louis (6), 1941 (24 July)
Spanish Game, Steinitz Defence Deferred [C75]

1. e4 e5 2. Nf3 Nc6 3. Bb5 a6 4. Ba4 d6 5. c3 The
favoured continuation of recent years has been 5 Bxc6+
bxc6 6 d4. 5 … Bd7 (Varying from 5 … f5 in the game
between the same opponents in the preliminary tournament. AW) 6. d4 Nf6 7. Bg5 A weak pseudo-developing
move, inferior to the other moves 0–0, Nbd2, Qe2 or even
d5. 7 … h6 8. Bh4 Be7 If 8 … g5, 9 dxe5 maintains
material equality. 9. Nbd2 exd4 If this pawn is recaptured, then 10 … Nxe4 wins a pawn. Hence the ensuing
exchanges, which leave Black with two bishops against two
knights. 10. Bxc6 Bxc6 11. Bxf6 Bxf6 12. cxd4 The
following play proves once more that the "classical pawn
centre" can prove quite weak when under observation by
two strong bishops. 12 … 0–0 13. 0–0 Re8 14. Qc2
g5! Very well played. The move is typical of the struggle of
the bishop against the knight, as it increases the scope of
the bishop, and correspondingly cuts down the scope of the
knight. 15. d5 Bb5 16. Rfc1 g4 17. Ne1 Bg5! One can
readily see that the bishops are being manoeuvred by a master! 18. a4 Bd7 19. Ra3 19 Rd1 was somewhat better.
19 … c6 20. Rd1 Losing quickly. 20 dxc6 and, if 20 …
Bxc6, 21 f3 had to be played. 20 … cxd5 21. exd5 Re2
Menacing the win of a piece with … Bxd2. If now 22 Qc1
Qe7 23 Ra1 Re8 24 Kf1 Bxa4 and wins. Or 22 Nd3 Qe7
23 Raa1 Re8 24 g3 Bf5 winning easily. 22. Qd3 Qe7
White resigned! If 23 Raa1 Bxd2 wins. If 23 Nc2 Bxd2 24
Rxd2 Re1+ coming out a piece ahead. 0–1 Reinfeld, BCM
1942, 15.

(587) Fine—Marchand, E

U.S. Open finals Saint Louis (7), 1941 (24 July)
French Defence, Winawer Variation [C18]

1. e4 e6 2. d4 d5 3. Nc3 Bb4 4. e5 c5 5. a3 Bxc3+
6. bxc3 b6 7. Qg4 Kf8 8. Bd3 f5 9. exf6 Nxf6
10. Qg3 Ba6 11. Nf3 Bxd3 12. cxd3 Nc6

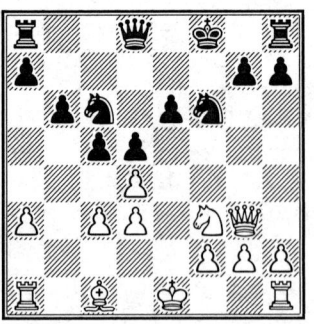

*Position after
Black's 12th move*

13. 0–0 cxd4 14. cxd4 h6 15. Bd2 g5 16. Rae1 Kf7
17. Ne5+ Nxe5 18. Qxe5 Qd7 19. f4 g4 20. f5 Rhe8
21. Qxf6+ Kxf6 22. fxe6+ Black resigned. 1–0

(588) Sturgis, G—Fine

U.S. Open finals, Saint Louis (8), 1941 (25 July)
Grünfeld Defence, 4 Bf4 [D96]

1. d4 Nf6 2. c4 g6 3. Nc3 d5 4. Bf4 Bg7 5. Nf3
0–0 6. Qb3 dxc4 7. Qxc4 c6 8. e3 Qa5 9. Be2
Nd5 10. 0–0 Nxf4 11. exf4 Be6 12. Qa4 Qc7
13. g3 Nd7 14. Qc2 Nb6 15. Rfd1 Rad8 16. b3 Bf5
17. Qd2 Bg4

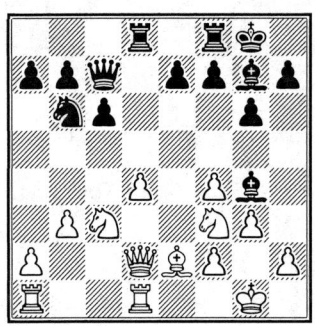

Position after
Black's 17th move

18. Ne5 Bxe2 19. Qxe2 Nd5 20. Rac1 Nxc3 21. Rxc3
Rd5 22. Rcd3 Rfd8 23. Qe3 Qd6 24. Nc4 Qd7
25. Ne5 Bxe5 26. fxe5 c5 27. f4 cxd4 28. Qe4
Qf5 29. Qe2 f6 30. exf6 exf6 31. Qd2 Qd7 32. Qb4
a5 33. Qb6 Qc6 34. Qa7 Rc5 White resigned. 0–1

(589) FINE—ANDERSSON, F

U.S. Open finals, Saint Louis (9), 1941 (26 July)
Petroff Defence [C43]

1. e4 e5 2. Nf3 Nf6 3. d4 Nxe4 4. Bd3 d5 5. Nxe5
Be6 6. 0–0 Nd7 7. Nxd7 Qxd7 8. Re1 f5 9. f3 Nd6
10. Nc3 0–0–0 11. Bf4 g6 12. Be5 Rg8 13. a4 Bg7
14. Nb5 Bxe5 15. Rxe5 Nf7 16. Re2 c6 17. Nxa7+
Kb8 18. Qe1 Rge8 19. Nb5 cxb5 20. axb5 b6 21. Qh4
Nd6 22. Rae1 Bg8 23. Re7 Rxe7 24. Rxe7 Qc8
25. Qf6 Bf7 26. Rxf7 Nxf7 27. Qxf7 Qc7 28. Qe6
Qd6 29. Qxd6+ Rxd6 Draw agreed. ½–½

63rd New York State
Chess Association Championship,
Hamilton, August 16–23, 1941

		1	2	3	4	5	6	7	8	9	10	11	
1	Fine	*	½	½	½	1	1	½	1	1	1	1	8
2=	Denker	½	*	½	0	1	½	1	1	½	1	1	7
2=	Kashdan	½	½	*	½	½	1	½	1	½	1	1	7
2=	Reshevsky	½	1	½	*	1	½	½	½	1	1	½	7
5	Willman	0	0	½	0	*	1	1	1	1	1	1	6½
6	Santasiere	0	½	0	½	0	*	½	1	1	0	1	4½
7=	Cruz	½	0	½	½	0	½	*	0	½	½	1	4
7=	Seidman	0	0	0	½	0	0	1	*	½	1	1	4
9	Shainswit	0	½	½	0	0	0	½	½	*	1	0	3
10	Hewlett	0	0	0	0	0	1	½	0	0	*	1	2½
11	Evans	0	0	0	½	0	0	0	0	1	0	*	1½

In a tough field at the annual tournament of the
strongest of the States, held for this year on the campus of

Colgate University, Fine drew with the grandmasters and
beat the other players until a draw (in a winning position)
was sufficient to take the title in the final round.

(590) WILLMAN, R—FINE

NYSCA, Hamilton (1), 1941 (17 Aug.)
Sicilian Defence [B40]

1. e4 c5 2. Nf3 e6 3. c4 Nc6 4. Nc3 Nd4 5. d3
Ne7 6. Be3 Nec6 7. g3 g6 8. Bg2 Bg7 9. Qd2 0–0
10. h4 h5 11. Bg5 f6 12. Bf4 d6

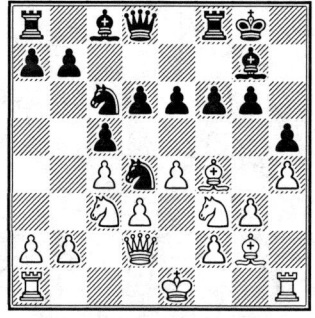

Position after
Black's 12th move

13. Nxd4 cxd4 14. Ne2 e5 15. Bh6 f5 16. exf5
Bxf5 17. Bd5+ Kh7 18. Bxg7 Kxg7 19. f3 Qa5
20. a3 Qxd2+ 21. Kxd2 Ne7 22. Be4 Bxe4
23. fxe4 Rf3 24. Rag1 Raf8

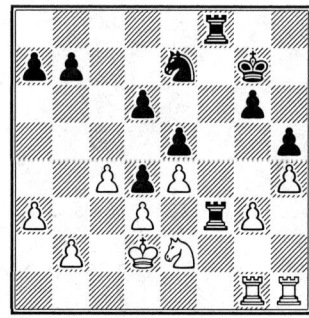

Position after
Black's 24th move

25. g4 Re3 26. Rh2 Kh6 27. gxh5 Kxh5 28. Ng3+
Kh6 29. h5 g5 30. Nh1 Ref3 31. Rhg2 Rg8 32. Nf2
Kxh5 33. Ng4?! Ng6 34. Rh2+ Nh4 35. Nf2 Rgf8
36. Nh1 R8f4 37. Ng3+ Kg6 38. Ne2 Rf2 39. Rxf2
White overstepped the time limit. 0–1

(591) FINE—SHAINSWIT, G

NYSCA, Hamilton (2), 1941 (17 Aug.)
Old Indian Defence [A28]

1. c4 e5 2. Nc3 Nf6 3. Nf3 Nc6 4. e4 d6 5. d4
Be7 6. h3 0–0 7. Be3 exd4 8. Nxd4 Nxd4
9. Bxd4 c6 10. Bd3 d5 11. cxd5 cxd5 12. e5 Ne8
13. 0–0 Nc7 14. Bc2 Be6 15. f4 f5 16. Qf3 Qd7
17. Rfd1 b5 18. Bb3 Qc6 19. Rac1 Qb7 20. Bf2
Rfd8 21. Ne2 Bf7 22. Nd4 g6 23. g4

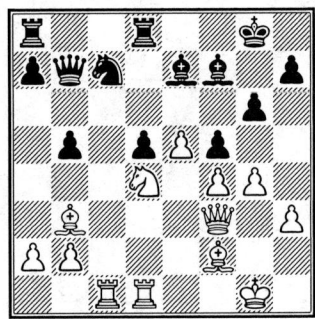

*Position after
Black's 23rd move*

23 ... f×g4 24. h×g4 a5 25. f5 g×f5 26. g×f5 Kh8
27. e6 Rg8+ 28. Kh1 B×e6 29. R×c7 Q×c7 30. N×e6
Black resigned. 1–0

(592) HEWLETT, C—FINE

NYSCA, Hamilton (3), 1941 (18 Aug.)
Sicilian Defence [B40]

1. e4 c5 2. Nf3 e6 3. d4 c×d4 4. N×d4 Nf6 5. Qf3
Be7 6. Nc3 d6 7. h3 0–0 8. Bd3 Nc6 9. Be3 Ne5
10. Qe2 d5 11. e×d5 N×d3+ 12. Q×d3 N×d5 13. N×d5
Q×d5 14. Ke2 e5 15. Nf3 Qe6 16. Ng5 B×g5 17. B×g5
b5 18. f3 Bb7 19. Kf2 Rac8 20. Rhe1

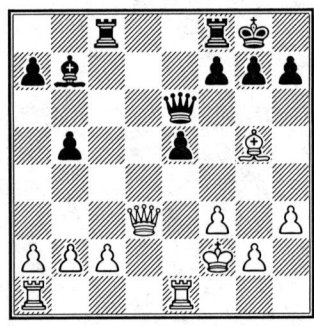

*Position after
White's 20th move*

20 ... e4 21. f×e4 f5 22. Kg1 B×e4 23. c3 Qg6
24. Qg3 f4 25. Qg4 h5 26. Qh4 Rc5 27. R×e4
R×g5 28. R×f4 R×g2+ 29. Kh1 R×f4 30. Q×f4 Qc6
White resigned. 0–1

(593) FINE—LASKER, ED

NYSCA, Hamilton (4), 1941 (19 Aug.)
Bogolyubov Indian Defence [E11]

1. d4 Nf6 2. c4 e6 3. Nf3 d5 4. g3 Bb4+ 5. Bd2 Qe7
6. Bg2 0–0 7. Qc2 b6 8. 0–0 Bb7 9. B×b4 Q×b4
10. Nbd2 c6 11. e4 d×e4 12. Ng5 Nbd7 13. Ng×e4
Rab8 14. a3 Qe7 15. c5 b×c5 16. d×c5 Ba6 17. Rfe1
Ne5 18. b4 Nd5 19. Nd6 Nd3 20. Red1 Qf6 21. N2e4
Qb2 22. Ra2 Q×c2 23. R×c2 Ne5 (*see diagram*) 24. Bf1
Nf3+ 25. Kg2 B×f1+ 26. R×f1 Nd4 27. Rd2 e5
28. Nc4 f6 29. Ned6 Rfd8 30. Rfd1 Ne7 31. Na5
Rd7 32. f4 Nd5 33. Re1 Re7 34. f×e5 R×e5 35. R×e5
f×e5 36. Nac4 Ne7 37. Rd3 Nd5 38. N×e5 Nc2

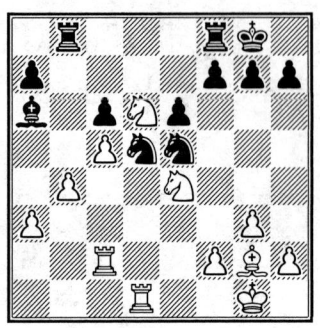

*Position after
Black's 23rd move*

39. Ndc4 Rf8 40. Nf3 R×f3 41. K×f3 Black resigned.
1–0

(594) DENKER, A—FINE

NYSCA Hamilton (5), 1941 (19 Aug.)
Grünfeld Defence [D97]

1. d4 Nf6 2. Nf3 g6 3. c4 Bg7 4. Nc3 d5 5. Qb3
d×c4 6. Q×c4 0–0 7. e4 b6 8. Bf4 c6 9. Qb3 Bg4
10. Rd1 Nbd7 11. Be2 Ne8 12. h3 B×f3 13. B×f3 e5
14. d×e5 Qe7 15. Qc4 N×e5 16. B×e5 B×e5 17. Q×c6
Nf6 18. 0–0 Rac8 19. Nd5 N×d5 20. Q×d5 B×b2
21. Qb5 Qf6 22. Rd7 Rc5 23. Qe2 a5 24. Rfd1 Be5
25. g3 Rfc8 26. Kg2 Rc3 27. R7d3 h5 28. R×c3
R×c3 29. h4 a4 30. Rd3 R×d3 31. Q×d3 Bd4 32. Qb5
a3 33. Qg5 Draw agreed. ½–½

(595) SEIDMAN, H—FINE

NYSCA, Hamilton (6), 1941 (20 Aug.)
Spanish Game, Steinitz Defence Deferred [C71]

1. e4 e5 2. Nf3 Nc6 3. Bb5 a6 4. Ba4 d6 5. d4 b5
6. Bb3 N×d4 7. N×d4 e×d4 8. Bd5 By no means as
strong as the pawn sacrifice 8 c3!, with which Yates had
much success. 8 Q×d4, of course, loses a piece (The Noah's
Ark Trap. AW). 8 ... Rb8 9. Q×d4 Nf6 10. Bc6+ Nothing constructive; Black meanwhile is consistently developing.
10 ... Bd7 11. B×d7+ Q×d7 12. 0–0 Be7 13. Nc3
0–0 14. Bg5 Rfe8 15. Rad1 h6 16. Bc1 16 Bh4
promised more. 16 ... b4

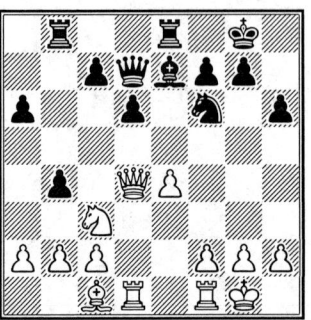

*Position after
Black's 16th move*

17. Ne2 This loses a pawn; 17 Nd5 was best. 17 ... Qc6
18. Ng3 Q×c2 19. Bf4 c5 20. Rd2 Qa4 21. Qc4

Qb5 22. Q×b5 a×b5 23. f3 Ra8 24. Nf5 R×a2 25. N×e7+ R×e7 26. B×d6 Rd7 27. Rfd1 c4 28. B×b4 R×b2! The charming conclusion of the middle game; the ending requires no comment. 29. R×b2 R×d1+ 30. Kf2 Rd3 31. Ke2 Nd7 32. Bd2 Rb3 33. R×b3 c×b3 34. Kd3 g5 35. Kc3 Nc5 36. Be3 b2 37. K×b2 Nd3+ 38. Kb3 Ne1 39. g4 N×f3 40. h3 Ne1 41. h4 g×h4 42. B×h6 h3 43. Bf4 Nf3 44. Kb4 h2 45. B×h2 N×h2 46. K×b5 N×g4 White resigned. Seidman had been very much pressed for time, and, towards the end, had someone keep score for him. Fine protested vehemently (A slight hypocrisy—Fine had done the same for Bernstein back in 1931. AW). Whether he was justified depends, I suppose, on whether the standards are professional or amateur. 0–1 Santasiere, ACB 1941, 77.

(596) FINE—KASHDAN, I

NYSCA, Hamilton (7), 1941 (21 Aug.)
Bogolyubov Indian Defence [E00]

1. d4 Nf6 2. c4 e6 3. g3 Bb4+ 4. Bd2 B×d2+ 5. N×d2 0–0 6. Bg2 Nc6 7. Ngf3 d6 8. 0–0 e5 9. e3 Ne8 10. d×e5 d×e5 11. Ne4 Bf5 12. Nh4 Q×d1 13. Rf×d1 Bg4 14. f3 Be6 15. b3 f5 16. Nc5 Bc8 17. f4 c4 18. g4 g6 19. g×f5 g×f5 20. Kf2 Nd6 21. Bf1 b6 22. Na4 Be6 23. Nc3 Ne7 24. Rd2 Kf7 25. Rc1 a5 26. Na4 Rad8 27. Rcd1 Nb7 28. R×d8 R×d8 29. R×d8 N×d8 30. c5 b×c5 31. N×c5 Bc8 32. Ng2 Nec6 33. Ne1 Ke7 34. Nc2 Kd6 35. Na4 Nb4 36. Nd4 N×a2 37. Bh3 Nc1 38. N×f5+ B×f5 39. B×f5 h6 40. B×e4 N×b3 41. Bc2 Draw agreed. ½–½

(597) RESHEVSKY, S—FINE

NYSCA, Hamilton (8), 1941 (21 Aug.)
Nimzowitsch-Indian Defence, Rubinstein Variation [E49]

1. d4 Nf6 2. c4 e6 3. Nc3 Bb4 4. e3 d5 5. a3! First played in the memorable Botvinnik–Capablanca game at the A.V.R.O. Tournament, 1938. The idea of the move is typically modern: to transpose into a favourable variation which would not be reached in any normal manner. The line White is anxious to obtain is a branch of the Sämisch Attack, which begins with 4 a3 (thus one move earlier) B×c3+ 5 b×c3. If Black now continues with 5 ... d5, we have the text position, but he has a far better reply in 5 ... c5!, for if then 6 e3 Qa5! 7 Bd2 Ne4 with at least equality. Incidentally, Reshevsky almost never prepares openings—this game is a rare exception. RF 5 ... B×c3+ 6. b×c3 c5 7. c×d5 e×d5 Judging from the further course of the game, Black might be better off with 7 ... Q×d5, as in Reshevsky–Levin, U.S. Championship, 1942. SR 8. Bd3 0–0 9. Ne2 b6! To exchange White's dangerous king's bishop. RF 10. 0–0 Ba6 11. B×a6 Contemporary practice has shown that this exchange is unnecessary: 11 f3 Re8 12 Ra2 Qc8 13 Bb1! Bc4 14 Rb2 Qa6 15 Re1 Nbd7 16 a4 and White went on to win

in 35 moves, Gulko–Ljubojevic, Moscow Olympiad, 1994. 11 ... N×a6 12. Qd3! Hoping for ... c4, which would stabilize the centre and lead to a powerful reaction later on with f3 and e4. SR 12 ... Qc8 In his excellent treatise *Dynamic Pawn Play in Chess*, Marović writes that this has been neutralized by 12 ... Nc7 (Fine himself played 13 d×c5 against Steiner, Dallas 1940) 13 f3 Qe8. Hence the continuation noted at move 11. 13. Bb2 The only drawback to White's potentially powerful position is that this bishop has to operate behind his own pawn structure. SR 13 ... c×d4 I had counted on the opening of the c-file to give me adequate counterplay, but this hope proved illusory. Consequently the cold-blooded 13 ... c4 14 Qc2 Re8 and if 15 Ng3 Ne4! was preferable. RF 14. c×d4 White's position is slightly more comfortable, PCO 251. 14 ... Nc7 15. Rfc1! Looks illogical, but is really a subtle manoeuvre designed to get the black pieces away from their best squares. On 15 f3 at once, Black can reply 15 ... Re8 16 Ng3 Qa6 17 Qd2 Nb5 18 Rae1 Nd6, when the advance e4 has been prevented and Black can get his knight to the strong square c4. RF 15 ... Qd7 Whereas if now 15 ... Qa6 16 Q×a6 N×a6 17 Rc6 Rac8 18 Rac1 R×c6 19 R×c6 and White's control of the c-file gives him a vastly superior game. SR 16. f3 Rfe8 17. Ng3 Ne6 So that if 18 e4? d×e4 18 f×e4 Nc5 winning the e-pawn. However, the advance of the e-pawn cannot be held back much longer. SR 18. Re1 Rac8 19. Rad1 It is important to give the queen additional protection, for if 19 e4? d×e4 20 f×e4 Nc5 21 Qf3 Na4 with good counterplay. SR 19 ... Qa4 And now 20 e4 would be answered by ... Qc2. One must admire the resourcefulness with which Fine makes the most of an inferior position. SR 20. Rd2 Qc4 21. Qb1 Qb3 I was still under the impression that the counter-action along the c-file was adequate. Since it is not, I should have tried 21 ... Red8, when it is still quite difficult for White to advance his e-pawn. RF 22. Nf5 Rc7 23. e4 Rec8 24. Rd3 Well-timed, as 24 ... Qc2? would cost the exchange after 25 Q×c2 R×c2 26 Ne7+. SR 24 ... Qa4 25. e5 Ne8 26. Ne3 Qb5 27. Rd2 Qb3 To prevent 28 Qa2. RF 28. Rd3 Qb5 29. Rd2 Qa5 Fine explains that he did not repeat moves here because he was afraid, that after 29 ... Qb3, Reshevsky would reply 30 Qf5, when Black would be forced to sacrifice material on the queenside to maintain the balance. However, he then goes on to say that Black would probably have held the game after 30 ... g6 31 Qg4 Rc2 32 R×c2 R×c2 33 N×c2 Q×c2 34 Ba1 Qd2 35 Rf1 Qe3+ 36 Kh1 Qd3 37 Rg1 Q×a3. For his part, Reshevsky apparently intended to build up his attack in the centre and on the kingside by g3 and f4. 30. Qd1 Qb5 31. g3 g6 Now this defence, although it weakens Black, is forced because of the threat of f4, h4 and f5, which would have left me without any counter-chances at all. RF 32. f4 f5 33. Qf3 Rd8 34. g4 N8g7 35. g×f5 N×f5 Black has little choice: after 35 ... g×f5 the manoeuvring scope of his pieces would be drastically restricted, and he could hardly hope to meet an attack based on the doubling of rooks on the g-file supplemented by the advance of White's h-pawn right down to h6. SR 36. Ng4 After 36 N×f5 g×f5 37 Rg2+ Rg7 Black would be much better off than in the previous note. SR **36 ... Rf7 37. Nf6+ Kh8 38. Rc1 Rxf6!?** At the time I was under the impression that the strongly posted knights would hold everything together, but again I was somewhat too optimistic. However, there seems to be nothing better than giving up the exchange: White is threatening Rg2 followed by Rxg6! at an appropriate moment. RF **39. exf6 Rf8 40. Re1 Rxf6 41. a4!!** A most ingenious sealed move. I had expected 41 Rde2 Qd7 42 Re5 Nc7 43 Rc1 Rf7, when Black's position is quite solid and White can only break through by means of a sacrifice. The great advantages of the move chosen lie in the fact that the square e5 is kept open for White's queen and that the bishop is brought into the game quickly. RF **41 ... Qd7** 41 ... Qxa4 42 Qxd5, opening the diagonal for the bishop, is obviously bad. RF **42. Rf2** If at once 42 Qe2 Kg7 43 Qe5 Nh4 44 Kh1 Nxf4 with adequate counterplay. RF **42 ... Nc7 43. Rc2 Rf7** Black has made it impossible for the white queen to get to e5, for 44 Qe2 would be answered by 44 ... Re7. RF **44. Recl Ne8 45. Ba3! Nf6?** This should have been fatal. Correct was 45 ... Kg7 46 Rc8 Rf6 followed by ... Re6; or 46 Qe2 Nf6 47 Qe5 Nh4—and in either event Black seems to have an adequate defence. SR **46. Rc8+ Kg7 47. Bf8+!!** A bolt from the blue. On 47 ... Rxf8 48 R8c7 wins Black's queen. RF **47 ... Kg8 48. Bd6+?** Overlooking a fairly simple win. The correct continuation was 48 Qxd5!!. If then either 48 ... Nxd5 or 48 ... Qxd5, 49 Bh6+ leads to mate. On 48 ... Nd6 49 Bxd6+ Kg7 50 Bf8+ is the simplest, while on 48 ... Ng7 49 Qxd7 (49 Be7+! Fritz) Rxd7 50 Bxg7+ Kxg7 51 R1c7 leads to an ending which is quite easily won. RF **48 ... Ne8 49. Be5** Looks strong, but the bishop is soon exchanged. RF **49 ... Ne7 50. Ra8** Fine reckoned that on 50 R1c7, 50 ... Qxa4 would be hard to counter. Reshevsky on the other hand believed that the position would be winning after 51 Ra8 a5 52 Rb7. Reshevsky, however, had just four minutes left for his next ten moves. **50 ... Nc6 51. h3 Nxe5 52. dxe5 Qxa4** Now Black has enough threats with his pieces to be able to draw. RF **53. Rcc8 Rf8 54. e6 Kg7 55. e7** 55 Qe3! would have won, for 55 ... Rxf4 56 Rxe8 Qd1+ 57 Kg2 Qf1+ 58 Kg3 Re4 59 Rh8+ wins; 55 ... d4 56 Qe1! wins. SR **55 ... Rxf4 56. Qd3 Rf5!** 57. Rc2 But not 57 Rxe8 Qa1+ 58 Kg2 Rg5+ 59 Kf3 Qf6+ and mates. SR **57 ... Qh4?** The comedy of errors continues. 57 ... Qa1+ 58 Kh2 Qe5+ 59 Qg3 Qxe7 would probably have won for Black. RF **58. Re2?** Most obliging. As Vera Menchik pointed out, 58 Rxe8 wins immediately because Black does not have perpetual check. RF **58 ... Rg5+ 59. Rg2 Rxg2+ 60. Kxg2 Qxe7 61. Qxd5** Both sides must be content with a draw. RF ½–½ Fine 1945, 49–53; Reshevsky, 205–8.

(598) Fine—Evans, H

NYSCA Hamilton (9), 1941 (22 Aug.)
French Defence, Rubinstein Variation [C10]

1. e4 e6 2. d4 d5 3. Nd2 dxe4 4. Nxe4 Nf6 5. Bd3 Nxe4 6. Bxe4 c5 7. Nf3 Nc6 8. Be3 Qb6 9. 0-0

Bd7 10. c3 0-0-0 11. b4 cxb4 12. cxb4 Qxb4
13. Rb1 Qa5 14. Ne5

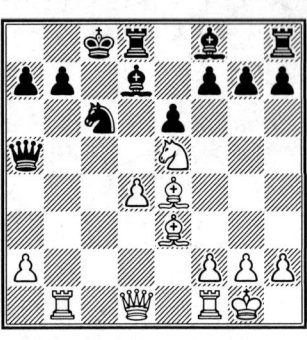

Position after White's 14th move

14 ... Qc7?! 15. Nxf7 Bd6 16. h3 g5 17. Qb3 h5
18. Nxd6+ 1–0

(599) Santasiere, A—Fine

NYSCA Hamilton (10), 1941 (23 Aug.)
Réti Opening [A12]

1. Nf3 d5 2. g3 Nf6 3. Bg2 Bf5 Old but strong. RF **4. c4 c6 5. b3 e6 6. Bb2 Bd6** The London Defence against the Réti System brings back to mind the New York tournament of 1924 and, of course, Réti the great dreamer who injected a fresh romantic spirit into the streams of decadent classicism. AES **7. 0-0 0-0 8. d3 Qe7 9. Nc3** Réti played 9 Nbd2, but later practice has proven the superiority of the text. AES **9 ... dxc4!** New and apparently quite good, the usual line is 9 ... e5, when 10 cxd5 cxd5 11 Nxd5! Nxd5 12 e4, gives White an excellent game. RF **10. e4 Bg4 11. dxc4 e5 12. Qc2 a5 13. h3** Loss of time—Black was going to exchange anyhow. RF; Loss of time; though, to tell the truth, I never expected Fine's simple reply. Best was Na4, followed by c5. AES **13 ... Bxf3! 14. Bxf3 Na6** Black has a clear positional advantage, PCO 313. **15. Rad1 Rfd8 16. Qc1** Or 16 Rd2 Nb4 17 Qc1 Bc5 18 Rfd1 Bd4 19 a3 Na6 and Black's game remains much superior. RF **16 ... Nc5 17. Rd2 Ne6 18. Kg2** Not 18 Ne2, because of 18 ... Ng5, winning a pawn. RF **18 ... Nd4 19. Rfd1 Bb4 20. Rd3 Nd7 21. Ne2?!** Loses quickly. The best chance was 21 Na4 Nc5 22 Nxc5 Bxc5 23 Bxd4 Bxd4, reducing Black's advantage to a minimum. RF; 21 Na4! should have been played. What deterred me was the expected reply 21 ... b5 but, after 22 cxb5 cxb5 23 Nc3, White threatens Nd5 with great effect. AES **21 ... Nc5 22. Re3** White should fight for the initiative with 22 Rxd4!? exd4 23 Nxd4 Ne6 24 Nf5. AW **22 ... Nxf3 23. Rxf3** Sad necessity. On 23 Kxf3 Rxd1 24 Qxd1 Rd8 25 Q- Bd2 wins the exchange. RF **23 ... Nxe4 24. Rfd3** He can get no real compensation for the pawn. If 24 Re3 f5 25 f3 Rxd1 26 Qxd1 Rd8 27 Qc2 Rd2 will soon decide. RF **24 ... Rxd3 25. Rxd3 Bc5 26. f4** The only hope. RF **26 ... exf4 27. Qxf4 Nf2 28. Rf3 Nd3!** But not 28 ... Qxe2?? 29 Qxf7+ and 30 Qxg7 mate. RF **29. Qd2 Re8 30. Kf1** On 30 Q or Rxd3 Qxe2+ wins a piece, while any knight move is refuted by 30 ... Ne1+. RF **30 ... Nxb2! 31. Qxb2 Qe4** White resigned. Since 32 Rf4 allows 32 ... Qh1+ with mate next move, White must give up the exchange, when his position falls apart: 32 Rf2 B×f2 33 K×f2 Qe3+ 34 Kf1 Qf3+ 35 Ke1 Q×g3+ 36 Kd1 Qd3+ 37 Ke1 Q×h3. RF; Coldly exact, yet not without charm; a splendid game above even Fine's usual high average. AES **0–1** Fine, BCM 1941, 290–1; Santasiere, ACB 1941, 77.

(600) FINE–CRUZ, W

NYSCA, Hamilton (11), 1941 (23 Aug.)
Catalan System [E02]

1. d4 Nf6 2. c4 e6 3. Nf3 d5 4. g3 dxc4 5. Qa4+ Bd7 6. Qxc4 Bc6 7. Bg2 Nbd7 8. 0–0 Be7 9. Nc3 Nb6 10. Qd3 Nbd5 11. Ne5 Nb4 12. Nxc6 Nxc6 13. Qb5 Rb8 14. Bxc6+ bxc6 15. Qxc6+ Qd7 16. Qxd7+ Kxd7 17. b3 Rhd8 18. Rd1 Nd5 19. Bb2 Nxc3 20. Bxc3 Rb5 21. Rac1 Ra8 22. Be1 a5 23. Rc4 c6 24. e4 g6 25. Kg2 h5 26. Rd3 Rab8 27. Bd2 R8b7 28. Be3 Rb8 29. Rdc3 Rc8 30. h4 Bb4 31. Rc2 Be7 32. Bd2 Bd6 33. R2c3 Be7 34. a4 Rbb8 35. Rf3 f5 36. exf5 gxf5 37. Bxa5 Rb7 38. Bd2 Rcb8 39. Bf4 Bd6 40. Bxd6 Kxd6 41. a5 Ra7 42. b4 Rg8 43. Rfc3 Ra6 44. Re3 Rg4 45. Re5
Draw agreed. ½–½

In a rapid transit (ten seconds a move) tournament on 8 October held to mark the opening of the new premises of the Manhattan Chess Club at 100 Central Park South, New York, Fine was relegated to second place by Jack Moscowitz. Moscowitz scored 7–2 to finish half a point ahead of Fine.

The other participants were George Shainswit, Israel A. Horowitz, Albert S. Pinkus, Edward S. Jackson, Isaac I. Kashdan and Arnold S. Denker. Fine started with a win over the eventual victor but then lost to Horowitz and Pinkus and had to win all of his games from rounds five to nine to keep in contention. Denker, Kashdan and Pinkus finished on 5½–3½.

In another rapid transit tournament held at the Marshall Chess Club around this time Fine won with a score of 10–2, losing to Louis Levy, Captain of the N.Y.U. chess team. Carl Pilnick also participated.

U.S. Speed Champion, 1942–1945

Fine was unable to attend the 4th United States Championship in 1942 because of his government job in Washington, working for the Foreign Broadcast Monitoring Service of the Federal Communications Commission. He was fluent in French, Spanish, Italian, Dutch, Yiddish, and German.

In 1942 a new series of tournaments was initiated—The United States Rapid Transit Championships. Both qualification and final rounds were held on a single day, games being played at the rate of ten seconds per move. The best players in the country, with the exception of Arthur Dake, took part in these events. Fine showed himself to be the supreme American exponent of the form, rarely losing while chalking up victories over his major rivals. He won the first four events, the only ones in which he participated, with a score around 95 percent. The games were apparently all recorded, but only a selection have surfaced so far.

During the height of the war Fine only participated in one strong event—the fifth United States Chess Championship. His friend Arnold Denker was, however, in devastating form and once more Reuben failed to get his name on the trophy.

New York Metropolitan League, April, 1942

Although now resident in Washington, Fine continued to represent his club occasionally. Arnold Denker essayed an enterprising sacrifice against the Fianchetto development which Fine used to counter his Sicilian Dragon. The play became rather wild, but Fine eventually consolidated his extra piece to win in the ending.

Fine   1   Denker   0

(601) FINE–DENKER, A

Metropolitan League, New York, 1942 (4 April)
Sicilian Dragon [B70]

1. e4 c5 2. Nf3 Nc6 3. d4 cxd4 4. Nxd4 Nf6 5. Nc3 d6 6. Nde2 g6 7. g3 Bg7 8. Bg2 0–0 9. 0–0 Bd7 10. b3 b5?! 11. Nxb5 Nxe4

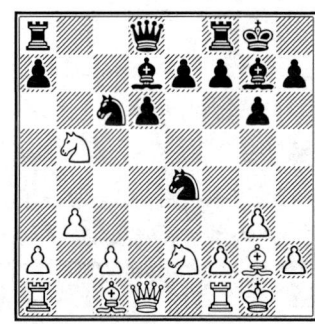

Position after Black's 11th move

12. Bxe4!? Bxa1 13. c3 Qa5 14. a4 a6 15. b4 Nxb4 16. cxb4 Qxb4 17. Bxa8 axb5 18. Bg2 Qxa4 19. Nf4 Bd4 20. Nd5 Re8 21. Be3 Bxe3 22. fxe3 Qd1 23. Rxd1 Kf8 24. Nb6 Bg4 25. Rb1 Kg7 26. Rxb5 Rb8 27. Kf2 Be6 28. Ke1 Bc4 29. Rb4 Be6 30. Kd2 Bf5 31. Nd5 Rxb4 32. Nxb4 Bd7 33. Kc3 Be6 34. Nd5

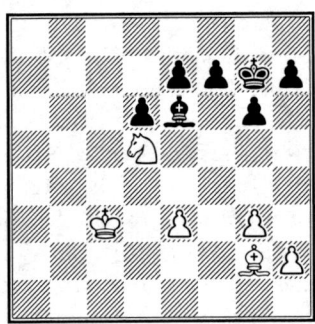

Position after
White's 34th move

34 ... Kf8 35. Kb4 Bd7 36. Ka5 Ke8 37. Kb6 Kd8
38. Nb4 Bg4 39. Nc6+ Kd7 40. Nd4 Bd1 41. Bc6+
Kd8 42. Bb5 h5 43. h3 g5 44. Bc4 e6 45. Kc6 Ke7
46. Be2 Bxe2 47. Nxe2 d5 48. Nd4 h4 49. gxh4
gxh4 50. Nf3 Kf6 51. Kc5 Kf5 52. Kd4 Kf6 53. Nxh4
Kg5 54. Nf3+ Kf5 55. Ne5 f6 56. Nd3 Kg5 57. Nc5
Kh4 58. Nxe6 Kxh3 59. Kxd5 Kg4 60. Nd4 Kg5
61. Ke6 Kg6 62. Nf3 Kg7 Black resigned. 1–0 Peter
Lahde

1st U.S. Speed
Championships Preliminaries,
New York, July 5, 1942

"In the United States Lightning Tourney the Federation added another major event to its program of championship tournaments. Held at the Capitol Hotel in New York
on July 5, 1942, this contest brought together 48 of the
country's finest players for 22 rounds of sizzling chess all
played in the course of a single day. Notwithstanding the
combined strain of the speed play, a move every 10 seconds,
and the pressure of tournament competition, the quality of
play was of a remarkably high order. Position judgment was
sound, while attack and defense alike were conducted brilliantly. Preliminary rounds were played in the morning
session for qualifying purposes." (U.S.C.F. Yearbook) Gamescores unavailable.

1st U.S. Speed Championships
Finals, New York, July 5, 1942

"Reuben Fine proved himself to be the champion of
the speed artists with 10 victories in the championship section, followed by U.S. Champion Samuel Reshevsky. They
met in the 10th round and Reshevsky, a half point down
had to play for a win or be content with second place. With
a draw in hand, Reshevsky tried to force a win, wavered in
the endgame and was finally numbered among Fine's victims. It was the tenth straight win for Fine. In the last round,
with the title already won, he relaxed and dropped his game
to Herbert Seidman." (U.S.C.F. Yearbook) All scores from
the U.S. Rapid Transit tournaments are taken from the
U.S.C.F. Yearbooks unless otherwise stated.

(602) Fine–Kashdan, I

U.S. Lightning championship, New York, 1942 (5 July)
Grünfeld Defence, 4 Bf4 [D93]

1. d4 Nf6 2. c4 g6 3. Nc3 d5 4. Bf4 Bg7 5. e3 0–0
6. Qb3 c6 7. Nf3 dxc4 8. Bxc4 Nbd7 9. Be2 Nb6
10. e4 Nfd7 11. 0–0 c5 12. dxc5 Nxc5 13. Qa3 Ne6
14. Bg3 Bd7 15. Rfd1 Qc8 16. Rac1 Qc5?! 17. b4
Qc8 18. Nd5 Qe8 19. Ne5 Nxd5 20. exd5 Ng5
21. Qe3 h6?! 22. Rc7 Bc8 23. Rdc1 Nh7 24. Qc5
b6 25. Qxe7 Nf6 26. Qxe8 Rxe8

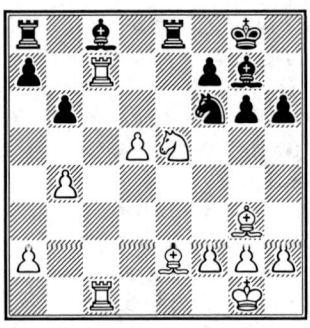

Position after
Black's 26th move

27. Bf3 Nh5 28. d6 Nxg3 29. hxg3 Bxe5 30. Bxa8
Be6 31. d7 Rf8 32. Rxa7 Bxd7 33. Rxd7 Rxa8 34. Re1
Bc3 35. Ree7 Rf8 36. a3 Bf6 37. Re3 Rc8 38. Rd6
Kg7 39. Rf3 Rc1+ 40. Kh2 Be7 41. Rxb6 1–0

(603) Fine–Shainswit, G

U.S. Lightning championship, New York, 1942 (5 July)
Catalan System [E07]

1. d4 Nf6 2. c4 e6 3. Nc3 d5 4. Nf3 Nbd7 5. g3
Be7 6. Bg2 0–0 7. 0–0 dxc4 8. a4 c5 9. Bf4 Nd5
10. Bd2 Nb4 11. Ne4 cxd4 12. Nxd4 a5 13. Nb5
Nb6 14. Be3 N6d5 15. Bc5 Bd7 16. Bxe7 Qxe7
17. Na3 Rac8 18. Qd4 Rfd8 19. Rfc1 e5 20. Qa7 f5
21. Nc3 Nxc3 22. bxc3 Nc6 23. Qxb7

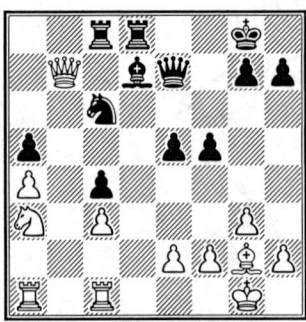

Position after
White's 23rd move

23 ... e4 24. Nxc4 Rb8 25. Qc7 Rdc8 26. Qd6 Qf7
27. Ne3 Be6 28. Rab1 Rxb1 29. Rxb1 Qd7 30. Qxd7
Bxd7 31. Rb5 g6 32. f3 exf3 33. Bxf3 Kf7 34. Nc4
Ke7 35. Nb6 Rd8 36. Nxd7 Kxd7 37. Rb7+ Kd6
38. Rb6 Rc8 39. Kf2 Kd7 40. Bxc6+ Rxc6 41. Rxc6
Kxc6 1–0

(604) PINKUS, A—FINE

U.S. Lightning championship, New York, 1942 (5 July)
French Defence, Tarrasch Variation [C08]

1. e4 e6 2. d4 d5 3. Nd2 c5 4. exd5 exd5 5. Ngf3
Nf6 6. Bb5+ Bd7 7. Bxd7+ Nbxd7 8. 0–0 Be7
9. dxc5 Nxc5 10. Re1 0–0 11. Nd4 Qd7 12. N2f3
Bd6 13. Ne5 Bxe5 14. Rxe5 Nfe4

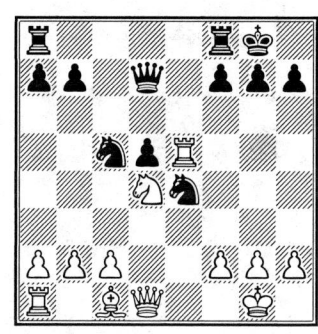

*Position after
Black's 14th move*

15. c3 (15 Nf5!) 15 ... f6 16. Rh5 g6 17. Rh4 Nd6
18. Bh6 Rf7 19. f3 Re8 20. Qc2 Rfe7 21. Rf1 Ne6
22. Qd1 Nc4 23. b3 Nd6 24. Bc1 Ng7 25. Bf4
Ndf5 26. Rh3 Nxd4 27. Qxd4 Ne6 28. Qd2 d4
29. Bg3 dxc3 30. Qxc3 Qd4+ 31. Qxd4 Nxd4
32. Bf2 Ne2+ 33. Kh1 Nf4 34. Rg3 Re2 35. Bxa7
Re1 36. Rg1 Rxg1+ 37. Kxg1 Ne2+ 38. Kf2 Nxg3
39. hxg3 Ra8 40. Bd4 Rxa2+ 41. Ke3 Rxg2 0–1

(605) FINE—RESHEVSKY, S

U.S. Lightning championship, New York (10), 1942 (5 July)
Grünfeld Defence, 4 Bf4 [D93]

1. d4 Nf6 2. c4 g6 3. Nc3 d5 4. Bf4 Bg7 5. Qb3
c6 6. e3 0–0 7. Nf3 dxc4 8. Bxc4 Nbd7 9. 0–0
Nb6 10. Be2 Bf5 11. Rfd1 a5 12. a4 Be6 13. Qc2
Nfd5 14. Be5 Nb4 15. Qd2 f6 16. Bg3 Nc4 17. Qc1
Nd6 18. e4 Qb6 19. Qd2 Rfd8 20. Rac1 Bb3
21. Re1 e5

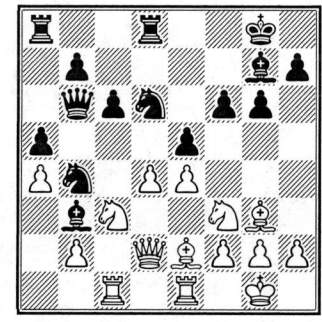

*Position after
Black's 21st move*

22. Qe3 Nc2 23. Rxc2 Bxc2 24. Rc1 Bb3 25. h4
Nc4 26. Bxc4+ Bxc4 27. dxe5 Qxe3 28. fxe3 fxe5
29. Nxe5 Be6 30. Nf3 Rd3 31. Bf4 Rad8 32. e5
R3d7 33. Kf2 Bd5 34. Nd4 Re8 35. Nxd5 Rxd5
36. Nf3 h6 37. Ke2 g5 38. hxg5 hxg5 39. Bxg5

Bxe5 40. Nxe5 Rexe5 41. Bf6 Re6 42. Bc3 Rg6
43. Rh1 b6?! 44. Rh8+ Kf7 45. Rb8 c5 46. Rb7+
Ke8 47. g4 Rd7 48. Rb8+ Rd8 49. Rb7 Rd7 50. Rb8+
Kf7 51. g5 Re6 52. Rh8 Rde7 53. Rh3 Kg6 54. Bf6
Rh7 55. Rxh7 Kxh7 56. Kd3 Kg6 57. e4 Re8 58. e5

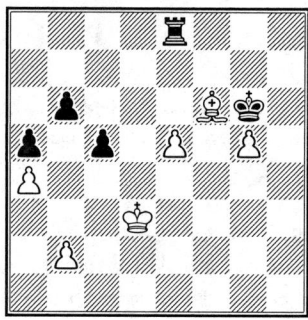

*Position after
White's 58th move*

58 ... Kf5 59. Kc4 Ke6 60. g6 Rc8 61. g7 Kf7
62. Kb5 c4 63. Kxb6 Rb8+ 64. Kxa5 Kg8 65. e6
Re8 66. Kb5 Rxe6 67. Bc3 Re4 68. a5 Kf7 69. a6
Re8 70. a7 Ke6 71. Kc6 Rd8 72. Bd4 Re8 73. Bb6
Rg8 74. Bc7 1–0

(606) SEIDMAN, H—FINE

U.S. Lightning championship, New York (11), 1942 (5 July)
French Defence, Burn Variation [C11]

1. e4 e6 2. d4 d5 3. Nc3 Nf6 4. Bg5 dxe4 5. Nxe4
Be7 6. Bd3 b6 7. Nf3 Bb7 8. Qe2 Nbd7 9. 0–0
0–0 10. Rfe1 h6 11. Bh4 Nd5 12. Bg3 Kh8 13. a3
f5 14. Nc3 f4 15. Qxe6 N7f6?! 16. Bh4 Bc8 17. Qe2
g5 18. Nxd5 Nxd5 19. Qe4 Rf7 20. c4 gxh4 21. cxd5
Rb8 22. Qg6 Qf8 23. Ne5 1–0 Peter Lahde

Match—Newcomers vs. Established Players, Chess Divan, Washington, 29 July, 1942

While stationed in the capital during the war years Fine was a member of the Washington Divan Chess Club. According to Dr. Richard Cantwell, the grandmaster often gave exhibitions and lectures in the capital.

His first recorded non-exhibition activity took the form of a match held over twenty-seven boards between players who had joined the Divan in 1942 and those who were already members of the club in 1941. Many people had moved to the capital to work for the government after the United States had entered the war in December 1941. Fine's opponent was to have been the former prodigy William Ewart Napier, but he was unable to play.

Mugridge 0   Fine 1

(607) MUGRIDGE, D—FINE

Team Match Washington, 1942 (29 July)
Queen's Pawn Opening [A45]

1. d4 Nf6 2. Bf4 e6 3. e3 c5 4. c3 d5 5. Nd2
Bd6 6. Bg3 0–0 7. Bd3 b6 8. e4 Be7 9. e5 Nfd7
10. f4 cxd4 11. cxd4 Ba6 12. Qc2 Bxd3 13. Qxd3
Nc6 14. Ngf3 Nb4 15. Qb3 a5 16. 0–0 a4 17. Qd1
b5 18. Qe2 Qb6 19. Rfc1 Rfc8 20. Rxc8+ Rxc8
21. a3 Nc2 22. Rc1 Rc6 0–1 *Washington Post*, 9 August,
1942.

Washington Divan Championship, October–December, 1942

John Hilbert has researched this event and uncovered
much detail about its course (Hilbert 2002, 65–94). As
usual when outside New York, Fine outclassed the field,
making a clean score in the Divan Championship of 1942.
The veteran Anglo-American William Ewart Napier (whose
father, one would assume, must have supported the Liberal
Prime Minister Gladstone) started this event but did not
complete his programme, he was involved in two car crashes
and then moved to Philadelphia. This was the third time
that Fine had been due to meet Napier in competition, and
the third time that the encounter did not take place. The
Divan President Donald Mugridge also started the event
but retired, on the advice of his doctor, after only two
rounds had been played. The unfortunate Eaton had scored
a win over Napier in Round 3 and a draw from Mugridge
in Round 1.

		1	2	3	4	5	6	7	8	
1	Fine	*	1	1	1	1	1	1	1	7
2=	Mengarini	0	*	½	0	½	1	1	1	4
2=	Shapiro	0	½	*	0	1	½	1	1	4
2=	Stark	0	1	1	*	½	0	½	1	4
5	Rousseau	0	½	0	½	*	1	½	½	3
6	Fox	0	0	½	1	0	*	1	0	2½
7	Eaton	0	0	0	½	½	0	*	1	2
8	Ponce	0	0	0	0	½	1	0	*	1½

Fine participated in a Rapid Transit tournament held
either during December 1942 or January 1943, possibly the
former as a similar event was held at the Divan in December 1943, when Fine scored seven wins and one draw (with
Mugridge) to take first place.

(608) EATON, V–FINE

Washington Divan Championship (1), 1942
Sicilian Defence [B33]

1. e4 c5 2. Nf3 Nc6 3. d4 cxd4 4. Nxd4 Nf6
5. Nc3 e5 6. Nxc6 bxc6 7. Bc4 Bc5 8. 0–0 d6
9. h3 Be6 10. Qe2 0–0 11. Be3 Nd7 12. Bd3 Qh4
13. Bxc5 Nxc5 14. Rad1 a5 15. a4 Rad8 16. Qe3 f5
17. exf5 Bxf5 18. Bxf5 Rxf5 19. Rd2 Qb4 20. Rfd1
d5 21. g4 Rff8 22. Qxe5 Qxb2 23. Qe3 Qb4
24. Rd4 Qb8

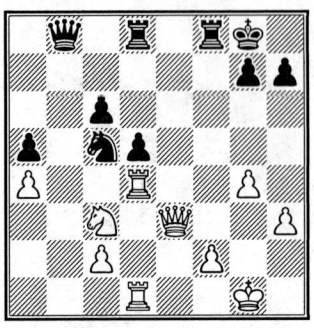

Position after
Black's 24th move

25. Qe7 Qd6 26. Qxd6 Rxd6 27. Ne4 Nxe4
28. Rxe4 Rdf6 29. Re2 Rf4 30. Rb1 Rxa4 31. Rb7
Raf4 32. Ra7 h5 33. gxh5 R4f5 34. Rxa5 Kh7
35. Ra7 Rg5+ 36. Kf1 Rf4 37. Re6 Rc4 38. Re2?!
(38 h6!) 38 … Rxh5 39. Rc7 Rh6 40. Ke1 Rc3
41. Ree7 Rg6 42. Kd2 Rxh3 43. Re3 Rxe3 44. Kxe3
Re6+ 45. Kd3 Kh6 46. c4 dxc4+ 47. Kxc4 Rf6
48. Kd4 Rxf2 49. Rxc6+ Rf6 50. Rc2 g5 51. Ke3
Kh5 52. Rh2+ Kg4 53. Rg2+ Kh4 54. Rh2+ Kg3
(White 2:49 Black 2:48) 0–1 *The Chess Review*, January 1943.

(609) FINE–MUGRIDGE, D

Washington Divan Championship (2), 1942
Caro-Kann Defence, Tartakower Variation [B12]

1. e4 c6 2. d4 d5 3. f3 e6 4. Nc3 Bb4 5. e5 c5
6. a3 cxd4 7. axb4 dxc3 8. bxc3 Qc7 9. f4 Ne7
10. Nf3 Bd7 11. Bd3 Qxc3+ 12. Bd2 Qc7 13. 0–0
Qb6+ 14. Kh1 Bb5 15. Bxb5+ Qxb5 16. Nd4 Qc4
17. Be3 0–0 18. Nb3 Na6 19. Na5 Qb5 20. c3
Rfc8 21. Qd2 Nf5

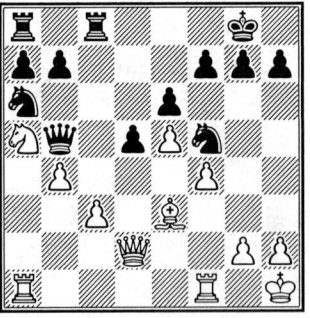

Position after
Black's 21st move

22. g4 d4 23. gxf5 dxe3 24. Qxe3 exf5 25. Qf3
Rc7 26. Rfd1 g6 27. c4 Qxb4 28. Rdb1 Qe7 29. Nxb7
Rb8 30. Nd6 Rxb1+ 31. Rxb1 Qd8 32. Qb3 Qa8+
33. Kg1 Qc6 34. Qc3 h5 35. Qd2 Kh7 36. Qd5
Nc5 37. Nxf7 (37 … Ne4! AW) 1–0 *The Chess Review*, Jan-
uary 1943, 13.

(610) ROUSSEAU, H–FINE

Washington Divan Championship (3), 1942
Sicilian Defence [B23]

1. e4 c5 2. Nc3 e6 3. g3 d5 4. exd5 exd5 5. d4 cxd4 6. Qxd4 Nf6 7. Bg5 Be7 8. Bg2 Nc6 9. Qd2 d4 10. Nce2 0–0 11. Bxf6 Bxf6 12. Nf3 Qb6 13. 0–0 Bf5 14. c4 dxc3 15. Nxc3 Rfd8 16. Nd5 Qxb2 17. Nxf6+ Qxf6 18. Qf4 Rd7 19. Nh4 Be6 20. Qxf6 gxf6 21. Rfb1 Rad8 22. Be4 Na5 23. Rb5 b6 24. Rh5 Rd1+ 25. Rxd1 Rxd1+ 26. Kg2 Bxa2 27. Bxh7+ Kf8 28. Bc2 Bd5+ 29. Kh3 Be6+ 30. Nf5 Bxf5+ 31. Rxf5 Rd6

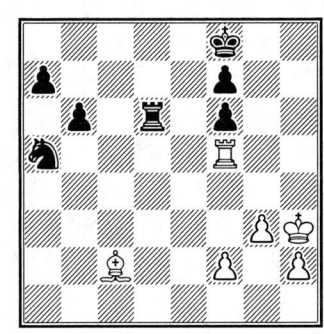

Position after
Black's 31st move

32. Kg4 Nc6 33. Be4 Nd4 34. Rd5 Rxd5 35. Bxd5 b5 36. Kf4 Ne2+ 37. Ke3 Nc3 38. Bf3 b4 39. Kd3 a5 40. Kc4 f5 41. Bc6 Kg7 42. f3 Kf6 43. f4 Ne4 44. Ba4 Nd2+ 45. Kd3 Nf3 46. Kc4 Nxh2 47. Kb5 Nf1 48. Kxa5 Nxg3 49. Kxb4 Ne2 50. Kc4 Nxf4 51. Kd4 Kg5 52. Ke3 Kg4 53. Kf2 Nd3+ 54. Ke3 Ne5 55. Bc2 f4+ 56. Kf2 f3 57. Bb1 Kf4 58. Bc2 Ng4+ 59. Ke1 f2+ 60. Ke2 Ne3 (White 1:40 Black 0:55) 0–1 Contributed by Mutchler (Lahde).

(611) FINE—STARK, M

Washington Divan Championship (4), 1942
Nimzowitsch-Indian Defence, Rubinstein Variation [E46]

1. d4 Nf6 2. c4 e6 3. Nc3 Bb4 4. e3 0–0 5. Nge2 d5 6. a3 Be7 7. Ng3 c5 8. dxc5 dxc4 9. Qc2 Bxc5 10. Bxc4 Nc6 11. 0–0 a6 12. b4 Be7 13. Bb2 Qc7 14. Bb3 Ne5 15. Qe2 Rd8 16. Nce4 Nxe4 17. Nxe4 Bd7 18. Rac1 Qb8 19. Nc3 Bc6 20. Ba1 Bf6 21. f4 Ng6 22. f5 exf5 23. Rxf5 Rd7 24. Nd5 Bxa1 25. Rxa1 Qd8 26. e4 Ne7

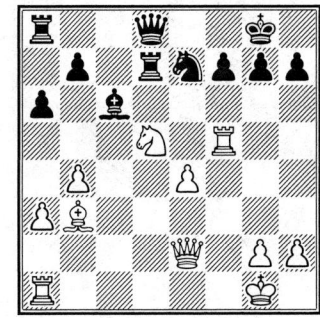

Position after
Black's 26th move

27. Rxf7! Nxd5 28. Rxd7 Qxd7 29. exd5 Bb5 30. Qe6+ Qxe6 31. dxe6 Kf8 32. a4 Bc6 33. Rf1+

Ke8 34. Rf7 Rd8 35. Rxg7 Rd3 36. Bc2 Rd2 37. Bxh7 1–0 *The Chess Review*, January 1943, 12.

(612) PONCE, L—FINE

Washington Divan Championship (5), 1942
Nimzowitsch-Indian Defence, Classical Variation [E33]

1. d4 Nf6 2. c4 e6 3. Nc3 Bb4 4. Qc2 Nc6 5. Nf3 d6 6. a3 Bxc3+ 7. bxc3 e5 8. h3 h6 9. e4 0–0 10. Bd3 Nh7 11. 0–0 Qf6 12. Be3 Bxh3 13. gxh3 Qxf3 14. Kh2 Ng5 15. Bxg5 hxg5 16. d5 Ne7 17. Rg1 Qf4+ 18. Kg2 Ng6 19. Kf1 Qh2 20. Rxg5 Nf4 21. Rd1 f5 22. exf5

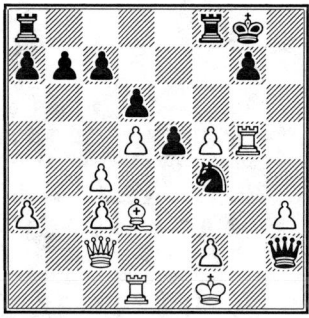

Position after
White's 22nd move

22 ... Qh1+ 23. Rg1 Qxh3+ 24. Ke1 Ng2+ 25. Kd2 Qh6+ 26. Ke2 Nf4+ 27. Ke1 Qh2 28. Rf1 Ng2+ 29. Ke2 e4 30. Bxe4 Rae8 31. Rh1 Qf4 32. Rd4 Rxf5 33. Kd1 Qxf2 34. Qxf2 Rxf2 35. Bxg2 Rxg2 36. Rd2 Rxd2+ 37. Kxd2 g5 (White 1:59 Black 1:32) 0–1 *The Chess Review*, January 1943.

(613) FOX, Λ FINE

Washington Divan Championship (6), 1942
Alekhine's Defence, Four Pawns Attack [B03]

1. e4 Nf6 2. e5 Nd5 3. c4 Nb6 4. d4 d6 5. f4 dxe5 6. fxe5 Nc6 7. Nf3 Bf5 8. Bd3?! Nxd4 9. Ng5 e6 10. 0–0 Be7 11. Nxf7 Kxf7 12. g4 Rf8 13. gxf5 Nxf5 14. Bxf5 Qxd1 15. Rxd1 exf5 16. b3 Bc5+ 17. Kg2 Rad8 18. Nc3 Bd4 19. Bb2

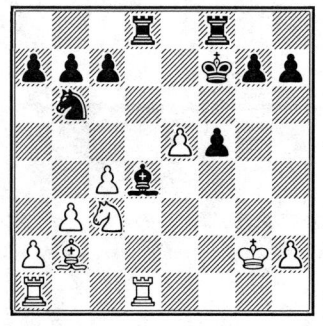

Position after
White's 19th move

19 ... Bxe5 20. Na4 Bxb2 21. Nxb2 Rfe8 22. Kf3 Nd7 23. Nd3 Kf6 24. Nf4 Ne5+ 25. Kg3 c6

26. h4 g6 27. c5 h6 28. Ng2 g5 29. Kf2 Nd3+
30. Kf3 Nxc5 31. Rac1 Nd3 32. Ra1 g4+ 33. Kg3
h5 34. Rf1 Rd4 35. Rad1 Ree4 36. Rd2 f4+
37. Nxf4 Nxf4 38. Rxd4 Rxd4 39. Rxf4+ Rxf4
40. Kxf4 c5 41. a4 b6 42. Ke4 a6 43. Kf4 b5
44. axb5 axb5 45. Ke4 c4 46. bxc4 bxc4 (White
1:55 Black 0:32) 0−1 *Washington Star*, 8 January, 1943.

(614) FINE—MENGARINI, A

Washington Divan Championship (7), 1942
Queen's Gambit Declined [D45]

1. d4 d5 2. c4 c6 3. Nc3 Nf6 4. e3 e6 5. Nf3 a6
6. c5 Nbd7 7. Na4 Qc7 8. Bd3 e5 9. Bc2 Be7
10. 0−0 e4 11. Nd2 Nf8 12. f3 exf3 13. Qxf3 Bg4
14. Qf2 Bh5 15. h3 Bg6 16. Bxg6 Nxg6 17. Nb6
Rd8

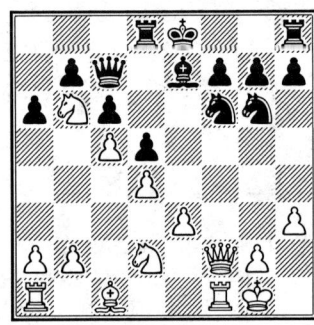

*Position after
Black's 17th move*

18. e4 dxe4 19. Nxe4 0−0 20. Nc3 Nh5 21. Be3 Ng3
22. d5 Bh4 23. d6 Qb8 24. Rfe1 Rde8 25. Nd7
Ne4 26. Qc2 (White 0:58 Black 1:59) 1−0 *The Chess
Review*, January 1943.

(615) FINE—SHAPIRO, O

Washington Divan Championship (8), 1942
Nimzowitsch-Indian Defence, Spielmann Variation [E22]

1. d4 Nf6 2. c4 e6 3. Nc3 Bb4 4. Qb3 Nc6 5. d5
exd5 6. cxd5 Bxc3+ 7. Qxc3 Nxd5 8. Qxg7 Qf6
9. Qxf6 Nxf6 10. f3 Rg8 11. g4 d5 12. Bf4 Nb4
13. Rc1 c6 14. a3 Na6 15. e3 Bd7 16. Bxa6 bxa6
17. Ne2 h5 18. h3 Ke7 19. Nd4 Rac8 20. Rc5 hxg4
21. hxg4

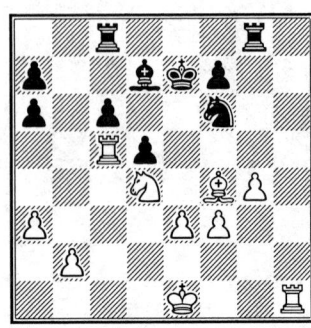

*Position after
White's 21st move*

21 ... Ne8 22. Rh6 Rg6 23. Rxg6 fxg6 24. b4 Ng7
25. Ra5 Ne6 26. Rxa6 Nxd4 27. exd4 Rf8 28. Bg5+
Kd6 29. Ke2 Ra8 30. Bf4+ Ke7 31. Kf2 Kd8 32. b5
cxb5 33. Rxg6 a5 34. g5 b4 35. axb4 a4 36. Rg8+
Be8 37. g6 Ra6 38. g7 Rg6 39. b5 Ke7 40. b6 1−0
Washington Star, 3 January,1943.

2nd U.S. Speed Championships
Preliminaries, New York, July 4, 1943

"The second Annual U.S. Lightning Tourney was
played at the Capitol Hotel in New York on July 4, 1943.
    The event, which captured the public imagination the
year before, was well attended and attracted 48 players. The
morning play was given over to preliminary rounds to determine who should be entitled to participate in the championship division." (*U.S.C.F. Yearbook*)

2nd U.S. Speed Championships Finals,
New York, July 4, 1943

"Reuben Fine repeated his triumph of the year before
in even more convincing fashion by winning every one of
his games from the cream of the country's chess talent.
Fine's games were an exemplification of master play even
without regard to time, and at 10 seconds per move were
marvels of efficiency." (*U.S.C.F. Yearbook*) First prize was $50,
second prize $25.

(616) FINE—ADAMS, W

National Rapid Transit, New York, 1943 (4 July)
Fianchetto Grünfeld [D02]

1. Nf3 Nc6 2. d4 d5 3. g3 g6 4. Bg2 Bg7 5. 0−0
Nf6 6. c4 dxc4 7. Qa4 0−0 8. Rd1 Be6 9. Nc3
Nd5 10. e4 Nb6 11. Qc2 Nxd4 12. Nxd4 Bxd4
13. Nd5 c6?! 14. Rxd4 cxd5 15. Bh6 Re8 16. exd5
Bf5 17. Qc3 f6 18. g4 Bd7 19. g5 Kf7 20. Re1 Bf5
21. Re6

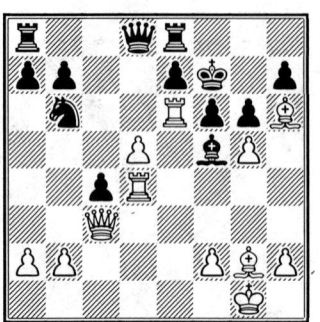

*Position after
White's 21st move*

21 ... Nxd5?! 22. Bxd5 Qxd5 23. Rxf6+ exf6
24. Rxd5 Re6 25. Rd7+ Ke8 26. Rxh7 Rc8 27. Rh8+
Kd7 28. Rxc8 1−0

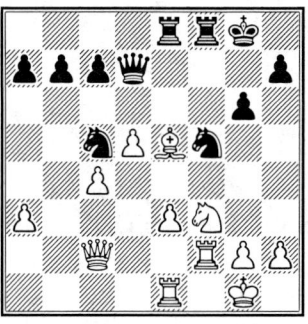

Position after White's 23rd move

23 ... Qd8?! 24. Ba1 Ne4 25. Qb2
Qf6 26. Qxf6 Nxf6 27. Bxf6 Rxf6
28. e4 Ne7 29. Nd4 Ra6 30. Ne6
Rxa3 31. Ref1 h5 32. Rf8+ Rxf8
33. Rxf8+ Kh7 34. Rf7+ Kh6
35. h4 g5 36. hxg5+ Kg6 37. Rg7
Mate. 1–0

(618) FINE—KUPCHIK, A

National Rapid Transit, New York, 1943
(4 July)
French Defence [C05]

1. e4 e6 2. d4 d5 3. Nd2 Nf6 4. e5
Nfd7 5. Bd3 c5 6. c3 Nc6 7. Ne2
Qb6 8. Nf3 Be7 9. 0–0 h6 10. a3
c4 11. Bc2 Na5 12. Rb1 Nb3 13. Be3
a5 14. a4 Nb8 15. Nd2 Nxd2
16. Qxd2 Bd7 17. f4 g6 18. g4
h5 19. f5 gxf5 20. gxf5 Nc6
21. Nf4 0–0–0 22. b3 cxb3
23. Rxb3 Qc7 24. Rfb1 Rdg8+
25. Kh1 Nd8 26. f6 Bf8 27. R3b2
Bc6 28. h3 Bh6 29. Kh2 h4
30. Bd1 Rg3 31. Bf2 Rhg8 32. Bxg3
Rxg3 33. Bg4 Bd7 34. Rc1 Nc6
35. Rg1

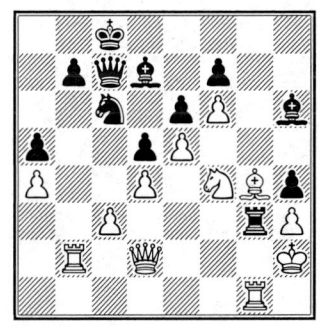

Position after White's 35th move

35 ... Rxg1 (35 ... Nxe5!) 36. Kxg1 Nxe5 37. dxe5
Qxe5 38. Qd4 Qe1+ 39. Kg2 Qg3+ 40. Kf1 Bxf4
41. Qc5+ Bc6 42. Qf8+ Kc7 43. Qxf7+ Kb8 44. Qf8+
Kc7 45. Qe7+ Bd7 46. Qc5+ Bc6 47. f7 Qd3+

Fine on the cover of the leading U.S. chess periodical with his trophy for winning the National Rapid Transit tournament for the second time. He made a perfect 11–0 score in the finals to win ahead of Reshevsky and Kashdan among others.

(617) FINE—GREEN, M

National Rapid Transit, New York, 1943 (4 July)
Nimzowitsch-Indian Defence, Rubinstein Variation [E40]

1. d4 Nf6 2. c4 e6 3. Nc3 Bb4 4. e3 d5 5. a3 Bxc3+
6. bxc3 Nc6 7. cxd5 Qxd5 8. c4 Qd6 9. Nf3 e5
10. d5 Ne7 11. Bb2 Nd7 12. Bd3 f6 13. Nh4 g6
14. 0–0 Nc5 15. Bc2 0–0 16. f4 Bd7 17. Qd2 Ba4
18. fxe5 fxe5 19. Nf3 Bxc2 20. Bxe5 Qd7 21. Qxc2
Nf5 22. Rae1 Rae8 23. Rf2

48. Re2 Qd1+ 49. Re1 Qd3+ 50. Re2 Qd1+ 51. Kg2 d4+ 52. Qxc6+ bxc6 53. f8Q Be3 54. Rxe3 1–0

(619) FINE—SUSSMAN, H

National Rapid Transit, New York, 1943 (4 July)
Queen's Indian Defence [E15]

1. d4 Nf6 2. Nf3 b6 3. c4 Bb7 4. g3 e6 5. Bg2 c5 6. d5 exd5 7. Nh4 d6 8. 0–0 g6 9. cxd5 Bg7 10. e4 0–0 11. Nc3 Nbd7 12. f4 a6 13. a4 c4 14. Be3 Rc8 15. h3 Nc5 16. Qc2 Nh5 17. Kh2

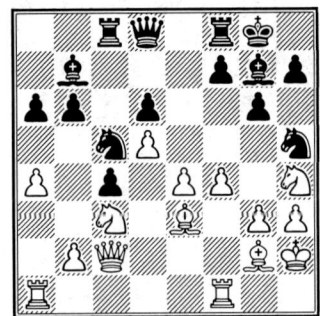

Position after White's 17th move

17 ... f5 18. exf5 gxf5 19. Nxf5 Nb3 20. Rae1 Qf6 21. g4 Bh8 22. Be4 Ng7 23. g5 Qd8 24. Nh6 Mate. 1–0

(620) KASHDAN, I—FINE

National Rapid Transit, New York, 1943 (4 July)
Nimzowitsch-Indian Defence, Classical Variation [E33]

1. d4 Nf6 2. c4 e6 3. Nc3 Bb4 4. Qc2 Nc6 5. Nf3 d6 6. g3 0–0 7. Bg2 e5 8. dxe5 dxe5 9. 0–0 Bxc3 10. Qxc3 Ne4 11. Qc2 Nd6 12. Rd1 Bf5 13. Qa4 Qe7 14. Be3 Bd7 15. Rac1?!

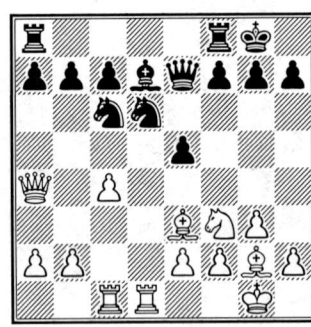

Position after White's 15th move

15 ... Nd4 16. Qa3 Nxe2+ 17. Kh1 Nxc1 18. Rxc1 Bc6 19. Qc3 Rae8 20. b4 a6 21. Qb3 Kh8 22. a4 Nf5 23. Bc5 Nd6 24. b5 axb5 25. cxb5 Bxf3 26. Bxf3 b6 27. Bb4 e4 28. Bg2 f5 29. Rc6 f4 30. Bxd6 cxd6 31. Rxb6 e3 32. fxe3 fxe3 33. Qc3 e2 34. Qe1 Qf6 35. Rc6 Qf1+ 36. Bxf1 Rxf1+ 0–1

(621) RESHEVSKY, S—FINE

National Rapid Transit New York, 1943 (4 July)
Queen's Gambit Accepted [D28]

1. d4 d5 2. c4 dxc4 This defence was chosen because I needed only half a point to clinch the title, and because Reshevsky has always found it difficult to refute. 3. Nf3 Nf6 4. e3 e6 5. Bxc4 c5 6. 0–0 a6 7. Qe2 In our game at Semmering-Baden 1937, Reshevsky tried 7 a4, but the results were none too good. 7 ... cxd4 8. Rd1 b5 8 ... Nc6 transposes into more regular lines. 9. Bb3 Be7 10. a4 10 Nxd4 offers little real hope of an advantage. 10 ... bxa4! The simplest way to preserve equality. 11. Rxd4 Qc7 12. Bxa4+ Bd7 13. Nc3 After 13 Bxd7+ Nbxd7 the a-pawn is indirectly defended. 13 ... Bxa4 14. Raxa4 0–0

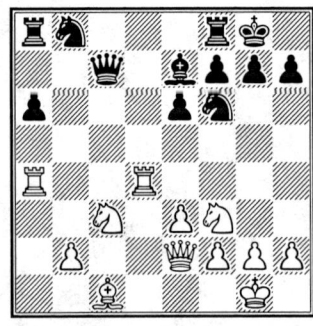

Position after Black's 14th move

15. e4 The only way he can play for an attack, but the advance is two edged. 15 ... Nc6 16. Rdc4 Rfd8 17. e5 Nd5 18. Nxd5 Rxd5 19. h3 If 19 Qc2, Qd7 is more than enough. 19 ... Qd7 20. Bf4 a5 Black has now managed to consolidate the centre and queenside, and has a little the better of it. 21. Ra1 Nb4 After which doubling rooks would be uncomfortable. 22. Kh2 Rd8 23. Bg5 A desperate exchange, but he feels compelled to be aggressive. 23 ... h6 24. Bxe7 Qxe7 Note how the strongly centralized black rook dominates the board. 25. Rac1 Nd3 26. R1c3 Qb7 27. b3 Qb8 28. Rc7 Qb4 Time pressure! I was confident that consistent hammering at the white pawns would pay dividends, but could not find the most exact method. 29. g3 His best drawing chance was 29 Rc8. 29 ... Qb6 30. Kg2 Fine suggested 30 Kg1, but that loses the exchange to 30 ... Nc5. AW 30 ... Qb5 30 ... Nc5 is still the simplest, but Fine was simply trying to keep up the pressure on the e-pawn and threaten ... Nf4+. 31. Qe4 Nxe5 32. Qf4 f5 White's attack is easily stopped, despite his apparent command of the seventh rank. 33. Nxe5 Rxe5 34. Re7 The sacrifice 34 Rxg7+ would have been hopeless. 34 ... Qd5+ 35. Kh2 Re1 36. Rf3 His best chance was 35 Qf3, but he still had visions of a mating attack, since a draw was no better than a loss. 36 ... Qd1 37. Rxg7+ Despair. If 37 g4, g5! wins the queen or mates soon. 37 ... Kxg7 38. g4 Qd6 0–1
Fine 1945, 61–3.

(622) SEIDMAN, H—FINE

National Rapid Transit, New York, 1943 (4 July)
Sicilian Defence, Nimzowitsch Variation [B29]

1. e4 c5 2. Nf3 Nf6 3. e5 Nd5 4. Nc3 Nc7 5. d4
cxd4 6. Nxd4 Nc6 7. f4 g6 8. Bc4 Bg7 9. Be3 0-0
10. 0-0 d6 11. Nxc6 bxc6 12. exd6 exd6 13. Bd4
Bf5 14. Bxg7 Kxg7 15. Qd4+ Qf6 16. Rad1 d5
17. Qxf6+ Kxf6 18. Bd3 Rfe8 19. Bxf5 Kxf5 20. Rfe1
Re6 21. Ne2 c5 22. b4 Kf6 23. bxc5 Rae8 24. Kf1
Re4 25. g3 Rc4

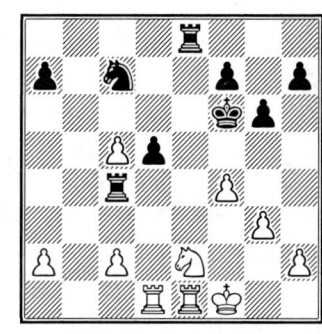

*Position after
Black's 25th move*

26. c6 Rxc6 27. Nd4 Rxe1+ 28. Kxe1 Ra6 29. Ra1
Ne6 30. Nxe6 fxe6 31. Kd2 Kf5 32. Kd3 Kg4
33. c3 Kh3 34. Re1 Kxh2 35. g4 Kg3 36. f5 exf5
37. gxf5 gxf5 38. Re5 f4 39. Rg5+ Kf2 40. Rxd5
f3 41. Rh5 h6 42. c4 Kg2 0-1

Match with Herman Steiner,
Washington, March, 1944

In March Fine had a short warm up before the U.S.
Championship, playing a practice match with Herman
Steiner, against whom he had not lost since Pasadena 1932.
Fine won the first three games, the third being an excellent
illustration of play with the bishops. In the fourth and final
game Steiner missed his only chance for some consolation
in a complicated position.

	1	2	3	4	
Fine	1	1	1	½	3½
Steiner	0	0	0	½	½

(623) STEINER, H—FINE

Match, Washington (1), 1944 (March)
Torre Attack [A46]

1. d4 Nf6 2. Nf3 e6 3. Bg5 h6 4. Bxf6 Qxf6 5. e4
c5 6. Nc3 cxd4 7. e5! Qd8 8. Qxd4 Nc6 9. Qe3 d5
10. exd6 Bxd6 11. 0-0-0 Qe7 12. Kb1 Bc5 *(see
diagram)* 13. Qe4 Bxf2 14. Bb5 0-0 15. g4 Qc5
16. Rhf1 Qe3 17. Rxf2 Qxf2 18. g5 hxg5 19. Nxg5
f5 20. Qc4 Qxh2 21. Bxc6 bxc6 22. Qxc6 Qh6
23. Qxa8 Qxg5 24. Qxa7 f4 25. Ne4 Qe5 26. Rg1

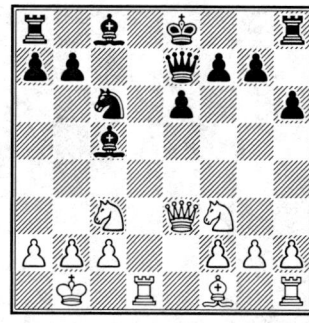

*Position after
Black's 12th move*

f3 27. a4 Rf7 28. Qa8 Qc7 29. Ng5 f2 30. Rf1 Qc4
31. Qh1 Qxf1+ 32. Qxf1 Ba6 33. Qxa6 f1Q+
34. Qxf1 Rxf1+ 35. Ka2 Rf5 36. Nxe6

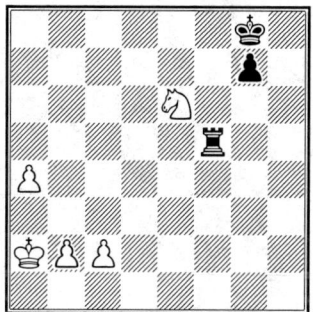

*Position after
White's 36th move*

36 ... g5 37. Nxg5 Rxg5 38. b4 Kf7 39. a5 Rg3 40. a6
Ke6 41. a7 Rg8 42. b5 Kd6 43. c4 Kc5 0-1

(624) FINE—STEINER, H

Match, Washington (2), 1944 (March)
Catalan System [E00]

1. d4 d5 2. c4 e6 3. Nf3 Nf6 4. g3 Nbd7 5. Bg2
Bb4+ 6. Bd2 Be7 7. 0-0 0-0 8. Qc2 Ne4 9. Bf4
c6 10. Nfd2 Nxd2 11. Nxd2 f5 12. f3 g5 13. Be3 f4
14. Bf2 Nf6 15. e4 Bd7 16. Rae1 Bb4 17. exd5 exd5
18. Re5 Kh8 19. c5 Bxd2 20. Qxd2 Ng8 21. gxf4
gxf4 22. Qe1 Rf7 23. Bh4 Qf8 24. Kh1 Rg7 25. Rg1
Qf7 26. Rg5 Re8 27. Qf2

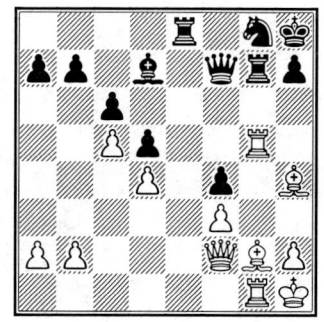

*Position after
White's 27th move*

27 ... Rxg5 28. Bxg5 Ne7 29. Qh4 Ng6 30. Bf6+
Kg8 31. Bf1 Re3 32. Qxf4 Re6 33. Qb8+ Qf8
34. Qxb7 Re1 35. Qb8 Be8 36. Qd8 Re6 37. Be5

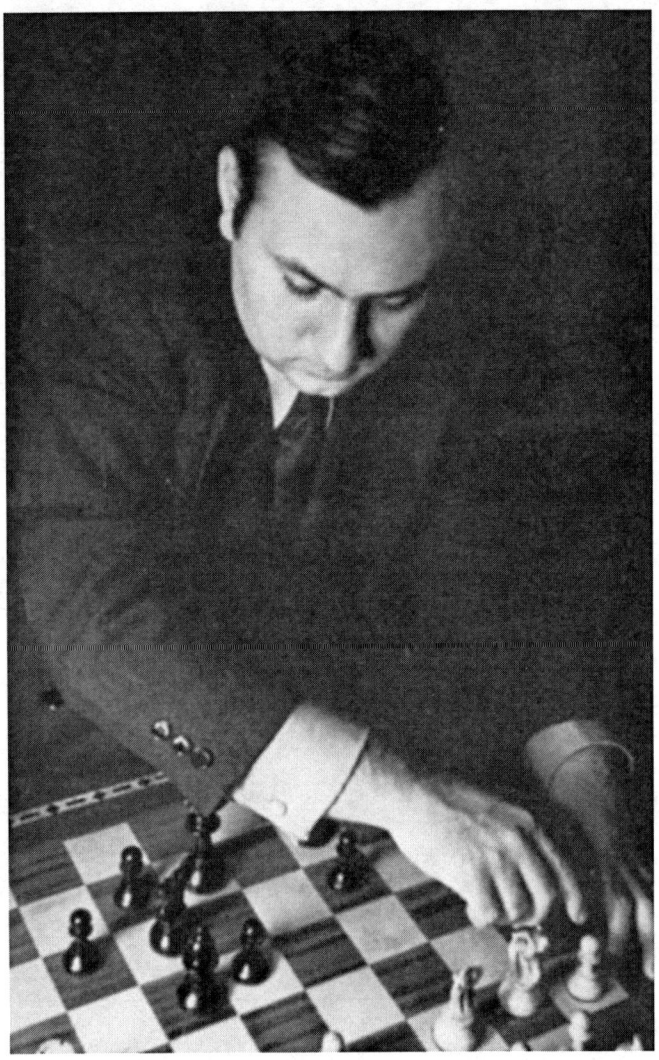

Analysing a position

Qxf3+ 38. Bg2 Qe2 39. Qc7 Bf7 40. Qc8+ Re8
41. Qxc6 Rxe5 42. dxe5 Qxe5 43. Qd6 Qd4 44. c6
Kg7 45. c7 1–0

(625) STEINER, H—FINE

Match, Washington (3), 1944 (March)
Torre Attack, Wagner Gambit [A46]

1. d4 Nf6 2. Nf3 e6 3. Bg5 An inferior continuation.
3 ... c5 In the first match game I tried 3 ... h6 with satisfactory results. However, the text is better because White will
be compelled to exchange sooner or later in any case. **4. e4!**
Qa5+ On the alternative 4 ... Qb6 5 Bxf6! gxf6 6 d5!
Qxb2 7 Nbd2 White has enough compensation for the
pawn. **5. Nbd2** This came as a surprise. I had expected
5 Bd2 Qb6 6 e5 Ne4 (6 ... cxd4!? Fritz) 7 Bc1! cxd4 8 Qxd4
Qxd4 9 Nxd4 Bc5 10 Be3 Nc6 11 Nxc6 Bxe3 12 fxe3 dxc6
with a slight advantage for Black. **5 ... cxd4** 5 ... Nxe4 is
tempting. This could then force a draw—a sufficient refutation of White's strategy—with 6 b4! Qxb4 7 Rb1 Qa5 8 Rb5

Qc3 9 Rb3 Qa5 10 Rb5, but after 6 b4! Qxb4 7 Rb1 he can
also play for more with 7 ... Nc3! 8 Rxb4 Nxd1 9 Rb3! Nxf2
10 Kxf2 Nc6—the three pawns are enough for the piece.
However, it is doubtful whether either side can win the ending. **6. Bxf6 gxf6 7. Nxd4 Nc6 8. N4b3** After this
White remains on the defensive for the rest of his life. More
energetic was 8 Nxc6 bxc6 (9 ... dxc6 was good enough for
equality, but stodgy) 9 Bd3 d5 10 0-0 Bb7 11 Qe2 0-0-0
with an interesting struggle in sight. **8 ... Qe5!** Compelling
a favourable simplification. **9. c3** Despite the traditional
taboos, on 9 Bd3 I would have pounced upon the b-pawn
with gusto and enjoyed the meal. **9 ... f5 10. Qe2** Forced.
10 ... fxe4 11. Qxe4 d5 To play on the c-file. The alternative procedure would be an attempt to force ... d4, but on
11 ... Qxe4+ 12 Nxe4 d5 13 Nf6+! Ke7 14 Nh5 is frustrating.
12. Qxe5 Nxe5 13. Bb5+ A welcome offer. Since Black's
queen's bishop has only potential value, 13 Be2 would have
been harder to meet. **13 ... Bd7 14. Bxd7+ Kxd7**

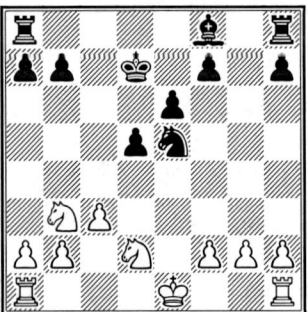

*Position after
Black's 14th move*

15. Ke2 Black with eventual command of the half-open
g- and c-files, undoubtedly has the better of it, but the technical problems are none too easy. There are two main plans
possible: one, play on the g-file with ... Rag8, ... h7-h5-h4, ...
Rh6, the other a break on the queenside, with c4 as a pivot.
At first I intended to adopt the first plan, but later decided
that the break on the kingside is too hard to execute, and
not decisive in any case. **15 ... Bd6** To reply to f4 with
immediate pressure against the kingside. However, it would
undoubtedly have been better to forget the kingside entirely
for the time being and play ... Rc8 at once. **16. Nd4** White
is reduced to passivity; he cannot even improve his position significantly. A break with f4-f5 would merely serve to
strengthen Black's centre pawns. **16 ... Rac8 17. Rad1 a6**
Preparing the queenside advance. **18. g3 b5 19. f4 Nc4**
20. Nxc4 Rxc4 21. a3

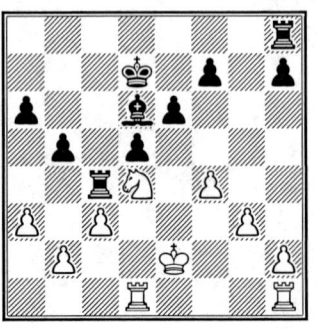

*Position after
White's 21st move*

21 ... a5! Finally the thrust ... b4 cannot be stopped. **22. Nb3** By far the best. After 22 Nxb5 Rb8 23 Nxd6 Rxb2+ 24 Rd2 Rxd2+ 25 Kxd2 Kxd6 26 Rb1 Kc7! 27 Kd3 Ra4 28 Rb3 h5, the rook and pawn ending would be won for Black. **22 ... Ra8** Unwelcome but necessary. On 22 ... b4 23 cxb4 axb4 24 a4! Ra8 25 a5 Bc7 26 Rd2! the pawn cannot be taken and White suddenly has strong counterplay. **23. Ra1 Bf8** Regrouping to increase the pressure against the white queenside. Now we see why the bishop should have gone to g7 immediately. **24. Rhd1 Bg7 25. Rd3 Ke7** The pin is uncomfortable; under certain circumstances ... d4 might be desirable. **26. Kf3 h5 27. Re1?** White is in a peculiar dilemma; there is no direct threat, there is not even any obvious breakthrough plan for Black, and yet pure passivity does not look too good. Steiner does not like positions where he has to wait for the other fellow to force the issue, and so decides to invite complications, which were most agreeable to me. After 27 Ke2, or 27 Nd2, there is no clear win in sight for Black, although he undoubtedly retains the upper hand. **27 ... b4 28. Rxd5** On 28 Nd2 instead, the sacrifice 28 ... bxa3! wins; 29 Nxc4 dxc4 30 Rd2 Rb8! and Black will get at least bishop and two connected passed pawns for the exchange. **28 ... bxc3 29. Rxa5** Or 29 Nxa5 Rc7! for if then 30 bxc3 Bxc3 and the knight is lost. **29 ... Rd8** The simplest: the passed c-pawn will decide. **30. Ra7+ Kf8**

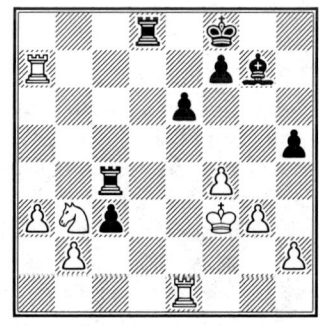

Position after Black's 30th move

31. Na5 Here we see the weakness of the knight in such positions. 31 bxc3 Rxc3+ 32 Re3 Rdd3! costs a piece. Consequently the knight cannot take part in the attack, and must rush off to a useless corner to save its skin. Meanwhile the bishop can both support the passed pawn and defend the king position. **31 ... Ra4 32. b3** On 32 b4 Rxa3 the knight is defended, but ... c2+ is too strong. **32 ... Rxa3 33. f5!** A last try, which looks promising, but ... 33 ... exf5! Not 33 ... Bd4? 34 fxe6 fxe6 35 Nc6!, and White can probably save himself. **34. Ree7 Bd4!** Simple and conclusive. All White's pieces are now *en prise*. **35. Rxf7+ Kg8 36. Rad7** The seventh rank is useless because the bishop commands the vital g7 square. **36 ... Rxd7 37. Rxd7 Bb6** Quickest; 37 ... c2 is also good enough. **38. Nc4 c2** White resigned. **0–1** Fine 1945, 64–7.

(626) FINE—STEINER, H

Match, Washington (4), 1944 (March)
Two Knights Defence [C59]

1. e4 e5 2. Nf3 Nc6 3. Bc4 Nf6 4. Ng5 d5 5. exd5 Na5 6. Bb5+ c6 7. dxc6 bxc6 8. Be2 h6 9. Nf3 e4 10. Ne5 Bc5 11. c3 Qc7 12. f4 Nb7 13. d4 exd3 14. Qxd3 0–0 15. Nd2 Nd6 16. Bf3 Bf5 17. Qe2 Nd5 18. Nb3 Bb6 19. c4 Nb4 20. c5 Nc2+ 21. Kf2 Bxc5+ 22. Nxc5 Nxa1 23. g4 Bh7 24. Na6 Qe7 25. f5 Qh4+ 26. Kg2 Rae8 27. Bf4 Nxf5 28. Rxa1 Nd4 29. Qf2 Nxf3 (29 ... Qxf2+ 30 Kxf2 f5!) 30. Qxf3 f6 31. Bg3 Qg5 32. Bf4 Qh4 33. Bg3 Qg5 34. Bf4 Draw agreed. ½–½

5th U.S. Championship, New York, April 15–May 7, 1944

Amongst those invited to play in this, the 5th biennial tournament, Reshevsky, the four time champion, preferred to concentrate on his accountancy examinations, and Kashdan, vice champion in 1942, had to decline on doctor's orders.

"The first three rounds of play found Denker and Horowitz in the lead with scores of 3–0 apiece, while Fine was at their heels, handicapped by his 1st round draw with Pinkus. In the 4th Denker set the pace by winning from Horowitz a game that the latter could have drawn, save for an impulsive move. Thence onwards it was a five-man race with Denker ever in the lead and Fine, Horowitz, Steiner and Pinkus pounding after him. While Denker was taking undisputed first place in the 4th, Fine was gaining a brilliant victory over Shainswit (a game which won Fine the Second Brilliancy Prize), and Steiner was fighting a difficult draw with Weinstock. In the 2nd Steiner and Pinkus had met and drawn. In the 7th Round the critical moment came when Denker met Fine in what proved to be the deciding game of the tournament. Playing aggressively, Denker built up a strong attack that had Fine squirming so that he resigned in 25 moves. This game gained Denker the First Brilliancy Prize. While Shainswit was holding Denker to a draw, Fine defeated Steiner and moved into a tie with Pinkus for second place. Then in the 12th Horowitz and Pinkus drew, leaving Fine in undisputed possession of the second spot, one point behind Denker. But Fate gave both leaders a scare then, for the youthful Rothman had a forced win against Denker but failed to make the right continuation and lost the game, while Weinstock had Fine caught in a trap but let the experienced veteran wiggle out of it and gain victory. In the 13th Denker hurdled one of the last barriers when he bested Pinkus in a hard fought battle. In the 15th Horowitz and Fine met in a tussle that wavered long in the balance. First Horowitz won the exchange and could have won the game, then Fine missed a winning continuation and the fireworks then sputtered to a well earned draw. In the 16th Steiner held Denker to a draw while Fine was winning from DiCamillo, and again the two leaders were separated by only one point. But in the final round Denker offered a draw to Altman after fourteen moves, and when Altman accepted, the title was Denker's. Thereupon Fine agreed a draw with Neidich and was content with second place." (*U.S.C.F. Yearbook*)

		1	2	3	4	5	6	7	8	9	10	11	12	13	14	15	16	17	18	
1	Denker	*	1	1	½	1	½	½	1	1	1	1	1	1	1	1	1	1	1	15½
2	Fine	0	*	½	1	½	1	1	1	1	1	1	½	1	1	1	1	1	1	14½
3=	Horowitz	0	½	*	0	½	1	1	1	1	1	1	1	1	1	1	1	1	1	14
3=	Steiner	½	0	1	*	½	½	1	1	1	1	1	½	1	1	1	1	1	1	14
5	Pinkus	0	½	½	½	*	½	1	1	1	½	1	1	1	1	1	1	1	1	13½
6	Shainswit	½	0	0	½	½	*	1	½	0	1	½	½	1	1	1	½	1	1	10½
7	Altman	½	0	0	0	0	0	*	½	0	1	0	1	1	1	1	1	1	1	9
8=	Adams	0	0	0	0	0	½	½	*	1	0	1	1	½	0	1	½	1	1	8
8=	Almgren	0	0	0	0	0	1	1	0	*	0	0	1	0	1	1	1	1	1	8
10=	DiCamillo	0	0	0	0	½	0	0	1	1	*	½	½	½	0	0	1	1	1	7
10=	Weinstock	0	0	0	½	0	½	1	0	1	½	*	0	0	½	1	0	1	1	7
12=	Isaacs	0	0	0	0	0	½	0	0	0	½	1	*	1	½	0	1	1	1	6½
12=	Neidich	0	½	0	0	0	0	0	½	1	½	1	0	*	0	1	1	½	½	6½
12=	Rothman	0	0	0	0	0	0	0	1	0	1	½	½	1	*	1	½	0	1	6½
15	Stromberg	0	0	0	0	0	0	0	0	0	1	0	1	0	0	*	1	1	1	5
16	Chernev	0	0	0	0	0	½	0	½	0	0	1	0	0	½	0	*	1	1	4½
17	Gladstone	0	0	0	0	0	0	0	0	0	0	0	0	½	1	0	0	*	1	2½
18	Persinger	0	0	0	0	0	0	0	0	0	0	0	0	½	0	0	0	0	*	½

(627) FINE—PINKUS, A

U.S. Championship, New York (1), 1944 (15 April)
Nimzowitsch-Indian Defence [E20]

1. d4 Nf6 2. c4 e6 3. g3 d5 4. Bg2 Bb4+ 5. Nc3 0–0 6. Nf3 dxc4 7. 0–0 c5 8. dxc5 Bxc5 9. Qa4 Nc6 10. Qxc4 Be7 11. Rd1 Qa5 12. g4 Rd8 13. Bd2 Qb4 14. Qxb4 Bxb4 15. g5 Ne8 16. Ne4 Bxd2 17. Nfxd2 Kf8 18. Nc4 Rd5 19. Ne3 Rxd1+ 20. Rxd1 Ke7 21. Nc4 Rb8 22. Nc5 Nd8 23. Ne5 Nd6 24. Rc1 f6 25. gxf6+ gxf6 26. Nc4 Nf5 27. Rc3 b6 28. Nb3 Ba6 29. Ne3 Nxe3 30. Rxe3 Rc8 31. Rh3 Bxe2 32. f4 h5 33. Nd4 Bg4 34. Ra3 a5 35. h3 Rc4 36. hxg4 Rxd4 37. gxh5 Rxf4 38. Rb3 Rh4 39. Rxb6 Rxh5 40. a4 Rc5 41. b4 axb4 42. Rxb4 f5 43. Rb5 Rc1+ 44. Bf1 Ra1 45. a5 Nc6 46. a6 Kd6 47. Rb6 e5 48. Kf2 Kc5 49. Rb5+ Kd4 50. Rb6 Ra2+ 51. Kg3 Kc5 52. Rb5+ Kd4 53. Rb6 Ra3+ 54. Kf2 Kc5 55. Rb5+ Kd4 56. Rb6 Kd5 57. Rb5+ Kd6 58. Rb6 Kc7 59. Rb7+ Kc8 60. Bc4 Nd4 Draw agreed. **½–½**

(628) FINE—ADAMS, W

U.S. Championship, New York (2), 1944 (16 April)
Albin Counter Gambit [D08]

1. d4 d5 2. c4 e5 3. dxe5 d4 4. Nf3 Nc6 5. Nbd2 Bb4 6. a3 Bxd2+ 7. Qxd2 Bg4 8. b4 Bxf3 9. exf3 Nxe5 10. Bb2 Qe7 11. 0–0–0 0–0–0 12. f4 Nc6 13. g3 f5 14. b5 Nb8 15. Bh3 Nh6 16. Rhe1 Qf7 17. Qb4 a5 18. Qb3

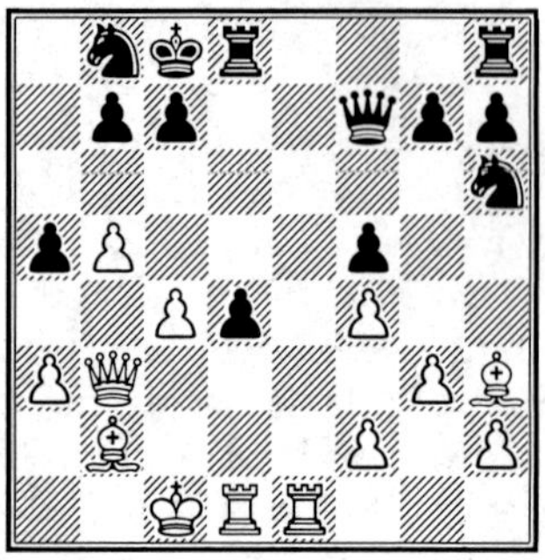

Position after White's 18th move

18 ... Rhe8 19. Rxe8 Rxe8 20. Bxd4 Qh5 21. Bg2 Qe2 22. c5 c6 23. bxc6 Nxc6 24. Be5 Qa6 25. Bxg7 Ng8 26. Qf7 Black resigned. **1–0**

(629) ALMGREN, S—FINE

U.S. Championship, New York (3), 1944 (17 April)
Queen's Gambit Declined [D43]

1. d4 Nf6 2. c4 e6 3. Nf3 This move is not considered to be as strong as 3 Nc3, because White cannot make use of the Pillsbury Attack to secure such a tight grip on the game as usual, should Black transpose into the Queen's Gambit Declined as here. Also Black has reasonably good equalizing chances with 3 ... b6; whereas after 3 Nc3, neither 3 ... Bb4 4 Qb3!, nor 3 ... d5 4 Bg5, leave Black an easy task to secure an equal game. The alternative 3 g3, which prevents the Queen's Indian, is a more promising line if White wants to avoid the humdrum book lines. **3 ... d5 4. Bg5** Now White should have taken advantage of Black's failure to play the Queen's Indian by playing 4 g3, for it has not yet been conclusively demonstrated that Black has any way of securing absolute equality against this modern line which gives White considerable pressure. **4 ... h6!** This practically forces the exchange of the white bishop at once, and after 5 Bxf6 Qxf6 6 Qb3 c6 7 Nc3 Nd7 8 e4 dxe4 9 Nxd4 Qf4 10 Bd3, Black may either play 10 ... e5 11 0–0 Be7 as in the game Euwe–Fine, A.V.R.O. 1938, or 10 ... Nf6 11 Ng3 Be7 12 0–0 0–0 13 Rad1 Rd8 14 Bb1 Qc7 15 Qc2 Bd7 16 Ne5 Be8 as in Purdy–L. Steiner, Sydney 1937. Black then has a very solid and safe position, and can play to open the game by ... c5, whereupon his bishops would become a potent factor. **5. Bh4** Now Black may take and hold the gambit pawn without disadvantage, thus securing early winning prospects. **5 ... Bb4+** The correct move. If 5 ... dxc4 (given in MCO as advantageous) 6 Qa4+ recovers the pawn with a satisfactory game. **6. Nc3** After 6 Nbd2, 6 ... dxc4 threatening ... c3 appears to be equally satisfactory. **6 ... dxc4 7. e3 b5 8. a4** The only way to try to weaken the Black queenside pawns, but he no longer has f3 free for the queen to attack on the long diagonal, and that makes a lot of difference between the present variation and the Queen's Gambit proper. **8 ... c6 9. Be2** 9 Nd2 Bb7 10 Be2 Nbd7 11 Bf3 Qc8 12 0–0 a6 leaves Black quite comfortably placed. **9 ... a6 10. 0–0** It is clear that his best chance is to develop as quickly as he can and try to make something of the occupation of the centre by e4, but Black is not seriously embarrassed by this plan. **10 ... Bb7 11. Qc2 Be7** The bishop has new work to do, and his purpose in going to b4 has been accomplished with the firm establishment of the queenside pawns. **12. e4 0–0 13. e5** An impetuous move from which White cannot expect to derive any great advantage since he leaves his d-pawn very weak and his pieces are not well placed for an immediate assault on the black king. 13 Rad1, followed by Ne5 and f4 would be the best way of working up an enduring attacking position. **13 ... Ne8** It was advisable thus to prevent White from occupying d6 with Ne4-d6, after the exchange of bishops. **14. Bxe7** There was still less to be gained from retreating the bishop, which would be unable to take any effective part in the game for a long time thereafter. **14 ... Qxe7 15. Ne4** Black was now threatening to undermine White's centre pawns with ... c5, but as is quickly apparent he could no longer be effectively prevented from carrying out this freeing advance, and White, therefore, no longer has anything tangible to show for his pawn. **15 ... Nd7 16. Rad1 c5 17. dxc5** The exchange only enhances the liberation of the black position. Somewhat better would be 17 Rd2, and if 17 ... cxd4 18 Rxd4 Nc5 19 Nxc5 Qxc5 20 Rfd1, but his position would still be inadequate in the long run. **17 ... Nxc5 18. Nxc5 Qxc5 19. Qc3** He must protect the e-pawn, which Black threatens to win by 19 ... Bxf3. **19 ... Nc7** Black's game almost plays itself. White is hopelessly weak on the light squares and has not the ghost of an attacking chance. If now 20 Rd7 Rfd8 21 Rfd1 Bd5, and White can only exchange rooks. **20. Nd2** In order to try to play f4 with some attacking prospects, but it only allows Black to pile on the attack. 20 Rd2 Nd5 21 Qd4 would put up a longer resistance. **20 ... Nd5 21. Qg3 Nb4** Preventing 22 Ne4 and threatening ... Rad8 followed by ... Nd3. **22. Kh1 Rad8 23. f4 Nc2** White has attained his objective of advancing the f-pawn, but only at the cost of weakening another square (e3). The text at once exploits this new weakness, and the threat of ... Ne3 leaves White without any satisfactory move, for if 24 Rf2 Ne3 wins at least the exchange. **24. Bf3**

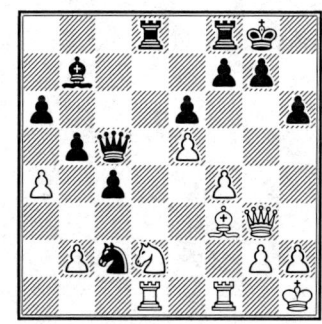

Position after White's 24th move

24 ... Ne3! 25. Qf2 For if 25 Bxb7 Nxf1 26 Rxf1 Rxd2 winning easily. **25 ... Qd4 26. Nb3** If now 26 Bxb7 Nxd1 (not 26 ... Nxf1 27 Qxf1) 27 Qxd4 Rxd4 29 Rxd1 Rfd8 and wins. **26 ... Qxf4 27. Rxd8 Rxd8 28. Re1 Nxg2!** A crushing reply. White has no better reply than to capture the knight, for if 29 Rf1 Bxf3 30 Qxf3 Qxf3 31 Rxf3

cxb3 32 Kxg2 bxa4 and Black clearly wins the ending with the greatest of ease. **29. Kxg2 Qg4+ 30. Kf1 Bxf3 31. Nc5 Qh3+ 32. Kg1 Rd4 33. Qf1 Rg4+ 34. Kf2 Rg2+** White resigned. **0–1** W. Ritson-Morry, *BCM* 1944, 256–8.

(630) FINE—SHAINSWIT, G

U.S. Championship, New York (4), 1944 (18 April)
Queen's Gambit Declined, Slav Defence [D17]

1. Nf3 Nf6 2. c4 c6 3. d4 d5 4. Nc3 dxc4 5. a4 Bf5 6. Ne5 A move which received a good deal of attention some years ago. RF **6 ... Nbd7** This is believed to be refuted; correct is 6 ... e6 and if 7 f3 Bb4. RF **7. Nxc4 Qc7 8. g3 e5 9. dxe5 Nxe5 10. Bf4 Nfd7 11. Bg2 Be7** White gained the advantage after both 11 ... Be6 12 Nxe5 Nxe5 13 0–0 Be7 14 Qc2 Rd8 15 Rfd1 0–0 16 Nb5 Alekhine–Euwe, match game 1, 1935, and 11 ... f6 12 0–0 Rd8 13 Qc1 Be6 14 Ne4! Bb4 15 a5 0–0 16 Nxe5 Nxe5 17 Nc5 Euwe–Alekhine, match game 1, 1937. AW **12. 0–0 Be6 13. Nxe5 Nxe5 14. a5** A strong alternative is 14 Qc2, threatening 15 Nb5 (for example 15 ... Qb8 16 Bxe5 Qxe5 17 Bxc6+ bxc6 18 Qxc6+ winning the rook). However, Black could parry the threat by 14 ... 0–0. **14 ... a6 15. Ne4 Rd8 16. Qc2**

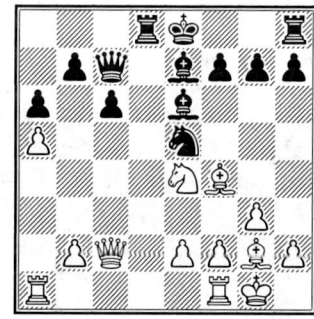

Position after White's 16th move

16 ... 0–0 17. Ng5 To get the two bishops and to weaken the kingside. RF (White stands slightly better, *PCO* 206.) **17 ... Bxg5 18. Bxg5 f6 19. Bf4 Rfe8 20. Be4 g6 21. Bd2** Now that the long diagonal has been shorn of most of its defenders, the bishop will try to take possession. **21 ... Bd5 22. Bc3 Bxe4 23. Qxe4 Qf7 24. Rad1 Rd5** Hoping to build up a solid position in spite of the isolated pawn if White captures. **25. Rxd5 cxd5 26. Qf4**

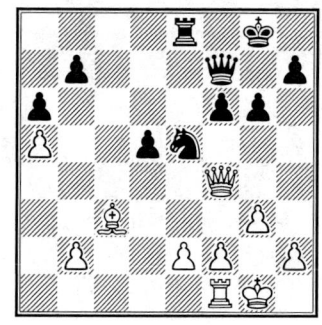

Position after White's 26th move

26 ... Nc6 27. e3 Kg7 28. Rd1 Qe6? Allowing the combination. However, on 28 ... Rd8 29 g4 should win in the long run. 29. Rxd5!! The whole of the [following] combination is based on the weakness of the long black diagonal, and the insecure position of the black king which is its consequence. In itself this sacrifice is obvious enough, but over the board it is hardly possible to calculate that it leads to a forced win for White. ME 29 ... Qxd5 30. Qxf6+ Kh6 31. Qg7+ White repeats moves here to gain time. In practice a player has to contend not only with the problems on the board, but also with his clock; that is to say he must keep an eye on how much time he has in hand. ME 31 ... Kg5 Black is compelled to repeat moves. If 31 ... Kh5 32 h3! is conclusive (but not 32 Qxh7+?? Kg4! 33 Qxg6+ Kf3 and Black should win). After 32 h3 the main variation is 32 ... Ne5 33 Qxh7+ Kg5 34 f4+! (but not 34 Bxe5 Rxe5 35 f4+ Kf5 which only draws) Kf5 35 fxe5 Qd1+ 36 Kf2 Qc2+ 37 Ke1! Qc1+ 38 Ke2 Qc2+ 39 Bd2. Now Black has only one more check. With three pawns for the exchange and Black's king in the centre of the board, White wins without any trouble. RF 32. Qf6+ Kh6 33. Qf4+ The strongest continuation. ME 33 ... Qg5 If instead 33 ... g5 34 Qf6+ Kh5 35 h3! wins: 35 ... Qe6 36 g4+ Kh4 37 Qf3 Qd6 38 Kg2! and mate cannot be stopped; or 35 ... Re6 36 Qf7+; or 35 ... Ne5 36 Bxe5; or finally 35 ... g4 36 hxg4+ Kxg4 37 Qf4+ Kh5 38 g4+ Kh4 39 Bf6+ and mate next. RF (It seems that 35 ... Re4!! would have allowed Black to avoid the mate: 36 Qg7 h6 37 g4+ Rxg4+ 38 hxg4 Kxg4 39 Qxh6, but the ending would be lost. AW) 34. Bg7+ Kh5 35. Qf3+ Qg4 36. Qd5+ Qf5 If 36 ... g5 37 Qf7 mate. But the best defence was 36 ... Ne5! Then after 37 Bxe5 Qf5 38 Qd1+ Kh6 39 Bc3 it is still by no means easy for White to convert his advantage into a win. ME 37. Qd1+ Qg4 There is no choice, for if 37 ... Kg5 38 h4 mate. ME 38. f3 Qe6 The queen must stay on the diagonal to prevent 39 f4 mate. RF 39. g4+ Kg5

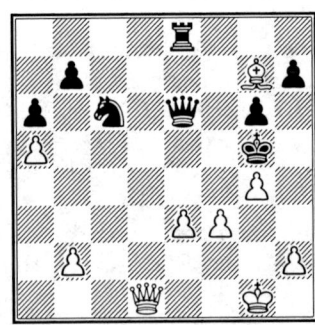

Position after Black's 39th move

40. Kg2!! A quiet move, with deadly effect. ME 40 ... Qxe3 41. h4+ Kxh4 41 ... Kf4 also leads to mate after 42 Qd6+. AW 42. Qh1+ and mate next move. ME Black resigned. This amazing combination is comparable in its length and complexity to Lasker's great win from Pillsbury at St. Petersburg 1896. Mugridge 1–0 Fine 1945, 25–8; *U.S.C.F.* 1944, 31–3; *BCM* 1945, 208–9; Kahn & Renaud, 62–4; Euwe & Kramer 1965, 77–8.

(631) GLADSTONE, D—FINE

U.S. Championship, New York (5), 1944 (20 April)
Sicilian Defence [B29]

1. e4 c5 2. Nf3 Nf6 3. Nc3 Nc6 4. Be2 d5 5. exd5 Nxd5 6. 0–0 Nc7 7. b3 g6 8. Bb2 Bg7 9. Re1 0–0 10. Qc1 e5 11. d3 b6 12. Bf1 Ne6 13. Ne4 Bb7 14. g3 Qd7 15. Bg2 Rae8 16. Qe3 f5 17. Nc3 Ned4

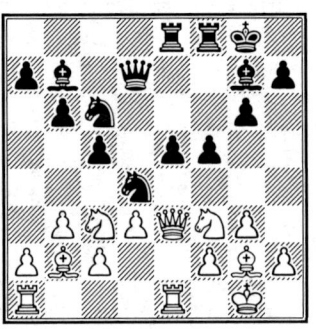

Position after Black's 17th move

18. Qd2 Nxf3+ 19. Bxf3 Nd4 20. Bd1 Qc6 21. f3 Nxf3+ 22. Bxf3 Qxf3 23. Rf1 Qh1+ 24. Kf2 Qxh2+ 25. Ke1 Qxg3+ 26. Kd1 e4 27. Kc1 e3 28. Qe2 Qg2 29. Qe1 e2 30. Rg1 Qxg1 White resigned. 0–1

(632) FINE—ROTHMAN, A

U.S. Championship, New York (6), 1944 (21 April)
Reversed Grünfeld [D02]

1. Nf3 d5 2. g3 c5 3. Bg2 g6 4. d4 cxd4 5. Nxd4 Bg7 6. c4 Nc6 7. Nxc6 bxc6 8. cxd5 Qb6 9. dxc6 Bxb2 10. Bxb2 Qxb2 11. Nd2 Be6 12. Rb1 Qxa2 13. c7 Rc8 14. Rb8 Nf6 15. Bb7 Black resigned. 1–0

(633) DENKER, A—FINE

U.S. Championship, New York (7), 1944 (22 April)
Nimzowitsch-Indian Defence, Rubinstein Variation [E43]

1. d4 Nf6 2. c4 e6 3. Nc3 Bb4 4. e3 b6 5. Bd3 Bb7 6. Nf3 Ne4 7. 0–0! An ingenious pawn sacrifice, of a kind which is very promising in over-the-board play. RF 7 ... Nxc3 Fine apparently decided to accept the sacrifice because at the time he was at least half a point behind Denker (subject to the result of his adjourned game for round 1). In a relatively weak field it was necessary to score as many points as possible in order to win the title. Denker was in tremendous form during the tournament and eventually finished on 15.5/17, allowing two draws against lesser lights in the final two rounds. This bid for a win was therefore justified on sporting grounds, though, as it turned out, actually cost Fine any hope of winning the tournament. Denker was not only in excellent form but also rode his luck courageously, saving two lost positions, and even scoring a win in the process. Fine later recommended either 7 ... Bxc3 8 bxc3 0–0 with equality, or 7 ... f5 8 Bxe4 fxe4 9 Nd2

Bxc3 10 bxc3 Qh4. **8. bxc3 Bxc3 9. Rb1 Ba5?!** Bobby Fischer says that 9 ... Nc6! refutes the gambit. Perhaps, but most players prefer to avoid it. Even in defeat White has all the fun. Moreover, a couple of games form the 1970s suggest that White keeps a strong initiative even after Fischer's suggestion. Balashov–Romanishin (Lvov 1978) continued 10 Rb3 Ba5 11 e4 h6 12 d5 Ne7 13 Bb2 0–0 14 Ne5!, when White is doing fine. AD &LP (9 ... 0–0 10 Qc2, returning the pawn, looks good for a draw after 10 ... Bxf3 11 Bxh7+ Kh8 12 gxf3 Qg5+ 13 Kh1 Qh5, but Fine was trying to win.) **10. Ba3 d6 11. c5! 0–0 12. cxd6 cxd6 13. e4 Re8 14. e5 dxe5 15. Nxe5 Qg5?** Later published analysis by both players established that 15 ... g6!? 16 Bb5 Qd5 17 f3 Bc6 18 Ng4 Kg7! 19 Qc1 Bxb5 20 Qh6+ Kh8 21 Rxb5 Qxd4+ 22 Kh1 Nd7 would have given Black reasonable chances. **16. g3 g6** 16 ... Rc8 fails to 17 Nxf7. **17. Qa4! Qd8 18. Rfc1 b5 19. Bxb5 Qd5 20. f3 Bb6 21. Rc5!! Bxc5?** Black's last chance was 21 ... Qxa2 22 Rd1 Bxc5 23 dxc5 Nc6 24 Nd7 Ne5 25 Nxe5 Red8. **22. Bxc5 Rf8 23. Bc4 Bc6 24. Bxd5 Bxa4 25. Bxa8** Black resigned. 1–0 Denker 135–9; Fine 1948, 27–31; Soltis and McCormick 68–71; Denker & Parr 340–1.

(634) FINE—PERSINGER, L

U.S. Championship, New York (8), 1944 (23 April)

The score of this game is not available. 1–0

(635) CHERNEV, I—FINE

U.S. Championship, New York (9), 1944 (25 April)
Marshall Defence [D06]

1. d4 Nf6 2. c4 d5 3. cxd5 Nxd5 4. e4 Nf6 5. Bd3 g6 6. Ne2 e5 7. 0–0 exd4 8. Nxd4 Bg7 9. Nf3 0–0 10. Bg5 h6 11. Bh4 g5 12. e5 gxh4 13. exf6 Qxf6 14. Nc3 Bg4 15. Qa4 Bxf3 16. gxf3 Nc6 17. Qe4 Rfe8 18. Qh7+ Kf8 19. Be4 Nd4 20. Nd5 Qe5 21. Rae1 c6 22. f4 Qd6 23. Nc3 Qxf4 24. Re3 Re7 25. Kh1 Be5 26. Rh3 f5 27. Qg6 fxe4 28. Qh5 Bf6 29. Rg1 Nf3 30. Ne2 Qe5 31. Qxh6+ Bg7 32. Qg6 Nxg1 33. Rxh4 Nxe2 0–1 *Christian Science Monitor*, June 10, 1944.

(636) FINE—STEINER, H

U.S. Championship, New York (10), 1944 (27 April)
Dutch Defence [A98]

1. Nf3 f5 2. g3 Nf6 3. Bg2 e6 4. 0–0 Be7 5. c4 I considered 5 d3 here; on 5 ... d5 6 Nc3 0–0 7 e4! c5 8 exf5 exf5 9 Re1 White has some pressure, but 5 ... d6 6 Nc3 0–0 7 e4 fxe4 8 dxe4 e5 looked too strong. **5 ... 0–0 6. Nc3 Qe8 7. d4 d6?!** Weak here; 7 ... d5 is essential, though 8 Nb5! Bd8 9 Bf4 Na6 10 Qb3 gives White a strong game. **8. Qc2 Nc6?!** Known to be weak since Bogolyubov tried it against Fine at Nottingham 1936. Alekhine calls 8 ... Qh5 the logical move. Mugridge **9. d5 Nd8** Inferior to Bogolyubov's manoeuvre of ... Nc6-b4-a6-c5. Mugridge **10. Nd4**

Qh5 **11. dxe6 Nxe6** Black has no choice. On 11 ... Bxe6 12 Nd5! is crushing. **12. Nxf5 Bd8 13. f3 Kh8 14. e4 Qf7 15. Ne2 a5 16. b3 Nd7 17. Bb2 Bf6 18. Rad1 a4 19. Bxf6 Qxf6 20. Nc3 axb3 21. axb3 Ne5 22. f4 Nc6 23. Nd5 Qf7 24. b4** Preventing ... Nc5 and threatening b5 followed by b6. **24 ... b6 25. g4 Bd7 26. Qb2 Ra4 27. Ra1 Rxa1 28. Qxa1 Rc8** To free his knight at e6. **29. g5 Qf8 30. h4**

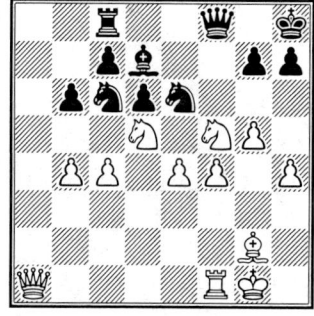

Position after White's 30th move

30 ... Ra8 31. Qb2 Ra4 32. h5 Ned8 33. h6 Bxf5 34. exf5 Kg8 Too pressed for time to resign. **35. Re1 gxh6 36. Nf6+ Kf7 37. Bd5+** Black resigned. 1–0 Fine, *The Chess Review* in U.S.C.F. 1944, 38.

(637) ALTMAN, B—FINE

U.S. Championship, New York (11), 1944 (29 April)

The score of this game is unavailable. 0–1

(638) FINE—WEINSTOCK, S

U.S. Championship, New York (12), 1944 (30 April)
French Defence, Winawer Variation [C15]

1. e4 e6 2. d4 d5 3. Nc3 Bb4 4. Bd3 dxe4 5. Bxe4 Nf6 6. Bf3 0–0 7. Nge2 c5 8. a3 Bxc3+ 9. bxc3 Nc6 10. 0–0 Qa5 11. Qd3 Rd8 12. Rb1 Ne5 13. Qe3 Nxf3+ 14. Qxf3 cxd4 15. cxd4 Qh5 16. Qe3 b6 17. Bd2 Ba6 Fine was reputed to be worried here. His position is fair, but so is his opponent's—and that accounts for it. Fine had to win! **18. Nf4 Qf5 19. Rfc1 Rac8 20. c3 Ne4 21. Be1 Nd6 22. Qg3 Nc4 23. h4 e5 24. dxe5 Nxe5 25. f3 Nd3 26. Nxd3 Bxd3 27. Rb4 Rc4?** Why offer to swap a good rook for a bad one? 27 ... Bc4 would be effective. **28. Rd1**

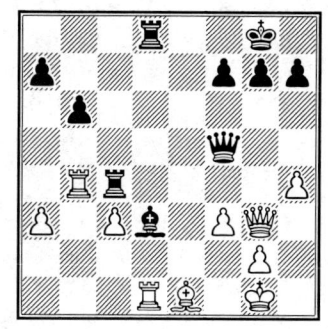

Position after White's 28th move

28 ... Rdc8? 29. Qd6 With one fell swoop the game changes hands. For no reason at all, Black has succeeded in tying himself into a knot. 29 ... Qc5+? 30. Qxc5 bxc5 31. Rb7 Bg6 32. Rxa7 Rf4 33. a4 Bc2 34. Ra1 h6 35. a5 Rf6 36. Bf2 Bd3 37. a6 Kh7 38. Ra4 Rcc6 39. c4 Bc2 40. Ra3 Bg6 41. Ra8 Black resigned. 1–0 Horowitz in *The Chess Review* from *U.S.C.F.* 1944, 35–6.

(639) STROMBERG, B—FINE

U.S. Championship, New York (13), 1944 (1 May)

The score of this game is unavailable. 0–1

(640) FINE—ISAACS, L

U.S. Championship, New York (14), 1944 (3 May)
Grünfeld Defence [D97]

1. d4 Nf6 2. c4 g6 3. Nc3 d5 4. Nf3 Bg7 5. Qb3 dxc4 6. Qxc4 0–0 7. e4 c6 8. Qb3 b6 9. Bc4 b5 10. Be2 e6 11. 0–0 Nbd7 12. Bg5 Qb6 13. e5 Nd5 14. Nxd5 exd5 15. Be3 Re8 16. Ne1 Nf8 17. f4 Ne6 18. Rd1 Nf8 19. g4 f5 20. h3 Bd7 21. Rf2 Qd8 22. Rg2 a5 23. Qc2 Rc8 24. Nf3 a4 25. Bd3 fxg4 26. hxg4 Bh6 27. Qd2 Kh8 28. f5 Bxe3+ 29. Qxe3 Re7 30. Qh6 Rg7 31. Ng5 Be8 32. f6 Rf7 33. Nxf7+ Bxf7 34. Qg7 Mate. 1–0 *Christian Science Monitor*, July 1, 1944.

(641) HOROWITZ, I—FINE

U.S. Championship, New York (15), 1944 (4 May)
Spanish Game, Steinitz Defence Deferred [C71]

1. e4 e5 2. Nf3 Nc6 3. Bb5 a6 4. Ba4 d6 5. c4 Bd7 6. d4 An innovation of Duras in a similar position, and also successfully tried by Keres in a game with Alekhine. The idea is to permanently restrain Black from playing ... d5, the liberating move in such positions. 6 ... g6 If 6 ... exd4 7 Nxd4 Nxd4! 8 Bxd7+ Qxd7 9 Qxd4 Nf6 (or 9 ... Ne7 10 0–0 Nc6 11 Qc3 Qg4 12 f3 Qg6 13 Qb3 Eliskases–Thomas, Hastings 1936/7 and now 13 ... 0–0–0!) 10 0–0 Be7 11 Nc3 0–0 12 b3 Rfe8 13 Bb2 Bf8 with equality, PCO 373. 7. dxe5 To fix Black's pawn at e5 so that the king's bishop, when fianchettoed, will be posted behind an immobile barrier. 7 ... Nxe5 If 7 ... dxe5 8 Be3 Bg7 9 Bc5 with a strong bind on the position. 8. Nxe5 dxe5 9. 0–0 9 Qd5, simultaneously attacking the b-pawn and e-pawn with threat on the rook, at first sight seems to win a pawn, but it is easily refuted by 9 ... Bxa4 10 Qxe5+ Be7 and White cannot capture the rook as Black is threatening 11 ... Qd1 mate. 9 ... Ne7 10. Nc3 Nc6 11. Nd5 Bg7 12. f4 A double-edged move, consistent with my style, which opens the f-file but leaves weaknesses in the ranks of White's pawns. 12 ... exf4 A choice of evils: if he does not thus open up lines for White he will have to face f5! Mugridge 13. Bxf4 Ne5 Leading to unfavourable complications. The unsavoury

looking 13 ... Rc8, defending the c-pawn, as a temporary expedient, has much in its favour in that Black may castle safely and later exploit the weaknesses of White's pawn position. 14. Bxd7+ Qxd7 15. Bh6! White's position is distinctly superior, PCO. 15 ... 0–0 Losing the exchange but with a fair amount of counterplay. The alternative 15 ... Kf8 is out of the question. Not only would Black forfeit the privilege of castling, and hence lose co-operation between his forces, but his king would be in the direct line of fire of the opposition. 16. Nf6+ Bxf6 17. Bxf8 Qe6 He could hardly afford to trade the balance of forces and remain an exchange behind. (17 ... Nd3! threatening 18 ... Qd4+ seems to recover the exchange with a good game. AW) 18. Bc5 Nxc4 19. Qb3 What I failed to realize was that after 19 Bd4 Rd8 I should play 20 Bxf6. Then Black has no better than 20 ... Rxd1 21 Radl Nd6 22 e5 Ne8 23 Rd8 and Black is tied in a knot. Also, against 19 Bd4 Nxb2 (19 ... Bg5!? Fritz) would not do on account of 20 Rxf6 Nxd1 21 Rxe6 fxe6 22 Rxd1 and while Black gets two pawns for the piece minus the prospects favour White. 19 ... b6 20. Rac1 Bxb2 21. Rxc4 bxc5 22. Kh1 Bd4 The bishop supported by a passed pawn is practically as strong as a rook. Mugridge 23. Qd3 Rb8 24. Rc2 Rb4 25. Rfc1 h5 26. Re2 Qf6 27. Rec2 a5 28. Qf3 Qe6 29. e5 Bxe5 30. Rxc5 Bd6 31. Rxa5 Re4 32. Rf1 Better would be 32 Ra8+ Kh7 33 Qc3 threatening mate and attempting interference with Black's plans. (Fritz seems to believe that after 33 ... Be5 it is not easy to find a sensible continuation for White.) 32 ... Rf4 33. Ra8+ 33 Qd3! may still hold, for example 33 ... Qe4! 34 Qd1! Rh4 35 Qf3 Rxh2+ 36 Kg1 without a clear win. AW 33 ... Kh7 34. Qd1 Not 34 Qd3 Qd5! and White is helpless against the threat of ... Qxd3 and ... Qxa8. 34 ... Qd5 34 ... Rh4 was a winning line: 35 Qb3 Rxh2+ 36 Kg1 Qe5! and White exhausts after a check or two, he cannot meet the threat of either 37 ... Rh1+ followed by mate at h2 or 38 ... Bc5+. However the text should also win. 35. Rd8 Rf2! 36. Rg1 Qe5 Fine could win by 36 ... Rxg2 37 Rxd6 (forced, for on 37 Qxd5 Rxh2 mate, or on 37 Rxg2 Qxd1+) Rxg1+ 38 Kxg1 Qg5+ and if 39 Kh1 cxd6 40 Qxd6 Qc1+ followed by 41 ... Qb2+, the capture of the a-pawn with two pawns plus. 37. Rxd6 cxd6 38. Qb3 Kg7 39. a4 Rf4 40. Qc2 Rh4 41. h3 Re4 42. a5 Re2 43. Qc4! Not 43 Qa4 on account of 43 ... Qd5 followed by 44 ... Ra2, winning the a-pawn. 43 ... d5 44. Qa4 d4 45. a6 Qd5 46. a7 Ra2 47. a8Q Qxa8 48. Qxd4+ Kg8 Now that the important pawns are swapped, the position is a book draw. But White still has to be careful. 49. Qe5 Ra5 50. Qc7 Qd5 51. Qb8+ Kh7 52. Qg3 Ra2 53. Rf1 g5 54. Qf3 Qxf3 55. Rxf3 Kg6 56. Rb3 g4 57. hxg4 hxg4 58. g3 Kf5 59. Rb4 Draw agreed. ½–½ Horowitz, *The Chess Review* in *U.S.C.F. Yearbook* 1944, 36–8.

(642) FINE—DiCAMILLO, A

U.S. Championship, New York (16), 1944 (6 May)
Nimzowitsch-Indian Defence, Rubinstein Variation [E44]

1. d4 Nf6 2. c4 e6 3. Nc3 Bb4 4. e3 b6 5. Nge2 Bb7 6. a3 Bxc3+ 7. Nxc3 d5 8. Be2 0-0 9. 0-0 Nbd7 10. Bf3 c6 11. b3 Qe7 12. e4 Nxe4 13. Nxe4 dxe4 14. Bxe4 Rad8 15. Qf3 Nf6 16. Bxc6 Bxc6 17. Qxc6 Rxd4 18. a4 Rfd8 19. Be3 Qd7 (19 ... R4d6!) 20. Qxd7 R4xd7 21. a5 Rd6 22. axb6 axb6 23. Ra6 Nd7 24. b4 Kf8 25. c5 Rc6

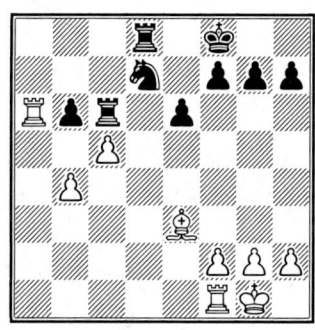

Position after Black's 25th move

26. Rd1 Ke8 27. h3 h6 28. cxb6 Nb8 29. Rxd8+ Kxd8 30. Ra7 Nd7 31. Ra8+ Rc8 32. b7 Black resigned. **1-0**

(643) NEIDICH, L—FINE

U.S. Championship, New York (17), 1944 (7 May)

The score of this game is not available. ½-½

In 1997 Soltis and McCormick calculated the following statistics for Fine's U.S. Championship appearances: he shared 10th to 14th place for most finishes in the top three places (4), he had the second highest winning percentage, after Robert Fischer, of players who had played in three or more tournaments (78 percent) and that he had the fifth lowest percentage of draws (28.6 percent), of players who had played in two or more tournaments. In May 1944 Fine began research work for the Department of the Navy as part of a team employed to determine likely surfacings of U-Boats. This work later extended to attempts to determine the locations of Japanese Kamikaze attacks upon Allied ships. These attacks, which began on 13 October 1944 at the Battle of Leyte Gulf, in the Philippines, were so damaging to morale, not to mention lives and ships, that Admiral Nimitz ordered that they be the subject of a news blackout.

3rd U.S. Speed Championships Preliminaries, New York, June 25, 1944

"The third annual U.S. Lightning Tourney was played at the Hotel Astor in New York City on June 25th. The ever growing popularity of this one-day chess event was signalized by an entry of sixty eager contestants, including such recognized Chess Masters as Fine, Reshevsky, Kashdan,

Denker, Horowitz, Kevitz, Pinkus, Mugridge, Chernev and Edward Lasker. In Group B Fine romped through with eleven victories, Denker was second with a score of 8½-2½, and J. Partos was third with 7½-3½." (*U.S.C.F. Yearbook*)

3rd U.S. Speed Championships Finals, New York, June 25, 1944

"Reuben Fine again demonstrated his almost unchallenged superiority at rapid chess, winning the title for the third successive year and thereby taking permanent possession of the Sturgis-Stephens Trophy. Horowitz (*the only player other than Fine to score 11-0 in the preliminaries—AW*) led the field until the 9th round. Exhibiting a choice display of tricky openings, including such forgotten gems as the Schliemann Defence to the Ruy Lopez, he had disposed of Reshevsky, Kashdan and several other strong threats to his challenge for the title. He had been nicked slightly in his encounter with U.S. Champion Denker when forced to a brilliant draw, but had won all his other games. In the meantime Fine was playing brilliant chess but had lost one game in an early round to Partos. Passing into first place at the end of the 9th round by virtue of his victory while Horowitz was losing to Kevitz, he remained the pacesetter to the end. In the semi-finals Fine and Horowitz met in a thriller that decided the title, and Fine won it narrowly in a game which was remarkable for the precision and skill considering the rigid limitations under which it was played. In the final round Fine defeated his old rival Reshevsky to clinch his hold on the title for the third successive year." (*U.S.C.F. Yearbook*)

(644) FINE—DENKER, A

National Rapid Transit, New York, 1944 (25 June)
Bogolyubov Indian Defence [E00]

1. d4 d5 2. c4 e6 3. Nf3 Nf6 4. g3 Bb4+ 5. Nbd2 0-0 6. a3 Bxd2+ 7. Nxd2 dxc4 8. e3 b5 9. Bg2 c6 10. 0-0 Qb6 11. a4 Bb7 12. a5 Qc7 13. Qc2 Rd8 14. b3 cxb3 15. Nxb3 Nbd7 16. a6 Bc8 17. Na5 Nd5 18. Qxc6 Qxc6 19. Nxc6 Re8 20. e4 Nc7 21. Ba3 Nb6 22. Bd6 Nxa6 23. Ne7+ Rxe7 24. Bxe7 Bb7 25. e5 Bxg2 26. Kxg2

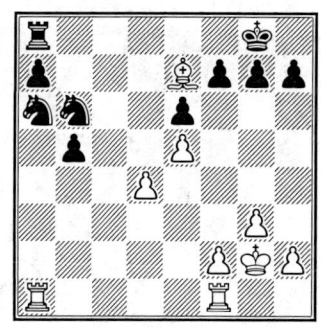

Position after White's 26th move

26 ... Nc7 27. Bc5 Ncd5 28. Ra6 b4 29. Rb1 Nc7
30. Raa1 Ncd5 31. Bxb4 Nxb4 32. Rxb4 Nd5
33. Rxa7 Rf8 34. Rb5 Nc3 35. Rc5 Ne4 36. Rcc7
h5 37. h4 g5 38. f3 Nd2 39. hxg5 1–0

(645) FINE—HOROWITZ, I

National Rapid Transit New York, 1944 (25 June)
Nimzowitsch-Indian Defence, Spielmann Variation [E22]

1. d4 Nf6 2. c4 e6 3. Nc3 Bb4 4. Qb3 Nc6 5. Nf3
0–0 6. a3 Bxc3+ 7. Qxc3 a5 8. g3 d6 9. Bg2 e5
10. d5 Ne7 11. 0–0 Ne4 12. Qc2 f5 13. Ng5 Nc5
14. f4 e4 15. Be3 a4 16. Nh3 Qe8 17. Nf2 b6
18. g4 fxg4 19. Nxe4 Nf5 20. Bf2 Bd7 21. Rad1
Qg6 22. Nxc5 bxc5 23. e4

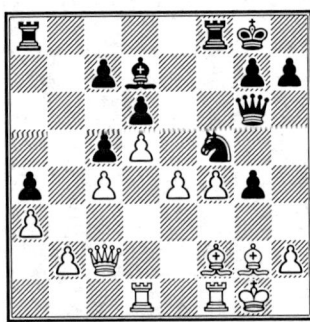

*Position after
White's 23rd move*

23 ... g3! 24. hxg3 Nxg3 25. Bxg3 Qxg3 26. Rd3
Qh4 27. f5 Rf6 28. Qd2 Re8 29. Rh3 Qg4 30. Kh2
Rxe4!? (Note: a photograph of the game at this position,
courtesy of the Russell Collection, is incorrectly captioned
as the game Fine–Horowitz, U.S. Championship 1944, post
mortem, in Soltis and McCormick. Instead of the text, 30 ...
Bxf5 would have offered Black excellent winning chances.)
31. Bxe4 Qxe4 32. Qf4 Qxf4+ 33. Rxf4 Bxf5
34. Re3 Kf7 35. b3 g5 36. Rf2 axb3 37. Rxb3
h5?! 38. a4 Kg6 39. Rbf3 g4 40. Rxf5 Rxf5 41. Rxf5
Kxf5 42. a5 Kf4 43. a6 Kf3 44. a7 1–0

(646) FINE—KEVITZ, A

National Rapid Transit, New York, 1944 (25 June)
Budapest Defence [A52]

1. d4 Nf6 2. c4 e5 3. dxe5 Ng4 4. e4 Nxe5 5. f4
Ng6 6. Be3 Bb4+ 7. Kf2 d6 8. Nf3 Qf6 9. Qc1
Nc6 10. Bd3 0–0 11. g3 Bg4 12. Nc3 Bxf3 13. Nd5
Qd8?! 14. Kxf3 Ba5 15. Rf1 Nge7 16. Kg2 Bb6
17. h3 Re8 18. Bxb6 axb6 19. Qc3 Ng6 20. Rae1
Nce7 21. Ne3 Nf8 22. Ng4 Qd7 23. a3 Nc6
24. Bc2 Re7 25. Rd1 Rae8 (*see diagram*) 26. e5 Qc8
27. exd6 cxd6 28. Rxd6 h5 29. Nf2 Re3
30. Rd3 Re2 31. Bd1 R2e7 32. Bxh5 Ne6 33. b4
Ncd4 34. Rxd4 Nxd4 35. Qxd4 Re3 36. Rd1 Rxa3
37. Qd7 Qxd7 38. Rxd7 g6 39. Bf3 Ree3 40. Bd1
Rxg3+ 41. Kf1 Rgc3 42. Rxb7 Rxc4 43. f5 gxf5
44. Rxb6 Rf4 45. Rd6 Ra2 46. Be2 Rxb4 47. Rd3

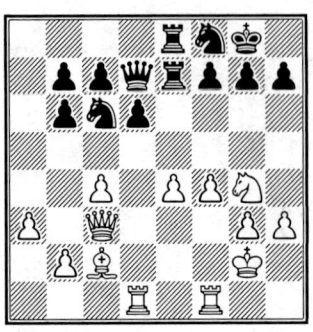

*Position after
Black's 25th move*

Rbb2 48. Re3 f4 49. Re8+ Kg7 50. Nd3 Rd2
51. Nxf4 Ra1+ 52. Kf2 Ra4 53. Ke3 Rb2 54. Bd3
Kf6 55. h4 Kg7 56. Nh5+ 1–0

(647) FINE—RESHEVSKY, S

National Rapid Transit, New York, 1944 (25 June)
Two Knights Defence [C59]

1. e4 e5 2. Nf3 Nc6 3. Bc4 Nf6 4. Ng5 d5 5. exd5
Na5 6. Bb5+ c6 7. dxc6 bxc6 8. Be2 h6 9. Nf3 e4
10. Ne5 Bd6 11. d4 exd3 12. Nxd3 Qc7 13. h3 0–0
14. 0–0 c5 15. b3 c4 16. bxc4 Nxc4 17. Nd2 Ba6
18. Nxc4 Bxc4 19. Be3 Rad8 20. Qc1 Rfe8 21. Re1
Nd5 22. Bd2 Re7 23. Bf3 Rde8 24. Rxe7 Rxe7 25. a4
Re8 26. Nb2 Be5 27. Nxc4 Qxc4 28. Bxd5 Qxd5

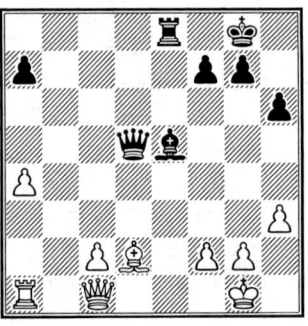

*Position after
Black's 28th move*

29. Ra3 Re6 30. Rd3 Qc6 31. Bf4 Bc3 32. Bd2 Rg6
33. f3 Qc5+ 34. Kf1 Be5 35. Qd1 Qc4 36. a5 Rc6
37. Be3 a6 38. Kg1 Kh7 39. Rd5 Bc7 40. Qd3+
Qxd3 41. cxd3 Rc3 42. Kf1 Rc2 43. Rc5 Rxc5
44. Bxc5 Bxa5 45. d4 Kg6 46. Ke2 Kf5 47. Kd3
Bc7?! 48. d5 Ke5 49. Kc4 g6 50. Bf8 h5 51. Kc5
a5?! 52. Kc6 Bd8 53. d6 Ke6 54. d7 a4 55. Ba3
h4 56. Bd6 g5 57. Bc5 f5 58. Ba3 f4 59. Bd6 Ba5
60. Bc7 a3 61. d8Q 1–0

(648) FINE—RIVISE, I

National Rapid Transit, New York, 1944 (25 June)
Nimzowitsch-Indian Defence, Rubinstein Variation [E44]

1. d4 Nf6 2. c4 e6 3. Nc3 Bb4 4. e3 b6 5. Nge2
Bb7 6. a3 Bxc3+ 7. Nxc3 d5 8. cxd5 Nxd5 9. Qg4
0–0 10. Bd3 Nf6 11. Qh4 c5 12. 0–0 Nc6 13. Rd1

Qc8 14. dxc5 Ne5 15. cxb6 Bf3 16. Be2 Bxe2 17. Nxe2
Qc2 18. Bd2 Ng6 19. Qb4 axb6 20. Nd4 Qc7
21. Rac1 Qe5 22. Qb5 Nd5 23. Nc6 Qf6 24. Bc3
Qh4 25. Qe2 Ra4 26. Bd4

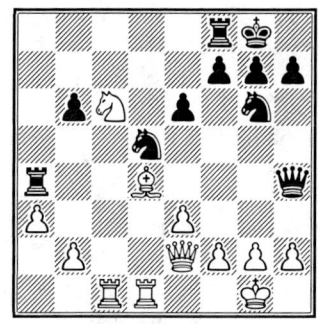

Position after
White's 26th move

26 ... e5 27. Nxe5 Nxe5 28. Bxe5 Nf6 29. Qf3 Ng4
30. Bg3 Qg5 31. Rd5 Qg6 32. Rd6 Nf6 33. h3 h5
34. Be5 Ra7 35. Bxf6 gxf6 36. Rxf6 Qg5 37. Rf5
Qe7 38. Qg3+ 1–0

(649) GREEN, M–FINE

National Rapid Transit, New York, 1944 (25 June)
Queen's Gambit Declined, Lasker Variation [D53]

1. d4 Nf6 2. c4 e6 3. Nc3 d5 4. Bg5 Nbd7 5. e3
Be7 6. Nf3 Ne4 7. Bxe7 Qxe7 8. cxd5 Nxc3 9. bxc3
exd5 10. Qb3 c6 11. c4 dxc4 12. Bxc4 0–0 13. 0–0
Nb6 14. Bd3 h6 15. Rac1 Be6 16. Qb2 Rac8 17. e4
Rfd8 18. Rfe1 Na4 19. Qa1 Qa3 20. Re3 Qb2 21. Qxb2
Nxb2 22. Bb1 Nc4 23. Rec3 Nb6 24. h3 Kf8 25. Kf1
Na8 26. Ke2 Re8 27. a4 Bd7 28. Kf1 Rcd8 29. a5
Nc7 30. Bd3 Ne6

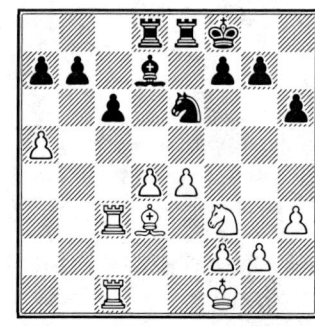

Position after
Black's 30th move

31. d5 Nf4 32. Bb1 cxd5 33. Rc5 b6 34. axb6
axb6 35. Rxd5 Nxd5 36. exd5 Bb5+ 37. Kg1 Rxd5
38. Ba2 Rc5 39. Rb1 Rb8 40. Nd4 Bc4 0–1

(650) KASHDAN, I–FINE

National Rapid Transit, New York, 1944 (25 June)
Semi-Tarrasch [D41]

1. d4 Nf6 2. c4 e6 3. Nf3 d5 4. Nc3 c5 5. cxd5
Nxd5 6. Nxd5 Qxd5 7. g3 Nc6 8. dxc5 Qxd1+ 9. Kxd1
Bxc5 10. e3 e5 11. Be2 Be6 12. Bd2 Rd8 13. a3

Na5 14. Ke1 Nb3 15. Rd1 f6 16. Bc3 Ke7 17. Nd2
a6 18. Ne4 Kf7 19. Nxc5 (19 Bxe5!) 19 ... Nxc5
20. f3 Na4 21. Kf2 Nxc3 22. bxc3 Rc8 23. c4 Rc7
24. Rd6 Re8 25. Rb1 Bd7 26. e4 Ke7 27. Rdb6
Bc6 28. Ke3 Rd8 29. R6b2 g6 30. f4 Rd4 31. Bd3
Rcd7 32. Rb3 Kd6 33. Rf1 Ke7 34. Rc3

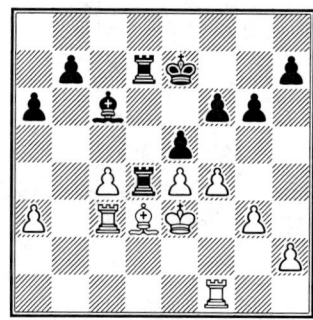

Position after
White's 34th move

34 ... b5! 35. fxe5 fxe5 36. Rfc1 bxc4 37. Bb1 Bb5
38. a4 Bxa4 39. Rxc4 Rxc4 40. Rxc4 Bb5 41. Rc5
Kf6 42. g4 g5 43. Rc8 Rd1 44. Bc2 Re1+ 45. Kf3
Rc1 46. Ke3 Ba4 47. Rc4 Bxc2 48. Kd2 Rg1 49. Kxc2
Rxg4 50. Rc6+ Kg7 51. Kd3 Rh4 52. Re6 Rxh2
53. Rxe5 h6 0–1

(651) PARTOS, J–FINE

National Rapid Transit, New York, 1944 (25 June)
King's Indian Defence [E90]

1. d4 Nf6 2. c4 g6 3. Nc3 Bg7 4. Nf3 0–0 5. e4
d6 6. Bd3 Nbd7 7. 0–0 e5 8. dxe5 dxe5 9. Bc2 c6
10. Bg5 h6 11. Bh4 Qe7 12. Qe2 Nc5 13. Bg3 Nh5
14. Rad1 Ne6 15. Qd2 Nd4 16. Nxd4 exd4 17. Ne2
Rd8 18. Bd3 Be6 19. f4 Nxg3 20. Nxg3 Bg4
21. Rde1 Bd7 22. e5 Re8 23. Ne4 c5 24. Nd6
Reb8 25. f5 Bxe5?! 26. fxg6 Qxd6 27. Qxh6 Be6
28. gxf7+ Bxf7 29. Qh7+ Kf8 30. Qxf7 Mate. 1–0

(652) SEIDMAN, H–FINE

National Rapid Transit, New York, 1944 (25 June)
Spanish Opening, Steinitz Defence Deferred [C71]

1. e4 e5 2. Nf3 Nc6 3. Bb5 a6 4. Ba4 d6 5. d4 b5
6. Bb3 Nxd4 7. Nxd4 exd4 8. c3 Nf6 9. cxd4 Be7
10. 0–0 0–0 11. Nc3 Bb7 12. Re1 b4

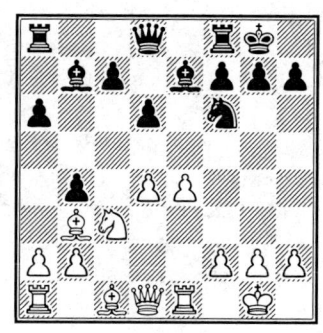

Position after
Black's 12th move

13. e5 bxc3 14. exf6 cxb2 15. Bxb2 Bxf6 16. Rc1
Qd7 17. Qc2 Rac8 18. d5 Bxb2 19. Qxb2 Rfe8
20. Bc4 Rxe1+ 21. Rxe1 c6 22. Qd4 h6 23. f3 cxd5
24. Bxd5 Bxd5 25. Qxd5 Qa7+ 26. Kh1 Qf2 27. Rb1
Qc5 28. Qd1 d5 29. h3 d4 30. Rb7 Qd5 31. Rb4 d3
32. Qd2 Rc2 33. Rb8+ Kh7 34. Qd1 Qc4 35. Kh2
Qf4+ 0–1

Team Match, Chess Divan, Washington, 1944

This game was kindly supplied by Jack O'Keefe. Unfortunately at this time there is no further information to go along with it.

Turover 0   Fine 1

(653) TUROVER, I—FINE

13th McCoy-Hatfield Match, Divan CC, Washington, 1944
  (7 June)
English Opening [A48]

1. d4 Nf6 2. Nf3 g6 3. b3 Bg7 4. Bb2 0–0 5. Nbd2
c5 6. e3 cxd4 7. Nxd4 d5 8. c4 e5 9. N4f3 d4
10. exd4 exd4 11. Bd3 Re8+ 12. Kf1 Nc6 13. a3 Ng4
14. Qc2 Nge5 15. Be4 Nxf3 16. Bxf3 d3 17. Qc1 Nd4
18. Qc3 Be5 19. Bd5 Nc2 20. Qxe5 Rxe5 21. Bxe5
Nxa1 22. Bxa1 Qe7 23. Ne4 Qxa3 24. Nf6+ Kh8
0–1 *Christian Science Monitor*, 15 July 1944.

Exhibition Game with Hugh Alexander, Washington, October 9, 1944

On a two-month visit to the U.S. capital (his second of the year, as he had already visited in February according to Hugh Sebag-Montefiore writing in *Enigma*) Alexander, who was carrying out cryptanalytical and administration work at Bletchley Park, played an exhibition game with Fine, who was himself involved in work for his government as part of the war effort. In his obituary of Fine in *BCM* Bernard Cafferty even suggested that Fine may have been involved in work on early computers during his years in Washington (possibly the American version of Alan Turing *et al.*'s "Bombe"). The first electronic computer, built by Turing's team at Bletchley to decode Enigma messages, was dismantled, for security reasons, after the war on Churchill's orders. But until valve technology was superseded the machines were both enormous and relatively slow. Hartston recorded "When the occasional opportunity presented itself to escape from work to the chessboard, Alexander was naturally delighted to take advantage of the chance. [The Game] against Reuben Fine is an excellent example of the type of exciting tussle which can occur when imaginative players have been too long starved of chess." (Golombek & Hartston)

Alexander ½   Fine ½

(654) ALEXANDER, C—FINE

Exhibition Game, Washington, 1944 (9 Oct.)
Philidor's Defence [C41]

1. e4 e5 2.Nf3 d6 Philidor's Defence is better than its reputation. RF 3. d4 Nd7 3 ... Nf6 is generally considered preferable, reaching a position similar to that in the game after 4 Nc3 Nbd7 5 Bc4, but avoiding the possibility mentioned in the note to move 5. WH 4. Bc4 c6 A trap for the unwary is 4 ... Be7? 5 dxe5 Nxe5 (5 ... dxe5? 6 Qd5!) 6 Nxe5 dxe5 7 Qh5 winning a pawn. The frequency with which players fall into this is one of the principal reasons for the unpopularity of the Philidor. WH 5. a4 5 0–0! is better, leading to White's advantage after 5 ... Be7 6 dxe5 dxe5 7 Ng5! Bxg5 8 Qh5. WH 5 ... Be7 6. Nc3 Ngf6 7. 0–0 h6 Fine chooses the aggressive continuation, planning a pawn advance on the kingside. While positionally suspect, this may be playable and is, at any rate, more exciting than the conventional 7 ... 0–0. WH 8. Ba2 8 Nh4!? is more active, White does not need to fear 8 ... Nxe4, which is met by 9 Nxe4 d5 (9 ... Bxh4 10 Nxd6+) 10 Nf5. WH 8 ... g5 9. dxe5 dxe5 10. Qe2 Here 10 Qd3 appears to be a bit better to prevent 10 ... Bd6. Thus if 10 ... Qc7 11 Qc4 Rh7 12 Nd5 is strong. RF 10 ... Bd6 11. Rd1 Qe7 12. Be3 Nc5 This was too tempting. 12 ... Nf8 may have been preferable. RF 13. Nd2 Ne6 I considered 13 ... Bg4 14 f3 Bh5 and later g5-g4, but after 15 Nc4 Bc7 16 Qf2 White's pressure is annoying. RF 14. Nc4 Bc7 In view of what follows, it would have been more prudent to retreat the bishop to b8, but that was difficult to see at this stage. WH 15. Qd2! I had underestimated this continuation. RF 15 ... Ng4 16. Nd5! Well played! This sacrifice is not only sound, it gives White a clear advantage. RF 16 ... cxd5 17. exd5 0–0! 17 ... Nd4 is refuted by 18 Bxd4 exd4 19 Re1 Bxh2+ 20 Kh1 Be5 21 d6 Qf3 22 Qxd4. RF 18. d6 Bxd6 19. Qxd6 Qxd6 20. Rxd6 Ng7! The only effective way to untangle the black pieces. WH 21. Bc5 Be6 22. Rxe6 A little simplifying manoeuvre to leave White ultimately with an extra pawn. WH 22 ... Nxe6 23. Bxf8 Kxf8 24. h3 Nf6 25. Nxe5 Rd8! Black must rely on aggressive counterplay. RF 26. Re1 Inviting the following complications, but the simple 26 Bxe6 fxe6 27 Nd3 was better. WH 26 ... Rd2 27. Nxf7 The point of his previous move, but now Fine shows great resourcefulness in defence, giving up yet another pawn to give his pieces maximum mobility. WH 27 ... Nf4! 28. Nxh6 The alternative is 28 Bb3, but 28 ... g4 still leaves Black with dangerous counterplay. WH 28 ... Rxc2 29. Re5 Rxb2 30. Bc4 Rb4 31. Bf1 Rxa4 32. Rxg5 Now the game should probably end in a draw; the two black passed pawns being fully as strong as White's three on the opposite side. The reason for this lies in the fact that Black's king is already well placed to obstruct the white pawns, while his own are more difficult to stop. WH 32 ... Ra1 33. Rf5 Ne2+ 34. Kh2 Rxf1 35. Rxf6+ Kg7 36. Ng4 Rb1! The right square for the rook; now the a-pawn threatens to rush forward. WH 37. Re6 Nd4 38. Re4 Rb4 39. Ne3 Nc6

40. Rxb4 Nxb4 41. Kg3 a5 42. Kf4 a4 43. Nc4 b5 44. Nd2! 44 Na3 Nd5+ 45 Ke5 b4 would give Black distinct winning chances. After the text a draw was agreed. Black could still try for a trap with 44 ... Na2 45 Nb1? b4 46 h4? Nc3 with good prospects of winning, but White simply brings his king to the queenside in good time to halt the pawns, and the game must be drawn. ½–½ Hartston in Golombek and Hartston, 87–9; Fine, *BCM* 1945, 20–21 from *Divan News*.

New York Metropolitan League, 1945

In one of his increasingly rare appearances in the Metropolitan League, Fine overcame Alexander Kevitz.

Fine   1   Kevitz   0

(655) FINE—KEVITZ, A

Metropolitan Chess League, New York, 1945
Budapest Defence [A52]

1. d4 Nf6 2. c4 e5 3. dxe5 Ng4 4. e4 Nxe5 5. f4 Ng6 6. Nf3 Bb4+ 7. Nc3 Qf6 8. e5 Qb6 9. Qd3 d6 10. a3 Bxc3+ 11. Qxc3 0–0 12. Be3 Qc6 13. 0–0–0 dxe5 14. fxe5 Nd7 15. Re1 Nc5 16. Nd4 Qa4 17. Nb5 Nb3+?! 18. Kb1 c6 19. Nd6 b5 20. Ka2 Photograph, *NiC* 1993/4 69. **20 ... Na5 21. Bc5 bxc4 22. Nxc4 Nxc4 23. Bxc4**

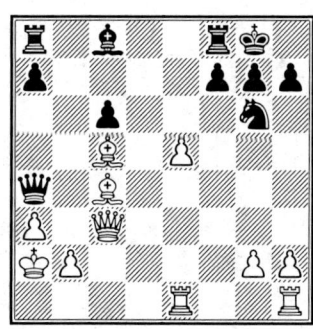

*Position after
White's 23rd move*

23 ... Be6 On a rook move, 24 b3 wins the queen. **24. Bxe6 fxe6 25. Bxf8 Rxf8 26. Rhf1 Rb8 27. b3 Qb5 28. Qc4 Qxc4 29. bxc4 h6 30. g3 c5 31. Rb1 Rxb1 32. Rxb1 Nxe5 33. Re1 Nxc4 34. Rxe6 Nd2 35. Ra6 Nf1 36. Rxa7 Nxh2 37. Rc7 Nf1 38. a4 1–0** Fine in *The Chess Review*, April 1945.

4th U.S. Speed Championships Preliminaries, New York, June 24, 1945

"There was little doubt in any mind at the finish of the Fourth Annual U.S. Lightning Tourney about one specific fact. Reuben Fine remains the uncontested monarch of 'ten-second' chess, and no challenger has as yet cast even a shadow on the horizon. For the fourth successive year

Fine has exhibited superiority over all the other contenders for the title, and in the four final contests compiled the impressive score of forty wins, two draws and two losses. In a single game he may be out-generalled (remember J. Partos in 1944), but so far no other player has shown the stamina to last out against him in the pressure and flurry of a tournament of rapid chess. The fourth of these popular Lightning Chess events was held at the Hotel Astor in New York on June 24th before a small but very enthusiastic audience. Once again L. Walter Stephens, originator of this event, served as tournament Director. There were forty-eight entries for the championship event and nine more modest contestants who entered a special non-championship section. In group A Fine qualified brilliantly with eleven wins. Pinkus was second with a score of 8½–2½. Lasker and Mugridge tied for third with scores of 8–3, but under the rules Lasker had to be content with the Class B Finals since he had lost his individual game with Mugridge." (*U.S.C.F. Yearbook*)

(656) LASKER, ED—FINE

U.S.-ch Lightning preliminaries, New York, 1945 (24 June)
Ragozin Variation [D38]
1. d4 Nf6 2. c4 e6 3. Nc3 Bb4 4. Nf3 d5 5. e3 c5 6. a3 cxd4 7. axb4 dxc3 8. bxc3 0–0 9. Nd4 e5 10. Nb3 Be6 11. Nc5 Qc7 12. cxd5 Bxd5

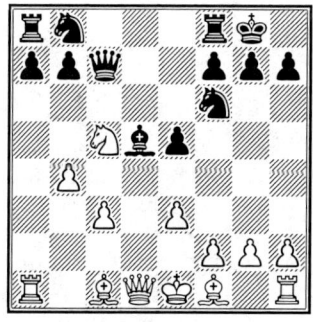

*Position after
Black's 12th move*

13. Bb2?! b6 14. Nd3 Rd8 15. Qc1 Bc4 16. Qc2 Nc6 17. Rc1 a5 18. Be2 a4 19. 0–0 a3 20. Ba1 Na7 21. Ne1 e4 22. Bxc4 Qxc4 23. g3 Ng4 24. Ng2 Ne5 25. Nh4 Nb5 26. Rcd1 Rd3 27. Nf5 Rad8 28. Nd4 Nxd4 29. exd4 Nf3+ 30. Kg2 Nxd4 31. Rxd3 exd3 32. Qd2 Nb3 33. Qe3 d2 34. Qxb6 Qxf1+ 0–1

4th U.S. Speed Championships Finals, New York, June 24, 1945

"Fine was the pacemaker throughout the final championship contest from the very first game, although he did not dare to falter so closely did Shainswit pursue him, drawing their individual game. Fine's other draw went to Moskowitz in the final round of play. In the semi-final round Fine clinched the title by a victory over Horowitz since thereafter Shainswit could no longer tie his score." (*U.S.C.F. Yearbook*)

(657) BYRNE, D—FINE

U.S. Lightning Championship finals, New York, 1945 (24 June)
Catalan System [E02]

1. d4 Nf6 2. c4 e6 3. Nf3 d5 4. g3 dxc4 5. Qa4+ Bd7 6. Qxc4 Bc6 7. Bg2 Bd5 8. Qc2 Nc6 9. a3 Bxf3 10. Bxf3 Nxd4 11. Qa4+ b5! 12. Qa5 Nxf3+ 13. exf3 c6 14. Qc3 Qd7 15. 0-0 Be7 16. Be3 0-0 17. Nd2 Nd5 18. Qc2 Nxe3 19. fxe3 c5 20. Racl Qc6 21. Nb3 c4 22. Nd4 Qb6 23. Rfd1 Bc5

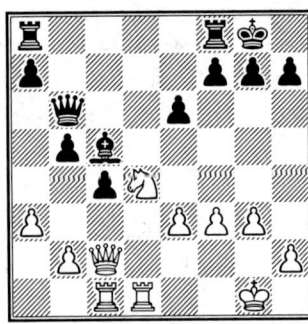

Position after
Black's 23rd move

24. b3? Bxa3 25. Ra1 cxb3 26. Qxb3 Bc5 27. Nxb5 a6 28. Racl Bxe3+ 0-1

(658) FINE—HOROWITZ, I

U.S. Lightning Championship finals, New York, 1945 (24 June)
Grünfeld Defence [D81]

1. d4 Nf6 2. c4 g6 3. Nc3 d5 4. Qb3 dxc4 5. Qxc4 Be6 6. Qa4+ c6 7. Nf3 Bg7 8. e4 0-0 9. Be2 Bc8 10. 0-0 b6 11. Bf4 Bb7 12. Rfd1 Nbd7 13. Racl Nh5 14. Be3 Qe8 15. Ba6 Qc8 16. Be2 e5 17. d5 c5 18. b4 Qd8 19. Nb5 Nf4 20. Bxf4 exf4 21. Nd6 Qc7 22. Nxb7 Qxb7 23. Ba6 Qc7 24. d6 Qd8 25. Bb5 a6 26. Bxd7 b5 27. Qc2 Qxd7 28. bxc5

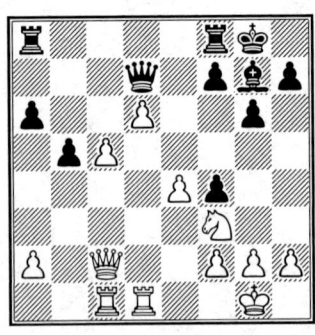

Position after
White's 28th move

28 ... Qc6 29. e5 Rfd8 30. Qd2 Bh6 31. Qd5 Rac8 32. Qxc6 Rxc6 33. Nd4 Rcc8 34. e6 fxe6 35. Nxe6 1-0

(659) FINE—PAVEY, M

U.S. Lightning Championship finals, New York, 1945 (24 June)
Budapest Defence [A52]

1. d4 Nf6 2. c4 e5 3. dxe5 Ng4 4. Bf4 Nc6 5. Nf3 Bb4+ 6. Nc3 Qe7 7. Qd5 f6 8. exf6 Bxc3+ 9. bxc3 Nxf6 10. Qd3 d6 11. e3 0-0 12. Be2 Ne4 13. 0-0 Nc5 14. Qd2 Bd7 15. Nd4 Rae8 16. Rfe1 Ne5 17. Nb3 Ne6 18. Bg3 Bc6 19. f3 Nd7 20. Nd4 Nec5 21. Bf1 Qf7 22. Nxc6 bxc6 23. e4 Nf6 24. e5 dxe5 25. Rxe5 Rxe5 26. Bxe5 Re8 27. Bd4 Ne6 28. Re1 Nh5 29. Qf2 Nhf4 30. g3 Ng6 31. c5 Ng5 32. Rxe8+ Qxe8 33. h4 Nf7 34. Qe3 Qf8 35. Bc4 Kh8 36. h5 Ne7 37. Qf4 Nd5 38. Bxd5 cxd5 39. h6

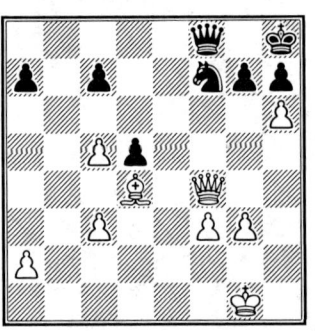

Position after
White's 39th move

39 ... Qe7 40. Kf2 Nd8 41. Bxg7+ Kg8 42. Bd4 Ne6 43. Qe5 Kf7 44. Qxd5 Kg6 45. Be3 Qf6 46. Qe4+ Qf5 47. Qxf5+ Kxf5 48. g4+ Ke5 49. Ke2 c6 50. Kd3 Nc7 51. f4+ Ke6 52. Ke4 Nd5 53. f5+ Ke7 54. Bd4 Nc7 55. g5 Kf7 56. g6+ Kg8 57. Ke5 Nd5 58. Kd6 Nf4 59. Kxc6 hxg6 60. fxg6 Nxg6 61. Kd5 1-0

(660) FINE—SHAINSWIT, G

U.S. Lightning Championship finals, New York, 1945 (24 June)
Queen's English [A30]

1. Nf3 Nf6 2. g3 b6 3. Bg2 Bb7 4. 0-0 e6 5. c4 c5 6. d4 cxd4 7. Nxd4 Bxg2 8. Kxg2 Nc6 9. Nb5 d5 10. Qa4 Qd7 11. Rd1 Be7 12. cxd5 exd5 13. Bg5 0-0 14. N5c3 d4 15. Nb5 Qb7?! (15 ... Qd5+!) 16. f3 Nd5 17. Bc1 Bf6 18. e4 Nc7 19. Nd6 Qa6 20. Qxa6 Nxa6 21. Na3 Nab4 22. f4 d3 23. e5 Be7 24. Nf5 Bc5 25. Be3 Bxe3 26. Nxe3 Nd4 27. Nac4 Rac8 28. Nd6 Ndc2 29. Nxc8 Nxe3+ 30. Kh1 Rxc8 31. Rxd3 Nbc2?! 32. Rc1 Ra8 33. Rc3 g5 34. R3xc2 Nxc2 35. Rxc2 gxf4 36. gxf4 Rd8 37. Kg2 Rd3 38. Kf2 Kg7 39. f5 Rd5 40. Re2 f6 41. exf6+ Kxf6 42. Re6+ Kxf5 43. Re7 Rd2+ 44. Kg3 Rxb2 45. Rxa7 h5 46. a4 Rb4 ½-½

(661) KASHDAN, I—FINE

U.S. Lightning Championship finals, New York, 1945 (24 June)
Catalan System [D77]

1. d4 Nf6 2. Nf3 g6 3. g3 Bg7 4. Bg2 0–0
5. 0–0 d5 6. c4 e6 7. Nbd2 b6 8. Ne5 Bb7 9. Qc2
Nbd7 10. f4 c5 11. cxd5 exd5 12. e3 Rc8 13. Qa4
Nxe5 14. dxe5 Ng4 15. Nf3 f6 16. h3 Nh6 17. exf6
Rxf6

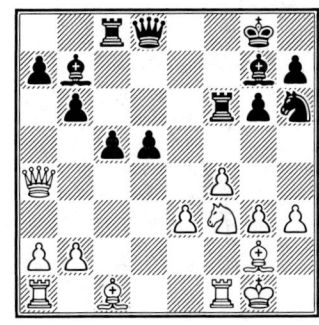

*Position after
Black's 17th move*

18. Bd2?! Qc7 19. Bc3 Rf7 20. Bxg7 Rxg7
21. Ng5 Nf5 22. Ne6?! Qd7 23. Qxd7 Rxd7
24. Kf2 Re8 25. Ng5 Nxe3 26. Rfe1 Rde7 27. Bf3
h6 0–1

(662) MUGRIDGE, D–FINE

U.S. Lightning Championship finals, New York, 1945
    (24 June)
English Opening, Anti-Grünfeld [A16]

1. c4 Nf6 2. Nf3 g6 3. Nc3 d5 4. cxd5 Nxd5
5. Qb3 Nb6 6. g3 Bg7 7. Bg2 0–0 8. 0–0 c5
9. d3 Nc6 10. Be3 Nd4 11. Qd1 Bg4 12. h3 Bxf3
13. exf3 Rc8 14. f4 Qd7 15. Ne4 f5 16. Ng5 h6
17. Nf3 Nd5 18. Ne5 Bxe5 19. fxe5 Nxe3 20. fxe3
Nc6 21. Bxc6 Rxc6 22. Qb3+ Kg7 23. Rad1 Qc7
24. d4 cxd4 25. exd4 Rd8 26. Rf2 e6 27. Rfd2
Rd5 28. Kf2 Qe7 29. Qe3 Rc7 30. Rd3 Qb4
31. Qd2 Qb5

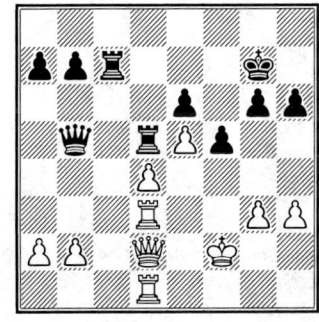

*Position after
Black's 31st move*

32. Rc3 Rcd7 33. Rd3 Qb6 34. Kf3 Qd8 35. Qe3
g5 36. Kg2 Rf7 37. Rf1 Qa5 38. a3 Rd8 39. Rc3?!
Qd5+ 40. Kh2 Qxd4 41. Qxd4 Rxd4 42. Rf2 Re4
43. Rc5 Rd7 44. Rfc2 Kg6 45. Kg2 h5 46. Kf2 h4
47. gxh4 Rxh4 48. Rc7 Rhd4 49. Rc8 Rd2+ 50. Ke3
R7d3 Mate. 0–1

International Tournaments and Matches, 1945–1951

Fine was divorced from his first wife in 1944, but remarried in 1946. His second wife, Sonya Lebeaux, bore him a son and a daughter. Fine was still a resident of Washington at the time of the Pan-American tournament, but moved to California in September 1945. There he studied at the University of Southern California, gaining a Ph.D. in Clinical Psychology in 1948.

During his years as a graduate student Fine played almost no serious chess at all. His studies would have commenced after the U.S.A.–U.S.S.R. radio match of 1945. In the three years following he played two games with Keres in Moscow 1946 and six with Herman Steiner in October 1947. On graduation Fine returned to New York City. In December 1948 and early January 1949 he gained victory in a strong event ahead of former World Champion Max Euwe and future Candidate Miguel Najdorf, who some, including Najdorf himself, thought should have been invited to the 1948 match-tournament for the World Championship. A fortnight later, in mid–January, Fine and Najdorf contested a hard-fought match in which honours were ultimately shared. In the next two years Fine played just four more competitive games.

Fine's swan song came in 1951. Although he was not in practice, and apparently lacked fighting spirit, Reuben managed to share first place with rising star Larry Evans in a short tournament held between February and April at the Marshall Chess Club. During June he made a last attempt in a major event. Handicapped by his workload during the event, he managed a rather moderate fourth place, and then bowed out of international chess.

First Pan-American Chess Congress, Hollywood (L. A.), July 28–August 12, 1945

"Chess-conscious movie stars such as Charlie Chaplin, Humphrey Bogart, Charles Boyer, Basil Rathbone, Myrna Loy, Linda Darnell, Maureen O'Sullivan and many others were largely responsible for the phenomenal growth of Steiner's Hollywood Chess Group and inspiration for a chess congress in the film city. Steiner worked zealously for six months lining up players from North and South America. With the attractive prizes offered by the *Los Angeles Times* ($1,000, $750, $500, $350, $200) his task was an easy one. Few tournaments can boast such a fund.

"The fifteen rounds were scheduled to open July 28th at 8 P.M. With rounds being played nightly at 7 P.M. Sunday rounds at 2 P.M. The event was to conclude August 11th with special features of the festival slated for Sunday, August 12th. All adjournments were scheduled for 10 A.M. each day. Unfortunately the original list of players did not attend.

America was still at war in the Pacific and travel was difficult if not impossible. Pinkus and Lasker withdrew as they could not obtain reservations. Weaver Adams, a last minute replacement, was delayed *en route* and arrived three days late with Dr. Cruz of Brazil. Herman Pilnik, another replacement from Argentina, lost his plane reservation and proceeded by car. He crashed into an unlighted truck at night and woke up in Yuma, Arizona hospital. He arrived in Hollywood three days late with his head swathed in bandages. Thus a rather hectic situation presented itself to the tournament committee. With only nine players on hand the event was started with possible entrants yet to arrive. Therefore for most of the two weeks allotted to play players were busy catching up with their postponements. It was impossible to get an accurate estimate of the leaders until late in the tournament. For a time Fine and Horowitz shared the lead as Reshevsky had several postponements. Eventually he caught up as he challenged Fine in the crucial 11th round. Both players were in time trouble with Fine having the advantage most of the time. Had the latter been able to win he would have tied for first place. Reshevsky also had a poor game against Adams but salvaged a win as Adams made a mistake during the time pressure struggle. The rest of the field offered few problems to America's No. 1 grandmaster. The race for runner-up developed late in the tournament between Fine and Pilnik. The latter played remarkably chess in spite of his recent injuries (In *How to Get Better at Chess* Pilnik recollected the tournament and felt that he might have won had he not lost to Reshevsky when still suffering from the effects of the crash). He made a game bid for second by defeating Kashdan in the last round but the Horowitz–Fine draw clinched second for the latter.

"Herbert Seidman found that his leave was shortened the last few days of the event and he had to forfeit to Kashdan, Steiner and Reshevsky.

"Many movie stars attended the special events and the tournament games. A living chess game was won by a team of Reshevsky, Fine, Horowitz, Steiner, Adams and Borochow. They defeated Pilnik, Rossetto, Cruz, Araiza, and Camarena. Hollywood's pleasant contribution to this spectacle consisted of the "living chess pieces" as Earl Carroll girls in White bathing suits were white pieces while Latin American beauties in formal gowns were the black pieces. Bud Williams and Barbara Hale of RKO were the black king and queen; Lt. P. B. Clagett and Rosanne Murray of MGM were the white king and queen. Linda Darnell of 20th Century Fox announced the moves. A suggestion that each team keep the captured pieces was turned down by the tournament committee! A gala dinner was attended by 150 chess fans who listened to Gregory Ratoff as toastmaster and participated in the distribution of prizes as conducted by Linda Darnell ... The first brilliancy prize went to Fine for his game with Steiner." (Spence)

		1	2	3	4	5	6	7	8	9	0	1	2	3	
1	Reshevsky	*	½	1	½	1	½	1	1	1	1	1	1	1	10½
2	Fine	½	*	½	½	1	½	1	1	½	½	1	1	1	9
3	Pilnik	0	½	*	½	1	½	1	½	½	1	1	1	1	8½
4	Horowitz	½	½	½	*	½	1	0	1	½	½	1	1	1	8
5	Kashdan	0	0	0	½	*	1	1	1	½	½	½	1	1	7
6	Rossetto	½	½	½	0	0	*	0	1	1	½	½	1	1	6½
7	Adams	0	0	0	1	0	1	*	½	0	0	1	1	1	5½
8	Steiner	0	0	½	0	0	0	½	*	1	1	1	1	½	5½
9	Cruz	0	½	½	½	½	0	1	0	*	½	0	½	1	5
10	Araiza	0	½	0	½	½	½	1	0	½	*	0	½	1	5
11	Broderman	0	0	0	0	½	½	0	0	1	1	*	0	½	3½
12	Seidman	0	0	0	0	0	0	0	0	½	½	1	*	1	3
13	Camarena	0	0	0	0	0	0	0	½	0	0	½	0	*	1

(663) FINE–BRODERMAN, A

Pan-American Congress, Hollywood (1), 1945 (28 July)
Queen's Indian Defence [E16]

1. d4 Nf6 2. c4 e6 3. Nf3 Bb4+ The Bogolyubov Variation. Best is 4 Bd2 Bxd2+ 5 Nbxd2 d6 6 g3 0–0 7 Bg2. On 4 ... Qe7 5 g3 Nc6 6 Bg2 Bxd2+ 7 Nbxd2 d6 8 0–0 leaves White with a slight advantage. **4. Nbd2** In PCO Fine admits his fourth is tame. The line 4 ... 0–0 5 a3 Bxd2 6 Qxd2 b6 7 Qc2 Bb7 8 Bg5 d6 9 e3 Be4 leads to equality. **4 ... b6 5. g3 Bb7 6. Bg2 0–0 7. 0–0 Bxd2** Incorrect. The exchange develops White's game too quickly. Best is 7 ... Re8 or better still 7 ... Ne4 8 Nxe4 Bxe4 9 Ne1 Bxg2 10 Kxg2 Re8 11 Nd3. **8. Qxd2 d6 9. b3 Nbd7 10. Ba3 Re8 11. Rfd1 Ne4 12. Qc2 f5**

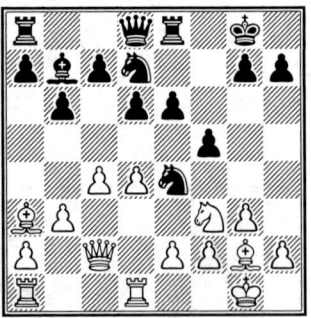

Position after Black's 12th move

13. d5 A potent thrust which opens the centre while Black is still completing his development. Broderman is forced to attempt a combination as the knight must not reach e6. **13 ... exd5 14. cxd5 Ndf6 15. Nd4! Nxd5 16. Nxf5 Qf6 17. Bxe4 Ne3 18. Nxe3 Rxe4** 18 ... Bxe4 is not as good as 19 Qxc7 Rac8 20 Qxd6 forces 20 ... Qxd6. **19. Qxc7 Rf8 20. Rf1 Ba6 21. Qxd6 Rd8** Black has no choice as White threatens Qxf8+ winning the exchange. **22. Qxf6 gxf6 23. Rfe1 Rd2 24. Kf1 h5 25. Bc1 Rd7 26. Bb2 h4 27. Rad1 Rc7 28. Nd5** Black resigned. A nice little tactical game. The piece ahead decides quickly. (Times taken—Fine 1:50, Broderman :50) **1–0** Spence 1952, 2.

(664) SEIDMAN, H—FINE

Pan-American Congress, Hollywood (2), 1945 (29 July)
Alekhine's Defence [B04]

1. e4 Nf6 2. e5 Nd5 3. d4 d6 4. Nf3 g6 5. c4 Nb6
6. exd6 cxd6 7. Nc3 Bg7 8. Be3 0–0 9. Be2 Bg4
10. 0–0 Nc6 11. b3 e5 12. d5 Ne7 13. Rc1 Nf5 14. Bg5
f6 15. Bd2 Qe7 16. Ne4 Nd7 17. Bb4 b6 18. Nfd2
Bxe2 19. Qxe2 Nd4 20. Qe3 Nc5 21. Rfe1 f5

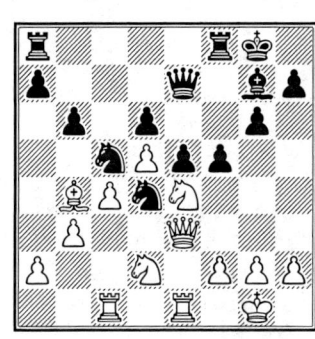

Position after
Black's 21st move

22. Nxc5 bxc5 23. Bc3 Qh4 24. b4 Bh6 25. Qd3
e4 26. Qg3 Qxg3 27. hxg3 cxb4 28. Bxb4 Rab8
29. Bc3 Bxd2 30. Bxd2 Rb2 31. Rcd1 Rc8 32. Bf4
Rxc4 33. Bxd6 Rb5 34. Rb1 Rxd5 35. Rb8+ Kf7
36. Bf4 Rd7 37. Reb1 Ne2+ 38. Kf1 Nxf4 39. gxf4
Rc2 40. R1b7 Ke7 41. Rxd7+ Kxd7 42. Rh8 Rxa2
43. Rxh7+ Ke6 44. Rg7 Kf6 45. Rc7 a5 46. Ra7
a4 47. g3 a3 48. Kg1 Ke6 49. Rg7 Rb2 50. Rxg6+
Kf7 51. Ra6 a2 Times taken—Seidman 2:00, Fine 1:59
0–1

(665) FINE—PILNIK, H

Pan-American Congress, Hollywood (3), 1945 (8 Aug.)
Queen's Gambit Declined, Lasker Variation [D55]

1. d4 Nf6 2. c4 e6 3. Nc3 d5 4. Nf3 Be7 5. Bg5
0–0 6. e3 Ne4 7. Bxe7 Qxe7 8. Rc1 c6 9. Bd3 f5
10. 0–0 Nd7 11. Nd2 Kh8 12. f4 g5?! 13. fxg5 Qxg5
14. Qe2 Nxd2 15. Qxd2 Nf6 16. Rf3 Bd7 17. Rcf1
Rg8 18. cxd5 cxd5 19. Rg3 Qh6 20. Rff3 Ng4 21. h3
Nf6 22. Ne2 Rgc8!? (*Incorrectly given as 22 ... Rac8 in
some sources*) 23. Nf4 a5 24. Rf1 b5 25. Rgf3 b4
26. Rc1 Rxc1+ 27. Qxc1 Rc8 28. Qd2 Nh5 29. Nxh5
Qxh5 30. a3 Rg8 31. Kh2 Qg5 32. axb4 axb4 33. Qf2
Qe7 34. Rg3 Qd6 35. Qf4 Qxf4 36. exf4 Rc8
37. Rf3 Kg7 38. Rf1 Ba4 39. Kg3 Kf6 40. Kf3 h5
41. g3 Times taken—Fine 2:19, Pilnik 1:46 ½–½

(666) CAMARENA, J—FINE

Pan-American Congress, Hollywood (4), 1945 (31 July)
King's Indian Attack [A08]

1. Nf3 d5 2. g3 c5 3. Bg2 g6 4. 0–0 d4 5. d3 Or
5 c3 to try to break up the centre. 5 ... Bg7 6. a4 Nf6

7. Na3 0–0 8. Nc4 Nd5 9. Bd2 Nc6 10. Qc1 A frequent manoeuvre to get rid of Black's king bishop. 10 ... e5
11. Bh6 f6 12. Bxg7 Kxg7 13. Nfd2 Be6 14. e4 dxe3
15. fxe3 Qe7 16. c3 Rad8 17. Qc2 Rd7 18. Rad1
Nb6 19. Nxb6 axb6 20. Nc4 Qd8 21. Bf3 Na7
22. e4 b5 23. axb5 Nxb5 24. Ne3 f5 25. exf5
gxf5 26. Qe2 Bb3 27. Rd2

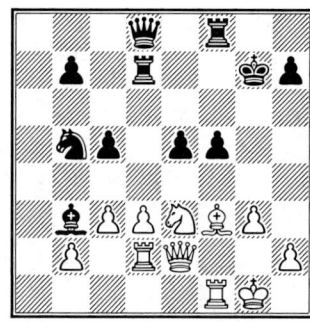

Position after
White's 27th move

27 ... Qg5 Not 27 ... e4? because of 28 Bxe4! fxe4
29 Qg4+ Kh8 30 Rxf8+ Qxf8 and 31 Qxd7! 28. Rf2
Protecting himself from the threat of ... f4. 28 ... Kh8?!
Nevertheless, 28 ... f4 looks best. AW 29. Nc4 White
could have played 29 d4! with advantage. AW 29 ... e4
30. dxe4?? 30 Bxe4 might lead to 30 ... Bxc4 31 dxc4
Nxc3 32 bxc3 Rxd2 33 Qxd2 Qxd2 34 Rxd2 fxe4 with a
probable draw. 30 ... Bxc4 31. Qxc4 Rxd2 32. Qxc5
Nd6 33. Rxd2 Qxd2 34. Qe5+ Kg8 35. Qe6+ Nf7
BCM (where the player of White is identified as Camara)
has 35 ... Kh8 36 exf5 Ra8? (36 ... Re8. AW) 37 Bg2?
(37 Qe5+!) Ra1+ 38 Bf1 Qd3 and wins. 36. exf5 Ra8
37. Bg2? Ra1+ 38. Bf1 Qd3 39. Qc8+ Kg7 40. f6+
Kxf6 41. Qh3 White resigned. A lucky win for Fine. 0–1
Dr. J. A. Seitz, BCM 1945, 243–4.

(667) FINE—CRUZ, W

Pan-American Congress, Hollywood (5), 1945 (1 Aug.)
English Opening, Flohr-Mikenas Variation [A19]

1. c4 Nf6 2. Nc3 e6 3. e4 c5 4. e5 Ng8 5. g3?! Nc6
6. f4 d6 7. Nf3 Nge7 8. exd6 Nf5 9. Bg2 Bxd6
10. 0–0 0–0 11. Ne4 Nfd4 12. d3 Be7 13. Be3 f5
14. Nc3 Bf6 15. Qd2 Qe7 16. Rfe1 Rd8 17. Bf2 Qd6
18. Rad1 Bd7 19. Ne2 Be8 20. Nexd4 Nxd4 21. Nxd4
Bxd4 22. Bxd4 Qxd4+ 23. Qf2 Kf7 24. Re5 Rac8
25. Bf1 Rd6 26. Rde1 Qxf2+ 27. Kxf2 Bd7 28. Ke3
Ra6 29. Ra1 Rb6 30. Rb1 a5 31. d4 cxd4+ 32. Kxd4
Rd6+ 33. Ke3 b6 34. Rc1 Rc5 35. Be2 Kf6 36. Rxc5
bxc5 37. Rc3 e5 38. Ra3 a4 39. b3 exf4+ 40. gxf4
Re6+ Draw agreed. ½–½

(668) ADAMS, W—FINE

Pan-American Congress, Hollywood (6), 1945 (2 Aug.)
French Defence, Burn Variation [C11]

1. e4 e6 2. d4 d5 3. Nc3 Nf6 4. Bg5 dxe4 A very

popular line today as it avoids the many complicated lines of attack which abound in the French Defence, not the least of which is the Alekhine-Chatard Attack 4 ... Be7 5 e5 Nfd7 6 h4! **5. Nxe4** Alternatives are 5 Bxf6 Qxf6 (5 ... gxf6 6 Nxe4 f5 7 Nc3 Bg7 8 Nf3 0–0 9 Qd2) 6 Nxe4 Qd8 7 Nf3 Nd7 8 Bd3 Be7 with even chances. The text follows *PCO* page 80 column 26. **5 ... Be7 6. Bxf6 gxf6** 6 ... Bxf6 7 Nf3 Nd7 8 c3 Qe7 9 Qc2 c5 10 dxc5 Nxc5 leads to a slight pull for White. **7. g3** Adams deviates from 7 Qd2 f5 8 Nc3 c6 9 0–0–0 Nd7. **7 ... b6 8. Bg2 c6 9. Qd2 Bb7 10. Ne2 Qc7 11. Qh6** Adams goes astray due to his refusal to castle when he has anything else to do as he says. Here 11 0–0–0 was best. The queen excursion was a waste of time. **11 ... Nd7 12. Qg7 Rf8 13. N4c3 f5 14. Qxh7 0–0–0 15. Bf3 c5 16. Bxb7+ Qxb7 17. 0–0–0 Nf6**

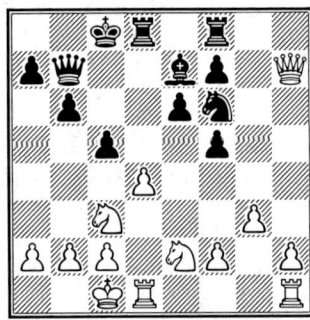

Position after Black's 17th move

18. Qh3 Capturing the Black's h-pawn was a loss of time justifiable only after a rapid advance of his own h-pawn. Since this was not possible the counterattack against the queen was worth the pawn. **18 ... cxd4 19. Nb5** 19 Nxd4 loses to 19 ... Rxd4 20 Rxd4 Qxh1+!. **19 ... Ng4 20. Qf1 e5 21. h3 Nf6 22. Nexd4** Desperation. Black threatens ... a6 forcing Na3 and ... Bxa3 with a winning position. **22 ... exd4 23. Qc4+ Kb8 24. Nxd4 Rc8 25. Qa4 Bc5 26. Nb5 a6 27. Qf4+ Ka8 28. Nc3 Rc6 29. g4 fxg4 30. hxg4 Ng8 31. Rh8 Rfc8 32. Ne4 Ne7 33. Rxc8+ Nxc8 34. f3 Ka7 35. Nf6 Bd6 36. Qf5 Ne7 37. Qe4 Ng6 38. Kb1 Be5 39. Nd5 Rd6 40. c4 Rd7** Here White sealed 41 Rd1 which was impossible. Analysis shows he has a difficult game which would go downhill after ... b5 dislodging the knight. (Times taken— Adams 2:24, Fine 1:58) **0–1** Spence 1952, 19.

(669) Fine—Steiner, H

Pan-American Congress, Hollywood (7), 1945 (4 Aug.)
Queen's Gambit Accepted [D29]

1. d4 d5 2. c4 dxc4 3. Nf3 Nf6 4. e3 e6 5. Bxc4 c5 6. 0–0 a6 All book so far. Black's decision to liberate the queenside immediately is probably playable but dangerous. **7. Qe2 b5 8. Bb3 Bb7 9. a4!** As played by Dr. Euwe against Alekhine in the Bad Nauheim Tournament of 1937, but 9 Rd1 is more usual, *PCO* 157. **9 ... c4?** Weak. On 9 ... Nbd7 Ståhlberg's 10 e4! gives White a clear positional advantage after 10 ... cxd4 11 axb5 Qb6 12 e5 Nd5

13 Bc4 a5 14 Bd2 Bc5 15 Na3 0–0 16 Bd3, *PCO*. **10. Bc2 Nc6 11. axb5 axb5 12. Rxa8 Qxa8 13. Nc3 Qa5**

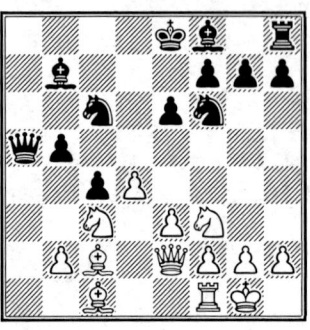

Position after Black's 13th move

14. e4 The position I had in mind. Black is now unable to develop normally because of the threat of d5. **14 ... Nd7** It is difficult, if at all possible, to find an adequate defence. On 14 ... b4 15 d5 Nd8 (surely 15 ... Nb8, allowing a knight to interpose on d7, would be better. AW) 16 Ba4+ is decisive. The text would be good if it were not for the sacrifice. **15. d5 Nd8** Now Black's game does not look so bad; he threatens ... Be7, ... 0–0, ... b4, with easy equality, for dxe6 at any time can be met by ... Nxe6. Still, there is a way to exploit his lack of development. **16. Nd4! b4 17. Ncb5!** Loses a piece, but obtains a winning attack, which is the idea. **17 ... e5** The main variation. On 17 ... b3, which stops Re1 at a later stage (as in the game), White replies 18 dxe6 fxe6 19 Qh5+! Ke7 (otherwise Nd6+) 20 Bb1, with a decisive attack. **18. Qxc4 exd4 19. Nc7+ Ke7**

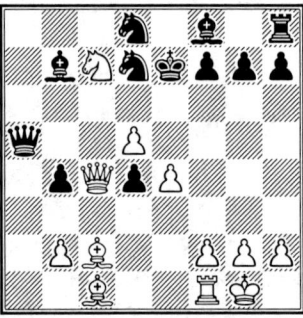

Position after Black's 19th move

20. e5! Not 20 Bd2 Ne5! 21 Bxb4+ Kd7 and Black gets out. **20 ... Nxe5 21. Re1 f6 22. d6+! Kxd6 23. Nb5+**

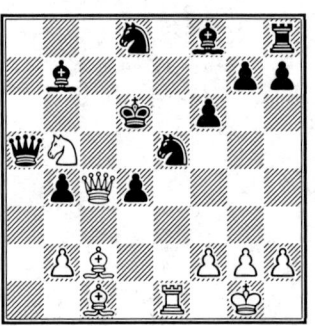

Position after White's 23rd move

23 ... Qxb5 It is a pity Steiner did not allow the continuation which is really the crux of the entire combinative series beginning with White's sixteenth move. It runs 23 ... Ke7 24 Rxe5+ fxe5 25 Bg5+ Ke8 26 Nc7+ Kd7 27 Bf5+ Kd6 (or 27 ... Ne6 28 Bxe6+) 28 Ne8 mate. **24. Qxb5 Kc7 25. Qa5+** Black resigned. One of the most pleasing games I have ever played. **1–0** Fine, 1948, 38–41.

(670) KASHDAN, I—FINE

Pan-American Congress, Hollywood (8), 1945 (5 Aug.)
Alekhine's Defence [B02]

1. e4 Nf6 In recent master play 1 e4 has proved so successful that Fine apparently feels the need for some novelty. **2. e5 Nd5 3. c4 Nb6 4. d4 d6 5. exd6 Qxd6** Can it be that Fine's long association with Emanuel Lasker has resulted in a weakness for psychological moves?! The text is demonstrably bad. AD **6. Nc3** 6 Be3 (not 6 c5 Qe6+) Qd8 7 Bd3 g6 8 Nf3 Bg7 9 Nc3 0–0 10 h3 is also good as in Zubarev–Grünfeld, Moscow 1925. PCO **6 ... Qd8 7. Nf3 Bg4 8. c5** He advances the pawn after all, but under less favourable circumstances. If now 8 ... Nd5 9 Qb3 Nxc3 (9 ... Bxf3 10 Qxb7 leads to similar variations) 10 Qxb7 Bxf3 11 gxf3 Qxd4 (11 ... Qd5! AW) 12 Be3 Qd5 13 c6! wins. Hence Fine replies carefully. **8 ... N6d7 9. h3 Bh5 10. g4 Bg6 11. Bg2** The pawn advances have given White a very aggressive position; but if his initiative ever sags, his pawn position may lead to difficulties. **11 ... c6 12. Bf4** White's position is distinctly superior, *PCO*. **12 ... e6 13. 0–0 Be7**

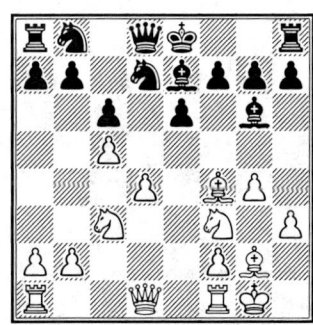

Position after Black's 13th move

14. Qe2 A superfluous routine move. 14 b4 at once would have saved useful time. **14 ... 0–0 15. b4 Na6 16. b5 Nb4 17. bxc6 bxc6** 17 ... Bd3 loses material after 18 Qb2. But now 18 ... Bd3 is threatened. **18. Qd2 Qc8 19. Nb5 Nd5** The posting of the wandering queen's knight on this solid square has of course greatly improved Black's game. **20. Nd6 Qa6 21. Bg3 Bd8 22. Rfd1 Qa4** Not 22 ... Ba5 23 Bf1! and Black's game looks pretty bleak. The text is played with a view to 23 ... Ba5 followed by 24 ... Nc3. **23. Nb7 Qa6 24. Nxd8** Kashdan jumps at the opportunity to obtain two bishops for two knights. However, his endgame position will be slightly inferior because of the rapidity with which Black can double rooks on the d-file. Consequently, it would have been more prudent to play 24 Nd6; Black would then hardly have anything better than a draw by repetition. **24 ... Rfxd8 25. Nh4 N7f6 26. Nxg6 hxg6 27. a4 Rd7 28. Bf1 Qc8 29. Qa5 Ne4 30. Bh2 Qd8**

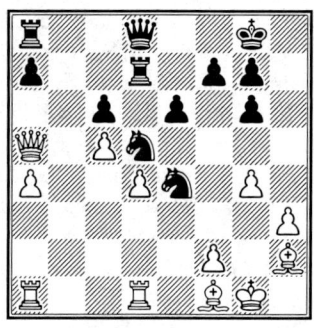

Position after Black's 30th move

31. Qxd8+ Hardly in the spirit of the position. White seems to be entirely unaware of the danger to his d-pawn, or else he is counting too heavily on his two bishops. More aggressive and full of possibilities where the bishops come into their own, would be the following sacrifice: 31 Qa6 N5c3 32 Qxc6 Nxd1 (32 ... Rc8! AW) 33 Rxd1! a likely continuation is 33 ... Nc3 34 Rc1 Rc8 35 Qa6 Ne4 36 f3 Rxd4 37 c6 Qf8 38 Qxc8 Qxc8 39 Rb1!! and wins. **31 ... Raxd8 32. Bg2?!** Missing his last chance. 32 f3 would still have given him a chance to regroup his pieces and hold his game together. From now on White's position becomes steadily more helpless in the face of Fine's pitilessly accurate play. **32 ... Ndc3 33. Re1 Rxd4 34. Be5 Rc4 35. Bxc3 Nxc3 36. Bxc6 Rxc5 37. Bg2 Rd2 38. a5** If instead 38 Kf1 Rc4 39 Rac1 Rf4 40 f3 Nd5 and White's position is a sorry mess. **38 ... Ne2+ 39. Kf1 Nf4 40. Rec1 Rxc1+ 41. Rxc1 Ra2** Winning still another pawn, for if 42 Rc5?? Ra1+ forces mate. **42. Rc8+ Kh7 43. Kg1 Rxa5** White's resignation is now in order. The rest is played methodically by Fine. **44. Kh2 g5 45. Bc6 Ng6 46. Be4 f5 47. Bc2 Nf4 48. Bb3 Ra3 49. Rb8 g6 50. Rb7+ Kg8 51. f3 a5 52. Kg3 a4 53. Bc4 Rc3 54. Rb4 Rc2 55. Bf1 Nd5 56. Rb8+ Kg7 57. h4 f4+ 58. Kh3 Rf2 59. Rb7+ Kf6 60. hxg5+ Kxg5 61. Bg2 a3** White resigned. Times taken—Kashdan 3:00, Fine 2:50. **0–1** Denker from *The Chess Review* in Spence 1952, 25–6.

(671) FINE—RESHEVSKY, S

Pan-American congress, Hollywood (9), 1945 (7 Aug.)
Grünfeld Defence, Russian Variation [D81]

1. d4 Nf6 2. c4 g6 3. Nc3 d5 4. Qb3 c6 5. cxd5 Nxd5 6. e4 Nb6 7. Nf3 Bg7 8. Qd1 An inaccuracy which works out well. 8 h3!, to sacrifice the pawn, was better, for example, 8 ... Bxd4 9 Bh6 c5 10 Bb5+ Bd7 11 0–0 with a strong attack. RF **8 ... 0–0** But this allows White to rectify the omission. Correct was 8 ... Bg4. If then 9 Be3 e5! 10 d5 cxd5 11 exd5 0–0 with the better game for Black (12 Be2 f5). RF **9. h3!** Now Black's light-squared bishop has no good square and his game begins to deteriorate. RF **9 ... Qc7 10. Be2 Rd8 11. Qc2!** N8d7 11 ... Bxd4 can be answered either by 12 Nxd4 Rxd4 13 Nb5 winning rook for knight and pawn (Fine) or by the immediate 12 Nb5 winning a piece for a pawn. AW **12. 0–0 e5** Black has managed to play the first essential freeing manoeuvre; the question now is will he be able to get all his pieces out? RF **13. Bg5** To develop with tempo, or to block the diagonal of Black's dark-squared bishop. RF **13 ... Re8 14. Rad1** For the moment White's primary purpose is to maintain his lead in development. RF **14 ... exd4 15. Nxd4 Nf8** Black seems to be freeing himself; he already threatens ... Bxd4 followed by ... Ne6, and on a move such as 16 Be3 Ne6 17 Nb3 Nf4 is satisfactory. RF **16. Bh4! 16 ... a6** The need for this time consuming move demonstrates the force of White's bishop retreat. On 16 ... Ne6 17 Nxe6 Bxe6 18 Nb5! and wins the exchange, for example, 18 ... Qe5 19 Bg3 (the simpler 19 Nd6 Rf8 20 Rd2 is also strong) Qxb2 20 Qxb2 Bxb2 21 Nc7 and the a-pawn may not be taken, so that Black's compensation is inadequate, or 18 ... Qb8 19 Nd6 Rf8 20 Be7. RF **17. Bg3 Qe7 18.f4** The vital tempo gained gives this attack its force. RF **18 ... Ne6 19. Nb3** Black's knight is out, but the remainder of his pieces are still badly posted. RF **19 ... c5** The difficulties are great. If 19 ... Nc5 20 Nxc5 Qxc5+ 21 Bf2 Qa5 22 e5! with a clear advantage (the threat is b4), for example, 22 ... Bf5 23 Qb3 Nd7 24 Bc4 and wins. RF **20. e5 c4 21. Nd4 Nxd4 22. Rxd4 Bf5 23. Qd2** Black has managed to develop, but his c-pawn has become fatally weak. RF **23 ... f6 24. Rd6 Rad8** At this stage of the game Reshevsky had little more than a couple of minutes to complete his 40 moves. It is indeed remarkable that he maintained his composure under the circumstances. IH **25. Rd1** And here with a win for the asking I begin to falter. Simplest was 25 Nd5!, which wins a pawn without complications and maintains the superiority of the position: 25 ... Nxd5 26 Qxd5+ Kh8 27 Bxc4 and Black has no real counterplay. The text was still good enough, however. RF **25 ... Rxd6 26. Qxd6** Again second best, but again still good enough. Stronger was 26 exd6 Qd8 27 Bf2 followed by Qd4. RF **26 ... Qxd6**

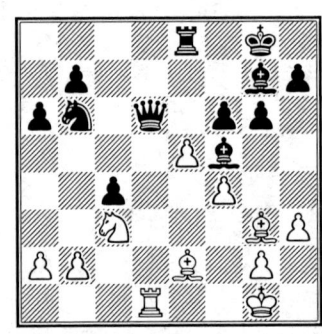

*Position after
Black's 26th move*

27. Rxd6? But this definitely throws away the win. 27 exd6 was still sufficient, since a pawn goes. If, for example, 27 ... Be6 28 Bf3 Rb8? 29 d7! wins a piece (threats f5 and Rd6). RF **27 ... Nc8 28. Bxc4+ Kf8!** Avoiding the last trap: 28 ... Kh8? 29 Rd2 fxe5 30 fxe5 Bxe5 (if 30 ... Nb6 31 Bf7) 31 Rd8!! and wins the exchange (Chernev). RF **29. Rd1 fxe5 30. fxe5 Bxe5 31. Bxe5 Rxe5 32. g4 Be6** Not 32 ... Bc2 33 Rd2. Hereabouts we were both in terrible time pressure, and in accordance with the rules of the tournament every once in a while the clocks would be stopped to bring the scores up to date. Very amusing for the spectators, and a welcome breather for the players, but the laws of tournament chess should be clarified to prevent such spectacles. RF **33. Rd8+ Ke7 34. Rh8 Bxc4 35. Rxc8 Bd5 36. Rc7+**

Kf6 **37. Nxd5+** 37 Rxh7 Bc6 is a better try; however, a draw is still the probable result. RF **37 ... Rxd5 38. Rxb7 Rd2 39. a4 Kg5 40. Rxh7 Rxb2 41. Rd7 Ra2 42. Rd4 Kh4** Draw agreed. ½-½ Fine 1948, 42–7; Horowitz from *The Chess Review*, October 1945 in Gordon, 105–6.

(672) ARAIZA, J—FINE

Pan-American Congress, Hollywood (10), 1945 (8 Aug.)
Nimzowitsch-Indian Defence, Classical Variation [E33]

1. d4 Nf6 2. c4 e6 3. Nc3 Bb4 4. Qc2 Nc6 5. Nf3 d6 6. Bg5 h6 7. Bxf6 Qxf6 8. a3 Bxc3+ 9. Qxc3 0–0 10. e4 e5 11. d5 Nd4 12. Nxd4 exd4 13. Qd2 c5 14. Bd3 Qg6 15. f4 Re8 16. 0–0 f5 17. e5 dxe5 18. fxe5 Rxe5 19. Rae1 Draw agreed. Times taken— Araiza 1:10, Fine 0:55. ½-½

(673) FINE—ROSSETTO, H

Pan-American Congress, Hollywood (12), 1945 (10 Aug.)
The score of this game is not available. ½-½

(674) HOROWITZ, I—FINE

Pan-American Congress, Hollywood (13), 1945 (11 Aug.)
The score of this game is not available. ½-½

Radio Match with Isaac Boleslavsky, U.S.A.–U.S.S.R., September 1–4, 1945

"Years before the American magazine *Chess Review* proposed a match, pitting the Soviets against the U.S. team that had won four straight Olympiads. But the war intervened and efforts were revived only after Nikolai Romanov was named chairman of the Sports Committee in March 1945. Arrangements for a match in September 1945 quickly fell into place and the two sides agreed that ten players from each team would play two games each, with moves transmitted by radio. Nikolai Zubarev and members of the United States and British embassies would head a judges' panel to enforce the rules in Moscow, while a member of the Soviet consulate in New York joined the panel on the other side of the Atlantic. The games began at 5 P.M. in Moscow but 10 A.M. in New York—and dragged on because of transmission errors in virtually every game as well as other delays. Igor Bondarevsky said that it took more than 10 minutes for a full move to be sent back and forth, adding more than six hours to the length of a 40-move game. With a time control at move 32, eight of the games had to be adjourned." (Soltis 2000)

According to the 1945 U.S.C.F. Yearbook (*U.S.C.F. 9,* 54–5) " ... the practical difficulties demanded much careful thought and ingenuity. Transmission difficulties were ably solved by the Mackay Radio Company, which did the sending and receiving, with a competent staff under the supervision of Henry Leleu. Time involved in sending or receiving a move was reduced to five minutes, of which only one minute was needed for the actual transmission and the other four consumed in coding or decoding, receiving an acknowledgement and other details."

The result of the match was a shock for many Americans, who expected that a team headed by United States Champion and containing six members of successful pre-war Olympiad teams would at least provide tough opposition for the acknowledged rising force of world chess. Herman Steiner was the only American to win his individual encounter, gaining a win and a draw against former Soviet Champion Igor Bondarevsky on board 6; Horowitz had a win and a loss in his match with Flohr and Pinkus made two draws with Lilienthal (these two were now naturalized citizens of the U.S.S.R.). The presence of Dake and Simonson, had they been available, in place of Santasiere and Seidman would undoubtedly have strengthened the American team. The *British Chess Magazine* commented "On another page we give the detailed result of the Radio match between the U.S.A. and the U.S.S.R. The result 15½–4½ in favour of the Russians is more overwhelming than most people expected, and will no doubt give our friends over the water much food for thought. What is the reason for this debacle? Are the Russians more talented than their rivals to the extent of 15½–4½? Emphatically no. We publish elsewhere a letter from J. Hannak, which contains some very hard criticism of the trend of American chess. Although we disagree with a good deal of what Mr. Hannak says, the opinion of a former editor of the *Wiener Schachzeitung* cannot be treated lightly. His strictures are partly directed against our contemporary the *Chess Review*. In their praiseworthy and successful efforts to create new adherents, the *Chess Review* has recourse to many devices known to modern journalism. Moreover, it has the difficult task of catering for the beginner as well as the expert. But we hardly think that the fact that they publish photographs of pretty ladies and good looking film stars playing at chess has anything to do with the result of the match. We prefer to think that the reason is inadequate training. It is a well-known fact that you cannot improve your strength except by hard games with players stronger than yourself if possible, or at least in the same class.

Now for the last thirty years Russia has had the advantage of the active support of their Government. Chess is being taught at school by experts and even masters. Everything is done, even after the school years, to continue the training of everyone who shows talent. In result we find in Russia today over one million "registered" players, well over fifty qualified masters, more, probably, than in the rest of the world. Of these, at least eight can claim to be in the grandmaster class. In the U.S.S.R. there is a keen rivalry

between provinces and towns. A continuous round of tournaments culminates in a yearly championship contest. This, including eliminating tournaments, brings together some sixty outstanding players. The final invariably is the equal in strength of a strong International Masters' tournament, and the participants must necessarily at all times be at the top of their form. Moreover, such is their enthusiasm, that after each game all the various points are discussed and examined, so that their knowledge of the most subtle points in the opening and practiced skill in the endgame must give them the advantage over players here and in America, of whom the majority care little for their last game except the result. What do we find in America? Two grandmasters of the top class, Reshevsky and Fine. We have not heard that, as preparation for the radio match, they indulged in a practice match, their only chance of getting into real form. Lightning tournaments, and even ordinary tournaments, in which most of the participants are a class below them will hardly fit them for a contest against their equals."

		1	2	
Boleslavsky		½	1	1½
Fine		½	0	½

(675) FINE—BOLESLAVSKY, 1

U.S.A.-U.S.S.R. radio-match board 3 (1), 1945 (1 Sept.)
King's Indian Defence, Fianchetto Variation [A53]

1. d4 Nf6 2. c4 d6 3. g3 g6 4. Bg2 Bg7 5. e4!? In PCO Fine later wrote "5 e4 at once exposes White to counterplay," and recommended instead 5 Nc3 0-0 6 Nf3 Nbd7 7 0-0 e5, followed by either 8 b3 or 8 e4. **5 ... 0-0 6. Ne2 e5!** Much better than 6 ... Nbd7, since it reserves the possibility of ... Nc6. HK **7. 0-0** The game continuation shows that 7 Nbc3 should have been preferred. HK **7 ... exd4!** With this move Black gives up his strong-point in the centre, with the aim of gaining free play for his pieces. DB **8. Nxd4 Nc6! 9. Nc2** This is why White should have played 7 Nbd2. If he had done so he could now have played 9 Nde2 Be6 10 b3. HK **9 ... Be6 10. Ne3 Ne5 11. Na3 Nfg4** The attack on the c4 pawn has forced the white knights to take up somewhat awkward positions, and now Black intends to attack the white centre by advancing his f-pawn. DB **12. Nd5 c6 13. Nf4 Bc8 14. Bd2 f5 15. Qb3 fxe4 16. Bxe4 Nf6** A pity. After the game Boleslavsky showed that with 16 ... Nd7 (a typically King's Indian move), aiming for the fine post at c5, Black could have fully justified his opening strategy. The point is that 17 Ne6, for example, can be answered by 17 ... Qe7 18 Nxf8 Nc5 19 Qd1 Qxe4 20 f3 Qd4+ 21 Kg2 Ne5, when the white knight is lost, and Black's two minor pieces are much superior to White's rook and pawn. DB (This seems to be an accurate appraisal, in which case White might be forced to play 17 Nd3 with a slightly worse position. AW) **17. Bg2 Qc7 18. Rad1 Bg4 19. f3 Bf5 20. Bb4** Now White centralizes his pieces and with the attack on the weak d6 pawn he forces Black onto the defensive. DB **20 ... Nf7**

21. g4 Bd7 22. Nc2 The tempting 22 B×d6 N×d6 23 R×d6 (so that if 23 … Q×d6? 24 c5+) allows Black good counterplay with 23 … Ne8. Now Black makes a desperate attempt to gain some play on the queenside, but at the cost of weakening his position in the centre. DB **22 … a5! 23. Be1 a4 24. Qb4 b5! 25. c×b5 Qb6+ 26. Bf2 c5! 27. Rfe1 Rfb8 28. Qd2 B×b5** Black has play against the b2 pawn, but White is very strong on the central files. DB **29. g5** Impatiently played. White could have increased the positional pressure with 29 h4 followed by 30 g5 and 31 Nd5, or 29 Ne6 Be8 30 g5 followed by 31 Ne3 and 32 Nd5, in each case occupying the weak d5 square. DB **29 … N×g5** Forced, for if 29 … Nf6 would allow White to play 30 Nd5, with a great advantage. HK **30. N×g6! h×g6 31. Q×g5 Be8 32. f4 Ra7** Here the game was adjourned. HK **33. Ne3 Bf7 34. f5** Black's position looks critical, but his king's defences, with the g7 bishop playing a major role, prove surprisingly resilient. DB **34 … Nh7! 35. Qg4 g5 36. Nd5 Qd8 37. h4 R×b2** Black's plan of counterplay has succeeded, and the worst for him is now over. DB **38. Be3** On 38 B×c5 d×c5 39 Ne7+ Q×e7 40 R×c7 R×c7 Black would have plenty of material for the queen. HK **38 … g×h4 39. Bh6 B×d5 40. B×d5+ Kh8 41. Bc1** Black's defences also hold after 41 Qh5 (threatening Re8+) 41 … Rb8, e.g. 42 Bc6 Qg8 43 Kh1 B×h6 44 Q×h6 Qg4. DB **41 … Rb4 42. Qh5 Be5 43. Kh1 Rd4** Black has defended strongly, however, the situation has become critical and he can risk no more. The text breaks White's attack but also renders Black's extra pawns worthless. HK **44. R×d4 c×d4 45. Bf4 d3!** This tactical resource saves the game. Black's defences hold after 46 R×e5 d×e5 47 B×e5+ Rg7 48 Qf7 Qf8, while after 46 B×e5+ d×e5 47 R×e5 Re7 48 Q×h4 d2 he even wins. DB **46. f6 d2 47. B×d2 Q×f6 48. Rc1 Qf8 49. Q×h4 Rc7 50. Rg1 Rg7 51. R×g7** An extraordinarily difficult game, worthy of two great masters. HK ½–½ Bronstein 1999, 14–7; Kmoch 1945, 14–5.

(676) BOLESLAVSKY, I—FINE

U.S.A.-U.S.S.R. radio-match board 3 (2), 1945 (3 Sept.)
Spanish Game, Steinitz Defence Deferred [C71]

1. e4 e5 2. Nf3 Nc6 3. Bb5 a6 4. Ba4 d6 5. c4 The continuation of the Czech Grandmaster Duras, introduced into contemporary practice by Keres; for several years it was considered the strongest retort to the improved Steinitz Defence. IB **5 … Bd7** After this passive defensive move, White carries out d4 and obtains a good game. A telling blow for the move 5 c4 was a game of the 15th U.S.S.R. Championship Leningrad 1947, Goldenov–Yudovich, in which Black continued 5 … Bg4!, exploiting the weakening of the d4 square. The continuation was 6 Nc3 (In PCO—but not MCO—Fine quotes the game Wojcikowski–Pirc, Jurata 1937: 6 h3 B×f3 7 Q×f3 Ne7 8 Nc3 Ng6 9 0–0 Be7 10 Nd5 0–0 11 B×c6 b×c6 12 Ne3 Nh4! 13 Qd1 f5 with equality. AW) Nf6 7 h3 B×f3 8 Q×f3 Be7 9 d3 0–0 10 Be3 Nd7 11 Nd5 Nc5 12 B×c5 d×c5 13 B×c6 d×c6 14 N×e7+ Q×e7 and, despite the pawn structure, Black's position is preferable. IB

6. Nc3 6 d4 is a bit more precise, since Black may now play 6 … Nd4. RF **6 … g6** This risky move I chose mainly because of the score. 6 … Nf6 is sufficient for equality: after 7 d4 N×d4 8 N×d4 e×d4 9 B×d7+ Q×d7 10 Q×d4 Be7 11 0–0 0–0 12 Re1 b5! Black can free himself. RF **7. d4 e×d4** The surrender of the centre is premature, better is 7 … Bg7 (as occurred earlier in Boleslavsky–Goldberg, U.S.S.R. Championship, Moscow 1945, a game won by Boleslavsky. AW). IB **8. N×d4** And here 8 … N×d4 9 B×d7+ Q×d7 10 N×d4 f6 was safer. RF **8 … Bg7 9. N×c6** The usual continuation here is 9 Be3, but practice has shown that in this case it is difficult for White to count on obtaining an advantage. IB (The line is assessed by Fine as equal after 9 … Nge7 10 0–0 0–0 11 Bc2 Ne5, PCO 376. AW) **9 … b×c6?** A mistake, leading to serious consequences. Necessary was 9 … B×c6 10 B×c6+ b×c6 11 Be3 Ne7. After 12 Bd4 White stands a little better, but the greatly simplified game eases Black's defence. IB **10. 0–0 Ne7?** On 10 … c5 would follow 11 Nd5, and Black is forced to play 11 … c6 or 11 … h6, compromising his position. IB **11. c5!** A strong move, after which Black gets into a difficult position. If 11 … d×c5, then 12 Be3; if 11 … d5, then 12 e×d5 c×d5 13 N×d5 N×d5 14 Q×d5 B×a4 15 Qe4+ to White's advantage. IB **11 … Nc6** From here on life was a question of lesser evils. RF **12. Be3 0–0 13. Qd2 Qe7** Black holds on to the material not because he wants to but because there is no good way to give it up. RF (Kmoch suggests 13 … f5 as a possible alternative. AW) **14. Rad1 Be8?** With this move, Black once and for all breaks the interaction of his pieces. He should prefer 14 … Rd8. IB **15. f4! f5** In the hope that the g-file might eventually offer some counterplay. 15 … f6 is a bit more cautious but condemns Black to pure passivity. RF **16. e×f5 g×f5** On 16 … R×f5 there might follow 17 Bc2 Rf8 18 e×d6 c×d6 19 f5 with powerful effect. HK **17. Rfe1 d×c5** So as to have the possibility of bringing out the knight c8. IB **18. Qf2 Nd6 19. B×c5 Qd8** Black's position is clearly unsatisfactory. White only needs to find the correct plan to realize his advantage. IB **20. Bd4!** White could win a pawn by 20 Qf3, but Black would obtain counterchances and confuse the game. With the move 20 Bd4, White exchanges Black's only active piece—the bishop g7, after which Black is defenceless against the combinational attack in the centre and on both flanks. The weakness of the kingside forces Black to go in for an exchange of queens but the endgame is very bad for him because of the broken pawn structure. IB **20 … B×d4 21. Q×d4 Qf6** Although the endgame is theoretically lost, it offers some chances—endgames always do. RF **22. Bb3!** Precise as ever. Inferior is 22 Q×f6 R×f6 23 Re7 Rf7 24 Bb3 Kf8! RF **22 … Kh8 23. Q×f6+ R×f6 24. Re7 Rc8 25. Rde1** In order to transfer the rook to the fifth rank. 25 Na4 Ne4 26 Be6 Rb8 27 B×f5 would also be good here. IB **25 … Bg6** The best drawing hope is an ending with rook and bishop against rook and bishop. If 25 … Bf7 26 B×f7 R×f7 27 R×f7 N×f7 28 Re7 Kg7 29 Na4 Black remains bottled up, and White wins easily. RF **26. R1e6 R×e6** If 26 … Rff8, then 27 Re5 and Black does not save the pawns on the queenside. IB **27. B×e6 Re8 28. R×e8+ B×e8 29. Na4!** Fixing the queenside pawns. Black has miraculously managed to preserve material equality but the bad pawns cost him the game. RF **29 ... Kg7 30. Nc5 a5 31. Kf2 Bf7** A minor trap: ... Ne4+; N×e4 B×e6. RF **32. B×f7 K×f7 33. b3 h5 34. Ke2 Ke7 35. Ke3 Nb5** Other moves also lead to the speedy loss of a pawn. HK **36. Nb7 c5 37. N×a5 Kd6 38. Nc4+ Kd5 39. Kd3 Nd6** Not a mistake but desperation. HK **40. N×d6! c×d6 41. a3** The sealed move, which was radioed "open for inspection." Against a careless continuation such as 41 Ke3 Kc6 42 Kf3 d5 Black has drawing hopes, but after the text the queenside pawns will be exchanged and White will walk in on the kingside. Black resigned. I have lost such games only to the very greatest masters. RF **1–0** Fine 1948, 270–3; Boleslavsky from Adams, 65–6 & 68–9; Kmoch 1945, 30–1.

In his chess column of 30 September Herman Steiner recorded that Fine gave a talk about the reasons for the United States' loss to the Soviet Union. On this same occasion he played four games of chess at 10 seconds a move without the sight of the board, losing the first to Harry Borochow, he played a second which he won. In November and December Fine gave talks at and directed the championship of Steiner's Hollywood Chess Group. In May 1946 he acted as referee at the match between Arnold Denker and Herman Steiner for the United States Championship.

Match with Paul Keres, U.S.A.–U.S.S.R., Moscow, September 12–15, 1946

"The U.S.A. teams did rather better in this match than in the Radio Match a year ago. The score of the first round was 7 to 3, but the U.S.A. team made a fine recovery in the second round, though they lost this also by 5½ to 4½. Curiously enough, all the American stars failed badly and success came on the lower boards. The top five boards scored two half-points during the match, or 1 to 9, while the last five scored 6½ to 3½! In the second round they actually scored 4 to 1." (BCM) "The radio match of 1945 led immediately to the arranging of an over-the-board match, which has proved no disappointment. Everybody can be satisfied—the Russians with their second victory, the Americans with their improved showing and the whole chess world with the quality of the games. The 15½–4½ result of the 1945 match was a bit too grim. Nobody believed that the Russians were quite so much better, in spite of the admittedly exceptional standing of Russian Chess. The U.S.S.R. is clearly stronger than the U.S.A., but the situation is not hopeless. The war was allowed to interfere with first-class chess much more severely in the U.S.A. than in Russia. It is pleasing news that it has been agreed to have these meetings annually.

The match was an eventful one. It was particularly well organized. Remarkable was the obstinacy with which most of the games were fought; nine out of ten had to be adjourned at the end of the first session, and great inroads were made into the time of the adjournment session, as is

well illustrated by the lengths of the games (66 on board 4, 64 on board seven, 71 on board eight, and 118 on board ten!). The Russians were actually lucky to win the second round, several good games being thrown away by the Americans in time pressure." (Euwe in Wood (ed) 1946, 3)

On the way to the match several of the American team played in a Rapid Transit tournament in Stockholm with a number of Swedish internationals. The event was won by Reshevsky with +7 –1 =1. Fine did not participate.

During the stay in Moscow Fine lobbied for a match tournament for the World Championship (an idea he had first suggested in the October 1944 issue of *The Chess Review*), to feature Fine himself, Reshevsky, Euwe, Botvinnik, Smyslov and Keres. The U.S.C.F. wanted to replace Fine, who had attempted with some other masters to set up a rival organization for U.S. chess with more concentration on improving conditions for professional players, with Kashdan. The Soviets backed out after a report in a Dutch newspaper suggested that there might be collusion amongst their players. Steiner reported in his column that Fine had to play his second round match early in order to fly back to California for the start of the fall term—he was to teach a class in Clinical Psychology at the University of Southern California.

	1	2	
Keres	½	1	1½
Fine	½	0	½

(677) FINE—KERES, P

U.S.S.R.-U.S.A. (board 2), Moscow (1), 1946 (12 Sept.)
Nimzowitsch-Indian Defence [E40]

1. d4 Nf6 2. c4 e6 3. Nc3 Bb4 4. e3 d5 5. a3 Be7 6. Nf3 b6 7. Bd3 0–0 8. Qe2 c5 9. 0–0 Nc6 10. Rd1 c×d4 11. e×d4 Ba6 12. Bg5 d×c4 13. B×c4 B×c4 14. Q×c4 Rc8 15. Qa6 Nd5 16. B×e7 Nd×e7 17. Ne5 N×e5 He is forced to unisolate White's d-pawn owing to the pressure on his own a-pawn and the possibility of d4-d5. ME **18. d×e5 Qc7 19. Qe2 Ng6 20. Re1 Rfd8 21. g3 Qc4 22. Q×c4 R×c4 23. Rad1 Rcd4 24. f4 Ne7 25. R×d4 R×d4 26. Rd1 R×d1+ 27. N×d1** Very correctly played by both sides. ME **½–½** Euwe in Wood (ed), 1946 7–8; Olde, 182.

(678) KERES, P—FINE

U.S.S.R.-U.S.A. (board 2), Moscow (2), 1946 (15 Sept.)
English Opening, Symmetrical Variation [A34]

1. c4 c5 2. Nf3 Nf6 3. Nc3 d5 4. c×d5 N×d5 5. e3 N×c3 6. b×c3 g6 7. Qa4+ Nd7 8. Ba3 White had originally thought he could continue very strongly with 8 Bc4 but now he notices that Black could reply simply 8 ... Bg7, the sacrificial line 9 B×f7+ K×f7 10 Ng5+ Ke8! 11 Ne6 Qb6 12 N×g7+ Kf7! achieves nothing. ME **8 ... Qc7 9. Be2**

Bg7 10. 0–0 0–0 11. d4 a6?! 11 ... b6 was simpler, when Black can continue with 12 ... Bb7 and then ... e5. PK 12. c4 e5! 13. Rad1 White cannot play 13 d5 because of 13 ... e4. PK 13 ... exd4 14. exd4 b6 The possibility of winning the queen by 14 ... b5 15 cxb5 axb5 16 Qxa8 Bb7 17 Qa7 Ra8 does not appeal to Black since after 18 Qxa8+ Bxa8 19 dxc5 White clearly stands better. Now White gets in d5 and obtains an advantage in the centre. PK 15. d5 Bb7 The game is quite even. White's protected passed pawn counts for little, for Black can always isolate it by ... b5. ME 16. Qb3 Rab8 17. Bc1? 17 Bb2 would have been very strong here, exchanging off the powerful enemy bishop. After 17 ... Bxb2 18 Qxb2 b5 19 cxb5 axb5 20 Bxb5 Ba6 21 a4 Bxb5 22 axb5 Qb7 Black does win back the pawn, but he remains in a difficult plight on account of the strong enemy passed pawns and his weakened king position. PK 17 ... b5! Very well played. ME 18. cxb5 axb5 19. Bxb5 Ba6 20. a4 Bxb5 21. axb5 Qb7 21 ... Qa5! 22 Ng5 Rxb5 23 Qh3 Nf6 and now White cannot win a tempo with 24 Bf4. PK 22. Ng5! A surprise attack on the other wing. ME 22 ... Qxb5 22 ... h6!? 23. Qh3 Nf6 After 23 ... h6 24 Ne4, Nunn reckoned that Black could activate his pieces and equalize by 24 ... Qa4 25 Rde1 f5 26 Ng3 Rb4, preventing Bxh6 and threatening to trap the queen with ... Rh4. 24. Bf4 Rbc8? Black overlooks his opponent's next move, winning a pawn. Keres explained that 24 ... Rbd8 would be answered by 25 Bc7 Rc8 26 Be5 Qd7 27 Qc3 Qf5 28 f4, when Black cannot play 27 ... Nxd5 because of 28 Bxg7! Nxc3 29 Rxd7 Kxg7 30 Ne6+. Keres recommended instead 24 ... Rb7 25 Be5 Qd7 26 Qc3! Qf5 (Nunn and Keres both thought 26 ... Nxd5 could be refuted by 27 Rxd5! Qxd5 28 Bxg7 Qxg5 29 Bxf8 Kxf8 30 Qh8+ Ke7, but it is not clear that Black could not simply move the attacked rook on move 28) 27 f4. The computer suggests that Black might also hold out by 24 ... Rb6. AW 25. Nxf7! Qd7 26. Qxd7 Nxd7 27. Nd6 Rcd8 28. Be3! Nb6 29. Bxc5 Na4 30. Ba3! Nc3 31. Nb7! Confounds all Black's plans. 31 Rd2 Rf4 would have given him drawing chances. ME 31 ... Nxd1 32. Nxd8 1–0 Keres, 1996 200–3; Euwe, Wood (ed), 1946 27–9.

Match with Herman Steiner, Los Angeles, October, 1947

"Fine and Reshevsky have been staging exhibition games and matches in preparation for the Championship contests. With due deference to their opponents, it would seem to us more to the point if they had met each other in a long set match. It would have been worth almost any sacrifice. In a match of six games R. Fine beat H. Steiner by the convincing score of 4 wins and 2 draws and, what is more, his play against Steiner's strong opposition was masterly as can be seen in the following, the first game of the match." (BCM 1948, 81)

	1	2	3	4	5	6	
Fine	1	1	1	½	1	½	5
Steiner	0	0	0	½	0	½	1

(679) STEINER, H–FINE

Match, Los Angeles (1), 1947 (14 Oct.)
Grünfeld Defence [D71]

1. d4 Nf6 2. c4 g6 3. g3 Bg7 4. Bg2 d5 5. Nc3 dxc4 6. Nf3 c6 7. Ne5 Be6 8. 0–0 Nbd7 9. Nf3 h6 10. e4 0–0 11. h3 b5 12. Qc2 Nb6 13. Ne2 Qc8 14. Kh2 Rd8 15. Be3 Ne8 16. Nf4 Nd6 17. Ne5 Bd7 18. g4 Be8 19. Nf3 Nb7 20. Rad1

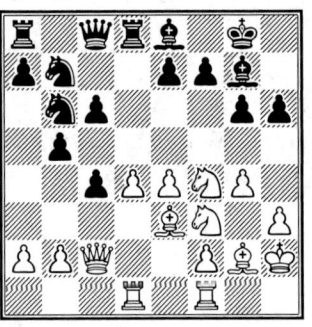

Position after White's 20th move

20 ... e6 21. b4 Qc7 22. Kh1 a5 23. a3 axb4 24. axb4 Ra4 25. Ne2 Rda8 26. Rb1 Ra2 27. Rb2 Rxb2 28. Qxb2 c5 29. Qc1 cxb4 30. Bxh6 Bh8 31. Bf4 Qe7 32. h4 b3 33. h5 b4 34. Bg5 f6 35. Be3 c3 36. d5 b2 37. Qc2 Ra1 38. Bxb6 Ba4! 39. Qd3 c2 40. Qc4 Rxf1+ 41. Bxf1 b1Q 42. Qc8+ Qe8 White resigned. 0–1

(680) FINE–STEINER, H

Match, Los Angeles (2), 1947 (Oct.)
Spanish Opening, Bird's Counterattack [C61]

1. e4 e5 2. Nf3 Nc6 3. Bb5 Nd4 4. Nxd4 exd4 5. 0–0 g6 6. c3 Bg7 7. f4 Ne7 8. f5 gxf5 9. exf5 Bf6 10. Na3 a6 11. Bd3 d5 12. Nc2 c5

Position after Black's 12th move

13. cxd4 c4 14. Be2 Bxf5 15. d3 Qb6 16. dxc4 dxc4 17. Bxc4 Rg8 18. Bf4 Rc8 19. Bd3 Bxd4+ 20. Kh1 Qg6 21. Ne1 Bxb2 22. Rb1 Bc3 23. Bxf5 Nxf5 24. Rxb7 Kf8 25. Qf3 Rg7 26. Rc7 Re8 27. Qxc3 Gillam 1–0

(681) STEINER, H—FINE

Match, Los Angeles (3), 1947 (Oct.)
Giuoco Pianissimo [C50]

1. e4 e5 2. Nf3 Nc6 3. Bc4 Bc5 4. d3 Nf6 5. Nc3 d6 6. Be3 Bb6 7. Qd2 Nd4 8. Bxd4 exd4 9. Ne2 c5 10. 0–0 Be6 11. Bxe6 fxe6 12. Ng5 Qd7 13. Nf4 h6 14. Ng6 Rg8 15. Nf3 Qf7 16. Nfh4 0–0–0 17. c3 dxc3 18. bxc3

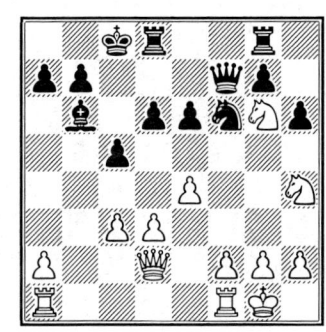

*Position after
White's 18th move*

18 ... c4 19. d4 Nxe4 20. Qe2 d5 21. Rac1 Qf6 22. Qb2 Rd7 23. Ne5 Qxh4 24. Nxd7 Kxd7 25. a4 Rb8 26. f4 g6 27. Rf3 Qf6 28. Kh1 Bc7 29. Re1 a6 30. Ref1 h5 31. Qc1 Ba5 32. Rh3 Qf5 33. Qe1 b5 34. axb5 Rxb5 35. Qa1 Nf2+ 0–1
(Gillam)

(682) FINE—STEINER, H

Match, Los Angeles (4), 1947 (Oct.)
Budapest Defence [A51]

1. d4 Nf6 2. c4 e5 3. dxc5 Nc4 4. Nd2 Bb4 5. a3 Bxd2+ 6. Bxd2 f6 7. Nf3 fxe5 8. g3 Nc6 9. Bg2 0–0 10. 0–0 Nxd2 11. Nxd2 d6 12. e3 Be6 13. Qe2 Qd7 14. Ne4 h6 15. Rad1 Qf7 16. b3 Rae8 17. Nc3 Kh8 18. Nd5 Na5 19. b4 Nxc4 20. Qxc4 c6 21. Qd3 cxd5 22. Bxd5 Qc7 23. Bxe6 Rxe6 24. Qd5 Ref6 25. Rc1 Qd7 26. f4 Qe7 27. Rf2 exf4 28. exf4 Re6 29. Rd1 Re8 30. f5 Re1+ 31. Rxe1 Qxe1+ 32. Kg2 Re2 33. Rxe2 Qxe2+ 34. Kg1 ½–½ (Gillam)

(683) STEINER, H—FINE

Match Los Angeles (5), 1947 (Oct.)
Giuoco Pianissimo [C50]

1. e4 e5 2. Nf3 Nc6 3. Bc4 Nf6 4. d3 Bc5 5. Nc3 d6 6. Be3 Bb6 7. Qd2 0–0 8. 0–0–0 Na5 9. Bb3 Nxb3+ 10. axb3 Ng4 11. d4 Nxe3 12. fxe3 exd4 13. exd4 a5 14. Qf4 f6 15. h4 c6 16. d5 c5 17. h5 Bc7 18. Nh4 Qe8 19. g4 a4 *(see diagram)* 20. bxa4 Rxa4 21. Nxa4 Qxa4 22. Kb1 b5 23. Rd3 b4 24. Rg3 Bd7 25. b3 Qa6 26. Qc1 c4 27. bxc4 Bb6 28. Nf3 Qxc4 29. Nd2 Qe2 30. Nb3 Qxe4 31. Re1 Qc4 32. Re7 Bxg4 33. h6 g6 34. Qe1 Bf5 35. Rd3

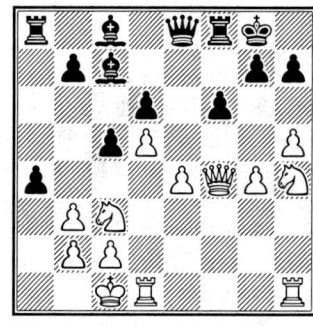

*Position after
Black's 19th move*

Bd8 36. Nd4 b3 37. Rg7+ Kh8 38. Rxb3 Bxc2+ 39. Kb2 Bxb3 40. Nxb3 Qxd5 41. Qe3 f5 0–1
(Gillam)

(684) FINE—STEINER, H

Match Los Angeles (6), 1947 (Oct.)
Catalan System [E08]

1. d4 Nf6 2. c4 e6 3. Nf3 d5 4. g3 Be7 5. Bg2 0–0 6. 0–0 Nbd7 7. Qc2 Ne4 8. Nc3 Nxc3 9. Qxc3 c6 10. b3 f5 11. a4 a5 12. Ba3 f4 13. Ne1 Bxa3 14. Rxa3 Qe7 15. Ra2 dxc4 16. bxc4 e5 17. Nd3 fxg3 18. hxg3 e4 19. Ne1 Nf6 20. Nc2 Qf7 21. f3 exf3 22. exf3 Qg6 23. g4 h5 24. Ne3 hxg4 25. fxg4 Bxg4 26. Raf2 Be6 27. d5 Bd7 28. Nf5 Nxd5 29. cxd5 Rxf5 30. Rxf5 Bxf5 31. dxc6 bxc6 32. Qxc6 Rd8 33. Qxg6 Bxg6 34. Rc1 Rd4 35. Bc6 Be4 36. Bb5 Bd5 37. Rc7 Bb3 38. Ra7 Bxa4 39. Rxa5 Bb3 40. Be2 ½–½
(Gillam)

The World Championship match-tournament eventually took place from 1 March to 16 May 1948 at The Hague and Moscow. Fine ultimately declined to participate as he did not wish to take time away from his dissertation research.

Cable Match with Dr Ossip Bernstein, U.S.A.–France, December 19, 1948

"The Cable Match between France and the U.S.A. proved a disappointment. Either insufficient time was allowed for the contest or the transmission of moves was much slower than had been anticipated. Be that as it may, the longest game lasted 23 moves and the shortest 15. Practically all had to be adjudicated (by Najdorf), and the match was drawn at 4 each ... " (BCM 1949, 50)

Fine ½   Bernstein ½

(685) BERNSTEIN, O—FINE

U.S.A.-France Cable Match, New York/Paris, 1948 (19 Dec.)
Two Knights Defence [C55]

1. e4 e5 2. Nf3 Nc6 3. d4 exd4 4. Bc4 Nf6 5. 0–0 Bc5 6. e5 Ng4 Steinitz's move. 7. Bf4 0–0 8. h3 Nh6

9. Bg5 Dr. Bernstein's move. Better than 9 B×h6 at once as it forces Black's king's bishop to abandon its strong post at c5. **9 ... Be7 10. B×h6 g×h6 11. Bd5** To prevent 11 ... d6. **11 ... Kh8** In a friendly game Bernstein–Llorens, Barcelona 1945, Black did play 11 ... d6; and the game went; 12 B×c6 b×c6 13 N×d4 d×e5 14 N×c6 Qd6 15 Qf3 Ba6 16 Rd1 Qf6 (16 ... Qe6 17 Qg4+) 17 Rd7 Resigns, as he loses a piece. **12. B×c6 d×c6 13. Q×d4 Q×d4 14. N×d4 f6 15. e×f6 B×f6** Here Black offered a draw, which White accepted, for after 16 c3 B×d4 17 c×d4 Rd8 18 Rd1 Be6 19 Nc3 Rd7 20 Rd2 Rad8 21 Rad1 neither side can make any headway. ½–½ BCM 1949, 50.

New York International, December 23, 1948–January 2, 1949

"[The tournament] was not planned a long time in advance, but organized spontaneously by the Manhattan Chess Club when it was learned that Euwe, Najdorf and Ståhlberg by mere chance would all be in New York at about the same time in December 1948. Ståhlberg, on his return from Sweden to Argentina, hoped to come, but could not meet the schedule. Euwe arrived at the La Guardia airport on the 22nd of December in the late afternoon. The rate of play was to be 20 moves per hour to be controlled after the first two hours, then after each hour. This and the tight schedule were necessary since the days of the tournament were the only days on which all participants would be present in New York. Some players also had to carry on their normal duties, for example Fine was employed as a psychologist in a local hospital. A decade of almost complete abstinence from tournament play had done no harm to [Fine's] fighting power; on the contrary, it looked as if Fine had lost a great deal of the nervousness from which he used to suffer occasionally before the war. He gave a wonderful performance, keeping his place in the very small group of the best players of our time. The last event of the tournament, a banquet combined with the distribution of the prizes, took place on January 4 at the home of the promoter of the tournament, Mr. Maurice Wertheim." (Kmoch 1950) Each participant received $250 for expenses in addition to which there were four prizes amounting to $1,000, $750, $500 and $250.

		1	2	3	4	5	6	7	8	9	10	
1	Fine	*	1	½	1	1	1	½	1	1	1	8
2	Najdorf	0	*	1	½	½	1	½	1	1	1	6½
3	Pilnik	½	0	*	½	½	1	½	1	½	½	5
4	Euwe	0	½	½	*	½	1	1	½	½	½	5
5	Horowitz	0	½	½	½	*	½	½	0	1	1	4½
6	Kramer	0	0	0	0	½	*	1	1	1	1	4½
7	Bisguier	½	½	½	0	½	0	*	½	½	1	4
8	Kashdan	0	0	0	½	1	0	½	*	1	1	4
9	Denker	0	0	½	½	0	0	½	0	*	½	2
10	Steiner	0	0	½	½	0	0	0	0	½	*	1½

(686) FINE—EUWE, M

New York (1), 1948 (23 Dec.)
Catalan System [E00]

1. d4 Nf6 2. c4 e6 3. Nc3 d5 4. g3 Kmoch calls this the Queen's Catalan on the basis of White's third move. He goes on to say "The Queen's Catalan is the oldest but least usual form of the opening. Developing the queen's knight first has the merit of preparing e2-e4 most effectively, possibly in connection with f2-f3. On the other hand it exposes the knight to the possible attack of Black's b-pawn, which most players seem to dislike. The pros and cons may keep the balance.". **4 ... d×c4 5. Qa4+ Nbd7** 5 ... Bd7 6 Q×c4 Bc6 7 f3! Be7 8 Bg2, as played in the inaugural game of the Catalan Queen's Gambit, Tinsley–Schlechter, Hastings 1895, is favourable to White. Opposing the queen's bishop on the long diagonal is commendable only in the King's Catalan (i.e. with 3 Nf3. AW) and Orthodox Catalan (3 Nf3 d5 4 Nc3 Be7 5 g3. AW) when the knight on f3 prevents White from playing f2-f3. **6. Bg2 a6 7. Q×c4** White wants to keep his fianchettoed bishop's diagonal open as long as possible. After 7 Nf3, which leads to a well-known position of the King's Catalan, Black can equalize by 7 ... Rb8, for example, 8 Q×c4 b5 9 Qe3 Bb7 10 0–0 c5 (Petrovs–Alekhine, Margate 1936). Less clear is 7 ... Bd6 (Petrovs–Fine, Semmering-Baden 1937) because of 8 e4. **7 ... b5** Or 7 ... c5!? 8 Nf3 b5 9 Qd3 Bb7 10 0–0 Rc8 11 Rd1 c4 12 Qc2 b4 13 Nb1 Qb6 with the initiative, Mancini–Dorfman, France 1994. AW **8. Qd3 Rb8 9. a4!?** Sacrificing two tempi in order to create holes in Black's pawn formation on the queenside. White employs a somewhat double-edged strategy. **9 ... b4** An interesting alternative is 9 ... b×a4 with the idea of avoiding the hampering pawn on b4 and getting more manoeuvring space for the pieces. As in some variations of the ordinary Queen's Gambit, it may be sufficient for an approximately even game. **10. Nb1 Be7** If 10 ... c5 11 Bf4 Rb6 12 Nd2 White has the initiative. Chekhov **11. Nd2 0–0** Or 11 ... c5!? Chekhov **12. Nb3 c5 13. Bf4!** This move justifies White's strategy. It is strong, though not quite as strong as it looks.

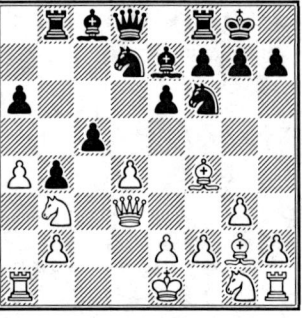

Position after White's 13th move

13 ... Bb7 The only good answer. If 13 ... Rb6? then White forcibly wins the exchange: 14 d×c5 N×c5 15 Q×d8 R×d8 16 N×c5 B×c5 17 Bc7. **14. B×b7 R×b7 15. Q×a6** So far so good. With a mighty passed pawn ahead, White seems to have a winning position. However, closer investigation of the situation proves that Black has fine counter-chances because of his lead in development. Utilizing these chances very effectively in the ensuing part of the game, Euwe succeeds in holding his own. **15 ... Rb6 16. Qc4 cxd4 17. Nf3 Qa8 18. 0–0 Nd5 19. Qxd4 Bf6 20. Be5** It is important to deny Black the free use of both the bishop's diagonal and the d-file. After 20 Qd2 Nxf4 21 gxf4 Rd8, White's position is critical. **20 ... Nxe5 21. Nxe5 Rd8 22. f4** 22 e4? is no good because of 22 ... Qb8! **22 ... Ra6 23. a5 Ne7!** Very well played. By temporarily giving up a second pawn, Black greatly increases the activity of his pieces. **24. Qxb4 Rb8 25. Qc4 Qa7+ 26. Rf2!** Otherwise the king would remain dangerously exposed to checks. **26 ... Bxe5 27. fxe5 Nc6 28. Qc3** A necessary security measure. Sure of getting back at least one pawn in any event, Black can afford this loss of tempo. **28 ... h6 29. e3 Rb5 30. Nd4 Nxd4 31. exd4** After 31 Qxd4 Rbxa5 White would soon lose his foremost e-pawn too. **31 ... Rbxa5** With the most dangerous of White's pawns gone, Black can feel rather safe. The presence of only major pieces and the particular pawn formation makes it almost sure that he will find ample opportunity to keep the balance by means of an attack. **32. Raf1 Ra1 33. Qc8+ Kh7 34. Qc2+ Kg8 35. Qc8+ Kh7 36. Qc5 Rxf1+ 37. Rxf1 Qb7 38. Qc2+ Kg8 39. Qg2 Qd5??**

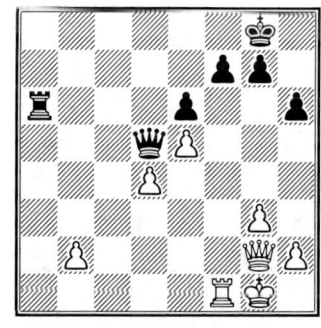

Position after Black's 39th move

A pernicious hallucination due to time pressure and nervous strain. Euwe simply overlooked that the queen could be taken. A good move was 39 ... Qa7. **40. Qxd5 exd5** This ending is hopeless for Black. The great struggle between two Grandmasters and old rivals of many European tournaments ends in a fizzle. The game was adjourned here. **41. b4! Kf8 42. b5 Ra8 43. b6 Ke7 44. Rc1 Ra2 45. Rb1 Ra8 46. Rb5 f6 47. b7 Rb8 48. exf6+ Kxf6 49. Kf2 1–0** Kmoch, 18–20.

(687) BISGUIER, A—FINE

New York (2), 1948 (24 Dec.)
French Defence, Winawer Variation [C18]

1. e4 e6 2. d4 d5 3. Nc3 Bb4 4. e5 c5 5. a3 Bxc3+ 6. bxc3 Ne7 A good alternative is 6 ... Qc7 (Reshevsky–Botvinnik, World's Championship 1948) with the idea 7 Qg4 f5. **7. Qg4 Nf5 8. Bd3 h5 9. Qf4** An interesting possibility, leading to difficult complications, is 9 Qh3 cxd4 10 g4!. **9 ... Qh4** By exchanging queens Black definitely stops any danger on the kingside. **10. Ne2** 10 Qxh4 Nxh4

11 g3 Nf5 12 dxc5 is no good since White's extra pawn remains too weak, for example, 12 ... Nd7 13 Bb5 Ke7 14 Bxd7 Bxd7. This action would only spoil White's pawn formation. **10 ... Qxf4** This is perfectly safe although it involves the definite sacrifice of a pawn. **11. Nxf4** Threatening 12 Bxf5 exf5 13 Nxd5. Black's reply is practically forced. **11 ... Ne7 12. Be3** In this position, White can take the pawn and maintain it: 12 dxc5 Nbc6 13 Bb5 Bd7 14 Bxc6 (there is no other remedy against 14 ... Nxe5) Bxc6 15 Be3, followed if necessary by Nd3. The result, however, is an almost immediate draw because of bishops of opposite colour as well as the tripled pawn. **12 ... Nbc6 13. Rb1 cxd4 14. cxd4 b6 15. Kd2 Na5 16. Rhc1 Bd7 17. c4** This leads to a lifeless position with bishops of opposite colour. However, waiting until Black's knight appears on f5 would bring White into difficulties. **17 ... dxc4 18. Bxc4 Nxc4+ 19. Rxc4 Bc6 20. Rbc1 Kd7 21. h4 Rac8 22. g3 Bb7 23. Rxc8 Nxc8 24. Kd3 Ne7 25. Bd2 Nf5 26. Nh3 a5 27. Ng5 f6 28. Nh3** White proposed a draw, Black accepted by repeating moves. **28 ... Ba6+ 29. Ke4 Bb7+ 30. Kd3 Ba6+ 31. Ke4 ½–½** Kmoch, 23–4.

(688) FINE—PILNIK, H

New York (3), 1948 (25 Dec.)
Grünfeld Defence [D96]

1. d4 Nf6 2. c4 g6 3. Nc3 d5 4. Qb3 Botvinnik's move which has been tested and is frequently played today, although for a period of years it had been considered premature. (This is the opinion again, nowadays White plays 4 Nf3 Bg7 and only then 5 Qb3. AW) **4 ... dxc4 5. Qxc4 Bg7** The line which seemed to shake Botvinnik's 4 Qb3 is 5 ... Be6 6 Qb5+ Nc6 7 Nf3 Nd5! with a good game for Black (Feigins–Flohr, Kemeri 1937). Bad for Black is 6 ... Rb8? on account of 7 e4! (Najdorf–Szabo, Mar del Plata 1948), which favours White far more than 7 Ne5 (Euwe–Alekhine, match 1935, game 2). However, White can avoid Flohr's line by 6 Qd3! and gets a good game himself. (Uhlmann assesses this line as favourable to Black after 6 ... c5! AW) **6. Nf3 0–0 7. g3** Fine evades the difficult problems arising from 7 e4 (reaching the main line of the "Russian System." AW) and goes his own way, which is less pretentious but safe. **7 ... c6** A more active line, leading to equality is 7 ... Be6 (Fine–Najdorf, match 1949, game 5). **8. Bg2 Nbd7 9. 0–0 Nb6 10. Qd3 Be6 11. Qc2 h6 12. e4** There is no time for further preparations. After 12 h3 Qc8 13 Kh2 c5! Black has a good game. **12 ... Qc8 13. Ne5** The best chance of getting a lasting initiative. With 13 Rd1 White would walk into the annoying pin 13 ... Bg4. **13 ... Nfd7 14. f4!** The only consistent move. If 14 Nxd7 Qxd7 White must give up the d-pawn for the h-pawn which is a dubious bargain, for example, 15 Rd1 Bxd4 16 Bxh6 Rfd8 17 Ne2 c5 18 Nxd4 cxd4 and Black's passed pawn is very strong. **14 ... Nxe5 15. dxe5** At the cost of a slight weakening of his pawn front White has secured chances for attack. Henceforth he will operate with the threat of breaking through on the kingside with f5. **15 ... Bc4 16. Rf3** Less energetic, but still quite good, is 16 Rd1 anticipating any danger on the d-file and enabling White to retain the king's bishop which may get good activity on h3. **16 ... Qe6 17. b3 Ba6 18. Bb2 Rad8 19. Bf1** This exchange is necessary since White needs f1 for the queen's rook. **19 ... B×f1 20. Ra×f1 Qd7 21. Nb1** Preventing 21 ... Qd2. Besides, White wants to use his knight for an additional protection of the foremost e-pawn. **21 ... Qc7 22. R3f2 Nd7** Keeping White's foremost e-pawn under pressure is the remedy against f5. However, f5 is not the only danger. **23. Nd2 Rfe8 24. Nf3** The knight has reached its destination, but f5 is still out of the question since it would lead to the loss of the foremost e-pawn. **24 ... e6** Black must do something, so he opens a way out for his bishop, aiming for a more active counterplay on and around the d-file. This has the drawback of loosening the grip on White's e-pawn, thereby increasing the danger for f5. However, a waiting attitude may enable White to suddenly switch to the queenside himself, taking advantage of his far greater freedom of movement. **25. h4 Bf8 26. Kg2** Not 26 f5? because of 26 ... Bc5 When Black wins either the exchange or the pawn on e5. **26 ... Nc5** Threatening 27 ... Nd3 but releasing the pressure on the e-pawn almost entirely. **27. Nd4 Qd7 28. Kh2** The crisis of the game. White is apparently anticipating the possible check on d5 and intending 29 f5 with even more effect. But Black is now able to strike first. (Kmoch believed that White could safely play 28 f5, citing lines such as 28 ... g×f5 29 e×f5 Qd5+ 30 Kh2 Bg7; 28 ... Na6 29 f×g6 f×g6 30 Rf6 or 28 ... e×f5 29 e×f5 Qd5+ 30 Kh2. In this last line Fritz reckons 30 ... g5! 31 e6 Bd6 32 h×g5 Ne4! 33 e×f7+ Q×f7 34 g6 B×g3+ 35 Kg2 Qd5 is at least unclear, if not favourable to Black. AW) **28 ... Na6!** Threatening 29 ... c5 followed by ... Qd3 or ... Nb4. **29. Qc4!** Fine took a great deal of time for this move. Realizing that he has to play for safety, he is going to stop and eliminate Black's majority on the queenside. **29 ... c5 30. Nb5! Qd3!** Not 30 ... b6? on account of 31 Nd6 B×d6 32 Rd1 which gives White a great advantage. Black has no time for saving the a-pawn. **31. N×a7 Q×c4 32. b×c4 Nb4 33. a3 Nd3 34. Rc2 N×b2 35. R×b2 Rd4 36. Rc1 R×e4 37. Rcc2 g5!** Excellent. Black demolishes the enemy formation on the kingside and gets full activity for his pieces. **38. h×g5 h×g5 39. f×g5** Other moves are bad. It is important to keep the pawn on g3 which can be easily protected and serves well by preventing Black from getting two connected passed pawns. **39 ... R×e5 40. R×b7 R×g5 41. a4** White's last move was sealed. Neither of the opponents succeeded in finding a reasonable winning chance. ½–½ Kmoch, 38–40.

(689) DENKER, A—FINE

New York (4), 1948 (26 Dec.)
Nimzowitsch-Indian Defence [E33]

1. d4 Nf6 2. c4 e6 3. Nc3 Bb4 4. Qc2 Nc6 5. e3 An unpretentious though steady line. The usual 5 Nf3 has the advantage of being a little more flexible since for the moment it conceals White's intention concerning the development of the bishops. **5 ... 0–0 6. Nge2 d5** Simple and perfect. With the white queen's bishop locked in Black easily gets a satisfactory game by turning it into a kind of Queen's Gambit. **7. c×d5** This frees the black queen's bishop, yet it is not as co-operative as it looks; otherwise Black gets even more freedom of movement by ... e5, if necessary preceded by ... d×c4 and ... Bd6. **7 ... e×d5 8. a3** Although driving the bishop to a better square, this move is indispensable as a protection against ... Nb4. After 8 Ng3 g6 9 Bd3 Bd6 White must evidently play 10 a3, which leads by transposition of moves to the game. **8 ... Bd6 9. Ng3 g6 10. Bd3 a6 11. Bd2 Be6 12. Nce2 Qd7 13. 0–0 Ne8** Preparing for ... f5 so as to thwart White's obvious intentions in the centre, consisting of Bd3, f3, and finally e4. **14. f3** Instead of stubbornly clinging to his plan White would have done much better to adjust himself to Black's counterplay. He should try to take advantage of either 13 ... Ne8 by pushing the e-pawn directly, or of the expected ... f5 by preparing to get a knight anchored to e5. Though not particularly effective, each of these ideas seems to guarantee White a satisfactory game, for example, 14 e4 B×g3 15 h×g3 d×e4 16 B×e4 (16 ... N×d4? 17 N×d4 Q×d4 18 B×b7 favouring White); or 14 Kh1 f5 15 Ng1 Nf6 (15 ... f4!? AW) 16 f4 Ne4 17 Nf3. **14 ... f5**

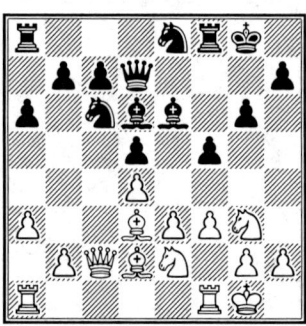

Position after Black's 14th move

15. e4?! Reckless consistency. White plays this key move even at the cost of a pawn and a weakening of his king position as well. He succeeds in causing Black difficulties, but this is hardly enough of a compensation. Patient manoeuvring starting with Bd2-e1-f2 was indicated. White should have retained the slight chance for playing e4 under more convenient circumstances. **15 ... B×g3 16. h×g3 d×e4 17. f×e4 N×d4 18. N×d4 Q×d4+ 19. Kh2?** This is disastrous since it enables Black to mobilize his knight with check. 19 Kh1! is necessary, for example, 19 ... Rd8 20 Rf3 when Black must play 20 ... Nd6 21 Bc3 Qc5 protecting the f-pawn, not 20 ... Nf6? because of 21 Bc3 Qc5 22 e×f5 when White's attack becomes too strong (22 ... g×f5 23 B×f5 Bd5 24 B×h7+ or 23 ... B×f5 24 R×f5 Rd5 25 Qb3!). **19 ... Rd8 20. Rf3 Nf6! 21. e×f5** Equally ineffective now is 21 Bc3 on account of 21 ... Ng4+ 22 Kh1 Qc5 (even 22 ... d3 looks playable). **21 ... B×f5 22. Qb3+** If 22 Bc3?, Black wins with 22 ... Ng4+! 23 Kh1 B×d3. And if 22 B×f5, Black has the choice between playing for the attack (22 ... g×f5) or remaining in a superior position with a pawn ahead (22 ... Q×d2 23 Qb3+ (23 Be6+ Kh8 24 Q×c7!? AW) Kg7 24 Bh3

Qd5). **22 ... Rf7 23. Bc3 Ng4+! 24. Kh1 Qc5 25. B×f5 g×f5 26. Rd1** Or 26 Q×b7 Qd6. Due to the ideal position of his knight, Black can work with mating threats anyhow. **26 ... Rd6!** Not 26 ... Nf2+? because of 27 R×f2 R×d1+ 28 Q×d1 Q×f2 29 Qd8+ Rf8 30 Qd5+. White having a draw by perpetual check. (In fact White even wins after 30 Q×c7 Rf7 31 Qd8+ Rf8 32 Qg5+ Kf7 33 Qf6+ Ke8 34 Qe6+ Kd8 35 Ba5+. AW) **27. R×d6** Or 27 Bd2 f4! **27 ... Q×d6 28. Kg1 Qh6** White exceeded the time limit. Black wins anyway. He threatens mate in six by 29 ... Qc1+. The only reasonable move is 29 Bd4, but this loses at least the exchange: 29 ... c5! 30 Be3 Qh2+ 31 Kf1 Qh1+ enforcing 32 Bg1 Nh2+, for if 32 Ke2 Q×g2+ 33 Bf2 then 33 ... c4!! wins much quicker (34 Q×c4 Q×f3+!). **0–1** Kmoch 49–50. Also see Fine 1953, 147–8.

(690) FINE–STEINER, H

New York (5), 1948 (28 Dec.)
Dutch Stonewall [A90]

1. d4 d5 2. c4 e6 3. Nf3 c6 4. Qc2 f5 5. g3 A rather surprising transposition into the main variation of the Dutch Defence: The Dutch Stonewall which is marked by the fianchetto of White's king's bishop. **5 ... Nf6 6. Bg2 Bd6** In old-timer style. For about twenty years, that is since Botvinnik has been playing this variation successfully, experts have preferred ... Be7, which is much better. The king's bishop is the most precious of Black's minor pieces, and standing on d6 it is more exposed to possibilities of attack and exchange. **7. 0–0 0–0 8. c5** White hopes to profit from Black's king's bishop by adopting a system which is normally (with the bishop standing on e7) hardly commendable. **8 ... Bc7** 8 ... Be7 leads to the game Reshevsky–Botvinnik, Nottingham 1936, but with an extra tempo for White. **9. Nc3 Nbd7 10. Bf4!** The exchange of the enemy king bishop yields White supremacy on the dark squares in the central zone. **10 ... h6** So as to compel White, if necessary by means of ... g5, to play B×c7 sooner or later. If Black exchanges bishops himself, he loses the chance of getting any counterplay by either ... e5 or ... g5, for example, 10 ... B×f4 11 g×f4 Nh5 12 e3 h6 13 Qe2! with a winning position for White (13 ... g5? 14 N×g5!). **11. e3** After this White can answer ... B×f4 with e×f4, which is even better than g×f4. **11 ... Ne4 12. B×c7 Q×c7 13. Ne2** Having exchanged bishops White faces the problem of how to meet ... e5 effectively. **13 ... g5** If 13 ... e5 then 14 Ne1!, which favours White distinctly. 14 N×e5 N×e5 15 d×e5 Q×e5 16 Nd4 is also good, but 14 d×e5 is dubious because of 14 ... Nd×c5. **14. Ne1!** Preventing 14 ... e5 which would lose a pawn because of 15 f3 Nef6 16 Q×f5, the point being that 16 ... N×c5? fails against 17 Qg6+. **14 ... Kg7** Making 15 ... e5 feasible by eliminating the possibility of Qg6+. **15. f3** White stands on the crossroads. Shall he prevent ... e5 definitely by f2-f4, or rather try to profit from it by getting a knight on d4? For the latter, he should have played 15 Nd3 at once. **15 ... Nef6 16. Nd3** Apparently afraid that 16 f4 may concede Black chances on the kingside,

White decides on the second plan. The text has the merit of leading to a more open position, which is desirable because of Black's weakened king position. However, White remains hampered by his backward e-pawn. It seems that Fine had underestimated this factor, for the ensuing part of the game is certainly not a justification of his decision. The other line (16 f4) looks more logical, but there is one annoying reply: 16 ... g4! which prevents Nf3 and threatens h6-h5-h4. That breakthrough White is unable to stop safely; here is a possible continuation: 17 Bh1 h5 18 Ng2 Rh8 19 Nc1 Nf8 20 Nd3 Ng6 21 Ne5 Nd7 22 N×g6 K×g6 23 Nh4+ Kg7 24 Bg2 Nf8. The conclusion is twofold, first; 8 c5 is little promising even when played with tempo, second: White's best chance would have been 15 Nd3. **16 ... e5 17. d×e5?** 17 f4 leads to a game with about even chances: 17 ... e×f4 18 e×f4 g4 19 Ne5 Ne4. White wants more, but the text seriously weakens his pawn position. **17 ... N×e5 18. Nd4 Bd7 19. N×e5** After a very long consideration White failed to find any effective plan. At any rate, we see him from here on assuming a more or less waiting attitude. **19 ... Q×e5 20. Qc3** It is important to protect not only the e-pawn but also the knight. 20 Rad1 looks more natural but is questionable because of 20 ... f4. **20 ... Rae8 21. Rae1 Kg6** The beginning of a strange-looking manoeuvre, which however serves well. Black posts his king on g6 in order to bring his queen there. The king must help protect the f-pawn before the queen arrives. **22. Re2 Qe7 23. b4 Qh7 24. Qc2 Kg7 25. Qb2 Kg8** Miraculously, the king returned to its penates. **26. Rff2 Re7 27. Rf1** White has no good moves. **27 ... Qg6 28. Bh3** Obviously dissatisfied with his position, White wants to complicate matters by provoking 28 ... g4 29 Bg2 g×f3. **28 ... Rfe8 29. Qb3 f4?** An ill-calculated combination which should lead to a considerable improvement of White's game. **30. B×d7 N×d7**

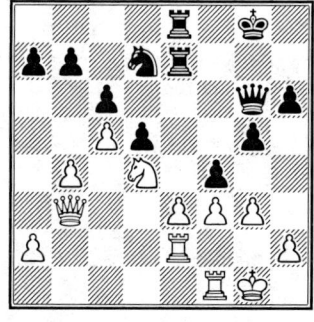

Position after Black's 30th move

31. g×f4? Heavily pressed for time, both sides are cherishing rosy dreams. White is entitled to have some, but not to the extent of winning the queen (31 ... g×f4+ 32 Rg2) or at least a pawn. He should play 31 e4!, threatening both 32 g×f4 and 32 Nf5, possibly followed by 33 Nd6. That would make his game very promising all of a sudden. With the text, White overlooks what Black was dreaming of. **31 ... R×e3!** A painful surprise for White, who now loses a pawn in a very critical position. **32. R×e3 R×e3 33. Qb2 g×f4+ 34. Kh1 Re5 35. b5** The only chance.

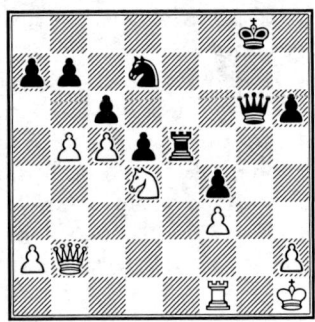

*Position after
White's 35th move*

35 ... Rg5? A waste of time. With 35 ... Qd3! Black must win, for example, 36 Rg1+ Rg5 37 Re1 cxb5 38 Qxb5. **36. bxc6 bxc6 37. Re1 Ne5??** This loses. Correct is either 37 ... Qd3 or 37 ... Nf8 with some winning chances for Black. **38. Qb8+ Kh7 39. Qc7+ Nf7** Or 39 ... Kh8 (39 ... Qg7 40 Qxg7+) 40 Qd8+ Kh7 (40 ... Qg8 41 Qf6+) 41 Qe7+ Kh8 42 Ne6. **40. Ne6 Rg2** Shortening the story. **41. Nf8+** Black resigned. **1–0** Kmoch, 63–6.

(691) KRAMER, G—FINE

New York (6), 1948 (29 Dec.)
Réti Opening [A09]

1. Nf3 d5 2. c4 dxc4 3. e4 This unusual move was first played by Kevitz. The ordinary continuations are 3 Qa4+, 3 Na3 and 3 e3. **3 ... c5** 3 ... e6 4 Bxc4 c5 5 d4 a6 6 0-0 cxd4 7 Nxd4 b5 8 Bb3 Bb7 9 Nc3 Nc6 10 Nxc6 Qxd1 11 Rxd1 Bxc6 12 Be3 Nf6 13 f3 gave White a slightly better position, Makarov–Ibragimov, Smolensk 1991. AW **4. Bxc4 Nc6 5. b4** A very interesting gambit; the main idea seems to be 5 ... cxb4 6 d4 with an excellent game for White or 5 ... Nxb4 6 d4 cxd4 7 Ne5 e6 8 Bb5+ with a great advantage for White. **5 ... e6** A wise decision; Fine avoids all vague complications and plays for a sound development. It may be remembered that Alekhine used to practice the same attitude toward gambits of all kinds. **6. b5** 8 bxc5 Bxc5 9 Bb2 Nf6! favours Black (7 ... Bxf2+ 8 Ke2 is less clear). **6 ... Nce7 7. Nc3** Much more natural is 7 d4 which gives White a rather good game (7 ... cxd4 8 Qxd4!). **7 ... Nf6 8. 0-0 Ng6**

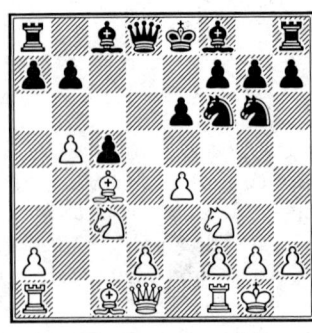

*Position after
Black's 8th move*

9. d3 This backward pawn is nothing to be proud of, although it does appear in some playable variations first of all in the Sicilian Defence. Its main disadvantage in this game is that it hinders the white rooks on the d-file and, indirectly the c-file. There is scarcely a chance that another file will be opened, and so throughout the game we see these rooks inactive. White should play 9 Bb2 with d4 to follow as soon as possible. 9 d4 directly is not good on account of 9 ... cxd4 10 Qxd4 Qxd4 11 Nxd4 Bb4 or 10 Nxd4 Bb4 when the poorly protected state of White's e-pawn and minor pieces can easily cause trouble. **9 ... Be7 10. h3 0-0 11. a4 Kh8 12. Re1 Nd7** There is an aggressive idea behind Black's seemingly very passive manoeuvring: [... f5]. There is also a defensive one of immediate significance: 13 d4? fails on 13 ... cxd4 14 Nxd4 Qc7! 15 Qb3 Nc5 16 Qa2 Ne5 threatening first of all 16 ... Ncd3. Even worse is 14 Qxd4 because of 14 ... Bf6 15 Qe3 Qc7. **13. Qb3 b6 14. Be3 Bb7 15. a5** Finally, White realizes that he must somehow get his rooks into action. However, the a-file proves a poor substitute for the d-file. Besides, it costs White several tempi to regain the pawn. **15 ... bxa5 16. Ra2 Bd6 17. Rea1 Bc7 18. Ne2 Qe7 19. Bd2 Nb6 20. Bxa5**

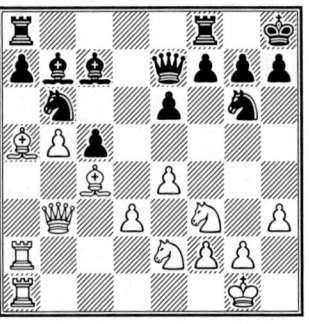

*Position after
White's 20th move*

20 ... f5! Black's better view on the question of opening lines decides the game. While White's pieces are queuing for a bit of activity on and around the remote a-file, Black breaches the pawn wall in the most vital sector and gets a winning attack. It is remarkable how early in the game Fine started working for this breakthrough (see note to Black's 12th move). It pays to have a sound plan. **21. Bxb6** If 21 exf5, Black would neither close the f-file (21 ... exf5) nor enter into obscure complications (21 ... Bxf3 22 fxg6). Instead, he would sacrifice the e-pawn (21 ... Rxf5!) the capture of which loses almost instantly (22 Bxe6 c4! 23 Bxc4 Bxf3 or even 23 ... Rxf3). **21 ... Bxb6 22. Ng3** Again 22 exf5 Rxf5! 23 Bxe6 loses because of 23 ... c4!! This time there is the alternative 24 Qxc4, but all the same Black obtains a crushing attack, for example, 24 ... Rxf3 25 gxf3 Ne5 26 Qb3 Nxf3+ 27 Kf1 Re8. **22 ... Nf4 23. Rb1 fxe4 24. dxe4 Rad8** What a difference in activity between Black's and White's rooks! And there are similar distinctions between the other pieces. From here on White's king's knight is immobilized because of ... Rd4, and so is his bishop because of ... c4. **25. Qe3 Qf6 26. Kh2** In view of a possible ... Nxh3. **26 ... g5!** Brutally threatening ... h5 and ... g4, probably combined with ... Rd8-d7-h7. **27. e5** This opens the black light-squared bishops diagonal and causes a quick collapse. **27 ... Qg7** Threatening ... Nxg2. **28. Rh1** White overlooks the threat, but he is lost anyway. After 28 Ne1 Rd4 he can resist longer but not for long. **28 ... N×g2 29. K×g2 R×f3 0–1** Kmoch, 77–9.

(692) FINE–NAJDORF, M

New York (7), 1948 (30 Dec.)
Sicilian Najdorf [B91]

1. e4 c5 2. Nf3 d6 3. d4 c×d4 4. N×d4 Nf6 5. Nc3 a6 Najdorf likes the Sicilian Defence, but instead of the much favoured Dragon he always plays the Paulsen System (... Nbd7) or one of its descendants such as the Scheveningen Variation (... Nc6). The text belongs to this system and can be made at various points. But for the particular purpose which Black has in mind, it must be played very early. **6. g3** The more modern system of attack. The conservative one is 6 Be2. **6 ... b5** The System of The Hague, as it is called in Holland. It was analyzed in the Dutch capital about twenty-five years ago and has been popular there ever since. So far, very little attention has been paid to this variation in international chess, the feeling being that Black's immediate action on the queenside must be premature. Nonetheless, it seems to be very playable. 6 ... e5 leads to a variation of the Tcheppy System (similar to Yanofsky–Tartakower, Hastings 1946/7). From 6 ... e6 arise the more common lines of the Paulsen. In this latter case Black has to watch the possibility g3-g4, for example, 7 Bg2 Qc7 8 0–0 Bd7? 9 g4! with a considerable advantage for White (Szabo–Stoltz, Zaandam 1946). **7. Bg2 Bb7 8. 0–0** In a note to the game Horowitz–Denker from the next round of the same tournament this is what Kmoch had to say about 8 a4: "This is more enterprising than 8 0–0 and probably stronger, too. At any rate it hits the weak spot of Black's system.". **8 ... e6** Threatening to win the e-pawn. **9. Qe2 Nbd7 10. a3 Qc7 11. f4 Rc8 12. h3 Qc4** "An unusual but strong defence—Black neglects the development of his kingside and concentrates on the centre." (Fine in *The Chess Review*, January 1949) **13. Qf2!** Played after a long consideration spent on the question of whether White can avoid the exchange of queens, which is highly desirable, without bringing the e-pawn into danger. This pawn is safe, as Fine points out in *The Chess Review*. If 13 ... e5 then 14 Nb3!, threatening 15 Na5, while 14 ... N×e4?? costs a piece because of 15 N×e4 B×e4 16 Nd2. And if 13 ... Nc5 14 Re1 e5 15 Nf3! (15 Nf5!? Nf×e4 16 B×e4. AW), Black loses two pieces for a rook if he takes the pawn: 15 ... Nf×e4 16 N×e4 N×e4 17 R×e4!! B×e4 (17 ... Q×e4?? 18 Ne1) 18 Nd2. A remark may be added about 18 ... Qc7 which, it seems to me, offers Black considerable fighting chances, for example, 19 N×e4 (19 B×e4? d5!) d5 20 Ng5 (forced) Bc5 21 Be3 d4 22 Bd2 d3 23 Be3 d×c2 24 Rc1 e×f4 25 g×f4 0–0. **13 ... d5 14. e5 Bc5?** An error. Correct is 14 ... Ne4 15 N×e4 d×e4 16 Be3 Be7 17 Rad1 Qc7 leading to a position where the chances are very difficult to judge; Fine claims some superiority for White, Najdorf a distinct advantage for Black. I cannot decide. **15. Be3 Ne4 16. N×e4 d×e4**

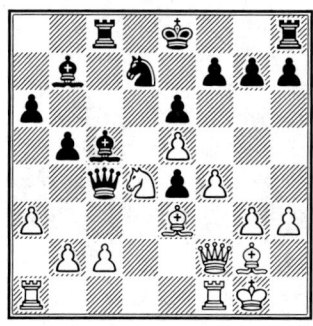

*Position after
Black's 16th move*

17. Nb3! Says Fine: Even I was taken by surprise by the strength of this move. It wins at least a pawn. (*The Chess Review*) White threatens first of all 18 Na5 B×e3 (18 ... Qd5?? 19 Rfd1!) 19 Q×e3 Qc7 20 N×b7 Q×b7 21 B×e4. Not so good is 18 B×c5 N×c5 19 Na5 Qd5 20 Rfd1 because of 20 ... e3!!. **17 ... Q×c2** To avoid the loss of his foremost e-pawn, Black has nothing better than the text, which yields material parity indeed, but is hopeless from the positional point of view. Hopeless from the material point of view is 17 ... f5 18 e×f6 B×e3 19 Q×e3 N×f6 20 Rac1 0–0 21 Nd2; or 17 ... B×e3 18 Q×e3 when Q×c2? fails on 19 Rac1 Q×b2 20 Na5! while there is otherwise no defence against Rac1 followed by Nd2. **18. N×c5** 18 Q×c2 B×e3+ favours Black. **18 ... Q×f2+ 19. R×f2 N×c5 20. Rc1 Nd7** Fine gives this remark: "If the knight ventures too far, it may not get back, 20 ... Na4? 21 R×c8+ B×c8 22 Rc2 Bd7 23 b3 and the knight is gone; or 20 ... Nd3? 21 R×c8+ B×c8 22 Rc2 Bd7 23 B×e4 Ne1 24 Rc1. Black has an alternative defence in 20 ... Nb3 21 R×c8+ B×c8 22 Rc2 0–0. The resulting position is then similar to that reached in the game except that Black's knight is somewhat better placed; but White should still win." He certainly should. **21. R×c8+ B×c8 22. Rc2** Conclusive. White wins the pawn back and obtains a very great advantage, thanks to his formidable bishops and the ideal activity of his remaining rook. **22 ... 0–0 23. B×e4 f6 24. Bd4 f×e5 25. f×e5 Rd8** Fine remarks ingeniously: " ... in such positions, one is happy to be able to make a legal move." Indeed, Black's resistance is a mere formality. **26. Rc7 Nf8 27. Bc5 Bd7 28. Ra7 Be8 29. Bd6 Bg6 30. Bc6 Bd3 31. b4 h5 32. R×a6 Rc8 33. Kf2 h4 34. g×h4 Ng6 35. Kg3 Kh7 36. h5 Nh8 37. Kf4 Nf7 38. Bc5** Threatening 39 Bd7. **38 ... Rc7 39. Bf3 Bc4 40. Be4+ Kh6 41. Bf5** Not 41 Bg6 at once because of 41 ... Nh8 when 42 Bf5?? fails on 42 ... Rf7. RF **41 ... Ng5 42. Bg6 N×h3+ 43. Kg3 Ng5 44. Ra8!** Black resigned. Mate in a few moves is inevitable. **1–0** Kmoch, 83–5.

(693) KASHDAN, I–FINE

New York (8), 1949 (1 Jan.)
Queen's Gambit Accepted [D25]

1. d4 d5 2. Nf3 Nf6 3. c4 d×c4 4. e3 a6 5. B×c4 b5 At this stage an irregular continuation believed to be premature. The regular line is 5 ... e6. **6. Bb3?!** This is harmless. Only 6 Bd3! offers whatever chances of profiting from 5 ... b5 there may be in the opening. An attempt to disorganize Black's queenside with a4 being indicated, the bishop must stand on d3, not on b3. Remember that forcing Bb3 constitutes one of the points of the regular line. **6 ... e6 7. a4 c6!** Thanks to 6 Bb3 Black is able to maintain his b-pawn on the fourth rank keeping the important square c4 under control. **8. 0–0 Nbd7 9. Qe2 Be7 10. e4 0–0 11. Bg5** More enterprising is 11 Nc3 intending 12 Rd1. If 11 ... b4 12 Nb1. Ineffective is 12 e5 because of 12 ... b×c3 13 e×f6 N×f6! (not 13 ... c×b2?? which loses on account of 14 f×e7 b×a1Q 15 e×d8Q R×d8 16 Bb2!). **11 ... Bb7 12. Nbd2 h6 13. Bh4?!** Much better is 13 Bf4. **13 ... Nh5!** Annoying in view of the possibility ... Nf4. **14. B×e7** With 14 Bg3 N×g3 15 h×g3 White can maintain some superiority in controlled space sufficient to compensate for Black's pair of bishops. But Kashdan would never allow a bishop to be exchanged in that way. **14 ... Q×e7 15. g3** The situation is uncomfortable to White who must watch the three possibilities ... Nf4, ... c5, and ... Qb4. With the text he speculates on the unprotected state of Black's king's knight. 15 Qe3 looks more natural, but it has the drawback of relieving the pressure on Black's b-pawn with the effect of allowing 15 ... c5!, also with a better game for Black. **15 ... Qb4!** Pinning down a number of White's pieces and preparing for ... c5. **16. Ne1** With this combination White transposes from a troublesome middlegame into an unfavourable endgame. But there is no line leading safely to equality. **16 ... Q×d4! 17. Q×h5 Q×d2 18. Rd1 Nf6! 19. Q×f7+ K×f7 20. R×d2 Rfd8 21. R×d8 R×d8 22. f3**

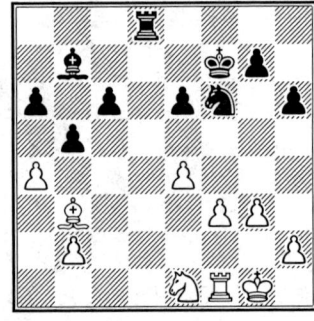

Position after White's 22nd move

22 ... c5 With all his pieces in action and his queenside majority on the move, Black obviously has an advantage. **23. a×b5 a×b5 24. Ng2 Rd2** In order to keep White's rook from the a-file. **25. Rf2 Rd4 26. Kf1 Nd7 27. Bc2 c4** A strong alternative is 27 ... b4 intending 28 ... Ba6(+). **28. Ke2 Ne5 29. Ke3 Rd8 30. h3** Preparing for f4. White's counter-measures proceed in a tormentingly slow tempo. A little better is 30 Ne1 directly, possibly followed by 31 Rd2. **30 ... Ke7 31. Ne1 Nc6 32. f4** He could better try 32 Rd2 Ra8 33 Rd1. However, there is very little hope for White anyway. **32 ... b4 33. e5** An improvement as far as White's bishop is concerned. Unfortunately it involves an even greater improvement for Black who now controls the vital square d5. The latter factor is decisive. **33 ... Na5 34. Rd2**

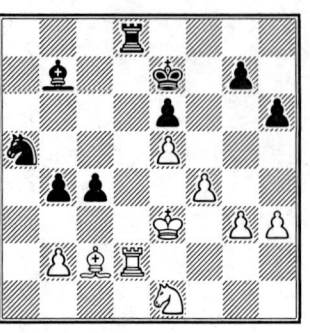

Position after White's 34th move

34 ... b3 Intending 35 R×d8 b×c2! winning a piece. However, 34 ... Bd5, threatening first of all 35 c3, followed by 36 ... Nc4+, wins more simply. **35. Bg6** The battle is over, for after 35 ... Bd5! White cannot stop 36 c3! and must lose a piece within a few moves since Black's passed pawn is too strong, for example, 36 Kd4 Be4+!, or 36 Rd1 c3 37 b×c3 Nc4+ 38 Ke2 Ra8. **35 ... c3?** A grave miscalculation in time-pressure. By winning a piece in that way, Black scores only a Pyrrhic victory. **36. R×d8 K×d8** No intermediate move is obviously playable. **37. b×c3 Nc4+ 38. Kd4 Bd5** So far so good. The threat of winning a piece with 39 ... b2 is irremediable. **39. Nf3?** Also time pressure. Correct is 39 Nd3! b2 (there is nothing else) 40 Nb4 Na3 41 N×d5 e×d5 42 K×d5 b1Q 43 B×b1 N×b1 44 c4 or 44 Ke6. With three mighty pawns for a knight, White has good chances for a win and can, if he wishes, draw at will. **39 ... b2 40. Bb1 Na3** White resigned. Instead of three pawns for a knight, White would now have two pawns for a bishop, more the bishop of the proper colour with regard to the h-pawn: 41 Nd2 N×b1 42 N×b1 Ba2. This is hopeless. **0–1** Kmoch 100–2.

(694) FINE–HOROWITZ, I

New York (9), 1949 (2 Jan.)
Queen's Gambit Declined [D35]

1. d4 Nf6 2. c4 e6 3. Nf3 d5 4. Bg5 c6 An attempt to avoid the most common lines. 4 ... h6 and 4 ... Bb4+ are also possible. **5. e3 Nbd7** With 5 ... Qa5+, he can indeed reach an irregular line which is, however, quite satisfactory for White: 6 Nbd2! Ne4 7 Bh4. White cannot play 6 Nc3 because of Ne4! which is stronger than transposing into the Cambridge Springs: 6 ... Nbd7. **6. c×d5 e×d5 7. Nc3** The Classical Exchange Variation. This line offers White a slight initiative and, if he wishes, an easy draw. Fine was satisfied with a draw since he needed only half a point to secure the undivided glory of becoming winner of the tournament. **7 ... Bd6** A move that Horowitz prefers to ... Be7. But the usual 7 ... Be7 is safer. **8. Bd3 0–0 9. 0–0 Re8 10. Qc2** Since the bishop stands on d6, White threatens 11 B×h7+. This, however, is an insignificant detail. Much more important is Black's inability to get some relief with the usual ... Ne4. **10 ... Nf8 11. Rfe1 Bg4** A loss of time. Better 11 ... Be6 at once, or repentantly 11 ... Be7. **12. Nd2 Be6 13. Nf1** White has a good position though, of course, by no means a winning one. Before starting any major action, Fine offered a draw. **13 ... Ng6?** Black has nothing other than either to accept the draw or play for it with 13 ... Be7. With the weak text, Horowitz refuses both. He felt obliged to put up a tough fight, anticipating any reproach that U.S. masters would favour U.S. masters. This is high sportsmanship, mediocre chess, and bad business. Business is not everything in this country. **14. f4!** Forced to fight, Fine starts in at once with grim energy. First he threatens to win a piece: 15 f5. **14 ... Bd7 15. Ng3! Rc8?!** Apparently intending ... c5, Black misses the last opportunity to play ... Be7, thereby diminishing the effect of e4. The alternative 15 ... h6? is erroneous and can be refuted two ways, first if 16 Bxf6 Qxf6 17 Nh5! followed by 18 Bxg6 which wins a pawn; second 16 Bxh6 gxh6 17 Bxg6 fxg6 18 Qxg6+ Kf8 19 e4, which yields White a winning attack. **16. f5 Nf8 17. e4!** This is decisive in view of the following combination. **17 ... dxe4 18. Ncxe4 Be7 19. Bxf6!**

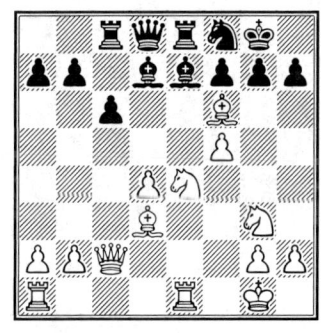

Position after White's 19th move

19 ... Bxf6 Taking with the pawn is obviously hopeless. **20. Nd6!** Not only attacking both the rooks but also threatening 21 Nxf7!. This puts too much strain on Black. **20 ... Rxe1+ 21. Rxe1 Qa5 22. Kf1 Rb8 23. Nxf7!** Winning a pawn at least, in a superior position. White threatens 24 Bc4 or 24 Qb3. **23 ... h6** The knight is immune: 23 ... Kxf7 24 Qb3+ Be6 25 fxe6+ Ke8 26 e7! Bxe7 27 Nf5. **24. Qb3** Oddly enough, there seems to be no direct win, and so 24 Ne5 may serve even better than the text. **24 ... Kh7?** This loses quickly. A much better defence is offered by 24 ... Qd5! when White, as Fine himself points out in *Chess Review*, March 1949, has nothing stronger than 25 Ne5, allowing the exchange of queens, the continuations 25 Nxh6+ Kh7 or 25 Bc4 Qxd4 being too obscure. **25. Nh5! Bxf5** Or 25 ... Bxd4 26 f6+ g6 27 Ng5+ hxg5 28 Qf7+ and White mates in five. **26. Nxf6+ gxf6 27. Re7 Kg6** If 27 ... Ng6, White mates in two. **28. Ne5+ Kg5 29. h4+** Black resigned. It is mate in a few moves, for example, 29 ... Kf4 30 g3+; or 29 ... Kxh4 30 Bxf5 fxe5 31 Rg7 Qb5+ 32 Qxb5 cxb5 33 g3+ Kh5 34 Bg4 mate. **1–0** Kmoch 105–6; *BCM* 1949, 46–8.

Match with Miguel Najdorf, New York and New Jersey, January 15–26, 1949

A match was arranged between the two top prizewinners from the international tournament held at the turn of the year. Fine started well, winning the first two games, after which he perhaps underestimated his opponent. In the third game the opening went reasonably for the American grandmaster, but inaccuracies in the middlegame led to an inferior ending, which the author of the "endgame bible" treated rather carelessly. Najdorf's excellent opening preparation for game four gave him a strong initiative, which he ultimately converted into a won game. Games five and six both featured early simplification leading to an even position. The penultimate game of the match was a truly magnificent battle in which both players missed winning chances in hair-raising complications. In the final game Fine playing with the black pieces managed to reach a favourable looking ending, but his decision to exchange both pairs of rooks produced a knight ending with no real prospects. Games were played in New York with the exceptions of game four which was held at Englewood, New Jersey, and game seven at West Orange, New Jersey.

	1	2	3	4	5	6	7	8	
Najdorf	0	0	1	1	½	½	½	½	4
Fine	1	1	0	0	½	½	½	½	4

(695) Fine—Najdorf, M

Match New York (1), 1949 (15 Jan.)
Grünfeld Defence [D93]

1. d4 Nf6 2. c4 g6 3. Nc3 d5 4. Bf4 A continuation which is more ambitious than its innocent appearance leads one to suppose. Its strategic meaning has been elucidated in a game Tartakower–Frydman, Łódź 1935. **4 ... Bg7 5. e3 0–0 6. Qb3** White can win a pawn by 6 cxd5 Nxd5 7 Nxd5 Qxd5 8 Bxc7, but then most players would prefer Black's game with its superior development, which is well worth a pawn. This is shown in a game Swihart–Hall, correspondence, U.S.A. 1950: 8 ... Nc6 9 Nf3 Bf5 10 a3 Rac8 11 Bg3 Bc2 12 Qd2 Na5 13 e4 Qxe4+ 14 Qe3 Nb3 15 Ra2 Qxe3+ 16 fxe3 Bb1 White resigned: he loses the rook. An amusing finish. **6 ... c6 7. Nf3 b6** A surprising move for a player of Najdorf's temperament. By allowing White to exchange pawns, he virtually surrenders an open c-file and condemns his own queen's bishop to comparative inactivity. He should himself exchange pawns. After 7 ... dxc4 8 Bxc4 Nbd7 9 0–0 Nb6 10 Be2 Be6 Black has a satisfactory game. **8. Rc1 Bb7 9. cxd5 cxd5 10. Be2 Nc6 11. 0–0 Rc8 12. h3 h6 13. Qa4 a6** The queenside is evidently Black's weak point. **14. Ne5 Nxe5 15. Bxe5 Nd7 16. Bxg7** On positional grounds this move is open to question. White's queen's bishop was much more effective than Black's king's bishop. Moreover, White's efforts are clearly centred on the queenside, and, as the exchange in the text solves all Black's kingside problems, Black can now concentrate on redressing the balance on the queenside. One would have expected 16 Bg3, contributing to the pressure on the queenside. **16 ... Kxg7 17. Rc2 e6 18. Qb4 Nb8 19. Rfc1 Nc6 20. Qa3**

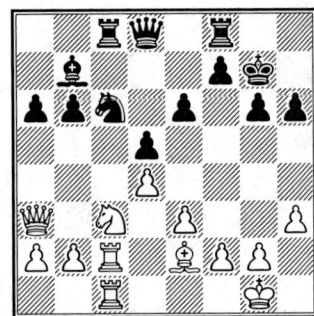

*Position after
White's 20th move*

20 ... Qe7 Tartakower and du Mont recommend 20 ... b5 21 Nb1 Qa5. Golombek however reckons that, in the event of 20 ... b5 21 Nb1, White would gain the advantage by way of the manoeuvre Nb1-d2-b3-c5. **21. Na4!** An excellent move! If now 21 ... b5 22 Qxe7 Nxe7 23 Nc5 Black has no adequate reply. **21 ... Qxa3 22. bxa3 b5 23. Nb6** Now better than 23 Nc5 Na5 24 Nxb7 Rxc2 25 Rxc2 Nxb7 26 Rc7 Rb8 and Black can hold out. **23 ... Rc7 24. a4 bxa4** He cannot play 24 ... b4 25 Bxa6 Bxa6 26 Rxc6. **25. Nxa4** His threat is 26 Nc5, winning the a-pawn. **25 ... Rfc8** In order to prevent 26 ... Nc5. If, for instance, 25 ... Ra8 26 Nc5 Nd8 27 Nxe6+ Nxe6 28 Rxc7 Nxc7 29 Rxc7, White wins a valuable pawn. **26. Nb6 Rb8 27. a4** Undue precipitancy here would have untoward consequences, for example, 27 Bxa6 Bxa6 28 Rxc6 Rxc6 29 Rxc6 Bb5 30 Rd6 Kf8 31 Nd7+ Bxd7 32 Rxd7 Rb1+ 33 Kh2 Rb2 and Black has established equality. After the text, however, the threat Bxa6 is real and unanswerable. **27 ... Rd8 28. Bxa6** Q.E.D.! The fight for Black's a-pawn during the last five moves has been dramatic. **28 ... Bxa6 29. Rxc6 Rxc6 30. Rxc6 Rb8 31. a5 Rb7** This will cost a second pawn, but at least the rook will get into play. **32. Nxd5 Rb1+ 33. Kh2 Bd3 34. Rb6 Ra1** Not 34 ... exd5 35 Rxb1 Bxb1 36 a6 and the pawn queens! **35. Nb4 Bc4 36. a6 f5 37. Rc6 Bb3 38. Rc7+ Kf6 39. a7 g5** Black puts up a desperate defence, which, however, is of no avail against his opponent's consummate technical skill. **40. Nc6** Black resigned because of the threat 41 Ne5 g4 42 h4 with an unavoidable mate by Rf7. **1–0** (*BCM* 1949, 220-1) Tartakower & du Mont 1955, 139-40.

(696) NAJDORF, M—FINE

Match New York (2), 1949 (16 Jan.)
Nimzowitsch-Indian Defence, Classical Variation [E34]

1. d4 Nf6 2. c4 e6 3. Nc3 Bb4 4. Qc2 d5 5. cxd5 5 a3 is more promising. **5 ... Qxd5** 5 ... exd5 is also good. **6. Nf3** The text is considered to be more solid than 6 e3, which was used several times in the Euwe–Alekhine match of 1937. In the event of 6 e3, Black can reply 6 ... c5 7 a3 Bxc3+ 8 bxc3 when White cannot claim any advantage. **6 ... c5 7. Bd2 Bxc3 8. Bxc3 0–0!** The 7th U.S.S.R. Championship match game Levenfish–Botvinnik, Moscow–Leningrad, 1937 continued 8 ... cxd4 9 Nxd4 e5 10 Nf3 (10 Nf5!? Capablanca–Euwe, A.V.R.O. 1938) Nc6 11 Rd1

with a double edged position. 8 ... Nc6 9 Rd1 0–0 10 a3 (10 e3 b6, Capablanca–Fine, A.V.R.O. 1938) cxd4 11 Nxd4 Nxd4 12 Rxd4 Qc6 13 e4 gave White the advantage in Capablanca–Najdorf, Margate 1939. AW **9. dxc5** If 9 a3 then 9 ... cxd4 10 Nxd4 10 e5, and Black has won an important tempo, or 10 Bxd4 Nc6 11 Bc3 Rd8 12 g3 e5 Bg2 Nd4. **9 ... Qxc5 10. Rc1 Nc6 11. Qb1 Qe7 12. g3** In order to be able to answer 12 Ng5 with 12 ... e5. **12 ... e5 13. Bg2 Nd5** Black has overcome his opening problems and now seizes the initiative. **14. 0–0 Nxc3 15. bxc3?!** It would have been less compromising to play 15 Rxc3 e4 16 Nd2 Nd4 17 Re1 f5 followed by 18 Nf1, and not 18 f3 exf3 19 exf3? Ne2+ 20 Kh1 Nxc3. By attempting to strengthen d4, White simply weakens the c4-square, a circumstance which Fine immediately exploits. **15 ... Be6 16. Rfd1** He should have preferred e2-e4, in order to secure an outpost in the centre and hinder the advance f7-f5. **16 ... Rac8 17. Ne1 Bc4**

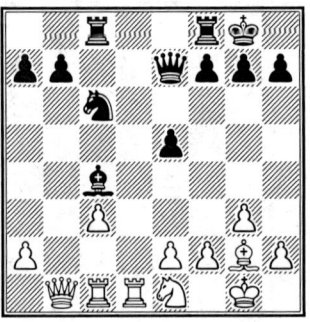

*Position after
Black's 17th move*

18. Nd3! f5! 19. e4 Now this move is too late and only encourages Black's attack. **19 ... f4! 20. Bh3 Rcd8 21. Nb4 Qf7!** There is no defence against the intrusion of the queen on f2 or h5. **22. Rxd8 Nxd8 23. Qc2 Ne6 24. Bf5** White hoped to provoke 24 ... g6, closing the queen's path to h5. **24 ... Nc5! 25. Rd1 Qh5 26. Nd5 g6 27. Bd7 Nxd7** White resigned in view of 28 Ne7+ Kh8 29 Rxd7 Qh3, after which Black delivers mate. **0–1** Levenfish, *Shakhmaty za 1947-1949 gg*, 270-2.

(697) FINE—NAJDORF, M

Match New York (3), 1949 (20 Jan.)
Spanish Opening, 8 d3 [C90]

1. e4 e5 2. Nf3 Nc6 3. Bb5 a6 4. Ba4 Nf6 5. 0–0 Be7 6. Re1 b5 7. Bb3 0–0 8. d3 With the score 2–0 in his favour one can easily understand Fine's desire to play solidly and safely. Nevertheless, 8 c3 is best here; since the Marshall Counterattack (8 ... d5) is in White's favour. HG **8 ... d6 9. c3 Na5 10. Bc2 c5 11. Nbd2 Nc6 12. Nf1 d5** Rather too soon and leading to a difficult game for Black. Correct is first 12 ... Be6. HG **13. exd5 Qxd5 14. Bg5 Bb7** Weakening the square f5 (see White's 17th move) but at any rate yielding counter chances on the long diagonal. HG **15. Ne3 Qd7 16. d4!** Strongly played; the pawn sacrifice is only a temporary one and Black's pieces are driven back. HG **16 ... exd4 17. Nf5! Bd8** Golombek points out that Black cannot play 17 ... dxc3 because of 18 Qxd7. His second idea, that Black cannot play 17 ... Rfd8 because of 18 Ne5 Nxe5 19 Nxe7+ Qxe7 20 f4, is however inaccurate as Black has the resource 20 ... dxc3!. Instead White can retain his advantage by 18 cxd4 cxd4 19 Qd3! AW **18. cxd4 cxd4 19. N3xd4** Too hasty. Golombek recommends 19 Qd2 and Levenfish, 19 a3 followed by Qd3 or Qd2. **19 ... Nxd4 20. Qxd4 Qxd4 21. Nxd4 h6 22. Bf4 Bb6** Black has emerged from his troubles and the game should now be drawn. HG **23. Nf5 Rfe8 24. Bb3** Threatening Bf7+ followed by Nd6+. HG **24 ... Bc5 25. Bd6?!** Mistimed aggression. He should give his king a loophole by 25 h3 or, if intent on the draw, play simply 25 Be3. He has clearly overlooked Black's reply. HG **25 ... Ne4! 26. Bxc5** If 26 Rxe4 Bxe4 27 Ne7+ Rxe7 28 Bxe7 Bxe7 29 Re1 Rc8 30 g3 Bf3 winning a piece. HG **26 ... Nxc5 27. Bc2** Bad for White is 27 Nd6 Nxb3 (27 ... Rxe1+ 28 Rxe1 Nxb3 29 Nxb7 is more accurate—AW) 28 axb3 (White has the intermezzo 28 Rxe8+ Rxe8 29 axb3—AW) Rxe1+ 29 Rxe1 Bd5 30 b4 g6, the bishop being much superior to the knight in this open position. HG **27 ... Rxe1+ 28. Rxe1 Rd8** Here Fine offered a draw and, this being refused, the quality of his play took a marked turn for the worse—as quite frequently happens on such occasions. HG **29. b4 Ne6 30. Bb3 Kf8 31. Rd1** If 31 Bxe6 fxe6 32 Ng3 Rd2 33 Rxe6 Rxa2 34 Rb6 Ra1+ 35 Nf1 Bd5 followed by 36 ... Bc4. HG **31 ... Rxd1+ 32. Bxd1 Be4 33. Nd6** 33 Ne3 is better, although after 33 ... Nd4 with ... f5 to follow, Black's pieces would dominate the board. GL **33 ... Bd5 34. a4 Nd4! 35. axb5 axb5 36. f3 Ke7 37. Ne4 Bc4** No more than a draw results after 37 ... Bxe4 38 fxe4 Kd6 39 Kf2 Ke5 40 Ke3 Nc6 41 Be2. HG **38. Kf2** The best chance in this position, White intends to liquidate the pawn on b5. GL **38 ... Nc6 39. Be2 Nxb4 40. Nc3** Winning the b-pawn but eventually yielding in return a pawn on the other wing. HG **40 ... Nd3+ 41. Ke3** If 41 Kg3 b4 42 Bxd3 bxc3!. HG **41 ... Ne1 42. Nxb5 Nxg2+ 43. Kf2 Bxe2 44. Kxe2** Knight and two pawns against knight and three on the same side should usually draw. This position should be no exception; but perhaps neither player is well acquainted with the relevant chapter in *Basic Chess Endings*. HG **44 ... Kf6 45. Nd6 Ke6 46. Nc4 Kd5 47. Nb2 Kd4 48. Nd3 f5 49. Nb4 Nf4+ 50. Kd2** Not 50 Kf2 Nd3+ with a won pawn ending. HG **50 ... Ne6 51. Nc6+ Kd5 52. Ne7+ Ke5 53. Ke3 Kf6** With the idea of advancing the king along the h-file and so pin down White to the defence of the h-pawn. HG **54. Nd5+ Kg5 55. Kf2 Kh4 56. Kg2 g6 57. Ne7 Kg5** A forced retreat; for if 57 ... Nf4+ 58 Kf2 Kh3 59 Ke3 Ne6 60 Nxg6 Kxh2 61 Ne7 drawing easily. HG **58. Kg3 f4+** Black cannot do without this move, it does, however, reduce the possibility of an intrusion and therefore the chance of a win. GL **59. Kf2 Nd4 60. Nd5 Nc6 61. Nc3 Kh4 62. Kg2 Ne7 63. Ne4** Santasiere suggested 63 Ne2! Nd5 64 Ng1 with a draw. AW **63 ... Nf5 64. h3?** Providing the ingenious Najdorf with the opportunity of winning a neat endgame study. Black can now win the pawn, even at the cost of giving up the knight and force

his own pawn to queen. Correct is 64 Nf2 Ne3+ 65 Kg1 g5 66 Nd3 h5 67 Ne5 g4 68 fxg4 hxg4 69 Nd3 when Black can have no hope of winning. HG **64 ... Ne3+ 65. Kh2 Nc2 66. Kg2** Or 66 Nd2 Ne1 and White is in *Zugzwang*. HG **66 ... Ne1+ 67. Kf2 Kxh3! 68. Kxe1 Kg2 69. Ke2** Edward Lasker's suggestion 69 Nd6 loses to the advance of the h-pawn. AW **69 ... h5 70. Ng5 h4 71. Ne6 g5!** Not 71 ... h3 72 Nxf4+ and draws. Now if 72 Nxg5 h3 73 Nxh3 Kxh3 74 Kd3 Kg2! 75 Ke2 Kg3. Therefore White resigned. **0–1** Golombek, BCM 1949, 221–3; Levenfish, *Shakhmaty za 1947-1949 gg*, 272–3.

(698) NAJDORF, M—FINE

Match New Jersey (4), 1949 (21 Jan.)
Nimzowitsch-Indian Defence, Rubinstein's Variation [E44]

1. d4 Nf6 2. c4 e6 3. Nc3 Bb4 4. e3 b6 5. Nge2 Bb7 6. a3 In my game against Furman (16th U.S.S.R. Championship, Moscow 1948) I showed that the continuation 6 ... Bxc3+ 7 Nxc3 0–0 8 d5 exd5 9 cxd5 c6 10 Bc4 cxd5 11 Nxd5 Nc6 12 0–0 Ne5 13 Nxf6+ Qxf6 14 Be2 is completely satisfactory for Black. GL **6 ... Be7 7. d5! 0–0 8. Ng3** On 8 g3 Black has a strong reply in 8 ... b5!, for example, 9 b3 bxc4 10 bxc4 and one of his knights will reach c5. 8 e4! is perhaps best: 8 ... d6 9 g3 c6 10 dxe6 fxe6 11 Nd4 Bc8 (as occurred in Euwe–O'Kelly, Groningen 1946) and now 12 Bh3 e5 13 Bxc8 Qxc8 14 Nf5 would have given White a clear positional advantage according to Euwe. G&G **8 ... d6** 8 ... b5 is also possible here: 9 dxe6 fxe6 10 Nxb5 c5 and now not 11 Nd6 (Botvinnik–O'Kelly, Groningen 1946), but 11 f3 followed by Be2 and 0–0. G&G **9. Be2 c6 10. e4 Na6** Fine copies Ragozin in his game with Botvinnik (Sverdlovsk 1943), which continued 11 dxc6 Bxc6 12 b4 Nc7 13 0–0 Qb8! 14 Be3 b5!, and Black has a good game. Najdorf strengthens the whole variation. GL **11. 0–0 Nc7 12. Re1! Qd7** Black gains nothing by 12 ... cxd5 13 exd5 exd5 14 Bf3, and White regains the pawn and retains the pressure. GL **13. Bf3 cxd5** Grooten & Gijssen suggest 13 ... Rb8, preparing ... b5. AW **14. exd5 exd5 15. cxd5 Rfe8 16. Bg5!** Black cannot take the pawn on d5, as the following variations show: A 16 ... Nfxd5 17 Rxe7!; B 16 ... Ncxd5 17 Rxe7! Nxe7 18 Bxb7 Qxb7 19 Bxf6 gxf6 20 Nce4. GL **16 ... h6 17. Be3! Bf8 18. Qd4! Nb5** On 18 ... Re5 White would answer 19 Bf4 (GL) or 19 Red1 Ncxd5 (19 ... Nfd5 20 Nxd5 Bxd5! AW) 20 Bxd5 Nxd5 21 Bf4 Nxf4 22 Qxe5 (G&G). In the Dutch analysts' line it is not clear that White is better after 22 ... Nxg2, even disregarding the possibility at move 19, therefore Levenfish's move is surely better. AW **19. Nxb5 Qxb5 20. a4 Qc5 21. Qd2 Qc7 22. Rec1 Qd8 23. a5! bxa5 24. Rxa5 a6 25. b4 Rc8 26. Rca1 Qc7 27. b5! axb5 28. Rxb5 Ra8** Otherwise 29 Ra7 would follow. G&G **29. Rc1! Qd7 30. Rcb1! Ba6 31. R5b4 Qd8 32. Bb6 Qd7 33. Bd4 Qd8 34. Ra1! Nd7 35. h3 Nc5** Black might have held out longer with 35 ... Ne5, as suggested by Grooten & Gijssen. AW **36. Nh5 f5** The patient manoeuvring game begins to bear fruit. White threatened 37 Qc3 Qg5 36 Nf6+ gxf6 39 Bxc5 dxc5

40 Rg4. Black frees the 7th rank in order to be able to defend the pawn on g7, but this weakens e6. GL **37. Nf4 Qg5 38. h4!** White concludes the struggle in an efficient manner. GL **38 ... Qxh4 39. Ne6 Qe7** Interesting complications result from 39 ... Nxe6 40 dxe6 d5!, but they also lead to White's advantage: 41 e7! Bxe7 42 Bxd5+ Kh7 43 Rba4 Rad8 44 Bb6. GL (Fritz prefers 44 Be3, in view of 44 Bb6 Bc4! 45 Bxd8 Rxd8 46 Rd1 Rxd5 47 Qxd5 Bxd5 48 Rxh4 Bxh4. AW) **40. Bxc5 dxc5 41. d6 Qxd6?** Losing immediately to 41 Qxd6 Bxd6 42 Bxa8 Rxa8 43 Rb6. Black had to play 41 ... Qe6 42 Bxa8 Rxa8 43 Rb6 when 43 ... Rd8 may be the best chance (if 43 ... Qc4 44 d7! Be7 45 Qe3 Kf8 46 Qf3 or if 43 ... Bb7 44 Rxa8 Bxa8 45 d7 Qxb6 46 d8Q Qxd8 47 Qxd8 winning), for example 44 Raxa6 c4! 45 Qd4 Qe1+ 46 Kh2 Qe6 with some compensation in the insecure position of the white king. AW **1–0** Grooten & Gijssen, Postma 99–101; Levenfish, *Shakhmaty za 1947-1949 gg*, 273–5.

(699) Fine—Najdorf, M

Match New York (5), 1949 (22 Jan.)
Grünfeld Defence [D96]

1. d4 Nf6 2. c4 g6 3. Nc3 d5 4. Qb3 dxc4 5. Qxc4 Bg7 6. Nf3 0–0 7. g3 Fine was always keen on fianchetto variations in the queen pawn openings. **7 ... Be6 8. Qd3** After 8 Qa4 Nc6 9 Bg2 Nd5 10 0–0 Nb6 11 Qd1 Nxd4 12 Nxd4 Qxd4 13 Qxd4 Bxd4 14 Bxb7 Rab8 15 Ba6 Nc4 Black's position is somewhat preferable according to Smyslov. **8 ... Qc8 9. Ng5 Bd7 10. Bg2 h6 11. Nf3** 11 Nge4 may be better. **11 ... Bh3 12. 0–0 Bxg2 13. Kxg2 c5 14. dxc5 Qxc5 15. Be3 Qh5 16. Rac1 Nc6 17. Na4 Qd5 18. Qxd5 Nxd5 19. Bd2 Rfd8 20. Nc5 Rdc8 21. Nxb7!? Rab8 22. Rc5 Nf6 23. Rfc1 Rxb7 24. Rxc6 Rxc6 25. Rxc6 Rxb2 26. Ra6 Ne4 27. Be3 Rxe2 28. Rxa7 Nc3 29. Nd2 Re1 30. a4 Ra1 31. a5 Nd5 32. Bc5** Perhaps White should have tried 32 Kf3!? **32 ... Ra2 33. Nb3 Be5 34. Ra6 Kg7 35. Rc6 Bc3 36. a6 Nb4 37. Bxb4 Bxb4 38. Nc1 Ra3 39. Kf1 e5 40. Ke2 e4 41. Kf1** Draw agreed. **½–½**

(700) Najdorf, M—Fine

Match New York (6), 1949 (23 Jan.)
Grünfeld Defence, Fianchetto Variation [D71]

1. d4 Nf6 2. c4 g6 3. g3 Bg7 4. Bg2 d5 5. cxd5 Nxd5 6. e4 Nb4 7. d5 0–0 Or 7 ... c6 8 Ne2 (8 a3 N4a6 9 Nc3 0–0 10 Nge2 cxd5 11 exd5 Nc7 R. Byrne–Najdorf, Mar del Plata 1961) cxd5 9 exd5 Bf5 10 0–0. **8. Ne2 c6 9. a3 N4a6 10. 0–0 e6 11. Nbc3 exd5 12. exd5 cxd5 13. Nxd5 Nc6 14. Nec3 Nc7 15. Nxc7 Qxc7 16. Nd5 Qd8 17. h4** An even position was reached by 17 Bf4 Bf5 18 Qd2 Qd7 19 Bh6 f6 20 Rfe1 Rae8, Averbakh–Ilivitsky, U.S.S.R. Championship Kiev 1954. **17 ... Be6 18. Bg5 Qc8 19. Qd2 Bxd5 20. Bxd5 Nd4 21. Qd3 Qd7 22. Bg2 h6 23. Bf4 Rad8 24. Rfe1 Ne6 25. Qxd7 Rxd7 26. Be5** Draw agreed. **½–½**

(701) Fine—Najdorf, M

Match New Jersey (7), 1949 (25 Jan.)
Grünfeld Defence, Fianchetto Variation [D75]

1. Nf3 Nf6 2. c4 g6 3. d4 Bg7 4. g3 0–0 5. Bg2 d5 By transposition of moves the Kemeri Variation (A sort of hybrid between the Grünfeld and King's Indian Defences: in the King's Indian proper the d-pawn is usually held back on d6, to support an assault on square d4 by either e5 or c5; in the Grünfeld proper White has played 3 Nc3, so that the black knight appearing on d5 can be exchanged off at once and the attack on d4 taken up by ... Bg7, ... c5 and possibly ... Bg4, with the black queen having a controlling interest on the d-file.) has been reached. WH **6. cxd5 Nxd5 7. 0–0 c5!** The book move—Flohr tried 7 ... Nc6 against Fairhurst in the Anglo-Soviet match of 1946. WH **8. dxc5** The advance 8 e4 is premature: 8 ... Nb6 9 dxc5 (9 d5!?) Qxd1 10 Rxd1 Na4 leaves Black with the better game (Alexander); 8 ... Nb4 9 a3 N4c6 10 dxc5 Qxd1 11 Rxd1 Na6 and White cannot protect both c5 and b2, while after 10 d5 Nd4 Black has achieved his principal target, a vast expanse of black diagonal from the Atlantic to the Urals (Heidenfeld) or 8 ... Nf6 when White retains a minimal advantage (Mikhalchisin, EMCO 1998). **8 ... Na6 9. Qa4** An extremely interesting idea, and the only way to preserve any initiative at all. Any other line gives Black the advantage, for example, 9 e4? Ndb4 or 9 c6 bxc6 (Mikhalchisin's main line, in which he concludes that White retains some advantage. There is however room for improvement in Black's play.) followed by ... Rb8 and Black's open lines more than compensate for his pawn weaknesses. CHO'DA **9 ... Nxc5** The interesting idea 9 ... Nbd4 costs Black more time than White: 10 a3 Bd7 11 Qd1 Nc6 12 Be3! Bxb2 13 Ra2 Bg7 14 Rd2 would give White much the better play—it is peculiar how well his pieces are developed after all the "crooked" moves they had to make. WH **10. Qh4** White must try to create chances on the kingside; on the other wing, the black knights are beautifully placed and the black bishop on g7 has as much power as any King's Indian or Dragon bishop. WH **10 ... Qb6!** A vigorous counter-attack, threatening to win the queen's rook, and avoiding a pin on the d-file. CHO'DA **11. Nbd2** Alexander questioned this move stating that White should play boldly: 11 Nc3 Nxc3 (11 ... Nf6 12 Be3!) 12 bxc3. He considered that it would be too dangerous for Black to accept the material by 12 ... Bxc3 13 Be3, and suggested Black should play 12 ... Qc7, with equal chances after 13 Bh6. However, in the main line after 13 ... Bxa1 14 Rxa1 Qd6 it is unclear how White will generate a winning attack. Another suggestion was 11 Ng5, which also does not look clear. Fine's move is therefore perfectly reasonable, though 11 Na3 may be even better. AW **11 ... Qb4! 12. e4** If White exchanges queens he will have a very bad game, owing to Black's threat of ... Nc2 and ... Bf5. CHO'DA **12 ... Nf6 13. a3 Qa4 14. b4** Alexander awards this move an exclamation mark, whereas Heidenfeld makes no comment. In view of some later tactical points, the slightly surprising 14 b3! may have been best: 14 ... Nxb3 (14 ... Qe8 15 e5!) 15 Nxb3 Qxb3

16 e5! Nd5 17 Bh6 with compensation. AW **14 … Nd3!** Black "retreats to the front"—and the point of his queen manoeuvre. 14 … Ncxe4 15 Nxe4 Nxe4 16 Bh6! Bxa1 (16 … Nf6 17 Rfe1 Re8 18 Ne5 with ample positional compensation—Alexander) 17 Rxa1! would win a pawn (White regains the rest of his material since two black pieces are attacked), but Black's most important weapon, the dark-squared bishop, would be gone. WH **15. e5 Ng4 16. Qxe7** In view of a previously overlooked shot on move 19, White should probably play 16 Ne4 Ngxe5 17 Nxe5, which is quite murky. AW **16 … Re8 17. Qh4 Ndxe5** White had to sacrifice tempi to remove the important e-pawn (the weakness of f6 will be an important motif later on), whereas Black gets e5 in the course of the day's business, so to speak. As a result, the white position now looks endangered; Black threatens … Bf6 as well as … Nxf3+, followed by … Bxa1. Both sides now display their ingenuity—their knight play in particular is of fantastic complexity. WH **18. Ng5 h6 19. Nge4**

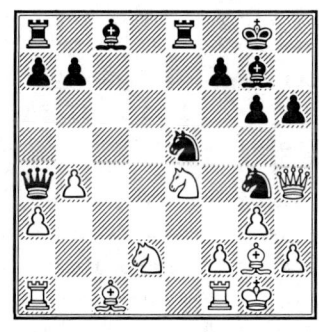

Position after White's 19th move

19 … Qc2 Alexander suggested 19 … Bf5, which probably is good for Black, but even more to the point is the explosive 19 … Nxh2!!, threatening … Nf3+ or … Neg4, which gives Black a won game. AW **20. h3 Nd3 21. Rb1 Nge5** It is amusing how the horses follow each other—a sort of parade that White is going to copy immediately. WH **22. Nd6 Rf8** Now Alexander, who, like Kurt Richter, underestimated White's next move, suggests 23 Be4 f5 24 Bd5+ Kh7 25 Nf3!, with the idea 25 … Qxb1 26 Bxh6 Nxf3+ 27 Bxf3, which would appear to be finely balanced after 27 … Qb3 28 Bxg7+ Kxg7 29 Qd4+ Kh7 30 Be2! AW **23. N2e4!**

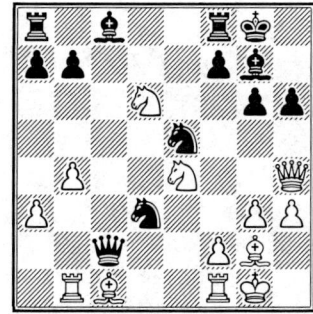

Position after White's 23rd move

23 … Nxc1! Can Black take the rook? 23 … Qxb1 24 Bxh6 Qb2!, and now: a) 25 Ng5 Nc6 26 Ndxf7 Rxf7 27 Bd5 Nd8!

and White gets insufficient value for his sacrifices (Heidenfeld); b) 25 Bxg7 Kxg7 26 Qf6+ Kg8 27 Qe7 Be6 28 Nf6+ Kh8 29 Nde8 Nd7! (rather than Heidenfeld's 29 … Rfxe8 30 Nxe8 Nc6! 31 Qf8+ Kh7 32 Nf6+ Qxf6 33 Qxa8); c) 25 Nf6+ Bxf6+ 26 Qxf6 Nc6 (26 … Nc4 27 Ne4) 27 Ne4 Qe5 (27 … Qxf6 28 Nxf6+ Kh8 29 Bxf8 Bxh3 30 Bh6 with a favourable ending) 28 f4 Qd4+ 29 Qxd4 Nxd4 30 Nf6+ Kh8 31 Bxf8 Bxh3 32 Be7 Ne2+ 33 Kh2 Bxg2 34 Kxg2 Kg7 35 Rh1 Rh8 36 Rxh8 Kxh8 37 Kf3 with a good ending for White. AW **24. Rbxc1 Qb2 25. Rc7 Be6** At last this bishop has a chance of being developed, and from now on it will play a significant part in the proceedings. WH **26. Kh1** 26 Nc5! threatening 27 Nxe6 fxe6 28 Qe7, or 27 Qe7 at once would make things very difficult for Black. CHO'DA **26 … Rad8! 27. f4 Nd3** Back to familiar pastures! WH **28. f5 Bd5!** Threatening 29 … Rxd6, which would also follow 29 f6—after 29 … Rxd6 30 fxg7 Kxg7 White would be a pawn down with no attack left. If then 31 Rcf7+ Rxf7 32 Rxf7+ Bxf7 33 Nxd6 g5!, and White can only save his queen at the expense of a piece: 34 Nf5+ Kf6 35 Qxh6+ (simply 35 Qd4+ retains the equilibrium. AW) Kxf5 with a winning position. WH **29. Nxf7!** White again crosses his opponent's plan. The disappearance of the f-pawn and the time lost in the retreat of the bishop make all the difference. WH **29 … Bxf7** Not 29 … Bxe4 30 Qxe4 Rxf7 Qe6 and wins. CHO'DA **30. f6! g5!** And not 30 … Bh8? 31 Qxh6 when Black has no real defence against the threat Ng5. WH **31. Qg4 Ne5 32. Qf5 Bh8 33. Nxg5! hxg5!** On 33 … Bg6? the simplest win is 34 Bd5+! Rxd5 35 Qe6+ Nf7 36 Nxf7. AW **34. Qxg5+ Bg6** If 34 … Ng6 35 Rxf7 (Heidenfeld's 35 Be4 is refuted by 35 … Qe2 attacking the bishop and threatening mate in one) Rxf7 36 Qxg6+ Kf8 and a draw by perpetual check. AW **35. f7+!** Now 35 … Nxf7 would be answered by 36 Qxg6+ Qg7 37 Qf5 Rd6 38 Rxb7 and White should win. AW **35 … Kg7 36. Qf6+?** White could now win by 36 Qxd8 Rxf7 37 Rf4!! (Fritz, which improves on a trickier winning line suggested by Horowitz: 37 Qf6+ Kh7 38 Rxf7+ Bxf7 39 Be4+ Bg6 40 Bxg6+ Nxg6 41 Qxb2 Bxb2 42 Rf7+ Kg8 43 Rxb7 Bxa3 44 b5). Black is in *Zugzwang*. AW **36 … Kh7 37. Qh4+** 37 Qxd8 Rxf7 38 Rf4! would win in a similar fashion to the last note. AW **37 … Kg7 38. Qf6+** Draw agreed. ½–½ Heidenfeld 1982, 97–9; Alexander, BCM 1949, 126–8.

(702) NAJDORF, M—FINE

Match New York (8), 1949 (26 Jan.)
Queen's Gambit Declined, Semi-Tarrasch [D42]

1. d4 d5 2. c4 e6 3. Nc3 Nf6 4. Nf3 c5 5. cxd5 Nxd5 6. e3 Be7 7. Bd3 0–0 8. 0–0 cxd4 9. exd4 Nc6 10. Qe2 Nf6 11. Rd1 Nb4 12. Bc4 b6 13. Ne5 Bb7 14. a3 Nbd5 15. Ba6 Qc8 16. Bxb7 Qxb7 17. Qf3 Rac8 18. Bg5 h6 19. Nxd5 Qxd5 20. Qxd5 Nxd5 21. Bxe7 Nxe7 22. Rac1 Rxc1 23. Rxc1 Rc8 24. Rxc8+ Nxc8 25. Kf1 f6 26. Nc4 Kf7 27. Ke2 Ke7 28. Kd3 Kd7 29. Ne3 Nd6 30. Nd1 Nf5 ½–½

Radio Match with Vasja Pirc, U.S.A.–Yugoslavia, February 11–13, 1950

"Jugoslavia once again demonstrated its great chess strength by decisively beating the U.S.A. in a radio match that lasted for four days from February 11th to February 14th. What would have happened if the U.S.A. had been able to field its original and strongest team is not clear, though, personally, I would still rather back the Jugoslavs." (*BCM* 1950) The U.S.A scored only two wins in the match—on board 10, Bisguier from Ivkov in the first round and, on board 4, Denker from Rabar in the second. Meanwhile Milan Vidmar, Jr., defeated Ulvestad 2–0, Puc beat Dake by 1½–½ and Matanovic whitewashed Pinkus 2–0, for a final score 11½–8½. Kashdan had to withdraw from the team when he went down with a perforated ulcer a week before the match and Herman Steiner, then U.S. Champion, was dissatisfied with the board he was assigned and declined to participate. They were replaced by Ulvestad and Bisguier. Larry Evans, then three time Marshall Club Champion, was available but had finished a point and a half behind Ulvestad in the 1948 U.S. Championship, however, he won the next, held in summer 1951, ahead of Reshevsky. Later that year, in September in the absence of the Soviet Union, Yugoslavia won the Hamilton-Russell Trophy in Dubrovnik. In the later match between these two countries, at the International Team Tournament, Reshevsky beat Gligoric on top board and Horowitz beat Pirc, however Shainswit and Kramer both lost, to Trifunovic and Vidmar respectively. Surprisingly Evans was only second reserve, he scored 9/10.

	1	2	
Fine	½	½	1
Pirc	½	½	1

(703) PIRC, V–FINE

U.S.A.–Yugoslavia Radio Match board 2 (1), 1950 (11 Feb.)
King's Indian Attack [A07]

1. Nf3 d5 2. g3 Nf6 3. Bg2 g6 4. 0–0 Bg7 5. d4 Nbd7 The usual move is 5 ... 0–0. SV **6. c4 dxc4 7. Nbd2 Nb6!?** Black would indeed equalize after 7 ... c5. VP **8. Nxc4 Nxc4!?** Now White gains a considerable advantage. 8 ... 0–0 was correct. VP **9. Qa4+ c6 10. Qxc4 Be6** 10 ... 0–0 is better. VP **11. Qb4** With pressure on b7 and e7. VP **11 ... Qc8 12. Re1 Ne4!** Control of e4 is an important theme in the position. SV **13. Bf4 a5** Weakening his position, but it is essential to chase the white queen. VP **14. Qa3 Qd8 15. Qd3 Nd6 16. Ng5 Bc4 17. Qc2 Ba6** The bishop is out of the game here. There was, however, no choice because of the threat of 18 Bxd6. VP **18. Be5! 0–0 19. Bxg7 Kxg7 20. Rad1 a4 21. Qc3** White starts to play inexactly. 21 e4 was correct, for example, 21 ... Bc4? (21 ... Qb6!? Fritz) 22 e5 Bxa2 23 exd6 Bb3 24 dxe7. VP

21 ... Nb5 22. Qe3 Qc7 23. a3?! A loss of time which probably costs White the full point. 23 Nf3, followed by Qc1 and e3, would have been correct. VP **23 ... Rad8 24. Nf3 Rd6** Now Black gains activity and emerges from his difficulties. VP **25. Qe5+ f6 26. Qc5 Qd8** Black now exerts pressure along the d-file. VP **27. e3 e5 28. Bf1 Rf7 29. Qc2 exd4 30. Bxb5 Bxb5 31. Rxd4 Rfd7 32. Red1 Qe7 33. Qc5** Agreed drawn on Black's suggestion. White's advantage is insignificant as the opponent's queenside pawns are unassailable. VP ½–½ Pirc, 56; *Sahovski Vjesnik* 1950, 64.

(704) FINE–PIRC, V

U.S.A.–Yugoslavia Radio Match board 2 (2), 1950 (13 Feb.)
King's Indian Defence, Fianchetto Variation [E72]

1. d4 Nf6 2. c4 g6 3. Nc3 Bg7 4. e4 d6 5. g3 0–0 6. Bg2 e5 7. Nge2 Nc6 8. d5 Nd4 9. 0–0 On 9 Nxd4 exd4 10 Ne2 (10 Nb5!? Fritz) there would follow 10 ... Re8 11 f3 c5 12 dxc6 bxc6 13 Nxd4 Qa5+ 14 Bd2 Qb6, or the immediate 13 ... Qb6, and Black has adequate compensation for the pawn sacrificed. **9 ... Nxe2+ 10. Nxe2** White is planning the advance f2-f4, but this does not turn out to be a happy choice in this position. **10 ... Re8 11. h3 Bd7 12. Be3 b6 13. Qd2 a5 14. Rac1 Kh8 15. g4 Ng8 16. f4** Carrying out his idea, though it yields him no advantage. **16 ... exf4 17. Nxf4 Qe7 18. Bd4 Bxd4+ 19. Qxd4+ Qe5** The e5-square is firmly under Black's control, Fine therefore acquiesces to the draw. **20. Qf2 f6 21. b3 Rf8 22. a3 Qe7 23. Qd4 Qe5 24. Qf2 Qe7** Draw agreed. ½–½ *Sahovski Vjesnik* 1950, 68.

New York Metropolitan League, June, 1950

In the final competitive game contested between these old rivals, and possibly Fine's final game after twenty years representing the Marshall Chess Club in the Metropolitan League, Fine notched up another win. The game was typical of many of their encounters; Denker attempted to complicate the game, while Fine strove to keep positional control.

Fine	1	Denker	0

(705) FINE–DENKER, A

Metropolitan Chess League, New York, 1950 (June)
Sicilian Defence, Fianchetto Najdorf [B91]

1. e4 c5 Denker's favourite defence; he likes its fighting possibilities. **2. Nf3 d6 3. d4 cxd4 4. Nxd4 Nf6 5. Nc3 a6** The modern "Paulsen." In the original version Black used to play this on his fourth move, when White can get in 5 c4, which gives Black a very cramped game. **6. g3** In this position Horowitz played 6 Be2, followed by a4 against Denker in the 1936 United States Championship. It is also playable, but the king's fianchetto is good for White once Black has disclosed his intention to advance his queen-side pawns. **6 ... b5 7. Bg2 Bb7 8. 0–0 e6 9. a3 Qc7 10. g4!** An original conception! This impudent little pawn advances on its own to g5, where it stays, very effectively, until the end of the game. **10 ... Nc6** If 10 ... h6 White starts a dangerous attack with 11 f4. **11. g5 Nd7 12. Nde2 g6 13. Be3 Bg7 14. Qd2 Nde5 15. b3 0–0 16. Rad1 Rfd8** The advanced g-pawn has created serious problems for Black. To challenge it with 16 ... f6 leaves the e-pawn critically weak, and so Black decides to contest the centre, but the g-pawn remains to the end a serious hindrance. **17. h3 b4** An ingenious attempt to free himself. **18. axb4 d5 19. exd5 Nxb4**

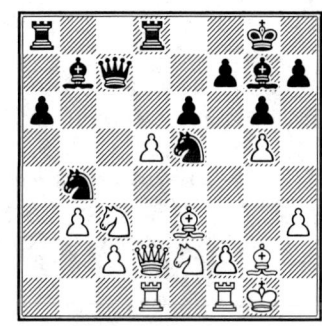

Position after Black's 19th move

20. d6! White's refutation. He now has two advanced pawns in the enemy camp. **20 ... Qc8 21. Ne4 Nd5 22. Bd4 Nd7 23. c4 e5 24. Ba1 f5 25. cxd5 fxe4** A curious position, but it still is the g-pawn which hinders Black the most. **26. Ng3 Nc5 27. Qe3 Nd3 28. Qxe4 Nf4 29. Rc1 Qb8 30. Rc7 Re8** If 30 ... Rc8 then equally 31 Rxg7+ Kxg7 32 Qxe5+. **31. Rxg7+** Black resigned. If 31 ... Kxg7 32 Qxf4, a good game by Fine. **1–0** Julius du Mont, *BCM* 1950, 300, from the *Manchester Guardian*.

Capablanca Chess Club of Havana vs. Marshall Chess Club, Havana, February 10–12, 1951

"The weekend of February 10–12 was utilized for a match on seven boards between the Marshall CC and the Capablanca CC of Havana at the rooms of the latter, the outcome being a tie, with 3½ points for each side, ... Senor Aureliano Sanchez-Arango's private plane carried the visitors from Miami to Havana ... " 1. Fine 1 Planas 0, 2. Ed. Lasker ½ Aleman, 3. Kmoch ½ Broderman, 4. Mengarini 0 Florido 1, 5. McCormick 1 Bucelo 0, 6. Bowman 0 Meylan 1, 7. Bino ½ Sanchez-Arango. Fine also gave an exhibition, winning four games and drawing one. (*ACB* 1951, 1)

Fine   1   Planas   0

(706) FINE—PLANAS GARCIA, F

Marshall CC vs. Havana, Havana (1), 1951 (10 Feb.)

The score of this game is not available. **1–0**

Marshall Club Sextangular, New York, 25 February–1 April, 1951

"The sextangular tournament at the Marshall Club ended in a tie between Reuben Fine and Larry Evans with 4 points—a noteworthy success for the latter. They drew with each other and both drew with Lasker, who was third with 2½, followed by Simonson 2, Santasiere 1½, and Hanauer 1." (*BCM* 1951) A few months after the event, which is also known as the Marshall Chess Club Special Masters Tournament, Evans managed to do what Fine had thrice failed to do himself—he won the United States Championship ahead of Reshevsky.

		1	2	3	4	5	6	
1=	Fine	*	½	½	1	1	1	4
1=	Evans	½	*	½	1	1	1	4
3	Lasker	½	½	*	1	0	½	2½
4	Simonson	0	0	0	*	1	1	2
5	Santasiere	0	0	1	0	*	½	1½
6	Hanauer	0	0	½	0	½	*	1

(707) SANTASIERE, A—FINE

Marshall Club Sextangular, New York (1), 1951 (25 Feb.)
Alekhine's Defence [B02]

1. e4 Nf6 2. Nc3 d5 3. e5 Nfd7 4. e6 (Santasiere sacrifices a pawn to disrupt Black's development, but he never really gets value for his investment. AW) **4 ... fxe6 5. d4 c5 6. Nf3 Nc6 7. dxc5** (7 Bb5 [Wollmann–Nitsche, 24th German correspondence chess championship preliminaries 1992–4] cxd4 is unclear, Bagirov, EMCO 1996, 284–5) **7 ... Nxc5 8. Be3 Nd7 9. Bb5 g6 10. Nd4 Ndb8 11. Nxc6 bxc6 12. Bd4 Rg8 13. Bd3 Qd6 14. Qe2 Nd7 15. f4 Qxf4**

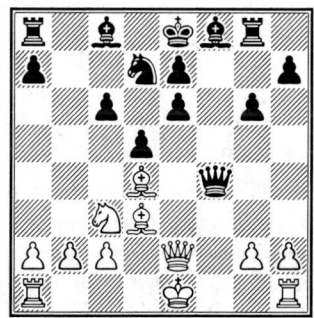

Position after Black's 15th move

16. Be3 (Possibly White had intended 16 Qxe6 Qxd4 17 Qxg8, which would, however, be well met by 17 ... Nf6!, trapping the queen. AW) **16 ... Qe5 17. 0–0 d4 18. Bf4 Qxe2 19. Nxe2 Bg7 20. h4 e5 21. Bh2 Nc5 22. Ng3 Nxd3 23. cxd3 Be6 24. Ne4 Bd5** (*see diagram*) **25. Rae1 Bxa2 26. Ng5 Bd5 27. Bxe5 Kd7 28. Rf4 Bxe5 29. Rxe5 Rab8 30. Re2 Rb3 31. Ne4 Rb5 32. Ng5**

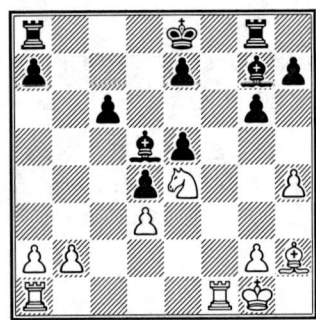

Position after
Black's 24th move

Rgb8 33. Nxh7 Rxb2 34. Rxb2 Rxb2 35. Rg4 a5
36. Nf8+ Kc7 37. Nxg6 a4 38. Nxe7 a3 0–1 ACB
March 1951.

(708) Fine—Lasker, Ed

Marshall Club Sextangular, New York (2), 1951 (4 March)
Nimzowitsch-Indian Defence, Rubinstein System [E12]

1. d4 Nf6 2. c4 e6 3. Nc3 Bb4 4. e3 Rubinstein's
answer to the Nimzowitsch-Indian. Everybody plays it nowadays but all it proves is that Black's resources are adequate.
CL 4 ... c5 5. Nge2 d5 Excellent! An improvement over
5 ... cxd4 6 exd4 d5 7 c5! *CL* 6. a3 Bxc3+ 7. bxc3 Against
Reshevsky, in the recent exhibition game he played at the
Manhattan Chess Club, Fine obtained no advantage with the
continuation 7 Nxc3. But the text cannot be good because
development is delayed. *BCM* 7 ... cxd4 8. cxd4 dxc4
9. Qa4+ Nc6 10. Qxc4 So Black is left with a queenside
pawn majority which proved itself many times a winning
advantage in endgames. *CL* 10 ... 0–0 11. Nc3 Bd7
12. Be2 Rc8 13. Qd3 Na5 This manoeuvre with the
queen's knight seems faulty. 13 ... Ne7 to free the bishop
and the file would be more to the point or perhaps 13 ... a6
to prevent White's Nb5. *CL* 14. Rb1 Qc7 15. Bd2 b6 He
is forced to exchange or lose the valuable a-pawn. But now
White has two bishops and that is too many against two
knights. *CL*; With this move Black throws away the considerable superiority he has secured in the opening. Correct was
15 ... a6 followed by b5 and Nc4. *BCM* (The game looks
about equal after 15 ... a6 16 0–0 b5 17 Rfc1 Nc4 18 a4! AW)
16. Nb5 Bxb5 17. Qxb5 Rfd8 The idea is that Black
hopes White will play 18 Bxa5 Rd5! and he would be happy.
CL 18. 0–0 18 Rc1 looks to be worth investigation. AW 18
... Nc6 Now 19 Bxa5 is a threat, and although 18 ... Ne4
looks better, it would be a blunder as 19 Bxa5 Rd5 20 Bxb6!
(the simple 20 Qd3 may be even better, and 19 ... bxa5 may
also be playable. AW) and 20 ... Rxb5 cannot be played. *CL*
19. Qa4 Ne4 20. Be1 Nb8 This move prevents White
from chasing his knight away with 21 f3 as 21 ... Nc3 forces
22 Bxc3. Also White was threatening to play 21 Ba6, forcing
the rook to move from the open file. *CL* 21. Rb3 Qe7
21 ... Qd7 would be preferable as he will do it later anyway.
CL 22. f3 Nf6 23. Bh4 Qd7 A risky play, giving up his
queenside pawns. *CL* 24. Bb5 Qd5 25. Rb2 e5 A combination intended to get rid of all queenside pawns and thus

to nullify the advantage of the two bishops. *BCM* 26. Qxa7
exd4 27. Qxb6 Qe5 28. exd4 Qe3+ 29. Bf2 Qxa3
Black is now a pawn down and he is playing against two
bishops. Quite an advantage for White, and yet ... *CL*
30. Be2 Nd5? A blunder in time pressure. 30 ... Nc6! was
indicated, threatening Re8 as well as Nxd4. *BCM* 31. Qb3
Qxb3 32. Rxb3 Nf4 33. Bb5 Nc6 34. Rd1 Rb8
35. Kf1 It would not be wise to play 35 Bc4 because of
35 ... Rxb3 36 Bxb3 Ne2+ 37 Kf1 Nexd4. *CL* 35 ... Na5
36. Rbb1 Nd5 37. Rdc1 Kf8 38. Be1 Nc4! Fine had
completely overlooked this move when analyzing the adjourned
position. When he saw the sealed move (37 ... Kf8) he
remarked "This loses right away. The only move to hold
your game together was Nf7, I think." He now must give up
one bishop, in view of the threat ... Na3. *BCM* 39. Bxc4
Rxb1 40. Rxb1 Ne3+ 41. Ke2 Nxc4 42. Bb4+ Ke8
43. Kd3 Ne5+ 44. Ke4 Nc6 45. Bc5 f5+! 46. Kxf5
Much better chances were offered by Kd3. Apparently Fine
overlooked that Black can save himself with 48 ... Rd8. *BCM*
46 ... Nxd4+ 47. Bxd4 Rxd4 48. Ke6 Rd8 49. h4
Kf8 50. h5 Ra8 51. Rb6 h6 52. g4 Kg8 53. f4 Re8+
54. Kf5 Rf8+ 55. Ke5 Re8+ 56. Re6 Ra8 57. Re7
Kf8 58. Rd7 Kg8 59. g5 Ra5+! Producing a book draw.
If White advances his pawn to g6, the black king either gets
stalemate or goes to g8 in reply to h5-h6. If White does not
advance the g-pawn, Black plays so as to occupy f7 whenever
White threatens to invade g6 with his king. *BCM* 60. Rd5
Rxd5+ 61. Kxd5 hxg5 62. fxg5 Kf7 63. Kd6 Kf8
64. Ke6 Ke8 65. Ke5 Ke7 66. Kf4 Kf8 67. Kg4
Ke7 68. Kf5 Kf7 Draw agreed. ½–½ *BCM* 1951, 254;
Chess Life, July 5, 1951.

(709) Hanauer, M—Fine

Marshall Club Sextangular, New York (3), 1951 (11 March)
English Opening, Rubinstein Variation [A34]

1. c4 Nf6 2. Nc3 c5 3. g3 d5 4. cxd5 Nxd5 5. Bg2
Nc7 6. Qa4+ Nd7 7. Nf3 g6 8. d4 cxd4 9. Qxd4 e5
10. Qa4 Bg7 11. Bg5 f6 12. Be3 0–0 13. Rd1 Qe7
14. Qc4+ Ne6 15. Bh3 f5 16. Ng5 Nb6 17. Qb3 Kh8
18. Nf3 e4 19. Nd4 Nc5 20. Qb5 f4

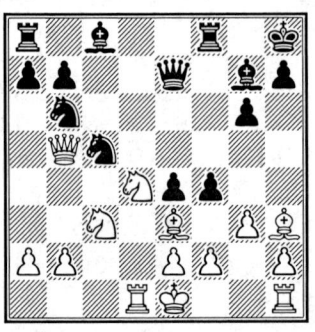

Position after
Black's 20th move

21. Nf5 Rxf5 22. Bxf5 fxe3 23. Bxc8 exf2+ 24. Kxf2
Rxc8 25. Kg2 Bxc3 26. bxc3 Nca4 27. Qb4 Qxb4
28. cxb4 Nc3 29. Rd4 Nbd5

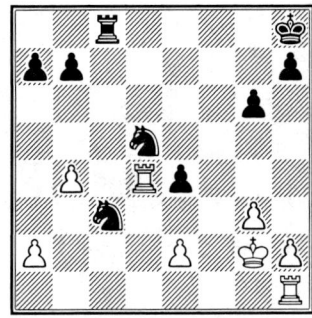

Position after Black's 29th move

30. a4 Kg7 31. Rc1 Rc7 32. Kf2 Kf6 33. e3 Ke5 34. Rd2 Nxb4 35. Ra1 Rf7+ 36. Kg1 Nbd5 37. a5 Nxe3 38. a6 bxa6 39. Ra5+ Ned5 40. Rc2 Rc7 41. Rxa6 e3 White resigned. 0–1 *ACB* March 1951.

(710) EVANS, L—FINE

Marshall Club Sextangular, New York (4), 1951 (25 March)
Fianchetto Grünfeld [D75]

1. d4 Nf6 2. c4 d5 3. cxd5 Nxd5 4. Nf3 g6 5. g3 Bg7 6. Bg2 0–0 7. 0–0 c5 8. dxc5 Na6 9. Ne1 (Kalinichenko, *EMCO* 1998, 67, prefers 9 Ng5 or 9 c6, both of which he assesses as leading to a slightly better position for White, or even 9 Qa4 which he reckons to be unclear. Evans' move is not even quoted to show Fine's refutation. AW) **9 ... Nf4!** The two bishops constitute a powerful weapon—but they are not inherited: an active effort must be made to "win" them in the middle game. If a knight is also worth 3.5 units, one may well be justified in demanding to know why all this fuss about the "two bishops." The truth is, a bishop is actually worth about 3.75 units—this is what a century of chess theory has taught us! Also good is 9 ... Ndb4 10 Qxd8 Rxd8 11 a3 Nxc5! 12 Nd2 (if 12 axb4 Nb3 regains the piece most favourably {13 Nc2 Nxc1 (13 ... Nxa1 14 Nxa1 is good for White) 14 Rxc1 Bxb2 15 Nba3 Bxa1 16 Rxa1 does not look worse for White in view of the pressure on the queenside. AW}), Nc6. In this variation Black retains only a slight advantage. The text not only recaptures the pawn—but wins the two bishops in the process. **10. Qc2** Not 10 Qxd8 Nxe2+ 11 Kh1 Rxd8 and White must lose at least a pawn owing to the double threat of 12 ... Nxc1 or 12 ... Nxc5. (12 Be3 leaves the b-pawn hanging.) **10 ... Nxg2 11. Nxg2 Qa5 12. Bd2** White should not attempt to hold onto the pawn with 12 Be3 Bf5 13 Qc1—Black regains the pawn and his pieces spring into dynamic play. **12 ... Qxc5** Black regains the pawn with the better game. **13. Qxc5 Nxc5 14. Bc3** Exchanging would lose the two bishops. **14 ... e5 15. Bb4 b6 16. Nc3** And White managed to equalize. **16 ... Ba6 17. Rfd1 Rfc8?!** (17 ... Rad8!? AW) **18. Ne3 Ne6 19. Ned5 Bf8 20. Ne7+ Bxe7 21. Bxe7 Nd4 22. e3 Nf3+ 23. Kg2 Bb7 24. e4** Draw agreed. ½–½ *ACB* March 1951; Notes from Evans, 80.

(711) FINE—SIMONSON, A

Marshall Club Sextangular, New York (5), 1951 (1 April)
Grünfeld Defence, Russian Variation [D81]

1. d4 Nf6 2. c4 g6 What, no Budapest!? **3. Nc3 d5 4. Qb3** One of many good lines 4 cxd5 (preferred by Bronstein), 4 Bf4 (the most usual) and 4 g3 or 4 Qa4+ are also plausible. **4 ... c6** 4 ... dxc4 is an interesting alternative. Then after 5 Qxc4 Be6 White can attempt 6 Qb5+, 6 Qa4+ or 6 Qd3. The latter is the most popular nowadays. **5. cxd5 Nxd5** On 5 ... cxd5 6 Bg5 is annoying. **6. e4 Nxc3** 6 ... Nb6 is more usual and stronger. After the text Black must (unlike the variations following 4 cxd5) lose a tempo in order to enforce ... c5 (he has already played 4 ... c6). **7. bxc3 Bg7 8. Nf3 0–0 9. Be2 c5 10. 0–0** Here Fine offered a draw to the astonishment of everyone. It must be admitted that only a fighting, determined player like Simonson could have refused such an offer from a Grandmaster! **10 ... cxd4 11. Nxd4** At first sight 11 cxd4 appears better, but by this move White hopes to profit by the open d-file and his strongly centralized pieces—good enough reasons! **11 ... a6** Black has a difficult game. This move is played to restrict White's queenside activity and to prevent the possibility of Bb5 after ... Re8. **12. Ba3 Re8 13. Rad1 Qc7 14. f4 Nc6 15. Nxc6 Qxc6 16. f5!** White's threats are very strong. Black takes a pawn in order to compensate for his lack of development. **16 ... Qxe4 17. fxg6 Qxg6 18. Bd3 Qe6** On 18 ... Qh5? White crashes through in masterful fashion by 19 Rxf7!! Qxf7 (White would have to work a little harder after 19 ... Kh8. AW) 20 Bxh7+! Kf8 (on 20 ... Kxh7 21 Qxf7) 21 Rf1! Bf6 22 Rxf6 Qxf6 23 Qg8 mate. **19. Bc4 Qe3+ 20. Kh1**

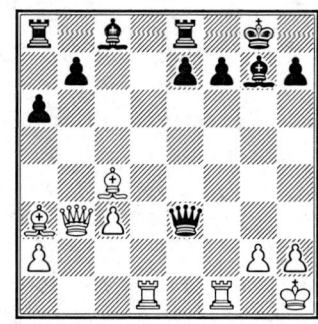

Position after White's 20th move

20 ... e6 The losing move. 20 ... Be6 is obviously forced. After 21 Bxe6 fxe6 (or 21 ... Qxe6 22 Qxe6 fxe6 23 Rd7 with pressure for White) 22 Rde1 Qxc3 23 Qxe6+ Kh8 there is no direct win for White, although the position is manifestly in his favour. (The line in parentheses looks good for Black. Fortunately for White, however, he can force the main variation by 21 Rde1, although his advantage appears minimal. AW) **21. Qa4 b5** Black must lose the exchange; the rook is "cooked." **22. Bxb5 axb5 23. Qxa8 Qb6** Black's only chance lies in the rapid utilization of his two bishops. **24. Qf3 f5 25. Qh5 Rd8 26. Qg5 Re8 27. Bd6 Kh8** 28 Be5 cannot be allowed. **28. Rfe1 Rg8 29. Be7 Bb7** Not 29 ... Bxc3 30 Bf6+ Bxf6 31 Qxf6+ Rg7 32 Rd8+ and wins.

30. Re2! White must watch his step. On 30 Bf6 B×g2+ wins a pawn (31 K×g2 B×f6 wins; on 31 Q×g2 B×f6 is a hard win for White). **30 ... Bd5 31. Bf6 Qb7 32. Rd3 B×f6 33. Q×f6+ Qg7 34. Q×g7+ R×g7 35. Rg3 Ra7 36. Rd2 R×a2 37. R×a2 B×a2 38. Kg1** Here the game was adjourned. White's win is easier than it appears. **38 ... h6** If Black could get his bishop to g6 and pawn on e5 he might hold the position. However, if 38 ... e5 39 Rg5 is too strong. Thus Black attempts to prevent this "killer," however, now g6 is vulnerable. **39. h4 Kh7 40. h5 Bb3 41. Rg6 f4 42. Rf6 Kg7 43. Rg6+ Kh7 44. Kf2 Ba2 45. Rf6 Kg7 46. R×f4 Bb1 47. Ke3 Bc2 48. Kd4 Bd1 49. g4 Be2 50. Ke5** Black resigned since further resistance is useless. **1–0** *Chess Life*, May 20, 1951.

Wertheim Memorial Tournament, New York, June 3–17, 1951

		1	2	3	4	5	6	7	8	9	10	11	12	
1	Reshevsky	*	½	0	½	1	½	1	1	½	1	1	1	8
2	Najdorf	½	*	1	1	½	½	½	½	½	1	½	1	7½
3	Euwe	1	0	*	1	0	½	1	1	½	½	1	1	7½
4	Fine	½	0	0	*	½	1	½	1	1	1	½	1	7
5	Evans	0	½	1	½	*	1	1	0	½	0	1	1	6½
6	Horowitz	½	½	½	0	0	*	1	1	½	½	1	½	6
7	Byrne	0	½	0	½	0	0	*	1	1	1	1	1	6
8	Guimard	0	½	0	0	1	0	0	*	1	1	1	½	5
9	O'Kelly	½	½	½	0	½	½	0	0	*	½	½	1	4½
10	Bisguier	0	0	½	0	1	½	0	0	½	*	½	½	3½
11	Kramer	0	½	0	½	0	0	0	0	½	½	*	1	3
12	Shainswit	0	0	0	0	0	½	0	½	0	½	0	*	1½

Maurice Wertheim, Senior Partner in the firm H. Wertheim and Company, former publisher of *The Nation*, founder of the Theater Guild and instrumental in the Palestine Economic Foundation, died in May 1950 at the age of 64. His 1800 acre shooting preserve, Stealaway, near Brookhaven Long Island, was willed to the Department of the Interior as a wildlife sanctuary. Wertheim was also President of the Manhattan Chess Club, organizer of the American team visiting Moscow in 1946, and patron of many U.S. events, including several U.S. championships. Fine, Horowitz, Kramer and Shainswit were working during the day and could play only in the evening. Fine had to start his games at 7 P.M. and had no time available for adjournments. The time limit was set at 50 moves in 2½ hours with controls at move 30 (1hr 30m per player), 50, 70 (each hour after). Eliot Hearst in *Chess Review*, July 1951, wrote "Fine seemed to lack the necessary concentration in his games." His quick draw with Reshevsky prompted Tournament Controller Kmoch to ask the contestants to sign a statement promising no agreed draws in under 30 moves. Snacks were furnished free to all contestants. Old mechanical-time-keepers, as opposed to electric clocks, had to be used and

sometimes failed in time pressure. Kmoch in *Chess Review*, August 1951, called Fine's result more of a miracle than a failure, for he played the entire tournament in a state of exhaustion. (Spence, 1952b).

(712) FINE—EUWE, M

Wertheim Memorial, New York (1), 1951 (3 June)
Catalan System [E04]

1. d4 Nf6 2. c4 e6 3. g3 d5 4. Bg2 d×c4 5. Nf3 Nbd7 6. 0–0 c6 7. a4 b5 8. a×b5 8 b3 ought to be considered, leading either to the recovery of the pawn or substantial action on the queenside. JS **8 ... c×b5 9. Nc3 Qb6 10. b3 Bb4** Seemingly holding the pawn and giving White many problems, but Fine has a clever reply! JS **11. Na2 Be7 12. b×c4 b×c4 13. Nd2! Nd5** On 13 ... Q×d4 with 14 Bb2! White wins the exchange (Münninghoff *et al*). But this looks pretty unclear after 14 ... Q×b2 15 B×a8 Ba6 16 Rb1 Qa3 with compensation. AW **14. N×c4 Qa6 15. Na3** Spence, who proposes 15 Ne3 N×e3 (or 15 ... Bb7 16 Rb1 with equal chances according to Münninghoff *et al*, but according to Fritz 17 B×d5 B×d5 18 N×d5 is clearly advantageous for White) 16 B×e3 Rb8 17 Nc3 with adequate counterplay, incorrectly identifies this as the losing moment and Münninghoff *et al* call it the beginning of a dubious combination, but the mistake certainly comes later. **15 ... B×a3 16. B×d5 e×d5 17. Nc3 Qc6 18. B×a3??** (After the essential 18 R×a3 0–0 Euwe assesses Black's position as favourable.) **18 ... Q×c3 19. Qa4 Qc4 20. Qa5 f6! 21. Rfc1 Q×d4 22. Qb5 Rb8 23. Qc6 Kf7 24. e3 Qb6 25. Q×d5+ Qe6 26. Qd4 Re8 27. Rc7 Rb7 28. Rc3 Ne5 29. Qe4 Rd7 30. f4 Ng6 31. Q×e6+ K×e6 32. Bc5 a6 33. Bd4 Ne7 34. g4 Bb7 35. Kf2 Rc8 36. Rb3 Rc2+ 37. Kg3 h5** White resigned. **0–1** Euwe in Münninghoff *et al*, 433–4; Euwe 1955, 7–8; Spence 1952b, 3.

(713) KRAMER, G—FINE

Wertheim Memorial, New York (2), 1951 (4 June)
Nimzowitsch-Indian Defence [E43]

White held a slight advantage for most of the game in Kramer–Fine but the former was unable to convert it into any tangible advantage. Fine retained sufficient chances at all times to hold the position in balance. JS **1. d4 Nf6 2. c4 e6 3. Nc3 Bb4 4. e3 b6 5. Bd3 Bb7 6. Nf3 Ne4** Or 6 ... 0–0 7 0–0 B×c3 8 b×c3 Be4, PCO 254. **7. Qc2** The celebrated game Denker–Fine, U.S. Championship, New York 1944, continued with 7 0–0!. **7 ... f5 8. 0–0 B×c3 9. b×c3 0–0 10. Nd2** 10 d5 is a good alternative. JS **10 ... N×d2** 10 ... Qh4 11 f3 N×d2 12 N×d2 Nc6 13 e4 f×e4 14 f×e4 e5 15 d5 Ne7 16 c5 Ng6 17 d6 c×d6 18 c×b6 is unclear, Emms, NCO 485. **11. B×d2 Nc6 12. f3 Na5 13. e4 f×e4 14. f×e4 Qh4 15. g3 Qh5 16. Bf4 Rac8 17. Rab1** To transfer the queen's rook to the kingside with a minimum of moves. JS **17 ... Ba6 18. c5 B×d3 19. Q×d3 Nc6**

20. cxb6 axb6 21. Rb5 Qf7 22. d5 exd5 23. exd5
Ne7 24. d6 cxd6 25. Bxd6 Qxf1+ 26. Qxf1 Rxf1+
27. Kxf1 Kf7 Draw agreed. An interesting game worthy of
study. JS ½–½ Spence 1952b, 5–6.

(714) FINE—BISGUIER, A

Wertheim Memorial, New York (3), 1951 (5 June)
Queen's Gambit Declined [D30]

1. d4 d5 2. c4 c6 3. Nf3 e6 4. Qc2 A remarkable
idea. White avoids the complexities of the Semi-Slav and
obtains an acceptable position akin to the Catalan. 4 ...
Nd7 5. g3 Ngf6 6. Bg2 Ne4?! This occupation of e4
merely slows up Black's development. 6 ... Be7 7 0–0 0–0
8 Nbd2 b6 9 b3 Bb7 10 Bb2 Rc8 and a familiar position
from the Catalan has been reached in which both sides have
their chances. 7. 0–0 Bd6 8. Nbd2 f5?! Black's handling of the late opening leaves much to be desired. Here he
elects to play a kind of Dutch defence, whereas 7 ... Be7 was
called for. Now though White can exchange the poorly
placed knight on d2 to the detriment of the black pawn formation. 9. Nxe4! fxe4 10. Ng5 A very strong move with
the black king's bishop on d6 rather than e7. 10 ... Nf6
11. f3! This attack on the black pawn centre is the real
point of White's previous move. Black cannot now reply
11 ... h6 in view of the answer 12 fxe4 hxg5 13 e5! 11 ...
exf3 12. exf3 0–0 13. f4! Fixing the black e-pawn as
an object of attack. 13 ... Bd7 If Black wanted to save his e-
pawn, it was essential to play 13 ... h6. True, White would
retain the advantage after 14 Nf3, because of the weak
e-pawn and the strong square e5 available for his knight, but
Black would at least preserve the material balance. 14. c5
Bc7 15. Bh3 Qe8 16. Qe2 Qg6 17. Nxe6 Bxe6 On
17 ... Rfe8, simply 18 f5. 18. Qxc6+ Kh8 19. Qf5 Qh6
20. Bg2 Rae8

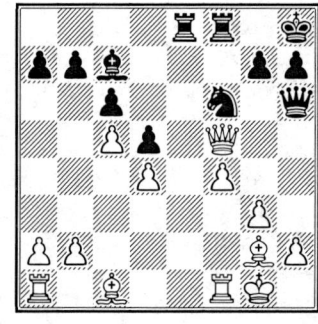

*Position after
Black's 20th move*

21. Qg5! Seemingly surprisingly, White allows a doubling
of his pawn by this queen exchange. However, he has evaluated the resulting position accurately. The advantage of the
bishop pair and the extra doubled pawn, which, nevertheless, is strategically important, guarantee him an endgame
advantage. 21 ... Qxg5 22. fxg5 Ne4 23. Rxf8+ Rxf8
24. Be3 Bd8 25. Bxe4! White exchanges the advantage
of the bishop pair for an advantage of another kind. On
account of the weak e-pawn, the ending is easily won. The
g5-pawn deprives the black bishop of the f6-square. 25 ...

dxe4 26. Bf4 Kg8 27. Re1 Re8 28. h4 Ba5 29. Re2
b6 If Black remains passive, White will first of all win the
e-pawn and eventually the game by playing Be5, either by a
central breakthrough (d4-d5) or by a breakthrough on the
queenside (b2-b4-b5). 30. Kf2 Kf7 31. Ke3 Re6 32. a3
Black resigned. On 32 ... bxc5 33 dxc5 followed by 34 b4
the pressure exerted by the rook along the d-file would eventually be decisive. 1–0 Euwe 1955, 13–4.

(715) EVANS, L—FINE

Wertheim Memorial, New York (4), 1951 (7 June)
Queen's Indian Defence [E45]

1. d4 Nf6 2. c4 e6 3. Nc3 Bb4 4. e3 b6 5. Nge2
Ba6 5 ... Bb7 6 a3 Be7 7 d5! 0–0 8 Ng3 d6 with advantage
to White, PCO 254. 6. Ng3 0–0 6 ... h5 (Bronstein) 7 h4
Bb7 8 Bd2 a6 9 Qc2 d5 10 cxd5 Nxd5 11 Nxd5 Bxd2+ 12
Qxd2 Qxd5 13 Rc1 with advantage to White, NCO 486.
7. Qb3 7 e4 d5 8 cxd5 Bxf1 9 Kxf1 exd5 (9 ... Nxc3
10 bxc3 exd5 11 e5 Ne4 12 f3 Nxg3+ 13 hxg3 and White
stands better, NCO) 10 e5 Ne4 11 Qg4 and White has a
strong attack, but on the other hand he is unable to castle.
Bronstein 7 ... c5 8. a3 Ba5 9. Be2 cxd4 10. exd4
d5 11. cxd5 Qxd5 12. Qxd5 Nxd5 13. Bd2 Bxc3
14. bxc3 Rc8 15. Rc1 Bxe2 16. Kxe2 Rc4 Spence is
slightly contradictory here saying that this move was premature before developing the queenside, and then that
blockading c4 was to be condoned. Both the text and
16 ... b5 look good for Black. 17. Kd3 Ra4 18. Ra1 Nc6
19. Rhc1 Rc8 20. c4 Nde7 21. Bb4 Rd8 22. Kc3
Rxd4 23. Rd1 Rxd1 24. Rxd1 h6 25. Kb3 Ra6
26. Ne4 Nf5 27. Rd7 Nfd4+ 28. Kc3 e5 29. Nd6
Ra4 30. Nxf7 Draw agreed. ½–½

(716) FINE—BYRNE, R

Wertheim Memorial, New York (5), 1951 (9 June)
Catalan System [E02]

1. d4 d5 2. c4 e6 3. Nf3 Nf6 4. g3 dxc4 5. Qa4+
Nbd7 6. Bg2 a6 7. Qxc4 b5 8. Qc2 Bb7 9. 0–0 c5
10. a4 Be7 11. Rd1 0–0 12. e3?! Qb6 13. Qe2 Rfc8
14. Nbd2 h6 15. axb5 axb5 16. Rxa8 Bxa8 17. dxc5
Nxc5 18. Nd4 Bxg2 19. Kxg2 b4 20. f3 Nfd7 Draw
agreed. ½–½

(717) FINE—O'KELLY DE GALWAY, A

Wertheim Memorial, New York (6), 1951 (10 June)
Queen's Gambit Declined [D06]

1. d4 d5 2. c4 c5 This, the Austrian (or Haberditz) Defence, is rightly unpopular. I doubt whether even O'Kelly,
who alone has for a long time used this defence himself, has
ever won a game with it—while he has lost a few and drawn
many. Black must play precisely in order to maintain the
balance, the slightest inaccuracy could push him over the

precipice. **3. cxd5 Nf6** An important improvement over the earlier 3 ... Qxd5 after which White can gain a considerable lead in development by 4 Nf3 cxd4 5 Nc3. ME **4. dxc5 Qxd5 5. Qxd5 Nxd5 6. Bd2** The strongest move, according to Euwe. Szabo won a famous miniature from O'Kelly at Groningen 1946 with 6 e4 Nb4 7 Na3 e5 8 Be3 a6? 9 Nf3 f6 10 Nd2 Be6 11 Bc4 Bxc4 12 Ndxc4 Bxc5 13 Bxc5 Nd3+ 14 Ke2 Nxc5 15 Nb6 Ra7 16 Rhc1 1–0, but the Belgian Grandmaster showed in his game with Bolbochan in Trencianske Teplice 1949, that Black has nothing to fear after 8 ... f6!, preparing ... Na6. **6 ... e5** Although the black e-pawn is rather vulnerable after this double advance, it would nevertheless have been difficult to choose 6 ... e6 instead. There would follow 7 Nc3!, when Black, since he cannot safely take first on c3, will be burdened with a weak isolated pawn after 7 ... Bxc5 8 Nxd5 exd5 9 Rc1 Nd7 10 e3. ME **7. Nc3** 7 Na3 Na6! 8 e4 Nbd4 9 Rc1 Bd7! Estrin–O'Kelly, Ragozin Memorial 1963–6, was drawn in 38 moves. AW **7 ... Nxc3 8. Bxc3 Nc6?!** This "natural" developing move does not meet the requirements of the position. Black must play f6, preserving the choice of development for the knight (Purdy's principle of greater choice!). It would be a mistake for White then to play 9 Rc1 Be6 10 a3 Bxc5 11 Bxe5 fxe5 12 Rxc5 Nd7 (O'Kelly) as Black would have a considerable advantage in development for the pawn. **9. Nf3 f6 10. Rc1** Not 10 b4 a5! 11 b5 Nb4 12 Bxb4 axb4 13 c6 b3!. **10 ... Bxc5 11. Bxe5 Bxf2+** The well-known desperado motif. ME **12. Kxf2 fxe5** After this move Black is lost. 12 ... Nxe5 was essential, although after 13 Nxe5 fxe5 14 e4! (and not 14 Rc5 0–0 15 Ke3 Re8 16 Ke4 b6 17 Rxe5 Bb7+ 18 Kf4 Rxe5 19 Kxe5 Rc8 with Rc1 to follow) 0–0 15 Ke3 Be6 16 Bc4 Black must still be careful, for example, 16 ... Bxc4 17 Rxc4 Rac8? (17 ... Rf7!) 18 Rhc1 Rxc4 19 Rxc4 Rf7 (or 19 ... h6 20 Rc5! Re8 21 Rc7) 20 Rc8+ Rf8 21 Rc5 Re8 22 Rc7 winning a pawn. **13. e4 0–0** After this move the knight becomes very strong. But Euwe's alternative from the tournament book, 13 ... Bg4 is likewise insufficient: 14 Bb5 Bxf3 15 Bxc6+! (and not as Euwe suggested 15 gxf3? Rac8 16 Rc5 0–0 17 Bxc6 Rxc6 18 Rxe5 Rc2+) bxc6 16 gxf3, and it is not clear how Black can protect both of the isolated pawns, for example, 16 ... Rb8 17 b3 Kd7 18 Rhd1+ Kc7 19 Rd5 Rhe8 20 Rcc5. **14. Bc4+ Kh8 15. Kg3!** In order to free the knight and more particularly to prevent ... Bg4. ME **15 ... Bd7 16. Rhd1 Be8 17. Bd5 Rd8** Black seems to have everything under control: 18 Bxc6 Rxd1! 19 Rxd1 Bxc6 20 Nxe5 Bxe4. But now there comes a little surprise.

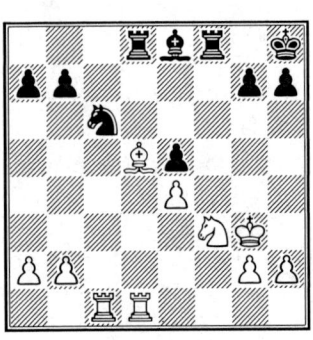

*Position after
Black's 17th move*

18. Rf1! Threatening both Bxc6 followed by Nxe5 (since without the exchange on the d-file a fork is threatened on f7) and also the immediate Nxe5 (because of the threat of mate on f8). Black has but a single defence to the two-fold threat. The rest is easily understood. **18 ... Rf6 19. Bxc6 bxc6 20. Nxe5 Rd2 21. Rcd1!** With the deadly threat of Rd8, in the event that the rook moves away. **21 ... Rxd1 22. Rxd1 Re6 23. Kf4 Kg8 24. Rd8 Kf8 25. Nc4 Ke7 26. Ra8** Black resigned. A ruthless exploitation of a small opening advantage. **1–0** Heidenfeld, 1983 62–4; Euwe 1955, 28–30.

(718) NAJDORF, M—FINE

Wertheim Memorial, New York (7), 1951 (11 June)
Queen's Gambit Accepted [D27]

1. d4 d5 2. c4 dxc4 3. Nf3 Nf6 4. e3 e6 5. Bxc4 c5 6. 0–0 a6 7. Qe2 cxd4 It would be better to defer this exchange (which commits him too soon to one line of play) and either develop a piece by 7 ... Nc6 or else play the aggressive 7 ... b5. HG; Fine follows in Steinitz' footsteps. In the 9th round Byrne played 7 ... b5 against Najdorf, with the continuation 8 Bb3 Bb7 9 Rd1 Nbd7 10 Nc3 Qc7. On 11 d5 Nxd5 12 Nxd5 Bxd5 13 Bxd5 13 Bxd5 exd5 14 Rxd5 Be7 chances were equal. 11 e4! would have been stronger, for example 11 ... cxd4 12 Nxd4 Bc5 13 Bxe6!! G&G **8. exd4 Be7** Again rather tame; 8 ... b5 followed by 9 ... Bb7 was preferable. HG **9. a4** Hindering ... b5 is more important than the effect on the b4-square. G&G **9 ... 0–0 10. Nc3 Nc6 11. Rd1** Threatening d5, so Black hastens to protect this square. HG **11 ... Nb4 12. Ne5 Nbd5** If 12 ... Bd7, 13 d5 is very strong, and if 12 ... Qc7 13 Bf4 Bd6 14 Rac1 with advantage to White. But for all that, the knight move is incorrect. He should move the other knight to d5 and then if 13 Ne4, 13 ... Bd7 can be played. HG **13. Rd3 Nb4 14. Rg3** White prefers to make a promising pawn sacrifice rather than submit to a repetition by 14 Rd1. HG **14 ... Qxd4 15. Bh6 Ne8 16. Rd1 Qc5 17. Bf4** So as to play Ne4 and thereby bring another piece into the kingside attack. HG (Grooten and Gijssen present half a page of analysis by Vuković from *Sahovski Vjesnik* purporting to show a forced win for White after 17 Qh5!. AW) **17 ... Nc6! 18. Bd3! Nxe5 19. Bxe5 g6** A weakening move that is inevitable since White can force it if he likes by Qe4. HG **20. b4!** A fine diversionary sacrifice to enable White to concentrate all his pieces on the attack. Black must accept since other moves merely allow White to achieve his objective without giving up the pawn. HG **20 ... Qxb4 21. Ne4 Ng7** The sort of move one makes, not because one believes it is good, but out of sheer desperation and inability to see a reasonable continuation. Nevertheless 21 ... f5 would give much greater chances of resistance. HG **22. Nf6+ Bxf6** Forced; for if 22 ... Kh8 23 Rh3, when Black must play 23 ... Bxf6, since he is mated after 23 ... h5 24 Nxh5 gxh5 25 Qxh5+. HG **23. Bxf6 Qf4** Golombek and Grooten & Gijssen assumed that this was forced, in view of the threat of Qe2-e3-h6, but 23 ... Qxa4 would prevent White from carrying out this manoeuvre. I'm not sure what they had in mind after the alternative queen move. AW **24. Qb2 Nh5 25. Bg5 Qc7!?** Vukovic thought this was the decisive mistake. Instead he recommended 25 ... Qxa4 26 Ra1 (or 26 Bc2 Qb5 27 Bb3, after which I don't see why Black doesn't play 27 ... Nxg3!! rather than the suggested 27 ... e5!) Qe8 27 Bh6 f6! 28 Bxf8 Qxf8 (again why not 28 ... Nxg3!) 29 Rf3 f5. AW **26. Bh6 e5** On 26 ... Rd8 27 Be2 Rxd1+ 28 Bxd1 Qa5 29 Re3! f6 (Vukovic) White's best might be 30 Qa3 rather than the analysts 30 g4, which does not look so clear after 30 ... Qd8 31 Bc2 Ng7 32 g5 Kf7!. AW **27. Rc1 Qe7** White wins after 27 ... Qb8 28 Rg5!. AW **28. Bxf8 Kxf8 29. Re3 Nf4** If, now or on the next move, ... f6 White plays Qb6 and Rc7. HG **30. Bf1 Bf5 31. Rxe5 Qg5** Threatening 32 ... Nh6+ 33 Kh1 Nxf2+, but White can meet this quite simply. HG **32. g3!** In his turn White menaces 33 Rxf5 gxf5 34 Qh8+. HG **32 ... Ne6 33. Re3 Kg8 34. Qxb7 Qd8 35. Bxa6 Nd4 36. Bc4 Bd7 37. Rd1** Black resigned. **1–0** Golombek, BCM 1951, 282–3; Grooten & Gijssen in Postma 135–8.

(719) FINE—RESHEVSKY, S

Wertheim Memorial, New York (8), 1951 (12 June)
Nimzowitsch-Indian Defence, Classical Variation [E33]

1. d4 Nf6 2. c4 e6 3. Nc3 Bb4 4. Qc2 Nc6 5. Nf3 d6 6. a3 Bxc3+ 7. Qxc3 a5 8. Bg5 h6 9. Bxf6 Qxf6 10. e3 e5 11. dxe5 Nxe5 Draw agreed. **½–½**

(720) SHAINSWIT, G—FINE

Wertheim Memorial, New York (9), 1951 (14 June)
Nimzowitsch-Indian Defence [E45]

1. d4 Nf6 2. c4 e6 3. Nc3 Bb4 4. e3 b6 5. Nge2 Ba6 6. a3 Be7 7. Nf4 d5 8. cxd5 (8 b3 0 0 9 Bb2 Botvinnik-Novotelnov, 19th U.S.S.R. Championship, Moscow 1951.) **8 ... Bxf1 9. Kxf1 exd5** (9 ... Nxd5 10 Ncxd5 exd5 11 Qh5 c6 12 Ne6 g6 13 Qe5 Bf6 14 Nxd8+ Bxe5 15 Nxf7 Kxf7 16 dxe5 Nd7 and Black can survive, Timman–Hübner, Montreal 1979.) **10. Qf3** (10 g4! g5 (10 ... c6 11 g5 Ne4!? (11 ... Nfd7 12 h4 Bd6?! Botvinnik-Smyslov, World Championship game 2, Moscow 1954) 11 Nh5 Nxh5 12 gxh5 Qd7 13 Qf3 c6 (not 13 ... Qc6—Botvinnik—because of 14 Nxd5!) with an unclear position.) **10 ... c6 11. g4 0–0** Black has a good position—Botvinnik. **12. Bd2 Na6 13. g5 Ne8 14. h4 Nd6 15. Rg1 Qd7 16. Qg4 Qxg4 17. Rxg4 Nc7 18. Nd3 Rac8 19. Ne5 Ne6**

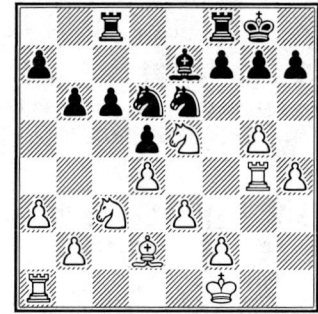

Position after Black's 19th move

20. Rc1 Rc7 21. Ke2 f6 22. gxf6 Bxf6 23. Nd3 Re7 24. Kd1 h5 25. Rg1 Bxh4 26. Ne5 Bxf2 27. Rh1 Rc7 28. Rxh5 Bg3 29. Ne2 Bxe5 30. Rxe5 Rf1+ White resigned. **0–1**

(721) GUIMARD, C—FINE

Wertheim Memorial, New York (10), 1951 (16 June)
Queen's Gambit Declined, Vienna Variation [D39]

1. d4 Nf6 2. c4 e6 3. Nf3 d5 4. Nc3 dxc4 5. e4 Bb4 6. Bg5 h6 7. Bxf6 Qxf6 8. Bxc4 0–0 9. 0–0 c5 10. e5 Qd8 11. Qe2!? cxd4 12. Rad1 Nc6 13. Nb5 Bc5 14. Qe4 Bd7?! 15. Nbxd4 Qe7?! 16. Bd3 g6 17. Nb3 Bb6 18. Qf4 Kg7 19. h4!? Nb4 20. Be4 Bb5 21. Rfe1 Rfd8 22. Nbd4 Ba4 23. b3 Be8 24. Qg4 h5 25. Qf4 Nxa2 26. g4 hxg4 27. Qxg4 Nc3

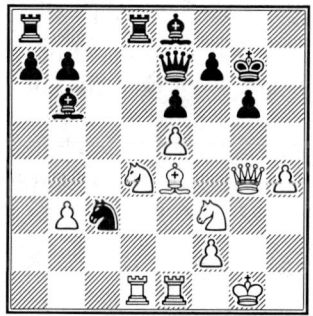

Position after Black's 27th move

28. h5 Nxe4 29. Rxe4 Bc6 30. hxg6 Bxe4 31. gxf7+ Bg6 32. Nh4 Qxf7 33. Nxe6+ Kh6 34. Rf1 Rd2 35. Qg5+ Kh7 36. Qg4 Rxf2 37. Ng5+ Kg7 38. Rxf2 Qxf2+ 39. Kh1 Qe1+ 40. Kg2 Qg1+ White resigned. **0–1**

(722) FINE—HOROWITZ, I

Wertheim Memorial, New York (11), 1951 (17 June)
Réti Opening [A09]

1. Nf3 d5 2. c4 d4 According to the current state of theory, this advance guarantees Black a decent game. **3. e3 c5** This manner of protecting the pawn on d4 is, however, antiquated. The correct method of play is 3 ... Nc6 4 exd4 Nxd4 5 Nxd4 Qxd4 6 Nc3 e5 with approximately equal chances. **4. b4** This is the great objection to protecting the pawn on d4 by ... c5. White immediately undermines the black pawn centre. **4 ... g6** On 4 ... f6 there would follow not 5 bxc5? e5 but 5 exd4! cxd4 6 c5!, with Bf4 to follow, and White has an excellent game (Alekhine). The text represents a new way of supporting the d4 square, which should at least improve Black's chances. **5. bxc5 Nc6 6. exd4 Nxd4 7. Bb2 Bg7 8. Nxd4 Bxd4 9. Qa4+** The introduction of a fine manoeuvre designed to wrest control of d4 from Black. **9 ... Bd7 10. Qb3 Bc6 11. Bxd4 Qxd4**

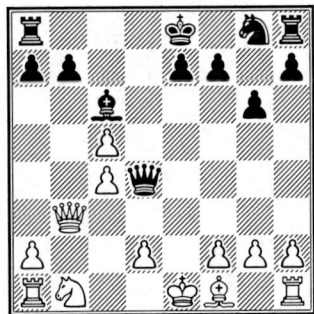

*Position after
Black's 11th move*

12. Qc3 The point of White's handling of the opening.
After 12 ... e5 White gains control of the centre and saddles
Black with a weak pawn on d4. The alternative 12 ... Q×c3
13 N×c3 0-0-0 leads to White's advantage after 14 Rd1 e5
15 Nb5! **12 ... e5 13. Q×d4 exd4 14. d3 0-0-0 15. Nd2
Nf6** (15 ... Re8+ followed by 16 ... Nh6 seems more reasonable. AW) **16. Nb3 Nh5** 16 ... Rhe8+ 17 Kd2 Ng4 was
seemingly stronger here, but there would follow 18 Be2! and
Black is driven backwards (18 ... N×f2 19 Rhf1). **17. Kd2
Nf4 18. Rg1** An excellent defensive move. White protects
the g-pawn and at the same time prepares g2-g3 and Bf1-h3.
18 ... Kc7 19. g3 Ne6 20. f4 Rhe8 21. Bh3 White
squashes any possible counterplay for Black, whose pieces
are tied to the defence of the d-pawn in addition to which
White has an extra pawn. **21 ... f5 22. Rge1** Preparing
to double rooks on the e-file. Before long Black is bound
hand and foot. **22 ... Re7 23. Re5 Rde8 24. Rae1
Kd7**

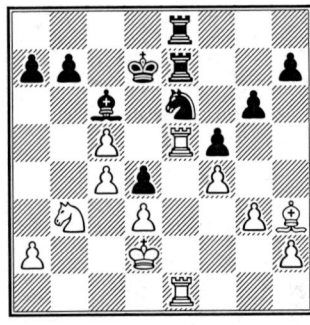

*Position after
Black's 24th move*

25. R1e2! A tempo-move which clearly demonstrates the
helplessness of Black's position. Black can still move a
couple of pawns (... h7-h5 and ... a7-a5), but after that he
will be left with only king moves. **25 ... a5** A desperate
shot. On 25 ... h5, for instance, White can win by Kd2-e1-f2
followed by Bh3-g2 exchanging the black bishop and walking
the king back over to b4. Meanwhile Black can only mark
time with his king until the white king reaches a5, at which
point White can force the transition to a winning endgame
with the little combination c5-c6+, b7×c6+; R×e6 followed
by Nc5+. **26. N×a5!** 26 ... Ra8 27. N×c6 b×c6 On
27 ... Ra2+ there would follow the very witty 28 Kc1! R×e2
29 Nb8+ Kc7 30 R×e2 K×b8 31 g4! and White wins easily.
28. Ke1 Ra5 29. g4 R×c5 30. g×f5 R×e5 31. R×e5
Black resigned. **1-0** Euwe 1955, 51-2.

Fine as a Correspondence Chess Player

The requirement for a professional player to actually earn
money at the game has led several players to take on games
by post for a fee. Fine's high profile as a member of the United
States Chess team in 1933 must have made him an attractive
opponent for those players in remote parts of the country. The
game is also potentially beneficial to the master too as it affords
great opportunities for experimentation and honing technical skills (Paul Keres developed his games during the early
1930s by playing hundreds of games by post).

Correspondence Chess Games, April 1934–November, 1935

Fine's notebooks in the Library of Congress, Washington, D.C., contain a record of 24 correspondence chess
games started by him as early as April 1934. Apparently only
13 or 14 of these were definitely completed (though Fiala
records a number where the result would not be in doubt
as completed), several getting no further than the opening
few moves. These were not part of an organized tournament, but probably games played as a professional exercise.
Fine advertised his services in the Correspondence Chess
League of America newsletter, for which he was a contrib-
utor. Reshevsky also used this method of supplementing
his income, between 1980 and 1992. These games were all
recorded in English descriptive notation, and some include
dates of posting and receipt.

(723) CARTER, R—FINE

Correspondence 1934/5
Caro-Kann Defence [B18]

**1. e4 c6 2. d4 d5 3. Nc3 dxe4 4. Nxe4 Bf5 5. Ng3
Bg6 6. f4 e6 7. Nf3 Nf6 8. Ne5 Bd6 9. Nc4 Bc7
10. Qe2 0-0 11. Bd2 Qxd4 12. c3 Qc5 13. b4 Qe7
14. Ne5 Nbd7** no result recorded

(724) COLBY, H—FINE

Correspondence 1934/5
Nimzo-Indian Defence, Classical Variation [E37]

**1. d4 Nf6 2. c4 e6 3. Nc3 Bb4 4. Qc2 d5 5. a3
Bxc3+ 6. Qxc3 Ne4 7. Qc2 Nc6 8. Nf3 e5 9. e3
Bf5 10. Bd3 exd4 11. exd4 0-0** unfinished

(725) FINE—CARTER, R

Correspondence 1934/5
Spanish Opening, Open Variation [C83]

1. e4 e5 2. Nf3 Nc6 3. Bb5 a6 4. Ba4 Nf6 5. 0–0
Nxe4 6. d4 b5 7. Bb3 d5 8. dxe5 Be6 9. c3 Be7
10. Nbd2 0–0 11. Qe2 Nc5 12. Nd4 Nxd4 13. cxd4
Nxb3 14. Nxb3 Qd7 unfinished

(726) FINE—COLBY, H

Correspondence 1934/5
Two Knights Defence [C58]

1. e4 e5 2. Nf3 Nc6 3. Bc4 Nf6 4. Ng5 d5 5. exd5
Na5 6. d3 h6 7. Nf3 e4 8. Qe2 Nxc4 9. dxc4
Bd6 10. Nd4 0–0 11. Be3 Ng4 12. Nc3 Nxe3?!
13. Qxe3 Bg4 14. h3 Qh4 15. Nde2 Bxe2 16. Nxe2
unfinished

(727) FINE—GLADNEY, W

Correspondence 1934/5
King's Gambit Accepted [C37]

1. e4 e5 2. f4 exf4 3. Nf3 g5 4. Bc4 d6 5. 0–0
Bg4 6. h3 h5 7. hxg4 hxg4 8. Nh2 g3 9. Ng4 Nf6
10. d4 Nbd7 11. Nc3 Bg7 12. e5 Nxg4 13. Qxg4
dxe5 14. Ne2 Qf6 15. Nxg3 1–0

(728) FINE—GLADNEY, W

Correspondence 1934/5
Marshall Defence [D06]

1. d4 d5 2. c4 Nf6 3. cxd5 Nxd5 4. e4 Nf6
5. Nc3 e6 6. Bd3 Be7 7. Nge2 0–0 8. 0–0 c5
9. dxc5 Bxc5 10. Bg5 Be7 11. e5 Nd5 12. Bxe7
Nxe7 13. Be4 Nbc6 14. Qxd8 Rxd8 15. f4 a6
16. Bf3 Bd7 17. Ne4 Nf5 18. Nc5 Rab8 19. Rfd1
Be8 20. Nxb7 1–0

(729) FINE—GLADNEY, W

Correspondence 1934/5
King's Gambit Accepted [C39]

1. e4 e5 2. f4 exf4 3. Nf3 g5 4. h4 g4 5. Ne5 Bg7
6. d4 Nf6 7. Nxg4 Nxe4 8. Bxf4 Qe7 9. Qe2 Bxd4
10. c3 d5?! 11. cxd4 Bxg4 12. Qxg4 Ng3+ 13. Be5
1–0

(730) FINE—GLADNEY, W

Correspondence 1934/5
Spanish Opening, Open Defence [C84]

1. e4 e5 2. Nf3 Nc6 3. Bb5 a6 4. Ba4 Nf6 5. 0–0
Nxe4 6. d4 Be7 7. Qe2 Nd6 8. Bxc6 bxc6 9. dxe5
Nb7 10. Nc3 Nc5 11. Nd4 0–0 12. Re1 Ne6 13. Be3
Re8 14. Rad1 Nxd4 15. Bxd4 d5 16. Na4 Bd7 17. c3
Bf8 18. Bc5 f6 19. f4

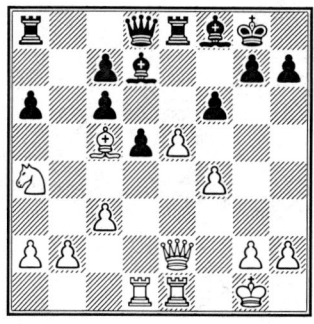

*Position after
White's 19th move*

19 ... Bf5?! 20. Bxf8 Kxf8 21. Qf2 Qe7 22. Nc5
fxe5?! 23. fxe5 Kg8 24. b4 Be6 25. Nb3 unfinished

(731) FINE—HAMPTON, L

Correspondence 1934/5
French Defence [C14]

1. e4 e6 2. d4 d5 3. Nc3 Nf6 4. Bg5 Be7 5. e5
Nfd7 6. Bxe7 Qxe7 7. Qd2 0–0 8. f4 c5 9. Nf3 a6
10. g3 b5 11. Bg2 Bb7 12. 0–0 Nc6 13. Rae1 cxd4
14. Ne2 Rac8 15. Nexd4 Nxd4 16. Nxd4 Nb6
17. b3 Qc5 18. Kh1 Qc3 19. Qf2 Rc7 20. f5 Qb4
21. fxe6 Re7 22. Bh3 1–0

(732) FINE—KILBURN, C

Correspondence 1934/5
Caro-Kann Defence [B13]

1. e4 c6 2. d4 d5 3. exd5 cxd5 4. c4 Nf6 5. Nc3
Nc6 6. Nf3 Bg4 7. cxd5 Nxd5 8. Bb5 Rc8 9. 0–0
e6 10. h3 Bxf3 11. Qxf3 Bb4 12. Nxd5 Qxd5 13. Qxd5
exd5 14. Be3 0–0 15. Rfc1 Na5 16. Rxc8 Rxc8 17. Rc1
Rxc1+ 18. Bxc1 Kf8 19. Kf1 Ke7 20. Ke2 Ke6 21. Bd3
g6 22. Be3 a6 23. h4 Be7 24. h5 Bf6 25. hxg6
hxg6 26. Bb1 Nc6 27. Kd3 ½–½

(733) FINE—LYNCH, M

Correspondence 1934/5
Dutch Defence [A95]

1. d4 f5 2. g3 e6 3. Bg2 Nf6 4. Nf3 d5 5. 0–0 Be7
6. c4 0–0 7. Nc3 c6 8. Bf4 Ne4 9. Ne5 Nd7 10. Nxd7
Bxd7 11. Qd3 Qe8 12. f3 Nxc3 13. bxc3 dxc4 14. Qxc4
Rd8 15. e4 Bc8 16. Rae1 Qf7 17. Rf2 Rfe8 18. Rfe2
g5 19. Bc1 h6 20. Qb3 Kf8 21. f4 g4 22. Kh1 Kg8
23. exf5 Qxf5 24. Re5 1–0

(734) FINE—MOORE, D

Correspondence 1934/5
Queen's Gambit Accepted [D21]

1. d4 d5 2. c4 dxc4 3. Nf3 e6 4. Nc3 a6 5. a4 c6
6. e4 Bb4 7. Bxc4 Bxc3+ 8. bxc3 Nf6 9. Bd3 Nbd7

10. 0–0 c5 11. a5 c4 12. Bc2 h6 13. Qe2 b5 14. axb6
Nxb6 15. Ba3 Bd7 16. Nd2 Qc7 17. e5 Nfd5 18. Ne4
Nc8 19. f4 Nce7 20. Rf3 0–0 21. Nf6+ gxf6 22. Rg3+
Ng6 23. Bxg6 fxg6 24. Rxg6+ 1–0

(735) FINE—PROSSER, E

Correspondence 1934/5
Queen's Gambit Declined [D63]

1. d4 Nf6 2. c4 e6 3. Nc3 d5 4. Bg5 Be7 5. Nf3
Nbd7 6. e3 0–0 7. Rc1 a6 8. cxd5 exd5 9. Bd3 c6
10. 0–0 h6 11. Bf4 Ne8 12. Bb1 f5 13. Qb3 Nb6
14. Ne2 Nc4 15. Rfd1 Ned6 16. Ne5 Nxe5 17. dxe5
Ne4 18. Bxe4 fxe4 19. Nc3 Qa5 20. Nxe4 Qb5
21. Nd2 Bf5 22. a4 Qb4 23. Qxb4 Bxb4 24. Nb3
Rad8 25. Bg3 a5 26. f3 Be6 27. Be1 Ra8 28. Bxb4
axb4 29. a5 Kf7 30. Rd4 Ke7 31. Rxb4 Rfb8
1–0

(736) FINE—SEEDS, J

Correspondence 1934/5
French Defence [C14]

1. e4 e6 2. d4 d5 3. Nc3 Nf6 4. Bg5 Be7 5. e5
Nfd7 6. Bxe7 Qxe7 7. Qd2 0–0 8. f4 c5 9. Nf3
unfinished

(737) FINE—WINK, T

Correspondence 1934/5
Colle System [D04]

1. d4 d5 2. Nf3 Nf6 3. e3 c5 4. c3 Nbd7 5. Bd3
g6 6. 0–0 Bg7 7. Ne5 0–0 8. f4 Re8 9. Nd2 c4
10. Bc2 e6 11. Qf3 Nf8 12. b3 1–0

(738) GLADNEY, W—FINE

Correspondence 1934/5
Queen's Gambit Declined, Cambridge Springs Defence [D52]

1. d4 d5 2. c4 e6 3. Nc3 Nf6 4. Bg5 Nbd7 5. Nf3
c6 6. e3 Qa5 7. Nd2 dxc4 8. Bxf6 Nxf6 9. Nxc4
Qc7 10. Bd3 Be7 11. 0–0 0–0 12. Rc1 Bd7 13. Ne5
Rfd8 14. Ne4 Be8 15. Qf3 Rac8 16. Ng5 Bd6 17. Ng4
Nxg4 18. Bxh7+ Kh8 19. Qxg4 g6 20. f4 f6 21. Nxe6
Qxh7 22. Nxd8 Rxd8 23. Qe6 Kg7 24. e4 Bf7
25. Qg4 Bc7 0–1

(739) GLADNEY, W—FINE

Correspondence 1934/5
Spanish Opening [C84]

1. e4 e5 2. Nf3 Nc6 3. Bb5 a6 4. Ba4 Nf6 5. 0–0
Be7 6. Nc3 b5 7. Bb3 d6 8. h3 Na5 9. d3 0–0

10. Ne2 c5 11. c3 Qc7 12. Be3 Bb7 13. Ng3 d5
14. Bc2 c4 15. exd5 Nxd5 16. d4 Nxe3 17. fxe3
exd4 0–1

(740) HAMPTON, L—FINE

Correspondence 1934/5
Spanish Game, Worrall Attack [C86]

1. e4 e5 2. Nf3 Nc6 3. Bb5 a6 4. Ba4 d6 5. c3
Nf6 6. Qe2 Be7 7. d4 Bd7 8. 0–0 0–0 9. d5 Nb8
10. Bc2 a5 11. Bd3 Na6 12. Nbd2 Nc5 13. Nc4 Ne8
14. Be3 Nxd3 15. Qxd3 f5! 16. Ncd2? f4 17. Bd4
exd4 18. Nxd4 Bf6 19. N2f3 Qe7 20. Rfe1 Be5
21. h3 Kh8 22. Rad1 g5 23. Nh2 Nf6 24. Nf5
Bxf5 25. exf5 Rg8 0–1

(741) KILBURN, C—FINE

Correspondence 1934/5
Nimzo-Indian Defence, Classical Variation [E37]

1. d4 Nf6 2. c4 e6 3. Nc3 Bb4 4. Qc2 d5 5. a3
Bxc3+ 6. Qxc3 Ne4 7. Qc2 Nc6 8. Nf3 e5 9. e3
Bf5 10. Bd3 exd4 11. exd4 0–0 12. 0–0 Re8 13. Re1
Qd7 14. cxd5 Qxd5 15. Be3 Nd6 16. Rac1 Re7
17. Bc4 Nxc4 18. Qxc4 Be4 19. Qxd5 Bxd5 20. Ne5
Nd8 21. Nd3 f6 22. Bd2 Rxe1+ 23. Rxe1 Kf7
24. Bc3 Ne6 25. f3 Rd8 26. Kf2 b6 27. Rd1 Bc4
28. Ke3 g5 29. g3 Ng7 30. g4 h5 31. Rd2 hxg4
32. fxg4 Rh8 33. Nb4 Ne6 34. d5 Nc5 35. d6
Rh3+ 36. Kf2 Ne4+ 37. Kg2 Rh8 38. Rc2 Nxd6
39. Rd2 Ke6 40. Rd1 c5 41. Re1+ Kf7 42. Nc2
Bd5+ 43. Kg1 Ne4 44. Re3 Nxc3 45. Rxc3 Be6
46. h3 Rd8 47. Ne3 Ke7 48. Rc2 Rd4 49. Kf2 Kd6
50. Ke2 Ke5 51. Kf3 c4 52. Re2 Kd6 53. Rc2 Kc5
54. Ke2 b5 55. b4+ Kd6 56. Rc3 Ke5 57. Nc2
Re4+ 58. Ne3 f5 0–1

(742) LYNCH, M—FINE

Correspondence 1934/5
Scottish Four Knights [C47]

1. e4 e5 2. Nf3 Nc6 3. Nc3 Nf6 4. d4 exd4 5. Nxd4
Bb4 6. Nxc6 bxc6 7. Bd3 d5 8. exd5 cxd5 9. 0–0
0–0 10. Bg5 Be6 11. Qf3 Be7 12. Rae1 Qd7 13. h3
c5 14. b3 Rab8 15. Re2 Rfe8 16. Rfe1 c4 17. bxc4
dxc4 18. Be4 Red8 19. Bf5 Rb6 20. Bxe6 Rxe6
21. Rxe6 fxe6 22. Qe3 Kf7 23. Bxf6 Bxf6 24. Qf4
Qd2 25. Re3 Qxc2 26. Qxc4 Qf5 27. Ne4 Qd5
28. Qc2 Qd1+ 29. Qxd1 Rxd1+ 30. Kh2 Bd4 31. Re2
½–½

(743) MOORE, D—FINE

Correspondence 1934/5
Two Knights Defence, Chigorin Variation [C59]

1. e4 e5 2. Nf3 Nc6 3. Bc4 Nf6 4. Ng5 d5 5. exd5
Na5 6. Bb5+ c6 7. dxc6 bxc6 8. Be2 h6 9. Nf3 e4
10. Ne5 Bd6 11. d4 Qc7 12. Bf4 0–0 13. c3 c5
14. Nd2 Bb7 15. 0–0 Rad8 16. Qc1 Nd5 17. Nxe4
Nxf4 18. Qxf4 f6 19. Nxd6 fxe5 20. Qxe5 Qxd6
21. Qh5 Qb6 22. Qxc5 Qxc5 23. dxc5 Rd2 24. Bd1
Rxb2 25. Bb3+ Kh8 26. Rab1 Rfxf2 27. Rxb2 Rxb2
28. Rf2 Rb1+ 29. Rf1 Rxf1+ 30. Kxf1 Nxb3 31. axb3
Kg8 32. g3 Kf7 33. Ke2 Ke6 34. Kd3 Kd5 35. b4
Ba6+ 36. Ke3 Kc4 37. Kd2 Bc8 38. Kc2 Bf5+
39. Kd2 g5 40. h4 a6 41. hxg5 hxg5 42. c6 Be4
43. c7 Bf5 0–1

(744) Prosser, E—Fine

Correspondence 1934/5
French Defence [C00]

1. e4 e6 2. d4 d5 3. Bd3 Nf6 4. Bg5 dxe4 5. Bxe4
c5 6. c3 cxd4 7. Bxf6 gxf6 8. Qxd4 Qxd4 9. cxd4
f5 10. Bf3 Bg7 11. Ne2 Nc6 12. Bxc6+ bxc6
13. Nbc3 Ba6 14. 0–0–0 Ke7 15. f4 Rhd8 16. Rd2
Rd7 17. Rhd1 Rad8 18. g3 h5 19. h4 Bf6 20. Kc2
Rg8 21. Rg1 Rb8 22. b3 Rc8 23. Rgd1 Rcd8
24. Kc1 Kf8 25. Kb2? c5 26. Kc1 cxd4 27. Ng1
Rc8 28. Rc2 Rdc7 0–1

(745) Seeds, J—Fine

Correspondence 1934/5
Queen's Gambit Declined [D30]

1. d4 d5 2. Nf3 Nf6 3. c4 e6 4. Bg5 Be7 5. e3 0–0
6. Nbd2 Nbd7 7. Bd3 c5 unfinished

(746) Wink, T—Fine

Correspondence 1934/5
King's Gambit Accepted [C33]

1. e4 e5 2. f4 exf4 3. Bc4 Qh4+ 4. Kf1 d5 5. Nf3
Qh5 6. Bxd5 Nf6 7. Nc3 Bb4 8. Qe2 0–0 9. d4
Bxc3 10. bxc3 Re8 11. Bxf7+ Qxf7 12. Ne5 Qh5
13. Bxf4 Qxe2+ 14. Kxe2 Nxe4 0–1

Correspondence Chess, 1940–1943

Fine resumed his practice of earning supplementary
income through correspondence games in the early 1940s,
charging $5 a game. Several have come to light, however, it
is unclear what level of activity he was engaged in and hence
whether there may be many more to be uncovered.

(747) Fine—Snethlage, J

Correspondence 1940,
French Defence, Rubinstein Variation [C10]

1. e4 e6 2. d4 d5 3. Nc3 dxe4 4. Nxe4 Nd7 5. Nf3
Ngf6 6. Nxf6+ Nxf6 7. Ne5 Qd5! 8. Be3 Bd6 9. Nf3
Bd7 10. Be2 b5!? 11. 0–0 Bc6 12. a4 a6 13. Ne1 e5!
The game is even, PCO 87. 14. b3 b4 15. Bc4 Qe4
16. Nf3 0–0 17. Re1 exd4 18. Bxd4 Qg4 19. Bxf6
gxf6 20. Bd5 1–0

(748) Fellner, A—Fine

Postal Game, 1941
Sicilian Defence [B30]

1. e4 c5 2. Nc3 Nc6 3. Nf3 e5 4. Bb5 d6 5. Ne2
Nf6 6. Bxc6+ bxc6 7. d3 g6 8. 0–0 Bg7 9. c3 0–0
10. Be3 Ng4 11. d4 Nxe3 12. fxe3 exd4 13. exd4
Qb6 14. b3 Ba6 15. Re1 Rfe8 16. Ng3 cxd4 17. cxd4
c5 18. Kh1 cxd4 19. Qd2 Rac8 20. Red1 d3 21. Rac1
h5 22. h4 Rxc1 23. Rxc1 Qb7 24. Qg5 Bb5 25. Qd5
Qxd5 26. exd5 Bh6 27. Rd1 Bf4 28. Nf1 Re2 29. a4
Ba6 30. N3d2 Kg7 31. b4 Bb7 32. Nf3 Bxd5
33. Rxd3 Be4 34. Rd1 Ra2 35. a5 Rb2 36. Rd4 d5
37. N1d2 Be3 0–1

(749) Fine—Fellner, A

Postal Game, 1941
Dutch Defence [A90]

1. d4 e6 2. c4 f5 3. g3 Nf6 4. Bg2 Bb4+ 5. Bd2
Qe7 6. Nh3 0–0 7. 0–0 Bxd2 8. Qxd2 Nc6 9. Nc3
Nd8 10. Nf4 d6 11. e4 e5 12. Nfd5 Nxd5 13. Nxd5
Qf7 14. dxe5 dxe5 15. exf5 Bxf5 16. Rae1 c6 17. Ne3
Be6 18. Qc3 Qf6 19. Nc2 Bf5 20. Na1 Nf7 21. Nb3
Rad8 22. Nc5 Qe7 23. Ne4 Qd7 24. Re3 Qd4
25. Qb3 Be6 26. Qxb7 Bxc4 27. Rfe1 Rb8 28. Qxc6
Rxb2 29. a3 Nd8 30. Qa4 Bb5 31. Qa5 Bc6 32. R3e2
Rxe2 33. Rxe2 Qd1+ 34. Qe1 Qxe1+ 35. Rxe1 Ne6
no result recorded or unfinished

(750) Fine—Hibbard

Postal Game, 1941
Spanish Game, Chigorin Variation (without h3)[C90]

1. e4 e5 2. Nf3 Nc6 3. Bb5 a6 4. Ba4 Nf6 5. 0–0
Be7 6. Re1 b5 7. Bb3 d6 8. c3 Na5 9. Bc2 c5 10. d4
Qc7 11. Nbd2 0–0 12. Nf1 h6 13. Ne3 cxd4 14. cxd4
Nc6 15. b3 Ng4? 16. Nd5 Qb7 17. Bb2 Nf6 18. dxe5
Ne8 19. exd6 Bxd6 20. e5 Bb4 21. Qd3 g6 22. e6
Ng7 23. Nf6+ Kh8 24. Nh5 1–0

(751) Fine—Potter, A

Postal Game, 1941
French Defence, McCutcheon Variation [C12]

1. e4 e6 2. d4 d5 3. Nc3 Nf6 4. Bg5 Bb4 5. e5 h6
6. Be3 Ne4 7. Nge2 c5 8. a3 cxd4 9. Bxd4 Nxc3

10. Nxc3 Bxc3+ 11. Bxc3 Nc6 12. Qg4 0–0 13. f4
Bd7 14. Bd3 Qb6 15. 0–0–0 Rac8 16. Rhf1 Qc7
17. Rf3 Kh8 18. Rg3 Rg8 19. Rh3 Ne7 20. Qg5
Rge8 21. Rxh6+ Kg8 22. Rh7 Ng6 23. Bxg6 fxg6
24. Rxg7+ Kxg7 25. Qf6+ 1–0

(752) POTTER, A—FINE

Postal Game, 1941
Grünfeld Defence [D85]

1. d4 Nf6 2. c4 g6 3. Nc3 d5 4. cxd5 Nxd5 5. e4
Nxc3 6. bxc3 Bg7 7. Ba3 Nd7 8. g3 c5 9. Bb2 Qa5
10. Nf3 0–0 11. Be2 cxd4 12. Nxd4 Nc5 13. Nb3
Bxc3+ 14. Kf1 Bh3+ 15. Kg1 Nxb3 16. axb3 Qe5
17. Bxc3 Qxc3 18. Rc1 Qe5 19. Bf3 Rac8 20. Rb1
Rfd8 21. Qe1 Rc7 0–1

(753) DE AGNEW, A—FINE

Postal Game, 1941
English Opening, Classical Variation [A29]

1. c4 e5 2. Nc3 Nf6 3. g3 d5 4. cxd5 Nxd5 5. Bg2
Nb6 6. Nf3 Nc6 7. 0–0 Be7 8. d3 0–0 9. Be3 Bg4
10. a4 a5 11. Rc1 Kh8 12. Nb5 Nd5 13. Bc5 Ndb4
14. Qd2 f6 15. Bxe7 Qxe7 16. Qe3 Rad8 17. Nd2
Rfe8 18. Nb3 Qf7 19. Nc5 Nd4 20. Nxd4 exd4
21. Qd2 b6 22. Ne4 Qd7 23. f3 Be6 24. Qe1 c5
25. g4 Qxa4 26. Qh4 Qd7 27. Bh3 Nd5 28. Kh1
Qe7 29. Qg3 Ne3 30. Rg1 Bd5 31. Qf4 Qe5 32. Qxe5
fxe5 33. g5 Re7 34. Nd2 Rc7 no result recorded

(754) FINE—HAYES

Postal Game, 1942
Spanish Opening, Berlin Defence [C66]

1. e4 e5 2. Nf3 Nc6 3. Bb5 Nf6 4. 0–0 Be7 5. Re1

d6 6. d4 Bd7 7. Nc3 Nxd4 8. Nxd4 exd4 9. Qxd4
Bxb5 10. Nxb5 0–0 11. b3 a6 12. Nc3 Ng4 13. Nd5
Bf6 14. Nxf6+ Qxf6 15. Bb2 Qxd4 16. Bxd4 f6
17. c4 Ne5 18. f4 Nd3 19. Rf1 Rae8 20. Rf3 Nb4
21. Bc3 Nc6 22. Re1 a5 23. g4 b6 24. Kf2 h6
25. h4 Nd8 26. Rg3 Ne6 27. f5 Nc5 28. Kf3 Nd3
29. Re2 Re7 30. g5 fxg5 31. hxg5 hxg5 32. Rxg5
Ne5+ 33. Bxe5 Rxe5 After a few more moves the game
was agreed a draw. ½–½ *The Chess Correspondent*, May/June
1943, 14 (Lahde/Hilbert).

(755) FINE—HERZBERGER, M

Postal Game, 1942
Queen's Gambit Declined [D61]

1. d4 d5 2. c4 e6 3. Nf3 Nf6 4. Bg5 Nbd7 5. Nc3
Be7 6. e3 0–0 7. Qc2 c5 8. Rd1 Qa5 9. cxd5 Nxd5
10. Bxe7 Nxe7 11. Bd3 Nf6 12. 0–0 cxd4 13. exd4
Bd7 14. Ne4 Ned5 15. Ne5 Rfc8 16. Qe2 Be8 17. a3
Qd8 18. f4 Nxe4 19. Bxe4 f6 20. Nd3 Rc7 21. Qf3
f5 22. Bxd5 Qxd5 23. Qxd5 exd5 24. Rf2 a5 25. h3
Bb5 26. Ne5 Rac8 27. Rdd2 Ba4 28. Nd3 Bc2
29. Rfe2 Bxd3 ½–½ *The Chess Correspondent*, May/June
1943, 13 (Lahde/Hilbert).

(756) FINE—KILBURN, C

Postal Game, 1943
Caro-Kann Defence [B13]

1. e4 c6 2. d4 d5 3. exd5 cxd5 4. c4 Nf6 5. Nf3
Nc6 6. Nc3 Bg4 7. cxd5 Nxd5 8. Bb5 Rc8 9. 0–0
e6 10. h3 Bxf3 11. Qxf3 Bb4 12. Nxd5 Qxd5 13. Qxd5
exd5 14. Be3 0–0 15. Rfc1 Na5 16. Rxc8 Rxc8
17. Rc1 Rxc1+ 18. Bxc1 Kf8 19. Kf1 Ke7 20. Ke2
Ke6 21. Bd3 g6 22. Be3 a6 23. h4 Be7 24. h5 Bf6
25. hxg6 hxg6 26. Bb1 Nc6 27. Kd3 ½–½ Correspondence Chess League of America, 1943 (Lahde).

Simultaneous Exhibition Games and Miscellany

Throughout his career, and in common with most masters of the period, particularly professionals, Fine generated income by giving exhibitions of simultaneous play.

1932

| | Marshall C.C., New York | +10 | =2 | –2 | tandem with Reinfeld |
| 26 May | Marshall C.C., New York | +7 | =0 | –2 | as Zu-ux "the man from Mars" |

1933

| | Reading YMCA | +25 | =0 | –0 | (one blindfold) |
| | International CC, New York | +6 | =2 | –0 | (all blindfold) |

7 October	Chicago Chess and Bridge	+9	=1	−2	tandem with Dake
16 December	Boston City Club	+26	=4	−3	

1934

16 November	Club De Ajedrez "Mexico"	+24	=4	−5	
22 November	Carlos Torre Club	+18	=2	−0	

1936

12 September	Oslo	+25	=5	−0	
November	(The Netherlands)				
December	Bussum	+23	=2	−0	
December	The Hague	+31	=2	−2	
December	Arnhem	+28	=3	−2	
December	Amsterdam	+39	=0	−1	
December	Rotterdam	+33	=5	−2	
December	Eindhoven	+39	=1	−0	
December	Arnheim	+51	=0	−0	
December	Steenwijk	+41	=0	−0	
December	The Hague	+7	=3	−0	Clock simul
December	Delft	+36	=3	−1	

1937

9 January	Metropolitan C.C., London	+31	=4	−0	
13 January	Göteborg	+23	=4	−4	
14 January	Stockholm	+25	=5	−5	
26 January	Örebro	+5	=2	−1	(consultation games)
27 January	Örebro	+18	=10	−1	
28 January	Västerås	+30	=3	−3	
15 February	Helsingborg	+34	=4	−3	
16 February	Helsingborg	+8	=1	−0	(clock match)
8 March	Moscow	+1	=1	−3	(clock simul, 1st categorniks)
March	Leningrad	+33	=7	−6	
13 April	Eton Manor, Hackney				35 games
26 April	The Hague (A.V.R.O.)				
27 April	Rotterdam (A.V.R.O.)				
28 April	Haarlem (A.V.R.O.)				
29 April	Utrecht (A.V.R.O.)				
1 May	Nijmegen (A.V.R.O.)				
3 May	Arnhem (A.V.R.O.)				
4 May	Amsterdam (A.V.R.O.)				

(A.V.R.O. sponsored tour with Alekhine, Bogolyubov, Euwe, Flohr, Lasker, Tartakower. Fine scored +257 =5 −3, 97.9 percent)

1939

18 May	City College, New York	+20	=3	−2	

1940

27 January	Philadelphia	+5 =3		(blindfold)
29 January	Richmond	+21 =1		
31 January	St. Louis	+20 =1; +1		(blindfold)
2 February	Tulsa	+14 =1; +1		(blindfold)
4 February	Dallas	+27; +1		(blindfold)
10 February	Mexico City	+5 =1		(serious games)
12 February	Mexico	=1		(Araiza and Soto-Larea consulting)
13 February	Mexico City	+19 =1		
15 February	Mexico City	+22 −1		
16 February	Mexico City	+7 =1		(serious games [sic], ?clock games)
17 February	Mexico City	+47 =4		
18 February	Cuernavaca	+18 =1		
19 February	Monterrey	+14; +2		(blindfold)
22 February	Denver	+12; +2		(blindfold)
24 February	Chicago	+26 −1 =4; +1 =1		(blindfold)
25 February	Detroit	+25		
27 February	Minneapolis	+34 −1 =2		
28 February	Winnipeg	+29; +2		(blindfold)
2 March	Montreal	+15; +1		(blindfold)
4 March	Ottawa	+21; =1		(blindfold)
13 April	Marshall C. C., NY	+13 =2		
	Denver, Colorado	+4 −1 =1		(blindfold)
	Sacramento, California	+13 =1		
	San Francisco, California	+18 =1		
	Carmel, California	+23 =1		
	Los Angeles, California	+29 =3		
	Hollywood, California	+14 =4		
	Santa Barbara	+15 =1		
	Albuquerque, New Mexico	+11 =1		
	San Antonio, Texas	+19 =2		
	Baton Rouge, Louisiana	+12 =0		
	Springfield, Missouri	+20 =0		
	Omaha, Nebraska	+16 =1		
	Sioux City, Arizona	+13 −1		
	Winnipeg, Manitoba	+29 −1 =2		
	Minneapolis, Minnesota	+13 −1		
	Washington, D.C.	+11		

1941

3 March	Capitol Hotel, New York	+24	for the Emanuel Lasker Memorial Fund
17 November	Marshall Chess Club, NY		
1 December	Washington, D.C.	+31 =4	

(Willard Mutchler of the *Washington Post* wrote "Playing with a speed and accuracy which left everyone awestruck, Fine disposed of 35 adversaries in exactly 3 hours and 4 minutes (*Also reported as 3 hours and 22 minutes with a twenty minute break. AW*). The master had offered a copy of his *Basic Chess Endings* to the first two to defeat him, but the books are still for sale." The four who drew were Mutchler himself, Martin Stark, Vincent Eaton and Nathaniel Weyl. The exhibition was held at the Hotel Gordon under the auspices of the Capital City Chess Club)

1942

23 April	New Haven		
3 May	Washington, D.C.	+87 =17 −6	

(The exhibition took nine hours and twenty five minutes. All the players in the 1941 Washington Championship took part. Mugridge was one of the winners. The drawing players included Mengarini, Stark and Ponce.)

| 6 June | Washington, D.C. | | |

1943

4 September	Guatemala	+41 =5 −1	
6 September	Guatemala	+12	Clock games against first class players
7 September	Guatemala	+9 =1	Blindfold exhibition
8 September	Guatemala	+40 =6 −2	
9 September	Guatemala	+36 =3	
10 September	Guatemala	+34 =5 −1	(Black on all boards)
10 November	Washington Chess Divan	+9 =1	clock simultaneous exhibition.

(Fine's 10 opponents were required to play at a rate of 36 moves in the first two hours and 18 moves an hour thereafter. According to the club's statistician they collectively consumed 20 hours and 22 minutes 30 seconds. Except for a lone draw, credited to editor Le Roy Thompson, Fine made a clean sweep. He started at 8:02 pm and finished at 12:40 am, with five brief rests for coffee. Fine defeated Stark, Shapiro, Cheney, Burdge, Korfstrom, Fox, Long, Hesse and Johnson.)

December	Washington, D.C.	+37 =2 −1	For the benefit of the U.S.C.F.
21 December	Washington, D.C.	+39 =1	For the benefit of the U.S.C.F.

(Fee was $1 for membership of the United States Chess Federation. The result of the second exhibition was also reported as +40 =1.)

1944

22 February	City Chess Club, Boston	+40 =4 −2	
July	Washington	+9 =1	blindfold/10 seconds a move

(Fine's opponents included Klein, Mugridge and two strong teenagers—Richard Cantwell and Hans Berliner)

1945

7 January Richmond Chess Club, Richmond, VA	+10	blindfold simul
25 April Washington Chess Divan, Blindfold	8½–1½	(played two at a rate of 10 s per move)
23 June Marshall Chess Club, NY	+20 −2 =3	
27 June Washington	+3 =3	two sets of three simultaneous blindfold rapid

1946

May	Los Angeles	+28 −0 =0	(after the end of the Denker–Steiner match, completed in 1 hour and 50 minutes)
5 November	Santa Monica	+39 −2 =2	(also reported as +39 −3 =2)

Simultaneous Exhibition Games

(757) FINE—ROBEY, P

Simultaneous exhibition, Marshall Chess Club, New York, 1932
Semi-Slav Defence [D46]

1. d4 d5 2. c4 c6 3. Nc3 Nf6 4. Nf3 e6 5. e3 Nbd7 6. Bd3 Be7 7. 0-0 0-0 8. Qe2 dxc4 9. Bxc4 b5 10. Bd3 b4 11. Na4 Qa5 12. b3 c5 13. Nb2 cxd4 14. exd4 Bb7 15. Ne5 Qd5 16. Nf3 Ne4 17. Nc4 Nc3 18. Qc2 Qh5 19. Nfe5 Rfd8 20. Be3 Rac8 21. a3 Nxe5 22. dxe5 Rxd3 23. Qxd3 Ne2+ 24. Qxe2 Qxe2 25. axb4 a6 26. Rad1 Rd8 27. Nd6 Bd5 28. Bc5 Qxe5 29. Nc4 Qf6 0-1 Partially reconstructed score. The 18th move was repeated in the score in the paper. *Brooklyn Daily Eagle*, 21 January 1932 (Lahde).

(758) FINE & REINFELD—CHRISTY, K

Tandem Simultaneous Exhibition, Marshall Chess Club, 1932 (April)
Spanish Opening [C66]

1. e4 e5 2. Nf3 Nc6 3. Bb5 d6 4. d4 Bd7 5. Nc3 Nf6 6. 0-0 Be7 7. Re1 exd4 8. Nxd4 0-0 9. Bxc6 bxc6 10. b3 Qb8 11. Bb2 Qb6 12. Qd3 Qc5 13. Rad1 Qh5 14. h3 Qg6 15. Nf5 Rfe8 16. Re3 Nh5 17. Ne2 Bf6 18. Bxf6 gxf6 19. g4 Qg5 20. Kh2 Nf4 21. Qd2 Bxf5 22. exf5 Rxe3 23. Qxe3 Nxe2 24. Qxe2 Qf4+ 25. Kg2 Kf8 26. Re1 Qe5 27. Qd2 Qd5+ 28. Qxd5 cxd5 29. Rd1 c6 30. Kf3 Re8 31. Rd4 Re5 32. Ra4 Re7 33. Ra6 Rc7 34. Ke3 Ke7 35. Kd4 Kd7 36. b4 Rb7 37. c3 Kc7 38. b5 Rxb5 39. Rxa7+ Rb7 40. Rxb7+ Kxb7 41. f4 Kc7 42. g5 Kd7 43. h4 1-0 *Bethlehem Globe Times*, 10 May 1932 (Brennen/Lahde).

(758A) FINE,R—REX, A

Simultaneous exhibition Rialto Rooms, Allentown, Pennsylvania, 1933 (4 Oct.)
Spanish Opening, Steinitz Defence [C62]

1. e4 e5 2. Nf3 Nc6 3. Bb5 d6 4. d4 exd4 5. Nxd4 Bd7 6. 0-0 Ne5 7. Nc3 Nf6 8. Be2 h6 9. f4 Nc6 10. Bf3 Nxd4 11. Qxd4 c5 12. Qf2 Bc6 13. e5 Nd7 14. Bxc6 bxc6 15. exd6 Bxd6 16. Re1+ Be7 17. Qe2 Nf6 18. b3 Rb8 19. Bb2 Rb7 20. Rad1 Qc7 21. Ne4 Nxe4 22. Qxe4 0-0 23. Rd3 Bd6 24. Rf1 c4 25. Qxc4 Rb4 26. Qxb4? Bxb4 27. Rg3 Qb6+ 28. Kh1 Rd8?! 29. Rxg7+ Kh8?! 30. Rxf7+?! Rd4? 31. Rd1 c5 32. Rd7 Kg8 33. Re1?? Rxd7 0-1 *Allentown Morning Call*, 16 April, 1933 (Peter Lahde/Neil Brennen).

(759) FINE—FELDMAN, N

Blindfold Exhibition, Hungarian Chess Club, New York, 1933
Double Fianchetto Opening [A00]

1. g3 e5 2. Bg2 d5 3. b3 Nf6 4. Bb2 Nc6 5. Nf3 Bd6 6. 0-0 Bd7 7. d4 e4 8. Ne5 Qe7 9. Nxd7 Nxd7 10. e3 0-0 11. c4 b6 12. cxd5 Nb4 13. Nc3 f5 14. Qe2 Nd3 15. Bc1 Nf6 16. Bd2 Bb4 17. d6 Bxd6 18. f3 Nb4 19. fxe4 fxe4 20. Rxf6 gxf6 21. Nxe4 Nd5 22. Qc4 c6 23. Qxc6 Nxe3 24. Bxe3 Rad8 25. Re1 Bb4 26. Rf1 Kh8 27. Bh6 Rg8 28. Qxf6+ Qxf6 29. Nxf6 Rg6 30. Be3 Bc3 31. Nd5 Bb2 32. Rb1 Ba3 33. b4 Rc6 34. Bf4 Rc2 35. Be5+ Kg8 36. Bh3 Bc1 37. Bf5 Rc4 38. Bd3 Rcc8 39. Ne7+ Kf7 40. Nxc8 Rxc8 41. Kf1 Ke7 42. Ke2 Ba3 43. h4 Rc3 44. g4 Bc1 45. Bxh7 Black resigned. 1-0 Fine 1958, 30-4.

(760) FINE—HESTERLY & SANDFORD

Blindfold Exhibition, Hungarian Chess Club, New York, 1933
French Defence, Winawer Variation [C15]

1. Nc3 d5 2. e4 e6 3. d4 Bb4 4. Nge2 dxe4 5. a3 Bxc3+ 6. Nxc3 f5 7. f3 exf3 8. Qxf3 Qxd4 9. Bd3 Ne7 10. Be3 Qf6 11. 0-0-0 Nd7 12. Qg3 c6 13. Bc4 0-0 14. Bd4 Qh6+ 15. Kb1 Nd5 16. Qd6 N7f6 17. h3 Qf4 18. Qxf4 Nxf4 19. g4 fxg4 20. hxg4 Ng6 21. Bc5 Re8 22. g5 Nd5 23. Ne4 b6 24. Bd6 Bb7 25. Rh2 Nf8 26. Rdh1 Ne7 27. Rxh7 Nxh7 28. Bxe6+ Kh8 29. Bf7 Rf8 30. g6 Rxf7 31. Rxh7+ Kg8 32. gxf7+ Kxf7 33. Bxe7 Kg6 34. Rh4 Re8 35. Bd6 c5 36. Nc3 and wins. 1-0

(761) FINE—MULLONEY

Simultaneous Exhibition, Boston City Chess Club, 1933
Evans Gambit Accepted [C52]

1. e4 e5 2. Nf3 Nc6 3. Bc4 Bc5 4. b4 Bxb4 5. c3 Ba5 6. d4 exd4 7. 0-0 dxc3 8. Qb3 Qf6 9. e5 Qg6 10. Nxc3 Nge7 11. Ba3 0-0 12. Rad1 a6 13. Nd5 Nxd5 14. Bxd5 Re8 15. Bb2 h6 16. Nh4 Qh5 17. Qg3 Nxe5 18. f4 Ng4 19. h3 Bb6+ 20. Kh1 Nf2+ 21. Rxf2 Qxd1+ 22. Kh2 g5 23. Bb3 Qe1 24. Qd3 d5 25. Bxd5 Be6 26. Rf1 Qxh4 27. Qc3 Kf8 28. Qg7+ Ke7 29. Bxe6 Qxf4+ 30. Rxf4 gxf4 31. Qxf7+ Kd6 32. Qd7+ Kc5 33. Ba3 mate 1-0

(762) FINE & DAKE—JACKS, D

Simultaneous Exhibition, Chicago, 1934 (12 Sept.)
English Opening, Classical Variation [A21]

1. c4 e5 2. Nc3 Bc5 3. e4 Nf6 4. Nf3 Nc6 5. Nxe5 d6 6. Nxc6 bxc6 7. d4 Bb4 8. Bd3 0-0 9. 0-0 c5 10. d5 Bb7 11. Bg5 c6 12. dxc6 Bxc6 13. Nd5 Bxd5 14. exd5 Ba5 15. Qf3 Rb8 16. b3 Bc3 17. Rac1?! Be5 18. Qh3 g6 19. Qh4 h5 20. Rfe1 Kg7 21. Rc2 Rb7 22. Rce2 Bd4 23. Re4? Nxe4 24. Rxe4 Bf6 25. f4 Bxg5 26. fxg5 Re7 27. Rf4 Re5 28. Rf6

Rxg5 29. Rf4 Qe7 30. g4 Qe3+ 31. Qf2 Qxd3 0–1
Illinois State Chess Association (Lahde).

(763) FINE—GALINDO

Simultaneous Exhibition, Mexico, 1934 (Nov.)
Caro-Kann Defence [B14]

1. e4 c6 2. d4 d5 3. exd5 cxd5 4. c4 Nf6 5. Nc3
g6 6. Bg5 Be6 7. Bxf6 exf6 8. Nf3 Bb4 9. c5! Nc6
10. Rc1 0–0 11. Be2 b6! 12. a3 Bxc3+ 13. Rxc3 bxc5
14. Rxc5 Qd6 15. 0–0 Rfc8 16. Qd2 Kg7 17. Rfc1
Ne7 18. Rxc8 Rxc8 19. Rxc8 Bxc8 20. Qc3 Ba6
21. Qd2 Bxe2 22. Qxe2 Nf5 23. Kf1 Qf4 24. Qd1
Kg8 25. g3 Qe4 26. b4 Nxd4 On 27 Nxd4 Qh1+
28 Ke2 Qe4+. ½–½ *L'Echiquier*, March/April 1935 (Lahde).

(764) FINE—BRUNNER, J

Simultaneous Exhibition, Mexico City, 1934 (16 Nov.)
Sicilian Defence, Pin Variation [B40]

1. e4 c5 2. Nf3 Nf6 3. Nc3 e6 4. d4 cxd4 5. Nxd4
Bb4 6. Bd3 e5 7. Nde2 d5 8. exd5 Nxd5 9. 0–0
Bxc3 10. bxc3 0–0 11. Ba3 Re8 12. Qd2 Nc6 13. Rab1
Qa5 14. Bd6 Nd4 15. Nxd4 exd4 16. Qg5 h6 17. Qh5
Qd8 18. Qxd5 Re6 19. Rfe1 Black resigned, for if 19 …
Rxd6 20 Qxd6 Qxd6 21 Re8+ Qf8 22 Rxf8+. 1–0 ACB
1934, 157.

(765) FINE—GONZALES ROJO, E

Simultaneous Exhibition, Mexico City, 1934 (22 Nov.)
Queen's Indian Defence [E16]

1. d4 Nf6 2. c4 e6 3. Nf3 b6 4. g3 Bb7 5. Bg2
Bb4+ 6. Bd2 Qe7 7. 0–0 Bxd2 8. Qxd2 Ne4 9. Qc2
d5 10. Nc3 f5 11. Ne5 0–0 12. Nxe4 dxe4 13. f3
exf3 14. Bxf3 Bxf3 15. Nxf3 Nd7 16. e4 f4 17. e5
g5 18. g4 Rf7 19. Qe4 h5 20. h3 Rg7 21. Kg2 Rd8
22. Rad1 Nf8 23. d5 Qc5 24. dxe6 Rxd1 25. Rxd1
Nxe6 26. Qd5 Qe7 27. a3 Rf7 28. Qe4 hxg4 29. hxg4
Kg7 30. Rh1 Kg8 31. Qd5 Nf8 32. Rh5 Nh7 33. e6
Rf6 34. Qe4 Rg6 35. Nd4 Qe8 36. Nf5 Kh8 37. Qe5+
1–0

(766) FINE—RAMIREZ

Simultaneous Exhibition, Mexico City, 1934 (22 Nov.)
French Defence, Rubinstein Variation [C10]

1. e4 e6 2. d4 d5 3. Nc3 dxe4 4. Nxe4 Nf6 5. Bd3
Be7 6. Nf3 0–0 7. 0–0 Nxe4 8. Bxe4 c6 9. Qe2
Nd7 10. c4 Nf6 11. Bc2 b6 12. b3 Ba6 13. Bb2 Qc7
14. Rad1 Rfd8 15. Rfe1 g6 16. Ne5 Nd7 17. Nxf7
Nf8 18. Nh6+ Kg7 19. d5+ Kxh6 20. Qe3+ Kh5
21. Qh3+ Bh4 22. g3 Qe7 23. Rd4 g5 24. gxh4
gxh4 25. Rxh4+ Black resigned. For if 25 … Qxh4

26 Bd1+ Kg5 27 Qxh4+ Kxh4 28 Bf6+ Kh3 29 Re3 mate.
1–0 *ACB* 1934, 157.

(767) FINE—BEKKER, J

Simultaneous Exhibition, 1936 (Nov.)
King's Indian Defence [A31]

1. Nf3 g6 2. c4 Nf6 3. Nc3 c5 4. d4 cxd4 5. Nxd4
Bg7 6. e4 d6 7. Be2 0–0 8. 0–0 Nc6 9. Nc2 Nd7
10. Qd2 Nc5 11. f3 f5 12. exf5 Bxf5 13. Ne3 Nd4
14. Nxf5 Rxf5 15. Bd1 Rc8 16. b3 b5! 17. Bb2 bxc4
18. bxc4 Nce6 19. Bb3 Nxb3 20. axb3 Nd4 21. Ra2
Qb6 22. Qf2? Nxf3+! 23. Kh1 Nd4 24. Qe1 Rxf1+
25. Qxf1 Rf8 26. Qd3 Nf5 27. h3? Ng3+ 28. Kh2
Be5 29. Nd5 Ne2+0–1 *Nieuwe Rotterdamsche Courant*,
Wednesday 25 November, 1936 (Fiala).

(768) FINE—FONTEYN, G

Simultaneous Exhibition, 1936 (Dec.)
Spanish Opening, Worrall Attack [C86]

1. e4 e5 2. Nf3 Nc6 3. Bb5 a6 4. Ba4 Nf6 5. 0–0
Be7 6. Qe2 d6 7. c3 0–0 8. d4 Bd7 9. Bc2 Re8
10. Rd1 Bf8 11. d5 Ne7 12. c4 Ng6 13. Nc3 Nh5
14. Ne1 Nhf4 15. Qe3 Be7 16. g3 Nh3+ 17. Kf1 Rf8
18. Qe2 Qc8 19. Be3 h6 20. Rac1 Bg5 21. Rd2 b6
22. a3 Bg4 23. f3 Bd7 24. Bxg5 hxg5 25. Qe3 g4
26. Kg2 Qd8 27. Nd1 gxf3+ 28. Nxf3 Bg4 29. Nf2
Bxf3+ 30. Kxf3 Nxf2 31. Rxf2 a5 32. b3 Qd7
33. Kg2 Ne7 34. Rcf1 Qg4 35. Bd1 Qg6 36. Bc2 f6
37. h4 Kh7 ½–½ (Fiala)

(769) WEIL, W—FINE

Exhibition Game, Vienna, 1937
Nimzowitsch-Larsen Opening [A06]

1. Nf3 d5 2. b3 c5 3. Bb2 Nc6 4. e3 Qc7 5. Bb5
a6 6. Bxc6+ Qxc6 7. d3 f6 8. Qe2 e5 9. c4 Ne7
10. 0–0 Bg4 11. Re1 0–0–0 12. e4 dxe4 13. dxe4
Ng6 14. g3 Qd7 15. Nc3 Qd3 16. Kg2 Qxe2 17. Rxe2
Rd3 18. Re3 Rxe3 19. fxe3 Bd6 20. a4 Kc7
21. Ba3 Ne7 22. Rf1 ½–½

(770) FINE—STIEL, T

Simultaneous Exhibition, 1937
Slav Defence [D18]

1. d4 d5 2. c4 c6 3. Nf3 Nf6 4. Nc3 dxc4 5. a4
Bf5 6. e3 e6 7. Bxc4 Nbd7 8. 0–0 Be7 9. Qe2 Nb6
10. Bb3 Nfd5 11. e4 Nxc3 12. bxc3 Bg4 13. h3
Bxf3 14. Qxf3 0–0 15. Bb2 c5 16. d5 exd5 17. Bxd5
Nxd5 18. exd5 Qd7 19. c4 Bd6 20. Rfe1 Rfe8 21. Kf1
Rxe1+ 22. Kxe1 Re8+ 23. Kf1 Be5 24. Bxe5 Rxe5
25. Qc3 Qc7 26. Rb1 Re8 27. Kg1 Kf8 28. Qb3 b6

29. Qb5 Rb8 30. a5 Qd6 31. Qa6 Qc7 32. axb6 Rxb6 33. Rxb6 Qxb6 34. Qxb6 axb6 35. Kf1 Ke7 36. Ke2 Kd6 37. Kd3 h6 38. h4 g5 39. hxg5 hxg5 40. g4! b5 41. cxb5 Kxd5 42. Kc3 c4 43. b6 Kc6 44. Kxc4 Kxb6 45. Kd5 Kc7 46. Ke5 Kd7 47. Kf6 Ke8 48. Kxg5 1–0 (Fiala)

(771) FINE—RUPP

Simultaneous Exhibition, 1937
Rousseau Gambit [C50]

1. e4 e5 2. Nf3 Nc6 3. Bc4 f5? 4. 0–0? fxe4 5. Nxe5 Nxe5 6. Qh5+ Ng6 7. Bxg8 Rxg8 8. Qxh7 Kf7 9. Qh5 d5 10. Nc3 c6 11. d3 Rh8 12. Qd1 Qh4 13. h3 Bxh3 14. g3 Qh7 15. dxe4 Bg4 0–1 P. F. van Hoorn in *De Schaakwereld* 1e Jaargang, game 40, 2–3.

(772) FINE—EKELUND AND PETTERSSON

Simultaneous Exhibition, Orebro, 1937 (26 Jan.)
Slav Defence [D17]

The old masters often gave odds to encourage their hopelessly outclassed opponents. The contemporary form of odds-giving is the simultaneous exhibition, which is suited to modern notions of mass entertainment. The play is on even material terms, but the master is nevertheless handicapped by the physical effort of walking several miles; by having seconds instead of minutes in which to plan and execute; by having to rely on routine rather than on imagination. The combination of these factors increases the possibility of blunders. FR 1. d4 Nf6 2. c4 c6 3. Nc3 d5 4. Nf3 dxc4 5. a4 Bf5 6. Ne5 Nbd7 7. Nxc4 Qc7 8. g3 e5 9. dxe5 Nxe5 10. Bf4 Nfd7 11. Qb3? An experiment which turns out badly. The "book" move 11 Bg2 leaves White with a comfortable game. FR 11 ... Be6! 12. e3? White should have tried 12 0–0–0 Nc5 13 Qa2 Bxc4 14 Qxc4 Nxc4 15 Bxc7. AW 12 ... Nf3+ 13. Kd1 Likewise after 13 Ke2 Nfe5 White has a miserable position. FR 13 ... Qd8! Threatening ... Nc5+. FR 14. Kc1 Nc5 15. Qd1 Qxd1+ 16. Kxd1 0–0–0+ 17. Ke2 Bg4 Black's game is so superior that even the exchange of queens did not ease the pressure very much. FR 18. h3 Or 18 Bg2 Ne5+ 19 f3 Nxc4 20 fxg4 Rd2+ winning easily. The text allows a problem-like finish. FR 18 ... Rd2+ On 19 Nxd2 there follows 19 ... Nd4+ 20 Ke1 Nc2 mate! SJ 0–1 Reinfeld 1948, 120–1; Jonasson, 50–1.

(773) AXELSSON & LAETI—FINE

Simultaneous Exhibition, Orebro, 1937 (26 Jan.)
Nimzowitsch-Indian Defence, Spielmann Variation [E23]

1. d4 Nf6 2. c4 e6 3. Nc3 Bb4 4. Qb3 c5 5. dxc5 Nc6 6. Nf3 Bxc5 7. Bg5 h6 8. Bxf6 Qxf6 9. Ne4 Bb4+ 10. Qxb4 Nxb4 11. Nxf6+ gxf6 12. Nd4 Ke7 13. g3 Nc6 14. Rd1 b6 15. Bg2 Bb7 16. 0–0 Rac8

17. Nb5 Ba8 18. Rd2 a6 19. Nd6 Rc7 20. Rfd1 Ne5 21. f4 Ng4 22. Bxa8 Rxa8 23. h3 Ne3 24. Rc1 Rc6 25. Kf2 Rxd6 26. Rxd6 Kxd6 27. Kxe3 Rc8 28. Rd1+ Ke7 29. b3 Rg8 30. Kf3 h5 31. Rd4 f5 32. e4 fxe4+ 33. Rxe4 f5 34. Re3 Kd6 35. Rd3+ Kc6 36. Ke2 b5 37. cxb5+ axb5 38. a4 bxa4 39. bxa4 Ra8 40. Ra3 Kc5 41. Rc3+ Kd4 42. Rd3+ Ke4 43. Rxd7 Rxa4 44. Rd2 h4 45. g4 fxg4 46. hxg4 Kxf4 47. Kf2 Kxg4 0–1 *Los Angeles Times*, 7 March, 1937 (Lahde).

(774) FINE—NILSSON, H

Clock Exhibition, Helsingborg, 1937 (16 Feb.)
Spanish Game, Møller Defence [C78]

1. e4 e5 2. Nf3 Nc6 3. Bb5 a6 4. Ba4 Nf6 5. 0–0 Bc5 6. c3 Ba7 7. d4 Nxe4 8. dxe5 0–0 9. Qe2 f5 10. Nbd2 d5 11. exd6 Nxd6 12. Bxc6 bxc6 13. Nc4 Re8 14. Nce5 Qf6 15. Bg5 Qe6 16. Be3 Bxe3 17. Qxe3 Ne4 18. Rfe1 c5 19. Nd3 c4 20. Nf4 Qb6 21. Nd5 After the game Fine suggested that 21 Qxb6 would have been better, giving the following variation: 21 ... cxb6 22 Nd5 Rb8 23 Nd4 Bd7 24 f3 Nd6 25 Rxe8+ Nxe8 26 Nxf5 winning a pawn in view of the threatened fork Ne7+. 21 ... Qc6 22. Rad1 Be6 23. Nf4 Bf7 24. Nd4 Qf6 25. f3 Nc5 26. Qd2 g5 27. Rxe8+ Rxe8 28. Nh3 f4 29. Nf2 Bg6 30. Re1 Rxe1+ 31. Qxe1 Nd3 32. Nxd3 cxd3 33. Kf2 Kf7 34. b4 Qd6 ½–½ Jonasson, 51.

(775) FINE—CHISTYAKOV, A

Clock Exhibition (1st Category Players), Moscow, 1937 (6 March)
Dutch Defence, Stonewall Variation [A95]

1. d4 e6 2. Nf3 f5 3. g3 Nf6 4. Bg2 Be7 5. 0–0 0–0 6. c4 d5 7. Nc3 c6 8. Bf4 Qe8 9. Qc2 Qh5 10. Rab1 Nbd7 11. c5 Ne4 12. b4 g5 13. Bc7 Rf6 14. h3 Rh6 15. Rfe1 g4 16. hxg4 fxg4 17. Nh4 Nxf2! 18. Kxf2 Bxh4 19. gxh4 Qxh4+ 20. Ke3 e5! 21. dxe5 d4+ 22. Kxd4 Qf2+ 23. Kd3 Nxe5+ 24. Bxe5 Bf5+ 25. e4 Rd8+ 26. Bd6 Rdxd6+ 27. cxd6 Rxd6+ 28. Nd5 Qg3+ 29. Kd2 Rxd5+ 30. Kc1 Qxe1+ 31. Kb2 Qxb4+ 32. Ka1 Qd4+ 33. Qb2 Qxb2+ 34. Kxb2 Rb5+ 35. Kc1 Rxb1+ 36. Kxb1 Bg6 37. Kc2 Kf7 38. Kd3 Ke6 39. Kd4 b6 40. Bf1 c5+ 0–1 64

(776) FINE—KOGAN

Clock Exhibition (1st Category Players) Moscow, 1937 (6 March]

(See diagram at top of next page.) 1. f5 Kf6 2. Ra6+ Ke5 3. Kg3 Ke4 4. Ra3 Re2 5. Kh4 Kf3 6. Kh5 Rh2+ 7. Kg5 Rg2 8. f6 gxf6+ 9. Kf5 Kg3 10. e4+ Kh4 ½–½ 64

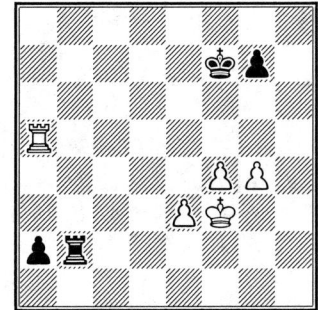

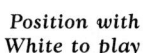
*Position with
White to play*

(777) FINE—ZAGORYANSKY, E

Clock Exhibition (1st Category Players) Moscow, 1937 (6
   March)
Queen's Gambit Declined, Orthodox Variation [D62]

1. d4 d5 2. c4 e6 3. Nc3 Nf6 4. Bg5 Nbd7 5. e3
Be7 6. Nf3 0-0 7. Qc2 c5 8. cxd5 cxd4 9. Nxd4
Nxd5 10. Bxe7 After the logical 10 ... Nxe7

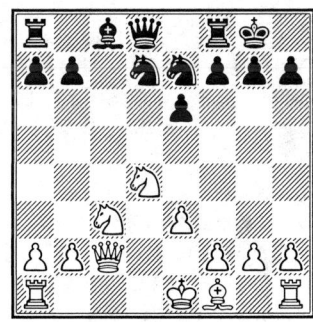
*Position with
White to play*

   I was unable to gain any kind of advantage. My opponent simply did not allow the creation of a weak pawn on
d5. True, he did have quite a cramped position, however,
he defended well and continually presented me with technical difficulties. RF

   A picture of the game printed in *64* appears to show
a position where Zagoryansky has his king on h8, rook on
f8, queen on e7 and pawns on h6, g7, f5 and e5, while Fine's
queen stands on h3. Although much of the board is obscured it seems the minor pieces may have been exchanged.

(778) KOTS—FINE

Clock Exhibition (1st Category Players), Moscow, 1937 (6
   March)
Colle System [A46]

1. d4 Nf6 2. Nf3 e6 3. e3 c5 4. Nbd2 b6 5. c3
Bb7 6. Bd3 Nc6 7. 0-0 Be7 8. e4 cxd4 9. Nxd4
Ne5 The start of an incorrect manoeuvre, here he should
have played 9 ... Nxd4 or 9 ... 0-0 equalizing. 10. Bc2 Ba6
11. Re1 Nd3? Overlooking White's 13th move. 12. Bxd3
Bxd3 I must admit that, having the two bishops, I thought
I stood well. However I was in for an unpleasant surprise.

RF 13. c4! White threatens to win a piece in short order by
Qb3 or Re3. RF 13 ... Bb4 Black manages to ward off the
principal threat, however he obtains a bad position and
White conducts the game in the manner of a master. RF
14. e5! White pushes back his opponent's pieces and gains
a positional advantage by force. Black would have had counterchances after 14 N4f3 b5!! *64* 14 ... Ng8 15. Qb3 Forcing the following exchange, which leads to a weakening of
the dark squares in Black's camp. 15 ... Bxd2 16. Bxd2
Bg6 17. Nb5! Ne7 18. Nd6+ Kf8 19. Bg5 h6 20. Bh4
Qc7 Black attempts to free himself from the unpleasant
pressure. *64;* I wanted to play 20 ... Kg8 in order to free
myself somewhat by ... Kh7, however in that event there
follows 21 Qf3 (threatening Bxe7) Rb8 (not 21 ... Kh7
because of 22 Bxe7) 22 Qa3 Ra8 23 Nb5 Kf8 24 Rad1 and
Black has run out of moves. RF 21. Qa3! White finds a way
to take the game into a winning ending. He now threatens
22 Bxe7+ followed by a discovered check. Black's reply is
forced. 21 ... Qc5 22. b4 A subtle positional move; after
the exchange of queens Black will advance his pawn to b5 in
order to create a passed b-pawn. RF 22 ... Qc6 22 ... Qd4
would be bad because of 23 Bxe7+ Kxe7 24 Rad1. 23. b5
Qc5 24. Qxc5 bxc5 25. Bxe7+ A quicker route to
the win was 25 f3 Nf5 26 Bf2 Nxd6 (26 ... Nd4 27 Rad1)
27 Bxc5. 25 ... Kxe7 The ending is won for White in view
of the queenside majority supported by the ideally-placed
knight. Black's bishop, on the other hand, has no prospects.
26. a4 f6 27. f4 Rhf8 Black tries to generate counterplay
along the f-file. 28. a5 Rab8 29. Re3 Now White threatens 30 Rg3 followed by Rb3 supporting the queenside
pawns. 29 ... Bh7 30. Ra2 fxe5 30 ... g5 31 g3 Rg8
32 Rg2 would be a little sharper. 31. fxe5 Rf4 32. Rf2
Rd4 This loses straight away. However, even after 32 ...
Rxf2 33 Kxf2 Rf8+ 34 Rf3 Rxf3+ 35 Kxf3 Kd8 36 b6 axb6
(or 36 ... a6 37 Nb7+) 37 a6 White must win. 33. Rf7+
Kd8 34. Rf8+ Kc7 35. b6+ Black resigned. After 35 ...
axb6 36 axb6+ neither 36 ... Rxd6 nor 36 ... Kxb6 is possible because of the hanging rook on b8. 1-0 *64* March 1937,
game 678; Fine, "A Meeting with First Category Players," *64*,
March 1937.

(779) FINE—ROOSEVELT & FORSBERG

Simultaneous Exhibition, New York, 1939
Spanish Game, Worrall Attack [C86]

1. e4 e5 2. Nf3 Nc6 3. Bb5 a6 4. Ba4 Nf6 5. 0-0
b5 6. Bb3 Be7 7. Qe2 0-0 8. c3 d6 9. d4 Bg4
10. Rd1 Qc8 11. a4 b4 12. a5 Qb7 13. Bc4 Rfe8
14. d5 Nb8 15. Nbd2 Nbd7 16. Nb3 Nf8 17. h3
Bh5 18. Ra4 bxc3 19. bxc3 Qc8 20. Bd3 N8d7
21. Be3 h6 22. Nbd2 Nh7 23. g4 Bg6 24. Nf1 Ng5
25. Nxg5 Bxg5 26. Bxg5 hxg5 27. Qe3 Nc5 28. Rb4
f6 29. Nd2 Rb8 30. Bc2 Kf7 31. Nc4 Rh8 32. Kg2
Ke7 33. Rdb1 Rxb4 34. cxb4 Nd7 35. Rc1 Be8
36. Bd3 Qb7 37. Qd2 Nf8 38. Ne3 Ng6 39. Nf5+
Kd8 40. Bf1 Nf4+ 41. Kh2 g6 42. Ne3 Bb5 43. Nc4
Qa7 44. Qe3 Qd4 45. Rc3 Kd7 ½-½ (Lahde)

(780) FINE—SEIDMAN

Simultaneous Exhibition, New York, 1939
Sicilian Dragon [B74]

1. e4 c5 2. Nf3 d6 3. d4 cxd4 4. Nxd4 Nf6 5. Nc3
g6 6. Be2 Bg7 7. Be3 Nc6 8. 0–0 0–0 9. Nb3 a5
10. a4 Be6 11. Nd4 Nxd4 12. Bxd4 Rc8 13. Bd3
Bc4 14. Qe2 Bxd3 15. Qxd3 Nd7 16. Bxg7 Kxg7
17. Nd5 e6 18. Ne3 Nc5 19. Qd4+ Qf6 20. Qxf6+
Kxf6 21. f3 Rc6 22. Rfd1 Ke7 23. Rd4 h5 24. b3
b6 25. Rad1 Rd8 26. Kf2 Na6 27. e5 Nb4 28. c4
Na6 29. Nf1 Nc5 30. Nd2? dxe5 31. Rxd8 Kxd8
32. Ne4+ Ke7 33. Nxc5 bxc5 34. Re1?! f6 35. Ke3
Rb6 36. Rb1 f5 37. h4 Rd6 38. g3 Rd4 39. Rg1 e4
40. fxe4 Rxe4+ 41. Kf3 Rd4 0–1

(781) FINE—WOLFF

Simultaneous Exhibition, New York, 1939
Nimzowitsch-Indian Defence, Rubinstein's Variation [E43]

1. d4 Nf6 2. c4 e6 3. Nc3 Bb4 4. e3 b6 5. Bd3
Bb7 6. f3 d5 7. Nge2 0–0 8. 0–0 c5 9. Qe1 cxd4
10. exd4 Ba6 11. b3 Nc6 12. a3 dxc4 13. Bxc4 Bxc4
14. bxc4 Ba5 15. Be3 Rc8 16. Qh4 h6 17. h3 Ne7
18. c5 Nf5 19. Qf2 bxc5 20. dxc5 Qd3 21. Nd1
Nxe3 22. Nxe3 Bd2 23. Nd1 Nd5 24. Kh1 Ne3
25. Rg1 Rxc5 26. Ra2 Rb8 27. Nf4 Nxd1 28. Rxd1
Bxf4 0–1

(782) FINE—NOVICK

Simultaneous Exhibition, City College, New York, 1939 (18
May)
Sicilian Dragon [B73]

1. e4 c5 2. Nf3 Nc6 3. d4 cxd4 4. Nxd4 Nf6
5. Nc3 d6 6. Be2 g6 7. 0–0 Bg7 8. Be3 Bd7
9. Kh1 0–0 10. f4 Nxd4 11. Bxd4 Bc6 12. Bf3 Qd7
13. Qe2 b5 14. Rad1 Qb7 15. e5 dxe5 16. fxe5 Nd7
17. e6 Bxf3 18. Rxf3 Bxd4 19. exd7 Bf6 20. Qxb5
Qxb5 21. Nxb5 Rfd8 22. Nc7 Rab8 23. Rb3 Rxb3
24. axb3 Bxb2 25. Nb5 Be5 26. Nxa7 Bd6 27. Nb5
Rxd7 28. c4 Rd8 29. g3 Rb8 30. Kg2 Kf8 31. Kf3
f5 32. Ra1 Bc5 33. Ra6 e5 34. Rc6 Bg1 35. Kg2 Be3
36. Rc7 h5 37. Rd7 Ra8 38. Nc7 Ra2+ 39. Kf1
Rf2+ 40. Ke1 Rxh2 41. c5 Bf2+ 42. Kf1 Bxg3
43. c6 e4 44. Ne6+ Kg8 45. c7 Bxc7 46. Rxc7
Rb2 47. Rg7+ Kh8 48. Rxg6 Rxb3 49. Rg5 Rf3+
50. Ke2 f4 51. Rxh5+ Kg8 52. Re5 Re3+ 53. Kd2
Rd3+ 54. Kc2 Ra3 55. Nxf4 e3 56. Nd5 Ra2+
57. Kb3 Re2 58. Nxe3 Re1 59. Kc3 Kf7 60. Kd4
Rh1 61. Ke4 Rh4+ 62. Kf5 Ra4?? 63. Kg5 Ra1
64. Ng4 Rg1 65. Re2 Rg3 66. Kf5 Rf3+ 67. Kg5
Rb3 68. Nh6+ Kf8 69. Nf5 Rb6 70. Re3 Ra6
71. Re7 Ra5 72. Rb7 Ke8 73. Kf6 Kd8 74. Ke6
Ra6+ 75. Nd6 1–0 *ACB*

(783) FINE—SCHMOLKA, I

Simultaneous Exhibition, City College, New York, 1939
(18 May)
French Defence, Tarrasch Variation [C05]

1. e4 e6 2. d4 d5 3. Nd2 Nf6 4. e5 Nfd7 5. Bd3
c5 6. c3 Nc6 7. Ne2 Be7 8. 0–0 0–0 9. Nf3 cxd4
10. cxd4 Qb6 11. a3 f5 12. exf6 Nxf6 13. Qc2 Bd7
14. Bg5 h6 15. Bh4 Rac8 16. Qb1 Na5 17. Ne5 Be8
18. b4 Nc4 19. Bxc4 dxc4 20. Rc1 c3 21. Qb3 a5
22. Rab1 axb4 23. axb4 g5 24. Bg3 Ne4! 25. Nc4
Qa6 26. Nxc3 Nxg3 27. b5! Bxb5 28. Qxb5 Rxc4
29. hxg3 Rfc8 30. Qxa6 bxa6 31. Ne2 a5 32. Rxc4
Rxc4 ½–½ *ACB*

(784) FINE—ZEITLIN, S

Simultaneous Exhibition, City College, New York, 1939
(18 May)
Queen's Gambit Declined, Exchange Variation [D35]

1. d4 Nf6 2. c4 e6 3. Nc3 d5 4. Bg5 Be7 5. e3
0–0 6. Nf3 Nbd7 7. cxd5 exd5 8. Bd3 c6 9. 0–0
h6 10. Bf4 Nh5 11. Be5 Nxe5 12. dxe5 g6 13. Nd4
Ng7 14. f4 c5 15. Nc2 a6 16. Be2 Be6 17. Bf3 d4
18. exd4 cxd4 19. Ne4 d3 20. Ne1 Qd4+ 21. Kh1
Rad8 22. Qd2 Bb4 23. Nc3 Nf5 24. Bxb7 Ne3
25. Rf3 Nc4 26. Qxd3 Qb6 27. Qe4 Nd2 28. Qc6
Qxc6 29. Bxc6 Nxf3 30. Nxf3 Bxc3 31. bxc3 Bd5
32. Nd4 Bxc6 33. Nxc6 Rd7 34. c4 Rc8 35. Nb4
Rxc4 36. Nxa6 Rxf4 37. h3 Rd2 38. a4 Rff2 39. Rg1
Ra2 40. Nc5 Rfc2 41. Ne4 Rxa4 42. Nf6+ Kg7
43. Ne8+ Kf8 44. Nd6 Rca2 45. Kh2 Ra1 46. Rxa1
Rxa1 47. Kg3 Ke7 48. Nb7 Rb1 49. Nc5 Rb5 0–1
ACB

(785) FINE—LITTLE, P

Blindfold display Chicago, 1940
Queen's Gambit Accepted [D20]

1. d4 d5 2. c4 dxc4 3. Qa4+ Bd7 4. Qxc4 e6 5. e4
c6 6. Nc3 Be7 7. e5 Na6 8. Nf3 Nc7 9. Be2 b5
10. Qb3 Rb8 11. 0–0 a5 12. Bd2 Nd5 13. Ne4 Bb4
14. Bxb4 axb4 15. Nd6+ Kf8 16. a3 h6 17. axb4
Ra8 18. Nd2 Nge7 19. N2e4 Nf5 20. Nxf5 exf5
21. Nd6 Be6 22. Qc2 Ne7 23. Qc5 g6 24. Bf3
Rxa1 25. Rxa1 Kg7 26. Bxc6 Nxc6 27. Qxc6 f4
28. Qe4 Qg5 29. g3 fxg3 30. hxg3 Qd2 31. Qf4
Qxb2 32. Ra7 Rf8 33. Re7 Bd5 34. Ne8+ Rxe8
35. Qf6+ Kf8 36. Rxf7+ Bxf7 37. Qh8+ ½–½ Ultimate Games Collection III

(786) FINE—YANOFSKY, D

Simultaneous Exhibition, Canada, 1940 (March)
French Defence [C07]

1. e4 e6 2. d4 d5 3. Nd2 c5 4. exd5 cxd4 5. Bb5+
Nc6 6. Ngf3 Bd6 7. 0–0 exd5 8. Nxd4 Bd7 9. N2f3
Nge7 10. Be3 0–0 11. c3 Nxd4 12. Nxd4 Nf5
13. Nxf5 Bxf5 14. Bd3 Be6 15. Qh5 f5 16. Bd4 Qe8
17. Qxe8 Rfxe8 18. Rfe1 a6 19. Rad1 Bd7 20. g3 Kf7
21. f4 g6 22. Kf2 Rxe1 23. Rxe1 Re8 24. Rxe8 Bxe8
25. Ke3 Ke6 26. b4 Bc6 27. Bb6 Be7 28. Bc2 Bb5
29. a4 Bf1 30. Bc5 Bf6 31. Bd4 Bd8 32. a5 Bb5
33. Be5 b6 34. axb6 Bxb6+ 35. Bd4 Bd8 36. Bd3
Bc4 ½–½ *ChessBase Big Database 2002.*

(786A) FINE—CHAPMAN

Simultaneous exhibition Sacramento, California, 1940 (4 Sept.)

1. e4 e5 2. f4 d6 3. Nf3 Nc6 4. Bc4 Nf6 5. 0–0
Be7 6. d4 Bg4 7. c3 Nxe4 8. fxe5 d5 9. Bd3 Ng5
10. Nbd2 0–0 11. Qe1 f5 12. Nxg5 Bxg5 13. Nf3 Be7
14. Bf4 Qd7 15. Qg3 Nd8 16. Rae1 Ne6 17. Bd2 Rf7
18. h3 Bh5 19. Ng5 Bxg5 20. Bxg5 Bg6 21. Bf4
Raf8 22. Rf2 c6 23. Ref1 Qe7 24. b4 b5 25. a4 a6
26. Ra1 Qb7 27. Rfa2 Ra8 28. axb5 cxb5 29. Bf1
Qb6 30. Ra5 Rfa7 31. Qf2 Be8 32. Be3 g6 33. Kh2
Qc7 34. Bd2 Bc6 35. Bd3 Qf7 36. Rf1 Qg7 37. Qh4
½–½ *Los Angeles Times,* 15 September, 1940.

(787) ENIVRE—FINE

New York, 1940
King's Gambit Declined [C30]

1. e4 e5 2. f4 Bc5 3. Nf3 d6 4. Nc3 Nf6 5. Bc4
Nc6 6. d3 Bg4 7. Na4 Bxf3! 8. Qxf3 Nd4 9. Qg3
exf4! 10. Qxg7? Rf8 11. Bb3 Qe7 12. Bxf4 Nh5
13. Qg5 Nxf4 14. Qxf4 f5 Black has the better game,
PCO 120.

(788) FINE—WEYL, N

Simultaneous Exhibition, Washington, 1941 (1 Dec.)
Sicilian Defence [B32]

1. e4 c5 2. Nf3 Nc6 3. d4 cxd4 4. Nxd4 e5 5. Nb3
Nf6 6. Nc3 Bb4 7. Bd3 Bxc3+ 8. bxc3 0–0 9. c4
d6 10. 0–0 Bg4 11. f3 Bh5 12. Ba3 a5 13. Be2 a4
14. Nc1 Qb6+ 15. Kh1 Nd4 16. Bd3 Ne6 17. Ne2 g5
18. Qd2 Kh8 19. Nc3 Rg8 20. Rab1 Qc7 21. Nb5
Qd8 22. Bxd6 Nd7 23. Ba3 Ndc5 24. Nc3 Nxd3
25. cxd3 g4 26. fxg4 Rxg4 27. Nd5 Nf4 28. Nxf4
Qg5 29. Bc1 Rxf4 30. Rxf4 Qxf4 31. Qxf4 exf4
32. Bxf4 Be2 33. Rxb7 Bxd3 34. c5 Bxe4 35. Rxf7
Kg8 36. Re7 Bd5 37. a3 Rf8 38. Be3 Rf1+ 39. Bg1
Ra1 40. Re3 Ra2 41. Rg3+ Kf7 42. h3 Rb2 43. Bd4
Rb3 44. Rxb3 axb3 45. Kg1 Ke6 46. Kf2 Kf5 47. a4
Ke4 48. Bh8 Kd3 49. g4 Kc4 50. Ke3 Kxc5 51. h4
Kb4 52. h5 Kxa4 53. Bb2 Kb4 54. Kf4 Bc4
55. Ke4 Kc5 56. g5 Bf7 57. g6 Bxg6+ ½–½ John
Hilbert. *Washington Post,* 7 December, 1941.

(789) FINE—BASS, A

Simultaneous Exhibition, Washington, 1941 (1 Dec.)
King's Gambit Accepted [C38]

1. e4 e5 2. f4 exf4 3. Nf3 g5 4. Bc4 Bg7 5. 0–0
h6 6. d4 Ne7 7. Nc3 0–0 8. g3! fxg3 9. Bxg5! d5
10. Nxd5 Nbc6 11. Bf6 Bg4 12. Qd2 Re8 13. c3
Qd7 14. Qf4 Nxd5 15. Bxd5 Bh3 16. Bxg7 Kxg7
17. Nh4 Re7 18. Rf3 gxh2+ 19. Kxh2 Be6 20. Rg1+
Kh7 21. Bxe6 fxe6 22. Qxh6+ Kxh6 23. Rh3 1–0
Washington Post, 7 December, 1941.

(790) FINE—STARK, M

Simultaneous Exhibition, Washington, 1941 (1 Dec.)
French Defence [C08]

1. e4 e6 2. d4 d5 3. Nd2 c5 4. exd5 exd5 5. Ngf3
Nf6 6. Bb5+ Bd7 7. Bxd7+ Nbxd7 8. 0–0 Be7
9. dxc5 Nxc5 10. Nd4 Qd7 11. Qf3 0–0 12. N2b3
Nxb3 13. axb3 Rfe8 14. Bf4 Bc5 15. Rfd1 Re4
16. Ne2 Qf5 17. Be3 Qxf3 18. gxf3 Ree8 19. Nd4
Rad8 20. c3 h6 21. b4 Bb6 22. Rd3 Rd7 23. Nf5
Bxe3 24. fxe3 a6 25. Kf2 Kh7 26. Rg1 g6 27. Nd4
Red8 28. Ne2 Re7 29. Nf4 Ree8 30. Ra1 Re7
31. Ra5 Red7 32. b5 g5 33. Ne2 axb5 34. Rxb5
Re8 35. Ng3 Kg6 36. e4 dxe4 37. Rxd7 e3+ 38. Ke2
Nxd7 39. Rxb7 Nc5 40. Rb6+ f6 41. b4 Nb3 42. Ne4
Kg7 43. Rb7+ Kg6 44. Rb6 Kg7 45. Rb7+ Kg6
½–½ *Washington Star,* 3 December, 1941.

(791) FINE—JENSEN

Simultaneous Exhibition, New Haven, 1942 (23 April)
Ragozin System [E51]

1. d4 d5 2. c4 e6 3. Nc3 Nc6 4. Nf3 Bb4 5. e3
Nf6 6. Bd3 0–0 7. 0–0 Qe7 8. Qe2 e5 9. Nxd5
Nxd5 10. cxd5 Nd8 11. Nxe5 Qg5 12. e4 Qf6 13. f4
Qh6 14. f5 Qb6 15. Be3 f6 16. Nc4 Qb5 17. Rf3
Nf7 18. Rh3 Ng5 19. Bxg5 fxg5 20. Rf1 Qe8 21. e5
Bd6 22. exd6 Bxf5 23. Qxe8 Rfxe8 24. Bxf5 Kf7
25. Bxh7 mate 1–0 *The Chess Correspondent,* November/
December 1943, 25 (Lahde contributed by Hilbert & Ansel).

(792) FINE—FOX, A

Exhibition Game, Washington, D.C., 1942 (May)
Queen's Gambit Declined, Grau Variation [D06]

1. d4 d5 2. c4 Bf5 Fox had recently tried this line, a personal favourite, against Herman Steiner, and lost. 3. Nc3
Nf6 4. Nf3 Nc6 5. Bf4 e5!? 6. Nxe5 Nb4 7. Rc1
dxc4 8. e4 Bg6 9. Bxc4 Be7 10. 0–0 0–0 11. a3
Nc6 12. Nxg6 hxg6 13. e5 Nh7 14. d5 Na5 15. Ba2
b6 16. Nb5 Rc8 17. b4 Nb7 18. Nxa7 Ra8 19. Nc6
Qd7 20. e6 fxe6 21. dxe6 Qe8 22. Nxe7+ Kh8
23. Rxc7 Rxf4 24. Rxb7 Nf8 25. Nd5 Rf5 26. e7
Rg5 27. g3 1–0 *Washington Post,* May 31, 1942.

A display at the Marshall Chess Club, December 7, 1942. Fine gave many simultaneous exhibitions in aid of the fledgling U.S.C.F. during the 1940s.

(793) FINE—FOX, A

Exhibition Game, Washington, D.C., 1942 (6 June)
Sicilan Defence, Nimzowitsch Variation [B29]

1. e4 c5 2. Nf3 Nf6 3. e5 Nd5 4. c4 Nb4 5. Nc3 g6
6. d4 cxd4 7. Nxd4 Bg7 8. f4?! 0–0?! 9. a3 N4c6
10. Nxc6?! Nxc6 11. Be2 d6 12. exd6 exd6 13. 0–0
Be6 14. Be3 Na5 15. Qa4 Rc8 16. Nd5 Bxd5 17. cxd5
Re8 18. Rf3 Rxe3! 19. Rxe3 Qb6 20. Qe4 Bd4 21. Kf2
Nc4 22. Bxc4 Qxb2+ 23. Kg3 Qxa1 24. Re1 Qxa3+
25. Bd3 Rc3 26. Rd1 Qc5 27. h3 Bf6 28. Kh2 Qf2
29. Qb4 Rc5 30. Rf1 Qd4 31. Qxd4 Bxd4 32. Rb1
Rc3 33. Rd1 a5 34. Bb5 Be3 35. Kg3 Bd2+ 36. Kf2
Bxf4 37. Ra1 Rc5 38. Be2 Bd2 39. Rb1 Bb4 40. Bf3
b5 41. Ke3 Bc3 42. Kd3 a4 43. Bd1 a3 44. Bb3 Be5
45. Ba2 Rc3+ 46. Kd2 Rg3 47. Kc2 Rxg2+ 48. Kb3
and White soon resigned. **0–1** *Washington Post*, 14 June 1942.

(794) FINE—LEWIS, H

Simultaneous Exhibition, Washington, 1942 (3 May)
English Opening, Classical Defence [A20]

1. c4 e5 2. Nf3 e4 3. Nd4 Nc6 4. Nc2 f5 5. g3 Bc5
6. Bg2 Nf6 7. 0–0 0–0 8. d3 Qe8 9. Nc3 a6 10. dxe4
fxe4 11. Nxe4 Be7 12. Nc3 d6 13. e4 Ne5 14. b3 c6
15. h3 Qg6 16. Ne3 Nh5 17. Kh2 Bxh3 18. Bxh3
Rxf2+ 19. Rxf2 Qxg3+ 20. Kh1 Qxf2 21. Qxh5
Nf3?! 22. Qxf3? Qxf3+ 23. Bg2 Qf2 24. Nf1 Bf6
25. Bd2 Bd4 **0–1** *Washington Post*, 17 May, 1942.

(795) EVANS, H—FINE

Washington, 1943
Queen's Gambit Accepted [D27]

1. d4 d5 2. c4 dxc4 3. e3 Nf6 4. Bxc4 e6
5. Nc3 c5 6. Nf3 a6 7. a4 Nc6 8. 0–0
Bc7 9. Qe2 cxd4 10. Rd1 d3 11. Bxd3
Qc7 12. e4 Ng4 13. h3 Nge5 14. Nxe5
Nxe5 15. Bf4 Bd6 16. Bb5+ Ke7
17. Rac1 Qb8 18. Rxd6 Qxd6 19. Rd1
Qb8 20. Nd5+ exd5 21. exd5 f6
22. d6+ Ke6 23. Bc4+ Kd7 24. Bxe5
fxe5 25. Qxe5 Re8 26. Qxg7+ Kc6
27. Bd5+ Kxd6 28. Bf7+ Ke7 29. Bg8
mate **1–0** Ultimate Games Collection III

(796) FINE—BARBALES, M

Simultaneous Exhibition, Guatemala, 1943 (4 Sept.)
King's Gambit Declined [C31]

1. e4 e5 2. f4 d5 3. exd5 Qxd5 4. Nc3
Qe6 5. Nf3 exf4+ 6. Kf2 Bd7 7. d4 Nf6
8. Bxf4 Ng4+ 9. Kg1 Bd6 10. Qd2 0–0
11. Bd3 Bxf4 12. Qxf4 Qe3+ 13. Qxe3
Nxe3 14. Re1 Nf5 15. Nd5 Nc6 16. c3
Rac8 17. Kf2 Be6 18. Nf4 Bd7 19. Re2
Rfe8 20. Rhe1 Kf8 21. Nd5 Nfe7 22. Nxe7 Rxe7
23. Rxe7 Nxe7 24. Ne5 Be6 25. Bxh7 Bxa2 26. Be4
Bd5 27. Nd7+ Kg8 28. Bh7+ Kxh7 29. Rxe7 Kg8
30. g4 Be6 31. g5 g6 32. d5 Bxd7 33. Rxd7 Kf8
34. d6 cxd6 35. Rxb7 Rc5 36. h4 a5 **½–½** Cohn 1947.

(797) FINE—BARBALES, M

Simultaneous Exhibition, Guatemala, 1943 (8 Sept.)
Queen's Gambit Declined [D37]

1. d4 Nf6 2. c4 e6 3. Nc3 d5 4. Nf3 Be7 5. g3
Nbd7 6. Bg2 c6 7. Qd3 0–0 8. 0–0 Re8 9. e4
dxe4 10. Nxe4 e5 11. dxe5 Nxe4 12. Qxe4 Bd6
13. Rd1 Bc7 14. Bf4 Qe7 15. Re1 Nc5 16. Qc2 Ne6
17. Be3 Nf8 18. Bd4 Bg4 19. h3 Bxf3 20. Bxf3
Qd7 21. Qe4 Qxh3 22. Bg4 Qh6 23. Kg2 Qg5
24. Bh3 Qe7 25. Bc3 Rad8 26. f4 a5 27. Bg4 b5
28. Redl b4 29. Bel c5 30. Bf2 f6 31. Qc6 fxe5
32. Bxc5 Qf7 33. Bxf8 Kxf8 34. Rd7 Re7 35. Rxd8+
Bxd8 36. fxe5 Rxe5 37. Qd6+ Qe7 38. Rf1+ Kg8
39. c5 h5 40. Bd1 Rxc5 41. Bb3+ Kh7 42. Qd3+
Kh8 43. Rf7 Qe8 44. Qf3 Bf6 45. Ra7 Qc6 46. Qxc6
Rxc6 47. Rxa5 Bxb2 **½–½** Cohn 1947.

(798) FINE—HIDALGO, E

Simultaneous Exhibition, Guatemala, 1943 (8 Sept.)
Sicilian Defence, Pin Variation [B40]

1. e4 c5 2. Nf3 e6 3. d4 cxd4 4. Nxd4 Nf6 5. Nc3
Bb4 6. e5 Ne4 7. Qg4 Nxc3 8. Qxg7 Rf8 9. a3 Nc6
10. axb4 Nxd4 11. bxc3 Nf5 12. Qf6 Qxf6 13. exf6
Rg8 14. h4 b6 15. Rh3 Bb7 16. f3 Rg3 17. Rxg3 Nxg3
18. Bd3 Nh5 19. Bg5 h6 20. Bxh6 Nxf6 21. Bd2

a5 22. Bb5 Bc6 23. Bxc6 dxc6 24. Rb1 Nd7 25. g4 f6 26. h5 a4 27. Ke2 Kf7 28. f4 f5 29. g5 b5 30. Be3 e5 31. g6+ Kf6 32. Rg1 Rg8 33. h6! 1–0 Cohn 1947.

(799) Fine—Vela, D

Simultaneous Exhibition, Guatemala, 1943 (8 Sept.)
Sicilian Defence [B45]

1. e4 c5 2. Nf3 Nc6 3. d4 cxd4 4. Nxd4 Nf6 5. Nc3 e6 6. Be2 a6 7. 0-0 Bc5 8. Nb3 Ba7 9. Bg5 h6 10. Bh4 b5 11. Kh1 g5 12. Bg3 e5 13. Bd3 h5 14. h4 Ng4 15. Nd5 gxh4 16. Bh2 Ne7 17. Qf3 Nxd5 18. exd5 d6 19. Nd2 Rh6 20. Bg1 f5 21. Qe2 Nf6 22. a4 Nxd5 23. f4 Bxg1 24. Kxg1 Qb6+ 25. Kh1 Qe3 26. fxe5 Qxe2 27. Bxe2 dxe5 28. axb5 Ne3 29. Rf2 Bb7 30. bxa6 h3 31. axb7 Rxa1+ 32. Kh2 Rb6 33. Nc4 Nxc4 34. Bxc4 hxg2 35. Rxg2 Rxb7 0–1 Cohn 1947.

(800) Fine—Hidalgo, E

Simultaneous Exhibition, Guatemala, 1943 (9 Sept.)
Sicilian Defence, Pin Variation [B40]

1. e4 c5 2. Nf3 e6 3. d4 cxd4 4. Nxd4 Nf6 5. Nc3 Bb4 6. e5 Ne4 7. Qg4 Nxc3 8. Qxg7 Rf8 9. a3 Nb5+ 10. axb4 Nxd4 11. Bd3 Nbc6 12. c3 Nf5 13. Bxf5 exf5 14. Bg5 Ne7 15. h4 Qb6 16. Qxh7 Qg6 17. Qxg6 fxg6 18. 0-0-0 b6 19. h5 gxh5 20. Rxh5 Ng6 21. Rh6 Rg8 22. f4 Bb7 23. Rh7 Bc6 24. Rd6 Rc8 25. Rxg6 Rxg6 26. Rh8+ Kf7 27. Rxc8 Bxg2 ½–½ Cohn 1947.

(801) Fine—NN

Simultaneous Exhibition, Guatemala, 1943 (11 Sept.)
Evans Gambit [C51]

1. e4 e5 2. Nf3 Nc6 3. Bc4 Bc5 4. b4 Bxb4 5. c3 Be7 6. d4 Bf6 7. 0-0 Nge7 8. dxe5 Nxe5 9. Nxe5 Bxe5 10. Qh5 Ng6 11. f4 Bf6 12. Ba3 d6 13. Rf3 0-0 14. Nd2 Nh4 15. Rg3 Be6 16. Rf1 Re8 17. e5 dxe5 18. fxe5 Ng6 19. Rd3 Bd7 20. exf6 gxf6 21. Bxf7+ Kxf7 22. Qxh7+ Ke6 23. Qxg6 1–0 *The Chess Correspondent*, November–December, 1943.

(802) Fine—NN

Simultaneous Exhibition, Guatemala, 1943 (11 Sept.)
Bird's Opening [A03]

1. f4 d5 2. Nf3 Nf6 3. e3 b6 4. d4 Ba6 5. Bxa6 Nxa6 6. c4 Nb8 7. cxd5 Qxd5 8. Nc3 Qb7 9. 0-0 e6 10. f5 exf5 11. Ne5 g6 12. e4 Bg7 13. exf5 Nbd7 14. Qb3 Rf8 15. Bg5 0-0-0 16. Rae1 Rde8 17. Nxd7 Kxd7 18. Rxe8 Nxe8 19. f6 Bh8 20. Bh6 1–0 *The Chess Correspondent*, November–December 1943.

(803) Fine—Vela

Simultaneous Exhibition, Guatemala, 1943 (Sept.)
English Defence [B00]

1. e4 b6 2. d4 Ba6 3. c4 c5 4. Nf3 g6 5. Nc3 Bg7 6. d5 Nh6 7. Bd3 0-0 8. 0-0 d6 9. Bf4 Nd7 10. Nd2 Bc8 11. Bg3 Ne5 12. Be2 f5 13. f4 Neg4 14. Qb3 Bd4+ 15. Kh1 Ne3 16. Rf3 fxe4 17. Ncxe4 Nhf5 18. Be1 e6 19. h3 exd5 20. cxd5 Bb7 21. g4 Bxd5 0–1 Fatbase 2000

(804) Fine—Vela, Rodriguez & Ruiz

Simultaneous Exhibition (blindfold), Guatemala, 1943 (7 Sept.)
Sicilian Defence [B45]

1. e4 c5 2. Nf3 Nc6 3. d4 cxd4 4. Nxd4 Nf6 5. Nc3 e6 6. Be2 Bc5 7. Ndb5 0-0 8. Bf4 Ne8 9. 0-0 a6 10. Nd6 e5? 11. Nxe8 Rxe8 12. Bg3 b5 13. a4 b4 14. Nd5 d6 15. Kh1 Ne7 16. Bc4 Bb7 17. f4 Nxd5 18. Bxd5 Bxd5 19. Qxd5 Qe7 20. f5 Qf6 21. Bf2! Rac8 22. Rad1 Red8 23. h3 h5? 24. Rd3 Kh7 25. Qb3 a5 26. c3 Rb8 27. Qd1 Qg5 28. f6 Rg8 29. Rg3 Qh6 30. Bxc5 dxc5 31. Rxg7+ Rxg7 32. fxg7 Kxg7 33. Qd5 Qe6 34. Qxc5 bxc3 35. bxc3 Rb2 36. Qxa5 f6 37. Qa7+ Kg6 38. Qe3 Ra2 39. Qg3+ Kf7 40. Qh4 Rxa4 41. Qxh5+ Kg7 42. Rf3 Rxe4 43. Rg3+ Kf8 44. Qh8+ Ke7 45. Qh7+ 1–0 Cohn 1947.

(805) Fine—Fox, A

Simultaneous Exhibition, Washington, 1943 (10 Nov.)
Grau Variation [D06]

1. d4 d5 2. c4 Bf5 3. Nc3 e6 4. Nf3 Nf6 5. Qb3 Nc6 6. c5 Qd7 7. Bf4 Be7 8. e3 a6 9. Be2 0-0 10. 0-0 Rab8 11. Qd1 Qc8 12. Rc1 Nh5 13. a3 Nxf4 14. exf4 Bf6 15. b4 Qd8 16. Qd2 Bg4 17. Ne5 Bxe2 18. Nxe2 Bxe5 19. fxe5 Ne7 20. f4 c6 21. g4 g6 22. Ng3 Kh8 23. Rc3 Rg8 24. Rcf3 Qf8 25. Kh1 Qh6 26. Qg2 Rbf8 27. Qf2 Qg7 28. f5 gxf5 29. gxf5 exf5 30. Nxf5 Nxf5 31. Rxf5 Qg6 32. Rg1 Qxg1+ 33. Qxg1 Rxg1+ 34. Kxg1 Kg7 35. Rf6 Re8 36. Rd6 Re7 37. Kf2 Kf8 38. Kf3 Re6 39. Rd8+ Re8 40. Rxe8+ Kxe8 41. Kg4 Kf8 42. Kg5 Kg7 43. h3 Kf8 44. Kf6 h6 45. h4 Ke8 46. Kg7 Ke7 47. Kxh6 f6 48. exf6+ Kxf6 49. h5 Kf7 50. Kg5 Kg7 51. h6+ Kh7 52. Kh5 Kg8 53. Kg6 Kh8 54. h7 1–0 *ACB* November–December 1943 (Lahde)

(806) Fine—Hesse, C

Washington simul, 1943 (10 Nov.)
Queen's Gambit Declined [D51]

1. d4 Nf6 2. c4 e6 3. Nc3 d5 4. Bg5 Nbd7 5. e4!?

dxe4 6. Nxe4 Bb4+ 7. Nc3 c5 8. Nf3 Bxc3+
9. bxc3 b6 10. Bd3 Bb7 11. 0–0 0–0 12. Ne5 cxd4
13. cxd4 Qc7 14. Bf4 Qc8 15. Qe2 Rd8 16. Rad1
Nf8 17. Bc1 Ng6 18. f4 Rb8 19. f5 exf5 20. Bxf5
Qc7 21. Nxf7 Re8 22. Be6 Rxe6 23. Nh6+ Kh8
24. Qxe6 Re8 25. Qh3 Qxc4 26. Nf5 Ne4
27. Nxg7 Kxg7 28. Bh6+ Kh8 29. Qd7 Re7
30. Rf8+ Nxf8 31. Qxe7 Qg8 32. Qe5+1–0 *ACB*
November-December 1943 (Lahde).

(807) FINE—LONG, N

Simultaneous Exhibition, Washington, 1943 (10 Nov.)
Evans Gambit [C52]

1. e4 e5 2. Nf3 Nc6 3. Bc4 Bc5 4. b4 Bxb4 5. c3
Ba5 6. d4 d6 7. Qb3 Qe7 8. d5 Nd4 9. Nxd4 exd4
10. Qa4+ Bd7 11. Qxa5 Qxe4+ 12. Kd1 Bg4+ 13. f3
Bxf3+ 14. gxf3 Qxf3+ 15. Kc2 Qxh1 16. Qxc7 Qe4+
17. Kb3 Qe7 18. Qxe7+ Nxe7 19. Bf4 0–0–0 20. cxd4
a6 21. Nc3 Nf5 22. Bd3 Nxd4+ 23. Kc4 Nb5
24. Nxb5 axb5+ 25. Kxb5 Rhe8 26. Rf1 g6 27. Kb6
1–0 *ACB* November-December 1943 (Lahde).

(808) FINE—SHAPIRO, O

Simultaneous Exhibition, Washington, 1943 (10 Nov.)
Nimzowitsch-Indian Defence, Rubinstein Variation [E42]

1. d4 Nf6 2. c4 e6 3. Nc3 Bb4 4. e3 c5 5. Nge2
d6 6. a3 Bxc3+ 7. Nxc3 0–0 8. g3 Nc6 9. Bg2
Na5 10. b3 Rb8 11. 0–0 a6 12. d5 b5 13. cxb5
axb5 14. b4 cxb4 15. axb4 Nc4 16. e4 e5
17. Qd3 Qb6 18. Bg5 Nd7 19. Rfc1 h6 20. Bd2
Qd4 21. Qxd4 exd4 22. Nxb5 Nxd2 23. Nxd4
Rxb4 24. Nc6 Rc4 25. Ne7+ Kh7 26. Nf5 Ne5
27. Nxd6 Rxc1+ 28. Rxc1 Bg4 29. f4 Ndf3+
30. Kh1 Nd3 31. Rf1 Rb8 32. Bxf3 Bxf3+
33. Rxf3 Rb1+ 34. Kg2 Ne1+ 35. Kf2 Nxf3
36. Kxf3 Rb3+ 37. Kg4 Kg8 38. Nf5 Rd3 39. d6
Kf8 40. e5 Kg8 41. Ne7+ Kf8 42. Kf5 Rd2 43. h4
Rd3 44. g4 Rd4 45. h5 Rd1 46. Ke4 Ke8 47. Nf5
Rf1 48. Kd5 Rd1+ 49. Nd4 1–0 *ACB* November-
December 1943 (Lahde).

(809) FINE—STARK, M

Simultaneous Exhibition, Washington, 1943 (10 Nov.)
King's Fianchetto Opening [A45]

1. d4 Nf6 2. g3 g6 3. Bg2 d5 4. Nh3 Bg7 5. 0–0
0–0 6. Nf4 c6 7. Nd2 e5 8. dxe5 Ng4 9. e6
fxe6 10. e4 e5 11. Nd3 Qd6 12. b3 d4 13. a4 c5
14. Ba3 Na6 15. h3 Nh6 16. f4 Be6 17. g4 exf4
18. e5 Qe7 19. Nxf4 Rae8 20. Qe2 Bc8 21. Nc4
Nc7 22. Nd6 Bxe5 23. Nxe8 d3 24. Qxd3 Bxa1
25. Nxc7 Bd4+ 26. Qxd4 1–0 *ACB* November-
December 1943 (Lahde).

(810) FINE—HURVITZ, J

Simultaneous exhibition, Washington, 1943
Sicilian Defence [B40]

1. e4 c5 2. Nf3 e6 3. d4 d5 4. exd5 exd5 5. Bb5+
Bd7 6. Bxd7+ Nxd7 7. 0–0 Ngf6 8. Re1+ Be7
9. dxc5 Nxc5 10. Nd4 0–0 11. Nc3 Nce4 12. Nce2
Re8 13. f3 Nd6 14. Bf4 Rc8 15. c3 Qb6 16. Qc2
Nc4 17. b3 Na3 18. Qd2 Bc5 19. Kh1 Bxd4 20. Nxd4
Nb5 21. Nxb5 Qxb5 22. Be3 Qc6 23. Bd4 a6
24. Qf4 Nd7 25. Qg3 f6 26. h4 Re6 27. Rxe6
Qxe6 28. Re1 Qf7 29. h5 Qxh5+ 30. Kg1 Re8
31. Rxe8+ Qxe8 32. Qc7 Qe1+ 33. Kh2 Qh4+
½–½ *Christian Science Monitor*, 8 January 1944.

(811) FOX, A—FINE & HELMS

1944
Spanish Opening, Caro Variation [C70]

1. e4 e5 2. Nf3 Nc6 3. Bb5 a6 4. Ba4 Bc5 5. c3
Nf6 6. d3 b5 7. Bb3 d5 8. Qe2 0–0 9. Bg5 dxe4
10. dxe4 h6 11. Bh4 Qe7 12. Nbd2 Be6 13. 0–0 g5
14. Bg3 Nh5 15. Bd5 Bd7 16. Rfe1 Rae8 17. Nf1 Nf4
18. Qc2 Nd8 19. Rad1 Kg7 20. Bb3 Nb7 21. Nxe5
Qxe5 22. Rxd7 Bd6 23. Ne3 Nc5 24. Ng4 Qf5
25. Rxd6 cxd6 26. f3 Qg6 27. Ne3 Kh7 28. Rd1
Re5 29. Nf5 Rd8 30. Qd2 Nxb3 31. axb3 Rxf5
32. exf5 Qxf5 33. Bxf4 gxf4 34. Qd3 Kg6 35. Qxf5+
Kxf5 36. Rd5+ Ke6 37. Rd4 Kf5 ½–½ *Christian Science
Monitor*, 11 March, 1944. (No actual date or circumstance
given)

(812) FINE—EVANS, H

Washington, 1944
Queen's Gambit Declined, Cambridge Springs Defence [D52]

1. d4 d5 2. c4 e6 3. Nc3 Nf6 4. Bg5 Nbd7 5. e3
c6 6. Nf3 Qa5 7. Nd2 Bb4 8. Qc2 0–0 9. Be2 e5
10. dxe5 Ne4 11. Ndxe4 dxe4 12. 0–0 Bxc3 13. bxc3
Nxe5 14. Bf4 Re8 15. Qxe4 Bf5 0–1 Ultimate Games
Collection III

(813) FINE—LILLING, W

Simultaneous Exhibition, New York, 1944
Nimzowitsch-Indian Defence [E58]

1. d4 Nf6 2. c4 e6 3. Nc3 Bb4 4. e3 d5 5. Nf3 c5
6. Bd3 Nc6 7. 0–0 0–0 8. a3 Bxc3 9. bxc3 b6
10. Ne5 Bb7 11. f4 Na5 12. cxd5 Qxd5 13. Qe2 c4
14. Bc2 Ne4 15. Bb2 g6 16. Nf3 Qh5 17. Rad1 b5
18. Qe1 Qg4 19. h3 Qg3 20. Qxg3 Nxg3 21. Rfe1 Ne4
22. Nd2 Nxd2 23. Rxd2 f5 24. e4 fxe4 25. Rf2 e3
26. Rxe3 Bd5 27. g3 Rf7 28. Rfe2 Rd8 29. Kh2
Nc6 30. Bc1 a5 31. Bd2 Rb8 32. Rf2 b4 33. axb4
axb4 34. cxb4 Nxb4 35. Bxb4 Rxb4 36. g4 Rfb7

37. Kg3 Kg7 38. Rc3 Rb2 39. Re2 ½–½ *Brooklyn Daily Eagle*, 2 March, 1944

(814) FINE—DALY, H

Simultaneous Exhibition, City Club Boston, 1944 (22 Feb.)
Sicilian Dragon [B70]

1. e4 c5 2. Nf3 Nc6 3. d4 cxd4 4. Nxd4 Nf6 5. Nc3
d6 6. Be2 g6 7. 0–0 Bg7 8. Nb3 0–0 9. f4 a5
10. Be3 a4 11. Nd4 Ng4 12. Bxg4 Bxd4 13. Bxd4
Bxg4 14. Qd2 Be6 15. Be3 Qa5 16. Qf2 Bc4 17. Rfd1
a3 18. Bc1 axb2 19. Bxb2 Rfd8 20. Nd5 Qc5 21. Qxc5
dxc5 22. Nb6 Rxd1+ 23. Rxd1 Be2 24. Ra1 Rd8
25. Bc3 f6 26. Kf2 Bg4 27. f5 gxf5 28. h3 Bd1
29. exf5 Bxc2 30. g4 Rd3 31. Be1 Rxh3 32. Rc1
Be4 33. Rxc5 Ne5 34. Rc7 Nxg4+ 35. Ke2 Rh2+
36. Kd1 Ne3+ 37. Kc1 Rc2+ 38. Rxc2 Nxc2 39. Bf2
Nb4 40. Kd2 Bxf5 0–1 Lyman and Dann, 32–3.

(815) KLEIN, H—FINE

Blindfold rapid transit, 1944 (Aug./Sept.)
King's Indian Defence [E90]

1. d4 Nf6 2. Nf3 g6 3. c4 Bg7 4. Nc3 0–0 5. e4 d6
6. h3 Nbd7 7. Be3 e5 8. d5 Ne8 9. Bd3 Nc5
10. Bxc5 dxc5 11. Rc1 Nd6 12. Qc2 f5 13. 0–0 a6
14. Rce1 f4 15. Qd1 Qf6 16. a4 Bd7 17. b3 g5
18. Nh2 Qg6 19. f3 h5 20. Kh1 Rf6 21. Rg1 Qh6
22. Ne2 g4 23. fxg4 hxg4 24. Rgf1 Rf7 25. Kg1
Kh8 26. Nxg4 Bxg4 27. hxg4 Bf6 28. Nc3 Bh4
29. Re2 Bg3 30. Rf3 (Presumably Fine now announced
mate. AW) 0–1 *Los Angeles Times*, 22 October, 1944 (Lahde);
Christian Science Monitor, 23 September, 1944 (O'Keefe).

(816) FINE—KNAPP

Simultaneous blindfold exhibition, Richmond, VA (1), 1945
    (7 Jan.)
English Opening, Classical Variation [A22]

1. c4 e5 2. Nc3 Nf6 3. g3 Bc5 4. Bg2 Nc6 5. e3
d6 6. Nge2 0–0 7. 0–0 Bg4 8. h3 Bf5 9. d4 exd4
10. exd4 Bb6 11. g4 Bc8 12. Bg5 h6 13. Bh4 g5
14. Bg3 Nh7 15. Nd5 Ne7 16. Nec3 Nxd5 17. Nxd5
c6 18. Nxb6 axb6 19. Qb3 Kg7 20. Rad1 Nf6 21. f4
Re8 22. fxg5 hxg5 23. Rd2 Ne4 24. Bxe4 Rxe4
25. Qf3 f5 26. gxf5 d5 27. f6+ Kg6 28. f7 Qf8
29. Qf6+ Kh7 30. Bd6 Re6 31. Bxf8 Rxf6 32. Rxf6
1–0 *Reuben Fine in Richmond (01/07/1945)* from "More Early
History of Virginia Chess" (Internet)

(817) FINE—SCOTT

Simultaneous blindfold exhibition, Richmond, VA (2), 1945
    (7 Jan.)
Schlechter/Gruenfeld [D81]

1. d4 Nf6 2. c4 g6 3. Nc3 d5 4. Qb3 c6 5. Bf4
Bg7 6. e3 Qa5 7. Nf3 0–0 8. Nd2 Nbd7 9. Be2
Qb6 10. Qc2 Re8 11. Nf3 Qd8 12. cxd5 cxd5
13. 0–0 a6 14. Ne5 Nb6 15. Rac1 Be6 16. Qb3 Rc8
17. a4 Nc4 18. Nxc4 dxc4 19. Qxb7 Qa5 20. Bf3
Bd7 21. b4 cxb3 22. Qxb3 e6 23. Rc2 Bc6
24. Bxc6 Rxc6 25. Ne4 Rxc2 26. Nxf6+ Bxf6
27. Qxc2 e5 28. dxe5 Bxe5 29. Bxe5 Qxe5 30. g3
Rb8 31. Rb1 Rd8 32. Qc4 Qd6 33. Rb7 Qf6
34. Kg2 Rd2 35. Qf4 Qe6 36. Rb4 Qc6+ 37. Qf3
Qc7 38. Qe4 Qd7? 39. Rb7 Qd5 40. Qxd5 Rxd5
41. Rb6 Ra5 42. Rb4 f5? 43. Kf3 g5 44. g4 Kg7
45. Kg3 Kg6? 46. Rb6+ Kg7 47. gxf5 h5?
48. Rg6+ Kf7 49. Rxg5 h4+ 50. Kxh4 Rxa4+
51. Kg3 Kf6 52. h4 a5 53. f3 Rb4 54. e4 a4
55. Kf4 a3 56. Rg6+ Kf7 57. Ra6 Rb3 58. Ra7+
Kg8 59. e5 Rb4+ 60. Kg5 Rb3 61. Kg6 Kf8 62. f6
Ke8 63. e6 Kd8 64. e7+ 1–0 *Reuben Fine in Richmond
(01/07/1945)* from "More Early History of Virginia Chess"

(818) FINE—PECK

Simultaneous blindfold exhibition, Richmond, VA (3), 1945
    (7 Jan.)
Nimzowitsch Defence [B00]

1. e4 Nc6 2. d4 d5 3. e5 Bf5 4. c3 f6 5. f4 e6
6. Bd3 Nh6 7. Nf3 Be7 8. Bxf5 Nxf5 9. g4 Nh6
10. exf6 gxf6 11. f5 Bf8 12. Qe2 Qe7 13. fxe6 Nxg4
14. Nh4 Bh6 15. Nf5 Qf8 16. Bxh6 Nxh6 17. Qh5+
Nf7 18. exf7+ Qxf7 19. Qxf7+ Kxf7 20. Nd2 Rae8+
21. Kf2 Kg6 22. Ne3 Ne7 23. Rae1 c6 24. Nf3 Kf7
25. Ng2 Rhg8 26. Ngh4 b6 27. Re2 Rd8 28. Rhe1
Rd7 29. Rg1 Rxg1 30. Kxg1 Rd6 31. Nd2 Rd7 32. Nf1
Rd8 33. Ng3 Rg8 34. Kf2 Rg4 35. Ng2 Rg5 36. Re1
Rg4 37. Rg1 Kg6 38. Ne3 Rg5 39. h4 Rxg3 40. Rxg3+
Kf7 41. Rf3 h5 42. Kg3 Kg6 43. Kf4 Kf7 44. Nf5
Ng6+ 45. Kg3 Nf8 46. b3 Ng6 47. c4 Nf8 48. cxd5
1–0 *Reuben Fine in Richmond (01/07/1945)* from "More Early
History of Virginia Chess"

(819) FINE—LINFIELD

Simultaneous blindfold exhibition, Richmond, VA (4), 1945
    (7 Jan.)
Bird's Opening [A03]

1. f4 d5 2. Nf3 Nf6 3. e3 e6 4. Bd3 Bd6 5. b3 0–0
6. Bb2 Nc6 7. 0–0 Bd7 8. Ne5 Ne7 9. Nc3 Ng6
10. Ne2 c5 11. Ng3 Qc7 12. Nxd7 Nxd7 13. Nh5 e5
14. Qg4 exf4 15. exf4 d4 16. Rf3 Kh8 17. Rh3 Rfe8
18. Rf1 Re7 19. c3 Rae8 20. Qd1 Nxf4 21. Nxf4
Bxf4 22. Rxh7+ Kg8 23. Qh5 Bh6 24. Rxh6 gxh6
25. Qxh6 f6 26. Bc4+ Re6 27. Rf3 Kf7 28. Rg3
Ke7 29. Bxe6 Kxe6 30. cxd4 cxd4 31. Qg6 Re7
32. Qg4+ Kf7 33. Qg8 mate 1–0 *Reuben Fine in Richmond (01/07/1945)* from "More Early History of Virginia
Chess"

(820) FINE—LEVY

Simultaneous blindfold exhibition, Richmond, VA (5), 1945 (7 Jan.)
Sicilian Defence [A36]

1. c4 e6 2. e4 c5 3. Nc3 Nc6 4. g3 g6 5. Bg2 Bg7 6. Nge2 Nge7 7. 0–0 0–0 8. d3 d6 9. Be3 b6 10. d4 cxd4 11. Nxd4 Nxd4 12. Bxd4 Bb7 13. Bxg7 Kxg7 14. Qd4+ e5 15. Qd2 Qd7 16. Rad1 Rad8 17. f4 Qc7 18. f5 f6 19. b3 gxf5 20. exf5 Qc5+ 21. Kh1 Bxg2+ 22. Qxg2 a6 23. Nd5 Nxd5 24. Rxd5 Qc7 25. Rfd1 Rf7 26. g4 h6 27. R5d3 Kh7 28. Qd2 b5 29. Rh3 Kg8 30. Qxh6 Rh7 31. Qxh7+ Qxh7 32. Rxh7 Kxh7 33. c5 Kg7 34. cxd6 Kf7 35. d7 Ke7 36. h4 Rxd7 37. Rxd7+ Kxd7 38. g5 fxg5 39. hxg5 Kd6 40. Kg2 e4 41. g6 Ke7 42. g7 Kf7 43. f6 a5 44. Kf2 Kg8 45. Ke3 Kf7 46. Kxe4 1–0 *Reuben Fine in Richmond (01/07/1945) from "More Early History of Virginia Chess"*

(821) FINE—MICHIE

Simultaneous blindfold exhibition, Richmond, VA (6), 1945 (7 Jan.)
Albin Counter-Gambit, Alapin Variation [D08]

1. d4 d5 2. c4 e5 3. dxe5 d4 4. Nf3 Nc6 5. Nbd2 f6 6. exf6 Qxf6 7. g3 Bf5 8. Bg2 Bb4 9. 0–0 Nge7 10. Nb3 0–0–0 11. a3 Bd6 12. Bg5 Qg6 13. Nbxd4 Nxd4 14. Qxd4 Nc6 15. Qc3 Rde8 16. Be3 Bg4 17. Rad1 a6 18. b4 Qf7 19. b5 axb5 20. cxb5 Be5 21. Nxe5 Nxe5 22. Qa5 c6 23. Qa8+ 1–0 *Reuben Fine in Richmond (01/07/1945) from "More Early History of Virginia Chess"*

(822) FINE—KAFKO

Simultaneous blindfold exhibition, Richmond, VA (7), 1945 (7 Jan.)
Spanish Opening, Steinitz Defence Deferred [C73]

1. e4 e5 2. Nf3 Nc6 3. Bb5 a6 4. Ba4 Nf6 5. 0–0 d6 6. Bxc6+ bxc6 7. d4 Bg4 8. dxe5 Bxf3 9. Qxf3 dxe5 10. Bg5 Be7 11. Nd2 h6 12. Be3 Qd7 13. Rad1 Qe6 14. b3 Nd7 15. Nc4 0–0 16. Qe2 Rad8 17. f3 f5 18. exf5 Rxf5 19. Bf2 c5 20. Bg3 h5 21. Rfe1 Bf6 22. Ne3 Rg5 23. Qc4 Qxc4 24. Nxc4 Kf8 25. Re2 Ke8 26. Red2 Rf5 27. Ne3 Rg5 28. Nd5 Rc8 29. f4 Rg6 30. fxe5 Bg5 31. Bf4 Nxe5 32. Re2 Bxf4 33. Nxf4 Rd6 34. Rxe5+ Kd7 35. Rde1 Rf8 36. Nd3 1–0 *Reuben Fine in Richmond (01/07/1945) from "More Early History of Virginia Chess"*

(823) FINE—CLEEK

Simultaneous blindfold exhibition, Richmond, VA (8), 1945 (7 Jan.)

Bird's Opening [A03]

1. f4 Nf6 2. g3 d5 3. Bg2 Bf5 4. Nf3 e6 5. 0–0 Nbd7 6. b3 Bd6 7. Bb2 c6 8. d3 0–0 9. e3 Re8 10. Nbd2 e5 11. fxe5 Nxe5 12. Nxe5 Bxe5 13. Bxe5 Rxe5 14. d4 Bg4 15. Qe1 Re7 16. Qf2 Qd6 17. Rae1 Bd7 18. h3 Ne4 19. Nxe4 dxe4 20. Qf4 Qxf4 21. gxf4 f5 22. Kf2 h6 23. h4 Be6 24. Rg1 Bf7 25. Bh3 Be6 26. Rg3 Kh7 27. Reg1 Rg8 28. Rg6 Bf7 29. R6g3 g6 30. h5 Re6 31. hxg6+ Bxg6 32. Rxg6 Rge8 33. Rxe6 1–0 *Reuben Fine in Richmond (01/07/1945) from "More Early History of Virginia Chess"*

(824) FINE—SHERMAN

Simultaneous blindfold exhibition, Richmond, VA (9), 1945 (7 Jan.)
Queen's Pawn Game [A45]

1. d4 Nf6 2. e3 d5 3. Bd3 Bg4 4. Ne2 e6 5. c4 Bd6 6. Qb3 b6 7. Nbc3 dxc4 8. Bxc4 Bxe2 9. Bxe2 0–0 10. e4 e5 11. d5 a6 12. 0–0 Nbd7 13. Be3 Nc5 14. Qc2 Ne8 15. g3 Qc8 16. Kg2 f5 17. exf5 Qxf5 18. Qxf5 Rxf5 19. b4 Nd7 20. a3 Rf7 21. Bg4 Nf8 22. Ne4 Be7 23. Rac1 Nf6 24. Nxf6+ Bxf6 25. Rc6 e4 26. Re1 Rd8 27. Be6 Nxe6 28. dxe6 Re7 29. Bf4 Rd3 30. Rxe4 Rc3 31. Rxc3 Bxc3 32. Bxc7 b5 33. Bd6 Re8 34. Re2 Bf6 35. f4 g6 36. Bc5 Kg7 37. Kf3 Be7 38. Bxe7 Rxe7 39. g4 h6 40. h4 Kf6 41. g5+ hxg5 42. hxg5+ Kg7 43. Kg4 Kf8 44. f5 gxf5+ 45. Kxf5 Kg7 46. g6 Kg8 47. Kf6 Kf8 48. Rh2 1–0 *Reuben Fine in Richmond (01/07/1945) from "More Early History of Virginia Chess"*

(825) FINE—HARRINGTON

Simultaneous blindfold exhibition, Richmond, VA (10), 1945 (7 Jan.)
Bishop's Opening [C24]

1. e4 e5 2. Bc4 Nf6 3. d3 Nc6 4. f4 d5 5. exd5 Nxd5 6. fxe5 Nxe5 7. Qe2 Bb4+ 8. Kf1 Qf6+ 9. Nf3 Bg4 10. Qxe5+ Qxe5 11. Nxe5 Be6 12. c3 Bd6 13. Nf3 0–0–0 14. Kf2 Bf4 15. Bxd5 Bxc1 16. Bxe6+ fxe6 17. Rxc1 Rxd3 18. Nbd2 Rf8 19. Nf1 g5 20. Ke2 Rd5 21. Ne3 1–0 *Reuben Fine in Richmond (01/07/1945) from "More Early History of Virginia Chess"*

(826) FINE—STARK

Washington Chess Divan, 1945 (13 Jan.)
Slav Defence [D15]

1. d4 d5 2. c4 c6 3. Nc3 Nf6 4. Nf3 dxc4 5. e3 b5 6. a4 b4 7. Nb1 e6 8. Bxc4 Nbd7 9. 0–0 Bb7 10. Qe2 c5 11. Rd1 Qc7 12. Nbd2 Be7 13. a5 0–0 14. Bd3 Rfd8 15. Nc4 Ng4 16. h3 Ngf6 17. Bd2

Be4 18. Rac1 Qb7 19. Bxe4 Nxe4 20. Be1 Qa6 21. Qc2 Ndf6 22. Nfe5 cxd4 23. exd4 Rdc8 24. Qa4 Nd5 25. Qb3 Nef6 26. Rc2 Rc7 27. Rdc1 Rac8 28. Qd3 h6 29. b3 Qb5? 30. Nxf7 Nf4 31. Qf3 Nxh3+ 32. Qxh3 Kxf7 33. Ne5+ 1−0 *The Chess Review*, February 1945, 21 (Lahde).

(827) Jackson—Fine

Manhattan Chess Club, Blindfold, 1945
Alekhine's Defence [B04]

1. e4 Nf6 2. e5 Nd5 3. d4 d6 4. c4 Nb6 5. Nf3 Nc6 6. e6 fxe6 7. Be3 d5 8. c5 Nd7 9. Ng5 Nf6 10. Bd3 e5 11. Nxh7 e4 12. Nxf6+ exf6 13. Be2 Be6 14. Nc3 Qd7 15. Bh5+ Bf7 16. Bxf7+ Qxf7 17. Qb3 0−0−0 18. Nb5 a6 19. a4 g5 20. Qc3 Be7 21. b4 f5 22. Nxc7 Kxc7 23. b5 f4 24. bxc6 fxe3 25. Qa5+ Kxc6 26. Qb6+ Kd7 27. fxe3 Qe6 28. Qxb7+ Ke8 29. Rb1 g4 30. Rb6 Qc8 31. Qa7 Rd7 32. Qxa6 Qxa6 33. Rxa6 Rb7 34. 0−0 Bd8 35. Re6+ Re7 36. Rg6 Rf8 37. Rxf8+ Kxf8 38. Rxg4 Ba5 39. Rf4+ Rf7 40. Rxf7+ Kxf7 41. Kf2 Kf6 ½−½ *The Chess Review*, February 1945 (Lahde).

(828) Fine—Helms, H

Blindfold Rapid Transit, New York, 1945
King's Indian Defence [E72]

1. d4 Nf6 2. c4 g6 3. Nc3 Bg7 4. e4 d6 5. g3 0−0 6. Bg2 e5 7. Nge2 Bg4 To block the diagonal of White's king's bishop. 8. f3 Be6 9. b3 c6 10. 0−0 Qc7 10 ... exd5 and 11 ... d5 was interesting. 11. d5 Bd7 12. Be3 Too routine. 12 dxc6 and 13 Ba3 was more aggressive. 12 ... c5 13. Qd2 a6 14. a4 To prevent ... b5, although Black has the option of blocking the queenside completely with ... a5. 14 ... b6 15. h3 Ra7 16. Bh6 Re8 17. g4 Bc8 18. Ng3 Nbd7 White has all the play. Eventually the kingside attack must break through, but as long as Black defers ... a5 there is always the possibility of play on the queenside. 19. Kh2 Nf8 20. Rg1 Qe7 21. Bf1 There is plenty of time for Nf5. 21 ... N8d7 22. Bxg7 Otherwise 22 ... Qf8 forces the exchange under less favourable circumstances. 22 ... Kxg7 23. Bd3 Ng8 24. Rg2 Kh8 25. Qe3 Nf8 26. a5! The simplest—and simplicity is a virtue in rapid transit blindfold. 26 ... bxa5 27. Rga2 Qb7 28. Rxa5 Qxb3 Loses the exchange, but he probably felt that the position was untenable in the long run. 29. Nb5 axb5 If 29 ... Rb7 30 Rb1 wins the queen. 30. Rxa7 bxc4 31. R7a3 Saves the bishop and leads to an easy ending. 31 ... Qb2+ 32. Qe2 c3 33. Qxb2 cxb2 34. Rb1 Bd7 35. Rxb2 Rc8 36. Rb6 c4 37. Bc2 Kg7 38. Rxd6 c3 39. Ne2 f5 40. gxf5 gxf5 41. exf5 Nf6 42. Rxc3 Ra8 43. Ng3 Ra2 44. Kg1 Bb5 45. Rc7+ N8d7 46. Ne4 Nxe4 47. Bxe4 1−0 Fine 1948, 54−7.

(829) Fine—Helms, H

New York, 1945
Spanish Opening, Marshall Gambit [C83]

1. e4 e5 2. Nf3 Nc6 3. Bb5 a6 4. Ba4 Nf6 5. 0−0 Nxe4 6. d4 b5 7. Bb3 d5 8. dxe5 Be6 9. c3 Be7 10. Nbd2 Nxd2 11. Qxd2 Na5 12. Bc2 Nc4 13. Qf4 c5 14. a4 0−0 15. Qg3 Re8 16. b3 Nb6 17. Bh6 g6 18. Ng5 Nd7 19. Nxe6 fxe6 20. Bxg6 Nf8 21. Bf7+ Kxf7 22. Qg7 mate 1−0 *The Chess Review*, April 1945, 28.

(830) Shipman, W—Fine

Blindfold rapid transit, New York, 1945
Nimzowitsch-Indian Defence, Rubinstein Variation [E43]

1. d4 Nf6 2. c4 e6 3. Nc3 Bb4 4. e3 b6 5. Bd3 Bb7 6. Nf3 Ne4 7. 0−0 Probably hoping for a repetition of may game with Denker in the last championship. I was sorely tempted to oblige. 7 ... Bxc3 8. bxc3 0−0 9. Qc2 f5 10. Ba3 d6 Black now has a little the better of it. 11. Nd2 Nxd2 12. Qxd2 Nd7 13. f3 Qe7 14. e4 fxe4 15. fxe4 e5 The counterplay is directed against the e-pawn. 16. Qe3 Rxf1+ 17. Rxf1 Rf8 Heading for the endgame, where Black's advantage is clearest. 18. Rxf8+ Qxf8

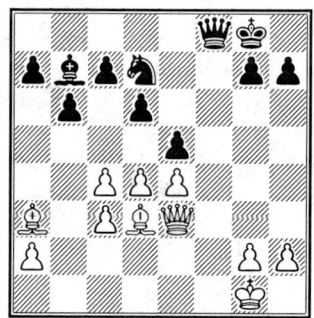

Position after Black's 18th move

19. Qf3 The exchange of queens was exactly what I had been hoping for. 19 Qh3 was preferable; 19 c5 was an interesting possibility. 19 ... c5 20. Qxf8+ Nxf8 21. Bb2 Ne6 22. d5 Nf4 23. Bc2 Ba6 24. Bb3 Kf7 25. h3 Violation of principle. The weakening of the kingside pawns facilitates the later entry of Black's king. 25 ... Ng6 26. Bc1 Kf6 27. g3 It would have been best to leave the pawns alone. 27 ... Nh8 28. Kg2 Nf7 29. Kf3 Nd8 30. Be3 Nb7 31. Ke2 Na5 32. Kd3 The position I had in mind. Now that White's pieces are tied up on the queenside, the next step is to break through with the king. 32 ... Bc8 33. g4 Better 33 h4. 33 ... h6 Necessary to keep White's dark-squared bishop out. 34. Ke2 34 Ba4 was more aggressive. 34 ... Kg6 35. Kd3 h5 36. Bd1 On 36 gxh5+ Kxh5 the position is hopeless. 36 ... hxg4 37. hxg4 If 37 Bxg4 Ba6. 37 ... Ba6 38. Bb3 Kf6 39. Bc1 Kg6 40. Be3 Kf6 41. Bc1 Nxb3 After which Black wins because the bishops are of opposite colours. 42. axb3 Bc8 43. g5+ The trouble is he cannot afford to give up the g-pawn because

the queenside pawns always remain exposed. **43 ... Kg6
44. Be3 Bg4** To keep White's king in place. **45. Bc1 Kh5
46. Be3 Bd1 47. b4 Kg4 48. Bc1 g6** To keep White's
bishop in place. The rest is dessert. **49. bxc5 bxc5 50. Be3
Kf3 51. Bc1 Be2+ 52. Kd2 Bxc4 0–1** Fine 1948, 58–60.

(831) COLON, M—FINE

Blindfold simultaneous (2-board), New York, 1945
Grunfeld Defence [D93]

1. d4 Nf6 2. c4 g6 3. Nc3 d5 4. Nf3 Bg7 5. Bf4
0–0 6. e3 c5 7. Be2 cxd4 8. exd4 dxc4 9. Bxc4
Nbd7 10. 0–0 Nb6 11. Bb3 Bf5 12. Rc1 a6 13. Qe2
Rc8 14. Rfd1 e6 15. Be5 Nfd5 16. h3 h5 17. Nh4
Qxh4 18. Bxg7 Kxg7 19. Nxd5 exd5 20. Qe5+ Qf6
21. Qe3 Nc4 22. Qc3 b5 23. a3 Rcd8 24. Bxc4
dxc4 25. Qa5 Rxd4 26. Rxd4 Qxd4 27. Qxa6 Qxb2
28. Re1 c3 29. Qc6 c2 30. Kh2 Rc8 0–1 *The Chess
Review*, April 1945 28.

(832) SIMON, E—FINE

Blindfold simultaneous (8-board), New York (1), 1945
Colle System [D04]

1. Nf3 d5 2. d4 c5 3. e3 Nf6 4. c3 Nbd7 5. Bd3
g6 6. Nbd2 Bg7 7. 0–0 0–0 8. e4 cxd4 9. cxd4
dxe4 10. Nxe4 Nxe4 11. Bxe4 Nf6 12. Re1 Nxe4
13. Rxe4 Bf5 14. Re1 Rc8 15. Be3 Qd5 16. b3 Bg4
17. Qe2 Rfd8 18. h3 Bxf3 19. gxf3 Qf5 20. Rac1
Qxh3 21. Rxc8 Rxc8 22. Rc1 Rxc1+ 23. Bxc1 Bxd4
24. Be3 Bxe3 25. fxe3 Qg3+ 26. Kf1 h5 27. Qg2
Qxg2+ 28. Kxg2 g5 29. Kg3 Kg7 30. e4 Kf6 31. f4
gxf4+ 32. Kxf4 e5+ 33. Kg3 Kg5 0–1 *The Chess
Review*, April 1945.

(833) FINE—RUBERL, C

Blindfold simultaneous (8-board), New York (2), 1945
Grünfeld Defence [D93]

1. d4 Nf6 2. c4 g6 3. Nc3 d5 4. Bf4 Bg7 5. e3 c6
6. Nf3 0–0 7. Rc1 Nh5 8. Be5 f6 9. Bxb8 Rxb8
10. cxd5 cxd5 11. Nxd5 Qxd5 12. Bc4 e6 13. Bxd5
exd5 14. 0–0 Bh6 15. Rc7 Ng7 16. Qb3 Be6 17. Rfc1
Nf5 18. Rxb7 Rxb7 19. Qxb7 Bg7 20. Rc7 Bf7
21. Qxa7 g5 22. h3 h5 23. g4 hxg4 24. hxg4 Nd6
25. a4 Ne4 26. a5 Kh7 27. Rxf7 1–0

(834) SIMONE, P—FINE

Blindfold simultaneous (8-board), New York (3), 1945
Réti Opening [A09]

1. Nf3 d5 2. c4 dxc4 3. e3 Nf6 4. Bxc4 e6 5. 0–0
Be7 6. d4 0–0 7. Nc3 c5 8. dxc5 Qa5 9. Bd2 Qxc5
10. Qb3 Nc6 11. a3 a6 12. Rac1 Na5 13. Qa2 Qxc4

14. Qxc4 Nxc4 15. Ne2 b5 16. Bc3 Bb7 17. Nfd4
Ne4 18. Nf4 Bf6 19. Nh3 Rac8 20. Rfe1 Nxc3
21. bxc3 Nxa3 22. f3 Rc7 23. e4 Rxc3 24. Rxc3
Bxd4+ 0–1

(835) FINE—VIDAL, J

Blindfold simultaneous (8-board), New York (4), 1945
Petroff Defence [C43]

1. e4 e5 2. Nf3 Nf6 3. d4 Nxe4 4. Bd3 d5 5. Nxe5
Be6 6. 0–0 Bd6 7. c4 0–0 8. cxd5 Bxd5 9. Qg4
Nf6 10. Qh4 Be7 11. Bg5 g6 12. Nc3 Bc6 13. Rae1
Qd6 14. Nc4 Qb4 15. Bxf6 Bxf6 16. Qxf6 Bd7
17. Nd5 b5 18. Nxb4 1–0

(836) LORIE, J—FINE

Blindfold simultaneous (8-board), New York (5), 1945
Queen's Indian Defence [E21]

1. d4 Nf6 2. c4 e6 3. Nc3 Bb4 4. Nf3 b6 5. g3 Bb7
6. Bg2 0–0 7. 0–0 Bxc3 8. bxc3 d6 9. a4 Nc6
10. Bb2 Na5 11. Ba3 Nxc4 12. Bc1 Qe7 13. Bg5 h6
14. Bxf6 Qxf6 15. Qd3 d5 16. Rab1 a5 17. Rfe1 Ba6
18. Qd1 Rad8 19. e4 dxe4 20. Rxe4 Bb7 21. Re1 Nd6
22. Ne5 Bxg2 23. Kxg2 Nf5 24. Qf3 Rd6 25. Re2
Rfd8 26. Nc6 Rf8 27. Rbe1 Nh4+ 28. gxh4 Qxf3+
29. Kxf3 Rxc6 30. Re3 Rc4 31. Rg1 Rxa4 32. Ke2
Kh7 33. Reg3 Rg8 34. Rf3 f6 35. h5 c5 36. Re3
cxd4 37. cxd4 Rxd4 38. Rxe6 Rb4 39. Re7 a4
40. Rg6 a3 41. Rxf6 a2 42. Ra7 a1Q 43. Rxa1 gxf6
0–1

(837) FINE—PERSINGER, L

Blindfold simultaneous (8-board), New York (6), 1945
Latvian Gambit [C40]

1. e4 e5 2. Nf3 f5 3. Nxe5 Qf6 4. d4 d6 5. Nc4
fxe4 6. Nc3 Qg6 7. Ne3 Nf6 8. Bc4 c6 9. d5 c5
10. Qe2 Be7 11. Bd2 0–0 12. h4 Nbd7 13. h5 Qe8
14. a4 Ne5 15. Ba2 Bg4 16. Nxg4 Nfxg4 17. Nxe4
Rc8 18. 0–0–0 Qxa4 19. Kb1 b5 20. Nc3 Qa6 21. f4
Nc4 22. Qxg4 Nxb2 23. Kxb2 b4 24. Qe6+ Rf7
25. Ne4 Rb8 26. Ra1 c4 27. Bxc4 Qxc4 28. Rxa7
Qd4+ 29. Kb1 Qxa7 30. Bc1 Ra8 31. Bb2 Re8 32. h6
Qc7 33. hxg7 Qc4 34. Nf6+ Kxg7 35. Rxh7+ Kf8
36. Qxf7 mate 1–0

(838) ECHEVERRIA, R—FINE

Blindfold simultaneous (8-board), New York (7), 1945
Sicilian Defence, Accelerated Dragon [B29]

1. e4 c5 2. Nf3 Nf6 3. d4 cxd4 4. Nxd4 Nxe4
5. Bd3 Nf6 6. 0–0 g6 7. Bg5 Bg7 8. Nc3 0–0
9. Qd2 Re8 10. Bh6 Bh8 11. Rae1 d5 12. Bg5 Nc6

13. Nxc6 bxc6 14. Re5 Ng4 15. Ree1 Ne5 16. Bf4
Nxd3 17. Qxd3 e5 18. Bc1 Bf5 19. Qg3 Bxc2
20. Bh6 Qd7 21. Rc1 Bf5 22. Na4 Rab8 23. Nc5
Qe7 24. b3 Bf6 25. Be3 d4 26. Bd2 e4 27. Na6
Rb6 28. Nc7 Be5 29. Bf4 Qxc7 30. Bxe5 Rxe5
31. b4 Qe7 32. Rc5 Rxc5 33. bxc5 Qxc5 34. Qc7
e3 35. fxe3 dxe3 36. Kh1 e2 37. Qd8+ Qf8
38. Qxf8+ Kxf8 39. Re1 Rb1 0–1

(839) FINE—TEARS, C

Blindfold simultaneous (8-board), New York (8), 1945
Spanish Opening [C70]

1. e4 e5 2. Nf3 Nc6 3. Bb5 a6 4. Ba4 Bb4 5. c3
Ba5 6. 0–0 Nge7 7. d4 exd4 8. cxd4 d5 9. exd5
Qxd5 10. Nc3 Qh5 11. d5 Bxc3 12. dxc6 b5 13. bxc3
bxa4 14. Re1 Be6 15. Rxe6 fxe6 16. Qd7+ Kf7
17. Ng5+ Kf8 18. Be3 Rc8 19. Nxe6+ Kf7 20. Ng5+
Kf8 21. Re1 Qe8 22. Bc5 Kg8 23. Rxe7 1–0

(840) FINE—FINKELSTEIN, M

Simultaneous Exhibition, Marshall Chess Club, New York,
    1945 (23 June)
Caro-Kann Defence, Steinitz Variation [B17]

1. e4 c6 2. d4 d5 3. Nc3 dxe4 4. Nxe4 Nd7 5. Nf3
Ngf6 6. Bd3 Nxe4 7. Bxe4 Nf6 8. Bd3 e6 9. 0–0
Be7 10. Qe2 0–0 11. c4 b6 12. Bd2 Bb7 13. Rad1
Rc8 14. Bc3 Qc7 15. Ne5 c5 16. dxc5 bxc5 17. f4
g6 18. Ng4 Nxg4 19. Qxg4 Qc6 20. f5 exf5 21. Bxf5
Rcd8 22. Bc2 Qc8 23. Qg3 Rfe8 24. Qe5 f6 25. Rxf6
Rxd1+ 26. Bxd1 Bxf6 27. Qxf6 Qd7 28. Qh8+ Kf7
29. Qxh7+ 1–0 *The Chess Review*, June-July 1945, 19
(Lahde).

(841) FINE—ROBEY

Simultaneous Exhibition, Marshall Chess Club, New York,
    1945 (23 June)
Nimzowitsch-Indian Defence, Spielmann Variation [E23]

1. d4 Nf6 2. c4 e6 3. Nc3 Bb4 4. Qb3 c5 5. dxc5
Nc6 6. Nf3 Ne4 7. Bd2 Nxc5 8. Qc2 f5 9. a3 Bxc3
10. Bxc3 0–0 11. g3 b6 12. Bg2 Bb7 13. 0–0 Rc8
14. Rfd1 Qc7 15. Rac1 Ne4 16. Be1 Ne7 17. Nd4 a6
18. f3 Nd6 19. Bb4 a5 20. Nxe6 dxe6 21. Bxd6 Qd7
22. b4 Qe8 23. Qb3 a4 24. Qe3 Qf7 25. Qxb6 Ba8
26. b5 Rfe8 27. Qa7 Qf6 28. Qd4 Qf7 29. Bb4
Ng6 30. c5 Bd5 31. c6 Bb3 32. Rd2 e5 33. Qd7
Qf6 34. b6 1–0 *The Chess Review*, June-July 1945, 19
(Lahde).

(842) FINE—CANTWELL, R

Simultaneous Speed Game, Washington, 1945 (27 June)
English Opening, Mikenas-Flohr Variation [A19]

1. c4 Nf6 2. Nc3 e6 3. e4 c5 4. e5 Ng8 5. f4 d5
6. cxd5 exd5 7. d4 Be6 8. Nf3 Nc6 9. Be2 Nh6
10. 0–0 Nf5 11. dxc5 Bxc5+ 12. Kh1 Rc8 13. g4 Nh4
14. f5 Nxf3 15. Bxf3 Bd7 16. Qxd5 Bb6 17. Bf4 Qe7
18. f6 Qe6 19. fxg7 Rg8 20. Qxe6+ Bxe6 21. Ne4
Bd8 22. Nf6+ Bxf6 23. exf6 Nd4 24. Rad1 Nxf3
25. Rxf3 Bxa2 26. Rfd3 Be6 27. Bc7 1–0 (O'Keefe)

(843) BOROCHOW, H—FINE

Exhibition Game, California Los Angeles, 1945 (Sept.)
Vienna Game [C29]

1. e4 e5 2. Nc3 Nf6 3. f4 d5 4. fxe5 Nxe4 5. Nf3
Be7 6. d4 0–0 7. Bd3 Nxc3 8. bxc3 Bg4 9. 0–0 c5
10. h3 Bh5 11. Rb1 Qc7 12. Bxh7+ Kxh7 13. Ng5+
Bxg5 14. Qxh5+ Kg8 If 14 … Bh6 15 Bxh6 gxh6 16 Rf6
mates. 15. Bxg5 cxd4 16. Bf6 1–0 Black resigned. *Los
Angeles Times*, 30 September 1945

(844) FINE—BOROCHOW, H

Exhibition Game, California Los Angeles, 1945 (Sept.)
Nimzowitsch-Indian Defence, Spielmann Variation [E23]

1. d4 Nf6 2. c4 e6 3. Nc3 Bb4 4. Qb3 c5 5. dxc5
Nc6 6. Nf3 Ne4 7. Bd2 Nxc5 8. Qc2 0–0 9. a3
Bxc3 10. Bxc3 f5 11. b4 Ne4 12. Bb2 b6 13. g4
Bb7 14. gxf5 exf5 15. Rg1 Rf7 16. Bh3 g6 17. Bxf5
Nf6 18. Bxg6 Rg7 19. Bxh7+ Kh8 20. Rxg7
1–0 Black resigned. *Los Angeles Times*, 30 September
1945

(845) FINE—BYRNE, R

Blindfold Rapid Transit (4-board), New York, 1945 (4 Sept.)
Zukertort Opening [D04]

1. d4 d5 2. e3 Nf6 3. Nf3 g6 4. Bd3 Bg7 5. 0–0
Nbd7 6. b3 0–0 7. Bb2 c5 8. Nbd2 a6 9. Qe2 b5
10. c4 cxd4 11. exd4 bxc4 12. bxc4 Nb6 13. Rab1
Na4 14. Ba1 dxc4 15. Nxc4 Be6 16. Nce5 a5 17. Bb5
Nb6 18. Nc6 Qd6 19. Ng5 Bg4 20. Qxe7 Nc8
21. Qb7 h6 22. Qxa8 hxg5 23. Ne5 Bf5 24. Rbc1
Ne7 25. Qxa5 Nfd5 26. Bc4 Nf4 27. Qc5 Qd8
28. Rfe1 Qa8 29. Bf1 Ned5 30. f3 Rc8 31. Qb5 Rf8
32. a4 Kh7 33. a5 f6 34. Nc6 g4 35. fxg4 Bxg4
36. a6 Nc7 37. Qb7 Nfd5 38. Qxa8 Rxa8 Black
resigned on move 48. 1–0 Fine 1958, 211–3; Korn 171;
Horowitz & Rothenberg, 128.

(846) FINE—EPSTEIN, M

Blindfold Rapid Transit (4-board), New York, 1945 (4 Sept.)
Two Knights Defence, Fegatello Variation [C57]

1. e4 e5 2. Nf3 Nc6 3. Bc4 Nf6 4. Ng5 d5 5. exd5
Nxd5 6. Nxf7 Kxf7 7. Qf3+ Ke6 8. Nc3 Nce7

9. d4 c6 10. 0–0 Kd6 11. dxe5+ Kc7 12. Bg5 Be6 13. Rad1 Qe8 14. Ne4 a5 15. Nc5 Ng6 16. Nxe6+ Qxe6 17. Bxd5 cxd5 18. Rxd5 Be7 19. Bc3 Rhf8 20. Qe4 Ra6 21. Rfd1 Rc8 22. Rd7+ Qxd7 23. Rxd7+ Kxd7 24. Qxb7+ Rc7 25. Qxa6 Nf8 26. g3 Ne6 27. Qxa5 Ke8 28. c4 h6 29. b4 Bd8 30. c5 Kf8 31. Qa6 Be7 32. Qxe6 1–0 Horowitz & Rothenberg, 128–9.

(847) Fine—Helander, B

Blindfold Rapid Transit (4-board), New York, 1945 (4 Sept.)
Spanish Opening, Caro Variation [C70]

1. e4 e5 2. Nf3 Nc6 3. Bb5 a6 4. Ba4 b5 5. Bb3 d6 6. 0–0 Be7 7. a4 Bg4 8. c3 Nf6 9. h3 Bh5 10. Qe2 b4 11. Rd1 0–0 12. d4 Bxf3 13. Qxf3 exd4 14. cxd4 Nd7 15. Bd5 Ndb8 16. Be3 Bf6 17. e5 dxe5 18. Bxc6 Nxc6 19. Qxc6 exd4 20. Bf4 Qe7 21. Nd2 Be5 22. Re1 Qd6 23. Qxd6 Bxd6 24. Bxd6 cxd6 25. Nf3 f6 26. Nxd4 Rac8 27. Rac1 a5 28. Nc6 Ra8 29. g3 h5 30. Re7 Rf7 31. Rce1 Rc8 32. Nxa5 Black resigned on move 46. 1–0 Horowitz & Rothenberg, 130.

(848) Fine—Fomin, A

Blindfold Rapid Transit (4-board), New York (3), 1945 (4 Sept.)
Queen's Gambit Accepted [D26]

1. d4 d5 2. c4 dxc4 3. Nf3 e6 4. e3 Nf6 5. Bxc4 Bb4+ 6. Nc3 0–0 7. 0–0 b6 8. Qe2 Bb7 9. Rd1 c6 10. e4 Qc7 11. Bg5 Be7 12. Rac1 Rd8 13. Bb3 Nh5 14. Nb5 Qd7 15. Ne5 Qe8 16. Nc7 Qf8 17. Qxh5 Bxg5 18. Qxg5 Rd6 19. Nxa8 Bxa8 20. Qg3 Rd8 21. d5 exd5 22. exd5 Rd6 23. dxc6 Nxc6 24. Nxf7 Rf6 25. Ne5+ Kh8 26. Nd7 Qc8 27. Nxf6 1–0 Fine 1958, 213–4; Horowitz & Rothenberg, 129.

(849) Fine—Lew, H

Simultaneous Exhibition, CCLA vs Masters, 1945
Queen's Gambit Declined [D53]

1. d4 Nf6 2. c4 e6 3. Nc3 d5 4. Bg5 Be7 5. e3 c6 6. Nf3 Nbd7 7. Qc2 Qa5 8. cxd5 Nxd5 9. Bxe7 Kxe7 10. Be2 h6 11. 0–0 Re8 12. Ne5 Nxc3 13. bxc3 Nxe5 14. dxe5 Qxe5 15. Rad1 b6 16. f4 Qxe3+ 17. Kh1 Bb7 18. Rd3 Qc5 19. f5 e5 20. f6+! gxf6 21. Rdf3 Rg8 22. Rxf6 Raf8 23. Bh5 Rg7 24. Qd2 Qd5 25. Qe2 c5 26. Bf3 e4 27. Rd1 Qg5 28. Rfd6 Rb8 29. Bxe4 Qe5 30. Rd7+ Kf8 31. Qb5 Re8 Reinfeld wrote "Correct was 31 ... Bxe4! 32 Rd8+ Ke7! 33 Qd7+ Kf6 34 Rd6+ Kg5 35 Rxc8 Bxg2+ forcing mate!". 33 Qe8+ would, however, win for White. Fortunately for Black, had he played 31 ... Bxe4, 32 Rd8+ could be answered by 32 ... Rxd8 33 Rxd8+ Ke7 and wins. 32. Bxb7 Qe1+ 33. Qf1 Qxf1+ 34. Rxf1 Re2 35. Bd5 Rd2 36. h3

Ke8 37. Rdxf7 Rxf7 38. Bxf7+ Ke7 39. Bc4 Rc2 40. Rf7+ Kd6 41. Rxa7 Rxc3 42. Ra4 Ke5 43. Bf1 Rc1 44. Kg1 Kd5 45. Kf2 c4 46. Rxc4 Rxf1+ 47. Kxf1 Kxc4 48. g4 Kc3 49. h4 Kd4 50. Ke2 Ke4 51. a4 The simplest win, as pointed out in the original notes, is 51 g5, when Black must play 51 ... hxg5, and there would follow 52 hxg5 Kf5 (not 52 ... Kf4, as given by the annotator, because of 53 g6) 53 Kd3 Kxg5 54 Kc4 Kf5 55 Kb5. 51 ... Kf4 52. g5? Contrary to the opinion of the above-mentioned annotator, White can still win by 52 Kd3! since, after 52 ... Kxg4 53 Kc4 Kxh4 54 Kb5 h5 55 Kxb6 Kg3 56 a5 h4 57 a6 h3 58 a7 h2 59 a8Q, Black cannot queen his pawn. 52 ... hxg5 53. hxg5 Kxg5 54. Kd3 Kf6 55. Kc4 Ke6 56. Kb5 Kd7 57. Kxb6 Kc8 ½–½ CCL, November 1945, 3 (Lahde).

(850) Fine—Suesman

Simultaneous Exhibition, New York, 1946
Sicilian Defence [B32]

1. e4 c5 2. Nf3 Nc6 3. d4 cxd4 4. Nxd4 d5 5. Bb5 dxe4 6. Nxc6 Qxd1+ 7. Kxd1 a6 8. Nd4+ axb5 9. Nxb5 Bg4+ 10. Ke1 Rd8 11. N1c3 f5 12. h3 Bh5 13. Nc7+ Kf7 14. g4 fxg4 15. Nxe4 gxh3 16. Ng5+ Kf6 17. Nge6 Rd1 mate 0–1

(851) Fine—Greene

Simultaneous Exhibition, Santa Monica, 1946 (5 Nov.)
Nimzowitsch-Indian Defence, Rubinstein Variation [E47]

1. d4 Nf6 2. c4 e6 3. Nc3 Bb4 4. e3 0–0 5. Bd3 Nc6 6. Nge2 b6 7. 0–0 Bb7 8. e4 d6 9. f4 Qd7 10. Qe1 Ne7 11. h3 Bxe4 12. Qd1 Bb7 13. Qc2 Rad8 14. Nd1 e5 15. a3 e4 16. axb4 exd3 17. Qxd3 Be4 18. Qg3 Rfe8 19. Ndc3 Nf5 20. Qf2 Bb7 21. Rxa7 Ne4 22. Nxe4 Bxe4 23. Nc3 Bd3 24. Rd1 Bxc4 25. d5 Bb3 26. Re1 Re7 27. g4 Rde8 28. Rxe7 Nxe7 29. Qd4 Nc8 30. Ra1 Re1+ 31. Kf2 Qe7 32. Ra8 Qh4+ 33. Kg2 Re8 34. Qd3 b5 35. Qxb5 Qe1 36. Qd7? Bxd5+ White resigned, for if 37 Nxd5 Re2+ 38 Kf3 Qf2 mate. 0–1 *Los Angeles Times*, 24 November 1946

(852) Fine—Lesser

Simultaneous Exhibition, Santa Monica, 1946 (5 Nov.)
English Opening, Classical Defence [A20]

1. c4 e5 2. Nf3 e4 3. Nd4 c5 4. Nc2 Nc6 5. Nc3 Be7 6. Nxe4 Nf6 7. Ng3 d5 8. cxd5 Nxd5 9. e3 0–0 10. Be2 Re8 11. 0–0 Qc7 12. b3 Bf6 13. Rb1 Bd7 14. Ba3 b6 15. Rc1 a5 16. Nh5 Be7 17. Bb2 Bd6 18. f4 Bf8 19. Qe1 Re6 20. Bf3 Nde7 21. d4 Rh6 22. dxc5 Re8 23. Nd4 bxc5 24. Rxc5 Qb6 25. Qc3 Nxd4 26. exd4 Nf5 27. Qxa5 Bxc5 28. Qxc5 Qg6 29. Ng3 Nxg3 30. hxg3 Qxg3 31. Qg5 Qh2+

32. Kf2 Rg6 33. Qc5 Rc8 34. Qa7 Bh3 35. Qb7
Qxf4 36. Kg1 Qg3 37. Bd5 Qe3+ 38. Kh2 Be6
39. Bxe6 Rh6+ 40. Bh3 Rxh3+ 41. gxh3 Rc2+
42. Kh1 Qxh3+ White resigned. 0–1 *Los Angeles Times*,
8 December 1946

(853) HOLTRICHTER, J–FINE

Simultaneous Exhibition, Santa Monica, 1946 (5 Nov.)
Ponziani Opening [C44]

1. e4 e5 2. Nf3 Nc6 3. c3 d6 4. d4 Bg4 5. Bc4
Na5 6. Bd3 Nc6 7. Be3 a6 8. Nbd2 Nf6 9. h3
Bxf3 10. Qxf3 Ne7 11. 0–0–0 Nd7 12. Nc4 b5
Perhaps White was hoping for ... c6 or ... c5 when 13 Nxd6
would be mate! 13. Nd2 g6 14. Nb3 Bg7 15. dxe5
Nxe5 16. Qe2 Nxd3+ 17. Qxd3 0–0 18. f4 Qb8
19. f5 Nc6 20. g4 a5 21. h4 b4 22. h5 bxc3
23. bxc3 a4 24. Nd2 Ne5 25. Qe2 Qb7 26. Kc2
Rab8 27. Rb1 Qc6 28. Bd4 a3 29. Nb3 Rb4
30. g5 Rfb8 31. hxg6 fxg6 32. f6 Bf8 33. Rh4
Rc4 34. Rbh1?! Rxd4 35. Rxh7 Qxe4+ 36. Qxe4
Rxe4 37. Rh8+ Kf7 38. R1h7+ Ke6 39. Nd4+ Kd5
40. Rxc7 Rg4 41. Kd2 Ke4 42. Nb3 Rg2+ 43. Ke1
Rxa2 White resigned. 0–1 *Los Angeles Times*, 24 November
1946

(854) FINE–ESTEIGER, O

Clock Simultaneous Exhibition, Havana, Cuba, 1951 (Feb.)
Queen's Gambit Declined, Exchange Variation [D51]

1. d4 e6 2. c4 Nf6 3. Nc3 d5 4. Bg5 c6 5. e3 Nbd7
6. cxd5 cxd5 7. Bd3 Be7 8. Nf3 a6 9. Qc2 b5
10. 0–0 Bb7 11. Rac1 Rc8 12. Qe2 0–0 13. a4 b4
14. Nb1 Qa5 15. Ne5 Nb6 16. b3 Rxc1 17. Rxc1 h6
18. Bf4 Rc8 19. Rxc8+ Nxc8 20. Qc2 Bf8 21. Nxf7
Kxf7 22. Bc7 Nb6 23. Bg6+ Kg8 24. Nd2 Be7
25. Nf3 Nfd7 26. Be8 Nc5 27. Qg6 Bf6 28. Ne5
Nxb3 29. Ng4 Bxd4 30. exd4 1–0 www.games-of-
chess.de

Miscellany

(855) CAPABLANCA, J– MANHATTAN CHESS CLUB

Simultaneous Exhibition, New York, 1931 (12 Feb.)
Queen's Gambit Declined [D53]

(By way of explanation I should state that the "others" all
deserted me after we manoeuvred ourselves into a lost position.) The others were MacMurray, Schwartz and Stephens.
AW 1. d4 Nf6 2. c4 e6 3. Nc3 d5 4. Bg5 Nbd7
5. e3 Be7 6. Nf3 At the time my ignorance of the openings was abysmal. I did not know that this variation had
been explored to the depths in the Alekhine–Capablanca
match of 1927. 6 ... c5? A blunder made because I knew

no better. **7. cxd5 cxd4?** Another mistake 7 ... Nxd5 is
relatively best. **8. Qxd4 exd5 9. Bb5** Preparing to win
the queen's pawn. **9 ... 0–0 10. Bxd7 Bxd7 11. Bxf6
Bxf6 12. Qxd5** Capa now has a won game, but Black's
two bishops and superiority in development make trouble.
12 ... Qc8 If instead 12 ... Bxc6 13 Qxd8 Rfxd8 14 Rc1 is
too strong for White. **13. Nd4** White must lose time; if
13 Rc1 Bc6 14 Qc4 Bxf3 15 Qxc8 Raxc8 16 gxf3 Rc4 the
ending is not easy for White to win. **13 ... Rd8 14. 0–0
Bc6 15. Qc5 Be8** The decision to try for compensation in
the endgame is the correct one. On 15 ... Bxd4 16 exd4 Qg4
15 d5 is unanswerable. **16. Qxc8 Raxc8 17. Rfd1 g6** At
this point I had the audacity to offer Capa a draw, which
was curtly refused. **18. Nde2?** Here, however, Capa begins
to go wrong, no doubt lulled into security by his opponent's
previous weak play. The king should go to the centre as
soon as possible: 18 Kg1-f1-e2, Rd2, and so on. **18 ... Kf8
19. Rxd8 Rxd8 20. Rd1 Rxd1+ 21. Nxd1 Ke7
22. Ndc3** To prevent ... Bb5. But now the Black king gets
in; Kf1 was imperative, here or on the next move. **22 ...
Bg7** To play ... Kd6 without fear of Ne4. **23. Nd4?** Serious loss of time. **23 ... Kd6 24. Kf1 Kc5 25. Nde2**
Or 25 Nce2 Kc4 26 Ke1 Kd3 27 Kd1 Bxd4 with similar
variations. **25 ... Kc4 26. Ke1 Kd3 27. Kd1 Bxc3!**
The key move, which keeps Black's king prancing around
in White's vitals. **28. Nxc3 Bc6 29. Ne2** Protecting the
g-pawn indirectly (Nf4). **29 ... Ba4+!** To weaken the pawns.
30. b3 Bc6 31. h4 White is already in trouble. If, instead,
31 Nf4+ Kc3 32 Kc1 g5 33 Nh3 (best) h6 34 f3 Kd3. **31 ...
f6** The position is most unusual. In spite of being a pawn
down, Black has a winning endgame

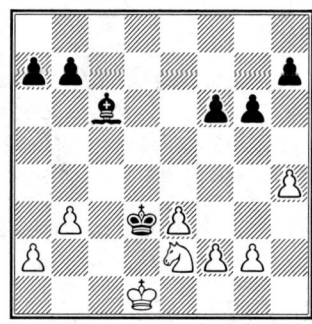

*Position after
Black's 31st move*

**32. Nf4+ Kc3 33. Kc1 g5! 34. hxg5 fxg5 35. Ne6
Bxg2 36. Nxg5 h5!** It is in endgames like these which
yield to exact calculation that the single player has a hard
time. Black has correctly counted out the position, and wins
in all variations. **37. Kd1** It does no good to advance the
pawns, for if 37 f4 h4 38 f5 h3 39 Nxh3 (on 39 f6 Black
queens first with check) Bxh3 40 f6 Be6 the rest is easy.
37 ... h4 38. Ke2 h3 39. f3 h2 40. Ne4+ Kb4 I still
had to avoid one last trap: if 40 ... Kb2 41 Nf2 h1Q 42 Nxh1
Bxh1 43 Kf2 Kxa2? 44 e4. **41. Nf2 h1Q 42. Nxh1 Bxh1
43. Kf2 Kc3 44. e4 Kd4 45. a3 a5 46. a4 b6
47. Kg3 Ke3 48. e5 Bxf3 49. e6 Bc6 50. e7 Kd3
51. Kf4 Kc3 52. Ke5 Kxb3 53. Kd6 Be8 54. Kc7
Kxa4 55. Kxb6 Kb4** White resigned. 0–1 *Fine 1958,*

3–6; Denker & Parr, 36–7 (included in the chapter on MacMurray, suggesting, perhaps, that Denker did not believe Fine played the game alone after the consultants got into a lost position); Fiala *QCH3* 1999, 444–5 from Benko in *Chess Life*, 1993, December, 20.

(856) FINE–MARSHALL & MISS HOPPE

Marshall Chess Club, New York, 1933
King's Indian Defence [A30]

1. c4 Nf6 2. Nf3 g6 3. b3 Bg7 4. Bb2 0–0 5. g3 b6 6. Bg2 Bb7 7. 0–0 c5 8. d4 cxd4 9. Nxd4 Bxg2 10. Kxg2 d5 11. Nd2 Qd7 12. Rc1 Nc6 13. Nxc6 Qxc6 14. cxd5 Qxd5+ 15. Nf3 Qb7! White's conservative opening would lead to a small edge after 15 ... Qxd1 16 Rfxd1 Rac8 17 Nd4. Fine now makes a curious decision. **16. Bxf6?! Bxf6 17. Qd3 Rfd8 18. Qe3** Soltis prefers 18 Qb5, but I think the point of Fine's move was to prevent 18 ... Rd2, after which Black's advantage would be at least as great as in the game. AW **18 ... Rd6 19. Rfd1 Rad8 20. Rxd6 Rxd6 21. Qf4?! e5! 22. Qc4 e4 23. Qc8+** A natural effort to reduce the tactical dangers but 23 Ne1 offered better drawing chances. **23 ... Qxc8 24. Rxc8+ Kg7 25. Ne1 Rd2 26. Rc2 Rd1 27. Kf1 Be7 28. Rc4 a5!** 0–1 Soltis 1994, 347.

(857) FINE–ARAIZA & GONZALEZ ROJO

Consultation Game, Mexico City, 1934 (6 Dec.)
English Opening, Classical Variation [A28]

1. c4 e5 2. Nf3 Nc6 3. Nc3 Nf6 4. e4 Bb4 5. d3 d6 6. Be2 h6 7. 0–0 Bxc3 8. bxc3 g5 9. Ne1 Ne7 10. Nc2 Ng6 11. Re1 c5 12. Ne3 Nf4 13. Bf1 h5 14. Nf5 Kf8 15. g3 Ne6 16. h4 Rg8 17. Bg2 Ng4 18. f3 Nf6 19. hxg5 Nxg5 20. f4 exf4 21. Bxf4 Bxf5 22. exf5 Ng4 23. d4 Qc7 24. dxc5 Qxc5+ 25. Qd4 Rd8 26. Rad1 Qxf5 27. Bxd6+ Rxd6 28. Qxd6+ Kg7 29. Qd4+ Kh6 30. Rf1 Qg6 31. Qf4 Qb6+ 32. Qd4 Qg6 33. Qd6 Ne6 34. Qe7 Rg7 35. Rde1 Ng5 36. Qf8 h4 37. Qc8 Kh5 38. Rf4 Nh7 39. Bf3 Nhf6 40. Qh8+ Qh6 41. Re5+ Kg6 42. Be4+ Nxe4 43. Rxg4+ 1–0

(858) GLICCO & ACEVEDO–FINE

Consultation Game, Mexico City, 1934 (6 Dec.)
Queen's Gambit Declined, Semi-Tarrasch [D41]

1. d4 Nf6 2. Nf3 d5 3. c4 e6 4. Nc3 c5 5. cxd5 Nxd5 6. e4 Nxc3 7. bxc3 cxd4 8. cxd4 Bb4+ 9. Bd2 Bxd2+ 10. Qxd2 0–0 11. Be2 b6 12. 0–0 Bb7 13. Qf4 Nd7 14. Nd2 e5 15. dxe5 Nxe5 16. Rfd1 Qe7 17. Rac1 Rac8 18. Qe3 Nd7 19. f4 Rc5 20. Rxc5 Qxc5 21. Qxc5 Nxc5 22. e5 Ne6 23. g3 Nd4 24. Bd3 Rd8 25. Nc4 Ba6 26. Kf2 Kf8 27. Ne3 Bxd3 28. Rxd3 g6 29. Nc2 Ne6 ½–½

(859) FINE–JOHN, W

"Centrum" Amsterdam, 1936 (16 Nov.)
French Defence [C00]

1. e4 e6 2. d4 d5 3. Bd3 dxe4 4. Bxe4 Nf6 5. Nc3 Nxe4 6. Nxe4 Qd5 7. Qe2 f5 8. Qh5+ Kd7 9. Qf7+ Kc6 10. Nf3? Qxe4+ 11. Be3 b6 12. Ne5+ Kb7 13. 0–0 Nc6 14. Bf4? Qxf4 15. f3 Nxe5 16. dxe5 Qxe5 17. Qe8 g6 18. Rfe1 Bc5+ White resigned. 0–1

(860) FINE–MRS. KORFMAN

Amsterdam, Friendly, 1936 (?22 Nov.)
Philidor Defence [C41]

1. e4 e5 2. Nf3 d6 3. Bc4 Be7 4. Nc3 Nf6 5. 0–0 Bg4 6. h3 Bd7 7. Re1 0–0 8. d4 Nc6 9. Nd5 Nxd5 10. Bxd5 a5 11. dxe5 dxe5 12. Bxc6 Bxc6 13. Qxd8 Rfxd8 14. Nxe5 Bb5 15. Be3 Bf6 16. Bf4 Re8 17. Nd3 c6 18. Rab1 Bc1 19. b3 Bxd3 20. cxd3 Rad8 21. e5 Be7 22. Rbd1 Bb4 ½–½

(861) MRS. KORFMAN–FINE

Amsterdam, Friendly, 1936 (?22 Nov.)
Queen's Pawn Game [D04]

1. d4 d5 2. e3 Nf6 3. Nf3 Bf5 4. Nc3 Nc6 5. Ne5 Nb4 6. Bb5+ c6 7. Ba4 Nd7 8. a3 Na6 9. Qh5 g6 10. Qh4 Nxe5 11. dxe5 Nc5 12. Qd4 e6 13. Qb4 Nd3+ 14. cxd3 Bxb4 15. axb4 Bxd3 16. b5 Qb6 17. bxc6 bxc6 18. Ra3 Bc4 19. e4 d4 20. Ne2 0–0 21. g3 Qb4+ 22. Kf1 d3 23. Kg2 dxe2 24. Bxc6 e1Q 25. Ra4 Qxe4+ 26. Bxe4 Qxa4 27. Bxa8 Rxa8 28. Re1 Bd5+ 29. Kh3 Bf3 30. Bf4 g5 31. Re3 Bh5 32. Bxg5 Qg4+ 0–1

(862) LANDAU, S–FINE

Exhibition, Ermelo, 1937 (29 Sept.)
Queen's Gambit Declined, Marshall Defence [D06]

1. d4 d5 2. c4 Nf6 3. cxd5 Nxd5 4. e4 Nb6 5. Nf3 Bg4 6. Be3 c6 7. Be2 e6 8. 0–0 Be7 9. Nc3 0–0 10. Qc2 Bxf3 11. Bxf3 Nc8 12. d5 e5 13. Rad1 Nd6 14. Bc5 Re8 15. dxc6 bxc6 16. Ne2 Qc7 17. Ng3 g6 18. Bg4 Na6 19. Be3 Rad8 20. f4 exf4 21. Bxf4 Qb6+ 22. Kh1 Nb5 23. e5 Qc5 24. Qe4 Rxd1 25. Rxd1 f5 26. exf6 Bxf6 27. Qxe8+ 1–0

(863) CRUZ, W–FINE

Clock Game New York (1), 1940 (20 June)
Grünfeld Defence, 4 Bf4 [D84]

1. d4 Nf6 2. c4 g6 3. Nc3 d5 4. Bf4 Bg7 5. e3 0–0 6. cxd5 Nxd5 7. Nxd5 Qxd5 8. Bxc7 Nc6 9. Ne2 Bg4 10. f3 Rac8 11. Nc3 Qe6 12. Bf4 Nxd4 13. fxg4

Rfd8 14. Bd3 Nc6 15. Qe2 Nb4 16. Rd1 Bxc3+
17. bxc3 Nxa2 18. 0–0 Nxc3 19. Qb2 Nxd1 20. Rxd1
Qxg4 21. Rd2 Qh4 22. Bf1 b6 23. g3 Qf6 24. Rd4
a5 25. Qd2 Rxd4 26. exd4 Rd8 27. d5 a4 28. Qb4
Rxd5 29. Qxa4 Qd4+ 30. Qxd4 Rxd4 31. Be3 Rb4
32. Kf2 e5 33. Kf3 f5 34. h4 Kg7 35. Ba6 Rb2
36. Bc8 b5 37. g4 fxg4+ 38. Bxg4 b4 39. Ke4 b3
40. Be6 Rb1 41. Kxe5 Re1 0–1

(864) FINE—CRUZ, W

Clock Game New York (2), 1940 (25 June)
Spanish Opening, Steinitz Defence Deferred [C72]

1. e4 e5 2. Nf3 Nc6 3. Bb5 a6 4. Ba4 d6 5. 0–0
Nge7 6. c3 g6 7. d4 b5 8. Bb3 Bg7 9. dxe5 dxe5
10. Be3 Qxd1 11. Rxd1 Na5 12. Bc5 Nxb3 13. axb3
Bb7 14. Re1 Nc6 15. Nbd2 Nd8 16. b4 Ne6 17. Nb3
0–0–0 18. Be3 f6 19. Nfd2 Bf8 20. Re2 Be7 21. Nc5
Bxc5 22. bxc5 Rd3 23. f3 Rhd8 24. Nb3 Rd1+
25. Re1 Rxe1+ 26. Rxe1 c6 27. Kf2 Kc7 28. g3 Bc8
29. f4 g5 30. f5 Ng7 31. h4 g4 32. h5 Rg8 33. h6
Ne8 34. Na5 Rf8 35. Rh1 Rg8 36. Ke2 Bd7 37. Kd3
Kc8 38. Kc2 Nc7 39. Rd1 Rd8 40. Rd2 Be8 41. Rd6
Rxd6 42. cxd6 Nd5 43. exd5 cxd5 44. Kb3 Bd7
45. Kb4 Bxf5 46. Kc5 Be4 47. Nc6 Kd7 48. Nb8+
1–0

(865) CRUZ, W—FINE

Clock Game New York (3), 1940 (26 June)
Nimzowitsch-Indian Defence, Sämisch Variation [E26]

1. d4 Nf6 2. c4 e6 3. Nc3 Bb4 4. a3 Bxc3+
5. bxc3 c5 6. e3 Qa5 7. Qc2 cxd4 8. exd4 e5
9. Bd2 0–0 10. Be2 Re8 11. d5 d6 12. Nf3 Bg4
13. 0–0 Nbd7 14. Rfb1 Qc7 15. Be3 b6 16. a4 a5
17. Rb5 Rec8 18. Rab1 Rab8 19. Bd3 Nc5 20. Bxc5
bxc5 21. Bf5 Bxf5 22. Qxf5 Re8 23. Nd2 h6
24. R1b2 e4 25. Nf1 Rxb5 26. Rxb5 Nd7 27. Qf4
Nb6 28. Ne3 Nxa4 29. Nf5 Nxc3 30. Qg4 g6
31. Rb3 Rb8 32. Rxb8+ Qxb8 33. h4 h5 34. Qg5
Qb1+ 35. Kh2 Ne2 0–1

(866) PHILLIPS, SHAPIRO & TUROVER— FINE, W K WIMSATT & EATON

Consultation game, Washington, Wimsatt residence, 1942
(2 Oct.)
Sicilian Defence [B45]

1. e4 c5 2. Nf3 e6 3. d4 cxd4 4. Nxd4 Nf6 5. Nc3
Nc6 6. g3 Bc5 7. Nxc6 bxc6 8. e5 Nd5 9. Qg4 Kf8
10. Nxd5 exd5 11. Qf4 d6 12. Be3 Bxe3 13. Qxe3
dxe5 14. Qxe5 Bg4 15. Qf4 h5 16. f3 Qe7+ 17. Kd2
Be6 18. Re1 Rh6 19. Bh3 Re8 20. Re5 Rf6 21. Rxh5
Qb7 22. Qd4 Bxh3 23. Rxh3 Kg8 24. Rh5 Qe7
25. Rd1 Rxf3 26. Kc1 Qe4 27. Rh4 Qf5 28. Rg4 f6

29. Rf4 Rxf4 30. gxf4 Re2 31. Rd2 Re4 32. Qg1
Rxf4 33. Rd1 Rf2 0–1 *ACB 1943, 15.*

(867) TUROVER, WIMSATT, JR. & EATON— FINE, WIMSATT, SR. & SHERIDAN

Consultation game, Washington, Wimsatt residence, 1942
Spanish Opening, Steinitz Defence Deferred [C71]

1. e4 e5 2. Nf3 Nc6 3. Bb5 a6 4. Ba4 d6 5. d4 b5
6. Bb3 Nxd4 7. Nxd4 exd4 8. Bd5 Rb8 9. Qxd4
Nf6 10. Qa7 Bd7 11. Qxa6 Be7 12. Be3 0–0 13. Nc3
b4 14. Ne2 Bb5 15. Qa7 c6 16. Bb3 c5 17. e5 Nd7
18. exd6 Bxd6 19. 0–0–0 Qe7 20. Ng3 Be5 21. Bxc5
Qxc5 22. Rxd7 Qxa7 23. Rxa7 Bd4 24. Re7 Bxf2
25. Ne4 Be3+ 26. Kb1 Rbe8 27. Rxf7 Rxf7 28. Bxf7+
Kxf7 29. Nd6+ Kf8 30. Nxb5 Bb6 31. Rf1+ Kg8
32. c3 Re2 33. cxb4 Rxg2 34. Rh1 g5 35. h3 h5
36. a4 Rg1+ 37. Rxg1 Bxg1 38. Nd6 Kg7 39. a5 Kg6
40. Kc2 g4 41. hxg4 h4 42. Ne4 h3 43. Kd3 h2
44. Ng3 Kg5 45. Ke2 Kxg4 46. Nh1 Kf4 47. Kf1
Ke4 48. Ng3+ Kd4 ½–½ *Washington Post, 26 July, 1942.*

(868) FINE—MENGARINI, A

Speed tournament, Washington, 1942?
Queen's Gambit Declined [D44]

1. d4 d5 2. c4 c6 3. Nc3 Nf6 4. Nf3 e6 5. Bg5 dxc4
6. e4 Qa5 7. Bxf6 gxf6 8. Bxc4 b5 9. Bb3 Rg8
10. 0–0 e5 11. dxe5 Bh3 12. g3 Bxf1 13. Kxf1 Nd7
14. Bxf7+ Kxf7 15. Qxd7+ Kg6 16. Nh4+ Kh6 17. Qf7
Kg5 18. Qxf6+ Kh5 19. Ne2 Rd8 20. Nf4+ Kg4
21. f3 Mate 1–0 *Washington Post, 10 January, 1943.* (The
actual date the game was played is unclear, it was described
as "recent," which could mean either late 1942 or January
1943. I recorded it as 1942 as I know that there were speed
tournaments in late December at the Divan in 1943 and
1944).

(869) FINE—MUGRIDGE, D

Speed Game Washington, 1944 (Dec.?)
Queen's Gambit Accepted [D22]

1. d4 d5 2. c4 dxc4 3. Nf3 a6 4. e3 Bg4 5. Bxc4 e6
6. Qb3 Bxf3 7. gxf3 b5 8. Be2 Nf6 9. a4 b4 10. Nd2
Nbd7 11. Nc4 Be7 12. Qc2 0–0 13. e4 c5 14. dxc5
Nxc5 15. Be3 Rc8 16. a5 Qc7 17. Nb6 Rcd8 18. Rc1
Nfd7 19. Nxd7 Rxd7 20. Bxc5 Rc8 21. Qa4 Bxc5
22. Rxc5 Qxc5 23. Qxd7 Qc1+ 24. Bd1 Rb8 25. Qd6
Rc8 26. 0–0 Qxb2 27. Qxa6 g6 28. Qxc8+ 1–0
Christian Science Monitor, 16 December, 1944. (O'Keefe)

(870) FINE—JOHNSON, R

Blitz Game, Washington, 1944
English Opening, Classical Defence [A21]

1. e3 e5 2. c4 d6 3. Nc3 Nc6 4. g3 Nf6 5. Bg2 Be7
6. f4 0–0 7. Nf3 exf4 8. gxf4 Bg4 9. 0–0 d5 10. cxd5
Nxd5 11. Qe1 Nf6 12. Qg3 Qd3 13. Ne5 Qf5 14. e4
Qh5 15. Nxc6 bxc6 16. d4 Be2 17. Nxe2 Qxe2 18. Be3
Rab8 19. b3 Nh5 20. Qh3 g6 21. f5 Qd3 22. Rad1
Qa6 23. Bh6 Rfe8 24. fxg6 hxg6 25. Qf3 Bf6
26. e5 Kh7 27. Bc1 Bg7 28. Qxf7 Rf8 29. Qe6
Rbe8 30. Qg4 Qxa2 31. Be4 1–0

(871) FINE—PAVEY, M

Blitz, Manhattan, 1945 (22 Jan.)
Alekhine's Defence [B03]

1. e4 Nf6 2. e5 Nd5 3. d4 d6 4. c4 Nb6 5. Nf3 Bg4
6. exd6 exd6 7. Be2 Be7 8. 0–0 0–0 9. h3 Bh5
10. Nc3 Nc6 11. b3 Bf6 12. Be3 Re8 13. Qd2 d5 14. c5
Nc8 15. Rad1 N8e7 16. Bg5 Bxf3 17. Bxf3 Bxd4
18. Nxd5 f6 19. Be3 Nxd5 20. Bxd4 Nde7 21. Rfe1
Qc8 22. Bg4 Qd8 23. Be6+ Kh8 24. Qb2 Ng6
25. Bc3 Qe7 26. Bd7 Nge5 27. Bxc8 Rxc8 28. b4
Qf7 29. b5 Nd8 30. Bxe5 fxe5 31. Rxe5 Rf8
32. Rde1 Qf4 33. Re8 h6 34. Rxf8+ Qxf8 35. Qe5
c6 36. Qe7 1–0 *The Chess Review*, February 1945 (Lahde).

(872) FINE—MUGRIDGE, D

Washington Divan, Blindfold, Blitz, 1945 (25 April)
Sicilian Defence [B45]

1. e4 c5 2. Nf3 e6 3. d4 cxd4 4. Nxd4 Nf6 5. Nc3
Nc6 6. Nxc6 bxc6 7. e5 Nd5 8. Ne4 f5 9. exf6 Nxf6
10. Nd6+ Bxd6 11. Qxd6 Qa5+ 12. Bd2 Qd5 13. Qxd5
cxd5 14. Bd3 0–0 15. Bb4 Re8 16. 0–0–0 a5 17. Bc3
Ba6 18. Rhe1 Bxd3 19. cxd3 Rec8 20. Kd2 a4 21. Rc1
Rc6 22. Bd4 Rac8 23. Rxc6 Rxc6 24. Rc1 Rxc1
25. Kxc1 d6 26. Kd2 e5 27. Ba7 d4 28. Bb8 Ne8
29. b3 axb3 30. a4! Nf6 31. Bxd6 Nd7 32. Kc1
Kf7 33. Kb2 Ke6 34. Bb4 Kd5 35. f3 1–0 *The Chess
Review*, May 1945, 8 (Lahde).

(873) FINE—HOROWITZ, I

Exhibition game, 1947 (31 Jan.)
Queen's Gambit Accepted [D25]

1. d4 d5 2. c4 dxc4 3. Nf3 Nf6 4. e3 g6 5. Bxc4
Bg7 6. 0–0 0–0 7. Nc3 c5 8. d5 Ne8 9. e4 Nd6
10. Bd3 e5 11. dxe6 Bxe6 12. Ng5 Nc6 13. Nxe6
fxe6 14. f4 Nd4 15. Be3 e5 16. Bxd4 cxd4 17. Nd5
exf4 18. Nxf4 Qe7 19. Qb3+ Kh8 20. Ne6 Rxf1+
21. Rxf1 Re8 22. Nxg7 Qxg7 ½–½ *Los Angeles Times*,
9 February 1947 (Lahde).

(874) RESHEVSKY, S—FINE

Blindfold exhibition, 1950 (8 Oct.)
Catalan System [E00]

1. d4 Nf6 2. c4 e6 3. g3 d5 4. cxd5 exd5 5. Bg2
Bd6 6. Nc3 c6 7. Nh3 0–0 8. 0–0 Re8 9. Nf4 Bf5
10. Nd3 Nbd7 11. Bf4 Nf8 12. Bxd6 Qxd6 13. Rc1
Ne6 14. e3 h5 15. Ne5 c5 16. Nf3 c4 17. Ne5 Nc7
18. e4 dxe4 19. Nxc4 Qd8 20. Ne3 Bd7 21. Qb3
Bc6 22. d5 Ncxd5 23. Rfd1 Nxc3 24. Rxd8 Ne2+
25. Kf1 Nxc1 26. Rxe8+ Rxe8 27. Qc4 Nd3 28. Qd4
Re5 29. b4 Ng4 30. Nxg4 hxg4 31. Ke2 g6 32. Ke3
a6 33. h3 gxh3 34. Bxh3 Rd5 35. Qf6 Nxb4 36. Be6
Rd3+ 36 ... Nc2+! 37 Kf4 g5+ 38 Kg4 fxe6 should win. AW
37. Ke2 fxe6 38. Qxg6+ Kf8 39. Qf6+ Ke8 40. Qxe6+
Kd8 41. Qf6+ ½–½ Gordon, 131.

(875) FINE—RESHEVSKY, S

Exhibition game, New York, 1951 (28 Jan.)
Nimzowitsch-Indian, Rubinstein Variation [E42]

1. d4 Nf6 2. c4 e6 3. Nc3 Bb4 4. e3 c5 5. Nge2 d5
6. a3 Bxc3+ 7. Nxc3 cxd4 8. Qxd4 An eccentric variation from the usual 8 exd4. Though it avoids an isolated
pawn it loses valuable time. In consequence Black has no
difficulty in equalizing. BCM (A recent example is 8 exd4
dxc4 9 Bxc4 Nc6 10 Be3 0–0 11 0–0 b6 12 Qf3 (12 Qd3
Bb7 13 Rad1 Ne7 (13 ... h6!) Botvinnik–Tolush, 1965) Bb7
13 Qh3 Ne7 17 Rad1 Nfd5 18 Bg5 and White has retained
his slight advantage, Morovic–Rivas, Leon 1995. AW) 8 ...
Nc6 9. Qh4 dxc4 10. Bxc4 Ne5 11. 0–0 Nxc4
12. Qxc4 0–0 13. e4 Qa5 14. b4 Qh5 15. Bb2 Bd7
16. Rad1 a6 17. Rd3 e5 18. f4 White's 18 f4 is a rash
move that he can ill-afford in view of Black's excellent development; preferable is 18 Rfd1. BCM. 18 ... Rac8 19. Qb3
Be6 20. Nd5 20 Nd5 is forced since 20 Qd1 loses the exchange after 20 ... Bc4. 20 ... Nxe4 21. Rel f5 22. Bxe5
Qf7 23. Qd1 Rcd8 24. Nc3 Bb3 25. Qb1? 25 Qf3 was
essential. (The game would be equal after 25 Qf3 Bc2
26 Rxd8 Rxd8 27 Nxe4 Bxe4 28 Rd1 Rxd1 29 Qxd1. AW)
25 ... Nd2 26. Rxd8 Nxb1 27. Rxf8+ Kxf8 28. Bd6+
White's pieces may have been a little better coordinated
after 28 Rxb1, but the position is probably still lost for him.
AW 28 ... Kg8 29. Nxb1 Qd5 30. Bc5 Qd3 31. h3
Bc2 32. Re8+ Kf7 33. Re7+ Kf6 34. Re3 Qd1+
35. Kh2 Bxb1 36. Be7+ Kf7 37. Bc5 Be4 38. Rg3
Qe2 39. Bd4 g6 40. h4 b5 41. h5 Qc2 42. hxg6+
hxg6 0-1 BCM 1951, 254–5.

(876) FINE—FISCHER, R

Manhattan Chess Club, New York, 1963
Grünfeld Defence, 4 Bf4 [D83]

1. d4 Nf6 2. c4 g6 3. Nc3 d5 4. Bf4 Bg7 5. e3 0–0
6. Qb3 c6 7. Rc1 dxc4 8. Bxc4 b5 9. Be2 Be6 10. Qc2
b4 11. Na4 Qd5 12. b3 Nh5 13. Bf3 Qa5 14. Ne2 Bd5
15. e4 Nxf4 16. Nxf4 Bh6 17. exd5 Bxf4 18. dxc6
Bxc1 19. Qxc1 Na6 20. 0–0 Nc7 21. Rel e6 22. Re5
Nd5 23. Bxd5 exd5 24. h4 Rac8 25. h5 Qb5 26. c7
Qd7 27. Qe3 Rxc7 28. Nc5 Qg4 29. h6 Rc6 30. Rxd5

Rf6 31. Nd7 Re6 32. Re5 Qd1+ 33. Kh2 Rxe5
34. Qxe5 1–0 Boiky, Krylova & Soloviev (eds) 1993, 308.

(877) FISCHER, R—FINE

Manhattan Chess Club, New York, 1963
Philidor's Defence [C41]

1. e4 e5 2. Nf3 d6 3. d4 Nd7 4. Bc4 c6 5. 0–0 Be7
6. dxe5 dxe5 7. Qe2 Ngf6 8. Rd1 Qc7 9. Ng5 0–0
10. Bxf7+ 1–0 Boiky, Krylova & Soloviev (eds) 1993, 308.

(878) FINE—FISCHER, R

Manhattan Chess Club Celebration, New York, 1963
Nimzowitsch-Indian Defence, Rubinstein Variation [E40]

1. d4 Nf6 2. c4 e6 3. Nc3 Bb4 4. e3 d5 5. Nge2
dxc4 6. a3 Bd6 7. e4 e5 8. f4 exd4 9. Qxd4 Nc6
10. Qxc4 0–0 11. Be3 Be6 12. Qd3 Na5 13. e5? Bxe5
14. Qb5 Bxc3+ 15. Nxc3 c6 16. Qg5 Bc4 17. Rd1 Qe8
18. Kf2 Bxf1 19. Rhxf1 Nc4 20. Bc5 Ne4+ 21. Nxe4
Qxe4 22. Kg1 f6 23. Qg4 Rf7 24. Rd4 Qe3+ 25. Kh1
Qb3 26. Qe6 Nd2 27. Qd6 Nxf1 28. Qd8+ Rf8
0–1 Boiky, Krylova & Soloviev (eds) 1993, 309.

(879) FINE—FISCHER, R

Skittles, New York, 1963 (March)
Sicilian Defence [B87]

1. e4 c5 2. Nf3 d6 3. d4 cxd4 4. Nxd4 Nf6 5. Nc3
a6 6. Bc4 e6 7. Bb3 b5 8. Qe2 Be7 9. g4?! b4
10. Nb1 d5! 11. e5?! Nfd7 12. Bf4 Qb6 13. Nf3 a5!
14. Ba4 0–0 15. Be3 Qc7 16. Bd4 Ba6 17. Qe3 Nc5
18. Bxc5 Bxc5 19. Nd4 Qb6 0–1 Donaldson and Tangborn, 77–8.

(880) FISCHER, R—FINE

Skittles, New York, 1963 (March)
Evans Gambit [C52]

1. e4 e5 2. Nf3 Nc6 3. Bc4 Bc5 4. b4!? Bxb4 5. c3
Ba5 6. d4 exd4 7. 0–0 dxc3 8. Qb3 Qe7 9. Nxc3
Nf6? 10. Nd5! Nxd5 11. exd5 Ne5 12. Nxe5 Qxe5
13. Bb2 Qg5 14. h4! Qxh4 15. Bxg7 Rg8 16. Rfe1+
Kd8 17. Qg3! 1–0 Fischer 1969, 276–9.

(881) FINE—BENKO, P

Offhand Speed Game, Manhattan Chess Club, New York, 1963
King's Indian Defence [E72]

1. d4 Nf6 2. c4 g6 3. Nc3 Bg7 4. e4 d6 5. g3 c5
6. Nge2 cxd4 7. Nxd4 Nc6 8. Nc2 0–0 9. Bg2
Bg4 10. f3 Be6 11. b3 a6 12. a4 Qb6 13. Rb1 Ng4
14. fxg4 Bxc3+ 15. Bd2 Bxd2+ 16. Qxd2 Bxc4
17. Ne3 Be6 18. g5 Ne5 19. 0–0 Rac8 20. Kh1 Rc7
21. h4 Rfc8 22. h5 Rc3 23. Nc4 Nxc4 24. bxc4
Qa5 25. Rxb7 Qe5 26. Rxe7 Rxg3 27. c5 dxc5
28. Rfxf7 Rxg2 29. Qxg2 Qa1+ 30. Rf1 Qe5 31. Rf6
Rd8 32. hxg6 Rd1+ 33. Rf1 Rxf1+ 34. Qxf1 Qxe4+
35. Qg2 Qh4+ 36. Kg1 Qe1+ 37. Kh2 Qh4+ 38. Kg1
Qd4+ 39. Qf2 Qg4+ 40. Qg2 Qd4+ ½–½ BCM 1964,
15.

(882) FINE—RESHEVSKY, S

Hall of Fame Game, Somerset, 1986 (10 Aug.)
Queen's Indian Defence [E19]

1. d4 Nf6 2. c4 e6 3. Nf3 b6 4. g3 Bb7 5. Bg2 Be7
6. Nc3 Ne4 7. Qc2 Nxc3 8. Qxc3 0–0 9. 0–0 c5
10. Rd1 Bf6 11. Qc2 Nc6 12. dxc5 bxc5 13. Be3 Qe7
14. Rd2 Rfd8 15. Rad1 d6 16. h3 h6 17. Bf4 e5
18. Be3 Nd4 19. Bxd4 exd4 20. Ne1 Bxg2 21. Nxg2
Bg5 22. Rd3 h5 23. h4 Bh6 24. e3 dxe3 25. Nxe3
Bxe3 26. Rxe3 Qd7 27. Qe2 Qf5 28. Qf3 Qxf3
29. Rxf3 Rd7 30. Rf5 Re8 31. Kf1 Rde7 32. Rxd6
Re1+ 33. Kg2 R1e2 34. Rd7 f6 35. Rxa7 Rxb2
36. a4 Re5 37. Rxe5 fxe5 38. Rc7 Rb4 39. a5
Rxc4 40. a6 Ra4 41. a7 Kh7 42. Kf3 Kg6 43. Rxc5
½–½ Gordon, 375.

Career Results Tables

Tournaments

Year	Place	Games	+	–	=	Score	Event
'29–30	1	?	?	?	?	(2½–½)[1]	Marshall CC, Junior Tournament
'29–30	1	16	?	?	?	13–3	Marshall CC, B Tournament
'30	?	?	?	?	?	(1–2)	Marshall CC, Handicap Tournament
	?	18	?	?	?	(3–0)	Manhattan CC, Handicap Tournament
	?	12	?	?	?	(4½–2½)	Rice Club, New York Junior Masters
	6	7	2	3	2	3–4	Marshall CC, Preliminaries
'31	1–2	?	?	?	?	?	Marshall CC, Summer Tournament
	2	11	6	1	4	8–3	Rome, New York State Championship
'31–2	1	13	10	2	1	10½–2½	15th Marshall Club Championship
'32	1	11	8	0	3	9½–1½	Minneapolis, Western Championship
	7–10	11	2	3	6	5–6	Pasadena
'32–3	1	13	10	0	3	11½–1½	16th Marshall Club Championship
'33	1	10	7	1	2	8–2	New York, Team Trial
	3–4	11	7	2	2	8–3	Syracuse
	1	13	12	1	0	12–1	Detroit, Western Championship
'33–4	1	11	8	0	3	9½–1½	17th Marshall Club Championship
'34	–	2	1	1	0	1–1	Chicago, Preliminaries
	1	7	6	1	0	6–1	Chicago, Preliminary Section
	1–2	9	7	1	1	7½–1½	Chicago, Finals
	3–4	14	8	2	4	10–4	Syracuse
'34–5	1–3	12	11	1	0	11–1	Mexico City
'35	1	9	6	0	3	7½–1½	Milwaukee, Preliminaries A
	1	10	6	0	4	8–2	Milwaukee, Finals
	2–3	9	3	0	6	6–3	Łódź
'35–6	1	9	6	0	3	7½–1½	Hastings
'36	3–4	15	7	1	7	10½–4½	U.S. Championship, New York
	1	11	6	0	5	8½–2½	Zandvoort
	3–5	14	5	0	9	9½–4½	Nottingham
	1	7	6	0	1	6½–½	Oslo
	1	4	4	0	0	4–0	Bussum, Section "Fine"
	1	3	3	0	0	3–0	Amsterdam Jubilee [ASB]
	1–2	7	4	1	2	5–2	Amsterdam [AP]

Year	Place	Games	+	–	=	Score	Event
	?	3	1	2	0	1–2	V.A.S. Winter Tournament
'36–7	2	9	7	1	1	7½–1½	Hastings
'37	1	9	7	0	2	8–1	Stockholm
	1	7	4	1	2	5–2	Moscow
	1	5	3	0	2	4–1	Leningrad
	1–2	9	6	0	3	7½–1½	Margate
	1–3	9	6	3	0	6–3	Oostende
	1	3	2	0	1	2½–½	V.A.S. Tournament
	8	17	6	5	6	9–8	Kemeri–Riga
	2	14	2	0	12	8–6	Semmering–Baden
'37–8	4–5	9	3	0	6	6–3	Hastings
'38	2	16	11	2	3	12½–3½	U.S. Championship, New York
	1–2	14	6	3	5	8½–5½	A.V.R.O.
'39	1	6	3	0	3	4½–1½	New York, Preliminaries
	1	11	10	0	1	10½–½	New York, Finals
'39–40	1	16	13	1	2	14–2	23rd Marshall Club Championship
'40	2	16	10	1	5	12½–3½	U.S. Championship, New York
	1–2	8	5	0	3	6½–1½	Dallas, Preliminaries
	1	8	8	0	0	8–0	Dallas, Finals
	1	7	7	0	0	7–0	Salt Lake City
	1	6	4	0	2[2]	5–1	Los Angeles
'40–41	1	15	13	0	2	14–1	24th Marshall Club Championship
'41	1	5	3	0	2	4–1	St. Louis, Preliminaries
	1	9	7	0	2	8–1	St. Louis, Finals
	1	11	7	0	4	9–2	Hamilton
'42	1	7	7	0	0	7–0	Washington Divan Championship
'44	2	17	13	1	3	14½–2½	U.S. Championship, New York
'45	2	12	6	0	6	9–3	Los Angeles
'48–9	1	9	7	0	2	8–1	New York
'51	1–2	5	3	0	2	4–1	Marshall Club Sextangular
	4	11	5	2	4	7–4	New York
TOTAL		356	43	157		458½–129½[3]	(588)
%		62.2	7.5	27.4		78%	

1. Figures in parentheses in the scores column indicate incomplete data.
2. The result of the last round game at Los Angeles 1940 is not absolutely certain.
3. Includes the known part scores of note 1.

Individual Matches

Opponent	Year	Result	Wins	Losses	Draws	Score
Croney	'30	won	2	0	0	2–0
Forsberg	'30	won	3	0	0	3–0
Forsberg	'30	?	?	?	?	(1–0)[1]
Dake	'31	lost	0	2	0	0–2
Reinfeld	'31	won	3	2	1	3½–2½
Reinfeld	'32	lost	0	1	1	½–1½
Steiner, H	'32	won	4	3	3	5½–4½
Dake	'33	won	4	2	3	5½–3½

Opponent	Year	Result	Wins	Losses	Draws	Score	
Horowitz	'34	won	4	1	4	6–3	
Denker	'34	lost	2	3	4	4–5	
Torre	'34	won	1	0	1	1½–½	
Ståhlberg	'37	won	4	2	2	5–3	
Jonsson	'37	won	2	0	1	2½–½	
Larsson	'37	won	3	0	0	3–0	
Steiner, H	'44	won	3	0	1	3½–½	
Steiner, H	'47	won	4	0	2	5–1	
Najdorf	'49	drew	2	2	4	4–4	
Planas	'51	won	1	0	0	1–0	
TOTAL			42	18	27	56½–31½[2]	(88)
%			45	22	33	(64%)	

1. Figures in parentheses in the scores column indicate incomplete data.
2. Includes the known part scores of note 1.

International Team Tournaments

Olympiads

	Year	Board	Wins	Losses	Draws	Score	Team Placing
Folkestone	'33	#3	6	1	6	9–4	1st
Warsaw	'35	#1	5	4	8	9–8	1st
Stockholm	'37	#2	9	1	5	11½–3½	1st
TOTAL			20	6	19	29½–15½	(45)
%			44.4	13.3	42.2	(65.6%)	

Other International Matches

Opponent	Year	Result	Wins	Losses	Draws	Board	
Boleslavsky	'45	lost	0	1	1	#3	Radio, USA–USSR
Keres	'46	lost	0	1	1	#2	Moscow, USA–USSR
Bernstein, O	'49	drew	0	0	1	#1	Cable, USA–France
Pirc	'50	drew	0	0	2	#2	Radio, USA–Yugoslavia
TOTAL			0	2	5	2½–4½	(7)
%			0	28.6	71.4	(35.7%)	

New York Metropolitan Chess League

Opponent	Year	Wins	Losses	Draws
Steiner, H	'31	1	0	0
Bloch	'32	0	1	0
Kevitz	'32	0	1	0
Cutler	'33	1	0	0
Kashdan	'33	0	1	0
Jaffe	'34	0	1	0

Opponent	Year	Wins	Losses	Draws	
Kashdan	'34	0	0	1	
Rubin	'36	1	0	0	
Simchow	'36	1	0	0	
Simonson	'36	1	0	0	
Treysman	'36	1	0	0	
Beckhardt	'38	1	0	0	
Kashdan	'38	1	0	0	
Horowitz	'38	1	0	0	
Kupchik	'39	1	0	0	
Simchow	'39	1	0	0	
Moscowitz	'40	1	0	0	
Fajans	'40	1	0	0	
Friedman	'40	1	0	0	
Maisel	'41	1	0	0	
Pinkus	'41	0	1	0	
Denker	'42	1	0	0	
Kevitz	'45	1	0	0	
Denker	'50	1	0	0	
TOTAL		18	5	1	18½–5½ (24)
%		75	20.8	4.2	(77.1%)

Miscellaneous Match Games

Opponent	Year	Wins	Losses	Draws	
Everding	'30	1	0	0	Manhattan CC vs Philadelphia
Goldstein	'31	1	0	0	Manhattan CC vs Philadelphia
?	'31	1	0	0	City College Alumni vs Varsity
Gustafson	'34	1	0	0	Brooklyn League vs Marshall CC
Mugridge	'42	1	0	0	Team match, Washington
Turover	'44	1	0	0	Team match, Washington
Total		6	0	0	6–0
%		100	0	0	100%

Overall record in tournament and match games where game results are known +442 −74 =209 (75.4%)
Overall record in tournament and match games where results are known 571.5/758 (75.4%)

Correspondence Games

Opponent	Year	Wins	Losses	Draws	
Carter	'34–5	–	–	–	unfinished × 2
Colby	'34–5	–	–	–	unfinished × 2
Gladney	'34–5	5	–	–	unfinished × 1
Hampton	'34–5	2	0	0	
Kilburn	'34–5	1	0	1	
Lynch	'34–5	1	0	1	
Moore	'34–5	2	0	0	
Prosser	'34–5	2	0	0	

Opponent	Year	Wins	Losses	Draws	
Seeds	'34–5	–	–	–	unfinished ×2
Wink	'34–5	2	0	0	
Snethlage	1940	1	0	0	
Potter	1941	2	0	0	
de Agnew	1941	–	–	–	unfinished ×1
Fellner	1941	1	–	–	unfinished ×1
Hibbard	1941	1	0	0	
Hayes	1942	0	0	1	
Herzberger	1942	0	0	1	
Kilburn	1943	0	0	1	
TOTAL		20	0	5	22½–2½
		80	0	20	90%

U.S. Speed Championships

Year	Result	Wins	Losses	Draws	
'42	?	?	?	?	New York, preliminaries
	1st	10	1	0	New York, finals
'43	1st	9	0	2	New York, preliminaries
	1st	11	0	0	New York, finals
'44	1st	11	0	0	New York, preliminaries
	1st	10	1	0	New York, finals
'45	1st	11	0	0	New York, preliminaries
	1st	9	0	2	New York, finals
TOTAL		71	2	4	(77)
%		92.2	2.6	5.2	(94.8)

Appendices

1. Biographical Data about Fine's Opponents

As a reader I have always been interested in knowing something about the people encountered by the subject of a biography. Naturally many of the names in this work are very familiar to all chess readers, and therefore require minimal introduction. Some of the minor masters, however, will be more familiar either to European or American readers, according to circumstances. For this reason the entries for lesser players are not necessarily briefer than those for the more well known. The information provided may also help to clear up any future confusion about which Adams, Bernstein, Evans, Fox, Lasker, Steiner, or Thomas is involved, not to mention the names which only appear once herein, but which occur more than once in the chess world in general.

Unfortunately it is not easy to track down data about the less well-known figures. It may be that it would not be difficult for readers to find out more about players local to their own area. I would be most interested to hear from anyone who can add to or improve the information offered herein.

The biographies of the players involved naturally reflect the history of the period under consideration, there being a great deal of upheaval in Europe in the first half of the last century. The effect was also seen in the Americas, since many of the players were migrants, either around the late 1930s to the South American continent fleeing Nazi Germany, or, in the case of many players from the United States and Canada, and particularly New York, from families leaving tsarist Russia earlier in the century.

Players about whom nothing more than surname and initials are known are omitted from the list.

Adams, Edward Bradford (28 July 1878, Westport, CT—12 January 1972, Pasadena, CA) New York State Champion 1934.

Adams, Weaver Warren (28 April 1901, Dedham, MA—06 January 1963, Cedar Grove, NJ) U.S. Master and author who believed that White had a decisive advantage in the initial position.

Aguirre, Alfonso (dates unknown)

Alatortsev, Vladimir Alekseyevich (15 May 1909, Turki (Saratov)—13 January 1987, Moscow, USSR) IM (1950), IGM (emeritus) 1983, Elo HR 2480, USSR Championship—10 time participant, 1933 2nd after Botvinnik.

Alekhine, Alexander Alexandrovich (31 October 1892, Moscow, Russia—24 March 1946, Estoril, Portugal) World Champion 1927–35, 1937–46, Grandmaster, Elo HR 2690. A model player for the "Soviet School of Chess."

Alexander, Conel Hugh O'Donel (19 April 1909, Cork, Ireland—15 February 1974, Cheltenham, England) IM (1950), Elo HR 2475, British Champion 1938 and 1956. Played in six Olympiads from 1933 to 1958. A cryptanalyst at Bletchley Park working on the decoding of Enigma messages, he took over running the section from Alan Turing.

Allentharp, R (dates unknown)

Almgren, Sven Elias (14 May 1900, Eskilstuna, Sweden—31 January 1973, Los Angeles, CA)

Altman, Benjamin (dates unknown) Queens Chess Club Champion 1939.

Andersen, Erik (10 April 1904, Gentofte, Denmark—27 February, 1938 København, Denmark) Elo HR 2480. Many time Danish Champion of the 1920s and 1930s. Winner of the Nordic Chess Congress Stockholm, 1930.

Andersson, Fred (dates unknown)

Appel, Izaak (c1905–c1941) Polish Master, Łódź City Champion 1934. Active during the 1920s and '30s. Participated in Polish Championships. 1st at Łódź 1930 ahead of Kolski,Regedziński and Frydman.

Apšenieks, Fricis (Franz Apscheneek) (07 April 1894, Tetele, Latvia—25 April 1941, Riga, USSR) Elo HR 2430, Latvian Champion 1926–7, 1934.

Araiza Munoz, José Joaquin (23 March 1900, Guadalajara, Mexico—27 September 1971) Perhaps the strongest of the Mexican players after Torre. A Captain in the Mexican army when he first encountered Fine he had risen to the rank of Major by 1945. Playing strength equivalent to U.S. Master. Mexican Champion.

Aviles Solares, Dr. José (dates unknown)

Barnes, George (dates unknown) of Minneapolis, Minnesota State Champion.

Barron, Ted (dates unknown) of Flushing.

Becker, Georg Albert(o) (05 September 1896, Vienna, Austria—17 May 1984, Vicente Lopez, Argentina) IM 1953, noted theoretician.

Beckhardt, Nathan (dates unknown) A college contemporary of Fine, Bernstein and Levenstein. A New York player of the 1930s.

Belavenyets, Sergey Vsevolodovich (18 July 1910, Smolensk, Russia—07 March 1942, Novgorod, USSR) Soviet Master of Sport, Moscow Champion 1932, 1937–8.

Belson, Harold (dates unknown) Canadian Champion of 1934.

Benko, Pal Charles (born 15 July 1928, Amiens, France) International Grandmaster (1958). Best 5-year average Elo rating 2570. Represented Hungary at the Moscow Olympiad, 1956. Settled in the United States and became a World Championship Candidate in 1959 and 1962. Played for the US in six Olympiads.

Bentz, David (dates unknown)

Bergkvist, Nils Valentin (13 August 1900, Södertälje, Sweden—1993) Three time Swedish international team tournament member—1936, 1939, 1950. Stockholm City Champion.

Bergs, Teodors (27 July 1902, Riga, Latvia—03 October 1962, Riga, Latvian SSR) Riga City Champion 1934. Second equal in the 2nd Latvian Chess Championship, Riga 1926.

Bernstein, Jacob (dates unknown) New York State Champion 1920, 1921 and 1922.

Bernstein, Dr. Ossip Samoilovich (02 October 1882, [Gregorian] Zhitomir, Ukraine/Russia—30 November 1962, France) Grandmaster (1950), Elo HR 2590.

Bernstein, Sidney Norman (born 13 July 1911, New York) U.S. Master. Tied with Smirka for the Marshall Club Championship of 1930, with Hanauer in 1939, he won outright in 1957 and 1958. He also tied with Reinfeld for the Manhattan Chess Club Championship in 1942. Nine time U.S. Championship finalist 1936–62. Captained the U.S. team in the 1952–3 Postal Olympiad.

Bigelow, Horace Ransom (born 06 March 1898, St. Paul, Minnesota) Marshall Chess Club Champion 1929.

Bisguier, Arthur Bernard (born 08 October 1929, New York, NY) IM (1950) GM (1957). U.S. Champion 1954. Seven times made a plus score in the U.S. Championship. Manhattan Chess Club Champion 1947–8, 1948–9.

Black, Roy T. (14 February 1888, Brooklyn, NY—27 July 1962, Williamstown, NY) of Buffalo.

Bloch (dates unknown) (possibly Dr. Benedict Bloch of Empire City Chess Club).

Blumin, Boris (born 29 December 1907, Saint Petersburg, Russia) Canadian Champion 1936 and 1937. U.S. Master.

Bogolyubov, Efim Dimitrijewitsch (14 April 1889, Stanislavsk/Kiev, Ukraine—18 June 1952 Triberg, Germany) Grandmaster, Elo HR 2610. Contested two World Championship matches with Alekhine.

Boleslavsky, Isaak Yefremovich (09 June 1919, Zolotonosha, Poltava, RSFSR—15 February 1977, Minsk, Belarus, USSR) GM (1950). One of the strongest players in the world in the 1940s and early 1950s, equal first with David Bronstein—his future son-in law—at the Candidates tournament of 1950, he lost the play-off match. A noted theoretician, his collection of his best games had an important influence on Robert Fischer. Best 5 year average Elo 2650.

Bondarevsky, Igor Zakharovich (12 May 1913, Samsonov village near Rostov-on-Don, Ukraine (Russia)—14 June 1979, Piatigorsk, USSR) Grandmaster, USSR Champion 1940.

Böök, Eero Einar (09 February 1910, Helsinki, Finland—07 January 1990, Helsinki) Grandmaster (emeritus). Active from the 1930s to the 1960s. Best five-year average Elo rating 2500.

Borochow, Harry (born 15 June 1898, Poltava, Russia) U.S. Master. Started his chess career in New York, like Fine he attended the College of the City of New York, but later moved to the West Coast. Western Champion.

Borsodi, Ralph (dates unknown) (In the 1890s the *American Chess Magazine* had a publisher by the name of William Borsodi)

van den Bosch, Johannes Hendrik Otto (born 12 April 1906, 's-Gravenhage, The Netherlands) Winner of the 3rd Keus Cup 's-Gravenhage 1928, 1st= with Landau at Zwolle, 1928 and 1st ahead of Landau at The Hague 1929–30.

Botvinnik, Mikhail Moiseevich (17 August 1911, Kuokkala (Repino), Russia—05 April 1995, Russia) World Champion 1948–57, 1958–60, 1961–63. Often described as the Patriarch of Soviet Chess.

Bourbeau, Charles H (dates unknown) of New York City.

Broderman, Dr. Alfredo (dates unknown) Playing strength equivalent to a U.S. Expert.

Budo, Alexander (dates unknown)

B[u]erger, Victor (29 January 1904, Nikolaevsky, Russia—March 1996) Internationalist in Cable matches. Participated at London 1927 and Margate 1937, when he defeated Alekhine.

Byrne, Donald (12 June 1930, New York, NY—08 April 1976, Philadelphia, PA) IM (1962). U.S. Open Champion 1953, played three times in Olympiads.

Byrne, Robert Eugene (born 20 April 1928, New York, NY) IM (1952) GM (1964) U.S. Open Champion 1960, U.S. Champion 1972. World Championship Candidate 1973. Eight time representative of the USA at Olympiads. U.S. Speed Champion 1948.

Camarena, Joaquin (dates unknown) Playing strength equivalent to a Class A player.

Capablanca y Graupera, José Raúl (19 November 1888 Havana, Cuba—08 March 1942, New York, NY) World

Champion 1921–27. Elo HR 2725. Champion of Cuba at the age of eleven, he was already clearly of World Championship class in his early twenties. Tried for nearly fifteen years to arrange a return match with his successor to the World title.

Cass, Alvin Cushing (11 May 1886, Boston, MA—08 March 1950, New York, NY) Frequent participant in the Marshall Club championships.

Chernev, Irving (29 January 1900, Priluki, Russia—29 September 1981, San Francisco, CA) Prolific chess author.

Chevalier, Frederick Richmond (born 14 September 1907 Boston, MA) Boston Champion 1927. Harvard College Champion and editor of a chess column in *The Christian Science Monitor*.

Chistyaskov, ?Alexander Nikolaevich? (born 22 January 1914, [Gregorian] Moscow, Russia)

Cohen, S. S. (dates unknown) U.S. Master.

Collett, John (born 1909?)

Collins, Jack (born 23 September 1912, Newburgh, NY) Author, coach and player.

Cruz, Walter Oswaldo (1910, Petropolis, Brazil—1967, Rio de Janeiro) Many time Brazilian champion. Playing strength equivalent to a U.S. Master.

Cutler, Harold (dates unknown) of New York University.

Dahlstrom, Burton O. (born 23 September 1913, Amery, WI)

Dake, Arthur William (born Darkowski 08 April 1910, Portland, OR—April 2000, Reno, NV) GM (emeritus) Elo HR 2470. Marshall Club Champion 1930/31. Three time member of victorious U.S. teams at Chess Olympiads. Fourth on the first USCF rating list.

Danielsson, Gösta [Erik Vilhelm] (1912–1978) a heavy scorer for Sweden on board four in four international team tournaments from 1935 to 1939. Resident of Stockholm.

Dekker, C. L. (?L. C. Dekker, member of B.S.G. Bussum, played in Dutch Championship 1942–3)

Denker, Arnold Sheldon (born 21 February 1914, New York, NY) IM 1950, GM (emeritus) 1981. U.S. Champion 1944. Elo HR 2470.

DiCamillo, Attilio (28 May 1917, Philadelphia, PA—17 February 1962, Philadelphia) U.S. Master. Three times a U.S. Championship finalist. One of Robert Fischer's teachers in his early years. According to Sidney Bernstein DiCamillo was a fine endgame player.

Donovan, Jeremiah (dates unknown) U.S. Master.

Drummond, Frank Redpath (born 30 April 1914, Toronto, Canada)

Dunkelblum, Arthur (23 April 1906, Podgorze, Poland—27 June 1979, Anvers, Belgium) IM 1957. Elo HR 2400.

Dunst, Theodore Alexander (Ted) (11 April 1907, New York, NY—18 December 1985, Lambertville, NJ) The opening 1 Nc3 is sometimes named for him. Won the Marshall Chess Club summer tournament of 1935 with Smirka.

Dyner, Israel (27 September 1903, Warsaw, Poland—13 February 1979, Rishon Lezion, Israel) Belgian Champion 1932 and 1935.

Eastman, [Charles John] George (né Karl Johan Georg Ostman) (04 March 1903, Stockholm, Sweden—16 May 1975, Detroit, MI) U.S. Master. Tied for first in the Canadian Championship of 1932.

Eaton, Vincent Lanius (born 31 August 1915, Puerto Cabello, Venezuela—1962) Graduated from Harvard at the age of eighteen. Chess problemist. District of Columbia Champion 1942.

Ekelund, Jakob [Emanuel] (20 September 1890, Västerås, Sweden—12 December 1975 Örebro, Sweden)

Eliskases, Erich Gottlieb (15 or 27 February 1913, Innsbruck, Austria—? February 1997, Cordoba, Argentina) GM 1952. Elo HR 2560. First player to represent three different countries in Olympiads (Austria, the Greater German Chess Union and Argentina). Suggested by Alekhine as a possible title contender around 1941, but never really of the same class as the AVRO players.

Elison, Charles F (né Karl) (24 February 1888, Berlin, Germany—02 August 1939, Chicago, IL) Member of the German Chess Club of Chicago. Took second place, behind Factor, at the 1930 Chicago Championship Tournament.

Elo, Arpad Emrick (né Imre Arpad Elö) (25 August 1903, Egyházaskeszö, Hungary—05 November 1992, Milwaukee, WI) Deviser of the international rating system and prime mover in the formation of the USCF in 1939. Best 5-year average Elo rating 2230. Wisconsin State Champion.

Enevoldsen, Jens (23 September 1907, Copenhagen, Denmark—23 May 1980) IM 1950, Elo HR 2430.

Engholm, Nils (dates unknown) Member of the Swedish Chess Club of Chicago.

Euwe, Dr. Machgielis (Max) (20 May 1901, Watergrafsmer, The Netherlands—26 November 1981, Amsterdam). World Amateur Champion 1928. World Champion 1935–7. GM 1950. Elo HR 2650, President of FIDE 1970–78.

Evans, Harry (dates unknown)

Evans, Larry Melvyn (born 22 March 1932, New York) IM (1952) GM (1957) U.S. Champion 1951 (successfully defending the title in a match with Herman Steiner in 1952), 1961–2, 1968 and 1980 (he was also second on four occasions), U.S. Open Champion 1951, '52, '54, and '71. Eight times a participant at Olympiads. U.S. Speed Champion 1950.

Factor, Samuel D. (22 September 1892, Łódź, Poland—11 January 1949, Chicago, IL) President of the Roosevelt Chess and Bridge Club, Chicago. Many time Chicago City Champion and Illinois State Champion during the 1920s and '30s. Western Championship 1922 and 1930 (tied with Norman Whitaker). Board 3 behind Kashdan and Steiner at The Hague International Team Tournament 1930.

Fairhurst, Dr. William Albert (21 August 1903, Alderley Edge, England—13 March 1982, New Zealand) IM 1951. Elo HR 2440. An eminent civil engineer. Scottish Champion eleven times between 1932 and 1962, British Champion 1937, Commonwealth Champion 1951. Played for Scotland and New Zealand in Olympiads.

Fajans, Harry (born 08 May 1905) of New York University.

Feigins, Movsa (28 February 1908, Daugavpils, Latvia—11 August 1950, Buenos Aires, Argentina) Latvian Champion 1932, first equal at the Latvian Chess Federation Congress, Section 2, Riga, 1930.

Fink, Adolf Jay (01 July 1890, San Francisco, California—15 December 1956, San Francisco) California State Champion 1928, 1929 and 1945 (with Steiner).

Finkelstein, Milton (03 May 1920, New York, NY—2001) Marshall Chess Club member, and later President, who also attended Townsend Harris High School.

Fischer, Robert James (born 09 March 1943, Chicago, IL) International Grandmaster (1958). Won the FIDE World Championship in 1972 but could not agree to terms for a defence of the title in 1975. Peak Elo rating 2780. Many people consider him the finest player who ever lived.

Flohr, Salo [Salomon Mikhailovich] (21 November 1908, Gorodenka (Horodenka), Ukraine/Russian Poland—18 July 1983, Moscow, USSR) GM. Elo HR 2620. Considered a contender for the World Championship in the early 1930s and officially nominated as the FIDE candidate after making the best first board score at the Stockholm Team Tournament of 1937. Born within the boundaries of the Russian Empire, he was orphaned and fled to Czechoslovakia in 1916; as a result of the rise of Nazism in the 1930s he made the U.S.S.R. his home for the later part of his life.

Foerder, Heinz (later Yosef Porat) (born 07 June 1909, Breslau/Wrocław) 14th Silesian Chess Federation Champion 1927, 1st place at the 17th Schleswig Chess Union Congress 1930, 1st Upper Silesian Champion 1932, 2nd Israeli Champion 1937.

Foltys, Jan (13 October 1908, Svinov, Czechoslovakia—11 March 1952, Ostrava, Czechoslovakia) IM, Elo HR 2530. Czech champion 1940 and 1943. Second board for the Czech teams of 1937 and 1939. Qualified for the Saltsjöbaden Interzonal 1952. His best results suggest he was of grandmaster strength.

Forsberg, Bruno Christian (26 August 1892 Finland—10 February 1961 New York, NY) Marshall Chess Club Champion 1920–21. Active during the 1920s, '30s and '40s.

Fox, Albert Whiting (29 April 1881, Boston, MA—29 April 1964, Washington, DC) Champion of the Manhattan Chess Club and of the Brooklyn Chess Club.

Fox, Maurice (born 14 January 1898, Ukraine) Canadian Chess Champion 1927, 1929, 1931, 1932, 1935 and 1938.

Frere, Walter (19 January 1874, New York, NY—24 April 1943) Member of the Brooklyn Chess Club and the Marshall Chess Club. He was a correspondent for the *American Chess Monthly*. Son of Thomas Frère, who assisted in the founding of the Brooklyn Chess Club and the Manhattan Chess Club.

Friend, Bernard (dates unknown)

Frydman, Paulin[o] (26 May 1905, Poland—03 February 1982, Buenos Aires, Argentina) IM (1955) Elo HR 2500. Several time Warsaw champion, twice runner up in the Polish Championship, seven time Olympiad team member. Won the

Helsinki Tournament 1935 ahead of Keres and Ståhlberg and Sopot, 1930, ahead of Rellstab, Appel and Stoltz.

Garfinkel, Boris (dates unknown)

Glass, Eduard (dates unknown) 1929 Austrian co–Champion.

Glicco, Moises (dates unknown)

Goldstein, M (dates unknown) (Possibly S. M. Goldstein of Providence, R.I.)

Goldwater, Walter Delmar (29 July 1907, New York, NY—24 June 1985, NY) Marshall Chess Club member, and later President, who also attended Townsend Harris High School.

Golombek, Harry (01 March 1911, London, England—07 January 1995) IM 1950, GM (emeritus 1985) Elo HR 2450. Three-time British champion, and once runner-up after play-off. Also a noted writer and International Arbiter. Nine times a member of the Olympiad team for B.C.F./ England.

Gonzales Rojo, Enrique (dates unknown) Mexican master, playing strength equivalent to that of a U.S. Master.

Grau, Roberto Gabriel (18 March 1900, Buenos Aires, Argentina—12 April 1944, Buenos Aires) Elo HR 2430, Argentine Champion 1924, 1926, 1934. South American Champion 1921/2, 1928.

Green, Matthew (born 28 December 1915) U.S. Master. Graduate of New York University, master level player, a notable exponent of lightning chess. USCF Grading 2306.

Grigorieff, W (Vladimir?) (dates unknown) Illinois State Chess Champion, who apparently had European experience. A player identified as W. Grigorieff in ChessBase played in a simultaneous exhibition against Alekhine at Geneva in 1925, if this is the same player it suggests he was a Russian émigré.

Grob, Henry (04 June 1904, Braunau, Austria/Bohemia—03 July 1974, Zollikon, Switzerland) IM 1950, 2440. Author of *Angriff g2-g4*. Probably the player to play the greatest number of games by correspondence, both in total and simultaneously.

Grossman, Nat (born circa 1910) New York City High School Student Champion 1926, active in the late 1920s and early 1930s. New York State Chess Association Champion 1932.

Grünfeld, Ernst Franz (21 November 1893, Vienna, Austria—03 April 1962, Vienna) GM (1950), Elo HR 2550. Noted theoretician and innovator in the openings. One of the strongest players in the world during the 1920s and, with Fine, a second to Euwe in his 1937 match with Alekhine.

Guckemus, R. J. (15 August 1874, Utica, NY—9 May 1935, Utica) of Utica.

Gudmundsson, Jon (dates unknown) Icelandic champion 1932, 1936 and 1937.

Guimard, Carlos Enrique (born 06 April 1913, Santiago del Estero, Argentina) IM (1950) GM (1960). Argentine Champion.

Halper, Nathan (Nat) (14 July 1907, New York, NY—26 June 1983, Hyannis, MA)

Hamermesh (dates unknown) (?Morton Hamermesh of El Paso Chess Club and City College)

Hanauer, Milton Loeb (05 August 1908–16 April 1988) United States Master. USCF rating 2300. Author, frequen participant in Marshall Club tournaments and U.S. Championship tournaments of the 1930s and 1940s. New York State Champion 1926. Won tournaments at Ventnor City 1939, ahead of Reinfeld, and 1940, with Sidney Bernstein. Marshall Chess Club Champion 1950–51. Reserve on the United States team at the 1928 Olympiad. Attended Townsend Harris High School.

Harris, Jacob (dates unknown) Six time Minnesota State Champion up to 1930 and again in 1934.

Hartsfield, Edgar (dates unknown) Texas State Chess co-Champion 1936.

Hassialis, M. D. (dates unknown) of West Side Chess Club.

Havasi, Kornél (10 January 1892, Budapest, Hungary—15 January 1945, Bruck/Leitha, Austria) Elo HR 2460. Hungarian Champion 1922, in seven Olympiads from 1927–37 he scored 61/90.

Hazard, Fred (dates unknown) of Minneapolis.

Hazenfuss, Volfgang R. (Wolfgang Hasenfuss) (dates unknown)

Heal, Edwin (dates unknown)

Heiestad, Sigurd (born 10 April 1903)

Hellman, Arne (dates unknown)

Hermann, Gabriel (dates unknown)

Herzberger, Dr. Max (dates unknown) Played in the Experts Section at Hamilton 1941.

Holland, Kirk D. (dates unknown) Player, organizer and benefactor of chess in the 1930s and 1940s.

Holm, Gösta (dates unknown)

Horowitz, Israel Albert (I. A., Al) (15 November 1907, New York, NY—18 January 1973, New York NY) IM (1950) Elo HR 2510. Founder of *The Chess Review*. Olympiad team member 1931, '35, '37 and '50 scoring 38.5/51.

Howard, Kenneth Samuel (12 April 1882, LeRoy, NY—20 July 1972, Morristown, NJ) Problem composer, high scorer in the New York Metropolitan League for the Marshall Chess Club from 1927–38.

Ilyin-Genevsky, Alexander Fedorovich (28 November 1894, St. Petersburg, Russia—03 September 1941, Novaya Ladoga, USSR) Elo HR 2460. 1st= at the Caucasian Championship Tiflis, 1928, 1st at the 7th (Soviet) City Championship Leningrad, 1929.

Isaacs, Lewis J (dates unknown) Member of the City Club of Chicago, participant in the Chicago City Championship.

Jaffe, Charles (c 1879 Dubrovno, Russia—12 July 1941, New York, NY) Elo HR 2430.

Jefferson, Bradford B. (08 July 1874, Memphis, TN—14 May 1963, Memphis)

John, Walter (1879, Thorn, Poland—c 1940, Berlin) Elo HR 2460.

Johnsen, Eugen (dates unknown) 1932 Norwegian Champion.

Jonsson, Eric (01 October 1903, Göteborg, Sweden—19 September 1974, Göteborg) Göteborg City Champion 1936.

Kahn, Victor (1889, Moscow, Russia—06 October 1971, Nice, France) Author and master, French Champion 1934.

Kan, Ilya Abramovich (04 May 1909 Samara, Russia—12 December 1978) IM 1950. Elo HR 2510.

Kashdan, Isaac (19 November 1905, New York, NY—20 February, 1985 Los Angeles CA) GM (1954), Elo HR 2570. The strongest player in the USA in the early to mid-thirties until surpassed by Fine and Reshevsky by 1936. Was unable to arrange a match for the U.S. championship with Marshall because of the financial demands. Playing on board one ahead of Marshall for the U.S. teams of 1930, '31 and '33 he made a higher percentage score than the then U.S. champion. Set up *The Chess Review* in 1933.

Kavli-Jørgenssen, Olaf (dates unknown) Norwegian Champion 1938.

Keres, Paul Petrovich (07 January 1916, Narva, Estonia—05 June 1975, Helsinki, Finland) GM 1950, Elo HR 2670. Three times USSR Champion, four times placed second or second equal in World Championship Candidates Tournaments (in addition to which he placed first on tiebreak in the 1938 AVRO tournament, which should have produced a world title challenger). From 1935 to 1965 one of the elite, continuing his success right until his final tournament just before his death.

Kevitz, Alexander (Al, Alex) (01 September 1902, New York, NY—24 October 1981, New York) U.S. Senior Master. Manhattan Chess Club Champion 1927, 1928/9 and 1935/6 and Brooklyn Club Champion. The 1951 USCF rating list placed Kevitz third amongst U.S. players (based on their results in American tournaments), behind only Fine and Reshevsky, and ahead of Dake, Denker, Kashdan, Simonson, and Horowitz. He defeated Bondarevsky in the USA–USSR match, Moscow 1946.

Kilburn, Dr. Carl J (dates unknown) President of the Collinsville Chess Club in Connecticut.

Kmoch, Hans (Johann Joseph) (25 July 1894, Vienna, Austria—13 February 1973, New York, NY) IM 1950, Elo HR 2475. Of Czech parentage, Kmoch three times played for Austria in team tournaments, emigrated to The Netherlands in the 1930s and to the USA in 1947. He was a respected writer on the game.

Knudsen, John (dates unknown)

Kolski, Josek (1900–1941) Third equal in the 1st Polish Championship, Warsaw 1926. Winner of a Łódź quadrangular tournament 1935.

Koltanowski, George (born 17 September 1903, Anvers, Belgium) IM (1950) Elo HR 2450.

Kramer, George Mortimer (born 15 May 1929, New York, NY) U.S. Senior Master. U.S. Speed Champion 1949.

Kraszewski, Clarence (dates unknown)

Kreznar, Steve (dates unknown)

Kupchik, Abraham (15 May 1892, Brest-Litovsk, Russia—26 November 1970, Montclair, NJ) Elo HR 2480. Manhattan Club Champion 1924/5. First equal with Marshall at the 9th American Chess Congress, Lake Hopatcong 1923. New York State Chess Association Champion 1915 and 1919.

Kussman A. S. (dates unknown) District of Columbia Champion 1941.

Landau, Salo (01 April 1903, Bochnia, Poland—Auschwitz) Elo HR 2480. Champion of The Netherlands 1936.

Lardo de Tejada, Major Juan (dates unknown)

Larsson, Erik (born 20 May 1915) Winner of the Swedish Chess Federation tournament 1935, Göteborg City Champion 1938.

Lasker, Dr. Edward (03 December 1885, Kempfen, Poland—23 March 1981, New York) IM (1963), U.S. Master. The only player to arrange a match with Marshall for his United States title, he lost narrowly 9½–8½ in 1923.

Lasker, Dr. Emanuel (24 December 1868, Berlinchen, Germany—11 January 1941, New York, NY) World Chess Champion 1894–1921, Elo HR 2720.

Lessing, Norman (born 24 June 1911, Philadelphia, PA) Member of the Empire City Chess Club. Tied for first with Santasiere at the New York State meeting at Utica 1930, but lost the play off.

Levenfish, Grigory Yakovlevich (09 March 1889 [Gregorian], Poland—09 February 1961, Moscow, USSR) GM 1950 Elo HR 2540. USSR Champion 1935 and 1937, in the absence of Botvinnik, but held his title by drawing a match +5 −5 −3 in late 1937 with Botvinnik.

Levenstein, Robert (dates unknown) Educated at Brooklyn Boys' High School and City College of New York (Class of '34). Interborough High School Chess League of New York individual champion 1930. New York State Champion 1934.

Levy, Louis (born 10 February 1921 New York, NY)

Lew, H. A. (dates unknown) Played in the Saint Louis City Championship.

Lilienthal, Andor (born 05 May 1911 [Gregorian], Moscow, Russia) GM (1950) Elo HR 2570, of Hungarian Jewish descent, he was for many years a resident of the USSR, 1st equal in the 12th USSR Championship, Moscow 1940.

List, Paul (1887 Klaipeda, Lithuania—09 September 1954, London, England) A player of master strength, he left Russia for Germany in the 1920s and Germany for England in 1938. British Lightning Chess Champion 1953.

Littman (Drexel), Gustave (dates unknown) Florida State Champion. Southern Chess Association Champion 1939, 1944 and 1945. U.S. Championship participant 1946.

Lundin, Erik Ruben (02 July 1904, Stockholm, Sweden—05 December 1988, Stockholm) IM (1950) GM (1983) Elo HR 2530. Ten times Swedish Champion and eight time participant at international team tournaments.

MacMurray, Donald (14 November 1914, East Schadack, NY—03 December 1938, New York) A fine natural talent. Died of a mystery illness.

Marchand, Erich Watkinson (born 07 July 1914, Hartford CT) of Harvard ('36).

Margolis, Albert Charles (21 February 1908, Pittsburgh, PA—03 January 1951, Chicago, IL) Western Chess Association Champion 1927, Chicago Champion 1933 and 1945.

Maróczy, Géza (03 March 1870, Szeged, Austro-Hungary—29 May 1951, Budapest, Hungary) Grandmaster, Elo HR 2620. Highly successful tournament player between 1899 and 1908, placing first, second or third in fourteen out of fifteen tournaments he played during the period. Was scheduled to play Lasker in a World Championship match from October 1906 but for political reasons (both chess and international) the match fell through. Manhattan Chess Club Champion 1926/7.

Marshall, Frank James (10 August 1877, New York, NY—09 November 1944, Jersey City, NJ) Elo HR 2570. U.S. Champion 1909–1935. Captained the United States at five Olympiads 1930–35, bringing home the gold medals on four occasions. Opened "Marshal's Chess Divan" in 1915, from which sprang the Marshall Chess Club.

Medina, Joaquin (dates unknown) Champion of Zacatecas.

Menchik, Vera (16 February 1906, Moscow, Russia [of Czech descent]—27 June 1944, London, England) Elo HR 2350, Women's World Champion 1927–44.

Mengarini, Ariel Aldace Anteo (born 19 October 1919, Roma, Italy) U.S. Master. District of Columbia Champion 1940. Like Fine he worked as a psychiatrist for the Veterans Administration.

Michell, Reginald Pryce (09 April 1873, Penzance, England—20 May 1938, London) Elo HR 2420. British Amateur Champion 1902. First at the British Chess Federation Congress, London 1922. City of London Champion 1925–6.

Michelsen, Einar (1885, Odense, Denmark—15 May 1952, Chicago, IL) Tied with Reshevsky for third in the Chicago City Championship 1932.

Mikenas, Vladas Ionovich (17 April 1910 [Gregorian], Revel, now Tallinn, Estonia—Autumn 1992) International Master, International Correspondence Chess Master, Elo HR 2540. Lithuanian Champion 1945, 1947, 1948, 1964 and 1968; Georgian Champion (hors concours) 1945. Ten times participant in the USSR Championship.

Milner-Barry, Sir Philip Stuart (P. S.) (20 September 1906, London, England—25 March 1995). Played for BCF at the international team tournaments of 1937, '39, '52 and '56. Worked at Bletchley Park.

Montgomerie, John (born 04 September 1911, Glasgow, Scotland)

Monticelli, Mario (16 March 1902, Venezia, Italy—30 June 1995) Grandmaster (emeritus). Three time Italian Champion. Equal first at Budapest 1926 with Grünfeld ahead of Rubinstein, Réti and Tartakower.

Morgan, Dale (dates unknown)

Morton, Harold (10 January 1906, Providence, RI—17 February 1940, Arcadia, IA) Several time New England Champion and partner of Horowitz on the Chess Review. Died in a car crash while driving Horowitz on a promotional tour.

Moskowitz or **Moscowitz**, Jakob (born 19 October 1912, New York, NY) U.S. Master. Bronx County Champion 1936–8, Manhattan Club Champion 1939.

Mugridge, Donald Henry (23 April 1905, Chicago, IL—03 November 1964, Washington, DC) Harvard College and District of Columbia Champion. President and Champion of the Washington Divan Chess Club in 1942.

Muir, Walter (born 07 August 1905, New York, NY) International Master of Correspondence Chess (1971).

Mulder, Emile (1910–?1990) Member of V.A.S, played in the

Dutch Championship in 1929, 1933, 1936, 1938 (as a student played under the pseudonym Molenaar).

Muller, W.C. (dates unknown) Member of B.S.G. Bussum

Myhre, Erling (11 January 1903, Kristiania/Oslo, Norway—12 April 1971) Norwegian Champion 1946 and 1950.

Naegeli, Oskar (25 February 1885, Ermatingen, Switzerland—19 November 1959, Fribourg) Elo HR 2450.

Najdorf, Moishe Mieczsław (later Miguel) (15 April 1910, Warsaw, Poland—04 July 1997, Spain) GM (1950) Elo HR 2635, twice World Championship Candidate (1950 and 1953).

Nash, Edmund (dates unknown)

Neidich, Leon (dates unknown)

Nilsson, Harald (dates unknown)

Norcia, Frederico (31 March 1904, Lugo di Romagna, Italy—15 July 1985, Modena)

Ohman, Reverend Howard Elmer (17 July 1899, Omaha, NE—25 February 1968, Omaha) Nebraska State Chess Association Champion for twenty-four years from 1917 to 1940.

O'Kelly de Galway, Albéric (17 May 1911, Bruxelles, Belgium—03 October 1980, Bruxelles) GM (1956) Elo HR 2530. Belgian Champion. World Champion of Correspondence Chess.

Opočenský, Karel (07 February 1892, Bruch/Most, Czechoslovakia—16 November 1975, Praha) IM (1950) Elo HR 2460. Four times Czech champion. Made the absolute best score at the Folkestone Team Tournament. Unlucky in opening nomenclature! The Opočenský Gambit was later renamed the Benko Gambit, the Opočenský Opening is more popularly known as the Trompowsky and the Opočenský Variation of the Sicilian Defence is now called the Najdorf Variation.

Osher, Seymour (dates unknown) of Chicago.

Ozols, Karlis (born 09 August 1912, Riga, Latvia) International Correspondence Chess Master. Became a naturalised citizen of Australia in the 1950s.

Page, George (27 October 1890, Glasgow, Scotland—26 June 1953, Edinburgh) Scottish Champion in 1925.

Palmer, Marvin (born 20 November 1897, Cedar Rapids, IA) of Detroit, first equal at the Michigan State meeting of 1934 and 1937, clear first 1940.

Panov, Vasily Nikolaevich (01 November 1906 [Gregorian], Kozelsk, Russia—18 January 1973, Moscow, USSR) IM Elo HR 2470.

Partos, Julius (26 July 1916, New York, NY—07 December 1968, New York) of Hungaria International Chess Club. Queens County Champion 1937.

Pavey, Max (05 March 1918, Boston, MA—04 September 1957, New York) U.S. Senior Master. Scottish Champion 1939, New York State Champion 1949. Died of Radium poisoning.

Peckar, Mark (dates unknown)

Pedersen, Henry (dates unknown)

Perez, Abel (dates unknown)

Perrine, Professor G. H. (dates unknown) of Clinton.

Persinger, Louis J (dates unknown) Noted violinist, teacher of Yehudi Menuhin and Ruggiero Ricci.

Petrovs, Vladimirs Mikhailovich (27 September 1909 [Gregorian], Riga, Latvia—26 August 1943, Vorkuta, Lithuanian SSR) Elo HR 2520. First equal at the Latvian Chess Federation Congress, Section 1, Riga, 1930, second equal in the 2nd Latvian Championship, Riga 1926.

Pettersson, Einar "Spielmann" (born 09 September 1901) 1929 Swedish Chess Federation champion.

Pilnik, Herman (08 January 1914, Stuttgart, Germany—12 November 1981, Caracas, Venezuela) IM (1950) GM (1952).

Pinkus, Albert Sidney (20 March 190, New York—04 February 1984, New York) U.S. Master. Champion of both the Marshall and the Manhattan Chess Clubs. Five times a participant in the U.S. Championship between 1940 and 1951, made the fifth highest winning percentage (62.3%) of players taking part three or more times up to 1996. Outside of chess, during the 1930s he made ten trips to South America in search of exotic species. He started a career in stockbroking in 1939.

Pirc, Vasja (19 December 1907, Idria, Austro-Hungary—02 June 1980, Ljubljana) GM (1953) Elo HR 2540. First or first equal in the Yugoslav championship 1935, '36, '37, '48 and '53.

Planas Garcia, Francisco (born 06 April 1908)

Polak, Joseph August Jean (24 January 1915–1943)

Polland, David S. (dates unknown) U.S. Senior Master active during the 1930s and '40s, eleventh on the 1951 USCF rating list. New York State Chess Association Champion 1937.

Ponce, Luis Neftali (born 05 February 1908, Quito, Ecuador) Champion of Quito in 1930, District of Columbia Champion 1937. Participated in a subsidiary event at the Nottingham Chess Congress 1936. A member of the Ecuadorian Diplomatic Service.

Prins, Lodewijk (27 January 1913, Amsterdam, The Netherlands—11 November 1999) IM (1950) GM (1982, emeritus), Elo HR 2480. Dutch champion in 1965, played in every Olympiad from 1939 to 1968.

Rabinovich, Ilya Leontievich (11 May 1891, St. Petersburg, Russia—23 April 1942, Kirov, USSR) Elo HR 2530, 1st= USSR Championship 1934. Leningrad Champion 1920, '25, '28 and '40.

Ragozin, Viacheslav Vasilievich (08 October 1908, St. Petersburg, Russia—11 March 1962, Moscow, USSR) GM 1950 Elo HR 2550, 2nd World Champion at correspondence chess.

Rauch, Joseph Lyon (born 07 February 1916, Montréal, Canada)

Rauzer, Vsevolod Alfredovich (16 October 1908 [Gregorian]—1941 Leningrad, USSR) Soviet Master (1929). A strong player but most notable for his early development work in certain openings, in particular the "Yugoslav" Attack (6 Be3, 7 f3, 8 Qd2 and 0-0-0) in the Dragon Sicilian, the idea 6 Bg5, 7 Qd2 and 8 0-0-0 in the Scheveningen Sicilian.

Regedziński, Teodor (later Theodor Reger) (28 April 1894, Aleksandrów, Łódzki—02 August 1954, Łódź) Several times a member of the Polish Olympiad team between 1928 and 1939. Third equal in the first Polish Championship, Warsaw 1926.

Reilly, Brian Patrick (12 December 1901, Menton, France—December 1991, England) Two times Irish Champion (1959 and 1960). Long time editor and owner of *British Chess Magazine*. Keres' first victim in international chess.

Reinfeld, Fred (27 October 1910, New York—29 May 1964, Long Island) New York State Champion 1931 and 1933. Ranked sixth on the first USCF rating list. Made a plus score against Reshevsky during the 1930s. A prolific, and excellent, chess author, he is unfortunately remembered by many simply for the sheer number of his books. A collaborator with Fine on some interesting early works.

Rejfír, Josef (22 September 1908, Prague, Czechokoslovakia—04 May 1962) IM (1956) Elo HR 2480. Czech Army Champion 1937.

Rellstab, Ludwig Adolf Friedrich Hans (23 November 1904, Berlin-Schöneberg, Germany—14 February 1983, Wedel, Holstein, FDR) IM (1950) Elo HR 2490. Winner of two tournaments at Berlin 1930.

Reshevsky, Samuel Herman (born Schmul Rzeschewski, also in the early 1930s Reshefsky, from the mid-thirties the version given in the main header was invariably used) (26 November 1911, Ozorkow, Poland—04 April 1992, Suffern, NY) GM 1950 Elo HR 2680. First or first equal in the U.S. Championship 1936, '38, '40, '42, '46, '69, and '72 (Robert Byrne won the play-off but Reshevsky was second ahead of Kavalek and thus qualified for the interzonals). World Championship candidate 1948, 1953 and 1967. In a more "normal" political situation he would also have taken part in 1950 and 1956.

Reynolds, Arthur (Spring 1910, Solihull—29 November 1943, transport ship "Suez" *en route* from Java)

Richman, Joseph (dates unknown) of Chesapeake Chess Club.

Riello, Michele (04 October 1894, Voltri, Italy—12 June 1971, Savona)

Rivise, Irving (05 March 1918, Philadelphia, PA—27 September 1976, Los Angeles, CA)

Rossetto, Hector Decio (born 08 September 1922, Bahia Blanca, Argentina) IM (1950) GM (1960).

Rousseau Henry A (dates unknown) One-time champion of the Capital City Chess Club, originally from Georgia. Renowned as an attacking player.

Ruth, William Allen (18 September 1886, Wilmington, DE—03 February 1975, Marlton, NJ) Pennsylvania Champion 1918, 1920, 1923 and 1935 and New Jersey Champion 1934.

Sacconi, Antonio (05 October 1895, Roma, Italy—22 December 1968, Roma) IM (1951) Elo HR 2420, Italian Champion 1935.

Sanchez Lamego, (dates unknown) Playing strength equivalent to a U.S. Expert.

Santasiere, Anthony Edward (09 December 1904, New York—13 January 1977, Hollywood, FL) U.S. Master. Four times U.S. Championship finalist 1938–51. New York State Champion 1928 and 1930. Marshall Chess Club Champion 1921–2, 1925–6 and 1935–6. Attended Townsend Harris High School.

van Scheltinga, Tjeerd (Theo) Daniel (06 March 1914, Amsterdam—1994) International Master (1950). Best five-year average Elo 2440.

Schmidt, Bruno (14 January 1910, Happenheim, Germany—08 December 1976, Daytona Beach, FL)

Schmidt, Paul Felix (11 October 1916, Narva, Estonia—11 August 1984, Allentown, PA) IM 1950 Elo HR 2500. Estonian Champion 1936 and 1937. Scored +6 –6 =5 in games with Keres between 1933 and 1943.

Schwartz, Edward (dates unknown) U.S. Master.

Seidman, Herbert (born 17 October 1920, New York) U.S. master, 15th on the 1951 USCF rating list. Marshall Chess Club Champion 1941-2, 1943-4, 1944-5, 1945-6 (with Santasiere).

Seitz, Jakob Adolf (14 February 1898, Mettlingen, Germany—06 April 1970, Switzerland) Elo HR 2410.

Shainswit, George (born 03 January 1918, New York) U.S. Master, 16th equal on the 1951 USCF rating list. Manhattan Chess Club Champion 1949–50 (with Denker).

Shapiro, Oscar (born 18 March 1909, Boston, MA—died circa 2000, Washington, D.C.) City of Boston Champion 1941, Massachusetts State Champion 1939.

Simchow, Alexander (dates unknown) leading player of the Empire City Chess Club.

Simonson, Albert C. (26 December 1914, New York—16 November 1965, San Juan, Puerto Rico) Elo HR 2430. Placed 2nd, 3rd and 4th= in the first three U.S. Championship tournaments, making him the third highest scorer in the pre–War tournaments with 32 points out of 47. Placed fifth on the first USCF rating list.

Smirka, Rudolph (12 February 1887, Wien, Austria—1947+) New York State Champion 1923 and 1927. Marshall Chess Club co–Champion 1930 and Summer co–Champion 1935.

Sørensen, Ernst (dates unknown) (Denmark)

Soto Larrea, Colonel Manuel (dates unknown) Mexican player active during the 1920s and 1930s.

Spielmann, Rudolf (05 May 1883, Wien, Austria—20 August 1942, Stockholm, Sweden) Elo HR 2560. Made an even score (+2 –2 =8) with Capablanca over his career.

Spinhoven, Frederik Antonius(?) (dates unknown) Played in the Dutch Championship of 1933.

Ståhlberg, [Anders] Gideon [Tom] (26 January 1908, Angered, Surte, Sweden—26 May 1967, Leningrad, USSR) GM (1950) Elo HR 2590. Swedish Champion from 1929 to 1939. Played in seven Olympiads. Resident in Argentina 1939 to 1948. Two times a World Champion Candidate. Was in Leningrad in 1967 to take part in a tournament, but died before play started.

Stark, Martin Charles (born 20 December 1912, North Plainfield, NJ) HYPD individual champion four times from 1929–33. Capital City Chess Club Champion 1935 and 1937, District of Columbia Champion 1935, '39, '44, '45, '52 and '53 and three time Divan Champion. Fine annotated a win of Stark's over Weaver Adams for *Chess Marches On!*

Steiner, Endre or Andreas (27 June 1901, Budapest, Hun

gary—29 December 1944, non-combatant labour corps) Elo HR 2490. Participant in five Olympiads—1927, 1928, 1930 (Hungary finished second), 1931 and 1937 and also the unofficial team tournament of 1936—making the best score on board four in 1927 (in the winning team); best score on board two in 1928 (again in the winning team) and highest score on any board in 1937 (when Hungary finished second). Brother of Lajos Steiner.

Steiner, Herman (15 April 1905, Dunaiskoi Stredi, Hungary now Czechoslovakia—25 November 1955, Los Angeles, CA) IM (1950) Elo HR 2450. First equal U.S. Open 1943, first place U.S. Open 1946, U.S. Champion 1948.

Steiner, Lajos (14 June 1903, Nagyvarad, Hungary now Oradea, Romania—22 June 1975, Sydney, Australia) IM (1950) Elo HR 2480. Champion of the Saxonian Chess Federation 1924 and 1927, Hungarian champion 1931 and '36, Australian Champion 1945, '46, '46–7, '52–3 and '58–9.

Stephens, Llewellyn Walter (16 August 1883[?], St. Louis, MO—30 September 1948, New York) Player and organizer.

Stolcenberg or **Stolzenberg**, Leon (18 October 1895, Tarnopol, Austria—25 October 1974, Detroit, MI) Western Chess Association Champion (U.S. Open) 1923, 1926 and 1928.

Stoltz, Gösta (09 May 1904, Stockholm, Sweden—25 July 1963, Stockholm) IM (1950) GM (1954) Elo HR 2520. Three times Swedish champion, played in nine olympiads. Defeated Flohr in a match in 1931.

Stork, possibly a mistranscription for J. C. Sterk, 1938 Champion of the Amsterdamsche Schaakbond.

Stromberg, Bernard or Barnet (dates unknown)

Sturgis, George (31 May 1891, Boston, MA—20 December 1944, Boston) Unanimously elected first President of the U.S.C.F. on the merger of N.C.F and A.C.F. in 1939.

Suesman, Walter Bradford (19 September 1918, Providence, RI—11 November 1984, Providence) U.S. Master.

Sundberg, Bertil (07 July 1907, Mariehäll, Sweden—20 July 1979, Stockholm) Stockholm City Champion 1947 and 1948.

Sussman, Dr. Harold (born September 1911) of the Marshall Chess Club.

Szabó, László (19 March 1917, Budapest, Hungary—08 August 1998, Budapest) GM (1950) Elo HR 2610. Eight times Hungarian champion. Three times World Championship Candidate (placing third in the Candidates tournament of 1956). Played in eleven Olympiads.

Tartakower, Savielly (Xavier) Grigorievich (21 February 1887 [Gregorian], Rostov na Donu, Ukraine/Russia—05 February 1956, Paris, France) GM (1950) Elo HR 2560. Played for Poland six times in Olympiads from 1930 to '39 (He was a Jew of Austrian and Polish parentage) and for France in 1950.

Tholfsen, Erling (born 12 January 1904, New York, NY) Marshall Chess Club Champion 1922–3, 1923–4, and second on tie break 1926–7. Board 4 at The Hague Olympiad, 1928.

Thomas, Andrew Roland Benedick (11 October 1904–16 May 1985, Tiverton, England) Player, author and academic.

Thomas, Sir George Alan (14 June 1881, Constantinople (Istanbul), Turkey—23 July 1972, London, England) IM (1950) Elo HR 2470, British Champion 1923 and 1934, 1st with Euwe and Flohr at Hastings 1934/5 ahead of Botvinnik and Capablanca. The heir to a Baronetcy—he was the 7th (and last) Baronet Thomas of Yapton—and private means, he played tennis at Wimbledon from 1919 to 1926 and was a highly successful badminton player, winning the All-England (effectively the World Championship) title four times consecutively from 1920 to 1923—the Thomas Cup is named in his honour.

Thomas, Professor C. K. (dates unknown) of Ithaca.

Thorvaldsson, Einar (dates unknown) Icelandic Champion 1928 and 1940.

Torre Repetto, Carlos (23 November 1905, Merida, Yucatan, Mexico—19 March 1978, Merida) IM (1963) GM (1977) Elo HR 2560. New York State Champion and Western Champion in 1924, Mexican Champion 1926. After a brief career, retired from chess at the age of 21 by which time he had already showed himself to be among the top ten players of the time.

Towsen, A. N. (dates unknown) Central Pennsylvania Champion 1931.

Treysman or, occasionally, **Treystman**, George Nelson (1880–February 1959) A professional coffee-house player whose first tournament was the 1936 U.S. Championship for which he qualified at the age of 55. U.S. Senior Master, eleventh on the 1951 USCF rating list.

Turover, Isador Samuel (08 July 1892, Warsaw, Poland—16 October 1978, Washington, D.C.) Participated in domestic tournaments from the 1920s to 1940s. District of Columbia champion 1921.

Tylor, Sir Theodore Henry (T. H.) (13 April 1900, Bournville, England—23 October 1968, Oxford) Near-blind. Placed second in the British Championship of 1933. Represented the British Chess Federation at the 1930 Hamburg Olympiad.

Ulvestad, Olav (27 October 1912, Tacoma, WA—24 August 2000, Washington Old Soldiers home, Retsil nr Bremmerton, WA) U.S. Master. Washington State Champion 1934 and 1952. Played for Andorra at the 1970 Olympiad after retiring to Spain.

Vaitonis, Povilas (Paul) (15 August 1911, Užpaliai, Lithuania—23 April 1983, Hamilton, Canada) IM (1952) Elo HR 2430. Lithuanian Champion (1933), Canadian Champion (1951 and 1957). Played in the Olympiads of 1933–9 for Lithuania and 1954 and '58 for Canada; represented the Canadian zone at the 1952 Interzonal.

Vidmar, Dr. Milan (22 June 1885, Laibach/Ljubljana, Austro-Hungary—09 October 1962, Ljubljana, Yugoslavia) GM (1950) Elo HR 2600. An amateur, an electrical engineer by profession, he was a strong tournament and match player from 1909 to 1939, when he won the Yugoslav Championship. Also a noted writer and correspondence chess player.

Vistanetskis or **Vistaneckis**, Isakas (Itzchak Vistanietsky) (29 September 1910 [Gregorian], Kapsukas, Lithuania—01

January 2001, Israel) Soviet Master of Sport, International Correspondence Chess Master. Emigrated to Israel in 1980. Professional player, trainer and journalist. Played in five pre–War Olympiads from 1930–37 (as well as Munich 1936). He was apparently prevented from playing at Buenos Aires 1939 after a falling out with Mikenas. Baltic Champion 1946.

Vos, [F. de?] (born 01 September 1893) Well-known Dutch problemist.

Weil, Dr. Wolfgang (born 23 November 1912)

Weiner, J (dates unknown) Philadelphia player.

Williams, Mrs. Russell J. (dates unknown) Manager of the Chicago Beach Chess Club.

Willman, Robert (born 03 January 1908, New York, New York) U.S. Master. Manhattan Chess Club Champion 1933/4, New York State Chess Association Champion 1940.

Winter, William (11 September 1898, Medstead, England—17 December 1955, London) IM (1950) Elo HR 2460. British Champion 1935 and 1936. Represented the B.C.F. in four Olympiads from 1930–35. His results had a decisive effect on the placings at Nottingham 1936. He had a winning position against Capablanca, in a game he eventually lost by making a hasty 37th move not realising he had already passed the time control, and agreed a draw with Botvinnik in the last round in a favourable position.

Woliston, Philip (born circa 1920) California State Champion in 1939 ahead of Harry Borochow, Herman Steiner, and Koltanowski.

Wood, Arthur W. (dates unknown) of Syracuse.

Woods, Henry M (dates unknown) North Carolina Chess Association Champion.

Yanofsky, Daniel Abraham (Abe) (26 March 1925, Brody, Poland—05 March 2000, Winnipeg, Canada) Best five-year average Elo rating 2530. His family emigrated to Canada when he was eight months old. Eight times Canadian Champion, British Champion 1953. Played in 11 Olympiads from 1939 (when he was 14 years of age) to 1980.

Yudovich, Mikhail Mikhailovich (Sr) (08 June 1911 [Gregorian], Roslavl, Russia—19 September 1987, Moscow, USSR) IM (1950) Elo HR 2480. Correspondence Chess Grandmaster (1972), USSR Correspondence Chess Champion 1965–6.

---

2. Time Controls and Rates of Play

From the 1920s Capablanca's favoured time limit of 40 moves in two-and-one-half hours became the standard rate of play for international chess. It remained so until fairly recently when a rate of 40 moves in two hours became popular. In the last few years attempts have been made to speed up play, but these have not been supported by the majority of players and it seems that the trend may reverse somewhat. During the 1930s and '40s there was a considerable degree of experimentation with non-standard time controls, in many cases for logistical reasons—not all organisers could afford to run tournaments at the rate of a game a day with adjournment and rest days. Players, therefore, often had to accustom themselves to differing rates of play in different locations. Rates of play varied between sixteen and twenty moves an hour, with time controls at two or two-and-a-half hours initially, followed, in most cases, by controls every hour thereafter. Below is a list of the known time controls of some of the events in which Fine participated, in ascending order of speed:

32 moves in 2 hours Moscow 1937 (then 16 moves an hour thereafter).

40 moves in 2½ hours—Kemeri/Riga 1937.

40 moves in 2½ hours—Semmering/Baden 1937.

40 moves in 2½ hours—A.V.R.O. 1938.

40 moves in 2½ hours (then 24 moves for every 1½ hours thereafter)—1st U.S. Championship, New York 1936.

40 moves in 2½ hours (then one hour for the next 16 moves)—Amsterdam International 1936.

34 moves in 2 hours (17 per hour thereafter)—Margate 1937.

34 moves in 2 hours—Hastings 1937/8.

36 moves in 2 hours—Intercollegiate Team Tournament, New York, 1931.

36 moves in 2 hours—Folkestone Team Tournament 1933.

36 moves in 2 hours—Warsaw Team Tournament 1935.

36 moves in 2 hours—Nottingham 1936.

36 moves in 2 hours (then 18 moves an hour thereafter)—Zandvoort 1936.

36 moves in 2 hours (then 18 moves an hour thereafter)—3rd U.S. Championship, New York 1940.

45 moves in 2½ hours—Stockholm International Tournament 1937.

20 moves per hour to be controlled after the first two hours, then after each hour—New York International, 1948/9.

40 moves in 2 hours—2nd U.S. Championship, New York 1938.

40 moves in 2 hours—U.S.C.F. Open Championship, New York 1939.

50 moves in 2½ hours—United States Team Trial, New York 1933.

50 moves in 2½ hours—Stockholm Olympiad 1937.

50 moves in 2½ hours with controls at move 30 (1hr 30m per player), 50, 70 (each hour after)—Wertheim Memorial, New York 1951.

3. Fine's Notebooks at the Library of Congress, Washington, D.C.

On 10 October 1945 Reuben Fine made a gift to the Library of Congress (shelf 21, 669) of a collection of his chess notebooks. They contain 523 games and fragments, largely from tournaments and matches, from the period 1931–1941. The games were presumably transferred from primary sources, probably during or soon after the event. I have also acquired a few other games, from at least three other researchers, for which the source is identified as Fine's Notebooks. They do not, however, appear in my copy, nor are they at the Library of Congress according to Patrick Kerwin.

The games in the notebooks are recorded in a variety of forms of notation, ofttimes conforming to the location or type of event in which Fine was participating. The early notebooks (1931–5) generally switch between the English descriptive and German algebraic forms of notation. A few games, but not the postal games, are however entered in the numeric form (as used in international correspondence chess). Most of the games from Mexico appear in the Spanish descriptive form. Hastings 1935/6 and the first US Championship are recorded in English descriptive, but from Zandvoort onwards the recording is exclusively in German or Dutch algebraic. The out-of-sequence games from Dutch events in 1936, which appear during 1941, are written in a somewhat more attractive calligraphic hand, possibly that of Emma Fine.

Note that there is no notebook to cover the bulk of 1935. Notebook 3 is, however, numbered as starting at game 51, but during the period of missing record Fine actually played fifty-one, and not fifty, games. The absence of two games from Oslo (in my copy) is not caused by the changeover from one book to another, since notebook 3 contains three games from the Norwegian tournament and notebook 4 a further two games. Note also that Schaakboekje (1936–1937) numbered #102–131 whereas the previous is numbered #51–100, which may indicate that a further gamescore from the Oslo tournament was included on a loose sheet. The games numbered #400–#424 do not appear in my copy, the games being numbered only as far as #399.

Notatieboek voor 50 Genummerde Schaakpartien (1937) numbered #182–231

Notatieboek voor 50 Genummerde Schaakpartien (1937–1939) numbered #232–281

Notatieboek voor 50 Genummerde Schaakpartien (1939–1940) numbered #282–331

Spiral bound notebook inscribed Gift, Reuben Fine, Oct 10 1945 numbered #332–381

Notatieboek voor 50 Genummerde Schaakpartien (1941–) numbered #382–424

4. Results of the A.V.R.O. Participants During the 1930s

Chessplayers and enthusiasts have for a long time been fascinated by the question of which player is, or was, the stronger. In spite of the attempts of some statisticians, it is in reality impossible to compare players of different eras in any meaningful fashion. The only truly valid comparisons are those made between contemporaries, which nevertheless, still suffer from the same problems. Any player who has matured, but not yet aged to a point of deterioration of stamina or concentration, is likely to score well in the period considered. Younger players may not have reached their peak, older ones are likely to suffer not only from the aforementioned problems, but also, usually, though not always, from a reduction in ambition.

Under normal circumstances, it would have been interesting to make a comparison of results of the top players during the 1940s. There were, however, restricted opportinities for meetings during this period. A meaningful sample of games only really exists between the participants of the 1948 match tournament for the World's Championship, in which Fine did not participate.

While this work was being edited, I was shown Jeff Sonas's website Chessmetrics. His figures rate Fine the number one player in the world 1940–1942, number two in 1937, 1939 and 1949–1951, number three for 1946–1947, and number six for 1938—presumably an effect of his poor 1937 results. Fine is listed as inactive for 1943, 1944 and 1948 and there is no plot for 1945.

Results During the Period 1930–1940

	JRC	AAA	ME	SF	MMB	SHR	RF	PPK
Capablanca	—	+1 −1 =1	+3 −1 =10	+2 −1 =8	+1 −1 =5	+1 −1 =4	+0 −0 =5	+0 −1 =1
Alekhine	+1−1=1	—	+21 −18 =30	+5 −0 =7	+0 −1 =2	+2 −1 =2	+2 −3 =4	+2 −1 =5
Euwe	+1 −3 =10	+18 −21 =30	—	+6 −3 =19	+2 −0 =3	+1 −1 =2	+1−1=3	+7 −7 =5
Flohr	+1 −2 =8	+0 −5 =7	+3 −6 =19	—	+2 −3 =14	+0 −1 =8	+0 −2 =8	+1 −1 =9
Botvinnik	+1 −1 =5	+1 −0 =2	+0 −2=3	+3 −2 =14	—	+1 −0 =2	+0 −1 =2	+0 −0 =2
Reshevsky	+1 −1 =4	+1 −2 =2	+1 −1 =2	+1 −0 =8	+0 −1 =2	—	+4 −1 =10	+2 −3 =3
Fine	+0 −0 =5	+3 −2 =4	+1 −1 =3	+2 −0 =8	+1 −0 =2	+1 −4 =10	—	+1 −2 =7
Keres	+1 −0 =1	+1 −2 =5	+7 −7 =5	+1 −1 =9	+0 −0 =2	+3 −2 =3	+2 −1 =7	—

	"matches"	wins (%)	losses (%)	draws (%)	games	score %
Capablanca	+2 −1 =4	8 (15.4)	6 (11.5)	38 (73.1)	51	51.9
Alekhine	+4 −2 =1	33 (30.3)	25 (22.9)	51 (46.8)	109	53.7
Euwe	+2 −1 =4	36 (25)	36 (25)	72 (50)	144	50
Flohr	+0 −5 =1	7 (7)	20 (20)	73 (73)	100	43.5
Botvinnik	+3 −2 =2	6 (14.3)	6 (14.3)	30 (71.4)	42	50
Reshevsky	+2 −3 =2	10 (20)	9 (18)	31 (62)	50	51
Fine	+3 −2 =2	9 (16.4)	8 (14.5)	38 (69.1)	56	50
Keres	+3 −1 =3	15 (23.4)	13 (20.3)	36 (56.3)	64	51.6

Results in the Period 1934–1940

	JRC	AAA	ME	SF	MMB	SHR	RF	PPK
Capablanca	—	+1 −1 =1	+1 −1 =2	+2 −1 =8	+1 −1 =5	+1 −1 =4	+0 −0 =5	+0 −1 =1
Alekhine	+1 −1 =1	—	+21 −18 =28	+2 −0 =5	+0 −1 =2	+1 −1 =2	+2 −3 =3	+2 −1 =5
Euwe	+1 −1 =2	+18 −21 =28	—	+3 −0 =6	+2 −0 =3	+1 −1 =2	+1 −1 =3	+7 −7 =5
Flohr	+1 −2 =8	+0 −2 =5	+0 −3 =6	—	+0 −1 =6	+0 −1 =8	+0 −2 =7	+1 −1 =9
Botvinnik	+1 −1 =5	+1 −0 =2	+0 −2 =3	+1 −0 =6	—	+1 −0 =2	+0 −1 =2	+0 −0 =2
Reshevsky	+1 −1 =4	+1 −1 =2	+1 −1 =2	+1 −0 =8	+0 −1 =2	—	+2 −1 =10	+2 −3 =3
Fine	+0 −0 =5	+3 −2 =3	+1 −1 =3	+2 −0 =7	+1 −0 =2	+1 −2 =10	—	+1 −2 =7
Keres	+1 −0 =1	+1 −2 =5	+7 −7 =5	+1 −1 =9	+0 −0 =2	+3 −2 =3	+2 −1 =7	—

	"matches"	wins (%)	losses (%)	draws (%)	games	score %
Capablanca	+1 −1 =5	6 (15.8)	6 (15.8)	26 (68.4)	38	50
Alekhine	+3 −2 =2	29 (29)	25 (25)	46 (46)	100	52
Euwe	+2 −1 =4	33 (29.2)	31 (27.4)	49 (43.4)	113	50.9
Flohr	+0 −5 =1	2 (3.2)	12 (19)	49 (77.8)	63	33.3
Botvinnik	+3 −2 =2	4 (13.3)	4 (13.3)	22 (73.4)	30	50
Reshevsky	+2 −2 =3	8 (17)	8 (17)	31 (66)	47	50
Fine	+3 −2 =2	9 (17)	7 (13.2)	37 (69.8)	53	51.9
Keres	+3 −1 =3	15 (23.4)	13 (20.3)	36 (56.3)	64	51.6

Capablanca

The former World Champion from Cuba demonstrated that he was able to hold his own against the new generation. He was, however, no longer the peerless player of earlier times. Furthermore his health was starting to fail, a point which was particularly evident during the tiring schedule of the A.V.R.O. tournament. After recovering his form during 1934–5, he had an excellent year in 1936 winning the very strong Moscow International, with only Botvinnik, a point behind, anywhere near his score, and the Nottingham Tournament, with Botvinnik, half a point ahead of the World

Champion Euwe, Fine and Reshevsky. Under the right conditions Capablanca would probably have proved a worthy challenger to either Euwe or Alekhine.

Alekhine

In the early 1930s the Russian World Champion was clearly the strongest active player. Euwe's thorough preparation for their first title contest, which he did not reproduce for the rematch, caught Alekhine in a down turn in form. His positive score in the games quoted in the tables above is in large part the result of his resounding success in the 1937 World Championship match. Of the younger players, he dominated Flohr and made a small plus score with Keres, which was increased significantly in 1942 (this however might be a result of a downturn in Keres' form and his unhappy war years).

Euwe

During the period 1934–7 Euwe's tournament and match results include: 2nd= with Flohr after Alekhine at Zurich '34, 1st= at Hastings '34/5 with Flohr ahead of Capablanca and Botvinnik, defeating Alekhine in the world title match (+9 =13 –8, agreeing a draw in the final game in a won position), 2nd at Zandvoort '36 after Fine, ahead of Keres, 3rd= with Reshevsky and Fine at Nottingham '36 half a point behind Capablanca and Botvinnik but ahead of Alekhine and Flohr, 1st= with Fine at Amsterdam '36 ahead of Alekhine, 1st at Nauheim-Stuttgart-Garmisch '37 ahead of Alekhine and third highest board 1 score at the Stockholm Olympiad behind Flohr and Keres. He also beat Flohr (official FIDE challenger) in an exhibition match, placed ahead of him in another tournament, beat Fine in a practice game in '38 and in '39–40 narrowly lost to Keres in a match.

Flohr

Salo Flohr was the official FIDE challenger in the late 1930s. From Hastings 1931/2 onwards he had many successes in tournaments, placing first in 18 from 1932 to 1939. However, he achieved this result more by dominating tail enders (that he had a quick sight of the board is borne out by his results in exhibition play and speed chess) than by defeating his closest rivals. His result at the A.V.R.O. tournament must have been disappointing, but in light of his previous results, should not have been as surprising as some contemporary commentators suggested.

Botvinnik

Botvinnik had a low number of games played, but his match result against Levenfish and his placing in the 1940

U.S.S.R. Championship suggest that he made a significant improvement later, from 1941, having his peak years from 1941 to 1948. Botvinnik, contrary to the suggestion in some of his biographies, did not show superiority over other grandmasters in the period under consideration.

Reshevsky

From 1931 to 1940 Reshevsky was 1st or 1st= in 12 tournaments, including three United States Championships where he finished ahead of Fine. All told he finished ahead of Fine on seven occasions (including Pasadena 1932), behind him five times and on the same score twice, and defeated him four times in individual encounters (again including Pasadena). He played only about two hundred and fifty games during the period, compared to over six hundred played by Fine. On the one hand this meant he did not suffer from staleness, on the other hand he was occasionally slow to start.

Fine

Fine had a significantly higher percentage of games with the black pieces than with the white pieces, so, his score is perhaps better even than it appears at first sight. He was highly successful in tournament play: from 1931 to 1940 he had forty-two finishes of 3rd= or higher, one 4th= and only two lower placings. He was improving rapidly, and towards the end of the period in question was increasing his technical knowledge and his aggressive instincts.

Keres

The Estonian Grandmaster had a plus score against each of the two Americans and a slight negative score in games with Alekhine. He had had little contact with master players before the Warsaw Olympiad. Numerous tournament wins were interspersed with poorer results, such as Dresden 1936 and Leningrad–Moscow 1939. Keres was improving quickly and completed his studies in 1940. Like Fine, being in his mid-twenties when war broke out, he could otherwise have expected a period of significant improvement during the 1940s, rather than the stagnation which actually occurred.

Conclusions

It is clear that there was actually very little between the players, with the possible exception of Flohr, the official FIDE candidate, in the late 1930s. Mindful of Herman Melville's warning in *Billy Budd, Sailor*—"the *might-have-been* is but boggy ground to build on"—we can draw some conclusions. Any match, under the right conditions, between the top seven players would have been extremely interesting.

indeed it would have been almost impossible to pick a favourite. The younger players, Keres and Fine, had not matured as much as Botvinnik and Reshevsky, although both Fine and Keres played more games during the 1930s than their slightly older rivals. With such a wealth of youthful talent the 1940s should have been one of the most interesting periods of chess history.

It seems that the evidence is really rather inconclusive. Readers may, and surely will, make up their own minds about the *might-have-been*.

---

5. Historical Elo Ratings and U.S.C.F. Ratings

Elo Historical Ratings

Arpad Elo's work on the early development of a rating system for the U.S.C.F. also led to the production of a selection of historical ratings. These are a measure of chess results and not of chess strength. Fine's best five year average was calculated to be 2660 (some sources seem to assume his best years were 1935–39, but I am sure they would have been during the period 1938–1949; if the former was used by Elo it probably underrates Fine, but of course he played far fewer games and had minimal international competition during the latter period), Reshevsky's 2680 (though bizarrely the graph on pages 88–9 of Elo 1978 puts his peak rating at 2650), Botvinnik's 2720 (already, and contrary to the evidence, which does not indicate any superiority over the top half dozen players, 2700 by 1938), Keres' 2670 (in his case the graph clearly shows arrested development during the war years, in contrast to Botvinnik), Euwe's 2650, Alekhine's 2690 (about 2680 in 1938), Flohr's 2620 and Capablanca's 2725 (about 2650 in 1938).

The U.S.C.F. Rating List

In February 1951 the *British Chess Magazine* reported the recently published rating list of the U.S.C.F. This first list was based on performances in 582 tournaments from the previous thirty years in America only and contained 2306 players. The players were categorised as Grandmaster, 2700 or higher; Senior Master, 2500–2699; Master, 2300–2499; Expert 2100–2299; Class A–C in descending blocks of 200 grading points and Class D below 1500.

The American players included—
- Grandmasters: Fine 2817 and Reshevsky 2770;
- Senior Masters: Kevitz 2610, Dake 2598, Simonson 2596, Reinfeld 2593, Kupchik 2583, Denker 2575, Kashdan 2574, Horowitz 2558, Polland and Treysman 2521;
- Masters: Levin 2485, Evans 2484, Seidman 2451, Pavey, Shainswit and Pinkus 2442, Willman 2414, Moscowitz 2410, Bisguier, Kramer and Steiner 2394, D Byrne and Schwarz 2392, Adams 2383, Hahlbohm 2376, Borochow 2374, Santasiere 2368, Cohen 2353, R Byrne and Hesse 2352, Blumin 2351, DiCamillo 2347, Jackson 2345, Lasker 2336, Eastman 2333, Levy 2332, Bernstein 2322, Donovan 2317, Ulvestad 2311, Mengarini 2310, Green 2306, Sussman 2304, Hanauer 2300.

A list of foreign competitors in U.S. tournaments was also compiled and featured—
- Najdorf 2786, Euwe 2620, Pilnik 2521, Rossetto 2471, Flores 2383, Gonzales 2366, Cruz 2354, Cuellar 2330, Araiza 2320, Sanchez 2249, Broderman 2221, Camarena 2011.

In November 1952 BCM published the top ten in the U.S.C.F. Rating System results (as of July 31). They were:
- 1 S Reshevsky 2751; 2 R Fine 2676; 3 L Evans 2660; 4 G Kramer 2564; 5 I A Horowitz 2545; 6 A S Denker 2538; 7 Max Pavey 2502; 8 A W Dake 2475; 9 D Byrne 2465; 10 R Byrne 2465.

---

6. Fine as Author

Chess Works, Chronologically

FINE 1931–41 Notebooks (Unpublished) (Library of Congress)
    An unannotated collection of games played between 1931 and 1941. See Appendix 4 for further information.

FINE & REINFELD (eds) 1934 *A. Alekhine vs E. D. Bogoljubov, World's Chess Championship 1934* David McKay and Company, Philadelphia
    Edited by Fred Reinfeld and Reuben Fine. Biographical sketches of the World Champion and his challenger are followed by a summary of their career results. A summary of the course of the match precedes a full complement of the games, annotated with accompanying diagrams. An excellent record of the match appearing soon after its completion. 56 pages in hardback.

FINE & REINFELD 1935 *Dr. Lasker's Chess Career, Part I: 1889–1914* Black Knight Press
    Annotations by Fred Reinfeld and Reuben Fine, with a biographical introduction by Fred Reinfeld. Preface, Acknowledgment (of pre-publication subscriptions), Contents, Index of Openings, Emanuel Lasker—Summary of Results 1889–1914, Appreciations by Kmoch, Nimzowitsch, Réti, Spielmann and

Tartakower, Biographical Introduction and seventy-five games from Breslau 1889 to Saint Petersburg 1914 annotated by the authors with occasional diagrams. Part II never appeared. The authors make good use of earlier sources to provide detailed analysis of the second official World Champion's career up to the outbreak of the First World War. ix plus 165 pages.

FINE & LANDAU 1936 *Schaak Sleutel* Amsterdam

EUWE & FINE 1937 *Schach-Schlüssel* Amsterdam

The British Chess Magazine of January 1938 contains a review of a work by Fine, Euwe and Landau described as *The Chess Key*: "This ingenious device provides for beginners and those innocent of book-knowledge an automatic method for finding out the standard variations in each opening. It consists of a circular chart inserted between two stout pieces of cardboard on which the openings are indexed. One twirls the chart to the number of the opening required and through apertures cut in the cardboard appears the requisite variation. The idea seems to be derived from the cinema and has similar defects and advantages—rigid but striking, inelastic but informative." Harry Golombek.

FINE & RESHEVSKY 1938 *De Revanchwedstrijd om het Wereld-kampionschap Schaken. Najaar 1937* Rotterdam (Reprinted from *Nieuwe Rotterdamsche Courant* Oct.–Dec. 1937)

Portraits of the players, an introduction by Fine. A comprehensive account of the 1937 return match for the World Championship between Dr. Alexander Alekhine and Dr. Machgielis Euwe. Compiled from newspaper accounts and containing annotations and introductions to all twenty five games of the match and the five exhibition games played to complete the program of thirty scheduled games. 131 pages in softcover.

FINE 1937 *Amsterdam Chess Congress 1936* London

Crosstable, all twenty eight games by the finishing players (but none of those by Prins) annotated with detailed text notes, variations and occasional diagrams. The 1980 reprint also contains a preface by B. G. Dudley and a wedding portrait of Reuben and Emma Fine. The original edition, limited to two hundred and eighty copies, was number twelve in E. G. R. Cordingley's series. It was also apparently the first of Cordingley's productions to be provided with diagrams, letters being used for the pieces, those of Black being underlined.

FINE, GRIFFITH & SERGEANT 1939 *Modern Chess Openings* (*by Griffith and White*), *6th edition (completely revised)* Leeds

Tabular display of the principal opening variations, arranged and indexed in alphabetical order by main lines. Enlarged over the 5th edition which had been published in 1932 (1,215 columns compared with 1,060 in the earlier edition). Fine's preface was dated December 1938. The work includes games played at the A.V.R.O., Hastings 1938/9 and Leningrad–Moscow tournaments, the latest of which finished on 1 February 1939. Although Fine apparently fell out with his collaborators over recognition of the work as his own, their preface makes it clear that he was the principal author. vi plus 324 pages in hardcover.

FINE 1941 *Basic Chess Endings* Philadelphia

Written in three months with many positions composed by Fine himself for didactive purposes. The first comprehensive single volume work about the endings in the English language. Fine concentrates on providing general rules for the practical player. Still in print, this is certainly one of the best works of its kind, though some of the analysis and commentary require updating. xiv plus 573 pages in hardcover.

FINE 1942 *Chess the Easy Way* Philadelphia

A basic primer containing the chapters: The moves, rules and notation; Checkmating the lone king; The three basic principles of chess; The opening; After the opening, what then?, Basic positions in the endgame and Ten rules for the ending; and in addition a Glossary of chess terms, Bibliography and Index. vi plus 186 pages in hardcover.

FINE 1943 *The Ideas Behind the Chess Openings* Philadelphia

Eight chapters explaining the basic variations and principles behind the openings: General principles; King pawn openings (Open games); King pawn openings (Semi-open games); Queen pawn openings (1 d4 d5); Queen pawn openings (other replies); the Réti and English Openings; Bird's Opening and the Nimzowitsch Attack; Irregular openings. An appendix relates the positions to those in MCO 6. The openings considered are indexed alphabetically. vii plus 240 pages in hardcover.

FINE 1944 *Reshevsky–Kashdan 1942–43 United States championship chess match*

Story and annotations by Reuben Fine, International Grand Master, published by the Correspondence Chess League of America. Contributors, foreword, results of the games, short biography of the contestants, games with analysis, conclusions. 28 pages in softcover.

FINE 1945 *Chess Marches On!* Philadelphia

Twenty five deeply annotated games from Fine's "Game of the Month" column in *The Chess Review* (initiated in May 1942) with an additional twenty five games, all arranged by theme: Chess in the United States; The National Game of Russia; Chess in the Old World and Chess below the Border. Index of openings. A three page biography of Fine rounds out the book. An excellent collection of games from 1941 to 1944 with introductory remarks by chapter and by game, thorough text and analytical notes. v plus 221 pages in hardcover.

FINE 1948 *Practical Chess Openings* Philadelphia

A single volume tabular openings encyclopaedia. Effectively an updated, revised, and expanded version of MCO 6 in 1220 columns. There seem to be very few entries later than 1945. ix plus 470 pages in hardcover.

FINE 1948 *The World's a Chessboard* Philadelphia

A follow up to *Chess Marches On!* Fifty games and ten positions taken from events played between 1943 and 1947. As with the earlier work, the basis of the book was supplied by Fine's "Game of the Month" column. The format is similar to the earlier work, with a few added short humorous articles by other writers. An excellent source for annotated games of the period. xi plus 323 pages in hardcover.

FINE 1951 *The World's Great Chess Games* Philadelphia

A collection of games from the time of Philidor to Fine's retirement from active chess. See Fine 1976.

FINE 1953 *The Middle Game in Chess* London

A logical progression from *MCO 6*, *PCO* and *BCE*. A treatise on the most difficult stage of the game in fourteen chapters: A few ideas; The elements of combinations; The mating attack; The combinative art; How to analyze a position; Material advantage; Compensating for a material disadvantage; Superior pawn structure; Command of space—superior mobility; The attack against the king; The art of defense; Equal positions; Continuing the opening and Entering the endgame, with 378 diagrams. Index of players. Index of openings and variations. Using many examples from his own games and those of Alekhine, Capablanca, Lasker, Euwe, Reshevsky, Rubinstein, Botvinnik and Nimzowitsch among others. vi plus 442 pages in hardcover.

FINE 1956 "Psychoanalytical Observations on Chess and Chess Masters" *Psychoanalysis*, Monograph I, 1956, *4*, No. 3 (see Fine 1967)

FINE 1958 *Lessons from my Games: A Passion for Chess* New York

Fine's own collection of his games and reminiscences. Contents, Foreword: A passion for chess, Tournament and match record and fifty chapters containing forty five tournament or match games, five blindfold games, four positions and one game from a simultaneous exhibition against Capablanca. xxii plus 225 pages.

FINE & Reinfeld 1963 *Lasker's Greatest Chess Games, 1889–1914* New York (Dover edition of Fine & Reinfeld 1935)

FINE 1965 "The Psychology of Blindfold Chess: an Introspective Account" *Acta Psychologica*, *24*, 352–70

See Appendix 8.

FINE 1965 *The Teenage Chess Book* New York

Not seen.

FINE 1967 *The Psychology of the Chess Player* New York

Dover edition of Fine's monograph published in *Psychoanalysis*. A Freudian examination of the motives of chess players. Contents: Review of the literature; General remarks on chess; The World Champions; Psychoses among chessplayers; Summary: Theory of chess; Appendix: Two letters by Ernest Jones; Bibliography. Although Fine defended his thesis in an interview with Pandolfini, it is not a particularly well-regarded work among chess players. Relies heavily on anecdotal evidence, some of which is certainly inaccurate. iii plus 74 pages in softcover.

FINE 1971 *The Final Candidates Match: Buenos Aires, 1971, Fischer–Petrosian* Jackson, Wyoming

Contents: Game results and games index; Introduction;

About the author; Annotated games 1 to 9. All of the games of the match with introductions, text comments and annotations. 32 pages in softcover.

FINE 1975 *Bobby Fischer's Conquest of the World's Chess Championship; the Psychology and Tactics of the Title Match* London

Contents: Preface; Part I The Players and the Setting (92 pages), The history of the World Championship, The preliminary skirmishes, Bobby Fischer—American Folk Hero, Boris Spassky—The ex-champion, The psychology of chess: Part II The Match (14 pages), Review of the match; Part III The Games (187 pages), all 21 games annotated with text and variations. The notes are not generally deep, and Fine occasionally shows he is not up to date on the theory. xiii plus 294 pages in hardcover.

FINE 1976 *The World's Great Chess Games* (Revised and expanded edition) New York

A new edition of Fine 1951. A collection of games of the most notable players from Philidor to Karpov. Contents: The game of kings; From Philidor to Morphy; The age of Morphy; The age of Steinitz; The age of Lasker; The age of Capablanca; The age of Alekhine; The age of Euwe; A brief interlude; The age of Botvinnik; The age of Soviet Champions; The age of Fischer; The age of Karpov. The games of eighty notable players, generally of Grandmaster class, with text and analysis. Chapters with general introductions and a prose section about the individuals themselves. ii plus 397 pages in softcover.

In addition to the above, Fine also contributed notes to: Kashdan and others *Book of Folkestone 1933 International Chess Team Tournament* Leeds (1933), and Reinfeld with annotations by Chernev, Fine, Janowski, Tarrasch, Chigorin and others *The Book of the Cambridge Springs International Tournament*, New York (1935) Black Knight Press.

By the end of the 1940s he had sold over 100,000 copies of his books, a figure which rose to in excess of 500,000 in ten languages by 1976. According to Pandolfini, by 1984 *Chess the Easy Way* had sold over 250,000 copies. In 2002 the following were still in print: *Basic Chess Endings*, *The Ideas Behind the Chess Openings*, *The World's Great Chess Games*.

In addition to his chess writings Fine was also a prolific author in his second career. His works included: *Freud: A Critical Re-evaluation of His Theories* (1962), *The Healing of the Mind: The Technique of Psychoanalytic Psychotherapy* (1971), *The Development of Freud's Thought: From the Beginnings (1866-1900) through Id Psychology (1900-1914) to Ego Psychology (1914-1939)* (1973), *Psychoanalytic Psychology* (1975), *A History of Psychoanalysis* (1979), *The Intimate Hour* (1979), *The Psychoanalytic Vision* (1982), *The Logic of Psychology: a Dynamic Approach* (1983), *The Meaning of Love in Human Experience* (1985), *Narcissism, the Self, and Society* (1986), *The Forgotten Man: Understanding the Male Psyche* (1987), *Troubled Men: The Psychology, Emotional Conflicts, and Therapy of Men* (1988), *Current and Historical Perspectives on the Borderline Patient* (1989), *Love and Work: The Value*

System of Psychoanalysis (1990), and *Troubled Women: Roles and Realities in Psychoanalytic Perspective* (1992) as well as many papers for journals.

---

7. Further Research Possibilities

As explained in the main introduction, the principal aim of this work has been to present a comprehensive collection of Reuben Fine's tournament and match games, with annotations from contemporary sources where possible. There are still many games missing, particularly during the period 1929 to 1933. In addition to the games identified in this volume, it is possible that there are further games to be found, particularly from further, unidentified, club tournaments or New York Metropolitan League matches.

In addition there are aspects of Fine's career which merit further study, for example: his contribution to endgame and middlegame theory, his methods and style of play (implicitly, but not explicitly, considered in this volume), his exhibition play, a comprehensive bibliography including his writings in journals.

While compiling the book, I was also considering including an appendix which would address the question of the value of his tournament prize monies. I decided, however, that I had insufficient data to make a meaningful assessment of his earnings—there being too many blanks in the record. To properly assess the financial position of chessplayers through the years it would be essential to know, first of all, their income generated from prize money (place money and supplementary prizes); second, their income from exhibition play; third, their income from writing articles and books; fourth, the extent to which their travel and accommodation was subsidized. Furthermore, to make these data meaningful it would be essential to compare their income to that of contemporaries in various trades and professions. The whole subject is complicated by the fact that a player may reside for long periods outside of his home country. This is, nevertheless, a fruitful area for future research with the aim of putting the lives of chessplayers into social and economic perspectives.

Missing Gamescores

Marshall Club Junior Championship, 1929–30 MacMurray and other participants unknown

Marshall Club B Championship, 1929–30 Levenstein, MacMurray and others

Marshall Club Handicap Tournament, 1930 Participants unknown

Manhattan Club Handicap Tournament, 1930 Schwartz, McGinnis, Belhoff and others

Marshall Club Championship preliminaries, 1930 Wright, Croney, Bentz, Tholfsen, Bernstein,

Croney–Fine match, 1930 1, 2, 3

Forsberg–Fine, 1930 1, 2, 3

Forsberg–Fine, 1930 1

Rice Club Junior Masters, 1930 Bartha, Cohen, Denker, Fajans, Gerrity, Dr. Kline, Kussman, Lessing, MacMurray, Newburger and Reinfeld

Dake–Fine match, 1931 #1

Rome New York State Chess Association Championship, 1931 August 17–22 Polland

Marshall Club Summer Championship, 1931 Sidney Bernstein, other participants unknown.

Manhattan CC vs Philadelphia, February 23, New York, 1931 Goldstein

City College Alumni–Varsity chess match, New York, 1931 unknown

Match with Reinfeld, New York, July 25– August 9, 1931 #1, #2, #3, #4, #5, #6

Consultation game with Reinfeld, New York, September 17, 1931 Details unknown

15th Marshall Club Championships, 1931–2 Smirka, Tholfsen, Cass, Dunst, Bigelow, Croney, Morton

Intercollegiate Team Tournament, 1931, 28–31 December Paul (Pittsburgh), Horwitz (Brown), Cutler (NYU)

Match with Reinfeld, New York, June, 1932 #1, #2

Pasadena, 1932, August 15–28 Bernstein J, Kashdan, Reshevsky

Folkestone Olympiad, 1933 Kahn, Appel, Petrovs, Winter, Havasi

Syracuse, 1933, New York State Chess Association Championship, August 21–26 Denker, Polland, Reinfeld, Black, Muir, Guckemus, Perrine, Thomas, Wood, Bourbeau

Detroit, 1933, 23 September–1 October Barnes

17th Marshall Club Championships, 1933–4 Reinfeld, Santasiere, Simonson, Costa-Rivas, Hamermesh

Denker–Fine match, 1934, ?June/July #1, #2, #3, #4, #5, #6, #7, #8, #9

Syracuse, 1934, August 13–25 Araiza, Martin

Milwaukee 1935, Western Open Finals Morton

Oslo, 1936, September 13–21 Heiestadt

24th Marshall Club Championships, 1940–41 Marshall, Forsberg

NY 1944, April–May, 5th U.S. Ch Altman, Neidich, Persinger, Stromberg

Hollywood 1945, August, Pan-American Championship Rossetto, Horowitz

Match New York–Havana, 1950 Planas

U.S. Speed Championships

New York 1942, July 5 Preliminaries, Section
Participants unknown **Finals** Denker, Green, Helms, Horowitz, Nadell, Yanofsky,

New York 1943, July 4 Preliminaries, Section
Participants unknown **Finals** Feldman, Heitner, Horowitz, Schwartz

New York 1944, June 25 Preliminaries, Section B
Denker, Partos, Platz, Chernev, Lasker, Ed., Almgren, Tabatznik, Jackson, Finkelstein, Barzin, Michael **Finals** Pavey, Willman

New York 1945 Preliminaries, Section A Pinkus, Mugridge, Marder, Rivise, Finkelstein, Almgren, Friedman, Shipman, Smith, Battell **Finals** Tenner, Moskowitz, Pinkus, Saltzberg, Helms

Hollywood 1945, Speed ch Reshevsky, Borochow, Rossetto, Cruz, Horowitz, Steiner and other participants unknown

Missing Crosstables

Marshall Club Junior Championship, 1929–30; Marshall Club B Championship, 1929–30; Marshall Club Handicap Tournament, 1930; Manhattan Club Handicap Tournament, 1930; Rice Club Junior Masters, 1930; Marshall CC Summer Tournament, 1931; Reinfeld–Fine match 1931; Reinfeld–Fine match 1932; Bussum, 1936; VAS Winter Tournament, 1936; VAS Tournament, 1937; USCF Preliminary Section 2, 1940; Utah State Championship, Salt Lake City, 1940; Hollywood four-cornered Tournament, 1940; USCF Preliminaries, 1941.

In addition detailed crosstables for the United States Lightning tournament preliminaries and finals are not available.

Endings

Fine composed a number of positions for his 1941 work *Basic Chess Endings*. Almost fifty of these can be found in the five volume Yugoslav *Encyclopaedia of Chess Endings*, along with many practical examples of his play. These, and other examples of his play, could provide the basis for an article "Fine on the Endgame."

Tournament Details

Details of some tournaments have been difficult to come by. Further data, which in some cases would include, for example, rates of play, time controls, dates, round numbers, full list of participants, prize funds, special prizes, details of organization, are sought.

Exhibition Play

I have not made a great effort to seek details of Fine's exhibition play, but simply included such information as has been available to me. There are many gaps in the record of Fine's exhibition play, and many hundreds of games as yet undiscovered.

Player Biographies

Many of these are incomplete and for some of the subjects I have uncovered no information at all.

I would be most pleased to hear from anyone who could correct any errors or fill any of the gaps in this volume. I can be contacted through the publisher, or by e-mail at aidanwoodger@yahoo.co.uk.

---

8. Fine on Blindfold Play

In 1965 Fine published an account of his experience in blindfold chessplay and his thoughts about the process (REUBEN FINE, Ph.D. 1965, "The Psychology of Blindfold Chess: An Introspective Account," *Acta Psychologica*, 24, 352–70). In his introductory remarks Fine notes that a considerable interest has been shown in blindfold play ever since Philidor gave the first recorded blindfold exhibition against two opponents in London in 1783.

He then notes, "The classic study on blindfold chess is the one by the famous French psychologist, Alfred Binet, which was published in 1892. Binet himself was not a chess expert and based his account on the introspective report of the chess masters whom he interviewed. While there are many excellent points made by Binet in his paper, it deserves to be supplemented for several reasons. First, the art of blindfold chess has advanced considerably since that date. At that time the world's record was 16 games played simultaneously, while today the world's record is 45, and other special records have been made. Second, none of the people whom Binet interviewed were specialists in blindfold play as such, which differs in some essential respects from ordinary play. And third, Binet's subjects were not trained introspectionists.

"In as much as the writer is both a chess master and a psychologist, it would therefore seem to be of some interest and value to give an introspective account of his experiences with blindfold chess."

Recording his own early experiences in blindfold play,

starting at the age of 14 while at High School, he notes that he only drew with a player he would normally expect to beat, suggesting some reduction in playing strength when blindfold compared to play when the board is in sight. He records that shortly thereafter he joined the Marshall Chess Club and was rated about knight odds (expected to score about 50 percent in games with a master) against the leading American players. He estimated that this would be the minimum strength requirement to be able to play without sight of the board.

He gave his first blindfold exhibition in 1930 when he was about 16 and of approximately master strength. He had been asked to give a simultaneous exhibition at a small club in New York. Only six players appeared, so rather than give a simultaneous exhibition he suggested that he play blindfold. He did so and won all six games. About a year later he gave his first planned exhibition on eight boards (later he played as many as twelve). In order to ease the task, he asked the organizers to provide him with a blank chess board, onto which to project the pieces, a technique described by Koltanowski. However, unlike Koltanowski, he did not find it helpful and never used the method in future.

Later Fine introduced a number of new forms to the display; in 1943 blindfold chess at ten seconds per move, in 1944 clock chess against five opponents (the opponents were all of master strength), in 1945 four games blindfold at ten seconds per move. Fine notes that the blindfold player can repeat the entire game with absolute accuracy after completing the exhibition.

In an attempt to quantify the task Fine then discusses Miguel Najdorf's world record of 45 games played blindfold: "When more than one game is played the blindfold player remembers all the positions in the course of evening and can usually reproduce all the games after the exhibition is over. If we take the world's record of 45 games set by Najdorf in 1945 [sic], this means that Najdorf was able to keep separate three thousand six hundred positions in the course of the evening, and to repeat these after the exhibition ended [This event is remembered in "Najdorf's legendary blindfold simul: A World Record to be remembered forever" Herman van Riemsdijk, New in Chess 1998/1 66–75. Najdorf conducted the exhibition from 8 p.m. 24 January to 7:25 p.m. 25 January 1947. The average length of the games was more like 25 moves, with 2,287 positions appearing on the boards). There are comparable feats in other fields; for example: musicians can reproduce a symphony after they have heard it once. Nevertheless, the impression is that such abilities are rarer even among musicians than the capacity to remember games among chessplayers."

Fine remarks that Binet and others have concluded that the blindfold player conducts his games by visualization. Here Fine reckons that the blindfold player's problem is to distinguish the different games (for this reason unusual moves by the sighted player make the task of the master easier). To ease this task he was in the habit of opening on the first board with 1 c4, the second with 1 d4, the third with 1 e4 and the fourth with 1 f4, repeating the same sequence for boards five to eight, and so on as necessary. Once the positions had diverged mistakes became rare, perhaps four or five errors in a ten board exhibition over the course of a seance.

Fine here notes a particular instance where an error could occur and draws a conclusion about the visualization process: "Towards the end of the game a problem arises at times in that I know the approximate place where a piece is situated, but not the exact one. This can come about, let us say, where there is a long series of king moves and I do not recall precisely whether the king is already at e3 or has gone to d4. This point is particularly important since it shows, as will be stressed later, that the Gestalt of the board is temporal as well as spatial. In such cases I often make a move which would satisfy both possibilities.... For example, if I am not sure whether the king is at e3, or d4, I play Ke4 or Kd3, both of which are possible from either position."

Fine notes that Djakow, Petrowski and Rudik and also de Groot had concluded that the way in which the master differs from amateurs is in their ability to recall chess positions which they had not encountered before. Fine believed that "this ability is related to the more general process of concept formation, as well as problem solving and scientific method."

In the next section of the paper Fine elaborates on different aspects of the chess master's ability to rapidly appraise a position. Firstly he discusses *The Chessboard*. He describes the associations the master has for the ranks, files, with individual squares or combinations of squares and their relationship to the pieces. Secondly, *The Pieces*: he describes how the master perceives pawn formations and the relationship of the pieces to pawns and to the squares of the board. He concludes that the squares and the pieces both have many associations which the master has built up through experience.

Thirdly, *Notation: the language of chess*; he describes how greater familiarity with the game also leads to a natural affinity with the notation and notes that N. R. Hanson (*Patterns of Discovery*) has shown that advances in notation are frequently associated with advances in scientific knowledge. He notes that to play over a game from the score requires more of an effort than conducting a blindfold game. He hypothesizes that in one of his own games "all the spatial and temporal Gestalten are provided by me, while in someone else's game they have to be inferred." He then goes on to write "These observations indicate that the notation becomes an integral part of the whole game. Each move has a symbol attached to it and each symbol is attached to a move. This point will be seen to be particularly important in the evaluation of what is meant by visualization."

Fourthly, *Spatial Gestalten*: Fine explains that it is necessary to "sort out the relevant from the irrelevant aspects of the position. The spatial Gestalt will thus be hierarchically organized, first centring around the king, second around the pieces attacking or defending the king, third, about the discrepancy of material, if any, and fourth, around the rest of the position."

He goes on to say that the spatial Gestalt includes the entire board, is based on dynamic interrelationships, there are minor Gestalten in various areas of the board which are related to the rest of the position and yet may not change for a long time and that only one part changes at a time. He notes that "similar items are remembered more readily than different ones; in fact this is one of the cardinal contributions of Gestalt psychology, and yet in chess the reverse seems to be the case."

He concludes that "the capacity to visualize spatial Gestalten depends upon the ability to perform a rapid linguistic summary of any position. This linguistic summary is verbalized in the learning process, but is dropped later. The essential point is that visualization is a shorthand summation of many previous steps."

Fifthly, *Temporal Gestalten*: Fine starts by noting that "there is nothing but spatio-temporal Gestalten." In other words this is an aspect that cannot properly be divided from the spatial Gestalt. Something of the history of a game can be determined from the current position, which itself is the basis for further calculation. This projection into the future may be based on variations of just a few moves or many. It is generally harmful to attempt to over-analyze because of the problem of interference: "The skill of the chess master thus involves the capacity to single out the most relevant aspects of any position and to pursue those to a logical conclusion." Chess masters therefore rely on feeling for position rather than exhaustive analysis.

Sixthly, *The goal-directed character of the position*: Fine explains that the evaluation of a position is never static. A player is continually asking questions such as is this a desirable pawn structure? Is this a good position for such and such a piece? What is the thought behind the opponent's last move?

Seventhly, *Shift brought about by the last move*: "No position changes in toto. One piece moves at a time and all the others remain where they are. If there is a capture the positions of two pieces change, but no more."

From the above Fine hypothesizes that visualization is a summation of many learned skills. He summarizes this process: (1) "Both the board and the pieces acquire a wealth of associations for the player as a result of long experience with the game ... visualization is part of the associative process which leads to skill at chess." (2) "A special notation exists which provides a language for the chess player. This language is learned as thoroughly as ordinary language." (3) "A spatio-temporal Gestalt is formed of the entire board." (4) "Every position is summed up dynamically." (5) "Once such a summation is made, the visual image reaches consciousness."

In the light of his theory he attempts two explain certain elements of blindfold play: 1. *Level of skill required to play blindfold*—he suggests that a minimum level of knight odds player is needed to play one game bilndfold, while the master can play several; 2. *Visualization of the board and pieces*—he suggests that it is a hindrance to use a blank chessboard to assist visualization since this interferes with the capacity to visualize free from non-essential associations; 3. *Level of strength in one game blindfold*—the temporal Gestalten shifts during play and analysis. Mistakes are caused by failure to return to a mental image of the current position (a problem not associated with sighted play, where one can look at the position in front of one after calculation); 4. *Level of strength in more than one game*—When more than one game is played at the same time, the level of strength falls off, because (a) interferences occur in similar game positions, (b) playing quickly may lead to inaccuracies, (c) the memory problem may become too great as the number of games increases; 5. *The memory feat in blindfold chess*—although many positions are encountered in play they are interrelated, reducing the strain on memory, particularly in view of the unconscious aspects of summation caused by familiarity with the task and the notation. Constant review of the positions during the game reinforces memory; 6. *The memory feat in more than one game*—the number of discrete items to be recalled is reduced by the use of key phrases, perhaps six per game, to sum up the course of a game; 7. *Speed of blindfold chess*—since the ability to quickly sum up a position is fundamental to the task, having more time would not improve the ability of the master to undertake the task. If you cannot do it quickly you cannot do it at all.

References

Binet, A., *Psychologie des grands calculateurs et des joueurs d'échecs.* Paris, 1894

De Groot, A. D., *Het denken van der schaker.* Amsterdam, N.V. Noord-Hollandsche Uitgevers Maatschappij, 1946.

Djakow, Petrowski and Rudik, *Psychologie des Schachspiels.* Walter de Gruyter & Co. Berlin, 1927.

Bibliography

Tournament Books

1932 **Pasadena**: Kashdan *Twenty-Five Best Games from the International Chess Congress of 1932 at Pasadena, California, August 15–28* Beverly Hills: Chess Reporter (1932)

1933 **New York**: Spence *1933 New York: United States Team Trial Tournament* Nebraska (1956)

Folkestone: Kashdan and others *Book of Folkestone 1933 International Chess Team Tournament* Leeds (1933)

Pokorny *Sachova Olimpiada ve Folkstonu* Brno (1934)

1935 **Milwaukee**: Lahde *Sopot 1935, Lodz 1935, Milwaukee 1935* Nottingham, The Chess Player (2001)

Warsaw: Reinfeld and Phillips *Book of the Warsaw 1935 International Chess Team Tournament* New York, Black Knight Press (1936)

Litmanowicz *VI Olimpiada Szachowa* Brno (1996)

Hastings: Kübel *Das Internationale Schachmeister-turnier zu Hastings 1935/36* (1973)

1936 **New York**: Hilbert & Lahde *New York 1936: The First Modern United States Chess Championship* Sands Point, NY: Chess Archaeology Press (2000)

Zandvoort: Kmoch *Officieel Wedstrijdboek Internationaal Meestertournooi Zandvoort 1936* Leiden (1936)

Nottingham: Alekhine *The Book of the Nottingham International Chess Tournament, 10–12 August 1936 with Annotations and analysis by A. Alekhine* Watts (ed) London: Printing Craft (1937) Unabridged corrected reprint New York: Dover (1962)

de Marimon and Ganzo *Torneo de Nottingham, 1936* Madrid (1949)

Nottingemsky Mezhdunarodny Shakhmatny Turnir Special Issue. Moscow: 64, 14 Aug.–6 Sept. 1936

Amsterdam: Fine *Amsterdam Chess Congress 1936* London (1937) corrected edition Coraopolis Chess Enterprises (1980)

Hastings: Brandreth (ed) *Hastings 1936/7 International Chess Tournament* Yorklyn, DE: Caissa (1992)

1937 **Stockholm**: Jonasson *Stockholm 1937* Uppsala (1992)

Ostende: Diemer *Das Internationale Schachmeister-turnier Ostende, 1937* Kecskemét (1937)

Kemeri/Riga: Betins, Petrovs & Kalnins *Das Grosse Internationale Schachmeister Turnier zu Kemeri in Lettland 1937* Riga (1938)

Reinfeld & Bernstein *Kemeri Tournament 1937* New York (1938)

Lopez Esnaola & de Marimon *Gran Torneo de Kemeri, 1937* Madrid (1958)

Stockholm Olympiad: Cozens *The Lost Olympiad–Stockholm 1937* BCM Quarterly 22 (1985)

Semmering-Baden: Hannak *Semmering-Baden 1937* Kecskemét (nd)

Lopez Esnaola & de Marimon *Gran Torneo de Semmering-Baden, 1937* Madrid (1957)

Reinfeld *Semmering-Baden 1937* New York (1938)

Wood *Semmering-Baden, 1937* Sutton Coldfield (nd)

Hastings: Lachaga *Internationales Schachmeisterturnier Hastings 1937–38* Argentina (1975)

Hastings 1937/38 Amsterdam (1938) Schaakwereld tournooiboeken: 1

1938 **New York**: Lahde (ed) *USA Championship New York 1938* (2001) Nottingham

A.V.R.O: Euwe *Analysen van A.V.R.O.'s Wereldschaak-Toornooi* Amsterdam: Algemeene Vereening Radio Omroep (1938)

1940 **New York**: Hilbert *New York 1940: United States Chess Championship* Yorklyn (2002)

1945 **Hollywood**: Spence *Hollywood Pan-American Chess Congress, 1946* Omaha (1952)

Radiomatch USA–USSR: Kmoch *De Eerste Schaakmatch U.S.A.-U.S.S.R.* Amsterdam (1945)

1948 New York: Kmoch *The Book of the International Chess Tournament held at the Manhattan C. C., New York, 1948–1949* New York (1950)

1951 New York: Euwe *New York 1951* Het Schaakhuis, Hilversum (1955)

Spence *Wertheim Memorial Tournament, New York 1951* Omaha (1952b)

United States Chess Federation Yearbooks

I   The Milwaukee Congress, 1935: 60 games *annotated by I. Kashdan*

V   The New York Open Tournament 1939: 32 games *annotated by F. Reinfeld*

VI   The New York U.S. Championship Tournament 1940; The Dallas Open Tournament, 1940: 27 games *annotations by A. Santasiere, C. J. S. Purdy, Fred Reinfeld, H. Golombek and others*

VII   Tournaments of 1941 1942 1943

VIII   Tournaments of 1944

IX   Tournaments of 1945

Soviet Chess Yearbooks

Шахматный Ежегодник Том 1 (1932–5) Grekov and Maizelis (eds) (1937)

Шахматный Ежегодник Том 2 (1936) Grekov and Maizelis (eds) (1938)

Шахматы за 1947–1949 гг Abramov (ed) (1951) Moscow

Biographical Games Collections

Alatortsev   Linder, I, and Linder, V *Dve Zhizni Gross meistera Alatortseva* (1994) Moscow (Russian)

Alekhine   Alekhine, A A, with Alexander, C H O'D, and Nunn, Dr J D M *Alexander Alekhine's Best Games* (1996) London; Skinner, L M, and Verhoeven, R G P *Alexander Alekhine's Chess Games, 1902–1946* (1998) Jefferson

Alexander   Golombek, H, and Hartston, W *The Best Games of C. H. O'D. Alexander* (1976) London

Boleslavsky   Adams, J *Isaac Boleslavsky: Selected Games* (1988) London

Botvinnik   Baturinsky, V *Shakhmatnoe Tvorchestvo Botvinnika I* (1965) Moscow (Russian); Soloviov, S (ed) *Mikhail Botvinnik Games I 1924–1948* (2000) Sofia

Bernstein, O   Cena, J *O.S. Bernstein. (Gran maitre international d'Echecs): 64 parties d'échecs* (nd)

Bernstein, S   Bernstein, S *Combat: My 50 Years at the Chessboard* (1977) New York

Capablanca   Soloviev, S (ed) *Jose Raul Capablanca II Games 1927–1942* (1997) Sofia; Winter, E G *Capablanca: A Compendium of Games, Notes, Articles, Correspondence, Illustrations and Other Rare Archival Materials on the Cuban Chess Genius José Raúl Capablanca, 1888–1942* (1989) Jefferson

Dake   Bush, C *Grandmaster from Oregon: The Life and Games of Arthur Dake* (1991) Portland

Daly   Lyman, H, & Dann, S *75 Years of Affection for Chess: A Tribute to Harlow B. Daly* (1975) USA

Denker   Denker, A *My Best Chess Games 1929–1976* (1981) New York

Euwe   Münninghoff, A *Max Euwe: The Biography* (2001) Alkmaar; Münninghoff, A, and Welling, J with analyses by Euwe *Max Euwe: Biografie van een Wereldkampioen* (1976) Amsterdam

Fine   Fine 1931–1941 Notebooks (Unpublished) Library of Congress, Washington, D.C.; Fine, R *Lessons from My Games: A Passion for Chess* (1958) New York; Fiala, V "Historical Database: Reuben Fine 1914–1935" in *Quarterly for Chess History 3/ 1999 Autumn* 433–514 (2000) Olomouc; Fiala, V (in preparation) *The Early Chess Career of Reuben Fine (1914–1935)*

Fischer   Soloviev, S (ed) *Bobby Fischer 3 1968–1992* (1993) Madrid

Foltys   Foltys, J *Zivotny Dilo* (1956) Prague (Czech)

Keres   Keres, P (with additional material by Golombek H, Nunn J and Burgess G) *Paul Keres: The Road to the Top* (1996) London; Keres, P *Ausgewählte Partien: 1931-1958* (1964) Amsterdam (German); Olde, H *Paul Keres–Photographs and Games* (1995) Demerlen Ltd; Varnusz, E *Paul Keres' Best Games, Volume 1: Closed Games* (1994) Cadogan; Varnusz, E *Paul Keres' Best Games, Volume 2: Open & Semi-Open Games* (1990) Pergamon; Reinfeld, F *Keres' Best Games of Chess 1931-1940* (1946) London

Lasker, Ed   Lasker, Ed *Chess Secrets I Learned from the Masters* (1952) London

Lasker, Em   Soloviov, *Emanuel Lasker 2: Games 1904–1940* (1998) Sofia

Levenfish   Levenfish, G *Izbrannie Partii i Vospominaniya* (1967) Moscow (Russian)

Marshall   Soltis, A *Frank Marshall, United States Chess Champion: A Biography with 220 Games* (1994) Jefferson

Muir   Muir, W *My 75 Year Chess Career* (1997) USA

Najdorf   Postma, S *Schaakromanticus Miguel Najdorf* (1996) Venlo/Antwerp (Dutch)

Panov Estrin, Ya (ed) *Vasily Panov* (1986) Moscow (Russian)

Pirc Pirc, V *Sto Izbranih Partij* (1967) Ljubljana (Slovenian)

Reshevsky Reshevsky, S *Reshevsky on Chess* (1948) Chess Review; Gordon, S W *Samuel Reshevsky: A Compendium of 1768 Games with Diagrams, Crosstables, Some Annotations, and Indexes* (1997) Jefferson

Ståhlberg Ståhlberg, G *i kamp med världseliten* (1958) Stockholm (Swedish)

Tartakower Tartakower, Dr S G *My Best Games of Chess 1931-1954* (1956) London

Ulvestad Donaldson, J *Olaf Ulvestad: An American Original* (2002) Davenport IA

Vidmar Vidmar, Dr M *Pol Stoletja ob Sahovnici* (1951) Ljubljana

Winter Winter, W *William Winter's Memoirs* (1997) Pulbrough

Yanofsky Yanofsky, A *Chess the Hard Way* (1953) London

General Works

Abrahams, G *The Chess Mind* (1951, 2nd edition 1964) Penguin

Averbakh, Yu *Chess Tactics for Advanced Players* (1984a) Berlin

Averbakh, Yu *Comprehensive Chess Endings, Volume 2: Bishop Against Knight Endings, Rook Against Minor Piece Endings* (1984b) London

Averbakh, Yu, & Chekhover, V *Comprehensive Chess Endings, Volume 1: Bishop Endings, Knight Endings* (1983) London

Averbakh, Yu, Henkin, V, & Chekhover, V *Comprehensive Chess Endings, Volume 3: Queen and Pawn Endings, Queen against Rook Endings, Queen against Minor Piece Endings* (1986) London

Averbakh, Yu, & Maizelis, I *Comprehensive Chess Endings, Volume 4: Pawn Endings* (1987) London

Bisguier, A, & Soltis, A *American Chess Masters from Morphy to Fischer* (1974) Macmillan

Bondar, L *Strategy, Tactics, Style: A Treasury of Chessplayers of Byelorussia* (1979)

Bronstein, D *Zurich International Chess Tournament 1953* (1979) New York (translation by Jim Marfia of *Mezhdunarodny Turnir Grossmeiterov; Kommentarii k Partiyam Turnira Pretendentov na Match Chempionom Mira*, 1960)

Bronstein, D *Bronstein on the King's Indian* Everyman (1999)

Bronstein, D, and Smolyan, G *Chess in the Eighties* (1982) Oxford (translation of *Prekrasnyi i yarostnyi mir*, 1978, published by Znanie)

Cohn, H *Ajedrez en Guatemala* (1947) Guatemala

Coles, R *Battles Royal of the Chessboard* (1995) Cadogan

Denker, A, & Parr, L *The Bobby Fischer I Knew and Other Stories* (1995) San Francisco

Donaldson, J, and Tangborn, E *The Unknown Bobby Fischer* ICE (1999) Seattle

De Groot, A *Thought and Choice in Chess* (1965)

Euwe, M *Meet the Masters* (2nd edition, 1945) London

Euwe, M, & Kramer, H *The Middle Game Book 1 Static Features* (1964) London

Euwe, M, & Kramer, H *The Middle Game Book 2 Dynamic and Subjective Features* (1965) London

Evans, L *New Ideas in Chess* (1958) Pitman

Fine, R 1939 *Modern Chess Openings*, 6th edition (Griffith and White) Leeds

Fine, R 1941 *Basic Chess Endings* Philadelphia (reprint of June 1967)

Fine, R 1945 *Chess Marches On!* Philadelphia

Fine, R 1948 *Practical Chess Openings* Philadelphia

Fine, R 1948 *The World's a Chessboard* Philadelphia

Fine, R 1951 *The World's Great Chess Games* Philadelphia; revised 1976, New York

Fine, R 1953 *The Middle Game in Chess* London

Gaige, J *A Catalog of USA Chess Personalia* (1980) Worcester, Massachusetts

Gaige, J *Chess Tournaments: A Checklist* (1985) Philadelphia

Gaige, J *Chess Personalia: A Biobibliography* (1987) Jefferson, North Carolina

Hajenius, W, and van Riemsdijk, H *The Final Countdown* (1997) London

Heidenfeld, W *Draw!* (1982) London

Heidenfeld, W *Damen sind Luxus* (1983) Bamberg

Hilbert, J *Essays in American Chess History* (2002) Yorklyn

Hooper, D, and Whyld, K *Oxford Companion to Chess* (1992) Oxford

van Hoorn, Th *Gedenkboek P. F. van Hoorn* (1937) Amsterdam

Horowitz, I, & Rothenberg, P *The Complete Book of Chess* (1969, edition of *The Personality of Chess* 1963)

Kahn, V, & Renaud, G *Les Six Candidats au Championnat du Monde des Echecs 1948* (1948) Le Triboulet–Monaco

Karpov, A (ed) *Shakhmaty: Entsiklopedichesky Slovar* (1990) Moscow

Karpov, A (ed) *Encyclopaedia: Modern Chess Openings–Open Games* (1994) Moscow

Karpov, A (ed) *Encyclopaedia: Modern Chess Openings–Semi-Open Games* (1996a)

Karpov, A (ed) *Encyclopaedia: Modern Chess Openings–Sicilian Defence* (1996b)

Karpov, A (ed) *Encyclopaedia: Modern Chess Openings–Closed Games* (1998)

Keene, R *Flank Openings: A Study of Réti's Opening, the Catalan, English and King's Indian Attack Complex* (2nd ed. 1970) BCM Quarterly 13

Korn, W *America's Chess Heritage: From Benjamin Franklin to Bobby Fischer and Beyond* (1978) McKay

Kotov, A *Think Like a Grandmaster* (fifth impression 1978, reprinted 1980) London

Lalić, B *Queen's Gambit Declined: Bg5 Systems* (2000) London

Matanović, A (ed) *Encyclopaedia of Chess Openings: A–E* Belgrade

Matanović, A (ed) *Encyclopaedia of Chess Endings: I–V* Belgrade

Polugaevsky, L, and Damsky, Ya *The Art of Defence in Chess* (1988) Oxford

Przewoznik, J, and Soszynski, M *How to Think in Chess* (2001) Russell Enterprises, Milford, CT USA

Reinfeld, F *Relax with Chess* (1948) London

Romanovsky, P *Chess in Russia* (1946) London

Saariluoma, P *Chess Players' Thinking: A Cognitive Psychological Approach* (1995) London

Schmidt, P *Schacmeister denken* (1985) Düsseldorf

Shereshevsky, M *Strategiya Endshpilya* (1988) Moscow

Shereshevsky, M, & Slutsky, L *Mastering the Endgame Volume 2: Closed Games* (1992) London

Soltis, A, & McCormick, G *The United States Chess Championship, 1845–1996* (2nd edition 1997) Jefferson, North Carolina

Soltis, A *The 100 Best Chess Games of the 20th Century, Ranked* (2000) Jefferson, North Carolina

Tartakower, S, & Du Mont, J *500 Master Games of Chess* (1952)

Tartakower, S, & Du Mont, J *100 Master Games of Modern Chess* (1955)

Trifunović, P, Gligorić, S, Marić, R, and Janošević, D *Yugoslav Chess Triumphs* (1976) Belgrade

Vainstein, B *David Bronstein—Chess Improviser* (1983) Oxford

Vuković, V *The Art of Attack in Chess* (1979) Oxford

Watson, J *Secrets of Modern Chess Strategy* (1998) London

"Наша система" на практике? (*"Our System" in Practice?*) (1997) Moscow

Periodicals

Ideally I would have searched through all significant publications for the relevant years, however that was not possible. I have been fortunate to receive assistance from other researchers and organizations in the production of this work. Many of the sources below have been supplied to me, at least in part, in the form of copied pages.

American Chess Bulletin 1930–51 (O'Keefe and Lahde)

Australasian Chess Review (1930s) (Whyld)

British Chess Magazine 1931–2001

The Chess Review 1933–40 (Gillam)

Chess 1935–51 (Gillam, Whyld and Howson)

Chess Life 1946, March and October 1984, 1993 and 1996 (The Royal Dutch Library)

Sahovski Vjesnik 1950 (Gillam)

New in Chess

64 1937 (Gillam)

De Schaakwereld 1935–9 (Gillam)

CCLA Newsletter (Lahde)

Tijdschrift van den Nederlandschen Schaakbond 1935–9 (Gillam)

In addition, Peter Lahde, Jack O'Keefe, Tony Gillam, Erik Osbun and John Hilbert have supplied me with many games from newspaper columns, in particular: *Brooklyn Daily Eagle, Washington Post, Washington Star, New York Sun, New York Sun Times, New York Times, Christian Science Monitor, Tilburgse Courant, Evening Sun, New York Evening Post, New York Herald Tribune.*

Openings Index—Descriptive (to game numbers)

Openings are listed, under three categories, alphabetically according to their classical names.
Game numbers in **bold** *indicate that Fine had the white pieces.*

Open Games

Bishop's Opening 542, 554, **825**
Evans Gambit **140, 761, 801, 807,** 880
Four Knights Game 46, 50, 414, 469, **509,** 742
Italian Game 30, 205, 251, **319,** 379, 504, 681, 683
King's Gambit Accepted **727, 729, 746, 789**
King's Gambit Declined 787, **796**
Latvian Gambit **837**
Petroff Defence 142, 216, **252,** 320, **552, 589, 835**
Philidor's Defence **550,** 654, **860,** 877
Ponziani Opening 38
Rousseau Gambit **771**
Scottish Game 853
Spanish Game 254, **425, 551,** 774, **758a, 811, 839, 847**
Spanish Game, Berlin Defence 269, **754**
Spanish Game, Bird's Counter-attack **680**
Spanish Game, Chigorin Defence 215, 329, **470, 697, 750**
Spanish Game, Closed Defence 739
Spanish Game, Exchange Variation **680**
Spanish Game, Old Steinitz Defence **758**
Spanish Game, Open Defence 467, 475, **481,** 516, **545, 725, 730,** 829
Spanish Game, Steinitz Defence Deferred 7, 76, 149, 171, 368, 372,

398, 400, **474,** 520, 580, 586, 595, 641, 652, 676, **822, 864,** 867
Spanish Game, Worrall Attack **178,** 181, 192, 271, 460, **468, 484, 513,** 561, 740, **768, 779**
Two Knights Defence **82, 529, 626,** 647, 685, **726,** 743, **846**
Vienna Game 1, **18,** 437, 537, 843

Semi-Open Games

Alekhine's Defence 48, 69, 71, **204,** 364, 395, 433, 476, 526, 613, 664, 670, 707, 827, **871**
Caro-Kann Defence 151, 174, 184, **194, 303,** 453, **501, 609,** 723, **732, 756, 763, 840**
English Defence **803**
French Defence 210, 321, 391, 744, **859**
French Defence, Advance Variation **80,** 132, 182, 198, 232
French Defence, Burn Variation 5, **173,** 606, 668
French Defence, Chatard-Alekhine Attack 130, 166, 358
French Defence, Classical Variation 3, 66, 105, 196, 731, 736
French Defence, Exchange Variation 32, 138, 203, 230, 265, 282
French Defence, McCutcheon Variation **751**
French Defence, Rubinstein Variation **598, 747, 766**

French Defence, Steinitz Variation 187, 554
French Defence, Tarrasch Variation 374, 604, **618, 783, 786, 790**
French Defence, Winawer Variation 183, **462, 464, 466,** 581, **587, 638,** 687, **760**
Nimzowitsch Defence 307, **438,** 818
Sicilian Defence 2, 25, 52, 120, **158, 162,** 201, **220,** 245, 253, 255, 308, 397, 477, **478,** 480, 491, 496, 500, 514, 518, 540, 547, 556, 567, 570, 590, 592, 608, 610, 748, **764, 788,** 798, **799, 800, 804, 810, 850,** 866, **872**
Sicilian, Nimzowitsch 622, 631, **793,** 838
Sicilian Defence, 2...d6 and 5 f3 **405, 431, 503, 577**
Sicilian Dragon 19, 74, 296, 369, 442, **523, 601, 780, 782, 814**
Sicilian, Fischer-Sozin Variation 879
Sicilian Najdorf, Fianchetto Variation **692, 705**
Sicilian Scheveningen 21, 125, 155, 189, 199, 238, 261, 348, 352, 386

Closed Games

Albin Countergambit **486, 628, 821**
Barnes Opening 1 f3 **37**
Clemenz Opening 1 h3 **84**
Double Fianchetto Opening g3/Bg2 and b3/Bb2 **759**

Openings Index—ECO
(to game numbers)

Openings are listed according to the Encyclopaedia of Chess Openings *classification.*
Game numbers in **bold** *indicate that Fine had the white pieces.*

Players Index
(to game numbers)

The index includes Fine as consultant or tandem simultaneous partner.
*Game numbers in **bold** indicate that Fine had the white pieces.*

Annotators Index
(to game numbers)

The source of annotations alone is quoted where there is uncertainty as to personality.

Sources Index
(to game numbers)

Games with named annotators and games from the notebooks are excluded.

General Index
(to page numbers)

Page numbers in italics indicate photographs.